OHIO COUNTY (WV) INDEX
VOLUME 7

Index to the
County Court Order Books (Part 7)

Civil Lawsuit Plainfiffs
& Misc. Entries for Surnames T-Z
with Corresponding Defendants
& Other References Covering Surnames A-Z

1777–1881

From the collection of the
West Virginia and Regional History Collection
West Virginia University
Morgantown, West Virginia

PLUS 1871 Map of the Panhandle

from the map collection of
the Library of Congress
Washington, D.C.

Compiled by
Kenneth Fischer Craft, Jr.

Heritage Books
2011

HERITAGE BOOKS
AN IMPRINT OF HERITAGE BOOKS, INC.

Books, CDs, and more—Worldwide

For our listing of thousands of titles see our website
at
www.HeritageBooks.com

Published 2011 by
HERITAGE BOOKS, INC.
Publishing Division
100 Railroad Ave. #104
Westminster, Maryland 21157

Copyright © 2001 Kenneth Fischer Craft, Jr.

Other Heritage Books by the author:

Ohio County (W.Va.) Index, Volume 1: Index to County Court Order Books, 1777-1881 [Part 1]

*Ohio County (W.Va.) Index, Volume 2: Index to County Court Order Books, 1777-1881 [Part 2]
Plus Gazetteer and Map Book*

Ohio County (W.Va.) Index, Volume 3: Index to County Court Order Books, 1777-1881 [Part 3]

Ohio County (W.Va.) Index, Volume 4: Index to County Court Order Books, 1771-1881 [Part 4]

Ohio County (W.Va.) Index, Volume 5: Index to County Court Order Books, 1771-1881 [Part 5]

Ohio County (W.Va.) Index, Volume 6: Index to County Court Order Books, 1771-1881 [Part 6]

*Ohio County (W.Va.) Index, Volume 7: Index to County Court Order Books, 1771-1881 [Part 7]
Plus an 1871 Map of the Panhandle*

*Ohio County (W.Va.) Index Volume 7C: Cumulative 'Personal Time Line' Index to Volumes 1-7,
Pages 1-1876, Index to County Court Order Books, 1777-1881*

Ohio County (W.Va.) Index, Volume 8: Card Index to All Ohio County Courts' Case Files and Loose Papers, Part 1; 1776-1825

Ohio County (W.Va.) Index, Volume 9: Card Index to All Ohio County Courts' Case Files and Loose Papers, Part 2; 1826-1836

Ohio County (W.Va.) Index, Volume 10: Card Index to All Ohio County Courts' Case Files and Loose Papers, Part 3; 1837-1841

Ohio County (W.Va.) Index, Volume 11: Card Index to All Ohio County Courts' Case Files and Loose Papers, Part 4; 1842-1851

Ohio County (W.Va.) Index, Volume 12: Card Index to All Ohio County Courts' Case Files and Loose Papers, Part 5; 1852-1856

Ohio County (W.Va.) Index, Volume 13: Card Index to All Ohio County Courts' Case Files and Loose Papers, Part 6; 1857-1861

Ohio County (W.Va.) Index, Volume 14: Card Index to All Ohio County Courts' Case Files and Loose Papers, Part 7; 1862-1872

All rights reserved. No part of this book may be reproduced or transmitted in any form or by any means, electronic or mechanical, including photocopying, recording or by any information storage and retrieval system without written permission from the author, except for the inclusion of brief quotations in a review.

International Standard Book Numbers
Paperbound: 978-0-7884-1750-4
Clothbound: 978-0-7884-8685-2

CONTENTS 1545

Subject	Page #
Contents	1545
Maps & County Formation Dates Chart	1546
Preface - Volume 7	1547
'T-Z' Key Table Index	1549
'T' Surnames - Plaintiffs	1551
'U' Surnames - Plaintiffs	1569
'V' Surnames - Plaintiffs	1570
'W' Surnames - Plaintiffs	1576
'Y' Surnames - Plaintiffs	1604
'W' Named Corporations & Firms	1607
'Y' Surnames - Plaintiffs	1608
'Z' Surnames - Frequently Occurring	1610
'Z' Surnames - Plaintiffs	1616
'W' Named Corporations & Firms	1617
'Z' Named Corporations & Firms	1618
T' Named Corporations & Firms	1620
'W' & 'V' Named Corporations & Firms	1624
'W' Named Corporations & Firms	1626
'Z' Named Corporations & Firms	1632
'T' Surnames - Frequently Occurring	1634
'U' Surnames - Frequently Occurring	1642
'W' Surnames - Frequently Occurring	1644
Wheeling - City of - Plaintiffs	1672
'T' Surnames - Miscellaneous Entries	1674
'U' & 'V' Surnames - Miscellaneous Entries	1683
'V' Surnames - Miscellaneous Entries	1684
'W' Surnames - Miscellaneous Entries	1687
'Y' Surnames - Miscellaneous Entries	1708
'Z' Surnames - Miscellaneous Entries	1710
Appendix - Table of Contents	1712
Appendix - 1871 'Map of the Panhandle' - 4 Counties	1713
Appendix - 1852 'Hempfield Railroad Map & Bond Prospectus'	1817
Appendix - 1852 'Brooke County Landowner Map'	1828
Appendix - 'Panoramic Maps in Library of Congress'	1855
Appendix - 1822 'Map of Wheeling City - with Original Layout'	1860
Appendix - 1916 'The National Road' Book - Ohio Co. extracts	1861
Appendix - Ohio Co. Microfilms at WVU & State Archives	1871
Appendix - Preview of 'OCI' Volume 8	1873
Appendix - Hints for Interpreting 'Misc. Entries ' & Abbreviations	1875
Appendix - Preview of 'OCI' Volume 7A - **CUMULATIVE INDEX**	1876
'Personal Time Line' Index with every Name, Stream, or Place	I

MAPS AND COUNTY FORMATION DATES CHART

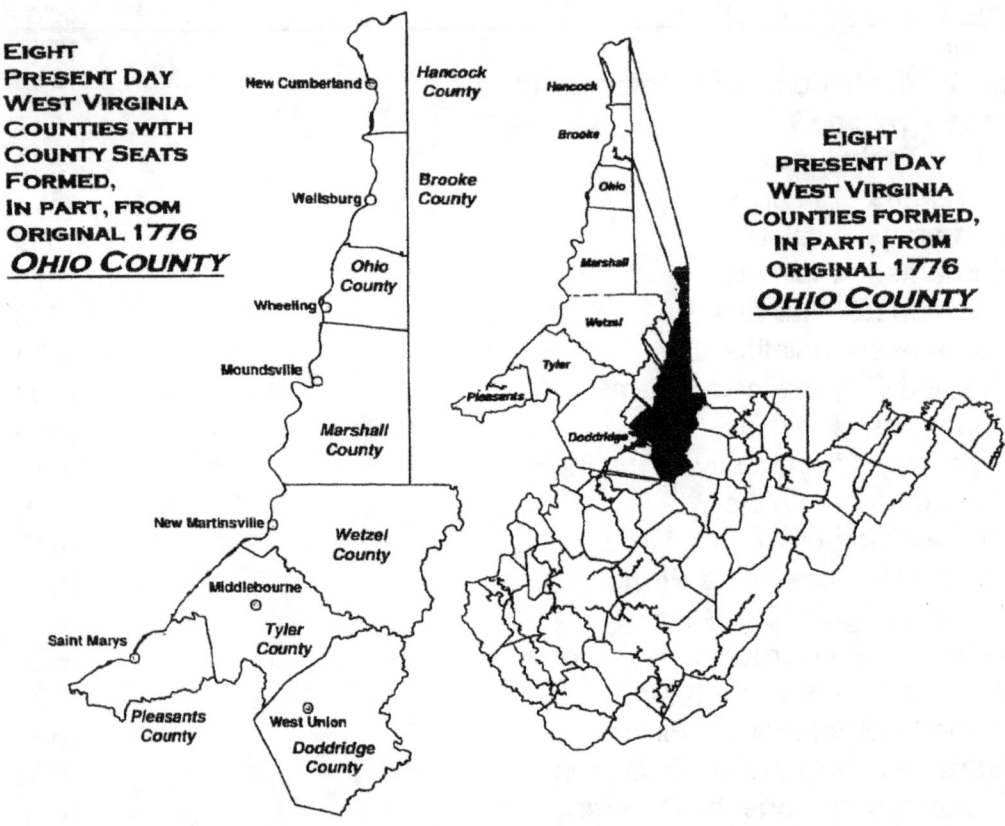

Eight Present Day West Virginia Counties with County Seats Formed, In Part, From Original 1776 **Ohio County**

Eight Present Day West Virginia Counties Formed, In Part, From Original 1776 **Ohio County**

County Formation Dates of Eight Counties
... formed (in part) from Original Ohio County

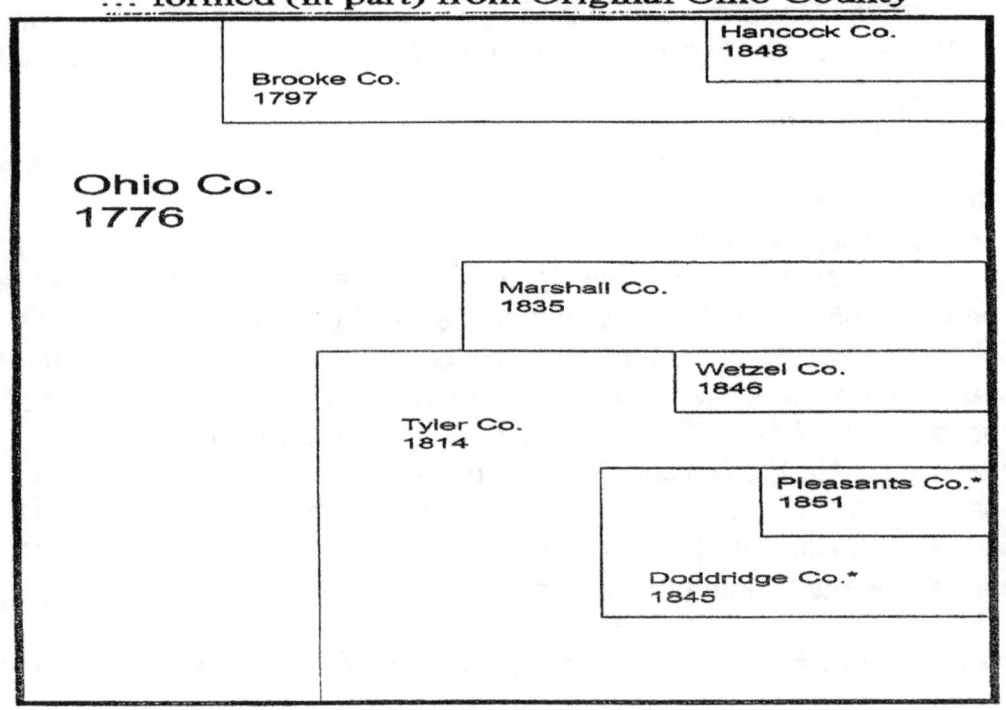

* Formed from other Counties also.

PREFACE to VOLUME 7

Introduction

Volume seven continues the **Ohio County Index** series by publishing the final records from the index to Ohio County (Virginia) West Virginia County Court Order Books from 1777 – 1881 as originally extracted during the 1930's. As part of an on ongoing series, the introductory comments from volume one will not be repeated. However, the reader needs to remember that the original Ohio County covered parts of eight present-day Northern West Virginia panhandle counties. As new counties were formed over the years the geography covered by the records was decreasing. One should pay special attention to what area the records covered during the time period of interest (See preface maps and county formation chart.) Volume 8 starts a new series of records.

Civil Lawsuits and Miscellaneous Entries

This volume continues to index the massive listing of civil lawsuits handled in the county court covering individuals, banks, firms and corporations. In addition, miscellaneous entries for the selected surnames are included and could cover almost any subject. As discussed in volume 1 (pages vi-vii and 1), these misc. entries are the last type of records that the indexers encountered so they had to make a place to put them.

These pages are very rich with names since they index both the plaintiff (for the selected surnames) and the corresponding defendant (regardless of surname) in each case. In addition, anyone's name could be mentioned in the miscellaneous entries.

Volume 7 Records

Covered in this volume are:
Plaintiffs with surnames starting with T through Z.
Defendants and misc. entries with surnames A through Z.

The original pages are included with a reference to the source County Court Order Book and page number. There are a few mentions of Chancery (i.e.C1) and Law Order Books (i.e. L4). Information on these original records is discussed in the appendix. Some index entries include only one entry per year per person per page – so check for multiple entries.

Also included is the 1871 Map of the Panhandle [covering Hancock, Brooke, Ohio & Marshall Cos.] by F. W. Beers from the map collection of the Library of Congress with _over 11,000 names_ indexed. All the major cities & towns show landowners – except Wheeling [covered by city directories]. There is some overlap among the cut up sections – so the same name may appear on two pages and might be indexed twice. The map makers often used initials – which refer to nearby landowners. The following abbreviations were found: 'hrs.'=heirs; 'B.S.S.'=Blacksmith Shop. A few names were not legible but are partially indexed as best as possible. Also some initials could not be identified – so the initials were indexed. Also indexed is an 1852 landowner Map of Brooke County, an 1822 Wheeling map and part of the 1916 book, The National Road.

PREFACE

Planned Future Volumes In The 'OHIO COUNTY INDEX' Series

This volume completes the Ohio *County Court* Order Book indexes. Future volumes will publish other primary Ohio County records. You will notice that the pagination continues from volume to volume – like a quarterly journal. Periodically, cumulative indexes will be published (see volume 7A below) to cover all the volumes of the series with one continuous page numbering system – superceding the indexes in each individual volume.

Volume 7A Preview

Volume 7A will be a **Cumulative** 'Personal Time Line' Index to vols. 1-7 with *110,000* entries !

Volume 8 Preview

Volume 8 will start an exciting new series of records – the 'index card files' to court case files and loose papers at the "WV and Regional History Collection" in Morgantown. See appendix for details. These files are the answer to the question: "Are there any papers from the lawsuit?". These cards also index many court papers besides lawsuits. These indexes also cover all courts [including criminal] in the county !

Acknowledgements

I would like to thank Mr. John Cuthbert, Curator of the West Virginia and Regional History Collection at West Virginia University for his support on this project. The 1871 Map of the Panhandle is from the collection of the Map & Geography Division, Library of Congress. The 1852 Brooke Co. Map is courtesy of the Brooke Co. Genealogical Society. The 1822 Wheeling Map is reproduced through the kindness of Mr. Ophir E. Vellenoweth of Wheeling.

I Need Your Help Too – Again !

Thank you for your wonderful support of this series of books.

As always, all name spelling variations should be carefully checked since the original source indexes were 1930's interpretations of various eighteenth and nineteenth century clerks' handwriting. In working with this data, I have added many duplicate, hopefully corrected, entries which I have marked with parentheses and question marks, i.e. (?Caldwell?). Some of the firm names were easily confused with first and last names so they were indexed in every combination. Please let me know if you find any errors and I will correct them in future volumes.

Also, I'd like to hear any other comments about the book. If you send along your query, family group sheet and an SASE – I might be able to help you in some way. Please write again !

Kenneth Fischer Craft, Jr. December 2000
5600 Clinchfield Trail
Norcross, Georgia 30092-2029

'T-Z' KEY INDEX TABLE (Ignore original page numbers below)

204 'T-Z' KEY TABLE INDEX – PAGE 1 OF 2 (Ignore original pages numbers below)

FIRST, SEARCH FREQUENTLY OCCURRING NAMES BELOW
Because of their frequent entry, all common and other active surnames or family names and the page on which they are separately grouped should be entered in proper ruled block below, according to large alphabet divisions.
COTTCO UNIVERSAL INDEX No. 54 (U.S. Pat. No. 1857181—U.S. Copyright No. 15600—1930) The Cott Index Company, Columbus, Ohio

KEY TABLE FOR MIXED NAMES
TO WHICH REFER IF NAME IS NOT FOUND IN RULED SPACES TO LEFT

Column 4	PAGE	Column 3	PAGE	Column 2	PAGE	Enter Names First in Column 1	PAGE	Alphabet Div.	First Letters of Surnames	Page
(MISCL)		Taa to Tay-Taz	105			Tayler / Taylor	85		Taa to Tay-Taz	1
Tax Commissioner	114	Tea – Tem				Thompson	86B		Tea to Tem	3
		Ten – Tez	107			Thomson	87		Ten to Tez	5
Tavern Rates	114	Tia to Tim							Tia to Tim	7
		Tin to Tiz	108						Tia to Tiz	9
		Th – Tk	109			Tomlinson	5	T	Th-Tk	11
		Toa – Tol							Toa to Tol	13
Toll Collector	115	Tom – Toz	111						Tom to Toz	15
		Tra-Tre-Tri-Try	112						Tra-Tre-Tri-Try	17
		Tro – Tru							Tro-Tru	19
		Ts – Tu – Tw – Ty	113						Ts-Tu–21 Tw-Ty–	23
								Odd	Names beginning T not above classified	23
		U	117			Udegraff / Udegraff / Udegrff	89	U	U	25
		Va(Except Van)	117						Va (except Van)	27
		Van	118			Van Buskirk	28		Van	29
		Ve – Vi – Vy	119					V	Ve-Vi-Vy	31
		Vo – Vr – Vu	120						Vo-Vr-Vu	33
								Odd	Names beginning V not above classified	33
		Waa to Wag to Wak	121			Walker	34		Waa to Wag to Wak	35
		Wal	122			Wayt / Wayts	36		Wal	37
		Wam – Wan				Weaver	39	Wa	Wam-Wan	39
		Wao – Wap				Webb	52		Wao-Wap	39
		War	123						War	41
		Was-Wat to Waz	125						Was-Wat to Waz	43
		Wea-Web-Wec-Wed	123						Wea-Web-Wec-Wed	45
		Wee to Wek	123						Wee to Wek	45
Wells	135	Wel	127			Wells / Wills	91	We	Wel	47
		Wom-Wen to Wer	129						Wem-Wen to Wer	49
		Wes-Wet to Wez	129						Wes-Wet to Wez	51
	138	Wia to Wik	123			Wickham	40		Wia to Wik	45
Wilson	139	Wil	127			Williamson	55		Wil	47
		Wim-Win to Wir	129			Wills / Wells	91	Wi	Wim-Win to Wir	49
		Wis-Wit to Wiz	129			Wilson / Willson	93		Wis-Wit to Wiz	51
						Williams	95			
White	135	Wh – Wl	131			Whetzel / Whetzell	96B	Wh	Wh-Wl	53
Whitten / Whittam Whitham	137	Woa to Wol-Wom	132			White	97	Wo	Woa to Wol-Wom	55
Whittingham / Whettingham	137	Won-Woo to Woz	133			Wheat (E)	99	Wr	Woa-Woo to Woz	57
Wood	141	Wr – Wu	134			Wood / Woods	101	Wu	Wr-Wu	59
Wheeling	142	Wy – Wz	134					Wy	Wy-Wz	59
Weights & Measures	143							Odd	Names beginning W not above classified	59
Wolf Scalp Rates	143	X						X	X	59
West Liberty	143	Ya	145						Ya	61
		Ye / Yi	146					Y	Ye / Yi	63 / 65
		Yo – Yu	146						Yo-Yu	65
		Za – Zi	147						Za	67
			148					Z	Za-Zi	69
		Zo – Zu – Zy	148						Zo-Zu-Zy	69
								Odd	Names beginning Y and Z not above classified	71

1550 'T-Z' KEY INDEX TABLE (Ignore original page numbers below)

'T-Z' KEY TABLE INDEX – PAGE 2 OF 2 (Ignore original pages numbers below)   205

FREQUENTLY OCCURRING CORPORATIONS, FIRMS, ETC.

Column 2	PAGE	Enter Names First in Column 1	PAGE	Group
				Ta to **Ti**, Tj-Tk, Tl-Tm, Tn — Page 73
				To to **Ty**, Tz — Page 75
				U / V — Page 77
		Warden & Edwards	60	**Wa** to **We**, Wf-Wg — Page 79
MISCL				
W H	130	Wheeling Town Of / City of	103	
Wheeling	142	Wilson & Waddle	70	**Wh** to **Wy**, Wz — Page 81
West Liberty	143	Woods & Caldwell	64	
		Zane & Petoney	71	**X / Y / Z** — Page 83

PLAINTIFF INDEX TO ORDER BOOKS — Ohio County, W. Va.

SURNAME	PLAINTIFFS GIVEN NAMES ABCDEFGH	GIVEN NAMES IJKLMNO	GIVEN NAMES PQRSTUVWXYZ	DEFENDANTS		YEAR	ORDER BOOK									
Tate	Assignee of	Wm. Martin James &	et al Thomas	James Whetzell et al	L	1807	11 49	11 64								
Tarries		John		John Pettis	L	1816	15 329	15 407								
Tappan	Benjamin			Joseph Majors	L	1818	16 291									
Tanner	Deborah &	James		Patience Graham et al	L	1827	22 63	22 69	22 82	22 194						
Tar			Peter	James Madison	C	1828	22 363									
Tarr			Peter, Jr.	James C. Madison, Jr.	C	1828	23 18									
Tawsey		Joseph		Bernard Wiedman	L	1828	22 330	22 404	22 469							
Tappan	Benjamin			John Parriott	L	1833	25 485									
Tappan	Benjamin			John Parriott et al	L	1834	26 129									
Taggart		Michael	et al	John Sexton	L	1836	27 122									
Talbot			Upton L.	Henry Parson	L	1838	27 411									
Tallant	Drury J.			Aaron Varney	L	1838	27 405									
Talbott			Richard	Andrew W. McColloch et al	L	1839	28 155	28 206								
Tanner		James		John Brooks	L	1839	28 171									
Talbott	Elisha	Assignee of Edward Smith		Warren Wheatley	L	1840	28 367									
Taleant	D. J.			Bancroft Woodcock	L	1840	28 428	28 495								
Tallant	Drury	et al		Robert Hamilton	L	1840	28 355									
Tallant	Drury J.			James M. Wheat	L	1840	28 358									
Tarr	Campbell	et al		William Chapline	L	1840	28 363	28 437								
Tarr	Campbell	et al		Noah Zane Chapline	L	1840	28 421									
Tassey		John	et al	Charles Ensell	L	1840	28 356									
Tallant	Drury J.		et al	John Gilchrist	L	1841	29 58	29 116								
Tallant	Drury J.	et al		George Dulty et al	L	1841	29 59									
Tallant	Drury J.			Zinn & Rohan	L	1841	28 505									
Tallant	Drury J.			Charles Ensell	L	1841	28 596									
Tallant	Drury J.	et al		James Sweeney	L	1842	29 60									
Tallant	Drury J.	et al		Andrew C. Huoston	L	1842	29 60									
Tallant	Drury J.	et al		Charles Ensell et al	L	1842	29 67									
Taggert	Henry			C. Belville	L	1846	30 114									
Tallant	Drury J.	et al		David Echols	L	1846	30 105									
Tanner		James		Martin Jennings	L	1853	33 19									
Tallant			William	Jacob E. Bier	L	1854	33 164									
Taylor		J. H. & E.		James H. Robinson	L	1854	34 8	34 20	34 36	34 84	34 119	34 139	34 173	34 193	34 218	34 231	34 263
do		do		do	L	1854	34 282	34 313	34 327	34 375	34 387					
Tarr	Campbell			Jesse Stobridge (Stowbridge)	L	1854	33 181									
Tarr			Peter, etal	Hughes & Campbell, et al	C	1833	25 493									

PLAINTIFF INDEX TO ORDER BOOKS — Ohio County, W. Va.

Surname	Given Names ABCDEFGH	Given Names IJKLMNO	Given Names PQRSTUVWXYZ	Defendants	L/C	Year	Order Book (Vol/Page)
Tallant	Henry &		William	Simeon D. Woodrow	L	1855	34/145
do	Henry &		William	William McMechen	L	1855	34/287
Tanner		James		Martin O'Neal	L	1855	34/202, 34/221, 34/254, 34/263, 34/296, 34/304, 34/313, 34/327, 34/375, 34/398
Taylor		J. E. & E.		James H. Robinson	L	1856	35/16, 35/51, 35/71, 35/89, 35/107, 35/136, 35/184, 35/199, 35/247, 35/271
do		do		do	L	1856	35/283, 35/318, 35/345, 35/392, 35/410, 35/434, 35/440, 35/469, 35/507
Tallant	Henry &		Wm. et al	Edmund Hobbs et al	L	1856	35/27
Tallant	Henry &		Wm. et al	George Hardman et al	L	1856	35/27, 35/98
Tanner		James		Martin O'Neal	L	1856	35/35, 35/51, 35/71, 35/89, 35/107, 35/136, 35/184, 35/199, 35/247, 35/271
do		do	et al	do	L	1856	35/283, 35/318, 35/344, 35/398, 35/410, 35/434, 35/440, 35/493, 35/506
Tallant	Henry &		William	John & Robert Ferrell	L	1856	35/294, 35/338
Tallant	Henry &		Wm. et al	Andrew Muldrew, Jr. et al	L	1857	35/365
Taggart		James H.		J. M. Tiernan	L	1857	36/74, 36/87, 36/109
Talcott			William H.	William Riheldaffer & Co.	L	1857	35/360
Tanner		James		Martin O'Neal	L	1857	36/73, 36/92
Tallant	Henry &		Wm. et al	Zernie Myers	L	1858	37/65
Tallant	Henry &		Wm. et al	James M. Todd et al	L	1858	36/177, 36/263
Tallant	Henry &		Wm.	John Dulty	L	1858	36/182
Tallant	Henry &		William	Joseph Hallam	L	1858	36/185
Tallant	Henry &		William	James Wayt	L	1858	36/187
Tallant	Henry &		William	Hans W. Phillips et al	L	1858	36/322, 36/414
Tallant	Henry &		Wm. et al	Charles Dankvirt	L	1859	37/139
Tallant	Henry &		Wm. et al	Thomas Gray et al	L	1859	37/139
Tanner	Deborah Adm'r. of		James	George Forbes	L	1859	37/346
Tallant			William	James Wayt et al	L	1860	38/279, 38/280
Taggart		Isaac	et al	Manfred T. Hullihen	L	1861	38/524
Tallant	Henry &		William etal	Adam Foose	L	1861	38/355
Tasker			Thomas T. & Stephen P.M. et al	Hans W. Phillips	L	1861	38/436, 38/472, 38/481
Tallant	Henry &		William	Mathew H. Houston	L	1863	39/199
Tallman			Peter	Charles Fisher	L	1873	L1/171, L1/205, L1/214, L1/294
Tappe	Henry			A. Ackerman et al	L	1878	L4/113, L4/118
Tarbett			Robert A.	James B. Tarbett	L	1878	L3/490
Tappe	Charles			Lewis Hahne	L	1879	L4/214, L4/301, L4/304

PLAINTIFF INDEX TO ORDER BOOKS — Ohio County, W. Va.

PLAINTIFFS			DEFENDANTS		YEAR	ORDER BOOK							
SURNAME	GIVEN NAMES ABCDEFGH	GIVEN NAMES IJKLMNO	GIVEN NAMES PQRSTUVWXYZ										
Templeton		James		Hisaciah Crosbey	L	1795	5 / 24						
Teal	Charles	Assignee of	John Sutt	John Patton et al	C	1797	6 / 5						
Templeton		James		Gilbert Hector	L	1800	6 / 471						
Teghardin		Jacob		John Stewart et al	L	1803	8 / 297	8 / 298					
Tegarden		John		Patrick Ray	L	1812	13 / 132						
Tegarden		John		Austin Nichols et al	L	1813	14 / 60						
Teagarden		Jacob	et al	Joseph Wilson	L	1816	15 / 408						
Templeton			William	Wm. & James Patton	L	1817	16 / 34	16 / 299	16 / 364				
Teables		Michael		Wm. Chapline	L	1818	16 / 480						
Teal		Nicholas		John Arnold	L	1820	17 / 200						
Teirn (Teirnan		Luke	et al	Andrew Howlet et.al	C	1820	17 / 260	17 / 335	17 / 393				
Templeton			Wm, et al	Van Caldwell et al	L	1823	20 / 38						
Teeters		Joseph		Augustus Maswie et al	L	1829	23 / 311						
Teeters		Joseph		Ambrose Palmer	L	1831	25 / 26	25 / 57					
Teal		Nicholas		George Dulty	L	1832	25 / 56						
Teeters		Joseph		John Wheeler	L	1832	25 / 53						
Teeters		Joseph		Peter Shipley	L	1832	25 / 184						
Teeters		Joseph		John Pierson	L	1833	25 / 329	25 / 335					
Teeters		Joseph		E. Spurnaugle et al	L	1834	26 / 52						
Teeters		Joseph		John Pierson	L	1834	26 / 127						
Teeters		Joseph		T. P. Robinson	L	1834	26 / 192						
Templeton			Thomas	D. Kennedey	L	1835	26 / 332	26 / 572					
Teeters		Joseph		T. P. Robinson Adm'rs.	L	1836	27 / 112						
Teeters		Joseph		Samuel Brentlinger	L	1836	27 / 168						
Teater	H.			Fieldon Berry	L	1839	28 / 68						
Tedford			Susanna	Murry & Reed	L	1841	29 / 11						
Templeton			Wm, et al	Jacob Berger	L	1843	29 / 298						
Templeton			William	Abner Black	L	1844	29 / 376	29 / 403					
Temple		Joseph E.	et al	John L. Maxwell	L	1851	31 / 467						
Teagarden			William	A. Biggs et al	L	1857	36 / 112						
Tesce	Arthur M.			Henry Schmulbach	L	1874	12 / 19	12 / 21	12 / 22				

'T' SURNAMES - PLAINTIFFS

PLAINTIFF INDEX TO ORDER BOOKS — Ohio County, W. Va.

SURNAME	PLAINTIFFS GIVEN NAMES ABCDEFGH	GIVEN NAMES IJKLMNO	GIVEN NAMES PQRSTUVWXYZ	DEFENDANTS	L/C	YEAR	ORDER BOOK						
Terel		James	et al	Ezecial Boggs	L	1789	3/119						
Terrell	George			Sarah Terrell et al	C	1803	9/113						
Terrel	Ebert			Walter Lewis	L	1807	11/124						
Terrel	Daniel	et al		Joseph Wilson	L	1824	20/103	20/298	20/368				
Tennis	Anthony			Reason Pumphrey et al	L	1826	22/18	22/50					
Tennan	Francis &	Michael		James H. Palmer	L	1830	24/270						
Terrell	Calvin	et al		Benjamin Rodgers et al	L	1836	27/48						
Terry	Eli	et al		Joseph Brentlinger et al	L	1836	27/91	27/131					
Tevis	Use of Hugh E. Fergus	John		Samuel G. Robinson	L	1840	28/429	28/491					
Terry		James		John C. Snider et al	L	1848	29/209	29/232					
Tevis		John		James W. Hamilton	L	1847	30/299						
Tevis		Joseph D.		Daniel M. Stockton	L	1852	32/305						
Tewhee		James		City of Wheeling	L	1853	33/26	33/76	33/95	33/102			
Terry		John P.		Eliphalet C. Dewey	L	1856	35/152	35/210					
Teusbury			R. M. etal	Eliphalet C. Dewey	L	1856	35/152	35/210					
Terrell		J. W.		Foreman & Dunlap	L	1861	38/431	38/468					
Terrell		John Adm'r.		James Wayt	L	1879	L4/241						
Terrill		Mary M.		John L. Tarrill et al	C	1880	C1/471	C1/495					
Tomlinson		Joseph		Lawrence Buskirk	L	1784	1/203						
do		Joseph		Frederick Lamb	L	1785	1/275						
do		Joseph		Richard Yeats	L	1789	3/146	3/148					
do		Joseph		Charles Barkshew	L	1795	5/19a						
do			Robert	George Beymer et al	L	1799	6/314						
do	Elizabeth &	Joseph		Jacob Chambers et al	L	1800	7/42	7/136	7/158	7/224	7/228	7/282	7/321
do		Joseph		Wm. Ward	L	1800	7/48	7/136	7/158	7/222	7/243		
do		Joseph		Litta Dickson et al	L	1800	6/467	6/500					
do		Joseph	(Sheriff)	Abenezer Zane	L	1801	7/252						
do		Joseph		Thomas Moore	L	1803	9/79						
do		Isaac		William Perrine	L	1805	10/189						
do		Joseph		Moses & Wm. Chapline	L	1805	10/11	10/127					
do		Joseph		William Chapline	L	1807	11/142						
do		Joseph		Lazarus Harris	L	1807	11/196	11/216	11/418	11/489			
do		Joseph	Dec'd.	Joseph Tomlinson	C	1808	11/383	11/406					
do		Joseph		Lazerus Harris	L	1809	12/16	12/92					

PLAINTIFF INDEX TO ORDER BOOKS — Ohio County, W. Va.

SURNAME	PLAINTIFFS GIVEN NAMES ABCDEFGH	GIVEN NAMES IJKLMNO	GIVEN NAMES PQRSTUVWXYZ	DEFENDANTS		YEAR	ORDER BOOK		
Tomlinson		Joseph		Moses & Wm. Chapline	L	1809	12 33	12 135	
do		Joseph	et al	Lucy Baker	C	1809	12 80		
do		Joseph	et al	Joseph Kerr	L	1812	13 316	13 367	
do		Joseph, Jr.	et al	Archibald McClean		1813	2 112	2 127	2 142
do		Joseph	et al	Joseph Kerr	L	1814	14 231		
do		Joseph		Edward Dowler	L	1816	2 313	2 333	
do		Nathaniel	et al	Henry Sockman et al	L	1816	364		
do		Nathaniel	et al	Wm. Chapline	L	1818	16 388		
do		James	et al	George Cafruthers	L	1823	19 365		
do		Jesse		Nathan Riggs	L	1823	19 494		
do		Nathaniel & Jesse	et al	Nathan Riggs	L	1823	20 57		
do		Margaret & Nathaniel	et al	Wm. Wilson et al	L	1828	23 52		
do		Nathaniel		George Wilson et al	L	1829	23 157		
do		Nathaniel	Adm'r.	George Wilson et al	L	1829	23 157		
do		Margaret & Nathaniel	et al	George Wilson et al	L	1829	23 229	23 230	
do	Elisabeth			Alexander Morrison	L	1831	24 462		
do	Elizabeth			Samuel Cockayne et al	L	1831	24 482		
do	Elizabeth			George Michael Wilson	L	1831	24 482		
do	Elizabeth			Alexander Morrison et al	L	1831	25 11		
do		Margaret &	Samuel	George W. Wilson et al	L	1831	25 6		
do	Elizabeth			George Wilson et al	L	1832	25 58		
do			Samuel	Susanna Parrott et al	L	1833	25 450	25 458	
do			Samuel	Susanna Parrott et al	L	1833	25 450	25 459	
do			Samuel	Richard Knight	L	1834	26 23		
do		Margaret		John N. Jacob	L	1840	28 366		

PLAINTIFF INDEX TO ORDER BOOKS — Ohio County, W. Va.

Surname	Given Names ABCDEFGH	Given Names IJKLMNO	Given Names PQRSTUVWXYZ	Defendants	L/C	Year	Order Book					
Tilton		John		John Badkin	L	1778	2/20					
do		John		Robert Black	L	1784	1/216					
do		John		Charles Wells et al	L	1784	1/223	1/236	1/237	1/239	1/274	1/275
do		John		Robert Harrison	L	1784	1/245					
do		John		James Parks	L	1785	1/254	1/262				
do			Thomas	Jacob Frissell	L	1785	1/252					
do		John		Thomas Selman	L	1787	3/14	3/110	3/111	3/114	3/159	
do		John		Charles Wells	L	1787	3/24					
Tibergan	Charles			Macom Colman	L	1788	3/91					
Tibugan	Charles	et al		John Pollock	L	1791	3/243					
Tigart	Francis			Isaac Kelley	L	1791	3/263	3/309A	3/336			
Tilton		John		Ephriam Bilderbach, Jr.	L	1791	3/254					
Tigert	Francis			Isaac Kelley	L	1792	4/13	4/41	4/62			
Tilton		John		Richard Powers	L	1795	5/204					
Tilton			William	John Bisell	L	1796	5/151					
Tilton		John	et al	Beelor Adm'rs	L	1798	6/207					
Tibugin	Charles			James Powell et al	L	1799	6/376					
Tilton			Richard	John Relfe	L	1799	6/345	6/357	6/354			
Tibergin	Charles	Assignee of Philip Dodridge		Isaac Newland	L	1800	7/95					
Tibugin		Assignee of Phillip Boddridge	Isaac	Isaac Newland	L	1800	6/509					
Tilton			Richard	John Tilton	L	1800	7/14					
Tilton			Richard	George Beymer	L	1800	6/472					
Tilton		John		Daniel Brown et al	C	1802	8/271					
Tieran		Luke		Joseph Kerr	L	1805	10/19					
Tilton		John		Christopher Burr et al	L	1805	10/180					
Tilton		John		Gideon Forsyth	L	1806	10/318					
Tilton			William	Joseph Palmer et al	L	1806	10/311					
Tiernan		Luke	et al	John Lee	L	1807	11/152					
Tilton		John		Gideon C. Forsythe et al	L	1807	11/23					
Tilton		John		James Brown et al	L	1808	11/257					
Tiberghin	Charles			William Robinson et al	L	1813	14/26	14/133	14/199			
Tiberghin	Charles			George Stotts et al	L	1813	14/36	14/95				
Tilton		John		James Brown et al	C	1814	14/311					
Timmons	Amos	(Black Slave)		Elizabeth Wayts	L	1818	2/492					
TilYord		James		George White	L	1820	17/386					

PLAINTIFF INDEX TO ORDER BOOKS — Ohio County, W. Va.

SURNAME	GIVEN NAMES ABCDEFGH	GIVEN NAMES IJKLMNO	GIVEN NAMES PQRSTUVWXYZ	DEFENDANTS		YEAR	ORDER BOOK					
Tilden			Wm. et al	J. L. Skinner	L	1821	18 87	18 88				
Timmons	Henry			David Miller	L	1822	19 165	19 351				
Timmons		Jesse		Benjamin Kelly	L	1826	21 405					
Timmons		Jesse		Benjamin Kelly	L	1827	22 196	22 268	22 270			
Tiffany	Comfort &	Osmond C.	et al	John Sexton	L	1833	25 595					
Tilden			Thomas E.	Gregg & Edwards	L	1838	27 507	27 507	509			
Tilden			Thomas	Morgan H. Gregg	L	1838	28 16	28 52				
Tilden			Thomas E.	William Bishop	L	1839	28 132					
Tiffany	Henry			John Hull	L	1841	28 534					
Tiffany	Henry			James M. Wheat	L	1841	28 534					
Tiffany	Henry			Robert T. Kendall & Co.	L	1841	28 563					
Tilton	David			F. H. Cooly et al	L	1842	29 45					
Tiernan		Miles J.		Samuel F. Black	L	1858	36 273	36 321	36 322	36 325		
Tiffany	Henry	et al		Mason M. Dunlap	L	1861	38 435					
Tierney		Joseph		David F. Swartz	L	1874	L1 334					
Tifft	B. E.			Henry Helling	L	1874	L1 260	L1 263	L1 288	L1 351	L1 354	L1 360
Tiernan	Henry			Peter Wendel et al	L	1879	L4 209					

PLAINTIFF INDEX TO ORDER BOOKS — Ohio County, W. Va.

SURNAME	GIVEN NAMES ABCDEFGH	GIVEN NAMES IJKLMNO	GIVEN NAMES PQRSTUVWXYZ	DEFENDANTS		YEAR	ORDER BOOK			
Tingle	Ebinezer			George Henry	L	1804	9 / 271			
Tiernan		Michael	et al	Hezekiah Simms	D	1824	20 / 170			
Tittle		Lemuel		Joseph S. Graham	L	1833	25 / 403			
Tinson	Aaron			Allen Wallace	L	1834	26 / 49			
Tittle		Lemuel		Ebenezer Zane et al	L	1838	27 / 450	27 / 454		
Tittle		Lemuel		John Hamilton	L	1838	27 / 470			
Tittle		Lemuel		Robert Marshall	L	1838	27 / 470			
Tittle		Lemuel		John Moffitt	L	1838	27 / 515			
Tittle		Lemuel		Robert G. Martin	L	1838	27 / 515			
Tittle		Lemuel		Simon P. Hullihen	L	1838	27 / 516			
Tittle		Lemuel		Josiah H. Hawkins	L	1838	27 / 516			
Tittle	For use of William B. Trump & Co.		Samuel et al	Robert L.S. Martin et al	L	1838	28 / 7			
Tinges	George W.	et al		M. Wheat	L	1839	28 / 108	28 / 156	28 / 172	28 / 207
Tingle	George	et al		Robert Guy	L	1842	29 / 131			
Tingle	George T.	et al		Orloff A. Zane	L	1843	29 / 209			
Tingle	George	et al		John Gilchrist et al	L	1844	29 / 329			
Tingle	George T.	et al		James Tanner et al	L	1844	29 / 375			
Tingle	George T.			Elijah C. Jeffers	L	1855	34 / 289			
Tingle	George	et al		Josiah W. Chapline	L	1856	35 / 209			
Tipper			William	Joseph Lancaster	L	1858	37 / 77			
Tisdale		Mace		Albert Rice	L	1862	39 / 106	39 / 155		
Tingle	George R.			James Godfrey	L	1874	L1 / 381			
Tingle	George R.			John Scott	L	1876	L2 / 379			
Tingle	George R.	et al		William H. Sheib	L	1876	L3 / 89	L3 / 124	L3 / 166	L3 / 189
Tingle	George R.	et al		Moses Ray	L	1877	L3 / 161			
Tingle	George R.	et al		J. C. Alderson	L	1877	L3 / 245	L3 / 389	L3 / 433	
Tingle	George R.	et al		Samuel M. Clemens et al	C	1877	C1 / 269	C1 / 281	C1 / 299	
Tingle	George R. (Sheriff)			Daniel F. Zane	L	1879	L4 / 195	L4 / 223		

PLAINTIFF INDEX TO ORDER BOOKS — Ohio County, W. Va.

SURNAME	PLAINTIFFS GIVEN NAMES ABCDEFGH	GIVEN NAMES IJKLMNO	GIVEN NAMES PQRSTUVWXYZ	DEFENDANTS		YEAR	ORDER BOOK								
Thomas			William	Michel Steele	L	1788	3 61								
Therrill	George	et al		Jonathan Right	L	1802	8 80								
Thomas	Francis			Reuben Martin	L	1805	10 12	10 129							
Thursbey	Edward	et al		Jacob Whetzel	L	1806	10 255								
Thomas	Francis			Reuben Martin	L	1808	11 257								
Thomas	Ellis			George Gregg	L	1810	12 316								
Thomas	Ellis	et al		John Williamson et al	L	1810	12 285	12 500							
Thomas	Ellis	et al		Wm. Wells	L	1810	12 371	12 459							
Thumb			Tom	Jack Longfingers et al	L	1812	2 90	2 107	2 109						
Thumb			Tom	James Kerr	L	1813	2 109	2 152	2 219						
Thomas	Ellis	et al		Jos. Kerr	L	1814	14 231								
Thistle			Thomas	John P. Hider et al	L	1817	16 120	16 150							
Thomas	Henry			Richard Hutchison	L	1818	16 360	16 524	16 602						
Thatcher		Jonas		Henry Sockman	L	1820	17 380	18 115							
Thistle	Assignee of Wm. Baker		et al Sampson	George Baker, Sr. et al	L	1822	19 14	19 169							
Thomas			Thomas	Elijah Burris	L	1822	19 236	19 517							
Thornburg			Thomas	Mary Dye et al	L	1822	19 295								
Thatcher	Charles &	Jonas		John H. Irwin	L	1823	19 494								
Thistle			Sampson et al	Henry Sockman et al	L	1823	20 6	20 327							
Thornburgh			Thos. et al	John D. Seamon	L	1823	20 129								
Thatcher	Charles &	Jonas	et al	John H. Irwin	L	1824	20 158	20 236							
Thomas			Thomas	Elijah Burris	L	1824	20 111	20 122							
Thatcher		Jonas		Wm. Cunningham	L	1830	24 18								
Thatcher		Jonas		Robert F. Ford et al	L	1833	25 302								
Thayer			et al Zipheon	John Parriott	L	1835	26 498	26 538							
Thomas	Asaeel			John Yearby	L	1837	27 271								
Tharp	Daniel V.			John Harvey	L	1840	28 364								
Thistle	Benjaman T.			David Agnew	L	1840	28 357								
Thornburg			Thomas	James McKean	L	1840	28 262								
Thornburg			Thomas	Redick McKee	L	1840	28 431	28 512							
Thomas	Henry E.	et al		James H. Robinson	L	1854	33 180	33 221	33 222	33 258	33 230	33 232	33 395	33 431	33 479
Thomas		Jacob C.	et al	Michael Sweeney et al	L	1855	34 146								
Thomas		Jacob C.	et al	John Wayt	L	1855	34 148								
Thomas		Jacob C.	et al	D. W. C. McKinley et al	L	1856	35 124								
Thomas		Jacob C.	et al	William Gregg et al	L	1856	35 142								

PLAINTIFF INDEX TO ORDER BOOKS — Ohio County, W. Va.

SURNAME	GIVEN NAMES ABCDEFGH	GIVEN NAMES IJKLMNO	GIVEN NAMES PQRSTUVWXYZ	DEFENDANTS		YEAR	ORDER BOOK								
Thomas			et al Washington	Edward W. Edwards et al	L	1856	35 295								
Thornburgh	H. S.			Lewis Walter	L	1856	35 249	35 272	35 325						
Thibalett	Francis	et al		John Bishop	L	1857	36 118	36 127	36 177	36 317					
Thieriot	Ferdinand			John Bishop	L	1858	36 334								
Thomas		Jacob C.		Andrew Mitchell	L	1858	36 389								
Thomas			William Beazon	Wm. Irwin	L	1858	37 76								
Thomas		Jacob	et al	John Jones	L	1859	37 294	37 479							
Thomas		Jacob	et al	Absalom Ridgly	L	1859	37 343	37 359							
Thomas	Daniel &	John & John M.	et al	James M. Todd et al	L	1859	37 296								
Tharp	Daniel V.			H. Q. Loomis	L	1860	38 188	38 212	38 235	38 281	38 341	38 364	38 374	38 385	38 402	38 418
do	do			do	L	1860	38 424	38 445	38 465	38 488	38 500	38 530	38 541			
Tharp	Daniel V.			Robert Guy	L	1861	38 500								
Thomas		Jacob C.		Andrew F. Ross et al	L	1862	39 30								
Thomas		Jacob C.		Andrew F. Ross	L	1862	39 30								
Thornburg	Harriet			Lydia L. Cruger	L	1862	39 48								
Thornburgh	Daniel S.	et al		W. C. Thornburgh	L	1873	L1 220								
Thornburgh	David M.			Alexander M. Jacob	L	1873	L1 164								
Thomas		Jacob C.		William H. Chapman et al	L	1873	L1 82								
Thomas		Jacob C.		John Nolan	L	1874	L1 516								
Thornburgh	Daniel S.	et al		H. S. Thornburgh	L	1874	L1 258								
Thornburgh	Daniel S.	et al		James Padgett	L	1874	L1 258								
Thornburgh	Daniel S.	et al		William Alton	L	1874	L1 259								
Thornburgh	Daniel S.	et al		Andrew Vance	L	1874	L1 259								
Thornburgh	D. S.			Mary & W. Beitzer	L	1874	L1 268								
Thornburgh	H. S. & E.			Jane Schneider	L	1877	L3 301	L3 331							
Thornburg		John M.		Patrick Kennedy	L	1877	L3 331								
Thornburg		John		W. J. W. Cowden	L	1877	L3 332								
Thalman	Andrew			Thomas Tag	L	1878	L3 454	L4 214							
Thallmane		Joseph		Adolph Botts et al	L	1878	L4 75	L4 126	L4 127	L4 128					
Thorburg		John	et al	Jane Schneider et al	C	1878	C1 333	C1 334	C1 337						
Thorburg		John	et al	H. S. Thorburg et al	C	1878	L3 468								
Thornton			W. H.	Enoch Hughes	L	1879	L4 338	L4 387	L4 428						
Thornburgh	H.		S. et al	John Thornburgh	L	1873	L1 31	L1 34	L1 35	L1 36	L1 38				

PLAINTIFF INDEX TO ORDER BOOKS — Ohio County, W. Va.

SURNAME	GIVEN NAMES A-H	GIVEN NAMES I-O	GIVEN NAMES P-Z	DEFENDANTS		YEAR	ORDER BOOK							
Tobin		Josiah		George Beelor et al	L	1804	9/216							
Todd			Samuel	Harmon Greathouse	L	1811	13/62							
Todd			Samuel	John Fosbinder	L	1816	15/311	15/327	16/599					
Todd			William	John Smith	L	1819	16/576							
Todd			Wm. et al	John Smith et al	L	1819	17/85	17/122						
Toland			William	Nancy Burt	L	1820	17/435							
Todd			William	Hugh Dixon	L	1821	18/73							
Todd			Wm. et al	Jas. McCoy et al	L	1821	18/75	18/194	18/258	18/449				
Toland			William	James Morgan	L	1823	19/331	20/156						
Todd		Martin L.		Susan Parrott	L	1832	25/186							
Todd	Assignee of Alexander Rogers et al	Martin L.		Robert T. Ford et al	L	1833	25/338	25/410						
Todd		Martin L.	et al	John A. Roe	L	1834	26/203							
Todd	Archibald S.			Joseph Moore	L	1836	27/134	27/551						
Todd	Archibald L.			Alexander Shellcross	L	1837	27/237							
Todd			William F.	James Dare	L	1841	28/536							
Todd	A. S.			James Caldwell et al	L	1842	29/193							
Todd	Archibald S.			James Tanner	L	1843	29/515							
Todd			Wm. et al	Thomas Myers	L	1847	30/249							
Todd		James M.		Sherrard Clemens	L	1852	32/203							
Todd			Thomas	Jesse Wheat	L	1852	32/204							
Todd			Thomas	John Bowers	L	1852	32/300	32/394						
Tolford	D. W.			Francis B. Hornbrooks etal	L	1853	33/22	33/76	33/109	33/125				
Tolford	D. W.			Rachel Hornbrook	L	1853	32/457							
Todd			Thomas	John Bowers	L	1853	33/50							
Todd			Thomas	Edward Coulter	L	1853	32/390							
Todd		James C.		Jacob Hull et al	L	1854	33/159	33/337						
Todd		James M.	et al	Sherrard Clemens et al	L	1855	34/132							
Todd		James M.	et al	Daniel Dean	L	1855	34/286							
Todd		James M.	et al	Benjamin S. Gregg	L	1855	34/287							
Todd		James C.		Paul Cook	L	1855	34/329							
Todd	A. S.			George K. Zinn	L	1856	35/105							
Todd	A. S.			Elizabeth Green	L	1857	36/55	36/74	36/94	36/130	36/156	36/193	36/206	36/222
Todd	A. S.			Elizabeth Green	L	1857	35/393	35/410	35/435	35/441	35/469	35/507		
Todd		James C.		Lucius O. Ackley	L	1857	35/479							
Todd		James M.		Pollard McCormick	L	1858	36/340							

PLAINTIFF INDEX TO ORDER BOOKS — Ohio County, W. Va.

PLAINTIFFS				DEFENDANTS		YEAR	ORDER BOOK	
SURNAME	GIVEN NAMES ABCDEFGH	GIVEN NAMES IJKLMNO	GIVEN NAMES PQRSTUVWXYZ					
Todd		James M.	et al	Thomas Painter	L	1858	36 396	38 197
Todd		James M.	et al	William H. Russell	L	1858	36 396	
Todd		James M.		S. H. Glenn	L	1874	12 6	
Todd	A. S. Dr.		et al	John Roemer	L	1875	12 313	
Tolen			Thomas	Isaac Snedeker et al	L	1877	13 133	

PLAINTIFF INDEX TO ORDER BOOKS — Ohio County, W. Va.

SURNAME	GIVEN NAMES ABCDEFGH	GIVEN NAMES IJKLMNO	GIVEN NAMES PQRSTUVWXYZ	DEFENDANTS		YEAR	ORDER BOOK							
Tonihill	Adamson	et al		John Hambleton	L	1792	4/24	4/69	4/98	4/141	4/168	4/169	4/196	4/208
Tovrill	Joseph			John McDonald	L	1799	6/336	6/362						
Tompson			Thomas	John Mills	L	1812	13/287	13/420						
Towson	Jacob T.			Thomas Conally	L	1812	13/145							
Tonner			Thos. et al	Alexander McClain	L	1814	14/318							
Toullerton		Matthew		Caleb Reeves et al	L	1814	2/227							
Tonner			Thomas	Solomon Wardle	L	1816	15/178							
Tonner			Thomas	Israel Updegraff et al	L	1816	2/360	2/362	2/403	2/453	2/488			
Tonner			Thomas	Joseph Clingan	L	1820	17/374							
Tonner			Thomas	Peter Wolf et al	L	1821	18/37							
Tonner			Thomas	Joseph Clingan	L	1821	18/104	18/294						
Tonner			Thomas	David Moore	L	1821	18/131							
Towers	George			John Allen	L	1825	21/138							
Tonner			Thomas	James Relfe et al	C	1826	21/327	21/407						
Townsend		Jeremiah		Moses Shepherd	L	1826	21/486							
Towsey		Joseph		Bernard Wiedman	L	1828	23/67	23/144	23/313					
Tonner			Thomas	John Hendricks	L	1829	23/401							
Town	David A.			Elias Scribner	L	1834	26/72							
Tonge			et al Samuel D.	Philip Fisher	L	1837	27/298							
Tompkins		John H.		John L. Newby	L	1838	28/21							
Tonge			et al Samuel D.	Henry Echols	L	1838	5							
Tonge			Samuel D.	Ebenezer Zane	L	1838	27/458							
Tonge			Samuel D.	John Sexton	L	1838	27/459							
Tonge			Samuel D.	Robert C. Martin	L	1838	27/459	27/522						
Tonge			et al Samuel D.	John Moffit	L	1838	27/468							
Tonge			Samuel D.	Henry Echols	L	1838	27/512							
Townsend	Assignee of John W. Weaver		Thomas	Levi H. Rose	L	1839	28/68							
Townsend			Thomas	James A. McClean	L	1839	28/127							
Townsend	Abel W.			Henry C. Wickham	L	1840	28/249							
Townsend			Thomas	George Swearingen	L	1840	28/308							
Tonge			Samuel D.	Joseph Junkin	L	1841	28/339							
Townsend			Thomas	William C. Piper	L	1841	28/495							
Tonner			Thomas	Wm. Cunningham	L	1842	29/64	29/103	29/134	29/169	29/203			
Toulman	Charles			Johnston & Glassford	L	1851	31/580							
Townsend			et al Solomon	Louis Kells		1854	33/410							

PLAINTIFF INDEX TO ORDER BOOKS — Ohio County, W. Va.

SURNAME	PLAINTIFFS GIVEN NAMES ABCDEFGH	GIVEN NAMES IJKLMNO	GIVEN NAMES PQRSTUVWXYZ	DEFENDANTS		YEAR	ORDER BOOK						
Towles			Wm. P. et al	Morgan H. Gregg	L	1855	34 150						
Torreyson			Wm. D.	William E. Russell et al	L	1857	35 488	35 491					
Towell		James F.		Thomas W. Gillis	L	1861	38 480						
Towers	E. W.			John D. M. Carr	L	1862	39 159						
Tonini		Joseph		George Roberts et al	L	1873	L1 68	L1 262	L1 321	L2 10	L2 109	L2 138	L2 263	L2 362
Tonner			William	Henry Hellebrand	L	1877	L3 332						
Toppe	Charles			Louis Hahne	L	1877	L3 398						
Tonini		Joseph		Pryor Boyd & Co.	L	1878	L4 29	L4 55	L4 87	L4 88	L4 93	L4 95		
Topp	Christiana J. & Adm'r Carle Earnest Dec'd.			Peter Wendel	L	1879	L4 308						

PLAINTIFF INDEX TO ORDER BOOKS — Ohio County, W. Va.

SURNAME	GIVEN NAMES ABCDEFGH	GIVEN NAMES IJKLMNO	GIVEN NAMES PQRSTUVWXYZ	DEFENDANTS		YEAR	ORDER BOOK									
Trimble		John		David Warley	L	1787	3/30	3/59								
Tremble		Mathew		Robert Jones	C	1826	21/364									
Trestler		Jacob		John Gasmier	L	1829	23/169									
Treesdale	Calvin	et al		James B. Sinclair	L	1831	24/462									
Trever		John B.	et al	James M. Thompson	C	1835	26/490	26/554								
Trissell		John		John Sexton	L	1839	28/115	28/174								
Trewartha		William		Samuel Hamilton	L	1843	29/284									
Trimble		William		Smith & Forlees	L	1843	29/335									
Trimble		Walter et al		William Brown	L	1851	31/432									
Trail	Edward H.			Ira Ransam	L	1852	32/317	32/348	32/366	32/394	32/442	32/461	32/477			
do	do			do	L	1853	33/27	33/45	33/76	33/109	33/130	33/158	33/199			
Tryon	Francis & Edmund		et al	Morgan H. Gregg et al	L	1854	33/483	33/484	34/149							
Triplett		Isabel		Francis Freeman	L	1856	35/69	35/94	35/109	35/177	35/272	35/248	35/321	35/385	35/406	35/436	35/448
Tracy	Erastus			Thomas Parker	L	1858	37/84									
Tripler		Thos. etal		Frederick Yahrling et al	L	1858	37/11	36/326								
Tripler		Thomas C.		James Tanner	L	1858	36/343									
Trimble		Samuel		M. M. Sanders	L	1859	37/300									
Trissler		Susan		John Russell	L	1860	38/281	38/341	38/374	38/402	38/418	38/430	38/445	38/465	38/489	38/494
Trissler		do		do	L	1860	38/506	38/541	38/385							
Trisler		Susan		John Russell	L	1862	39/2	39/50	39/55	39/66	39/81	39/111	39/122	39/136	39/149	39/155
Trisler		do		do	L	1862	39/175	39/180	39/186							
Tracey	Elizabeth M.			Stephen P. Tracey	L	1874	11/390									
Tracey		James		F. A. Brentlinger et al	L	1874	11/468									
Tracey		James		F. A. Brentlinger et al	L	1875	12/18									
Tracey		M. F.		George Grumbacker	L	1875	12/131	12/142								
Tracy			M. F.	James McCannon	L	1876	13/5									
Tracy		M. F.		S. J. Ellifritz	L	1877	13/134									

PLAINTIFF INDEX TO ORDER BOOKS — Ohio County, W. Va.

SURNAME	GIVEN NAMES ABCDEFGH	GIVEN NAMES IJKLMNO	GIVEN NAMES PQRSTUVWXYZ	DEFENDANTS		YEAR	ORDER BOOK							
Troy			Rosanna	Thomas Stanford	L	1808	11 420	11 480						
Troxwell	Frederick	et al		Martin Coons	C	1815	14 446							
Truxel		John & Jacob		Hugh Nichols	L	1827	22 83	22 90						
Truax		John F.	et al	Alexander Mager	L	1831	24 323							
Trussell	Charles			Joseph Alexander	L	1831	24 313							
Truax		John F.	et al	Henry & John Hupp	L	1832	25 260							
Truesdell	Calvin	Assignee of	Francis & David, Jr.	James B. Sinclair	L	1832	25 68							
Truax		John F.	et al	James Adams	L	1833	25 333							
Truax		John F.	et al	Samuel Knode	L	1833	25 339							
Truax		John F.	et al	John Sexton	L	1833	25 343	25 395						
Truax		John F.	et al	William Gregg	L	1833	25 388							
Truax		John F.	et al	John W. Berry	L	1833	25 396							
Truax		John F.	et al	James Adams et al	L	1834	26 5							
Truax	Hamilton &	John F.	et al	Daniel Murray	L	1835	26 444	26 515						
Truly			Simon	George Applegarth	L	1839	28 66	28 113	28 114	28 154	28 195	28 261	28 324	28 360
Truxell	Catherine	& Mary		Abraham Allman	L	1842	29 209	29 211	29 214					
Truitt	Charles B. &		Robert W. D.	Michael Sweeney et al	L	1855	34 147							
Troll			et al Valentine	Januar Fisher	L	1857	36 126	36 134	36 136					
Trull			William E.	William H. Stello	L	1873	L1 146							
Truxell		John C.		David Kull	L	1875	L2 309	L2 310	L2 318					
Truax		Nicholas		Jacob F. Luikert	L	1876	L2 425							
Truxell		John C.		Daniel W. Berry	L	1877	13 187	13 212	13 274	13 337	13 364	13 455		
Truschell		John P.		Isaac Freese	L	1873	L 1 205							

PLAINTIFF INDEX TO ORDER BOOKS --- Ohio County, W. Va.

SURNAME	PLAINTIFFS GIVEN NAMES ABCDEFGH	GIVEN NAMES IJKLMNO	GIVEN NAMES PQRSTUVWXYZ	DEFENDANTS	L	YEAR	ORDER BOOK								
Tumlinson		Joseph		Samuel Mason	L	1778	1 / 28	1 / 30							
Tupper	Edward W. Assignee of Michael Barker et al			James Potts	L	1793	4 / 240								
Tucker		James		John Fitton	L	1799	6 / 311								
Tucker			Wm. et al	Henry Smith	L	1801	7 / 220								
Turner	George	et al		George McColloch et al	L	1811	13 / 26	13 / 115							
Turner	George &	Mary		Samuel Anderson	L	1811	13 / 77	13 / 78							
Turner	George			George McColloch	L	1811	12 / 486								
Turner		John		Joseph S. Parrott	L	1829	23 / 237	23 / 317							
Turner		Joseph	et al	Ebenezer Zane	L	1834	26 / 203	26 / 261							
Turnbull		James		William Hayden	L	1838	27 / 485								
Tucker	Douglass A. & Jackson			James E. Wharton	L	1839	28 / 198	28 / 225							
Turnbull		James	et al	James E. Wharton	L	1841	28 / 535								
Turner	George			William Cunningham	L	1841	28 / 547								
Turner		Joseph		John Brotherton	L	1845	30 / 10								
Turpin		John		Franz Hegner	L	1855	34 / 227	34 / 235							
Turton		James		City of Wheeling	L	1855	34 / 202	34 / 309							
Turner			William A.	Robert C. Bonham et al	L	1857	35 / 486								
Turton		James		City of Wheeling	L	1857	36 / 67	36 / 87	36 / 81	36 / 155	36 / 209	36 / 231	36 / 271	36 / 292	36 / 357
Turton		James		City of Wheeling	L	1857	35 / 508								
Turton		James		City of Wheeling	L	1858	37 / 9	37 / 10							
Tucker	Charles	et al		Allen Hollowell	L	1859	37 / 275								
Turner			William	Exly & Bigerton	L	1859	37 / 196								
Turner			Samuel R.	Asa D. Johnston	L	1860	38 / 147	38 / 278							
Turton			Thomas	Thomas M. Parker	L	1860	38 / 108								
Turner	Alexander			J. W. Farrier & Co.	L	1862	39 / 6								
Turnipseed		John L.		Ephraim Trimble	L	1873	11 / 87								
Tuttle		Jesse		J. B. Ford	L	1874	11 / 388								
Tubby		J. T.		Michael W. Jordan	L	1875	12 / 342								

PLAINTIFF INDEX TO ORDER BOOKS — Ohio County, W. Va.

SURNAME	GIVEN NAMES ABCDEFGH	GIVEN NAMES IJKLMNO	GIVEN NAMES PQRSTUVWXYZ	DEFENDANTS		YEAR	ORDER BOOK					
Tygart		Michael		John McDonald	L	1784	1/188					
Tyler		James		John Good et al	L	1826	21/426					
Tyson			William B.	Alfred Harkins	L	1834	26/803					
Tyson			William B.	James Green	L	1837	27/344					
Tyson			Wm. et al	Enos W. Newton et al	L	1837	27/355	27/366				
Tweedie	David			William Lebaren	L	1838	28/17					
Tyson			William B.	Josiah W. Pomeroy	L	1838	27/403					
Tyson			William B.	James McConnell	L	1838	27/410					
Tyson			William B.	George W. Johnston	L	1840	28/366					
Tyson	Use of Hamilton Smith	Joseph W.		Alonzo Loring	L	1841	28/494	28/550				
Tydings		Louis L.	et al	John R. Howlett	L	1848	30/395	30/425				
Tydings		Lewis	et al	Mason M. Dunlap	L	1849	31/62					
Twinam		Leonard		Moses Ford	L	1850	31/246					
Tweehe		James		City of Wheeling	L	1852	32/329	32/349	32/365	32/421	32/434	32/462
Tywell			et al Robert S	Edward L. Pratt et al	L	1855	35/26	35/73				
Tyler			W. S.	Hanna & Clemens	L	1878	L4/82					

PLAINTIFF INDEX TO ORDER BOOKS — Ohio County, W. Va.

SURNAME	GIVEN NAMES ABCDEFGH	GIVEN NAMES IJKLMNO	GIVEN NAMES PQRSTUVWXYZ	DEFENDANTS		YEAR	ORDER BOOK				
Urie			Thomas, Sr.	James Marshall	L	1780	1 / 91				
Underwood			Samuel	Joseph Eastwood, et al	C	1803	9 / 161	9 / 175	9 / 303		
Underwood			Samuel	Joseph Estnood, et al	C	1805	10 / 27	10 / 253	10 / 258	10 / 256	10 / 266
Underwood			Samuel	Joseph Eastwood	C	1807	11 / 46				
Underwood		Joseph		George Cragg	L	1809	12 / 115				
Upp	Frances			Fredk. Beymer	L	1809	12 / 126				
Upp	Francis, et al			Frederick Beymer	L	1811	13 / 104	13 / 295			
Underwood			Samuel	Abner Martin	L	1814	14 / 311				
Underwood			Thomas	Charles Wells, et al	L	1814	2 / 164				
Uchtolf	Henry			J. C. Crowl	L	1838	27 / 481				
Uchtolf	Henry			J. C. Crowl	L	1838	27 / 551				
Uchtorf	Henry			J. W. Crawle	L	1839	28 / 35				
Umstadt			Richard S.	Hildebrand Charles	L	1856	35 / 137				
Uselton			Samuel	John Wolf	L	1856	35 / 24				
Unmussig		Joseph		Wm. Zane	L	1859	37 / 454				
Unmussig		Joseph		William Zane	L	1860	38 / 124	38 / 187	38 / 213	38 / 358	
Uhl	Charles		P. et al	Carrol & Burns	L	1861	38 / 516				
Uselton	George			Patrick Mahoney		1880	L / 486				

'V' SURNAMES - PLAINTIFFS

PLAINTIFF INDEX TO ORDER BOOKS — Ohio County, W. Va.

SURNAME	GIVEN NAMES A-H	GIVEN NAMES I-O	GIVEN NAMES P-Z	DEFENDANTS		YEAR	ORDER BOOK							
Valiley	Daniel			John Arnold	L	1816	2/342							
Vause(Vance) Adm'rs.			William, etal		L	1821	18/287							
Vause(Vance)	(Adm'r. of John McColloch, Dec'd)		Wm. et al	David Church	L	1821	18/405							
Vause(Vance)	(Adm'r. of John McColloch		William, et al	Garrison Jones	L	1821	18/280							
Vause(Adm'r.	John McCulloch,Dec'd)		Wm. et al	James McCord	C	1821	18/359							
Vause("	" "	" "	" ") Wm. et al	Samuel Saylor	L	1821	18/213	18/300						
Vause(Vanse)	" "	" "	William,etal	Dana Hubbard	L	1823	19/430							
Vause(Vance)	" "	" "	Wm. et al	Josiah McColloch, et al	C	1823	19/451							
Vause(Vanse)	" "	" "	Wm. et al	Wm. Young	C	1823	19/452							
Vause(Vanse)			William,etal	Joseph Willson	L	1824	20/237							
Valentine	C.			John Milligan	C	1826	21/463							
Vactor	Boston,etal			Griffith P. Edwards	L	1835	26/459	26/520						
Varney	Aaron,et al			Isaac Davis	L	1842	29/60	29/104						
Vail		John C.		John Goshorn	L	1846	30/142							
Vassal			William	John W. Glasscock	L	1846	30/142							
Vassall			William	John H. Armstrong	L	1847	30/294							
Varney	Edward,et al			Solon Austin	L	1854	33/488							
Varney	George			Solon Austin	L	1854	33/316							
Varney	Edwin			Solon Austin	L	1855	34/88							
Varney	Edwin			Knoke & Haman	L	1855	34/235							
Vail		I. C. etal		Joseph Abbott	L	1856	35/266							
Varney	George	M.		Jacob T. Smith	L	1857	35/507							
Varney	George	M.		Jacob J. Smith	L	1857	36/17							
Varney	Edwin			John Hazletts Committee	L	1858	36/177	36/309	36/363					
Varney	Edwin			John Hazlett	L	1858	37/55	37/129	37/149					
Vaas	Fred(Adm.)			James Hamilton	L	1877	L 3/152	L 3/252						
Vass	Fannie			William Taggart	L	1879	L 4/372	L 4/401						
Vaughan	George,et al			Franklin Insurance Co.	L	1879	L 4/396	L 4/413						
Vaughan	George,et al			Fire & Marine Insurance Co.	L	1880	L 4/414	L 4/396						

PLAINTIFF INDEX TO ORDER BOOKS — Ohio County, W. Va.

SURNAME	GIVEN NAMES ABCDEFGH	GIVEN NAMES IJKLMNO	GIVEN NAMES PQRSTUVWXYZ	DEFENDANTS		YEAR	ORDER BOOK							
Van Buskirk		Lawrence		Resin Pumfrey	L	1785	1/291							
Van Buskirk				Pumfry	L	1786	3/1							
Van Buskirk		Lawrence		John Jones	L	1787	3/30							
Van Buskirk			Thomas, etal	Robert Harrison	L	1787	3/44							
Van Buskirk		Lawrence		William Harrison	L	1788	3/58	3/82	3/106					
Van Buskirk		Lawrence		Thomas Roberts	L	1788	3/66							
Van Buskirk		Lawrence		Robert Moore	L	1789	3/113							
Van Buskirk		Lawrence		David Bradford	L	1790	3/211	3/249						
Van Buskirk		Lawrence		Michel Huff	L	1790	3/224							
Van Buskirk		Lawrence, Assignee of John Vanosdle		Benjamin Miller	L	1791	3/245							
Van Buskirk		Lawrence		Presley Peake	L	1791	3/238	3/245						
Van Buskirk		Lawrence		James Harrison	L	1792	3/305	3/285	3/335					

'V' SURNAMES - PLAINTIFFS

PLAINTIFF INDEX TO ORDER BOOKS — Ohio County, W.Va.

SURNAME	GIVEN NAMES ABCDEFGH	GIVEN NAMES IJKLMNO	GIVEN NAMES PQRSTUVWXYZ	DEFENDANTS		YEAR	ORDER BOOK		
Vanaman	George			Thomas Dickson	L	1788	3 / 53		
Vanmeter	Henry, etal			John Grayham	L	1789	3 / 132		
Vanosdle		John, etal		Benjamin Miller	L	1791	3 / 245		
Vanlear		Matthew, et al		Samuel Simms	L	1792	4 / 49		
Vanmetre		Morgan		George Humphreys	L	1793	4 / 92	4 / 141	4 / 169
Vanmetre		Morgan		Archibald Woods	L	1793	4 / 125		
Vanmetre		John		John Callaway	L	1794	4 / 219	4 / 234	
Vanmeatre		Morgan		John Nichols	L	1795	4 / 422		
Vanosdal		John		William Bonor	L	1795	4 / 407		
Vanmeater		Isaac, etal, Assgnee of John Bukey		Silas Hedges	L	1798	6 / 78		
Vanlear		Matthew		Claburn Simms	L	1802	8 / 171	8 / 204	8 / 312
Vanseyoc	Able			Wm. Dement, et al	L	1802	8 / 205	8 / 328	8 / 329
Vance	David, etal			Absolom Martin, Dec'd, et al	C	1803	9 / 115	9 / 122	9 / 154
Vanmetre		Isaac, for use of Robert Woods		John Nichols	L	1803	9 / 78	9 / 86	
Vansyock	Abel, et al			Jacob Durrant	C	1807	11 / 160	11 / 417	
Van Scyoc	Abel			Thomas Evans, et al	L	1808	11 / 422		
Van Scyoc	Abel			Thomas Evans, et al	L	1809	12 / 72		
Van Scyoc	Able, etal			Jacob Durant	C	1810	12 / 209		
Vanseyoc, et al				Thos. Evans, et al	C	1812	13 / 350		
Vanmeter		John		Rebeckah Nichols, et al	C	1814	14 / 424	14 / 471	
Vanmeter		Joseph		Andrew Craig	L	1814	14 / 409		
Vanmeter		Joseph		Ninian Beall	L	1815	14 / 480		
Vanmeter		Joseph		Ninian Beall	L	1815	15 / 32		
Vanmeter		Joseph		Robert Stewart	L	1816	2 / 350	2 / 374	
Vanmeter		Joseph		William Bently	L	1817	2 / 394		
Vanata			Samuel	James Burns, et al	L	1818	16 / 426	16 / 520	
Vance		James		William Pritchard	L	1819	16 / 616		
Vanmeter	Abraham			Robert Brown	L	1820	17 / 268	17 / 509	
Vance		John		Samuel Saylor	L	1821	18 / 427		
Vanse			et al Wm. Admrs.	Wm. Laughridge	L	1822	19 / 98		
Vanse (Vause)			et al Wm. Admrs.	George White	L	1822	19 / 110		
Vanse (Vause)	Adm. of Wm. McColloch, (Dec'd)		William, etal	Joseph Wilson, et al	L	1822	19 / 276		
Vanse (Vause)	" " " " "		William, etal	George McColloch	L	1823	19 / 417		
Vanse (Vause)			William, etal	Josiah McCollock, et al	C	1823	20 / 47	20 / 124	20 / 242
Vanse			William, etal	Wm. Young	C	1823	20 / 47	20 / 123	20 / 242

PLAINTIFF INDEX TO ORDER BOOKS — Ohio County, W. Va.

BURNAME	GIVEN NAMES A-H	GIVEN NAMES I-O	GIVEN NAMES P-Z	DEFENDANTS	L/C	YEAR	ORDER BOOK			
Vanmeter			William	John McCortney	L	1825	21 / 215	21 / 330		
Vandivender	C. et al			John Milligan	C	1827	22 / 288			
Vansyock	Aren			John Parrott, et al	L	1827	22 / 265			
Vanscyoc	Abel			Randolph Moore	L	1828	22 / 407			
Vansyock	Abel			Randolph Moore	L	1829	23 / 156	23 / 247	23 / 398	23 / 406
Vanmetre		Isaac, use of William Harris		Joseph Conner	L	1830	24 / 127			
Vansyock	Abel			Randolph Moore	L	1830	24 / 108	24 / 103		
Vanscoye		Lorenzo		James McDonald	L	1831	24 / 464			
Vanscyoc		Lorenzo, use of Simon Purdy		Ann McDonald, et al	L	1832	25 / 72			
Van Bonherst	Charles, et al			Samuel D. Harper	L	1833	25 / 333			
Vancyoc			William	William Minnix, et al	L	1833	25 / 483			
Vane		Assignee of Joseph C.(Dec'd) et al		Joshua Hunter, et al	L	1836	29 / 10			
Vance		James, etal		James McKean	L	1840	28 / 366			
Vanata			Thomas	Robert Sprowl	L	1846	30 / 58			
Van Sihn	B.			Jacob Butt	L	1850	31 / 248			
Vance		James, etal		Francis Lawson, et al	L	1851	32 / 25			
Vance		James N.		John Ferrell	L	1853	32 / 492			
Vanderpool	Frederick		S. et al	James Smylie	L	1855	34 / 286			
Vanmeter		(Adm'r)	Vincent H. et al	Hezekiah Foley	L	1856	35 / 212			
Vance		James		John Ferrell	L	1857	35 / 363			
Vance		James N.		James McConnell, et al	L	1857	36 / 29	36 / 100		
Vancurlen			et al Samuel W.	James W. Warden, et al	L	1860	38 / 296			
Vandyke	Augustus C. et al			Aaron Kelly, et al	L	1860	38 / 133			
Vance		J. N.		J. Wheeler	L	1861	38 / 420			
Vance		James N.		John Flood	L	1862	39 / 163			
Vance		James		Hiram Ray	L	1862	39 / 170	39 / 173		
Vanmeter			et al Vincent,	Daniel S. Forney	L	1862	39 / 102			
Vance	Andrew			Wheeling Pittsburgh & B. R. R. Co.	L	1876	L3 / 93	L3 / 371		
Vance	Andrew			A. H. Patterson	L	1878	L3 / 496	L3 / 512	L3 / 513	L3 / 514
Vanmetre			V. H.	John E. Wayt, et al	L	1879	L4 / 243			

PLAINTIFF INDEX TO ORDER BOOKS — Ohio County, W. Va.

SURNAME	PLAINTIFFS GIVEN NAMES ABCDEFGH	GIVEN NAMES IJKLMNO	GIVEN NAMES PQRSTUVWXYZ	DEFENDANTS		YEAR	ORDER BOOK					
Virgin			Rizon	Thomas Nichols	L	1776	1 22					
Vemmon	George			John Chapman	L	1805	10 59					
Vennum	George			Mark Douglass	L	1821	18 71	18 244	18 272			
Virtue			Samuel	Joseph Caldwell	C	1821	18 151					
Virtue			Samuel	Thomas Cordall, et al	L	1822	19 137					
Vennum	George			Wm. Clark	L	1825	21 231					
Vennium	George			Samuel Sprigg	L	1825	21 243					
Vennum	George			Henry Kirkpatrick	L	1829	23 103					
Vennum	George			Robert F. Digg	L	1830	24 171					
Veers	Asahel			Moses Ford	L	1833	25 344	25 411				
Venus			Samuel, etal Assgnee	Samuel P. Jones	L	1835	26 443					
Victor	D., et al			Ephraim Dagg	L	1836	27 120	27 198				
Vennum	Abigail			Lloyd Wright	L	1839	28 159					
Vees			Vincent	City of Wheeling	L	1853	32 439					
Vermilion, et al				Hughes	L	1854	33 148					
Vincent		J. A.		William Curry	L	1857	35 406					
Vincent		John A.		Joseph M. Stuart, et al	L	1857	36 29					
Veiwig	C.			Wm. Hughey	L	1858	36 361	36 380				
Vincent		John, Assgnee. of		A. A. Allison	L	1859	37 134					
Vincent		John, Assgnee. of		R. G. Gordan Co.	L	1859	37 134					
Vincent		John, Assgnee. of		James H. Roberts	L	1859	37 134					
Vincent		John A.		Pumphrey & Hull	L	1860	38 126					
Vincent		John A.		Dunlap, Atkinson & Co.	L	1862	39 137	39 111	39 163	39 202		
Vick			William	William H. Fleming	L	1873	L1 83	L1 127	L1 331	L1 338		
Vick			William	W. H. Fleming, et al	L	1874	L2 28					
Vick			William	William T. Chambers	L	1875	L2 255	L2 259	L2 277	L2 360	L2 416	L2 479
Vick			William	Isaac Linton	L	1875	L2 255	L2 260	L2 277	L2 360	L2 416	L2 479
Viewig	C.			G. G. Murdock	L	1878	L4 39					

PLAINTIFF INDEX TO ORDER BOOKS — Ohio County, W. Va.

SURNAME	GIVEN NAMES ABCDEFGH	GIVEN NAMES IJKLMNO	GIVEN NAMES PQRSTUVWXYZ	DEFENDANTS		YEAR	ORDER BOOK					
Vowel		John, et al		George Quinn	L	1809	12 119	12 148	12 196			
Voty	Charles	L. et al		Samuel D. Harper	L	1833	25 333					
Voorhees	Abraham	L.		Henry Helm	L	1840	28 357	28 437				
Vogleman		Jacob		J. L. Hargrave	L	1856	35 272	35 327	35 388	35 409	35 431	
Vollmer	Henry, etal			John Elliott	L	1856	35 19					
Von Kapff	Herman			William H. Russell, et al	L	1857	35 463					
Vockler		John		Moses Ford	L	1859	37 262					
Vockler		John		Wm. Saunders	L	1860	37 479					
Vogelsahne		Mena, et al		Louis Hahne	L	1877	L 3 262					
Voltz		Mrs. B.	V.	George Fritsch	L	1877	L 3 317	L 3 318	L 3 326	L 3 368		
Voltz	Bridget		V.	J. L. Hawley	L	1879	L 4 214	L 4 318				

PLAINTIFF INDEX TO ORDER BOOKS — Ohio County, W. Va.

SURNAME	GIVEN NAMES ABCDEFGH	GIVEN NAMES IJKLMNO	GIVEN NAMES PQRSTUVWXYZ	DEFENDANTS		YEAR	ORDER BOOK				
Walker			Robt.	Jno. Hanly	L	1778	1/20				
Walker		John		Jeremiah Williamson	L	1788	3/66				
Walker	Andrew, etal			Wm. Donnoldson	L	1797	5/221				
Walker	Andrew			Samuel Harris	L	1799	6/377	6/396			
Walker	Alexander			Thomas Mills	L	1800	6/516				
Walker	Andrew			James Satter	L	1800	6/495				
Walker	Daniel, etal			Ralph Smith	L	1800	7/171				
Walker		John, etal		Robert Beall, et al	L	1800	7/163				
Walker	Andrew			John Stewart, et al	L	1806	10/295				
Walker		Joseph		John Barker	L	1820	17/503				
Walker			Samuel D.	Benjamin F. Kelly	L	1835	26/374				
Walker		et al James D.		Silas Conner	L	1838	27/427				
Walker	George		W.	Charles L. Hoff	L	1840	28/247				
Walker		John, Admr. of John W. Kierle		James M. Wheat	L	1840	28/368				
Walker			et al Samuel D.	Josiah Z. Jefferson	L	1841	28/566				
Walker		Montgomery		Isaac Wilson	L	1847	30/169				
Walker		James D. use of		Frederick Beck	L	1852	32/303				
Walker		John		City of Wheeling	L	1853	33/27	33/77	33/100		
Walker		John		Daniel Morgan	L	1853	32/453				
Walker			Thomas	Thos. Slater	L	1853	32/442	32/458			
Walker		John		City of Wheeling	L	1854	34/12	34/26	34/42		
Walker			etal William, Admr.	Samuel F. Black, et al	L	1855	34/72				
Walker		Nathan	W.	Joseph A. Metcalf, et al	L	1857	35/483				
Walker		et al Samuel B.		David K. Irwin	L	1873	L1/43	L1/77	L1/94	L1/204	L1/367
Walker	Ann	L.		John Bashar	L	1874	L1/405	L1/412	L1/438	L1/453	L1/496
Walker	Ann	L.		Dorothea Bashar	L	1874	L2/60				
Walker		N.	W.	J. M. Brodie	L	1875	L2/254				
Walker	Annie			Jacob B. Hughes	L	1877	L3/250				
Walker			Robert	Thomas McEntee	L	1877	L3/180	L3/207	L3/267		
Walker			et al Philip A.	Franklin Insurance Co.	L	1880	L4/396	L4/413			
Walker			et al Philip A.	Fire & Marine Insurance Co.	L	1880	L4/396	L4/414			

PLAINTIFF INDEX TO ORDER BOOKS — Ohio County, W. Va.

SURNAME	GIVEN NAMES ABCDEFGH	GIVEN NAMES IJKLMNO	GIVEN NAMES PQRSTUVWXYZ	DEFENDANTS		YEAR	ORDER BOOK					
Waits		John		Henry Miller	L	1769	3 164					
Waits		John, etal		John Hanthorn	L	1790	3 192					
Waits		John et al		Andrew White	L	1790	3 171	3 175				
Waden		John, Dec'd		William Skinner	L	1800	7 162	7 220	7 274			
Waits		John, Assgnee. of Elizabeth Whittum		John Abrams, et al	L	1803	8 290					
Waddle			William	Samuel & Alex Mortin	L	1811	12 446					
Waddle			William	Samuel Martin, et al	C	1812	13 211	13 285	13 133	13 170	13 358	13 386
Wade		N.	Thomas	David Florack, et al	L	1818	16 289					
Waddle	Geo., etal			Lenard Carpenter, et al	L	1819	16 671	16 676				
Waddle	George, etal			Leonard Carpenter	L	1819	17 49					
Waddle		John, Assgnee. of		Arthur Pearce	L	1820	17 292	17 457				
Waddle		John, Dec'd		James Atkinson	L	1822	19 28					
Waddle		John, et al		Henry Giles, Adm. et al	L	1835	26 347					
Waesche	George Frederick, et al		Repold	Bushrod W. Price	L	1835	26 500	26 539	26 542			
Waddle		John		William Conner	L	1840	28 367					
Waddle		John		Stephen Foreman	L	1840	28 329	28 391	28 396			
Waddle		John		Wallace Hemphill	L	1840	28 366					
Waddle		John		Alfred S. Lauck	L	1840	28 366	28 413	28 415			
Waddle		John		Thomas Laws	L	1840	28 367	28 412	28 416			
Waddle		John, et al		Joseph Marshall	L	1840	28 357					
Waddle		John, etal		Levi Mills	L	1840	28 366					
Waddle		John, etal		William Wells	L	1840	28 366	28 451				
Waddle		John, etal		Henry Lewis	L	1841	28 547	28 588				
Waddle		John, etal		John Mooney	L	1841	28 573					
Waddle		John, etal		John Russell	L	1841	28 530	28 588				
Waddle		John, etal		Alexander W. Walker	L	1841	28 547					
Wagoner	Casper			Ensell & Stewart	L	1841	28 571					
Wagoner	Casper			Ensell & Stewart	L	1841	29 16	29 63	29 106	29 133		
Waddle		John, et al		Alexander Walker, et al	L	1842	29 155					
Waddle			William	Isaac Burkham	L	1842	29 433					
Waddle			William	John Ferrell	L	1844	29 378					
Waddle		James		Samuel Hames	L	1852	32 212					
Waite		Lorenzo, etal		Isaac Mast, (Mask)	L	1855	34 119	34 130	34 131			
Waddle			Dec'd William, etal	Francis Chesser	L	1856	35 131					
Wait		L, et al		James Moore	L	1857	36 50					

'W' SURNAMES - PLAINTIFFS

PLAINTIFF INDEX TO ORDER BOOKS — Ohio County, W. Va.

SURNAME	GIVEN NAMES ABCDEFGH	GIVEN NAMES IJKLMNO	GIVEN NAMES PQRSTUVWXYZ	DEFENDANTS	L/C	YEAR	ORDER BOOK				
Waddle			Sarah A.	Isaac Bentley	L	1858	36 212				
Wagner	C.			Adam Armant	L	1862	39 36	39 101	39 137	39 176	39 198
Waddle	A.			R. S. & W. B. Norman	L	1873	L1 57				
Waddle			William H.	Alexander M. Jacob	L	1873	L 1 164				
Waddle	Archibald			James Padgett, et al	L	1874	L 1 280				
Waddle	Archibald			P. Edward Peirson	L	1875	L 2 167				
Wagener	David, et al			Patrick Byrne, et al	L	1875	L 2 206	L 2 208	L 2 379		
Wagner		Joseph		Clinton Browning	L	1875	L 2 101				
Waddle			Robert	Wesley Bowman	L	1879	L 4 290	L 4 313	L 4 357		
Wayt		John		Elizabeth & Joseph Whitham et al	L	1800	7 178				
Wayt		John		Thomas Moran	C	1811	12 518				
Wayt		John		Saml. Buchanon	L	1811	13 17	13 80			
Wayt		John, et al		Thomas, William, Elenor Moran	C	1811	13 87				
Wayts (Heirs)	et al			Wayts Exectors	C	1820	17 489				
Wayt	Fanny			Adam Faris, et al	C	1820	17 211				
Wayt		John, Dec't, et al		John Faris, et al	C	1821	18 211	18 219	18 297	18 298	
Wayt	Fanny, et al			Adam Faris, Exectr. of, et al	C	1822	19 270	19 514			
Wayt		John, et al		John Poak, et al	C	1822	19 321	19 422			
Wayt		Nathaniel		Fanny Wayt, et al	C	1827	22 207	22 256			
Wayt		Nathaniel		John Wayt, (Dec'd) Heirs	C	1830	24 51	24 52			
Wayt		Nathaniel		Fanny Wayt, et al	C	1830	24 137				
Wayt		Nathaniel		Wm. Keenan, et al	C	1834	26 143	26 173	26 551	26 569	
Wayt		James		Hezikiah Degarmorer	L	1840	28 265				
Wayts		James		Hezekial Degarmo, et al	L	1842	29 233				
Wayt		James (Admr.)		John Maxwell, Sr.	L	1857	35 411	35 436	35 451		
Wayt		James, et al, for use of)		Robert Mozingo, et al	L	1860	38 133	38 140	38 183		
Wayt		James		Silas W. Wharton	L	1862	39 105				
Wayt		Martha		Esther Martin, et al	C	1876	C 1 180	C 1 192	C 1 202	C 1 220	C 1 230
Wayt			Robt. B.	James Wayt	L	1879	L 4 336				

PLAINTIFF INDEX TO ORDER BOOKS — Ohio County, W. Va.

SURNAME	GIVEN NAMES ABCDEFGH	GIVEN NAMES IJKLMNO	GIVEN NAMES PQRSTUVWXYZ	DEFENDANTS	L/C	YEAR	ORDER BOOK				
Wallace		James		Enocks Enock	L	1800	7/115				
Wallace		James, et al		Andrew Rodgers	L	1801	7/242				
Wallace		James, et al		Ralph Smith	L	1801	7/206	7/243	7/244	7/278	
Wallace		James, et al		Daniel Watson	L	1801	7/244	7/246			
Waller		Jesse, et al		Frederick Beeler	L	1801	7/304	7/307			
Walt	Elizabeth, et al			James Walt	C	1801	7/328				
Waln		Nicholas &	Caleb Cresson)	John Clark	L	1803	9/47	9/62			
Wallace	David	(Pyatt), et al		Joseph Palmer	L	1805	10/25	10/131			
Walters	George			James Ogle	L	1808	11/398				
Waller		Jesse		Frederick Beeler	L	1809	12/6	12/124			
Walters	George			James Ogle	L	1809	12/25				
Wallace	David			John Camnitz	L	1811	12/515				
Wallace	David			John Camnitz	L	1811	13/89				
Waller		Jesse		Frederick Beeler	L	1812	13/326				
Walters	George			Elizabeth Rogers, et al	C	1815	15/2				
Wallace		John		Thomas Moore, et al	L	1817	16/7				
Wallace	Henry &	Irwin		Dyer Fitch	L	1820	17/398	17/421			
Walton			Thornton	John Gilmore, et al	L	1820	17/417	17/448			
Wallace	Henry & Irwin			Zebediah Mix	L	1821	18/232				
Wallace		Jared		Jas. Wallace, et al	L	1821	18/130				
Waldren	Francis			Simms Dement, et al	C	1822	19/164				
Wallace	David,			Bukeys Heirs	C	1824	20/202				
Wallace	David			Joseph McKee	L	1824	20/144	20/243	20/256	20/328	
Waldin		John		George Carruthers	L	1825	21/233				
Wallace	David			Joseph McKee, et al	L	1825	21/8				
Walter		Jonathan		Mary Messeger	L	1826	21/535				
Wallace	David			Ana Bukey, et al	L	1827	22/174				
Wallace			Volney, etal	R. W. Randall & Co.	C	1827	22/210	22/254			
Wallace			Volney, etal	R. W. Randall & Co.	C	1830	24/189	24/516			
Wallis	B. E.			Thomas McComick	L	1833	25/465				
Walden		John, Assgnes. et al		Thomas G. Moore	L	1834	26/73	26/387	26/495		
Wallace			V. et al	R. W. Randall, et al	C	1834	26/12	26/93	26/317		
Wallis	Benjamin			Thomas McCormic	L	1835	26/520				
Waller	Abraham B.			John Borland	L	1836	27/159	27/206	27/255	27/299	27/398
Wallace			Stewart	Joseph M. Coppin	L	1838	27/551				

PLAINTIFF INDEX TO ORDER BOOKS — Ohio County, W. Va.

SURNAME	GIVEN NAMES ABCDEFGH	GIVEN NAMES IJKLMNO	GIVEN NAMES PQRSTUVWXYZ	DEFENDANTS		YEAR	ORDER BOOK				
Wallace			Stewart	William Donaldson	L	1838	27 551				
Walravin	Elias			Daniel Burris	L	1838	27 404				
Wallace			Stewart	Joseph M. Coppins	L	1839	28 35	28 44	28 79		
Wallace			Stewart	William Donaldson	L	1839	28 35	28 41			
Walton			William, etal	William Chapline	L	1841	28 494				
Walton			Wm.	Stephen Rice	L	1841	29 13				
Walton			William, etal	William Chapline, et al	L	1846	30 87				
Walgamuth	Francis F. et al			John Elliott	L	1856	35 19				
Wallace			William	William H. Russell, et al	L	1857	35 483				
Walter	Fraz, etal			Januar Fischer, et al	L	1857	36 126	36 134	36 136		
Walter			Stephen, et al	Januar Fischer, et al	L	1857	36 126	36 134	36 136		
Wallace		John		George A. Cracraft, et al	L	1860	38 195				
Walters	George Jr.			David K. Irwin	L	1873	L1 44	L1 77	L1 94	L1 204	L1 365
Wallace			Spaulding K.	F. C. Winship & Co.	L	1875	L 2 338	L 2 354			
Wallace	H. et al			George Crumbacker	L	1876	L 2 434	L 2 478			
Walters			et al William B.	Henry Gunther	L	1877	L 3 370				
Walke	Frank			John Hahne	L	1878	L 3 498				
Wallace	Henry			George Crumbacker, et al	L	1878	L 3 478				
Wallace	Alex Jr.			Henry Shmulbach	L	1880	L 4 480				

'W' SURNAMES - PLAINTIFFS

PLAINTIFF INDEX TO ORDER BOOKS — Ohio County, W. Va.

SURNAME	PLAINTIFFS GIVEN NAMES A-H	GIVEN NAMES I-P	GIVEN NAMES P-Z	DEFENDANTS		YEAR	ORDER BOOK					
Wandelhour	Frederick A.			Michael Wagner	L	1835	26 371					
Wandelohr	F. A.			Michael Wagner	L	1836	27 111	27 156				
Wandeloher	Frederick A.			Joseph W. Sample	L	1836	27 98					
Wandelhor	Frederick A.			William B. Reynolds	L	1838	27 550					
Wanchope	Eleanor			John Porter	L	1852	32 213					
Wame	Edward			Hugh Devine	L	1855	34 296					
Weaver	Henry			Frederick Beymer	L	1813	14 144					
Weaver	Henry			Christiana Beymer, Adm. et al	L	1815	15 101					
Weaver	Henry			Bartholamew McDonald, et al	L	1821	18 307					
Weaver	Henry			Charles McFadden	L	1821	18 445					
Weaver		John		Robert C. Thompson	L	1821	18 199					
Weaver	Henry			William Mathers	L	1822	19 109					
Weaver	Henry			Bartholomew McDonald, et al	L	1822	19 125					
Weaver		Jacob		Ezra W. Doase or (Doaye)	L	1822	19 235					
Weaver		Jacob		Solomon King	L	1823	20 4	20 380	20 230	20 290	20 297	20 503
Weaver	Henry			John Clark	L	1824	20 130	20 243	20 381	20 483		
Weaver		Jacob		Solomon King	L	1825	21 65	21 71	21 86			
Weaver	Henry			John Probasco	L	1827	22 269					
Weaver	Henry			John Thompson	L	1828	22 341	22 450				
Weaver	Henry			Peter W. Gale	L	1829	23 234					
Weaver	Henry			Joseph McCallister, et al	L	1829	23 345	23 457				
Weaver	Henry			John Smith	L	1829	23 409					
Weaver	Henry			William Mathers	L	1830	24 111					
Weaver	Hanse, et al			John A. Roe	L	1835	26 552					
Weaver		John	W.	Levi Rose	L	1839	28 68					
Weaver		Jacob		William A. Moysten	L	1848	30 394	30 425				
Weaver		Jacob Jr.		E. C. Dewey	L	1853	33 50	33 156	33 225	33 396	33 413	
Weaver		Jacob		Thomas Moore	L	1853	32 398	32 476	32 479			
Weaver		Jacob Jr.		Henry E. Parker	L	1853	33 52					
Weaver	Emmor, et al			McCormick Pollard	L	1858	36 332					

PLAINTIFF INDEX TO ORDER BOOKS — Ohio County, W. Va.

SURNAME	GIVEN NAMES ABCDEFGH	GIVEN NAMES IJKLMNO	GIVEN NAMES PQRSTUVWXYZ	DEFENDANTS		YEAR	ORDER BOOK				
Wickham			Warner	Samuel Logan	L	1819	16 604				
Wickham			William S.	John Settle	L	1834	26 268	26 363			
Wickham			William S.	John Farrow	L	1837	27 175				
Wickham	H. C. et al			George Harrison	L	1840	28 391				
Wickham	Dec'd Henry C.			John Carothers	L	1841	28 486				
Wickham			William S.	Bancroft Woodcock, et al	L	1848	30 345				
Wickham	Assgnee. of George E.			William Over	L	1854	33 232				
Wickham			W. S. Adm	S. M. Bell	L	1854	33 396	33 485			
Wickham			William S. etal	S. M. Bell	L	1855	34 79	34 140	34 233		
Wickham			William S.	Conrad Cotts	L	1855	34 220				
Wickham			William S.	Joseph Fowler	L	1856	35 206				
Wickham			William S.	Jacob Amick	L	1857	36 118	36 177			
Wickham			William S.	Conrad Broadrick	L	1857	35 445				
Wickham			William S.	William Dulty	L	1857	36 123				
Wickham			Wickham S.	Thomas M. Parker	L	1857	36 75				
Wickham			William S.	John J. Yarnall & Bro.	L	1857	35 445	35 450			
Wickham	Charles			Edward Morgan	L	1859	37 338	37 369			
Wickham	George E.			Isaac Hazlett	L	1859	37 341	37 355	37 367	37 375	
Wickham			William	The City of Wheeling	L	1859	37 173	37 225	37 262	37 313	37 403
Wickham			W. S.	City of Wheeling	L	1860	38 18	38 42	38 72	38 545	
Wickham	George E.			City of Wheeling	L	1862	39 49	39 59			
Wickham	Conrad			W. James Johnson	L	1877	L 6 281	L 3 392			

PLAINTIFF INDEX TO ORDER BOOKS — Ohio County, W. Va.

PLAINTIFFS SURNAME	GIVEN NAMES ABCDEFGH	GIVEN NAMES IJKLMNO	GIVEN NAMES PQRSTUVWXYZ	DEFENDANTS		YEAR	ORDER BOOK									
Warfield	Gerrard			John Coalman	L	1786	3/5									
Ward		Matthyas		John Greer	L	1788	3/60									
Ward		Joseph		Jacob & Catherine Chambers	L	1800	7/42									
Ward	of George Beeler, Dec'd, etal		William, Adm'r	John Clark	L	1800	6/513									
Ward			Wm. et al	Peter Terrell, et al	L	1800	7/185									
Ward			Wm. et al	Thomas Davis	L	1802	8/207	8/272								
Warrant		Jack, et al		Jacob Ankarum, et al	L	1802	8/269	8/315	8/316							
Ward			William, et al	Robert Wood, et al	L	1803	9/46									
Warrant		John, on the Demise of		Jacob Ankrum	L	1803	9/9	9/51	9/54							
Warnock		John		Reuben McSherry	L	1806	10/346									
Warring		John		James Robinson	L	1806	10/296									
Wartenbe			William	James Gamble, et al	C	1809	12/23	12/197								
Ward	Edward, etal			Lemuel Leghorn, et al	L	1810	2/327	2/378	2/412	2/431	2/44	2/57	2/76	2/90	2/111	2/127
do	do			do do	do	do								2/152	2/277	2/301
Warnock			William	Joseph Keer	L	1811	13/74									
Wareham		John		Wm. Downing	L	1812	13/279									
Wartinbe			William	Robert Gamble	L	1812	13/139	13/230								
Wareham		John		Wm. Downy	L	1813	14/53									
Warner			Peter	Basil Beell, Adm. et al	L	1815	15/70									
Warden			Samuel, etal	Dunker Henderson	L	1816	15/391									
Warden			Saml.	Dunkin Henderson	L	1817	16/159	16/195								
Warner			Peter	Basil Beal, Admr. et al	L	1817	16/41	16/54								
Warner			Peter	Basil Beal, et al	L	1818	2/460	2/470								
Warden			Samuel	Amos Miles	L	1821	18/169									
Warner	Dennis, Assgnee of			Wm. Killen	L	1826	21/428									
Ward	Allen			Wm. Huey	L	1829	23/134	23/318								
Wardle			Sarah	David White	L	1829	23/415	23/417								
Warden			Samuel	Reuben F. Hedges	L	1830	38/436									
Wardle			Sarah	David White	L	1830	24/19									
Warner			Thomas	Dana Hubbard	L	1832	25/256	25/303								
Wardle			Wm.	Pearly Sharp	L	1836	27/112	27/197	27/299	27/397						
Warden		James		Fielder Berry, et al	L	1837	27/248									
Warren		Matthew		Duke & Davis	L	1837	27/172									
Warden		James		Enos W. Newton, et al	L	1838	28/26									
Wardner	Allen, et al			William W. Prescott, etal	L	1838	27/375	27/355								

PLAINTIFF INDEX TO ORDER BOOKS — Ohio County, W. Va.

SURNAME	GIVEN NAMES ABCDEFGH	GIVEN NAMES IJKLMNO	GIVEN NAMES PQRSTUVWXYZ	DEFENDANTS		YEAR	ORDER BOOK				
Warren		Matthew		Merchant Deford	L	1839	28/156	28/207			
Warren		Mathew		William C. Piper Co.	C	1841	29/6				
Warden		Jacob M.		Benjamin M. Carr	L	1842	29/111				
Warner	George			Sarah Boram	L	1843	29/270				
Warnock		John &	William	William Templeton, et al	L	1844	29/409	29/484	29/517	29/542	
Warden		Jacob	W.	William Watson	L	1853	32/424				
Warden	Catherine			John H. Tappan	L	1855	34/130				
Warden		Jacob M. et al		Sherrard Clemens	L	1855	34/138				
Warden		Jacob, et al		Martin L. Fink	L	1855	34/113				
Warden		Jacob M. et al		Bentley Moore	L	1855	34/153				
Warden		Jacob M. et al		James H. Dodgson	L	1856	35/211				
Warden		Jacob M. et al		Noah T. Harris	L	1856	35/203				
Warden		Jacob M.		Robert G. Bonham	L	1857	35/480				
Warden		Jacob M.		Daniel M. Edgington	L	1857	35/480				
Warden		Jacob M. et al		Andrew Mitchell	L	1857	35/360				
Warden		Jacob M. et al		Johnston Mulrine	L	1857	35/478				
Warden		Jacob M.		George A. Cracraft	L	1858	36/179				
Warden		Jacob M.		David Luke	L	1858	36/390				
Warne	Edward A.			James Murphy	L	1858	36/328				
Warner	Griswold E.			George E. Caldwell	L	1858	36/181				
Warren		Mathew, et al		George Pumphrey, et al	L	1858	37/38				
Ward			Rachel	John Russell, et al	L	1859	37/345	37/460	37/464		
Warden		Jacob, et al		Edward Gilfillan	L	1859	37/133				
Warden		James	W.	John Phillips	L	1860	38/118				
Warren	George, et al			McKeen, Patton & Co.	L	1860	38/131				
Warner		et al	Richard C.	James W. Warden, et al	L	1861	38/478				
Warren		John T. et al		David K. Irwin	L	1873	L1/41	L1/77	L1/94	L1/204	L1/369
Warren		L. Maria, et al		John Marling	L	1876	L2/432	L2/516			
Warren		L. Maria, Admrx.		John Marling	L	1877	L3/344				
Ward		J.	W.	J. C. Hervey	L	1878	L4/113				
Warren		Isiah		G. G. Murdock	L	1878	L4/105				
Warfield	B. H.			Frank Watters	L	1879	L4/234	L4/237	L4/469		
Warner	Greagory			Ambros Holden	L	1879	L4/255	L4/274			
Warsinsky			Theodore	Hazlett & Ford	L	1879	L4/294				
Ward	D. A. et al			Fire & Marine Insurance Co	L	1880	L4/396	L4/414			
Ward	D. A. et al			Franklin Insurance Co.	L	1880	L4/396	L4/413			

PLAINTIFF INDEX TO ORDER BOOKS — Ohio County, W. Va.

SURNAME	PLAINTIFFS GIVEN NAMES ABCDEFGH	GIVEN NAMES IJKLMNO	GIVEN NAMES PQRSTUVWXYZ	DEFENDANTS		YEAR	ORDER BOOK							
Watson		James, etal use of William Sutherland		William Crawford	L	1796	5 40							
Watson	Hugh			Peter Bormsley	L	1799	6 269	6 318	6 370	6 434				
Watt	Elizabeth, et al			James Watt	C	1801	8 58	8 122						
Watterman	Charles, etal			George Henry	L	1807	11 128							
Washam		John		Henry Sterret	L	1809	12 69							
Wayman			Thomas	Joseph Ward	L	1809	12 133							
Waters	Hanson			et al Mordecai Yarnall, Dec'd	L	1811	2 58	2 80						
Waters	Hanson			Basel Beall, Jr.	L	1812	13 222							
Watkins		Sarah, etal		Archibald Hamilton	L	1812	2 85	2 96						
Wayman			Zachriah	Thomas Catlet	L	1812	2 95	2 100						
Wayman			Zacheriah	Nimrod Catlet	L	1812	2 96	2 100	2 102	2 110				
Way	Abishai			Wm. Chapline	L	1817	2 389							
Way	Abisha			Wm. Chapline, et al	L	1818	16 502							
Way	Abisha, for the use of			Wm. Chapline, et al	L	1819	17 41							
Watt		Jane, et al		Henry Sockman, et al	L	1820	17 408							
Wason	George			Benjamin Cole	L	1821	18 346							
Wason	Geo.			Benjh. Cole	L	1822	19 101							
Watson		John, et al		Wm. Williamson, et al	C	1824	20 221							
Watts		Richard, etal		Josiah Chapline	L	1824	20 150							
Watson		John, et al		Wm. Williamson, et al	C	1825	21 29							
Wayman			Samuel	Jesse Burch, et al	C	1827	22 137							
Waterson		use of James, etal		John Sexton	L	1828	22 344	22 423						
Way		Joshua, etal		May Dye	L	1829	23 410	23 412						
Watson			Wm. et al	Andrew W. McColloch	L	1832	25 182							
Wayman			Zachariah, etal	Morgan Jones, Jr.	L	1832	25 193							
Watson			Thomas	Fielder Berry	L	1833	25 486							
Watson			William	Joseph Foreman	L	1833	25 420							
Watson			William	Joseph Foreman	L	1834	26 51							
Watkins	Enoch			Miller & Haynes	L	1839	28 87	28 154	28 195	28 261	28 324	28 360	28 426	28 501
Washington	Lawrence	W.		Alexander McCortney	L	1840	28 330	28 374						
Waugh		Richard		Zacheus Biggs	L	1840	28 367							
Washington	Lawrence A.			George W. Berry	L	1841	28 547							
Washington	Lawranc, et al			William F. Gordon	L	1841	29 114							
Watt		John, et al		Robert T. Kendall, et al	L	1841	29 10							
Watt		John		Samuel G. Robinson	L	1841	28 563	28 565						

PLAINTIFF INDEX TO ORDER BOOKS — Ohio County, W. Va.

SURNAME	GIVEN NAMES ABCDEFGH	GIVEN NAMES IJKLMNO	GIVEN NAMES PQRSTUVWXYZ	DEFENDANTS		YEAR	ORDER BOOK						
Watt		John, et al		Samuel L. Robinson, et al	L	1841	29 28						
Watt		John		Wheat & Kendall	L	1841	28 565						
Washington		Lawrence A., et al		Daniel M. Edgington	L	1842	29 329						
Washington		Lawrence	W. et al	Alexander J. Laidley	L	1843	29 173						
Waterhouse			Stephen	Charles Steuben	L	1842	29 239						
Waterhouse			Stephen	E. C. Jeffers	L	1850	31 285						
Wates			Thomas	Francis Lawson	L	1850	31 353						
Watson		James		Frances Lally	L	1852	32 316						
Watterhouse			Stephen	Mat Jeffers	L	1853	32 489						
Waterhouse			Stephen	Matthias Jeffers	L	1853	33 50	33 156	33 225	33 415	33 495		
Waterbury		et al	Stephen W.	Morgan H. Gregg	L	1855	34 150						
Waterhouse			Stephen	Mathias Jeffers	L	1855	34 89	34 151	34 244	34 284	34 293	34 342	34 374
Watson		Jacob		Joel Wall	L	1855	34 193	34 197					
Waterhouse			Stephen	Mathias Jeffers	L	1856	35 17	35 137	35 202	35 303	35 348		
Way			T. G. et al	William Howard	L	1856	35 148						
Watson	Benjamin H.			Margaret Bole	L	1857	35 479						
Watson	Benjamin H.			Margaret Bole	L	1857	36 48	36 74	36 94	36 109			
Watson	Benjamin H.			George A. Cracraft	L	1857	36 37						
Wayman		Martin F. et al		John H. Downs	L	1857	35 341						
Wayman		Martin T. et al		John Rankin	L	1857	36 121						
Waters		Joseph H.		Joseph Liston	L	1858	36 361	36 378					
Waterhouse		John		George Marshall	L	1859	37 153						
Waters		Joseph H.		Samuel Carter	L	1859	37 341						
Wayne		Julius		David Armstrong, et al	L	1859	37 263						
Watson	George			L. C. Curtis	L	1873	L1 16	L1 19	L1 26	L1 32	L1 46		
Watson			Thomas	O. D. Thompson	L	1874	L 1 412						
Watson			Thomas	O. D. Thompson	L	1874	L2 29	L 2 379					
Waterhouse		et al John		John Fitzpatrick	L	1877	L 3 239						
Waymer		John		David B. Sherrod	L	1877	L 3 355	L 3 366					

PLAINTIFF INDEX TO ORDER BOOKS — Ohio County, W. Va.

SURNAME	PLAINTIFFS ABCDEFGH	PLAINTIFFS IJKLMNO	PLAINTIFFS PQRSTUVWXYZ	DEFENDANTS	L/C	YEAR	ORDER BOOK			
Webster		John	Porter	James Hall	L	1791	3 240			
Webster		John	Porter	John Mitchell	L	1791	3 245	3 313		
Webster		John	Portor	John Mitchell	L	1792	4 33			
Weeks			William	James Welch	L	1794	4 290	4 324	4 358	4 402
Webster		John	Porter	James Potts	L	1796	5 209			
Weeks			William	Stephin Abrams	L	1796	5 35			
Wear			Thomas, etal	Joseph McHenry	L	1804	9 289			
Wikoff		Jacob C.		George McCreary, et al	L	1804	9 187			
Weir			Thomas	Joseph McHenry	L	1805	10 13			
Webster		John, etal		John Lee	C	1809	12 34			
Weakly			Thomas, etal	Jones Dixon, et al	L	1810	12 366			
Weekly			Thomas, etal	Wm. Wells	L	1811	13 73			
Weems	Henry			Elijah Church	L	1818	16 457			
Widech			Samuel, etal	Zebediah Mix	L	1820	17 469			
Wedick		for use of	John Sockman) Samuel,)	Zebediah Mix	L	1821	18 97			
Weems	Henry			Sarah Robinson,	C	1821	18 105			
Weeks	Cornelius			Saml. Biggs, et al	L	1822	19 200			
Weems	Henry, Assghee of John McLure			David Church	L	1822	19 248			
Weems	Henry			Bennett Logdson	L	1822	19 203			
Weir		John		Richard Hardesty	L	1822	19 179	19 250		
Weaks	Cornelius, etal			Van Caldwell, et al	L	1823	20 38			
Weins	Henry			Peter Conrod Coltz, et al	C	1826	21 337			
Weir		John, etal, use of		Nathaniel Atkinson, et al	L	1827	22 141			
Weddle	Henry			Henry Beckley, et al	C	1828	22 348			
Weems	Henry			Wm. Donaldson	C	1828	23 22			
Widdle	Henry, et al			Rosana Bently, et al	C	1828	22 468			
Wedle(Weddle)	Henry, et al			Rosanna Bentley, et al	C	1829	23 155	23 260	23 302	23 464
Weddle	Henry, et al			Rosanna Bentley	C	1830	24 191			
Wier			Thomas	Wm. Mathews, et al	L	1832	25 118			
Webster		et al Joshua E.		Mundican Duvall	L	1835	26 503			
Weizell			Wm.	Clark Haines	L	1839	28 194			
Wiggins	Ely			Dennis Hobtitzell	L	1839	28 147			
Weber		John, et al		William Cunningham	L	1840	28 247			
Wickham			William S.	Philo W. Stocking	L	1841	29 18			
Webster			Samuel, etal	Abraham Allman, et al	L	1844	29 434			

PLAINTIFF INDEX TO ORDER BOOKS — Ohio County, W. Va.

SURNAME	PLAINTIFFS GIVEN NAMES ABCDEFGH	GIVEN NAMES IJKLMNO	GIVEN NAMES PQRSTUVWXYZ	DEFENDANTS	L/C	YEAR	ORDER BOOK							
Webster	George, et al			William Brown	L	1852	32/308							
Wehner		John Michael		City of Wheeling	L	1853	33/77	33/103	33/109	33/203				
Weisgard	Daniel			Return W. Hill	L	1853	32/483							
Wead		Jacob		Nehemiah T. Harris	L	1855	34/156							
Weidebush	August			Frederick M. Krakenburg	L	1855	34/232	34/243						
Weil			Theresa	Henry Dice	L	1855	34/89	34/159	34/255					
Weisoabber		John		City of Wheeling	L	1855	34/268	34/308						
Wick		James	R.	John Gill, et al	L	1855	34/249	34/289						
Wealer		John C.		William Dunnevon	L	1856	35/152	35/154						
Weber	E. A.			Mary Wardell	L	1856	35/219	35/300	35/304	35/352				
Wier		Martha		Richard Moore	L	1856	35/284							
Wier			Thompson	Michael Daves (Davis)	L	1856	35/137							
Wohler			Wilhelm, et al	Januar Fischer, et al	L	1857	36/126	36/134	36/136					
Weigett	Frederick, et al			January Fischer, et al	L	1857	36/126	36/134	36/136					
Weiller	Hermann, et al			Wattson Carr	L	1857	35/357							
Weirig			Peter	William Defibaugh	L	1857	35/318							
Weisgerber		John		John Jones	L	1857	36/51	36/74	36/94	36/109	36/156	36/168	36/208	36/222
Weidebush	August			W. M. Donley	L	1858	37/30							
Weidebush		John		David McGannon	L	1858	37/31	37/65	37/109					
Weiller	Hermann			Herman Renner	L	1858	36/334							
Widabush			William	David McGannon	L	1858	37/27							
Webster	George F.			J. R. Jones	L	1859	37/113							
Weidebush	August			Andrew Metz	L	1859	37/262							
Weidebush			William	John Duffy	L	1859	37/160	37/177	37/243	37/256	37/200	37/230	37/321	37/385	37/444
Weidman		J. G.		B. A. Biggs	L	1859	37/153	37/186						
Weber	Christian			George W. Pumphrey, et al	L	1860	37/494							
Weidebush	August			Wm. Briceland	L	1860	38/42	38/67						
Widabush			William	John Heindmarsh	L	1860	38/17	38/42	38/81	38/100				
Weikel	George	W. et al		W. A. Edwards & Bro.	L	1861	38/478							
Wiedebusch	A.			G. Grayson	L	1876	L2/380	L2/414	L2/423	L2/424	L2/427			
Weidebush	August			John Audlinger	L	1879	L4/293							
Weister	George			Alex T. Garden, Admr. et al	C	1879	C1/429							

PLAINTIFF INDEX TO ORDER BOOKS — Ohio County, W. Va.

SURNAME	PLAINTIFFS ABCDEFGH	GIVEN NAMES IJKLMNO	GIVEN NAMES PQRSTUVWXYZ	DEFENDANTS		YEAR	ORDER BOOK					
Welman		John		John Tilton	L	1784	1/218	1/219				
Welman		John		Andrw Zane	L	1784	1/216					
Welch		James		William Spencer	L	1788	3/57	3/60	3/67	3/82	3/229	3/250
Welch		James		James Nevit	L	1790	3/236					
Welch			Wm.	Wm. Shawal	L	1792	4/78					
Welsh				Shewell	L	1792	3/387					
Welsh, et al				Van Swearingen	L	1793	4/139	4/175				
Welsh		James		Wm. Week	L	1793	4/114					
Welch		James		Samuel Fulton	L	1796	5/145					
Welch	James (Use of Richard Spear)			James McConnell, Executors	L	1796	6/195					
Wilcoxon	Henry Hardy, Dec'd			George Dement, Dec'd, etal	C	1803	9/126					
Willing		John		Aaron Hedges	L	1803	8/297					
Weller			Peter	William Chapline	L	1806	10/441					
Wilds	George, etal			Richard Carson	L	1806	10/349					
Weller			Peter	William Chapline	L	1807	11/100					
Willets		Jesse, etal		John Bound	L	1807	11/95					
Weller			Peter	William Chapline	L	1809	12/77	12/435				
Weller			Peter	Frederick Beymer	L	1810	12/212					
Willis		Isaac, Assgnee. of (Robert Willis, who was Assgnee. of James Perigo)		Benjamin Gassaway	L	1818	16/274					
Willis			Peter	Wm. Shaw, et al	C	1818	16/275					
Willis,			Robert, Assgnee. of James Parigo	Benjamin Gassaway	L	1818	16/274					
Weller			Peter	William Shaw	C	1819	16/602	16/681				
Weller			Peter	William Shaw	C	1820	17/402					
Weller			Peter	Wm. Shaw, et al	C	1821	18/38					
Weller			Peter	William Shaw, et al	C	1824	20/160					
Wilie			William, et al	Levi Prescott, et al	L	1829	23/430					
Wilcox		Loyd, et al		Reason Pumphrey	L	1832	25/73					
Welch		James		Zepheus Biggs	L	1833	25/434	25/439	25/475			
Wilcox	Alfred			William McDonald	L	1834	26/144					
Wilcox		Imri		Samuel Shipler	L	1834	26/68					
Wiley		Joshua C.		James H. Forsyth	L	1837	27/304	27/321				
Welchons		Joseph		H. D. Hart	L	1838	27/399					
Weld	Assgnee. of Moses Thompson Z. A. et al			John Cummings	L	1841	28/574					
Wiley			Thomas, etal	Hugh McCurdy	L	1841	29/174	29/188				
Wiley			William, etal	John Feay	L	1847	30/168					

PLAINTIFF INDEX TO ORDER BOOKS — Ohio County, W. Va.

PLAINTIFFS SURNAME	GIVEN NAMES ABCDEFGH	GIVEN NAMES IJKLMNO	GIVEN NAMES PQRSTUVWXYZ	DEFENDANTS		YEAR	ORDER BOOK					
Welshons	Henry			John Douglas	L	1849	31 211					
Wiley			William, et al	John Feay	L	1850	31 227					
Welsh		Michael		City of Wheeling	L	1852	32 271					
Welsh			Philip	Richard Mayger	L	1852	32 211					
Welsh		Michael		City of Wheeling	L	1853	33 26	33 74				
Welty	Christian			City of Wheeling	L	1854	33 447					
Weltey	Christian			City of Wheeling	L	1854	34 12	34 26	34 41	34 120	34 173	34 202
Wilcock			William, et al	James Murphy	L	1855	34 240					
Wilcock			William, et al	William C. Thornburg	L	1855	34 239					
Wilcox			et al William T.	Wheeler & Larkin	L	1855	34 68					
Willis		James C.		N. L. Dorsey	L	1856	35 145	35 145				
Willison	Andrew			Isaac T. Conn	L	1857	36 69					
Wilden			Shubal	James M. Todd	L	1858	36 388	36 389				
Wilder			Shubal	The Crescent Mfg. Co.	L	1858	36 393					
Wilder			Shubal, et al	James M. Todd	L	1858	37 39	37 40	37 64	37 119		
Wilkins		Lefferts		Thomas Parker	L	1858	37 84					
Willis		James, et al		N. S. Dorsey	L	1858	37 14	37 30				
Williston			et al William G.	Jacob G. Metcalf	L	1858	36 180					
Welch		John, et al		S. G. W. Morrison	L	1859	37 347					
Welsh			Thomas	Josiah W. Chapline	L	1859	37 135					
Wilkins			et al Willard C.	David K. Irwin	L	1873	L1 42	L1 77	L1 94	L1 204	L1 370	
Welty	C. et al			August Rust	L	1874	L1 454	L1 471				
Wilkinson		Nathan, et al		John Marling	L	1875	L2 294	L2 309	L2 319			
Welty		M. et al		Bernard Shanley, et al	L	1876	L3 65					
Wilhelm		Ludwig		Charles Wagenkaucht, et al	L	1876	L3 83					
Willard	Adaline			James Butler	L	1876	L3 49					
Welty			S. & P.	Pryor Boyd, et al	L	1877	L3 409					
Welshaus	B. G.			Jacob Lash	L	1879	L4 284	L4 287				

PLAINTIFF INDEX TO ORDER BOOKS — Ohio County, W. Va

SURNAME	GIVEN NAMES ABCDEFGH	GIVEN NAMES IJKLMNO	GIVEN NAMES PQRSTUVWXYZ	DEFENDANTS	L/C	YEAR	ORDER BOOK						
Winters	Henry			Nathan Parr	L	1792	4 60	4 99	4 141	4 162			
Winter		James		James Knox	L	1799	6 261						
Winters		John		James Knox	L	1801	8 63	8 175	8 205				
Windsor			Thomas, et al	Alexander Love	L	1807	11 12						
Windsor			Use of Thomas I., et al	Nicholas Lewis	L	1814	14 418						
Winters	Henry, Assgnee. of Joseph Richmond, who was Assgnee. of John Farley			Wm. Anguish	L	1818	16 473						
Winters.	Benjn.			Joseph Hamon	L	1819	16 675	16 696					
Wimms	Henry			Sarah Robinson	L	1820	17 413						
Wing		Josiah		James Green	L	1820	17a 372						
Wing		Isaiah		James Green	L	1821	18 125						
Winters	Daniel (For use of Thomas Johnston)			Zebediah Mix	L	1821	18 346						
Wims (Weems)	Henry		et al	Arch. Hamilton, et al	L	1822	18 491	18 499					
Wims	Henry, Assgnee. of Thos. Johnston,			David Miller, et al	L	1823	19 334						
Wims	Henry			Wm. Donaldson	C	1824	20 401	20 492					
Wimms	Henry			Eli Quinter	L	1824	20 177						
Wims	Henry, et al			Daniel Zane	L	1824	20 379						
Wimms	Henry			William Donaldson	C	1828	22 398						
Wims	Henry			John Watson	L	1828	22 420						
Wims	Henry			Frederick Goldenburgh	L	1829	23 411						
Wims	Henry			James Higgins	L	1829	22 196	22 275					
Wims	Henry			John Watson	L	1829	23 160						
Wims	Henry			Samuel Knode, et al	L	1830	29 193						
Wims	Henry			Joshua Laskey	L	1832	25 174						
Wims	Henry			Samuel McGave, et al	L	1832	25 262						
Wims	Henry			Jacob Singleton	L	1832	25 66	25 175					
Werdebaugh			et al Samuel,	Moses Ford	L	1833	25 421						
Wimms	Henry			Adam Kemp, et al	L	1834	26 218						
Wimms	Henry			Joshua Lashley	L	1834	26 47	26 132	26 189	26 550			
Wimms	Henry			Pearley Sharp	L	1834	26 64	26 137	26 173				
Wimms	Henry			Jacob Singlemon	L	1834	26 56						
Wims	Henry, Assgnee. &		Thomas	Lewis Lemasters	L	1835	26 446						
Wims	Henry, et al			Hiram Martin	L	1835	26 485						
Wims	Henry, Assgnee., et al			David Miller, et al	L	1835	26 567	26 570	26 571				
Wims	George, et al			John Sexton	L	1836	27 122						
Wims	Henry			F. Gemmell	L	1836	27 45	27 116	27 196	27 211	27 397	27 466	27 509
Wims	Henry &		(Assgne. of) Thomas	William Lambdin et al	L	1836	27 123						

'W' SURNAMES - PLAINTIFFS

PLAINTIFF INDEX TO ORDER BOOKS — Ohio County, W. Va.

SURNAME	GIVEN NAMES ABCDEFGH	GIVEN NAMES IJKLMNO	GIVEN NAMES PQRSTUVWXYZ	DEFENDANTS		YEAR	ORDER BOOK									
Wims	Henry			Hiram Martin	L	1836	27 28									
Wims		Thomas, etal		Adam Kemp, et al	L	1837	27 210									
Wimms	Henry			F. Gemmell & Co.	L	1838	28 17	28 66	28 114	28 154	28 195	28 261	28 324	28 360	28 428	28 502
do	do			do	do	do									28 533	28 568
Winters		Valentine, etal)		Zedekiah B. Curtis	L	1838	27 505									
Winters		Valentine, etal)		Zedirish B. Curtis	L	1838	28 27									
Wintenger		John		William Prall	L	1839	28 127									
Winters		John		Robert Goldenburg	L	1841	28 575									
Wims		Thomas H.		Hiram Martin	L	1842	29 135									
Wingard	Adam			Wm. H. Cecil	L	1842	29 106	29 133	29 172	29 208	29 240					
Winters	David			S. D. Russell	L	1843	29 299									
Wertman		Phebe A.		Klieves & Kraft	L	1846	30 147									
Wind	Henry			Haley & Keltz	L	1854	33 137									
Winship	Franklin			Edward Westwood	L	1855	34 352									
Winship			T.	John Martin	L	1856	35 217	35 248	35 266							
Werdebaugh	Henry J. et al			Aaron Kelly, et al	L	1857	36 114	36 115								
Winship	Franklin			John A. Elliott	L	1857	35 481									
Went	Ernst			Mason M. Dunlap	L	1858	37 69									
Winship	Franklin			Joseph Perry	L	1858	37 31									
Wims		Martin B.		John Stewart	L	1860	38 236	38 272								
Winship	Franklin			Abraham Ray	L	1860	37 502									
Winship	Franklin			Abraham Ray	L	1860	38 7									
Winsdor		Joshua	R.	Mason M. Dunlap	L	1861	38 353	38 371	38 385	38 402	38 418	38 448	38 430	38 465	38 489	38 494
do		do	do	do	do	do									38 506	38 541
Winters	Elisabeth			John E. Mix	L	1861	38 373	38 396								
Windsor		J.	R.	M. M. Dunlap	L	1862	39 2	39 50	39 57	39 66	39 82	39 111	39 122	39 217	39 227	39 241
do		do	do	do	do	do					39 141	39 149	39 155	39 175	39 180	39 186
Wingerter (Winones)	Ferdinand			Robert H. Cotson	L	1862	39 32									
Winans			Thomas	James S. Wheat	C	1873	C1 21	C1 23	C1 25	C1 26	C1 27	C1 44	C1 50	C1 76		
Wenzel	George H.			August Fisher	L	1875	L 2 276	L 2 314	L 2 317							
Worner		Joseph		Kimberly & Co.	L	1875	L 2 255									
Windsor		J.	R.	Thomas Curren	L	1876	L 2 431									
Winters	Frank			George McCombs	L	1876	L 2 449									
Werner		Joseph		Kimberly & Co.	L	1878	L 3 505									
Werner		Joseph		Kimberly & Co.	L	1878	L 4 17									

PLAINTIFF INDEX TO ORDER BOOKS — Ohio County, W. Va.

SURNAME	PLAINTIFFS GIVEN NAMES ABCDEFGH	GIVEN NAMES IJKLMNO	GIVEN NAMES PQRSTUVWXYZ	DEFENDANTS		YEAR	ORDER BOOK						
Wingrove	Henry		S.	John Ebbert	L	1878	L 4 126	L 4 175					
Winship	F. C.			Geo. L. S. Corner	L	1878	L 3 476						
Winship	F. C.			Lewis Gravey.	L	1878	L 3 476						
Winship	F. C.			Wm. Leach	L	1878	L 3 476						

'W' SURNAMES - PLAINTIFFS

PLAINTIFF INDEX TO ORDER BOOKS — Ohio County, W. Va.

SURNAME	PLAINTIFFS GIVEN NAMES ABCDEFGH	GIVEN NAMES IJKLMNO	GIVEN NAMES PQRSTUVWXYZ	DEFENDANTS		YEAR	ORDER BOOK			
Withroe		of John McIngtier	Robert, Assgnee	Matthew Alexander	L	1798	6 196			
Withrou		Usee Richard Spears	Robert	Elzay Swearingen	L	1798	6 127			
West			Samuel, etal	Daniel Beacon	L	1806	10 310			
West	Amos			Hosea Morgan, et al	L	1807	11 99	11 384		
West	Amos			Geo. W. Day	L	1808	11 266	11 267		
Wister	Bartholamus, et al			Alexander S. Berryhill	L	1819	17 6			
Withrup		John		George White	L	1819	17 56			
Withurup		John		George White	L	1821	18 450			
Witten		John		Chas. McFadden	L	1821	18 235	18 432		
Wister			Richard Jr.	Alexander Caldwell	L	1823	19 491			
Withrup		John		George Pannell	L	1823	19 493			
Witherup		John		George Pannell	L	1824	20 146	20 158	20 236	20 384
Westcott			Samuel	Philip Fisher	L	1825	21 154			
Witten		Joseph		Timothy Adams	L	1828	23 77			
Weshart		John		David White	L	1832	25 124			
Wise	Adam			Wm. Chapline	L	1832	25 260			
Weston		Isabel		Alexander Caldwell	L	1837	27 260	27 320		
Wise	G., et al			Alexander McCortney	L	1840	29 18			
Withers	Charles A. et al			James M. Wheat	L	1840	28 421			
Wise	G. &	M		John McCortney	L	1841	28 573			
Wishart		John		William Newlove	L	1841	28 541	28 571		
Wishart		John		William Newlove	L	1841	29 10			
Withers	Ezekiel D.			Josiah Z. Jefferson	L	1841	28 566			
Wishart		John		Thomas Hughey	L	1842	29 106	29 133	29 171	
Wittenbrok	E. et al			Frederick Vosmen, etal	L	1842	29 163			
Withers	E. D.			William Hosack	L	1843	29 250			
Westwood	E.			E. Burkett	L	1853	32 341			
Weyman	George			Mifflin Marsh	L	1854	33 235			
Wisegerber, et al				City of Wheeling	L	1854	33 449			
Wisegerber			William	City of Wheeling	L	1854	33 448			
Witten	Arthur, Dec'd			Alexander Garden	L	1854	33 161	33 229	33 242	33 487
Witten's (Admrs) Arthur				Alexander Garden's Admrs et al	L	1855	34 89	34 154		
Withers		Joseph N.		Samuel B. Bushfield,	L	1856	35 23			
West	Henry			G. W. Wilson	L	1874	L2 6			
Weston			Sarah	William Ritz	C	1874	C1 59	C 1 144		

PLAINTIFF INDEX TO ORDER BOOKS — Ohio County, W. Va.

SURNAME	GIVEN NAMES A-H	GIVEN NAMES I-O	GIVEN NAMES P-Z	DEFENDANTS		YEAR	ORDER BOOK	
West	A. H.			Michael Stein	L	1875	L 2 278	
West		J.	W.	Wm. Richardson	L	1878	L 3 411	L 3 433
Westwood	A.			Dr. D. B. McLain	L	1879	L 4 240	L 4 291
Webb			William	John Rawland	L	1811	12 490	
Webb			Wm. et al	Henry Gosney	L	1811	13 15	13 88
Webb			William	John Rowland	L	1812	13 210	
Webb			William, et al	Nicholas Lewis	L	1814	14 273	14 418
Webb			Wm. et al	Wm. McConnell	L	1815	2 298	
Webb			William, et al	Nicholas Lewis, et al	L	1816	15 375	
Webb		of John Brooks	Wm. Assgnee.	Samuel Cockayne	L	1818	16 541	
Webb			Wm. et al	Lewis Perrine	L	1829	23 154	23 247
Webb			William, et al	Enos W. Newton	L	1837	27 342	
Webb		John A. et al		Jacob Orner	L	1838	29 137	
Webb			William, et al	Samuel Carter	L	1841	29 284	
Webb			William, T. E. (Adm'r)	Alexander McCortney	L	1841	28 505	
Webb			William, et al	Samuel H. B. Carter	L	1846	30 91	
Webb		Joseph		Leek Shabourday	L	1877	L 3 328	
Webb		Joseph		John Cooper, et al	L	1878	L 3 501	

'W' SURNAMES - PLAINTIFFS

PLAINTIFF INDEX TO ORDER BOOKS — Ohio County, W. Va

SURNAME	GIVEN NAMES ABCDEFGH	GIVEN NAMES IJKLMNO	GIVEN NAMES PQRSTUVWXYZ	DEFENDANTS	L/C	YEAR	ORDER BOOK		
Whiteford	Hugh,(Dec'd) Executors			Robert Giffen	L	1787	3/43	3/67	
Whitelock	Charles, et al			William B. Hays	L	1795	4/475		
Whiteford	Hugh, Assgnee of John Whiteford			Samuel Letten	L	1797	5/312		
Whitelash	Charles			Joseph Morton	L	1798	6/96		
Whitton			Thomas	David Parks	L	1802	8/231		
Whittum	Elizabeth, et al			John Abrams, et al	L	1803	8/290		
Whittom		Joseph, etal		William Perrine	L	1804	9/250		
Wherry		John, Dec.& Joseph, Adm.		Wm. Chapline	L	1810	12/182	12/254	
Whitton		Joseph, et al		Wm. Dement, et al	C	1810	12/213		
Whitelock	Hannah, et al			Abraham Rowland, Adm.	C	1812	13/330		
Wharton	Andrew			John Arnold	L	1813	14/117	14/224	14/281
Whitham		Joseph, etal		Wm. Dement, et al	C	1814	14/426		
Whitilock	Hannah, etal			Chas. Whitilock, Dec'd, etal	C	1814	14/277	14/290	
Whitaker		Levi		Elijah Woods	L	1818	2/496		
Whithan		Joseph		Alex Brown, et al	C	1818	16/237	16/273	16/312
Whittingham		James		Benjamin Gassaway	L	1820	17/401		
Wheeler	Elias H.			Thos. Reynolds	L	1822	19/164	19/239	19/351
Wheeler		John, Assgnee.		David Yates	L	1822	19/50		
Whalen			Patrick	James Salisbury	L	1823	19/455		
Whalon			et al Patrick,	Wm. McCoy	L	1823	19/408	19/502	
Wheeler	Elias H.			Thomas Reynolds, et al	L	1823	20/20		
Whitham		Joseph		Alice Moreland, et al	L	1824	20/168	20/179	
Whitten		Joseph		Henry Sockman	L	1824	20/212	20/449	
Wheatley			Warren	Benjamin C. Wright	L	1832	25/251	25/279	25/290
Whitehead	(Assgnee. of Elisha Whitehead)		Samuel H.	James Morris	L	1832	25/132	25/203	
Whitney		Joseph, etal		James H. Stout, et al	L	1838	27/400	27/483	27/485
Wheatley			Samuel C.	William F. Gordon	L	1839	28/59		
Whitman			Peter	Robert Argle	L	1839	28/153		
Whiteman		Lewis, et al		John F. Clarke	L	1840	28/418		
Wharton		James E.		Samuel Elkins	L	1841	28/544	28/588	
Wheeler	Albert P.			John Eberts	L	1848	30/320		
Wheeler	C. H.			William Forsyth	L	1854	34/8	34/20	34/33
Wheeler	Albert		P, et al	John Brotherton, etal	L	1855	34/70		
Whissen		Joseph		John Bishop	L	1855	34/237	34/321	
Whiteman	Ezra, etal			W. D. Hardy	L	1855	34/79	34/151	

PLAINTIFF INDEX TO ORDER BOOKS — Ohio County, W. Va.

SURNAME	GIVEN NAMES ABCDEFGH	GIVEN NAMES IJKLMNO	GIVEN NAMES PQRSTUVWXYZ	DEFENDANTS	L/C	YEAR	ORDER BOOK			
Whaltman	Adam			City of Wheeling	L	1856	34 392			
Whaltman	Adam			City of Wheeling	L	1856	35 49			
Wheelwright		Jeremiah, et al		Enos R. Bartleson	L	1856	35 290			
Wharton	Gibson			McCurdy & Gregg	L	1857	35 373	35 475		
Wheeler	Albert		P.	Bolivar Ward	L	1858	36 341			
Wheeler	Hayden		W.	John Bishop	L	1858	36 348			
Whittaker		Joseph, et al		James M. Todd	L	1858	36 343			
Wheeler			Samuel, Adm. of	Richard H. Hubbell	L	1859	37 441			
Wheeler			Samuel, Adm. of	James McGee	L	1859	37 452	37 455		
Whitaker		Joseph, et al		James M. Todd, et al	L	1859	37 101			
Wheeler	et al		Samuel P. Admr. et al	Oscar D. Thompson	L	1860	38 237			
Wheeler	Charles H.			Samuel B. Bushfield	L	1861	38 353			
Wheeler	Charles, et al			Hans W. Phillips	L	1861	38 436	38 472	38 481	
Wheeler			Samuel P. et al	Daniel Dunbar	L	1861	38 431	38 434		
Wheeler			Samuel P.	Samuel H. B. Carter	L	1862	39 104			
Whitaker	George &	Joseph		Aaron Kelly	L	1862	39 29			
Wharton		Lewis		Eliza J. Zane, et al	L	1873	L1 59			
Whelan			Richard V.	Caroline Ritz, et al	C	1873	C1 12	C1 24	C1 29	C1 51
Wheeler		James		William Stoetzer	L	1874	L1 389	L1 465	L1 518	
Whitaker	George		P.	Arthur C. McKee	L	1874	L1 433			
Whiting		John L.		George Roberts	L	1874	L1 284			
Wheeler		Louis		Frances Garrison	L	1875	L2 95	L2 149	L2 363	
Wheeler		Louis		Frances Garrisons, Adm.	L	1876	L3 17	L3 227		
Whinn		Michael		Ed. Larkin	L	1876	L3 87	L3 88	L3 108	
Whiteside			S. M.	Samuel Swift	L	1876	L3 68			
Wherry		Mary A.		John McConnell	L	1878	L3 499			
Wheeler		James		Augt. Nortsman	L	1878	L3 487	L3 489	L3 495	
Whitham		et al Joseph D.		Joshua Shook, et al	C	1878	C1 362			
Wheeler		James		James W. Sweeney	L	1879	L4 358	L4 375		
Wheeler		James		Andrew Wilson	L	1879	L4 285			

PLAINTIFF INDEX TO ORDER BOOKS — Ohio County, W. Va.

SURNAME	PLAINTIFFS (A-H)	PLAINTIFFS (I-O)	PLAINTIFFS (P-Z)	DEFENDANTS	L/C	YEAR	ORDER BOOK
Woherton			Thomas, etal	Elizabeth & Peter Donnald	L	1800	6/528
Wolf			Peter	James Hutchinson, et al	L	1817	2/427
Wolf			Peter	Jas. Hutchison, et al	L	1818	16/358 16/451
Wolford	Adam, Dec'd			Samuel Cockayne	L	1818	16/497 16/658 16/669 16/707
Wolfoot, Dec'd	Adam			Samuel Cockayne	L	1819	17/138
Wolf			Peter	James Hutchison, et al	L	1820	17/201 17/382
Wolfe	et al Erasmus D.			Zedekiah B. Curtis	L	1833	25/334
Wolfe		John		Loyd Hughes	L	1834	26/137 26/169 26/191 26/264 26/272 26/367
Wolf		John		Dana Hubbard	L	1835	26/431
Wolf		John		Wm. F. Peterson	L	1836	27/120 27/200 27/205 27/256
Wolfe		John		Jeremiah Clemens	L	1838	27/514
Wolf		John, etal		Jerimiah Clemens, et al	L	1838	28/10
Wolfe	Erasmus D. et al			John B. Wilson, et al	L	1855	34/351
Wolfe	Erasmus D. et al			William McKinley, Admr. etal	L	1856	35/26
Wolf	Christian, Jr.			Charles Freckman	L	1857	36/94
Wolf		Jacob		Gill, Hardman & Stephens	L	1861	38/432
Williamson	David			Samuel Taylor	L	1784	1/163 1/173 1/176 1/177
Williamson		John, Assgnee. of John Stokler		Charles Tibergan	L	1789	3/133
Williamson	Davidson			Francis Keller	L	1792	3/312
Williamson	David, for use of			John Polloch	L	1792	4/69 4/165 4/202
Williamson		John, Assgnee. of		Charles Zibregin	L	1793	4/113
Williamson		John		William McConnell	L	1796	6/180 6/312
Williamson			William	George Beymer	L	1799	6/450
Williamson			William	John Hambleton, et al	L	1799	6/308
Williamson	David			Thomas Smith	L	1800	7/111 7/258
Williamson	Admr. of Elizabeth, et al			Robert McClure	L	1800	6/529
Williamson	Dec'd	John, etal		Robert McClure	L	1800	6/529
Williamson	Elizabeth, et al Admr.			Robert McIntire	L	1801	7/314
Williamson	Elizabeth, etal			Robert McLure	L	1801	7/226 7/273
Williamson	Elizabeth, etal Admrs. of			Robert McClure	L	1801	8/57
Williamson		John, Dec'd, et al		Robert McIntire	L	1801	7/314
Williamson		John, Dec'd		Robert McLure	L	1801	7/226 7/273
Williamson	Alex. &	Joseph		Wm. Patton	L	1802	8/266 8/319
Williamson		James		Brigg Steenrod	L	1803	8/284 8/295

PLAINTIFF INDEX TO ORDER BOOKS — Ohio County, W. Va.

SURNAME	GIVEN NAMES ABCDEFGH	GIVEN NAMES IJKLMNO	GIVEN NAMES PQRSTUVWXYZ	DEFENDANTS	L/C	YEAR	ORDER BOOK					
Williamson		James, etal		Henry Smith	L	1805	10/76	10/77	10/128	10/129	10/192	10/193
Williamson, et al				Archibald Wood, et al	L	1806	10/332					
Williamson	David, etal			Dick Holdfast	L	1806	10/257	10/332				
Williamson		James		Aberham Birkhead	L	1809	12/132					
Williamson			Sally, Assgnee. of Patrick Ray	Wm. Zane, et al	L	1810	12/303					
Williamson		Isabel		Wm. Bounds, et al	L	1811	13/9	13/145				
Williamson		Isabella		John Shepherd	L	1811	13/52	13/148				
Williamson		Isabella		Clabourne Sims	L	1811	13/52	13/146	13/148	13/76		
Williamson		Isabella		Peter Sockman	L	1811	13/49	13/145				
Williamson		Isabel		Robt. Stewart	L	1811	13/7					
Williamson		Isabel		Samuel Whitaker	L	1811	13/8					
Williamson		Isabel		Robt. Williamson	L	1811	13/7					
Williamson		Isabel		Thos. Williamson	L	1811	13/9					
Williamson		Isabel		Wm. Williamson, et al	L	1811	13/8	13/9				
Williamson	David &	Mary		Henry Dillon	L	1811	13/69					
Williamson		Isabella, etal		John & James Bell	L	1812	13/146	13/147				
Williamson		Isabella, etal		John & Moses Bell	L	1812	13/147					
Williamson		James		Caleb McNulty	L	1812	13/323					
Williamson			Wm. Dec'd et al	James Fluharty	L	1813	14/47					
Williamson	David, Dec'd, et al			Henry Dillon	L	1814	14/306					
Williamson		James		Richard Parriott	L	1814	14/286					
Williamson			Thomas, etal	Maria Montgomery, et al	C	1814	14/327	14/354	14/377			
Williamson	David, Dec'd			David Moore, et al	C	1817	16/53					
Williamson			Thomas	Wm. Morrison, et al	L	1818	16/473	16/608	16/646			
Williamson			William	Archibald McDonald	L	1818	2/489					
Williamson			Wm.	Hugh Stewart	L	1821	18/74					
Williamson		Moses, Dec'd et al		Richard Coster	L	1826	21/420					
Williamson	Bazel, etal			George L. Meredith	L	1834	26/153					
Williamson	Bazil, etal, Assgnee			Ebenezer Zane	L	1834	26/203	26/261				
Williamson	B.			William A. Clarke	L	1843	29/299					
Williamson			William, etal	John Herron, et al	L	1860	38/296					
Williamson		Jane		Baltimore & Ohio R. R. Co.	L	1876	L4/75	L4/114				

PLAINTIFF INDEX TO ORDER BOOKS — Ohio County, W. Va.

SURNAME	GIVEN NAMES ABCDEFGH	GIVEN NAMES IJKLMNO	GIVEN NAMES PQRSTUVWXYZ	DEFENDANTS	L/C	YEAR	ORDER BOOK					
Worley		Joseph		Elijah Huff	L	1780	1 56					
Workman			Samuel	Daniel Preston	L	1787	3 38					
Workman			Samuel	John Pollock	L	1788	3 78					
Workman			Samuel	Joseph Wilson	L	1788	3 68					
Workman			Samuel	Michael Stulse	L	1789	3 142					
Worth		Richard		John McGloughland	L	1789	3 119					
Worth		John		John Dainold	L	1790	3 303					
Woolle		Mellon		Sebastion Durr	L	1796	5 101					
Wosley		Joseph, Assgnee. of John Head		Benjamin Bond	L	1797	6 8					
Worher, et al				John Tilton	L	1798	6 178					
Worley			Samuel	Asahael Griffith, et al	L	1798	6 93					
Worts		John		James Moak	L	1800	6 482					
Worden		John,Dec'd,et al		William Skinner	L	1801	8 56					
Woodburn		John,Assgnee.Thomas Gray)		George Gorden Dement, et al	L	1802	8 280					
Worthington (Warwick)		Thomas, Assgnee. et al		Moses Shepherd	L	1805	10 205					
Wornoch			William	Paprick McMahan	L	1806	10 275					
Worthington		Mary Ann, et al		Rebecca Nichols	L	1806	10 332					
Wookman	Benjamin			Geo. Pannell	L	1815	15 129					
Woodmunsy		James		Adrian Manvill	L	1820	17 203	17 414				
Worley		Joseph		Wm. H. Johnston	L	1822	19 108					
Worrell	Edward			Joseph C. McMahon	C	1822	19 273					
Workman	Hugh, Jr.			Amos Wright	L	1823	19 357					
Worley		Jos.		Wm. T. Good	L	1832	25 242	25 482				
Workman		James		Francis T. Harley	L	1833	25 340					
Workman		James		William I. Dobbin, et al	L	1834	26 143					
Woodford		Oliver		Samuel P. Jones	L	1835	26 398					
Workman		Josiah, et al		Elisha Barker	L	1837	27 305					
Workman		Josiah, for use of David Bonar		Elisha Barker	L	1839	28 87					
Woodmansee		Joseph		James Y. Caldwell	L	1845	30 14					
Wortman			Phebe A.	John Kraft	L	1847	30 190	30 222	30 398			
Wortman			Phebe A.	William Klevis, et al	L	1849	31 144	31 179				
Woodwell		Joseph		John V. K. Ebbert, et al	L	1850	31 352					
Woodwell		Joseph		Day & Harkins	L	1852	32 103					
Work		John A.		George Elrick	L	1852	32 59					
Woodruff		Edward D, et al		James Smylie	L	1855	34 352					

PLAINTIFF INDEX TO ORDER BOOKS — Ohio County, W. Va.

SURNAME	PLAINTIFFS GIVEN NAMES ABCDEFGH	GIVEN NAMES IJKLMNO	GIVEN NAMES PQRSTUVWXYZ	DEFENDANTS		YEAR	ORDER BOOK					
Wormser	Ephriam, et al			Edward W. Edwards, et al	L	1856	35 295					
Woodmanse		Lewis		Hugh G. Crymble & Co.	L	1860	38 117	38 278				
Wooster	F.			M. H. Gregg	L	1873	L 1 148					
Worthen	E. E.			William J. Robb	L	1873	L 1 135					
Woodmansee		Lewis		James Dooling, et al	L	1878	L 4 69	L 4 120	L 4 135			
Woodmansee		Louis		E W Showman, et al	L	1878	L 4 69	L 4 120				
Woodmansee		Lewis		William Tait, et al	L	1878	L 4 69	L 4 120				
Woodword			Wm. H.	Chas. Fisher	L	1879	L 4 139	L 4 182	L 4 183	L 4 197		
Woodmansee		Lewis		E. J. Arrick	L	1879	L 4 349	L 4 359	L 4 360	L 4 361	L 4 362	L 4 363
Woodmansee		Louis		R. H. Cochran	L	1879	L 4 373					
Woodmansee		Lewis		T. J. Woodmansee	L	1879	L 4 362					
Woodmansee		Lewis		David Bly	L	1880	L 4 468					

PLAINTIFF INDEX TO ORDER BOOKS — Ohio County, W. Va.

SURNAME	PLAINTIFFS GIVEN NAMES ABCDEFGH	GIVEN NAMES IJKLMNO	GIVEN NAMES PQRSTUVWXYZ	DEFENDANTS		YEAR	ORDER BOOK								
Wright			Zadoc	James McCord	L	1807	11 124	11 281							
Wright		Nancy, et al		Joseph Wright, et al	C	1817	16 126								
Wycart	Admr. of Francis, et al			Harmon Greathouse	L	1818	16 345	16 393							
Wyms	Henry			Wm. McMillen, et al	L	1819	16 378								
Wyms	Henry, or (Nancey)			M. G. Reynolds, et al	L	1819	17 314								
Wyat			Robert	Mason	L	1820	17 310								
Wycart	Francis, et al			Samuel Simms, Dec'd, et al	L	1821	18 417								
Wright		John C.		Lewis Peterson	L	1822	19 47	19 187							
Wycart	Francis, et al			Matthew Brown, et al	L	1822	19 37	19 55	19 309						
Wright		Jesse		Charles Vermillion	L	1824	20 224	20 355	20 356						
Wycart	Frances			Wm. Baker	L	1824	20 200								
Wycart		Nicholas		Dana Hubbard	L	1824	20 380								
Wright		Loyd		William Johnston	L	1827	22 118								
Wright			Sarah	John Hedges	L	1828	23 38	23 401							
Wynaman	Henry			Wm. Chauffant, et al	L	1829	23 200								
Wright	Amos			Salathiel Dillir	L	1830	24 21	24 123							
Wright			Sarah	John Hedges	L	1830	24 22	24 106	24 317						
Wyman		Samuel, et al		Robert Hamilton, et al	L	1837	27 259								
Wright		Thomas		Otis Dexter	L	1839	28 266								
Wylie		William		John Fisher, et al	L	1841	29 17	29 62	29 112	29 144					
Wright		John		John Nichols	L	1852	32 202	32 241							
Wright		John J., et al		Z. S. & J. J. Yarnall	L	1855	32 145								
Wunderlick		et al Simon H.		Perry Tracy	L	1855	34 72	34 284	34 292	34 307					
Wykart		(Assgnee. of John Flanagan) Samuel M.		Stewart Tag	L	1855	34 345								
Wright			Robert	J. T. Gillespie, et al	L	1856	35 35	35 152							
Wynkoop	Francis		S.	Julius Minett	L	1856	35 4								
Wynkoop	Francis		S.	James Smylie	L	1856	35 4	35 340	35 345	35 393	35 410	35 435	35 447	35 469	35 507
Wright		et al Peter T.		McCormick Pollard	L	1858	36 384	36 411							
Wurts	Charles, et al			William T. Robinson	L	1858	36 326								
Wright	George		W.	Jefferson Langston	L	1859	37 317	37 460	37 464						
Wright		Richard, et al		Edmund Booking	L	1859	37 142								
Wylie		William		Henry Otto	L	1860	38 308								
Wyman		Samuel G.		Robert Moore & Bro.	L	1861	38 523								
Wright		Joseph		Isaac Cotts	L	1863	39 194								
Wright		John	R.	Christian Becker	L	1873	L 1 101								

'W' NAMED CORPORATIONS AND FIRMS

PLAINTIFF INDEX TO ORDER BOOKS — Ohio County, W. Va.

SURNAME	GIVEN NAMES ABCDEFGH	GIVEN NAMES IJKLMNO	GIVEN NAMES PQRSTUVWXYZ	DEFENDANTS		YEAR	ORDER BOOK									
Wurster	Fred			M. H. Gregg	L	1873	L1 98	L1 98	L1 204	L1 310	L1 477					
Wright		John	R.	William T. Frazier	L	1874	L1 432									
Wright		Moses B. C.		William Klieves	L	1874	L1 388									
Wright		Moses B.		John Nolan	L	1874	L1 516									
Wusthoff	Frederick			Hermann Lingen	L	1874	L1 469									
Wray			Robert	Hansen Eimer	L	1876	L2 493									
Wray			Robert	August Rolf, et al	L	1876	L3 111									
Wright		M. L.		J. C. Orr & Co.	L	1880	L4 480									
Warden & Edwards				James M. Kirker	L	1849	31 204									
Warden & Edwards				James Fichner	L	1851	31 495									
Warden & Edwards				John Walker	L	1853	32 341									
Warden & Edwards				Sherrard Clemens	L	1855	34 136									
Warden & Edwards				Day & Harkins	L	1855	34 343	34 355								
Warden & Edwards				Martin L. Fink	L	1855	34 113									
Warden & Edwards				Bentley Moore	L	1855	34 153									
Warden & Edwards				James H. Dodgson	L	1856	35 211									
Warden & Edwards				John E. Hall	L	1856	35 185	35 217	35 247	35 271	35 302	35 318				
Warden & Edwards				Noah T. Harris	L	1856	35 202									
Warden & Edwards				Robert C. Bonham	L	1857	35 480									
Warden & Edwards				Daniel M. Edgington	L	1857	35 480									
Warden & Edwards				Mathias Jeffers	L	1857	36 55	36 74	36 94	36 109	36 156	36 193	36 200	36 222	36 270	36 291
do	do			do	do	do								36 307	36 354	36 423
Warden & Edwards				Andrew Mitchell	L	1857	35 360									
Warden & Edwards				Johnston Mulrine	L	1857	35 478									
Warden & Edwards				John Brenton	L	1858	37 85	37 243	37 334	37 421	37 502					
Warden & Edwards				Sherrard Clemens	L	1858	36 354	36 376								
Warden & Edwards				George A. Cracraft	L	1858	36 179									
Warden & Edwards				Mathias Jeffers	L	1858	37 14	37 30								
Warden & Edwards				David Luke	L	1858	36 390									
Warden & Edward				Robert William	L	1858	37 85									
Warden & Edwards				Bentley Moore	L	1859	37 177	37 201	37 230	37 243	37 274	37 314	37 376			
Warden & Edwards				John Brinton	L	1860	38 187	38 295	38 351	38 432	38 473	38 514				
Warden & Edwards				John Varner	L	1861	38 420									
Warden & Edwards				John Brinton	L	1862	39 15									

PLAINTIFF INDEX TO ORDER BOOKS — Ohio County, W. Va.

SURNAME	PLAINTIFFS GIVEN NAMES ABCDEFGH	GIVEN NAMES IJKLMNO	GIVEN NAMES PQRSTUVWXYZ	DEFENDANTS	L/C	YEAR	ORDER BOOK								
Yaund			Silas	Edward Coen	L	1787	3 / 47								
Yates			Richard	Uriah McCluskey	L	1788	3 / 59								
Yarnall		Mordacia		Matthew Alexander	L	1800	7 / 31								
Yarnel		Mordico		Peter Ogden	L	1802	8 / 78								
Yarnall		Mordecai		Gideon C. Forsyth	L	1809	12 / 5	12 / 131							
Yarnall		Mordecai		Jonah Updegraff et al	C	1809	12 / 37	12 / 515							
Yarnalk		Mordicai		John Morgan	L	1810	12 / 333								
Yarnell		Mordecai &	Peter	Josiah Updegraff	C	1811	13 / 17	13 / 93	13 / 133						
Yarnall		Mordecai &	Peter	Josiah Updegraff et al	C	1814	14 / 426								
Yarnall			Peter	John Hicks et al	L	1820	17 / 312	17 / 421							
Yarnall			et al Peter	David Miller	C	1824	20 / 73	20 / 330	20 / 337						
Yarnall			et al Peter	David Miller	C	1825	21 / 174								
Yarnall		Mordicae &	Peter	Wm. Burns	L	1825	21 / 239								
Yates	Hetty			Lewis Thompson	L	1828	22 / 332								
Yancey			William	Thomas Echols	L	1832	25 / 195								
Yardley	Use of Neff & Brothers	Kerkbride		James P. Smith	L	1832	25 / 175	26 / 59	26 / 142	26 / 189	26 / 475				
Yates		Joseph		Levy Mills et al	L	1845	30 / 14								
Yates			Thomas	Francis Lawson et al	L	1851	32 / 25								
Yates			Thomas	Francis Lawson et al	L	1851	31 / 395								
Yarnall			et al ZachariahS.	Samuel Rogers	L	1853	32 / 399								
Yard	Edmund	et al		John Elliott	L	1856	35 / 24								
Yard	Edmund	et al		Hugh C. Devine	L	1856	35 / 24	35 / 98							
Yarnall		John J. &	Zachariah & Peter	City of Wheeling	L	1856	35 / 177								
Yard	Edmund			William Goodrich	L	1857	35 / 479								
Yager		John		Alexander Malcum	L	1857	36 / 68	36 / 89	36 / 93						
Yager		John		Alexander Malcume	L	1857	35 / 508								
Yarnell	E. F. C. & Ella			William H. Russell et al	L	1857	35 / 463								
Yarnell	Emma &		Peter	Peter Yarnell, Sr.	L	1858	36 / 189	36 / 193							
Yarnall			Peter	McCormick Pollard	L	1858	36 / 309								
Yarhling	Frederick			Robert Hooman	L	1859	37 / 370								
Yarhling	F.			A. J. Phillips et al	L	1860	38 / 73								
Yates			et al Thos. Q.	Reuben F. Hedges	L	1861	38 / 352								
Yahrling	Fred			Johnston & Berryhill	L	1862	39 / 43	39 / 48	39 / 49	39 / 56	39 / 65	39 / 86	39 / 91	39 / 98	39 / 110	39 / 121
Yater	Florence A.			Burton Hedges	L	1875	12 / 204								
Yates	Byon T.	et al		Albert C. Fowler	L	1876	13 / 73								

PLAINTIFF INDEX TO ORDER BOOKS — Ohio County, W. Va.

SURNAME	PLAINTIFFS GIVEN NAMES ABCDEFGH	GIVEN NAMES IJKLMNO	GIVEN NAMES PQRSTUVWXYZ	DEFENDANTS		YEAR	ORDER BOOK						
Yates			Thomas G.	Andrew F. Yates et al	C	1877	C1 244	C1 265					
Yates	Byers T.			L. B. Morgan et al	L	1879	L4 164	L4 177	L4 187				

PLAINTIFF INDEX TO ORDER BOOKS — Ohio County, W. Va.

SURNAME	PLAINTIFFS GIVEN NAMES ABCDEFGH	GIVEN NAMES IJKLMNO	GIVEN NAMES PQRSTUVWXYZ	DEFENDANTS		YEAR	ORDER BOOK		
Yeaman	Agnes			John Hays	L	1787	3 / 24	3 / 57	
Yeats			Richard	George Beelor	L	1793	4 / 153		
Yeats			et al Richard	William McMachan	L	1794	4 / 295		
Yeats			Richard	James Fulton	L	1797	5 / 320		
Yeats			Richard	James Fulton	L	1798	6 / 98	6 / 135	
Yeats	Use of Archibald Woods		Richard	James Fulton	L	1801	7 / 279		
Yeats			Thomas	Thomas Marlow	C	1807	11 / 139	11 / 211	11 / 447
Yingling			R. H.	H. L. Turvey	L	1879	L4 / 218		

PLAINTIFF INDEX TO ORDER BOOKS — Ohio County, W. Va.

PLAINTIFFS SURNAME	GIVEN NAMES ABCDEFGH	GIVEN NAMES IJKLMNO	GIVEN NAMES PQRSTUVWXYZ	DEFENDANTS		YEAR	ORDER BOOK						
Woods & Caldwell				William Moore	L	1798	6 / 120						
Woods & Caldwell				Samuel Beck	L	1799	6 / 386	6 / 399					
Woods & Caldwell				Phillip Dover	L	1799	6 / 374						
Woods & Caldwell				John Green	L	1799	6 / 281						
Woods & Caldwell				Samuel Harris	L	1799	6 / 311	6 / 463					
Woods & Caldwell				Samuel McClure	L	1799	6 / 375						
Woods & Caldwell				William Dement	L	1802	8 / 252						
Woods & Caldwell				Reuben Harris et al	L	1802	8 / 232						
Woods & Caldwell				Henry Hoover	L	1803	8 / 357						
Woods & Caldwell				Peter Ogden	L	1803	8 / 356						
Woods & Caldwell				Jacob Whitzel	L	1803	8 / 357						
Woods & Caldwell				John Black	L	1805	10 / 219						
Woods & Caldwell				George McColloch	L	1806	10 / 245	10 / 373					

PLAINTIFF INDEX TO ORDER BOOKS — Ohio County, W. Va.

SURNAME	PLAINTIFFS GIVEN NAMES ABCDEFGH	GIVEN NAMES IJKLMNO	GIVEN NAMES PQRSTUVWXYZ	DEFENDANTS		YEAR	ORDER BOOK						
Young		John		John Mitchel	L	1787	3 32						
Young	Alexander			James Miller	L	1788	3 74						
Young		James		Joseph Ross	L	1793	4 152						
Young	Henry			Samuel Grayham	L	1793	4 139	4 288	4 291	4 321			
Young		James		George Edgington	L	1795	5 18						
Young	George			Isaac Meek	L	1795	4 444	5 56					
Young		John Goodman et al		George Edgington et al	C	1796	5 97						
Young		Morgan et al		John Marshal et al	C	1804	9 266						
Young		Morgan et al		John Marshall et al	C	1805	10 186						
Young	Henry			James Curtis	L	1807	11 127	11 275					
Young	Henry			John Seybert	L	1807	11 127	11 281					
Young			Samuel	John Lee	L	1808	11 424						
Young			Samuel	John Lee	L	1809	12 25						
Young			William	James McKnight	L	1809	11 477						
Yoho	Henry	et al		Spencer Biddle	L	1811	13 85	13 18					
Younger		Nehemiah		Cornelius Dehart	L	1812	13 175						
Yoho	Henry	et al		Spencer Biddle	C	1813	14 112						
Young			William	John Arnold et al	L	1814	14 280						
Younger	Humphrey &	Mary		Wm. Williamson	L	1817	8 384						
Yoho	Henry, Sr.			Wm. Chapline	C	1822	19 164						
Yoho	Henry			Wm. Chapline	C	1824	20 136	20 248	20 337				
Young	Andrew			Samuel Smith	L	1832	25 256						
Young		et al Wm., Jr.		Wm. W. Jamison et al	L	1834	26 199						
Young	Elijah B.			Ephram Banning	L	1835	26 314						
Young		Judy et al		William Brown et al	L	1850	31 312						
Young		Judy et al		Franklin Williamson	L	1850	31 287						
Yonker		Lewis		Richard Knowles	L	1852	32 241						
Young		John	et al	James Smylie	L	1856	35 28						
Young			Thomas	City of Wheeling	L	1856	35 181	35 248	35 272	35 324	35 385	35 386	35 391
Young			Philip	Henry Thompson	L	1857	36 102						
Young			Simon	August Goetz Surv. & Co.	L	1859	37 454	37 502					
Yocke	A.			West Liberty Academy	L	1859	37 454	37 484					
Young		et al Wm. T.		Gordon Robinson	L	1859	37 425	38 24					
Yocke	Adolph			West Liberty Academy	L	1860	38 125	38 187	38 193	38 292	38 309		
Young			Simon	August Goetze	L	1860	38 126						

66 PLAINTIFF INDEX TO ORDER BOOKS — Ohio County, W. Va.

SURNAME	GIVEN NAMES ABCDEFGH	GIVEN NAMES IJKLMNO	GIVEN NAMES PQRSTUVWXYZ	DEFENDANTS		YEAR	ORDER BOOK								
Young			Philip	Ezekiel Rodgers	L	1873	L1 139								
Yocke	Adolph			John S. Creigton et al	L	1873	L1 155	L1 168							
Yocke	Adolph			Isaac G. Burkam et al	L	1873	L1 162								
Young	Edward B.			James McGannon et al	L	1874	L1 307	L1 365							
Young	Albert			Pittsburg, Wheeling & Ky. R.R. Co.	L	1874	L1 322								
Yocke	Adolph			Pittsburg, Wheeling & Ky. R.R. Co.	L	1874	L1 392								
Young		Louis		P. E. Zinn	L	1875	L2 134								
Yocke	Adolph			Pittsburg, Wheeling & Ky. R.R. Co.	L	1875	L2 147	L2 261	L2 274	L2 445	L2 446	L2 447	L2 450	L2 470	L2 471	L2 475
Young			Thomas P.	James McCluney	L	1875	L2 246								
Young			Wm. H. et al	Henry Knoke & Co. et al	L	1876	L3 7								
Young			Philip	Frank Muldoon et al	L	1876	L3 38								
Young	Edward B. & Alice B.			Mary E. Young et al	C	1876	C1 190	C1 197	C1 213						
Yocke	A.			John Conner	L	1876	L2 485								
Young			et al Peter B.	Jacob F. Luikert et al	C	1877	C1 256	C1 284	C1 300	C1 321	C1 334	C1 340	C1 347		
Young			Philip	Frank Muldoon, Adm'r.	L	1878	L4 49								
Young			Phillip	J. E. McKennan Adm'r.	L	1879	L4 277	L4 422							

'Z' SURNAMES – FREQUENTLY OCCURRING

PLAINTIFF INDEX TO ORDER BOOKS — Ohio County, W. Va.

PLAINTIFFS SURNAME	GIVEN NAMES ABCDEFGH	GIVEN NAMES IJKLMNO	GIVEN NAMES PQRSTUVWXYZ	DEFENDANTS	L/C	YEAR	ORDER BOOK Vol	Page	Vol	Page	Vol	Page
Zane	Andrew			James Clark	L	1783	1	180				
do	Andrew			Conrod Stroup	L	1783	1	180	1	239		
do			Silas	Gaspoe & Barbary Frush	L	1783	1	180				
do	E. B.	et al		Joseph Tomlinson, Jr.	L	1784	1	183	1	216		
do			Silas	Matthew Kerr	C	1784	1	248				
do			William	David Fitchgibans	L	1787	3	47				
do	Andrew	et al		Philip Dover	L	1788	3	57	3	78		
do		Janathan		Francis Hardisty	L	1788	3	83	3	84	3	87	3	94
do	Ebenezer			Nathan McFarland	L	1789	3	139	3	187		
do	Ebenezer			Samuel Hand et al	L	1797	6	5	6	6	5	282
do	Ebenezer			Joseph Tomlinson	L	1798	6	97				
do	Ebenezer			George Beymer	L	1799	6	360				
do	Ebenzer			William Coss	L	1801	7	231	7	291		
do	Ebenezer			William Dement	L	1801	7	260				
do	Ebenezer			Isaac Taylor	L	1801	7	274	7	283	7	285
do		Jonathan	et al	Absalom Martin	L	1802	8	116				
do	Ebeneazer		et al	Jane Beelor et al	L	1803	8	323	8	324	8	332
do		John	et al	Absolom Martin et al	C	1803	9	115	9	122	9	154
do		Jonathan		Absolam Marton	L	1804	9	265				
do	Ebenezar			Alexander Mitchel	L	1806	10	309				
do		Jonathan		Edward Nicholas	L	1806	10	371				
do		Noah	et al	John Bound	L	1807	11	95				
do		Jonathan		James Sewright	L	1808	11	335				
do		Noah		Dennis Cassat	L	1808	11	276				
do		John & Noah	et al	Gideon C. Forsyth	L	1808	11	278	11	416	11	487
do		Noah		Josiah Updegraff	L	1809	11	488				
do	Ebenezer	et al		Frederick Beymer	L	1810	12	217				
do	Ebenezer			Wm. Barton	C	1811	13	74	13	213		
do	Ebenezer			Gideon Forsythe	C	1811	13	74	13	213		
do	Ebenezer			Gidion Forsyth et al	C	1811	12	514				
do	Ebenezer			Wm. Barton et al	C	1811	12	515				
do		Jonathan		Thomas Thompson	L	1811	13	66				
do		Jonathan		Thomas Thompson	L	1811	12	507				
do	Daniel &	Noah &	Samuel	John Carr	L	1812	13	293	13	428		
do	Ebenezer	Dec'd.		Benjamin Strong	L	1812	13	212				

PLAINTIFF INDEX TO ORDER BOOKS — Ohio County, W. Va.

PLAINTIFFS SURNAME	GIVEN NAMES ABCDEFGH	GIVEN NAMES IJKLMNO	GIVEN NAMES PQRSTUVWXYZ	DEFENDANTS	L	YEAR	ORDER BOOK (Top: Volume / Bottom: Page)			
Zane	Daniel & Ebenezer & Elizabeth &	Noah &	Samuel	William Grove	C	1812	13 206			
Zane	Daniel & Ebenezer & Elizabeth &	Noah &	Samuel	Benjamin Mulligan	C	1812	13 207	13 370	14 33	
do	do	do	Samuel	William Barton	C	1812	13 246			
do	do	do	Samuel	Michael Humbert	C	1812	13 338	13 437		
do	do	do	Samuel	John Collender	C	1812	13 336	13 448		
do	do	do	Samuel	Benjamin Strong	L	1812	13 335			
do	do	do	Samuel	William Grove	C	1812	13 369			
do		Jonathan		Basil Beall et al	L	1812	13 357			
do	Daniel & Ebenezer &	Noah &	Samuel	William Barton et al	C	1813	14 38			
do	do	do	Samuel	Gideon C. Forsyth et al	C	1813	14 49	14 79	14 395	
do	do	do	Samuel	Wm. Chapline, Jr. et al	C	1813	14 51	14 174	14 336	
do	do	do	Samuel	Wm. McConnell et al	L	1813	14 59			
do	do	do	Samuel	James Salters	L	1813	14 75			
do	do	do	Samuel	Michael Humbert	C	1813	14 78	14 151		
do	do	do	Samuel	William Grove	L	1813	14 149			
do	do	do	Samuel	Thomas Collenger, Dec'd.	C	1813	14 137			
do	do	do	Samuel	Wm. McConnell	L	1813	13 427			
do		Noah	et al	Basil Beall, Sr. et al	L	1814	2 160			
do	Daniel &	Noah		Jonathan Zane	L	1815	2 254	2 289	2 306	2 335
do		Jonathan		Robert Barclay	L	1815	15 31	15 140		
do		Noah		William Chapline	L	1815	15 28			
do		Jonathan		Conrad Catz	L	1816	2 344			
do		Noah		Jonathan Zane	L	1816	2 357	2 398	2 422	
do		Jonathan		Robert Bostley	L	1817	16 46			
do		Jonathan		Basil Beall, Sr.	L	1817	2 397	2 412	2 437	2 481
do			Samuel	Jacob Hanes	L	1817	16 110	16 247		
do			Samuel et al	Thomas Lyles	L	1817	2 426			
do		Noah		John Zane	L	1818	16 419	16 425		
do		Jonathan		Amos Mix	L	1819	17 137			
do		Noah	et al	Benjamin Gassaway et al	L	1819	17 3	17 216		
do		Jonathan		Noah Zane et al	L	1820	17 340	17 354		
do		Jonathan		Joseph Wosley	L	1820	17 357			
do	Daniel &	Noah		William Johnston	L	1820	17 382			
do		Noah		Samuel Warden	C	1820	17 423	17 466	17 481	17 493
do		Noah	et al	Samuel Saylor et al	C	1820	17 509			

'Z' SURNAMES – FREQUENTLY OCCURRING

PLAINTIFF INDEX TO ORDER BOOKS — Ohio County, W. Va.

SURNAME	GIVEN NAMES ABCDEFGH	GIVEN NAMES IJKLMNO	GIVEN NAMES PQRSTUVWXYZ	DEFENDANTS	L/C	YEAR	ORDER BOOK					
Zane	Daniel	et al		Archibald Hamilton et al	L	1821	18/147					
do	Daniel &	Noah		Wm. Johnson	L	1821	18/221					
do		Jonathan		Joseph Worley	L	1821	18/97	18/234	18/425			
do		Noah	et al	Joseph Godfrey	L	1821	18/71	18/255	18/256			
do		Noah	et al	Thomas Bell	L	1821	18/71	18/257	18/296			
do		Noah		John Wisinall	L	1821	18/203	18/242	18/243	18/434		
do		Noah		David Miller	L	1821	18/260					
do		Noah		Thomas Tonner et al	L	1821	18/363	18/414	18/415	18/473	18/497	18/498
do		Noah	et al	Samuel Saylor et al	C	1821	18/367					
do		Noah	et al	James McCoy et al	L	1821	18/414					
do		Noah	et al	Wm. McClelland et al	L	1822	19/14	19/95				
do		Noah		Joseph Worley	L	1822	19/25	19/26				
do		Noah		William Templeton et al	L	1822	19/74					
do		Noah	(Sheriff)	Joseph Montgomery	L	1822	19/89					
do		Noah	(Sheriff)	Wm. Laughridge et al	L	1822	19/98					
do		Noah	et al	Moses Shepherd	L	1822	19/111	19/246				
do		Noah	(Sheriff)	Thomas Stead et al	L	1822	19/117					
do		Noah		Samuel Warden	C	1822	19/125					
do		Noah		Henry Willey	L	1823	20/10	20/244				
do		Noah	et al	George White et al	L	1823	20/31					
do		Noah		James Pemberton	L	1823	19/345					
do		Noah	et al	Wm. Crawford	L	1823	19/421					
do		Noah		John Fawcett	L	1823	19/426					
do		Noah	et al	Conrad Catz	L	1823	19/437					
do		Noah		William Greer	L	1823	19/526					
do	Daniel &	Noah		Solomon Lightcap et al	L	1824	20/165	20/302	20/387			
do		Noah	et al	David Miller	C	1824	20/73	20/330	20/337			
do		Noah		James Lynn et al	L	1824	20/130					
do		Noah		Wm. Crawford	L	1824	20/166					
do		Noah		Hannah Gooding	L	1824	20/250					
do	Cynthia & Daniel &	Noah	et al	Samuel Wells et al	C	1825	21/171					
do	do	do	et al	Samuel H. Wells et al	C	1825	20/512					
do	Daniel &	Jonathan	et al	Elijah Burris et al	L	1825	21/95	20/488				
do		Noah		Adam Carp	L	1825	21/98					
do		Noah		David Miller	C	1825	21/107	21/174				
do		Noah		Elijah Burris	L	1823	20/13	20/190				

PLAINTIFF INDEX TO ORDER BOOKS — Ohio County, W Va.

SURNAME	PLAINTIFFS GIVEN NAMES ABCDEFGH	PLAINTIFFS GIVEN NAMES IJKLMNO	PLAINTIFFS GIVEN NAMES PQRSTUVWXYZ	DEFENDANTS		YEAR	ORDER BOOK		
Zane		Noah	et al	Wm. Harkins	L	1825	21 235		
do		Noah		Thomas Baker	L	1825	20 515		
do	Daniel &	Jonathan	et al	Wm. Ann Clord et al	C	1826	21 262		
do	Daniel &	Jonathan		Noah Zane et al	L	1827	22 96	22 165	22 205
do		Noah		Abraham W. Clemans et al	L	1827	22 111	22 244	
do		Noah		Adam Carp	L	1827	22 148		
do		Noah		John Lowrie	C	1827	22 158	22 186	
do		Noah		John Hendricks	C	1827	22 159	22 177	
do	Daniel &	Jonathan	et al	Daniel Steenrod et al	C	1828	23 14		
do	Fanny			Benjamin Zane	C	1828	22 323		
do		Jonathan		William Clark & Wife	C	1828	22 419		
do		Noah		Adam Carp	C	1828	23 74		
do		Noah		John Clark et al	C	1828	22 323		
do		Noah		Joseph Matthias et al	L	1828	22 384		
do		Noah		Garrison Jones	L	1828	22 424		
do		Noah		David Miller	C	1828	22 430		
do		Noah		John Ridden	L	1828	22 490		
do		Noah		John Ridden	L	1828	22 490		
do		Noah		Thomas Carroll	L	1829	23 257		
do		Noah		Wm. Chaffant et al	L	1829	23 280		
do		Noah		Salathial Diller et al	L	1829	23 305		
do		Noah		Asa Richards	L	1829	23 316	23 391	
do		Noah	et al	John Gosney	L	1829	23 401		
do		Noah		Robert Baldwin	L	1830	24 27		
do		Noah		Robert Baldwin	L	1831	25 20	25 431	25 479
do		Noah		John Pierson	L	1831	25 21	25 415	
do	Ebenezer	et al		Enoch Watkins et al	L	1832	25 190		
do	Daniel			Moses Ford et al	L	1833	25 373		
do	Ebenezer			Hilliary Beall	L	1833	25 336		
do		Noah		John Graham	L	1833	25 431		
do	Ebenezer	et al		Moses Thornburgh	L	1834	26 199		
do	Ebenezer &	Noah		Patrick Yoho	L	1834	26 221		
do		Noah		John Graham	L	1834	26 50	26 132	26 189
do	Ebenezer			Solomon King	L	1835	26 378		
do	Ebenezer			James Hamilton	L	1835	26 383		

'Z' SURNAMES – FREQUENTLY OCCURRING

PLAINTIFF INDEX TO ORDER BOOKS — Ohio County, W. Va.

SURNAME	GIVEN NAMES A-H	GIVEN NAMES I-O	GIVEN NAMES P-Z	DEFENDANTS		YEAR	ORDER BOOK					
Zane	Ebenezer			James H. Forsyth	L	1836	27/48					
do	Ebenezer &	Noah	et al	William Cunningham	L	1836	27/101	27/356				
do		Noah		William Cunningham	L	1836	27/14					
do		N.		John Graham	L	1836	27/111	27/195	27/299	27/396	27/466	27/499
do	Ebenezer	et al		Robert G. Martin et al	L	1837	27/212					
do			et al Platoff	William F. Barnes	L	1837	27/213	27/214				
do			et al Platoff	David Lee	L	1837	27/291	27/321				
do			et al Platoff	James A. McClean	L	1837	27/303					
do			et al Platoff	William Gill	L	1837	27/303					
do	Ebenezer			Ely Dorsey	L	1838	28/15	28/48				
do	Ebenezer			John L. Newby	L	1838	27/497					
do	Ebenezer			John Farrow	L	1838	27/550					
do	Ebenezer	et al		John Farrow	L	1839	28/35	28/44	28/235			
do		John		David McCulloch	L	1839	28/158					
do			et al Platoff	George W. Sights	L	1839	29/63	29/265				
do			Platoff	Jeremiah Clemens	L	1839	28/110					
do			Platoff	David Echols	L	1839	28/110	28/206				
do			Platoff	Ely Dorsey	L	1839	28/145					
do			Platoff	John R. Hall	L	1839	28/165					
do			Platoff	Abraham W. Clemens	L	1839	28/168	28/304				
do			Platoff	Joseph Vance	L	1839	28/189	28/224				
do	Elizabeth & Cornelius			Moses Rhodes	L	1840	28/421					
do			Platoff	John W. Berry	L	1840	28/250					
do			Platoff	William Chapline	L	1840	28/250	28/304				
do			Platoff	Perry Deford	L	1840	28/261	28/308				
do			Platoff	David Victor	L	1840	28/354					
do			Platoff	James K. Wharton	L	1840	28/354					
do			Platoff	Isaac Farnesworth	L	1840	28/365					
do			Platoff	Robert Fisher	L	1840	28/365					
do			Platoff	James Manly	L	1840	28/365					
do			et al Platoff	James Tanner	L	1840	28/365					
do			et al Platoff	James Lloyd	L	1841	29/8					
do			et al Platoff	John E. Reeside	L	1841	29/9					
do			et al Platoff	John M. McCreary	L	1841	29/16	29/62				
do			Platoff	Thomas Townsend	L	1841	29/17					

PLAINTIFF INDEX TO ORDER BOOKS — Ohio County, W. Va.

SURNAME	PLAINTIFFS GIVEN NAMES ABCDEFGH	GIVEN NAMES IJKLMNO	GIVEN NAMES PQRSTUVWXYZ	DEFENDANTS		YEAR	ORDER BOOK						
Zane			Platoff et al	James Townsend	L	1841	29 17						
do	Ebenezer	et al		John W. Berry et al	L	1842	29 75	29 124					
do		Noah	et al	James McCluney et al	L	1842	29 68						
do	Hampden			Abraham Allman	L	1843	29 186						
do		M. S.		John W. Berry	L	1843	29 299						
do		Noah		Adam Carp	C	1844	29 336						
do		Noah		John Lowry	C	1844	29 336						
do		Noah	et al	Robert Woods et al	L	1845	29 532						
do			Virginia F.C.	Orloff A. Zane	L	1853	32 358	34 41					
do	Ebenezer			David Kull	L	1855	34 252						
do	Clark Leander			Hezekiah Hendon	L	1857	36 40						
do			Virginia F.C.	Orloff A. Zane	C	1857	35 430						
do	E. P.	et al		John L. Bonham	L	1858	36 272						
do	Clark Leander		et al	Jacob H. Timmanns	L	1861	38 352						
do			Virginia F.C.	Orloff A. Zane et al	C	1861	38 509						
do	C. L.			William C. Hanes	L	1862	39 136						
do	C. Leander	et al		John Booker	L	1863	39 197						
do	C. L.	et al		Adolph Yocke	L	1874	L2 20	L2 117					
do	Eliza J.	&	Platoff	Jacob Emsheimer, Jr.	L	1874	L2 41						
do	L. E.			H. W. Phillips	L	1874	L2 6						
do	L. E.			William Armstrong	L	1874	L2 50	L2 118	L2 311	L2 312	L2 314	L2 315	L2 414
do	C. L.	et al		Smith McDonald	L	1875	L2 251						
do	Edwin E.			William Armstrong	L	1877	L3 161						
do	Edwin E.			Joseph N. Parker et al	L	1878	L4 122						
do	Edwin E.			L. D. Williams	L	1879	L4 246						
do	Edwin			Han W. Phillips	L	1873	L1 204	L1 214					

'Z' SURNAMES - PLAINTIFFS

PLAINTIFF INDEX TO ORDER BOOKS — Ohio County, W. Va.

SURNAME	GIVEN NAMES A-H	GIVEN NAMES I-O	GIVEN NAMES P-Z	DEFENDANTS	L/C	YEAR	ORDER BOOK						
Zephford			Peter	Alexander Orr	L	1794	251	325					
Zim	Daniel			William Chapline	L	1817	2 419						
Zeagler		John		William R. McClure	L	1838	27 512						
Zeigler	Benjamin			James Stephenson	L	1841	29 55						
Zink		Mary		A. P. Woods	L	1841	29 16	29 64					
Zink		Mary		A. P. Woods	L	1841	28 571						
Zinn			Peter E.	Smith McDonald et al	L	1850	31 285	31 345					
Zimmer		John N.		James McLure	L	1852	32 202	32 240	32 249				
Zimmer		John N.		John Schuckman	L	1852	32 263						
Zinn			Peter E.	Charles Swarts	L	1854	34 41	34 113					
Zeigler	Frederick			T. C. Layton	L	1856	35 107						
Zeigler	Frederick			James Logan	L	1856	35 107						
Zeloh		John et al		John Young et al	L	1857	55 354						
Zeockler	Ernest			John O'Brien	L	1857	36 102						
Zillis	George			Jacob Zillis	L	1857	36 55	36 73	36 86	36 135	36 156	36 168	36 200
Zimmer		John N. et al		George Curry	L	1857	36 50						
Zinn			Peter E.	Mason M. Dunlap et al	L	1857	36 26	36 100					
Zinn			Peter E.	Joseph M. Stewart	L	1857	36 90						
Zinn			Peter E.	George E. Zinn et al	L	1857	35 487						
Zinn			Peter E.	Mason M. Dunlap	L	1857	35 488						
Zeigler	F. Ernest			Leonard Zeigler	L	1858	36 194	36 321	36 423				
Ziegler	Ernest F.			Leonard Ziegler	L	1858	37 74						
Zimmer		J. N.		E. L. & R. Pratt	L	1858	36 194	36 318					
Zinn			Peter E.	John Kirkpatrick	L	1858	36 345						
Zeigler		Lewis		Lewis Cook	L	1859	37 113						
Zimmerman	George			John Davis	L	1859	37 133						
Zeockler			Peter	Ann Bollinger	L	1860	38 282						
Zimmer		John N.		Daniel P. Martin	L	1860	38 128						
Zimmer		John N.		George Metcalf	L	1860	38 198						
Zink			William	J. N. Fordyce	L	1861	38 396						
Zimmer			William	N. N. Moses	L	1875	L2 173						
Zenglein	Barbara			Gottfried Ryer et al	L	1875	L2 278						
Zenglein	Barbara			Catharine Weiss et al	L	1875	L2 278						
Zenglein	Daniel	et al		Katherine Niedermeyer et al	C	1876	C1 224	C1 233	C1 305				
Zinn			P. E.	R. Savage et al	L	1877	L3 362	L3 391	L3 420	L3 422	L3 434		

'W' NAMED CORPORATIONS AND FIRMS

PLAINTIFF INDEX TO ORDER BOOKS — Ohio County, W. Va.

PLAINTIFFS SURNAME	GIVEN NAMES ABCDEFGH	GIVEN NAMES IJKLMNO	GIVEN NAMES PQRSTUVWXYZ	DEFENDANTS	L	YEAR	ORDER BOOK		
Zierowich	Gottlieb			William M. Thoburn	L	1878	L4 16	L4 26	
Zink			William	J. J. Roberts	L	1878	L4 99	L4 111	L4 217
Wilson & Waddle				Henry Giles	L	1835	26 347		
do				William Connor	L	1840	28 367		
do				Stephen Foreman	L	1840	28 329	28 391	28 396
do				Wallace Hemphill	L	1840	28 366		
do				Alfred S. Lauck	L	1840	28 366	28 413	28 415
do				Thomas Laws	L	1840	28 367	28 413	28 416
do				Joseph Marshall	L	1840	28 357		
do				Levi Mills	L	1840	28 366		
do				William Wells	L	1840	28 366	28 451	
do				William Hodge	L	1841	28 566		
do				Henry Lewis	L	1841	28 547	28 588	
do				John Mooney	L	1841	28 573		
do				A. Ridgely, Jr.	L	1841	28 505		
do				John Russell	L	1841	28 530	28 568	
do				Alexander W. Walker	L	1841	28 547		
do				George Wheatley	L	1841	28 575		
do				Alexander Walker et al	L	1842	29 155		

'Z' NAMED CORPORATIONS AND FIRMS

PLAINTIFF INDEX TO ORDER BOOKS — Ohio County, W. Va.

SURNAME	GIVEN NAMES ABCDEFGH	GIVEN NAMES IJKLMNO	GIVEN NAMES PQRSTUVWXYZ	DEFENDANTS		YEAR	ORDER BOOK								
Zonkler		Leus		Joseph Turner	L	1835	26/501								
Zoeckler		John		Leonard Randam	L	1842	29/138								
Zoeckler	Casper			City of Wheeling	L	1852	32/329	32/349	32/365	32/422	32/462				
Zoeckler		John		John J. Yarnall et al	L	1852	32/204	32/211	32/288						
Zoeckler	Casper			The City of Wheeling	L	1853	33/20	34/26	34/45	34/120	34/171				
Zoeckler	F. E.			City of Wheeling	L	1855	34/269	34/271	34/306	34/311					
Zoeckler			Peter	Henry M. Jamison	L	1855	34/243								
Zoeckler		John		J. L. Sangston	L	1861	38/402	38/418	38/430	38/448	38/466	38/489	38/494	38/565	38/541
Zoeckler		John		Jefferson S. Sangston	L	1862	39/2	39/50	39/56						
Zulauf		John		Peter Kreusch	L	1879	L4/204								
Zane & Pentoney				Jacob Atkinson	L	1830	24/32	24/104							
do				N. P. Atkinson	L	1830	24/123	24/162	24/187	24/263					
do				John S. Hendershot	L	1830	24/141								
do				Tobias Watkins	L	1831	24/358								
do				William Chapline	L	1832	25/132	25/180							
do				Jeremiah Clemins	L	1832	25/134								
do				Joel Zane	L	1832	25/134								
do				Enoch Watkins et al	L	1832	25/190								
do				John H. Lyons	L	1833	25/379								
do				Samuel C. Richards	L	1834	26/139								
do				Bushrod W. Price	L	1834	26/198								
do	et al			Abraham W. Clemens	L	1834	26/200								
do				George Dulty	L	1834	26/200	26/256							
do	et al			David Church	L	1834	26/201								
do	et al			James A. Cochran	L	1834	26/201								
do	et al			William Cunningham	L	1834	26/201	26/568							
do	et al			Mathias Jeffers	L	1834	26/201								
do	et al			Bushrod W. Price et al	L	1834	26/260								
do				John C. Hull	L	1835	26/391								
do	et al			Alfred Haskins et al	L	1835	26/488								
do				Joseph Pollock	L	1836	27/91								
do				William Forsyth	L	1837	27/203								
do				Wm. F. Barnes	L	1837	27/213	27/214							
do				David Lee	L	1837	27/291	27/521							

PLAINTIFF INDEX TO ORDER BOOKS — Ohio County, W. Va.

PLAINTIFFS SURNAME	DEFENDANTS		YEAR	ORDER BOOK			
Zane & Pentoney	William Gill	L	1837	27 303			
do	James A. McClean	L	1837	27 303			
do	John F. Truax	L	1838	28 35	28 44		
do	James F. McClean et al	L	1838	27 450	27 453		
do	John F. Truax	L	1838	27 551			
do	George W. Sights	L	1839	29 63	29 265		
do	Jeremiah Clemens	L	1839	28 110			
do	Ely Dorsey	L	1839	28 145			
do	Willis Conwell	L	1839	28 163			
do	John R. Hall	L	1839	28 165			
do	Abraham W. Clemens	L	1839	28 188	28 304		
do	Joseph Vance	L	1839	28 189	28 224		
do	William Chapline	L	1840	28 250	28 304		
do	John W. Berry	L	1840	28 250			
do	Perry Deford	L	1840	28 261	28 308		
do	David Victor	L	1840	28 354			
do	James E. Wharton	L	1840	28 354			
do	John Reeside	L	1840	28 360	28 428	28 502	28 533
do	Isaac Farnesworth	L	1840	28 365			
do	Robert Fisher	L	1840	28 365			
do	Henry Helm	L	1840	28 365			
do	James Manly	L	1840	28 365			
do	James Tanner	L	1840	28 365			
do	James Lloyd	L	1841	29 8			
do	John Reeside	L	1841	29 9			
do	John M. McCreary	L	1841	29 16	29 62		
do	James Townsend	L	1841	29 17			
do	James Clemens	L	1843	29 299			
do	Matthias Jeffers	L	1843	29 299			
do	Maria Truax	L	1843	29 299			

PLAINTIFF INDEX TO ORDER BOOKS — Ohio County, W. Va.

SURNAME	GIVEN NAMES ABCDEFGH	GIVEN NAMES IJKLMNO	GIVEN NAMES PQRSTUVWXYZ	DEFENDANTS	L	YEAR	ORDER BOOK									
Thompson & Maria				Patrick Ford	L	1808	11/128									
Thornburger Miller & Webster et al				Zebulon Steenrod et al	C	1815	15/41									
Thompson & Mares				Israel Updegraff	L	1818	2/452									
Tiffany Wyman & Co.				Andrew Howlet et al	C	1820	17/335	17/260								
Thompson & Kirkpatrick et al				Frederick Eckstien	L	1821	18/105									
Tiernan & Co.	Francis			Joseph C. McMahon	L	1822	19/188	19/281								
Thompson & Diven				Orville Hamilton	L	1824	20/87									
Tiffany Weyman & Co.				John Johnson	C	1825	20/465									
Terhune & Vanmeter				Ebenezer Zane	L	1830	24/161	24/237								
Thompson & Co.	James M.			Benjamin Riddings	L	1830	24/165									
Thompson & Co.	J. L.			Garrison Jones	L	1830	24/241	24/418								
Thompson & Co.	James			James O. Clase	L	1832	25/67									
Thompson & Co.			Robert	Samuel P. Baker	L	1833	25/342									
Thompson & Co.			Robert et al	William O. Powell	L	1833	25/386									
Thompson & Co.			Robert	John Turner	L	1833	25/465									
Thompson & Co.			Robert	Morgan Jones, Jr.	L	1833	25/486									
Tiffany, Weyman & Co.				John Johnston	C	1833	21/74	21/75	21/131	21/167						
Tiffany Shaw & Co. et al				John Sexton	L	1833	25/395									
Tiffany Shaw & Co. (Assignee of Truax & Hamilton)				Elijah Burris	L	1833	25/434									
Thompson & Co	James M.			Joshua J. Jones	L	1834	26/52									
Thompson & Co			Robert	Morgan Jones, Jr. et al	L	1834	26/129									
Tiffany Shaw & Co.	et al			Elijah Burris et al	L	1834	26/7									
Thompson & Co.			Samuel L.	Curtis Pearson	L	1840	28/246	28/324	28/361	28/428	28/501	28/533				
Tarr Mendell & Co.	C.			Noah Zane et al	L	1840	28/363	28/421	28/437							
Taylor & Kain				George Wakeman	L	1840	28/313	28/364								
Taylor & Keys				James M. Wheat	L	1840	28/358									
Tevis & Flannigen				Samuel G. Robinson	L	1840	28/429	28/491								
Tallman & Booker				Henry G. Merdy	L	1842	29/175									
Thompson & Co.			Wm. R.	William H. King et al	L	1843	29/202									
Taylor & Hamilton				Jacob Kemp	L	1848	31/27	31/58	31/66	31/82	31/110	31/126	31/153	31/176	31/185	31/211	31/233
Taylor & Hamilton				Jacob Kemp	L	1848	30/405	30/450								31/424
Thompson & Co.	David H.			Joseph Buchanan	L	1848	30/346									
Taylor & Hobbs et al				Return Hill	L	1850	31/367									
Temple & Barker				John L. Maxwell	L	1851	31/467									
Tallant & Delaplain				Steamboat Labelle	L	1854	33/156									

'T' NAMED CORPORATIONS AND FIRMS

PLAINTIFF INDEX TO ORDER BOOKS — Ohio County, W. Va.

Surname (Plaintiffs)	Given Names ABCDEFGH	Given Names IJKLMNO	Given Names PQRSTUVWXYZ	Defendants		Year	Order Book								
Tarr & Crothers				Jesse Stobridge	L	1854	32 / 181								
Talband & Delaplain				Simeon D. Woodrow	L	1855	34 / 145								
Tannant & Delaplain				Wm. McMechen	L	1855	34 / 287								
Tallant & Delaplain				Gill Hardman & Stephens	L	1855	34 / 289								
Tingle & Marsh				Gill Hardman & Stephens	L	1855	34 / 289								
Tingle & Marsh				Elijah C. Jeffers	L	1855	34 / 289								
Thomeson & Co.	Lawrence			John J. Yarnall et al	L	1856	35 / 307								
Tallant & Delaplain				George Hardman et al	L	1856	35 / 27	35 / 98							
Tallant & Delaplain				Edmund Hobbs et al	L	1856	35 / 27								
Tallant & Delaplain				John A. Ray	L	1856	35 / 282								
Tallant & Delaplain				John Ferrell et al	L	1856	35 / 294	35 / 338							
Tingle & Alman				Josiah W. Chapline	L	1856	35 / 209								
Thomson & Co.	Lawrence et al			Watson Carr	L	1857	35 / 352								
Talcott & Co.		William H.		William Riheldaffer & Co.	L	1857	35 / 360								
Tallant & Delaplane				Andrew Muldrew Sr.	L	1857	35 / 365								
Taylor Shelby & Co.				Lucius O. Ackley	L	1857	36 / 38								
Taylor, Foster & Co.				Stephtha Congill	L	1858	37 / 14	37 / 26							
Tallant & Dellaplain				James M. Todd	L	1858	36 / 177	36 / 263							
Tallant & Delaplain				John Dulty	L	1858	36 / 82								
Tallant & Delaplain				Joseph Hallam	L	1858	36 / 185								
Tallant & Delaplain				James Vayt	L	1858	36 / 187								
Tallant & Delaplain				Hans W. Phillips	L	1858	36 / 322	36 / 414							
Taylor & Foster Co.				Jeptha Cowgill	L	1858	36 / 412	36 / 416							
Tmitt Bros. Co.				Drakely & Sweeney	L	1859	37 / 261								
Tallant & Delaplain				Wm. F. Robinson	L	1860	38 / 504								
Tallant & Delaplain				G. W. Duvaull	L	1860	38 / 125	38 / 187	38 / 193						
Tallant & Delaplain				William T. Robinson	L	1860	38 / 125	38 / 187	38 / 294	38 / 351	38 / 432	38 / 473	38 / 514	38 / 533	38 / 584
Thoburn & Hadden				J. B. McGuire	L	1860	38 / 115								
Tayler & Lord				Heiskell & Swearingen	L	1861	38 / 477	38 / 511	38 / 530						
Tallant & Delaplain				William T. Robinson	L	1862	39 / 9	39 / 36	39 / 42						
Tallant & Delaplain				Mathew H. Houston	L	1863	39 / 199								
Taylor & Bennett				Hollister et al	L	1874	L1 / 437								
Tingle & Isham				James Godfrey	L	1874	L1 / 381								
Taylor & Co.	George R.			William Klieves	L	1874	L1 / 368								
Taylor & Co.	George R.			J. R. L. Hardesty	L	1875	L2 / 251								
Thompson & Hibbard				Sarah Higgins et al	L	1877	C1 / 21								
Thompson & Hibbard				P. H. Moore	L	1878	L4 / 34								
Taylor & Co.	George R.			J. R. L. Hardesty	L	1880	L4 / 385	L4 / 402							

'T' NAMED CORPORATIONS AND FIRMS

PLAINTIFF INDEX TO ORDER BOOKS — Ohio County, W. Va.

PLAINTIFFS SURNAME	GIVEN NAMES ABCDEFGH	GIVEN NAMES IJKLMNO	GIVEN NAMES PQRSTUVWXYZ	DEFENDANTS		YEAR	ORDER BOOK									
Torrence & McLeod				John Snyder	L	1825	21 144									
Tyson & Co.			William B.	Edmond I. Evans et al	L	1829	23 389									
Townsend & Frasun				James F. King et al	L	1830	24 104	24 125	24 406							
Truax & Hamilton				John Vance	L	1832	25 258									
Truax & Hamilton				Henry Bupp et al	L	1832	25 260									
Truax & Hamilton et al				John Sexton	L	1832	25 343	25 395								
Truax & Hamilton et al				James Adams	L	1833	25 333									
Truax & Hamilton et al				Samuel Knode	L	1833	25 339									
Truax & Hamilton et al				William Gregg	L	1833	25 388									
Truax & Hamilton et al				John W. Berry	L	1833	25 396									
Truax & Hamilton et al				Elijah Burris	L	1833	25 434									
Truax & Hamilton et al				Moses Ford et al	L	1833	25 475									
Truax & Hamilton				James Adams et al	L	1834	26 5									
Truax & Hamilton et al				Elijah Burris et al	L	1834	26 7									
Truax & Hamilton				Moses Ford et al	L	1834	26 21	26 39								
Truax & Hamilton et al				Moses Ford	L	1834	26 93									
Truax & Hamilton et al				Samuel Mills	L	1834	26 137	26 192	26 293							
Truax & Hamilton				Samuel Richards	L	1834	26 137	26 192								
Truax & Hamilton				George Hogg	L	1834	26 137	26 192	26 273							
Truax & Hamilton et al				Mathias Jeffers	L	1834	26 137	26 192	26 370	26 354						
Tyson & Co.			William B.	Danna Hubbard	L	1834	26 173	26 177								
Tyson & Co.			William B.	Redick McKee	L	1835	26 308									
Truax & Hamilton				Saml. Richards	L	1836	27 111	27 124	27 197	27 299	27 396	27 466	27 498			
Tong & Seevers				Philip Fisher	L	1837	27 298									
Tonge & Seevers				Ebenezer Zane	L	1838	27 458									
Tonge & Seevers				John Sexton	L	1838	27 459									
Tonge & Seevers				Robert C. Martin	L	1838	27 459	27 522								
Tong & Seevers				William Elliott	L	1838	27 466									
Tonge & Seevers				John Moffit	L	1838	27 468									
Tonge & Seevers				Henry Echols	L	1838	27 512									
Tonge & Seevers et al				Henry Echols et al	L	1838	28 5									
Truax & Hamilton				Mathias Jeffers	L	1838	28 17	28 66	28 113	28 154	28 195	28 261	28 324	28 360	28 428	28 502	28 533
Truax & Hamilton				Matthias Jeffers		1838	27 466									
Trump & Co.			Wm. B.	John Moffitt	L	1838	27 515									
Trump & Co.			William B.	Robert C. Martin	L	1838	27 515									

PLAINTIFF INDEX TO ORDER BOOKS — Ohio County, W. Va.

SURNAME	GIVEN NAMES ABCDEFGH	GIVEN NAMES IJKLMNO	GIVEN NAMES PQRSTUVWXYZ	DEFENDANTS		YEAR	ORDER BOOK (Top: Volume / Bottom: Page)								
Trump & Co.			Wm. B.	Lemuel Tittle	L	1838	27/516								
Trump & Co.			Wm. B.	Josiah H. Hawkins	L	1838	27/517								
Tucker & Co.	D. A.			James E. Wharton	L	1839	28/198	28/225							
Todd & Co.			William F.	James Dare	L	1841	28/536								
Truax & Hamilton				S. C. Richards	L	1841	29/11	29/54	29/106	29/138	29/169	29/208	29/240	29/265	29/297
Truax & Hamilton				Matthias Jeffers	L	1841	29/11	29/54	29/106	29/133	29/169				
Tonge & Seavers				David Armstrong	L	1843	29/299								
Turner & Wheelright				Robb et al	L	1844	29/333	29/376	29/433	29/484	29/517				
Tydings & Bailey				John R. Howlett	L	1848	30/395	30/425							
Tydings & Bailey				Mason M. Dunlap	L	1849	31/62								
Twinam & Co.		Leonard et al		Moses Ford	L	1850	31/246								
Todd & Mitchell				Sherrard Clemens	L	1852	32/203								
Todd & Mitchell				George Whaller	L	1852	32/209	32/240	32/283						
Todd & Mitchell				John P. Haley	L	1852	32/237	32/317	32/341	32/441	32/458	32/489			
Todd & Mitchell				John P. Haley	L	1853	33/15	33/42	33/68	33/109	33/130	33/167	33/192	33/217	33/258 33/298
Todd & Mitchell				John P. Haley	L	1853	33/329	33/395	33/431	33/479					
Todd & Howell				Jacob E. Bier	L	1853	32/117	33/156							
Todd & Mitchell				William Robertson	L	1854	33/229								
Tryon & Co.	E. W.			Morgan H. Gregg	L	1854	33/483	33/484							
Townsend, Clench & Dick				Louis Kells et al	L	1854	33/410								
Todd & Mitchell				John A. Haley	L	1854	34/11	34/20	34/35	34/60					
Todd & Mitchell				Sherrard Clemens et al	L	1855	34/132								
Truitt Brothers & Co.				Michael Sweeney et al	L	1855	34/147								
Tryon & Co.	E. W.			Morgan H. Gregg	L	1855	34/149								
Turners Association et al				Januar Fischer	L	1857	36/126	36/134	36/136						
Todd & Co.		J. M.		McCormick Pollard	L	1858	36/340								
Todd & Co.		J. M.		Thomas Painter	L	1858	36/396								
Todd & Co.		J. M.		William H. Russell	L	1858	36/396								
Todd & Smith				Edward Cain	L	1878	L4/4								
Todd & Smith				Martin Gates	L	1878	L4/5	L4/64	L4/155	L4/189					

PLAINTIFF INDEX TO ORDER BOOKS — Ohio County, W. Va.

SURNAME	GIVEN NAMES ABCDEFGH	GIVEN NAMES IJKLMNO	GIVEN NAMES PQRSTUVWXYZ	DEFENDANTS	L	YEAR	ORDER BOOK				
United States	et al			George Stringer	L	1802	8/110	8/112	8/163		
Updegraff & Farguhar				Wm. Bounds	L	1807	11/128	11/207			
United States	of America			William Chapline et al	L	1815	2/262	2/296	2/432		
United States	of America			James Hair et al	L	1816	2/314	2/348	2/380	2/434	
United States				Thos. Evans et al	L	1816	2/347	2/380			
United States	of America			James Hair et al	L	1817	16/45				
United States	of America			John Feay	L	1817	16/52	16/471			
United States				Lewis Sisson et al	L	1817	16/145	16/470	16/669		
United States				Nicholas Moreland et al	L	1817	16/166	16/328			
United States	of America			Thomas Caton et al	L	1818	2/456				
United States				Samuel Barr et al	L	1818	16/280				
United States				Henry Bell et al	L	1818	16/360				
United States				Thos. Thornburgh et al	L	1818	16/371				
United States	of America			Thomas Caton et al	L	1818	16/438				
United States				Wm. Templeton et al	L	1818	16/458				
United States				John Adams et al	L	1818	16/475				
United States	of America			Benjamin Jeffery et al	L	1818	16/487				
United States				Chass Scott et al	L	1819	17/9	17/241	17/301		
United States				Wm. Templeton et al	L	1819	17/45	17/239	17/240	17/241	17/327
United States				Wm. Bound et al	L	1819	16/384				
United States				Nathaniel F. Atkinson et al	L	1820	17/242				
United States				Henry Bell et al	L	1820	17/226				
United States				Thomas Boyles	L	1820	17/399				
United States				Thomas Caton et al	L	1820	17/288				
United States				Barnabas Clark et al	L	1820	17/229				
United States				John Feay et al	L	1820	17/301				
United States				Nicholas Moreland et al	L	1820	17/239	17/311			
United States				Wm. Parrott et al	L	1820	17/243	17/329			
United States				John Rodifer et al	L	1820	17/330				
United States				Cleaburn Simms	L	1820	17/176	17/191	17/238	17/331	
United States				Thomas Thornburgh et al	L	1820	17/326	17/327			
Varner, Caldwell & Co.				James Dobbins	L	1820	18/15				
United States				Thomas Boyles	L	1821	18/222				
United States	of America			Thos. Caton et al	L	1821	18/79				
United States				John Brady	L	1822	19/48				

PLAINTIFF INDEX TO ORDER BOOKS — Ohio County, W. Va.

Surname (Plaintiff)	Given Names A-H	Given Names I-O	Given Names P-Z	Defendants		Year	Order Book						
United States				Benjm. McMechen	L	1822	19/59	19/82					
United States				Joseph Wilson	C	1822	19/31						
United States				Archibald Woods	L	1822	19/60	19/82					
Verner & Co.	Fearn S.			Wm. Robinson	L	1822	19/15	19/179	19/236				
Vance & Jacob et al				Josiah McCollock et al	L	1825	21/232						
Uchtorf & Borgedin				L. W. Crawle	L	1828	23/14						
United States				B. McMechen	L	1838	27/550						
United States				Archibald Woods	L	1838	27/550						
United States				B. McMechen	L	1839	28/35	28/44	28/235				
United States				Archibald Woods	L	1839	28/35	28/44	28/235				
Verner & Brown				William Burnside	L	1839	28/200						
Varney & Echols				Isaac Davis	L	1840	28/261	28/312	28/361	28/488	28/502	28/533	28/568
Varney & Echols				Isaac Davis	L	1842	29/60	29/104					
Vanderpool, Smith & Co.				James Smylie	L	1855	34/286						
Von Kapff & Arons				William H. Russell	L	1857	35/463						
Van Dusen, Smith & Co.				Nehemiah T. Harris	L	1862	39/141	39/171	39/197				
Vance, Hughes & Co.				Samuel Bell	L	1878	L4/99						

'W' NAMED CORPORATIONS AND FIRMS

PLAINTIFF INDEX TO ORDER BOOKS — Ohio County, W. Va.

PLAINTIFFS SURNAME	GIVEN NAMES ABCDEFGH	GIVEN NAMES IJKLMNO	GIVEN NAMES PQRSTUVWXYZ	DEFENDANTS		YEAR	ORDER BOOK						
Wells & Son	Benjamin			William Hannah	L	1800	13/24						
Wells & Ross et al				John Bounds et al	L	1805	10/457						
Wells & Son	Benjamin			Samuel Potter	L	1807	11/72						
Wells & Son	Benjamin			Joseph Biggs	L	1809	12/85						
Wells & Son	Benjamin			Michell Cramlet	L	1809	12/127						
Wells & Son	Benjamin			Alex McCornell	L	1809	12/66	12/208	12/306	12/323			
Wells & Son	Benjamin			George McCollock	L	1809	12/129						
Wells & Son	Benjamin			Frederick Beymer	L	1810	12/255	12/373					
Wells & Son	Benjamin			James Robinson	L	1811	12/442						
Wells & Son	Benjamin			John Ewing et al	L	1812	13/4						
Wells & Son	Benjamin			William Mills	L	1812	13/4						
Wells & Son	Benjamin			Philip C. Sutton	L	1812	13/150						
Wells & Son	Benjamin			John Williamson	L	1812	13/367						
Waesche & Despadd				Buarod W. Price	L	1835	26/500	26/539	26/542				
Wardner & Sabin				Wm. W. Prescott	L	1838	27/375	27/355					
West Liberty Academy		Trustees		William Maple	L	1839	28/129						
Walker & Co.	George W.			Charles L. Hoff	L	1840	28/247						
Weber Kendall & Co.				William Cunningham	L	1840	28/247						
Walker & Co.			S. D.	Josiah Z. Jefferson	L	1841	28/566						
Walton & Fuller				Stephen Mice	L	1841	29/13						
Washington Hall Association				Nathaniel S. Dorsey	L	1852	32/132						
Weisgard & Sharp				Return W. Hill	L	1853	32/483						
Weisgerber & Hook				City of Wheeling	L	1854	34/12	34/26	34/40	34/202			
Wayt	L. & A.			James Moore	L	1856	35/248	35/272	35/302	35/318	35/345	35/423	35/506
Warren & Son				J. H. Taggart	L	1857	35/493						
Warren & Sons				J. H. Taggart & Co.	L	1857	36/26	36/47					
Weiller Kline & Ellis				Wattson Carr	L	1857	35/357						
Werdebaugh Smith & Co.				Aron Kelly et al	L	1857	36/114	36/115					
Washington Hall Association				Michael Edwards, Jr.	L	1858	36/193						
Washington Hall Association				Absalon Ridgely	L	1848	36/167						
Wayne & Co.		J. L.		Nicholas Denizot	L	1858	36/194						
Weaver & Graham				McCormich Pollard	L	1858	36/332						
Weiller & Ellis				Herman Renner	L	1858	36/334						
Wagner & Son Co.				A. Armault	L	1861	38/360	38/431	38/471	38/533			
Weiller & Ellis				Rosenthral & Horkeimer	L	1861	38/427						

PLAINTIFF INDEX TO ORDER BOOKS — Ohio County, W. Va.

SURNAME	GIVEN NAMES ABCDEFGH	GIVEN NAMES IJKLMNO	GIVEN NAMES PQRSTUVWXYZ	DEFENDANTS		YEAR	ORDER BOOK					
Weiller & Ellis				Conrad Stroble	L	1861	38 361					
Walter & Kraft				Henry Gunther	L	1870	L3 370					
Weed Sewing Machine Co.				Samuel G. Nayler et al	L	1873	L1 137					
Weil & Co.			Theodore	Rosa Baer	L	1873	L1 96					
Welty & Bro.	C.			Wm. Englehardt	L	1873	L1 227					
Weschler Brothers				John P. Foose	L	1873	L1 60					
Weed Sewing Machine Co.				John Burns	L	1874	L1 456					
Wagener & Co. et al				Patrick Byrne et al	L	1875	L2 206	L2 208	L2 379			
Warwick & Co.	N. E.			J. B. Drake	L	1876	L2 379					
Welty & Bro.	C.			Jas. Elliott et al	L	1876	L2 517					
Welty & Bro.	C.			Hanson & Henry Imer	L	1876	L2 492	L2 546				
Welty & Bros.	C.			Richard Nolan	L	1876	L2 396					
Welty & Brother	C.			B. Shanley	L	1876	L2 548	L2 549				
Welty & Brother	C.			George Watson	L	1876	L3 35					
Welty & Brothers			Peter	John Farley	L	1880	L4 467					

PLAINTIFF INDEX TO ORDER BOOKS — Ohio County, W. Va.

PLAINTIFFS SURNAME	GIVEN NAMES ABCDEFGH	GIVEN NAMES IJKLMNO	GIVEN NAMES PQRSTUVWXYZ	DEFENDANTS		YEAR	ORDER BOOK		
Winters & Rice				Francis Ryley	L	1786	1 / 299		
Woods & Co.		Joseph		Waitman Sipple	L	1803	9 / 35		
Withrow & Caldwell				Joshua Gumly	L	1804	9 / 307		
Worrell Jennings & Co.				Andrew Howlat et al	L	1817	2 / 415	2 / 440	2 / 451
Wyman & Co.				Andrew Howlat et al	C	1820	17 / 335	17 / 260	
Worrell & Jennings et al				Wm. Holliday et al	L	1821	18 / 139		
Woods & Montelius				Henry Weaver	L	1823	19 / 419		
Woods, Paul & Co.				Jacob Bently	L	1823	19 / 508		
Woods, Paul & Co.				Jacob Bently	L	1824	20 / 120		
Woods & Paull				Smith Cocke	L	1824	20 / 164	20 / 250	
Wharton & Grindage				Robert Davis	L	1825	20 / 495		
Wheeling Lancastrian Academy				Henry Sockman et al	L	1825	21 / 189	21 / 244	
Woods Paull & Co.				John Irwin	L	1826	21 / 469		
Wilson & Moore				William Murry	L	1829	23 / 334	23 / 392	
Whitehead & Son	E.			Josiah Chapline	L	1830	24 / 164	24 / 330	
Woods & Howard				Ezekiel Chapman	C	1830	24 / 112		
Wurtez & Reichard				Thomas Wilson et al	C	1831	24 / 465		
Wheeler & Co	Henry			Seth Purl et al	L	1832	25 / 165		
Wurts & Reinhard				Thomas A. Wilson et al	C	1832	25 / 221		
Wood & Cook				James McCracken	L	1833	25 / 473	25 / 477	
Wood & Co.		James		Zedekiah Curtis	L	1833	25 / 334		
Wood & Cook	et al			James McCrackin	L	1834	26 / 42		
Wood & Co.	et al		Phoenix N.	George Harrison	L	1835	26 / 147		
Wheat, Price & Co.				Abraham W. Clemens	L	1836	27 / 159		
Wilson, & Hadden (Endorsee of John List, Jr.)				Friend Cox	L	1836	27 / 85		
Wheeling Savings Institution et al				Ely Dorsey	L	1838	28 / 15	28 / 48	
White & Co. et al	Newkirk			Thos. J. Newton	L	1838	27 / 396		
Wheeling Savings Institution				James Ensley	L	1839	28 / 187		
Wheeling Savings Insitution				Thomas Morris	L	1839	28 / 58	28 / 128	
White & Chapline etal				John Fink	L	1840	28 / 313		
White & Chapline				Redick McKee	L	1840	28 / 420		
White & Chapline				William R. McLure	L	1840	28 / 263		
Williams & Co.		William H.		Charles Ensell	L	1840	28 / 356		
Withers & Carpenter				James L. Wheat	L	1840	28 / 421		
Wylie & Wilson et al				Benjamin Durbin	L	1840	29 / 110		

PLAINTIFF INDEX TO ORDER BOOKS — Ohio County, W. Va.

PLAINTIFFS SURNAME	DEFENDANTS		YEAR	ORDER BOOK									
Wylie & Wilson et al	John Hedges	L	1840	29/111									
Wheeling Rifle Corps et al	John Bauldin	L	1841	28/551									
Wheeling Savings Institution	Moses Good	L	1841	28/566									
Wheeling Savings Institution	Matthias Jeffers	L	1841	28/565									
Wheeling Savings Institution	Redic McKee	L	1841	28/563	28/567								
White & Cotts et al	Austin Peay et al	C	1841	29/8	29/29								
Williams Camp & Abbe et al	Stephen Rice	L	1841	29/10									
Wilson & Watt	Samuel G. Robinson	L	1841	28/563	28/565								
Wilson & Watt	Robert T. Kendall et al	L	1841	29/10									
Wilson & Watt	Samuel L. Robinson et al	L	1841	29/28									
Wilson & Watt	James Wheat & Kendall	L	1841	28/565									
Withers & Carpenter	J. G. Smith	L	1841	28/575									
Wylie & Wilson et al	Joseph Hemphill	L	1841	29/110									
Wylie & Wilson et al	Isaac Stewart	L	1841	29/111									
Williams & Dilworth	George A. Clutter	L	1843	29/209									
Wilson & Humes	Robert Sproul et al	L	1846	30/78									
Wheeling, West Liberty & Bethany Turnpike Co.	Absalom Ridgely	L	1848	31/8	31/12	31/13	31/36	31/53					
White & Coen	John Jones	L	1848	30/430	30/431								
Winson & Co. E.	George E. Zinn	L	1848	30/394									
Wheeling Female Seminary	William Anderson	L	1850	31/361									
Wheeling Female Seminary	Alfred Evans	L	1850	31/361									
Wheeling Female Seminary	George W. Pumphrey et al	L	1850	31/361									
Wheat & Chapline	Thos. Reed	L	1851	31/496									
Wilson Culbertson Co.	Wm. Charles et al	L	1841	31/456									
Wingard & Sharp	Hill & Bell	L	1854	33/412	33/431	33/479							
Wingard & Sharp	Hill & Bell	L	1854	34/11	34/20	34/35	34/61	34/119	34/139	34/173	34/194	34/218	34/231
do	do	L	1854	34/263	34/292	34/313	34/327	34/375	34/385				
Wood & Smith	Isaac W. Campbell	L	1854	33/215									
Wood, Wilson & Wood	Morgan H. Gregg et al	L	1854	33/483	33/498	33/499							
Wheat & Chapline	Porter E. Cutler	L	1855	34/83									
Wheat & Kemple	D. C. Cracraft	L	1855	34/235									
Wheeler & Lakin	Joseph B. Ford	L	1855	34/89	34/144								
Whiteman & Co. E.	W. D. Hardy	L	1855	34/79	34/151								
Wilcock, Rogers & Farley	James Murphy	L	1855	34/240									
Wilcock, Rogers & Farley	Wm. G. Thornburg	L	1855	34/239									

'W' NAMED CORPORATIONS AND FIRMS

PLAINTIFF INDEX TO ORDER BOOKS — Ohio County, W. Va.

SURNAME	GIVEN NAMES ABCDEFGH	GIVEN NAMES IJKLMNO	GIVEN NAMES PQRSTUVWXYZ	DEFENDANTS		YEAR	ORDER BOOK									
Winchester & Co.	O. K., et al			Morgan H. Gregg	L	1855	34 / 150									
Wolfe, Ballard & Co.				John B. Wilson	L	1855	34 / 351									
Wood & Co.				Eliphalet C. Dewey	L	1855	34 / 241	34 / 322								
Wright, Griffith & Co.				Z. S. & J. J. Yarnall	L	1855	34 / 145									
Wright, Pike & Co.				Joseph Moore's Admr.	L	1855	34 / 374									
Wheelwright & Mudge				Bartleson, Znoa R.	L	1856	35 / 290									
White, Sheffield & Co.				A. G. Robinson & Co.	L	1856	35 / 147									
Wingard & Sharp				Hill & Bell	L	1856	35 / 16	35 / 51	35 / 102	35 / 135	35 / 184	35 / 71	35 / 88	35 / 199	35 / 247	35 / 283
do				do	L	1856	35 / 318	35 / 392	35 / 410	35 / 434	35 / 440	35 / 469	35 / 506			
Wolfes, Ballard & Co.				William McKinley	L	1856	35 / 26									
Wood, Wilson & Wood				Stephen Rice	L	1856	35 / 209									
Wormser Burgraff & Co.				Edward W. Edwards et al	L	1856	35 / 295									
Wright Pike & Co.				Joseph Moore	L	1856	35 / 35	35 / 138	35 / 203	35 / 303	35 / 348	35 / 479				
Wheat & Chapline				A. M. Horniah	L	1857	36 / 117									
Wheat & Sons				Isaac T. Cown	L	1857	36 / 118									
Wheeler & Lakin				Henry C. Parker	L	1857	35 / 373	35 / 475								
Wilde & Bro.				Joseph J. Downs et al	L	1857	35 / 411	35 / 435	35 / 441							
Wilson Dunlevy & Co.				Franz Hegner	L	1857	36 / 81	36 / 109	36 / 156	36 / 168	36 / 208	36 / 270	36 / 289	36 / 348	36 / 354	36 / 360
Wilson & Heady				George Wilson	L	1857	36 / 39	36 / 113								
Wingard & Sharp				Hill & Bell	L	1857	36 / 17	36 / 73	36 / 86	36 / 108	36 / 151	36 / 168	36 / 200	36 / 222	36 / 270	36 / 291
do				do	L	1857	36 / 307	36 / 354	36 / 377							
Wright Pike & Co.				Joseph Moore's Admr.	L	1857	36 / 56	36 / 111	36 / 194	36 / 308	36 / 383					
Wheat & Sons	J. L.			John Cable	L	1858	36 / 361	36 / 380								
Whittakers & Cowden				James M. Todd	L	1858	36 / 343									
Wilson Dunlevy & Co.				F. E. Ziegler	L	1858	36 / 387									
Wingard & Sharp				Hill & Bell	L	1858	37 / 7	37 / 26	37 / 49	37 / 108	37 / 154	37 / 176	37 / 290	37 / 230	37 / 242	37 / 274
do				do	L	1858	37 / 313	37 / 328	37 / 385	37 / 402	37 / 445	37 / 478				
Wright & Co.				McCormick Pollard	L	1858	36 / 384	36 / 411								
Wright Pike & Co.				Joseph Moore	L	1858	37 / 55	37 / 129	37 / 334	37 / 415	37 / 483					
Wright & Co.			Peter	Pollard & Stephenson	L	1858	37 / 55	37 / 144	37 / 274	37 / 334	37 / 427	37 / 483				
Wurtz Austic & McVeigh				William T. Robinson	L	1858	36 / 326									
Wurtz Austic & McVeigh				Robinson & Clemens	L	1858	36 / 379									
Wheat & Kemple				James Moore	L	1859	37 / 160	37 / 172								
Wheeler & Lakin				Joseph Salyard	L	1859	37 / 334	37 / 417	37 / 508							
Wheeler & Lakin				Joseph Salyards	L	1860	38 / 188	38 / 212	38 / 429							
Williamson & Warn				M. Alt & Co.	L	1860	38 / 193									

'W' NAMED CORPORATIONS AND FIRMS

PLAINTIFF INDEX TO ORDER BOOKS — Ohio County, W. Va.

Surname (Plaintiffs)	Given Names ABCDEFGH	Given Names IJKLMNO	Given Names PQRSTUVWXYZ	Defendants		Year	Order Book (Top: Volume / Bottom: Page)									
Wingard & Sharp				Hill & Bell	L	1860	38/16	38/33	38/99	38/112	38/170	38/183	38/235	38/340	38/364	38/402
do				do	L	1860	38/417	38/445	38/385	38/430	38/465	38/488	38/500	38/506	38/541	
Wright & Co.		Peter F.		Pollar, Stevenson & Co.	L	1860	38/125	38/187	38/431	38/471	38/511					
Wright Pike & Co.				Jos. Moore adm.	L	1860	38/125	38/187	38/292	38/361	38/431	38/471	38/511			
Wilson, Dunlavy & Co.				Steamer Capitola et al	L	1861	38/346	38/373								
Woodborth & Brunel				Asa D. Johnston	L	1861	38/359	38/432	38/471	38/511						
Whitaker & Condon				Aaron Kelly	L	1862	39/29									
Wingard & Sharp				Hill & Bell	L	1862	39/2	39/49	39/55	39/82	39/91	39/122	39/149	39/154	39/175	39/179
do				do	L	1862	39/185	39/217	39/227	39/241	39/136					
Woodworth & Brunell				Asa D. Johnston	L	1862	39/13	39/96	39/137	39/163	39/189					
Wright & Co.		Peter T.		Pollard Stevenson & Co.	L	1862	39/13									
Wright Pike & Co.				Jos. Moore	L	1862	39/13	39/96	39/136	39/163	39/190					
Wilson & Co.	A.			William Spears	L	1863	39/192									
Wilson & Co	A.			M. & J. W. Sweeney	L	1863	39/193									
Wheeling Wagon & Carriage Co.				Young & Huseman	L	1893	L1/144	L1/179	L1/199	L1/223	L1/328	L1/336				
Wheeling Wagon & Carriage Co.				Edward B. Young	L	1873	L1/213	L1/223	L1/296							
Wheeling Library Association				O. C. Bray	L	1874	L1/478	L1/511								
Wheeling Library Association				George R. Leasure	L	1874	L1/478	L1/512								
Wheeling Pittsburgh & Cincinnati Trans. Co.				Thomas Seabrook et al	L	1874	L1/307									
Wheeling Window Glass Co.				George Roberts	L	1874	L1/284									
Whitaker Iron Co.				Swartz & Sons	L	1874	L1/288									
Wheat, Isett & Naylor				Rodelheimer & Cohn	L	1876	L3/33	L3/63								
Wheeling Iron & Nail Co.				Abbot Loring	L	1876	L2/493									
Williams Brothers				Lawrence Sickler	L	1876	L3/85									
Wheeler & Stephens				Joseph Robrecht et al	L	1877	L3/385									
Wheeling Iron & Nail Co.				T. C. Loff	L	1877	L3/134									
Wheeling Omnibus Co.				Wm. M. Curtis	L	1877	L3/254									
Wheeling Omnibus Co.				Fred Huseman	L	1877	L3/151	L3/152								
Wheeling Omnibus Co.				W. S. Thepps	L	1877	L3/350									
Wheeling Wagon & Carriage Co.				Samuel Braden	L	1877	L3/351	L3/352								
Wheat Isett & Naylor				John E. Wayt et al	L	1878	L4/162									
Wheeling Female Academy				Frank Walters	C	1878	C1/346	C1/408	C1/409							
Whitlock & Anderson				John F. Lakin	L	1878	L3/491									
Wiley & Co.	D. O.			Tarker Brothers	L	1878	L4/78									
Wheeling Female Academy				Frank Walters	L	1879	L4/249	L4/259	L4/449	L4/387	L4/451					
Wilkins & Co.		Joseph		John E. Tarker et al	L	1879	L4/164									

'Z' NAMED CORPORATIONS AND FIRMS

PLAINTIFF INDEX TO ORDER BOOKS — Ohio County, W. Va.

PLAINTIFFS SURNAME	GIVEN NAMES ABCDEFGH	GIVEN NAMES IJKLMNO	GIVEN NAMES PQRSTUVWXYZ	DEFENDANTS		YEAR	ORDER BOOK							
Zane & Knox				George White	L	1817	16/35	16/375	16/433					
Zane & Knox (Assignee of Samuel Zane)				Jacob Hanes	L	1817	16/110	16/247						
Zim Naddenbush & Co.				Wm. Chapline	L	1817	2/419							
Zane & Knox				Philip Beir	L	1818	16/442	16/511						
Zane & Knox				Garrison Jones	L	1821	18/338							
do				John Eoff, Jr. et al	C	1821	18/379	18/407						
do				Robt. J. Edney et al	C	1822	19/83							
do				John Feay	L	1822	19/96	19/278	19/313					
do				Nathaniel P. Atkison et al	L	1822	19/240							
do				Israel Updigraff	L	1822	19/240	19/314						
do				Wm. Young	L	1823	20/48	20/73	20/123	20/242				
do				John Eoff, Jr. et al	C	1823	20/55							
do				William Young	C	1823	19/453							
do				A. Mitchel	L	1823	19/503							
Zane, Knox & McKee				George Fannell	L	1824	20/119							
Zane & Knox				Garrison Jones	L	1828	22/424							
do				William Young	C	1829	23/141							
do				Salathiel Diller	L	1829	23/305							
Zane, Woods & Co.				John Gosney	L	1829	23/156							
do				John Gosney	L	1830	24/16	24/99						
Zane & Rohan				J. B. Hall	L	1839	28/113							
Yoho & Huff				Spencer Biddle	C	1844	29/336							
Zane & Knox				Young & McColloch	C	1844	29/336							
Yard, Gillmore & Co.				Hugh C. Devine	L	1856	35/24	35/98						
do				John Elliott	L	1856	35/24							
Yarnall & Co.			Z. S. & J. J.	City of Wheeling	L	1856	35/177							
Yard, Gillmore & Co.				William Goodrich	L	1857	35/479							
Yarnall & Co.			Z. S. & J. J.	J. Capstack	L	1857	35/345							
Zimmer & Ibbotson				George Curry	L	1857	36/50							
Yarnell & Co.	E. & F. C.			William H. Russell et al	L	1857	35/463							
Zimmer & Ibbotson				George Curry	L	1857	35/345	35/393	35/410	35/435	35/447	35/469	35/507	
Zimmer & Ibbotson				Stephen Hubbell	L	1859	37/230	37/282						
Zane & Co.	C. L.			Z. Wheat	L	1861	38/533							
Zane & Co.	C. L.			Z. Wheat	L	1862	39/8	39/23	39/42					
Young, Brothers & Co.				Homer A. Bushfield	L	1863	39/93							

PLAINTIFF INDEX TO ORDER BOOKS — Ohio County, W. Va.

SURNAME	GIVEN NAMES ABCDEFGH	GIVEN NAMES IJKLMNO	GIVEN NAMES PQRSTUVWXYZ	DEFENDANTS		YEAR	ORDER BOOK
Zane & Co.				John Booker	L	1863	39/197
Young & Co.	Albert			Pittsburgh Whg. & Ky. R. R. Co.	L	1874	L1/322
Zink & Son			Wm.	Wesley Crutchley	L	1877	L3/322

PLAINTIFF INDEX TO ORDER BOOKS — Ohio County, W. Va.

SURNAME	PLAINTIFFS GIVEN NAMES ABCDEFGH	GIVEN NAMES IJKLMNO	GIVEN NAMES PQRSTUVWXYZ	DEFENDANTS		YEAR	ORDER BOOK		
Tayler		Isaac		William Caldwell	L	1778	1/13	1/21	
Tayler		Isaac		Nathanl Templeton	L	1778	1/14	1/20	1/22
Taylor			Robert	David Williamson	L	1779	1/39	1/58	
do			Sarah	David Williamson	L	1780	1/101	1/112	
do		Isaac		John Luk	L	1795	5/27		
do		Isaac		Phillip Beall	L	1797	6/11	6/102	
do		Isaac et al		Peter Peterson	L	1797	5/220	5/264	
do			Robert	James Marks (Meaks) et al	L	1797	5/306		
do		Isaac		John McCown	L	1798	6/84		
do		Isaac		John Adams	L	1798	6/107		
do	(Assignee of Michael Coofft)	Isaac		Levi Smith	L	1798	6/220		
do		John		Amon Eastwood	L	1798	6/118		
do		John		James McDonnold	L	1798	6/119		
do			Septimus etal	John Butler	L	1798	6/108	6/198	6/297
do			Thomas	Samuel Eastwood	L	1798	6/119		
do			Thomas	John Nichols et al	L	1798	6/180		
do		Isaac		Nolley Hays	L	1799	6/308	6/352	
do		Isaac		Benjamin Mullican	L	1799	6/315		
do	(Assignee of John Carmichael)	Isaac		John Abrams	L	1799	6/130		
do		John		Nathan Gallion et al	L	1799	6/263	6/522	
do	(Assignee of Thomas Wherton) George			Elizabeth Donnald et al	L	1800	6/528		
do		John		Benjamin Mulligan	L	1800	7/30		
do		John		Thomas Millikan	L	1800	7/148	7/267	7/285
do			Thomas	John Relpe	L	1800	7/42	7/96	
do			Thomas	James Love	L	1800	7/178		
do			Thomas	John Relfe	L	1800	6/530		
do		Isaac		Michael Craft	L	1801	7/306		
do		Isaac et al		John Quinn	L	1801	7/336		
do			Thomas	Hugh McGuire et al	L	1801	7/215	7/271	
do		Isaac		Charles Robinson	L	1802	8/169	8/204	8/212
do		John		Thomas Smith	L	1802	8/91	8/133	
do		John		Fredk. Beymer	L	1802	8/92		
do		John		Job Malin	L	1802	8/148		
do		Isaac		Charles Robinson	C	1803	9/15	9/45	
do		Isaac		John Crawford	L	1803	9/130	9/171	9/173

PLAINTIFF INDEX TO ORDER BOOKS — Ohio County, W. Va.

SURNAME	GIVEN NAMES ABCDEFGH	GIVEN NAMES IJKLMNO	GIVEN NAMES PQRSTUVWXYZ	DEFENDANTS		YEAR	ORDER BOOK			
Taylor		Isaac		John Crofford	L	1803	8/314			
do		Isaac et al		James Taylor	L	1803	8/328			
do		Isaac		John Mitchell	L	1803	8/348			
do			Samuel et al	John Quinn	L	1803	8/345	8/353		
do	(Assignee of Edmund Rothburn) Isaac			Matthew Quinn	L	1804	9/261			
do	(Assignee of Edward Lynch) James			John Clark	L	1804	9/221			
do		Isaac		William Dament	L	1805	10/89			
do		Isaac		William Downing	L	1807	11/20	11/251		
do		Isaac		Henry Hull	L	1808	11/330			
do		Isaac		Wm. Downey	L	1808	11/343			
do		Isaac et al		William Downing	C	1808	11/315			
do		Isaac		Hercules Livens	L	1808	11/416	11/490		
do		Isaac		Alexander Caldwell et al	L	1808	11/440			
do		Jacob		Henry Conkle, Sr.	L	1808	11/272			
do		James et al		Edward Walker	L	1810	12/245	12/324		
do		James et al		John McHenry	L	1810	12/246	12/371	12/467	
do		James		Arthur Hieree et al	L	1810	12/247	12/313	12/364	12/468
do		James et al		Claburn Syms et al	L	1810	12/249	12/367		
do		Jonathan		Mordecai Yarnall	L	1811	12/523			
do			William	Moses Shephard	L	1812	13/364			
do		John		Edward Taylor et al	L	1813	14/69	14/166		
do	Edward			Wm. Burton et al	L	1814	14/266			
do			Thomas	Dorsey Baker	L	1816	2/343	2/351	2/356	
do		Jas.		John Clark	C	1817	16/211	16/245	16/454	
do	George et al			George Vennum	L	1820	17/380			
do	George			David Miller	L	1820	17/303			
do	George			Samuel George	L	1820	17/400			
do	Elizabeth et al			Job Prettyman	L	1822	19/157			
do		James		John Clark	C	1824	20/213			
do		James		Jeremiah Echols et al	L	1833	25/411			
do			Robert	Charles F. Peterson	L	1834	26/153			
do	(widow)			John Howlett	L	1836	27/90			
do		Isaac		George Kirkman	L	1838	27/380			
do		James et al		Alexander McCortney	L	1840	28/311	28/436		
do		James		George A. Wakeman	L	1840	28/364			

PLAINTIFF INDEX TO ORDER BOOKS — Ohio County, W. Va.

Surname	Given Names A-H	Given Names I-O	Given Names P-Z	Defendants		Year	Order Book								
Taylor		Joseph et al		James M. Wheat	L	1840	25 358								
do			Thomas	James Renforth	L	1841	28 575								
do			Thomas	Jonas Thatcher	L	1842	29 70								
do		Isaac		J. & D. Junkins	L	1844	29 335								
do	George			Robert Walters	L	1854	33 204								
do	Edward et al			James H. Robinson	L	1854	33 162	33 221	33 222	33 230	33 232	33 258	33 395	33 431	33 479
do		J. N. & E.		William T. Robinson et al	L	1854	33 397								
do	Alfred			Absolom Aikman et al	L	1855	34 70								
do	George R. et al			Sherrard Clemens	L	1855	34 138								
do	George R.			Nathaniel L. Dorsey et al	L	1855	34 238	34 32							
do	George R. et al			Michael J. Rohan	L	1855	34 238	34 323							
do	George R. et al			Henry Harris	L	1855	34 247								
do	George R. et al			Robert Walter	L	1855	34 247								
do			Thomas et al	Swearingen Taylor & Co.	L	1855	34 237								
do	George R. et al			Michael J. Rohan	L	1856	35 23								
do	George R.			Nathaniel L. Dorsey et al	L	1856	35 23	35 73							
do	George R.			John W. Boring	L	1856	35 25	35 99							
do	George R. et al			William W. Shriver	L	1856	35 140								
do	George R.			Josiah T. Chaplins	L	1856	35 210								
do	Henry et al			William McCurdy et al	L	1857	36 33								
do	E. et al			James H. Robinson	L	1857	36 17	36 73	36 86	36 108	36 151	36 168	36 200	36 222	36 270	36 291
do	do			do	L	1857	36 307	36 354	36 377						
do	Charles F.			Jephtha Cowgill	L	1858	36 412	36 416							
do	George			John Davis et al	L	1858	37 32	37 80	37 243	37 298	37 321	37 385	37 403	37 445	37 478
do	C	J. W. et al		James Robinson	L	1858	37 7	37 26	37 49	37 108	37 154	37 176	37 200	37 242	37 274
do		Mahlone		Gordon Robinson	L	1858	37 85								
do	George et al			Wm. Goudy et al	L	1859	37 348								
do	Charles F. et al			Gordon Robinson	L	1860	38 138								
do	George R. et al			William Reheldaffer	L	1860	38 127								
do	George R. et al			George E. Caldwell	L	1861	38 355	38 407							
do	George R.			Frederick Stanton	L	1862	39 128	39 112	39 142	39 164					
do	George R.			John Nolan	L	1874	L1 516								
do	George R.			William Klieves	L	1874	L1 386								
do	George R.			John Nolan	L	1874	L1 516								
Taylor		Joseph		Edwin P. Hubbard	L	1875	L2 87								
Taylor	Charles E.			Wm. Irwin	L	1880	L4 387	L4 392	L4 397						

'T' SURNAMES – FREQUENTLY OCCURRING

PLAINTIFF INDEX TO ORDER BOOKS — Ohio County, W. Va.

SURNAME	PLAINTIFFS ABCDEFGH	PLAINTIFFS IJKLMNO	PLAINTIFFS PQRSTUVWXYZ	DEFENDANTS		YEAR	ORDER BOOK		
Thompson		John		James Harper et al	L	1787	3/46		
Thomson		John		John Morris	L	1787	3/48		
Thompson	(Use of Thomas Deady)	John et al		William Spencer	L	1788	3/69		
do		John		Thomas Rouse	L	1788	3/72		
Thomson		John		John McDonald	L	1788	3/65	3/74	3/161
Thompson		John		Wm. Irwin	L	1790	3/218	3/222	
Thomson		John		Wm. Whitehead	L	1791	3/296		
do		Nancy		Samuel Rolston	L	1791	3/289	3/309	3/380
do (Thompson)			Wm.	John Henthorn	L	1794	4/226		
Thompson	George			Allen McDonnell	L	1803	9/106	9/225	
do		et al	Thomas McKean	Joseph Palmer	L	1803	8/322	8/324	
do	George et al			William Shepherd	L	1804	9/165	9/244	9/284
do	George			William Chapline	L	1804	9/295		
do	George			William Shepherd	L	1805	10/157		
do		John		James Robinson	L	1805	10/246		
do	George			James Ray	L	1806	10/250		
do			William	William Shepherd	L	1806	10/345		
do	George			William Chapline	L	1808	11/328		
do		Jno. et al		James Robinson	L	1808	11/254		
do		John		Mordecai Yarnell	L	1808	11/453		

'T' SURNAMES – FREQUENTLY OCCURRING

PLAINTIFF INDEX TO ORDER BOOKS — Ohio County, W. Va.

SURNAME	GIVEN NAMES ABCDEFGH	GIVEN NAMES IJKLMNO	GIVEN NAMES PQRSTUVWXYZ	DEFENDANTS		YEAR	ORDER BOOK				
Thompson			Thomas etal	William Dixon	L	1808	11/356	11/452			
do	(Assignee of Josiah Updegraff) John et al			Mordecia Yarnell	L	1809	12/14				
do	(Assignee of Frederick Beymer)		Thomas	William Dixon	L	1809	12/20				
do		John et al		Chas. Dean et al	L	1810	12/208				
do		Moses		Ford Patrick	L	1810	12/239				
do			Thomas	Joseph Kerr	L	1811	13/33				
do			Thomas et al	John Martin	C	1811	13/88	13/248			
do		John		Thomas Evans	L	1812	13/336				
do			Thomas M.	John Mills et al	C	1813	14/37	14/186	14/250	14/433	14/490
do	George			Thos. Evans	L	1814	14/394				
do			Robert	Jasper Mallory	L	1814	14/22				
do		John		Thos. B. Catlet	L	1817	16/218				
do			Thomas B.	William Grant	L	1817	2/399				
do	Edward	et al		Israel Updegraff et al	L	1818	2/452	2/486			
do	H. P. et al			Richard Dille et al	L	1818	2/300				
do		John		Joseph Day et al	L	1818	16/308				
do		John		Cornelius Steenrod et al	L	1818	16/525				
do			Robert etal	Richard Dille et al	L	1818	16/521				
do	(Assignee of Matthew Scott)		Thomas	David H. Blaine et al	L	1818	2/477				
do			Thomas	Wm. Patton	C	1818	16/539	16/553			
do			Robert	Thos. Huff et al	L	1819	16/651	16/680			
do			Thomas	William Patton	C	1819	17/31				
do		James L.		Elijah Church	L	1820	17/208				
do		John		Henry Sockman et al	L	1820	17/233	17/408	17/480		
do		Josias		Peregrine Ridgely	C	1821	18/377				
do		Josias		Peregrine Ridgely et al	C	1822	19/187				
do			R. C.	Henry Kirkpatrick	L	1822	19/102				
do			Thomas B.	Jesse Bailey	L	1822	19/275				
do			Thomas	Wm. Patton	C	1822	19/284	19/447			
do		James L.		Richard Cranswick	L	1823	19/392				
do		John, Jr.		Samuel H. Chapline	L	1823	19/421				
do	(Assignee of W. Hammond) John et al			George Fannell	L	1823	19/493				
do		John, Jr.		Samuel H. Chapline	L	1824	20/119				
do		John et al		George Fannell	L	1824	20/148				
do		Josiah		Richard Roe	L	1824	20/108				

PLAINTIFF INDEX TO ORDER BOOKS — Ohio County, W. Va.

SURNAME	PLAINTIFFS ABCDEFGH	PLAINTIFFS IJKLMNO	PLAINTIFFS PQRSTUVWXYZ	DEFENDANTS		YEAR	ORDER BOOK				
Thompson			Robert	James Pettit	L	1824	20/176				
do	Benjamin			Barney Sweeany et al	C	1825	21/202	21/318			
do		Jonas et al		William Patten	L	1825	20/484				
do		Josias		Wm. Patton	L	1825	21/146				
do			Samuel	James McCon	L	1825	20/464				
do		James M.		Philip Doddridge	L	1828	23/53				
do			Thomas	Wm. Patton	L	1828	23/8				
do		James M.		Edward S. Steenrod	L	1829	23/326				
do		James M.		George McCollock	L	1829	23/399				
do		James, Sr.		Levi Prescott et al	L	1829	23/429				
do		Jonas et al		Robert R. Clark et al	L	1829	23/178	23/179			
do		Josiah		Robert R. Clark	L	1829	23/163				
do	Archibald L.			Luke Griffith	L	1830	24/117				
do		J. M.		James Green	L	1830	24/240	24/322	24/379		
do		James M. (Use of Marcus Wilson)		Brice Howard	L	1830	24/344				
do		James M.		Frederick Fogle	L	1831	25/22	25/130			
do		James M. et al		Alexander Mager	L	1831	24/323				
do		Jonas		Robert R. Clark	L	1831	24/462				
do		Josiah		Robert R. Clark	L	1831	25/17				
do		Josiah		Jacob Brown	L	1831	24/423				
do		Josiah		Jacob Brown	L	1831	24/423				
do		James M.		Henry Hebin	L	1832	25/234	25/257			
do		James M.		Conrod Cats	L	1832	25/264				
do		John et al		Josiah Chapline	L	1832	25/259				
do		Moses		William Cunningham	L	1832	25/193				
do		Thomas		Peter W. Kenaday et al	L	1832	25/121				
do		James et al		Samuel P. Baker	L	1833	25/342				
do		John et al		John Turner	L	1833	25/485				
do		John et al		Morgan Jones, Jr.	L	1833	25/486				
do		James M. et al		Philip Bier et al	L	1834	26/41				
do		James M.		I. G. Clare (Claw)	L	1834	26/47	26/132	26/188		
do		J. M. et al		Lloyd Wright	L	1834	26/57	26/62	26/132	26/188	26/265
do		James M.		John Graham	L	1834	26/62	26/188			
do		James M.		Henry Stanley	L	1834	26/62				
do		James M.		Samuel Carter	L	1834	26/64	26/189			

PLAINTIFF INDEX TO ORDER BOOKS — Ohio County, W. Va.

SURNAME	PLAINTIFFS GIVEN NAMES ABCDEFGH	GIVEN NAMES IJKLMNO	GIVEN NAMES PQRSTUVWXYZ	DEFENDANTS		YEAR	ORDER BOOK (Top: Volume / Bottom: Page)									
Thompson		James M. et al		Francis L. Barnard	L	1834	26/69									
do		James M.		Dana Hubbard	L	1834	26/150									
do		James M.		John Moore	L	1834	26/90	26/180								
do		James M.		Samuel Carter	L	1836	27/22	27/111	27/296	27/395	27/196	27/466	27/498			
do		James M.		I. G. Clare	L	1836	27/22	27/111	27/196	27/299	27/395	27/466	27/498			
do		James M.		John Graham	L	1836	27/22	27/111	27/205	27/29	27/395	27/466	27/498			
do	George W. et al			Jacob Ormer	L	1838	29/137									
do		James M.		S. G. Clare	L	1838	28/17	28/66	28/113							
do		James M.		Samuel Carter	L	1838	28/17	28/66	28/114	28/154	28/195	28/261	28/324	28/360	28/428	28/502	28/533
do		James M.		John Graham	L	1838	28/17	28/66	28/113							
do		James M.		Philip Bier	L	1838	27/550									
do	George W.			Edward C. Crumbacker	L	1839	28/154	28/195	28/261	28/309	28/324	28/363	28/428	28/501		
do		James M.		Phillip Bier	L	1839	28/35	28/44								
do		James		Samuel Elkins	L	1839	29/211									
do		Moses		Thomas Dare	L	1839	28/126									
do		Moses		Thomas Morris	L	1839	28/196									
do		Moses		Willis S. Conwell	L	1839	28/205									
do	George W.			Jonathan Davis	L	1840	28/308									
do		James		Robert Morrison	L	1840	28/352									
do		Moses		David Lee	L	1840	28/236									
do		Moses		Thomas G. Moore	L	1840	28/306									
do		Moses		Alexander Laws	L	1840	28/334									
do		Moses et al		Charles Ansell	L	1840	28/357									
do		Isaac et al		William Farlenich	L	1841	28/545									
do		James M.		Samuel Carter	L	1841	29/11	29/63	29/106	29/128	29/172	29/208	29/246	29/284		
do		Moses et al		John Cummings	L	1841	28/574									
do			S. L.	Curtis & Pearson	L	1841	29/11	29/54	29/106	29/128						
do	Hilary			Cecilia N. Loomis	L	1842	29/69	29/249								
do		John H.		Alfred Caldwell	L	1842	29/167									
do		Mosey et al		William White	L	1842	29/150									
do		James et al		William H. King et al	L	1843	29/208									
do		Moses		P. W. Kenneday	L	1843	29/299									
do		Moses N.		Henry B. Sockman	L	1844	29/335									
do		James M. et al		Samuel H. B. Carter	L	1846	30/91									
do		Joseph R.		Alfred Caldwell	L	1846	30/90	30/112	30/146	30/189	30/222	30/296	30/341	30/395	30/429	

PLAINTIFF INDEX TO ORDER BOOKS — Ohio County, W. Va.

SURNAME	GIVEN NAMES ABCDEFGH	GIVEN NAMES IJKLMNO	GIVEN NAMES PQRSTUVWXYZ	DEFENDANTS	L/G	YEAR	ORDER BOOK				
Thompson	David H. et al			Thomas McKee	L	1847	30 277				
do		John N. et al		Markle, Augustus N. et al	L	1847	30 222				
do	David H. et al			Joseph Buchanan	L	1848	30 346				
do		James P.		Moses Ford	L	1848	31 28	31 136			
do			William B.	William M. Foster	L	1849	31 142				
do	George S. et al			John A. Ratcliff et al	L	1850	31 292	31 298			
do		John H.		Sheerard Clemens et al	L	1851	31 402	31 437			
do		James T. et al		Berger & Hoffman	L	1853	33 53				
do		O. D.		Ohio County	L	1853	33 91	33 120	33 155	33 265	33 316
do			Stephen	A. S. Crane	L	1853	32 490				
do	George S.			Abraham W. Clemens et al	L	1855	34 66	34 196			
do	George S. (Use of A. W. Clemens)			David McClane	L	1855	34 295				
do		James		James Smylie	L	1856	35 138				
Thomeson		Lawrence et al		John J. Yarnall et al	L	1856	35 307				
do		Lawrence		Yarnall & Botsford	L	1856	35 307				
Thompson	George S. et al			George A. Cracraft	L	1857	36 35				
do	Andrew			City of Wheeling	L	1858	37 32				
do	Alex			John McCoy	L	1859	37 202				
do	Alexander			Rebecca Witten	L	1859	37 395				
do		James		Isaac Lee	L	1859	37 153				
do	Alexander			Rebecca Witten	L	1860	38 225				
do		John F. et al		Morris, Faris & Co. et al	L	1861	38 527	38 529	38 530		
do	Alexander			Thos. W. Gilles	L	1862	39 65				
do		O. D.		John Stephens	L	1873	L1 148	L1 151	L1 168		
do		O. D.		Lewis Marshall	L	1873	L1 142	L1 152			
do			Samuel	Isaac Cotts	L	1875	L2 341				
do		John F. et al		Sarah Higgins et al	G	1877	C1 261				
do	Harriett			J. D. Prager	L	1879	L4 215	L4 386			

'U' SURNAMES – FREQUENTLY OCCURRING

PLAINTIFF INDEX TO ORDER BOOKS — Ohio County, W. Va.

SURNAME	PLAINTIFFS ABCDEFGH	PLAINTIFFS IJKLMN	PLAINTIFFS PQRSTUVWXYZ	DEFENDANTS		YEAR	ORDER BOOK				
Updegraff	(Use of William Brown) Israel et al			John Caston	L	1809	12 / 135	12 / 12			
do		Josiah et al		Mordecai Yarnell	L	1809	12 / 14				
do		Josiah		John Caldwell	L	1809	12 / 74	12 / 147			
do		Israel		Wm. Chapline	L	1810	12 / 183	12 / 261	12 / 367		
do		Josiah		Samuel Carpenter	L	1810	12 / 325				
do	(Assignee of Engle Cable) Josh.			Wm. Chapline	L	1810	12 / 254	12 / 360	12 / 310	12 / 447	12 / 511
do		Josiah		Michael Cresap	D	1810	12 / 185	12 / 283			
do		Josiah		Saml. Green	L	1810	12 / 326				
do		Josiah		John Kerr	L	1810	12 / 276				
do		Josiah		Jesse Hardesty	L	1811	12 / 434				
do		Josiah et al		Joseph Thomas Palmer	L	1811	12 / 444				
do		Josiah et al		Joseph Palmer	L	1811	13 / 18	13 / 19			
do		Josiah et al		Thos. Evans	L	1812	13 / 336				
Updgraff		Josiah		Russel Harrison	L	1813	2 / 127	2 / 153			
Updegraff		Josiah		John Pettis	L	1813	14 / 90				
do		Israel et al		Andrew Craig et al	L	1816	15 / 274	15 / 390			
do		Joseph et al		Zebediah Mix et al	L	1816	15 / 388				
do		Israel		George Pannell	L	1816	15 / 388				
do		Josiah et al		Archibald Hamilton et al	C	1816	15 / 227	15 / 429			
do		Israel		Zebediah Mix etal	L	1817	16 / 117				
do		Israil		George Pannel	L	1817	16 / 160				
do		Josiah et al		William Harkins et al	L	1818	2 / 412	2 / 434			
do		Israel		Morgan Jones et al	L	1818	16 / 248				
do		Israel		George Pannell	L	1819	17 / 159				
do		Israel		John Clark et al	L	1820	17 / 431				
do		Israel		William Amplett et al	C	1821	18 / 362	18 / 370			
do		Israel et al		Joshua Morton	L	1821	18 / 111	18 / 118			
do		Israel		William Amplett et al	C	1822	19 / 128				
do		Israel		Samuel Saylor	C	1822	19 / 288	19 / 451			
do		Israel		Thomas Smith	L	1822	19 / 20	19 / 22			
do		Israel		Thomas Smith	L	1825	20 / 495				
do		Israel et al		Josiah Chapline	L	1828	22 / 371				
do		Israel et al		Josiah Chapline	L	1829	23 / 262	23 / 285			
do		Israel et al		John Parrott	L	1829	23 / 288				
do		James H.		William R. McClure	L	1839	23 / 197				

PLAINTIFFS				DEFENDANTS		YEAR	ORDER BOOK								
SURNAME	GIVEN NAMES A-H	GIVEN NAMES I-O	GIVEN NAMES P-Z												
Updegraff		Joseph		Robert Pratt	L	1839	28 155								
Updigraff		Israel		John W. Berry	L	1840	28 309								
Updegraff		Israel et al		Robert C. Bonham	L	1840	28 360	28 428	28 501	28 533					
Updigraff		Israel		Andrew Cable	L	1840	29 309								
do		Israel		William Cahill	L	1840	28 309								
do		Israel		William Cunningham	L	1840	28 309								
Updegraff		Israel		Jonathan Davis	L	1840	28 309								
do		Israel		George Dulty	L	1840	28 364								
Updigraff		Israel		James C. Giffin	L	1840	28 310								
Updegraff		Israel		Lawson L. Hammond	L	1840	28 311								
do		Israel		George Harrison	L	1840	28 353								
do		Israel		David Morgan	L	1840	28 353								
Updigraff		Israel		Alexander McCortney	L	1840	28 309	28 436							
do		Israel		James McCluney	L	1840	28 309								
Updigraff		Israel et al		James McConnell	L	1840	28 311								
Updigraff		Israel		Frank McKee	L	1840	28 310								
Updegraff		Israel		Hugh Nichols	L	1840	28 368								
do		Israel et al		James Pearce	L	1840	28 361	28 428	28 502	28 539					
do		Israel et al		Patrick Roe	L	1840	28 312								
do		Israel		George W. Sights	L	1840	28 353								
do		Israel et al		William Stamm	L	1840	28 360	28 502	28 438	28 540					
do		Israel		James Trisler	L	1840	28 353								
Updigraff		Israel		David Victor	L	1840	28 309								
Updegraff	Charles			R. C. Bonham	L	1841	29 16	29 54	29 106	29 133	29 169	29 208	29 246	29 266	29 293
do	Charles et al			Wm. Stamm	L	1841	29 16	29 54	29 106	29 133	29 208	29 246	29 268	29 297	29 333
do		Israel		James Bell	L	1841	28 566								
do		Israel		Abraham Bennett	L	1841	28 541								
do		Israel		William F. Gordon	L	1841	28 546	28 588							
do		Israel		John Kraft	L	1842	29 138								
do		Israel et al		Robert G Bonham	L	1843	29 266								
do		Israel et al		A. H. Miller	L	1844	29 335								
do		Israel		William Stamm	L	1844	29 377	29 404							
do		Israel et al		John Kraft	L	1846	30 91								
do		Israel		Thomas Seabrook et al	L	1874	L1 348								
do		Josiah F.		George W. Steenrod	L	1875	L2 95	L2 127							
do		J. F. et al		Friend & Son et al	L	1876	L2 437								

PLAINTIFF INDEX TO ORDER BOOKS — Ohio County, W. Va.

PLAINTIFFS SURNAME	GIVEN NAMES ABCDEFGH	GIVEN NAMES IJKLMNO	GIVEN NAMES PQRSTUVWXYZ	DEFENDANTS		YEAR	ORDER BOOK				
Wells		Joseph		John Carpenter	L	1778	1/14	1/20	1/22	1/28	
do	Alexander			David Duncan et al	L	1787	3/71				
do	Alexander		V	Valentine Mendle	L	1787	3/25	3/34			
do	Charles			John Harris	C	1787	3/24				
do	Charles			Thomas Salmon	L	1787	3/16				
do	Absolom			Dewitt	L	1788	3/58				
do	Absolom			Uriah McClutchy	L	1788	3/66				
do	Alexander			David Dun	L	1788	3/79				
do	Absolom			Terrence Campbell	L	1789	3/160				
do	Absolom			James Harris	L	1789	3/131				
do	Absolom			Michel Talon	L	1789	3/123				
do	Absolom			Michell Tallon	L	1790	3/212				
do	Absolom			John Miller	L	1790	3/175				
do	Absolom			John Parrish	L	1790	3/236	3/266	3/287	3/303	3/331
do	Absolom			John Rommage	L	1790	3/187	3/197			
do	Amos			Zachariah Sprigg	L	1790	3/200				
do	(Use of John H. Anderson)	John		Nathan Griffith	L	1790	3/177				
do	Alexander			James Griffith	L	1791	3/264	3/309	3/333	3/339	
do	Absolam			John Parrish	E	1792	4/9	4/71			
do			Thos.	David Mash et al	L	1795	4/452				
do	Alexander			Jacob Ogle	L	1796	5/189	5/240			
do	Caleb et al			Alexander Wells, Jr.	L	1796	5/180	5/209	5/240		
do	Caleb			James Nevit	L	1798	6/106				
do	Charles			Aaron Hedges	L	1803	8/297				
do			Ross et al	Peter Darnell et al	L	1804	9/260				
do			Thomas	John Lee et al	C	1804	9/297				
do			William	Joseph Rice	L	1805	10/172	10/272			
Wills	Absolom			George McColrough	L	1806	10/355				
Wells	Absolom			Joseph Willison	L	1806	10/363	10/464			
do	Benjamin			Basil Beall	L	1806	10/304	10/457			
do	Benjamin et al			John Bounds et al	L	1806	10/457				
do	Absalom			Joseph Wilson et al	L	1807	11/24				
do	Benjamin			Basil Beall	L	1807	11/41				
do	Benjamin			William Bodwell et al	L	1807	11/146				
do	Benjamin			Henry Madden	L	1807	11/208				

PLAINTIFF INDEX TO ORDER BOOKS — Ohio County, W. Va.

SURNAME	GIVEN NAMES ABCDEFGH	GIVEN NAMES IJKLMNO	GIVEN NAMES PQRSTUVWXYZ	DEFENDANTS		YEAR	ORDER BOOK		
Wells	Benjamin			Joseph Palmer	L	1807	11 96		
Wills	Benjamin			Joseph Shaw	L	1807	11 187		
Wells	Benjamin			James Crosson	L	1808	11 455		
do	Benjamin			Joseph Shaw	L	1808	11 333		
do			Samuel	Wm. Burges	L	1808	11 403		
do	Benjamin			Joseph Biggs	L	1809	11 495		
do	Benjamin			John Carr	L	1809	12 83		
do	Benj.			John Crisson et al	L	1809	2 4	2 7	
do	(Assignee of Jacob Whitzell) Benjamin et al			Nathon Gutling	C	1809	12 20		
do	Benjamin			Charles Ellet (Elleot)	L	1809	2 3	2 7	2 16
do	Benjamin			Charles Rogers	L	1809	2 3	2 7	2 15
do			Wm.	Jacob Ankrom	L	1809	12 149		
do			William	Henry Smith	L	1809	12 130		
Wills	Benjamin			Gibson Forsyth	L	1809	12 44		
Wells	(Assignee of Richard Cain) Benjamin et al			Philip Sutton	L	1810	12 370		
do	Benjamin et al			Ebenezer Barns	L	1810	12 301		
do	Benjn.			Wm. Hannah	L	1811	12 510		
do		Mary		Wm. Merrick	L	1811	12 434		
do		John		Florenna Neely	L	1812	13 226		
do		Mary		Wm. Merrick	L	1812	13 382		
do	(Use Steubenville Bank) Bazaleel			George Beymer et al	L	1813	14 128	14 302	14 354
do	Benjamin			John Carr	L	1813	13 436		
do	Benjamin			Thos. Evans	L	1813	14 126	14 142	
do		John		Florenna Neely	L	1813	2 136	2 219	
do	Benjamin			John Ewing	L	1814	14 295	14 379	14 356
do	(For heirs of John Biddle) Benjamin			John Tegarden	L	1814	14 405		
do	(For use of Bank of Steubenville) Bazaleel			George Pannell et al	L	1815	15 121	15 391	
do	Bazaleel et al			William Chapline et al	L	1816	15 403	15 405	
do	Bazaleel et al			Christiana Beymer et al	L	1816	15 427		
do	Bazaleel et al			Cleaburn Simms	L	1816	15 238		
do	Bezulul (for use of Steubenville Bank)			Israel Updegraff	L	1816	2 358	2 376	2 387
do		John		Florenna Neely	C	1816	15 162	15 198	
do	Benjn. et al			Joseph Day	L	1816	2 513		
do	Benjamin et al			Morgan Jones	L	1816	15 260	15 343	
do	Bazelul			Wm. Chapline et al	L	1817	2 375	2 376	

'W' SURNAMES – FREQUENTLY OCCURRING

PLAINTIFF INDEX TO ORDER BOOKS – Ohio County, W. Va.

SURNAME	GIVEN NAMES ABCDEFGH	GIVEN NAMES IJKLMNO	GIVEN NAMES PQRSTUVWXYZ	DEFENDANTS	L	YEAR	ORDER BOOK (Top Line – Volume Number / Bottom Line – Page Number)
Wells	Bazelul (Use of Steubenville Bank)			Isaac Greathouse et al	L	1817	2/407 2/420
do		John		Florenna Neely	C	1817	16/179
do	Bazeleel (Use of Steubenville Bank)			William McConnell	L	1818	2/449
do	Bezalul (Use of Steubenville Bank)			Wm. McDonnell et al	L	1818	16/437
do	Bezalul (Use of Steubenville Bank)			Cleaburn Simms	L	1818	16/252
Wills (Wells)	Benjamin			John Ewing	L	1820	17/231
Wells	Chas. (Assignee of Jas. Brown)			Joseph Ferrell et al	L	1821	18/74 18/326
do	(Assignee of Richard Hardesty) Nicholas			I. L. Skinner	L	1821	18/344 18/349 18/417
do	Bazaleel (Use of Steubenville Bank)			Benjamin McMechen	L	1822	18/484
do	Eli et al			Geo. Baker, Sr. et al	L	1822	19/14 19/169 19/509
do		John		Floranna Neely	C	1822	19/153
do			William	Lewis Bonnett	L	1825	21/240
do	Charles			James Davis et al	L	1827	22/129
do			Washington	Basil Williamson	L	1834	26/291
do		Jessee		Dana Hubbard	L	1835	26/449
do			Zenas	James H. Forsyth	L	1839	28/188
do		John S.		Franklin H. Brooks	L	1841	29/19
do		John J.		Wm. Miller	L	1842	29/138 29/175
do		John J. et al		John A. Shipley	L	1842	29/113 29/144
do		Levi		Shepherd Moore	L	1845	29/532 29/543
do		Levi		Jacob Winesburg	L	1852	32/37 32/202
do		Mrs.		Wm. H. McBride	L	1861	38/166 38/489 38/500 38/507 38/542
do		Mrs.		W. H. McBride	L	1862	39/2 39/50 39/57 39/67 39/82 39/111
do	Dr. B. P.			Edward McCormack	L	1878	L3/421
do	Dr. B. P.			Ed. McCormack	L	1878	L4/27
do	Dr. B. P.			Chas. E. Wells	L	1878	L3/421
do	Dr. B. P.			Charles E. Wells	L	1878	L4/67

'W' SURNAMES – FREQUENTLY OCCURRING

PLAINTIFF INDEX TO ORDER BOOKS — Ohio County, W. Va.

SURNAME	PLAINTIFFS ABCDEFGH	PLAINTIFFS IJKLMNO	PLAINTIFFS PQRSTUVWXYZ	DEFENDANTS	L/C	YEAR	ORDER BOOK					
Wilson	Andrew			Samuel Fulton	L	1784	1/247					
do		John		John Combs	L	1784	1/207					
do		Joseph		John Green	L	1784	1/247					
do	Andrew et al			Arnold Evans	L	1786	1/298					
do	Andw.			Richd. Sutton	L	1786	1/298					
do	Adam			Robert Stuart	L	1789	3/142	3/216				
do	(Assignee of James Terel) Andrew			Ezecial Boggs	L	1789	3/119					
do	Adam			Robert Maxwell	L	1790	3/236	3/239	3/242			
do		John et al		John Chaney	L	1792	4/23					
do	Hugh			Wm. McMachan	L	1794	4/324					
do		James		Lenard Boyers	L	1797	5/246					
do		James		John McDonnald	L	1797	6/13					
do	Benjimin			Joseph Tomlinson	L	1798	6/97					
do		John		John Bonor	L	1798	6/132					
do			Samuel et al	David Fouts	L	1798	6/152					
do	Henry			Robert Musgrove et al	L	1799	6/251					
do		James		Benjamin Hardon et al	L	1799	6/344	6/518				
Willson		James		Morgan Hunt	L	1799	6/455					
do		James (Assignee of Stephen Abrahams)		John Relfe et al	L	1799	6/372					
Wilson		John et al		George Beymer et al	L	1799	6/439	6/519				
do	et al			Jacob Haines	L	1800	7/130					
do		James		John Caldwell	L	1800	7/22					
do		James		John Relfe et al	L	1800	7/98					
do	(Assignee of Stephen Abrams)	John et al		William McConnell et al	L	1800	7/120					
do			Samuel	John Caldwell	L	1800	7/17					
do	et al			Joseph Biggs	L	1801	7/248					
do	et al			Thomas Smith	L	1801	7/249					
Willson	Hugh			John Caldwell	L	1801	7/221					
do		John		James Moake et al	L	1801	7/248					
Willson		John		Robert Stuart	L	1801	7/189					
do		John		Able VanSyoc	L	1801	7/316					
do		John		Able Vansiock	L	1802	8/178					
do			Samuel	Benjamin Mulligan	L	1802	8/139					
do	Hugh et al			Absolom Martin et al	C	1803	9/115	9/122	9/154			
do		James		James Ogle et al	L	1802	9/63					

PLAINTIFF INDEX TO ORDER BOOKS — Ohio County, W. Va.

SURNAME	GIVEN NAMES ABCDEFGH	GIVEN NAMES IJKLMNO	GIVEN NAMES PQRSTUVWXYZ	DEFENDANTS		YEAR	ORDER BOOK					
Willson	(Assignee of David Griffith)		Stephen R.	John Caldwell	L	1803	9 14					
do		James		Isaac Tomlinson	L	1804	9 207					
Wilson		John		John Akins	L	1804	9 305					
do		John et al		John McCulloch	L	1805	10 69					
do	(For use of Matthew Kerr)	Joseph		Spencer Biddle	L	1805	10 216					
do		Joseph et al		John Gray	L	1805	10 252	10 264	10 265	10 371	10 391	10 452
do		Joseph		Abner Martin	L	1806	10 109					
do		Joseph		John Gray	L	1807	11 32					
do	(Assignee of John Ferrel et al)	Joseph		Robert Huston et al	L	1807	11 38					
do		James		William Patterson	L	1808	11 319					
do		Joseph		Spencer Biddle	L	1808	11 258	11 357	11 406			
do		Joseph		Spencer Biddle et al	G	1809	12 97	12 151				
do		Joseph		George Fryer	L	1809	12 6	12 78				
do		Joseph		Aaron Rulong	L	1809	12 143	12 214	12 258			
do		Joseph		Mary Knoup	L	1810	12 272	12 419				
do		Joseph et al		Allen McGreggar et al	L	1810	12 245	12 324				
do		Joseph et al		John McHenry	L	1810	12 246	12 274	12 467			
do		Joseph et al		Arthur Fierce et al	L	1810	12 247	12 313	12 364	12 468		
Willson		Joseph et al		Claburn Syms et al	L	1810	12 249	12 367				
Wilson		James et al		Richard Boone	L	1811	13 32					
do		James		Claburn Sims	L	1812	13 186	13 332				
do			William	Benjamin Bradley	L	1812	4 79					
do			William	Leo Tibergin	L	1812	2 79					
do	(Assignee of Wm. Downing)		Wm.	Josiah Patterson et al	L	1813	14 59					
do		Job		Alexander McConnell	L	1816	15 310					
do		Joseph, Jr.		Abraham McCulloch et al	L	1816	2 342					
do			Robert	Wm. Chapline et al	L	1816	2 313	2 340	2 377			
do			Wm.	James Crowley	L	1816	15 167					
do	(Assignee of Wm. Baker)	James et al		David McMechen	L	1817	16 121					
do			Samuel	William Wilson	L	1817	16 57					
do		et al	Stephen R.	Wm. Chapline	L	1817	2 405					
do			Stephen	Archibald Woods et al	C	1817	2 414					
do	Chas.			Mercer McFadden	L	1818	16 536					
do	Henry			Cleaburn Simms et al	L	1818	16 441	16 510				
do		Job		Alexr. McConnel, Jr.	L	1818	16 391					

PLAINTIFF INDEX TO ORDER BOOKS — Ohio County, W. Va.

PLAINTIFFS SURNAME	GIVEN NAMES A B C D E F G H	GIVEN NAMES I J K L M N O	GIVEN NAMES P Q R S T U V W X Y Z	DEFENDANTS		YEAR	ORDER BOOK		
Wilson		Joseph		Wm. Dixon et al	L	1818	16 393		
do		Joseph, Sr		Joseph Hollingsworth	L	1818	16 412		
do		Lewis		Joseph Alexander	L	1819	17 9		
do		Isaac et al		Isaiah Parlet	L	1820	17 187	17 278	
do	George			James McCoy	L	1821	18 224		
do		James et al		John Feay	L	1821	18 210	18 301	
Willson		Joseph		Wm. Chapline, Sr.	L	1821	18 209		
Wilson	Andrew et al			Joseph Wilson	L	1822	19 254		
do	Hans et al			Wm. Cunningham et al	L	1823	20 26	20 80	
do		James et al		Samuel Cooksyne	L	1823	20 19	20 132	
do	(Assignee of Garrison Jones)	Joseph et al		Morgan Jones	L	1823	19 348	19 538	
do		Joseph		Walter Brady (Charles)	L	1824	20 139	20 201	
do		Joseph		Wm. Deal	L	1824	20 245	20 287	382
do		Marcus et al		Mathew Adams	L	1825	20 317		
do		Marcus et al		Frederick Fogle	L	1824	20 111	20 113	249
do		Marcus		Frederick Fogle	L	1824	20 303	20 383	
do	Hugh			Daniel Peck	L	1825	20 499		
do	Hugh			Daniel Peck	L	1825	21 145		
do		Joseph, Jr.		John Caldwell	L	1825	21 94		
do		Joseph		Samuel Cuckler et al	L	1825	20 483		
do	(Assignee of James Wilson)	Joseph et al		John Echols	L	1825	21 130	21 228	
do		Joseph, Jr. et al		Joseph Wilson	L	1825	20 474		
do		Marcus		Abraham Clemmons	L	1825	20 506		
do		Marcus		Abraham Clemmons	L	1825	21 57	21 1453	
do			Thomas	Frederick Snider	L	1825	21 130	21 351	
do		Oliver		Israel Updegraff	L	1825	21 222	21 344	21 390
do	George			Fearley Sharp	C	1827	22 318	22 342	
do		J. et al		N. P. L. G. Atkinson	L	1827	22 87		
do		Marcus et al		James McDonald	L	1827	22 215	22 312	
do		Marcus et al		Joseph Parrott	L	1827	22 157		
do		Marcus		Jacob Bowman	L	1828	23 47		
do		Marcus		Jonah Chapline	L	1828	23 55		
do		Marcus		James F. King	L	1828	22 464		
do		Marcus		Edward Lane	L	1828	23 55		
do	Charles G.			Jonathan Zane	L	1828	23 417		

PLAINTIFF INDEX TO ORDER BOOKS — Ohio County, W. Va.

SURNAME	PLAINTIFFS GIVEN NAMES ABCDEFGH	GIVEN NAMES IJKLMNO	GIVEN NAMES PQRSTUVWXYZ	DEFENDANTS	L/E	YEAR	ORDER BOOK				
Wilson		Marcus		Edward R. Lane et al	L	1829	23 140				
do		Marcus et al		William Murry	L	1829	23 334				
do		Marcus		John Swyler	L	1829	23 353				
do		Marcus et al		George Vennum	L	1829	23 151				
do	George G.			James Green	L	1830	24 27				
do		Jos. et al		Moses Shepherd	L	1830	24 26	24 33	24 102	24 479	
do		Marcus		Jacob Atkinson et al	L	1830	24 32	24 158			
do		Marcus		Josiah Chaplin	L	1831	24 331				
do		Marcus		Robert R. Clark	L	1831	25 12				
do	(Assignee of Simon Culver)	Marcus		James Cunningham	L	1831	25 19				
do		Marcus et al		Frederick Fogle	L	1831	25 22	25 130			
do		Marcus		James Green	E	1831	24 480				
do		John et al		Joseph Teeters	L	1832	25 195	25 303			
do	George W.			Moses Ford	L	1833	25 480				
do	George et al			John Vance	L	1833	25 397				
do		John et al		Joseph S. Graham	L	1833	25 404				
do	(Assignee of Truax & Hamilton)	Marcus		Moses Ford et al	L	1833	25 475				
do	Alexander et al			Abraham Bennett	L	1834	26 74				
do	Alexander et al			Alexander Buchanon	L	1834	26 74	26 150			
do	Frederick A. et al			Josiah Chapline	L	1834	26 287				
do	George W.			M. J. Davis	L	1834	26 121				
do	George W. et al			John Vance et al	L	1834	26 38				
do		John L. et al		Jacob Amick	L	1834	26 67	26 147	26 228		
do		John L. et al		Graham & Helm	L	1834	26 66	26 147			
do		John L. et al		Jos. S. Graham et al	L	1834	26 272				
do		John L. et al		John R. Hall	L	1834	26 67	26 149			
do		John L. et al		David Victor	L	1834	26 67	26 147	26 191	26 273	
do		Marcus et al		Moses Ford et al	L	1834	26 21	26 39	26 93		
do		Marcus et al		Lloyd Wright	L	1834	26 57	26 62	26 132	26 188	26 265
do	Alexander et al			Henry Burdick et al	L	1835	26 447	26 560			
do	Colin			Henry Giles et al	L	1835	26 347				
do	George W. et al			Ebenezer Zane	L	1835	26 451	26 515			
do		Marcus et al		Dana Hubbard et al	L	1835	26 430				
do		Marcus et al		Loyd G. Hughes et al	L	1835	25 388				
do	Alexander et al			Mathias Jeffers	L	1836	27 81				

'W' SURNAMES – FREQUENTLY OCCURRING

PLAINTIFF INDEX TO ORDER BOOKS — Ohio County, W. Va.

SURNAME	PLAINTIFFS ABCDEFGH	PLAINTIFFS IJKLMNO	PLAINTIFFS PQRSTUVWXYZ	DEFENDANTS	L	YEAR	ORDER BOOK			
Wilson	Alexr. et al			David Victor	L	1836	27/44			
do		Marcus et al		Friend Cox	L	1836	27/85			
do			Paxton et al	Samuel G. Robinson	L	1836	27/40			
do			William et al	Henry Teater	L	1836	27/157			
do	Alexander			Joseph Jeffers	L	1837	27/297			
do	Alexander et al			Richard Pratt et al	L	1837	27/268	27/277		
do	George W.			Abm. Bennett	L	1837	27/205	27/255		
do	George W.			Matthias Jeffers	L	1837	27/305	27/319		
do		John J.		George Vennum	L	1837	27/348			
do		Lewis D.		James B. Hampson	L	1837	27/307			
do		Marcus et al		William Chapline	L	1837	27/301			
do		Marcus et al		Richard Pratt	L	1837	27/258			
do	Alexander et al			Jeremiah Clemens	L	1838	27/514			
do	Alexander et al			Jeremiah Clemens et al	L	1838	28/10			
do	Alexander et al			Michael Edwards	L	1838	27/515			
do	Alexander et al			Michael Edwards et al	L	1838	28/7			
do	Alexander et al			Ebenezer J. Mathers	L	1838	27/507			
do	Alexander et al			John L. Newly	L	1838	28/20			
do	Alexander			Robert M. Waterson	L	1838	27/513			
do	George J.			Jeremiah Y. Armstrong	L	1838	27/461			
do	George W. et al			George Berry	L	1838	27/440			
do	George W.			David Lee	L	1838	27/462	27/91		
do	George W.			John S. Mackey	L	1838	27/461	27/525		
do	George W.			Thomas Townsend	L	1838	27/454			
do	Alexander et al			Fielder Berry	L	1838	27/505			
do		Marcus		Robert Morrow	L	1838	27/366			
do	Alexander			W. Berry	L	1839	28/85	28/98		
do	Alexander			E. Mathers	L	1839	28/85	28/98		
do	Alexander et al			Richard Pratt	L	1839	28/69	28/126	28/128	
do	Alexander et al			Thomas Sweeney	L	1839	28/70			
do		John		S. & W. Bradley	L	1839	28/146	28/189		
do		John B.		Henry S. Strong	L	1839	28/67	28/114	28/153	28/195
do			Seth	Benjamin Smith	L	1839	28/159			
do	(Assignee of Humphrey Blakeway)		Thomas et al	Joseph D. Hager	L	1839	28/266			
do			Thomas	William R. McClure	L	1839	28/196			

PLAINTIFF INDEX TO ORDER BOOKS — Ohio County, W. Va.

SURNAME	PLAINTIFFS GIVEN NAMES ABCDEFGH	GIVEN NAMES IJKLMNO	GIVEN NAMES PQRSTUVWXYZ	DEFENDANTS	L/C	YEAR	ORDER BOOK									
Wilson	Alexander (Use of James McCoy)			Isaac Burt	L	1840	28/365									
do	Colin			William Connor	L	1840	28/367									
do	Colin			Stephen Foreman	L	1840	28/329	28/391	28/396							
do	Colin			Wallace Hemphill	L	1840	28/366									
do	Colin			Alfred S. Leuck	L	1840	28/366	28/413	28/415							
do	Colin			Thomas Laws	L	1840	28/367	28/413	28/416							
do	Colin et al			Joseph Marshall	L	1840	28/357									
do	Colin			Levi Mills	L	1840	28/366									
do	Colin			William Wells	L	1840	28/366	28/451								
do			Thomas	Robert Baldwin	L	1840	28/328									
do	Alexander			Timothy Adams et al	L	1841	29/28	29								
do	Collin			Henry Lewis	L	1841	28/547	28/588								
do	Colin			John Mooney	L	1841	28/573									
do	Collin			John Russell	L	1841	28/530	28/568								
do	Collin			Alexander W. Walker	L	1841	28/547									
do	George			Hiram Ray	L	1841	28/546									
do		James et al		Robert T. Kendall et al	L	1841	29/10									
do		James		Samuel G. Robinson	L	1841	28/563	28/565								
do		James et al		Samuel L. Robinson et al	L	1841	29/28									
do		James		James Wheat et al	L	1841	28/565									
do	Alexander et al			Fielder Berry	L	1842	29/69									
do	Alexander			William Eagle	L	1842	29/114									
do	Alexander			Charles Echols	L	1842	29/114									
do	Alexander			Wm. Wood	L	1842	29/106	29/133	29/172	29/208	29/246	29/268	29/293	29/334	29/377	29/433	
do	do			do	L	1842	29/484	29/516	29/546	29/560						
do	Collin et al			Alexander Walker et al	L	1842	29/155									
do		John et al		William K. Hammond et al	L	1842	29/172									
do			William et al	William Walker et al	L	1842	29/91									
do		James F.		Frederick H. Greer	L	1843	29/261									
do			William	William Webb et al	L	1843	29/290									
do	Ann			Andrew McMeans	L	1844	29/378									
do	A.			Wm. Wood	L	1845	30/13	30/49	30/90	30/112	30/146	30/189	30/222	30/296	30/341	30/394	30/430
do		John et al		Noah Chapline	L	1845	29/546									
do	Alexander et al			James M. Woodcock	L	1846	30/50									
do	George			Robert Sproul et al	C	1846	30/98									

'W' SURNAMES – FREQUENTLY OCCURRING

PLAINTIFF INDEX TO ORDER BOOKS — Ohio County, W. Va.

SURNAME	PLAINTIFFS GIVEN NAMES ABCDEFGH	GIVEN NAMES IJKLMNO	GIVEN NAMES PQRSTUVWXYZ	DEFENDANTS		YEAR	ORDER BOOK							
Wilson	J. et al (Use of James Y. Caldwell)			J. W. Chapline		L 1846	30 113							
do		John		Hugh Templeton		L 1846	30 92							
do	Alexander's Admr.			Joseph Wood		L 1848	31 45	31 98	31 142	31 162	31 202	31 245	31 285	
do			William P.	James Cunningham et al		L 1850	31 285							
do	Charles M. et al			William Charles et al		L 1851	31 436							
do	Alexander et al			Thomas O. Black et al		L 1851	31 439							
do	A.			William Wood		L 1852	32 304							
do	Alexander et al			William Wood		L 1852	32 203							
do	Henry et al			Artemas O. Fairchild		L 1852	32 213							
do		George		City of Wheeling		L 1854	34 44							
do		John V.		Morgan H. Gregg et al		L 1854	33 483	33 498	33 499					
do	Andrew et al			James Smylie		L 1855	34 66							
do	Andrew et al			Woods & Haley		L 1855	34 351							
do	George			Henry Otto		L 1855	34 245							
do	George			William D. Swift		L 1855	34 96							
do	Andrew et al			John Bishop et al		L 1856	35 24	35 99						
do	Andrew et al			John W. Gill et al		L 1856	35 144							
do	George			George Adams		L 1856	35 53	35 138	35 203	35 208	35 352			
do	George			City of Wheeling		L 1856	35 94	35 109	35 179					
do		John B. et al		Hezekiah Foley		L 1856	35 212							
do		John B.		Stephen Rice		L 1856	35 209							
do		Mary		John Grieshaber		L 1856	35 92	35 108	35 131					
do	Andrew			Isaac J. Conn		L 1857	35 436	35 450	35 508					
do	George			William Cowden		L 1857	36 88	36 130	36 156	36 193	36 307	36 361	36 377	36 208 / 36 222 / 36 270 / 36 291
do		Mary		Oscar D. Thompson et al		L 1857	36 122	36 372						
do	Andrew et al			Richard Blum		L 1858	36 324							
do	George			Wm. Cowden		L 1858	37 7	37 8	37 22					
do	James			Nathaniel C. Arthur		L 1858	36 344	36 423						
do	James			William Hastings		L 1858	36 329	36 355						
do	James			The Times Publishing Co.		L 1858	37 55							
do			R. H.	Elijah Merling		L 1858	36 349							
do			R. H.	David Snodgrass		L 1858	36 383							
do			William H.	Daniel Cushing		L 1858	36 181							
do	Andrew et al			Abraham Ditwiler et al		L 1859	37 141							
do		Mary		Jacob G. Metcalf		L 1859	37 442							

PLAINTIFF INDEX TO ORDER BOOKS — Ohio County, W. Va.

PLAINTIFFS SURNAME	GIVEN NAMES ABCDEFGH	GIVEN NAMES IJKLMNO	GIVEN NAMES PQRSTUVWXYZ	DEFENDANTS		YEAR	ORDER BOOK		
Wilson			J. O. et al	William Dillon et al	L	1860	37 492		
do		James		William S. Tippett	L	1860	38 196		
do		James		Math. H. Houston	L	1861	38 529		
do		James		Joseph H. Pendleton	L	1861	38 529		
do			William	Richard Radcliff et al	L	1861	38 369		
do		James		Mathew H. Houston	L	1862	39 9	39 120	
do		James		Joseph H. Pendleton	L	1862	39 10	39 18	
do	Andrew			John Jones	L	1863	39 194		
do	Andrew			John Nolan	L	1874	L1 515		
do		Margaret		City of Wheeling	L	1875	L2 149	L2 150	L2 333
do			William A.	Joseph Marshall	L	1875	L2 342		
do			Samuel McC.	George W. Wilson	L	1876	L2 514		
do			William A.	David W. Gibson	L	1876	L3 78		
do	Andrew			James Ashworth	L	1877	L3 320		
do	Andrew J.			Geo. C. McColloch	L	1877	L3 358		
do			William A.	Christian Frank	L	1877	L3 130		
do	Hugh			James Bodley	L	1879	L4 250	L4 283	

PLAINTIFF INDEX TO ORDER BOOKS — Ohio County, W. Va.

SURNAME	PLAINTIFFS GIVEN NAMES ABCDEFGH	PLAINTIFFS GIVEN NAMES IJKLMNO	PLAINTIFFS GIVEN NAMES PQRSTUVWXYZ	DEFENDANTS	L/C	YEAR	ORDER BOOK Vol/Page			
Williams	Charles			William Sutherland	L	1789	3/104			
do		Isaac		David Bradford	L	1789	3/139	3/139		
do		James		James Hambleton	L	1789	3/132			
do		James		James Marshall	L	1789	3/121			
do		John		Hugh McGloughland	L	1789	3/121			
do		John		Hugh McGuire	L	1789	3/130			
do	Charles			Thomas Deddy	L	1791	3/285			
do		Jeremiah		Joseph Tomlinson	L	1791	3/385			
do		Joseph		Wm. Barkshire	L	1792	3/343			
do	et al			James McCan	L	1793	4/99	4/129	4/141	
do		John		Andrew Wilson	L	1793	4/141	4/157	4/205	4/292
do	David (use of Wm. McKinley)			Danl. Cartor	L	1794	4/275			
do		John		Joseph Tomlinson	L	1796	6/96			
do	Hugh			Thomas Shepherd	L	1797	6/23			
William		John		John Relfe	L	1799	6/366			
Williams		Lewin		John Ustic	L	1799	6/366	6/397		
do			Swan	Jonathan Howell	L	1799	6/382	6/398	6/451	
do	(Assignee of John Meek)		Swan	John Ustick	L	1799	6/398			
do	(Assignee of Lewis Williams) Hugh			Benjamin Mulligan	L	1800	6/518			
do		Jeremiah		Jesse Bean et al	C	1800	7/90	7/229	7/323	
do		John		Joseph Tomlinson	L	1800	7/48			
do		Lewis et al		Benjamin Mulligan	L	1800	6/518			
William		Isaac		Lewis Dixson	L	1801	7/227			
Williams		Jesse		Lewis Dixson	C	1801	7/332			
do		Isaac		Lewis Dixson	L	1802	8/110	8/170		
do		Jeremiah		George Beelor	C	1802	8/176	8/331		
do		Jeremiah		Philip Wiggans	L	1802	8/54	8/204		
do	Charles			John Henthorn et al	L	1803	9/40	9/182	9/219	
do			Samuel	Philip Wiggans	L	1803	8/312			
do		Jeremiah et al		Richard Witherhead et al	L	1804	10/63			
do		Jeremiah et al		John Hupp et al	L	1805	10/52			
William		John et al		Benjamin Mills et al	L	1806	10/397			
do		John et al		Benjamin Mill et al	L	1806	10/397			
Williams		Mordecai et al		James Pettit	L	1806	10/347			
do		Matthews		Basil Beall	L	1808	11/369			

PLAINTIFF INDEX TO ORDER BOOKS — Ohio County, W. Va.

SURNAME	GIVEN NAMES ABCDEFGH	GIVEN NAMES IJKLMN	GIVEN NAMES PQRSTUVWXYZ	DEFENDANTS		YEAR	ORDER BOOK		
Williams			Matthews	John McClane	L	1808	11/419		
do			Jeremiah et al	George Gregg	L	1810	12/316		
do			Jeremiah et al	John Williamson et al	L	1810	12/285	12/500	
do			Jeremiah et al	Wm. Wells et al	L	1810	12/371	12/459	
do			Thomas	Edward Nichols	L	1812	13/227		
do	Hugh			Lewis Vinyard	L	1813	14/125		
do		John		James Downing et al	L	1813	14/18	14/94	
do		John et al		Job Prettyman	L	1816	8/346	8/379	
do			William	Lewis Helms	L	1816	15/381		
do			William	Lewis Helms	L	1817	16/163		
William		James		Isaac Greathouse	L	1818	16/443		
Williams		Lemuel		Samuel Saylor	L	1820	17/198	17/393	
do		Lemuel		George Wason	L	1820	17/198	17/396	17/449
do			Peter	Miles Cluney	L	1821	18/244	18/257	
do			Robert	Michael Graham	L	1823	20/30		
do	Benjamin et al			George Knox	C	1824	20/79	20/109	
do		Mary		John Moore	L	1825	20/475		
do		Mary		John Moore	L	1825	21/97		
do	Benjamin			George Knox	C	1826	21/391	21/485	
do		James		John S. Hendershot	L	1830	24/140		
do			Theodore	Noah Zane et al	L	1833	25/431		
do			Theodore	Noah Zane	L	1834	26/47	26/136	
do			Robert et al	David W. Harvey	L	1835	26/537		
do			William	James Maloney et al	L	1836	27/158		
do			Sarah	William Gill et al	L	1837	27/319		
do			William	Henry Echols et al	L	1837	27/179		
do			William	Thomas Hogg	L	1839	28/199	28/223	
do		et al	William H.	Charles Ensell	L	1840	28/356		
do	Alexander			Abraham Bennett	L	1841	29/210		
do	Austin F. et al			Stephen Rice	L	1841	29/10		
do	Harrison et al			William Farlinich	L	1841	28/545		
do			Robert	John W. Berry	L	1841	28/574		
do			Robert	John Hull	L	1841	28/573		
do			Robert et al	John W. Berry et al	L	1842	29/45		
do		et al	William H.	George A. Clutter et al	L	1843	29/209		

PLAINTIFF INDEX TO ORDER BOOKS — Ohio County, W. Va.

SURNAME	PLAINTIFFS ABCDEFGH	PLAINTIFFS IJKLMNO	PLAINTIFFS PQRSTUVWXYZ	DEFENDANTS		YEAR	ORDER BOOK					
Williams			Robert	Peter Yarnall et al	L	1846	30/45					
do			Robert	M. Sweeney	L	1847	30/189	30/222	30/296	30/341	30/394	
do			Robert	Dennis Fitzpatrick	L	1848	31/45	31/98	31/142	31/161	31/245	31/285
do			William	Daniel C. List et al	L	1850	31/311					
do			Robert	Dennis Fitzpatrick	L	1852	32/303					
do			Robert	M. Sweeney	L	1853	32/489					
do			Robert	Morgan Sweeney et al	L	1853	33/54					
do	Henry			John Nieninger et al	L	1856	34/389					
William			William W.	Aaron Kelly	L	1858	35/391					
Williams		Morgan et al		James M. Todd	L	1859	37/289	37/296				
do	George			Robert Samore	L	1875	L2/279	L2/292				
do	Charlotte			Peter Schlernitzauer	L	1876	L3/9	L3/34	L3/159	L3/256	L3/301	

PLAINTIFF INDEX TO ORDER BOOKS — Ohio County, W. Va.

PLAINTIFFS SURNAME	GIVEN NAMES ABCDEFGH	GIVEN NAMES IJKLMNO	GIVEN NAMES PQRSTUVWXYZ	DEFENDANTS		YEAR	ORDER BOOK (Top Line—Volume Number / Bottom Line—Page Number)			
Whetzell		Mary		Joseph Wilson	L	1788	3/95	3/97		
Whitsell		Louis		Gabriel Cox	L	1789	3/154			
do		Jacob		Robert McConnell	C	1800	6/525			
Whetzal		Jacob		James Ogle	L	1805	10/127	10/257		
do		Jacob et al		James Baird et al	L	1805	10/58			
do		Jacob et al		John McCaughy et al	L	1805	10/63			
Whetsal		Jacob et al		John Messer	L	1806	10/354	10/390		
do		Jacob et		William Perrine	L	1806	10/372	10/387	10/389	10/420
do		Jacob et al		James Warden	L	1806	10/334			
Whetzell		Jacob et al		Moses Shepherd	L	1806	10/434			
Whetsal (Whetzell)		Jacob		James Findale et al	C	1807	11/181			
Whetzell		Jacob et al		Moses Shepherd	L	1807	11/102	11/208	11/269	
Whetzel		Jacob		Joseph Biggs	L	1808	11/419			
do		Jacob		James Warden	L	1808	11/257			
do		Jacob		Robert Woods	L	1808	11/258	11/413		
do		John		Jacob Sailor	L	1808	11/453	11/496		
Whitzel		Jacob et al		Nathan Gutling	C	1809	12/20			
do		Jacob		James Findale et al	C	1809	12/29			
Whetzel		Jacob et al		Robert Woods et al	C	1809	12/155			
Whitzel			John et al	Jacob Sailor	L	1809	12/24			
Whetzel		Martin		John Hisey	C	1813	14/50			
Whitsell	Adam			George White	L	1822	19/26			
Whitzell	Adam et al			George White et al	L	1823	20/31			

PLAINTIFF INDEX TO ORDER BOOKS — Ohio County, W. Va.

SURNAME	PLAINTIFFS GIVEN NAMES ABCDEFGH	GIVEN NAMES IJKLMNO	GIVEN NAMES PQRSTUVWXYZ	DEFENDANTS	L/C	YEAR	ORDER BOOK (Vol / Page)
White				Wilson	L	1786	3/6
do		et al	William	Andrew Swearingen	C	1796	5/92 5/190 5/262 5/303 5/332
do		John		Henry Barton	L	1797	5/235
do		et al	William	Andrew Swearingen	C	1797	6/3
do		John		Fielding Beall	L	1804	8/246
do		John et al		Frederick Beymer	L	1804	9/248
do	Andrew et al			Yarnel Peter Nicewarger et al	C	1805	10/444
do		John		Fielding Beall	L	1805	10/22
do		John et al		Gideon Forsyth	L	1805	10/181 10/317 10/319
do	Bennet et al			Joseph Shaw et al	L	1806	10/416
do	Andrew et al			Peter Iriswonger et al	V	1807	11/34
do	Andrew et al			Peter Niswonger et al	C	1807	11/83 11/425
do		John		James Baird	L	1807	11/125 11/274
do		John		John Carr	L	1807	11/87
do		John		John Carr	L	1807	11/95
do		John		William Chapline	L	1807	11/40 11/134
do		John		George Bradshaw	L	1809	11/479
do		John		George Bratckey	L	1809	12/31
do			Thomas	Felty Holms	L	1809	12/84
do			Thomas	Valentine Holms	L	1809	12/26
do	(Assignee of Ebenezer Zane) John			Frederick Beymer	L	1810	12/217
do		John		Archibald Woods	L	1811	2/58 2/84
do	Edward			Samuel Todd	L	1816	15/318
do	Edward			Ezeriah Robinson	L	1817	16/42
do	Edward			Samuel Todd	L	1817	16/42
do	Edward			John Wilson	L	1817	16/43
do	(Use of Ohio Company) John			John Brady	L	1817	16/143 16/294 16/338
do	(Use of Ohio Company) John			Wm. Chapline et al	L	1817	16/161 16/293 16/394 16/448 16/508
do	(Use of Ohio Company) John			Benjamin Jeffery et al	L	1817	2/413 2/433
do	(Use of Ohio Company) John			Garrison Jones et al	L	1817	16/145 16/293 16/337
do	(Use of Ohio Company)			Abm. McColloch et al	L	1817	16/144
do	(Use of Ohio Company) John			Thomas Tonner et al	L	1817	16/162 16/302
do	(Use of Ohio Company) John			Artemas Baker et al	L	1818	16/295
do	(Use of Ohio Company) John			John Brady et al	L	1818	2/470 2/471 2/472 2/473 2/474 2/482 2/491
do	(Use of Ohio Company) John			John Flack et al	L	1818	16/497

PLAINTIFF INDEX TO ORDER BOOKS — Ohio County, W. Va.

SURNAME	PLAINTIFFS GIVEN NAMES ABCDEFGH	GIVEN NAMES IJKLMNO	GIVEN NAMES PQRSTUVWXYZ	DEFENDANTS		YEAR	ORDER BOOK		
White	(Use of Ohio Company)	John		Harmon Greathouse et al	L	1818	16 295		
do	(Use of Ohio Company)	John		Isaac Greathouse et al	L	1818	16 336		
do	(Use of Ohio Company)	John		Wm. Gunn et al	L	1818	16 505		
do	(Use of Ohio Company)	John		Wm. Harkins et al	L	1818	16 517		
do	(Use of Ohio Company)	John		Morgan Jones et al	L	1818	16 321	16 360	
do	(Use of Ohio Company)	John		Joseph Majors et al	L	1818	16 292	16 327	
do	(Use of Ohio Company)	John		Zebediah Mix et al	L	1818	2 443		
do	(Use of Ohio Company)	John		Wm. McConnell et al	L	1818	16 296		
do	(Use of Ohio Company)	John		Wm. Parrott et al	L	1818	16 497		
do	(Use of Ohio Company)	John		Josiah Patterson et al	L	1818	16 292		
do	(Use of Ohio Company) John	John		William Templeton et al	L	1818	16 395	16 447	
do	(Use of Ohio Company)	John		Nathaniel P. Atkinson et al	L	1819	16 613	16 644	
do	(Use of Ohio Company)	John		John Flack et al	L	1819	17 34		
do	(Use of Ohio Company)	John		Wm. Harkins et al	L	1819	17 33	17 34	
do	(Use of Ohio Company)	John		William Irwin	L	1819	17 50	17 75	
do	(Use of Ohio Company)	John		Wm. Parrott et al	L	1819	17 35		
do	(Use of Ohio Company)	John		Cleaburn Simms et al	L	1819	17 34		
do		John		James McCoy	L	1820	17 371		
do	George			George Burge	L	1821	18 97		
do	George			Thos. Crispin	L	1821	18 95		
do		John		James McCoy	L	1821	18 117		
do	Ebenezer et al			Andrew White	C	1822	19 227	19 318	
do	(Use of Ohio Company)	John		John Flack et al	L	1822	19 276		
do			Solomon	Peter Marlow	L	1823	19 341		
do			Solomon	Peter Marlow	L	1823	20 15		
do	George			Thomas Crispin et al	L	1824	20 367		
do	George			John Thompson, Sr.	L	1824	20 292	20 377	
do	George			Joseph Cline	L	1825	20 485		
do	George			Joseph Cline	L	1825	21 90		
do	George			Thomas Crispin et al	L	1825	21 96		
do		James et al		Lewis Perine	L	1826	22 15	22 314	22 343
do	Andrew et al			William Root et al	L	1827	22 324		
do	David			Redeek McKee	L	1831	24 299		
do		James H.		Mathias Jeffers	L	1837	27 259		
do		(Assignee of et al	John White) Robert	Robert G. Martin	L	1838	28 19		

'W' SURNAMES – FREQUENTLY OCCURRING

PLAINTIFF INDEX TO ORDER BOOKS — Ohio County, W. Va.

SURNAME	PLAINTIFFS GIVEN NAMES ABCDEFGH	GIVEN NAMES IJKLMNO	GIVEN NAMES PQRSTUVWXYZ	DEFENDANTS		YEAR	ORDER BOOK			
White			William	Thomas Bell	L	1838	27 501			
do			William	Henry Echols	L	1838	27 500			
do	Andrew			John Gilchrist	L	1840	28 353	28 412		
do		Joseph		William Shaw	L	1840	28 240			
do			Robert	Francis Plunkett	L	1840	28 325	28 357		
do (Use of Edward H. Fitzhugh)		et al	William	Redick McKee	L	1840	28 420			
do		et al	William	William R. McLure	L	1840	28 263			
do	Andrew			Austin Peay	L	1841	29 8	29 29		
do		Joseph et al		Ann Richards	L	1841	28 574			
do (Use of George Armstrong)			William	James Goudling	L	1841	28 451			
do		James H. et al		Thomas Townsend	L	1842	29 59	29 117		
do		James H. et al		Edie Stewart	L	1843	29 291			
do		Joseph et al		Ann Richards et al	L	1846	30 77			
do			Thayord et al	William Charles et al	L	1851	31 436			
do	Henry			John Cotts	L	1853	32 389			
do	John			Thomas Slater	L	1854	33 156			
do		Norman et al		Robert Bonham et al	L	1857	36 43			
do			Samuel et al	Mark Mellon	L	1857	35 406	35 436	35 450	35 459
Whyte		James C.		Nathaniel Wilkinson	L	1858	36 423			
do		James		John Healop et al	L	1858	37 7	37 15	37 31	37 53
White	Dennis			James Finety	L	1858	36 379			
do		Norman et al		John T. Davis	L	1858	36 397			
do		Norman et al		John Davis et al	L	1858	37 85	37 156		
do			Robert	David Armstrong	L	1858	36 407			
do			Robert	David Armstrong	L	1858	37 52			
do			Samuel	Alfred Hullihen et al	L	1858	37 68			
do		Norman et al		Francis W. Wright et al	L	1859	37 332			
do			Samuel et al	Manfred Hullihen et al	L	1859	37 213			
do		Jacob		Nancy White et al	C	1874	C1 74	C1 115		
do	Charles			William Stewart	L	1875	L2 195	L2 332		
do		James		L. H. Cox	L	1877	L3 301			
do		Mary		Thomas Buchanon	L	1877	L3 265	L3 388	L3 423	L3 519
do			Robert	Jacob F. Leukert	L	1879	L4 162	L4 182	L4 239	
do			Robt.	John E. Hayt	L	1879	L4 241			

'W' SURNAMES – FREQUENTLY OCCURRING

PLAINTIFF INDEX TO ORDER BOOKS — Ohio County, W. Va.

SURNAME	PLAINTIFFS GIVEN NAMES ABCDEFGH	GIVEN NAMES IJKLMNO	GIVEN NAMES PQRSTUVWXYZ	DEFENDANTS		YEAR	ORDER BOOK				
Wheat		Jesse et al		David Lane	L	1832	25 196				
do		Jessee et al		David Victor	L	1832	25 260				
do		Jesse		Moses Ford	L	1833	25 342				
do		Jesse		John Bramhall	L	1834	26 195	26 257			
do		Jessee		Isaac Krider	L	1834	26 296	26 318			
do		Jessee		Seth Earl	L	1834	26 58				
do		James M.		Henry Echols	L	1835	26 391				
do		Jessee		Michael J. Mohan	L	1836	26 373				
do		Jesse et al		Abraham S. Clemens	L	1836	27 159				
do		Jesse		George A. Buchanan	L	1837	27 258	27 277			
do			Thomas	John French	L	1837	27 348				
do		James S. et al		William B. Hubbard	L	1838	27 469				
do		James M.		John Ritchie	L	1838	27 459				
do		James S. et al		Ebenezer Zane	L	1838	27 401	27 446			
do		Jesse		John Fullmer	L	1838	28 19	28 99			
do		Jesse		William Hosack	L	1838	27 507				
do		Jessee		William Hosack	L	1838	28 18	28 67	28 114	28 153	28 195
do		Jesse		John Moffit	L	1838	27 406				
do		Jesse		Alexander McCortney	L	1838	27 405				
do		Jesse		Enos W. Newton	L	1838	27 406				
do		Jesse		James Shimer	L	1838	27 406				
do		James S. et al		Joseph Chapline	L	1839	28 198				
do		James et al		David Church	L	1839	28 198				
do		James S.		Alexander McCortney	L	1839	28 166	28 158			
do	(Assignee of Willis S. Conwell) James M. et al			John McCaskey	L	1839	28 71				
do		James M.		Lenard Bruel	L	1840	28 421				
do		James M.		Elijah Day	L	1840	28 358	28 436			
do		James et al		John Gilkerson	L	1840	28 237				
do		James S.		John Gilchrist	L	1840	28 352	28 414			
do		James S.		David Hull	L	1840	28 364				
do		James S.		Daniel Lady	L	1840	28 431				
do		James S.		Ross Brackson	L	1840	28 329				
do		James S.		John Sallyard	L	1840	28 329				
do		James S. et al		Ezekiel Steinhilber	L	1840	29 10	29 82			
do		James M.		Jeremiah Clemens	L	1841	28 418	28 492			

PLAINTIFF INDEX TO ORDER BOOKS — Ohio County, W. Va.

PLAINTIFFS SURNAME	GIVEN NAMES ABCDEFGH	GIVEN NAMES IJKLMNO	GIVEN NAMES PQRSTUVWXYZ	DEFENDANTS		YEAR	ORDER BOOK TOP LINE — Volume Number / BOTTOM LINE — Page Number							
Wheat		James M.		William H. F. Degge	L	1841	28/475							
do		James M.		John Frail	L	1841	28/502	28/540	28/566					
do		James M.		John Frail	L	1841	29/11	29/59						
do		James S. et al		William Cunningham	L	1842	29/172	29/208	29/246	29/293	29/333	29/377	29/433	29/484	29/517
do		James S. et al		George Forbes	L	1842	29/167							
do		James A.		Elizabeth Garwood et al		1842	29/113	29/114						
do		James S.		William F. Gordon	L	1842	29/113	29/138						
do		James S. et al		F. Griesmer	L	1842	29/172	29/208	29/246	29/268	29/333			
do		James S. et al		A. C. McCallam	L	1842	29/172	29/208	29/246	29/268	29/291			
do		James S.		Alexander Newman	L	1842	29/517							
do		James S. et al		Frederick Smith	L	1842	29/102							
do		James S.		Wm. Bukey	L	1843	29/250							
do		James S. et al		John C. Snider et al	L	1843	29/270	29/382						
do		Jesse		Cuthbert Stanley	L	1843	29/299							
do		James et al		Alf. Caldwell	L	1844	29/377	29/404						
do		James S.		Bancroft Woodcock	L	1844	29/335							
do		James S. et al		Alexander Newman	L	1846	30/97							
do	(Assignee of George Forbes) Jesse			James R. Buchanan	L	1851	32/30							
do		Jesse		George Forbes	L	1852	32/134	32/308						
Wheate		Jesse		R. Knowles & Co.	L	1852	32/329	32/348	32/417	32/441	32/460	32/489		
do		Jesse		Frances Roney	L	1852	32/321							
do		Jesse		Thomas Todd	L	1852	32/204	32/408						
Wheat		Jesse		Jerome Downs	L	1853	33/43	33/75	33/103					
do		Jesse		William Harvey	L	1853	33/109	33/130	33/160					
Wheate		Jessee		Richard Knowles et al	L	1853	33/15	33/42	33/68	33/95				
Wheat (Wheat)			Z.	City of Wheeling	L	1853	33/107							
Wheate	George K. et al			Porter E. Cutler et al	L	1855	34/83							
Wheat		Jesse		Dewit C. Cracraft	L	1856	35/140							
do	George K.			George A. Cracraft	L	1857	36/117							
do	George K.			A. M. Hornish	L	1857	36/117							
do	George K. et al			Isaac T. Conn	L	1857	36/118							
do		Jesse		Cracraft & Sangston	L	1857	36/25							
do		Jessee		Ebenezer McCoy	L	1857	35/478							
do		Jesse et al		Sherrard Clemens	L	1857	36/117							
Wheats		Jesse		Ed Schaffer	L	1859	37/279							

PLAINTIFF INDEX TO ORDER BOOKS — Ohio County, W. Va.

SURNAME	PLAINTIFFS GIVEN NAMES ABCDEFGH	GIVEN NAMES IJKLMNO	GIVEN NAMES PQRSTUVWXYZ	DEFENDANTS		YEAR	ORDER BOOK (Top: Volume / Bottom: Page)	
Wheat		et al	Zachariah	Ruben Foreman	L	1859	37 / 142	
do	George K.			William T. Robinson	L	1861	38 / 514	38 / 533
do	George K. et al			David Kennedy etal	L	1861	38 / 359	
do	George K.			William T. Robinson	L	1862	39 / 42	
do		James S.		George Storey	L	1862	39 / 111	39 / 135
do	George K.			James M. Wheat	L	1874	L1 / 325	
do	H. Bradley			J. H. Sheffield	L	1875	L2 / 287	
do	H. B.			James Ashworth et al	L	1877	L3 / 340	

'W' SURNAMES – FREQUENTLY OCCURRING

PLAINTIFF INDEX TO ORDER BOOKS — Ohio County, W. Va.

SURNAME	PLAINTIFFS ABCDEFGH	PLAINTIFFS IJKLMNO	PLAINTIFFS PQRSTUVWXYZ	DEFENDANTS		YEAR	ORDER BOOK						
Woods	Archibald			Lewis Frave	L	1788	3 / 85						
do	(Assignee of Jas. McCoy)		Robert	Peters Peterson	L	1788	3 / 57	3 / 214					
Wood			Robert	Geo. Striker	L	1788	3 / 55						
do			Robert	Joseph Wilson	L	1788	3 / 89	3 / 101					
do			Robert	Joseph Neely	L	1790	3 / 176	3 / 177					
Woods	(Assignee of John Anderson)		Wm.	Abraham Crooksdon	L	1791	3 / 275						
Wood	(Assignee of Thomas Morrison)		Wm.	Peter Peterson	L	1791	3 / 296	3 / 304	3 / 310				
Woods	Andrew			Alexander Orr	L	1794	4 / 225						
do	Andrew			William Barshire	L	1795	4 / 474						
do			Robert et al	Samuel Hand	L	1796	5 / 198						
do			Robert	Jesse Hollingsworth	C	1796	5 / 92	5 / 125	5 / 182	5 / 190	5 / 261	5 / 304	5 / 326
do			Robert	Jesse Hollingworth	C	1798	6 / 49B	6 / 50	6 / 52				
do			Robert	James Taylor	L	1798	6 / 261						
do	Andrew et al			John Abrams et al	L	1799	6 / 317	6 / 510					
do	Andrew			John Mitchell	L	1799	6 / 460						
do	Andrew			Joseph Tomlinson	L	1799	6 / 459	6 / 460	6 / 480				
do			Robert etal	Charles Cracraft	L	1799	6 / 284						
do			Robert etal	John Marton	L	1799	6 / 353						
do			Robert etal	John McConnell	L	1799	6 / 281						
do			Robert	James Ogle	L	1799	6 / 375						
do			Robert	Joseph Tomlinson	L	1799	6 / 396	6 / 439					
do			Robert	Timothy Welkins et al	L	1799	6 / 440	6 / 441					
do			Robert et al	Jonathan Wells et al	L	1799	6 / 356						
do			Robert etal	Samuel Wilson	L	1799	6 / 346						
do	Andrew			John Butler	L	1800	7 / 16						
Wood	Elijah et al			Andrew McFarland	L	1800	7 / 172						
Woods	Elijah et al			John Williams	L	1800	7 / 146	7 / 172	7 / 209	7 / 229			
do	(Assignee of James Ogle)	Jeremiah		Frederick Beelor	L	1800	7 / 74						
do		Jeremiah et al		Samuel Hand	L	1800	6 / 471						
do		Jeremiah		Samuel Harris	L	1800	7 / 15						
do			Robert etal	James Knox	L	1800	7 / 37						
do			Robert etal	Robert McClure	L	1800	6 / 529						
do			Robert et al	Caleb Reeves	L	1800	7 / 118						
do			Robert	Thomas Ritchards (Richards)	L	1800	6 / 475						
Wood			Robert et al	Thomas Smith	L	1800	7 / 83	7 / 145	7 / 210	7 / 213			

'W' SURNAMES – FREQUENTLY OCCURRING

PLAINTIFF INDEX TO ORDER BOOKS — Ohio County, W. Va.

SURNAME	PLAINTIFFS GIVEN NAMES ABCDEFGH	GIVEN NAMES IJKLMNO	GIVEN NAMES PQRSTUVWXYZ	DEFENDANTS	L/C	YEAR	ORDER BOOK		
Woods			Robert et al	Samuel Willson	L	1800	6/528		
do	Archibald			James Beard	L	1801	8/12	8/40	
do	Archibald			James Fulton	L	1801	7/279		
do	Elijah et al			James Wallace	L	1801	7/232		
do			Robert et al	Christopher Cunningham	L	1801	7/212	7/290	
do			Robert et al	Elias Dement	L	1801	8/52	8/178	
do			Robert et al	Robert McIntire	L	1801	7/314		
Wood			Robert et al	Robert McLure	L	1801	7/226	7/273	
Woods			Robert et al	Robert McLure	L	1801	8/57		
do			Robert et al	Andrew Sprowl	L	1801	7/273	7/335	
do	Andrew, Jr.			Richard Carter	L	1802	8/214		
do	Andrew			Christopher Dickson et al	L	1802	8/167	8/262	
do	Andrew			Benjamin Fort et al	L	1802	8/263		
do		Martha et al		Richard Finn	L	1802	8/167		
do			Robert et al	Henry Clark	L	1802	8/91		
do	Andrew et al			Samuel Hand	L	1803	8/346	8/358	
do	Andrew et al			Samuel Hand	L	1803	9/92		
do			Robert et al	Jane Beelor et al	L	1803	8/323	8/324	8/332
do			Robert et al	John Nichols	L	1803	9/78	9/86	
do			Robert	Wm. Ward et al	L	1803	9/48		
do	Archibold	(Assignee of Dennis Cassat)		Fielding Beall	L	1804	9/246		
do	Elijah et al			John Hickman et al	C	1804	9/290		
do	Archibald			Henry Gosney et al	L	1805	10/177	10/340	
do	Elijah et al			John Hickman et al	C	1805	10/30	10/448	
do			Robert et al	Henry Smith	L	1805	10/24		
do	Archibald et al			Fielding Beall	L	1806	10/379		
do			Robert	William Patton	L	1806	10/431		
do			Robert	Moses Shepheard et al	L	1806	10/435		
do			Robert et al	William Shepherd	L	1806	10/431		
do	Andrew et al			Richard Finn	L	1807	11/35		
Wood	Elijah et al			John Hickman et al	C	1807	11/147		
do			Robert et al	Robert Beall et al	L	1807	11/189	11/287	11/349
Woods			Robert	William Patton	L	1807	11/97		
do			Robert	Moses Shepheard et al	L	1807	11/60	11/365	
do	(Assignee of Matthew Howell)		Robert	William Shepherd et al	L	1807	11/98		

PLAINTIFF INDEX TO ORDER BOOKS — Ohio County, W. Va.

SURNAME	GIVEN NAMES ABCDEFGH	GIVEN NAMES IJKLMNO	GIVEN NAMES PQRSTUVWXYZ	DEFENDANTS	L/C	YEAR	ORDER BOOK (Vol/Page)
Wood	Andrew et al			Jacob Whetzel	L	1808	11/255 11/268
Woods	Archibald			William Patterson	L	1808	11/397
Wood	Elijah			Henry Smith	L	1808	11/293
do			Robert	Samuel Beall	O	1808	11/417
Woods	(Assignee of Thomas Evans) Archibald et al			William Patterson	L	1809	12/42
do	Eliza			John Gooding	L	1809	12/45
Wood			Robert	Samuel Beall et al	C	1809	12/53 12/447
do			Robert	Jonah Seamon	L	1809	12/119
do			Robert	Moses Shepherd	L	1809	12/71 12/79 12/84 12/138
Woods			Robert	Edmond Terrell	L	1809	11/513 11/514
Wood	Andrew et al			Philip Hupp	L	1810	12/192
do			Robert	Reubin Hays	C	1810	12/261 12/522
Woods			Robert	Joseph Tomlinson	L	1810	12/194
do	Elijah			Henry Gosney	L	1811	13/15 13/88
do			Robert	Moses Chapline	L	1811	2/62
do			Robert	Joseph Kerr	L	1811	2/60 2/85
Wood			Robert	Joseph Kerr	L	1811	12/432
do			Robt.	Moses Shepherd	L	1812	13/193
Woods			Robert et al	Robert Hardcastle et al	L	1813	2/138 2/152 2/155 2/219 2/252 2/259 2/290 2/308 2/338 2/367
do	Archibald et al			Basil Beall et al	L	1814	2/160
do			Robert	Richard Cuff et al	L	1815	2/283 2/290 2/290 2/308 2/338
do			Robert	George Selby et al	O	1815	15/144
do			Robert	Moses Shepherd	L	1815	15/135
do			Robert	John Taylor	L	1815	2/279
Wood	James et al			Wm. Chapline et al	L	1816	2/364 2/378
do			Robert	Josiah Patterson et al	L	1816	2/312
Woods	Archd. (Assignee of David Pierson)			Richd. Davis et al	L	1818	16/359
do	Archd. et al			Jonathan Zane	L	1818	16/419 16/425
do	Archd.			Thomas Howard	L	1819	16/682
do	Archibald			Wm. McKinley	L	1819	16/682
do	Archibald et al			John Caldwell et al	C	1819	17/108
do			Robert	George McCormick	L	1819	17/18
do			Robert	Wm. Chapline	L	1820	17/435 17/504
Wood			Robert	Wm. Chapline	L	1820	18/26 18/191 18/329
Woods	Archibald et al			Chapline Caldwell heirs et al	C	1821	18/468 18/484

'W' SURNAMES – FREQUENTLY OCCURRING

PLAINTIFF INDEX TO ORDER BOOKS — Ohio County, W. Va.

SURNAME	PLAINTIFFS GIVEN NAMES ABCDEFGH	GIVEN NAMES IJKLMNO	GIVEN NAMES PQRSTUVWXYZ	DEFENDANTS	L/C	YEAR	ORDER BOOK (Top: Vol / Bottom: Page)							
Woods	Archibold			Jacob Pottman et al	L	1821	18/138							
do	A. et al			John Caldwell et al	C	1821	18/55							
Wood			Thomas et al	Nathaniel F. Atkinson	L	1821	18/127							
Woods			Thos. et al	Jacob Marsilliot	L	1821	18/124							
Wood			Thomas	S. Scovill	L	1821	18/237	18/342						
do	Franklin			Edward G. Carlon	L	1822	19/111							
do	Archibald et al			James Caldwell et al	C	1822	19/138	19/508						
Woods			Robert	Wm. Chapline	L	1822	19/128	19/329						
Wood			Thomas	Jacob Atkinson et al	L	1822	18/493							
Woods			Thomas et al	Edward G. Carlin	L	1822	19/248	19/311						
Wood	George			Samuel W. Bostwick	L	1823	20/38							
Woods	A.	et al		John Caldwell et al	C	1823	20/349	20/380						
Wood			Robert	Wm. Chapline	L	1824	20/136							
Woods			Thomas et al	Samuel W. Bostwick et al	L	1824	20/395							
do			Robert	Isaiah Branson	L	1825	21/211	21/213	21/222	21/311	21/478	21/481		
do			Robert et al	John Caldwell	C	1825	21/33	21/34	21/37					
do	Andrew et al			Jonathan Nesbitt	C	1826	21/439	21/450						
do	Archebald et al			Joel Zane	C	1826	21/424	21/470						
do	Archibald et al			Joel Zane et al	C	1826	22/2	22/144	22/166	22/386	22/346			
do			Robert	Isiah Branson	L	1826	22/7	22/12	22/269	22/388	22/476	22/13	22/77	22/78
Wood			Robert	Robert Clagg	L	1826	21/884							
Woods			Thomas	James Orr	L	1826	21/433							
do	Andrew			Thomas Reynolds	L	1827	22/264							
do	Archibald			Thomas Hardesty et al	L	1827	22/249							
do			Robert	Susan Baker et al	C	1827	22/99	22/100	22/113	22/289	22/211	22/165		
do			Thomas et al	James Orr	L	1827	22/147	22/150	22/201					
do	Andrew, Sr			Wm. Riley et al	L	1829	23/439							
do	Archibald			Thomas Hardesty et al	L	1829	23/118	23/202						
do	Archibald			Jesse C. Smith et al	L	1829	23/280	23/384						
do		John		William Mack	L	1829	23/444							
do			Robert	Isaiah Branson	L	1829	23/315	23/317	23/329	23/336	23/257			
do		et al	Robert C.	Samuel Cookayne	L	1829	23/264							
do			Thomas etal	William Gunningham	L	1829	23/148							
do			William	James McCaskey	L	1829	23/195							
do			William	Robert Woods	L	1829	23/153	23/155						

PLAINTIFF INDEX TO ORDER BOOKS — Ohio County, W. Va.

SURNAME	PLAINTIFFS GIVEN NAMES ABCDEFGH	GIVEN NAMES IJKLMNO	GIVEN NAMES PQRSTUVWXYZ	DEFENDANTS		YEAR	ORDER BOOK	
Woods			Robert	Isaiah Branson	L	1830	24 / 15	
do			Robert C.	Samuel Cochran, Jr. et al	L	1830	23 / 460	
do			Robert	William Cunningham	L	1830	24 / 11	
do			Robert	Frederick A. Wilson et al	L	1830	24 / 242	24 / 297
do	(Use of George McMurry)		Samuel	Zachariah Pumphrey et al	L	1830	24 / 78	
do	Andrew et al			Eazchell Chapline et al	C	1831	24 / 471	
do	Andrew P.			James Patton et al	C	1831	24 / 401	
do	Andrew P.			James Patton et al	C	1831	25 / 37	
do			Robert C.	Wm. Cockayne et al	L	1831	24 / 319	24 / 402
do	Archibald			Jacob Atkinson et al	L	1832	25 / 235	
do	Archibald			Lewis Sisson et al	L	1832	25 / 193	
do		Thomas et al		Abraham Bennett	L	1832	25 / 197	
do		et al	Robert C.	Robert McHenry et al	L	1833	25 / 387	
do			Robert	Jonathan Roberts	L	1833	25 / 477	
do		Thomas		John Cauley	L	1833	25 / 330	
Wood		James et al		Zedekiah B. Curtis	L	1833	25 / 334	
Woods		Thomas et al		John Vance	L	1833	25 / 397	
do	Andrew			Shipley Martin et al	L	1834	26 / 385	
do	A. P. et al			George Whitzell et al	L	1834	25 / 127	
do	Archibald et al			Joel Zane et al	C	1834	26 / 63	
Wood		James et al		William Lambdin	L	1834	26 / 186	26 / 259
Woods			Robert et al	James Pelly	L	1834	26 / 197	
Wood		James et al		Zedekiah B. Curtis	L	1834	26 / 70	
Woods		Thomas et al		John Vance et al	L	1834	26 / 38	
do	Andrew			John Arnold et al	L	1835	26 / 553	
do	Archibald			John W. Hall	L	1835	26 / 440	
Wood		et al	Phoenix N.	George Harrison	L	1835	26 / 447	
Woods	Archibald			Joseph Moore	L	1836	27 / 134	27 / 551
do		James W. et al		John Sexton	L	1837	27 / 296	
Wood		Joseph		Charles B. Stickney	L	1837	27 / 214	
Woods	Andrew P.			John Banks	L	1838	27 / 550	
do	Andrew P.			James J. Pearce	L	1838	27 / 547	
do		James		James Temple	L	1838	27 / 512	
do			Robert W.	William Hollifield	L	1838	28 / 28	
do			Robert C.	Elijah Mix	L	1838	27 / 553	

PLAINTIFF INDEX TO ORDER BOOKS — Ohio County, W. Va.

SURNAME	PLAINTIFFS Given Names ABCDEFGH	Given Names IJKLMNO	Given Names PQRSTUVWXYZ	DEFENDANTS		YEAR	ORDER BOOK (Top: Volume / Bottom: Page)									
Woods	Andrew P.			John Banks	L	1839	28/35	28/44	28/235							
do		Robert C.		John Hull	L	1839	28/158									
do	(Assignee of Jacob Bruner) Archibald			Joseph Junkins	L	1840	28/366									
do	Andrew			Platoff Zane	L	1841	28/500									
do	Hamilton			Charles Ensell	L	1841	28/566									
do	Hamilton et al			William Lambdin	L	1841	28/574									
Wood	Hamilton et al			William Wells	L	1841	29/11	29/59								
Woods	Archibald et al			Platoff Zane	L	1842	29/298									
do		James		Vennum et al	L	1843	29/299									
do		et al	Theodore	Ely Dorsey	L	1844	29/378									
do	Archibald et al			James R. Buchanan et al	L	1847	30/238	30/239								
do	Hamilton et al			James R. Buchanan et al	L	1847	30/238	30/239								
do	Elizabeth			Jane James	L	1848	31/27	31/54								
do	Elizabeth			Wm. McKay	L	1848	31/54									
do	Hamilton et al			John Harvey et al	L	1848	30/397									
do			Theodore	John Frasher et al	L	1848	31/6									
do			Theodore	William Newlove	L	1848	30/358									
do	Hamilton et al			Josiah Harvey et al	L	1849	31/118									
do	Andrew P. et al			George Craft	L	1850	31/334									
do	A. P.			John F. Miller	L	1852	32/241	32/329	32/341	32/365	32/442	32/461	32/489			
do	Andrew P.			Ohio County	L	1852	32/321									
do	Andrew P.			John F. Miller	L	1853	33/27	33/42	33/75	33/120	33/202	33/265	33/316	33/338		
do	A. P. et al			City of Wheeling	L	1854	33/400									
do	Hamilton et al			Daniel Steenrod et a	L	1854	34/8	34/26	34/45	34/89	34/119	34/140	34/175	34/192	34/208	34/210
do	do			do	L	1854	34/216	34/255	34/267							
Wood		Joseph et al		Morgan H. Gregg et al	L	1854	33/483	33/498	33/499							
do	Albert et al			F. Rothacker & Co.	L	1855	34/352									
do		James		Eliphalet C. Dewey	L	1855	34/241	34/322								
Woods	Alexander et al			Josiah W. Chapline	L	1856	35/293	35/295								
Wood	George et al			James Smylie	L	1856	35/25	35/435	35/507							
Woods	Hamilton			Frederick Zeigler	L	1856	35/28	35/33	35/34	35/134						
Wood		Joseph et al		Stephen Rice	L	1856	35/209									
do	A & A.			George W. Anderson	L	1856	35/145	35/203	35/303	35/471						
do	A. & A.			George W. Anderson	L	1857	36/56	36/111	36/172	36/313						
Woods	Alexander C.			Hamilton Boone	L	1858	36/327									

PLAINTIFF INDEX TO ORDER BOOKS — Ohio County, W. Va.

SURNAME	PLAINTIFFS GIVEN NAMES ABCDEFGH	GIVEN NAMES IJKLMNO	GIVEN NAMES PQRSTUVWXYZ	DEFENDANTS		YEAR	ORDER BOOK						
Woods	Andrew I.			Elijah Marlin et al	L	1858	37 65						
Wood	George L.			William S. Tippett	L	1860	38 196						
Woods	Alfred			Charles Gregg	L	1862	39 16	39 18					
Wood		Joe et al		Annie Caldwell	L	1873	L1 161	L1 163	L1 204	L1 214	L1 484		
Woods		John		Alexander M. Jacob et al	L	1874	L1 433	L1 438	L1 481	L1 477			
Wood		Joseph		Annie Caldwell	L	1874	L2 63	L2 67	L2 263				
Woods		John F.		George Nau	L	1876	L2 421	L2 445	L2 463				
Woods	Amelia J. et al			Robert B. Woods et al	C	1878	C1 381	C1 419	C1 430				
do		John F. et al		Nicholas Zimmer	L	1878	L4 43	L4 269	L4 283	L4 295	L4 321	L4 387	L4 502
do			Wm. H.	George R. Thompson	L	1879	L4 339						
do		John F.		N. Zimmer et al	L	1880	L4 430	L4 387					

PLAINTIFF INDEX TO ORDER BOOKS — Ohio County, W. Va.

Surname (Plaintiff)	Given Names	Defendants	L/C	Year	Order Book (Vol/Page)
Wheeling, by City Mayor		Ezekiel Hildraith	L	1821	18/318, 18/380
Wheeling, The Mayor and Common. Atty. et al		Amos Mim	L	1824	20/333
Wheeling, The Mayor & Common. Atty. et al		Noah Zane et al	C	1826	22/8
Wheeling, Town of		John Baird	C	1827	22/56, 22/152
Wheeling, Town of		Robert Marshall	C	1827	22/56, 22/151
Wheeling, Town of		Patrick McNulty et al	C	1827	22/55
Wheeling, Town of		Alex. McConnell et al	L	1829	23/360
Wheeling, Town of		Isaac Cotts	L	1834	26/222
Wheeling, City of		Asa Polston	L	1838	27/522
Wheeling, City of		J. C. Bryan	L	1839	28/128
Wheeling, City of		Alexander McCartney	L	1839	28/153, 28/195, 28/261, 28/324, 28/361, 28/428, 28/502
Wheeling, City of		George Carruthers	L	1841	28/574
Wheeling, City of		Henry Helm	L	1841	28/522, 28/564
Wheeling, City of		Jos. Junkin & Sons	L	1841	28/571
Wheeling, City of		Joseph Junkin et al	L	1841	29/14
Wheeling, City of		Alexander McCortney	L	1841	28/532
Wheeling, City of		William Robinson et al	L	1841	28/519, 28/520, 28/554, 28/570
Wheeling, City of		James Caldwell	L	1842	29/187
Wheeling, City of et al		Thomas J. B. Tentoney et al	L	1842	29/202, 29/326
Wheeling, City of		McKee et al	L	1843	29/299
Wheeling, City of		Catherine Sockman	L	1846	30/131, 30/138, 30/198
Wheeling, City of		Peter Gartner	L	1851	31/461, 31/496
Wheeling, City of		Con McDonald	L	1851	31/496
Wheeling, City of		Peter Gartner	L	1852	32/39, 32/65
Wheeling, City of		Patrick Hughes	L	1854	33/489
Wheeling, City of		Thomas McDonald	L	1854	34/34
Wheeling, City of		John Pfeister et al	L	1855	34/209, 34/217
Wheeling, City of		James Moore	L	1856	35/185, 35/247, 35/266, 35/217
Wheeling, City of		Milo Adams	L	1859	37/447
Wheeling, City of		C. Basser	L	1859	37/447
Wheeling, City of	et al	John Burris	L	1859	37/443
Wheeling, City of	et al	E. W. Edwards	L	1859	37/443
Wheeling, City of et al		Samuel F. Faris	L	1859	37/444
Wheeling, City of	et al	Francis Flood	L	1859	37/362, 37/400
Wheeling, City of	et al	Joseph Forsyth	L	1859	37/444

PLAINTIFF INDEX TO ORDER BOOKS — Ohio County, W. Va.

PLAINTIFFS SURNAME	GIVEN NAMES ABCDEFGH	GIVEN NAMES IJKLMNO	GIVEN NAMES PQRSTUVWXYZ	DEFENDANTS		YEAR	ORDER BOOK									
Wheeling, City	of et al			Lawrence Hahn	L	1859	37 361									
Wheeling, City	of	et al		George Kennedy	L	1859	37 360									
Wheeling, City	of	et al		Frederick Miller	L	1859	37 444									
Wheeling, City	of			John Neininger	L	1859	37 360									
Wheeling, City	of			Thomas Pemberton	L	1859	37 360									
Wheeling, City	of			Henry Reckbrandt	L	1859	37 362									
Wheeling, City	of et al			Christopher Repp	L	1859	37 361									
Wheeling, City	of et al			Jacob Vogleman	L	1859	37 443									
Wheeling, City	of			N. Baltzell	L	1861	38 385	38 396								
Wheeling, Town	of			Wm. Travis	L	1861	38 341	38 373	38 385	38 402	38 416	38 430	38 465	38 483	38 494	38 506
do				do	L	1861	38 541	38 448								
Wheeling, City	of			George White	L	1861	38 403									
Wheeling, City	of			Hobbs & Barnes	L	1862	39 3	39 50	39 67	39 92	39 82	39 123	39 56	39 150	39 155	39 175
do				do	L	1862	39 180	39 191	39 217	39 226	39 256					
Wheeling, City	of			Exley & Bickerton	L	1862	69 3	39 50	39 67	39 56	39 92	39 82	39 123	39 150	39 155	39 175
do				do	L	1862	39 180	39 191	39 217	39 226	39 256					
Wheeling, Town	of			William Travis	L	1862	39 48									
Wheeling, City	of			Daniel Zane et al	L	1874	L1 248	L1 415								
Wheeling, City	of			Peter Phillips	L	1879	L4 215									
Wheeling, City	of			Hampden Shriver et al	L	1880	L4 439	L4 448	L4 479							
Wheeling, City	of			Sebastian Welty et al	L	1880	L4 429	L4 447	L4 448	L4 450	L4 453	L4 452	L4 454	L4 474		
Wheeling, Seargant	of			Thomas Sweeney et al	L	1843	29 106	29 133	29 172	29 208	29 246	29 263				

'T' SURNAMES - MISCELLANEOUS

PLAINTIFF INDEX TO ORDER BOOKS — Ohio County, W. Va.

MISCELLANEOUS

SURNAME	GIVEN NAMES ABCDEFGH	GIVEN NAMES IJKLMNO	GIVEN NAMES PQRSTUVWXYZ	DEFENDANTS / REMARKS	YEAR	ORDER BOOK (Vol/Page)	
Tade		Isaac	orphan	Bound to David Rodgers, Esq.	1777	1	4
Tayler		Isaac		Ear Marking of stock	1778	1	17
Tayler		Isaac		Paid for services rendered	1778	1	20
Taylor		Isaac		Paid for public building	1779	1	39
Taylor		John	orphan	Bound to Nicholas Rogers	1785	1	258
Tate		John		Exempt from Levies	1790	3	187
Tate		John		To be exempted from Militia duties and county Levies	1791	3	296
Taylor		Isaac		Allowed money for keeping poor man called James	1794	4	332
Taylor	Charles			Sheriff to condemn land for Grist Mill at Cross Creek	1796	5	149
Taylor		Isaac		Allowed fees as guard of Daniel Pearce	1797	5	275
Taylor		James		Released from paying fines	1798	6	99
Tarbill	Holmer			Exempted from working on road & County levy	1805	10	151
Taylor		Isaac		Fine for not attending as a Juryman	1806	10	357
Taylor		John		(Orphan) Guardian for Ebenezer Buchanan	1813	14	74
Taylor		John	estate	Adm'rs. & Appraisers	1814	14	325 / 14, 383
Tanner		James	orphan	Thomas Tanner-Guardian	1817	15	224
Taylor		James	estate	Danny Baker et al-Appraisers	1818	15	311
Taylor		Isaac		Exempt from road work-County Levies	1820	17	257
Taylor	George			Proved that he is a Resident of Ohio County	1820	17	465
Taylor	Elizabeth			Taylor Guardian of Heirs of James	1822	19	88
Taylor		James		Bound in Shaton(orphan boy)	1822	19	94
Taylor	Benjamin		estate	Adm'rs. & Appraisers	1823	19	584
Tanner		Michael		Certified age	1825	21	37
Taylor	Edward			Taylor Guardian for Thos. & Patty	1825	20	443
Taylor		John	estate	estate Michael Cresap et al to settle	1825	20	453
Taylor		Margaret & Martha &	Thomas & Patty	Edward Taylor-Guardian	1825	20	443
Taylor		John		Bound in John Daniels	1830	24	158
Taggart	Alex			Bound to Richard Hopkins	1834	26	19
Tayler	Alexander			Guardian of James Devinne	1836	27	28
Taylor		Isabelle	orphan	Bound to William B. Quarrier	1839	28	180
Taylor		estate	Robert G.	Obtaining letters of Adm'r.	1842	28	180
Tannor		James		Bound in Josephine Henet	1843	29	223
Taylor		Isabel		Bound to Wm. Quarrier-cancelled	1845	29	577
Tanner		James		Guardian for Harrison Caton Bound out to John W. Bouing	1847	30	173
Tanner		James		Guardian for William Myars	1847	30	258

PLAINTIFF INDEX TO ORDER BOOKS — Ohio County, W. Va.

MISCELLANEOUS

SURNAME	GIVEN NAMES ABCDEFGH	GIVEN NAMES IJKLMNO	GIVEN NAMES PQRSTUVWXYZ	REMARKS	YEAR	ORDER BOOK		
Tanner		Dr. James		return Exemption on tax bill-Tax	1851	31 380		
Taylor		estate	Thomas	Adm'rs. & Appraisers	1854	33 216		
Taylor			William Y.	Improperly taxed for 1854	1854	34 40	34 59	
Tanner		James		Tax refund	1860	37 470		
Taylor		John W.		Overseers of the Poor to send to the Poor house	1861	38 346		
Tayler		Lavina		Released from tax	1863	39 187		
Taylor	estate	Lewis	(Colored)	Adm'r. & Appraisers	1868	41 52		
Taggart		James	estate	Adm'rs. & Appraisers	1868	41 22		
Talbot	Eugene	Orphan		Joseph F. Mayes-Guardian	1874	L1 243		
Taney		estate	William H.	Adm'rs. & Appraisers	1877	L3 117		
Tappe			Sophia	Guardian of Emma Logan	1879	L4 380		
Tappe	Henry	estate		Executer appointed	1880	L4 462		

'T' SURNAMES – MISCELLANEOUS ENTRIES

PLAINTIFF INDEX TO ORDER BOOKS — Ohio County, W. Va.

MISCELLANEOUS

Surname	Given Names A-H	Given Names I-O	Given Names P-Z	Defendants / Remarks	Year	Order Book (Vol / Page)
Templeton		James		Ear Marks for stock	1781	1 / 113
Teal	Asey & Charles			Regarding damage if a mill dam was erected upon Cross Creek	1796	5/124 5/146
Teel	Charles			Purpose of condemning a Mill site	1797	5/212 5/215 5/227
Teeters	David			Bound to Marton Whetzell	1803	9/92
Teeter	George &	Mary		Bound to Jonothan Howell	1803	9/92
Teabler	George			Condemn to build water grist mill	1818	13/379 13/391
Teabler		Michael		To be released from payment of taxes on Negro woman	1822	19/59
Teel	Clarissa			Guardian of James Vansyock for purpose of binding James etc.	1827	22/61
Teeters	Henry			Bound in Andrew Fulton	1833	25/479
Tedford		John	estate	John Gilmore-Adm'r.	1838	27/444
Tedford		John	estate	Adm'r. & Appraisers	1839	28/114 28/213 28/270
Tedford		estate	Susanna	Adm'r. & Appraisers	1839	28/271 28/272 28/281 28/585
Teagarden		Isaac M.	estate	Adm'r. appointed	1863	40/25
Teece		estate	Sarah A.	Mary Teece-Curater	1875	L2/84
Teece		orphan	Sarah	George B. Caldwell-Guardian	1879	L4/178
Terrell	Calain &	Mary &		Indenture of apprenticeship to Samuel Cuckler	1818	16/340
Terytitan		Jacob		Thomas Watson bound to	1830	24/13
Terril	Daniel	estate		Jeremiah Terril et al Exec.	1847	30/195 30/196
Terrell	Elizabeth	estate		Adm'r. & Appraisers	1848	31/4
Terrell		Jane	estate	Adm'r. & Appraisers	1849	31/135 31/167 31/265 31/308
Terrell	Elizabeth &	Lucy & Olive &	(Infants) Sarah	Mathew Terrell-Guardian	1851	31/480
Terrell	Daniel G.	estate		Adm'r. & Appraisers	1854	33/473 33/474
Terril		estate	Wm. H.	Adm'r. appointed	1865	40/170
Terrel	C. S.			Guardian of Finley children	1879	L4/262

MISCELLANEOUS — PLAINTIFF INDEX TO ORDER BOOKS — Ohio County, W. Va.

SURNAME	GIVEN NAMES A-H	GIVEN NAMES I-O	GIVEN NAMES P-Z	DEFENDANTS / REMARKS	YEAR	ORDER BOOK Vol / Page		
Tilton		John		Ordered to appear in Court	1786	1 / 206		
Timmons		Nancy	orphan	Bound to Umphrey Younger	1810	12 / 338		
Timmons		Lazarus		Bound to Robert Caldwell	1812	13 / 163		
Timmins		Nancy		Bound to Nathan Strong	1814	14 / 262		
Timmons	Charlotte			Bound to Archibald Hamilton	1819	16 / 646		
Timmons		John	orphan	Apprenticed to Robert Thompson	1819	16 / 646		
Timmons		Lucinda		Bound to William Wilson	1819	16 / 646		
Timmons		orphan	Peter	Apprenticed to Edw. Carter	1819	16 / 646		
Timmons			Shartol	Bound to Samuel Flemming	1823	20 / 49		
Timmons		Jesse	(Black Man)	Sues for his freedom	1825	20 / 490		
Tilden			Sophia	Tax refund	1858	37 / 79		
Tiernan		M. J.		Excused from attending as Petit Juror	1862	39 / 129		
Tillman	(Colored)	estate	Susan	Adm'r. appointed	1873	11 / 139		
Tiernan	Ella &	orphans	William M.	M. J. Tiernan-Guardian	1874	11 / 288		
Tiernan		Michael	estate	Adm'r. appointed	1878	13 / 485		
Tippings	Elizabeth			Acknowledged land	1794	4 / 235	4 / 93	
Tingle			William	Allowed thirty dollars for carrying and transmitting records	1809	8 /		
Tinny		James		Discharged from recognizance	1811	13 / 110		
Titus	Elizabeth	Free Negro		To be bound to Richard Simms	1836	27 / 148	27 / 193	
Titus	Allen			Apprenticed to Samuel Knode — Transfer to John A. Good	1839	28 / 83		

'T' SURNAMES – MISCELLANEOUS ENTRIES

MISCELLANEOUS — PLAINTIFF INDEX TO ORDER BOOKS — Ohio County, W. Va.

SURNAME	PLAINTIFFS GIVEN NAMES A-H	GIVEN NAMES I-O	GIVEN NAMES P-Z	DEFENDANTS / REMARKS	YEAR	ORDER BOOK Vol/Page					
Thomson			Thomas	Exempted from paying tax	1800	7/82					
Thomson		John		Exempt from County Levies	1801	7/310					
Thompson		Moses		Indenture of apprenticeship from John Stewart	1813	12/60					
Thornburg			Thomas	Fined for not appearing as a witness	1813	2/107	2/115	2/124			
Thompson			Robert	Fined for not attending Petit Jury	1815	2/240					
Thompson		Josias		certified Slaves brought into state	1817	16/202					
Thompson		James M.		To bind Hillery Hays	1817	16/5					
Thompson			Robert C.	Apprentice Bound in John Fink as an	1819	17/30					
Thompson			Robert	Bound in John Timmons	1819	16/646					
Thompson		Moses		Hugh Carmichael bound to	1821	18/287					
Thompson		James M.		He to have liberty to retail ardent spirits in his store	1822	19/76					
Thompson		Moses		Guardian bound out Moses Harris to William Cunningham as an apprentice	1823	19/530					
Thatcher		Jones		Henry Jamison bound out to Hamilton-orphan	1826	22/10					
Thompson		Moses		Guardian-Bound in Sary Ann	1826	21/510					
Thompson		John		Failing to attend as a Juror discharged	1827	22/268					
Thompson		Moses		Guardian-Bound in Moses Harris & William Clark	1827	22/232					
Thatcher		Jonas		Bound in George Poyls	1828	23/16					
Thompson		Moses		Entered his account	1828	22/302					
Thompson			Samuel	Justice of the Peace entered his account	1828	22/303					
Thornburgh	David			Sarah E. Whittingham Guardian of James Whittingham	1828	23/8					
Thompson		estate	Robert	Charles D. Knox-Adm'r.	1831	24/292					
Thompson		James M.		Guardian of James Greenland	1831	25/35					
Thompson		Moses		Accounts Certified	1831	25/8	25/17	25/100	25/459	25/371	25/325
Thompson		Moses		Guardian of James A. Wender	1833	25/478					
Thompson		Moses		Account certified to Auditor	1834	26/228					
Thompson		Moses		Account certified to Auditor	1834	26/135					
Thompson		Moses		Account certified to Auditor	1834	26/40					
Thompson		Moses		Account certified to Auditor	1834	26/4	26/40	26/140	26/427	26/545	
Thompson		Josias	estate	Adm'r. & Appraisers	1835	26/474					
Thompson		James A.	estate	William Webb-Adm'r.	1836	27/111					
Thatcher		James		Daniel Hanke Guardian of Hammel orphans &	1838	27/419					
Thompson	George			Guardian of Wm. Thompson	1839	28/163					
Thompson		estate	Wm. P.	Adm'r. appointed	1839	28/164					
Thompson			William	Commonwealth Presents his acct. against	1840	28/392					
Thompson			William	Presents his account against County of Ohio for building bridge at mouth of McKinleyville	1841	28/557					

MISCELLANEOUS — PLAINTIFF INDEX TO ORDER BOOKS — Ohio County, W. Va.

110

SURNAME	GIVEN NAMES ABCDEFGH	GIVEN NAMES IJKLMNO	GIVEN NAMES PQRSTUVWXYZ	REMARKS	YEAR	ORDER BOOK			
Thompson		(Lunatic)		Removed to asylum	1843	29 260			
Thompson	George			Booth Guardian of Susana Jane et al	1844	29 481			
Thornburg			Thomas	Guardian to Waddle Orphan	1848	31 33			
Thornburg			Thomas	Tithables on Thos. Thornberg farm be exempt from work on rd.	1850	31 317			
Thoburn		Joseph		Bound in Gurtrude Dessell	1854	34 25			
Thompson	George			Guardian of Booth children	1857	35 449			
Thompson		Mary Virginia		Bound to John H. Downs	1860	38 180	38 336		
Thoburn		Joseph	estate	Adm'r. & Appraisers	1864	40 114			
Thomas		Louis	estate	Adm'r. appointed	1869	41 90			
Thompson	Catharine	estate			1870	41 143			
Thompson		estate	William	Adm'r. appointed	1870	41 115			
Thornburg		estate	Thomas	Adm'rs. & Appraisers	1871	41 174	41 183		
Thompson	Frances		estate	Will proved	1872	41 249			
Thomas	Andreas	estate		Adm'r. Appointed	1874	L1 468			
Thornburg		estate	Thomas	Adm'r. appointed	1874	L1 293			
Thornburgh		John	insane	W. J. Cowden-Committee	1874	L2 31			
Thomas		Mary E.	estate	orphans E. J. Stone-Guardian for	1875	L2 137			
Thornburgh		John		Habeas Corpus	1875	L2 275	L2 328	L2 338	
Thornburgh		estate	Thomas	Adm'r. appointed	1875	L2 219			
Thornburgh		John	Lunatic	W. J. W. Cowden-Committee	1876	C1 239	C1 267		
Thoburn	Alexander			Guardian of Ann Eliz. Watt	1877	L3 410			
Thornburg		John	Lunatic	John O. Pendleton-Committee	1878	L3 438			
Thompson	Armor	estate		Adm'r. & Appraisers	1879	L4 253			

PLAINTIFF INDEX TO ORDER BOOKS — Ohio County, W. Va.

MISCELLANEOUS

SURNAME	PLAINTIFFS GIVEN NAMES ABCDEFGH	GIVEN NAMES IJKLMNO	GIVEN NAMES PQRSTUVWXYZ	REMARKS	YEAR	ORDER BOOK		
Todd			William	Exempted from paying County Levy	1825	21 205		
Tolland		estate	William	Adm'r. & Appraisers	1827	22 184		
Todd		Martin		Guardian-Bound out James White to Mark Dunlap	1829	23 208		
Todd		estate	William	Adm'r. & Appraisers	1828	23 27		
Toland		James	estate	Adm'r. & Appraisers	1831	24 369		
Toland		James	estate	Francis C. Campbel-Commr. to settle, & audit estate	1834	26 38		
Todd	Archibald	Paull	orphan	Bound out to Nathan Chapman	1848	30 314		
Todd		James C.		Guardian Nancy Devol Todd-orphan	1853	32 345		
Todd		Nancy Devol	orphan	James Todd-Guardian	1853	32 345		
Todd	A. S. Dr.	et al		Bound out Mack-an orphan to James Caldwell	1854	35 226		
Toliver		Joseph		Account for clothing Margaret Dolan(Lunatic) certified etc	1861	38 409		
Todd	Eliza Jane & Margaret	Elizabeth		Samuel J. Ellifritz-Guardian	1866	40 320		
Todd		estate	William T.	Adm'r. appointed	1867	40 348	40 397	
Todd		Martin	Luther-Dec'd		1871	41 151		
Todd		estate	Thomas	Adm'r. named to settle estate	1872	41 227		
Todd	Genevieve		estate	Daniel Peck-Executor	1880	14 457		
Tomlinson		Joseph		Ear Marks for Stock	1784	1 206		
Tomlinson		Joseph		Oath of Allegiance	1789	3 138		
Tomlinson		Joseph		Exempt from road work and County levies	1789	3 149		
Tomlinson		Joseph	estate	Adm'r. & Appraisers	1807	11 67		
Tomlinson		Joseph		Exempt two tithables from work	1808	11 243		
Tomlinson		estate	Robert	Adm'r. & Appraisers	1810	12 193		
Tomlinson			Samuel	Fined for not attending Petit Jury	1815	2 240	2 246	
Tomlinson	Elizabeth Ann			Bound to John D. Seamon	1824	20 138		
Tomlinson		Joseph	estate	Adm'r. & Appraisers	1825	21 52	21 208	21 284
Tomlinson		Nathaniel	estate	Adm'r. & Appraisers	1827	22 128		
Tomlinson		Nathaniel	estate	Zachariah Jacob et al auditors	1829	23 231		
Tomlinson	Alfred & Ellen			Isaac Horkinson-Guardian	1830	24 89		
Tonner		estate	William	Adm'r. appointed	1841	29 37		
Tomison		estate	William	Adm'rs. & Appraisers	1848	30 391		
Tozzer		Mary Ann		Acct. for attending to Jane Powell	1849	31 137		
Tomison	(Tominison) Letitia		(Lunatic)	James Kellor made Committee	1850	31 265	31 448	
Townsend		estate	Thomas	Adm'r. & Appraisers	1851	3 412		
Townsend	Amos	estate		Samuel Irwin, Sheriff-Adm'r.	1857	36 9		

PLAINTIFF INDEX TO ORDER BOOKS — Ohio County, W. Va.

MISCELLANEOUS

Surname	Given Names ABCDEFGH	Given Names IJKLMNO	Given Names PQRSTUVWXYZ	Remarks	Year	Order Book						
Tompkins		James L.	estate	Adm'rs. & Appraisers	1860	38 307						
Tompkins		Lewis L.	estate	Adm'r. & Appraisers	1861	38 507	38 509	38 540				
Toothaere	Hannah L.	estate		Executor appointed	1873	L1 150						
Towers	Florence N.		orphan	Thomas Wilson-Guardian	1873	L1 49						
Topp	C. Ernest	estate		Adm'r. appointed	1877	13 125						
Tonini		Joseph	estate	Mary Tonini-Adm'r.	1879	L4 311						
Triadelphia				Josiah Thompson-laid off Town of Triadelphia	1829	23 150						
Trail	Daniel			Guardian of Wm. Rudiford-Orphan	1831	24 505						
Trimmell		Maria &	Sarah-orphan	Elijah Day- Guardian	1838	27 368						
Trisler		Martha &	Phebe	Homer Austin-Guardian	1841	29 52						
Travis		James		Released from payment of taxes fro year 1843	1844	29 331						
Trainer		John		Overseers ordered to remove pauper who is in jail to the poor house of this county	1853	33 94						
Trisler		James		Jailor-Presented his acct. for keeping & Dieting prisoners	1853	33 46	33 224	33 198	33 380	33 434	33 200	33 439
Travers	Bridget			James Travers-Guardian	1854	34 7						
Trisler	George			Guardian for Josephine Jones	1855	34 353	34 369					
Tracy		Julia & Margaret		Clothing furnished by Poor Commissioners for Margaret a crazy woman	1857	36 108						
Trimble		Harriet A.		(Orphan) Guardian for Harry Lincoln	1871	41 196						
Trimble		John B.	estate	Adm'r. & Appraisers	1871	41 195						

PLAINTIFF INDEX TO ORDER BOOKS — Ohio County, W. Va.

MISCELLANEOUS

Surname	Given Names A-H	Given Names I-O	Given Names P-Z	Defendants / Remarks	Year	Order Book
Truxel		Jacob	estate	Truxel — Letters of Adm'r. to Catharine	1833	25 / 461, 25 / 480
Truax		John F.	estate	William Webb, Sheriff-Adm'r.	1837	27 / 207
Trusschel	Ferdinand			Guardian of Reister orphans	1848	31 / 91
Trueschell	Ferdinand	estate		Adm'r. & Appraisers	1854	33 / 140
Tumbleton		Joseph		Appointed to examine Surveyors books & report	1788	3 / 58
Tumbelson		Joseph, Jr.		John Caldwell, Commr. to pay back money	1793	4 / 170
Tush	George		estate	John Rodiffer et al-appraisers	1805	10 / 398
Turk		Margaret		Guardian Turk children	1807	11 / 15
Turner	George		estate	Adm'rs. & Appraisers	1810	2 / 59
Tush	George		estate	Moses Shepherd et al appointed	1811	12 / 405, 12 / 410
Turner	George		estate	Mary Turner-Adm'r. Samuel McClure et al appointed	1814	14 / 250
Turner		John		Ordered to be exempt from paying County & Poor tax	1822	19 / 221
Turner		John		Exempt from County levy & Poor tax	1824	20 / 346
Tustler (Luatter)		Jacob		Joseph Gantz-Bound to	1827	22 / 84
Tuttle		Joseph & Jacob		Indenture of apprenticeship to Stephen Pollack	1828	24 / 355
Tucker		Joshua	orphan	Bound to Henry Pearson	1838	27 / 415
Turner	Alexander		estate	Adm'r. & Appraisers	1851	31 / 446
Turner		Mary		Discharged from Jail	1852	32 / 63
Tucker		Michael	estate	Adm'r. & Appraisers	1854	33 / 156, 33 / 158
Tucker		John		Account for furnishing clothing to Margaret Dolan (Lunatic) certified to Auditor	1860	38 / 302
Tucker		Mary Ann		Guardian of Tucker orphans	1868	41 / 46
Turner		estate	William	Executer appointed	1874	11 / 383
Turner	Mrs.	Lydia A.	estate	Adm'r. appointed	1875	12 / 240
Turner		estate	William	Alfred Turner-Executer	1875	12 / 113
Turner		John	estate	Elijah Day-Adm'r.	1880	14 / 508
Tweed		Isaac	estate	Adm'rs. & Appraisers	1830	24 / 46, 24 / 182
Tyson			William B.	Guardian of James Robb	1830	23 / 465

'U&V' SURNAMES – MISCELLANEOUS ENTRIES

MISCELLANEOUS PLAINTIFF INDEX TO ORDER BOOKS — Ohio County, W. Va.

SURNAME	GIVEN NAMES ABCDEFGH	GIVEN NAMES IJKLMNO	GIVEN NAMES PQRSTUVWXYZ	REMARKS / DEFENDANTS	YEAR	ORDER BOOK (Top: Volume / Bottom: Page)	
Updegraff		Josiah	estate	Execrs. & appraisers appt'd.	1815	15	90
Updegraff		Josiah	estate	Chas. D. Knox etal appointed	1818	16	313
Updegraff		Israel		Guardian for Barthold Shumire	1825	22 / 345	22 / 409
Updegraff		Asrial		To settle with sheriff	1826	21 / 289	21 / 348
Updegraff		Israel	(guardian)	Ritchie & Wilson. Binds G. Herrington to	1837	27	181
United States Hotel				Rental rates considered.	1839	28	96
United States Hotel				John McMillan, keeper. Rental & assessment be reduced	1842	29	80
Updegraff		Israel		Exempt from erroneous tax.	1860	38	179
Ubrecht	Charles		estate	Admr. & appraisers appointed	1864	40 / 103	40 / 104
Ubrecht		John	Orphan	Frederick D. Myer, guardian	1864	40	104
Ulrich	Aloes		estate	Admr. appointed.	1868	41	18
Unterzuber	Charles		estate	Admr. & appraisers appointed	1869	41	82
Urlamb	George		estate	Executor appointed	1874	L1	383
Updegraff		Israel	estate		1876	L2	507
Updegraff		Israel	estate	Admr. appointed	1876	L3	59
Updegraff		Josiah F.	estate		1876	L2	476
Updegraff		Mary A., Mrs.	estate	Administrator appointed	1876	L3	77
Varney			estate Royal	Administrators & appraisers app'td.	1838	28	8
Varney	Edward		Guardian	Matilda Hadden, bound to	1858	36	161
Valentine		Mary E.	(orphan)	David M. Blayney, guardian	1866	40	296
Valentine			estate Susan	Administrator appointed	1868	41	25
Vallentine	Benjamin		estate	Admr. & appraisers appointed	1869	41	88
Vaas			William	Guardian for orphan children of Louisa Schwenchueck	1872	41	203
Valentine		Mary E.	estate	Will proved	1872	41 / 256	41 / 257
Valentine		Mary E.	estate	Executor appointed	1873	L1 / 5	L1 / 150

'V' SURNAMES - MISCELLANEOUS ENTRIES

MISCELLANEOUS PLAINTIFF INDEX TO ORDER BOOKS — Ohio County, W. Va.

SURNAME	PLAINTIFFS Given Names A-H	PLAINTIFFS Given Names I-O	PLAINTIFFS Given Names P-Z	DEFENDANTS	YEAR	ORDER BOOK Vol.	ORDER BOOK Page
Van Metre		Joseph		1758-1759 Served as soldier in Ranging Co.	1780	1	69
VanMetre		Joseph	estate	John Mitchell, etal appraisers.	1781	1	132
VanMetre	Abram	estate		George McColloch, etal apprs.	1783	1	145
VanMetre		John		Ear Marks of stock	1784	1	242
VanMetre		John		Ear marks of stock	1784	1	242
VanMetre		Morgan (infant)		Jonah Seamon, guardian	1784	1	242
Vanmeter		Joseph		Jonah Seaman, guardian	1787	3	46
Van Buskirk			Tarrance, Jr.	admr. & appraisers appointed	1791	3	293
Van Buskirk			Samuel	Exempt from levies	1792	3	324
Vandine		estate	William	Admr. & appraisers appointed	1792	4	17
VanMetre		Morgan		Requested resurvey of land	1796	5	99
VanMetre		Morgan		Water grist mill	1796	5	141
VanMetre	Abraham			Exempt from taxes	1801	7	247
Vandwort		John		Bound to Hiram Hedges	1807	11	1
Van Scyoc	Abel	estate		Admrs. & appraisers appointed	1814	14	379
VanScyoc	Abel			J. Caldwell et al appointed	1816	15	268
Vance		John		Wm. Carmichael bound to	1821	18	287
VanMeter		Joseph	estate	Admrs. & appraisers appointed	1822	19	65
VanMeter		(orphan)	Robert	Salathiel Curtis, guardian	1822	19	89
VanMeter		John	estate	Proof of heirs	1825	20	450
Vansyock		James		Bound to John Laughten	1827	22	61
Vandman	Henry			Bound in Alex Files	1837	27	184
Vance		James		Guardian for Elizabeth Buchanan	1855	34	53
Vance		John		Improperly taxed	1856	35	238
Vance		estate	William	Admr. appointed	1872	41	230
Vance		James	estate	Executor appointed	1873	L1	226

MISCELLANEOUS PLAINTIFF INDEX TO ORDER BOOKS — Ohio County, W. Va.

SURNAME	GIVEN NAMES ABCDEFGH	GIVEN NAMES IJKLMNO	GIVEN NAMES PQRSTUVWXYZ	REMARKS DEFENDANTS	YEAR	ORDER BOOK
Virgin			Resin	Ear marks for stock	1776	1 / 16
Villars	Edward			Exempt from road work & levy	1807	11 / 181
Veasy		Noble	estate	Letters of Admr. granted	1811	12 / 405
Vennum	George			Sworn as grandjuror	1814	2 / 167
Vennum	George			& Andrew Woods. Bound in John Haslet	1816	15 / 271
Vannum	Geo.			Bound in James Carmichel	1817	16 / 5, 16 / 97
Vermilion	Charles			Exempt from paying county levy	1822	19 / 94
Vennum	George			Recommended as lumber inspector	1823	19 / 406
Vennum	George	estate		Abigail Vennum, admrx.	1838	27 / 545
Vennum	George	estate		James Pemberton etal appraisers	1839	28 / 39
Virginia Hotel				Jacob A. Kline, keeper Rental value be reduced.	1842	29 / 80
Vermilling	Charles			Exempt from county levy	1848	31 / 52
Vennum	David			Tax refund	1850	31 / 227
Veazey		estate	Richard	Admr. & appraisers appointed	1870	41 / 132, 41 / 160
Virdin		estate	William W.	Admr. appointed	1871	41 / 199
Veazey		et al	Richard W.	Orphans of Richard Veazey, decd	1872	41 / 204
Veazey		estate	Richard	Admr. & appraisers appointed	1873	L1 / 3
Veazey		decd.	Richard	children J. H. Hobbs, guardian of Minor	1875	L2 / 113
Vennum		Martha	estate		1876	L2 / 464

MISCELLANEOUS PLAINTIFF INDEX TO ORDER BOOKS — Ohio County, W. Va.

SURNAME	PLAINTIFFS GIVEN NAMES A-H	GIVEN NAMES I-O	GIVEN NAMES P-Z	REMARKS / DEFENDANTS	YEAR	ORDER BOOK (Vol/Page)
Voto		Jacob	estate	Admr. & appraisers appointed	1824	20 / 205
Vogler		John		Guardian of Catharine Neider.	1854	33 / 438
Vogler		John		Guardian Liebert orphans	1856	35 / 202
Voltz		Nicholas	estate	Administrator appointed	1864	40 / 77
Voelker	Charles H.	estate		Administrator appointed	1867	40 / 381
Vogler		John		Guardian of C. Kaiser, orphans.	1869	41 / 91
Vogler		Jacob		Guardian of Vogler children	1880	L4 / 464
Vogler	Andrew	estate		Jacob Vogler, admr.	1880	L4 / 464

MISCELLANEOUS — PLAINTIFF INDEX TO ORDER BOOKS — Ohio County, W. Va.

Surname	Given Names A-H	Given Names I-O	Given Names P-Z	Defendants / Remarks	Year	Order Book (Vol / Page)
Waits		John		Guardian of Wm. Price	1778	1 / 32
Waits		John		Ear Marks of Stock	1785	1 / 269
Waits		John		Exempt from Militia Duty	1787	3 / 27
Waer		Jane & James		Bound out to Wm. Waier	1798	6 / 117
Wadel		John	estate	Adm'r. & Appraisers	1818	16 / 484
Waddle		John	estate	Absalom Ridgely et al appointed	1821	18 / 442
Waddle		Mary	estate	Adm'r. & Appraisers	1825	20 / 431 20 / 448
Waddle		Joseph		Guardian for Rachel Waddle et al	1830	24 / 181
Waddle			William	Bound in David Johnson	1830	24 / 88
Waddle		estate	William Sr.	Wm. Hackins et al estate to settle	1830	24 / 206
Waddle		estate	William	Auditors & Executer	1835	26 / 329
Waddle	Elizabeth &	orphans	Sarah	Thos. Thornburg-Guardian	1848	31 / 33
Waddle		estate	William	Adm'rs. & Appraisers	1848	30 / 432 31 / 31
Waddle		estate	William	James Waddle-Adm'r.	1848	31 / 72 31 / 290
Wakeman	George A.	estate		Adm'r. & Appraisers	1850	31 / 253
Waddle		(orphans)	Pauline V. & William H.	Sarah Waddle-Guardian	1850	31 / 266
Wakeman	George A.	estate		A settlement presented in Court by Henry K. List-Adm'r.	1854	33 / 279
Wait	Albert	estate		Adm'r. & Appraisers	1868	41 / 10
Wait			Sarah	Guardian of Wait orphans	1868	41 / 11
Waddle		Joseph		Guardian for Ivea McColloch orphan	1871	41 / 184
Waddle		Joseph		Guardian for Ida McColloch	1873	11 / 19 12 / ?
Waddle		Jos.		Guardian of Iva McColloch	1875	12 / 204
Wagenknecht	Emilie &	Matilda		Philip Heinstein-Guardian	1875	12 / 243
Waddle		Joseph	estate	David Waddle-Executor	1878	14 / 100
Wagner		Louis	estate	Mary E. Wagner-Executor	1879	14 / 383

MISCELLANEOUS - PLAINTIFF INDEX TO ORDER BOOKS — Ohio County, W. Va.

SURNAME	GIVEN NAMES ABCDEFGH	GIVEN NAMES IJKLMNO	GIVEN NAMES PQRSTUVWXYZ	DEFENDANTS / REMARKS	YEAR	ORDER BOOK (Vol / Page)
Wall	Henry	estate		Thos. Waller et al-appraisers	1778	1/8 1/32 1/37
Waller			Thomas	Ear Marking of Stock	1778	1/17
Wallis		James		Deliver books to Able Johnstone	1794	4/353
Walker		Jacob		Resurvey for Jacob Walker of land requested	1796	5/115
Wallace		James		Age & Character certified	1796	5/82
Walker	Elenor &		Thomas	John Gooding appointed Guardian	1806	10/414
Walravin	Elias	orphan		Bound to James Roberts	1819	16/674
Waller	Elizabeth &	Kesiah		Confined to Poor house	1826	22/29
Walker	Hugh	orphan		Wm. Wilson-Guardian	1831	24/433
Walker		James		Restraining order	1831	25/13
Wallace		Mary	(Prisoner)	Jailor to furnish clothes	1835	26/337
Wallace			Thomas	Bound to Hugh McCurdy	1839	28/96
Wallace		orphan Margaret	Thomas Hastings &	Bound to Elizabeth Kelly	1844	29/469
Wallace	Eliza Jane	& Mary McCall		Alexander Rogers-Guardian	1851	31/393
Walker		John P.	estate	Adm'r. & Appraisers	1852	32/318
Walsh		Louisa		Order as to tax	1853	32/408
Walker		John P.	estate	An appraisement produced in Ct.	1854	33/431
Walter	Conrad			Released from tax for 1856	1856	35/278
Walter	Charles	estate		Fidel Mager-Curator P. Sweitzer et al-Appraisers	1857	36/82 36/141 36/152
Walter	Charles	estate		Fidel Mager-Adm'r.	1859	37/101
Walker		Montgomery		Guardian-Walker orphans	1866	40/313
Walls		John	estate	Adm'r. appointed	1868	41/51
Wallace		estate	Robert		1871	41/192
Wallace		estate	Samuel C.	Sheriff to administer estate	1872	41/247
Walters		John		Guardian for Charlotta Walters	1872	41/201
Waltermyer	A. J.	estate		E. T. Sheppard-Adm'r.	1875	L2/110
Walker	Carrie C.	(Insane)		Committee appointed	1876	L2/381 L2/413
Walker	Carrie C.	(Lunatic)		Jane A. Walker as Committee resigns as said Carrie Walker is restored to health.	1878	L4/154
Walters		John H.	estate	Thos. O'Brien et al-Appraisers Rev. John J. Kain-Executor	1880	L4/493 L4/494 L4/509

PLAINTIFF INDEX TO ORDER BOOKS — Ohio County, W. Va.

MISCELLANEOUS

SURNAME	GIVEN NAMES ABCDEFGH	GIVEN NAMES IJKLMNO	GIVEN NAMES PQRSTUVWXYZ	DEFENDANTS / REMARKS	YEAR	ORDER BOOK			
Warford		John		Ear Marks for Stock	1778	1 / 17			
Ward			William	Lieutenant 1760	1781	1 / 127			
Warpenby			William et al	Condemnation of land for Grist Mill	1795	4 / 428	4 / 441		
Ward			William	Adm'rs. John Bector-Dec'd.	1798	6 / 118			
Warden		James	orphan	John McColloch-Guardian	1799	6 / 245	6 / 299		
Warden		John	estate	Benjamin Biggs et al-Appraisers	1799	6 / 243	6 / 273	6 / 293	6 / 339
Warden		estate	Samuel	Auditors appointed	1803	3 / 132			
Warden		James		Auditors to settle Adm's acct.	1804	9 / 158			
Warnock		estate	Rebeckah	Letters of Testamentory granted to John Parison	1811	12 / 482			
Warnock		estate	Rebeckah	Adm'r. & Appraisers	1811	13 / 107			
Ward		Joseph		Joseph Ward fined for not attending Grand Jury	1812	2 / 89			
Ward		Joseph Jr.		Bound in Ann Hackham	1822	19 / 223			
Ward		Joseph	estate	Adm'r. & Appraisers	1826	21 / 377			
Ward		Joseph	estate	Auditors & Executor appointed	1827	22 / 43			
Wardell		estate	Solomon	Sarah Wardell took oath as Adm'r	1828	22 / 366			
Warden		James		Presents his acct. certified	1839	28 / 103			
Warden		estate	Samuel	Adm'r. & Appraisers	1839	28 / 161	28 / 168	28 / 184	
Warden			Samuel	Guardian of Hezekiah Clarke	1854	33 / 482			
Warren		Isiah		Witness	1857	35 / 348			
Ward		Jane		To be bound by Overseers of Poor to Wm. Henry Smith	1862	39 / 86			
Warnafeldt		John H.	estate	Adm'r. & Appraisers	1869	41 / 107			
Warden		estate	Samuel	Adm'rs. & Appraisers	1873	11 / 16	11 / 24	11 / 40	
Warden		Jacob M.	estate	Adm'r. & Appraisers	1874	11 / 381			
Warren	Dwight	estate			1876	12 / 434			
Ward	Annie	(Lunatic)		Thos. Byrnes-Committee	1879	14 / 366			
Weeks		Jane		Bound out to Henry Neff	1798	6 / 130			
Web				Bound in Wm. Fullerton	1812	13 / 267			
Webb			William	Indenture of apprenticeship of Geo. Quigley (Infant)	1813	13 / 396			
Wickham		Levi		Entered his account	1828	22 / 302			
Weasner			Thomas H.	To be bound to John Borland	1836	27 / 13			
Wickham	Henry C.			To bind in William Ritchie	1838	27 / 430			
Wickham		(Infant)	Robert	William S. Wickham-Guardian	1839	28 / 95			
Wickham			Wm. S.	Guardian of Robert Wickham (Infant)	1839	28 / 95			
Wickham		Mary		Guardian of Catherine Wickham	1855	34 / 52			

124 MISCELLANEOUS PLAINTIFF INDEX TO ORDER BOOKS — Ohio County, W. Va.

SURNAME	GIVEN NAMES ABCDEFGH	GIVEN NAMES IJKLMNO	GIVEN NAMES PQRSTUVWXYZ	REMARKS	YEAR	ORDER BOOK	
Wickham			William	tax reduction for 1856	1856	35 216	
Wiedebush			William	Guardian of Robert Pikarri	1858	36 353	
Wehner		Michael	estate	Sheriff to Adm'r. estate	1859	37 298	37 326
Weisgerber	Henry			Released from State tax	1859	37 452	
Wehner		M.	estate	Adm'rs. & Appraisers	1860	38 303	
Wickham		Jr. Mary Anne & Rebecca		Alonzo Toring Guardian	1860	37 482	37 486
Wickham		Mary Ann	Sr.	Guardian of Wickham Children	1860	37 486	
Wickham		estate	William	Adm'r. & Appraisers	1860	37 476	
Wickham		estate	William P.	Adm'r. appointed	1860	38 149	
Wickham		Mrs.	Sarah-Lunatic	Committee appointed	1863	39 187	
Wickham	Emma C.	orphan		Joseph Seybold-Guardian	1866	40 320	
Weed	Rev. Henry R.	estate			1871	41 156	41 159
Wehner	George, Jr.	John & Margaret		A. H. Britt-Guardian	1871	41 154	
Weisgarber		John	estate	Adm'r. appointed	1871	41 184	41 186
Wickham	George E.			Guardian of Helen A. Wright Geo. Mendel resigned	1872	41 229	
Weber	Frank S.			Guardian for Kullman Heirs	1873	L1 49	
Weber	Frank A.			Guardian for Peter Kuhleman	1873	L1 210	
Weed	H. R.	estate		Executor appointed	1873	L1 150	
Wickham	George A.	estate		Adm'r. appointed	1873	L1 36	
Wickham	George A.			Guardian for Helen A. Wright	1873	L1 162	
Wiesel	Henry J.	estate		Adm'r. appointed	1873	L1 221	
Weiske	Herman	estate		Adm'r. appointed	1874	L1 449	
Wicard		estate	Thomas	Adm'r. appointed	1874	L1 246	
Wiesel		Mary H.		Michael Wiesel-Guardian	1874	L1 427	
Wickham	G. W.			Guardian for Helen A. Wright	1875	L2 268	
Wier		Jane	estate		1875	L2 335	
Wickham	George E.			Guardian for Helen A. Wright	1876	L2 366	
Weitzel	Charles			Janitor-Fees for 8 days.	1878	L3 517	
Weitzel		estate	William	Executor & appraisers	1879	L4 143	L4 149
Weber	C. A. &	M. O. &	W. H.	E. A. Weber-Guardian	1880	L4 442	
Weiss		estate	William W.	Catherine Weiss-Adm'r.	1880	L4 458	

'W' SURNAMES – MISCELLANEOUS ENTRIES

PLAINTIFF INDEX TO ORDER BOOKS — Ohio County, W. Va.

SURNAME	GIVEN NAMES ABCDEFGH	GIVEN NAMES IJKLMNO	GIVEN NAMES PQRSTUVWXYZ	REMARKS DEFENDANTS	YEAR	ORDER BOOK					
Watkins	Ann	estate		Silas Hedges, etal appraisers	1795	4/435					
Watkins	Elizabeth & Anna			Isaac Meek, guardian	1795	4/447					
Watkins			Thomas	Nathan Shepheard, guardian	1795	4/447					
Watkins	Ann	estate		Admr. appointed	1798	6/85	6/120	6/160	6/330		
Watson	Daniel			Admr. of J. Milton, decd.	1799	6/273					
Wayman			Thomas	Exempt from road work	1811	12/404					
Wayman			Thomas	Exempt from County levy	1811	12/491					
Watson	Aaron	estate		Admr & appraisers appointed	1811	13/5					
Watson	Aaron			To be bound to suitable trade	1811	13/108					
Wayts		John	estate	Admr. & appraisers appointed	1818	16/484					
Watson	Aaron	estate		Auditors appointed	1819	17/152					
Wayman			Thomas	Bound in Eleanor Argo	1822	19/94					
Washington		Lawrence A.	estate	Mary Dorcas Washington, exerx.	1824	20/100					
Wayt		John	estate	Archd. Wood, etal to settle	1824	20/265	20/406				
Watson	Catharine et al			To be bound out	1827	22/190					
Watson		Catherine Ann etal		Bound in by suitable persons	1827	22/232					
Wayman		estate	Thomas	Executor appointed	1827	22/284					
Wayt		John	estate	Order to settle estate.	1827	22/55	22/68	22/179	22/110	22/404	22/339
Washington		Mary Dorcas		Guardian of L. Washington's children.	1828	23/7					
Wayt		John	estate	Money to be distributed	1829	23/98	23/235	23/393			
Wayt		John Joseph	estate estate	Children came into court & demanded settlement of estate.	1829	23/235	23/393				
Watson		(orphan)	Thomas	Bound to Jacob Terytitan	1830	24/13					
Wayne	Andrew			Exempt from levy & poor tax	1831	24/520					
Wayt		Mary	(idiot)	Jos. Waddle, etal, committee	1834	26/299	26/330				
Washington		Laurence A.	estate	Admr. & appraisers appointed	1835	26/542	26/565				
Watson		(Orphan)	Robert	To be bound to John Robinson	1836	27/192					
Watson		John	estate	Executor & appraisers apptd	1839	28/42					
Watson		John	estate	Comm. & admr. appointed	1842	29/160					
Wayt		Nathaniel	estate	Appraisers appointed	1849	31/194	31/329				
Waterson		estate	Robert	Admr. & appraisers appointed	1851	31/459					
Watkins		estate	Taxwell	Admr. & appraisers appointed	1853	33/5					
Wayt		James		Released from taxes	1853	32/433					
Watts		John S.	estate	Admr. & appraisers appointed	1854	33/229	33/414				
Wayt		Nathaniel	estate	Settlement presented in court.	1854	33/374					
Wayman			estate Samuel	Admr. & appraisers appointed	1856	35/237					

MISCELLANEOUS PLAINTIFF INDEX TO ORDER BOOKS — Ohio County, W. Va.

SURNAME	PLAINTIFFS GIVEN NAMES ABCDEFGH	GIVEN NAMES IJKLMNO	GIVEN NAMES PQRSTUVWXYZ	REMARKS	YEAR	ORDER BOOK
Waterhouse			Stephen	Tax refund	1859	37 / 416
Wauchope	Eleanor	estate		Administrator appointed	1860	38 / 113
Wassen		estate	Thomas	Administrator appointed	1866	40 / 306
Waters		Margaret		Guardian of Waters children	1866	40 / 314
Waters		Joseph H.	estate	Admr. & appraisers appointed	1866	40 / 297
Wassermeier		estate	William	Admr. & appraisers appointed	1869	41 / 101
Watson		Jacob	estate	Admr. & appraisers appointed	1872	41 / 239
Wayman		estate	Samuel	Admr. appointed	1872	41 / 240
Wayman		Martin		Guardian for Wayman Children	1872	41 / 240
Wassemann	Conrod	estate			1873	L1 / 48
Wasseman	Elizabeth	estate			1875	L2 / 256
Washington	Hannah	estate			1876	L2 / 504
Watt	Ann Elizabeth			Alexander Fhoburn, guardian	1877	L3 / 410
Watterson		Mary, Sr.	non compos	Mentia) Mary Watterson, Jr. committee	1878	L4 / 91
Watson		estate	Sadie	Admr. & appraisers appointed	1880	L4 / 461

MISCELLANEOUS PLAINTIFF INDEX TO ORDER BOOKS — Ohio County, W. Va.

SURNAME	GIVEN NAMES ABCDEFGH	GIVEN NAMES IJKLMNO	GIVEN NAMES PQRSTUVWXYZ	REMARKS	YEAR	ORDER BOOK			
Williamson		James	estate	Appraisers appointed	1782	1/148			
Williams	Enoch			Levy free	1785	1/270			
Welman		John		Earmarks of stock	1786	1/297			
Williamson	Ann	et al		Failed to give in tax returns	1787	3/20			
Welch			William	Exempt from levies etc.	1789	3/159			
Williamson		Moses	estate	Letters of administration granted.	1792	3/340			
Willcoxton	Henry Hardy	estate		Admrs. & appraisers appointed	1793	4/111	4/189	4/315	4/327
Williams		James		Take deposition	1793	4/110			
Williams		James	estate	Appraisers appointed	1793	4/210			
Williams		Moses	estate	Appriasement bill of estate	1793	4/180			
Williamson		Mary		Examination of right of dower	1794	4/365			
Williamson		John	estate	Appraisers & admrs. appointed	1795	4/416			
Welch		Margaret		Bound to Henry Beff	1798	6/130			
Williams	Azra			Exempt from tax	1800	7/82			
Willison		John		Exempt from taxes	1800	7/181			
Willcoxton	Henry Hardy	estate		Appraisers appointed	1801	8/50	8/136		
Williamson	Elizabeth	estate		Appraisers appointed	1803	9/76			
Williams	Elizabeth	estate		Auditors to settle estate	1805	10/147			
Williamson	Elizabeth	estate		Auditors appointed	1805	10/54			
Williamson		John et al (orphans)		Alexander Caldwell, guardian	1805	10/150			
Williamson		estate	William	Admr. & appraisers appointed	1810	2/40	2/47	2/72	
Williamson		estate	William	To bind Martin child	1810	12/342			
Williams		Jeremiah		Presented bill for accounting	1811	13/40	13/302		
Wilcoxon	Anthony			For not attending jury	1812	2/97			
Williamson		John	estate	Died intestate	1813	14/41			
Williamson		estate	Wm.	Order for partition of land	1813	14/5	14/22		
Williams			S. et al	Guardian of McCrery children	1817	15/67			
Welshons	David	estate		Admr. & appraisers appointed	1821	18/360			
Williamson			Robert	Released from taxes, etc.	1821	18/382			
Williams			Polly	Bound out to Thomas Conrad	1823	19/354			
Williamson			Sarah	Released from levy for 1822	1823	19/379			
Welch		estate	William	Thomas Conard, admr.	1824	20/335			
Williams	Daleliff			Exempt from county levy	1825	21/208			
William				Bound in Emily, a black child	1827	22/397			
Williamson			William	Exempt from county levy	1829	23/373			

'W' SURNAMES – MISCELLANEOUS ENTRIES

MISCELLANEOUS PLAINTIFF INDEX TO ORDER BOOKS — Ohio County, W. Va.

Surname	Given Names A-H	Given Names I-O	Given Names P-Z	Remarks (Defendants)	Year	Order Book	
Wilisalian	Society			Permission to use Courthouse.	1831	24/300	
Welling		Levi	(cripple)	Exempt from county levy.	1833	25/362	
Williamson			Robert	Acct. certified to auditor	1835	26/328	
Welch	et al	(orphans)	Philip	John Frazier, guardian	1837	27/184	
Welshhans		Joseph	estate	Admrs. & appraisers appointed	1839	28/168	
Williams	Charles Mortimer		(orphan)	James Flannagan, guardian	1840	28/345	
Welshhans		Joseph	estate	Comm. & admr. appointed	1842	29/149	
Wilda		Isaac		Released from payment of one titheable.	1844	29/508	
Williamson		estate	William	Appraisers appointed	1849	31/132	31/237
Williamson		Margaret	estate	Appraisers & exec. appointed	1851	31/454	
Williamson		Morgan	(orphan)	William McCoy, guardian	1851	31/460	
Williamson		John D.	estate	Sheriff to administer	1852	32/236	
Williamson		Margaret	estate	John Milligan, exec.	1853	32/455	
Willard		Emma		Overseers of Poor to send her home.	1854	33/340	
Williams	Frederick	estate		Admrs. & appraisers appointed	1855	34/220	
Williams	Ann Lucretia		(orphan)	Bound to William B. Morrow.	1856	35/277	
Williamson		Morgan	(orphan)	Wm. McCoy, guardian	1856	35/69	35/86
Williams	Charles H.	estate		Admr. & appraisers appointed	1858	36/369	
Williamson		Morgan		Josiah Brown, guardian	1858	37/36	37/267
Williamson		Morgan	(orphan)	Richard Carter, guardian	1868	41/41	
Welte		Mary Ann, Mary Catharine		Anthony Reymann, guardian	1869	41/60	
Welty	Christian	estate		Admr. & appraisers appointed	1870	41/112	41/161
Williams	David	estate		Administrator appointed	1871	41/195	
Welty		Mary estate		Administrator appointed	1872	41/237	
Willeke		John estate			1874	42/42	42/44
Willitts		John S.		August Wincher. To bind J. A. Willets to	1875	42/93	
Willitts		Joseph A.		Bound to August Wincher	1875	42/93	
Williams		Isaac Harrison		Guardian of Cummins Children	1878	44/13	
Welsh		John	estate	Michael Freismuth, admr.	1879	44/198	
Welty Schauber		John		Petition to change name	1879	44/129	
Wills		Leve	estate	Executor & appraisers appointed	1879	44/202	44/203
Welshaus		Mathilda	estate	Administrator appointed	1880	44/461	
Williamson	Elizabeth	estate		Executor & appraisers appointed	1880	44/461	44/462

'W' SURNAMES – MISCELLANEOUS ENTRIES

MISCELLANEOUS PLAINTIFF INDEX TO ORDER BOOKS — Ohio County, W. Va.

PLAINTIFFS SURNAME	GIVEN NAMES ABCDEFGH	GIVEN NAMES IJKLMNO	GIVEN NAMES PQRSTUVWXYZ	REMARKS / DEFENDANTS	YEAR	ORDER BOOK	
Wetsell		John	estate	Thos. Wetsell proved rightful heir.	1799	6/243	
Wetsell			Thos.	Heir to John Wetsell, decd.	1799	6/243	
Wethered			Richard	Man of good character; resided in Ohio County 1 yr. Certify to General Court of Commonwealth	1804	9/177	
West		John	estate	Curators appointed	1827	22/231	
Westcott		estate	Samuel A.	Admr. & appraisers appointed	1833	25/378	
Wittenbrock		estate	Rodolf	Admr. & appraisers appointed	1839	28/39	
Wisely			William	One titheable & 100% on real & personal property assessed to William Wisely.	1845	29/503	
Weymer	Adam	(orphan)		Bound out to John W. Berry	1846	30/121	
Weyman		John		Released from jail	1852	32/46	
West	(Free negro)		Walter	Leave to live in County	1854	33/491	
Westbrook	George & Eliza	(colored)		Petitioned the court to remain in commonwealth	1854	33/388	
Westbrook	Eliza			Guardian of Mary Hopkins	1868	41/47	
Witerholter		John	estate	Executrix appointed	1880	L4/462	
Winter		John		Return of Negro slave	1795	4/198	
Winter		James		Exempt from county levies etc.	1800	7/148	7/152
Wender		James A.	(infant)	Bound out to Charles Kemple	1833	25/478	
Winchel	Chas.			Bound to Peter Wilson	1838	27/430	
Wims	Henry	estate		Admrs. & appraisers appointed	1847	30/288	30/326
Wims		estate	William H.	Sheriff to administer	1854	33/311	
Winesburg	George			Improperly taxed	1856	35/238	35/315
Wingerter	Ferdinand	estate		Appraisers appointed	1867	41/2	
Winesburg	George &	Nancy		Landon Wharton, guardian	1868	41/101	
Winesburg	Elizabeth	estate		Administrator appointed	1869	41/87	
Wendel	Jacob			Guardian of Hess orphans	1870	41/136	
Werder			Rev. A. W.	Guardian for Ernestine Fritke.	1872	41/254	
Winesburg	Adaline	(orphan)		Bound to John O'Keefe	1873	L1/47	
Winesburgh	George &	Nancy	(orphans)	W.J.W. Cowden, guardian	1873	L1/97	L1/483
Wincher	August			To bind Joseph A. Willitts	1875	L2/93	
Wincher	Christian	E. estate		Executor appointed	1875	L2/229	
Winesburg	(Orphans)	Nancy et al		W. J. W. Cowden, guardian	1876	L2/485	
Winesburg	George	estate		J. R. Cowden, administrator	1878	L4/19	L4/46
Winesburg		Mary		Guardian of Yaus Children	1878	L4/47	
Winship	Franklin	estate		Administrator appointed	1878	L4/109	
Wendel		estate		Sheriff appointed admr.	1879	L4/360	

'W' SURNAMES – MISCELLANEOUS ENTRIES

MISCELLANEOUS PLAINTIFF INDEX TO ORDER BOOKS — Ohio County, W. Va.

PLAINTIFFS SURNAME	GIVEN NAMES ABCDEFGH	GIVEN NAMES IJKLMNO	GIVEN NAMES PQRSTUVWXYZ	REMARKS / Defendants	YEAR	ORDER BOOK			
Windsor	Ann et al (orphans)			Ellen Windsor, guardian	1879	L4 184			
Windsor		estate	Samuel C.	Ellen Windsor, administrator	1879	L4 184			
Wheeling Manufacturing Co. Incorporated				Charter accepted	1828	22 392	22 403	22 416	22 458
What, Price & Co.				Allan Hamat, bound to	1834	26 5			
Wharf				Daniel Zane to erect wharf.	1851	31 380	31 400		
Wheeling Female Academy				Improperly charged taxes	1853	32 402			
Wheeling Gas Co.				County to reduce tax on Gas Co's Real Estate	1856	35 217	35 270	35 273	
Wheeling Hotel Company				Tax Refund	1856	34 397			
Wheeling Saving Institution				Overcharged on state tax	1857	35 385			
Wheeling & Belmont Bridge Co.				Released from County Levy etc	1859	37 401			
Wheeling Hospital				Tax refund	1859	37 168			
Wheeling Gas Co.				State Taxes reduced	1860	38 282			
Wheeling Hospital				Exempt from erroneous tax	1861	38 384			
Wheeling Hospital				Bound in Hosie Parker (infant)	1878	23 515			

MISCELLANEOUS PLAINTIFF INDEX TO ORDER BOOKS — Ohio County, W. Va.

Surname	Given Names (A-H)	Given Names (I-O)	Given Names (P-Z)	Remarks	Year	Order Book
Wheat	Conrod	estate		Appraisers appointed	1781	1/138 1/159
Whitehill		John	estate	James McConnell et al apptd.	1786	3/3
Wheelor		Levy		Allowed fees as guard of Daniel Pearce	1797	5/275
Whetzell		John	estate		1797	5/312
Whetzell		Martin		Eldest son & heir of John Whetzell decd.	1797	5/312
Whetzel		Jacob		Bound in Lutz children	1800	7/3
Whetzell		Jacob		Guardian of Beelow orphans	1800	7/141
Whetzel		Marton		Proved himself son & legal heir.	1800	3/193
Whetzell		Jacob		Guardian for Mary Beelor	1802	8/189
Whetzell		Marton		Guardian of David Teeter	1803	9/98
Whetzel		John & Mary		Appraisers appointed	1804	9/161
Whetzel		Morton		Motion to resurvey land	1806	10/276 10/293 10/462
Whetzel		Marton		Fined for non-attendance as juror.	1808	11/357 11/358
Whitelock	Charles	estate		Auditors appointed	1811	12/392
Whiting		John		Negro slave brought in county and certified.	1814	14/326
Wheatly	George			Exempt from county tax, etc.	1814	20/415
Whitehead			Samuel H.	Certified to Judges, His residence and character	1824	20/329
Whitehead			Samuel	Guardian for McConnell children	1827	22/80
Wheeler	Garritt			Exempt from county levies, etc.	1828	22/338
Wheeler			Thomas	Exempt from county levy.	1829	23/119
Wheeler		Jared (lunatic)		Returned from Staunton asylum and placed on poor list	1834	26/169
Wharton		Meredith		Exempt from levy for this year	1838	28/27
Wheat		James S.		Binds J. Clayton to S. C. Jeffers.	1841	28/497
Whisson	Elizabeth			Guardian for Whisson orphans	1841	28/528
Wheat			James A.	Tax refund	1842	29/223
Whitney		John H.	estate	Administrator appointed	1842	29/83 29/90
Wheatley			Wm.	Levied with gold watch instead of silver watch.	1846	30/35
Whitelock	Benjamin F. (orphan)			Wm. M. Nichol, guardian	1849	31/193
Whelan	Catharine et al (orphans)			Martha Jane Keating, guardian	1852	32/325
Whealler	George			Appointed Deputy Clerk	1853	33/119
Wheeler	A. P.			Released from taxes	1854	33/202
Wharton	Bailey			Improperly taxed	1856	36/238 35/315
Whelan			Rev. Richard V.	Released from taxes 1855	1856	34/394
Whelan			Richard V.	Is Released from tax.	1856	35/269 35/301
Wheat		Jesse	estate	Administrator appointed	1857	36/13

'W' SURNAMES – MISCELLANEOUS ENTRIES

MISCELLANEOUS PLAINTIFF INDEX TO ORDER BOOKS — Ohio County, W. Va.

PLAINTIFFS SURNAME	GIVEN NAMES ABCDEFGH	GIVEN NAMES IJKLMNO	GIVEN NAMES PQRSTUVWXYZ	REMARKS DEFENDANTS	YEAR	ORDER BOOK (Top: Vol / Bottom: Page)	
Wheat		James		Sheriff to pay	1859	37 / 318	
Wheeler			Thomas	Guardian of Joseph Simmons	1859	37 / 94	
Whelan			Richard B.	Guardian of Quinlin children	1859	37 / 357	
Whedlier	George			Sheriff to pay for preparing poll books.	1860	38 / 279	38 / 349
Whelan			Richard V.	Guardian for Quinlan children	1861	38 / 454	
Whitehead	Elisha	estate		Executors appointed	1862	39 / 57	
Wheat		James M., Sr. estate		Admr. & Appraisers appointed	1865	40 / 152	
Wheat		Jessie S.		Guardian Frederick A. Gasmier	1865	40 / 213	
Wheat		George W. estate		Administrator appointed	1866	40 / 305	
Whiteman		Michael	(orphan)	Conrod Gotts, guardian	1866	40 / 270	
Wheat		Jesse S.		Guardian of Augustus Gasmire	1868	41 / 29	
Wheeler		estate	Thomas	Admr. appointed	1868	41 / 40	
Whitaker	Henry G.	estate		Admr. & appraisers appointed	1868	41 / 43	
Wharton		Landon		Guardian of Winesburg children	1869	41 / 101	
Whiteside			Samuel M.	Guardian for Virginia Whiteside	1872	41 / 227	
Wharton		Landon		Bound Adaline Winesburg. Guardian	1873	L1 / 47	
Wheat		Jesse S.		Guardian for Augustus Gasmire	1873	L1 / 49	
Whelan			Richard V.	Guardian for Rule children	1873	L1 / 50	
Wheat		James S.	estate	To draft a memorial	1874	L1 / 456	L1 / 458
Wheat		James S.	estate	Harry M. Russell	1874	L2 / 73	
Wheeler	Christian	estate		Executor appointed	1874	L1 / 240	L1 / 249
Whelan		estate	Richard V.	Executors & appraisers apntd.	1874	L1 / 425	
Whally	Feargus			Guardian of Chas Loyons	1879	L4 / 172	L4 / 187
Wolford	Adam	estate		Admr. appointed	1818	16 / 451	
Wolford	Adam	estate		Richard Simms et al to settle	1825	20 / 438	20 / 502
Wolf		John		Apprenticeship of N. Hughes	1831	24 / 407	
Wolff	Andrew			Erroneous tax certified	1861	38 / 531	
Woeber	Frank A.			Guardian for Kollman heirs	1871	41 / 170	
Wohlert	Henry	estate			1876	L2 / 469	
Wollenweber		estate	William F.	Administrator appointed	1877	L3 / 275	
Wolff	Harry	(orphan)		John Korne, guardian	1878	L4 / 12	
Wohuhas		John		Guardian for Almina Meder	1879	L4 / 366	

'W' SURNAMES – MISCELLANEOUS ENTRIES

MISCELLANEOUS INDEX TO ORDER BOOKS — Ohio County, W. Va.

SURNAME	PLAINTIFFS (A-H)	PLAINTIFFS (I-O)	PLAINTIFFS (P-Z)	REMARKS	YEAR	ORDER BOOK		
Worthington		estate	Thos.	Appraisers appointed	1779	1/36	1/122	1/167
Worth			Richard	Exempt from militia duty	1792	3/343		
Worley	David			Exempt from County levy	1794	4/294		
Wornock			Wm. estate	Show cause next term	1796	5/173		
Wornock		(Rebecca)	Rebeccah	Show cause next term.	1796	5/173		
Woodian		John	(estate)	Admr. appointed	1800	7/70		
Woodruff		Mary et al	(orphans)	Bound to suitable persons	1829	22/101		
Woodrow			Simon	Accounts certified	1833	25/378		
Woodburn		James	Decd. estate	Admr. & appraisers appointed	1834	26/100		
Woodrow			Simeon	Account certified to auditor	1834	26/145		
Woodcock	Bancroft			Assessed with one titheable	1840	28/416		
Woodburn		James	estate	Commissioners appointed	1843	29/231		
Woodrow		decd.	Simeon	Children certified for pension	1854	33/489	33/490	
Woodward			S. H.	Tax reduced	1854	33/144		
Workhouse				Committee appointed to make application.	1855	34/208		
Woodward		John		Bound to Joseph Sheppard	1863	39/244		
Work	Alfred D.			Guardian of Samuel M. Work.	1865	40/212		
Work	Alfred D.			Guardian of Mary Ann & Anna Laura Culp.	1866	40/296		
Woodward			S. H.	Guardian of Hersey children.	1867	40/341		
Woodward			S. H.	Guardian for Samuel S. Hersey.	1873	L1/206		

MISCELLANEOUS PLAINTIFF INDEX TO ORDER BOOKS — Ohio County, W. Va.

SURNAME	GIVEN NAMES ABCDEFGH	GIVEN NAMES IJKLMNO	GIVEN NAMES PQRSTUVWXYZ	REMARKS / DEFENDANTS	YEAR	ORDER BOOK								
Wright	Amos			Bound to Pollack Hamilton	1816	15 228								
Wright	Amos			Andrew Gants, bound to	1827	22 84								
Wright	Amos			Jailer: produced accounts	1829	-23 409								
Wright	Ann Maria	estate		Last will recorded	1846	30 34								
Wright		John		Guardian for Mary White, orphan	1852	32 110								
Wright		John		Erroneously taxed	1858	36 214	36 259							
Wright			Thomas	Erroneously taxed	1858	36 224								
Wright		John		Tax refund	1858	37 58	37 63							
Wright			Thomas	Tax refund	1858	37 61								
Wright	Amos			Exempt from tax	1861	38 383								
Wunderlich			Simon estate	Administrator appointed	1865	40 153								
Wright	Augustus			Bound to C. Leander Zane	1866	40 322								
Wright	Augustus	(infant)		C. Leander Zane, guardian	1869	41 79	41 80	41 103	41 104					
Wright	Helen A.			George E. Wickham, guardian	1872	41 229								
Wright	Helen A.			George A. Wickham, guardian	1873	L1 162								
Wright	Helen A.			C. W. Wickham, guardian	1875	L2 268								
Wright	Helen A.			Guardian appointed	1876	L2 366								
Wycart	Francis			Guardian of Simms children	1823	19 309								
Wykart	Francis	estate		Admr. & appraisers appointed	1825	21 51	21 123	81 307						
Wynkoop	Hannah	estate		Probate of will	1829	23 243	23 458							
Wykart		Nicholas		Produced accounts	1830	23 458								
Wynkoop	Hannah	estate		Commissioners appointed	1831	24 378								
Wynkoop	Hannah	estate		Executors appointed	1831	25 8	25 22							
Wylie			William	Collector of tolls	1856	35 3	35 41	35 68	35 80	35 181	35 193	35 277	35 121	35 225	35 253
do			do	do	1856	35 102	35 343	35 400	35 416	35 448	35 497	35 456			
Wylie		estate	William	Admr. & commissioners apptd.	1873	L1 145	L1 158							

'W' SURNAMES – MISCELLANEOUS ENTRIES

PLAINTIFF INDEX TO ORDER BOOKS — Ohio County, W. Va.

MISCELLANEOUS

SURNAME	PLAINTIFFS GIVEN NAMES ABCDEFGH	GIVEN NAMES IJKLMNO	GIVEN NAMES PQRSTUVWXYZ	DEFENDANTS / REMARKS	YEAR	ORDER BOOK (Vol / Page)		
Wells	Charles			Ear Marks of Stock	1779	1 / 42		
do	Charles	et al		Appraise money	1779	1 / 42		
do		Joseph		Ear Marks Stock	1779	1 / 42		
do	Enoch	estate			1784	1 / 202		
do	Charles	(His Negro	Marsh)	Exempt from County tax	1788	3 / 58		
do	Charles			Commissioners to value goods	1788	3 / 63	3 / 59	
do	Charles			To be paid for the year 1788 Working for County	1789	3 / 166		
do			Richard	Oath of Allegiance	1789	3 / 138		
do			Richard	Negro woman of Wells Exempt from levies	1790	3 / 191		
do	Baziel			Recommendation	1792	4 / 65		
do	Charles			For payment of services as Commissioner	1792	4 / 31		
do	Charles			Resigned as Commissioner	1793	4 / 81		
do	Charles			Resurvey two tracts of Land Ordered that they be filed against him.	1793	4 / 163		
do			Richard		1794	4 / 220		
do	Benjamin	estate		Benjamin Biggs et al Appraisers & Adm'rs.	1795	4 / 387		
do			Temperance	Exempt from paying Co. levies	1796	5 / 112		
do			William	Excused from paying fine in Higgins vs. Pollock case	1797	5 / 324		
do	Benjamin	estate		Charles Wells-Executor Benjamin Biggs et al to settle	1798	6 / 32	6 / 151	
do	Benjamin	estate		Robert Woods & Benjamin Biggs appointed to settle estate	1799	6 / 284		
do			et al Samuel	Ordered to appear at next term	1814	14 / 364		
do		Joseph		Exempt from paying county levy	1824	20 / 66		
do		Jesse, Sr.	estate	Adm'r. & Appraisers	1872	41 / 243	41 / 246	
do		Jesse	estate	Removal of Jesse Wells & Clark Wells as Executors	1876	13 / 40	13 / 62	
do		Jesse	estate	George R. Tingle-Sheriff-Adm'r.	1878	14 / 126	14 / 133	
do			estate William	Mary W. Wells-Adm'r.	1879	14 / 324		
White		estate	Samuel	James Miller & John Lemmon to settle estate	1785	1 / 253	1 / 255	
do		John		Took oath of allegiance to Commonwealth of Virginia	1792	6 / 239		
do		John		Sworn to give evidence pertaining to road from Honey's Point to State line	1802	8 / 107		
do			estate Robert	Alexander Pettit-Security Edw. Ward et al-Appraisers	1803	9 / 70	9 / 90	9 / 75
do	Andrew			Jailed for contempt and disturbing court	1805	10 / 242		
do	Charles	estate		Adm'r. & Appraisers	1808	11 / 465		
do	Alexander			Fined for not reporting for Petit Juror	1815	2 / 277	2 / 280	
do		Jacob		Order that Jacob White, Guardian of Providence Mounts settle estate with Reuben Foreman	1816	15 / 265		
do	Andrew			Guardian of James Stephens	1823	20 / 25	20 / 26	

PLAINTIFF INDEX TO ORDER BOOKS — Ohio County, W. Va.

MISCELLANEOUS

SURNAME	GIVEN NAMES A-H	GIVEN NAMES I-O	GIVEN NAMES P-Z	DEFENDANTS / REMARKS	YEAR	ORDER BOOK		
White		James		Was bound in by Mark Dunlap	1829	23/208		
do		John	estate	Adm'rs. & Appraisers out	1829	23/160	23/426	23/459
do		Jackson		Poor Overseers ordered to bind	1830	24/58		
do		James		Bound in Joseph Caldwell	1830	24/205		
do		John	estate	Executors & Appraisers	1831	24/293	24/309	
do	George W.	orphan		Bound out to Jos. S. Graham	1831	25/35		
do	Alexander	estate		Letters of Administration to Robert White et al	1832	25/160	25/288	
do		John	estate	George W. Wilson appointed to settle estate	1833	25/314	25/330	
do	Alexander	estate		John Feay et al to audit etc.	1834	26/120		
do		John	estate	John Feay et al to audit etc.	1834	26/120	26/128	
do		estate	Samuel	Adm'r. & Appraisers	1834	26/213		
do	Andrew J.			Bound to John Knote etc.	1835	26/537		
do		James H.		Guardian-Thos. Weasner to bind	1836	27/13		
do		John	estate	Appointed Commr. to settle est.	1839	28/144	28/163	
do			Sarah	Guardian of Mary White	1839	28/163		
do		estate	William	William M. Robb-Adm'r.	1839	28/98	28/553	
do		James H.		Released from paying for one tithable	1841	29/7		
do		James H.		Entered his account to be certified-Commrs. appointed to investigate account	1842	29/61		
do		estate	Solomon	Adm'rs. & Appraisers	1849	31/167	31/208	
do		Mary	orphan	John Wright-Guardian	1852	32/110		
do		Joseph	estate	Adm'rs. & Appraisers	1855	34/105		
do		(Orphan)	Thomas	Michael J. Rohan-Guardian	1855	34/172		
do	Andrew			Guardian of Isett Orphans	1856	35/238		
do			Washington	Fee for support from Overseers of Poor	1856	35/245		
do	Mrs. Eleanor			John W. Cummins-Committee	1857	35/344		
do	Mrs. Elanor	estate		Charles B. Cecil-Adm'r.	1857	36/149	36/278	36/301
do		(Pauper)	Washington	Alexander A. Allison-Keeper of Poor house account allowed	1857	36/85		
do	Elizabeth	estate		Adm'r. & Appraisers	1871	41/150	41/151	
do		estate	Robert		1871	41/176		
do	George & Arlena &	Nancy & James & Louisa &	Thomas T.	Jacob White-Guardian	1873	11/222		
do		John	estate		1875	12/342		

PLAINTIFF INDEX TO ORDER BOOKS — Ohio County, W. Va.

MISCELLANEOUS

SURNAME	GIVEN NAMES ABCDEFGH	GIVEN NAMES IJKLMNO	GIVEN NAMES PQRSTUVWXYZ	DEFENDANTS / REMARKS	YEAR	ORDER BOOK			
Whitten			Phillip	Duty – To be exempted from Militia	1791	3 / 293			
Whittam	Benjamin	estate		Adm'rs. appointed	1800	6 / 486			
Whithams	Elizabeth			Guardian of Whithams orphans	1801	8 / 33	8 / 34	8 / 95	
Whithams	Elizabeth & Benjamin &		Perrywine & William R.	Elizabeth Whithams-Guardian	1801	8 / 33	8 / 34	8 / 95	
Whithams		estate	Perrywine	Auditor & Appraisers	1801	8 / 33	8 / 34		
Whittam	Benjamin	estate		Geo. Knox et al-Auditors	1802	8 / 93			
Whitham		estate	Peregrine	Geo. Miller et al appointed	1816	15 / 249			
Whittam	Joseph	estate		Adm'rs. & Appraisers	1846	30 / 117			
Whitham	Emily	et al	orphans	Geo. D. Whitham-Guardian	1849	31 / 182			
Whittam		estate	William	Adm'r. & Appraisers	1849	31 / 188	31 / 380		
Whitham	D.			Guardian for Eliza J. Dakin etal	1874	12 / 1			
Whittingham		James	estate	Inventory and appraisement of the estate returned to Ct	1828	23 / 7	23 / 23	23 / 353	23 / 276
do		James &	Sarah Eliz.	David Thornburg-Guardian	1828	23 / 8			
do		James	estate	Adm'r. & Appraisers	1828	22 / 450			
do		James	estate	Appointed Auditors	1830	24 / 137	24 / 154		
do		Joanna		Guardian of Whittingham orphans	1832	25 / 117			
do	George	estate		Blake Robert et al-appraisers	1832	25 / 117			
do		Joanna &	Richard	James Holliday-Guardian	1846	30 / 71			

MISCELLANEOUS — PLAINTIFF INDEX TO ORDER BOOKS — Ohio County, W. Va.

SURNAME	GIVEN NAMES ABCDEFGH	GIVEN NAMES IJKLMNO	GIVEN NAMES PQRSTUVWXYZ	DEFENDANTS / REMARKS	YEAR	ORDER BOOK	
Wilson		Joseph		Ordered brought into Court to give evidence	1778	1 / 11	
do			William	Took oath of allegiance	1793	4 / 158	
do			William	Failed to appear for Grand Jury service fined-exempted	1803	9 / 2	9 / 22
do		John	estate	Auditors appointed	1803	9 / 33	
do	Daniel	estate		Wm. Gaskin et al appraisers	1804	9 / 257	
do	Daniel	estate		Auditors appointed	1806	10 / 403	
do			William	Examined as Surveyor	1808	11 / 346	11 / 349
do		estate	Sarah	Adm'r. & Appraisers	1810	12 / 238	
do	Daniel	estate		John Wilson-Adm'r.	1811	12 / 424	
do	David, Jr.	orphan		William Wilson-Guardian	1812	13 / 164	
do		estate	Sarah	Jacob Creis et al appointed	1812	13 / 164	
do		estate	Sarah	Absolam Ridgely et al appointed	1816	15 / 192	
do		Joseph	Jr.	Fined for not attending Grand Jury	1818	2 / 480	
do			William	Guardian of James Pearce	1818	16 / 501	
do		John	estate	Executor & Adm'r.	1819	17 / 4	
do			Robert	Brought slave into state	1819	17 / 8	
do			William	Bound Lucinda Timmons	1819	16 / 646	
do			William	Guardian for Pearce Orphans	1821	18 / 423	
do			William	Guardian for Stephen Foot	1822	18 / 478	
do		Job		Ordered that he be exempt from County Levy	1822	19 / 73	
do		John	estate	Claburn Simms to settle estate	1823	20 / 16	
do		Joseph	estate	Adm'r. & Appraisers	1825	20 / 441	20 / 442
do		Joseph	estate	John Snodgrass et al Auditors	1827	22 / 131	22 / 178 22 / 378

'W' SURNAMES – MISCELLANEOUS ENTRIES

PLAINTIFF INDEX TO ORDER BOOKS — Ohio County, W. Va.

SURNAME	GIVEN NAMES ABCDEFGH	GIVEN NAMES IJKLMNO	GIVEN NAMES PQRSTUVWXYZ	REMARKS	YEAR	ORDER BOOK			
Wilson			Job	et al	Court ordered Sheriff to hold inquest on their lands in regard to a road review	1828	23/83			
do		Lewis	estate	Appraisers & Executors	1828	22/360			
do		Lewis	estate	Appraisement Bill	1829	23/193			
do			William	Robt. Laughlin bound to him	1829	23/358			
do		Joseph	(Infant)	Overseers of Poor to bind out	1830	24/52			
do	Eugenius	estate		Appraisers appointed	1831	24/111			
do		Job	estate	Adm'r. & Appraisers	1831	24/294			
do			William	Guardian of Hugh Walker-Orphan	1831	24/433			
do	Catharine			Guardian of Wilson Infants	1832	25/42			
do	Frederick	A.	estate	Thos. Riggs et al-appraisers	1834	26/83	26/101	26/207	26/315
do	Frederick	estate		Auditors and Executor	1834	26/306			
do	Geo. W.	estate		Executor & Appraisers	1834	26/122			
do			William	Guardian of Maulding children	1834	26/61			
do	Henry	estate		Executors & Appraisers	1835	26/511			
do		Lewis	estate	Josiah Morgan et al appointed	1835	26/307			
do		(Lunatic)	William	Humphrey Boon-Committee	1835	26/403			
do		(Lunatic)	William	Humphrey Boon-Committee	1836	27/131			
do			Ritchie	To bind in David Brady et al son	1836	27/138	27/184		
do	Alexander			Guardian of Catherine E. Wilson	1837	27/209			
do	Catherine	E	orphan	Alexander Wilson -Guardian	1837	27/309			
do	David & Alexander & Elizabeth	& (Orphans)	Virginia	Alexander Wilson-Guardian	1837	27/293			
do	Catherine E. & Marcus		estate	Alexander Wilson et al-Adm'r	1837	27/293	27/478		
do	David E. & Elizabeth	& (Orphans)	Virginia	Alexander Wilson-Guardian	1838	27/416			
do			Peter	Bound in Chas. Winchel	1838	27/430			
do		Marcus	estate	Daniel Lamb, Esq.-Commr.	1839	28/136			
do		estate	William	Richard Simms et al-Commr.	1839	28/95			
do		Lavina	estate	Died intestate ordered that Sheriff act as Adm'r.	1840	28/384			
do	Emily &	Joseph & Margaret &	Rebecca & Rachel	David Atkinson-Guardian of orphans	1841	28/578			
do		estate	Rosana	John Snodgrass et al appraisers	1841	28/560			
do	Alexander			Summoned to appear	1842	29/120	29/134	29/147	29/156
do		Joseph	orphan	Commissioners appointed to settle account of David Atkinson-Guardian for J.Wilson	1843	29/279	29/289		
do		estate	Rosannah	Appraiser appointed	1843	29/273			
do	David E.	estate		Granted letters of Adm'r.	1844	29/345			
do		Lewis	estate	Auditors appointed	1844	29/369			
do		Margaret	Orphan	Commissioners appointed to settle accounts of David Atkinson as Guardian of M.Wilson	1844	29/399	29/437		

PLAINTIFF INDEX TO ORDER BOOKS — Ohio County, W. Va.

MISCELLANEOUS

SURNAME	GIVEN NAMES ABCDEFGH	GIVEN NAMES IJKLMNO	GIVEN NAMES PQRSTUVWXYZ	REMARKS	YEAR	ORDER BOOK (Top: Volume / Bottom: Page)	
Wilson	Alexander	estate		James A. Clarke appointed to settle with A. Caldwell-Admr	1846	30	
						41	
do	George W.			Resigned as acting Magistrate	1846	30	
						23	
do		Marcus	estate	Adm'rs. appointed	1847	30	
						189	
do		orphan	Rachel	David Atkinson-Guardian	1847	30	30
						227	257
do	David E.	estate		Richard Simms-Sheriff-Adm'r.	1848	30	30
						355	356
do		orphan	Rebecca	David Atkinson-Guardian	1848	30	
						439	
do	Elizabeth Ann & Ellen &	Mrs. Mary		Tax reduction on rental prop.	1848	31	
						35	
do	George W.&	John Wm. &	Roxaline	Peter Keith-Guardian	1849	31	
						105	
do	Catharine	estate		Appraisers appointed	1849	31	
						92	
do		estate	William	Peter Keith to administer	1853	32	
						377	
do		Emily		David Atkinson-Guardian	1854	33	33
						193	258
do		James		Improperly charged for tax	1855	34	
						104	
do		estate	Sarah	Adm'rs. & Appraisers	1855	34	34
						106	118
do		John	estate	Adm'r. & Appraisers	1856	35	
						173	
do			Rachel	Improperly charged for taxes	1856	34	
						394	
do		John	estate	Executors appointed	1859	37	37
						239	446
do	Andrew	et al		To examine report of Commrs. of Sinking Fund	1868	39	39
						71	73
do	George	estate		Adm'r. appointed	1866	40	
						318	
do			Sarah A.	Wilson Guardian of John & Sarah R. (Orphan)	1869	41	
						75	
do	Abram			Guardian of Joseph Wilson	1869	41	
						92	
do	Frances	estate			1871	41	
						177	
do			Thomas	Guardian for Florence N. Towers	1873	L1	
						49	
do		estate	William P.	Executor appointed	1873	L1	
						108	
do	Orphans			Sample Ford-Guardian	1874	L1	
						429	
do		John B.	estate	Executors appointed	1874	L1	L1
						422	430
do		James		Habeas Corpus	1875	L2	L2
						346	350
do		John A.	estate		1875	L2	
						385	
do	Henry	estate		Sheriff to adm'r. estate	1876	L3	
						430	
do		estate	Wm. M.	James P. Roger-Adm'r.	1880	L4	
						420	

'W' SURNAMES – MISCELLANEOUS ENTRIES

MISCELLANEOUS —— PLAINTIFF INDEX TO ORDER BOOKS — Ohio County, W. Va.

SURNAME	PLAINTIFFS (A-H)	PLAINTIFFS (I-O)	PLAINTIFFS (P-Z)	DEFENDANTS / REMARKS	YEAR	ORDER BOOK (Vol / Page)
Wood			Samuel	Ensign 1760	1781	1 / 127
Woods	Andrew			Commissioner to value goods	1788	3 / 63 ; 3 / 59
Woods			Robert	Oath of Allegiance	1789	3 / 138
Woods			Robert et al	Settle accts. John Bagga-late Sheriff	1792	4 / 71
Woods	Andrew			Received payment for services as Commissioner	1795	5 / 1 ; 5 / 170
Woods			Robert	Guardian of Nancy McClure	1796	5 / 57
Woods	Archibald			Recommended to the Governor for appointment	1799	6 / 344
Woods	Archibald			Relieved from County Levy etc.	1800	7 / 28
Woods	Archibald			Condemnation of land for Grist Mill	1801	7 / 299
Woods	Archibald			Condemnation of land of Thos. Mills property for erecting Dam	1801	8 / 17 ; 8 / 39
Wood	Arche.			Recommended as Escheator	1810	12 / 372
Woods		Jeremiah		Appointed guardian for Heirs of Hugh Carmichael	1815	15 / 113
Wood			Robert	Exempt from paying levy etc.	1815	14 / 472
Woods	Andrew	(Orphan)		Bound in by George Vennum	1816	15 / 271
Woods	Archibald			Allowed for services for making map of Ohio County	1816	15 / 276
Woods		Jeremiah		Refused to accept guardianship of the Carmichael Children — Edward Dowler-Guardian	1816	15 / 52 ; 15 / 113 ; 15 / 177 ; 15 / 238 ; 15 / 267
Woods			Thomas	Poor agent-entered accts.	1819	17 / 86
Woods	Archibald			Resigns his office as Escheator	1822	19 / 269
Woods	Franklin	estate		Adm'r. & Appraisers	1825	21 / 32 ; 21 / 53
Woods			Robert	Exempted from County Levy etc.	1825	21 / 360
Woods			Robert C.	Allowed $100 on County Levy for transcribing Entry Book	1829	23 / 137
Woods	Archibald			Enters protest against Sheriffs allowance on Delinquent Tithable	1830	23 / 77
Wood	Andrew	estate		Appointed Executors	1831	24 / 316
Woods		estate	Robert	Appraisers appointed	1831	24 / 451 ; 24 / 459
Woods	Ama & Henry & Edgar &	Lydia &	Theodore	Archibald Woods-Guardian	1832	25 / 99
Woods		estate	Robert	Robert C. Woods-Trustee	1832	25 / 214
Woods		estate	Thomas	Adm'r. & Appraiser	1832	25 / 99 ; 25 / 359 ; 25 / 427 ; 25 / 444
Wood		estate	Robert	William McConnell appointed to audit and settle estate	1834	26 / 4
Woods		estate	Robert	Wm. McConnell to audit estate	1835	26 / 537
Woods		estate	Robert C.	William McConnell	1837	27 / 338
Woods			Robert C.	Came into Court and gave notice that he would be a Candidate	1839	28 / 31 ; 28 / 77 ; 28 / 88
Woods		estate	Robert	William McConnell-Commr.	1839	28 / 124
Woods		Joseph	orphan	Bound to Denny Burns	1841	28 / 592
Wood		(Colored)	William	Produced Registry that proved satisfactory	1841	29 / 8
Woods		estate	Robert	Wm. McConnell-auditor of est.	1841	29 / 33 ; 29 / 161

MISCELLANEOUS PLAINTIFF INDEX TO ORDER BOOKS — Ohio County, W. Va.

SURNAME	PLAINTIFFS GIVEN NAMES ABCDEFGH	GIVEN NAMES IJKLMNO	GIVEN NAMES PQRSTUVWXYZ	REMARKS	YEAR	ORDER BOOK			
Yates			Richard	To examine surveyor's books	1788	3 58			
Yarnell		Mordecia		Bound in Rebeccah Cave	1808	11 380			
Yarnall		Mordecai	estate	Letters of Admr. granted	1811	12 530			
Yarnall			Peter	Retail ardent spirits in store	1822	19 75			
Yates			Thomas	Granted writ to assess damages for road thru land	1822	19 296			
Yarnall			Peter	To settle with sheriff	1826	21 289	21 348		
Yates	Adam	et al		Awarded Ad Quod Damnum.	1837	27 172	27 181		
Yates	Andrew			Overcharged for value on house.	1842	29 90			
Yarnell		Mordecai	estate	Appraisers & comm. appointed	1843	29 222	29 511	29 529	
Yarnall		Mordecai	estate	Zachariah S. Yarnall, admr.	1847	30 194			
Yarnall	Emma et al (orphans)			Peter Yarnall, guardian	1849	31 194			
Yarling		estate	Theodore	Admr. & Appraisers appointed	1854	33 239	33 240		
Yarnall		John J.		Improperly charged with taxes	1854	33 440			
Yates		estate	Thomas	Admrs. & appraisers appointed	1855	34 303			
Yahrling	Charles & Margaret			Elizabeth Yahrling, guardian	1857	35 471			
Yates		estate	William	Exectrx. & appraisers appointed	1857	35 418			
Yarnall	Emily Y.			Guardian of Yarnell children	1858	36 162	36 189	36 193	36 257
Yates		estate	Thomas	Andrew Yates, executor	1859	37 154			
Yates			Thomas Stockton	Guardian of Hugh Yates	1859	37 393			
Yarnall		John J.		Erroneous tax certified	1861	38 531			
Yarnall		estate	Zachariah S.	Alonzo Loring, administrator	1863	39 234			
Yater		Matthew		Guardian of Geo. Oliver Yater	1866	40 290			
Yager		Nicholas	estate	Will proved	1872	41 207			
Yagle	Francis	estate		Administrator appointed	1873	L1 12			
Yates		estate	William	Executors & comm. appointed	1874	L1 298			
Yager		John F. W.	estate		1875	L2 234			
Yates			Wm. L.	Guardian Thos. G. Yates	1875	L2 337			
Yates			Thomas G.	Guardian for Wm. Lester Yates	1877	L3 232			
Yaus	Andrew et al (orphans)			Mary Winesburg, guardian	1878	L4 47			

PLAINTIFF INDEX TO ORDER BOOKS — Ohio County, W. Va.

SURNAME	GIVEN NAMES ABCDEFGH	GIVEN NAMES IJKLMNO	GIVEN NAMES PQRSTUVWXYZ	REMARKS	YEAR	ORDER BOOK
Yeats			Richard	Received fees as collector	1778	1 / 32
Yeates			Thomas	Guardian of John Canon orphans	1818	16 / 506
Yeater	(female child)			Poor Overseers to take charge.	1850	31 / 233
Yeager		estate	Theodore	Will proved	1878	L3 / 506
Young		James		Exempt from county levy	1793	4 / 101
Yoho	Henry			Exempt from county levy	1799	6 / 417
Young		James		Exempt from road work etc.	1802	8 / 237
Young	Henry	estate		Administrator appointed	1810	12 / 384
Younger			Umphrey	Bound in Nancy Timmons	1810	12 / 338
Younger		Nehemiah		Mahala Barne Smith bound to	1811	12 / 491
Young	Catherine &		William	Indenture of apprenticeship to Wm. Holliday.	1812	13 / 252
Yoho		estate	Peter	Admr. & appraisers appointed	1823	19 / 534
Yoho		estate	Peter	Robt. C. Woods, etal to settle	1824	20 / 342
Young		John N.		Character and residence certified.	1827	22 / 97
Young	Catherine (lunatic)			Sent to Washington Co. Poor house	1846	30 / 104
Young	George C.			Pension	1856	35 / 104
Yuengling		Lucas	estate	Administrator appointed	1870	41 / 112
Young		James estate			1871	41 / 157
Young	Ed. S.	estate			1876	L2 / 357

'Z' SURNAMES - MISCELLANEOUS ENTRIES

MISCELLANEOUS PLAINTIFF INDEX TO ORDER BOOKS — Ohio County, W. Va.

SURNAME	PLAINTIFFS GIVEN NAMES ABCDEFGH	GIVEN NAMES IJKLMNO	GIVEN NAMES PQRSTUVWXYZ	REMARKS / DEFENDANTS	YEAR	ORDER BOOK (Top: Vol / Bottom: Page)			
Zane	Ebenezar			Ear marks for stock	1778	1 / 18			
Zane	Andrew			Bounty for 3 wolves.	1780	1 / 85			
Zane	Ebenezer	et al		Make list of taxable property	1784	1 / 249			
Zane	Mrs. Elizabeth			Examined concerning deeds.	1784	1 / 236			
Zane		Mariam		Bastard child of VanSwearinger	1784	1 / 185			
Zane	Ebenezer			Oath of allegianse	1789	3 / 151			
Zane	Ebenezor			Condemnation of land for a grist mill.	1794	4 / 320	4 / 330	4 / 349	
Zane		Joel		John McIntier, guardian	1798	6 / 154			
Zane (Ferryman)	Ebenezer			Exempt from county levy	1802	8 / 136			
Zane		Joel		Resurvey of land	1806	10 / 464			
Zane		John	estate	Admr. appointed	1806	10 / 226			
Zane		Noah		Guardian for Ebenezer Martin	1807	11 / 60			
Zane	Daniel	(infant)		Noah Zane, guardian	1811	13 / 139			
Zane	Ebenezer	estate		Executor and appraisers apptd	1811	13 / 111			
Zane		Jonathan		Fined for not reporting for grand jury.	1812	8 / 68			
Zane		Noah		Guardian of Daniel Zane	1812	13 / 139			
Zane	Ebenezer	estate		Admr. & executor appointed	1813	14 / 162			
Zane	Elizabeth	estate		Admr. & appraisers appointed	1814	8 / 151	2 / 162		
Zane	Daniel			Emancipation to negro slave.	1815	14 / 494			
Zane		Noah		Ear marks of stock	1816	15 / 363			
Zane		Jonathan	estate	Curator appointed	1823	19 / 427	19 / 439	19 / 536	
Zane		Joel	orphan	Ezekiel Hildraith, guardian	1824	20 / 407			
Zane		Jonathan	estate	Charles Knox, et al to settle	1825	21 / 255			
Zane		Nancy	(orphan)	Thomas McKay, guardian	1831	24 / 442			
Zane		Noah	estate	Admr. & appraisers appointed	1833	25 / 496	25 / 497		
Zane	Hampden	et al (orphans)		Mary L. Zane, guardian	1834	26 / 11			
Zane		Noah	estate	Appraisers appointed	1834	26 / 4	26 / 21		
Zane		Noah	estate	Appraisers appointed	1834	26 / 21			
Zane		Noah	estate	Admr. & auditors appointed	1835	26 / 402			
Zane		Noah estate		Moses C. Good appointed	1836	27 / 56			
Zane		Noah	estate	Bond given for administrator	1841	28 / 517			
Zane		Noah estate		Administrator appointed	1841	29 / 15	29 / 214		
Zane	Ebenezer	estate		Administrators appointed	1843	29 / 258			
Zane		Noah	estate	James A. Clarke, to settle est.	1845	30 / 5	30 / 54	30 / 286	30 / 354
Zane		Noah	estate	Admr. & commr. appointed	1849	31 / 201			

MISCELLANEOUS PLAINTIFF INDEX TO ORDER BOOKS. — Ohio County, W. Va.

SURNAME	PLAINTIFFS (A-H)	PLAINTIFFS (I-O)	PLAINTIFFS (P-Z)	REMARKS	YEAR	ORDER BOOK			
Zane	Edmund G.	et al (orphans)		Henry Moore, guardian	1852	32 289			
Zane	Daniel	estate		Admr. & appraiser appointed	1860	38 144	38 149		
Zane	C. Leander			Bound in Augustus Wright	1866	40 321			
Zane	Ebenezer	estate		Administrator appointed	1868	41 14			
Zane	C. Leander			Guardian of Augustus Wright	1869	41 79	41 80	41 103	41 104
Zane	Edward E.	et al (orphans)		R. G. Barr, guardian	1874	L1 248	L1 249		
Zane	Caroline V.	estate		Admr. & appraisers appointed	1880	L4 508			
Zimmies		Lazerus	(orphan)	Bound to John Campbell	1810	12 248			
Zian	George S.			Bound out to J. S. Graham	1831	25 34			
Zinn			Peter E.	Bound in Eliza Stewart	1846	30 103			
Zimmerman	Guido	estate		Admr. & appraisers appointed	1851	31 373			
Zimmerman	August			Erroneously taxed.	1857	36 105			
Zeockler		John		Exempt from erroneous tax	1861	38 339			
Zimmer		J. N.	estate	Admr. & appraisers appointed	1861	38 425			
Zimmer		J. N.	estate	Admr. allowed to withdraw note	1863	39 234			
Ziegler	F. B.			Guardian of John Strebel	1867	40 388			
Zimmerman		Leonard Frederick	estate	Admr. & appraisers appointed	1871	41 196			
Zimmermann		Mary		Guardian for Lindner orphans	1871	41 197			
Ziegenfelder		John M.	estate	Executrix appointed	1873	L1 15			
Zimmerman	Frederick			Guardian of Lizzie Hoffman	1879	L4 523			
Zinn	Ann	estate		Administrator appointed	1879	L4 185			
Zoeckler		John		Released from tax.	1863	39 247			
Zoeckler	George			Guardian of Dorothea Koch	1869	41 58			
Zoeckler		John		Guardian for Kircher orphans	1872	41 204			
Zoeckler		John		Guardian Kircher children	1875	L2 219			
Zoeckler	August			To bind Frederick Stengel	1876	L2 444			
Zoeckler	August			Released from all further responsibility of F. Stengel.	1877	L3 355			

APPENDIX – TABLE OF CONTENTS

ITEM	PAGE
1. BEER'S 1871 MAP OF THE PANHANDLE [4 counties]	
A. TITLE BLOCK	1713
B. OVERVIEW OF ORIGINAL MAP	1714
C. INDEX TO DETAIL MAP SECTIONS	1716
D. TOWNSHIP OVERVIEW MAPS	
1. HANCOCK CO.	1718
2. BROOKE CO.	1719
3. OHIO CO.	1720
4. OHIO CO / WHEELING WARDS AND TOWNSHIPS	1721
5. CITY OF WHEELING WARDS	1722
6. MARSHALL CO.	1724
E. DETAIL MAP SECTIONS OF COUNTY MAPS WITH SOME TOWN MAPS (SEE INDEX PAGES 1716-7)	1726
F. SELECTED ENLARGED CITY/TOWN & BUSINESS NOTICES (SEE INDEX FOR FULL LIST)	
1. HANCOCK CO.	1726
a. NEW CUMBERLAND	1766
2. BROOKE CO.	1772
a. WELLSBURG	1776
3. OHIO CO.	1779
a. WHEELING CITY	1786
4. MARSHALL CO.	1795
a. MOUNDSVILLE	1806
G. 'AIRLINE' DISTANCE - MILEAGE CHART	1815
H. POPULATION FROM 1870 CENSUS	1816
2. 1852 HEMPFIELD RAILROAD BOND PROSPECTUS & MAPS WITH 'TRIBUTARY' AND 'RIVAL' RAILROADS	1817
3. 1852 BROOKE CO. LANDOWNER MAP	1828
4. PANORAMIC MAPS AT THE LIBRARY OF CONGRESS	1855
A. 1882 BENWOOD, MARSHALL CO. MAP	1856
B. 1899 CAMERON, MARSHALL CO. MAP	1857
C. 1889 MOUNDSVILLE, MARSHALL CO. MAP	1858
D. 1870 WHEELING, OHIO CO. MAP	1859
5. 1822 WHEELING CITY MAP WITH *ORIGINAL* STREET LAYOUT [Streets were originally named 2nd from river, 6th from river, etc. This was later changed to current method with numbered streets running from North (Lowest #'s) to South (Highest #'s)	1860
6. 1916 'THE NATIONAL ROAD' BOOK - OHIO COUNTY EXTRACTS Detail maps, photos and points of interest are described.	1861
7. OHIO CO. MICROFILMS AT WV.UNIV. & STATE ARCHIVES	1871
8. PREVIEW OF *'OHIO COUNTY INDEX'* - VOLUME 8	1873
9. HINTS FOR INTERPRETING 'MISC. ENTRIES' & ABBREVIATIONS'	1875
10. PREVIEW OF *'OHIO COUNTY INDEX'* - VOLUME 7A The *CUMULATIVE INDEX* to volumes 1-7 with ***110,000*** entries !	1876

1871 MAP – BEERS' "MAP OF THE PANHANDLE" – TITLE BLOCK   1713

Map of the "PanHandle"
Embracing Counties of
HANCOCK, BROOKE, OHIO and MARSHALL
WEST VIRGINIA
From Actual Surveys and Records
By F. W. BEERS, C.E.
Assisted by
JAS. M. LATHROP
Published by
F. W. BEERS & CO.
GEO. NICHOLS, I. D. HALL, D. L. MILLER, W. R. DUMOND
I. F. MANCHESTER & C. J. CORBIN.
ASSISTANTS &c.

LOUIS E. NEUMAN
ENGRAVER
95 Maiden Lane N.Y.

1871
Scale - One inch to the mile

CHAS. HART
LITHOGRAPHER
36 Fulton St. N.Y.

```
                [Card catalog entry]
         [Library of Congress, Geography and Map Division]    PRELIMINARY

G3892
.P3      Beers, F   W    & Co.
1871        Map of the "Panhandle" embracing
.B4      counties of Hancock, Brooke, Ohio and
         Marshall. -- New York : Geo. Nichols,
         I.D. Hall, D.L. Miller, W.R. Dumond,
         I.F. Manchester and C.J. Corbin, 1871.
            1 map : col. ; 166 x 84 cm.
            Scale 1:63,360         Size 65 ½ x 33 inches
            Shows some residences.
            Includes table of airline distances
         and 25 insets.
            Joint author: Jas. M. Lathrop.
            LC has 2 copies.
            Land Ownership Map  1386
```

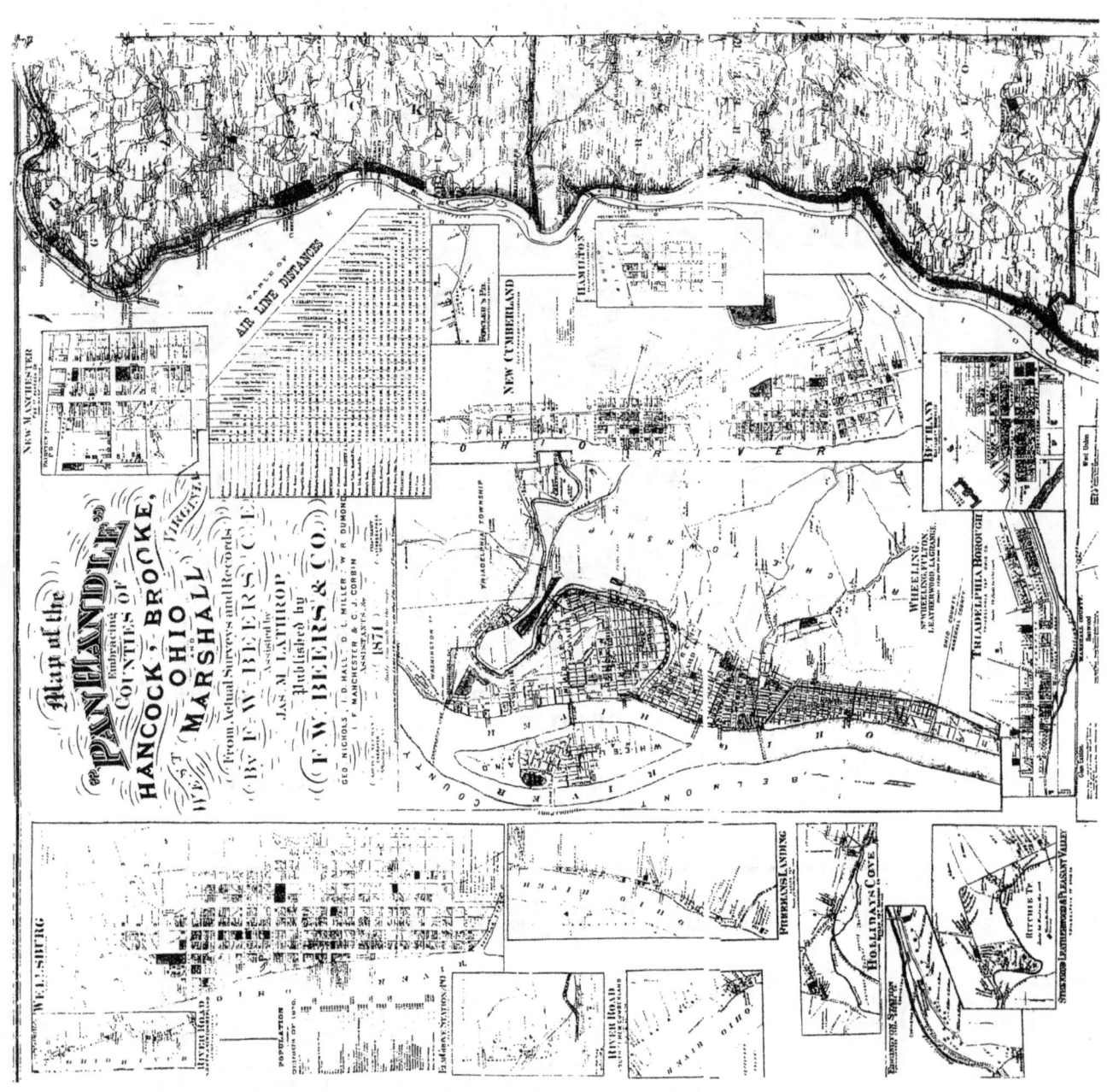

1871 MAP – OVERVIEW – BOTTOM HALF OF ORIGINAL MAP

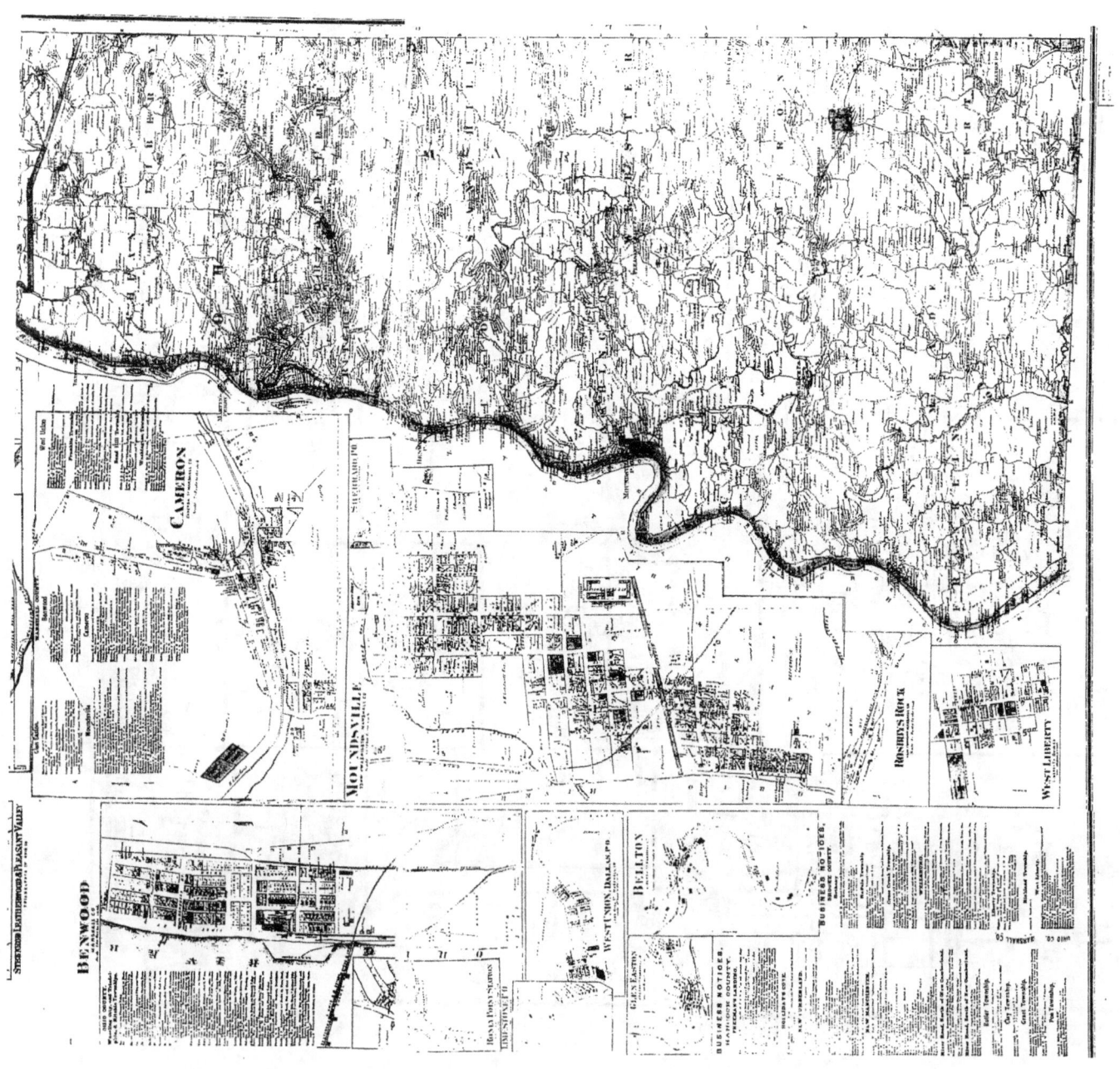

CAMERON
MOUNDSVILLE
BENWOOD
BELLTON
GLEN EASTON
WEST UNION, DALLAS P.O.
ROSEBY'S ROCK
WEST LIBERTY

1716   1871 MAP – OVERVIEW – TOP HALF – INDEX TO DETAILED MAPS

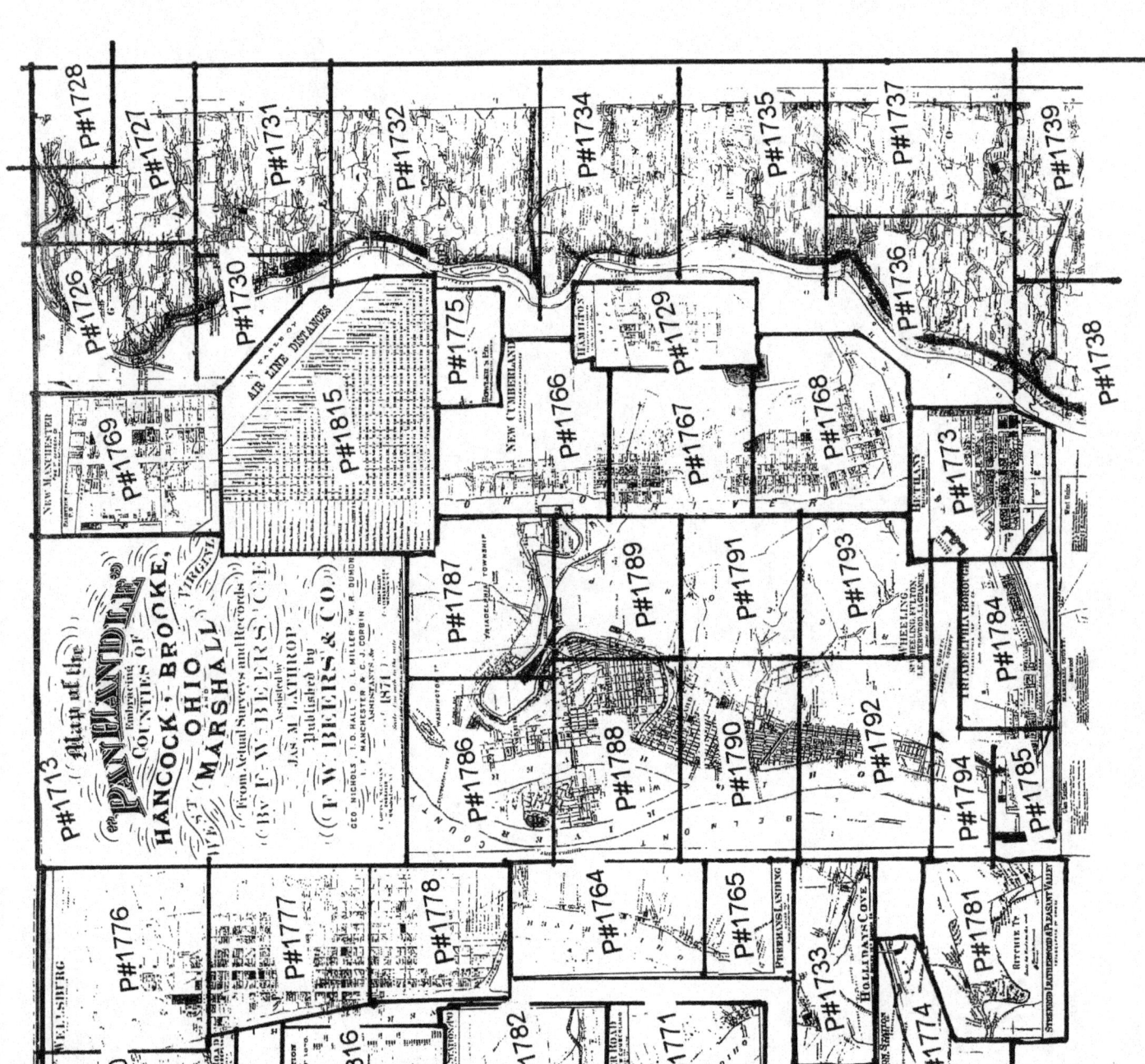

1871 MAP – OVERVIEW – BOTTOM HALF – INDEX TO DETAILED MAPS

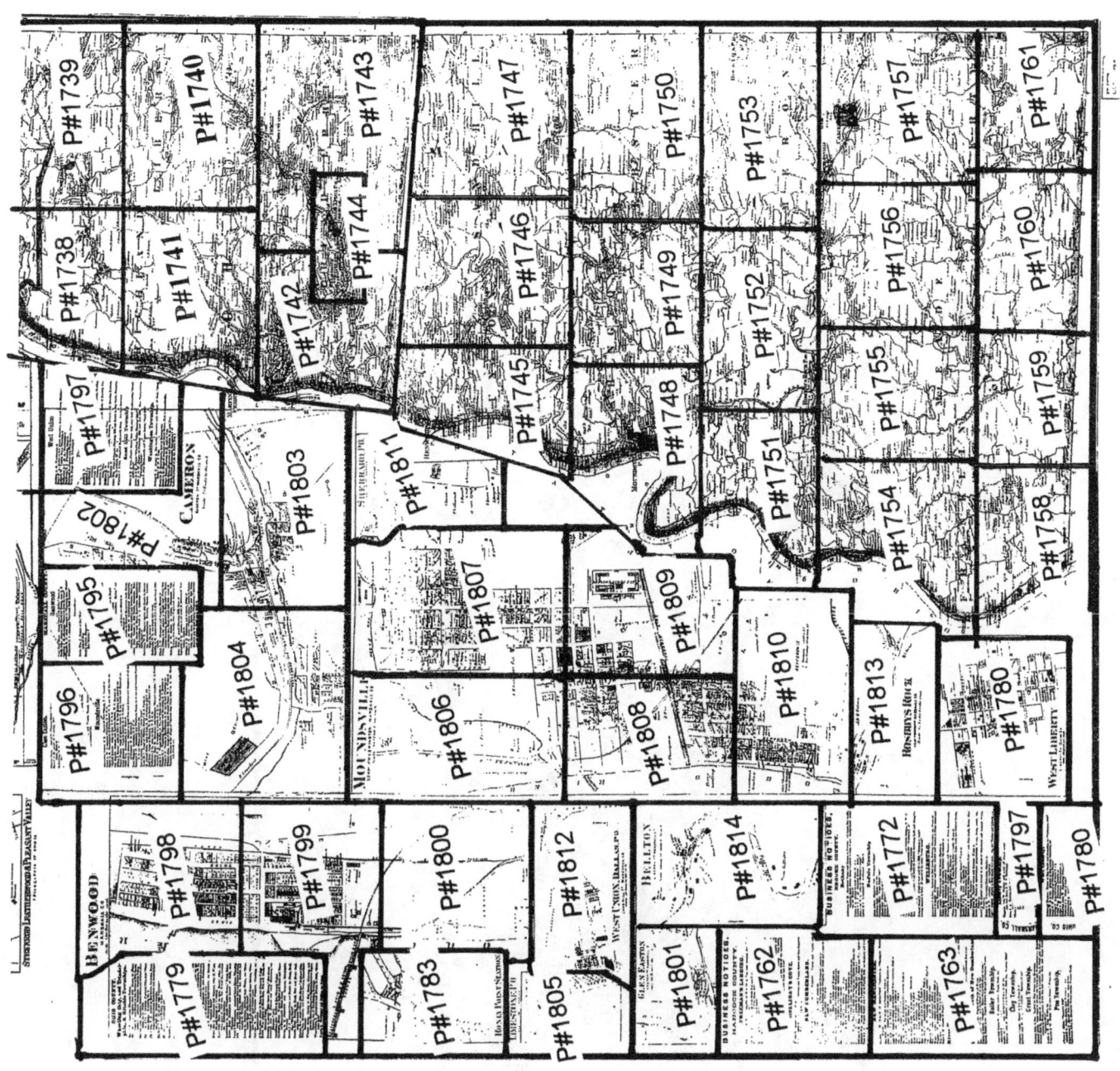

1718   1871 MAP – HANCOCK COUNTY TOWNSHIPS

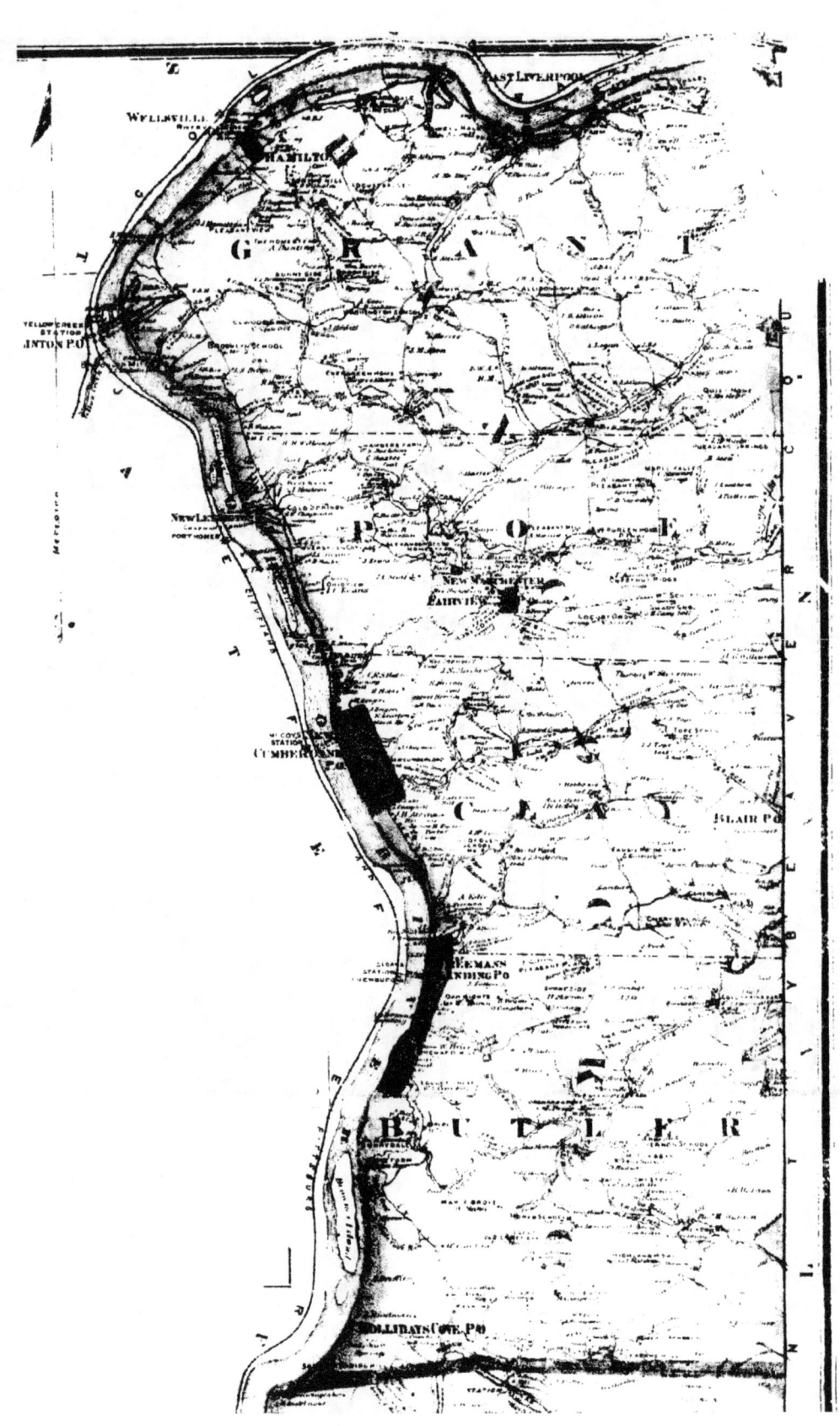

1871 MAP – BROOKE COUNTY TOWNSHIPS

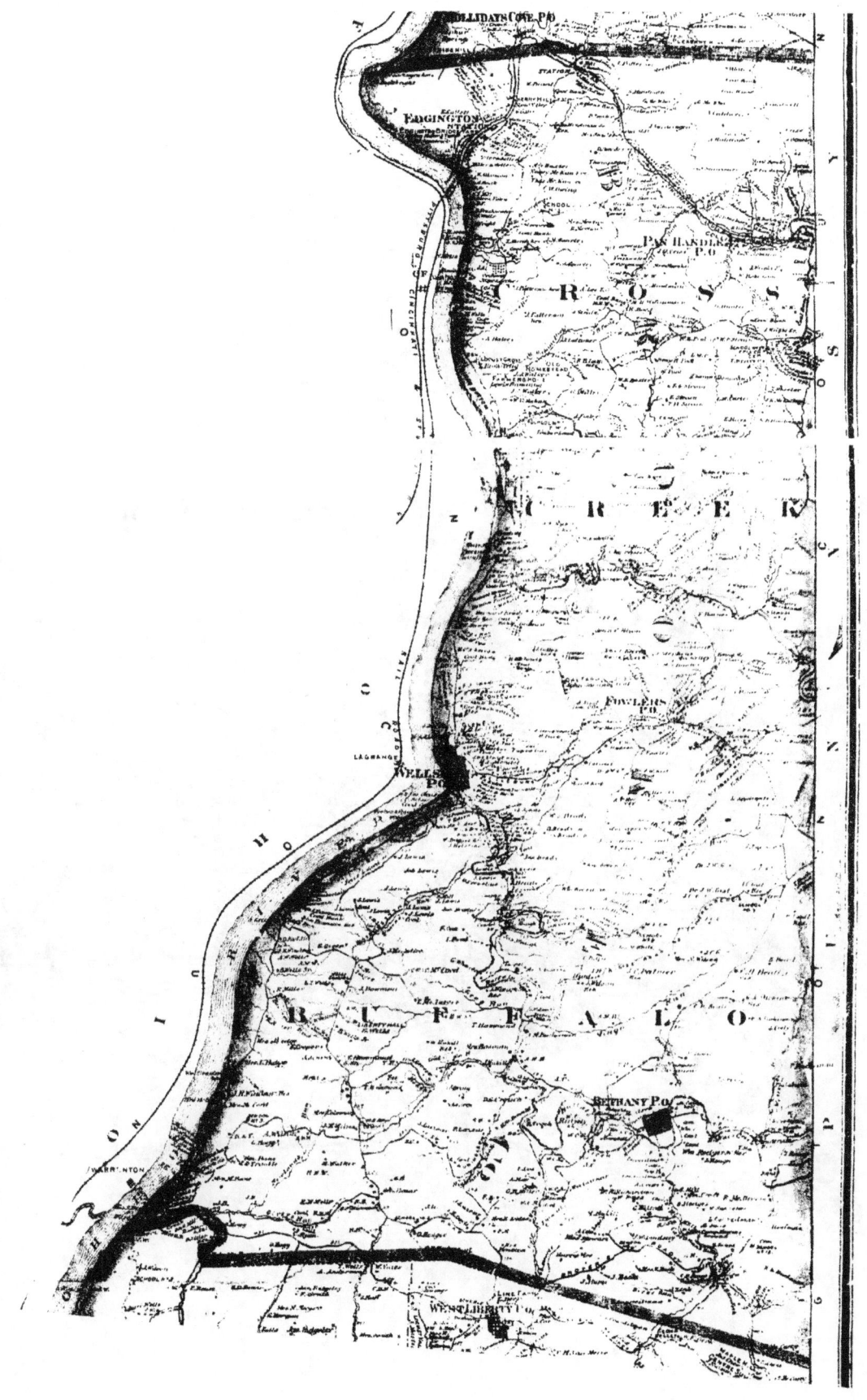

1720   1871 MAP – OHIO COUNTY TOWNSHIPS

Also see page 1721 for Wheeling City Townships and Wards

1871 MAP – OHIO COUNTY TOWNSHIPS – COUNTY AND WHEELING

1. Ohio County Townships – Outside of Wheeling City Limits
   (See also page 1720 plus detail maps)

   - Richland Twp
   - Liberty Twp
   - Triadelphia Twp
   - Ritchie Twp

2. City of Wheeling (See pages 1722-3 plus detail maps)
   [Source: Population...Census of 1870...shown on map]

Townships and Wards – From North to South

   - Washington Twp   - North of Corp. Line.
   - [no township listed] - 1st Ward
   - Madison Twp   - 2nd Ward
   - Clay Twp   - 3rd Ward
   - Union Twp   - 4th Ward
   - Centre Twp   - 5th Ward
   - Webster Twp   - 6th Ward
   - Madison Twp   - 7th Ward
     (Wheeling Island)

   - South Wheeling

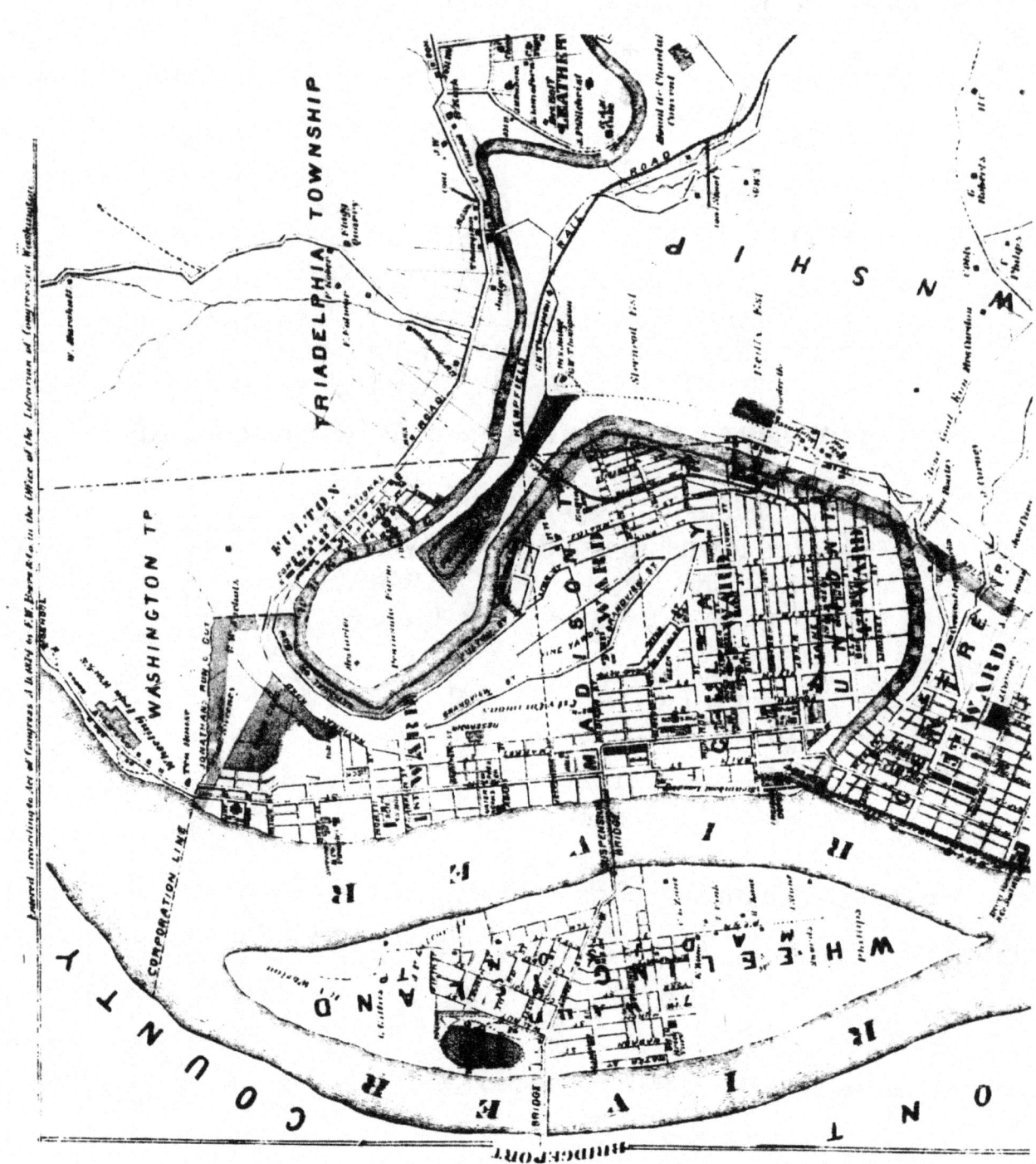

1871 MAP – WHEELING TOWNSHIPS & CITY WARDS – S. PART   1723

Note: Part of Ritchie Township to East of Wheeling City Boundary

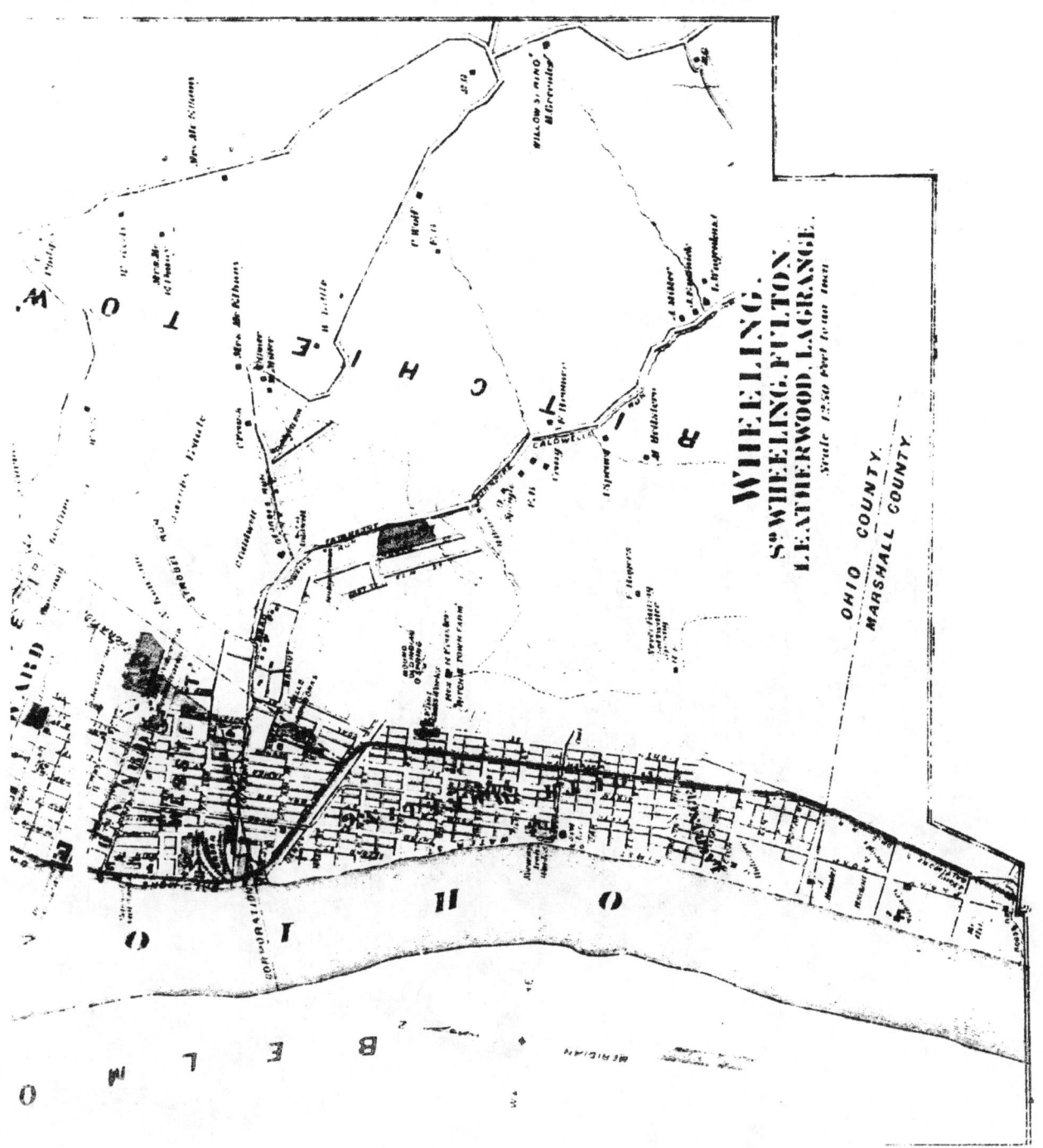

1724   1871 MAP – MARSHALL CO. TOWNSHIPS – N. PART

1871 MAP – MARSHALL CO. TOWNSHIPS – SOUTHERN HALF   1725

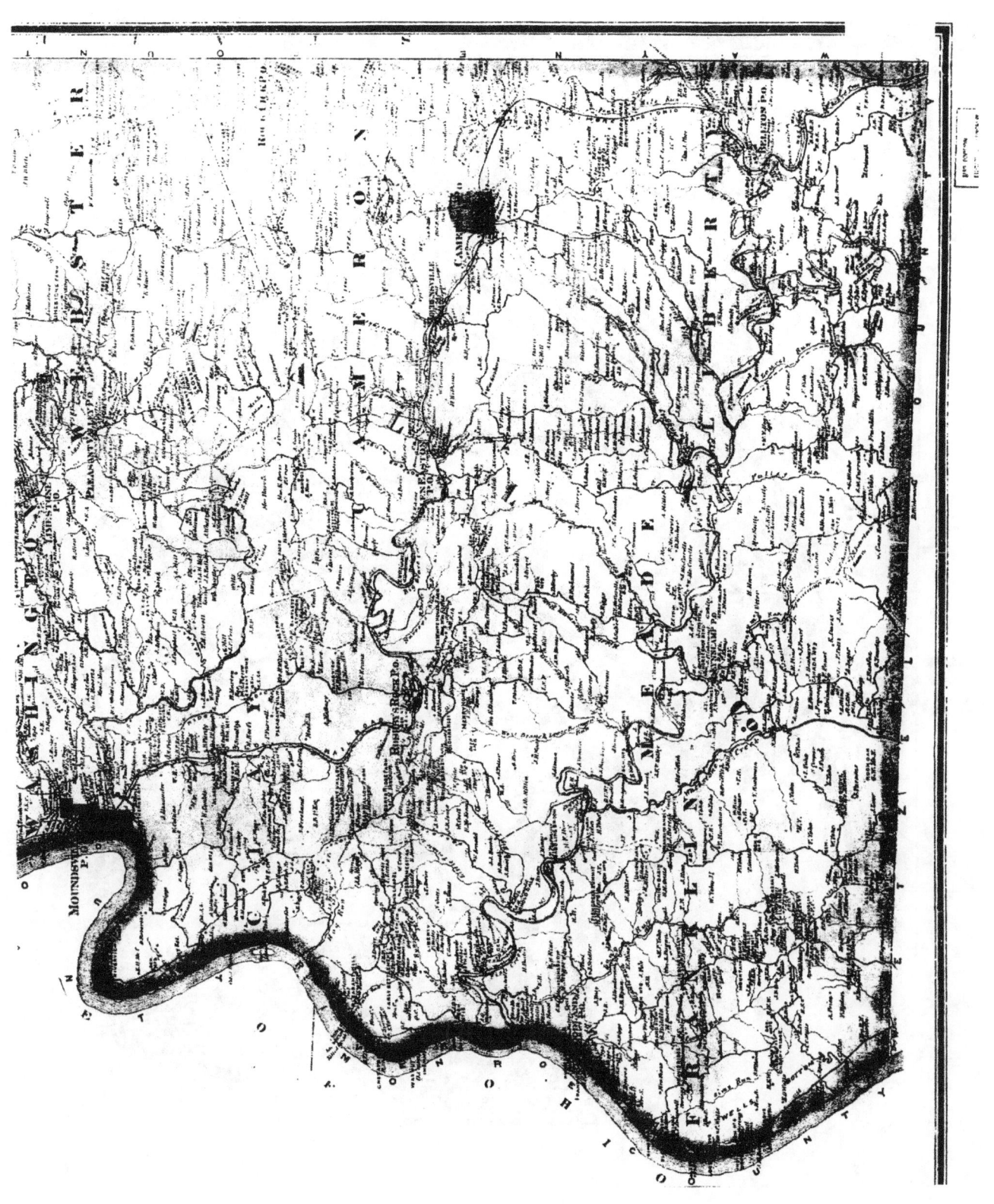

1871 MAP – HANCOCK CO. - NW. PART

1871 MAP – HANCOCK CO. – NE CORNER   1727

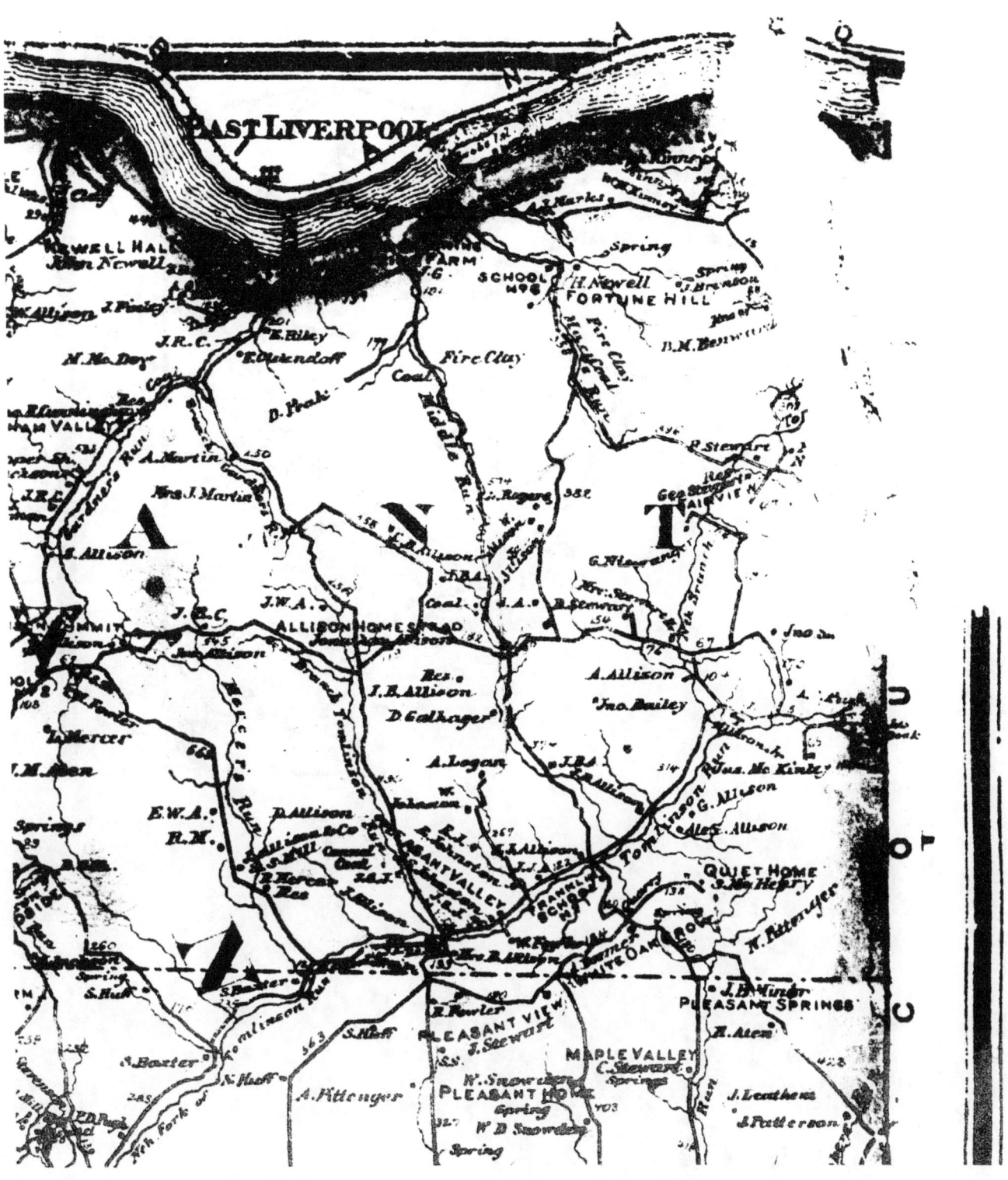

EAST LIVERPOOL
NEWELL HALL
John Newell
J. Finley
J.R.C.
E. Riley
SCHOOL No 6
H. Newell
FORTUNE HILL
Spring
Fire Clay
Coal
Middle Run
A. Martin
Mrs. J. Martin
Gardner's Run
S. Allison
J.R.C.
ALLISON HOMESTEAD
Jas. Allison
J.W.A.
P. Stewart
Rogers
G. Stewart
FAIRVIEW
J.B. Allison
D. Galhager
A. Allison
Jno. Bailey
A. Logan
L. Mercer
Mercer's Run
Jas. Mc Kinley
G. Allison
Alex. Allison
Tomlinson Run
D. Allison
E.W.A.
R.M.
PLEASANT VALLEY
QUIET HOME
S. Mc Henry
W. Pittenger
WHITE OAK
S. Baxter
S. Huff
J.B. Miner
PLEASANT SPRINGS
R. Aten
B. Fowler
PLEASANT VIEW
J. Stewart
MAPLE VALLEY
C. Stewart
W. Snowden
PLEASANT HOME
A. Pittenger
N. Huff
Springs
J. Leathem
J. Patterson
W. D. Snowden
Spring

1728   1871 MAP – HANCOCK CO. - NE. PART – MISSING PART

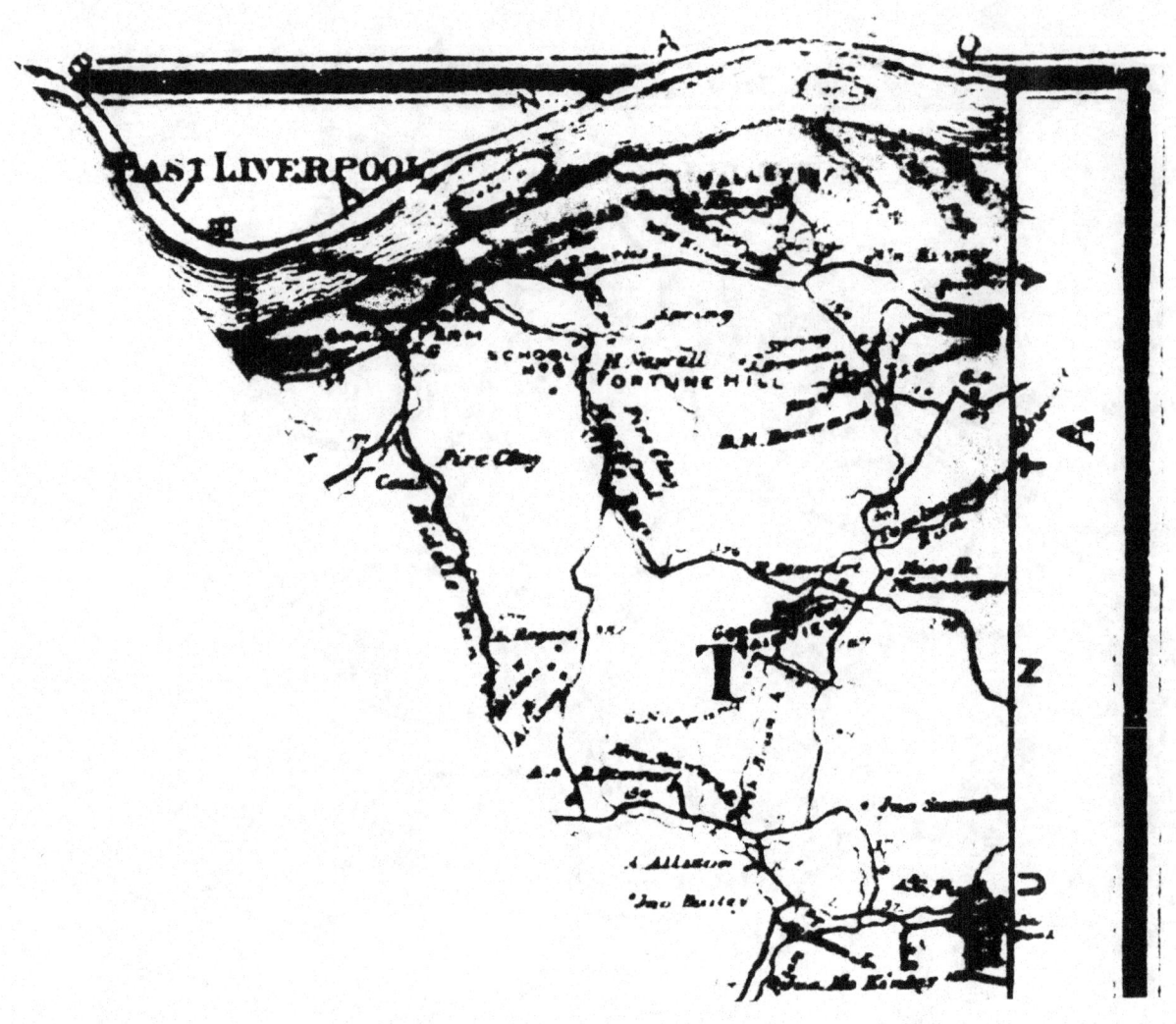

1871 MAP – HANCOCK CO. – HAMILTON TOWN 1729

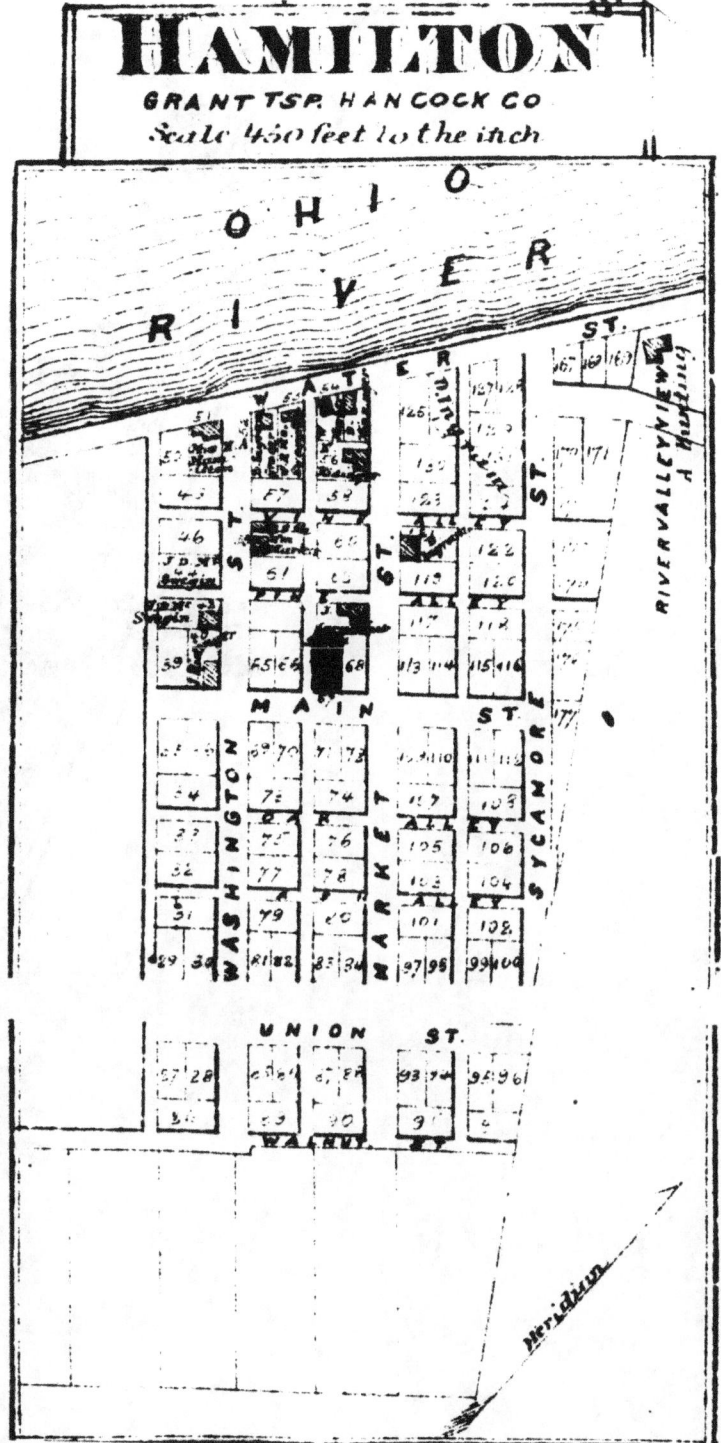

GRANT TSP. HANCOCK CO
Scale 450 feet to the inch
OHIO RIVER
WATER ST.
WASHINGTON ST.
MARKET ST.
SYCAMORE ST.
MAIN ST.
UNION ST.
RIVERVALLEY VIEW
Meridian

1730   1871 MAP – HANCOCK CO. - CUMBERLAND P.O. AREA

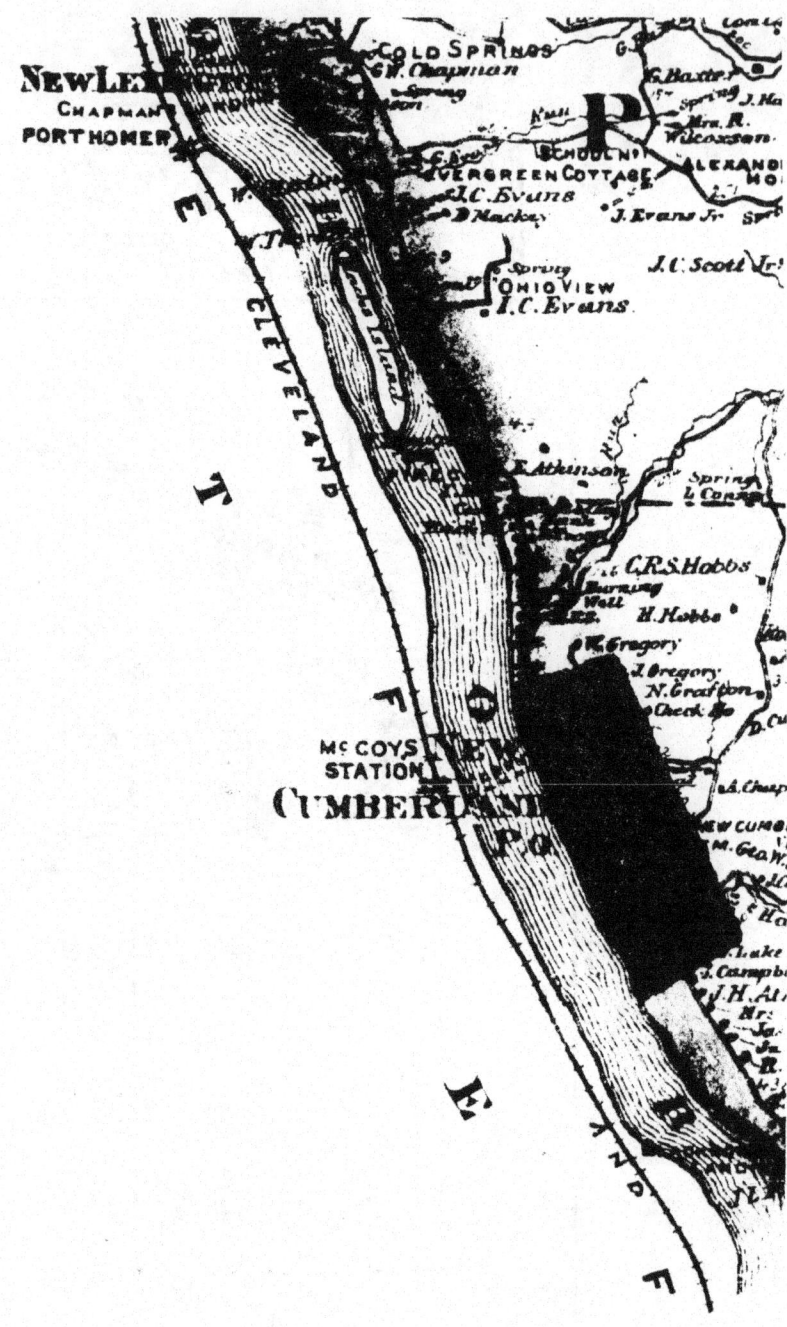

1871 MAP – HANCOCK CO. – NEW MANCHESTER AREA   1731

FAIRVIEW
PLEASANT HILL
EVERGREEN HOME
ROCKY POINT
Tomlinson Run
WHITE OAK
CHESTNUT RIDGE
Wm SCOTT HOMESTEAD
J.R. Scott
SHADY GROVE
LOCUST GROVE
N. Spivey
ROSE COTTAGE
Wm. Stewart
J.N. Mayhew
R. Herron
Thomas W. Stevenson
Jas Carson
A. Cunningham
J.J. Tope
TOPE SCHOOL No. 4
Edward Campbell
W. Luke
J. Grace
W. Herron
J.R. Hobbs
Coal Bros.
BLAIR P.
Geo. Chambers
SHADY GLEN SCHOOL No. 8
David Ward
Mrs. J.J. Anderson
FARMERS DELIGHT
L. Gardiner
James Chambers
CAMERON SCHOOL
A. Edie
H. Jenkins
CHERRY GROVE
Jno. N. Wylie
J. Pugh
J. Cameron
FREEMANS LANDING P.O.
J. Sutton
PLEASANT PLAINS
J. Sutton Jr.
SUNNY SIDE
R. Morrow
C.W. Owings
A. Eaton
COLD SPRING
R. Brown
D. Carothers
Mrs. Swearingen

1732   1871 MAP – HANCOCK CO. - BUTLER TOWNSHIP

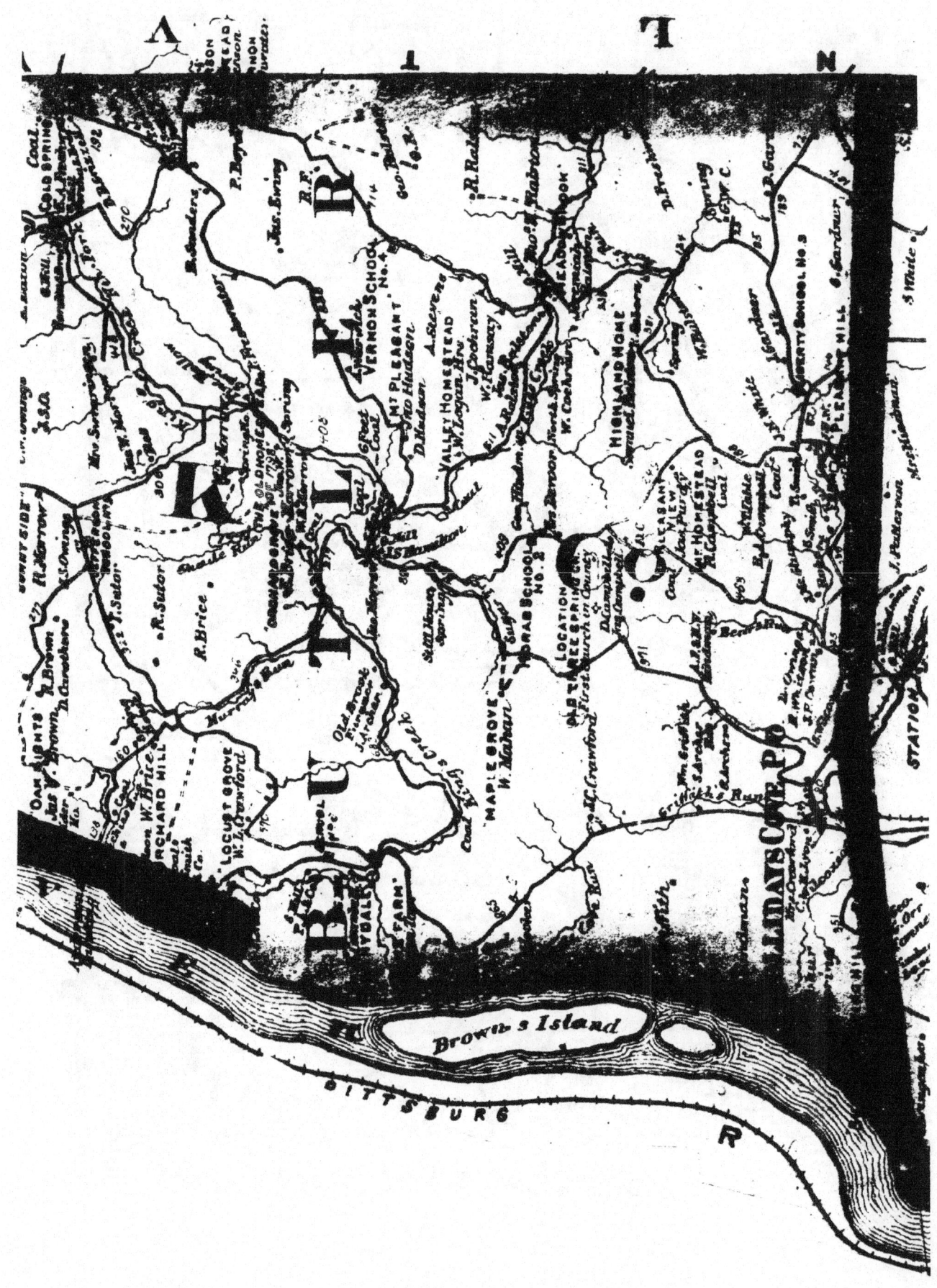

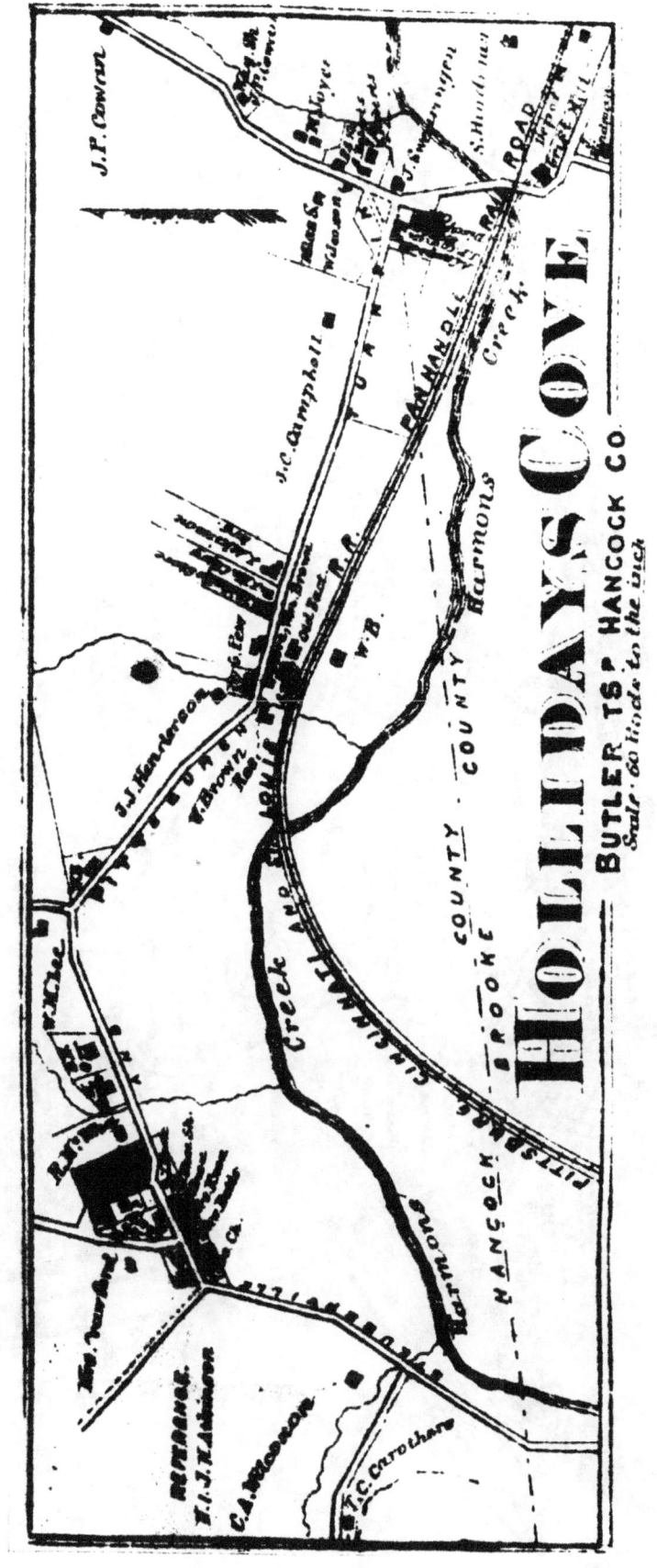
HOLLIDAYS COVE
BUTLER TSP. HANCOCK CO.
Scale 60 Rods to the inch
Harmons Creek
Harmons Creek
BROOKE COUNTY
HANCOCK COUNTY
PAN HANDLE RAIL ROAD
J.P. Cowan
S.C. Campbell
J.J. Henderson
C.A. Wilkinson
A.C. Carothers

1734   1871 MAP – BROOKE CO. – CROSS CREEK TOWNSHIP – N. PART

1871 MAP – BROOKE CO. – CROSS CREEK TOWNSHIP – S. PART   1735

1736   1871 MAP – BROOKE CO. – BUFFALO TOWNSHIP – W. PART

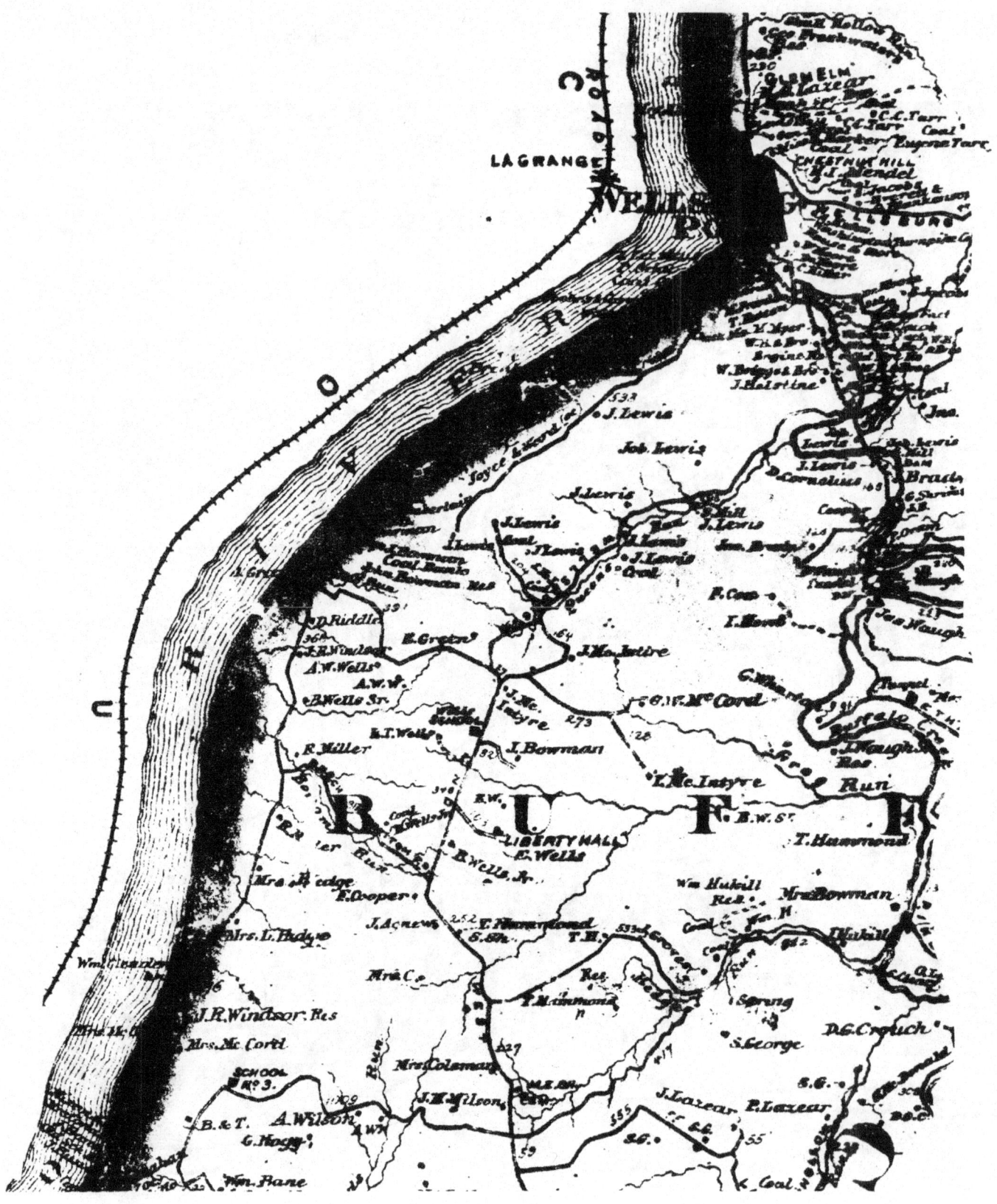

1871 MAP – BROOKE CO. – BUFFALO TOWNSHIP – E. PART 1737

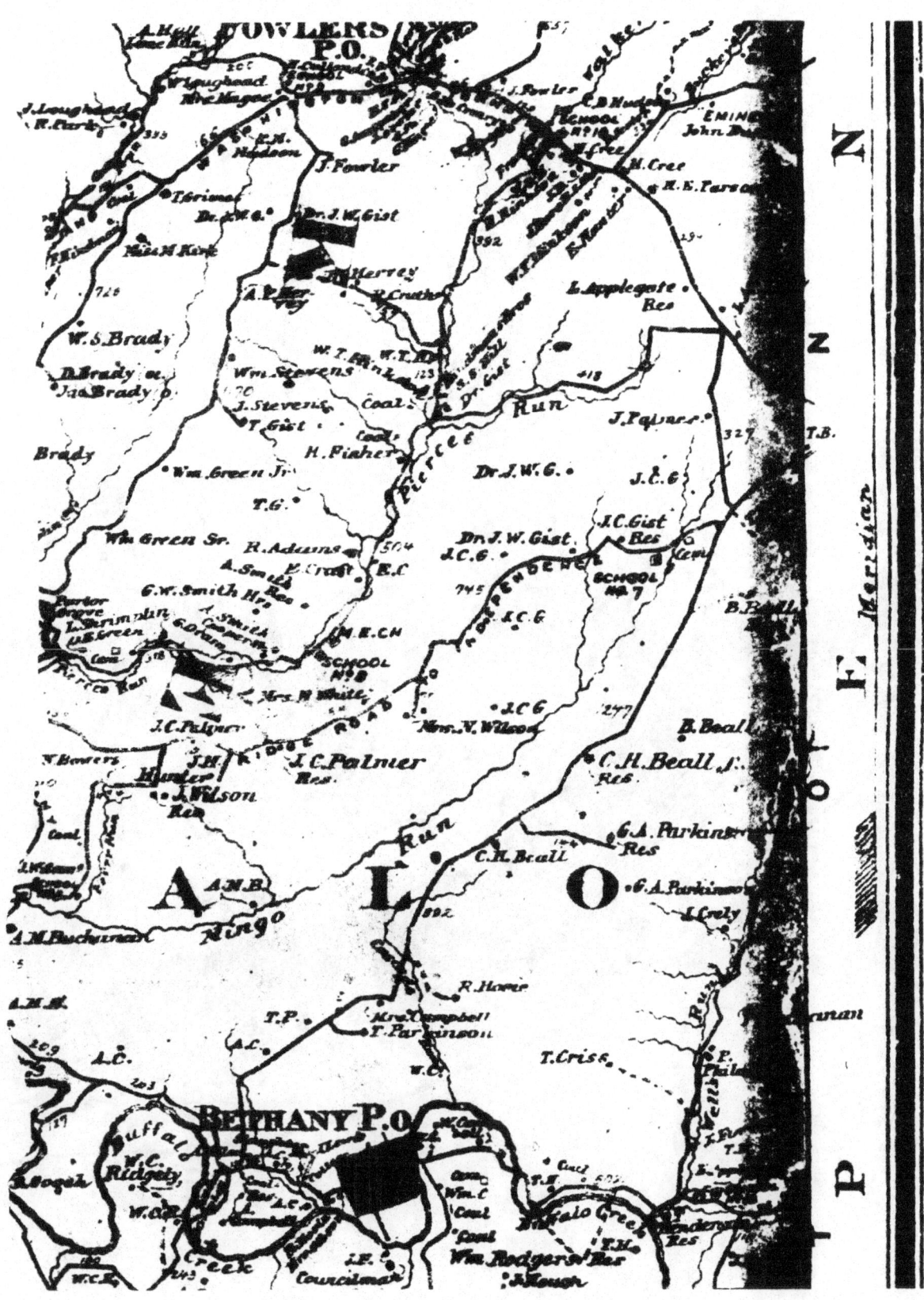

FOWLERS P.O.
J. Fowler
M. Cree
Dr. J. W. Gist
L. Applegate Res
W. S. Brady
Jas Brady
Brady
Wm. Stevens
J. Stevens
T. Gist
H. Fisher
Coal
Run
Pierce
J. Palmer
Dr. J. W. G.
J. C. G
Wm. Green Jr.
T. G.
Wm. Green Sr.
R. Adams
Dr. J. W. Gist
J. C. G.
J. C. Gist Res
SCHOOL No. 7
G. W. Smith Hrs.
M. E. CH
SCHOOL No. 8
Mrs. N. White
J. C. G
Mrs. N. Wilson
RIDGE ROAD
J. C. Palmer Res
J. C. Palmer
J. Wilson Res
C. H. Beall Jr. Res
B. Beall
G. A. Parkinson Res
C. H. Beall
G. A. Parkinson
Run
Mingo
A. M. Buchanan
R. Home
Mrs. Campbell
T. Parkinson
T. Criss
BETHANY P.O.
W. C. Ridgely
Buffalo Creek
Creek
Councilman
Wm. Rodgers Res
Z
Meridian

1738   1871 MAP – BROOKE CO. – SW. PART & OHIO CO. NW. PART

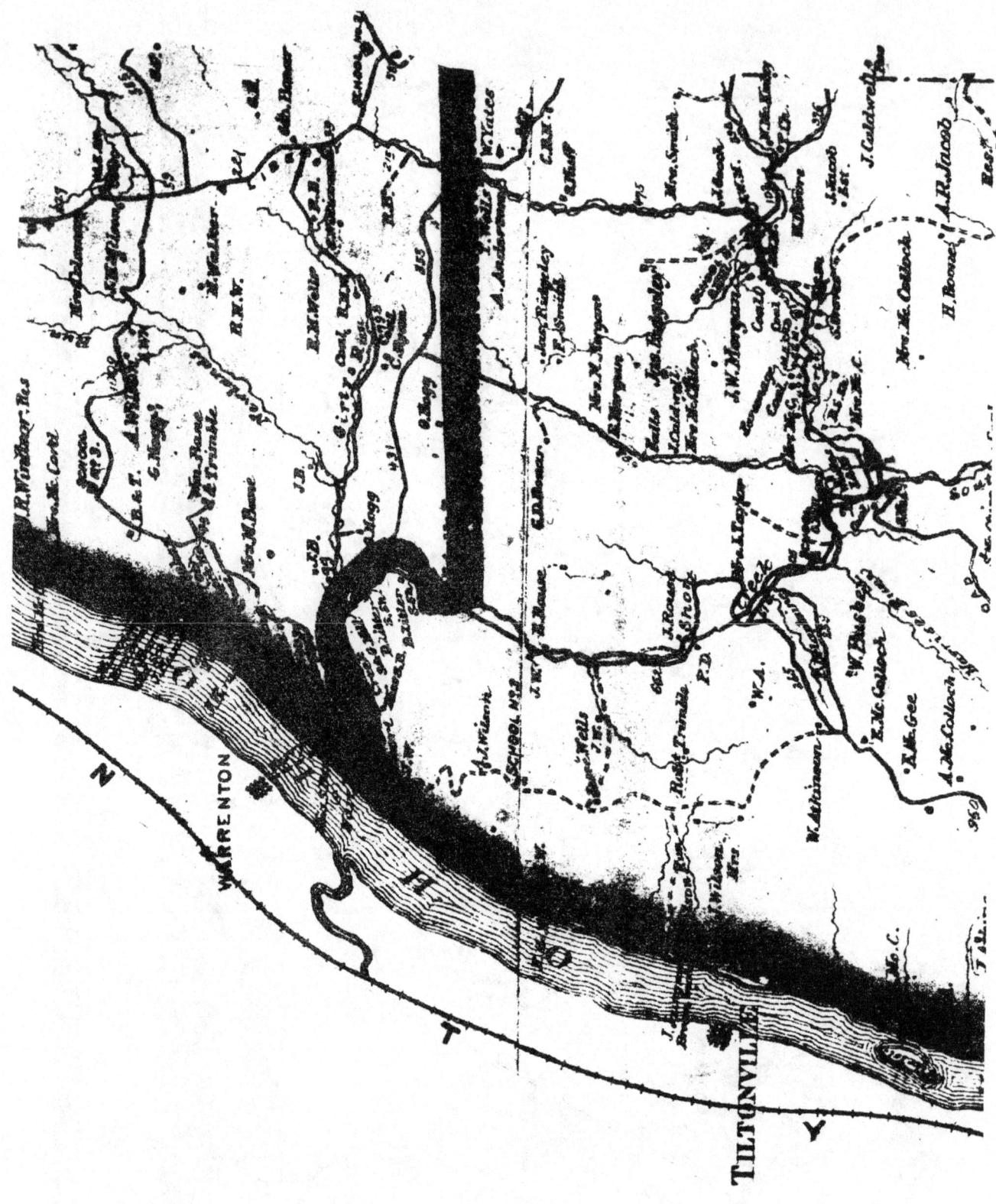

1871 MAP – BROOKE CO. – BETHANY & OHIO CO. – WEST LIBERTY

BETHANY P.O.
WEST LIBERTY P.O.
PROSPECT HILL
CENTRE SUMMIT
MAPLE HILL
"PINE GROVE"
LINE FARM
"LOCUST VALLEY"
"FAIRVIEW"
CHERRY HILL
Short Creek

1740   1871 MAP – OHIO CO. – LIBERTY TOWNSHIP

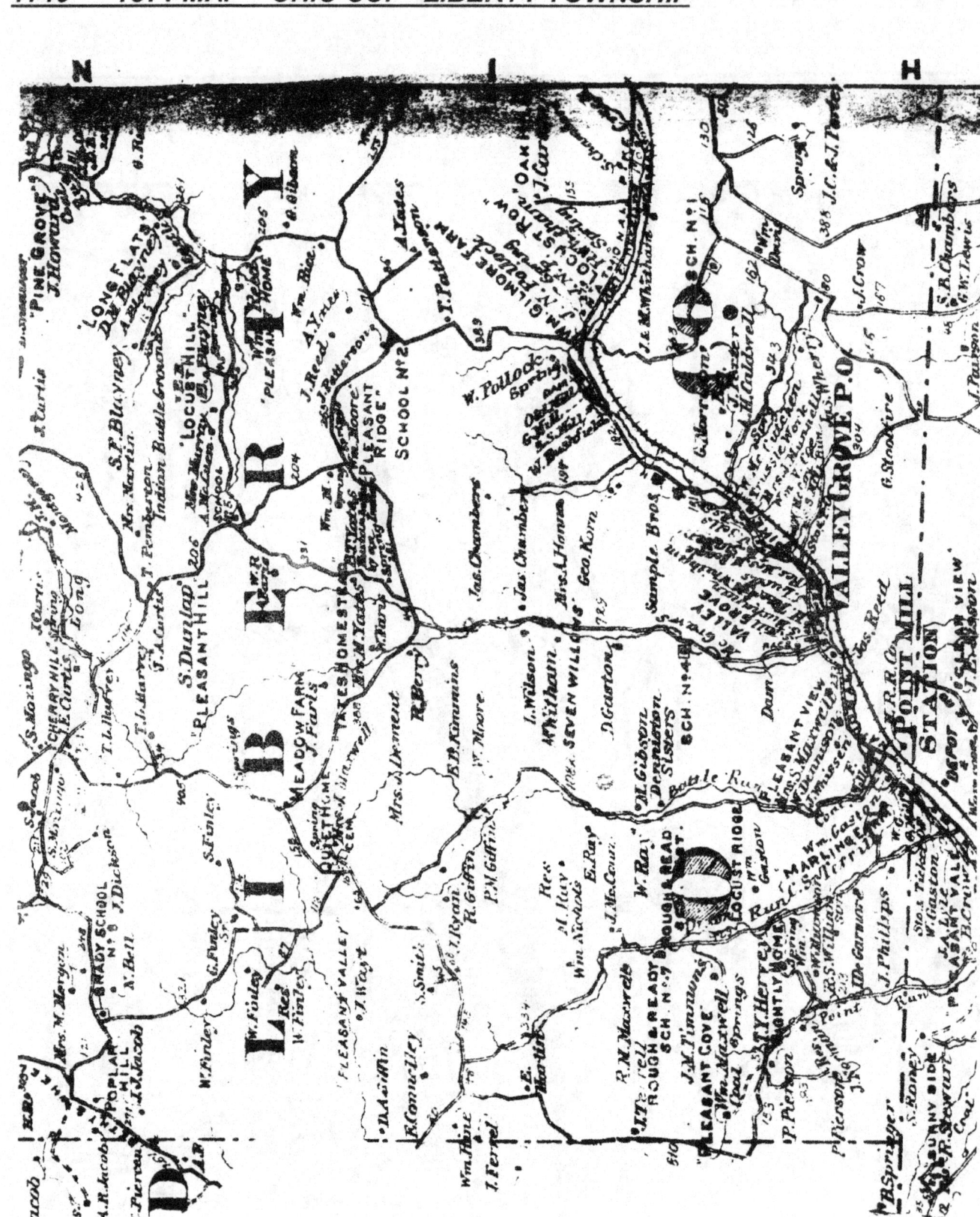

1871 MAP – OHIO CO. – RICHLAND TOWNSHIP 1741

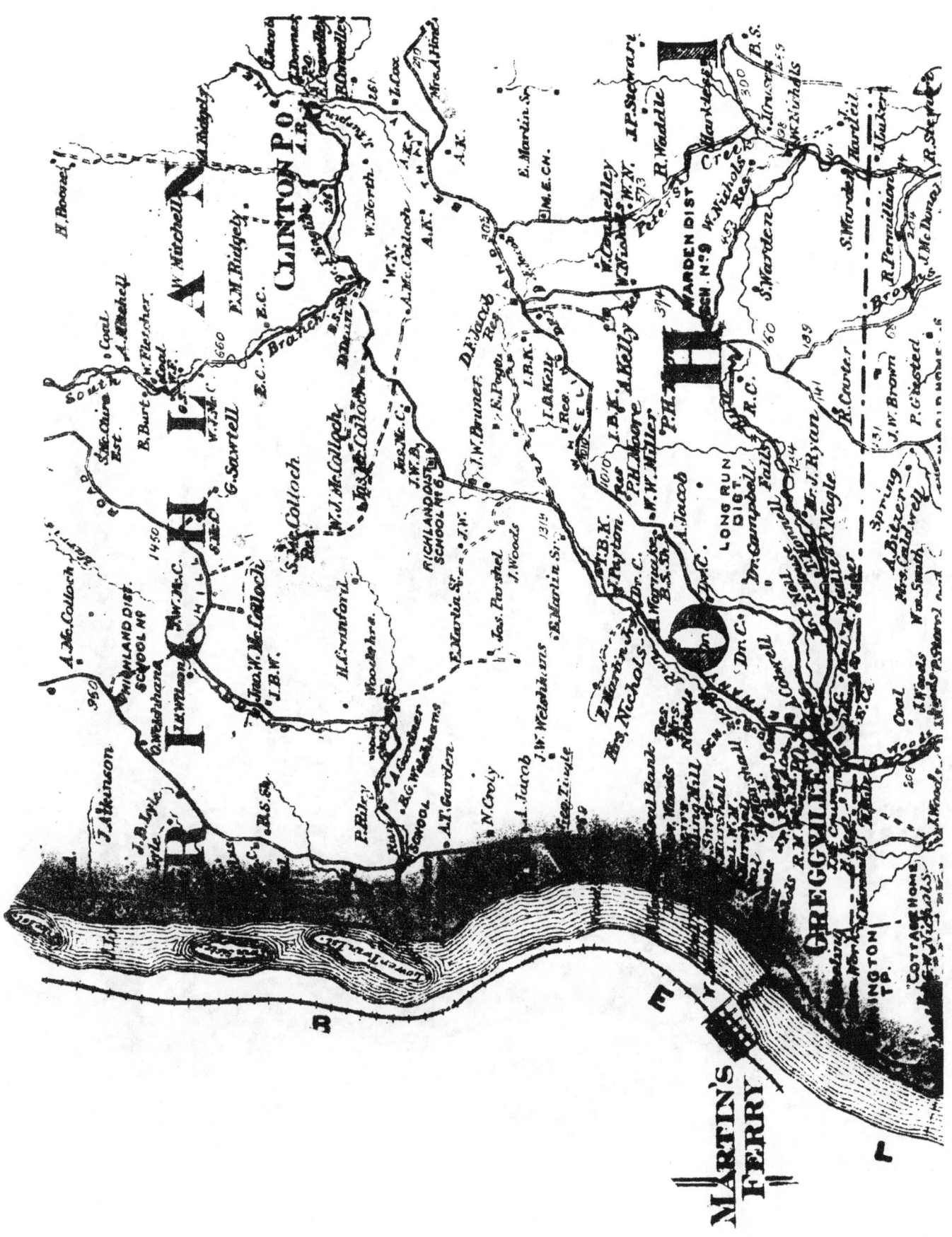

CLINTON P.O.
GREGGVILLE
MARTIN'S FERRY
RICHLAND DIST. SCHOOL No 6
WARDEN DIST SCH. No 9
LONG RUN DIST.

1742   1871 MAP – OHIO CO. – RITCHIE TOWNSHIP

1871 MAP – OHIO CO. – TRIADELPHIA TOWNSHIP 1743

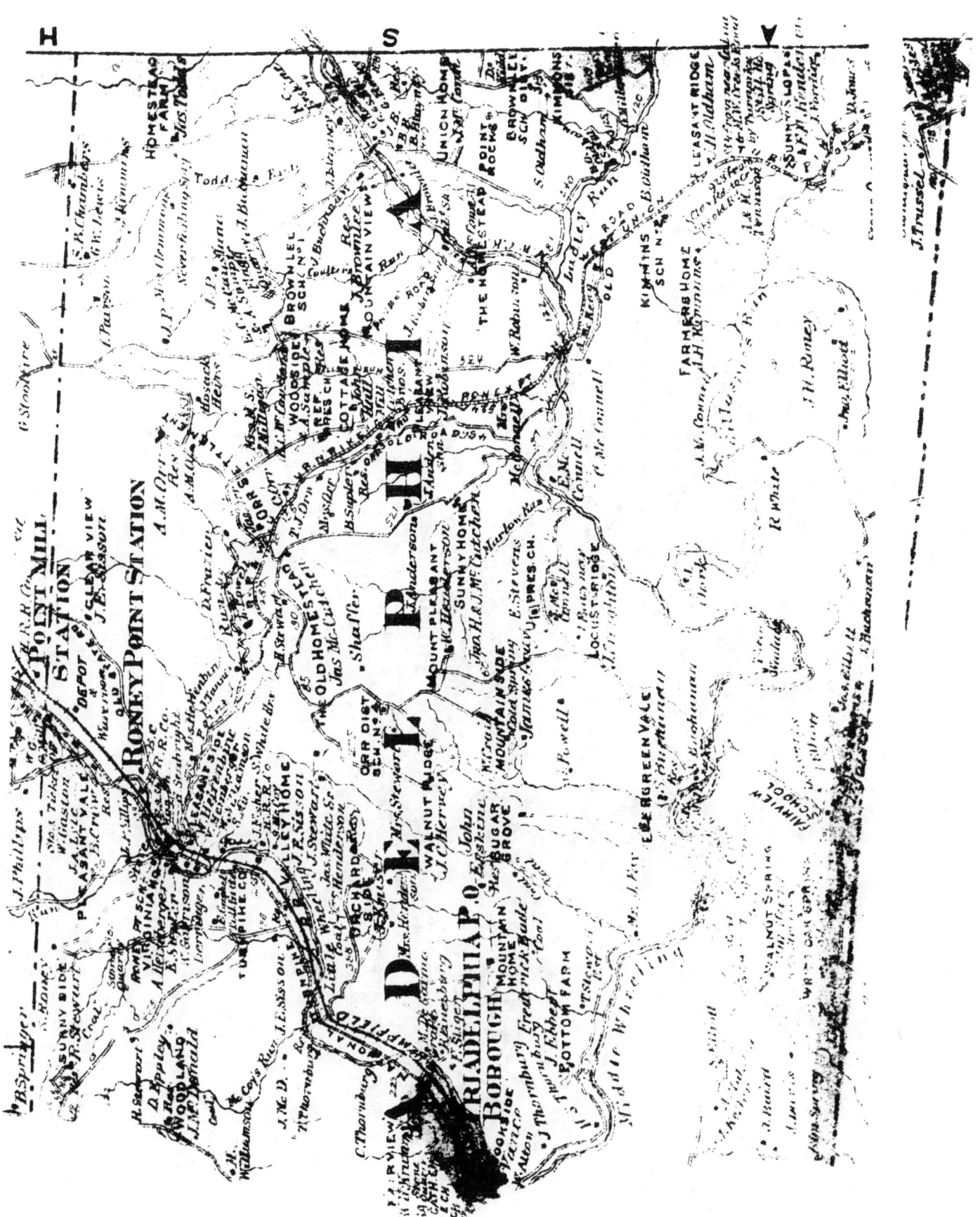

RONEY POINT STATION
POINT MILL STATION
TRIADELPHIA P.O.
TRIADELPHIA BOROUGH
Middle Wheeling
EVERGREEN VALE
WALNUT RIDGE
SUGAR GROVE
OLD HOMESTEAD
MOUNT PLEASANT
SUNNY HOME
MOUNTAIN SIDE
LOCUST RIDGE
FARMERS HOME
KIMMINS SCH. NO. 2
MOUNTAIN VIEW
UNION HOME
THE HOMESTEAD
J.H. Roney
FAIRVIEW SCHOOL
WALNUT SPRING

1744   1871 MAP – OHIO CO. – ELM GROVE – TRIADELPHIA BOROUGH AREA

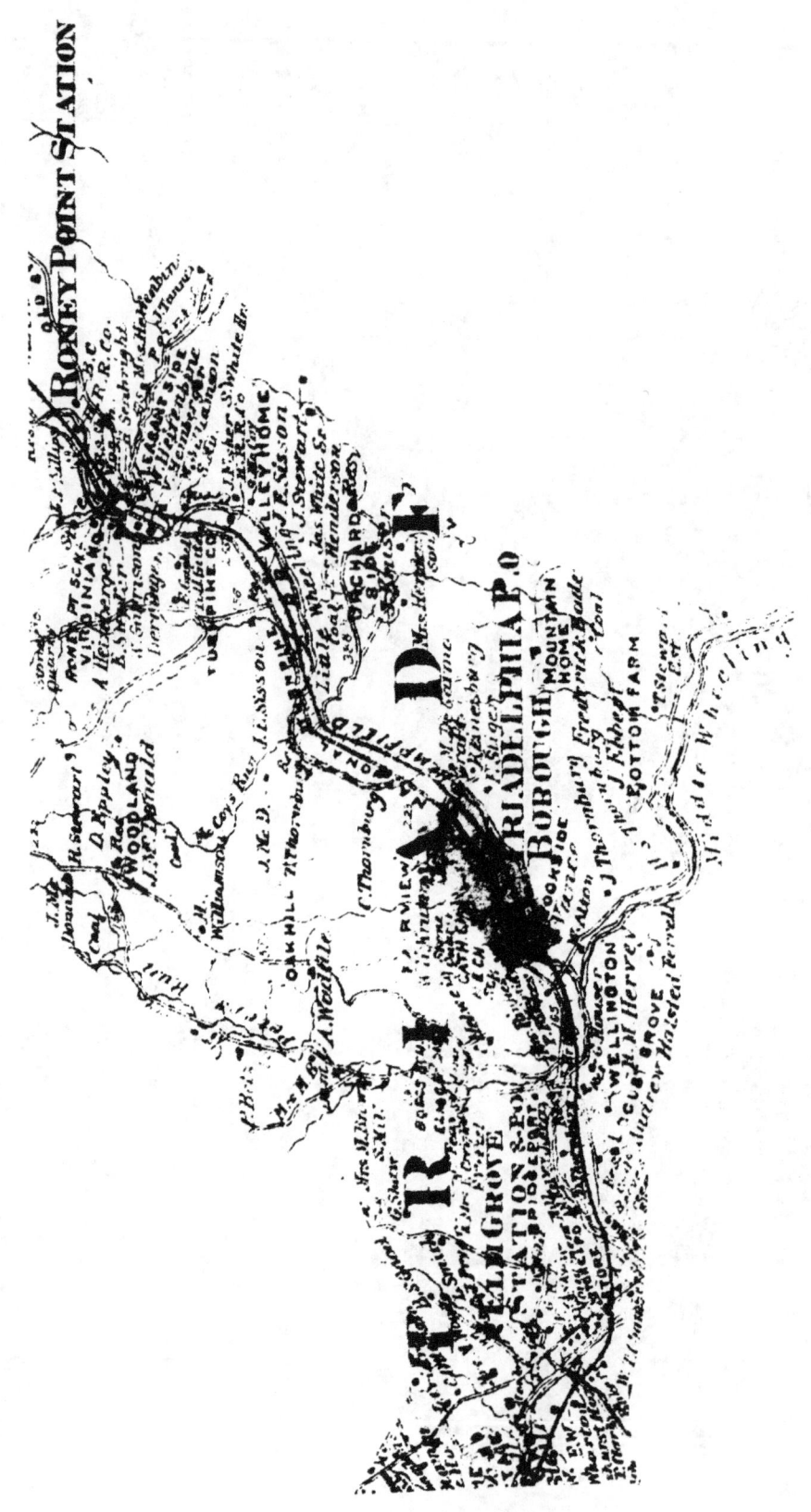

1871 MAP – MARSHALL CO. – UNION TOWNSHIP 1745

BENWOOD
P.O.
SUNNYSIDE
CH. MARSH
WAIT FARM
M.T. Weyman
H. Keltz
L. Davis
E. Baker
Gruppy
C. Goetze
B. Jurgens
H. Keltz
Freebolt
WHITEHOUSE HOME
CHESTNUT HILL
J.M. Brown
COTTAGE HOME
APPLE TREE COTTAGE
Mrs. M. Davidson
FAIRVIEW
Mrs. Bardo
CHESTNUT RIDGE
J. Kennedy
McMECHEN PATENT
RIVER VIEW
L. Seabright
J. Thatchers Heirs
S. Morris
H. Bumgardner
WHITE COTTAGE
GRAND VIEW
D. Dorsey
MOUNT ZION
W. Talbert
M.E.CH.
J. Price
PLEASANT POINT
CHERRY HILL FARM
CENTRE SUMMIT
J. Smith
J.H. Marple
HONEY BEE COTTAGE
HOME
E. Campbell
P. Markey
T. Markey
W. Yancy
W. Fisher
C. Ebert
C.T. Kleiner
J. Scanlan
C.T.K.
N. Dowler
Miss E. Caldwell
S. Jones
J. Flannagan
C. Clinor
P. Farrelly
Miss C. G. Pelley
G. Powell
J.F.B.
William Rogerson
P.C.
P. Crow
Little Grave Creek
Wilsons

1746   1871 MAP – MARSHALL CO. – SAND HILL TOWNSHIP – W. PART

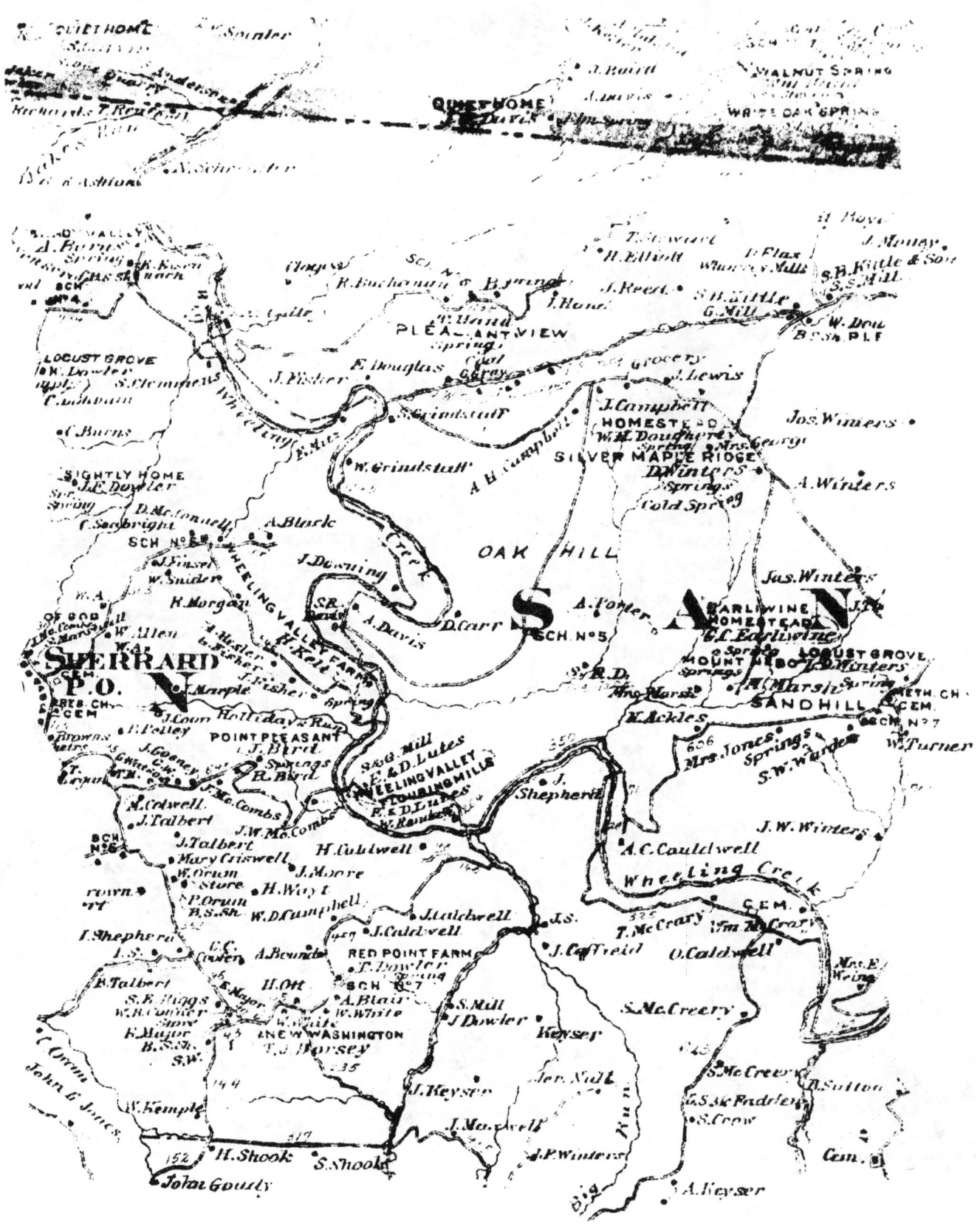

1871 MAP – MARSHALL CO. – SAND HILL TOWNSHIP – E. PART

Gillaspies Run
R.White
J.H.Roney
Fairview School
A.Siverts
J.Elliott
D.Jones
Wm.Buchanan
W.Kimmons
Roney
A.Money
WEST UNION
PRES.CH
CEM
J.Elliott
Springs
RURAL HOME
J.Trussell
J.Buchanan
E.Strickland
R.Buchanan
SHADY ORCHARD
J.Hand
Spring
J.Smith
W.Bellic
J.C.Armstrong
J.Winters
SCH.NO.1
S.Kimmons
A.Tompson
Turkey
Run
GREEN RIDGE
Geo.McCauslin
A.Thompson
Bruices Run
A.Kimmins
W.Rogers
J.Wilson
A.McCarithon
Mrs.Hamilton
J.Carroll
H.Thompson
W.Rosebery
J.Roseberry
J.McCracken
J.Rogers
J.Howard
J.Cole
J.Wilson
J.Thompson
W.Luke
H.Davis
T.Mitchel
SCH. NO.2
J.Beard
T.Steele
D.Craton
J.Huff
L.Simpson
J.Miller
W.Gardner
J.Wilson
J.Abercombie
G.Long
Mrs.Sivert
Taylor
J.Blake
W.Steele
W.Turner
A.J.Steele
M.Amos
H.Wilson
D.Ric
G.Tolen
Turkey Run
T.Scott
E.Ally
Coal
R.Taylor Hrs.
Wm.Kain
B.Richman
C.Cannon
W.Harsh
L.Croup
Mrs.Nixon
G.Mill
Mrs.Dague
SUGAR BOTTOM
D.Dague
Springs
W.Ruth
McCrary
R.E.Wallace
L.Candle
J.Harsh
J.Richman
NEW GERMANTOWN
H.Harsh
C.Lucas
L.Ludge
J.Cortes
Coal
Mrs.H.Woodruff
W.Riggle
J.Richey
Wilson
Jennings Heirs

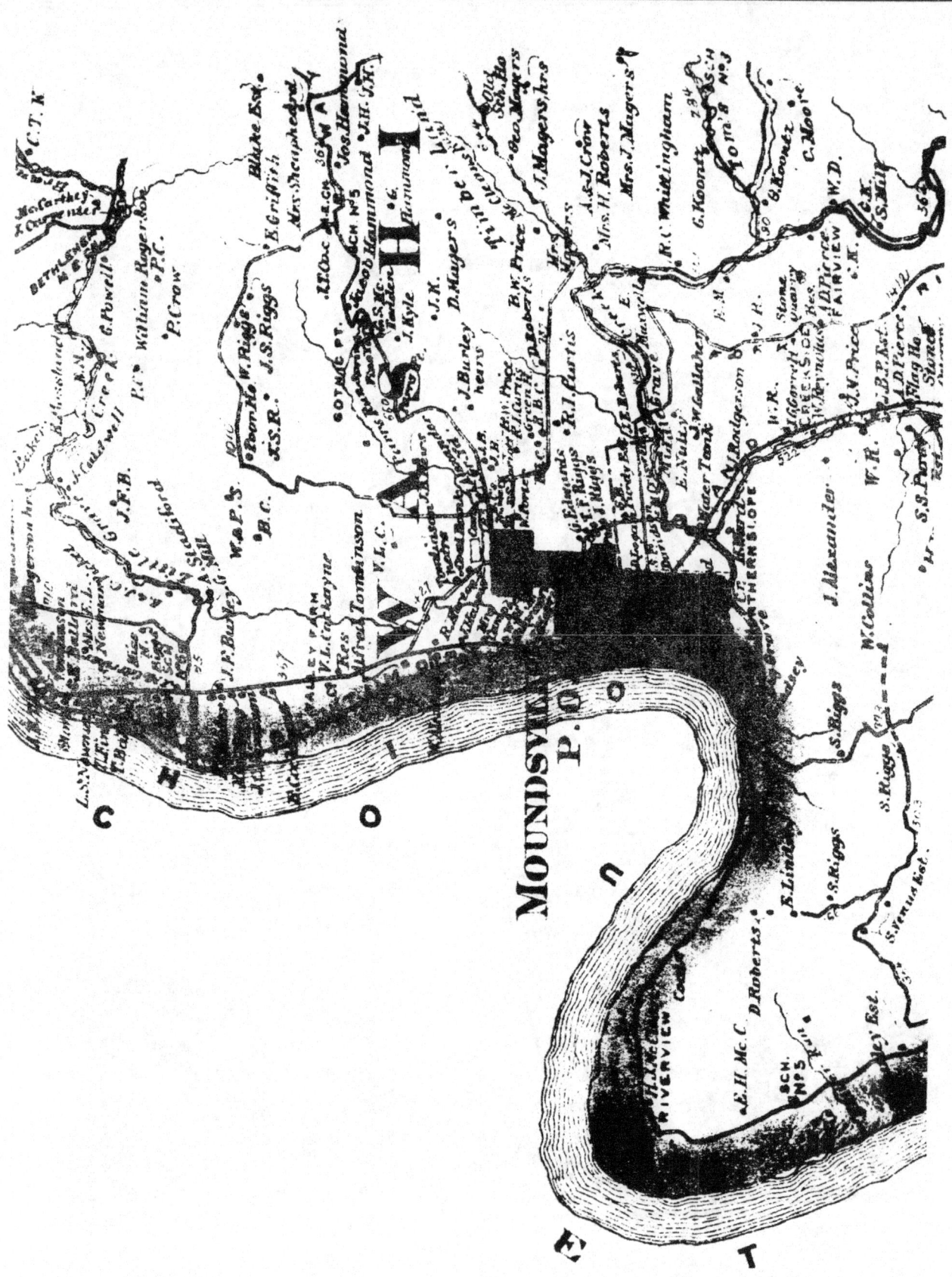

1871 MAP – MARSHALL CO. – WASHINGTON TOWNSHIP – E. PART

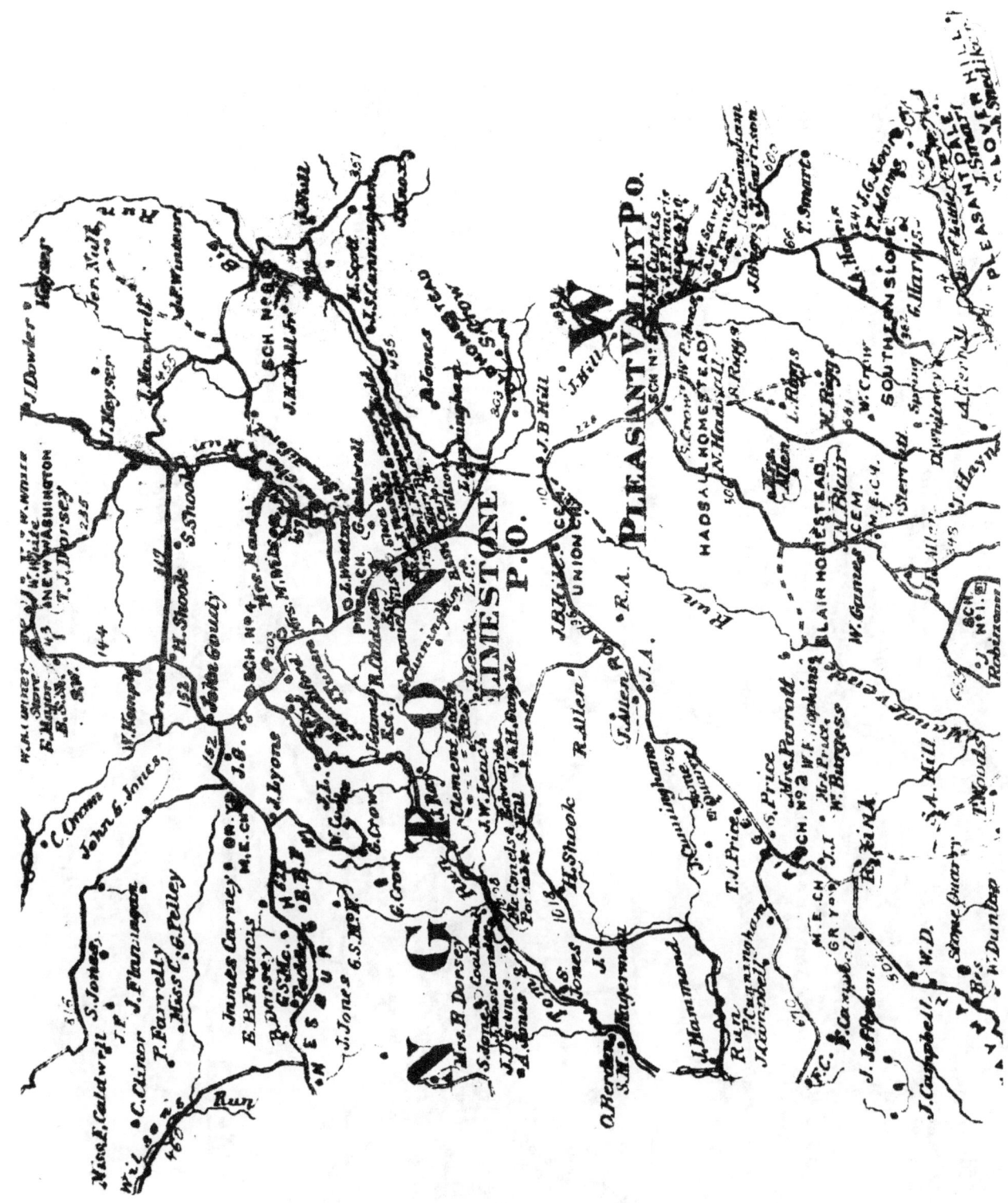

PLEASANT VALLEY P.O.
LIMESTONE P.O.
NEW WASHINGTON
BLAIR HOMESTEAD
HADSALL HOMESTEAD
SOUTHERN SLOPE

1750 1871 MAP – MARSHALL CO. – WEBSTER TOWNSHIP

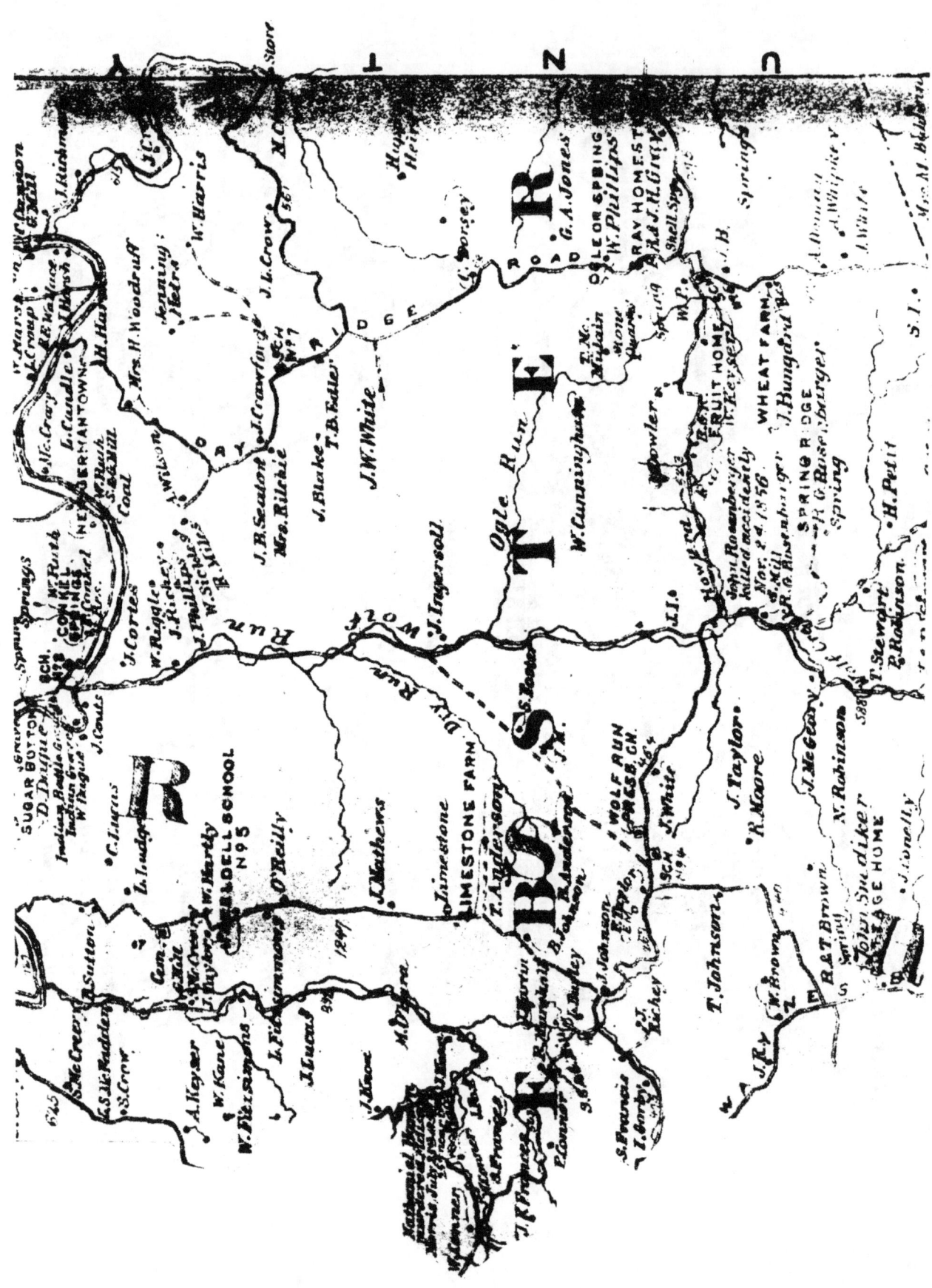

1871 MAP – MARSHALL CO. – CLAY TOWNSHIP   1751

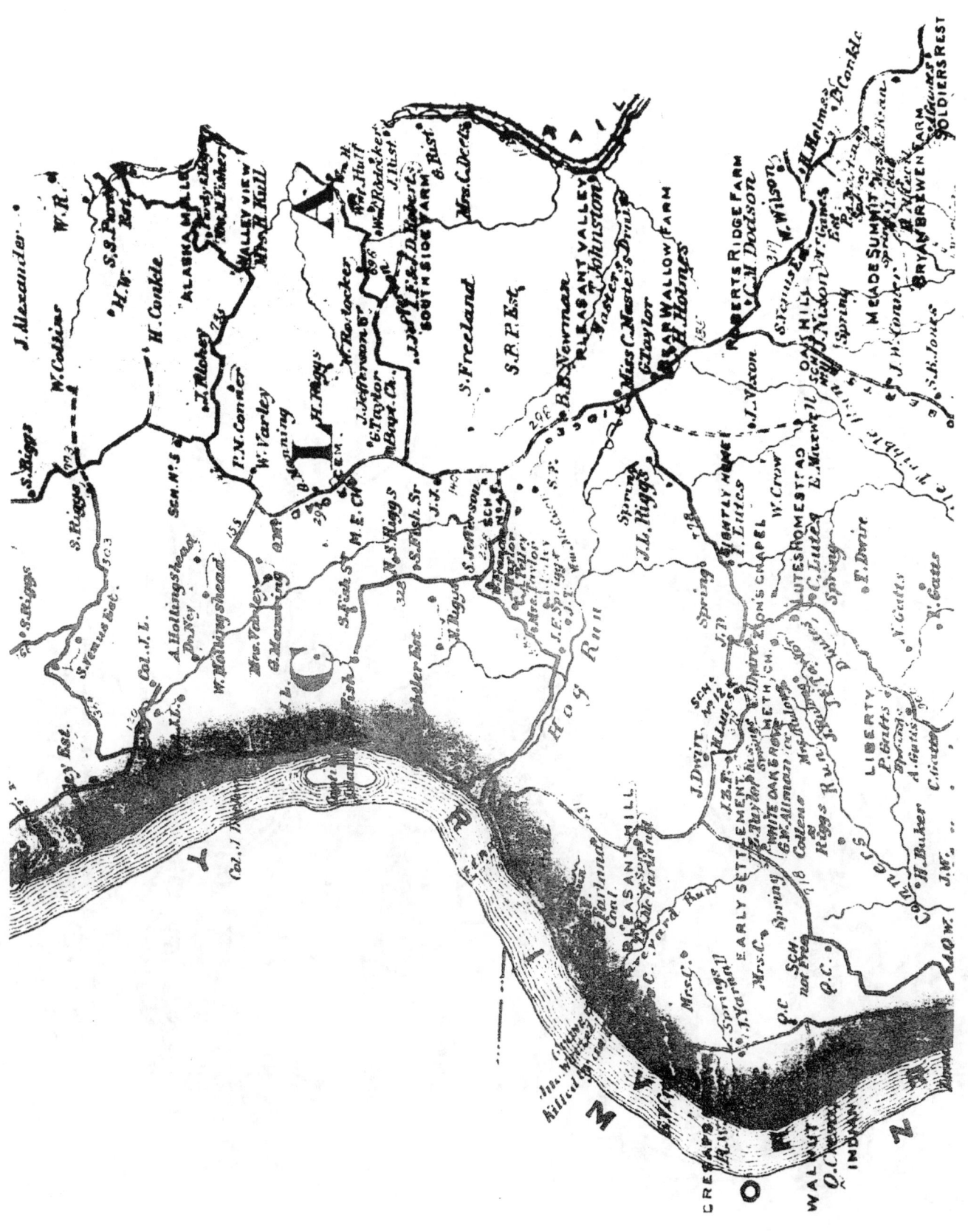

ROBERTS RIDGE FARM
PLEASANT VALLEY
MEADE SUMMIT
SOLDIERS REST
BRYAN BREWEN FARM
LIBERTY
Hog Run
EARLY SETTLEMENT
WHITE OAK GROVE
ZIONS CHAPEL
LUTES HOMESTEAD
PLEASANT HILL
VALLEY VIEW
SOUTH SIDE FARM
WALNUT
INDIANA
S.P.P. Est.
S. Freeland
H. Conkle
J. Alexander
W. Collins
H. Riggs
J.L. Riggs
W. Crow
T. Lutes
C. Lutes
W. Wilson
H. Holmes

1752   1871 MAP – MARSHALL CO. – CAMERON TOWNSHIP – W. PART

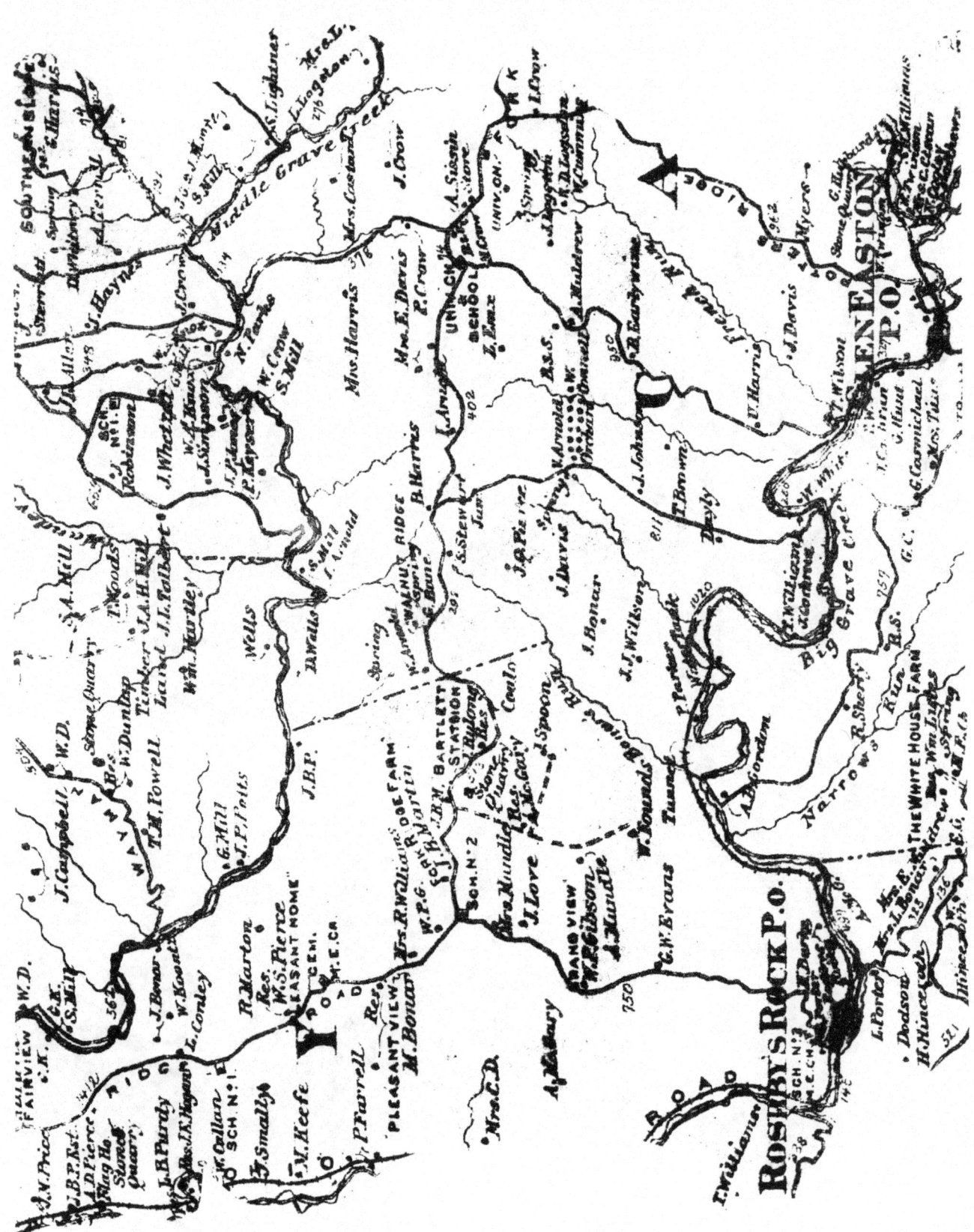

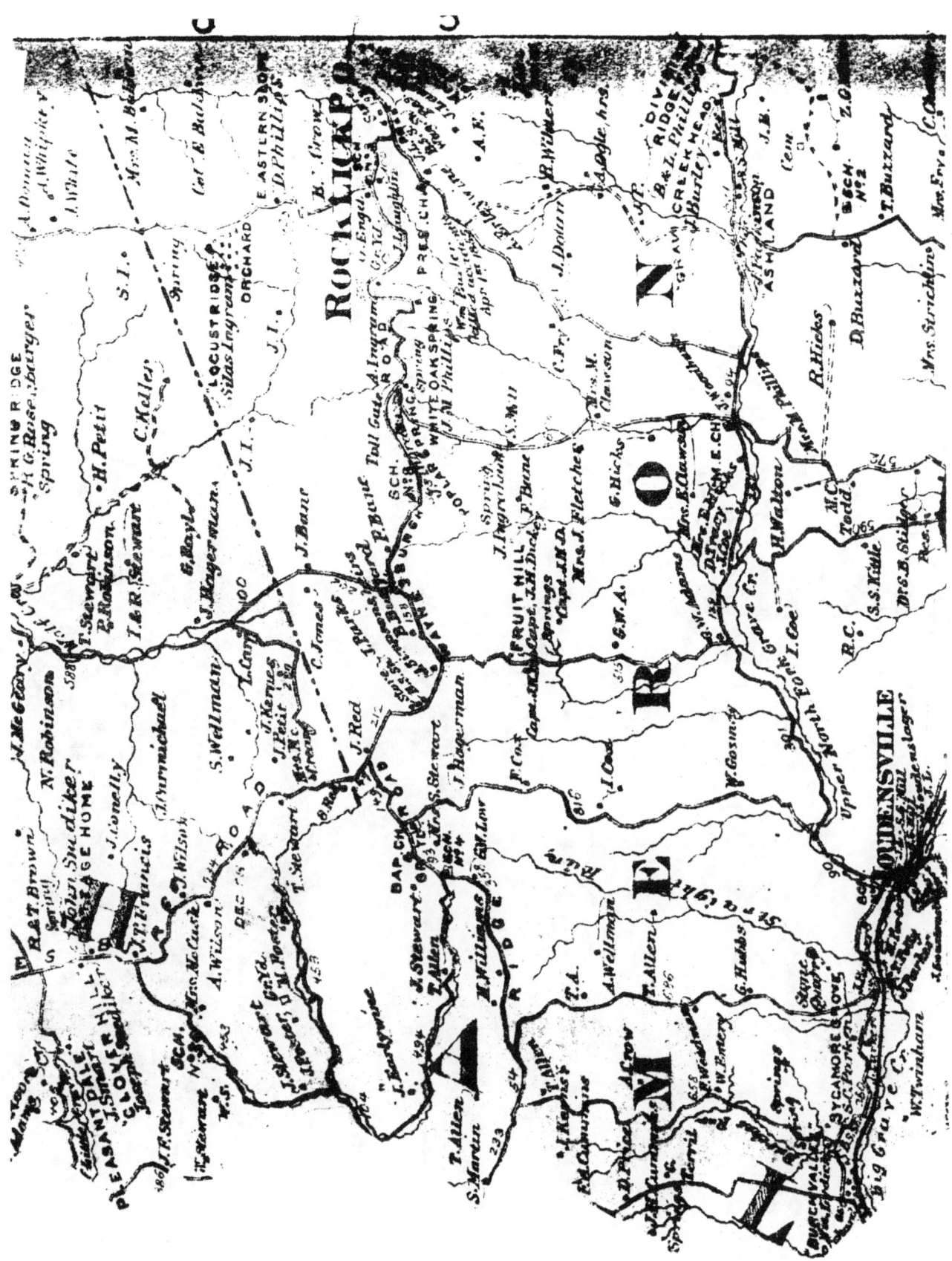
ROCKLICK P.O.
DIVIDE RIDGE
ASHLAND
FRUIT HILL
LOCUST RIDGE
SPRING RIDGE
WHITE OAK SPRING
PLEASANT DALE
SYCAMORE GROVE
Grave Cr.
Upper North Fork
Big Grave Cr.

1754   1871 MAP – MARSHALL CO. – FRANKLIN TOWNSHIP

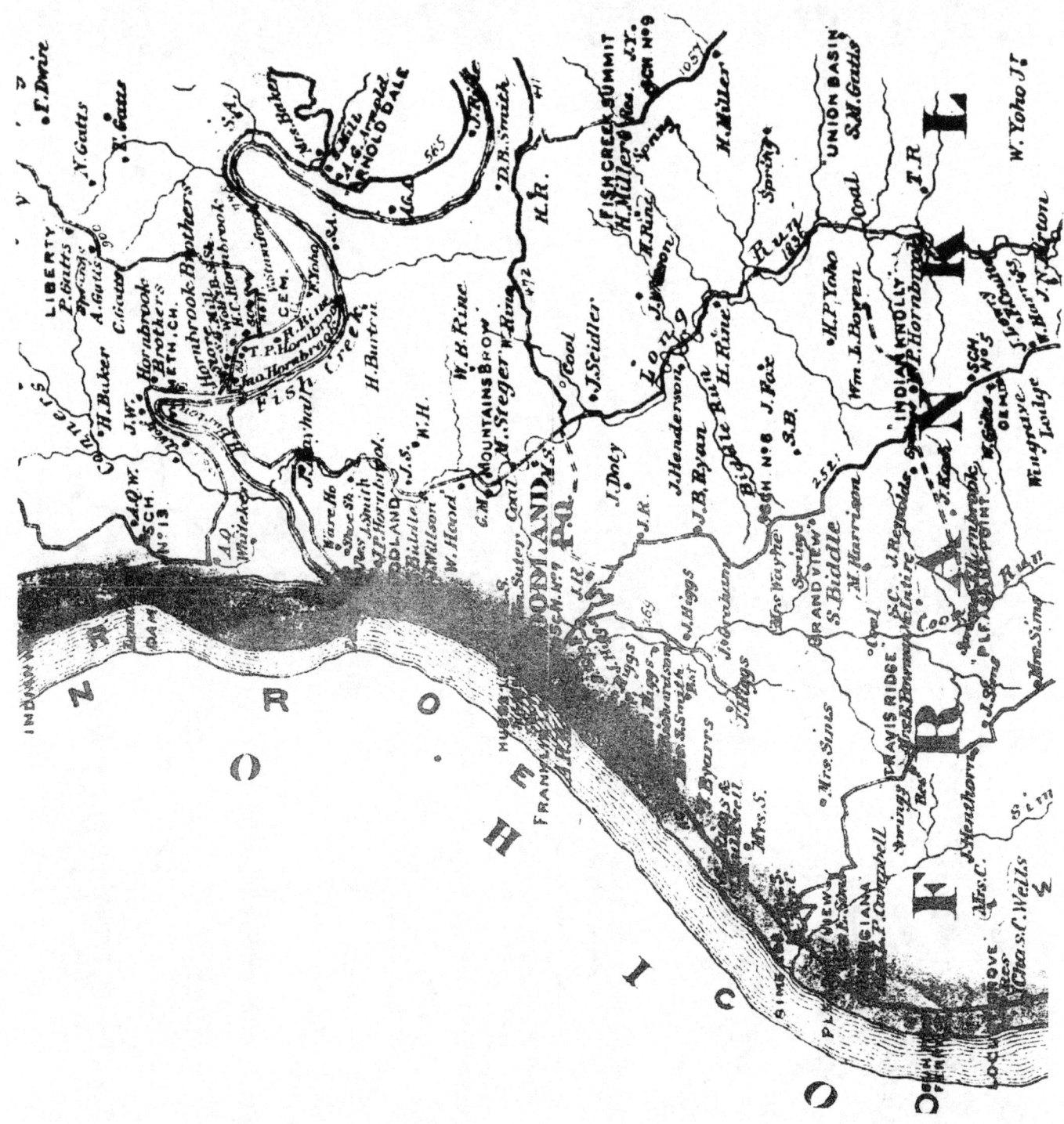

1871 MAP – MARSHALL CO. – MEADE TOWNSHIP – W. PART 1755

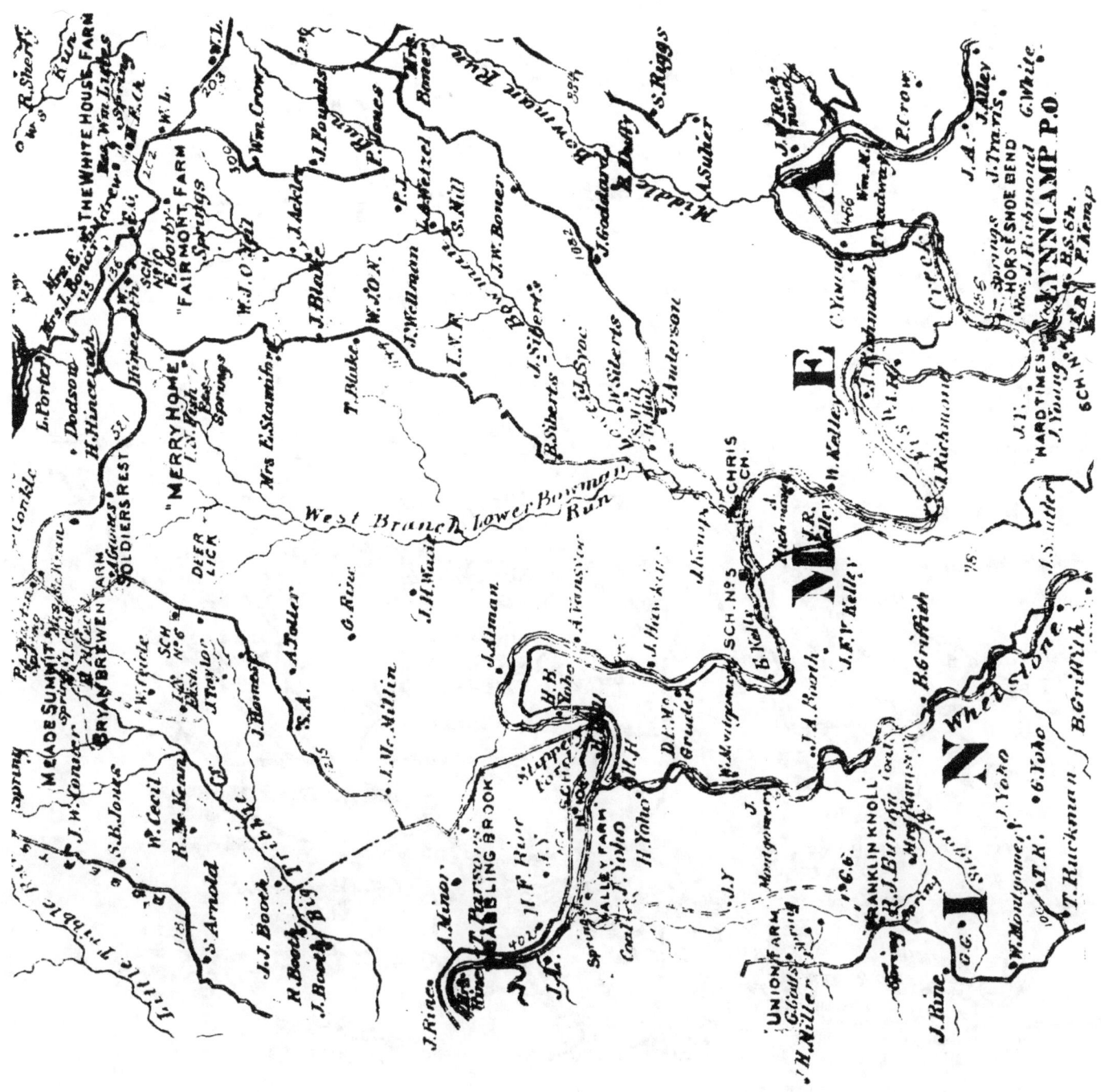

THE WHITE HOUSE FARM
FAIRMONT FARM
MERRY HOME
SOLDIERS REST
MEADE SUMMIT
BRYAN BREWEN FARM
DEER LICK
West Branch Lower Bowman Run
BABBLING BROOK
VALLEY FARM
UNION FARM
FRANKLIN KNOLL
HORSESHOE BEND
HARDYTIMES
LYNNCAMP P.O.

1756 1871 MAP – MARSHALL CO. – MEADE TOWNSHIP – E. PART

1871 MAP – MARSHALL CO. – CAMERON P.O. AREA   1757

S.S. Kittle
Todd
D. Buzzard
SCH. No. 2
T. Buzzard
Res.
Mrs. Strichlin
Mrs. Fry
R. Howard
B.S.
R. Dorsey
J.M. Howard
D. Mc. Cracken
J. Loudenslager
G.W. Thomp.
M. Barrel
Curtis
E. Dorsey
J. Grimes
G. Thompson
J. Thompson
Booher
C. Mc. Cracken
R. Dorsey
J.A. Chambers
G. Davis
J. Mc. Cracken
J.M.H.
J.A. Murphy
J.T.
J. Jones
B. Howard
S. Mellan
E. Dowler
J.T.
S. Ross
S. Howard
J.P.C. Hicks Est.
SCH No. 13
W. Mc. Conaughey
T.C.
J.W. Dowler
A. Wendt
J.M.H.
G. Kemp
Miss Chambers
A.C. Est.
J.A.C.
J.A. Chambers
T. Courtright
Mrs. Staley
T. Howard
SCH. No. 4
A. Wendt
W. Mathews
CEM.
CHRIS. CH.
SCH. No. 12
A. Chambers Est.
J. Mathews
D. Mc. Conaughy
M. Howard
J.M.
J. Mc. Cuskey
F.H. Woods
W.J. Davis
T. Fox
J. Riggle
R.R. Co.
FARMERS HOME
B.R. Harris
J. Harris Est.
S. Mc. Cuskey
C. Bonar
Wm. Marshall
W. Mathews
P. Morris
T.H. Genine, Est.
R.R. Co.
Wyatt
G.W. Low
Mrs. M. Fry
J. Quigley
Jas. C. Connelly
J. Turner
C. Harris
J.C.C.
Big Run
Mrs. Clouston
T.H.G. Est.
J. Reed
J. Lancaster
Jas. Reed
J. Sibert
B E R R Y
Four Mile Run
SCH. No. 14
T. Fox

1871 MAP – MARSHALL CO. – FRANKLIN TOWNSHIP – S. PART

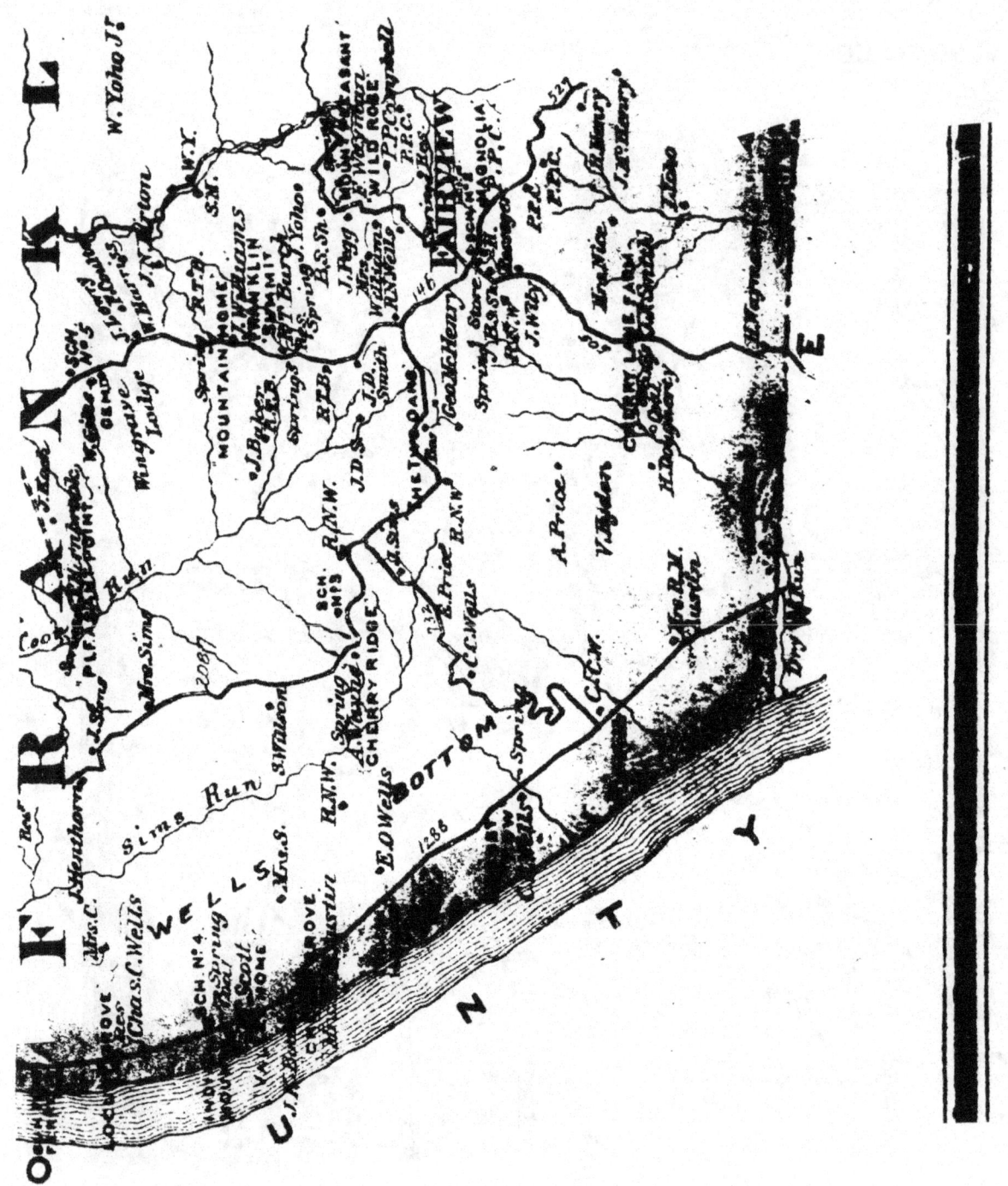

1871 MAP – MARSHALL CO. – LYNN CAMP P.O. AREA

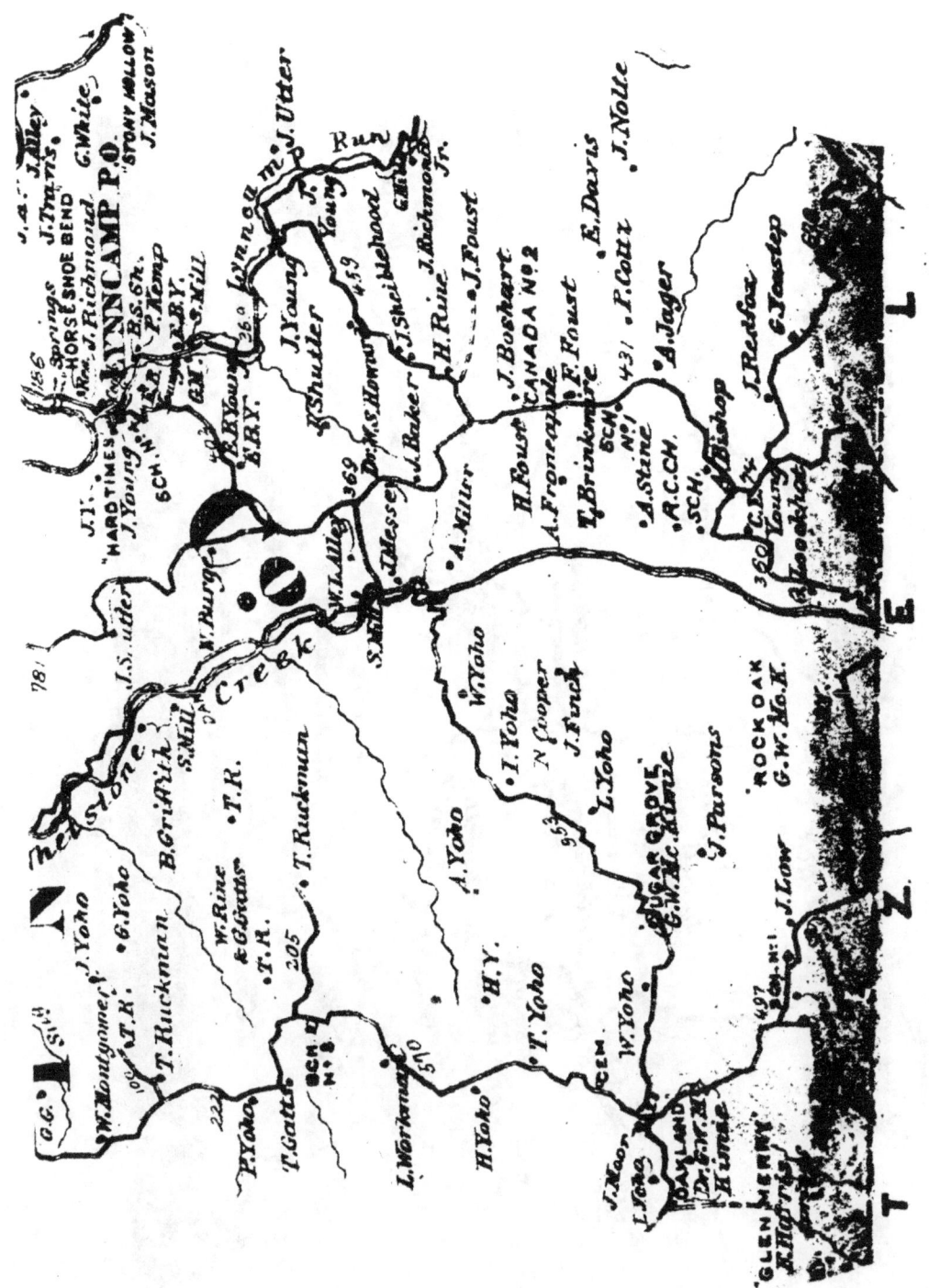

HORSESHOE BEND
STONY HOLLOW
HARDTIMES
CANADA No. 2
ROCK OAK
SUGAR GROVE
OAKLAND
GLEN MERRY
Creek

1760   1871 MAP – MARSHALL CO. – LIBERTY TOWNSHIP – W. PART

1871 MAP – MARSHALL CO. – LIBERTY TOWNSHIP – E. PART 1761

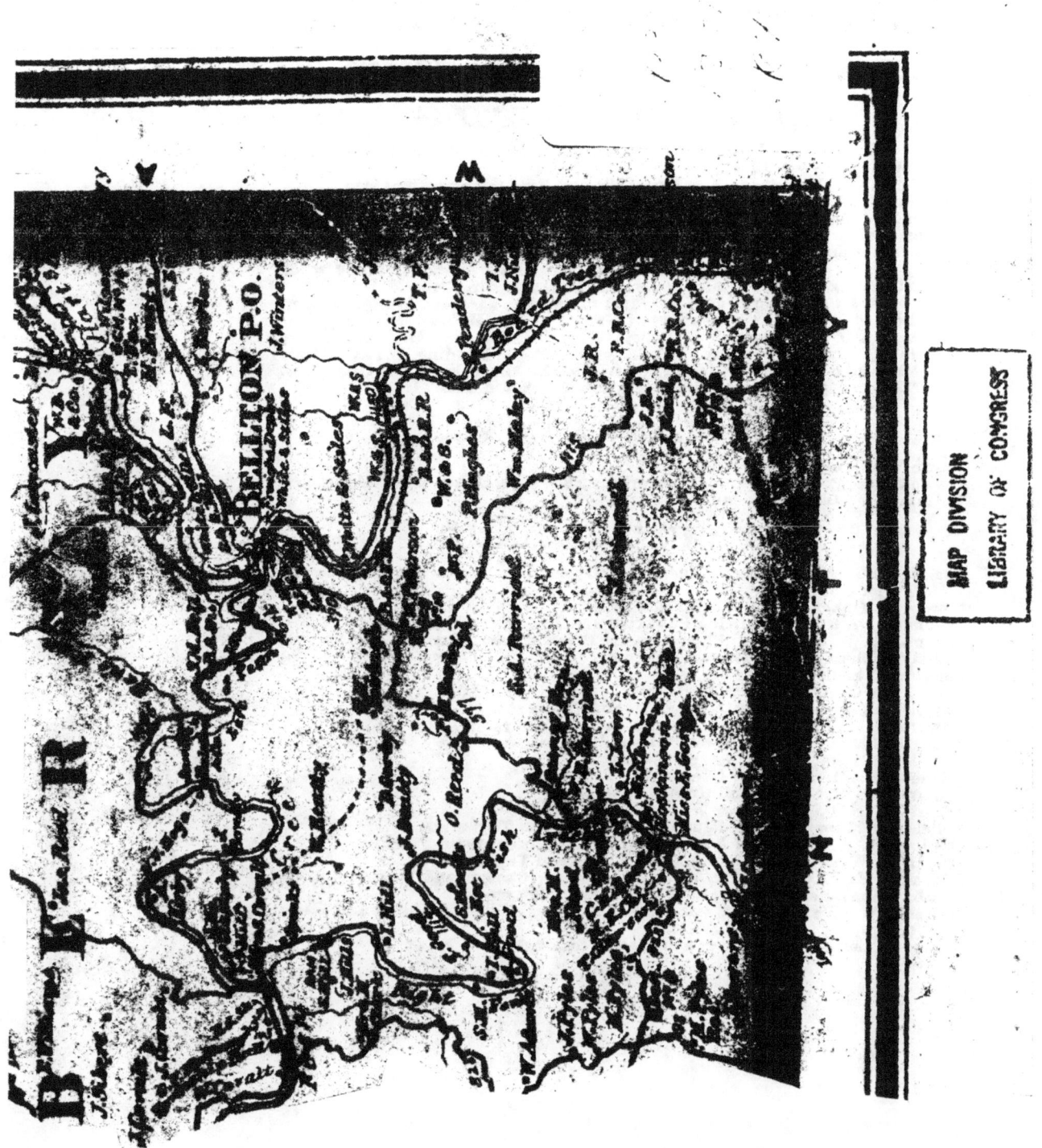

BUSINESS NOTICES.

HANCOCK COUNTY.

FREEMAN'S LANDING.

Anderson Thos & Co..Manufrs of Fire Brick Tile and Ground Fire Clay, "Anderson's Landing"

Campbell & Co..Manufrs of Fire Brick Tile and Fine Ground Fire Clay

Freeman W. B..Manufr of Fire Brick, Fire Clay and Tile, "Freeman's Landing." Res "Sloan's Station," Ohio

Hudson & Wilson..Manufrs of Fire Brick, Tile and Finely Ground Fire Clay

Magee & Wilson..Dealers in Genl Mdse, "Freeman's Landing"

Porter Anderson & Co..Propts "Kingston Fire Brick Works." Manufrs of Fire Brick and Tile of all Shapes and Sizes, also Fine Ground Fire Clay

Porter John & Co..Manufrs of Fire Brick of Square, Circular, Wedge or any Desired Shape. Every Variety of Tiles for Gas Houses, Oil Refineries, Stoves, Grates, Steam Boat Boilers, Fire Beds or any like purpose, and Finely Ground Fire Clay. Works at "Porter's Landing." Post Office, "Freeman's Landing." John Porter, Agt for the Sale of the Celebrated "Mt. Savage and Savage Mountain Fire Brick and Tiles"

HOLLIDAY'S COVE.

Brown W..Dealer in Genl Mdse

Cowan James P..Dealer in Genl Groceries, also Wagon Maker and Genl Repairer

Roberts Wm..Genl Blacksmith

NEW CUMBERLAND.

Borsell W. G..Music Dealer, Tuner and Repairer of Pianos and Organs, cor Taylor and Chesnut sts

Bowers C..Tinner, cor High and Fillmore sts

Beaumont Dr. G. L..Practicing Physician and Druggist, Chesnut st

Chapman B. W..Practicing Physician and Druggist, cor Pearl and Chesnut sts

Campbell John..Lumber Dealer, Water st

Colee C. C..Sadler, Chester st

Colee T. F..Cabinet Maker, Chester st

Daniels J. T..Dealer in Mdse, cor Pearl and Water sts

Edwards J. C..Blacksmith, cor Chester and Madison sts

Evans Jas. M. D..Carpenter, cor Pearl and Chester sts

Edie John..Pilot, cor Chester and Clay sts

Gibson J. H..Merchant, cor Chester and Pearl sts

Jenkins J. H. & S. B..Retail Grocers, Chester st

Lindsey Wm..Carpenter, cor Water and Harrison sts

Miller J. O..Propt of Stove Foundry, cor Water and Taylor sts

McClurg W. K..Manufr of Boots and Shoes, cor Chesnut and Pearl sts

Stewart G. W..Dealer in Genl Mdse, cor High and Taylor sts

Stevens B. H..Engine Builder and Machinist, cor Chester and Washington sts

Teesdale Wm..Retail Grocer, cor Fillmore and High sts

Thayer J. W..Wagon Maker and Propt of Planing Mill, cor Madison and Chester sts

Thayer Milton H..Brick Layer and Mason, Strait st

BUSINESS NOTICES.
HANCOCK COUNTY.

NEW MANCHESTER.

Allison J. W..Manufr of Agricultural Implements, "Champion Machine Works"
Andrews Robt..Physician and Surgeon, Main st
Beall H. C..Dealer in Dry Goods and Groceries, Market st
Burns Mrs. J. R..Propt Hotel, High st
Cain M..Dealer in Drugs, Medicines and Fancy Articles, High st
Donehoo Danl..Atty at Law, Market st
Durbin T..Genl Black-smith, Lynn st
Frank J. D..Tanner and Currier
Hobbs J. W. & Co..Dry Goods and Groceries, High st
Hunter J. S..Machinist, High st
Lloyd Thos..Tailor, Main st
Morrow Alex..Propt "Virginia House," Market st
Marshall Jas G..Atty at Law, High st
McFlanegin A..Recorder, High st
Moore S..Dealer in Dry Goods, High st
Melvin Jas..Dealer in Furniture, High st
Pugh Wm. H..Carpenter and Machinist, High st
Plattenburg J. W..Publisher "Hancock Courier," High st
Reilly J. W..Atty at Law, Wellsville, Ohio
Whims J..Clerk Circuit Court, High st
Wilson..Manufr Saddles and Harness, High st
Wilson S. W..Manufr Saddles and Harness, High st
Whitacre T. W..Propt "Whitacre House," Wellsville, Ohio
Yant D. H..Dealer in Drugs, Medicines and Hard-ware, High st

River Road, North of New Cumberland.

Atkinson & Shane..Manufrs of Fire Brick, Tile and Clay
Cullen M. M. & Bros..Manufrs of Fire Bricks, Tile and Fine Ground Fire Clay
Manypeny J. & A..Manufrs of Fire Brick, Furnace Lining, Tile and Fine Ground Fire Clay
Smith, Porter & Co..Propts of "Clifton Fire Brick Works"
Troup & Minor..Manufrs of Fire Brick, Tile and Fine Ground Fire Clay

River Road, South of New Cumberland.

Freeman J. L. & Co..Propts of Fire Brick Works
Moren John..Manufr of Fire Brick, Tile and Clay
Porter & Smith..Propts of "Black Horse Fire Brick Works,"
Smith, Porter & Co..Propts of Sewer Pipe and Terracotta Works

Butler Township.

Campbell James M..Manufacturer of Flour, Feed, &c
Carothers T. C..Teacher
Hamilton J. S..Manufacturer of Flour, Feed, &c
Ralston Thos. H..Manufacturer of Flour, Feed, &c, "Ralston Mills"

Clay Township.

Foster Joseph..Dealer in Mdse, Blair P. O
Stewart Geo. W..Propt of Vineyard, "Hardin's Run"

Grant Township.

Hudson John & Son..Dealers in Flag Stone, near Hamilton
Inman David..Genl Grocery Dealer, cor Water and Washington sts, Hamilton
Mahan John L..Manufr of and Dealer in Lumber, Lath, Flour and Feed and Grower of Wool, Grain, Fruit, &c, also Steam Boat and Barge Builder, "Brooklyn Mills"
Reilly J. W..Atty, Wellsville
Whitacre T. W..Propt "Whitacre House," Wellsville

Poe Township.

Allison J. Miller, "Foster's Mill"
Campbell J...Paper Maker, near Woolen Factory
Ferguson T..Manufr Fire Brick, near Ohio River
Ferguson John R..Dealer in Woolen Goods, Woolen Facty

1764 1871 MAP – HANCOCK COUNTY – FREEMANS LANDING – N. PART

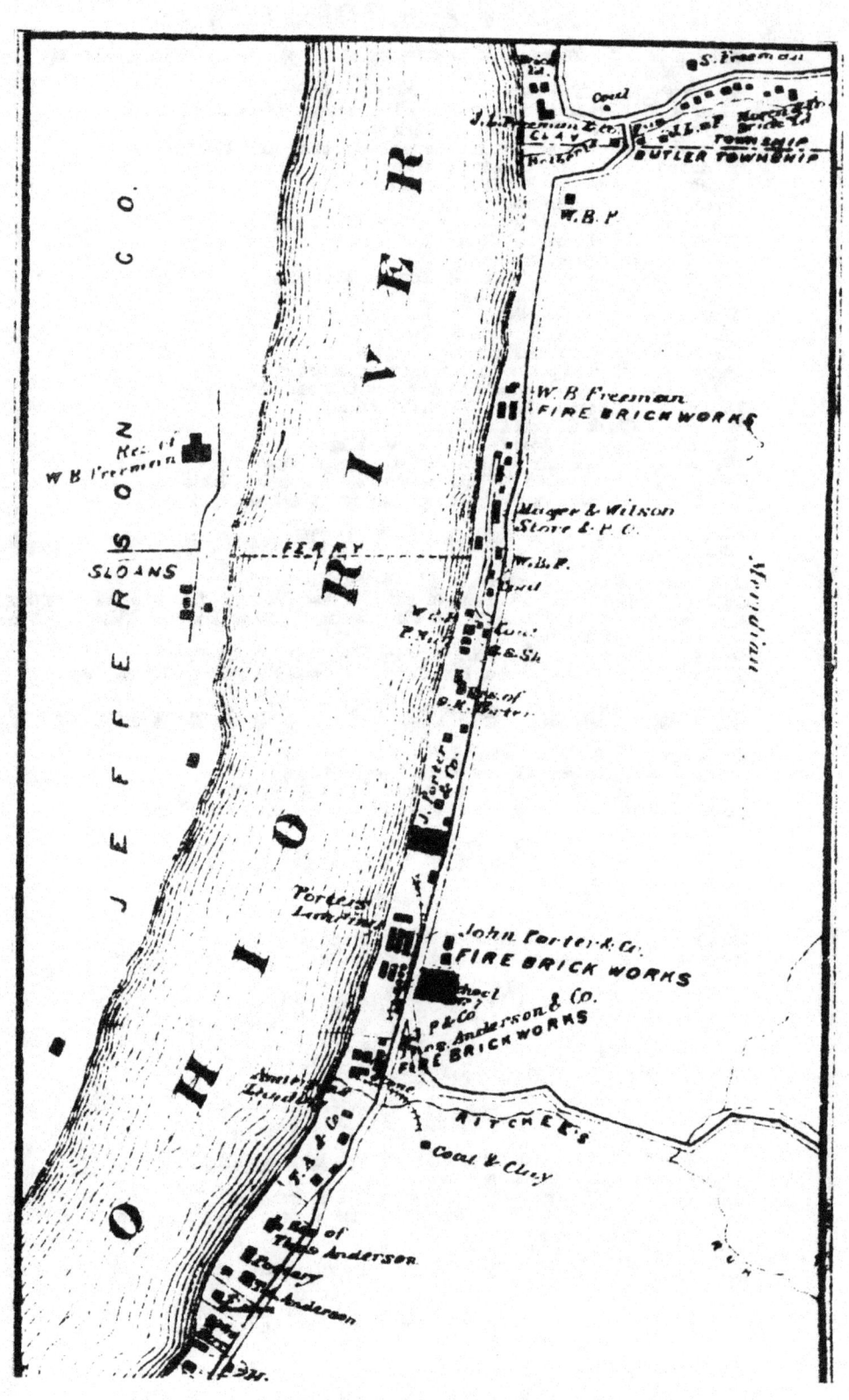

1871 MAP – HANCOCK CO. – FREEMANS LANDING – S. PART   1765

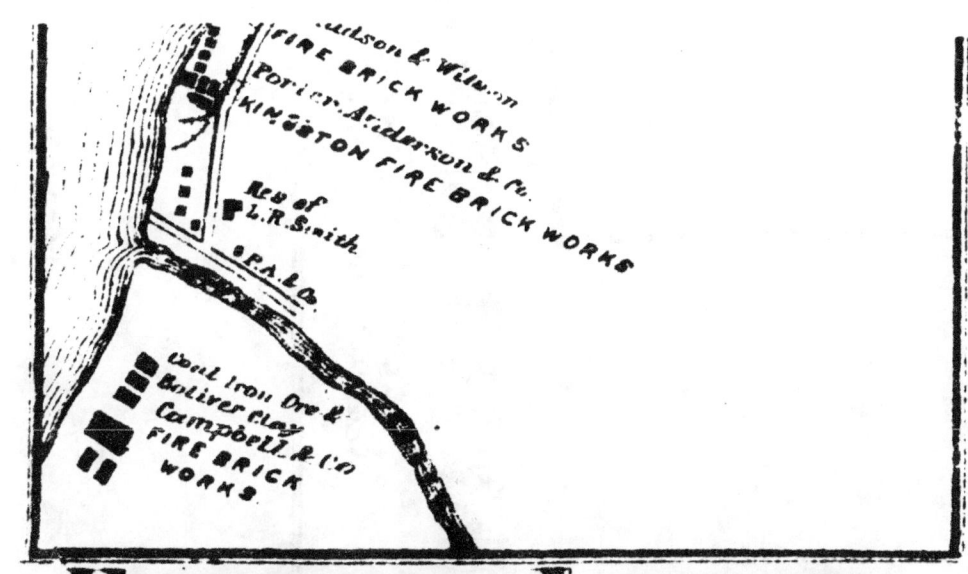

1766   1871 MAP – HANCOCK COUNTY – NEW CUMBERLAND – N. PART

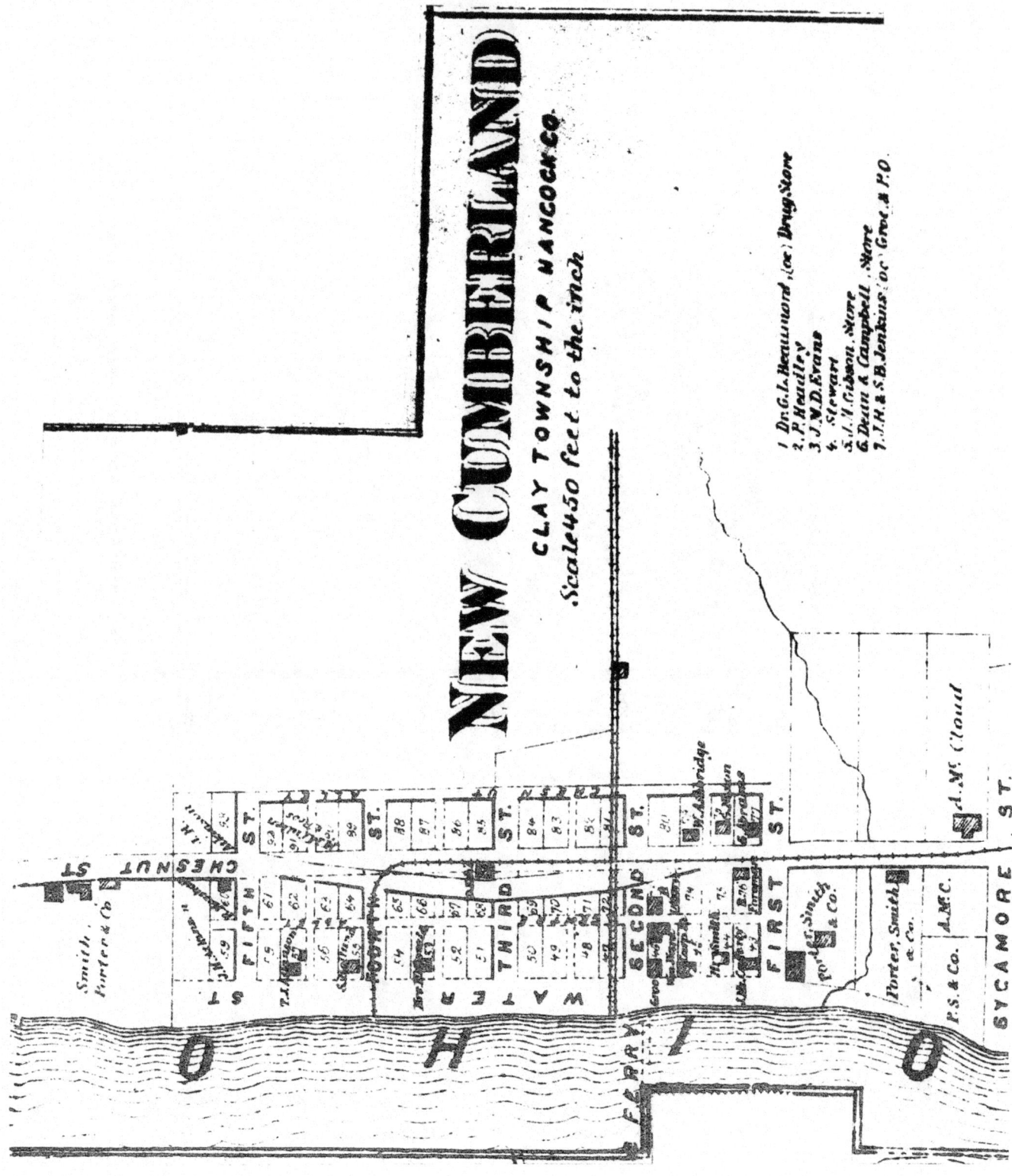

1871 MAP – HANCOCK CO. – NEW CUMBERLAND – MIDDLE PART   1767

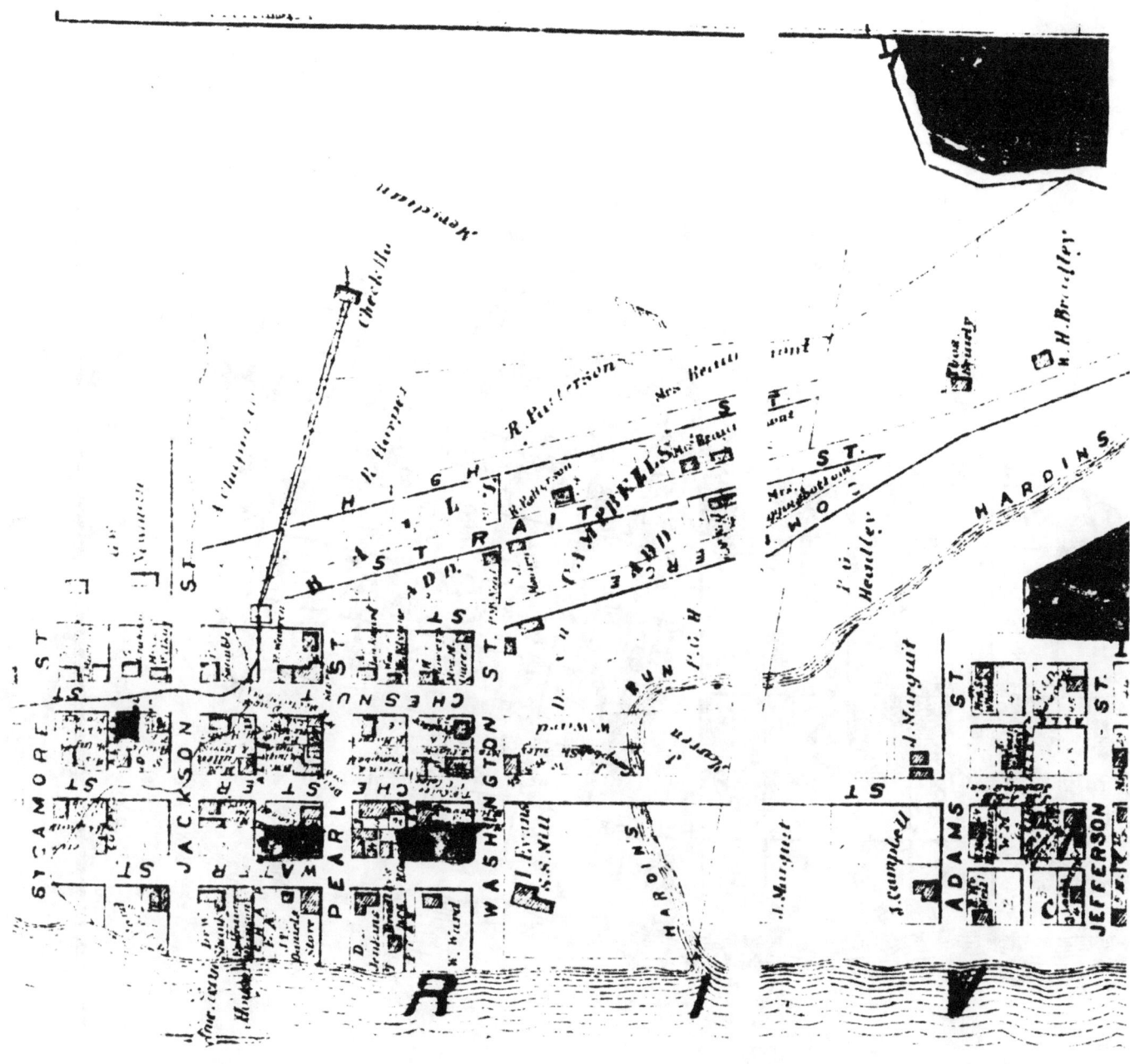

1768   1871 MAP – HANCOCK COUNTY – NEW CUMBERLAND – S. PART

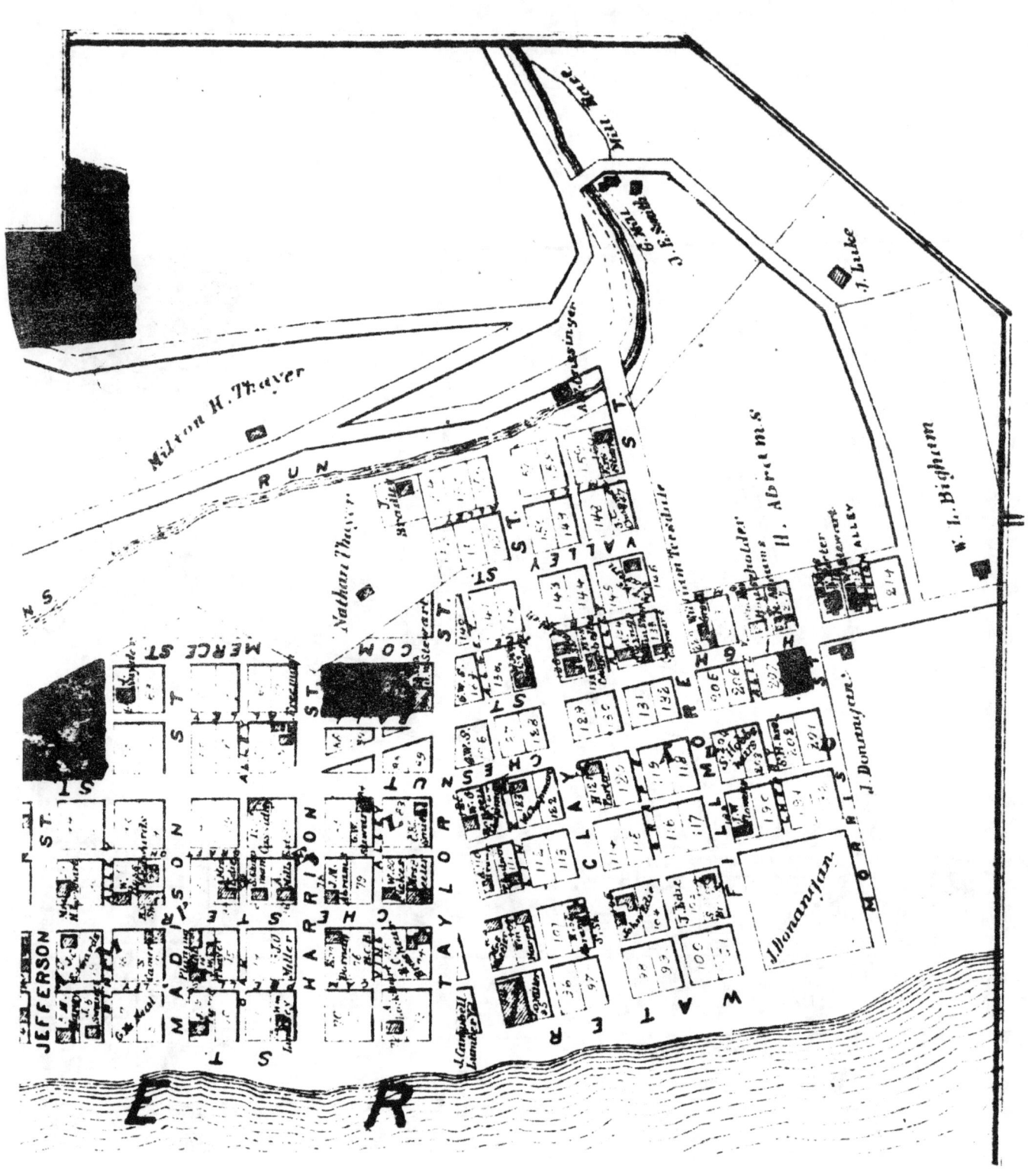

1871 MAP – HANCOCK CO. – NEW MANCHESTER   1769

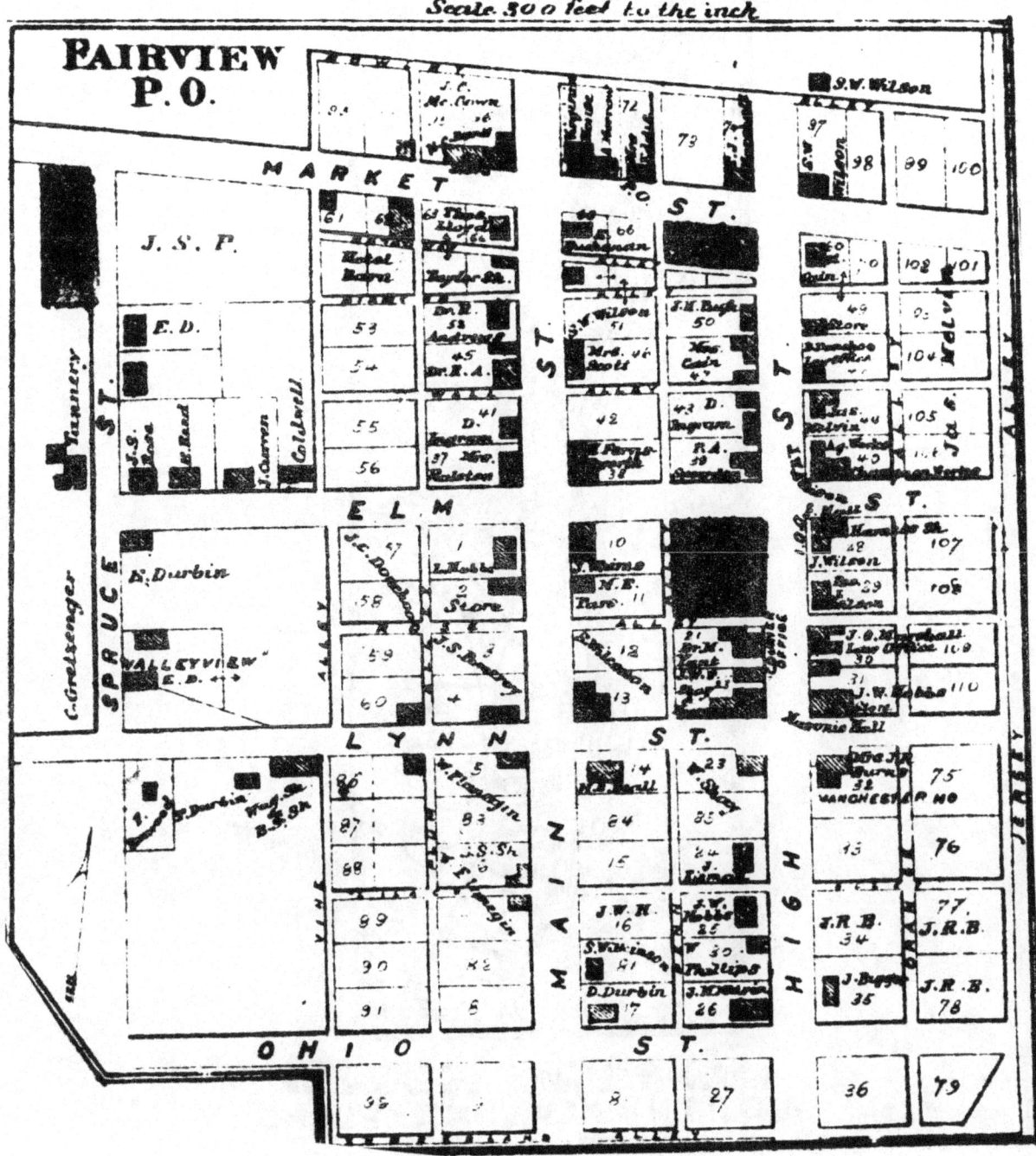

1770   1871 MAP – HANCOCK CO. – RIVER ROAD N. OF NEW CUMBERLAND

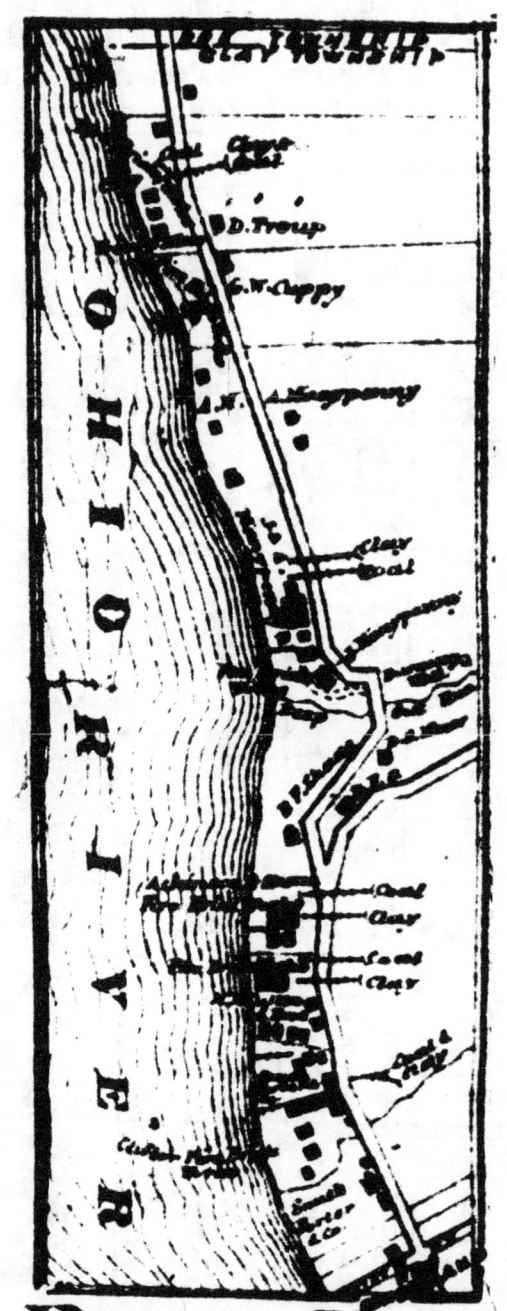

1871 MAP – HANCOCK CO. – RIVER ROAD – S. OF NEW CUMBERLAND   1771

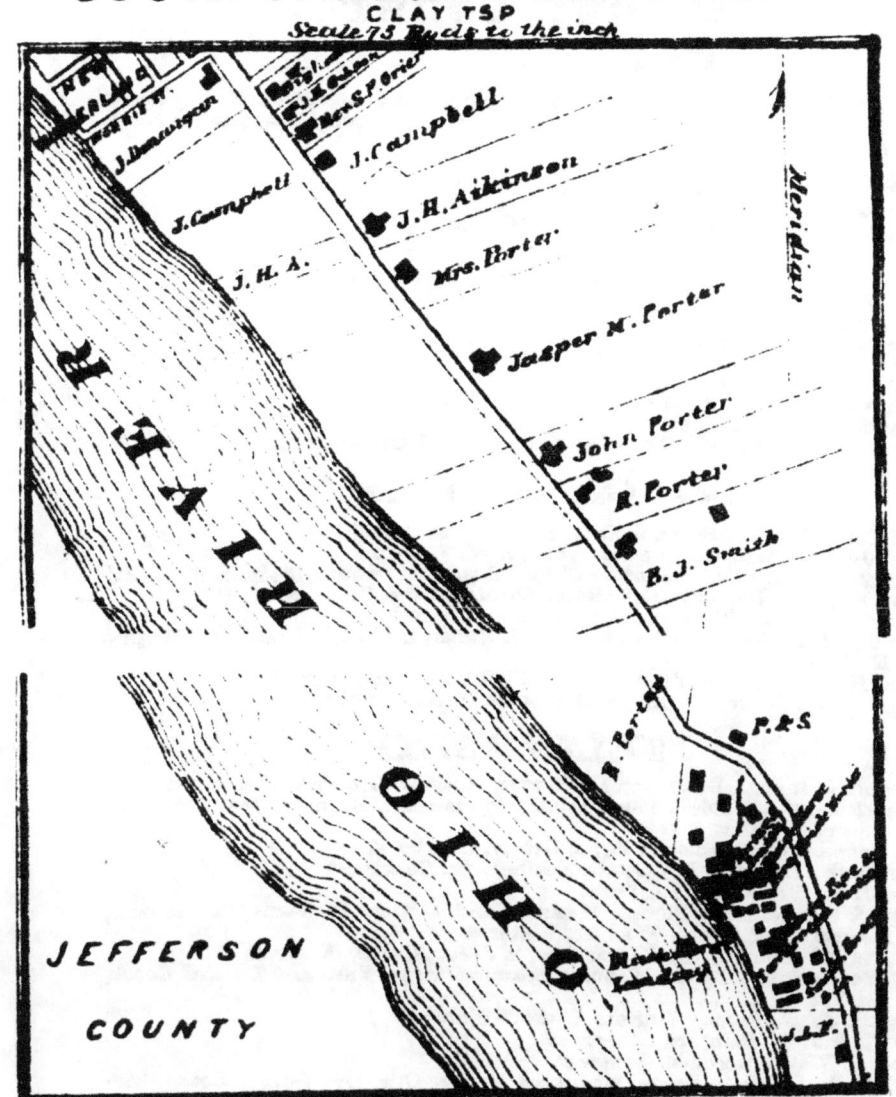

BUSINESS NOTICES, BROOKE COUNTY.

Bethany

Anderson W. H..Merchant Tailor and Dealer in Foreign and Staple Dry Goods, Groceries, Hats, Boots, Shoes, Carpets, Bacon, Flour, Ready-made Clothing, &c. Main st
Curtis J. E..Dealer in Genl Mdse, Main st
Lauck J. T..Propt "Bethany House," Main st
Pendleton W. K..Pres of "Bethany College"
Smith A. C..Publisher of "Guardian," Main st

Buffalo Township

Allen Albert..Financial Agt "Bethany College"
Bowman John..Dealer in Coal
Carnahan Thos..Propt Short Creek Coal Bank
Elliott Geo..Producer of Coal
Forbes & Carmichael..Coal Dealers
Shrimplin Wm. G..Cooper
Trimble Samuel..Propt "Short Creek House," and Dealer in Produce, Grain, &c

Cross Creek Township.

Antill Benj..Propt of Saw and Grist Mill, "Cross Creek"
Archer James..Farmer and Stock Grower, W. P. Twp
"Edgington Bridge Co"..Manufrs of Rail Road and County Bridges, N. W. P.
Fowler Wm. M..Dealer in Dry Goods, Groceries, &c', "Fowler's P. O"
Hindman Andrew..Black-smith, "Harmon's Creek"
Miller & Polen..Manufrs of all kinds of Lumber, including Lath and Shingles, N. W. P
Ryland Hugh P..Propt of Saw and Grist Mill, "Harmon's Creek"
Strong Samuel & Sons..Manufrs of Brooms, "Cross Creek".

WELLSBURG.

Applegate J. & Son..Dealers in Dry Goods, Notions, Groceries, &c, Water st
Barclay & Lloyd..Wholesale and Retail Grocers and Dealers in Flour, Grain and Bacon, Water st
Bentz Casper..Wholesale and Retail Grocer, Charles st
Barth Hugh..Dealer in Dry Goods, Notions, &c, Charles st
Cooper J. M..Physician, Yankee st
Everett & Blankensops..Plough Manufrs and Dealers in Farm Implements, Hard-ware, Produce, Wool &c, Water st
"First National Bank"..A. Kuhn, Pres, S. Jacob, Cashr, Water st
Gould, Pearce & Co..Cotton Manufrs, Seamless Bags, Yarn and Twisted Goods, Fleet st
Gelsthorpe John..Propt "Virginia House," Water st
Hagen T. & J. B..Painters, Liberty st
Haeemer C. W..Tobacconist, Water st
Kirker A. P..Dealer in Drugs, Medicines, Paints, Oils, Dye Stuffs, Books, Stationery, &c, Water st
Lloyd Thos. M..Variety Goods and Notions, Water st
Lewis Job, Jr..Dealer in Agricultural Implements, Grain, Fruit, Seeds, &c, Water st
Lloyd J. D..Manufr and Dealer in all kinds of Furniture and Cabinet Ware, Water st
Moore E. H..Practicing Physician, Charles st
Russell G. W..Teacher. Res Charles st
Tarr Campbell..Dealer in Dry Goods, Groceries, &c, cor Charles and Liberty sts
Wells Milton..County Supt of Schools. Res Yankee st

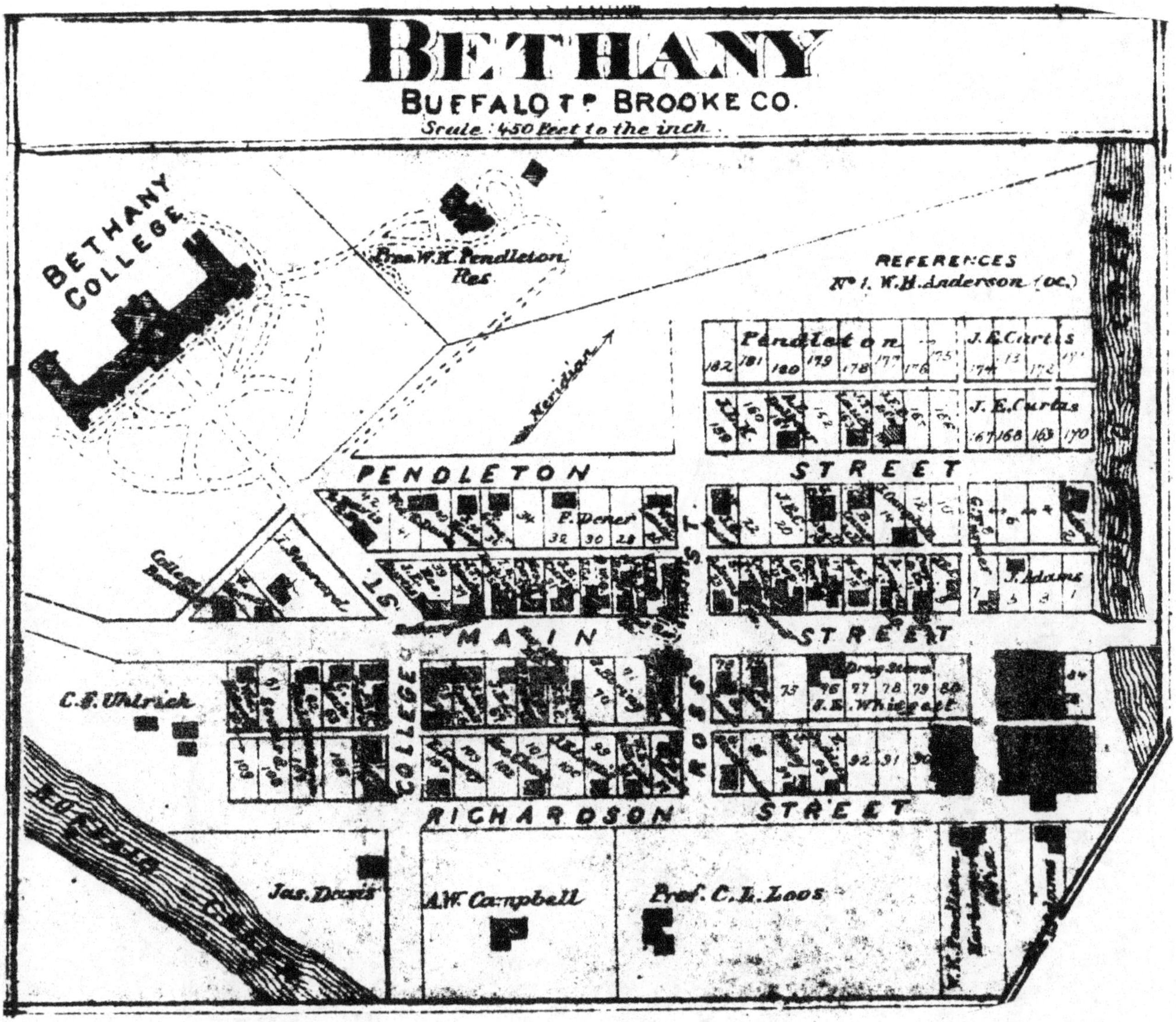

1871 MAP – BROOKE CO. – BETHANY   1773

BUFFALO TP. BROOKE CO.
Scale: 450 Feet to the inch
BETHANY COLLEGE
Pres. W. K. Pendleton Res.
REFERENCES
No. 1. W. H. Anderson (oc.)
Meridian
PENDLETON STREET
MAIN STREET
RICHARDSON STREET
COLLEGE ST.
ROSS ST.
J. E. Curtis
P. Dener
J. Adams
Drug Store
C. F. Uhlrich
Jas. Davis
A. W. Campbell
Prof. C. L. Loos
W. K. Pendleton
BUFFALO CREEK

1774   1871 MAP – BROOKE CO. – EDGINGTON STATION

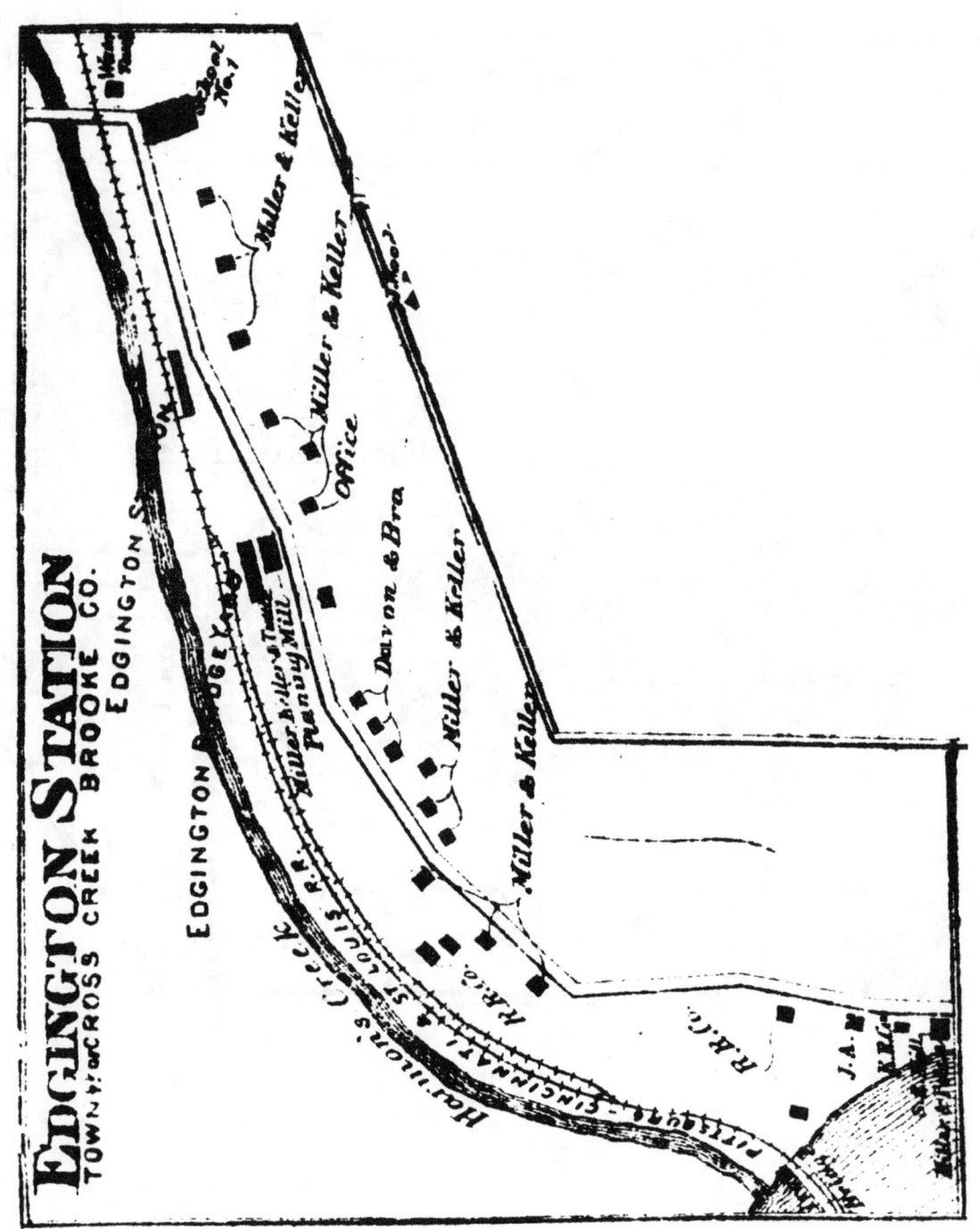

1871 MAP – BROOKE CO. – FOWLER'S P.O.

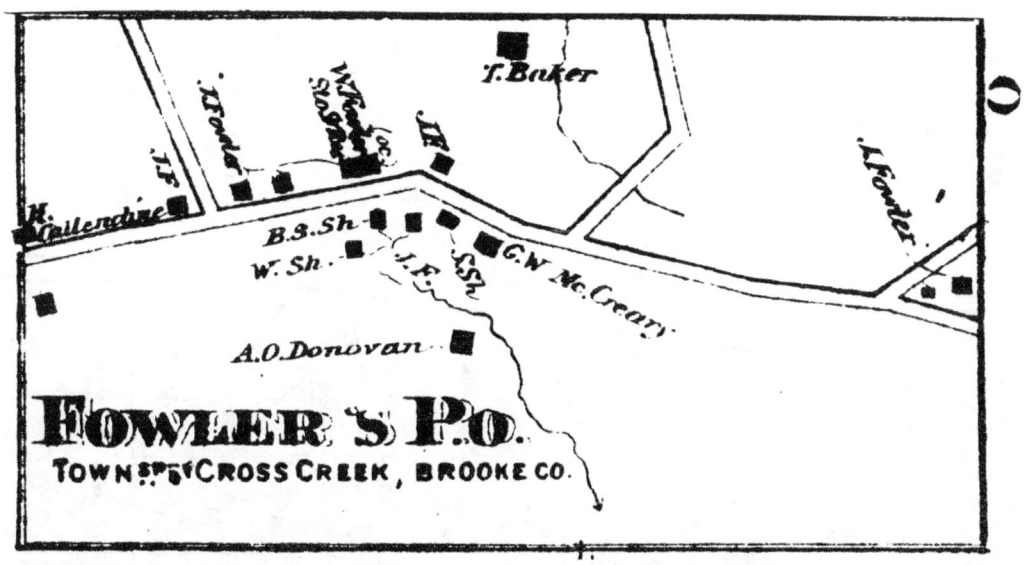

T. Baker
B.S.Sh
W. Sh.
G.W. Mc.Creary
A.O.Donovan
TOWNSP. OF CROSS CREEK, BROOKE CO.

1776   1871 MAP – BROOKE CO. – WELLSBURG – N. PART

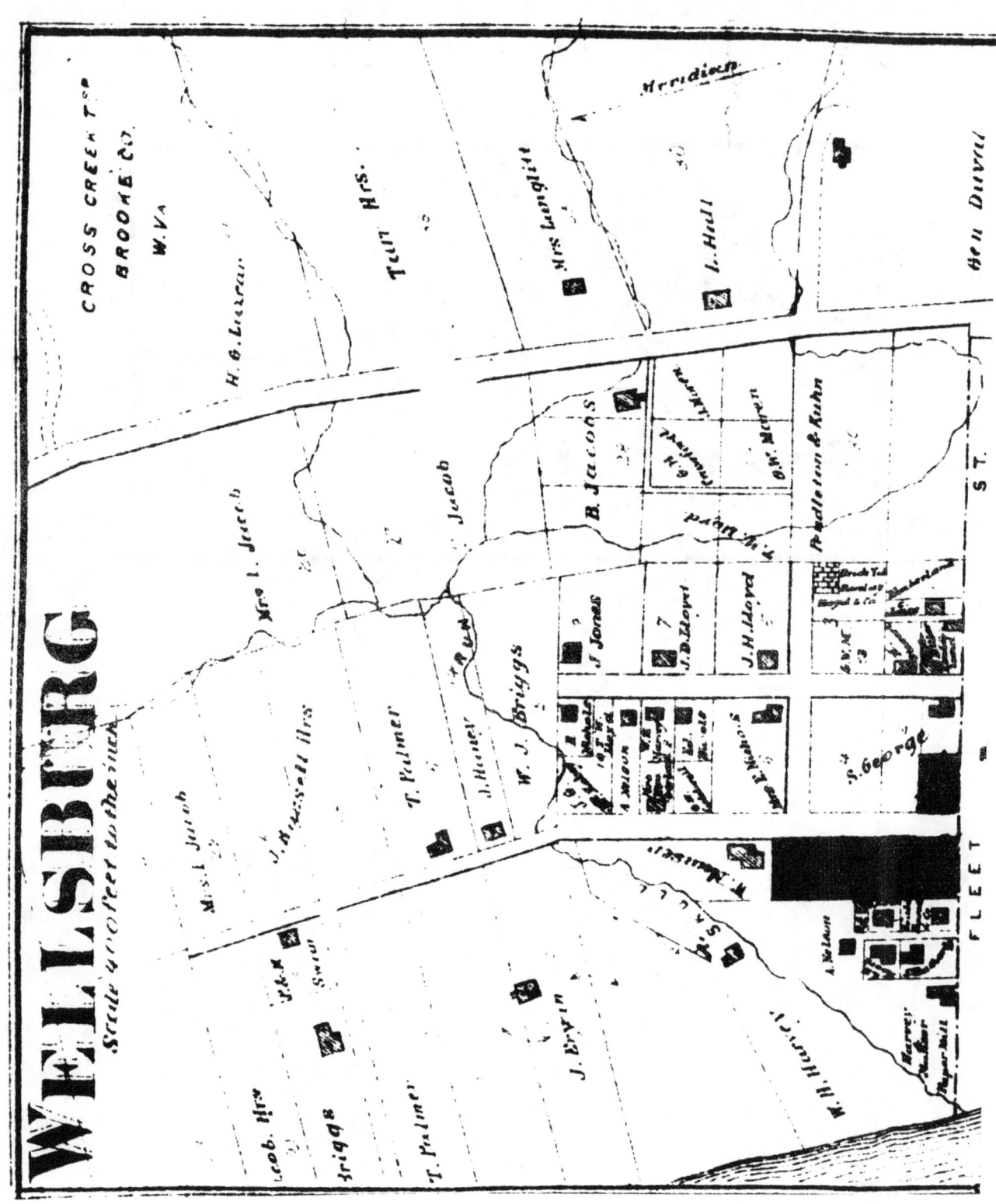

CROSS CREEK T.P
W.VA
Meridian
H. G. Lazear
Tell Hrs.
Mrs Langlitt
I. Hall
B. Jacobs
Jacob
J. Jones
J. D. Lloyd
J. H. Lloyd
Pendleton & Kuhn
W. J. Briggs
T. Palmer
R. George
J. Erwin
Swan
Briggs
T. Palmer
FLEET
ST.

1871 MAP – BROOKE CO. – WELLSBURG – MIDDLE PART 1777

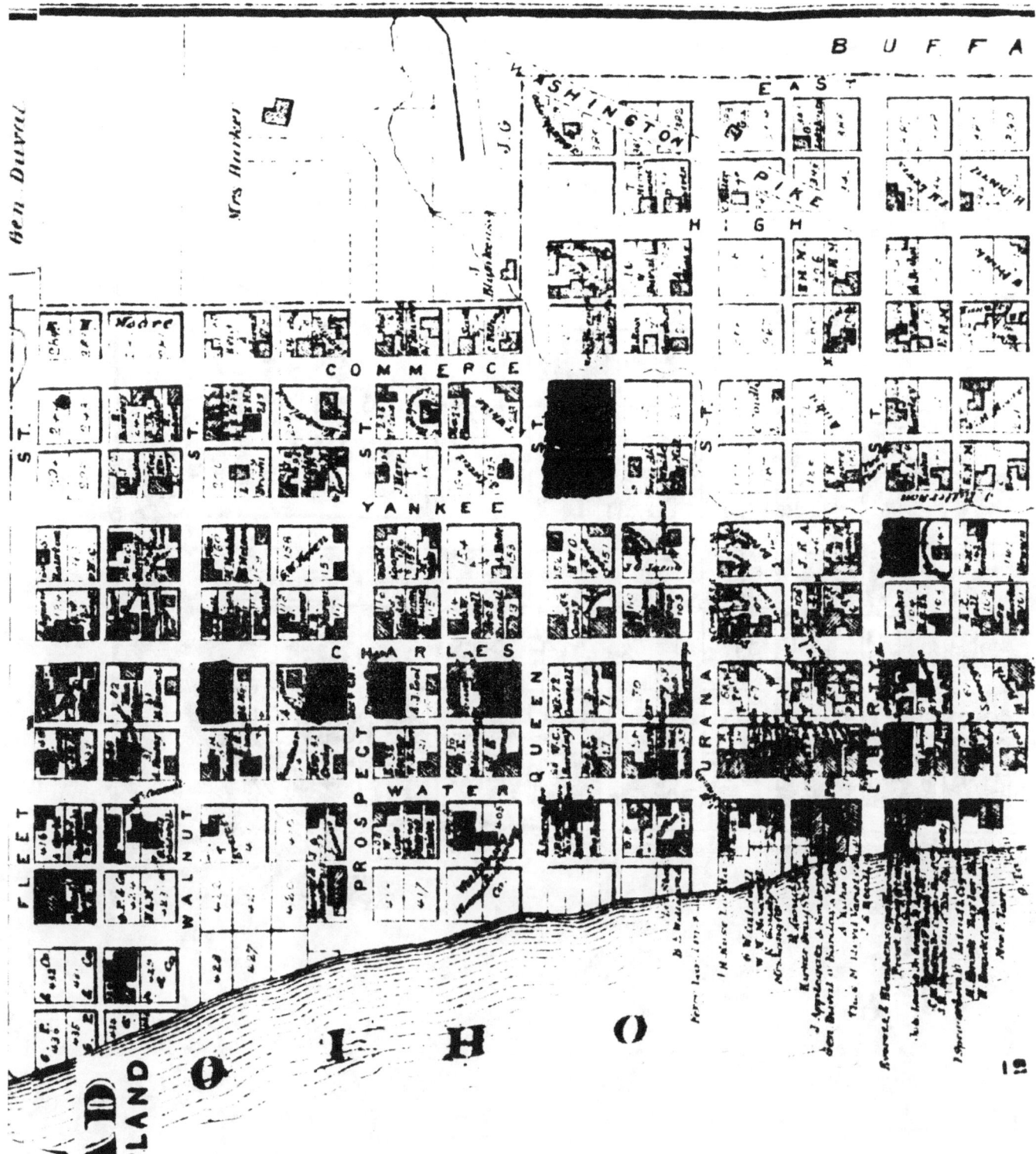

BUFFA
EAST
WASHINGTON
PIKE
HIGH
COMMERCE
YANKEE
CHARLES
WATER
FLEET
WALNUT
PROSPECT
QUEEN
URANA
LIBERTY
ST.
Ben Duvall
Mrs Hukes
OHIO
LAND
19

1778   1871 MAP – BROOKE CO. – WELLSBURG – S. PART

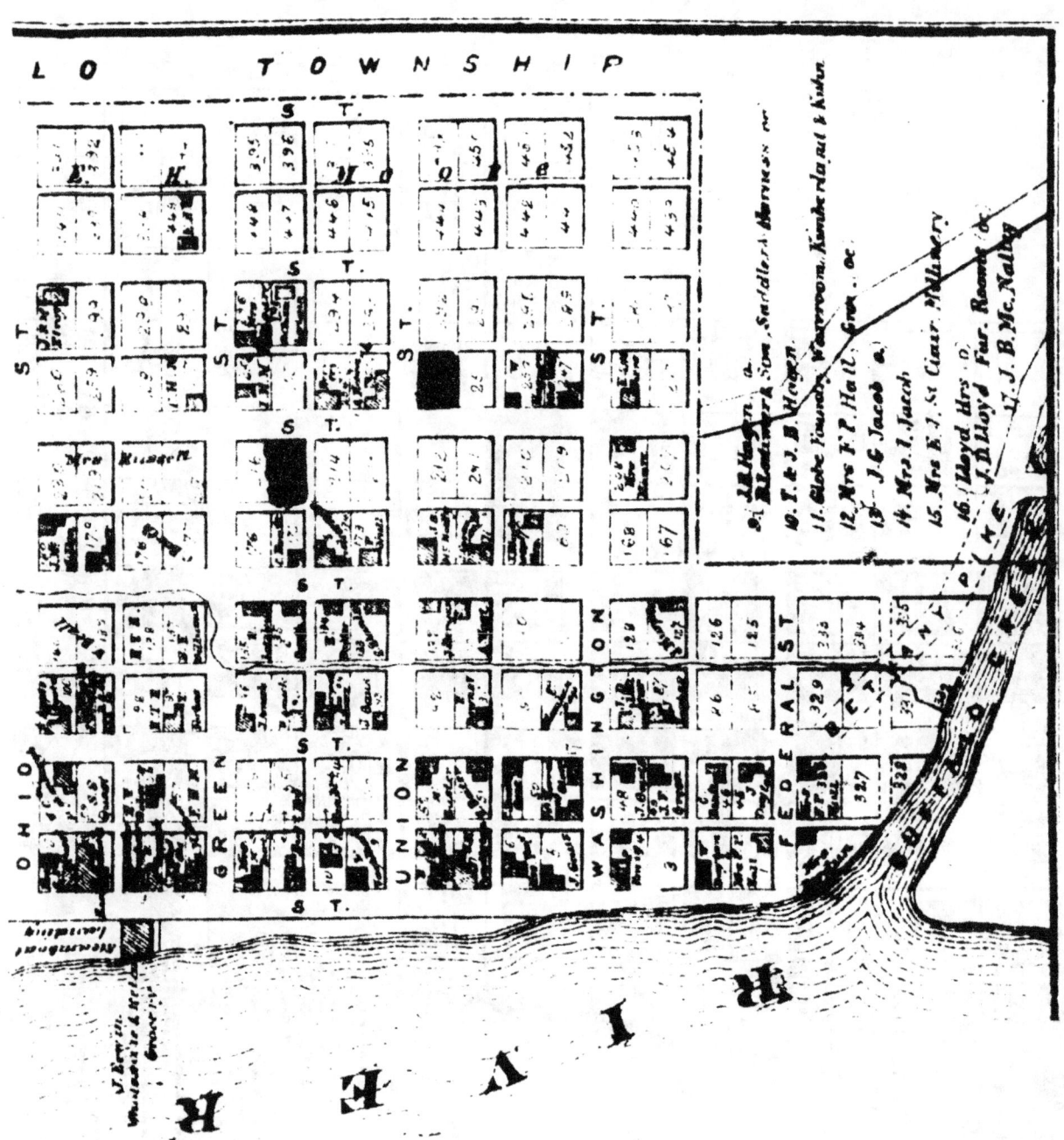

TOWNSHIP
OHIO
GREEN
UNION
WASHINGTON
FEDERAL ST
10. T. & J. B. Hogan
12. Mrs F.P. Hall
13. J.G. Jacob
14. Mrs I. Jacob
15. Mrs E.J. St Clair Millinery
17. J. B. Mc.Nally
R I V E R

OHIO COUNTY.
Wheeling City, and Triadelphia, & Ritchie Townships.

Ball, J. M..Gardener, Pleasant Valley
Bechtol, ? L..Manufacturer and Dealer in Flour, Feed, &c., also Dealer in Ice, Dealer in Dry Goods, Groceries, Crockery, Hardware, Pleasant Valley
Blayney, Jno..Tin-ware, Boots, Shoes and General Merchandise, Roney Point
Carney, R. & Co..Distillers, National Pike, near "Four Mile House," Distillery No. 3
Chambers, W. T..Dealer in Dry Goods, Groceries, Boots, Shoes, Queens-ware, Hard-ware and General Merchandise, Elm Grove Station
Du Bois, ? ? ..Secretary and Superintendent of Belmont Nail Works, ?s Leatherwood
Fr?..?armer and Grape Grower, "Ritchie Township"
Guenrie, Jno. P..President Wheeling Nail Co., res Leatherwood
Harvey, Jno. C..Insurance Agent, office Wheeling, res "Walnut Ridge"
Hodgson, J. P..Dealer in General Merchandise, Watches, Clocks, and Jewelry, also Postmaster and Agent for the Hempfield R R Co, also Agent for Seiberling's "Excelsior" Self Raking, Dropping, Reaping or Mowing Machine, also the Thomas Sulky Hay Rake, "Wheeler's Thresher and Cleaning Machine," and General Agent for the Cleveland Agricultural Works, Triadelphia, W.Va
Hopkins, E. L..Dealer in Dry Goods, Groceries, Queensware and General Merchandise, also Postmaster and Agent for Hempfield R R Co
Huss, Jno. Z..Gardener and Grape Grower, on County Line "Summit Farm"
Hupp, Jno. C..Physician and Surgeon, office N. W cor. 5th and Quincy St., Wheeling
Hornbrook, Thos..Dealer in Real Estate, office No. 1185 Main St., city res. No. 70 East St., country res. "Bellvue Retreat"
Heimberger, A..propt "Virginia House," Roney Point
Kober, Fred..Dairyman and Dealer in Milk, near Wheeling
Lewis & Woodmansee..propts of Grant House, Wheeling
Luke, Robt..propt Excelsior Sale and Livery Stables, also Dealer in Ice, Quincy St. bet. Market and Fourth St. Wheeling
Loring, A..Secretary Benwood Iron Works, res "Monument Place" Elm Grove
Montgomery, J. B..Gardener and Grape Grower, "Pleasant View" near County Line
McCabe, R. A..Wholesale Druggist, Wheeling, res Leatherwood
O'Keefe, Jno..Dealer in Horses, res Pleasant Valley
Porter, Wm..Dealer in Clean Coal, Nut and Block, res Pleasant Valley
Roettger, A..propt "Elm Grove House," Elm Grove
Steenrod, Geo. W..Farmer and Coal Merchant, res Pleasant Valley
Schellhase, Geo..Dealer in Ice, Pleasant Valley
Seabright, Henry..Wagon Maker and Ironer and General Black-smith, Roney Point
Storer, J. H..Physician and Surgeon, Triadelphia Borough
Smith, J. F..Manufacturer and Dealer in Flour, Feed, etc., "Elm Grove"
Stooch, Peter..Dealer in Hard, Nut and Clean Coal, near Pleasant Valley
Stoman, Wm..propt "Four Mile House," National Pike
Weiss, Jno..Huckster and Produce Dealer, Triadelphia Borough
Wheeler, Louis..Dealer in Dry Goods, Groceries and General Merchandise, also Manufacturer of Segars Factory, No. 15 Triadelphia Borough
Wagenknht, L..Dairyman and Dealer in Milk, "Caldwells Run"
Yacke, A..Contractor and Builder, res Fulton

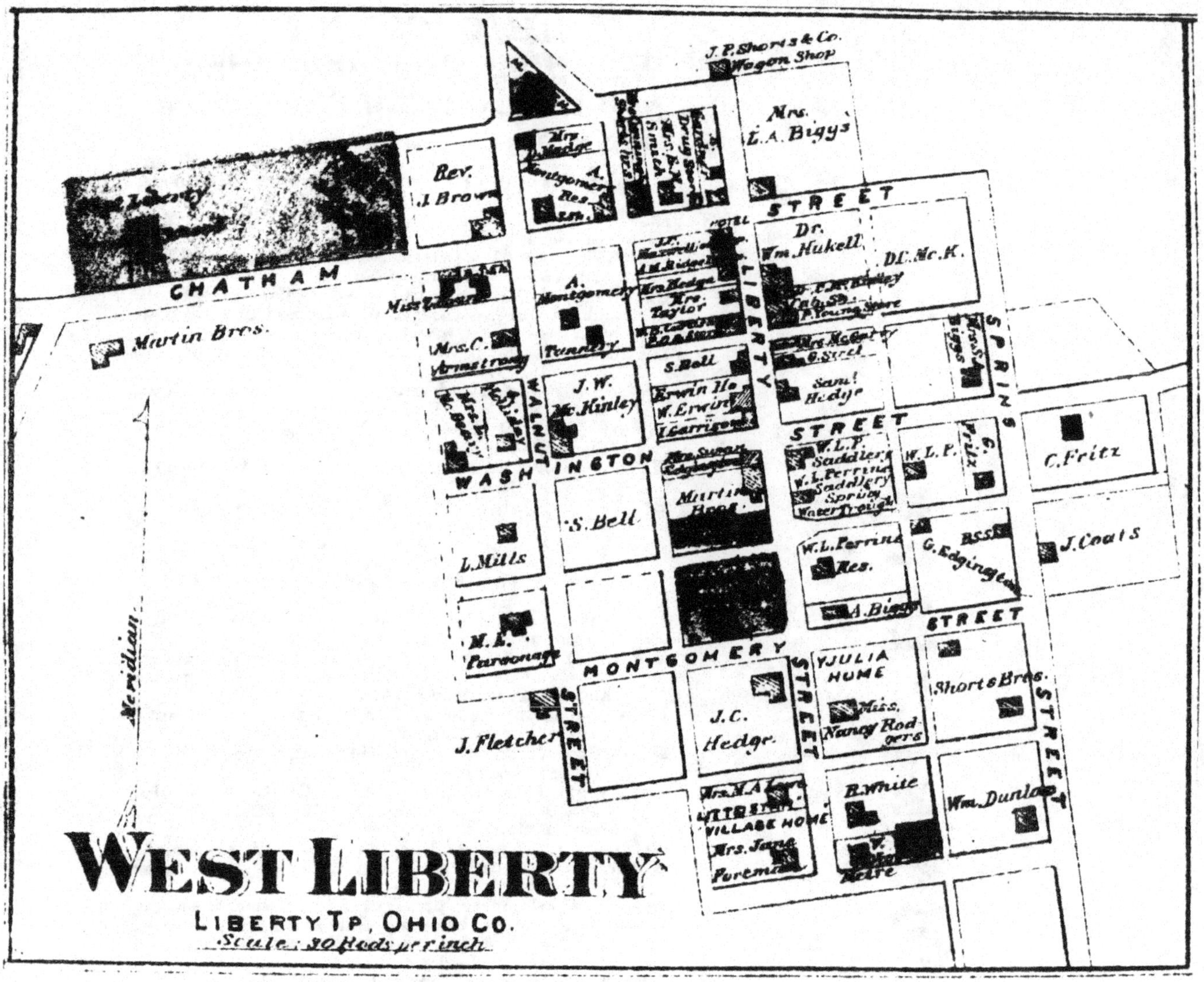

1871 MAP – OHIO CO. – WEST LIBERTY & BUSINESS NOTICES

WEST LIBERTY
Liberty Tp, Ohio Co.
Scale: 20 Rods per inch

BUSINESS NOTICES.

West Liberty.

Brisland Thomas..Dealer in Dry Goods and Groceries, on "Castleman Run"
Curtis W. B. & Son..Dealers in Dry Goods, Groceries, &c
Crago F. H..Principal of "Normal School"
Dunlap S..Nursery-man, Liberty T'w'p
Hukill Wm..Physician, Liberty st
Kelley S. H..Physician, Montgomery st
McKinley John W..Repairing Furniture, Walnut st
Maxwell J. C..Prop't of Hotel
Montgomery A..Tanner and Currier, Montgomery st
Perrine Wm. L..Saddler and Harness Maker
Ridgely A. M..Dealer in Dry Goods, Groceries, &c, Liberty st
Shorter J. E..Dealers in Dry Goods, Groceries, Hard-ware, &c
Young P..Dry Goods Merchant, Tailoring, &c, Liberty st

OHIO CO.

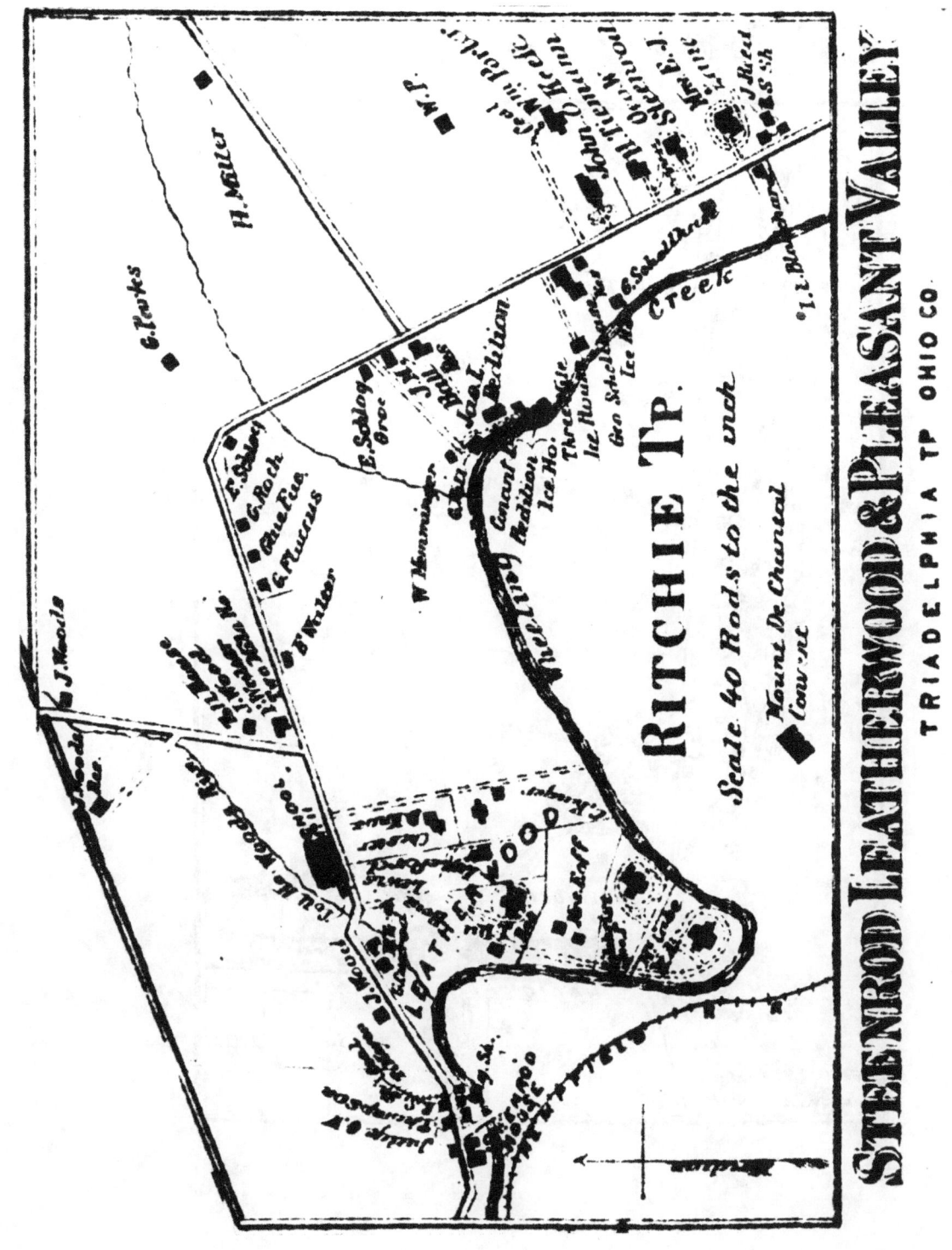
STEENROD LEATHERWOOD & PLEASANT VALLEY
TRIADELPHIA TP OHIO CO.
RITCHIE TP.
Scale 40 Rods to the inch
Mount De Chantal Convent
Wheeling Creek
H. Miller
G. Parks

1871 MAP – OHIO CO. – ELM GROVE STATION & P.O.

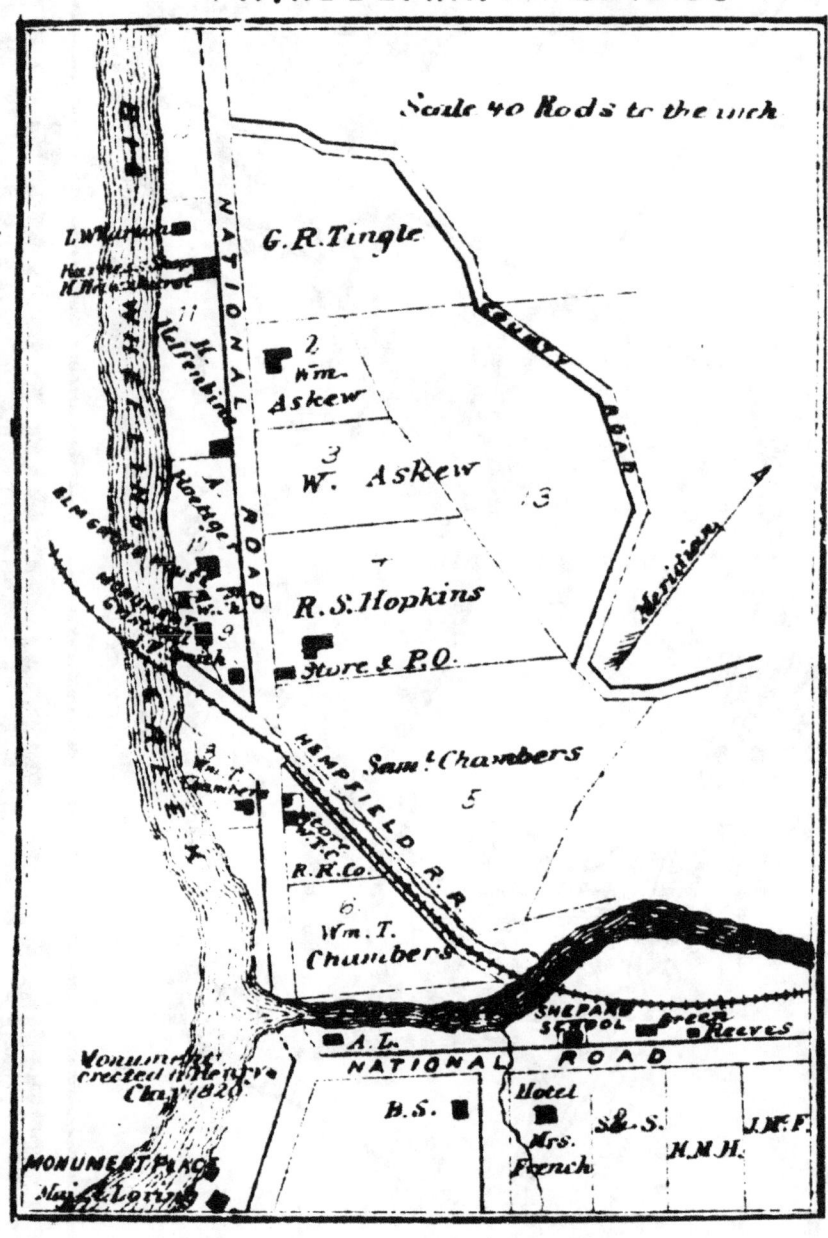

1871 MAP – OHIO CO. – RONEY POINT STATION 1783

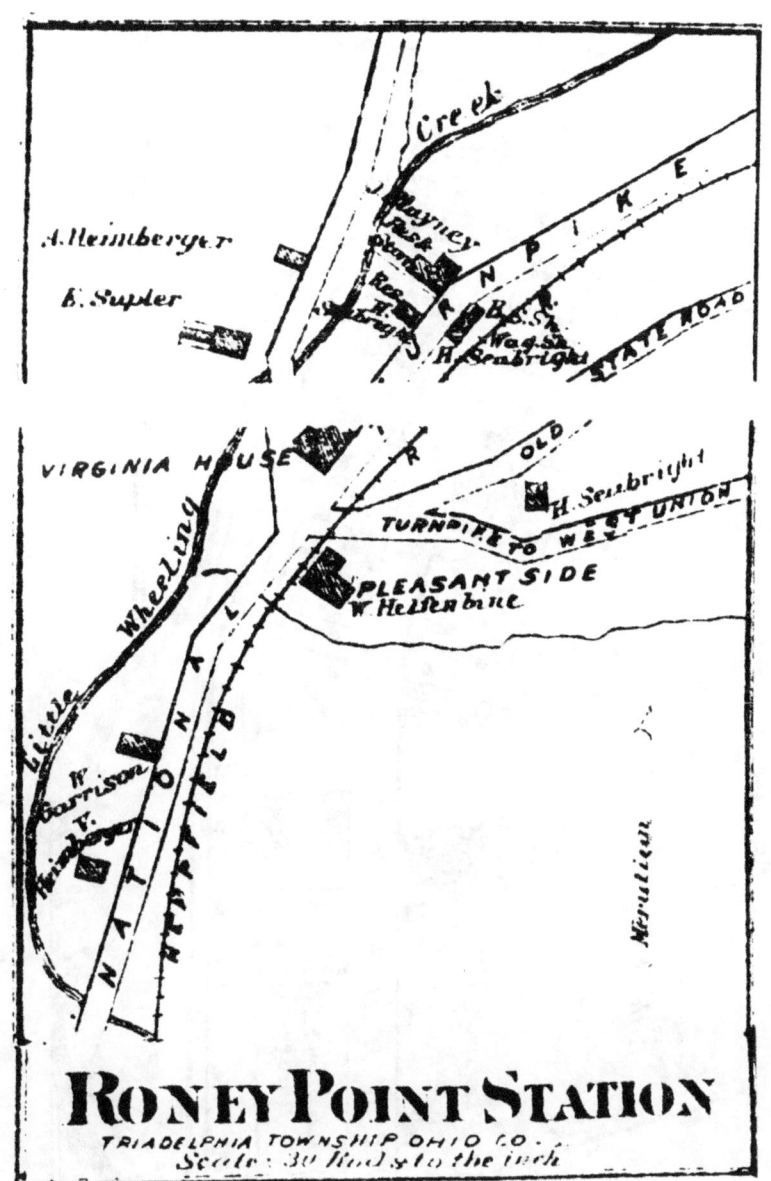

Creek
A. Heimberger
E. Supler
STATE ROAD
VIRGINIA HOUSE
OLD
H. Seabright
TURNPIKE TO WEST UNION
PLEASANT SIDE
Little Wheeling
W. Garrison
NATIONAL
HEMPFIELD
Meridian
TRIADELPHIA TOWNSHIP OHIO CO.
Scale: 30 Rods to the inch

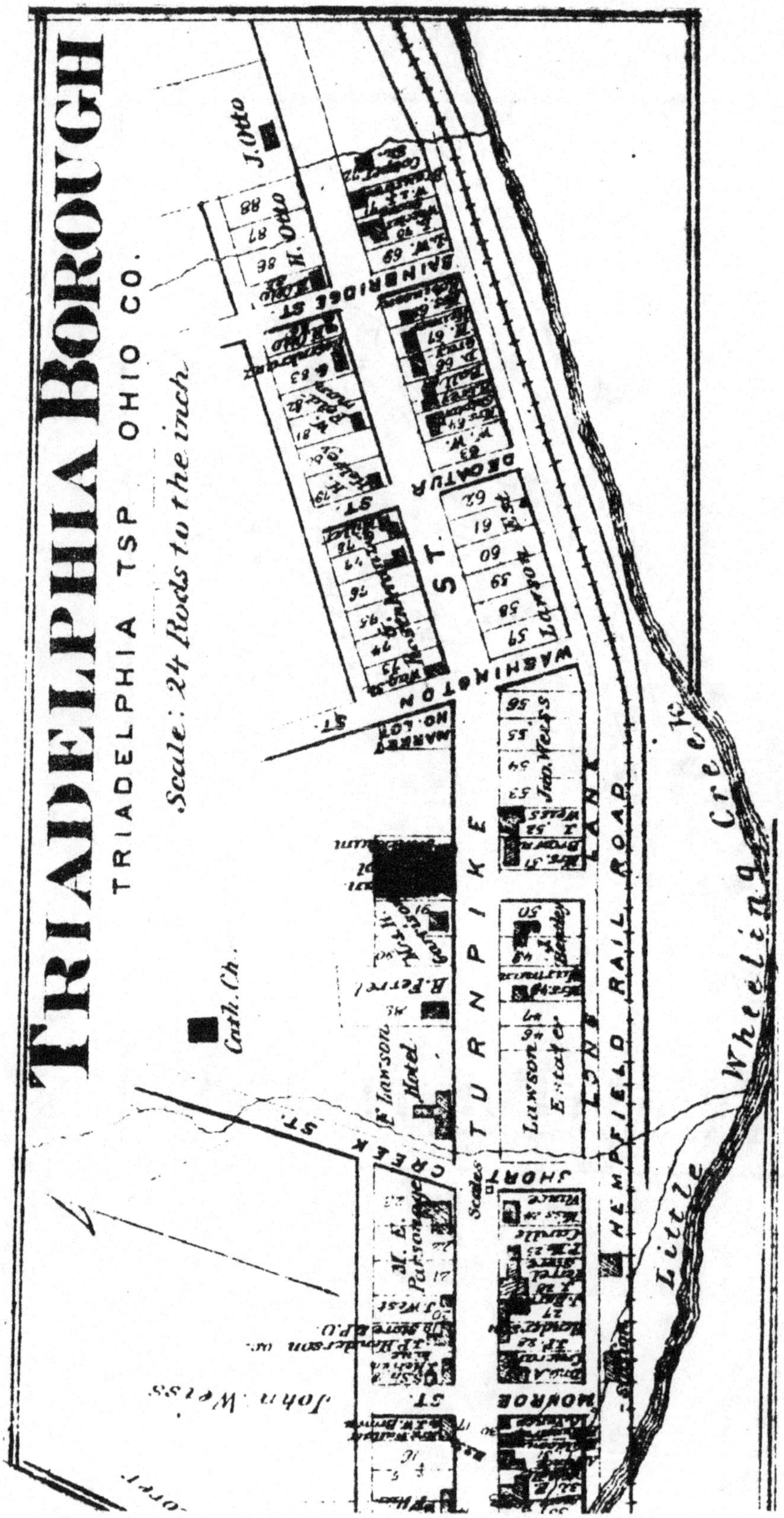

1784   1871 MAP – OHIO CO. – TRIADELPHIA BOROUGH – E. PART

1871 MAP – OHIO CO. – TRIADELPHIA BOROUGH – W. PART   1785

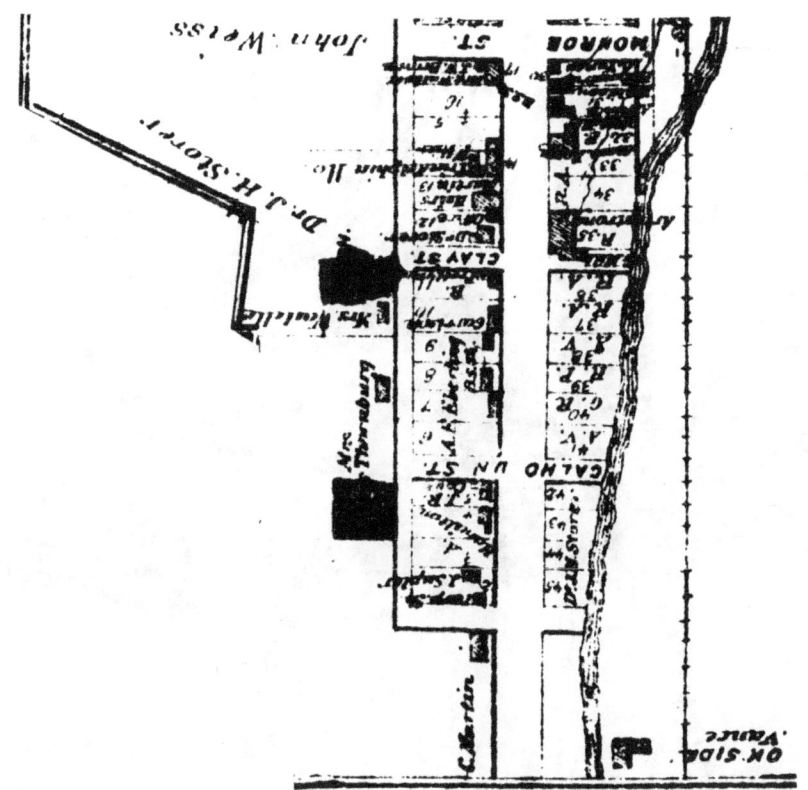

1786   1871 MAP – OHIO CO. – WHEELING CITY – NW. PART

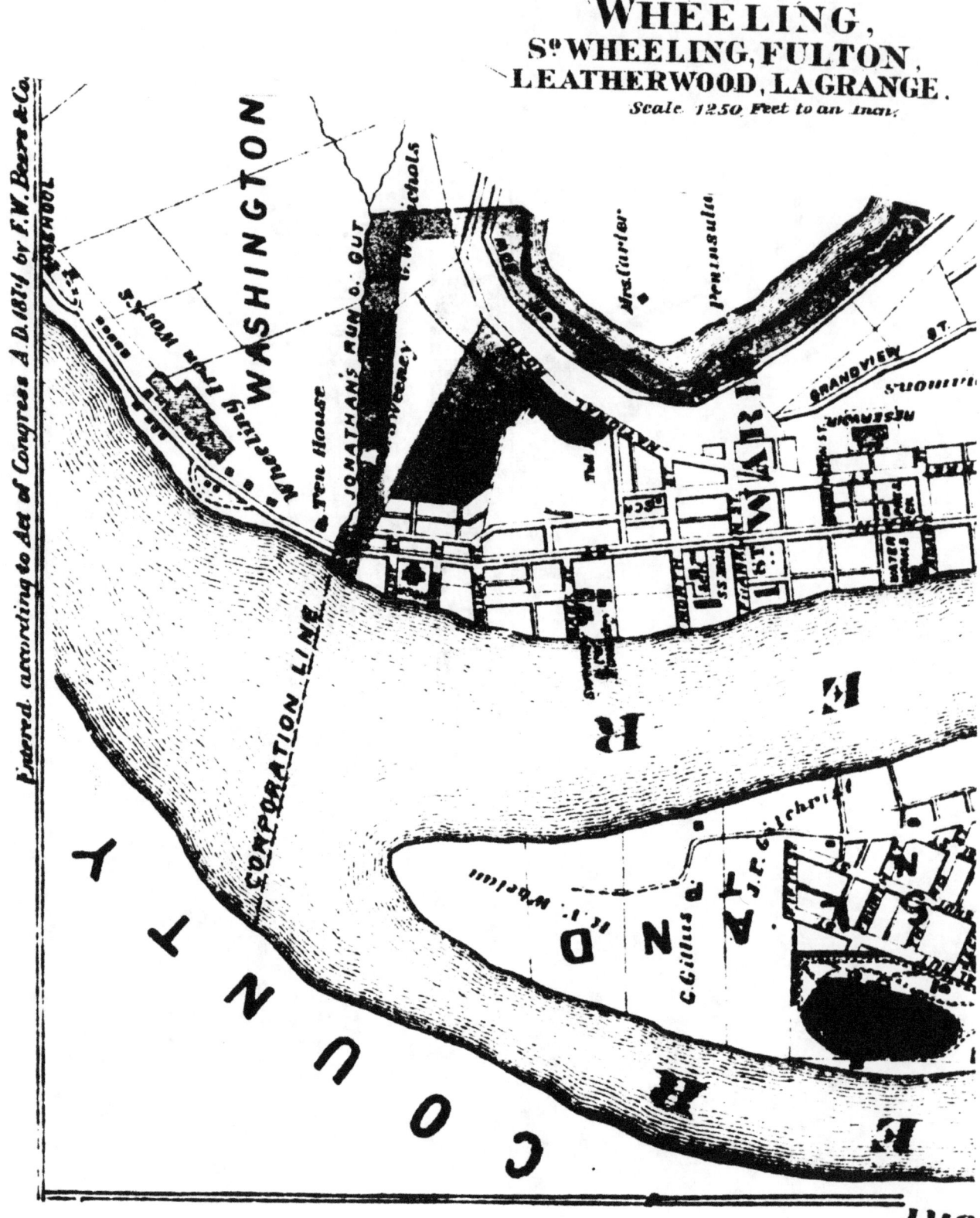

S.º WHEELING, FULTON,
LEATHERWOOD, LAGRANGE.
Scale 1250 Feet to an Inch
Entered according to Act of Congress A.D. 1871 by F.W. Beers & Co.
WASHINGTON
Wheeling Iron Works
Toll House
JONATHAN'S RUN O. CUT
Mrs. Carter
Peninsula
GRANDVIEW ST.
RESERVOIR
CORPORATION LINE
C. Gillus
J.P. Gilchrist
COUNTY
ORT

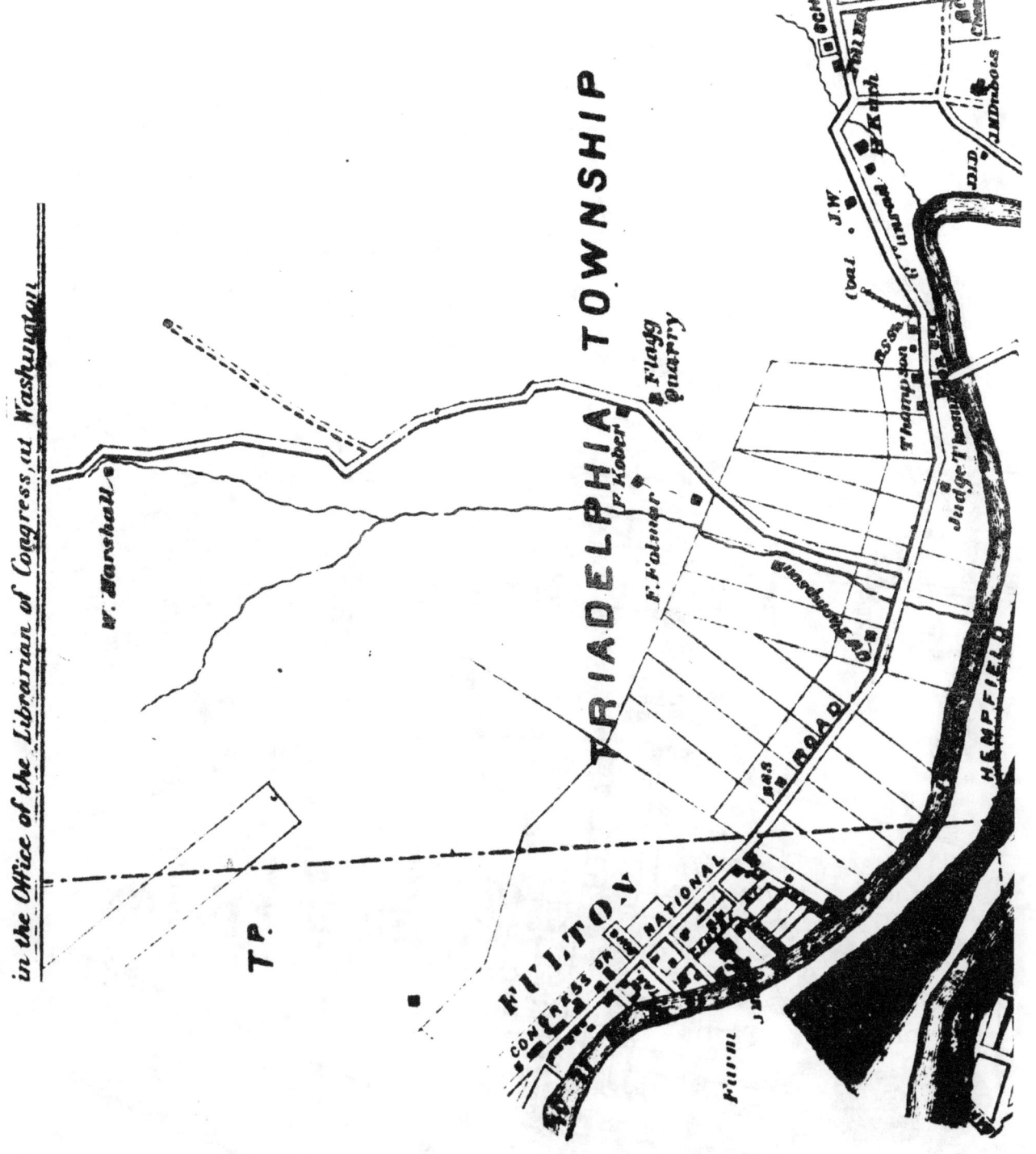
in the Office of the Librarian of Congress, at Washington
TRIADELPHIA TOWNSHIP
TP.
W. Marshall
F. Flagg Quarry
P. Kober
F. Folmer
Thompson
Judge Thompson
Coal
NATIONAL
ROAD
FULTON
CONGRESS
HEMPFIELD
Farm

1788   1871 MAP – OHIO CO. – WHEELING CITY – 1ST THRU 4TH & 7TH WARDS

Note: Wheeling Island is the 7th Ward and also Madison Township

1871 MAP – OHIO CO. – WHEELING CITY & LEATHERWOOD 1789

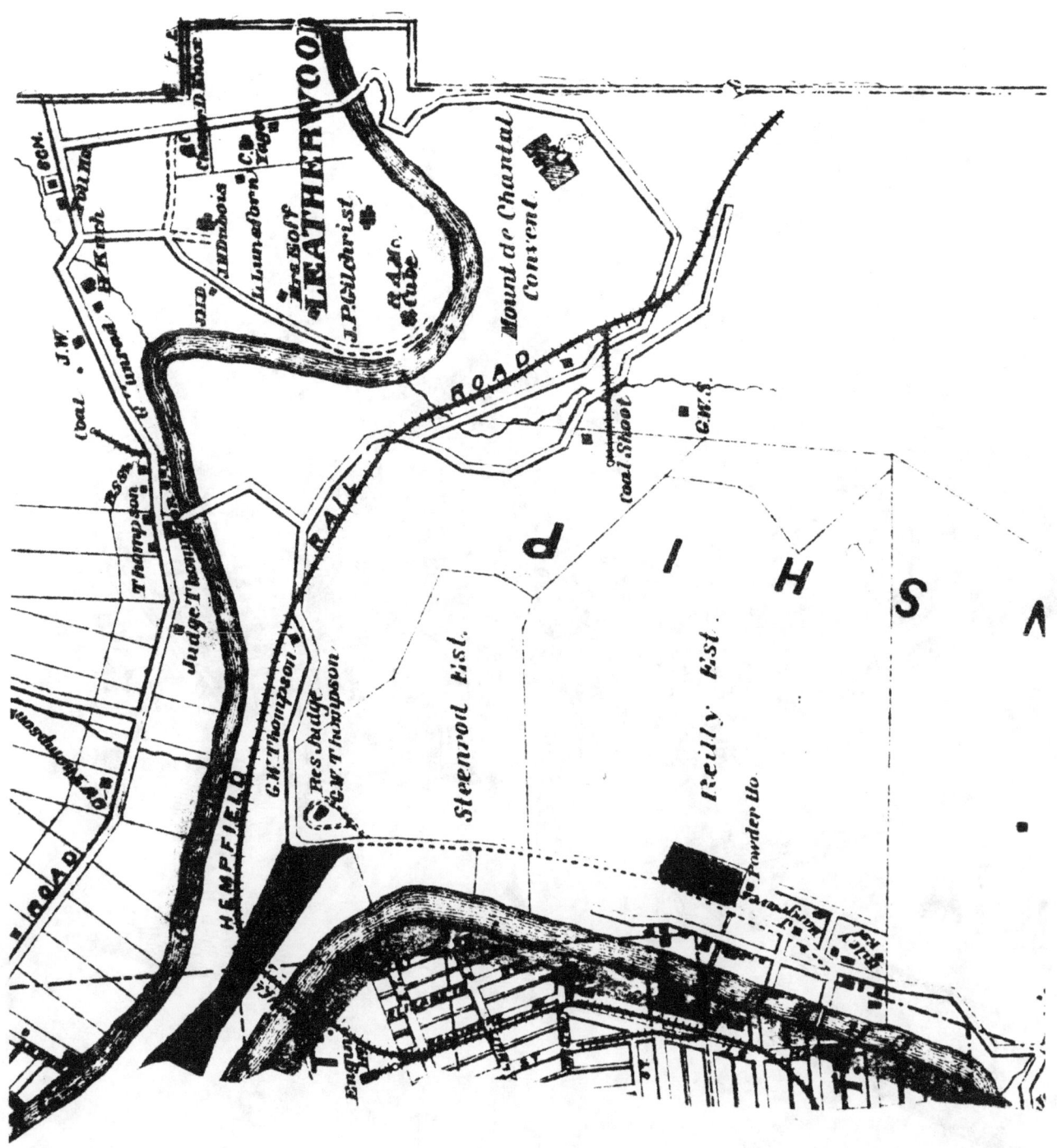

Mount de Chantal
Convent
ROAD
RAIL
Coal Shoot
Steenrod Est.
Reilly Est.
Powder Ho.
HEMPFIELD
Judge Thompson
G.W. Thompson
Res. Judge
G.W. Thompson
J.P. Gilchrist
Thompson

1790   1871 MAP – OHIO CO. – WHEELING CITY – 5TH AND 6TH WARDS

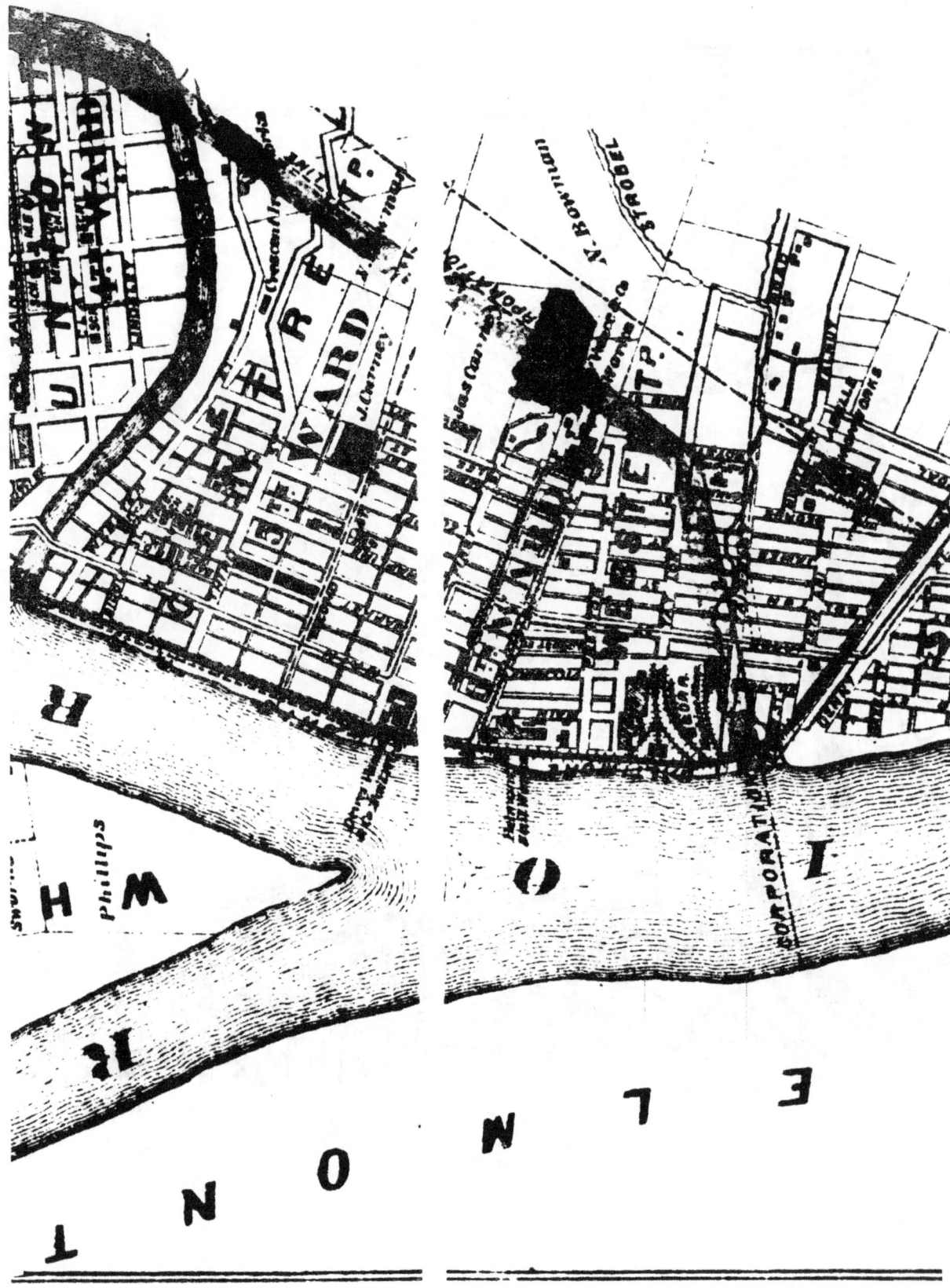

1871 MAP – OHIO CO. – WHEELING CITY – RITCHIE TWP – MIDDLE

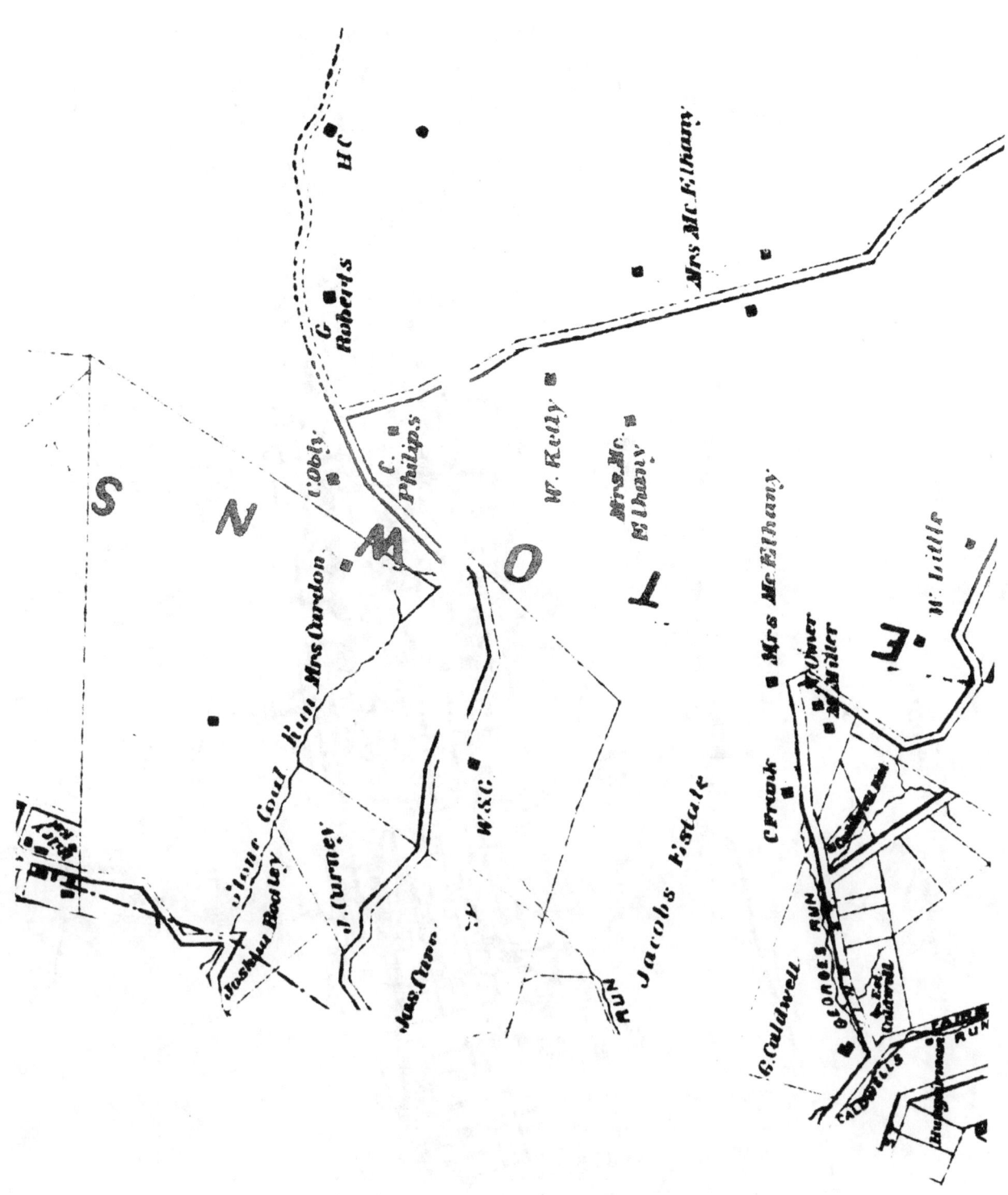

1792   1871 MAP – OHIO CO. – SOUTH WHEELING AND LAGRANGE

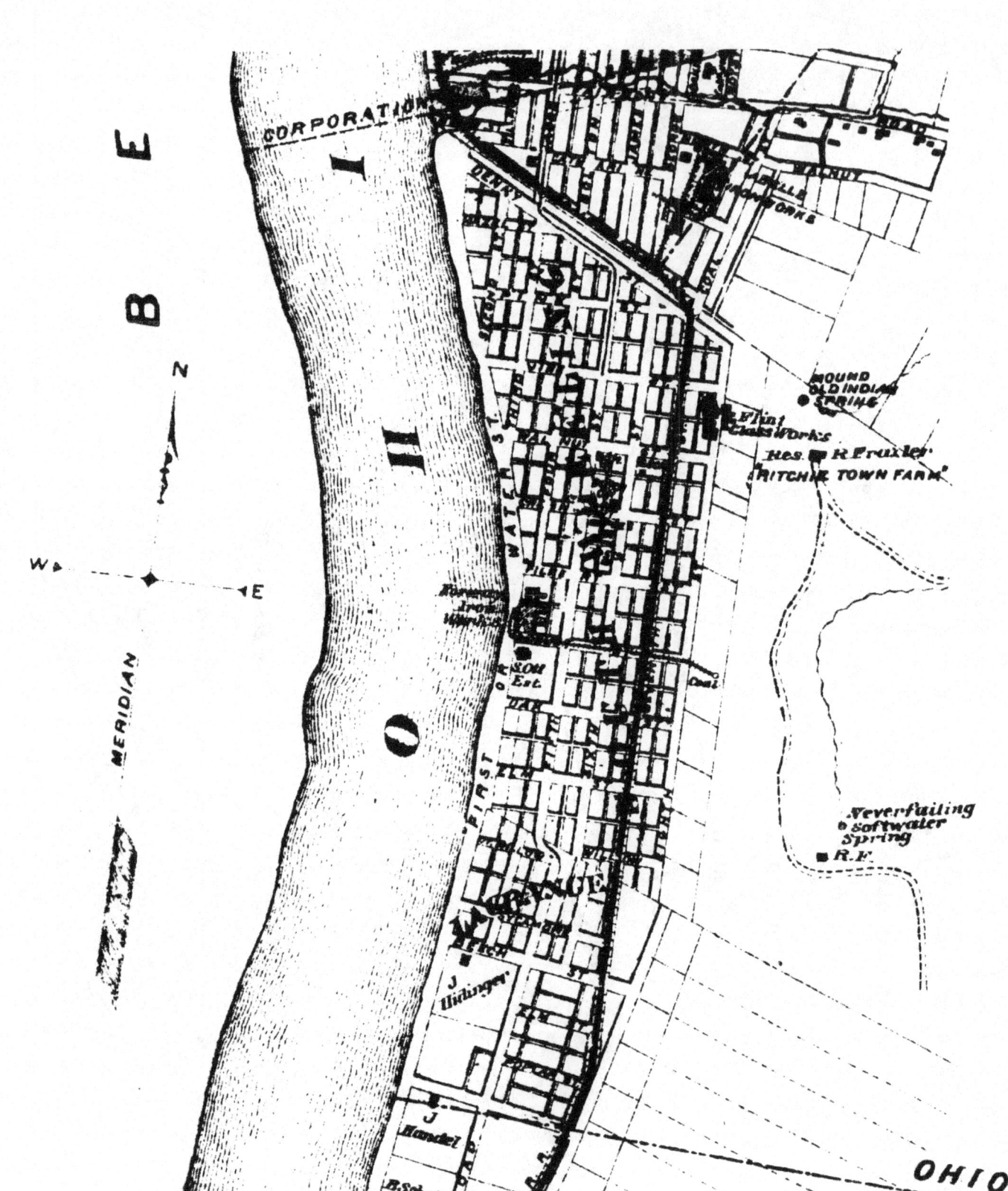

1871 MAP – OHIO CO. – WHEELING CITY – RITCHIE TWIP – SOUTH

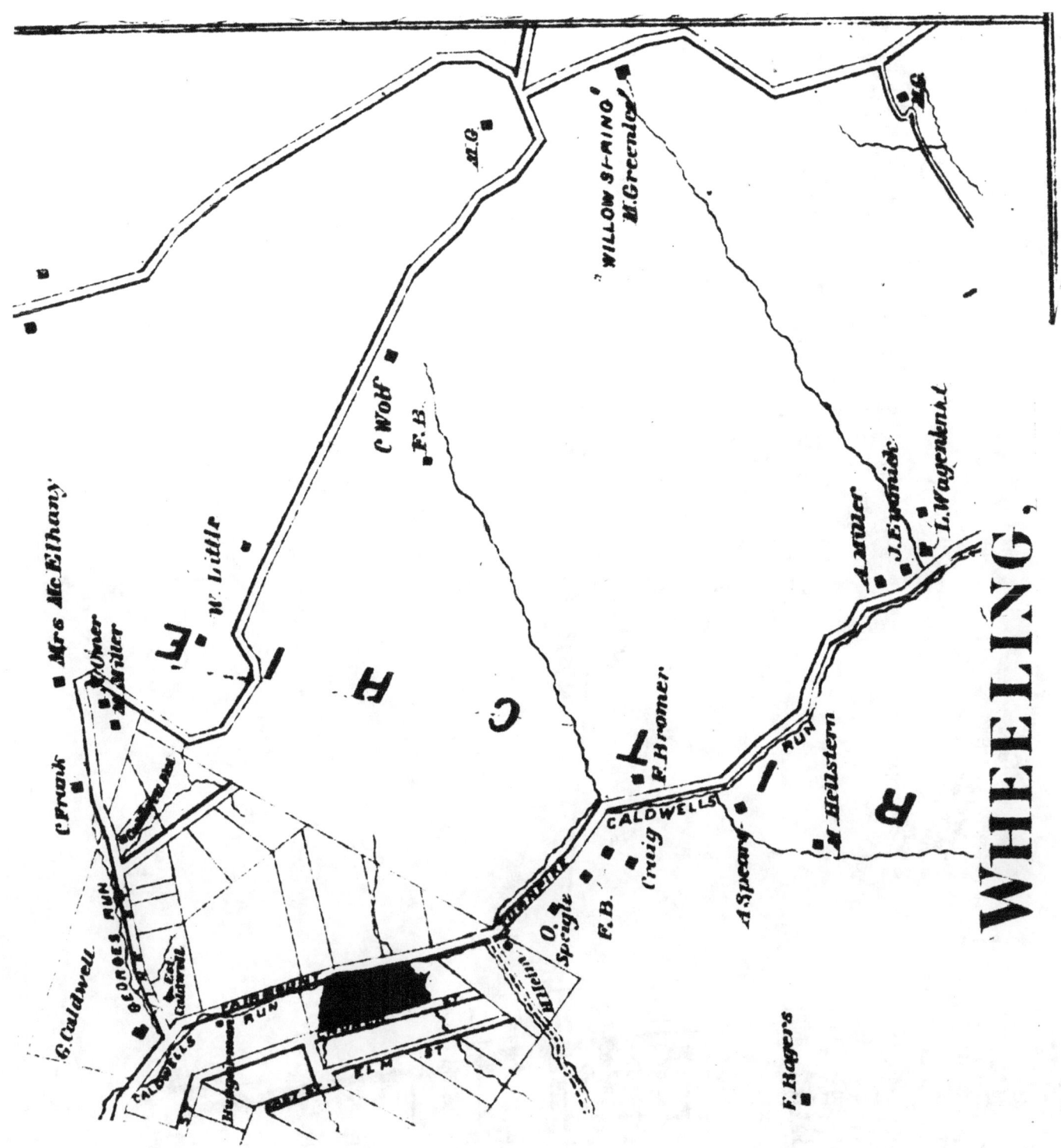

1794   1871 MAP – OHIO CO. – LAGRANGE

BUSINESS NOTICES.

MARSHALL COUNTY.

Benwood

Burr Mrs. Mary..Propt "Benwood Hotel," First st
Healy John..Grocer and Provision Dealer, near R. R.
Oglebay J. H..Manager "Benwood Iron Co Store"
Whipple H. D..Genl Manager of "Benwood Iron Works"
Whiteside R. J..Manager "Benwood Nail Factory"

Miscellaneous.

Davis Wm. J..Pastor of the "Church of God." Res South part of Twp
Ensley James..Grape Grower and Sheep-Skin Tanner. Res "Fertile Valley," Boggs Run

Cameron

Bosner, C. F..Manufacturer and Dealer in Boots and Shoes, Green st
Bentley, W. H..Agent B & O R R
Cunningham, James..Telegraph Operator at Depot
Dickey, John H..Notary Public, Main st
Fitzgerald, James B..propt "Cameron House," cor Ridge and Main sts
Hooton, J. E..Attorney at Law, res Church st
Hosock, E. P..res Church st
Loper, John..Dealer in General Hardware, Sash, Doors, Blinds, all kinds of Agricultural Implements, Paints, Oils, Glass, Cutlery and Notions, Main st
Miller, John..Dealer in Dry Goods, Groceries, Hats Caps, Boots and Shoes, Hard-ware, Queensware and everything found in a first-class country store, Main st
McGahan, W T..Express Agent, also Dealer in Groceries, Confectioneries, Tobacco, Cigars, Notions, Toys, &c, Main st
McDonald, W. R..res South Side Creek
Mackin, C. H..Conductor on B & O R R, res South Side Creek
Pipes, J. W..Physician and Surgeon, Church st
Penn, Phillips & Co..Dealer in Staple and Fancy Dry Goods, Groceries, Hardware, Hats and Caps, Boots and Shoes, &c., Stock always kept full. Green st
Rickey, J. W..Dealer in Drugs, Chemicals, Oils, Paints, Dye Stuffs, Pure Wines and Liquors, &c., Main st
Rees, Wm. H..propt Flouring Mill, Main st
Reynolds, F. M..Dealer in all kinds of Household Furniture, Main st
Stidger, S. B..Physician and Surgeon, Ridge st
White, J. H..propt "White's Hotel," Dealer in Paints, Oils, Glass, Sash, Doors, White and Red Lead, Mineral and Mixed Paints, Turpentine, Varnishes and all kinds of Hard-ware, Main st

BUSINESS NOTICES.

Glen Easton.

Blincoe, Mark..propt of St "Charles Hotel," Main st
Harris, J. M..propt of Flouring Mill and Dealer in Grain, Main st
McDonald, W. E..Dealer in Dry Goods, Groceries, &c. Main st
Wilson, Thomas..Dealer in Dry Goods, Groceries, Boots and Shoes, &c., Mechanic st

Miscellaneous.

Laughlin, John..Dealer in Stock, also in Dry Goods, Groceries, Grain and Country Produce, Rock Lick
Laudenslager, Joseph..Dealer in Grain, Dry Goods, Groceries, &c., also propt of Flouring Mill, Main st Loudensville
Lyclick, Wm..Blacksmith and Wagon Maker, Grone Creek, West Loudensville

Moundsville

Alexander James, D.D...Pastor of Pres Church, E. S. Second st
Bruce G. W..Practicing Physician, N. S. B. st
Baker A. O..Commissary of Penitentiary, N. E. cor E. and Market sts
Criswell Hanson..Atty at Law, S. S. B. st
Cox Harvey..Saddler and Harness Maker, W. S. Market st
Ewing J. Dallas..Atty at Law, N. E. cor Market and Liberty sts
Evans Walter..Clerk of Circuit Court, S. E. cor North and Marshall sts
Ernst Michael..Propt of Bakery, E. S. Water st
Elder Wm..Blacksmith, S. S. Main st
Edwards & Roberts..Dealers in Genl Mdse and Buyers and Shippers of all kinds of Produce, W. S. Market st
Finn Thomas..Recorder, N. S. C. st
Gallaher J. W..Merchant and Wholesale Dealer in Grain and Country Produce, S. E. cor Water and Liberty sts
Harms Joseph..Nurseryman, "River Road"
Keily M. C..Propt of "Clifton House," N. S. Purdy st
M. Connell Robt..Atty at Law, N. E. cor Second and C. sts
Neff Jesse..Propt of Tannery, N. E. cor North and Market sts
Parkinson J. L..Atty at Law, N. S. A. st
Robinson John H..Merchant and Gardener, "Sharp's Garden," N. S. Purdy st
Shattuck N. K..Principal of School, S. S. D. st
Slaib J. C..Wagon Maker, N. W., cor South and Mechanic st
Thomas E. C..Practicing Physician and Merchant, E. S. Market st
Woods J. F..Pastor of Epis Church, S. W. cor E. and Wheeling sts
Wharry John..Propt of Grist Mill and Woolen Facty, W. S. Water st
Webster, Brown & Co..Props of "Mound City Flour Mill," S. E. cor Marshall and Purdy sts

BUSINESS NOTICES.

West Union

Bedillon A. D..Washington st
Barry W. A..Dealer in Dry Goods, Groceries, Boots and Shoes, Washington st
Leller S. W..Variety Store, Wheeling st
McCracken S. C., M. D., Washington st
Marshman T. F..Physician, Main st
McDonell B..Farmer and Wool Grower, Washington st
Wirt B..Propt Hotel, Wheeling st

Franklin Township

Arnold A. G..Farmer and Propt of Saw Mill. Res Fish Creek
Campbell P. P..Farmer and Grazer. Res South part of Township
Hornbrook J. P..Dealer in Foreign and Domestic Dry Goods and all kinds of Produce, Woodland, W. Va
Hornbrook Brothers..Dealers in Dry Goods, Groceries, Flour, Grain, Country Produce, &c, Woodland, W. Va
Matthews A. R..Dealer in Dry Goods, Groceries and all kinds of Country Produce, Woodland, W. Va
McKimie G. W..Physician. Res near Fair View
Ressegger H..Dealer in Dry Goods, Groceries, Notions and Country Produce, Fairview, W. Va
Suter Wm..Propt of Custom Flouring Mill and Dealer in Dry Goods, Groceries, &c, Woodland, W. Va
Wayman F. & Son..Propts of Black-smith Shop. Res near Fairview

Sand Hill Township

Kittle S. B. & Son..Propts Steam Saw Mill, also Genl Black-smiths, "Grindstaff's Run"
Lutes E. & D..Propts "Wheeling Valley Flouring Mills"
Ruth J. & W..Propts of Flouring Mill and Saw Mill, New Germantown, "Wheeling Creek"
Rogers J..Genl Black-smith and Wagon Maker, "Sand Hill"

Washington Township.

Ballard C. K..Dealer in Dry Goods, Groceries and Shipper of Coal, "River Road," N. W. P. Twp
Curtis G. D..Nurseryman, East of Moundsville
Curtis R. B..Propt of Nursery and Green House, East of Moundsville
Carney James..Farmer, N. E. part of Twp
Goudy John..Carpenter and Farmer, N. E. part Twp
Wilson Daniel..Blacksmith, Limestone P. O
Keltz M..Sheriff of M. Co, Union Twp

Liberty Township.

Higgins, John W..Farmer and propt of Steam Grist and Saw Mills, S. W. P. Township
Rice, J. A..Farmer and Dealer in Lumber, S. W. P. Township
White & Stiles..Dealers and Manufacturers of Flour, Lumber, Brooms, Boots and Shoes, and Retail Dealers of General Merchandise and Shippers of Country Produce, Beilton

Richland Township.

Groves S..Black-smith

1798   1871 MAP – MARSHALL CO. – BENWOOD – N. PART

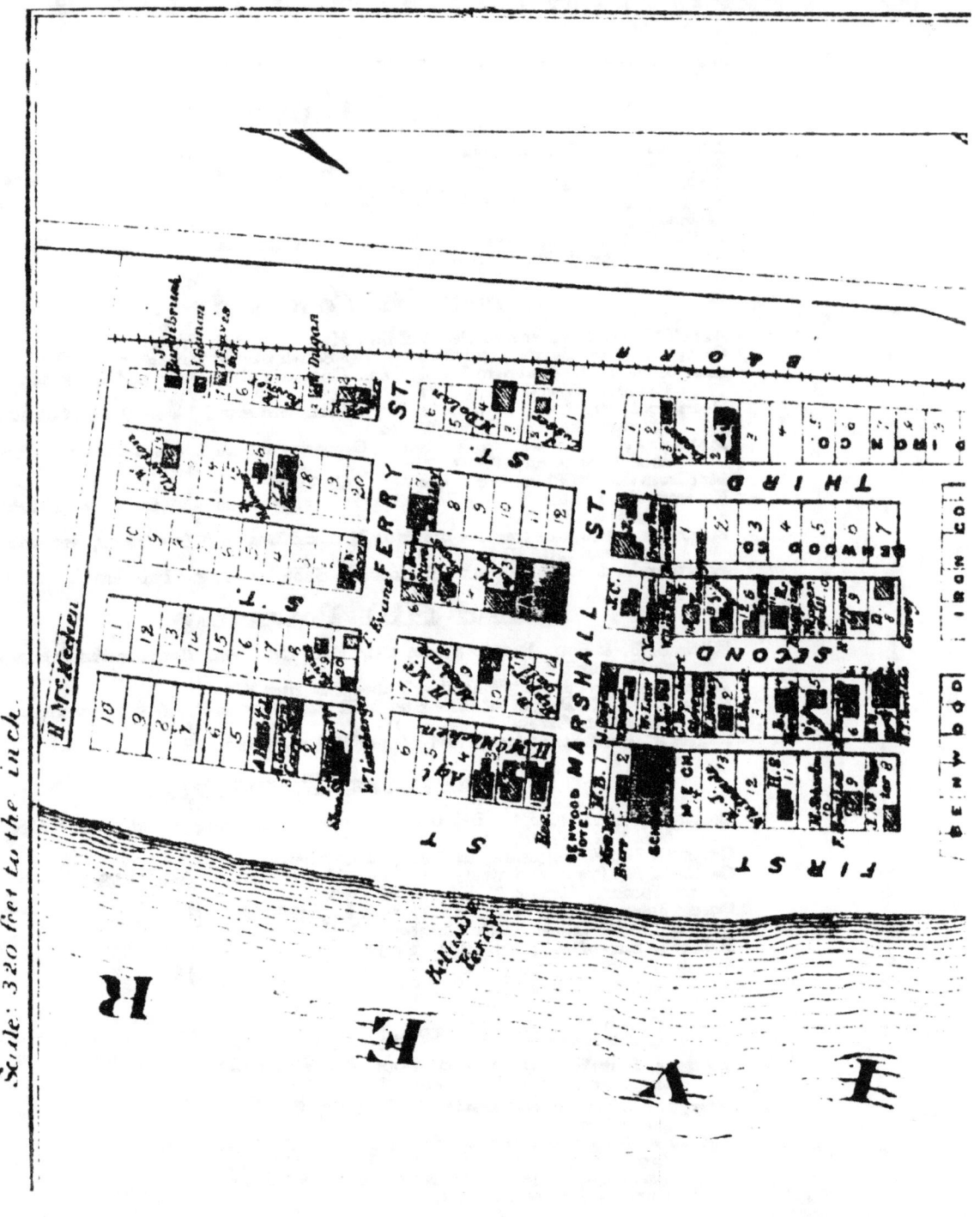

1871 MAP – MARSHALL CO. – BENWOOD – MIDDLE PART

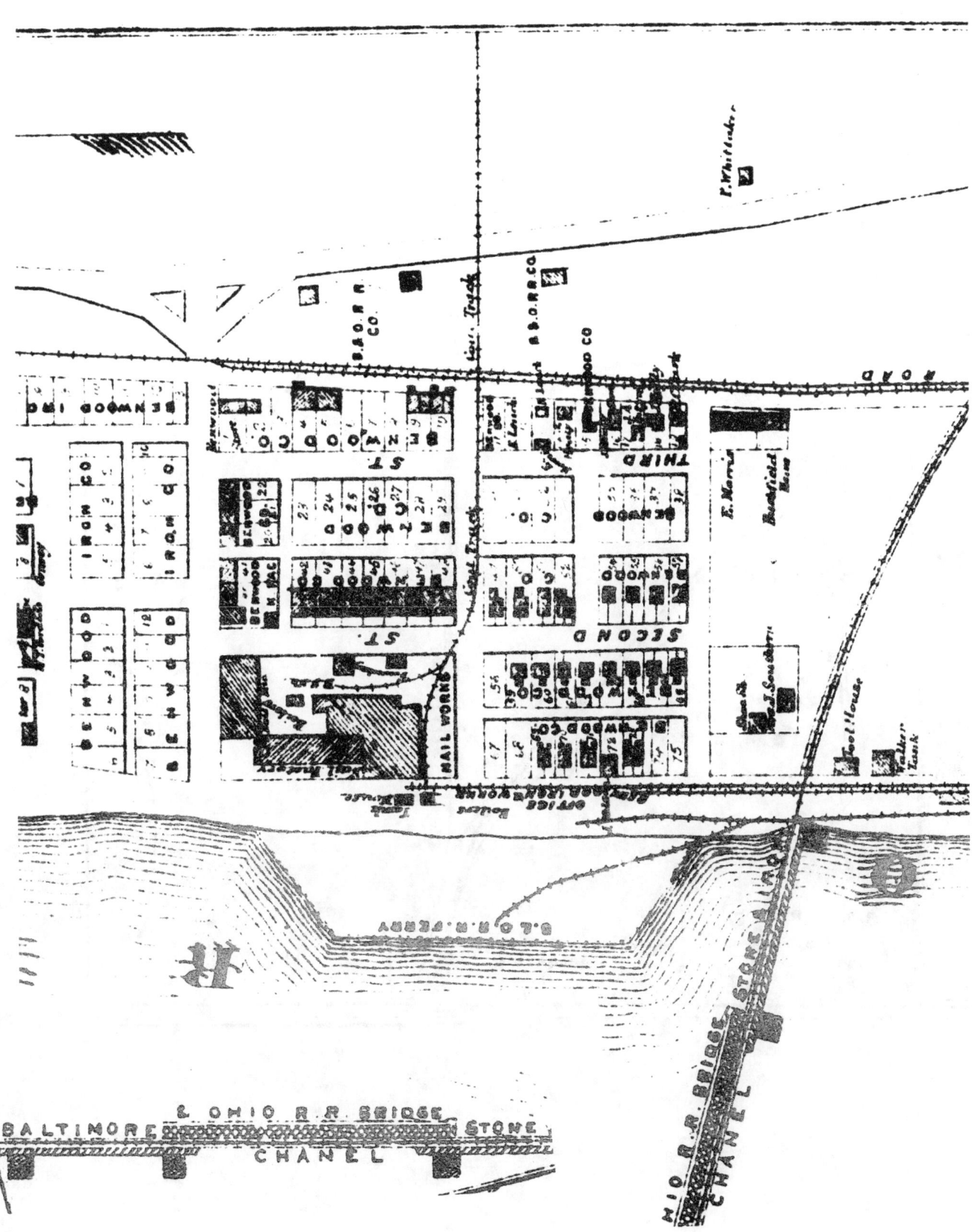

BALTIMORE & OHIO R.R. BRIDGE STONE
CHANEL
NAIL WORKS
B.&O.R.R. CO.
B.&O.R.R. CO.
BENWOOD CO
IRON CO
THIRD
SECOND
ST.
ROAD
Tool House
Water Tank
P. Whittaker
E. Morris

1871 MAP – MARSHALL CO. – BENWOOD – S. PART

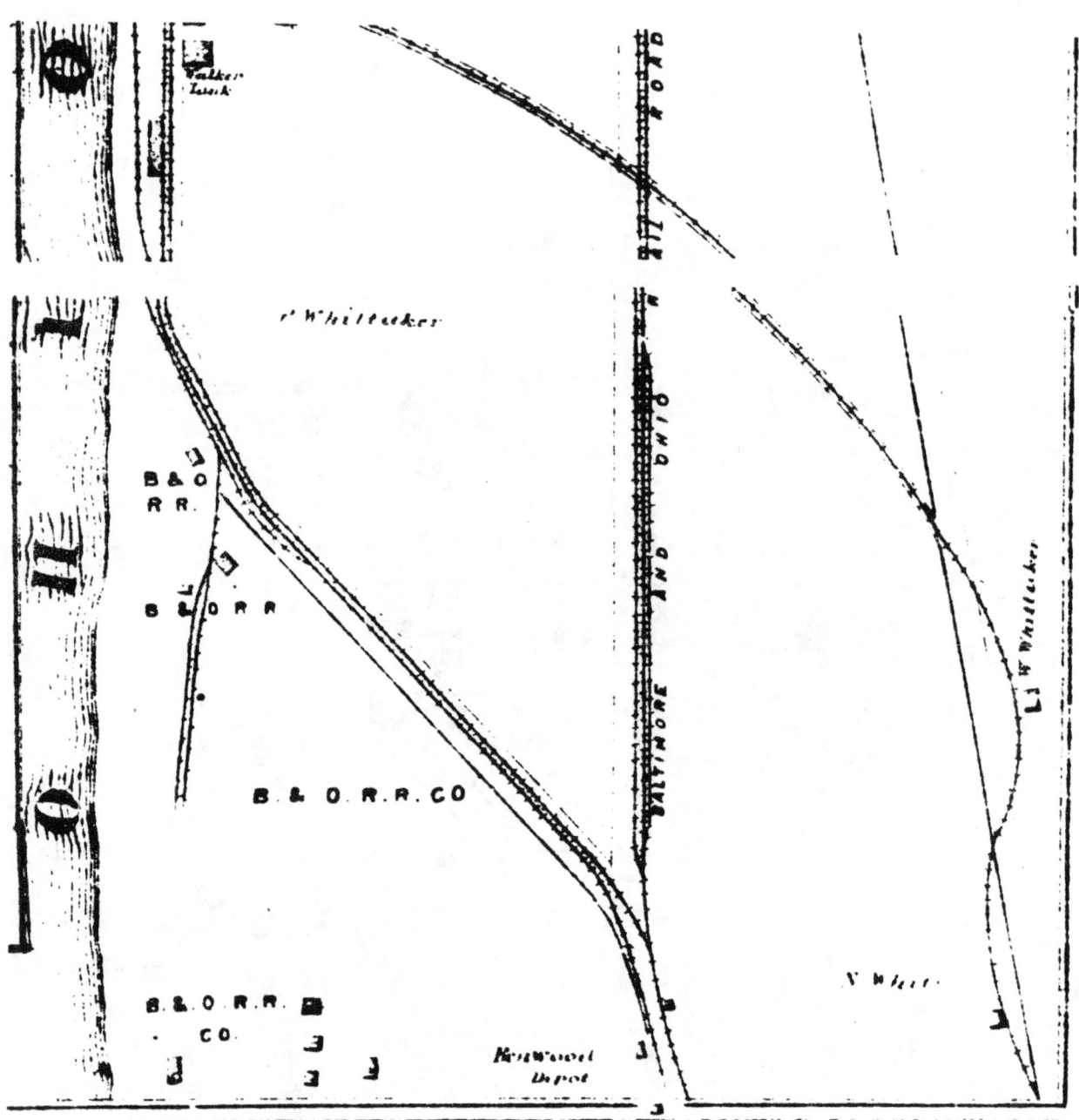

1871 MAP – MARSHALL CO. – GLEN EASTON   1801

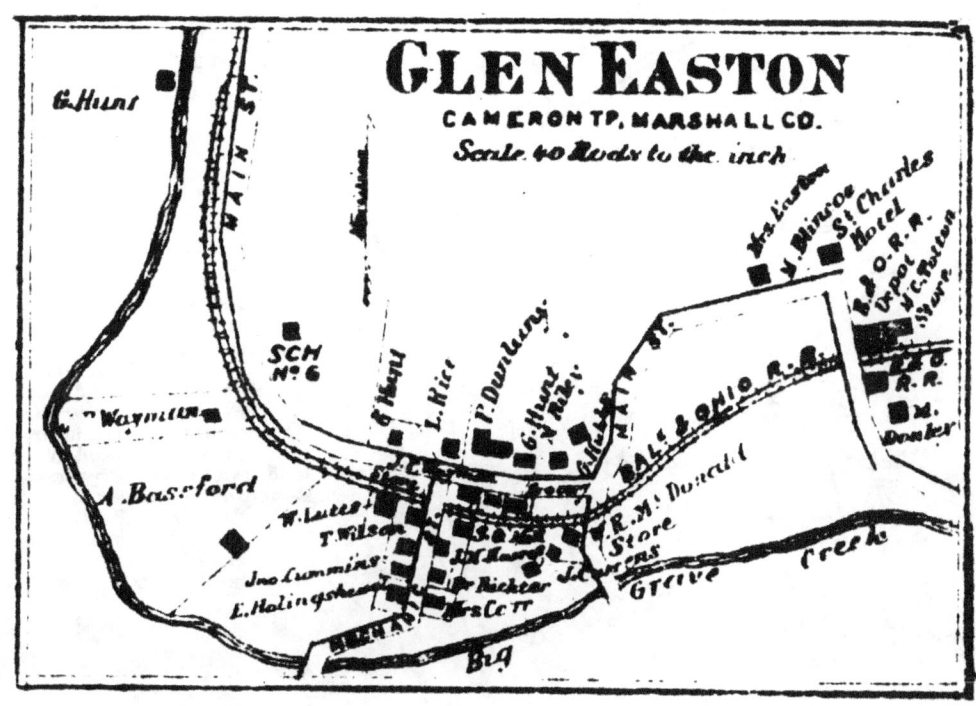

CAMERON TP, MARSHALL CO.
Scale 40 Rods to the inch
G. Hunt
MAIN ST.
SCH No 6
A. Bassford
W. Lutes
T. Wilson
Jno Cummins
E. Holingshead
L. Rice
P. Dunlany
G. Hunt
St. Charles Hotel
B. & O. R.R. Depot
BALT & OHIO R.R.
W. R. McDonald Store
Grave
Creek
Big
M. Donley
B & O. R.R.

1802   1871 MAP – MARSHALL CO. – CAMERON – N. PART

Business listings on this Page are not indexed – they are indexed on another page. They are shown here to show town boundary line only.

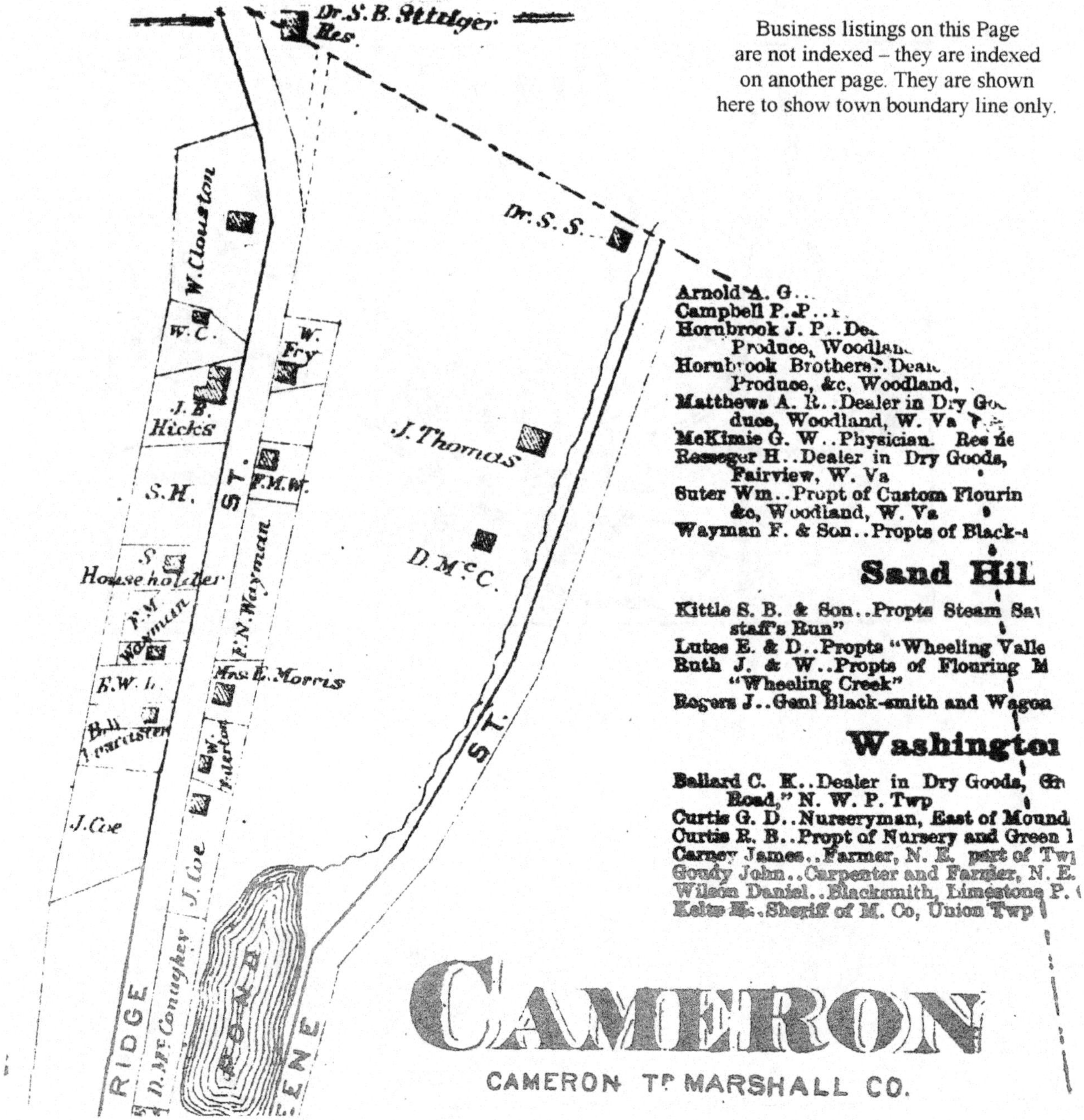

Arnold A. G...
Campbell P. P...
Hornbrook J. P..De...
   Produce, Woodlan...
Hornbrook Brothers..Deal...
   Produce, &c, Woodland,...
Matthews A. R..Dealer in Dry Go...
   duce, Woodland, W. Va...
McKimie G. W..Physician. Res...
Ressegger H..Dealer in Dry Goods,
   Fairview, W. Va
Suter Wm..Propt of Custom Flourin...
   &c, Woodland, W. Va
Wayman F. & Son..Propts of Black-...

Sand Hill

Kittle S. B. & Son..Propts Steam Sa...
   staff's Run"
Lutes E. & D..Propts "Wheeling Valle...
Ruth J. & W..Propts of Flouring M...
   "Wheeling Creek"
Rogers J..Genl Black-smith and Wagon...

Washingto...

Ballard C. K..Dealer in Dry Goods, G...
   Road," N. W. P. Twp
Curtis G. D..Nurseryman, East of Mound...
Curtis R. B..Propt of Nursery and Green...
Carney James..Farmer, N. E. part of Tw...
Goudy John..Carpenter and Farmer, N. E...
Wilson Daniel..Blacksmith, Limestone P...
Kelts M..Sheriff of M. Co, Union Twp...

CAMERON
CAMERON TP MARSHALL CO.

1871 MAP – MARSHALL CO. – CAMERON – E. PART   1803

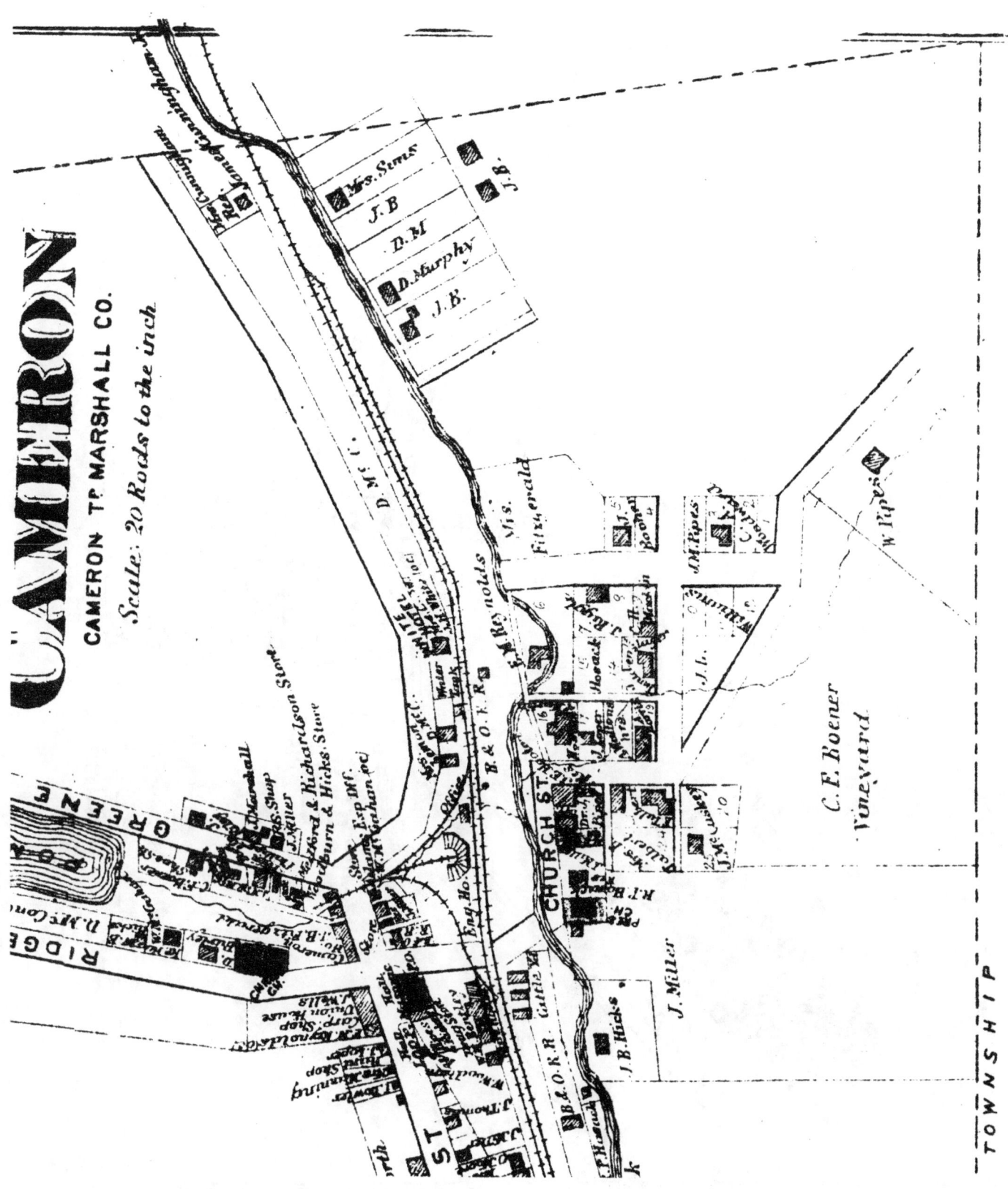

CAMERON Tp. MARSHALL CO.
Scale: 20 Rods to the inch
Mrs. Sims
D. Murphy
E.M. Reynolds
B.&O.R.R.
CHURCH ST
GREENE
RIDGE
Fitzgerald
W. Pipes
C.E. Roener
Vineyard
J. Miller
J.B. Hicks
TOWNSHIP

1804   1871 MAP – MARSHALL CO. – CAMERON – W. PART

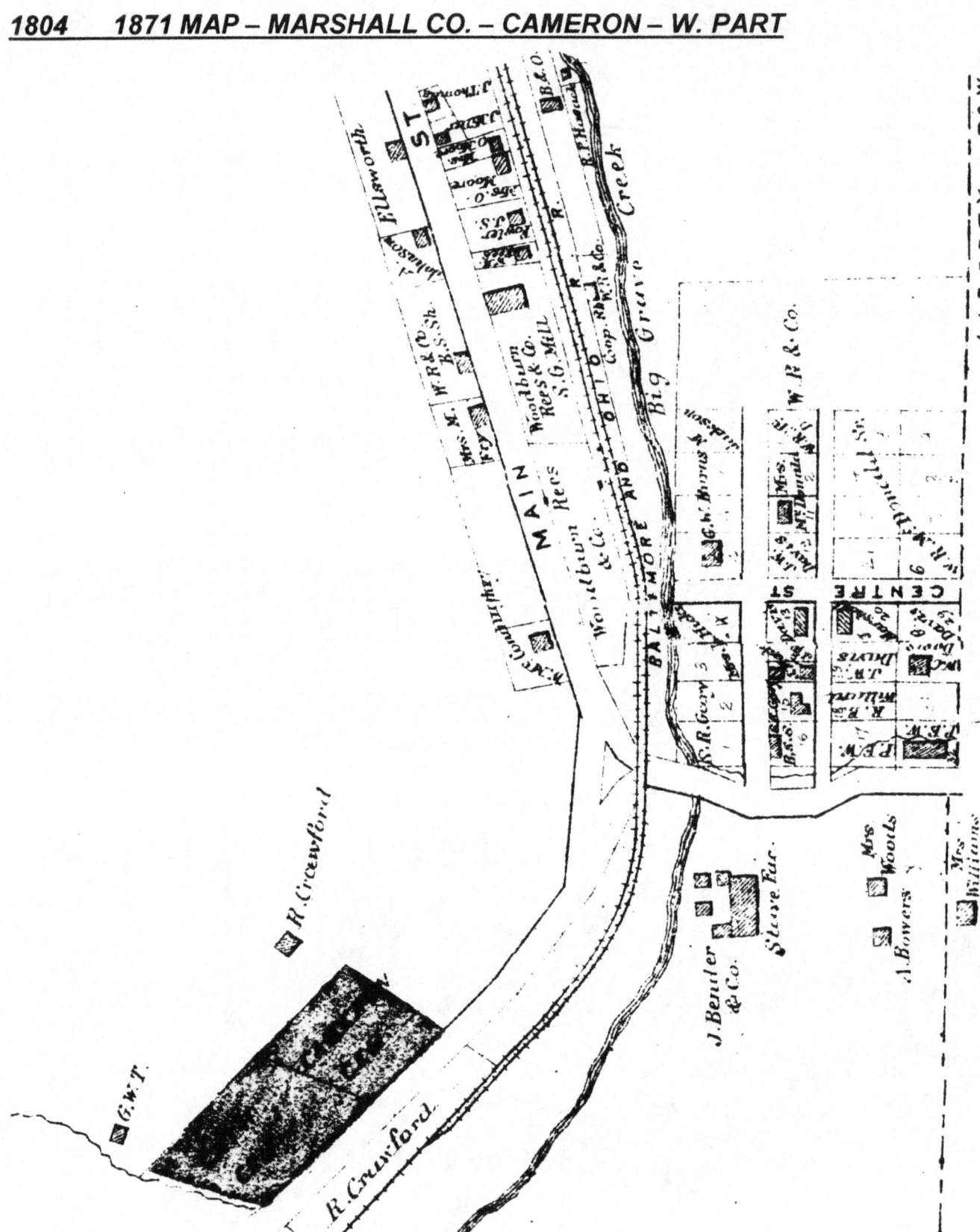

LIBERTY TOW
MAIN ST
BALTIMORE AND OHIO R. R.
Big Grave Creek
CENTRE ST
Ellsworth
Woodburn Rees & Co. S.G. Mill
Woodburn & Co.
Rees
W. R. & Co.
R. Crawford
R. Crawford
G.W.T.
J. Bender & Co.
Stave Fac.
A. Bowers
Mrs. Woods
Mrs. Williams

1871 MAP – MARSHALL CO. – LIMESTONE P.O.   1805

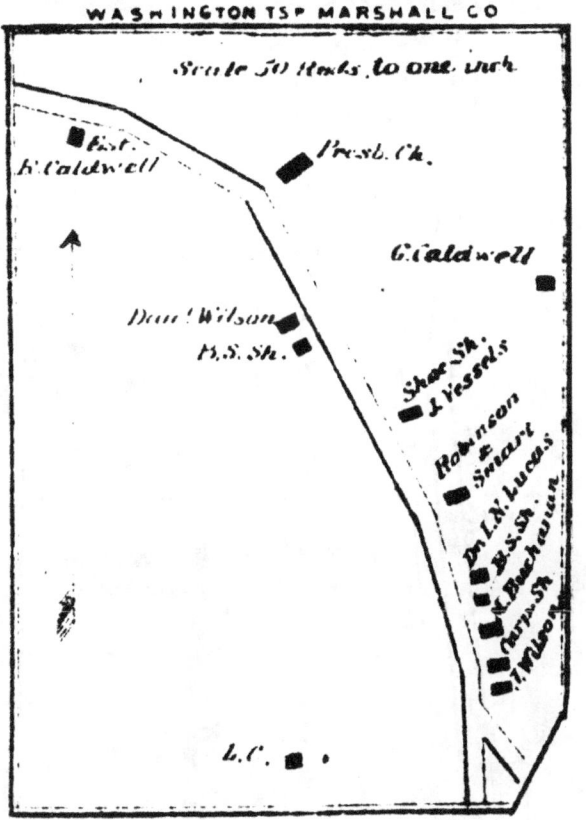

WASHINGTON TSP MARSHALL CO
Scale 50 Rods to one inch
Est. E. Caldwell
Presb. Ch.
G. Caldwell
Dan'l Wilson
B.S. Sh.
Shoe Sh.
J. Vessels
Robinson & Smart
Dr. I.N. Lucas
B.S. Sh.
K. Buchanan
Carp. Sh.
T. Wilson

1806   1871 MAP – MARSHALL CO. – MOUNDSVILLE – NW. PART

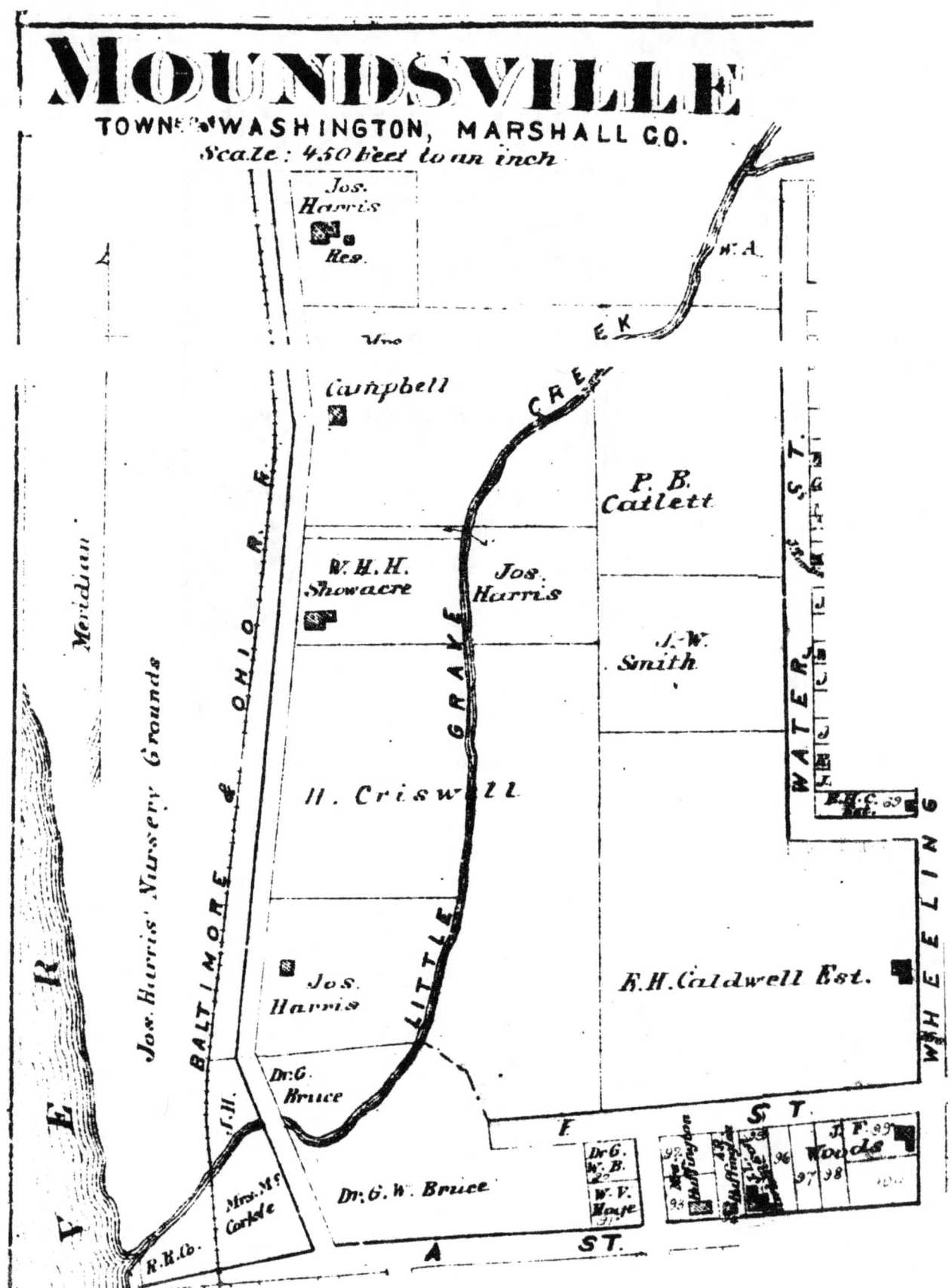

TOWNSP WASHINGTON, MARSHALL CO.
Scale: 450 feet to an inch
Jos. Harris
Res.
W. A.
Campbell
CREEK
P. B. Catlett
W. H. H. Showacre
Jos. Harris
J. W. Smith
WATER ST.
Meridian
Jos. Harris' Nursery Grounds
BALTIMORE & OHIO R.R.
LITTLE GRAVE
H. Criswell
E. H. Caldwell Est.
WHEELING
Jos. Harris
Dr. G. Bruce
F ST.
Dr. G. W. Bruce
Mrs. McCarlele
R. R. Co.
A ST.
W. V. Hoge
Woods
96
97
98
99
RIVER

1871 MAP – MARSHALL CO. – MOUNDSVILLE – NE. PART

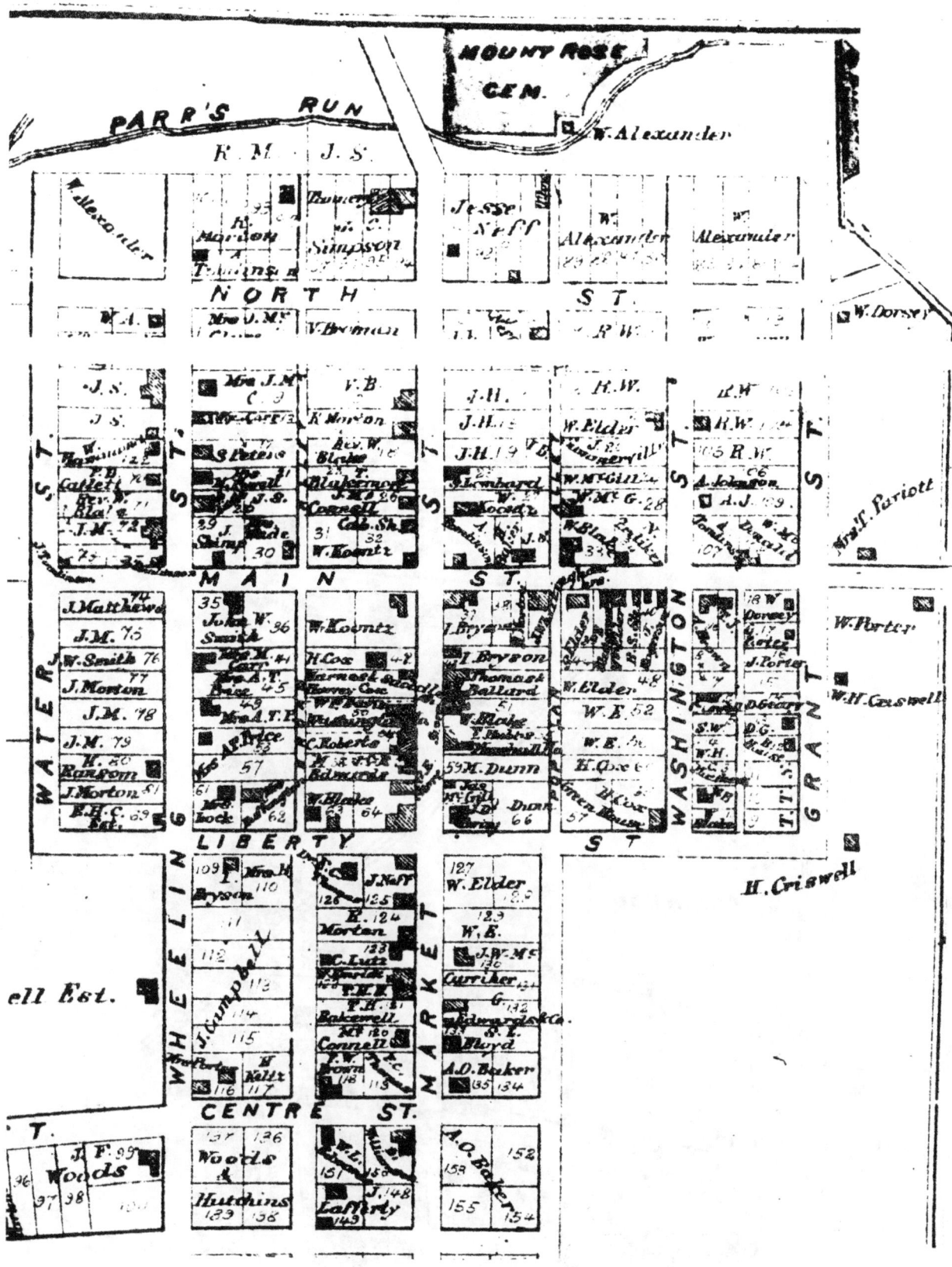

MOUNT ROSE CEM.
PARR'S RUN
W. Alexander
NORTH ST.
MAIN ST.
LIBERTY ST
CENTRE ST.
WATER ST.
WHEELING ST.
MARKET ST.
WASHINGTON ST.
GRANT ST.
Jesse Neff
Simpson
W. Dorsey
Mrs. T. Pariott
W. Porter
W. H. Criswell
H. Criswell
J. Matthews
J. W. Smith
J. Morton
John W. Smith
W. Koontz
H. Cox
I. Bryson
W. Elder
M. Dunn
ell Est.
J. Campbell
Morton
C. Lutz
A. O. Baker
A. D. Baker
Woods & Hutchins
Lafferty

1808 1871 MAP – MARSHALL CO. – MOUNDSVILLE – W. CENTRAL PART

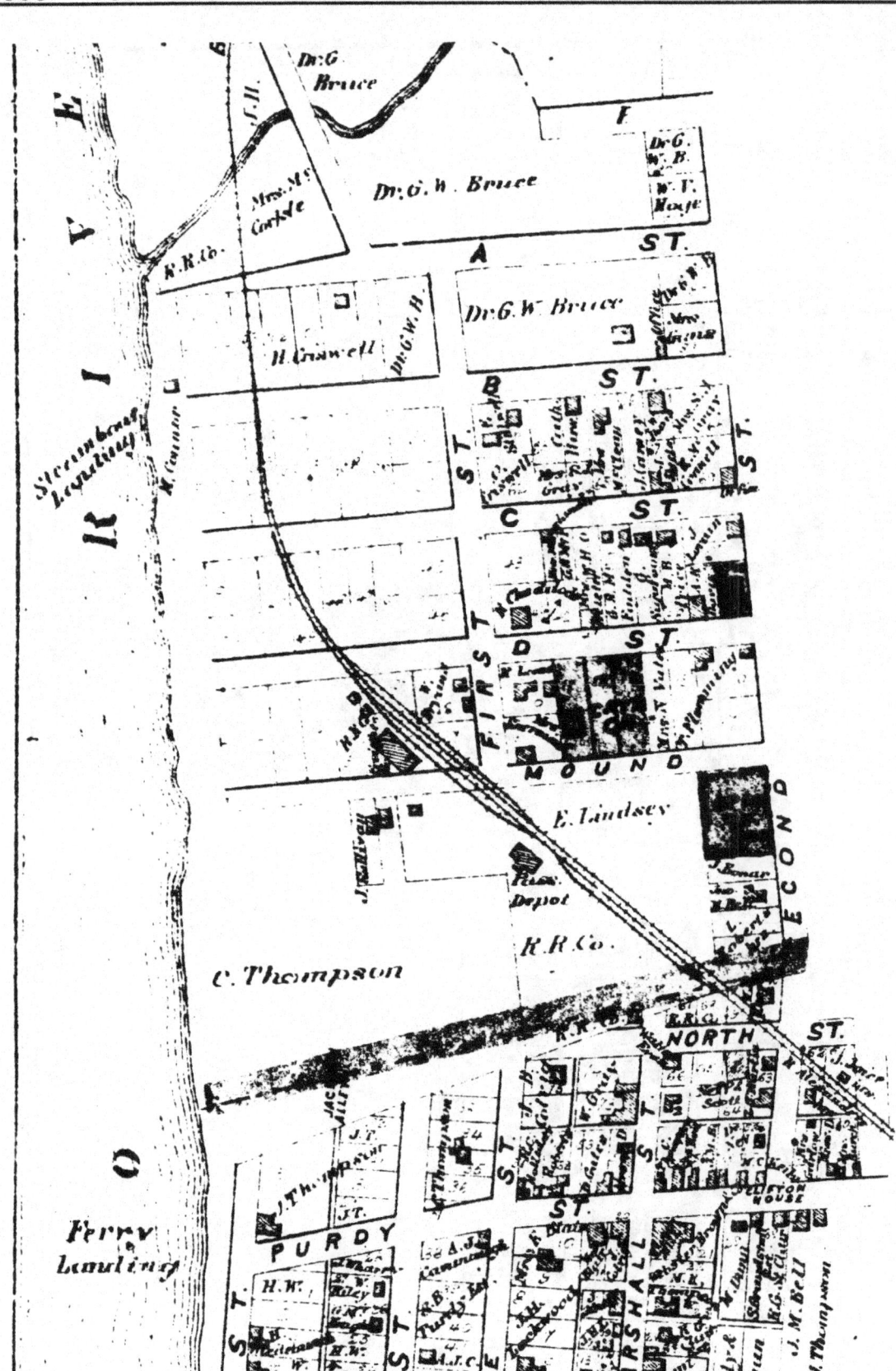

1871 MAP – MARSHALL CO. – MOUNDSVILLE – E. CENTRAL PART   1809

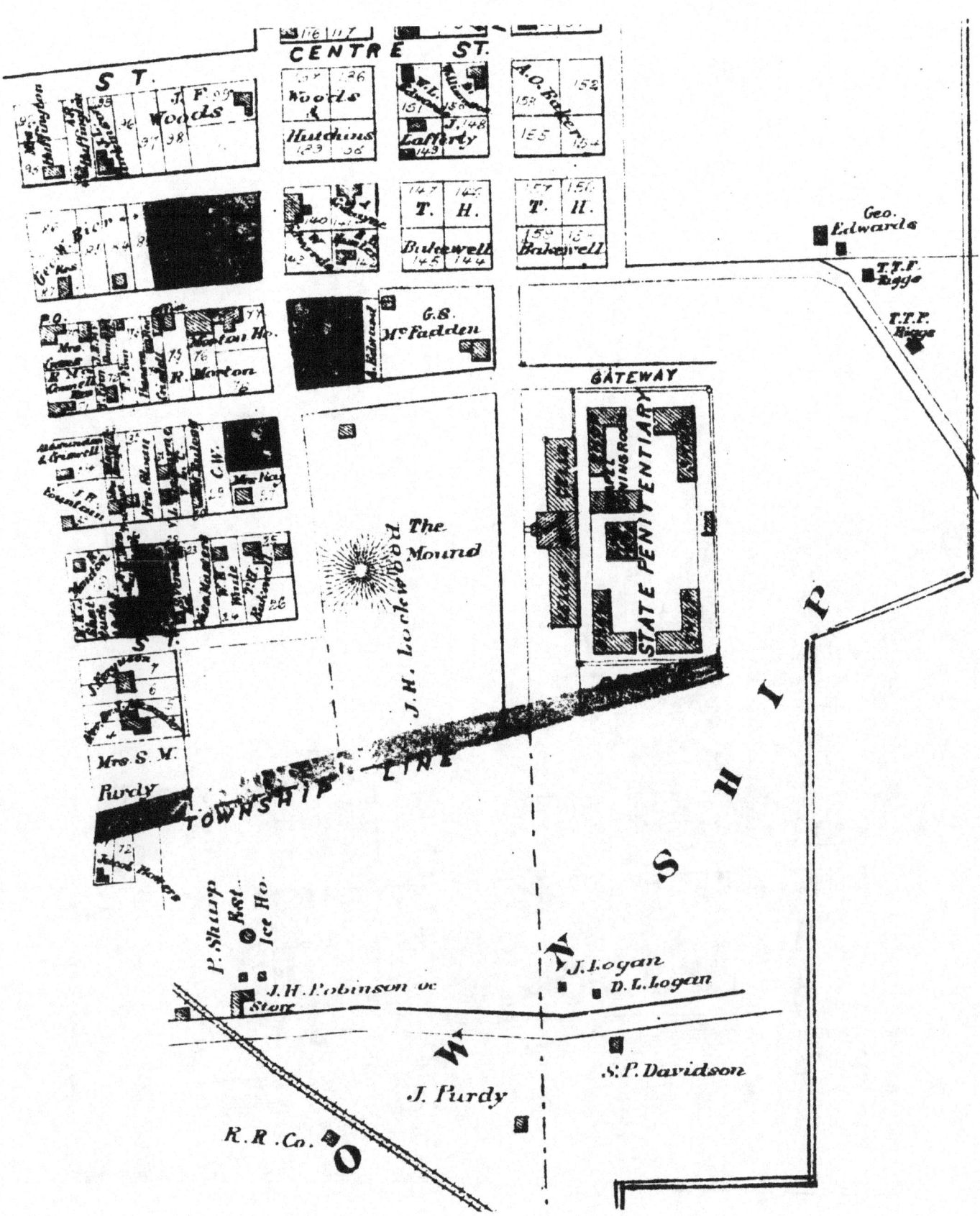

1871 MAP – MARSHALL CO. – MOUNDSVILLE – S. PART

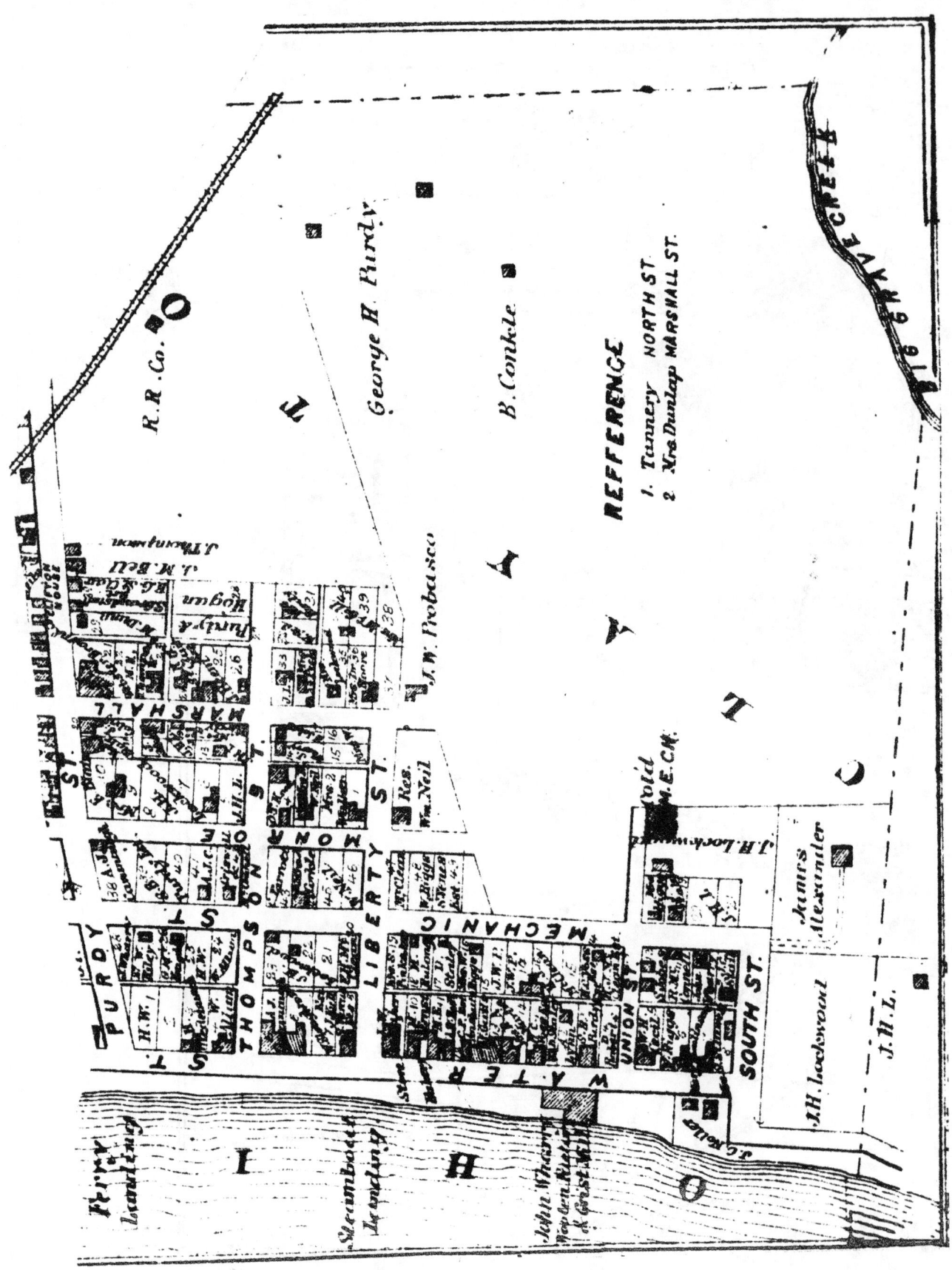

1871 MAP – MARSHALL CO. – SHERRARD P.O. 1811

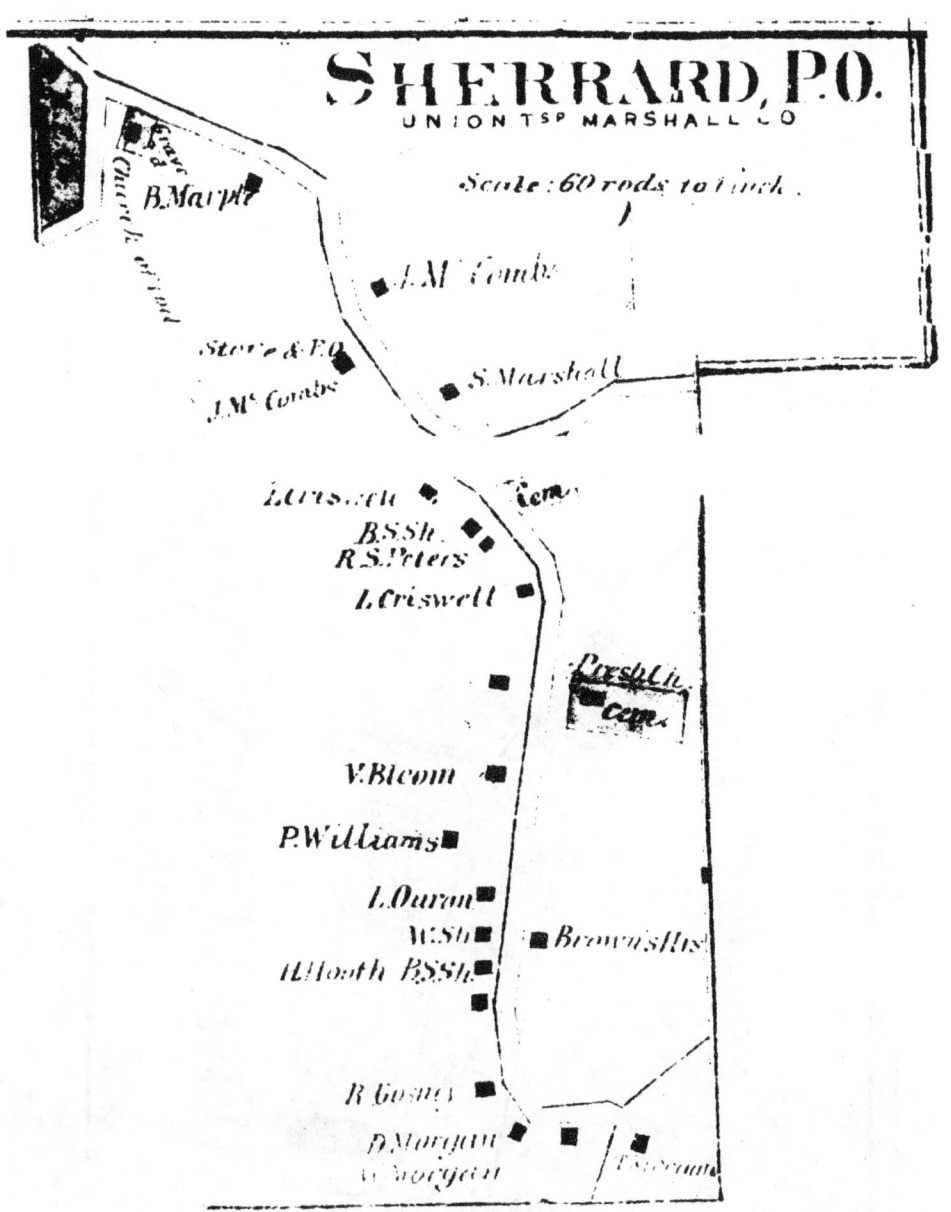

UNION TSP MARSHALL CO
Scale: 60 rods to 1 inch
B.Marple
Church
J.Mc Combs
Store & P.O.
J.Mc Combs
S.Marshall
B.S.Sh.
R.S.Peters
I.Criswell
Presb.Ch.
Cem.
V.Bloom
P.Williams
W.Sh.
Brown's Hs.
R.Gosney
D.Morgan

1812   1871 MAP – MARSHALL CO. – WEST UNION, DALLAS P.O.

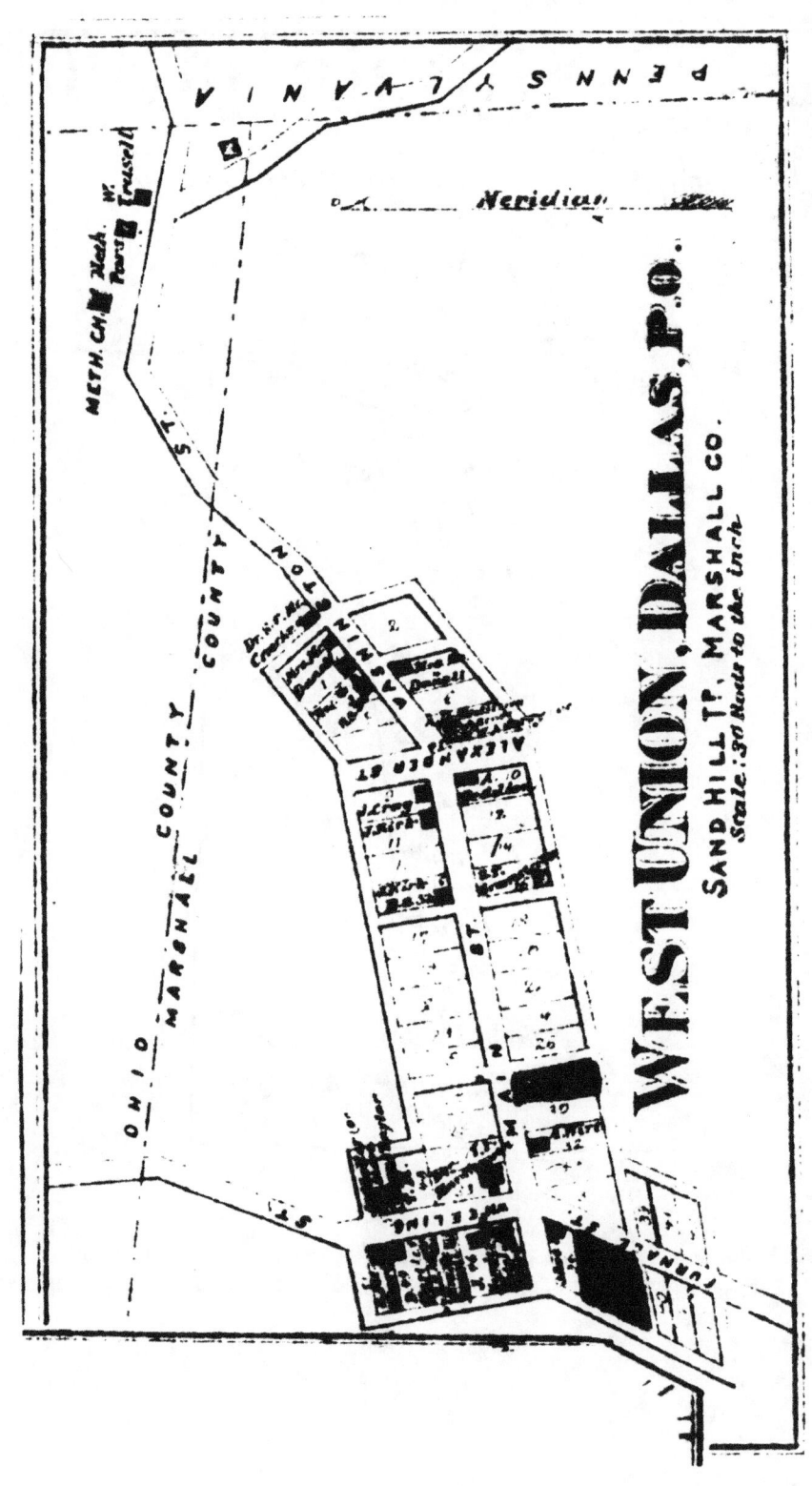

1871 MAP – MARSHALL CO. – ROSBBYS ROCK 1813

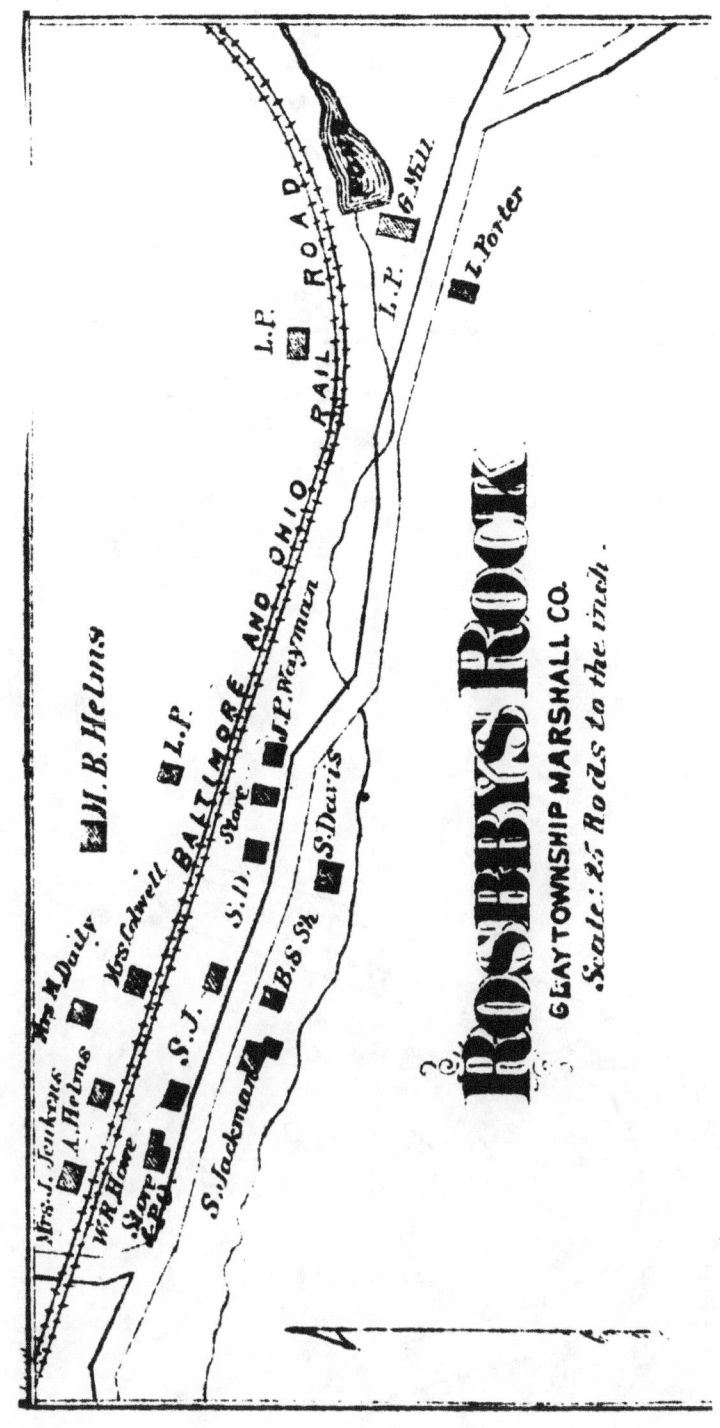

GLAY TOWNSHIP MARSHALL CO.
Scale: 25 Rods to the inch
BALTIMORE AND OHIO RAIL ROAD
H. B. Helms
L.P.
L.P.
L.P.
G. Mill
L. Porter
J.P. Wayman
S. Davis
S.D.
Store
S.J.
B.S. Sh
S. Jackman
Mrs. Colwell
A. Helms
W.R. Howe
Store
P.O.
Mrs. J. Jenkins

1814   1871 MAP – MARSHALL CO. – BELLTON

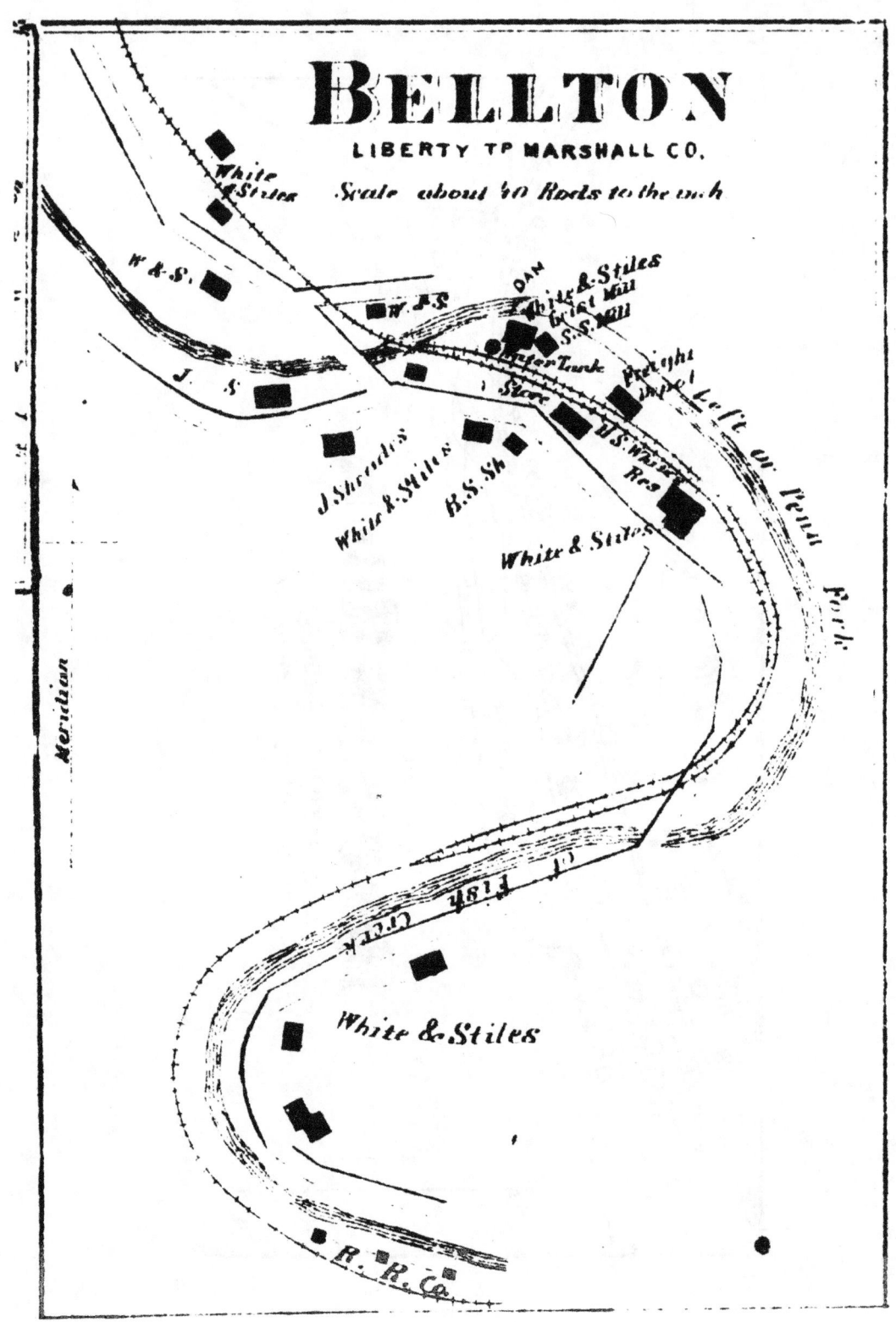

TABLE OF AIR LINE DISTANCES

	Belton	Benwood	Bethany	Blair.	Cameron.	Clinton, Brooke Co.	Edgington.	Elm Grove, Ohio Co.	Fowlers, Brooke Co.	Freeman's Landing.	Glen Easton.	Greggsville, Ohio Co.	Hamilton.	Holliday's Cove, Marshall Co.	Limestone.	MOUNDSVILLE	New Cumberland.	New Manchester, FAIRVIEW P. O.	Pleasant Valley, Marshall Co.	Rock Lick, Marshall Co.	Rosbby's Rock	STEUBENVILLE	Sherrard, Marshall Co.	Triadelphia Borough.	Valley Grove, Ohio Co.	WELLSBURG.	WHEELING.	West Union.	West Liberty.
Belton	0																												
Benwood	20.5	0																											
Bethany	32.3	18.	0																										
Blair	53.5	38.	21.2	0																									
Cameron	4.8	16.1	27.0	48.8	0																								
Clinton, Brooke Co.	27.	11.1	6.9	27.4	22.2	0																							
Edgington	48.7	29.2	13.4	8.9	40.9	19.	0																						
Elm Grove, Ohio Co.	31.6	5.5	13.	33.7	16.7	6.8	25.2	0																					
Fowlers, Brooke Co.	37.6	22.7	5.8	15.9	32.9	11.7	8.3	18.	0																				
Freeman's Landing	60.9	34.3	18.5	4.8	46.1	24.2	5.2	30.4	13.8	0																			
Glen Easton	7.7	18.2	27.4	48.6	4.0	21.8	40.3	15.8	32.7	45.6	0																		
Greggsville, Ohio Co.	25.2	7.	11.3	31.1	20.4	4.5	23.3	3.6	15.8	27.5	18.7	0																	
Hamilton	61.6	44.4	29.3	9.9	56.8	34.7	15.8	40.8	24.1	10.7	56.1	37.7	0																
Holliday's Cove, Marshall Co.	46.9	30.6	14.5	7.4	42.1	20.8	1.5	26.5	9.8	4.	41.6	23.7	14.7	0															
Limestone	18.7	7.1	20.6	41.6	9.1	14.8	33.3	8.2	25.8	38.5	7.1	11.6	49.	34.6	0														
MOUNDSVILLE	16.9	6.5	23.9	44.4	12.2	17.1	35.7	10.9	28.8	40.8	8.2	13.3	50.9	37.1	5.8	0													
New Cumberland	54.1	37.3	21.8	4.7	49.3	27.8	8.4	33.5	16.6	3.2	48.7	30.5	7.5	7.9	41.6	43.8	0												
New Manchester, FAIRVIEW P. O.	55.9	39.6	23.6	8.8	51.2	29.4	10.4	35.6	18.8	5.2	50.8	32.7	6.2	9.1	43.7	46.1	26.	0											
Pleasant Valley, Marshall Co.	11.9	9.	21.6	42.8	7.8	15.5	34.5	9.7	26.9	39.8	5.8	13.2	50.8	35.8	1.8	9.9	42.9	44.9	0										
Rock Lick, Marshall Co.	3.3	16.	24.1	45.1	4.1	19.2	37.5	14.4	29.4	42.6	7.2	18.	53.4	38.6	8.	12.8	45.9	47.7	6.2	0									
Rosbby's Rock	11.2	11.6	27.8	48.7	6.6	21.8	40.2	15.	32.9	45.4	4.	17.9	55.7	41.6	7.4	5.4	48.4	50.6	7.1	10.8	0								
STEUBENVILLE	48.5	26.9	11.5	11.2	38.8	16-7	3.3	23.9	6.6	7.4	38.1	20.	18.	8.8	31.1	33.3	10.5	12.7	32.4	35.4	37.9	0							
Sherrard, Marshall Co.	17.5	3.6	17.8	38.6	12.9	11.1	30.	4.8	22.9	35.2	10.7	8.	45.6	31.4	8.8	6.8	38.3	40.4	5.6	11.4	10.1	27.7	0						
Triadelphia Borough	22.	7.8	11.6	32.5	17.2	5.1	24.1	1.6	16.7	29.8	16.2	4.	39.9	25.4	9.1	12.5	32.5	34.5	10.4	14.4	16.2	21.9	6.9	0					
Valley Grove, Ohio Co.	24.	11.7	3.4	29.5	19.2	4.8	21.7	6.2	13.7	26.8	19.1	6.9	37.5	22.8	19.5	16.6	30.	31.9	18.8	15.8	19.8	19.6	10.2	4.4	0				
WELLSBURG	37.8	21.	5.5	17.	32.5	10.5	8.4	16.8	8.	13.6	31.9	14.1	24.2	9.7	24.8	27.4	16.8	18.8	26.1	29.2	31.8	6.2	21.6	15.7	18.8	0			
WHEELING	24.3	4.9	13.6	33.1	19.6	6.8	24.8	3.8	18.	29.4	17.5	2.8	39.5	25.7	10.6	11.4	32.8	34.6	12.8	17.7	16.3	22.	6.8	5.1	8.8	16.2	0		
West Union	18.3	11.8	18.1	35.1	13.7	9.9	27.5	7.6	19.8	[illegible]	14.5	10.5	43.4	28.5	9.	14.4	35.9	37.6	9.1	10.	16.1	25.5	8.7	6.1	6.	19.2	11.4	0	
West Liberty	29.6	14.5	3.5	24.3	24.8	8.8	16.	9.6	8.4	21.2	24.3	7.7	31.9	17.8	17.4	20.5	24.4	26.4	18.5	21.6	24.5	18.9	17.4	8.2	5.8	7.6	10.1	11.8	0

POPULATION
ACCORDING TO
CENSUS OF 1870.

Ohio County.
Richland	1,...
Liberty	1,...
Triadelphia	4,...
Ritchie	...

Wheeling City by Wards
1st Ward	2,971
2d "	1,...
3d "	3,...
4th "	3,...
5th "	2,070
6th "	3,...
7th "	1,...
South Wheeling	3,...
Washington Township	...

Total for City .... 22,...

Total for County 28,819

Brooke County
Buffalo Township, exclusive of Bethany	1,...
Bethany Town	...
Cross Creek Township	1,...
Wellsburg Township	1,...

Total for County .... 5,...

Hancock County
Butler Township	970
Clay "	1,...
Grant "	1,...
Fee "	...

Total for County .... 4,...

Marshall County
Clay Township	1,619
Franklin Township	1,511
Sand Hill Township	951
Union Township	2,700
Washington Township	...
Moundsville Town	1,...
Cameron, excluding Town	1,...
Cameron Township	...
Liberty Township	2,...
Meade Township	1,...
Webster	1,143

Total for County .... 14,...

Total for the Four Counties .... 59,...

THE

HEMPFIELD RAIL ROAD,

AND

THE BONDS

OF

OHIO COUNTY, VIRGINIA,

AND

WASHINGTON COUNTY, PENNSYLVANIA.

PHILADELPHIA:
JOHN C. CLARK, PRINTER, 66 DOCK STREET.
1852.

OFFICERS AND DIRECTORS

OF

THE HEMPFIELD RAIL ROAD COMPANY.

OFFICERS.

THOMAS M. T. M'KENNAN, *President*.
JOSEPH HENDERSON, *Secretary and Treasurer*.
CHARLES ELLET, Jr., *Chief Engineer*.

DIRECTORS.

S. BENTLEY, of Washington County.
HARRISON P. LAIRD, } Of Westmoreland County.
H. Y. BRADY, }
SAMUEL NEEL. }
ISAAC W. MITCHELL, } Of Wheeling.
JAMES PAULL. }

THE

HEMPFIELD RAIL ROAD.

THE HEMPFIELD RAIL ROAD is intended to afford an eastern outlet to the great lines of western roads which are concentrating on the Ohio river at Wheeling. It connects the City of Wheeling with the Pennsylvania Rail Road at the town of Greensburg. Its length will be a fraction greater or less than 76 miles.

The importance of this connecting link will be recognised by tracing the three great western and south-western rail roads, leading from the Mississippi river in the west, and the Cumberland and Tennessee in the south-west, towards the seaboard.

The conclusion of the mind will be strengthened, moreover, by observing on the annexed or any popular map, the boundaries of south-western Pennsylvania and north-western Virginia.

It will be noticed that *the western boundary of the State of Pennsylvania no where borders on the*

: THE HEMPFIELD RAIL ROAD ; [HEMPFIELD RAIL ROAD] THE HEMPFIELD RAIL ROAD, AND THE BONDS OF OHIO COUNTY, VIRGINIA, AND WASHINGTON COUNTY, PENNSYLVANIA. Philadelphia: John C. Clark, Printer, 68 Dock Street, 1852. 8vo, 31 pages, wrappers, large folding map in rear, entitled: "Map of the Western railroads Tributary to Philadelphia, With Their Rival lines." Map measures 32 x 18 inches, is hand colored in outline, shows the railroad routes westward to Jefferson City, Missouri. A few breaks along fold joints, rear cover detached, interior clean. ▫The Hempfield Rail Road was begun to join the city of Wheeling, (not-yet-West Virginia on the Ohio River to the Pennsylvania Rail Road line. Wheeling was apparently becoming a hub of railroad lines linking east and west.

Ohio river. A narrow strip of the territory of Virginia, lies between Pennsylvania and Ohio, and extends upwards, from the south-western angle of Pennsylvania, along the Ohio, until it reaches a latitude sixteen miles north of the City of Pittsburg.

It is of great importance that the geography of this section of Virginia and Pennsylvania should be appreciated; for *the charter granted to the Hempfield Rail Road Company is the only charter that has been conceded by the State of Virginia for any rail road passing through her territory from Pennsylvania into Ohio.*

This is the first advantage which the Hempfield road possesses in the active competition which is expected for the trade of the west. It has a complete and satisfactory charter from Virginia, to cross that neck of land belonging to Virginia, and separating south-western Pennsylvania from the Ohio river.

Attempts have been made to obtain other charters for lines running through the territory of Virginia, both north and south of Wheeling. But they have all been unsuccessful. After several months of extraordinary exertion, aided by gentlemen of great political and social influence, and commanding ability, the application for a charter for a road from Pittsburg to Steubenville, during the last session of the legislature, was signally defeated. It is believed that it could not challenge a single vote in the Virginia senate.

The fact that the Hempfield road possesses the only charter that has been granted, or is likely to be granted, through that portion of Virginia which lies west of Pennsylvania, is, as before stated, the first great advantage which it claims in the competition for the trade of the West.

WAY TRAFFIC.

The second important advantage of this line, consists in the wealth and fertility of the district through which the road passes. The counties of Westmoreland and Washington, in Pennsylvania, and that of Ohio, in Virginia, are among the richest and most productive of those two States. From the origin of the road at Greensburg, to its western termination at Wheeling, it passes through a fertile and most populous agricultural district, over large portions of which are found extensive beds of coal, already worked with profit, and certain to be more advantageously and extensively developed on the completion of the road. The WAY TRADE and WAY TRAVEL, which experience in this country has shown to constitute an important element of the success of every rail road, must therefore inevitably be large.

LOCAL TRIBUTARIES.

The next, in the list of peculiar advantages which this route possesses, is the importance of the tributaries which it must receive in its course.

At Greensburg, the Hempfield road takes up and produces westwardly, the PENNSYLVANIA RAIL ROAD—the great central artery, leading from Philadelphia into the western and south-western States. It must therefore carry beyond the Ohio, both because it is the only chartered road through Virginia, and because it is the shortest and best possible line—whatever trade and travel can circulate between Philadelphia and the country west and southwest of Wheeling.

About sixteen miles west of Greensburg it crosses the Yohiogeny, a stream which has been made navigable for steamboats, and is already supplied with an important trade.

About twenty-five miles from Greensburg, it crosses the Monongahela, where its borders abound in mineral wealth, and the stream is navigated by numerous steamboats, which already have an amount of freight and travel almost adequate to the support of the road.

At the borough of Washington it will receive a branch from Pittsburg, and offer the shortest possible connexion between that city and Cincinnati and St. Louis. This tributary will bring upon the Hempfield line the trade and travel of the Alleghany valley road.

TRADE OF THE OHIO RIVER.

These, however, are only the local contributions of the line. But it was not to accommodate the trade which these tributaries will supply, nor the way traffic of the country, that the Hempfield road was projected. Its great resources are found in the trade of the Ohio river, and the great rail ways which are approaching the Ohio river at Wheeling.

The trade of the Ohio river is a business already well developed, and has been found sufficient, of itself, to have stimulated the construction of several great lines of improvement, by canal or rail road, from tide water to the West. It is not practicable to estimate with any reasonable approach to accuracy, the magnitude of the commerce which is now borne upon this stream.

It has been ascertained, indeed, and fully established in an important trial before the Supreme Court of the United States, that there are annually *registered*, on the books of the wharf master at

Wheeling, no less than two hundred and thirty distinct steamboats, which touch more than three thousand times at the landings of that city, in the course of the year, to receive or discharge freight and passengers. This fact is true, beyond question; but the amount of trade which these boats actually carry, or which may be carried by those that pass without landing, and being entered on the register, has not been ascertained.

The smaller class of boats on the Ohio carry 100 tons, or sometimes less: the largest packets about 400 tons.

They are all, or nearly all, provided with accommodations for passengers, and on many of them the cabins are fitted up with every desirable comfort and elegance.

There are, however, no satisfactory data for determining either the number of tons or passengers actually carried by these boats. But it has been variously estimated, in the aggregate, at

From 400,000 to 700,000 tons of freight per annum;
From 250,000 to 500,000 passengers per annum.

The only specific evidence which we have on the subject is, that there are over 230 boats running on the upper Ohio, and that of these 58 are regular packets trading to the ports of Cincinnati and St. Louis.

It has also been shown by the testimony of persons engaged on these regular packets, that the average annual business amounts to

Freight carried by 58 boats, 170,000 tons.
Passengers carried by 58 boats, 168,000 persons.

The estimates of the business done by the 170 other boats, which do not run in regular lines, is wholly conjectural.

It is not necessary to speculate on the proportion of this trade and travel which will leave the boats at Wheeling and seek to reach Philadelphia by the Hempfield Rail Road. It is enough, or ought to be enough, to give every assurance of the success of the work, to know that the trade is there, and can only get to Philadelphia by the line which this company controls and is now constructing.

To follow the course of the river up to Pittsburg, and *there* take the Pennsylvania road, the trade must surmount the worst portions of the navigation of the Ohio, found in the 94 miles between Pittsburg and Wheeling. In overcoming the difficulties there encountered, a boat consumes ordinarily from 12 to 20 hours, during the brief season of navigation, on that portion of the river: while in about 16 hours the passenger will traverse, in the cars, the 398 miles between Wheeling and Philadelphia.

It requires, therefore, no argument to prove that on the completion of the Hempfield road, the trade of the Ohio river, destined to Philadelphia, will be landed at Wheeling, and go through by rail road. But until it is completed, this business must of necessity be monopolized by the Baltimore and Ohio road,—if that road is able to accommodate it all. In this age of enterprise, an unnecessary and superfluous river trip of 12 or 20 hours cannot be tolerated.

WESTERN RAIL ROADS.

The great lines of western and south-western rail roads, which are rapidly approaching and concentrating upon Wheeling, are represented on the annexed map. These roads are not all completed, but are in various stages of progress, from the Ohio to the Mississippi.

The rail road system of this country possesses a feature which, at this moment, is worthy of serious consideration; for it is unprecedented in the past history of the system here or abroad. It must be duly noted to enable us to anticipate, with any approach to correctness, the probable results which the future is to bring forth.

There are, essentially, two great systems of rail road enterprises now rapidly progressing towards completion: viz. a western system, spreading over the space between the Ohio and Mississippi, and between the northern lakes and the Cumberland mountains: and an eastern system, extending from the Alleghany mountains to the seaboard.

There appears to belong to this western system, about 6800 miles of road, finished, in actual progress, or on the point of being commenced. In fact, rejecting many hundred miles of road chartered, and in the hands of organized companies, there were, computed or in progress, according to the United States census of 1850,

In Ohio,	- -	2400 miles.
In Indiana,	- -	1300 ,,
In Illinois,	- -	1900 ,,

Total, in those three States, 5600 miles.

It is impossible to state the number of miles in these three States which are completed and in actual operation. The amount is changing every month, as sections of new road, upon all the lines, are thrown open to the public. It is probable, however, that nearly or quite one-half of the whole, will be in actual use before the close of the current year, and a total of more than 5000 miles in the next two years.

Three of these great western lines, it will be observed, radiate from Wheeling into different parts

of the west, and north-west, and south-west, and are designed to form the trunk roads leading to the Atlantic seaboard. As far as they have yet proceeded, the results are indicative of most extraordinary success: but no just estimate can be made of the ultimate value of any one of these primary lines, until the gaps which yet remain are filled up, and the routes are made continuous, at least from the Mississippi to the Ohio.

The other system of roads may be designated as the *seaboard system*, and embraces all those roads connecting the Atlantic cities with each other, as well as the great lines pushing out from New York, Philadelphia, Baltimore and Richmond, across the Alleghany mountains, into the Ohio valley.

Both of these immense systems of rail road are well advanced, and, in the aggregate, eminently successful. But, what constitutes the remarkable feature of the present state of things, is the fact, *that no connexion has yet been formed* between the great system of the east and the still greater system of the west.

The HEMPFIELD RAIL ROAD is designed to constitute one, and by far the most important, of these connecting links. We may glance, therefore, with profit, at the most prominent of its tributaries.

FIRST WESTERN TRIBUTARY.

Cleveland and Wheeling Road.

The rail road leading from Cleveland on Lake Erie to the City of Wheeling, was originally designed to extend from Cleveland to Pittsburg. The direction of the road has been recently changed, and it is now the purpose to extend it to the more central and prominent rail road focus at Wheeling.

That portion of the line extending from the City of Cleveland to the Ohio river, below Wellsville, having a length of 100 miles, is finished, and has been for several months in use.

That portion which is yet required to reach the City of Wheeling [38 miles] it is hoped to have opened in the course of the next season.

The division of this line which is finished, is operated at great disadvantage, but, nevertheless, very successfully. The roads with which it connects, running along the southern shore of Lake Erie, are still incomplete; and until they are finished, and the line is extended to Wheeling, its influence upon the traffic and travel of the northwest cannot be fully appreciated. The Cleveland road will be the most northern of the important feeders of the HEMPFIELD ROAD.

SECOND WESTERN TRIBUTARY.

The Alton, Terre Haute, Indianapolis, Columbus, Zanesville, and Wheeling Line.

This great central road is completed, or under contract, in all its parts, from the Mississippi river at Alton, through the States of Illinois, Indiana, and Ohio, to a point within about 50 miles of Wheeling. The balance, it is expected, will also be got under way in the course of the present summer.

It is useless to discuss the merits and importance of this route. It passes through the very heart of three of the richest and most prosperous of the States of this Union. It touches at nearly all the great central towns and cities of those States; and it receives tributaries from the lakes on the north, and the Ohio on the south. Many miles of the line, in detached portions, are now in use, and it will all be finished and in active operation before the Hempfield road can possibly be ready to receive, or to share with the Baltimore and Ohio road, the trade that it will bring forward from the fertile west.

THIRD WESTERN TRIBUTARY.

The St. Louis, Vincennes, Cincinnati, Zanesville, and Wheeling Line.

The whole of this line, with a very trifling exception, is under contract, from the Mississippi river at St. Louis, through Cincinnati to Zanesville. At Zanesville it unites with the Central road, where the united trade and travel of the two works will pass over the eighty miles of the central line from Zanesville to Wheeling.

This is the third great tributary of the Hempfield road, and is the shortest rail road line that can ever be obtained from Philadelphia to Cincinnati, and from Philadelphia to St. Louis.

FOURTH WESTERN TRIBUTARY.

The Nashville, Lexington, Maysville, Portsmouth, Marietta, and Wheeling Line.

This line is not all in progress of construction, but the preliminary legislation has been procured, the companies organized, surveys commenced, and large amounts of individual and municipal subscriptions obtained. Portions of the route are nearly completed, and other sections are in progress of construction.

By this line Philadelphia will obtain, through

the Hempfield and Marietta roads, a continuous and unbroken *gauge* as far as Nashville, in Tennessee.

FIFTH WESTERN TRIBUTARY.

The Line from Wheeling, through Marietta, Chilicothe, and Cincinnati.

This line is second to no other western road in its importance to Philadelphia, and as a feeder to the Hempfield road. It is one of the routes by means of which the trade of the Ohio and Mississippi road, extending from St. Louis to Cincinnati, can reach Philadelphia; and it is the *only route* through which the trade of Kentucky and Tennessee can approach that city.

In addition to its other claims, this tributary has the peculiar merit of affording an *unbroken gauge* from Philadelphia, through Wheeling and Cincinnati, to St. Louis; and, as before stated, through Wheeling to Lexington, Louisville, and Nashville.

It is unnecessary to enter into any detailed discussion of the amount of travel, or the value of the trade which will be concentrated at Wheeling by these immense feeders. The rail road distance from the Ohio to the Mississippi, across the three intervening States, is nearly 600 miles. The country traversed is fertile, to a proverb—prosperous beyond comparison, and already occupied by a population of four millions of persons.

The trade of these great works and their tributaries is seeking to approach the Ohio river at Wheeling, and will pass from thence exclusively to Baltimore until the Hempfield road is completed. It will then be divided, as the value of their respective markets, and the facilities of transportation afforded by their competing lines, may prescribe, between Philadelphia and Baltimore. It is not pretended that this trade, and the trade of the Ohio river, is all to be monopolized by the Hempfield road. Such a monopoly is impossible. It will be divided, in some proportion which experience is to decide, between our own line and that of our enterprising southern competitor. It is, however, scarcely to be doubted that the utmost capacity of both works will speedily be taxed to give free vent to it all.

The length of the Hempfield road, as already stated, will vary but little from 76 miles.

The steepest grade will be 66 feet per mile.

The cost of the work is estimated by the chief engineer, after careful and extensive surveys, at $35,500 per mile, or, in the aggregate, $2,700,000, for a single track. This estimate is intended to include the cost of obtaining the right of way and the running stock. In the opinion of the engineer the sum is ample.

OHIO COUNTY BONDS.

In payment of the subscription of $150,000 made to the stock of the Hempfield Rail Road Company by the County of Ohio, in the State of Virginia, the bonds of the said County have been received by the Company, under the authority of the following act, passed by the Legislature of Virginia.

From the Code of Virginia, Chapter 61; and Chapter 41, Session Acts of 1850-51.

SECTION 38. When a joint stock company shall have been incorporated to construct a rail road or turnpike through, by or near to any county likely to be benefitted thereby, the county court of such county may make an order requiring the sheriff and commissioners of elections, at the next general election for members of the General Assembly, or at any other time, not less than one month from the date of the order, which shall be designated therein, to open a poll, and take the sense of the persons qualified to vote for members of the General Assembly of such county, on the question whether the said court, on behalf of such county, shall subscribe to the stock of such company. The said order shall state the maximum amount proposed to be subscribed, which in no case shall exceed one-third part of the stock to be subscribed by others than the State.

SECT. 39. The commissioners of elections, after taking an oath fairly to take and return the poll, shall open poll books at the court house of the county, and at the other places therein at which separate elections for members of Assembly are held, and shall cause to be entered upon such books, in a column to be headed "subscription," the names of the persons qualified to vote for members of the General Assembly of the county, who attend and are in favour of the subscription; and shall cause to be entered upon said books, in another column to be headed "no subscription," the names of those persons qualified to vote for members of the General Assembly of the county, who attend and are opposed to the subscription. The commissioners who take the said polls shall certify them, and within five days after the day they were taken, return them to the clerk of such county court.

SECT. 40. If by the said poll books it shall appear that three fifths of the persons qualified to vote for members of the General Assembly of such county, voting upon the question, are in favour of the subscription, the said court, at its term next after taking the said polls, shall make an order requiring the sheriff to summon the acting Justices thereof to attend the next June term of the court, to carry out the wishes of the persons qualified to vote for members of the General Assembly.

SECT. 41. The acting Justices being summoned as directed in the preceding section, and a majority being present, shall have power to determine what amount of the capital stock (not exceeding the maximum mentioned in section thirty-eight of this chapter) shall be subscribed for on behalf of such county, and shall enter of record the amount so agreed to be subscribed; and thereupon shall appoint an agent to make the subscription, to be paid in such instalments as may be agreed upon by said court, or as may be called for by said company.

SECT. 42. For the purpose of paying the quotas on said stock as they may be called for, or the instalments of such subscriptions as they may fall due, the court, at its June term, shall have power

to appoint an agent or agents to negotiate a loan or loans, for and in the name of such county; and at the time at which it makes its county levy, shall levy on all the lands, and all other subjects liable to State tax and county levy in such county, without the limits of a town that provides for its poor and keeps its streets in order, such tax to pay the amount of such subscription, or of such loan or loans as may be authorized, and the interest thereon, as said court may deem necessary and proper; and from year to year repeat such assessments, until the subscription or loan made by such court, together with all interest, is fully paid. But such levy, for a year, shall not exceed one-fifth of the whole amount of such subscription.

SECT. 43. The right to stock in any company subscribed by any county, under the authority of the two preceding sections, shall vest in such county. And the court of the county shall have power, from time to time, to appoint a proxy to represent the stock in the meetings of the stockholders of the company, and also an agent to collect the dividends on its stock; which dividends, when collected, the said court shall annually apply to the diminution of the levy in such county.

Pursuant to the authority given by the above sections, the question of a subscription for three thousand shares of the capital stock of the Hempfield Rail Road Company, by the county of Ohio, was submitted to the people, and the vote resulted unanimously in favour of the subscription, with the exception of 23 persons. The justices of the county having been summoned in compliance with the 40th section, made the following order at its June term, 1851.

"*Virginia, Ohio County Court, June Term,* 1851.

"The justices having been summoned for the purpose, as appears by the return of the sheriff, and a majority of them being present, proceeded to vote for and against the subscription proposed to be made on behalf of this county, for a portion of the capital stock of the Hempfield Rail Road Company, which vote resulted as follows:—

"*For the subscription*—Andrew Yates, Jacob Gooding, William T. Selby, James Baker, James Kelley, Alexander Rogers, Samuel M'Collock, John Thornburgh, John Gilmer, Andrew P. Woods, Thomas Sweeney, Thomas Thornburgh, Samuel Oldham, John English, John Eoff, John Brady, Peter Yarnall, and Charles D. Knox—18 votes.

"*Against the subscription*—No votes.

"Whereupon it is ordered, that a subscription be made on behalf of this county for capital stock of the Hempfield Rail Road Company, to the amount of one hundred and fifty thousand dollars, or three thousand shares, payable in coupon bonds of this county, which shall be made payable to said company or its order, at twenty years from their date, with interest payable semi-annually; and James Baker, William T. Selby, Jacob Gooding, Thomas Thornburgh, and James Kelley, gentlemen, are hereby appointed agents and commissioners (a majority of whom shall have power to act in the premises) to make the said subscription, and to agree with the directors as to the terms on which the same shall be made; they may also agree with the said directors as to the place at which the said bonds, and the coupons for interest, shall be made payable; but the bonds for the principal shall not be in smaller sums each than one thousand dollars; they may also agree with said directors. before or at the time of making such subscription, as to the route on which the said Hempfield Rail Road shall be made through this county, or any part thereof, and as to the time or times when said bonds shall be called for by the said company; and the bonds may be issued under the direction of said agents, and under the seal of this court attested by the clerk thereof, the same being also signed by the said agents, or a majority of them; and it is ordered that the said Jacob Gooding be and he is hereby appointed the proxy to vote upon the said stock at all elections, and at other times when it may or shall be necessary or proper to vote the same."

The bonds of the county having been duly executed, the following order was made by the court at its May term, 1852:—

"Ordered, that the clerk of this court be authorized and required to sign the coupons or interest warrants attached to the bonds of this county, issued to the Hempfield Rail Road Company in payment of stock."

Bonds of Ohio County, State of Virginia.

These bonds, of $1000 each, are issued to the Hempfield Rail Road Company, in payment of subscriptions of stock to that road, made by said county, by authority of a vote of the people, unanimously, with the exception of but 23 votes. The county of Ohio is rich and populous, embracing a body of land unsurpassed in fertility in the State of Virginia. The assessor's report for 1850, exhibits the following:—

Taxable real estate, exclusive of the city of Wheeling, $1,750,545; real estate within the limits of said city added, gives the sum of 6,250,545, the assessment within the city being $4,500,000. This valuation is exceedingly low, as is also the rate of taxation in Virginia. Almost every part of the county is underlaid with exhaustless beds of coal, of which the value can scarcely be estimated. A proximate estimate of the real estate would be $9,000,000 or $10,000,000. This amount is exclusive of the whole personal property of the county, the value of which, from the fact that but one or two articles have ever been *valued* as the subjects of taxation in Virginia, cannot be satisfactorily ascertained, but must certainly furnish a taxable fund of not less, at a moderate estimate, than $3,000,000; making the whole taxable fund not less than $12,000,000 or $13,000,000. The flourishing city of Wheeling is located in this county, the *annual* value of whose manufactured products exceeds, as appears by the late census, $2,250,000. Her manufacturing facilities are, from her exhaustless coal mines, unlimited; and her population is now growing with great rapidity.

Wheeling is the terminus, on the Ohio river, of the Baltimore and Ohio Rail Road, and of the Hempfield Rail Road, on the east, and the proposed terminus of three rail roads, now rapidly progressing through Ohio, on the west. With the

concentration of these roads, in connexion with the Ohio river, and her extraordinary means of manufacturing, surrounded on all sides by a rich, populous, and fertile country, no city of the west has greater prospects of a rapid increase in wealth and population. The county of Ohio has a present population of about 18,000.

The present debt of the county is $37,452.

When it is considered that the annual *proceeds* of the *industry of the county* alone, agricultural and manufacturing combined, probably approach $3,000,000, and that the bonds now issued will be represented by an equal amount of stock in a road which will be a link in the main chain of rail roads connecting the West with the Atlantic seaboard, no doubt can remain of the entire safety of the investments which may be made in the bonds of this county.

WASHINGTON COUNTY BONDS.

Extract from a Law of Pennsylvania, entitled an Act in relation, among other things, to the Hempfield Rail Road Company, passed the   day of   1851.

SECTION 7. That at the next or some subsequent general election, as may be determined by the president and directors of the Hempfield Rail Road Company, it shall be lawful for the qualified voters of Washington County to decide, by ballot, whether or not the commissioners of said county shall subscribe, on its behalf, four thousand shares in the capital stock of said company; and it shall be the duty of the inspectors and judges of the several townships, boroughs and districts, in said county, at the said election, to receive from the citizens qualified to vote for members of the General Assembly, tickets, written or printed, labelled on the outside, "subscription of stock," and on the inside "for the subscription of stock," or "against the subscription of stock," and to deposite said tickets in a box to be provided for that purpose, as is now required by law in case of tickets for officers to be elected at such election; and at the close of said election, the votes so deposited shall be counted, and an accurate return made to the clerk of the Court of Quarter Sessions of said county, within three days thereafter.

SECT. 9. That it shall be the duty of the clerk of the Court of Quarter Sessions to lay the returns of said election before the judges of the said court, at the term succeeding such election, and the said judges shall thereupon examine the same and declare the result of the vote, and they shall also make out and file a certificate of such result in the office of the said clerk; and if it shall be ascertained by the said judges that a majority of votes has been given "for subscription of stock," it shall be their duty to make an order, that the commissioners of said county of Washington shall, in her name and behalf, subscribe four thousand shares in the capital stock of the said Hempfield Rail Road Company.

In pursuance of this act, an election was ordered by the directors of the Hempfield Rail Road Company, to be held at the time of the general election for governor and State officers, in October, 1851; and in a full vote, the majority in favour of subscription was 1798. The result was duly declared and certified by the judges of the Court of Quarter Sessions, and an order made upon the commissioners to make the subscription.

Extract from a Law of Pennsylvania, entitled "An Act authorizing the Boroughs of Washington and Monongahela City to make a Subscription to the Hempfield Rail Road Company, and for other purposes."

SECTION 3. That the commissioners of the county of Washington, or a majority of them, be and they are hereby authorized and empowered to subscribe four thousand shares in the capital stock of the Hempfield Rail Road Company, in the name and in behalf of said county, and to borrow money to pay therefor, and to make provision for the payment of the principal and interest of the money so borrowed, as in other cases of loans to corporations.

SECT. 4. That the commissioners of said county, or a majority of them, may issue certificates of loan or bonds in the name of said county, redeemable in not less than ten nor more than twenty-five years, bearing an interest of six per cent., payable semi-annually, which shall be transferable as may be directed by said com-

missioners, or a majority of them: and the said certificates of loan or bonds shall be received as cash by the said Rail Road Company, in payment of instalments on shares of stock subscribed for said county.

Sect. 5. That the Hempfield Rail Road Company is hereby authorized to guarantee the payment and interest of any of the certificates of loan or bonds to be issued under this act.

Pursuant to the authority granted in the above acts, the bonds of Washington County, to the amount of $200,000, have been duly executed and delivered to the company, and are guarantied, as well also as those of Ohio County, by the Hempfield Rail Road Company.

STATISTICS OF WASHINGTON COUNTY.

The assessed value of the real and personal estate of this county *for the purposes of taxation*, for the year 1852, is **$8,876,755**, as officially certified.

The following letter is appended, from the clerk of the commissioners:—

Dear Sir,

The valuation of Washington County for purposes of taxation, is as above stated; but this, as you are aware, is no criterion by which to determine the real value of the property in the county. It is notorious that the assessors, in making their valuation, generally put lands at not more than one-half of their real value. I feel safe in believing that the real and personal estate of the citizens of the county, which is subject to taxation, is fully equal to from fourteen to sixteen millions. I believe it is worth more.

Yours truly,
A. SILVEY.

To the Hon. Thos. M. T. M'Kennan,
President of Hempfield Rail Road Co.

The following facts are taken from a tabular statement furnished by the Census Bureau, exhibiting the returns in detail of the census of 1850, for the county of Washington, Pa.

Cash value of farms, $14,942,098

Productions for 1850.

Bushels of wheat,	558,082
Bushels of Indian corn,	804,540
Bushels of oats,	855,943
Pounds of butter,	860,563
Pounds of wool,	933,167

The annual value of these five products alone, is worth more than *one and a half million* of dollars.

The population of the county exceeds 48,000 persons.

A county of such magnitude, population, wealth and resources, in offering her securities, presents to the capitalist an investment of the very first class.

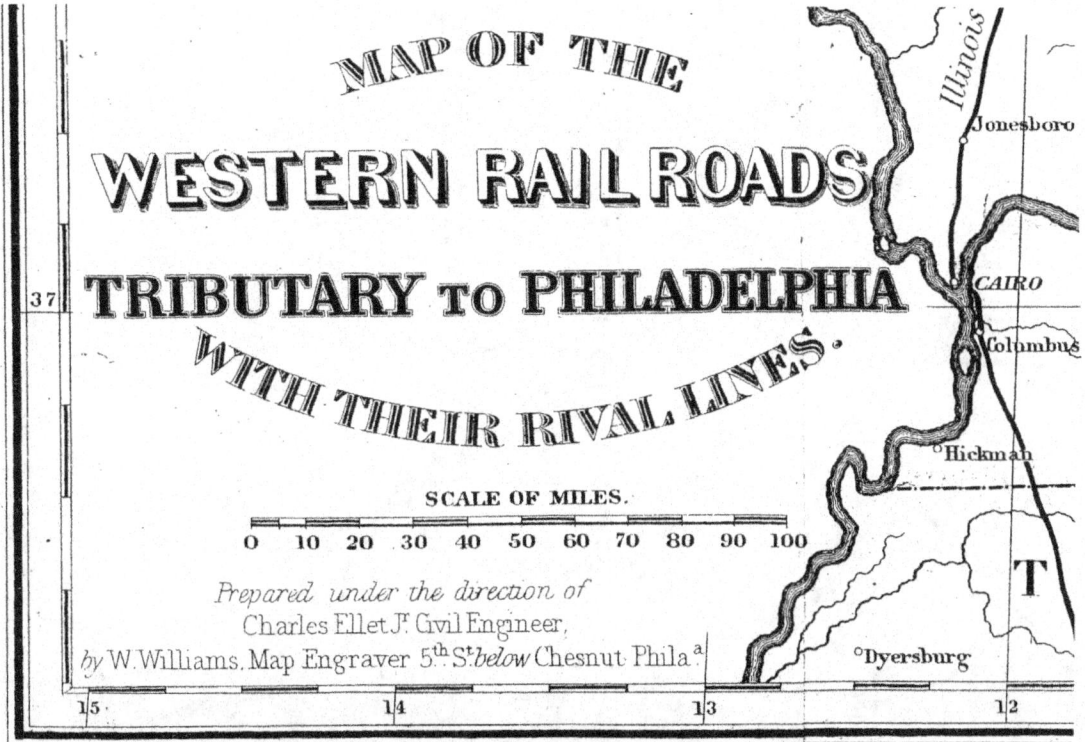

Entered according to Act of Congress, in the year 1851 by Charles Ellet Jr. in the Clerk's Office of the District Court of the eastern district of Pennsylvania

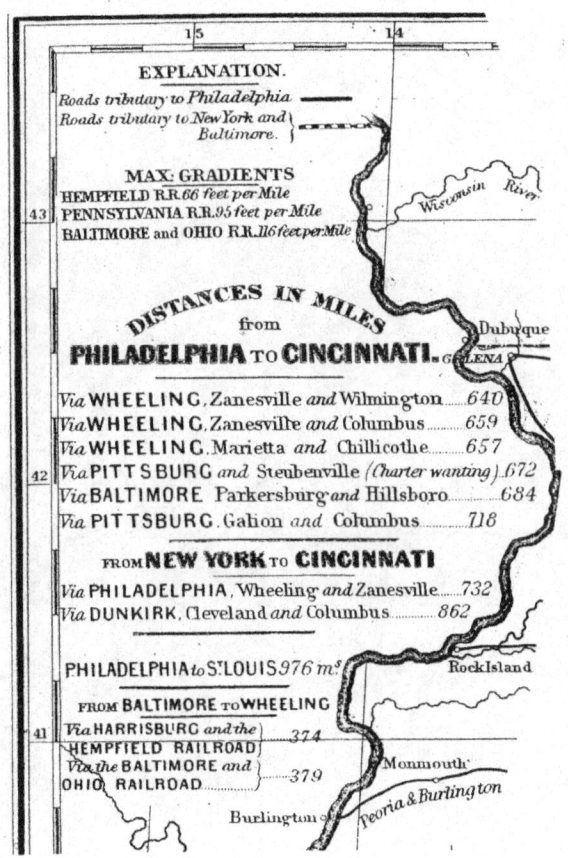

1826 1852 HEMPFIELD RAILROAD – OHIO RAILROADS

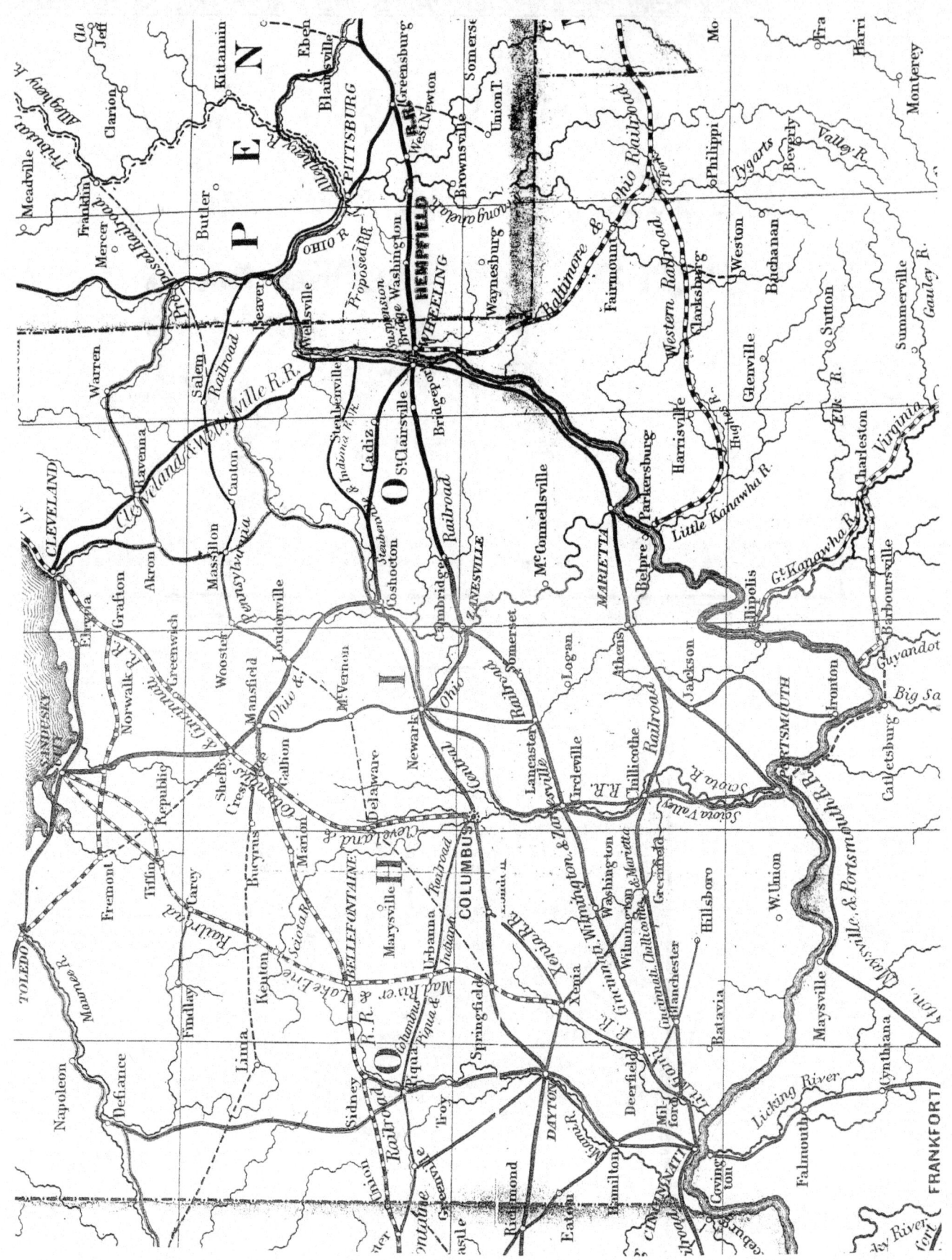

1852 HEMPFIELD RAILROAD BOND – PHILADELPHIA ROUTES / B&O

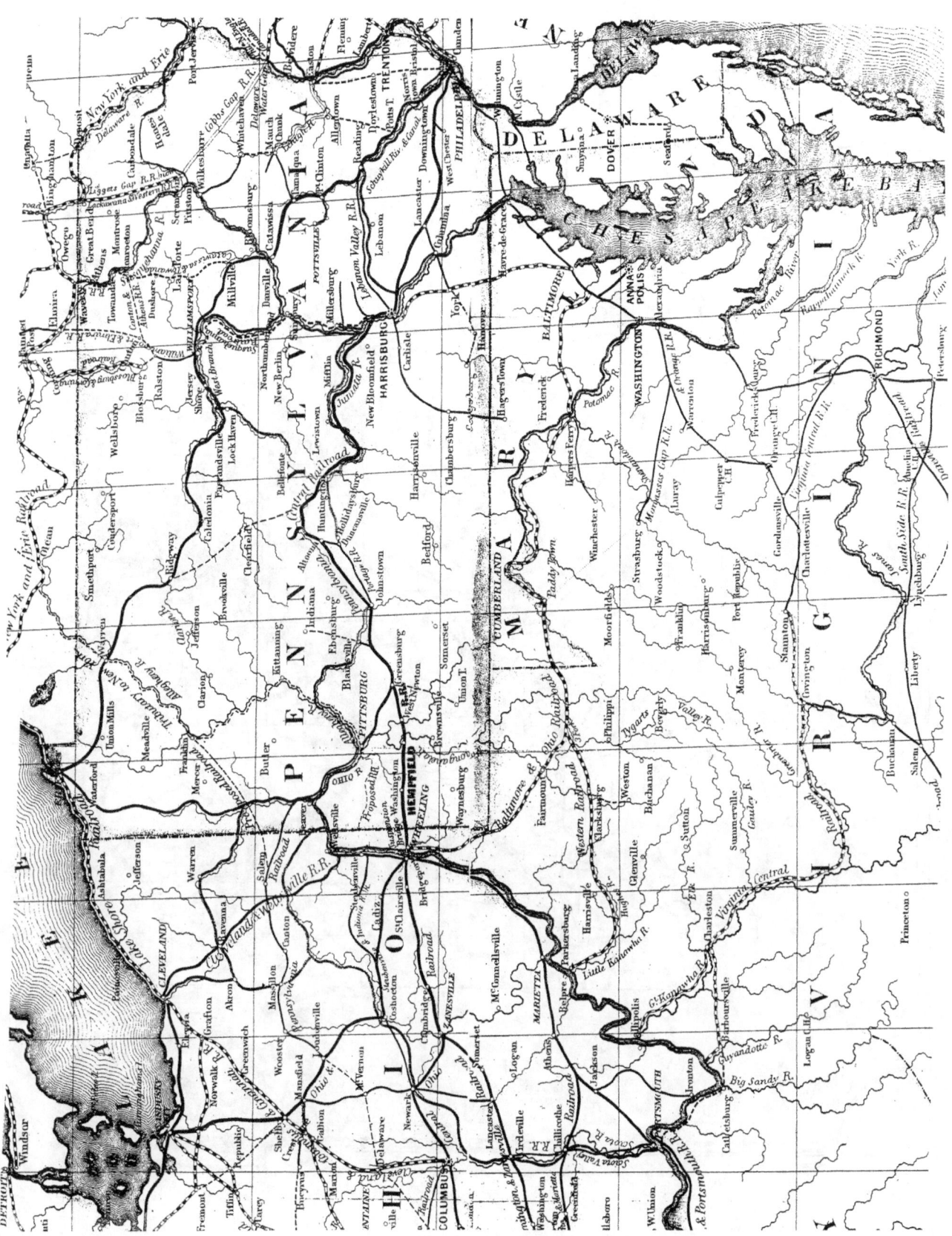

1828 1852 BROOKE COUNTY LANDOWNER MAP – OVERVIEW - S. HALF

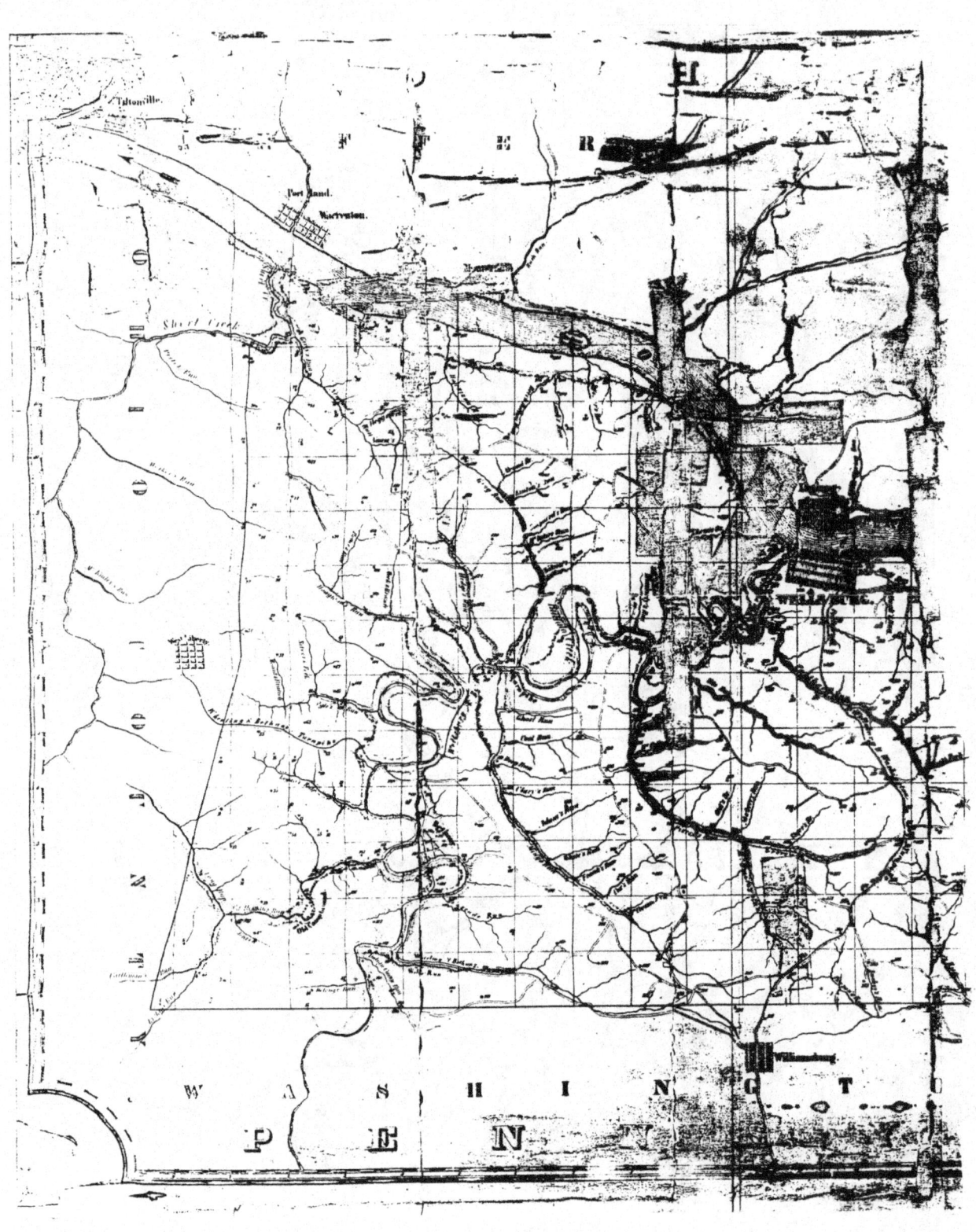

1852 BROOKE COUNTY LANDOWNER MAP – OVERVIEW - N. HALF

1830 1852 BROOKE CO. MAP – NUMBER INDEX TO LANDOWNERS...
...as determined by an anonymous donor to the Brooke County Genealogical Society
(Alphabetic index to names included in "Personal Time Line" Index)

MAP#	NAME
1	ERSKINE, WILLIAM
2	MCBROOM, ROBERT
3	RODGERS, WM.
4	ATKINSON'S MILL
5	ATKINSON, JOHN / ESQ.
6	ATKINSON, JOHN / ESQ.
7	ZINC, JOHN
8	ZINC, JOHN
9	LAUCK, REV. S. HEIRS
10	HUPP, JOSEPH & ISAAC
12	BANE, ROBERT / TAVERN,
13	BANE, ROBERT / WAREHOUSE,
14	BANE, ROBERT / SAW MILL
15	PRESBURY, OCTAY. / MILL
16	TRIMBLE, M. / HEIRS (MILL)
17	TRIMBLE, M. / HEIRS (MILL)
19	TRIMBLE, M. / HEIRS (MILL) / (GONE)
20	BRADY, WM. P.
22	BECK, SAMUEL
23	ANDERSON, THOMAS
24	MORGAN, EDWARD
25	SCHOOL - WALKERS
26	HEDGES, OTHO / ESQ.
27	HEDGES, OTHO / ESQ.
28	HEDGES, OTHO JR.
29	MCKINLEY, WM.
30	MCKINLEY, WM.
31	POAG, ELIJAH
32	PIERSON, DAVID
33	HUPP, JOSEPH & ISAAC
34	STEWART, ELIZABETH
35	SNEDEKER, GEO. / HEIRS
36	SCHOOL - HEDGES
37	HEDGES, MOSES
38	JONES, ELLIS JR.
39	STEWART, ELIZABETH
40	JONES, CHARLES
41	JONES, CHARLES / (MILL)
42	JONES, ABRAM
43	HOOTMAN, CHRISTIAN
44	HOOTMAN, CHRISTIAN
45	JONES, ELLIS C.
46	MCBROOM, ROBERT
47	JONES, WASHINGTON
48	LINDSEY, JOSHUA'S / HEIRS
49	LINDSEY, JOSHUA'S / HEIRS
50	LINDSEY, JOSHUA'S / HEIRS / (SAWMILL)
51	LINDSEY, JOSHUA'S / HEIRS / (SAWMILL)
52	PARKINSON, DAVID
53	PARKINSON, DAVID / (MILL)
54	HEDGES, MOSES
55	BROWN, JOSEPH
56	BROWN, JOSEPH
57	HEDGES, MOSES / (SMITHSHOP)
58	HEDGES, MOSES / (SMITHSHOP)
59	RICHARDSON, ROBERT
60	MILLER, GEORGE B.
61	STEWART, JAS. / HEIRS
62	MILLER, GEORGE B.
63	STEWART, JOHN
64	SCHOOL - NO NAME
65	STETTS, ISAAC
66	LEFLER, DAVID
67	SILVERS, JAMES
68	SMITH, FERGUS

MAP#	NAME
69	LEFLER, DAVID
70	BONER, GEORGE
71	GARRET, SAMUEL
72	WALKER, MONTGOMYRY
73	BECK, SAMUEL
74	HOGG, GEORGE
75	HOGG, GEORGE
76	HOGG, GEORGE
77	BRADY, WM. P.
78	BANE'S SAWMILL / GONE
79	PRESBURY, OCTAY. / MILL
80	PRESBURY, OCTAY. / MILL
81	BANE, ROBERT
82	BANE, ROBERT
83	BANE, ROBERT
84	BANE, ROBERT
85	BANE, ROBERT
86	BANE, ROBERT
87	MCKIM & CO. / (DIS'Y)
88	BANE, ROBERT
89	BANE, ROBERT
90	SCHOOL - BANES
91	BANE, ROBERT
92	WINDSOR, JOSHUA R.
93	WYKOFF, WM.
94	WYKOFF, WM.
95	WYKOFF, WM.
96	BANE, JOHN / HEIRS,
97	MCCORD, G. W. / ESQ.
98	HOGG, GEORGE
99	BANE, ROBERT
100	WALKER, MONTGOMYRY
101	MOORE, ISAIAH / HEIRS
102	EDGINGTON, JESSE / ESQ.
103	NEELY, HUGH D.
104	LAZAER, JESSE
105	COUNCILMAN, LEWIS J.
106	COUNCILMAN, LEWIS J.
107	COUNCILMAN, LEWIS J.
108	MAY, ALEXANDER
109	RIDGELY, FRANKLIN
110	CAMPBELL, ALEXANDER
111	COUNSELMAN, JOHN F.
112	COUNSELMAN, JOHN F.
113	BROWN, JOSEPH
114	BROWN, JOSEPH
115	COUNSELMAN, JOHN F.
116	HOUGH, JAMES
117	HEDGES, MOSES / (SMITHSHOP)
118	HENDERSON, ARTHUR / HEIRS
119	HENDERSON, ARTHUR / HEIRS
120	BUCHANAN, JONATHAN
121	BUCHANAN, JONATHAN
122	APPLEGATE, LEWIS
123	APPLEGATE'S MILL
124	LINDSEY, JOSH SR. / HEIRS
125	CAMPBELL, ALEXANDER
126	CAMPBELL, ALEXANDER
127	CAMPBELL, ALEXANDER / (STUDY)
128	CAMPBELL, ALEXANDER / SMITHSHOP
129	CAMPBELL, ALEXANDER
130	CAMPBELL, ALEXANDER / (MILL)
132	PENDLETON, W. K.
133	BETHANY COLLEGE
134	BETHANY COLLEGE INN
135	BETHANY COLLEGE BUILDING

1852 BROOKE CO. MAP – NUMBER INDEX TO LANDOWNERS

MAP#	NAME
136	CAMPBELL, ALEXANDER / (MILL)
137	CAMPBELL, ALEXANDER / (MILL)
138	ROSS
139	BETHANY PROP'TY SCHOOL
140	BETHANY PROP'TY SCHOOL
141	RIDGELY, FRANKLIN
142	CAMPBELL, J. C. / ESQ.
143	CAMPBELL, J. C. / ESQ.
144	CAMPBELL, J. C. / ESQ.
145	CAMPBELL, J. C. / ESQ.
146	WAUGH, RICHARD / HEIRS
147	CAMPBELL, J. C. / ESQ.
148	EDGINGTON, JESSE / ESQ.
149	GROVES, JOHN
151	COLEMAN, DAVID
152	BANE, ROBERT
153	BANE, ROBERT / (GONE)
154	BANE, ROBERT / (GONE)
155	MCCORD, G. W. / ESQ. / (OLD CABIN)
156	CLENDENIN, WM.
157	MCCORD, G. W. / ESQ. / (OLD CABIN)
158	CLENDENIN, WM.
159	CHAPEL, KATY'S
159	CLENDENIN, WM.
160	MCCORD, G. W. / ESQ. / (OLD CABIN)
161	HEDGES, SAMUEL
162	HEDGES, SAMUEL
163	HEDGES, SAMUEL
164	LAZAER, JOSEPH
165	AGNEW, JAMES
166	SCHOOL - AGNEWS
168	HAMMOND, TALBOT / ESQ
169	WELLS, BAZEL
170	HUKIL WM.
171	SCHOOL - HUKLE'S
172	MOORE, ROBERT
173	BOWMAN, S. & J.
174	BOWMAN, S. & J.
175	BOWMAN, S. & J. / (MILL)
176	BOWMAN, AB / HEIRS.
177	WAUGH, RICHARD / HEIRS
178	WAUGH, RICHARD / HEIRS
179	WAUGH, RICHARD / HEIRS
180	WAUGH, RICHARD / HEIRS
181	CAMPBELL, ALEXANDER / (MILL)
182	WAUGH, RICHARD / HEIRS
183	PARKINSON, BENJAMIN
185	CAMPBELL, ALEXANDER / (MILL)
186	CAMPBELL, ALEXANDER / (MILL)
187	CAMPBELL, ALEXANDER / (MILL)
188	BUCHANAN, THOMAS
189	SUTER, STROTHER, T.
190	PARKINSON, DAVID
191	CAMPBELL, ALEXANDER / (MILL)
192	BEALL, BAZEL / ESQ.
193	PALMER, JAMES
194	SHRIMPLIN, JOHN
195	WAUGH, RICHARD / HEIRS
196	HUKIL WM.
197	WELLS, BAZEL
198	MCINTYRE, ISAAC
199	BEALL, WILLIAM
200	BEALL, WILLIAM
201	WELLS, BAZEL

MAP#	NAME
202	WELLS, BAZEL / (GONE)
203	NICHOLLS, HUGH
204	NICHOLLS, HUGH
205	NICHOLLS, HUGH
206	NICHOLLS, HUGH
207	NICHOLLS, HUGH
208	NICHOLLS, HUGH
210	LINDSEY, SAMUEL
211	WELLS, BAZEL / (GONE)
212	WELLS, BAZEL / (GONE)
213	SCHOOL - WALNUT RIDGE
214	WELLS, BAZEL / (GONE)
215	GREEN, ELI
216	MCINTYRE, JOSEPNUS
217	WILSON, SAM'L / HEIRS
218	WAUGH, RICHARD / HEIRS
219	WAUGH, RICHARD / HEIRS / (UPPERMILL)
220	WILSON, JAMES
221	WILSON, JAMES
222	PALMER, JAMES
223	PALMER, JAMES
224	PALMER, JAMES
225	WHITE, WM. / (GONE)
226	WHITE, WM. / (GONE)
227	WHITE, WM. / (GONE)
228	GIST, JOSEPH / ESQ.
229	BEALL, JOHN
230	GEORGE, THOMAS
231	GEORGE, THOMAS
232	BEALL, BAZEL / ESQ.
233	BEALL, BAZEL / ESQ.
234	WAUGH, DAVID
235	BEALL, BAZEL / ESQ.
236	BEALL, BAZEL / ESQ.
237	GIST, JOSEPH / ESQ.
238	GIST, JOSHUA
239	BEALL, JOHN
240	BEALL, JOHN
241	PALMER, JAMES
242	SCHOOL - PIERCE'S RUN
243	BEALL, JOHN
244	SMITH, ANDREW
245	OREM, GEORGE
246	SMITH, ANDREW
247	OREM, GEORGE
248	OREM, GEORGE
249	BORING, ELI
250	GREEN, WILLIAM
251	GREEN, WILLIAM
252	GREEN, WILLIAM
253	SCHOOL - WAUGH'S
254	WAUGH, RICHARD / HEIRS / (UPPERMILL)
255	CASNER, JAS. / HEIRS / (DISTILLERY)
256	CASNER, JAS. / HEIRS
257	CASNER, JAS. / HEIRS
258	CASNER, JAS. / HEIRS / (MILL)
259	CASNER, JAS. / HEIRS / (MILL)
260	WAUGH, RICHARD / HEIRS / (UPPERMILL)
261	WAUGH, RICHARD / HEIRS / (UPPERMILL)
262	WAUGH, RICHARD / HEIRS / (UPPERMILL)

1832 1852 BROOKE CO. MAP – NUMBER INDEX TO LANDOWNERS

MAP#	NAME
264	WAUGH, RICHARD / HEIRS / (COOPERSHOP)
265	WAUGH, RICHARD / HEIRS / (LOWER MILL)
266	WAUGH, RICHARD / HEIRS / (LOWER MILL)
267	BRADY, JOHN
268	BRADY, JOHN
269	FLEMING, JOSEPH
269	WORTHINGTON, SJG
270	KIMBERLY, WILLIAM
270	LEWIS, JOHN
271	LEWIS, JOHN
271	LEWIS, JOHN
272	MCINTYRE, JOSEPNUS
273	MCINTYRE, JOSEPNUS
274	BROWN, J. & D.
275	BROWN, J. & D.
276	WELLS, BAZEL / (GONE)
277	WELLS, ROBT. M.
278	BROWN, J. & D.
279	KUHN, ADAM / ESQ.
280	KUHN, ADAM / ESQ.
282	BROWN, DANFORTH SR.
283	SALTWORKS
284	LEWIS, JOHN
285	LEWIS, JOHN
286	LEWIS, JOHN
287	LEWIS, JOHN
288	LEWIS, JOB
289	BAIRD, JAMES
290	ROBERTS, SAMUEL
291	MILLER, JOHN
292	MILLER, JOHN
293	LEWIS, JOB
294	LEWIS, JOB
295	LEWIS, JOB / (MILL)
296	MORROW, SAMUEL
297	NOLAND, MRS.
298	GREEN, WILLIAM
299	GREEN, WILLIAM
300	GIST, GEORGE
301	GIST, GEORGE
302	NUNEMAKER, DANIEL
303	FISHER, HILLARY
304	FISHER, HILLARY
305	SCHOOL - NO NAME
308	WAUGH, RICHARD / HEIRS / (LOWER MILL)
309	WAUGH, RICHARD / HEIRS / (LOWER MILL)
310	APPLEGATE, LEWIS
311	APPLEGATE, JOSEPH
312	SMITH, EDWARD / ESQ.
313	HINKSON, JOHN
314	HARVEY, DAVID / REV.
315	STEPHENS, WILLIAM
316	BRADY, JOHN / (GONE)
317	BRADY, JOHN / (GONE)
318	BRADY, JOHN / (GONE)
319	JACOB, SAMUEL / (GONE)
320	JACOB, SAMUEL / (GONE) / (GONE)
321	JACOB, SAMUEL / (GONE) / (GONE)
322	JACOB, SAMUEL / (GONE) / (GONE)
323	JACOB, SAMUEL / (GONE) / (MILL)
324	MILLER, JOHN
325	MARSHEL, E. & C.

MAP#	NAME
326	MILLER, JOHN
327	MILLER, JOHN / (FACTORY)
328	MORE, ROBERT
329	LEWIS, JOB / (MILL)
330	PATTON, THOS.
331	PICCARRA, JOHN
332	MORE, ROBERT
333	FRANK, HIGGINS
334	FRANK, HIGGINS
335	CUNNINGHAM, C. II
336	LEWIS, JOHN
337	MCCLANEY, WM.
338	ANTLE, BENJAMIN
339	LEWIS, JOHN
340	SCOTT, JOHN
341	SCOTT, JOHN
342	MORE, ROBERT
343	MORE, ROBERT
344	HARKER, EZEKIEL
345	KUHN, ADAM / ESQ.
346	TOLL-HOUSE
347	MENDEL, HENRY
348	JACOB, SAMUEL / (GONE) / (MILL)
349	BROWN, J. & D.
350	BROWN, J. & D. / (MILL)
351	BROWN, J. & D. / (MILL)
352	BROWN, J. & D. / (MILL)
353	KIRK, MARY
354	GRIMES, THOMAS P.
355	FOWLER, JOHN
356	FOWLER, JOHN
357	SMITH, EDWARD / ESQ.
358	HINKSON, WM. T.
359	HINKSON, WM. T.
360	SCOTT, ROBERT / HEIRS
361	APPLEGATE, LEWIS
362	DO.
363	BUCKEY, JOHN
364	SCOTT, ROBERT / HEIRS
365	SCOTT, ROBERT / HEIRS / (HAUNTED)
366	CHURCH, FRANKLIN
367	SMITH, EDWARD / ESQ.
368	FOWLER, WM / HEIRS
369	SMITH, EDWARD / ESQ.
370	SMITH, EDWARD / ESQ.
371	FOWLER, JOHN
372	FOWLER, JOHN
373	FOWLER, JOHN
374	FOWLER, JOHN / (SMITHSHOP)
375	FOWLER, JOHN / (SMITHSHOP)
376	FOWLER, JOHN / (TAVERN)
377	FOWLER, JOHN / (TAVERN)
378	CALENDINE, HENRY
379	WHITE, HUGH / (TAVERN)
380	JONES, JAMES
381	JONES, JAMES
382	GRIMES, THOMAS P.
383	LAUGHEAD, W & J / (GONE)
384	LAUGHEAD, W & J / (GONE) / (GONE)
385	LAUGHEAD, W & J / (GONE) / (GONE)
386	LAUGHEAD, W & J / (GONE) / (MILL)
387	PARK, ROBERT
388	PARK, ROBERT
389	PARK, ROBERT
390	TARR, CAMPBELL SR.
391	TARR, CAMPBELL SR.

1852 BROOKE CO. MAP – NUMBER INDEX TO LANDOWNERS

MAP#	NAME
392	TARR, CAMPBELL SR.
393	TARR, CAMPBELL SR.
394	TARR, CAMPBELL SR.
395	MILLER, W. L.
396	TARR, WILLIAM
397	TARR, WILLIAM
398	MEADE COL. INSTITUTE
399	NICHOLLS, ROBERT / ESQ.
400	PRATHER, JOHN
401	DISCIPLES / (GONE)
402	NELSON, ANDREW
403	LAMBDIN & CO.
404	CARLE & PERRY
405	CARLE & PERRY
406	LAMBDIN & CO. PAPERMILL
408	COX, GEORGE / ESQ.
409	TARR, WILLIAM
410	MILLER, W. L.
411	TARR, W. & C.
412	CLAYTON, RICHARD
413	PATTON, JAMES
414	JAMISON, JOHN
415	RAY, THOMAS / HEIRS
416	REEVES, REASON
417	STEPHENS, JACOB
418	FOWLER, ZADUE
419	DORSEY, MATILDA
420	HERRON, CHARLES
421	KELLY, THOMAS R.
422	MAGEE, JOHN
423	CLAYTON, STEPHEN
424	MAGEE, JOHN
425	FOWLER, JOHN / (TAVERN)
426	MCGUIRE, FRANK
427	MCGUIRE, FRANK / (MILL)
428	FOWLER, JOHN / (MILL)
429	FOWLER, JOHN / (MILL)
430	HEADINGTON, JOHN
431	MAGEE, JOHN
432	GIST, JOSEPH
433	SMITH, MISS ELISABETH
434	MAGEE, JOHN
435	CARTER, JOSEPH
436	SMITH, ANDREW
437	ENSOR, JOHN
439	CHURCHMAN, J. / HEIRS
440	HUSTER, NATHANIEL
441	HUSTER, NATHANIEL
442	ELSON, JOHN
443	HARRIS, MATHIAS / HEIRS.
444	REEVES, NATHAN
445	BRADY, BERNARD
446	ANTLE, JAMES
447	COX, GEORGE / ESQ.
448	COX, GEORGE / ESQ.
449	COX, JOHN
450	CLARK, SETH / MILL
451	CLARK, SETH / MILL
452	CLARK, SETH / MILL
453	CLARK, SETH / MILL
454	CLARK, SETH / MILL
455	CLARK, SETH
456	BAPTIST / (OLD)
457	HUSTER, NATHANIEL / (SMITHSHOP)
458	HUSTER, NATHANIEL / (SMITHSHOP)
459	HUSTER, NATHANIEL / (SAWMILL)
460	HUSTER, NATHANIEL / (SAWMILL)

MAP#	NAME
461	HUSTER, NATHANIEL / (MILL)
462	HUSTER, NATHANIEL / (MILL)
463	HUSTER, NATHANIEL / (COOPERSHOP)
465	MOONEY, PETER / HEIRS
466	CORNELIUS, ELIJAH
467	BAPTIST / (OLD)
468	CORNELIUS, ELIJAH
469	WIGGINS, W. & JOHN JR.
470	WIGGINS, W. & JOHN JR.
471	ENSOR, JOHN
472	SMITH, MISS ELISABETH
473	WIGGINS, JOHN SR.
474	WIGGINS, JOHN SR.
475	MURCHLAND, WM.
476	NEAL'S SAWMILL
477	MURCHLAND, WM. / (GONE)
478	ARMSPOKER, GEO. / ESQ.
479	MURCHLAND, JAS. / HEIRS
480	MURCHLAND, WM. / OF R. (?ROBERT?)
481	MURCHLAND, ROBT. SR.
482	SMITH, W. J. & R.
483	SMITH, W. J. & R. / (COOPERSHOP)
484	MCGUIRE, LUKE
485	BURGOYNE, JOSHUA
486	HEADINGTON, GREENBR'Y
487	MCKEEVER, WM.
488	MERRYMAN, J. / HEIRS
489	BOSLEY, WM / HEIRS
490	WILLIAMSON, JAMES
491	WILLIAMSON, JAMES
492	GRIFFITH, JAMES / HEIRS
493	JOHNSON, AMOS
494	MURCHLAND, ROBT. SR.
495	MURCHLAND, ROBT. SR.
496	ARMSPOKER, JNO. / HEIRS
497	CASSIDAY, ROBT. / HEIRS
498	MCCLEARY, EWING / (GONE)
499	STEEN, WM.
500	STEEN, WM.
501	HINDMAN, SAMUEL JR.
502	MURCHLAND, ROBT. SR.
503	HAYS, ENOCH
505	STRAIN, EBEN / (SAWMILL)
506	PATTERSON, JAMES
507	ELSON, ALEX. M.
508	THAWLEY, SAM'L / HEIRS
510	MAY, JASON
510	SCHOOL - MAY'S
511	MAHAN, WM.
512	BROWNING, LEWIS
513	CLARK, SETH
514	BROWNING, LEWIS
515	LOGE, JOHN
516	BROWNING, LEWIS
517	WALKER, JACOB / HEIRS
518	WALKER, JACOB / HEIRS
519	WALKER, JOHN
520	HENDRIX, TOBIAS
521	BAXTER, WILLIAM
522	STRAIN, EBENEZER
523	POOL, WILLIAM
524	CARTER, LEWIS
525	DONOVAN, THOMAS
526	DONOVAN, THOMAS
527	HEADINGTON, MRS. ELIZABETH

1834 1852 BROOKE CO. MAP – NUMBER INDEX TO LANDOWNERS

MAP#	NAME
528	WHEELER, THOS. C. / HEIRS
529	HINDMAN, WM.
530	HINDMAN, SAMUEL
531	WELLS, GREYBEARD / HEIRS
532	WELLS, GREYBEARD / HEIRS
533	HOOKER, GEORGE
534	SECEDER
535	SCHOOL - TENT
536	CAIRNS, SARAH
537	HOOKER, GEORGE
538	STRAIN, WM. P.
539	CARTER, SAMUEL
540	ST. JOHN'S
541	WALLACE, JAMES
542	SCHOOL - WALLACE'S / (LOUISA OF BROOKE)
543	HENDRIX, JOHN ESQ / HEIRS
544	PATTERSON, W. / (SMITH'P)
545	PATTERSON, W. / (SMITH'P)
546	PATTERSON, JAMES
547	WALKER, JOHN
548	CLARK, SETH
549	CLARK, SETH / (FERRY)
550	WELLS, NATHANIEL
551	WELLS, NATHANIEL / (SMITHSHOP)
552	WELLS, NATHANIEL / (FERRY & TAV)
553	ARCHER, SAMUEL / ESQ.
554	ARCHER, SAMUEL / ESQ. / (GONE)
555	BEATY, THOMAS
556	BEATY, THOMAS
557	PATTERSON, JAMES
558	STRAIN, JOHN
559	MARSHEL, THOS. / MRS
560	CAIRNS, MARY / HEIRS
561	THAWLEY, DAVID
562	WALLACE, SAMUEL
563	HINDMAN, W. & SAM'L
564	CARTER, SAMUEL
565	HINDMAN, JAS / HEIRS
565	HUSTER, NATHANIEL / (COOPERSHOP)
566	BAXTER, GEORGE
567	WELLS, GREYBEARD / HEIRS
568	WELLS, GREYBEARD / HEIRS
569	WELLS, GREYBEARD / HEIRS
570	PEARCE, DAVID'S / HEIRS
571	CRISWELL, JAMES
572	CRISWELL, MISSES
573	RYLAND, HUGH P. / (MILL)
574	RYLAND, HUGH P.
575	ROBINSON, WILLIAM
576	REEVES, REASON
576	ROBINSON, ELIJAH / HEIRS
577	SCHOOL - SYCAMORE
578	ROBINSON, JOHN
579	ADAMS, WILLIAM
580	MARSH, JAMES
581	FRESHWATER, REUBEN
582	FRESHWATER, WM.
583	MORETON, JOSEPH
584	MORETON, JOHN
585	LEE, ANDREW / HEIRS
586	SCHOOL - GORCLY'S
587	GORELY, JOHN / CAPT.
588	GORELY, JOHN / CAPT.
589	MONTGOMERY, DANIEL
590	MARSH, THOMAS

MAP#	NAME
591	SCHOOL - MARSH'S
592	WELLS, NATHANIEL / (FERRY & TAV)
593	WELLS, NATHANIEL / (FERRY & TAV)
594	WALLACE, JOHN
594	WELLS, NATHANIEL / (FERRY & TAV)
595	WELLS, NATHANIEL / (FERRY & TAV)
596	HANNA, THOMSON / & CO.
598	HANNA, THOMSON / & CO.
599	HANNA, THOMSON / & CO.
600	HANNA, THOMSON / & CO. / (PAPER MILL)
601	HANNA, THOMSON / & CO. / (PAPER MILL)
602	EDGINGTON, JESSE / ESQ.
603	EDGINGTON, JESSE / ESQ. / (FERRY)
604	EDGINGTON, JESSE / ESQ. / (WAREHOUSE)
605	ATKINSON, WILLIAM
606	MCKIM, MRS. NANCY
607	ATKINSON, JOSEPH
608	ATKINSON, JOSEPH
609	OWENS, CHARLES W.
610	SCHOOL - NO NAME
612	CAIRNS, MARY
613	MORETON, THOMAS
614	WELSH, SARAH / (GONE)
615	ELLIOT, WM A.
616	ELLIOT, THOMAS / HEIRS
617	SANDERS, B. D.
618	SANDERS, B. D. / (SAWMILL GONE)
619	SANDERS, B. D. / (SAWMILL GONE)
620	WELSH, SARAH / (GONE)
621	SANDERS, B. D. / (SAWMILL GONE)
622	SANDERS, B. D. / (SAWMILL GONE)
623	STANSBERRY, JOHN
624	STANSBERRY
625	STANSBERRY
626	HOLMES, THOMAS
627	WRIGHT, JACOB
629	WRIGHT, JACOB
630	CAMPBELL, THOMAS
631	HOLMES, THOMAS
632	HOLMES, THOMAS
633	MANARY, JAMES / ESQ.
634	FRESHWATER, REUBEN, JR.
635	STANSBERRY, NICHOLAS
636	STANSBERRY, NICHOLAS
637	SWEURENGEN, GEO. / ESQ.
638	SNIDER, DAVID / HEIRS
639	SNIDER, DAVID / HEIRS / (COOPERSHOP)
640	SNIDER, DAVID / HEIRS / (COOPERSHOP)
641	SNIDER, DAVID / HEIRS / (MILL)
642	SNIDER, DAVID / HEIRS / (MILL)
643	OWENS, EPHRAIM
644	CAIRNS, JAS.
645	CAIRNS, JAS.
646	EDGINGTON, JESSE / ESQ. / (WAREHOUSE)
647	SINCLAIR, JAMES
648	SWEURENGEN, G. D. / HEIRS
649	ORR, THOMAS ESQ.
650	ORR, THOMAS ESQ.
651	ORR, THOMAS ESQ.
652	ORR, SAMWEL

1852 BROOKE CO. MAP – NUMBER INDEX TO LANDOWNERS

MAP#	NAME
653	ORR, SAMWEL
654	POOL, BENJAMIN
655	HINDMAN, JOHN
656	HINDMAN, JOHN / (MILL)
657	HINDMAN, SAML
658	PATTERSON, JAS. / ESQ.
659	MAWHA, R. & G.
660	SWEURENGEN, GEO. / ESQ. / (GONE)
661	HINDMAN, JAMES
662	MAWHA, R. & G.
663	CAMPBELL, ALEX / CAPT.
664	HENDRIX, JACOB
665	HENDRIX, JACOB
666	HENDRIX, JACOB
667	BELL, PHILIP / HEIRS
668	BELL, PHILIP / HEIRS
669	BELL, PHILIP / HEIRS
670	BELL, PHILIP / HEIRS
671	BAXTER, RICHARD
671	HINDMAN, SAML
672	METHODIST
673	PATTERSON, JAMES
674	WIGGINS, JOHN JR.

1836   1852 BROOKE CO. MAP –INDEX TO "MISSING" LANDOWNERS...
...not on map - as determined by an anonymous donor to the Brooke County Genealogical Society
(Alphabetic index to names included in "Personal Time Line" Index)

"MISSING" NAMES ON MAP	WHERE LOCATED (LANDOWNER NUMBERS PLUS GRIDS FROM MARGIN OF ORIGINAL MAP)
ADAMS, WILLIAM	NORTH OF 580 & WEST OF 579 ON WEST OF ROAD
BLACKSMITH SHOP - JONES / CHARLES	0-1 N. 1-2 W. BELOW LONG RUN
BLAKCSMITH SHOP - MILLERS / J	BETWEEN 292 AND 324
BUCHANAN, JOHNATHAN	5-6 N. 1-2 W.
CLARK, SETH	20-21 N. 7-8 W. N OF ELDERSVILLE ROAD
COX, FRIEND	3-4 N. 5-6 W. ON WEST SIDE OGLES RUN
COX, JOHN	15-16 N. 7-8 W. FORK OF RIVER & CREEK ROAD
EUCIL, -	100 FT. E. OF 400
FARQUAR, JOHN	14-15 N. 7-8 W. ON NORTH OF REIDS RUN
GROVES, JAMES	NEAR INTERSECTION 5N. 8 W.
HARVEY, DAVID	NEAR 4 W. AND MIDWAY OF 11-12 N.
HINDMAN, SAMUEL	(NO NOTES)
HINKSON, J / (SAWMILL)	10-11 N. 2-3 W. IN FORKS OF GROVES' & M'GUIRE'S RUN
HINKSON, J / (SAWMILL)	SOUTH OF 313 AND ABOVE SAWMILL
HINKSON, W T / (C. SHOP)	NORTH OF 359 ON N. OF PIKE
HINKSON, W T / (C. SHOP)	ON SOUTH OF PIKE BETWEEN 359 AND 366
JACOB, SAMUEL	12 N. 6-7 W. EAST OF RUN
JONES, CHARLES / (SMITHSHOP)	0-1 N. 1-2 W. BELOW LONG RUN
JONES, CHARLES / (SMITHSHOP)	NEAR SMITHSHOP
JONES, JOSIAH	200 FEET S.E. OF NO 400
LARGE, -	N.E. OF 400 AND S. OF SKULL RUN
LATTIMORE, BROWN	20 N. 4-5 W.
LEFLER, DAVID / (SAWMILL)	300 FEET S. OF 66 ON BANK OF RUN
LEIPER, JOHN	15-16 N. 0-1 W.
MAHAN, WILLIAM	ON NORTH BANK OF MAHAN'S RUN 40 ROD BELOW MERRYMAN'S FORK
MAWHA, G / & R	300 FEET EAST OF 662
MAWHA, R / & G.	300 FEET EAST OF 662
MCDONALD, WILLIAM	16-17 N. 3-4 WEST, AND WEST OF JOHNSON'S RUN
MCGARTY, SAMUEL	S.E. OF NO. 1 NEAR THE COUNTY LINE
MILLER, J / (FINISHING HOUSE)	BETWEEN 325 AND 326
MILLER, J / (SMITHSHOP)	BETWEEN 292 AND 324
MOUNTS, DANIEL	1-2 N. NEAR LINE OF 6 WEST
MOUNTS, DANIEL	UP OGLE'S RUN ABOVE MOUNTS BRANCH
MOUNTS, DANIEL	UP OGLE'S RUN ABOVE MOUNTS BRANCH
NICHOLS, JOHN D	NORTH OF 399, SOME 200 FEET
NICHOLS, ROBERT JR.	NORTH OF 399, SOME 350 FEET
PATTON, JOHN	14 NORTH AND WEST OF ROAD TO 413
RIDGELY, FRANKLIN	3-4 N. 5-6 W. SOUTH BANK CREEK & W. OF PIKE
RIDGELY, FRANKLIN	3-4 N. 5-6 W. EAST OF OGLES RUN
RYLAND, HUGH P	EAST OF 573
SAWMILL - HINKSON / J	SOUTH OF 313 AND ABOVE SAWMILL
SILVERS, JAMES	WEST OF OGLE'S RUN AND N. OF 66
SMITIR, R / & W J	16-17 N. 5 W. EAST OF ROAD
SMITIR, W J / & R.	16-17 N. 5 W. EAST OF ROAD
SUTER, S T	EAST OF 189
TOLL HOUSE	ON BETHANY PIKE EAST OF 330 AT CREEK
WELLS, NATHANIEL	400 FEET N. OF 552
WELLS, NATHANIEL / (WAREHOUSE)	WEST OF 596, ON RIVER BANK
WILLIAMSON, SAMUEL	19-20 N. 2-3 W. AND ON WEST OF NAYLOR'S RUN
WYKOFF, WILLIAM	WEST OF 93 ON RIVER BANK.

1852 BROOKE CO. MAP – PAGE # INDEX GRID TO MAP SECTIONS 1837
Note: The top of this map is to the WEST – instead of North, like most maps

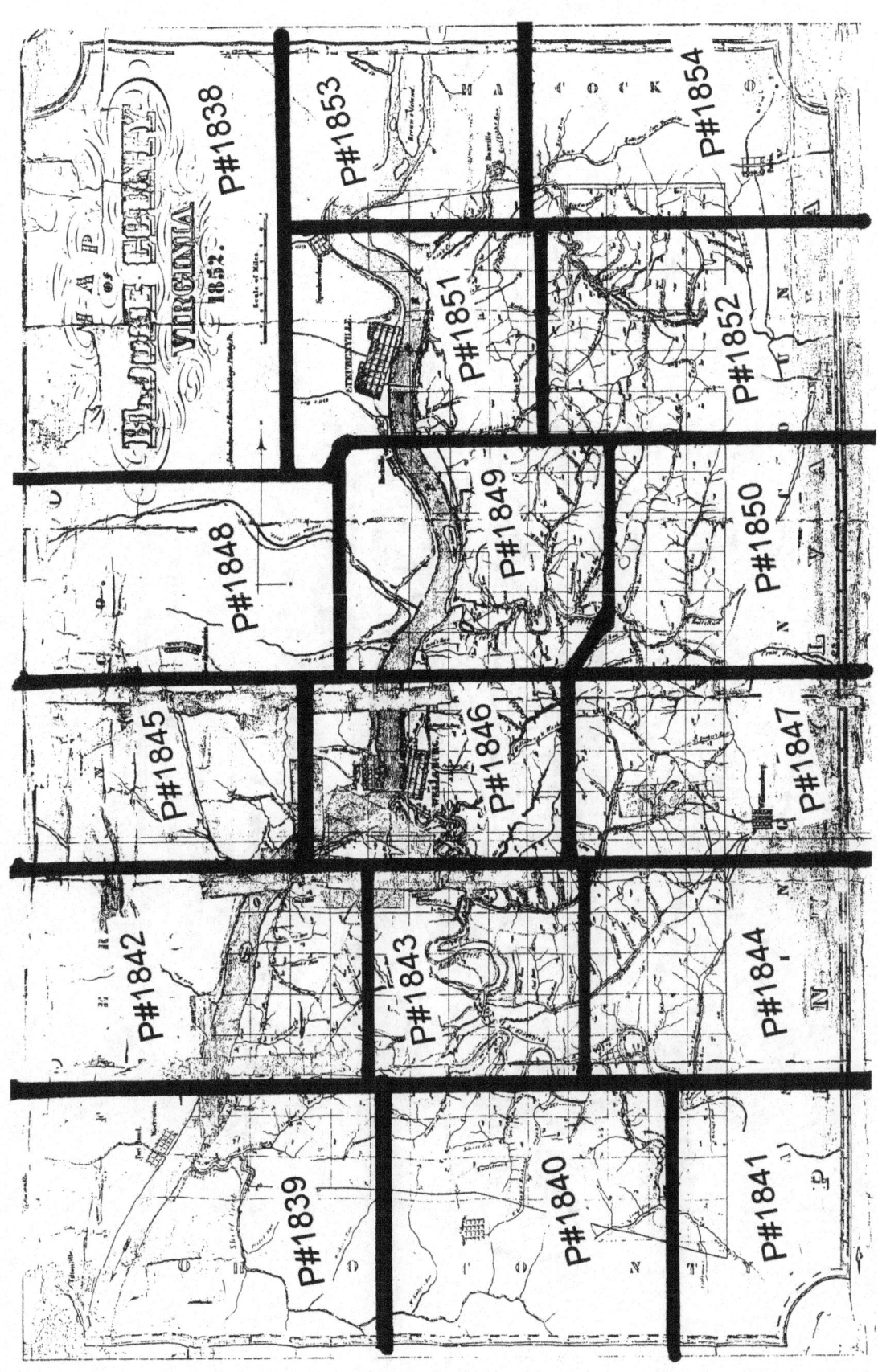

1838   1852 BROOKE CO. MAP – MAP TITLE BLOCK

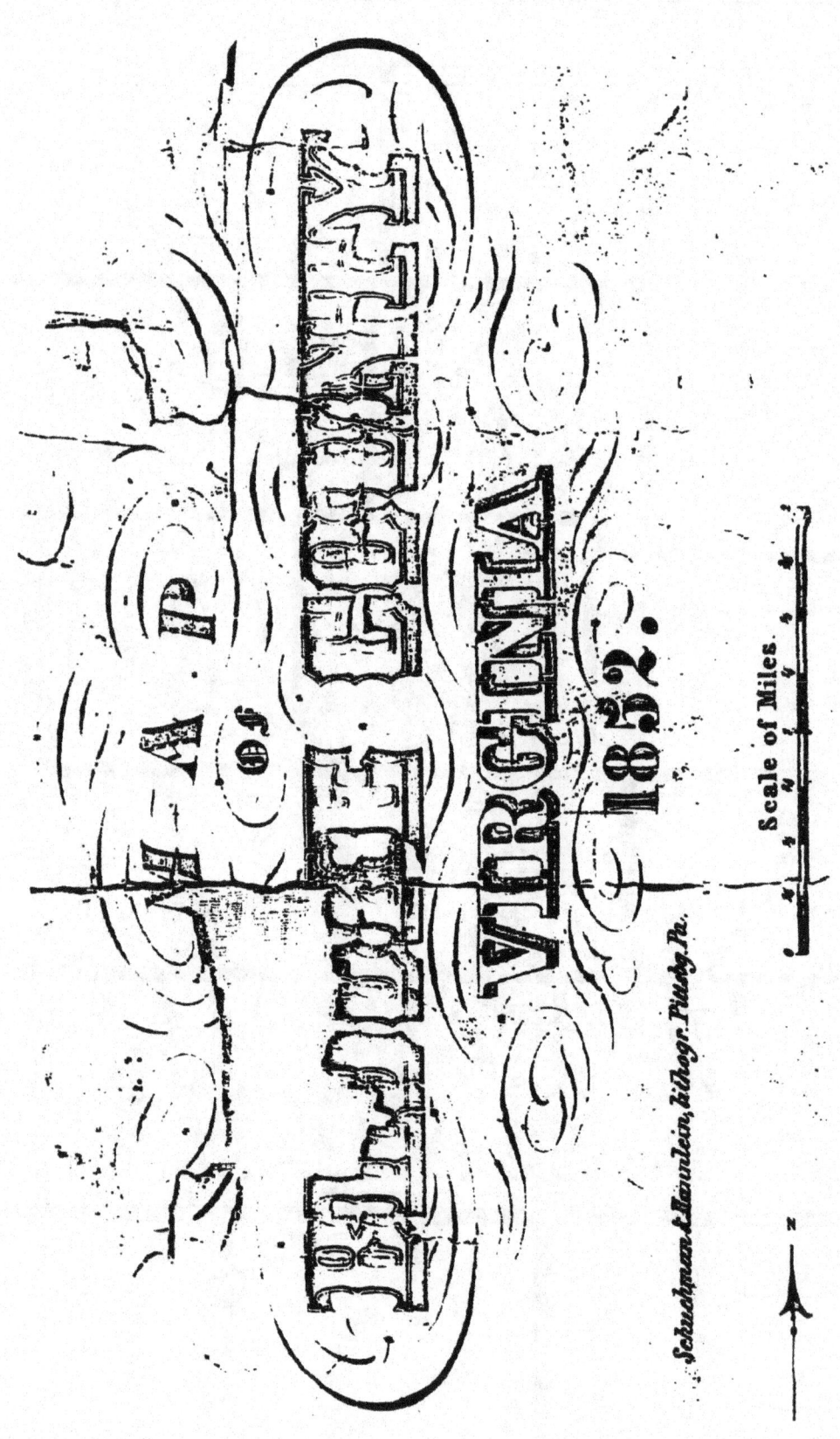

1852 BROOKE CO. MAP – SHORT CREEK AREA 1839
Note: Small #'s on maps are landowner #'s – see index p.1830.
Also alphabetical name index included in 'Personal Time Line' Index

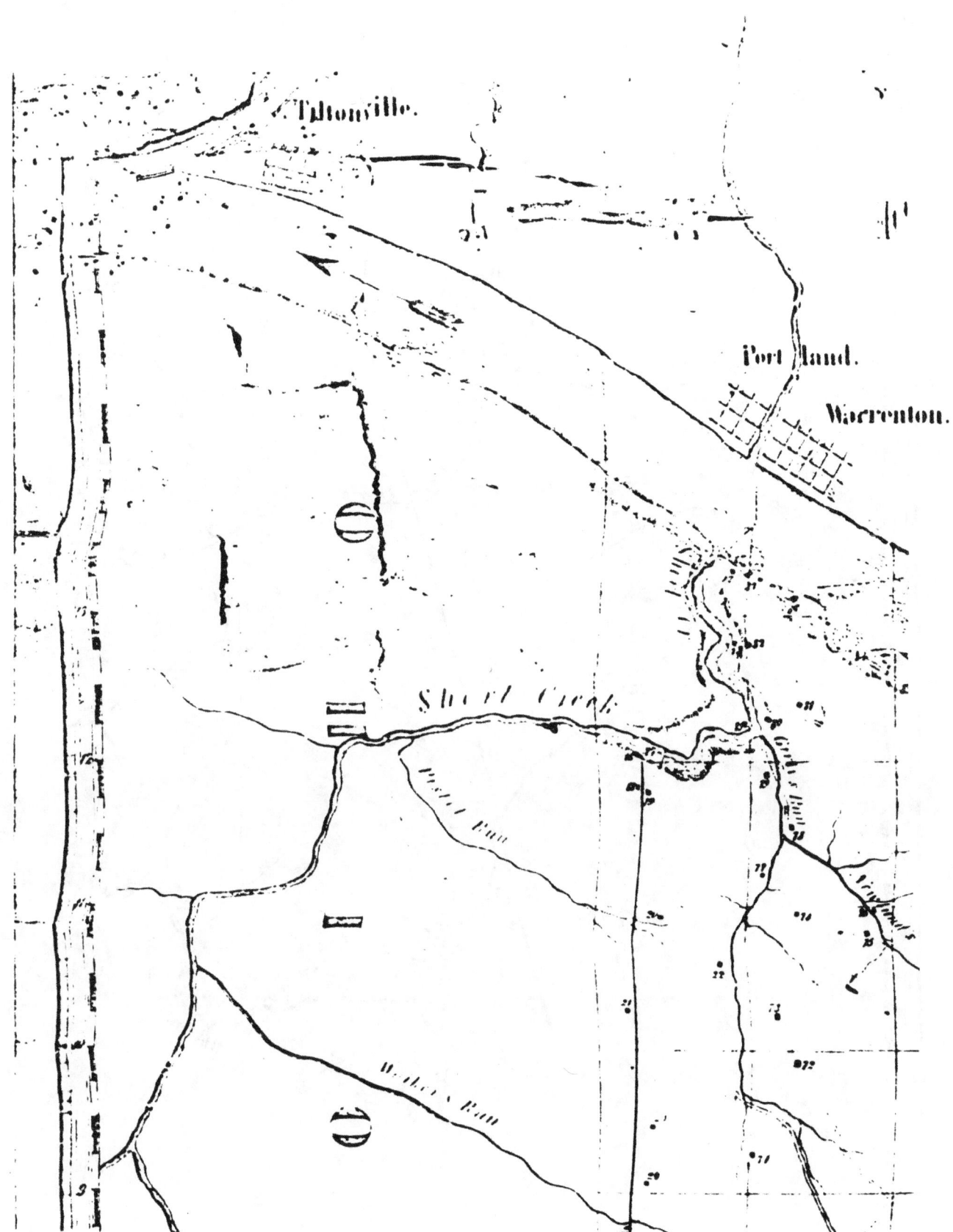

1840   1852 BROOKE CO. MAP – WHEELING & BETHANY TURNPIKE AREA

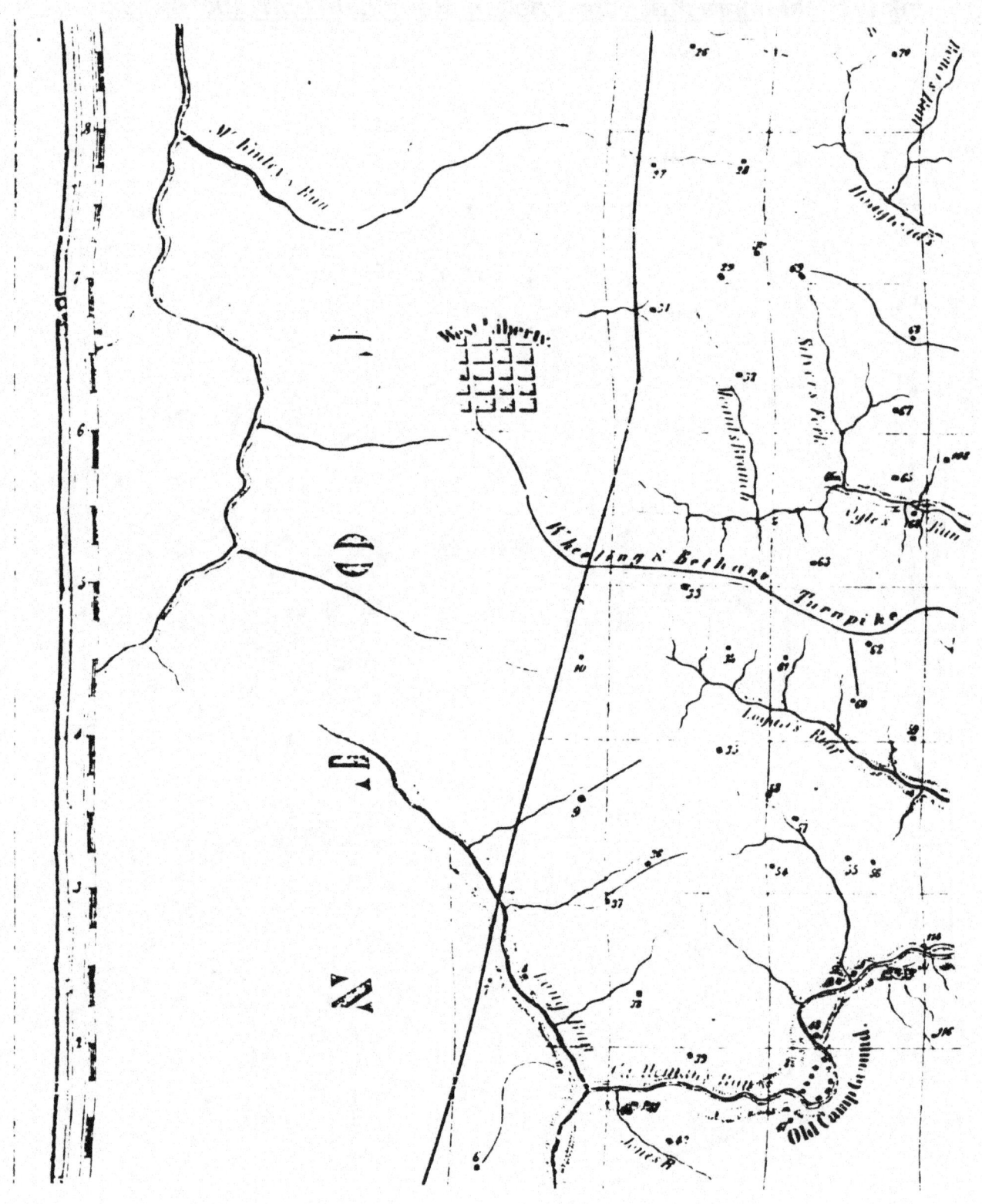

1852 BROOKE CO. MAP – CASTLEMANS RUN AREA   1841

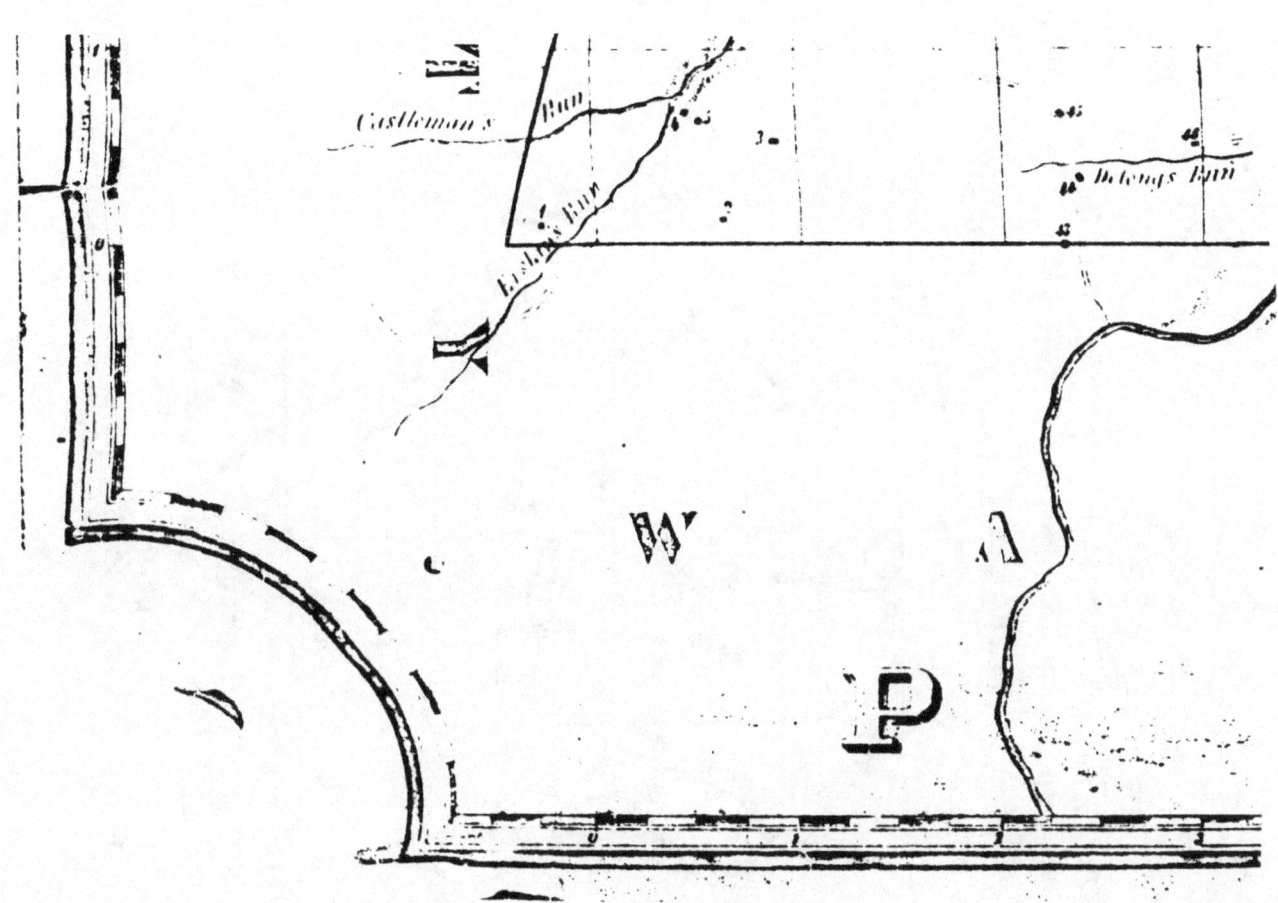

1842 1852 BROOKE CO. MAP – BEECH BOTTOM AREA

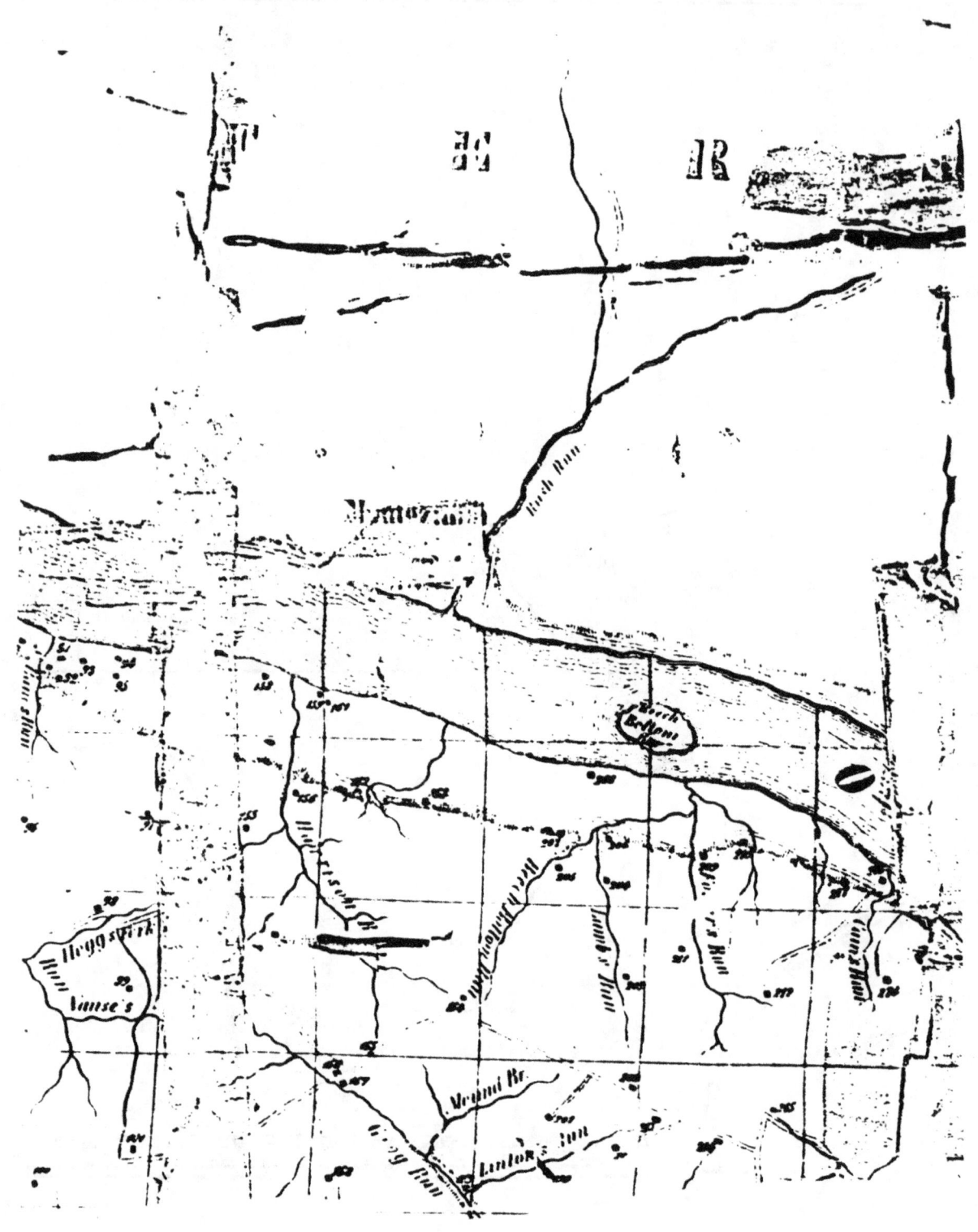

1852 BROOKE CO. MAP – BUFFALO CREEK AREA   1843

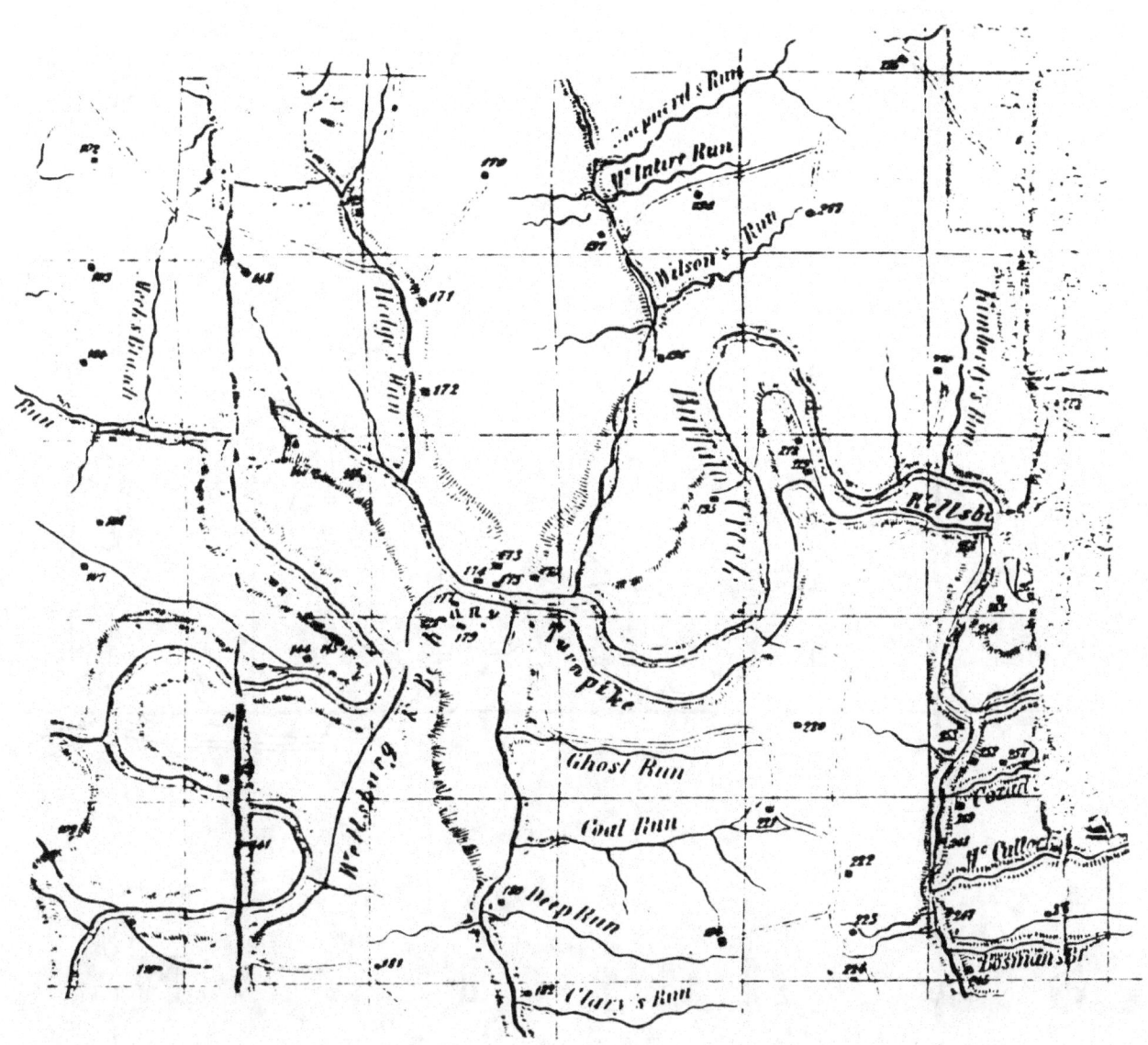

1844   1852 BROOKE CO. MAP – BETHANY AREA

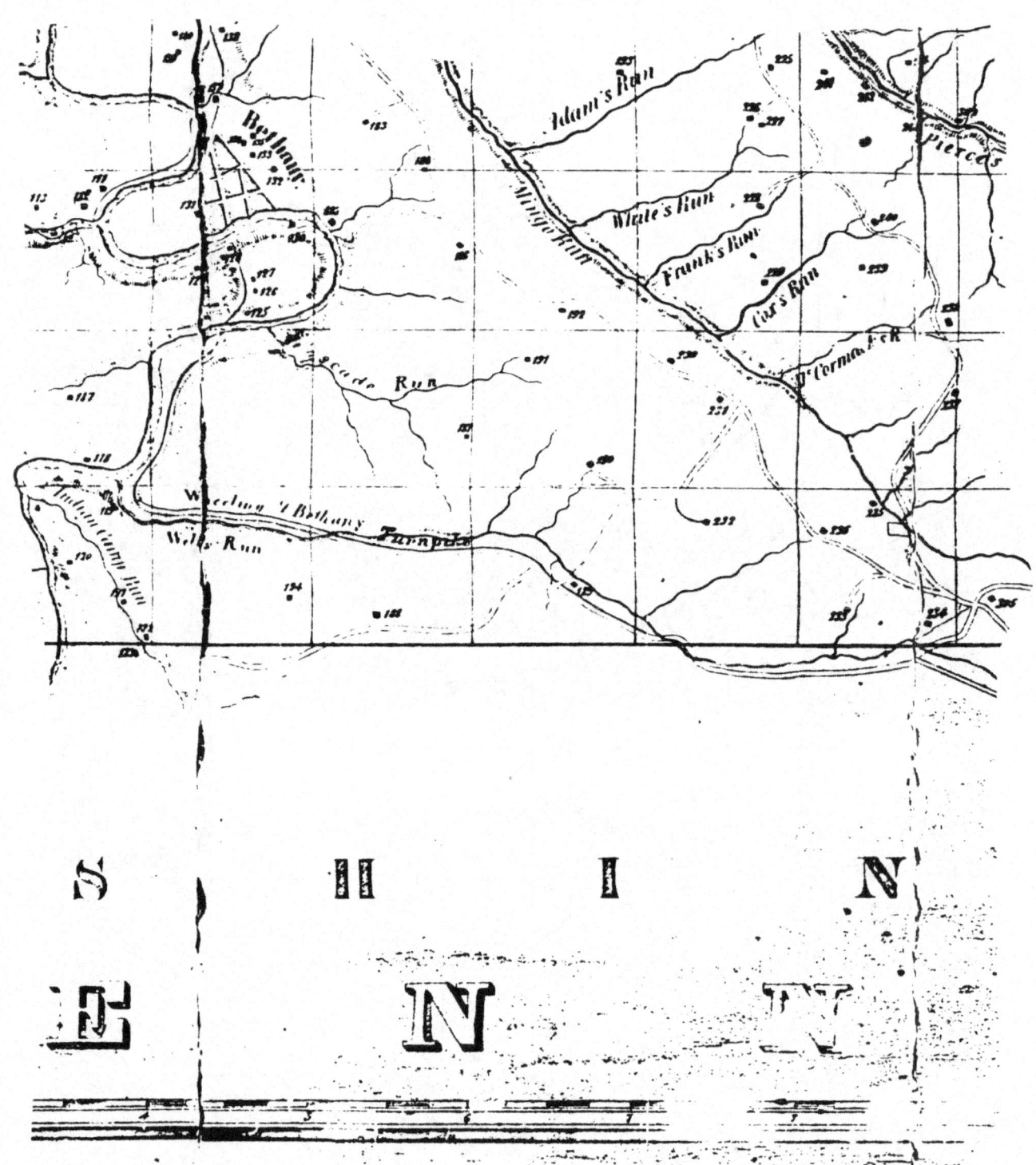

1852 BROOKE CO. MAP – STATE OF OHIO – W. OF WELLSBURG   1845

1846 1852 BROOKE CO. MAP - WELLSBURG AREA

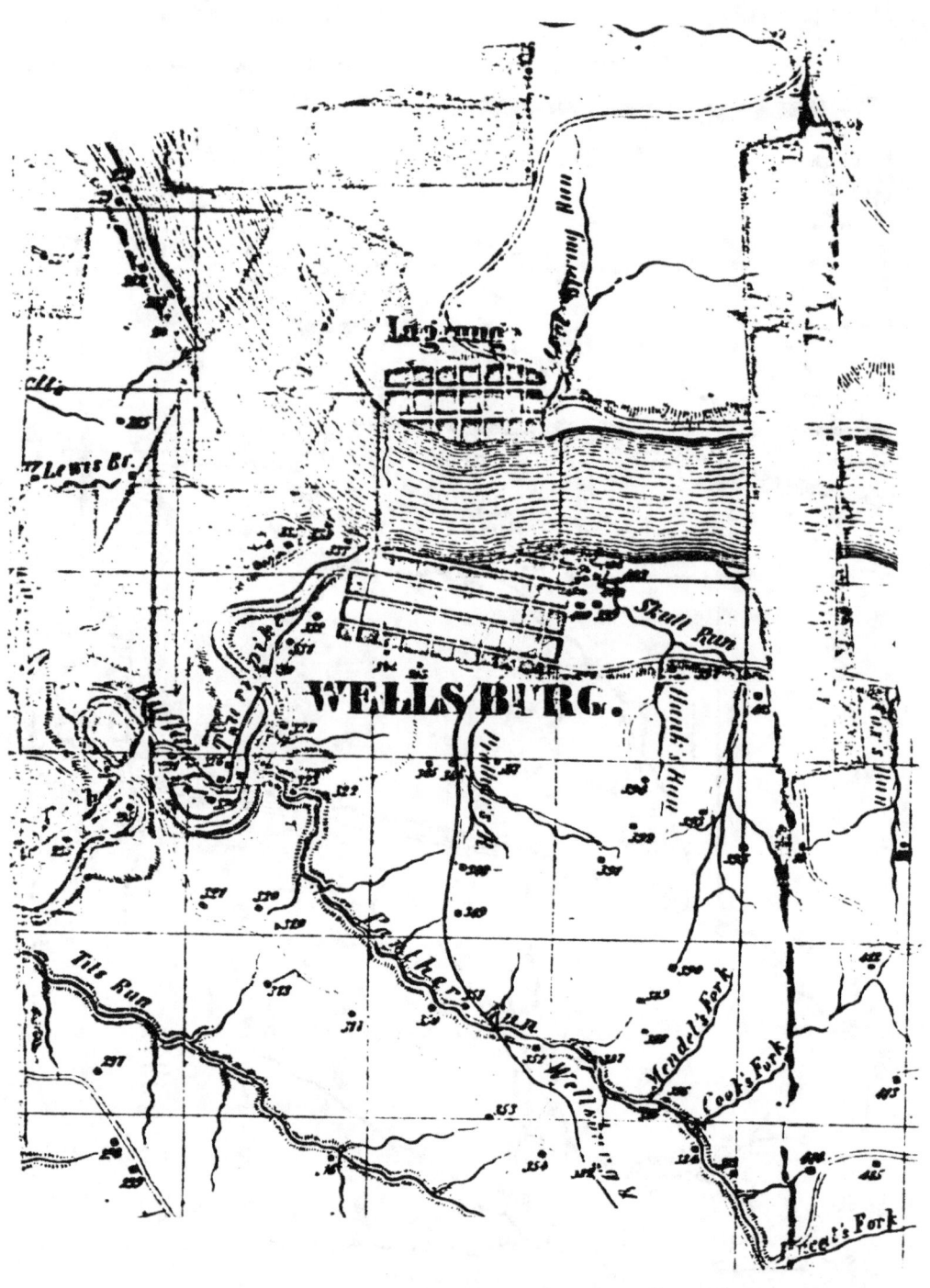

1852 BROOKE CO. MAP – WELLSBURG & WASHINGTON TURNPIKE 1847

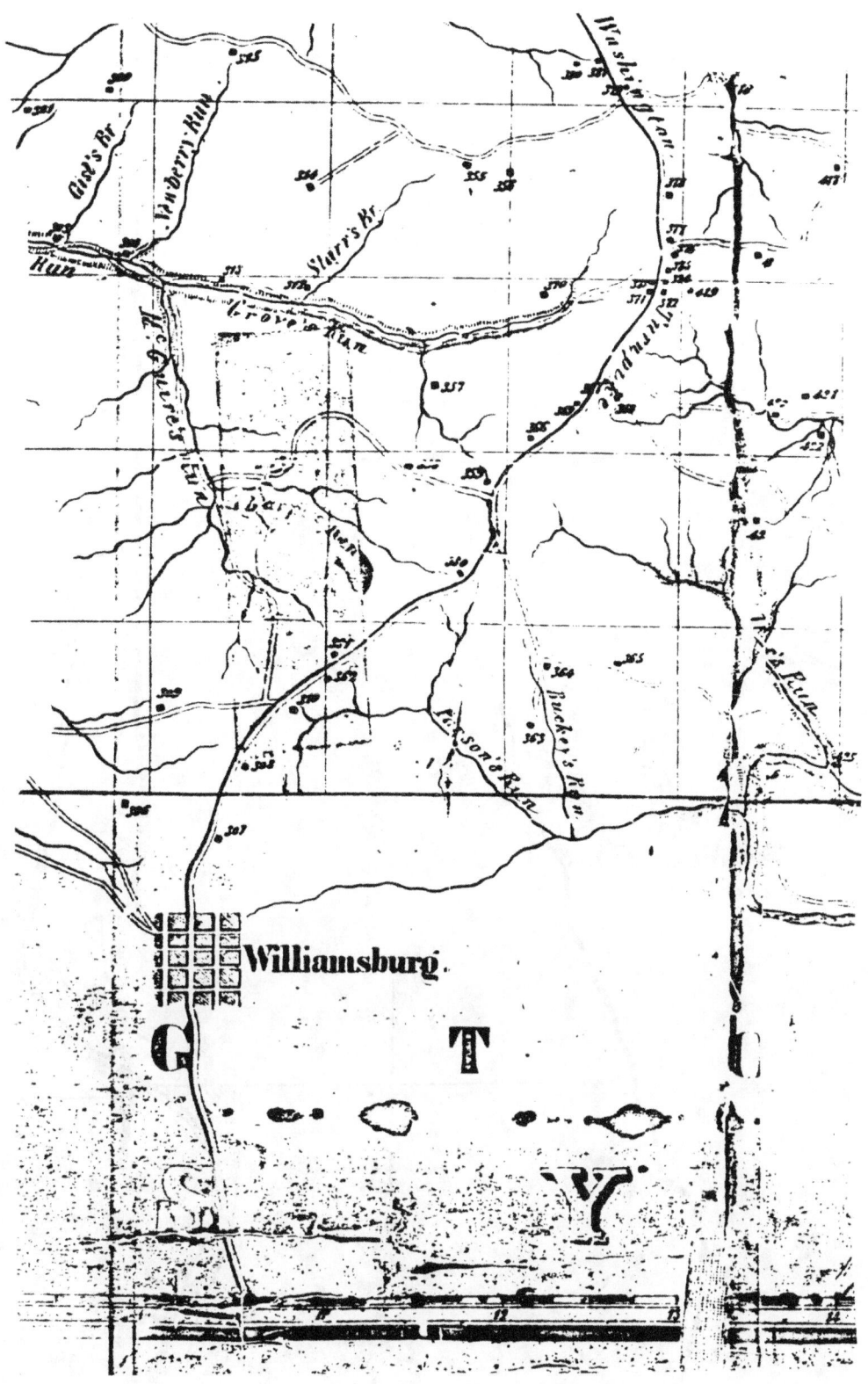

1848 1852 BROOKE CO. MAP - NEW ALEXANDRIA, OHIO AREA

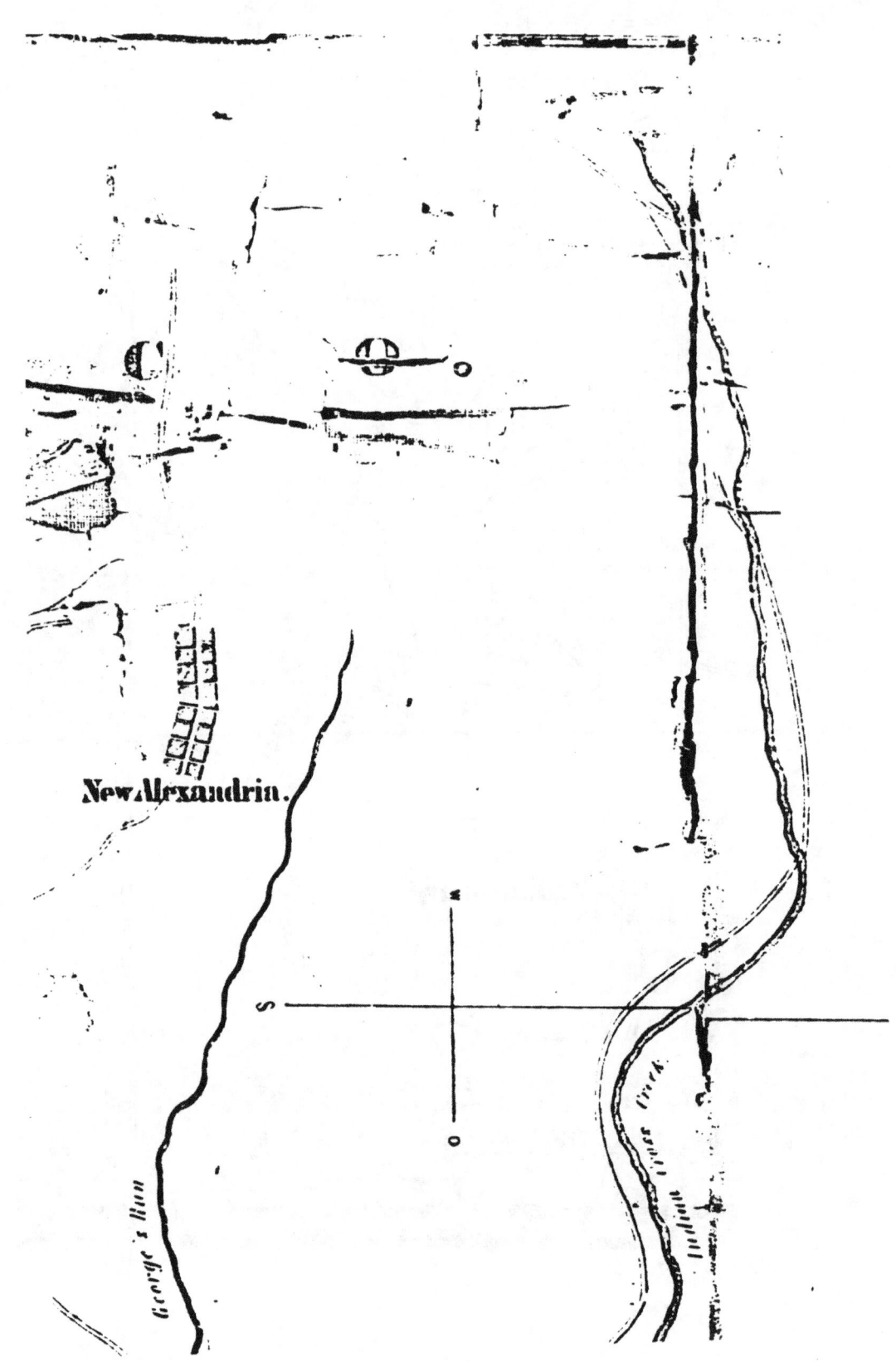

1852 BROOKE CO. MAP – CROSS CREEK / OHIO RIVER AREA   1849

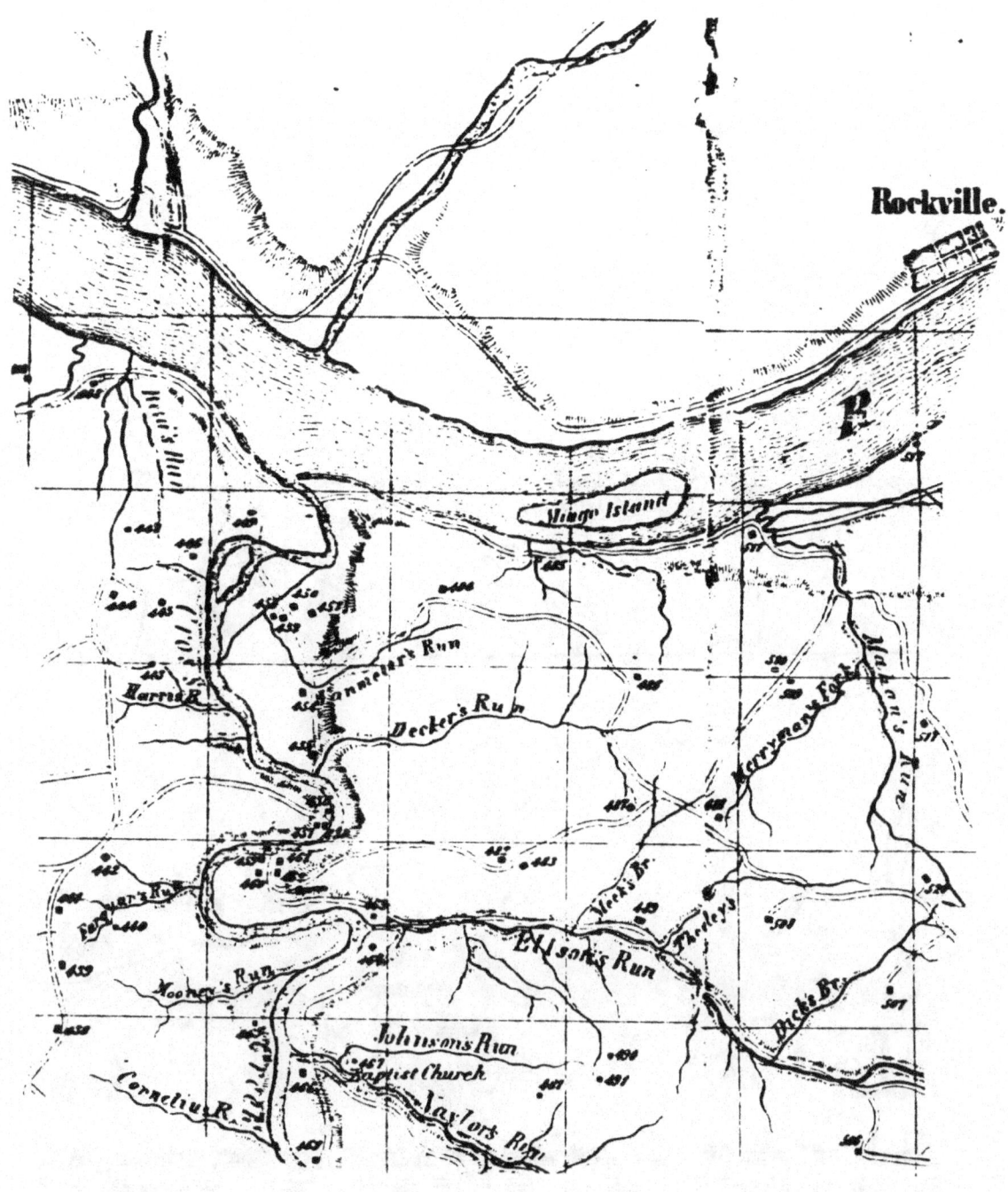

1850 1852 BROOKE CO. MAP - CROSS CREEK & PA. BORDER AREA

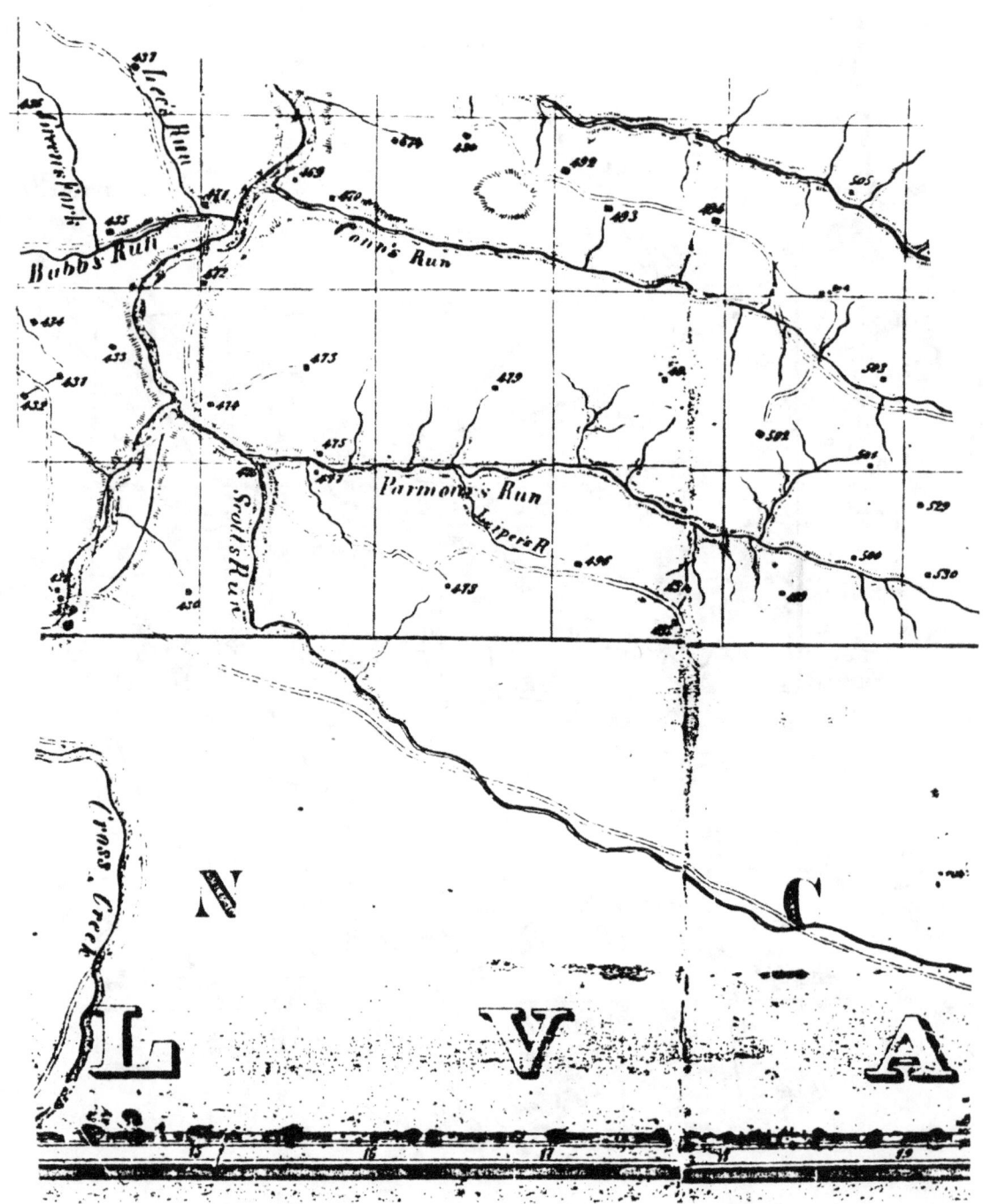

1852 BROOKE CO. MAP – STEUBENVILLE. OHIO / MCMAHANS RUN   1851

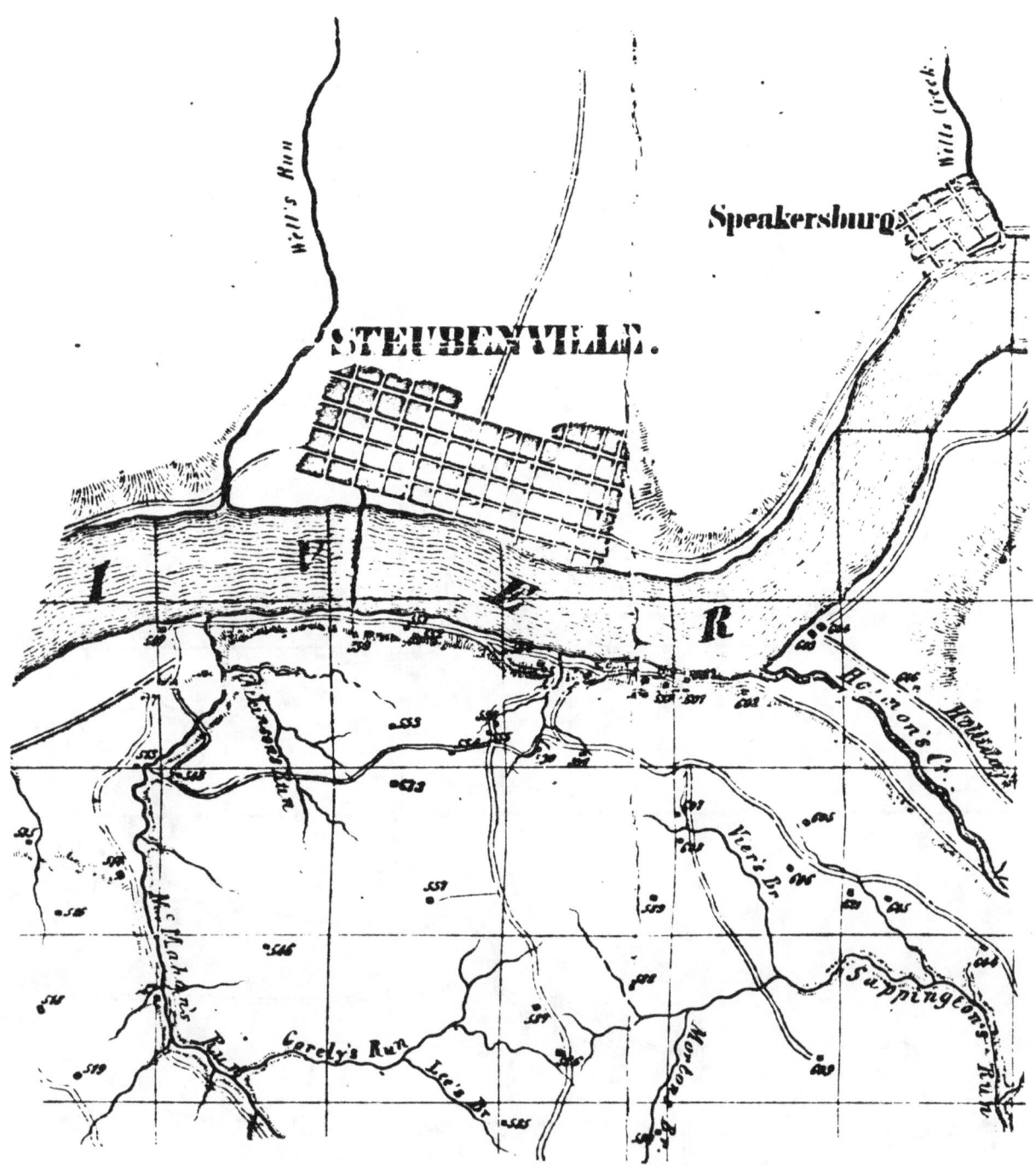

1852   1852 BROOKE CO. MAP - HARMONS CREEK AREA

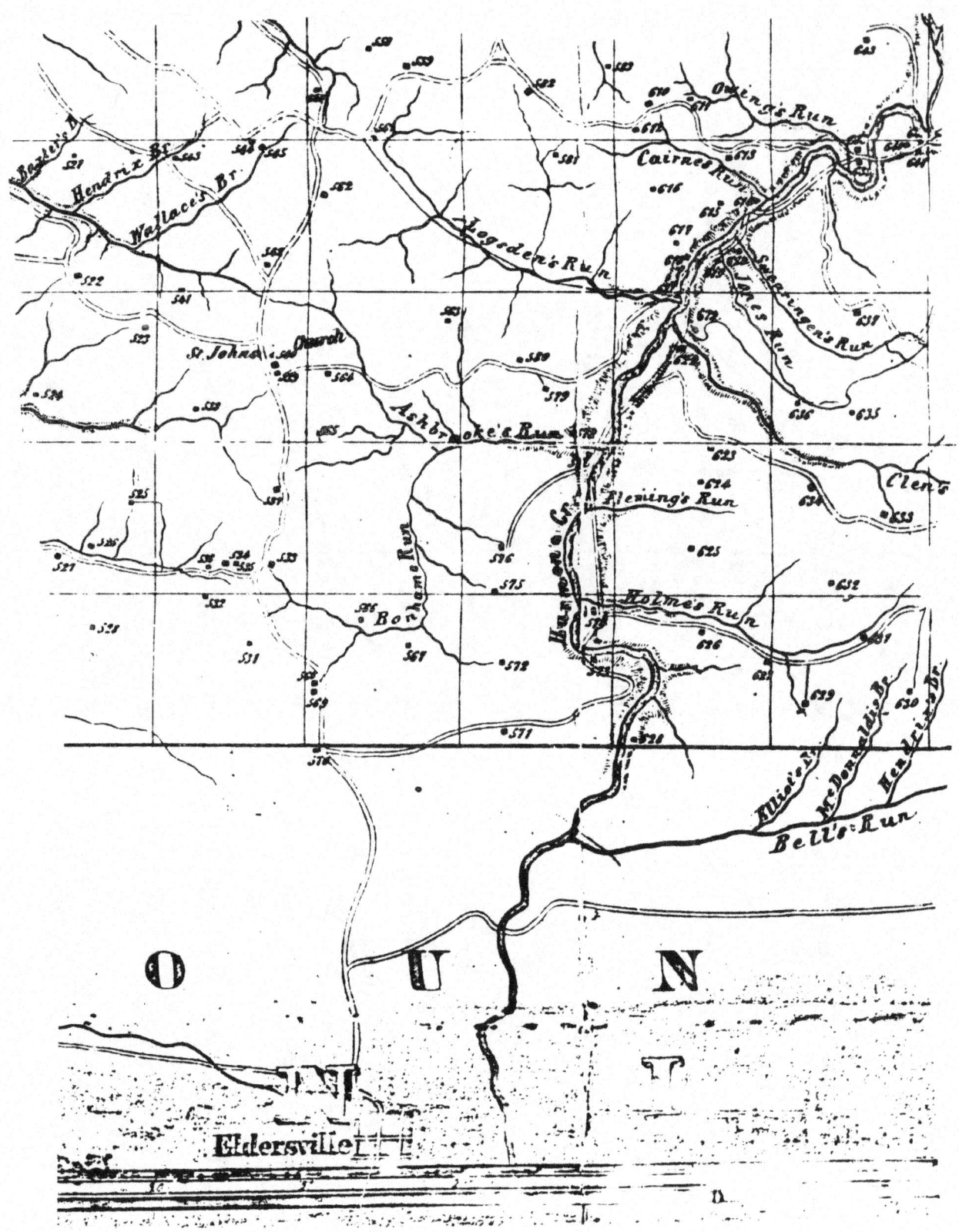

1852 BROOKE CO. MAP – DANVILLE / HOLLIDAYS COVE AREA   1853

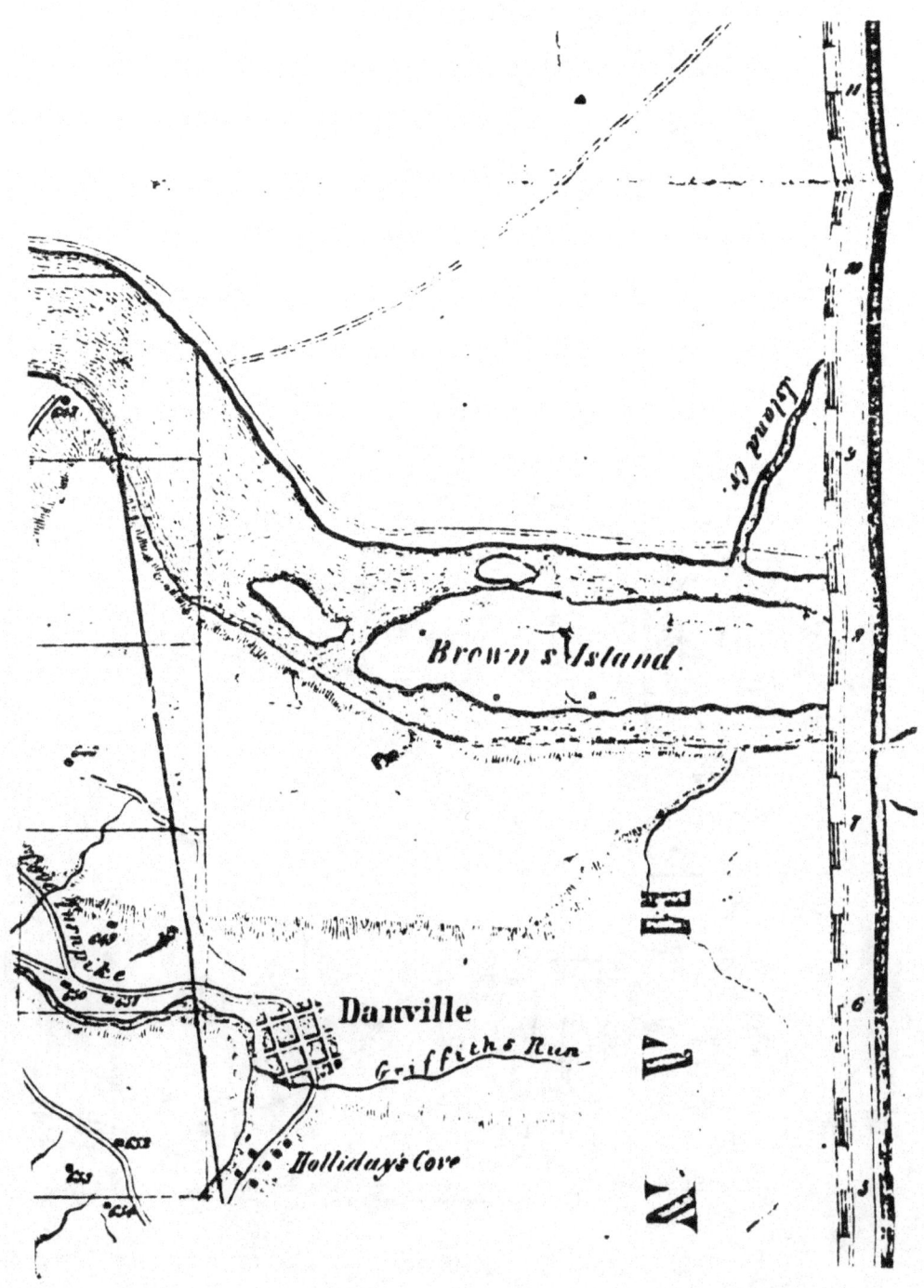

1854   1852 BROOKE CO. MAP - DEMAPOLIS / PARIS AREA

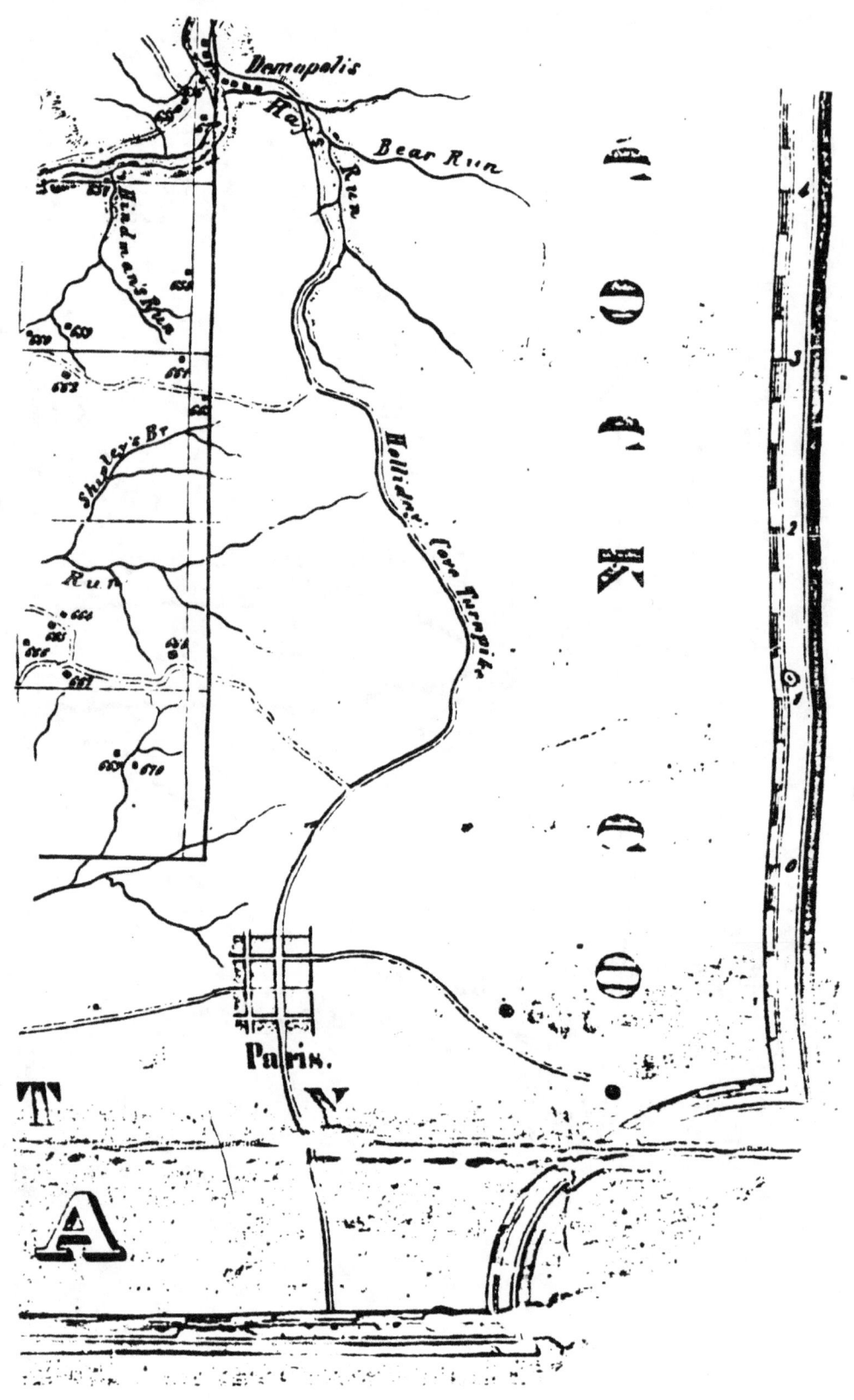

PANORAMIC MAPS OF PANHANDLE AT LIBRARY OF CONGRESS

Places in the News!

Map Collections: 1544-1999

Cities and Towns

Conservation and Environment

Discovery and Exploration

General Maps

Cultural Landscapes

Military Battles and Campaigns

Transportation and Communication

Geography and Map Division, Library of Congress

The panoramic maps on pages 1856-1859 come from the internet website of the
Geography and Map Division, Library of Congress, Washington, D.C.
The website address is   http://lcweb.loc.gov/rr/geogmap/
After that go to "online map collections", then "Cities & towns".
These online maps have 'zoom functions' where you can see street names and even see houses, churches, cemeteries, factories, etc.

It is interesting to see these 'panoramic views' of the same cities indexed earlier from the 1871 map of the panhandle.

Additional map information:

Page 1856 – An 1882 map of Benwood, Marshall Co. – enlarged from a much larger map of Bellaire, Ohio.

Page 1857 – An 1899 map of Cameron, Marshall Co.

Page 1858 – An 1889 map of Moundsville, Marshall Co.

Page 1859 – An 1870 map of Wheeling City with Wheeling Island in the foreground – showing only about half of the island inhabited ! Again, be sure and 'zoom in' with the 'online' version of this map.

1856   1882 MAP OF BENWOOD, MARSHALL CO. – FROM BELLAIRE, OH MAP

1899 MAP OF CAMERON, MARSHALL COUNTY

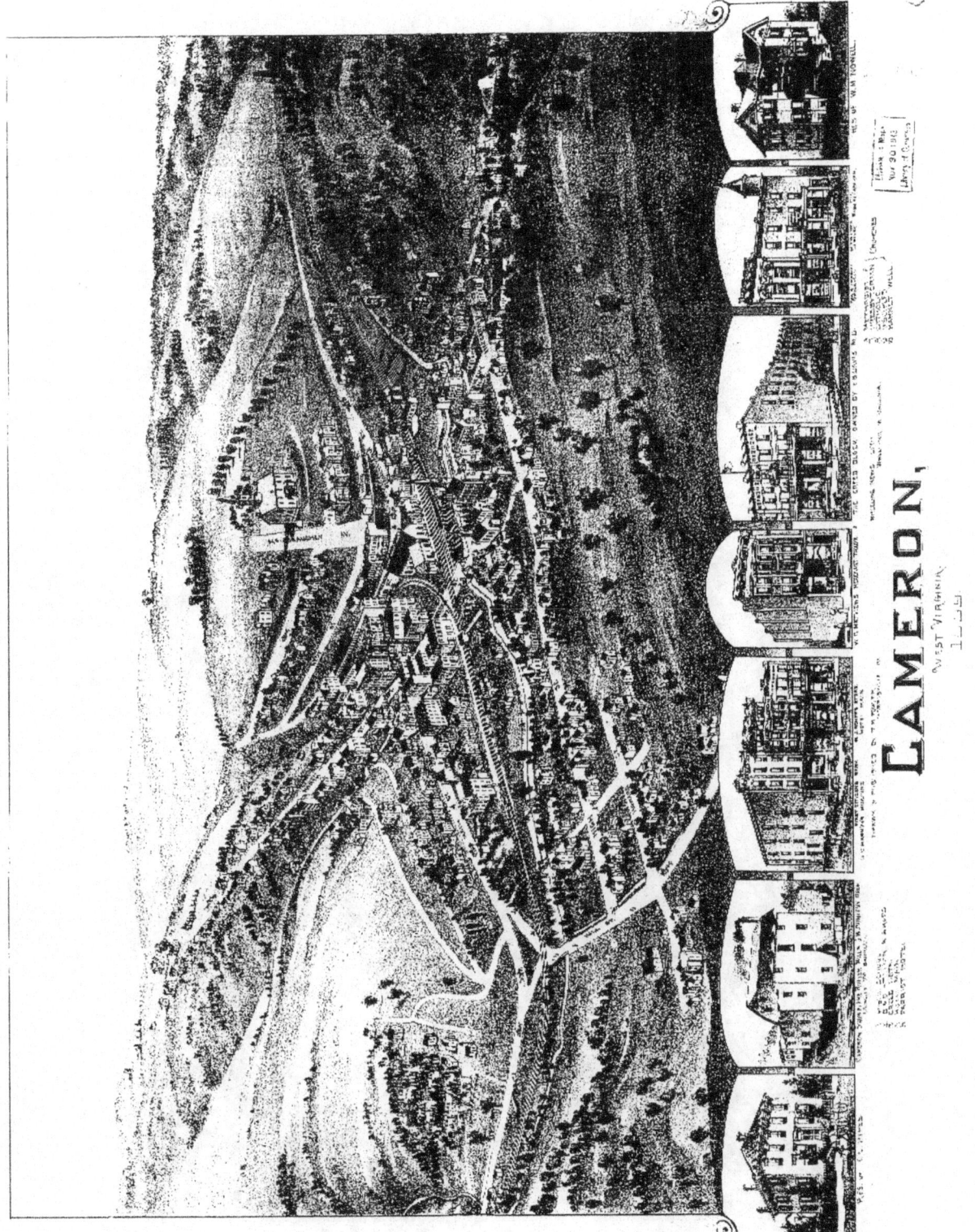

1858   1889 MAP OF MOUNDSVILLE, MARSHALL CO.

1870 MAP OF WHEELING CITY WITH WHEELING ISLAND   1859

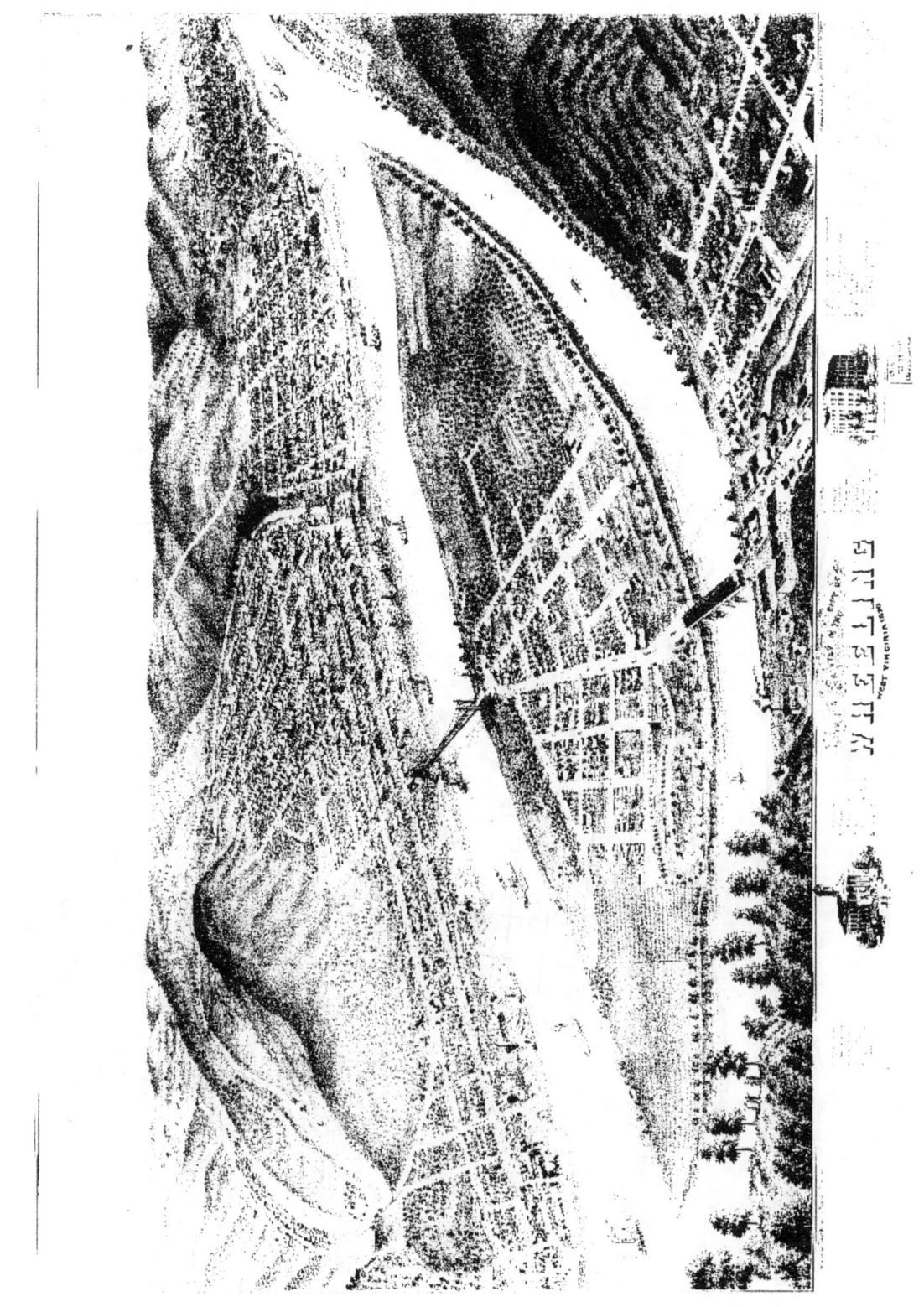

1860 1822 CITY OF WHEELING MAP –
WITH ORIGINAL STREET LAYOUT - 2ND ST. FROM RIVER, ETC.

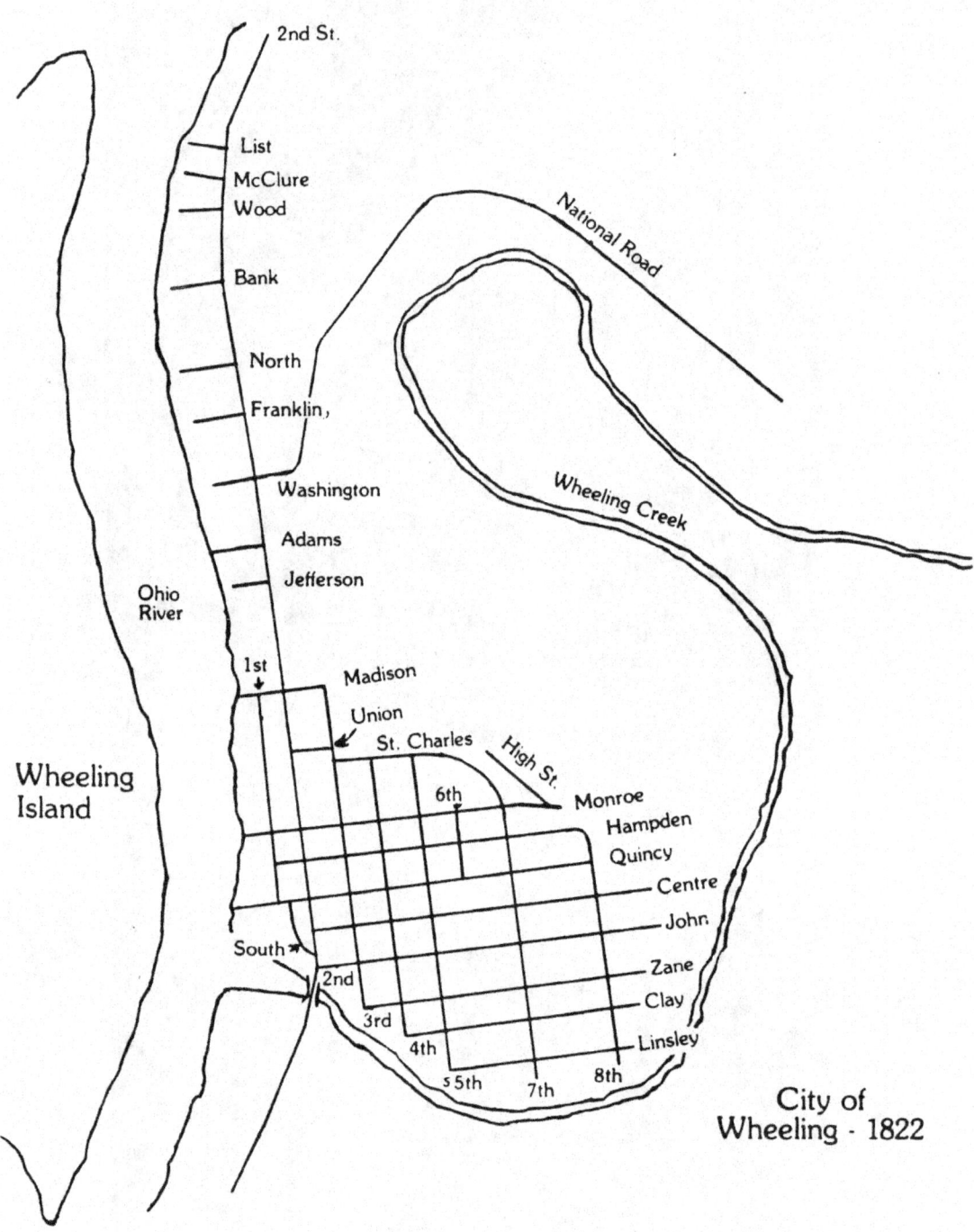

City of Wheeling - 1822

Source: Wheeling Union Chapter No.1 Royal Arch Masons 1822-1972; page 11; compiled by Ophir E. Vellenoweth, PHP. Used with compiler's permission.

Chapter 8: WASHINGTON, PA., ACROSS TO WEST VIRGINIA "PANHANDLE" TO WHEELING

T the intersection of Main Street, in Washington, our route turns right—nearly north on Main Street—up-grade, past the large and impressive Court House, which is at the corner of Beau Street. Perhaps there is an interesting story of how Beau and Maiden Street came to be so named; but that is outside the scope of the present series. Washington is the largest place between Cumberland and Wheeling, and was a popular stopping point for stage coaches and freight wagons; several of the celebrated taverns were located in this section, but they have now disappeared. At the second corner beyond the Court House, we turn left on Chestnut Street and start on the final westward stretch of 32½ miles to the Ohio River; in so doing, we run also into the main automobile route from Pittsburgh to Wheeling, which comes into Washington from the northeast to Main and Chestnut Streets. This Pittsburgh connection brings a great deal of additional travel into our route.

As usual, this identity of the old pike is partially lost in going through a city like Washington; but after crossing the Pennsylvania R. R. tracks, only a short distance out Chestnut Street, and the B. & O. further along, the National Road passes through West Washington (formerly Rankinville), and becomes itself again in the open country. Two miles out we cross Chartiers Creek over the three-arch stone bridge shown on page 76, this also illustrates the substantial way in which the bridges on the National Road were built over the smaller as well as the larger streams. A series of easy but continuous grades carries the old Pike past the old Miller House, a popular and well-remembered wagon stand situated on the north side of the road about five miles west of Washington; like many others that once catered to the traveling public, this is now a private residence. Along this portion of the road are several conspicuous old buildings, but not all of historical significance.

The next landmark of importance, and one of the most interesting features of this part of the route, is the low stone bridge over a branch of the Buffalo Creek, shown on page 77; on account of its peculiar shape, it is known far and wide as the "S-bridge." In early times there was a tavern at either end of it, though now travel goes by without stop, and the comparatively new building on the other side is a large private house. The old tavern on the west side of the "S-bridge" stood until it was burned in February, 1899, and was quite typical of the wooden buildings, in their last stages. The outside appearance of these old places was never very much of an index to the quality of the entertainment they afforded to the traveler of three-quarters of a century or more ago.

On the top of the hill beyond the "S-bridge," and on the south side of the road, is a large brick structure which was opened by John Cald-

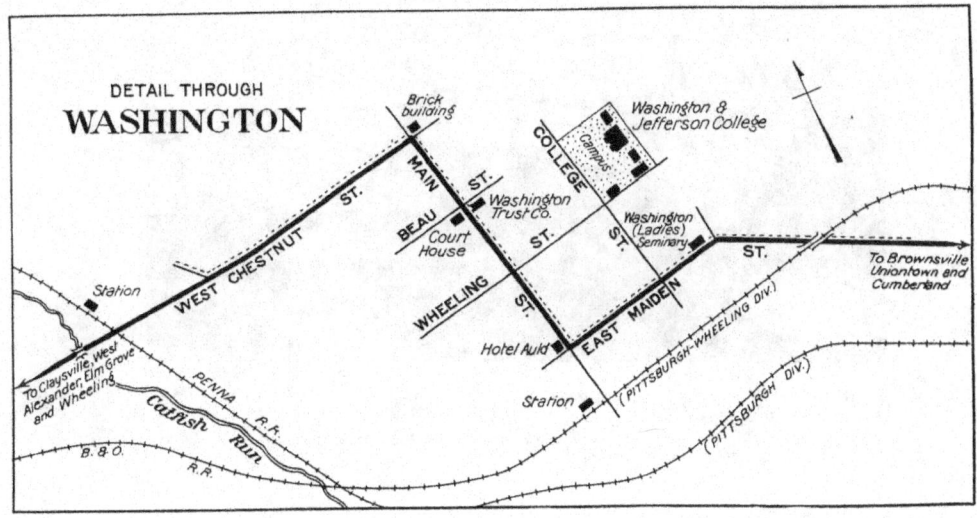

well as a tavern about the time the Pike was built through this section; he conducted it until 1838, and it was continued as a tavern until 1873. It was a favorite resort of pleasure-seeking parties; but like so many other of the old places, is now a private residence. At the foot of a grade about three-quarters of a mile beyond, the Pike crosses Buffalo Creek by another stone bridge, commonly known as the Clark Bridge; this creek becomes a considerable stream before reaching the Ohio near Wellsburg, W. Va.

About a half mile farther on, the road passes far above the Pittsburgh-Wheeling line of the B. & O. R. R., which here goes through a deep tunnel. Shortly the railroad comes alongside and is followed into Claysville, whose main street is the National Pike; the place was laid out in 1817 and named in honor of Henry Clay, the Kentucky statesman, who was one of the most ardent champions of the road. It was for many years an important stage station, well supplied with taverns, both for stage coach travelers and freight wagon drivers. The detailed map on page 77 shown the continuation of the route direct west across the railroad and past the hamlet of Vienna (once a relay for express wagons) better known as "Coon Island," to the old brick toll house.

This is the last toll house on our route in Pennsylvania, and is still owned by that state; of course, no toll has been collected for many years, and as long ago as 1875 the iron gates and posts were removed and sold for scrap iron. Almost in front of the toll house, the Pike turns right, and then left six-tenths of a mile beyond, direct to West Alexander which, laid out in 1796, became one of the important points of this great thoroughfare to the West; the original name of the community was "The Three Ridges," other names for it having been "Hard Scrabble," "Gretna Green" and "Saint's Rest." The two taverns, of which the "American Eagle," built in 1797 was probably the most celebrated, were patronized by the rival stage lines of the road. Today the tourist stopping at the Lafayette, on the left-hand side going west will probably be served by the proprietor or a member of his family; the meal is plain and substantial, the charge is only 35 cents, and the information quite likely volunteered that Marquis de Lafayette stopped here on his American visit in 1824.

Continue through the center of West Alexander, bearing right at the fork at farther end of the town; a short distance beyond the road turns right under the B. & O. R. R., and at the same time we pass from southwestern Pennsylvania into that irregular part of upper West Virginia, known as the "Panhandle." In so doing we are likely to miss one of the most interesting of the old milestones, which is on the right, almost under the railroad, and much more conspicuous as one travels east. It dates back to the time when there was no West Virginia; and the inscriptions are as follows:

(East side) "Penn'a 17 to Wheeling; to Tridelphia 8½."

(West side) "Virg'a 115 to Cumberland; to West Alexander ½."

Across the West Virginia "Panhandle"

We are now within 45 minutes' comfortable ride of the Ohio River; the 16 miles or so are almost level as compared with the route followed for the greater part of this trip, and there is a consciousness of having descended from the highlands to comparative lowlands.

Photograph Copyright J. K. Lacock

THREE SPAN STONE-ARCH BRIDGE, CARRYING THE NATIONAL PIKE OVER CHARTIERS CREEK, TWO MILES WEST OF WASHINGTON, PA.

This part of the road goes through one of the oil districts of southwestern Pennsylvania, as indicated by the derricks on the other side of the bridge

1916 'NATIONAL ROAD' BOOK – VALLEY GROVE (MAP P.1740)   1863

Photograph Copyright J. K. Lacock

THE "S-BRIDGE," WHICH CARRIES THE NATIONAL PIKE OVER BUFFALO CREEK ABOUT SIX MILES WEST OF WASHINGTON, PA.

This is one of the curious bridges along the route and bears some resemblance to the one across the Castleman River near Grantsville, Md.

West Virginia is the youngest state east of the Mississippi, and the only one formed as a direct result of a division of sentiment over the issues of the war between the states, having been cut off from the northwestern part of Virginia by representatives of 40 counties who rejected the ordinance of secession and met in convention, suggesting the new state of Kanawha. It was admitted into the Union June 29, 1863, as West Virginia, the most irregular state in the entire country; with an area of only 24,589 square miles, a line drawn from Harpers Ferry to Kenova will measure 574 miles. This section of it seems at once eastern, western, northern and southern, a conception which grows upon one with a closer geographical study of that section. One gains, however, only a very inadequate idea of West Virginia from the little buffer piece seen on this route; generally speaking, it is a state of great rivers, wild mountains, and picturesque valleys, with an abundance of coal, gas and oil, prime factors of industry and wealth. The climate also seems more genial; running across the "Panhandle" on a late fall day in 1914, the warmth and cheery brightness soon took away the last vestiges of chill left from going over the mountain ranges east of Uniontown a few hours before.

From now on, the Pike follows the general course of the railroad and trolley through to Wheeling; but the old road, first in the field, had its choice of right-of-way, the steam and electric lines being obliged to adapt themselves as best they could to the most natural route across this section. One result of this is the frequent crossings, especially of the trolley tracks, which are not encountered at as many places all the way from Baltimore to the West Virginia line. There are rather sharp curves across two small bridges to the little village of Valley Grove; the large frame tavern building on the north side of the road at this place was opened as a tavern in 1832, and was a station for the "Stockton" line of coaches.

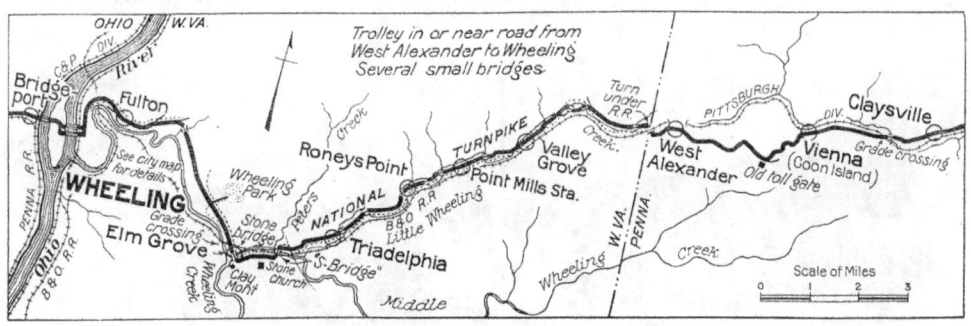

1864 1916 'NATIONAL ROAD' – RONEY'S POINT, TRIADELPHIA, ELM GROVE
(MAPS Pages 1782-4)

CHARACTERISTIC STRETCH OF GOOD ROAD ACROSS THE "PANHANDLE" OF WEST VIRGINIA, AND NEAR VIEW OF ONE OF THE MANY OIL DERRICKS FOUND THROUGHOUT THAT SECTION

Then comes Roney's Point where, on the north side of the road, we note the old stone tavern shown on page 80 erected in 1820, and a public house to this day; the "Simo" line of stages stopped here under one landlord and the "Good Intent" under another. Next is Tridelphia, another one of the many villages which grew up along the Pike. Two taverns of excellent reputation are said to have been conducted here when road travel was heavy; later on several of the old stage coach and freight wagon drivers retired and spent their declining years in this scattered little village. Today by the aid of the trolley, it is conveniently suburban to Wheeling, and automobiles outnumber all other vehicles over the road.

Less than a mile and a half beyond Tridelphia, the road turns across Middle Wheeling Creek, and then right along the south side of same into Main Street, Elm Grove village, past a sideroad leading to the stone Presbyterian Church, as shown by the map on page 77. That church was organized in 1787, and services were held under the large oak trees at the top of the hill about 1,000 yards from what was then, as it is now, the main thoroughfare and overlooking a considerable proportion of the surrounding country. In 1860 a church was rebuilt on the same site, and in 1914 a new structure was erected at the foot of the hill about 100 yards from the main street of the village.

Col. Moses and Lydia Shepherd, referred to in the following paragraphs, are buried in the cemetery attached to the old church on the hill. A short distance beyond one comes to the eastern edge of the three-arched stone bridge shown on page 80. In "Loring Place"—private grounds to the left of that bridge, and about 50 feet from the Pike—can still be seen what is left of the once famous Henry Clay monument, long worn by time and storm, and now very much dilapidated. One can scarcely view the present condition of this monument without feeling that Henry Clay and his services to the old Pike at

Photograph Copyright J. K. Lacock
WHERE THE ROAD AND TROLLEY CURVE IN GOING INTO TRIDELPHIA
The topography shown here is quite typical of the "Panhandle" of West Virginia

least deserves a better monument at this late day. Originally each of the four sides of the base column bore an elaborate inscription, though none of them is wholly legible now; one read:

> "This monument was erected by Moses and Lydia Shepherd, as a testimony of respect to Henry Clay, the eloquent defender of National rights and National Independence."

and another:

> "Time will bring every amelioration and refinement most gratifying to rational man; and the humblest flower freely plucked under the shelter of the Tree of Liberty, is more to be desired than all the wrappings of royalty: 44th year of American Independence, Anno Domini 1820."

Farther back in the spacious grounds is the old Shepherd mansion, where the Kentucky statesman and other notable travelers were frequently entertained on their trips between the Central West and the National Capital. Col. Moses Shepherd died in 1832, at the age of 68; the inscription on the monument at his grave refers to his part in the defence of that section when it was a frontier settlement and also to his public services in aiding the construction of the Cumberland or National Road across what was then the northwestern part of Virginia. Immediately beyond the grounds where one would stop to view the Clay Monument, the road turns square right to cross the arched stone bridge, and passes through the business center of Elm Grove; then we follow the trolley past the old stone building on the left, known in the busy days of the National Pike as Mrs. Gooding's, to Wheeling Park. Just opposite that park, about one and one-half miles west of Elm Grove, was Stamm's, and close to the two-mile post east of Wheeling, was Thompson's; both were noted road houses, but more patronized by teamsters than travelers on account of being so near Wheeling. These buildings are both standing and are in good repair, occupied as dwellings.

Into and About Wheeling

Many fine houses are noticed on either side of what is the most interesting and attractive as well as the most important thoroughfare of Wheeling; nor is the identity of the Pike as much lost here as in some smaller places farther east, for at least two of the milestones are noticed within the city limits. For a distance the trolley leaves the roadway, and before it returns there is a fine stretch of brick. After crossing a stone bridge over a tributary of Wheeling Creek, the road makes a left turn, and the trolley is followed through two or three suburban communities; then the tracks turn off to the left and we ascend Wheeling Hill over more brick pavement, some of it laid upon a high and expensive

Photograph Copyright J. K. Lacock

CLOSE VIEW OF THE HENRY CLAY MONUMENT, ERECTED IN 1820, JUST OFF THE ROAD AT ELM GROVE, W. VA.
Parts of the original design are now entirely gone and the rest is gradually crumbling

retaining wall built to assist travel up the grade. Considerable of this improvement was made possible through several thousands of dollars raised by or through the Ohio Valley Automobile Club, whose headquarters are at Wheeling.

From the top a very extensive bird's-eye view of Wheeling can be had, and especially of the great Ohio River Valley beyond, including the two bridges connecting the states of West Virginia and Ohio. One also gains some idea of this locality as an industrial center, with a large and valuable output, especially of iron and steel products, glass, tin-plate, enamel ware and tobacco. At about the start of the corresponding downgrade is the point shown on map, page 82, as "McColloch's Leap," so named from Samuel McColloch, who in September, 1777, during an assault on Fort Henry, escaped from the Indians by leaping from a point on the hillside into the creek at the foot. Curving around to the left, the Pike runs into Market Street to the intersection of 10th Street where, looking to the right across Main Street, one may see the historic suspension bridge shown on page 81.

We are now at the western terminus of that part of the National Road contemplated by the original act of Congress, March 29, 1806, though later extensions carried it to Zanesville, Columbus and Springfield, Ohio, Richmond, Indianapolis and Terre Haute, Indiana and Vandalia, Illinois, but never all the way to the "Father of Waters" at St. Louis. As early as 1805 there was a great deal of emigration through Wheeling, 800 wagons, carts and other vehicles crossing the Ohio here within three months on their way to the rich farming lands of what is now our Central West. The next year it was incorporated as a town, and one important event followed another, for in 1811 steam navigation was opened between Pittsburgh, Wheeling, Cincinnati, Louisville and New Orleans, and in 1818 the National Road was completed to the Ohio, providing through transportation from Baltimore, Hagerstown and Cumberland across the Alleghenies. Two years later, Congress made its first appropriation for continuing the survey of the National Road from Wheeling to the Mississippi River.

In the early days, the river was crossed by ferry, but in 1837 a covered wooden bridge was completed across the narrow or west channel between Wheeling Island and the Ohio shore at Bridgeport, though not across the east or main channel; and it may be interesting to know that it was replaced on the original piers by the present steel bridge only ten or twelve years ago. The main line of National Pike crossed this island over what is now known as Zane Street; the island was originally owned by Col. Ebenezer Zane, and tradition says that he purchased it from the Indians for a jug of whiskey.

The old wooden bridge was used until 1849, when the first suspension bridge—the first one across the Ohio, and at that time the longest in the world—was completed and opened to traffic. That one was blown down in 1854 and the present "suspension bridge," 1,010 feet long, was opened two years later. The "Steel Bridge" (1,600 feet long) can also be used by the westbound tourist, but this is owned by the traction lines and carries a very heavy traffic; it is also narrow, and requires taking a more circuitous route. So the old bridge that has accommodated most of the traffic for 59 years is still the best for the motorist of today.

Photograph Copyright J. K. Lacock
OLD STONE HOTEL AT RONEY'S POINT, W. VA., BUILT 1820, AND STILL DOING A LOCAL BUSINESS

Brief Historical Retrospect

The strategic location of Wheeling made it from the earliest days a point of more than ordinary historic importance; in his "Journals" (1751-52) Christopher Gist speaks of reaching the present site of the city, crossing the Ohio, probably near the suspension bridge, and mentions the "antique sculptures" (the work of the mound-builders) on the other side. It was settled, as Zanesburg, in 1769; and in 1774 Fort Fincastle, afterward called Fort Henry, in honor

Photograph Copyright J. K. Lacock
THREE-ARCHED STONE BRIDGE OVER LITTLE WHEELING CREEK AT ELM GROVE, W. VA., ABOUT FIVE MILES EAST OF WHEELING

of Patrick Henry, was established by General Dunmore to resist Indian outbreaks. An attack on that fort in 1782 was the last battle of the Revolutionary War.

After the nominal cessation of hostilities, but before the news reached the Ohio River, 260 Indians and 40 Queens Rangers, in command of Captain Brandt, attacked the settlement. Col. Ebenezer Zane, with four or five campanions was defending his barricaded house, when his supply of powder gave out. His daughter Elizabeth, who was in the fort, filled her apron with powder and ran from the fort to her father's house, over 100 yards, in the face of a brisk fire, but was unharmed. After a long fight the settlers were victorious. A tablet about two feet high, marking the site of Fort Henry, can be seen on the curb of Main Street, about a block south of the Suspension Bridge.

Wheeling was laid out by Colonel Zane in 1793, and the present name, about which there are conflicting legends, was adopted in 1795. Some claim that it was derived from the fact that the Creek, in its meandering course, "wheeled" around the hill near its junction with the Ohio; but the most generally accepted opinion is that it came from an Indian word meaning "The Head." It is said that on one occasion the Indians cremated a white man, placed his head on a pole and did a war-dance around it; this is supposed to have taken place at the head of Wheeling Creek and may account for the name.

It was incorporated in 1806, made a city in 1836, and was the capital of West Virginia from 1863 to 1870, and also from 1875 to 1885, before Charleston was made the permanent capital. The present population of Wheeling is about 50,000, and it is the center for a tri-state business district of about 200,000. It is slightly north of the Mason and Dixon line, and was the first point on the Ohio River reached by railway across the Alleghany Mountains.

The named streets run parallel with the Ohio River, while the numbered streets extend from the river to the eastern part of the city. One gains the impression that the streets in the downtown business center are narrow, possibly somewhat because the city itself is hemmed in between the river and the hills on either side of Wheeling Creek. But perhaps no place of its size in the United States has today as much through east and west travel as Wheeling. It has also now, as in the olden days, as large and important river commerce; and the tourist from the seaboard will probably be interested to note the characteristic boats on the Ohio, especially the large "tows" of soft coal, bound to points as far south as New Orleans.

On Main Street, half a square below the suspension bridge, is the site of Fort Henry, now occupied by a lunch room or restaurant. In 1860 there were only 100 slaves in Ohio County, in which Wheeling is situated; but there was a slave market on Market Street between 10th and 11th Streets, where the auditorium, a market and convention hall combined, now stands. Court was also held at this corner, and nearby at one time was an old-fashioned whipping post; of course, all these sites have since been occupied with modern buildings.

The most noted of the several old taverns was that of John McCortney, located on Main Street, running east on 14th Street to Alley B, parallel with and between Main and Market Streets. Ample grounds surrounding it afforded plenty of

Photograph Copyright J. K. Lacock

THE FAMOUS SUSPENSION BRIDGE ACROSS THE OHIO RIVER FROM WHEELING, WEST VIRGINIA, TO BRIDGEPORT, OHIO

This is now, as in the olden time, the principal means of connecting the eastern and western sections of the National Road

1868 1916 'NATIONAL ROAD' BOOK – WHEELING (MAP P.1788)

room for wagons and teams to stand; and in connection with his hotel, McCortney had a large commission business. As early as 1802, Capt. Fred Beymer kept a tavern near the site of Fort Henry; and in 1806 the Wheeling town council met there, the place having been kept subsequently by Mrs. Beymer. The two principal hotels of today are the McLure, on the southeast corner of 12th and Market Streets, and the Windsor, on the west side of Main Street, between 11th and 12th, both convenient to the National Road leading east or west, and to the several routes which diverge in other directions.

As a matter of mere driving, the Baltimore-Wheeling trip can be made in about fifteen hours, averaging probably eight from Baltimore to Cumberland and about seven from Cumberland to Wheeling. Spread over two fairly long days, and with such advance knowledge of the route and its chief points of interest as this series of articles is intended to supply, it should—in favorable weather—turn out to be a tour of unusual variety, and one full of memories well worth retaining. In running from the sea level of Chesapeake Bay across the entire Appalachian Range to the Ohio River, the tourist comes to know the different mountain ranges as would be possible in no other way except, of course, by primitive and slower means of transportation; and may frequently be surprised at the relative shortness of the trip and the little time needed to cover it as compared with the corresponding routes from the eastern seaboard to the Central West through Pittsburgh or Buffalo.

Probably a large portion of motor tourists who make this run from Baltimore arrive at Wheeling with a consciousness that their interest in the route would be increased rather than lessened if the trip were to be literally retraced on the two following days; but with a stronger inclination to follow the old road across the Ohio River, and part if not all the way to the Mississippi. It is quite possible that another year may see this series of articles carried from Wheeling to St. Louis or beyond, and ultimately to the Pacific Coast. But one making the tour, even so far as already covered by the detailed maps, will inevitably gain a new conception of the Old National Road—particularly its strategic location and deep historic interest; and is quite likely convinced that it is the most logical eastern part of the National Old Trails OCEAN-TO-OCEAN HIGHWAY.

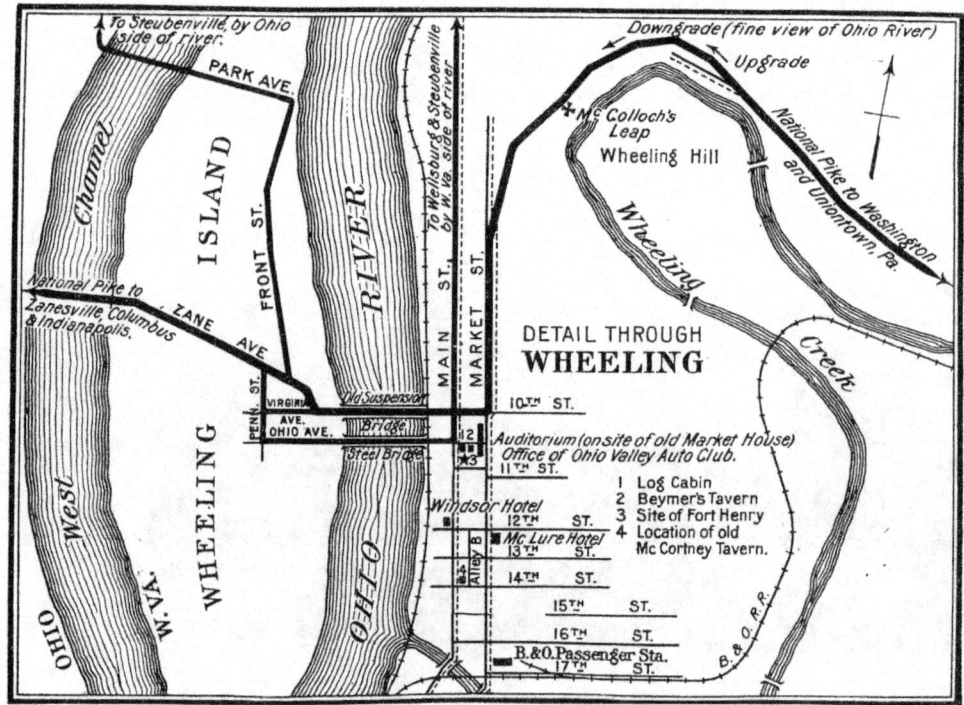

WHEELING, WEST VIRGINIA, IS THE NATURAL DIVIDING POINT BETWEEN THE GREAT EASTERN AND WESTERN SECTIONS OF THE NATIONAL ROAD, AND THE TERMINUS NAMED IN THE LAW UNDER WHICH IT WAS BUILT FROM CUMBERLAND TO THE OHIO RIVER

1916 'NATIONAL ROAD' BOOK — CUMBERLAND TO WHEELING MAP   1869

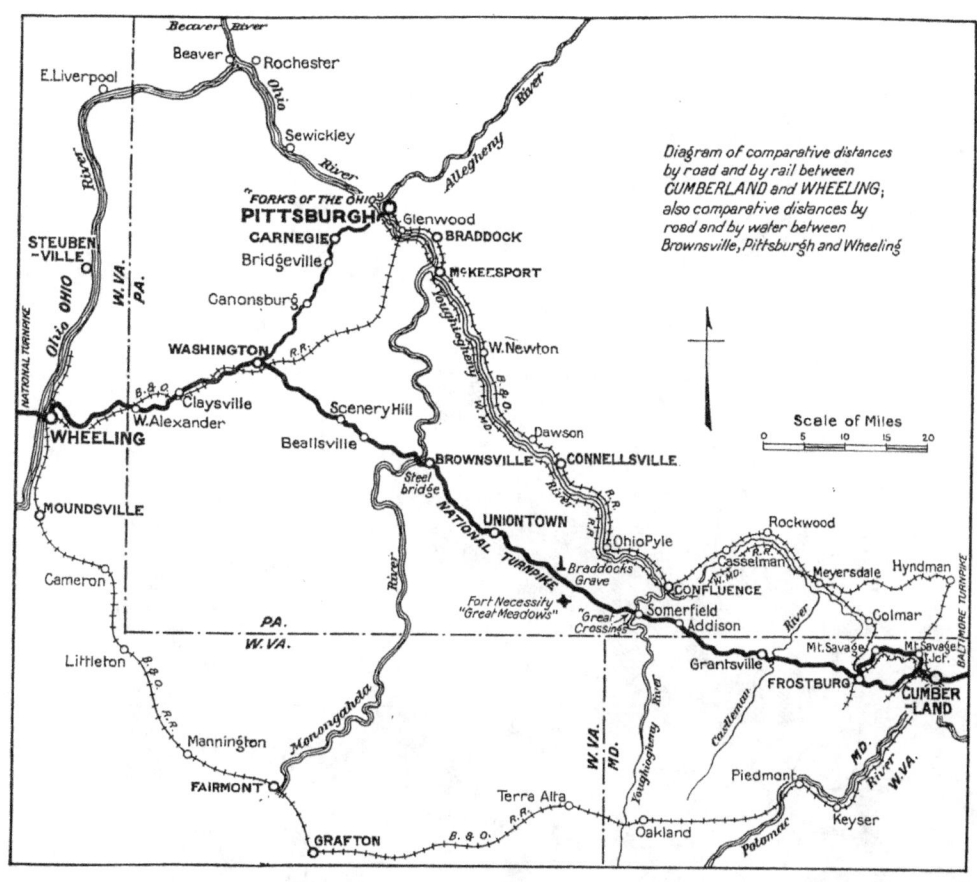

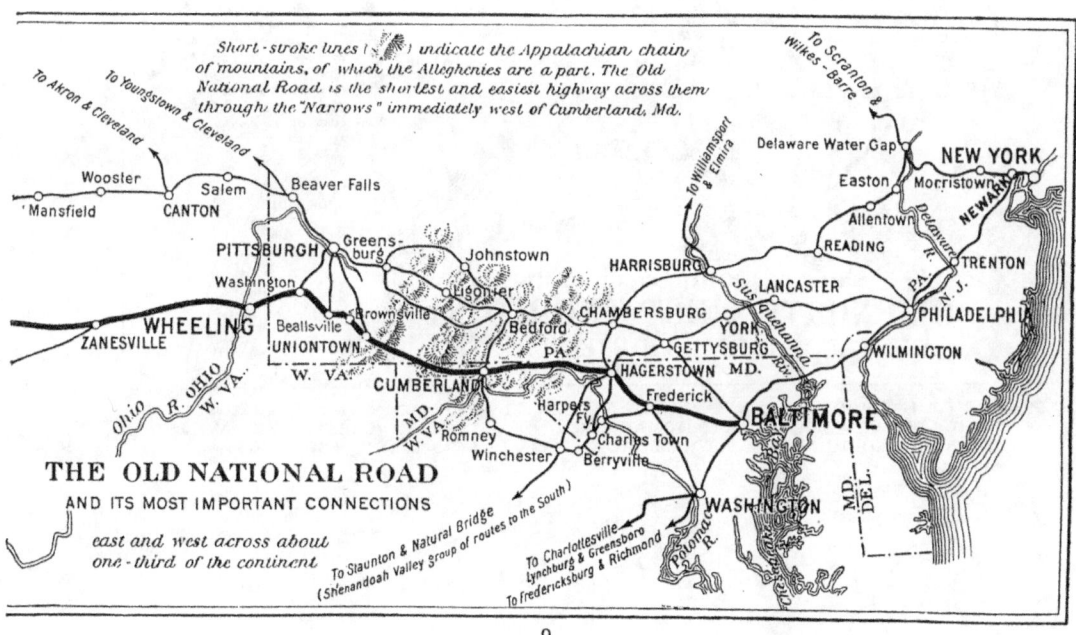

1870 1916 'NATIONAL ROAD' BOOK – OLD NORTH WEST TERRITORY

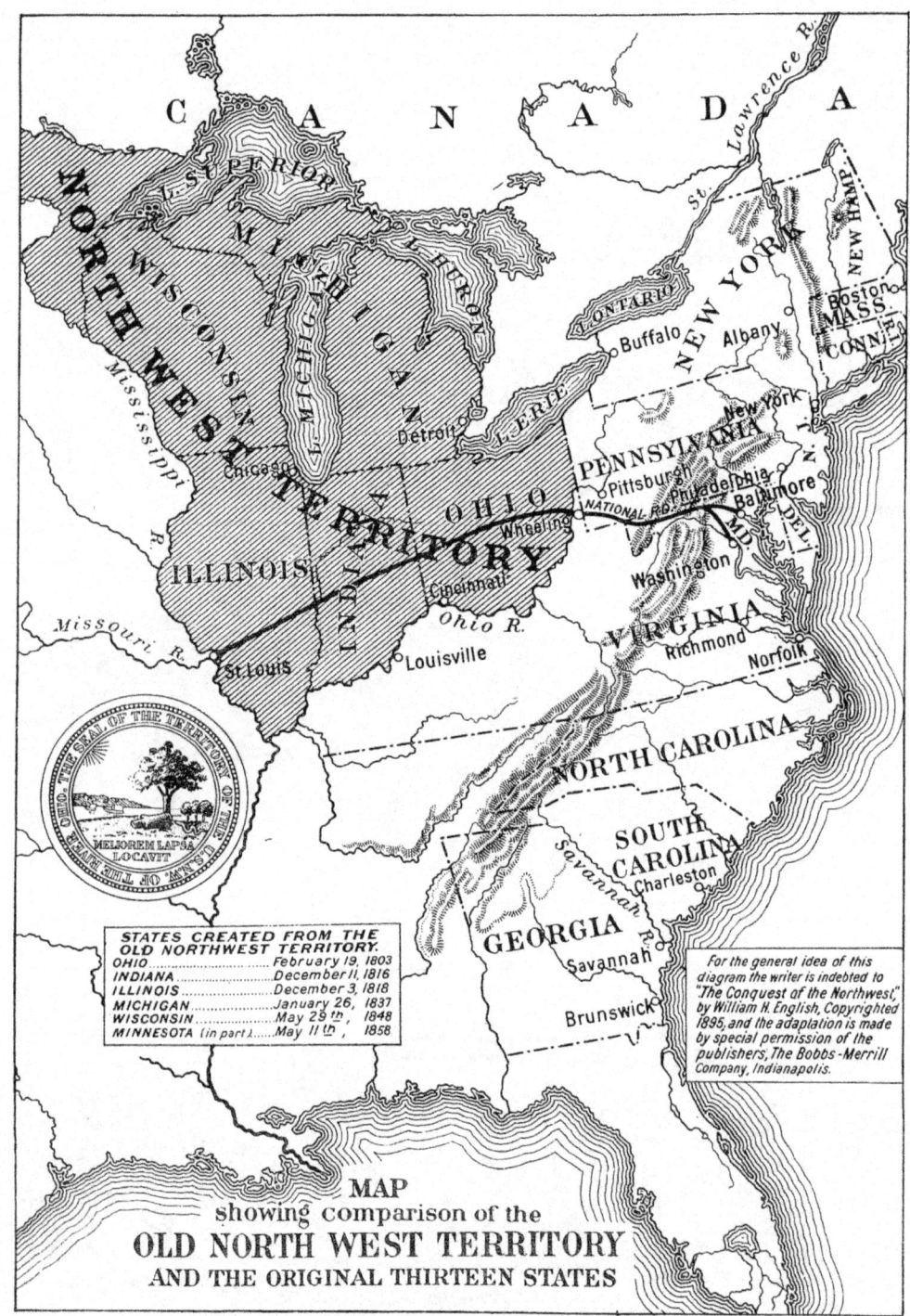

A GRAPHIC ILLUSTRATION OF THE SAVING OF DISTANCE BY THE OLD NATIONAL ROAD BETWEEN TIDEWATER AT WASHINGTON (POTOMAC RIVER) OR BALTIMORE (CHESAPEAKE BAY), AND THE OHIO RIVER AT WHEELING, W. VA., ALSO ITS DIRECTNESS ACROSS OHIO, INDIANA AND ILLINOIS

SOME OHIO CO. MICROFILMS AT WV & REGIONAL HISTORY COLL. 1871

Some Ohio County Microfilms at the West Virginia and Regional History Collection
The following microfilms can be viewed in person in Morgantown:

West Virginia & Regional History Collection
Colson Hall
West Virginia University
P.O. Box 6464
Morgantown, WV 26506-6464
Phone (304) 293-3536

Contents	Order Book #'s	Years	Film #
Order Books	1 - 3 (#2 non-existent)	1777 - 1792	**OHI 141**
Order Books	4 - 6	1792 - 1800	**OHI 142**
Order Books	7 - 9	1800 - 1804	**OHI 143**
Order Books	10 - 12	1805 - 1811	**OHI 144**
Order Books	13 - 15	1811 - 1816	**OHI 145**
Order Books	16 - 17	1817 - 1820	**OHI 146**
Order Books	18 - 20	1820 - 1825	**OHI 147**
Order Books	21, 23 & 24	1825 - 1826; 1828 - 1831	**OHI 148**
Order Books	22	1826 - 1828	**OHI 149**
Order Books	25 – 26	1831 - 1835	**OHI 150**
Order Books	27 – 28	1835 – 1841	**OHI 151**
Order Books	29 – 30	1841 – 1848	**OHI 152**
Order Books	31 – 32	1848 – 1854	**OHI 153**
Order Books	33 – 34	1853 – 1856	**OHI 154**
Order Books	35 – 36	1856 – 1858	**OHI 155**
Order Books	37 – 38	1858 – 1862	**OHI 156**
Order Books	39 – 41	1862 – 1872	**OHI 157**

(Originals for this book series below)

Contents	Years	Film #
Index Order Books Plaintiffs A - D	1777 – 1881	OHI 129
Index Order Books Plaintiffs E - K	1777 – 1881	OHI 131
Index Order Books Plaintiffs L - R	1777 – 1881	OHI 133
Index Order Books Plaintiffs T - Z	1777 – 1881	OHI 135

1872 SOME OHIO CO. MICROFILMS AT WV STATE ARCHIVES

This page provides additional information regarding where to find the original source documents for some index entries.

1. County Court Order Books 1873-1885

Below are the microfilms of the County Court Order Books from 1873-1885. These appear to be a continuation of the WV and Regional History Collection filming projects and most likely start with volume #42. The new volume numbers shown below seem to be incorrect so please order by year. All the following microfilm listings come from the WV State Archives in Charleston. Their film collection is comprised almost entirely of microfilms made by the LDS Family History Center (FHC) Library in Salt Lake City. As such, they are available for loan from your nearest Family History Center. There is also an archives film number in case you visit Charleston.

1	Record Title	Volumes	Dates of Film	FHC Film #*	Archives Film #**
2	Order Book (County Court)	V.1	1873-	857507	453
3	>Notes: [1] Continues WV & Regional History	V.2	1874-	857507	453
4	Collection film series.	V.3	1876-1878	857508	454
5	[2] These volume numbers look wrong -	V.4	1878-1880	857508	454
6	i.e. 1873 is probably Vol. 42, etc.	V.5	1881-1885	857509	455
7	* Family History Center Library (LDS)	** WV State Archives in Charleston, WV			

2. Chancery and Law Court entries in County Court Order Books

Included in the original indexes is a column referring to the type of court: 'C' Chancery; 'L' Law and 'S' State. In most instances, the 'C' Chancery, seems to mean that the county court was meeting 'in chancery session' to consider these important cases involving estates. So most of these 'C' entries are just included on a page of the normal County Court Order Books. Most of the 'L' Law cases also seem to be just regular cases and are found in the normal County Court Order Books. I have found no mentions of 'S' State court entries so far.

3. Special Chancery and Law Order Books shown in original indexes

In some index entries, however, 'C' Chancery and 'L' Law entries refer to specially marked volumes whose exact source has not been located. For more information see pages 738-740 in Ohio County (WV) Index, volume 3.

PREVIEW OF VOLUMES 8+ : A NEW SERIES OF COURT RECORDS   1873

Volume 8 will start a new series of unique Ohio County Records – the **Index Card Files to the Court Case Files** at the "WV and Regional History Collection" at WVU in Morgantown. During the 1930's, another massive project collected <u>all the existing</u> Ohio County Courts' *case files and loose papers* from 1776-1930. Thousands of <u>original court papers</u> (lawsuits and other court business, which have never been filmed) – from <u>every court</u>: County, Circuit, Superior, Circuit Superior, etc. – were collected and sorted. Then a massive index card file was made containing about <u>90,000 cards</u> describing persons involved and contents of the case file or other document. These index cards will be published for the first time ever *starting* with volume 8.

An early test of text files shows <u>most of the entries contain new names/data</u> – not included in **OCI** volumes 1-7. The entries for cases mentioned in **OCI** vols. 1-7 will guide to researcher to the original case document files for more details of the case. Below are some samples of the original 3"x5" cards that will be indexed starting with volume 8. Continued ·

Env. 25 B
Co. Ct.   Ohio Co.   1808

Chapline, Josiah; Chapline, William
vs
Inskeep, Abraham H.
Chancery Injunction

Bill of Complaint, 4 letters, 2 Interrogatories, 3 Depositions, Account, Injunction, Order

---

Env. 28-A
County Court   Ohio Co.   1808

Dille, Samuel
Dille, David
vs
Smith, Henry
Chancery

Nar., Agreement, Sum., 2 Ded., Notice, 2 Orders, Report, 2 Dep., Answer, Note, 5 Accounts

---

Env. 28
County Court   Ohio Co.   1808

Re: Anderson, Samuel; Spahr, John Jr.;
    Morgan, Daniel;   Spahr, John Sr.;
    Caldwell, John;   Neaff, Henry;
    Hughes, James;   Neelson, John;
    Willer, Peter;   Mauns, Providence

Summons to show cause, etc. (Road)

Env. 33 & 3
Cir. Sup. Ct.   Ohio Co.   1810
Re: Biggs, Ben   Tomlinson, Jos.
    Zane, Noah   McMechen, Benj.
    Williams, Jeremiah McColloch, John
    Buckey, John   Cross, Jacob
    Ridgely, Absolom   McKinley, Wm.
    McClure, John   Sims, Richard
    Ray, Patrick   Sims, Clabourn
    McClure, Samuel   Bofeman, Reuben
    Bounds, Wm.   Ryan, Jas.
    Erwin, Wm.   Eoff, John
    White, John   Evans, Thos.
    Burkett, Jacob,   Farquahar, Wm.
Grand Jury   / List.   J

Env. 36-A
County Court Chancery   Ohio Co.   1811

Alexander, Joseph &
McVicker, James
vs
Gregg's, George - Executors.
Foreclosure

Bill of complaint, 2 Answers, Original Grant, Decree, Copy of will, Copy of Grant, Deed, Decree for sale of land, Answer to sale, Agreement, Summon, Receipt, 2 notes, 2 Accts. Attorney's letter to Plaintiff, Attorney's Memo., Memo. on authorities, Memo on sale.

Env. 37
County Court   Ohio County   1811
Re: Carmicle, James)
    Carmicle, Hiram)
    Carmicle, Hugh)
    Carmicle, Eliz.) Children of

Carmicle, Hugh, Deceased

Order to Bind Out as Apprentices

1874 PREVIEW OF VOLUMES 8+ & ABBREVIATIONS USED IN THE INDEX

Below is a sample of the 'space-efficient' text page format listing the types of cards.
The usual 'Personal Time Line' Index will complete each volume.
Watch for volume 8!

CARD	ENV	CT	YEAR	PLAINTIFF VS DEFENDANT (OR ENTRY)	SUBJECT	ENV. CONTENTS
1		C	1776		DIVIDER	DIVIDER
2	1	C	1776	RE: MYERS, LUDWIG, CAPTAIN, FIRST LIEUTENANT	MILITARY AFFAIRS	2 BONDS OF COMMISSION
3		C	1777		DIVIDER	DIVIDER
4	1-A	C	1777	RE: MCCOLLOCH, JOHN, SHERIFF		2 BONDS
5		C	1778		DIVIDER	DIVIDER
6	1A-1	C	1778	HEDGES, SILAS; VS. DUNN, JERIMIAH; HARRISON, WM.; MILLS, LEVY	EX. (DEBT)	FIFA
7	1A-1	C	1778	DRENER, JACOB VS.JOLLY, PETER	EXECT, (DEBT)	FIFA
8	1	C	1778	RE: COX, ELEANOR; COX, ISRAEL; MCGUIRE, THOS., EXECUTORS; COX, GABRIEL, DEC.		BOND
9	1	C	1778	RE: HEDGES, SILAS TAKER UP.	ESTRAY-STEER	APPRAISEL & REPORT
10	1	C	1778	WHITE, JEMINA ; MEEK, ISAAC, ADMRS. WHITE, SAMUEL, DEC.		BOND
11	1	C	1778	RE: REAGER, JACOB, ADM. CALHOUN, A. DEC.		BOND
12	1	C	1778	RE: BUCKEY, JEMIMA; MILLS, LEVI, EXECUTORS; BUCKEY, JOHN, DEC.		BOND
13	1-A	C	1778	RE: SHEPHERD, DAVID, SHERIFF		BOND.
14	1-A	C	1778	RE: SHEPHERD, DAVID, SHERIFF		BOND
15	1-A	C	1778	RE: SPRIGG, ZACHARIAH, CORONER		BOND
16	1-A	C	1778	RE: SHEPHERD, DAVID, SHERIFF		2 BONDS
17		C	1779		DIVIDER	DIVIDER
18	1A-8	C	1779	CARPENTER, JOHN VS. KARR, JAMES; MCCONNAL, ARTHUR - GARNISHEE	DEBT - ATTACHMENT	ORDER OF ATTACHMENT (DEBT 60 POUNDS CURRENT MONEY)
19	1	C	1779	RE: LEPEN, MARGARET, EXECUTRIX; LEPEN, JAMES, DEC.		BOND
20	1	C	1779	RE: CLEMENS, JAMES, ADM. MILLER, JOSEPH, DEC.		BOND
21	1	C	1779	RE: MCCOLLOCH, GEORGE TAKER UP	ESTRAY - 2 HOGS	APPRAISEL & REPORT
22	1	C	1779	RE: HUFF, JOHN TAKER UP	ESTRAY-CALF	APPRAISEL & REPORT
23	1	C	1779	RE: WOLF, CHRISTY - TAKER UP	ESTRAY - STEER	APPRAISAL & REPORT
24	1	C	1779	RE: HUFF, JOHN TAKER UP	ESTRAY-CALF	APPRAISAL & REPORT

CARD	ENV	CT	YEAR	PLAINTIFF VS DEFENDANT (OR ENTRY)	SUBJECT	ENV. CONTENTS
74	1	C	1783	COMMONWEALTH VS. NEVIT, JOHN	PEACE ACTION	BOND
75	1	C	1783	RE: CHAPLINE, MOSES	LAND GRANT	DEED, SURVEY
76	1-A	C	1783	RE: HEDGES, SILAS, SHERIFF		BOND,
77	1A-3	C	1783	RE: DUNN, HEZEKIAH	SURVEY	<SEE LINE BELOW>
77A				PLAT AND SURVEY OF 400 ACRES ON BUFFALO CREEK. BOUNDED BY LANDS OF GEORGE HUMPHREYS, DAVID DEMENT, WILLIAM HUSTON, AND JAMES		
78		C	1784		DIVIDER	DIVIDER
79	1A-1	C	1784	HEITH, HENRY VS. PARKER, JAMES	EX.(DEBT)	FIFA
80	1A-1	C	1784	CULP, DANIEL VS. ZANE, ANDREW	EX.(DEBT)	FIFA
81	1A-1	C	1784	HAYDEN, MILES; HOOK, JAMES VS. BOERY, GEORGE	EX.(DEBT)	FIFA
82	1A-1	C	1784	COMMONWEALTH VS. MCFORSON, JOHN	EX.(DEBT)	FIFA, RECEIPT
83	1	C	1784	RE: ROGERS, DAVID, DEC'D.		MEMOS, AND SURVEYS OF LAND.
84	167 C-9	C	1784	RE: SMITH, SAMUEL	WILL	<SEE LINE BELOW>
84A				CIR. SUP. CT. OHIO CO. 1839 SEE: ALBRIGHT, MARGARET VS. BUCHANAN, WM. ET AL CHANCERY (INJUNCTION)		
85	1A-4	C	1784	RE: DEMENT, BENIJAH - OWNER BURCH, JESSE - FOR WOODS, ROBERT - SURVEYOR O.C.	SURVEY - 400 ACRES	<SEE LINE BELOW>
85A				PLAT AND SURVEY OF 400 ACRES, BOUNDED BY THE LANDS OF DAVID DEMENT, JAMES CALDWELL AND ROBERT HUMPHREYS.		
86	1A-4	C	1784	RE: HUMPHREYS, ROBERT HUMPHREYS, JOHN	SURVEY	<SEE LINE BELOW>
86A				PLAT OF 385 ACRES ON BUFFALO CREEK. BOUNDED BY THE LANDS OF DAVID DEMENT, HEZEKIAH DUNN, DAVID HUMPHREYS, GEORGE HUMPHREYS AND		

ABBREVIATIONS USED IN THE 'PERSONAL TIME LINE' INDEX

ABBREVIATION	DEFINITION
DEFENDANT	PERSON BEING SUED
MISC	MISCELLANEOUS ENTRY - NOT A LAWSUIT
PLAINTIFF	PERSON WHO BRINGS LAWSUIT

Hints for interpreting 'Miscellaneous Entries' notations and phrases

"Bound in" or "Bound out" – These relate the 'bound servants' or indentured servants. The usual reference is "Joseph Jones is bound out to William Smith". Because there are some separate mentions of 'apprentices', one could possibly assume this these 'bound servants' were of a lower status. However, sometimes there is an entry using both terms apparently interchangeably: "Fleming BILES bound out [his] son, John William BILES..as an apprentice to George FAUBEL". Apprenticeships had specific legal requirements and there are few mentions of these agreements regarding 'bound' children. But it seems likely that persons who were 'bound out' were poor and even sometimes recently orphaned – but this deserves study. Entries are sometimes cross-indexed under "Bound In" and "Bound Out".

"Certified age & residence" – People occasionally came into court and proved their age – possibly related to some lawsuit or just to have it 'in the record'.

"do" - An abbreviation for 'ditto' – or same as entry above.

"Ear marks for stock" – Livestock often roamed freely across the fields, so owners would 'mark' or 'brand' their animals. They would then go to the court and register their marks in order to prove ownership in case of a lost animal (sometimes referred to as 'estrays').

"et al" - Latin phrase meaning 'and others'. Unfortunately the names of the others were not transcribed by the original indexers.

"Exempt from Militia Duty" – Age of service was 18 to 45 (1849 Law) unless excused for a special occupation (Postmasters, sheriffs, professors, jailers, etc.) Could be a clue that he had reached the age of 45.

"Exempt from Road Work" – The court would exempt persons from road work due to age or other reasons. As discussed in detail in **OCI** volume 2 (page 233), road work was required (in the 1849 law) from most persons from ages 16 to 60 – so an exemption could mean the person had turned 60 years old. But use this only as a clue to further research.

"Released from paying county levy" – Presumably this is similar to being exempted from road work (discussed earlier) and could be a clue to the person's age. Age for levy tax was 16 years+ unless court excused (no upper age mentioned).

"Wolf Scalps" – A bounty was sometimes paid for wolf scalps – in order to rid the area of these predators.

1876 PREVIEW OF VOLUME 7A – 'CUMULATIVE INDEX' TO VOLUMES 1-7

Announcing the CUMULATIVE INDEX to volumes 1-7, with **110,000** entries !
Coming soon as **Volume 7A**, this will combine and re-sort **all the indexes in 'Personal Time Line' format** – showing the name, the date, the subject and the page number. What a great way to close out the County Court Order Book series (vols. 1-7) before starting the WVU Card Index in volume 8. Below is a sample for the BEYMER family, as first discussed on page 223 of *OCI* volume 1. We now have a much more complete view of this husband and wife - and future *OCI* volumes will add even more information and more entries to the never-ending cumulative index database.

FREDERICK BEYMER - CUMULATIVE INDEX VOLS. 1-7			
ENTRY	YEAR	SUBJECT	PAGE
BEYMER, FRED	1810	DEFENDANT	1033
BEYMER, FRED	1813	PLAINTIFF	527
BEYMER, FRED / CAPT. - TAVERN IN 1802	1916	NAT'L ROAD	1868
BEYMER, FREDERICH	1811	DEFENDANT	1071
BEYMER, FREDERICH	1814	DEFENDANT	1295
BEYMER, FREDERICK	1801	LICENSE	94
BEYMER, FREDERICK	1801	ROAD SUPV	254
BEYMER, FREDERICK	1802	DEFENDANT	1203
BEYMER, FREDERICK	1802	DEFENDANT	1311
BEYMER, FREDERICK	1802	DEFENDANT	1534
BEYMER, FREDERICK	1804	DEFENDANT	1659
BEYMER, FREDERICK	1804	DEFENDANT	685
BEYMER, FREDERICK	1805	DEFENDANT	579
BEYMER, FREDERICK	1805	DEFENDANT	696
BEYMER, FREDERICK / (?LISTED AS BEYLER?)	1805	DEFENDANT	636
BEYMER, FREDERICK	1807	DEFENDANT	1485
BEYMER, FREDERICK	1807	MISC	1527
BEYMER, FREDERICK	1808	LICENSE	95
BEYMER, FREDERICK	1808	DEFENDANT	1471
BEYMER, FREDERICK	1808	PLAINTIFF	527
BEYMER, FREDERICK	1809	PLAINTIFF	527
BEYMER, FREDERICK	1809	PLAINTIFF	527
BEYMER, FREDERICK	1809	DEFENDANT	1569
BEYMER, FREDERICK	1809	PLAINTIFF	1638
BEYMER, FREDERICK	1810	DEFENDANT	765
BEYMER, FREDERICK	1810	DEFENDANT	974
BEYMER, FREDERICK	1810	DEFENDANT	1589
BEYMER, FREDERICK	1810	DEFENDANT	1610
BEYMER, FREDERICK	1810	DEFENDANT	1626
BEYMER, FREDERICK	1810	DEFENDANT	1659
BEYMER, FREDERICK	1810	PLAINTIFF	527
BEYMER, FREDERICK	1810	DEFENDANT	533
BEYMER, FREDERICK	1811	PLAINTIFF	527
BEYMER, FREDERICK	1811	PLAINTIFF	527
BEYMER, FREDERICK	1811	DEFENDANT	884
BEYMER, FREDERICK	1811	DEFENDANT	1485
BEYMER, FREDERICK	1811	DEFENDANT	1569
BEYMER, FREDERICK	1812	DEFENDANT	765
BEYMER, FREDERICK	1812	DEFENDANT	957
BEYMER, FREDERICK	1812	PLAINTIFF	527
BEYMER, FREDERICK	1812	PLAINTIFF	527
BEYMER, FREDERICK	1812	PLAINTIFF	527
BEYMER, FREDERICK	1812	PLAINTIFF	527
BEYMER, FREDERICK	1812	DEFENDANT	533
BEYMER, FREDERICK	1813	PLAINTIFF	527
BEYMER, FREDERICK	1813	PLAINTIFF	527
BEYMER, FREDERICK	1813	DEFENDANT	555
BEYMER, FREDERICK	1813	MISC	615
BEYMER, FREDERICK	1813	DEFENDANT	968
BEYMER, FREDERICK	1813	DEFENDANT	1581
BEYMER, FREDERICK	1814	DEFENDANT	1449
BEYMER, FREDERICK	1814	PLAINTIFF	527
BEYMER, FREDERICK	1815	MISC	615
BEYMER, FREDERICK	1816	PLAINTIFF	527
BEYMER, FREDERICK	1817	PLAINTIFF	527
BEYMER, FREDERICK	1818	PLAINTIFF	527
BEYMER, FREDRICK	1804	DEFENDANT	1447
BEYMER, FREDRICK	1805	DEFENDANT	1098
BEYMER'S TAVERN - ON WHEELING MAP	1916	NAT'L ROAD	1868

CHRISTIANA BEYMER - CUMULATIVE INDEX VOLS. 1-7			
ENTRY	YEAR	SUBJECT	PAGE
BEYMER, C / (CHRISTIANA?)	1817	PLAINTIFF	527
BEYMER, C / (CHRISTIANA?)	1817	PLAINTIFF	527
BEYMER, C / (CHRISTIANA?)	1818	PLAINTIFF	527
BEYMER, C / (CHRISTIANA?)	1818	PLAINTIFF	527
BEYMER, C / (CHRISTIANA?)	1824	LICENSE	101
BEYMER, CHRISTENAH	1832	LICENSE	108
BEYMER, CHRISTIAN	1815	PLAINTIFF	527
BEYMER, CHRISTIAN	1825	LICENSE	102
BEYMER, CHRISTIANNA	1810	PLAINTIFF	527
BEYMER, CHRISTIANA	1813	MISC	615
BEYMER, CHRISTIANA	1814	DEFENDANT	1137
BEYMER, CHRISTIANA / (?NOT BAYMER?)	1814	MISC	1399
BEYMER, CHRISTIANA	1815	DEFENDANT	1581
BEYMER, CHRISTIANA	1815	PLAINTIFF	527
BEYMER, CHRISTIANA	1815	PLAINTIFF	527
BEYMER, CHRISTIANA	1815	MISC	615
BEYMER, CHRISTIANA	1816	DEFENDANT	592
BEYMER, CHRISTIANA	1816	DEFENDANT	1203
BEYMER, CHRISTIANA	1816	DEFENDANT	1645
BEYMER, CHRISTIANA	1817	PLAINTIFF	527
BEYMER, CHRISTIANA	1818	PLAINTIFF	527
BEYMER, CHRISTIANA	1819	LICENSE	96
BEYMER, CHRISTIANA	1819	DEFENDANT	870
BEYMER, CHRISTIANA	1819	DEFENDANT	1199
BEYMER, CHRISTIANA	1819	DEFENDANT	1295
BEYMER, CHRISTIANA	1819	DEFENDANT	1302
BEYMER, CHRISTIANA	1819	DEFENDANT	1353
BEYMER, CHRISTIANA	1819	DEFENDANT	1449
BEYMER, CHRISTIANA	1820	LICENSE	97
BEYMER, CHRISTIANA	1821	LICENSE	97
BEYMER, CHRISTIANA	1822	MISC	1002
BEYMER, CHRISTIANA	1827	LICENSE	103
BEYMER, CHRISTIANA	1829	LICENSE	106
BEYMER, CHRISTIANNA	1829	OVRSR POOR	160
BEYMER, CHRISTIANNA	1829	MISC	1399
BEYMER, CHRISTIANNA	1829	MISC	615
BEYMER, CHRISTINA	1822	LICENSE	98

'PERSONAL TIME LINE' INDEX TO VOLUME 7 OF THE *OHIO COUNTY INDEX*

ENTRY	YEAR	SUBJECT	PAGE
-, EMILY (BLACK CHILD)	1827	MISC	1693
-, JAMES (POOR MAN)	1794	MISC	1674
-, MACK (ORPHAN)	1854	MISC	1680
-, MARGARET (CRAZY WOMAN)	1857	MISC	1681
-, MARSH (NEGRO)	1788	MISC	1701
-, SHATON	1822	MISC	1674
__ALLS RUN / INCOMPLETE ?	1852	BRKE MAP	1846
__ALT RUN, OHIO / INCOMPLETE	1852	BRKE MAP	1645
__NEE_THS FORK OF PANTHER RUN / ? INCOMPLETE	1852	BRKE MAP	1846
2 MILE HOUSE	1871	OH CO. MAP	1742
3 MILE ICE HOUSE - WHEELING CREEK	1871	OH CO. MAP	1742
4 MILE HOUSE / WILLIAM STAMM	1871	OH CO. MAP	1742
6 FEET COAL	1871	HAN MAP	1732
888 FROM NEAR CO. LINE TO MIDDLE WHEEKING CREEK ROAD BY TURNPIKE	1871	OH CO. MAP	1743
923 FROM CLAY ROAD TO [MIDDLE WHEELING] CREEK BY OLD ROAD	1871	OH CO. MAP	1743
A, J / UNKNOWN INITIALS (?J.ATKINSON?) - EDG. STA.	1871	EDGINGTON STA.	1774
A, P / &CO (?ANDERSON?)	1871	HAN MAP	1732
A, P / &CO (?ANDERSON?)	1871	HAN MAP	1732
A, W C / UNKNOWN INITIALS - WELLSBURG	1871	WELLSBURG	1777
A.J. / INITIALS - J.ALLISON	1871	HAN MAP	1727
ABBE, -	1841	PLAINTIFF	1629
ABBOTT, JOSEPH	1856	DEFENDANT	1570
ABBREVIATIONS USED IN VOL.7 INDEX	1811	APPENDIX	1874
ABERCROMBIE, J	1871	MARH'L MAP	1747
ABRAHAM, J R / TIN SHOP (OC.)	1871	WELLSBURG	1777
ABRAHAMS, J R / CHARLES ST	1871	WELLSBURG	1777
ABRAHAMS, J R / INITIALS J.R.A.	1871	WELLSBURG	1777
ABRAHAMS, STEPHEN	1799	PLAINTIFF	1647
ABRAMS, G	1871	NEW CUMB'LD	1766
ABRAMS, H	1871	NEW CUMB'LD	1768
ABRAMS, H	1871	NEW CUMB'LD	1768
ABRAMS, J N	1871	NEW CUMB'LD	1768
ABRAMS, JOHN	1799	DEFENDANT	1634
ABRAMS, JOHN	1799	DEFENDANT	1665
ABRAMS, JOHN	1803	DEFENDANT	1577
ABRAMS, JOHN	1803	DEFENDANT	1596
ABRAMS, N / S SH. (?SHOE SHOP?)	1871	NEW CUMB'LD	1768
ABRAMS, STEPHEN	1800	PLAINTIFF	1647
ABRAMS, STEPHIN	1796	DEFENDANT	1587
ACKER, S / NEAR CHERRY ROW	1871	MARH'L MAP	1745
ACKERMAN, A	1878	DEFENDANT	1552
ACKLES, A / NE CORNER OF MAP	1871	OH CO. MAP	1743
ACKLES, A	1871	MARH'L MAP	1747
ACKLES, J	1871	MARH'L MAP	1755
ACKLES, J	1871	MARH'L MAP	1756
ACKLES, M	1871	MARH'L MAP	1746
ACKLES, R / MRS	1871	BKE/OH MAP	1739
ACKLEY, LUCIUS O	1857	DEFENDANT	1561
ACKLEY, LUCIUS O	1857	DEFENDANT	1621
ADAMS RUN	1852	BRKE MAP	1844
ADAMS, - / WATER ST	1871	WELLSBURG	1777
ADAMS, - / EXPRESS OFFICE & STORE	1871	CAMERON	1803
ADAMS, A	1871	WELLSBURG	1777
ADAMS, C	1871	MARH'L MAP	1756
ADAMS, G W	1871	MARH'L MAP	1753
ADAMS, G W / INITIALS G.W.A.	1871	MARH'L MAP	1753
ADAMS, GEORGE	1856	DEFENDANT	1653
ADAMS, J	1871	BETHANY	1773
ADAMS, J	1871	BETHANY	1773
ADAMS, JAMES	1833	DEFENDANT	1566
ADAMS, JAMES	1833	DEFENDANT	1622
ADAMS, JAMES	1834	DEFENDANT	1566
ADAMS, JAMES	1834	DEFENDANT	1622
ADAMS, JOHN	1798	DEFENDANT	1634
ADAMS, JOHN	1818	DEFENDANT	1624
ADAMS, MATHEW	1824	DEFENDANT	1649
ADAMS, MILO	1859	DEFENDANT	1672
ADAMS, R	1871	BRKE MAP	1737
ADAMS, S / LOT #23	1871	BETHANY	1773
ADAMS, T	1871	MARH'L MAP	1749
ADAMS, T / EDGE OF MAP - CUT OFF	1871	MARH'L MAP	1753
ADAMS, TIMOTHY	1828	DEFENDANT	1594
ADAMS, TIMOTHY	1841	DEFENDANT	1652
ADAMS, W	1871	MARH'L MAP	1761
ADAMS, WILLIAM	1852	NOT ON MAP	1836
AG. WORKS / AGRICULTURAL WORKS - J.W. ALLISON	1871	NEW MANCH.	1769

ENTRY	YEAR	SUBJECT	PAGE
AGENT - W.Y.HOGE	1871	MARH'L MAP	1760
AGNEW, - / SCHOOL / MAP#166	1852	BRKE MAP	1842
AGNEW, -	1871	WELLSBURG	1777
AGNEW, DAVID	1840	DEFENDANT	1559
AGNEW, J	1871	BRKE MAP	1736
AGNEW, JAMES / MAP # 165	1852	BRKE MAP	1842
AIKMAN, ABSOLOM	1855	DEFENDANT	1636
AIR LINE DISTANCES - TABLE OF MILEAGES - FROM TOWN TO TOWN	1871	DISTANCES	1815
AKINS, JOHN	1804	DEFENDANT	1648
ALASKA MILLS	1871	MARH'L MAP	1751
ALBRIGHT, MARGARET	1784	APPENDIX	1874
ALDERSON, J C	1877	DEFENDANT	1558
ALEXANDER & CRISWELL	1871	MDSVILLE	1809
ALEXANDER, - / MRS	1871	MARH'L MAP	1747
ALEXANDER, J	1871	MARH'L MAP	1748
ALEXANDER, J / GRAVE YARD - INITIALS GR.Y.D.	1871	MARH'L MAP	1748
ALEXANDER, J	1871	MARH'L MAP	1751
ALEXANDER, J / REV.DR.	1871	MDSVILLE	1809
ALEXANDER, JAMES / D.D. - PASTOR PRES.CHURCH	1871	MDSVL BUS	1796
ALEXANDER, JAMES	1871	MDSVILLE	1810
ALEXANDER, JOSEPH	1811	APPENDIX	1873
ALEXANDER, JOSEPH	1819	DEFENDANT	1649
ALEXANDER, JOSEPH	1831	DEFENDANT	1566
ALEXANDER, MATTHEW	1798	DEFENDANT	1594
ALEXANDER, MATTHEW	1800	DEFENDANT	1604
ALEXANDER, W	1871	MARH'L MAP	1748
ALEXANDER, W / INITIALS W.A.	1871	MDSVILLE	1806
ALEXANDER, W	1871	MDSVILLE	1807
ALEXANDER, W	1871	MDSVILLE	1807
ALEXANDER, W	1871	MDSVILLE	1807
ALEXANDER, W	1871	MDSVILLE	1807
ALEXANDER, W / INITIALS W.A.	1871	MDSVILLE	1807
ALEXANDERS, R / HRS -HEIRS	1871	MDSVILLE	1808
ALISON, A	1871	HAN MAP	1728
ALLEGHANY MOUNTAINS	1852	HEMPFIELD RR	1819
ALLEGHANY MOUNTAINS	1852	HEMPFIELD RR	1820
ALLEGHANY VALLEY ROAD	1852	HEMPFIELD RR	1818
ALLEGHENY MOUNTAINS	1916	NAT'L ROAD	1867
ALLEGHENY RIVER -P MAP	1916	NAT'L ROAD	1869
ALLEN, - / MRS	1871	MARH'L MAP	1749
ALLEN, A /W. OF BETHANY	1871	BRKE MAP	1737
ALLEN, A	1871	BKE/OH MAP	1739
ALLEN, ALBERT / BETHANY COLLEGE	1871	BUFF.TWP.BUS.	1772
ALLEN, J	1871	MARH'L MAP	1745
ALLEN, J	1871	MARH'L MAP	1745
ALLEN, J	1871	MARH'L MAP	1749
ALLEN, J / INITIALS J.A.	1871	MARH'L MAP	1749
ALLEN, J / INITIALS J.A.	1871	MARH'L MAP	1749
ALLEN, J R	1871	MARH'L MAP	1749
ALLEN, JOHN	1825	DEFENDANT	1563
ALLEN, R	1871	MARH'L MAP	1749
ALLEN, R	1871	MARH'L MAP	1752
ALLEN, R JR	1871	MARH'L MAP	1745
ALLEN, T	1871	MARH'L MAP	1753
ALLEN, T	1871	MARH'L MAP	1753
ALLEN, T	1871	MARH'L MAP	1753
ALLEN, T	1871	MARH'L MAP	1753
ALLEN, T / INITIALS T.A.	1871	MARH'L MAP	1753
ALLEN, W	1871	MARH'L MAP	1746
ALLEN, W / INITIALS W.A.	1871	MARH'L MAP	1746
ALLEN, W / INITIALS W.A.	1871	MARH'L MAP	1746
ALLEY, J	1871	MARH'L MAP	1755
ALLEY, J / INITIALS J.A.	1871	MARH'L MAP	1755
ALLEY, J	1871	MARH'L MAP	1759
ALLEY, J / INITIALS J.A.	1871	MARH'L MAP	1759
ALLEY, W L	1871	MARH'L MAP	1759
ALLGEHENY RIVER	1852	HEMP. RR MAP	1826
ALLISON HOMESTEAD	1871	HAN MAP	1727
ALLISON SUMMIT	1871	HAN MAP	1726
ALLISON, A	1871	HAN MAP	1727
ALLISON, A A	1859	DEFENDANT	1574
ALLISON, ALEX	1871	HAN MAP	1727
ALLISON, ALEXANDER A	1857	MISC	1702
ALLISON, B / MRS	1871	HAN MAP	1727
ALLISON, BURGESS JR	1871	HAN MAP	1726
ALLISON, C	1871	HAN MAP	1727
ALLISON, C B	1871	HAN MAP	1727
ALLISON, D	1871	HAN MAP	1727
ALLISON, E W	1871	HAN MAP	1726
ALLISON, E W / INITIALS E.W.A.	1871	HAN MAP	1726
ALLISON, E W	1871	HAN MAP	1727
ALLISON, E.W. / INITIALS E.W.A.	1871	HAN MAP	1727
ALLISON, G	1871	HAN MAP	1727

I

'PERSONAL TIME LINE' INDEX TO VOLUME 7 OF THE *OHIO COUNTY INDEX*

ENTRY	YEAR	SUBJECT	PAGE	ENTRY	YEAR	SUBJECT	PAGE
ALLISON, GEORGE / HIS SON JAMES'S LAND SHOWN	1871	HAN MAP	1731	ANDERSON, JAMES	1871	OH CO. MAP	1740
ALLISON, J	1871	HAN MAP	1727	ANDERSON, JOHN	1791	PLAINTIFF	1665
ALLISON, J / & CO.	1871	HAN MAP	1727	ANDERSON, JOHN H	1790	PLAINTIFF	1644
ALLISON, J / INITIALS J.A.	1871	HAN MAP	1727	ANDERSON, S	1871	OH CO. MAP	1742
ALLISON, J	1871	HAN-POE TWP	1763	ANDERSON, S	1871	MARH'L MAP	1746
ALLISON, J B / RESIDENCE	1871	HAN MAP	1727	ANDERSON, SAMUEL	1808	APPENDIX	1873
ALLISON, J J	1871	HAN MAP	1727	ANDERSON, SAMUEL	1811	DEFENDANT	1567
ALLISON, J J / INITIALS J.J.A.	1871	HAN MAP	1727	ANDERSON, T	1871	MARH'L MAP	1750
ALLISON, J W	1871	HAN MAP	1726	ANDERSON, T A	1871	FRE'MAN'S LDG	1764
ALLISON, J W / INITIALS J.W.A. ?	1871	HAN MAP	1727	ANDERSON, THOMAS / MAP # 23	1852	BRKE MAP	1839
ALLISON, J W / WEST SIDE OF MAP	1871	HAN MAP	1727	ANDERSON, THOMAS / & CO. - ANDERSONS LANDING	1871	FRE'MAN'S LDG	1762
ALLISON, J W	1871	NEW MANCH.	1763	ANDERSON, THOMAS / & CO. - FIRE BRICK WORKS	1871	FRE'MAN'S LDG	1764
ALLISON, J W	1871	NEW MANCH.	1769	ANDERSON, THOMAS / & CO. - INITIALS T.A. & CO.	1871	FRE'MAN'S LDG	1764
ALLISON, JAMES	1871	HAN MAP	1727				
ALLISON, JAMES / OF GEORGE	1871	HAN MAP	1728	ANDERSON, THOMAS / RES	1871	FRE'MAN'S LDG	1764
ALLISON, JAMES	1871	HAN MAP	1731	ANDERSON, W H	1871	BETHNY BUS.	1772
ALLISON, JOHN W / (?BLACKSMITH SHOP?)	1871	HAN MAP	1731	ANDERSON, W H / (O.C.)	1871	BETHANY	1773
ALLISON, JONATHAN	1871	HAN MAP	1727	ANDERSON, WILLIAM	1850	DEFENDANT	1629
ALLISON, S	1871	HAN MAP	1727	ANDERSONS LANDING	1871	HAN MAP	1730
ALLISON, T JR	1871	HAN MAP	1727	ANDERSON'S LANDING	1871	HAN MAP	1732
ALLISON, W	1871	HAN MAP	1727	ANDERSONS LANDING - FREEMANS LANDING	1871	FRE'MAN'S LDG	1762
ALLISON, W	1871	HAN MAP	1728				
ALLMAN, ABRAHAM	1842	DEFENDANT	1566	ANDERSONS LANDING - OHIO RIVER	1871	FRE'MAN'S LDG	1764
ALLMAN, ABRAHAM	1843	DEFENDANT	1615	ANDERSONS LANDING - THOMAS ANDERSON & CO.	1871	FRE'MAN'S LDG	1762
ALLMAN, ABRAHAM	1844	DEFENDANT	1587				
ALLMAN, G W	1871	MARH'L MAP	1751	ANDREWS, G	1871	HAN MAP	1731
ALLSION, J	1871	HAN MAP	1727	ANDREWS, J	1871	HAN MAP	1731
ALLSION, J B	1871	HAN MAP	1727	ANDREWS, R / DOCTOR	1871	NEW MANCH.	1769
ALLSION, J B / INITIALS J.B.A.	1871	HAN MAP	1727	ANDREWS, R / DOCTOR - INITIALS DR. R A	1871	NEW MANCH.	1769
ALLSION, T JR	1871	HAN MAP	1728				
ALLUM, W	1871	MDSVILLE	1808	ANDREWS, ROBERT	1871	NEW MANCH.	1763
ALLUM, W	1871	MDSVILLE	1808	ANGUISH, D	1871	MARH'L MAP	1756
ALLUM, W	1871	MDSVILLE	1810	ANGUISH, WILLIAM	1818	DEFENDANT	1591
ALLUM, W	1871	MDSVILLE	1810	ANKARUM, JACOB	1802	DEFENDANT	1583
ALLY, E	1871	MARH'L MAP	1747	ANKROM, JACOB	1809	DEFENDANT	1645
ALLY, E	1871	MARH'L MAP	1747	ANKRUM, JACOB	1803	DEFENDANT	1583
ALMAN, -	1856	PLAINTIFF	1621	ANSHUTZ, C P / EST	1871	MDSVILLE	1810
ALMAN, J	1871	MARH'L MAP	1755	ANTILL, B	1871	BRKE MAP	1735
ALT, M / & CO	1860	DEFENDANT	1630	ANTILL, BENJAMIN / SAW & GRIST MILL - "CROSS CREEK"	1871	CROSS CRK.BUS.	1772
ALTON, TERRA HAUTE, INDIANAPOLIS, COLUMBUS, ZANESVILLE AND WHEELING LINE	1852	HEMPFIELD RR	1820				
				ANTLE, BENJAMIN / MAP # 338	1852	BRKE MAP	1846
				ANTLE, JAMES / MAP #446	1852	BRKE MAP	1849
ALTON, W	1871	OH CO. MAP	1743	APPALACHIAN MOUNTAIN RANGE	1916	NAT'L ROAD	1868
ALTON, W	1871	OH CO. MAP	1744	APPENDIX CONTENTS - VOL.7	2000	APPENDIX	1712
ALTON, WILLIAM	1874	DEFENDANT	1560	APPLE TREE COTTAGE	1871	MARH'L MAP	1745
AMERICAN EAGLE - TAVERN - WEST ALEXANDER	1916	NAT'L ROAD	1862	APPLEGARTH, GEORGE	1839	DEFENDANT	1566
				APPLEGATE, - / MILL - MAP#123	1852	BRKE MAP	1844
AMERICAN HOUSE / HOTEL	1871	NEW CUMB'LD	1767	APPLEGATE, A / SON - DRY GOODS	1871	WELLSBURG	1777
AMICK, J	1871	WELLSBURG	1778	APPLEGATE, A	1871	WELLSBURG	1778
AMICK, JACOB	1834	DEFENDANT	1650	APPLEGATE, J / RES	1871	BRKE MAP	1737
AMICK, JACOB	1857	DEFENDANT	1582	APPLEGATE, J	1871	BRKE MAP	1737
AMICK, W	1871	WELLSBURG	1778	APPLEGATE, J / & SON	1871	WLSBRG BUS.	1772
AMOS, M	1871	MARH'L MAP	1747	APPLEGATE, J	1871	WELLSBURG	1777
AMPLETT, WILLIAM	1821	DEFENDANT	1642	APPLEGATE, JOSEPH / MAP #311	1852	BRKE MAP	1847
AMPLETT, WILLIAM	1822	DEFENDANT	1642	APPLEGATE, L	1871	BRKE MAP	1737
AMSPOKER, G	1871	BRKE MAP	1735	APPLEGATE, L	1871	BKE/OH MAP	1739
AMSPOKER, G / NE EDGE OF MAP	1871	BRKE MAP	1735	APPLEGATE, LEWIS / MAP #122	1852	BRKE MAP	1844
AMSPOKER, G	1871	BRKE MAP	1737	APPLEGATE, LEWIS / MAP #310	1852	BRKE MAP	1847
AMSPOKER, J	1871	BRKE MAP	1735	APPLEGATE, LEWIS / MAP #361	1852	BRKE MAP	1847
ANDERSON HOMESTEAD / R. ANDERSON	1871	HAN MAP	1732	APPRENTICES - DEFINED	2000	APPENDIX	1875
				ARBUCKLE, - / MRS	1871	HAN MAP	1726
ANDERSON J	1871	OH CO. MAP	1743	ARCHER, J / OLD BROOK FURNACE	1871	HAN MAP	1732
ANDERSON J	1871	OH CO. MAP	1743	ARCHER, JAMES / INITIALS J.A.	1871	BRKE MAP	1734
ANDERSON, - / SAW MILL - P.A. & CO / (?ANDERSON?)	1871	HAN MAP	1732	ARCHER, JAMES / ORCHARD	1871	BRKE MAP	1734
				ARCHER, JAMES	1871	CROSS CRK.BUS.	1772
ANDERSON, - / SEE ALSO (?P.A. & CO.?)	1871	HAN MAP	1732	ARCHER, S	1871	HAN MAP	1732
				ARCHER, S / RES.	1871	HAN MAP	1732
ANDERSON, - / MRS - S. BORDER OF BROOKE CO.	1871	BKE/OH MAP	1738	ARCHER, SAMUEL / ESQ - MAP #553	1852	BRKE MAP	1851
				ARCHER, SAMUEL / ESQ.- (GONE)- MAP #554	1852	BRKE MAP	1851
ANDERSON, - / PORTER, ANDERSON &CO	1871	FRE'MAN'S LDG	1762				
ANDERSON, - / PORTER, ANDERSON & CO	1871	FRE'MAN'S LDG	1765	ARGLE, ROBERT	1839	DEFENDANT	1596
				ARGO, ELEANOR	1822	MISC	1691
ANDERSON, - / PORTER, ANDERSON & CO - INITIALS P.A. & CO.	1871	FRE'MAN'S LDG	1765	ARMANT, ADAM	1862	DEFENDANT	1578
				ARMAULT, A	1861	DEFENDANT	1626
ANDERSON, -	1878	PLAINTIFF	1631	ARMSPOKER, GEORGE / ESQ. - MAP #478	1852	BRKE MAP	1850
ANDERSON, A / HOMESTEAD	1871	HAN MAP	1732				
ANDERSON, A	1871	BKE/OH MAP	1738	ARMSPOKER, JOHN / HEIRS - MAP #496	1852	BRKE MAP	1850
ANDERSON, B	1871	MARH'L MAP	1750	ARMSTRONG, C / MRS	1871	W.LIBERTY	1780
ANDERSON, GEORGE W	1856	DEFENDANT	1670	ARMSTRONG, DAVID	1843	DEFENDANT	1623
ANDERSON, GEORGE W	1857	DEFENDANT	1670	ARMSTRONG, DAVID	1858	DEFENDANT	1661
ANDERSON, J	1871	MARH'L MAP	1755	ARMSTRONG, DAVID	1858	DEFENDANT	1661
ANDERSON, J	1871	MARH'L MAP	1755	ARMSTRONG, DAVID	1859	DEFENDANT	1586
ANDERSON, J J / MRS.	1871	HAN MAP	1731	ARMSTRONG, GEORGE	1841	PLAINTIFF	1661

II

'PERSONAL TIME LINE' INDEX TO VOLUME 7 OF THE *OHIO COUNTY INDEX*

ENTRY	YEAR	SUBJECT	PAGE	ENTRY	YEAR	SUBJECT	PAGE
ARMSTRONG, J C	1871	MARH'L MAP	1747	ATKINSON, JACOB	1832	DEFENDANT	1669
ARMSTRONG, JEREMIAH Y	1838	DEFENDANT	1651	ATKINSON, JAMES	1822	DEFENDANT	1577
ARMSTRONG, JOHN H	1847	DEFENDANT	1570	ATKINSON, JOHN / ESQ.- MAP #6	1852	BRKE MAP	1840
ARMSTRONG, R	1871	TRIAD.BORO.	1784	ATKINSON, JOHN / ESQ. - MAP #5	1852	BRKE MAP	1841
ARMSTRONG, R / INITIALS R.A.	1871	TRIAD.BORO.	1784	ATKINSON, JOSEPH / MAP #607	1852	BRKE MAP	1851
ARMSTRONG, R / INITIALS R.A.	1871	TRIAD.BORO.	1784	ATKINSON, JOSEPH / MAP#608	1852	BRKE MAP	1851
ARMSTRONG, R / INITIALS R.A.	1871	TRIAD.BORO.	1784	ATKINSON, L G / & NP	1827	DEFENDANT	1649
ARMSTRONG, WILLIAM	1874	DEFENDANT	1615	ATKINSON, N P / & L G	1827	DEFENDANT	1649
ARMSTRONG, WILLIAM	1877	DEFENDANT	1615	ATKINSON, N P	1830	DEFENDANT	1618
ARNOLD DALE	1871	MARH'L MAP	1754	ATKINSON, NATHANIEL P	1820	DEFENDANT	1624
ARNOLD, A G	1871	MARH'L MAP	1754	ATKINSON, NATHANIEL P	1821	DEFENDANT	1668
ARNOLD, A G / INITIALS A.G.A.	1871	MARH'L MAP	1754	ATKINSON, W	1871	BRKE MAP	1734
ARNOLD, A G / SAW MILL - FISH CREEK	1871	FRKLN TWP-BUS.	1797	ATKINSON, W	1871	BKE/OH MAP	1738
				ATKINSON, W / INITIALS W.A.	1871	BKE/OH MAP	1738
ARNOLD, I	1871	MARH'L MAP	1752	ATKINSON, WILLIAM / MAP#605	1852	BRKE MAP	1851
ARNOLD, I / SAW MILL (?OR L?)	1871	MARH'L MAP	1752	ATKINSONS RUN	1852	BRKE MAP	1851
ARNOLD, JOHN	1813	DEFENDANT	1596	ATKINSONS RUN	1871	BRKE MAP	1734
ARNOLD, JOHN	1814	DEFENDANT	1608	ATKISON, NATHANIEL P	1822	DEFENDANT	1632
ARNOLD, JOHN	1816	DEFENDANT	1570	ATLANTIC SEABOARD	1852	HEMPFIELD RR	1823
ARNOLD, JOHN	1820	DEFENDANT	1553	ATTORNEY - DANIEL DONEHOO - NEW MANCHESTER	1871	NEW MANCH.	1763
ARNOLD, JOHN	1835	DEFENDANT	1669	ATTORNEY - HANSON CRISWELL - MOUNDSVILLE	1871	MDSVL BUS.	1796
ARNOLD, S	1871	MARH'L MAP	1754	ATTORNEY - J. DALLAS EWING - MOUNDSVILLE	1871	MDSVL BUS.	1796
ARNOLD, S / INITIALS S.A.	1871	MARH'L MAP	1754				
ARNOLD, S / INITIALS S.A.	1871	MARH'L MAP	1754	ATTORNEY - J.E.HOOTON	1871	CAMER'N - BUS.	1795
ARNOLD, S	1871	MARH'L MAP	1755	ATTORNEY - J.L.PARKINSON	1871	MDSVL BUS.	1796
ARNOLD, S / INITIALS S.A.	1871	MARH'L MAP	1755	ATTORNEY - J.W. REILLY - WELLSVILLE, OHIO	1871	HAN-GR'NT TWP	1763
ARNOLD, V / ORCHARD ?	1871	MARH'L MAP	1752				
ARNOLD, W	1871	MARH'L MAP	1752	ATTORNEY - J.W. REILLY - WELLSVILLE, OHIO	1871	NEW MANCH.	1763
ARONS, -	1857	PLAINTIF	1625				
ARRICK, E J	1879	DEFENDANT	1601	ATTORNEY - JAMES G MARSHALL - NEW MANCHESTER	1871	NEW MANCH.	1763
ARTHUR, NATHANIEL C	1858	DEFENDANT	1653				
ASH ALLEY - HAMILTON	1871	HAN MAP	1729	ATTORNEY - ROBERT MCCONNELL - MOUNDSVILLE	1871	MDSVL BUS.	1796
ASHBRIDGE, W	1871	NEW CUMB'LD	1766				
ASHBROORS RUN	1871	BRKE MAP	1734	AUDLINGER, JOHN	1879	DEFENDANT	1588
ASHBRPPLES RIM	1852	BRKE MAP	1852	AUGHIMBURGH, W C	1871	WELLSBURG	1778
ASHLAND	1871	MARH'L MAP	1753	AUSTIE, -	1858	PLAINTIFF	1630
ASHTON, R K	1871	MARH'L MAP	1746	AUSTIN, HOMER	1841	MISC	1681
ASHTON, R K	1871	MARH'L MAP	1746	AUSTIN, R M / MRS	1871	MARH'L MAP	1758
ASHWORTH, JAMES	1877	DEFENDANT	1654	AUSTIN, R M / MRS	1871	MARH'L MAP	1758
ASHWORTH, JAMES	1877	DEFENDANT	1664	AUSTIN, R M / MRS - INITIALS MRS. A	1871	MARH'L MAP	1758
ASKEW, W	1871	OH CO. MAP	1742	AUSTIN, SOLON	1854	DEFENDANT	1570
ASKEW, W	1871	OH CO. MAP	1744	AUSTIN, SOLON	1854	DEFENDANT	1570
ASKEW, WILLIAM	1871	ELM GROVE	1782	AUSTIN, SOLON	1855	DEFENDANT	1570
ASKEW, WILLIAM / ABBREV - W. ASKEW	1871	ELM GROVE	1782	B, D / UNKNOWN INITIALS - (?D.BRADY?)	1871	OH CO. MAP	1740
ATEN, H	1871	HAN MAP	1727	B, R / INITIALS - R. BONAR ?	1871	BKE/OH MAP	1738
ATEN, J M	1871	HAN MAP	1727	B.C. NURSERY / UNKNOWN INITIALS	1871	MARH'L MAP	1748
ATKINS, NATHANIEL P	1819	DEFENDANT	1660	B.R. CO. / PAN-HANDLE P.O.	1871	BRKE MAP	1734
ATKINSAN, NATHANIEL	1827	DEFENDANT	1587	B.S. / (?UNKNOWN INITIALS - BLACKSMITH?)	1871	ELM GROVE	1782
ATKINSON & SHANE	1871	RIV. RD N.OF N.C.	1763				
ATKINSON & SHANE - FIRE BRICK WORKS	1871	RIV. RD N.OF N.C.	1770	B.S. SH. / (?BLACKSMITH SHOP?)	1871	HAN MAP	1727
				B.S. SH. / (?BLACKSMITH SHOP?)	1871	HAN MAP	1727
ATKINSON, - / MILL - MAP#4	1852	BRKE MAP	1841	B.S.S. / INITIALS - BLACKSMITH SHOP ?	1871	HAN MAP	1731
ATKINSON, -	1862	DEFENDANT	1574				
ATKINSON, DAVID	1841	MISC	1705	B.S.SH / (?ABBREVIATION FOR BLACKSMITH SHOP?)	1871	HAN MAP	1729
ATKINSON, DAVID	1843	MISC	1705				
ATKINSON, DAVID	1844	MISC	1705	B.S.SH. / (?ABBREV. FOR BLACKSMITH SHOP?)	1871	BETHANY	1773
ATKINSON, DAVID	1847	MISC	1706				
ATKINSON, DAVID	1848	MISC	1706	B.W. SR / (?B. WELLS?)	1871	BRKE MAP	1736
ATKINSON, DAVID	1854	MISC	1706	BABBLING BROOK	1871	MARH'L MAP	1755
ATKINSON, E	1871	HAN MAP	1730	BABBS ISLAND / IN OHIO RIVER / SE OF EAST LIVERPOOL	1871	HAN MAP	1727
ATKINSON, E M	1871	OH CO. MAP	1742				
ATKINSON, E M / INITIALS E.M.A.	1871	OH CO. MAP	1742	BABBS ISLAND / IN OHIO RIVER / SE OF EAST LIVERPOOL	1871	HAN MAP	1728
ATKINSON, EPHRAIM	1871	NEW CUMB'LD	1767				
ATKINSON, EPHRAIM / INITIALS A.E.	1871	NEW CUMB'LD	1767	BABBS RUN	1852	BRKE MAP	1850
ATKINSON, J / HRS	1871	HAN MAP	1733	BABBS RUN	1871	BRKE MAP	1735
ATKINSON, J	1871	BKE/OH MAP	1738	BADE, FREDERICK	1871	OH CO. MAP	1743
ATKINSON, J / INITIALS J.A.	1871	BKE/OH MAP	1738	BADE, FREDERICK	1871	OH CO. MAP	1744
ATKINSON, J	1871	BKE/OH MAP	1739	BADKIN, JOHN	1778	DEFENDANT	1556
ATKINSON, J / INITIALS J.A.	1871	BKE/OH MAP	1739	BAER, ROSA	1873	DEFENDANT	1627
ATKINSON, J	1871	OH CO. MAP	1741	BAGGS, JOHN	1792	MISC	1707
ATKINSON, J / INITIALS J.A.	1871	OH CO. MAP	1741	BAILEY, -	1848	PLAINTIFF	1623
ATKINSON, J / ? UNKNOWN INITIALS J.A. - EDG. STA.	1871	EDGINGTON STA.	1774	BAILEY, -	1849	PLAINTIFF	1623
				BAILEY, JESSE	1822	DEFENDANT	1638
ATKINSON, J B	1871	BKE/OH MAP	1739	BAILEY, JOHN	1871	HAN MAP	1727
ATKINSON, J H	1871	HAN MAP	1730	BAILEY, JOHN	1871	HAN MAP	1728
ATKINSON, J H / W. SIDE OF MAP	1871	HAN MAP	1731	BAIRD, J	1871	OH CO. MAP	1743
ATKINSON, J H / REFERENCE N.1	1871	HAN MAP	1733	BAIRD, J	1871	MARH'L MAP	1746
ATKINSON, J H	1871	NEW CUMB'LD	1766	BAIRD, JAMES	1805	DEFENDANT	1658
ATKINSON, J H	1871	NEW CUMB'LD	1766	BAIRD, JAMES	1807	DEFENDANT	1659
ATKINSON, J H	1871	NEW CUMB'LD	1766	BAIRD, JAMES / MAP#289	1852	BRKE MAP	1846
ATKINSON, J H	1871	RIV. RD S.OF N.C.	1771	BAIRD, JOHN	1827	DEFENDANT	1672
ATKINSON, J H / INITIALS J.H.A	1871	RIV. RD S.OF N.C.	1771	BAIRDS, J / HRS	1871	OH CO. MAP	1742
ATKINSON, JACOB	1822	DEFENDANT	1668	BAKER ISLAND - OHIIO RIVER / #1	1871	HAN MAP	1726
ATKINSON, JACOB	1830	DEFENDANT	1618				
ATKINSON, JACOB	1830	DEFENDANT	1650				

III

'PERSONAL TIME LINE' INDEX TO VOLUME 7 OF THE OHIO COUNTY INDEX

ENTRY	YEAR	SUBJECT	PAGE	ENTRY	YEAR	SUBJECT	PAGE
BAKER ISLAND - OHIIO RIVER / #2	1871	HAN MAP	1726	BALTIMORE & OHIO RR - AT BENWOOD	1871	BENWOOD	1798
BAKER, - / MRS	1871	MARH'L MAP	1754	BALTIMORE & OHIO RR - AT BENWOOD	1871	BENWOOD	1799
BAKER, A O / PENITENTIARY	1871	MDSVL BUS.	1796	BALTIMORE & OHIO RR - AT BENWOOD	1871	BENWOOD	1800
BAKER, A O	1871	MDSVILLE	1807				
BAKER, A O	1871	MDSVILLE	1807	BALTIMORE & OHIO RR - AT CAMERON	1871	CAMERON	1803
BAKER, A O	1871	MDSVILLE	1809				
BAKER, A S	1871	MARH'L MAP	1745	BALTIMORE & OHIO RR - AT CAMERON	1871	CAMERON	1803
BAKER, ARTEMAS	1818	DEFENDANT	1659				
BAKER, D	1871	MARH'L MAP	1756	BALTIMORE & OHIO RR - AT CAMERON	1871	CAMERON	1804
BAKER, DORSEY	1816	DEFENDANT	1635				
BAKER, F	1871	MARH'L MAP	1745	BALTIMORE & OHIO RR - AT GLEN EASTON	1871	GLEN EASTON	1801
BAKER, G	1871	OH CO. MAP	1742				
BAKER, GEORGE SR	1822	DEFENDANT	1559	BALTIMORE & OHIO RR - AT LAGRANGE	1871	LAGRANGE	1792
BAKER, GEORGE SR	1822	DEFENDANT	1646				
BAKER, H	1871	MARH'L MAP	1751	BALTIMORE & OHIO RR - AT LAGRANGE	1871	LAGRANGE	1794
BAKER, H	1871	MARH'L MAP	1754				
BAKER, H	1871	MDSVILLE	1807	BALTIMORE & OHIO RR - AT MOUNDSVILLE	1871	MDSVILLE	1806
BAKER, J	1871	MARH'L MAP	1758				
BAKER, J	1871	MARH'L MAP	1759	BALTIMORE & OHIO RR - AT MOUNDSVILLE	1871	MDSVILLE	1808
BAKER, JAMES	1852	HEMPFIELD RR	1822				
BAKER, JAMES	1852	HEMPFIELD RR	1822	BALTIMORE & OHIO RR - AT ROSBBYS ROCK	1871	ROSBBYS RK	1813
BAKER, L	1871	OH CO. MAP	1742				
BAKER, LUCY	1809	DEFENDANT	1555	BALTIMORE & OHIO RR - AT WHEELING	1871	WHG CITY	1788
BAKER, SAMUEL P	1833	DEFENDANT	1620				
BAKER, SAMUEL P	1833	DEFENDANT	1639	BALTIMORE & OHIO RR - BELLTON - FREIGHT DEPOT	1871	MARH'L MAP	1761
BAKER, SAMUEL P	1871	MARH'L MAP	1745				
BAKER, SAMUEL P / TOP OF MAP	1871	MARH'L MAP	1748	BALTIMORE & OHIO RR - BENWOOD DEPOT	1871	BENWOOD	1800
BAKER, SUSAN	1827	DEFENDANT	1668				
BAKER, T	1871	BRKE MAP	1735	BALTIMORE & OHIO RR - BLDG - AT GLEN EASTON	1871	GLEN EASTON	1801
BAKER, T	1871	MARH'L MAP	1745				
BAKER, T / iNITIALS T.B.	1871	MARH'L MAP	1745	BALTIMORE & OHIO RR - BLDG - CAMERON	1871	CAMERON	1804
BAKER, T	1871	MARH'L MAP	1748				
BAKER, T	1871	FOWLERS P.O.	1775	BALTIMORE & OHIO RR - BLDG - W. OF GARRET STATION	1871	MARH'L MAP	1757
BAKER, THOMAS	1825	DEFENDANT	1613				
BAKER, WILLIAM	1817	PLAINTIFF	1648	BALTIMORE & OHIO RR - BLDG #1 - BENWOOD	1871	BENWOOD	1799
BAKER, WILLIAM	1822	PLAINTIFF	1559				
BAKER, WILLIAM	1824	DEFENDANT	1602	BALTIMORE & OHIO RR - BLDG #2 - BENWOOD	1871	BENWOOD	1799
BAKERS FORT	1871	HAN MAP	1726				
BAKEWELL, T H	1871	MDSVILLE	1807	BALTIMORE & OHIO RR - BLDG AT BENWOOD	1871	BENWOOD	1800
BAKEWELL, T H / INITIALS T.H.B.	1871	MDSVILLE	1807				
BAKEWELL, T H	1871	MDSVILLE	1809	BALTIMORE & OHIO RR - BLDG AT BENWOOD	1871	BENWOOD	1800
BAKEWELL, T H	1871	MDSVILLE	1809				
BAKEWELL, T H	1871	MDSVILLE	1809	BALTIMORE & OHIO RR - BLDG AT BENWOOD	1871	BENWOOD	1800
BALDWIN, E / COL.	1871	MARH'L MAP	1753				
BALDWIN, M / MRS	1871	MARH'L MAP	1750	BALTIMORE & OHIO RR - BLDG AT BENWOOD	1871	BENWOOD	1800
BALDWIN, M / MRS	1871	MARH'L MAP	1753				
BALDWIN, ROBERT	1830	DEFENDANT	1613	BALTIMORE & OHIO RR - BOARD TREE TUNNEL	1871	MARH'L MAP	1761
BALDWIN, ROBERT	1831	DEFENDANT	1613				
BALDWIN, ROBERT	1840	DEFENDANT	1652	BALTIMORE & OHIO RR - BUILDING - AT CAMERON	1871	CAMERON	1803
BALL LICK / STREAM	1871	MARH'L MAP	1757				
BALL, -	1871	TRIAD.BORO.	1784	BALTIMORE & OHIO RR - BUILDING - MOUNDSVILLE	1871	MARH'L MAP	1748
BALL, J M	1871	OH CO. MAP	1742				
BALL, J M	1871	OH CO.BUS.	1779	BALTIMORE & OHIO RR - BUILDINGS - AT BELLTON	1871	BELLTON	1814
BALL, J M / RES	1871	TRIAD.TWP.	1781				
BALLARD, -	1855	PLAINTIFF	1630	BALTIMORE & OHIO RR - CAMERON - AGENT	1871	CAMER'N - BUS.	1795
BALLARD, -	1856	PLAINTIFF	1630				
BALLARD, - / THOMAS & BALLARD	1871	MDSVILLE	1807	BALTIMORE & OHIO RR - CAMERON - CONDUCTOR	1871	CAMER'N - BUS.	1795
BALLARD, C K	1871	MARH'L MAP	1745				
BALLARD, C K	1871	MARH'L MAP	1748	BALTIMORE & OHIO RR - CATTLE YARD - AT CAMERON	1871	CAMERON	1803
BALLARD, C K	1871	WASH.TWP-BUS.	1797				
BALLS ADDITION / LAND LOTS IN NEW CUMBERLAND	1871	NEW CUMB'LD	1767	BALTIMORE & OHIO RR - DEPOT - AT GLEN EASTON	1871	GLEN EASTON	1801
BALTIMORE & OHIO RR	1852	HEMPFIELD RR	1819	BALTIMORE & OHIO RR - ENGINE HOUSE - CAMERON	1871	CAMERON	1803
BALTIMORE & OHIO RR	1852	HEMPFIELD RR	1822				
BALTIMORE & OHIO RR	1852	HEMP. RR MAP	1825	BALTIMORE & OHIO RR - FERRY - AT BENWOOD	1871	BENWOOD	1799
BALTIMORE & OHIO RR	1852	HEMP. RR MAP	1826				
BALTIMORE & OHIO RR	1871	OH CO. MAP	1742	BALTIMORE & OHIO RR - FREIGHT DEPOT - AT BELLTON	1871	BELLTON	1814
BALTIMORE & OHIO RR	1871	MARH'L MAP	1748				
BALTIMORE & OHIO RR	1871	MARH'L MAP	1751	BALTIMORE & OHIO RR - FRIEGHT HOUSE - MOUNDSVILLE	1871	MDSVILLE	1808
BALTIMORE & OHIO RR	1871	MARH'L MAP	1752				
BALTIMORE & OHIO RR / FLAG HOUSE - SW OF FAIRVIEW	1871	MARH'L MAP	1752	BALTIMORE & OHIO RR - GARRET STATION	1871	MARH'L MAP	1757
BALTIMORE & OHIO RR	1871	MARH'L MAP	1757	BALTIMORE & OHIO RR - GARRETT STATION	1871	MARH'L MAP	1761
BALTIMORE & OHIO RR	1871	MARH'L MAP	1761				
BALTIMORE & OHIO RR / BUILDING - E. OF J.REID	1871	MARH'L MAP	1761	BALTIMORE & OHIO RR - GARRETT STATION	1871	MARH'L MAP	1761
BALTIMORE & OHIO RR / BUILDING - NE OF J.REID	1871	MARH'L MAP	1761	BALTIMORE & OHIO RR - MACHINE SHOPS - WHEELING	1871	WHG CITY	1790
BALTIMORE & OHIO RR / BUILDING - W.OF T.FOX	1871	MARH'L MAP	1761	BALTIMORE & OHIO RR - MAP	1916	NAT'L ROAD	1869
BALTIMORE & OHIO RR / BUILDING NEAR WHITE & STILES	1871	MARH'L MAP	1761	BALTIMORE & OHIO RR - OFFICE - CAMERON	1871	CAMERON	1803
BALTIMORE & OHIO RR	1878	DEFENDANT	1599				
BALTIMORE & OHIO RR	1916	NAT'L ROAD	1861	BALTIMORE & OHIO RR - OFFICE - MAIN ST - CAMERON	1871	CAMERON	1803
BALTIMORE & OHIO RR - AT BELLTON	1871	BELLTON	1814				

'PERSONAL TIME LINE' INDEX TO VOLUME 7 OF THE *OHIO COUNTY INDEX*

ENTRY	YEAR	SUBJECT	PAGE
BALTIMORE & OHIO RR - OHIO RIVER CHANEL BRIDGE AT BENWOOD / STONE & IRON	1871	BENWOOD	1799
BALTIMORE & OHIO RR - PASSENGER DEPOT - MOUNDSVILLE	1871	MDSVILLE	1808
BALTIMORE & OHIO RR - PROPERTY - AT MOUNDSVILLE	1871	MDSVILLE	1806
BALTIMORE & OHIO RR - PROPERTY - MOUNDSVILLE	1871	MDSVILLE	1808
BALTIMORE & OHIO RR - PROPERTY - MOUNDSVILLE	1871	MDSVILLE	1808
BALTIMORE & OHIO RR - PROPERTY - MOUNDSVILLE	1871	MDSVILLE	1808
BALTIMORE & OHIO RR - PROPERTY - MOUNDSVILLE	1871	MDSVILLE	1808
BALTIMORE & OHIO RR - PROPERTY - S. OF MDSVILLE	1871	MDSVILLE	1809
BALTIMORE & OHIO RR - PROPERTY - S. OF MDSVILLE	1871	MDSVILLE	1810
BALTIMORE & OHIO RR - R.R.CO. / 3 - B&O RR BUILDINGS NEAR FARMERS HOME	1871	MARH'L MAP	1757
BALTIMORE & OHIO RR - STATION - WASHINGTON, PA.	1916	NAT'L ROAD	1861
BALTIMORE & OHIO RR - TOOL HOUSE AT BENWOOD / ?	1871	BENWOOD	1799
BALTIMORE & OHIO RR - TUNNEL - EAST OF ROSBY'S ROCK	1871	MARH'L MAP	1752
BALTIMORE & OHIO RR - TUNNEL - SE. OF CAMERON P.O.	1871	MARH'L MAP	1757
BALTIMORE & OHIO RR - WAREHOUSE AT TRACKS - CAMERON	1871	CAMERON	1803
BALTIMORE & OHIO RR - WATER TANK / ON B&O - SE OF MOUNDSVILLE	1871	MARH'L MAP	1748
BALTIMORE & OHIO RR - WATER TANK - AT BELLTON	1871	BELLTON	1814
BALTIMORE & OHIO RR - WATER TANK - CAMERON	1871	CAMERON	1803
BALTIMORE & OHIO RR - WATER TANK - E. OF P. PARKER	1871	MARH'L MAP	1752
BALTIMORE & OHIO RR - WHEELING	1871	WHG CITY	1790
BALTIMORE & OHIO RR - WHEELING	1871	WHG CITY	1790
BALTIMORE & OHIO RR - WHEELING & PITTSBURGH LINE	1916	NAT'L ROAD	1862
BALTIMORE & OHIO RR - WHEELING FREIGHT DEPOT	1871	WHG CITY	1788
BALTIMORE & OHIO RR - WHEELING PASSENGER DEPOT	1871	WHG CITY	1788
BALTIMORE & OHIO RR - WHEELING TO BALTIMORE MAP	1852	HEMP. RR MAP	1827
BALTIMORE TO WHEELING - NATIONAL ROAD MAP	1916	NAT'L ROAD	1869
BALTIMORE, MD	1852	HEMPFIELD RR	1820
BALTIMORE, MD	1852	HEMPFIELD RR	1821
BALTIMORE, MD	1852	HEMP. RR MAP	1825
BALTIMORE, MD	1852	HEMP. RR MAP	1827
BALTIMORE, MD	1916	NAT'L ROAD	1863
BALTZELL, N	1861	DEFENDANT	1673
BAMBRICK, T	1871	HAN MAP	1731
BANAN, T	1871	BRKE MAP	1735
BANE, - / SCHOOL - MAP#90	1852	BRKE MAP	1842
BANE, F	1871	MARH'L MAP	1753
BANE, G	1871	MARH'L MAP	1752
BANE, J	1871	BRKE MAP	1736
BANE, J	1871	BKE/OH MAP	1738
BANE, J	1871	BKE/OH MAP	1738
BANE, J / OHIO RIVER	1871	BKE/OH MAP	1738
BANE, J	1871	MARH'L MAP	1753
BANE, JOHN / HEIRS, - MAP#96	1852	BRKE MAP	1842
BANE, JOHN / INITIALS J.B.	1871	BKE/OH MAP	1738
BANE, JOHN / INITIALS J.B.	1871	BKE/OH MAP	1738
BANE, JOHN / RES - SHORT	1871	BKE/OH MAP	1738
BANE, M / MRS	1871	BKE/OH MAP	1738
BANE, P	1871	MARH'L MAP	1753
BANE, ROBERT / MAP#81	1852	BRKE MAP	1839
BANE, ROBERT / MAP#82	1852	BRKE MAP	1839
BANE, ROBERT / MAP#83	1852	BRKE MAP	1839
BANE, ROBERT / SAW MILL - MAP#14	1852	BRKE MAP	1839
BANE, ROBERT / TAVERN - MAP#12	1852	BRKE MAP	1839
BANE, ROBERT / WAREHOUSE - MAP#13	1852	BRKE MAP	1839
BANE, ROBERT / (GONE) - MAP#153	1852	BRKE MAP	1842
BANE, ROBERT / (GONE) - MAP#154	1852	BRKE MAP	1842
BANE, ROBERT / MAP#152	1852	BRKE MAP	1842
BANE, ROBERT / MAP#84	1852	BRKE MAP	1842
BANE, ROBERT / MAP#85	1852	BRKE MAP	1842
BANE, ROBERT / MAP#86	1852	BRKE MAP	1842
BANE, ROBERT / MAP#88	1852	BRKE MAP	1842
BANE, ROBERT / MAP#89	1852	BRKE MAP	1842
BANE, ROBERT / MAP#91	1852	BRKE MAP	1842
BANE, ROBERT / MAP#99	1852	BRKE MAP	1842
BANE, S / SAWMILL - GONE - MAP#78	1852	BRKE MAP	1839
BANE, S / INITIALS S.B. - MOUTH OF SHORT CREEK	1871	BKE/OH MAP	1738
BANE, S / MISS	1871	BKE/OH MAP	1738
BANE, S / MISS - INITIALS S.B.	1871	BKE/OH MAP	1738
BANE, S / MISS - O	1871	BKE/OH MAP	1738
BANE, WILLIAM	1871	BRKE MAP	1736
BANE, WILLIAM / & TRIMBLE / INITIALS B & T	1871	BRKE MAP	1736
BANE, WILLIAM / & TRIMBLE	1871	BKE/OH MAP	1738
BANE, WILLIAM / & TRIMBLE - INITIALS B. & T.	1871	BKE/OH MAP	1738
BANES RUN - MOUTH OF - AT OHIO RIVER	1852	BRKE MAP	1842
BANKS, JOHN	1838	DEFENDANT	1669
BANKS, JOHN	1839	DEFENDANT	1670
BANNING, EPHRAM	1835	DEFENDANT	1608
BAPTIST / (OLD) - MAP#456	1852	BRKE MAP	1849
BAPTIST / (OLD) - MAP#467	1852	BRKE MAP	1849
BAPTIST CHURCH - CLAY TWP	1871	MARH'L MAP	1751
BAPTIST CHURCH - JOHNSONS RUN	1852	BRKE MAP	1849
BAPTIST CHURCH - MARKET ST	1871	WHG CITY	1788
BAPTIST CHURCH - MARKET ST	1871	WHG CITY	1790
BAPTIST CHURCH - MONROE ST	1871	WHG CITY	1788
BAPTIST CHURCH & GRAVEYARD - FORK RIDGE ROAD	1871	MARH'L MAP	1753
BARCLAY & LLOYD	1871	WLSBRG BUS.	1772
BARCLAY, - / GENERAL DUVAL OF BARCLAY & LLOYD (GROC) O.C.	1871	WELLSBURG	1777
BARCLAY, LLOYD & CO. / BRICK YARD	1871	WELLSBURG	1776
BARCLAY, ROBERT	1815	DEFENDANT	1611
BARCLAY, W C	1871	WELLSBURG	1777
BARCLAY, W C	1871	WELLSBURG	1777
BARDNER, J / (?OR GARDNER?) - PROSPECT & WATER	1871	WELLSBURG	1777
BARDO, - / MRS	1871	MARH'L MAP	1745
BARKER, -	1851	PLAINTIFF	1620
BARKER, ELISHA	1837	DEFENDANT	1600
BARKER, ELISHA	1839	DEFENDANT	1600
BARKER, JOHN	1820	DEFENDANT	1576
BARKER, MICHAEL	1799	PLAINTIFF	1567
BARKSHEW, CHARLES	1795	DEFENDANT	1554
BARKSHIRE, WILLIAM	1792	DEFENDANT	1655
BARNARD, FRANCIS L	1834	DEFENDANT	1640
BARNES, -	1862	DEFENDANT	1673
BARNES, E	1871	WELLSBURG	1777
BARNES, F	1871	BRKE MAP	1735
BARNES, F	1871	BRKE MAP	1735
BARNES, R / HRS - HEIRS	1871	WELLSBURG	1777
BARNES, WILLIAM F	1837	DEFENDANT	1614
BARNES, WILLIAM F	1837	DEFENDANT	1618
BARNS, EBENEZER	1810	DEFENDANT	1645
BARR, J / CARPET FACTORY	1871	WELLSBURG	1778
BARR, J	1871	TRIAD BORO.	1784
BARR, R G	1874	MISC	1711
BARR, SAMUEL	1818	DEFENDANT	1624
BARR, W	1871	WELLSBURG	1777
BARRET, M	1871	MARH'L MAP	1757
BARRY, J	1871	MARH'L MAP	1756
BARRY, W A	1871	W.UNION-BUS.	1797
BARSHIRE, WILLIAM	1795	DEFENDANT	1665
BARTH, C	1871	WELLSBURG	1778
BARTH, C	1871	WELLSBURG	1778
BARTH, H	1871	WELLSBURG	1777
BARTH, HUGH	1871	WLSBRG BUS.	1772
BARTLEBRUSH, J	1871	BENWOOD	1798
BARTLESON, ENOS R	1856	DEFENDANT	1597
BARTLESON, ENOS R	1856	DEFENDANT	1630
BARTLETT STATION	1871	MARH'L MAP	1752
BARTON, H	1871	HAN MAP	1726
BARTON, H / ? - N. OF NEW LEXINGTON	1871	HAN MAP	1730
BARTON, HENRY	1797	DEFENDANT	1659
BARTON, WILLIAM	1811	DEFENDANT	1610
BARTON, WILLIAM	1811	DEFENDANT	1610
BARTON, WILLIAM	1812	DEFENDANT	1611
BARTON, WILLIAM	1813	DEFENDANT	1611

'PERSONAL TIME LINE' INDEX TO VOLUME 7 OF THE *OHIO COUNTY INDEX*

ENTRY	YEAR	SUBJECT	PAGE	ENTRY	YEAR	SUBJECT	PAGE
BASHAR, DOROTHEA	1874	DEFENDANT	1576	BEARS RUN	1871	HAN MAP	1732
BASHAR, JOHN	1874	DEFENDANT	1576	BEATTY, J	1871	MARH'L MAP	1761
BASSER, C	1859	DEFENDANT	1672	BEATTY, J	1871	MARH'L MAP	1761
BASSFORD, A	1871	GLEN EASTON	1801	BEATTY, W	1871	MARH'L MAP	1761
BASTERS BRANCH	1852	BRKE MAP	1852	BEATY, THOMAS / MAP#555	1852	BRKE MAP	1851
BATTLE RUN	1871	OH CO. MAP	1740	BEATY, THOMAS / MAP#556	1852	BRKE MAP	1851
BAULDIN, JOHN	1841	DEFENDANT	1629	BEAUMONT, - / MRS	1871	NEW CUMB'LD	1767
BAXTER, - / MRS	1871	BRKE MAP	1734	BEAUMONT, G L / DOCTOR & DRUGGIST	1871	NEW CUMB'LD	1762
BAXTER, A	1871	HAN MAP	1731				
BAXTER, E	1871	HAN MAP	1726	BEAUMONT, G L / DOCTOR & DRUG STORE	1871	NEW CUMB'LD	1766
BAXTER, G	1871	HAN MAP	1726				
BAXTER, G	1871	HAN MAP	1726	BEAVER, PA	1852	HEMP. RR MAP	1826
BAXTER, G	1871	HAN MAP	1726	BECK, E / MRS ?	1871	BKE/OH MAP	1739
BAXTER, G	1871	HAN MAP	1726	BECK, FREDERICK	1852	DEFENDANT	1576
BAXTER, G	1871	HAN MAP	1726	BECK, J	1871	BKE/OH MAP	1739
BAXTER, G	1871	HAN MAP	1726	BECK, L	1871	BKE/OH MAP	1739
BAXTER, G / N. PART OF MAP	1871	HAN MAP	1730	BECK, SAMUEL	1799	DEFENDANT	1607
BAXTER, GEORGE / MAP#566	1852	BRKE MAP	1852	BECK, SAMUEL / MAP#22	1852	BRKE MAP	1839
BAXTER, RICHARD / MAP#671	1852	BRKE MAP	1854	BECK, SAMUEL / MAP#73	1852	BRKE MAP	1839
BAXTER, S	1871	HAN MAP	1727	BECKER, CHRISTIAN	1873	DEFENDANT	1602
BAXTER, S	1871	HAN MAP	1727	BECKLEY, HENRY	1828	DEFENDANT	1587
BAXTER, S	1871	NEW CUMB'LD	1767	BECKS RUN	1871	BKE/OH MAP	1739
BAXTER, W E	1871	BRKE MAP	1734	BECTOR, JOHN	1798	MISC	1689
BAXTER, W E	1871	BRKE MAP	1735	BEDILION, - / CONANT & BEDILION ICE HOUSSE	1871	OH CO. MAP	1742
BAXTER, WILLIAM / MAP#521	1852	BRKE MAP	1852				
BAXTERS MILL	1871	HAN-POE TWP	1763	BEDILION, - / CONANT & BEDILION / ICE HOUSE	1871	TRIAD.TWP.	1781
BEACH GLEN SCHOOL NO.8 / (?BEECH GLEN?)	1871	OH CO. MAP	1742				
				BEDILION, A	1871	W.UNION	1812
BEACK, W F	1871	BKE/OH MAP	1739	BEDILION, A D	1871	W.UNION-BUS.	1797
BEACON, DANIEL	1806	DEFENDANT	1594	BEDILION, J	1871	OH CO. MAP	1742
BEAGLE, M / MRS - INITIALS M.B. ?	1871	OH CO. MAP	1740	BEDILION, J S / S. OF WHITE OAK SPRING	1871	OH CO. MAP	1743
BEAL, - / BROTHERS	1871	HAN MAP	1731				
BEAL, BASIL	1817	DEFENDANT	1583	BEDILION, J S	1871	MARH'L MAP	1746
BEAL, BASIL	1818	DEFENDANT	1583	BEDILION, JAMES L	1871	TRIAD.TWP.	1781
BEALL, B	1871	BRKE MAP	1737	BEDILLION, J L	1871	OH.CO.BUS.	1779
BEALL, B / RES	1871	BRKE MAP	1737	BEECH BOTTOM BAR - IN OHIO RIVER	1852	BRKE MAP	1842
BEALL, BASEL JR	1812	DEFENDANT	1585	BEECH BOTTOM ROAD	1871	BRKE MAP	1736
BEALL, BASIL	1806	DEFENDANT	1644	BEECH BOTTOM RUN	1852	BRKE MAP	1842
BEALL, BASIL	1807	DEFENDANT	1644	BEECH BOTTOM RUN	1871	BRKE MAP	1736
BEALL, BASIL	1808	DEFENDANT	1655	BEECH GLEN SCHOOL NO.8 / (?WRITTEN AS BEACH GLEN?)	1871	OH CO. MAP	1742
BEALL, BASIL	1812	DEFENDANT	1611				
BEALL, BASIL	1814	DEFENDANT	1667	BEELER, FREDERICK	1809	DEFENDANT	1579
BEALL, BASIL	1815	DEFENDANT	1583	BEELER, FREDERICK	1812	DEFENDANT	1579
BEALL, BASIL SR	1814	DEFENDANT	1611	BEELOR - ORPHANS	1800	MISC	1697
BEALL, BASIL SR	1817	DEFENDANT	1611	BEELOR, -	1798	DEFENDANT	1556
BEALL, BAZEL / ESQ. - MAP#232	1852	BRKE MAP	1844	BEELOR, FREDERICK	1800	DEFENDANT	1665
BEALL, BAZEL / ESQ. - MAP#233	1852	BRKE MAP	1844	BEELOR, FREDERICK	1801	DEFENDANT	1579
BEALL, BAZEL / ESQ. - MAP#235	1852	BRKE MAP	1844	BEELOR, GEORGE	1793	DEFENDANT	1606
BEALL, BAZEL / ESQ. - MAP#236	1852	BRKE MAP	1844	BEELOR, GEORGE	1800	PLAINTIFF	1583
BEALL, BAZEL / ESQ. - MAP#192	1852	BRKE MAP	1844	BEELOR, GEORGE	1802	DEFENDANT	1655
BEALL, C H	1871	BRKE MAP	1737	BEELOR, GEORGE	1804	DEFENDANT	1561
BEALL, C H JR / RES	1871	BRKE MAP	1737	BEELOR, JANE	1803	DEFENDANT	1610
BEALL, FIELDING	1804	DEFENDANT	1659	BEELOR, JANE	1803	DEFENDANT	1666
BEALL, FIELDING	1804	DEFENDANT	1666	BEELOR, MARY	1802	MISC	1697
BEALL, FIELDING	1805	DEFENDANT	1659	BEEM, J	1871	MDSVILLE	1808
BEALL, FIELDING	1806	DEFENDANT	1666	BEEM, J	1871	MDSVILLE	1810
BEALL, H C	1871	NEW MANCH.	1763	BEERS, F W / & CO - MAP PUBLISHER	1871	MAP	1713
BEALL, H C / STORE - MARKET ST	1871	NEW MANCH.	1769	BEERS, F W / & CO.- MAP PUBLISHER COPYRIGHT 1871	1871	WHG CITY	1786
BEALL, H C / LOT 14	1871	NEW MANCH.	1769				
BEALL, HILLIARY	1833	DEFENDANT	1613	BEIR, PHILIP	1818	DEFENDANT	1632
BEALL, J S / (O)	1871	WELLSBURG	1777	BEITER, E	1871	WELLSBURG	1778
BEALL, J S	1871	WELLSBURG	1778	BEITER, E	1871	WELLSBURG	1778
BEALL, JOHN / MAP#229	1852	BRKE MAP	1844	BEITZER, MARY	1874	DEFENDANT	1560
BEALL, JOHN / MAP#239	1852	BRKE MAP	1844	BEITZER, W	1874	DEFENDANT	1560
BEALL, JOHN / MAP#240	1852	BRKE MAP	1844	BELL, -	1854	DEFENDANT	1629
BEALL, JOHN / MAP#243	1852	BRKE MAP	1844	BELL, -	1856	DEFENDANT	1630
BEALL, NINIAN	1815	DEFENDANT	1572	BELL, -	1857	DEFENDANT	1630
BEALL, NINIAN	1815	DEFENDANT	1572	BELL, -	1858	DEFENDANT	1630
BEALL, PHILLIP	1797	DEFENDANT	1634	BELL, -	1860	DEFENDANT	1631
BEALL, ROBERT	1800	DEFENDANT	1576	BELL, -	1862	DEFENDANT	1631
BEALL, ROBERT	1807	DEFENDANT	1666	BELL, HENRY	1818	DEFENDANT	1624
BEALL, SAMUEL	1808	DEFENDANT	1667	BELL, HENRY	1820	DEFENDANT	1624
BEALL, SAMUEL	1809	DEFENDANT	1667	BELL, J M	1871	MDSVILLE	1808
BEALL, W	1871	WELLSBURG	1777	BELL, J M / INITIALS J.M.B.	1871	MDSVILLE	1808
BEALL, W	1871	WELLSBURG	1778	BELL, J M	1871	MDSVILLE	1810
BEALL, WILLIAM / MAP#199	1852	BRKE MAP	1842	BELL, JAMES	1812	DEFENDANT	1599
BEALL, WILLIAM / MAP#200	1852	BRKE MAP	1842	BELL, JAMES	1841	DEFENDANT	1643
BEALS RUN	1871	HAN MAP	1731	BELL, JOHN	1812	DEFENDANT	1599
BEAN, JESSE	1800	DEFENDANT	1655	BELL, JOHN	1812	DEFENDANT	1599
BEAR RUN	1852	BRKE MAP	1854	BELL, JOHN M	1871	MDSVILLE	1808
BEAR WALLOW FARM	1871	MARH'L MAP	1751	BELL, M / MRS	1871	MARH'L MAP	1753
BEAR, T	1871	MARH'L MAP	1745	BELL, MOSES	1812	DEFENDANT	1599
BEARD, H	1871	WELLSBURG	1777	BELL, N	1871	OH CO. MAP	1740
BEARD, J	1871	MARH'L MAP	1747	BELL, PHILIP / HEIRS - MAP#667	1852	BRKE MAP	1854
BEARD, J	1871	MARH'L MAP	1747	BELL, PHILIP / HEIRS - MAP#668	1852	BRKE MAP	1854
BEARD, JAMES	1801	DEFENDANT	1666	BELL, PHILIP / HEIRS - MAP#669	1852	BRKE MAP	1854

'PERSONAL TIME LINE' INDEX TO VOLUME 7 OF THE OHIO COUNTY INDEX

ENTRY	YEAR	SUBJECT	PAGE
BELL, PHILIP / HEIRS / MAP#670	1852	BRKE MAP	1854
BELL, S	1871	W.LIBERTY	1780
BELL, S	1871	W.LIBERTY	1780
BELL, S M	1854	DEFENDANT	1582
BELL, S M	1855	DEFENDANT	1582
BELL, S M	1871	MARH'L MAP	1757
BELL, S M	1871	MARH'L MAP	1761
BELL, S M	1871	MARH'L MAP	1761
BELL, SAMUEL	1878	DEFENDANT	1625
BELL, THOMAS	1821	DEFENDANT	1612
BELL, THOMAS	1838	DEFENDANT	1661
BELLAFONTAINE	1852	HEMP. RR MAP	1826
BELLAIRE FERRY - OHIO RIVER	1871	BENWOOD	1798
BELLEVUE RETREAT	1871	OH CO. MAP	1742
BELLIC, W	1871	MARH'L MAP	1747
BELLS RUN	1852	BRKE MAP	1852
BELLTON - BLACKSMITH SHOP	1871	BELLTON	1814
BELLTON - DETAIL MAP	1871	BELLTON	1814
BELLTON - FREIGHT DEPOT	1871	MARH'L MAP	1761
BELLTON - STORE NEAR B&O RR	1871	BELLTON	1814
BELLTON - WHITE & STILES	1871	LIB.TWP-BUS.	1797
BELLTON P.O.	1871	MARH'L MAP	1761
BELMONT CO, OHIO	1871	WHG CITY	1786
BELMONT CO, OHIO	1871	WHG CITY	1790
BELMONT NAIL WORKS	1871	WHG CITY	1790
BELTON	1871	DISTANCES	1815
BELVILLE, C	1846	DEFENDANT	1551
BELZ, P	1871	OH CO. MAP	1742
BELZ, P	1871	OH CO. MAP	1744
BENDER, J & CO - STAVE FACTORY - CAMERON	1871	MARH'L MAP	1757
BENDER, J & CO - STAVE FACTORY	1871	CAMERON	1804
BENGLE. M / MRS	1871	OH CO. MAP	1740
BENNETT, -	1874	PLAINTIFF	1621
BENNETT, ABRAHAM	1832	DEFENDANT	1669
BENNETT, ABRAHAM	1834	DEFENDANT	1650
BENNETT, ABRAHAM	1837	DEFENDANT	1651
BENNETT, ABRAHAM	1841	DEFENDANT	1643
BENNETT, ABRAHAM	1841	DEFENDANT	1656
BENS RUN	1871	MARH'L MAP	1761
BEN'S RUN	1871	MARH'L MAP	1757
BENTLEY, ISAAC	1858	DEFENDANT	1578
BENTLEY, J	1871	TRIAD.BORO.	1784
BENTLEY, ROSANNA	1829	DEFENDANT	1587
BENTLEY, ROSANNA	1830	DEFENDANT	1587
BENTLEY, S / WASHINGTON CO.	1852	HEMPFIELD RR	1817
BENTLEY, W H	1871	CAMER'N - BUS.	1795
BENTLEY, W H	1871	CAMERON	1803
BENTLY, JACOB	1823	DEFENDANT	1628
BENTLY, JACOB	1824	DEFENDANT	1628
BENTLY, ROSANA	1828	DEFENDANT	1587
BENTLY, WILLIAM	1817	DEFENDANT	1572
BENTZ, C	1871	WELLSBURG	1778
BENTZ, C	1871	WELLSBURG	1778
BENTZ, C / GROC	1871	WELLSBURG	1778
BENTZ, CASPER	1871	WLSBRG BUS.	1772
BENWARD, B M	1871	HAN MAP	1727
BENWARD, B M	1871	HAN MAP	1728
BENWOOD	1871	DISTANCES	1815
BENWOOD - BUSINESS NOTICES	1871	BENWOOD	1795
BENWOOD - CARPENTER SHOP	1871	BENWOOD	1798
BENWOOD - DETAIL MAP	1871	BENWOOD	1799
BENWOOD - DETAIL MAP	1871	BENWOOD	1800
BENWOOD - FERRY ST	1871	BENWOOD	1798
BENWOOD - FIRST ST	1871	BENWOOD	1798
BENWOOD - MARSHALL CO - DETAIL MAP	1871	BENWOOD	1798
BENWOOD - MARSHALL ST	1871	BENWOOD	1798
BENWOOD - NAIL FACTORY	1871	BENWOOD	1799
BENWOOD - NAIL WORKS	1871	BENWOOD	1799
BENWOOD - PANORAMIC MAP	1882	BENWOOD	1856
BENWOOD - SECOND ST	1871	BENWOOD	1798
BENWOOD - SECOND ST	1871	BENWOOD	1799
BENWOOD - SHOE SHOP	1871	BENWOOD	1799
BENWOOD - THIRD ST	1871	BENWOOD	1798
BENWOOD - THIRD ST	1871	BENWOOD	1799
BENWOOD - TOOL HOUSE	1871	BENWOOD	1799
BENWOOD - WALKER TANK / (?WATER TANK?)	1871	BENWOOD	1799
BENWOOD CO,	1871	BENWOOD	1798
BENWOOD CO.	1871	BENWOOD	1799
BENWOOD CO.	1871	BENWOOD	1799
BENWOOD CO.	1871	BENWOOD	1799
BENWOOD CO.	1871	BENWOOD	1799
BENWOOD CO.	1871	BENWOOD	1799
BENWOOD CO.	1871	BENWOOD	1799
BENWOOD CO.	1871	BENWOOD	1799
BENWOOD CO.	1871	BENWOOD	1799
BENWOOD CO.	1871	BENWOOD	1799
BENWOOD CO.	1871	BENWOOD	1799
BENWOOD DEPOT	1871	BENWOOD	1800
BENWOOD HOTEL - BENWOOD	1871	BENWO'D - BUS.	1795
BENWOOD HOTEL - FIRST ST	1871	BENWOOD	1798
BENWOOD IRON CO.	1871	BENWOOD	1798
BENWOOD IRON CO.	1871	BENWOOD	1798
BENWOOD IRON CO.	1871	BENWOOD	1799
BENWOOD IRON CO.	1871	BENWOOD	1799
BENWOOD IRON CO.	1871	BENWOOD	1799
BENWOOD IRON CO. STORE	1871	BENWO'D - BUS.	1795
BENWOOD IRON WORKS	1871	BENWO'D - BUS.	1795
BENWOOD IRON WORKS - BLACKSMITH SHOP	1871	BENWOOD	1799
BENWOOD IRON WORKS - BOILERS - BENWOOD	1871	BENWOOD	1799
BENWOOD IRON WORKS - FOUNDRY	1871	BENWOOD	1799
BENWOOD IRON WORKS - OFFICE - BENWOOD	1871	BENWOOD	1799
BENWOOD IRON WORKS - TANK HOUSE - BENWOOD	1871	BENWOOD	1799
BENWOOD K. FACTORY	1871	BENWOOD	1799
BENWOOD NAIL FACTORY	1871	BENWO'D - BUS.	1795
BENWOOD P.O.	1871	MARH'L MAP	1745
BENWOOD STORE	1871	BENWOOD	1799
BENWOOD, F	1871	NEW MANCH.	1769
BERDEN, O	1871	MARH'L MAP	1749
BERDEN, O / (?S.M.=SAW MILL?)	1871	MARH'L MAP	1749
BERGER & HOFFMAN	1853	DEFENDANT	1641
BERGER, J	1871	WELLSBURG	1778
BERGER, JACOB	1843	DEFENDANT	1553
BERRY, DANIEL W	1877	DEFENDANT	1566
BERRY, F	1839	DEFENDANT	1651
BERRY, FIELDER	1833	DEFENDANT	1585
BERRY, FIELDER	1837	DEFENDANT	1583
BERRY, FIELDER	1838	DEFENDANT	1651
BERRY, FIELDER	1842	DEFENDANT	1652
BERRY, FIELDON	1839	DEFENDANT	1553
BERRY, GEORGE	1838	DEFENDANT	1651
BERRY, GEORGE W	1841	DEFENDANT	1585
BERRY, JOHN W	1833	DEFENDANT	1566
BERRY, JOHN W	1833	DEFENDANT	1622
BERRY, JOHN W	1840	DEFENDANT	1614
BERRY, JOHN W	1840	DEFENDANT	1619
BERRY, JOHN W	1840	DEFENDANT	1643
BERRY, JOHN W	1841	DEFENDANT	1656
BERRY, JOHN W	1842	DEFENDANT	1615
BERRY, JOHN W	1842	DEFENDANT	1656
BERRY, JOHN W	1843	DEFENDANT	1615
BERRY, JOHN W	1846	MISC	1695
BERRY, R	1871	OH CO. MAP	1740
BERRYHILL, -	1862	DEFENDANT	1604
BERRYHILL, ALEXANDER S	1819	DEFENDANT	1594
BERSEY, H	1871	BENWOOD	1798
BEST, A W	1871	MDSVILLE	1810
BETHANY	1852	BRKE MAP	1844
BETHANY	1871	DISTANCES	1815
BETHANY - BROOKE CO	1871	POPULATION	1816
BETHANY - BUSINESS NOTICES	1871	BETHNY BUS.	1772
BETHANY - COLLEGE	1871	BETHANY	1773
BETHANY - DETAIL MAP	1871	BETHANY	1773
BETHANY - DRUG STORE - MAIN ST.	1871	BETHANY	1773
BETHANY - MAIN ST	1871	BETHANY	1773
BETHANY - MEAT SHOP / COLLEGE ST	1871	BETHANY	1773
BETHANY - PENDELTON ST	1871	BETHANY	1773
BETHANY - RICHARDSON ST	1871	BETHANY	1773
BETHANY - ROSS ST	1871	BETHANY	1773
BETHANY - SADDLER SHOP - MAIN ST	1871	BETHANY	1773
BETHANY - STORE - CORNER OF MAIN & ROSS STS	1871	BETHANY	1773
BETHANY - WELLSBURG & BETHANY TURNPIKE	1852	BRKE MAP	1843
BETHANY - WELLSBURG & BETHANY TURNPIKE / CUT OFF LEFT OF MAP	1852	BRKE MAP	1846
BETHANY - WHEELING & BETAHNY PIKE	1871	OH CO. MAP	1740
BETHANY - WHEELING & BETHANY PIKE	1871	OH CO. MAP	1741
BETHANY - WHEELING & BETHANY TURNPIKE	1852	BRKE MAP	1840
BETHANY - WHEELING & BETHANY TURNPIKE	1852	BRKE MAP	1844
BETHANY COLLEGE / MAP#133	1852	BRKE MAP	1844

VII

'PERSONAL TIME LINE' INDEX TO VOLUME 7 OF THE OHIO COUNTY INDEX

ENTRY	YEAR	SUBJECT	PAGE
BETHANY COLLEGE	1871	BRKE MAP	1737
BETHANY COLLEGE	1871	BKE/OH MAP	1739
BETHANY COLLEGE	1871	BETHANY	1773
BETHANY COLLEGE - ALBERT ALLEN, FINANCIAL AGENT FOR	1871	BUFF.TWP.BUS.	1772
BETHANY COLLEGE - PRES.W.H.PENDLETON	1871	BETHANY	1773
BETHANY COLLEGE - W.K.PENDLETON, PRESIDENT OF	1871	BETHNY BUS.	1772
BETHANY COLLEGE BOARDING HOUSE	1871	BETHANY	1773
BETHANY COLLEGE BUILDING / MAP#135	1852	BRKE MAP	1844
BETHANY COLLEGE INN / MAP#134	1852	BRKE MAP	1844
BETHANY COLLEGE PROPERTY - BOARDING HOUSE - LOT #21	1871	BETHANY	1773
BETHANY COLLEGE PROPERTY - LOT #19	1871	BETHANY	1773
BETHANY HOUSE - BETHANY / HOTEL	1871	BETHNY BUS.	1772
BETHANY HOUSE - BETHANY - HOTEL / MAIN ST	1871	BETHANY	1773
BETHANY P.O.	1871	BRKE MAP	1737
BETHANY P.O.	1871	BKE/OH MAP	1739
BETHANY PIKE / TUNNEL ON	1871	BRKE MAP	1736
BETHANY PIKE - TOLL HOUSE - NEAR NAT'L RD	1871	TRIAD.TWP.	1781
BETHANY PROPERTY SCHOOL / MAP#139	1852	BRKE MAP	1844
BETHANY PROPERTY SCHOOL / MAP#140	1852	BRKE MAP	1844
BETHLEHEM METHODIST EPISCOPAL CHURCH / UNION TWP	1871	MARH'L MAP	1745
BETHLEHEM METHODIST EPISCOPAL CHURCH / MARSH. CO.	1871	MARH'L MAP	1748
BETHLEHEM SCHOOL NO.2	1871	OH CO. MAP	1742
BETTS, - / MES	1871	HAN MAP	1733
BEYMER FAMILY - EXAMPLE IN CUMULATIVE INDEX	2000	APPENDIX	1875
BEYMER, - / MRS - TAVERN	1916	NAT'L ROAD	1868
BEYMER, CHRISTIANA	1815	DEFENDANT	1581
BEYMER, CHRISTIANA	1816	DEFENDANT	1645
BEYMER, FRED / CAPT. - TAVERN IN 1802	1916	NAT'L ROAD	1868
BEYMER, FREDERICK	1802	DEFENDANT	1634
BEYMER, FREDERICK	1804	DEFENDANT	1659
BEYMER, FREDERICK	1809	DEFENDANT	1569
BEYMER, FREDERICK	1809	PLAINTIFF	1638
BEYMER, FREDERICK	1810	DEFENDANT	1589
BEYMER, FREDERICK	1810	DEFENDANT	1610
BEYMER, FREDERICK	1810	DEFENDANT	1626
BEYMER, FREDERICK	1810	DEFENDANT	1659
BEYMER, FREDERICK	1811	DEFENDANT	1569
BEYMER, FREDERICK	1813	DEFENDANT	1581
BEYMER, GEORGE	1799	DEFENDANT	1554
BEYMER, GEORGE	1799	DEFENDANT	1598
BEYMER, GEORGE	1799	DEFENDANT	1610
BEYMER, GEORGE	1799	DEFENDANT	1647
BEYMER, GEORGE	1800	DEFENDANT	1556
BEYMER, GEORGE	1813	DEFENDANT	1645
BEYMER'S TAVERN - ON WHEELING MAP	1916	NAT'L ROAD	1868
BICKERTON, -	1862	DEFENDANT	1673
BIDDLE RUN / (?BRIDLE?)	1871	OH CO. MAP	1740
BIDDLE, JOHN	1814	PLAINTIFF	1645
BIDDLE, S	1871	MARH'L MAP	1754
BIDDLE, S	1871	MARH'L MAP	1754
BIDDLE, S / INITIALS S.B.	1871	MARH'L MAP	1754
BIDDLE, SPENCER	1805	DEFENDANT	1648
BIDDLE, SPENCER	1808	DEFENDANT	1648
BIDDLE, SPENCER	1809	DEFENDANT	1648
BIDDLE, SPENCER	1811	DEFENDANT	1608
BIDDLE, SPENCER	1813	DEFENDANT	1608
BIDDLE, SPENCER	1844	DEFENDANT	1632
BIDDLERUN	1871	MARH'L MAP	1754
BIDDLES RUN, OH	1852	BRKE MAP	1845
BIER, GEORGE W / RES	1871	MDSVILLE	1809
BIER, JACOB E	1853	DEFENDANT	1623
BIER, JACOB E	1854	DEFENDANT	1551
BIER, PHILIP	1834	DEFENDANT	1639
BIER, PHILIP	1838	DEFENDANT	1640
BIER, PHILLIP	1839	DEFENDANT	1640
BIG FOOT INDIAN / PLACE WHERE ADAM POE AND BIG FOOT INDIAN FOUGHT	1871	HAN MAP	1726
BIG GRAVE CREEK	1871	MARH'L MAP	1748
BIG GRAVE CREEK	1871	MARH'L MAP	1752

ENTRY	YEAR	SUBJECT	PAGE
BIG GRAVE CREEK	1871	MARH'L MAP	1753
BIG GRAVE CREEK	1871	MARH'L MAP	1756
BIG GRAVE CREEK - AT CAMERON	1871	CAMERON	1804
BIG GRAVE CREEK - AT GLEN EASTON	1871	GLEN EASTON	1801
BIG GRAVE CREEK - S. OF MOUNDSVILLE	1871	MDSVILLE	1810
BIG RUN / SAND HILL TWP	1871	MARH'L MAP	1746
BIG RUN	1871	MARH'L MAP	1749
BIG RUN	1871	MARH'L MAP	1757
BIG TRIBBLE CREEK	1871	MARH'L MAP	1755
BIG WHEELING CREEK	1871	MARH'L MAP	1746
BIG WHEELING CREEK - AT ELM GROVE	1871	ELM GROVE	1782
BIGERTON, -	1859	DEFENDANT	1567
BIGGER, J	1871	NEW MANCH.	1769
BIGGS, A	1857	DEFENDANT	1553
BIGGS, A	1871	W.LIBERTY	1780
BIGGS, B A	1859	DEFENDANT	1588
BIGGS, BEN	1810	APPENDIX	1873
BIGGS, BENJAMIN	1795	MISC	1701
BIGGS, BENJAMIN	1798	MISC	1701
BIGGS, BENJAMIN	1799	MISC	1689
BIGGS, BENJAMIN	1799	MISC	1701
BIGGS, JOSEPH	1801	DEFENDANT	1647
BIGGS, JOSEPH	1808	DEFENDANT	1658
BIGGS, JOSEPH	1809	DEFENDANT	1626
BIGGS, JOSEPH	1809	DEFENDANT	1645
BIGGS, L	1871	MARH'L MAP	1745
BIGGS, L	1871	MARH'L MAP	1748
BIGGS, L A / MRS	1871	W.LIBERTY	1780
BIGGS, M / MISS	1871	MARH'L MAP	1745
BIGGS, M / MISS	1871	MARH'L MAP	1748
BIGGS, S A / MRS	1871	W.LIBERTY	1780
BIGGS, SAMUEL	1822	DEFENDANT	1587
BIGGS, ZACHEUS	1833	DEFENDANT	1589
BIGGS, ZACHEUS	1840	DEFENDANT	1585
BIGHAM, - / PORTER & BIGHAM	1871	NEW CUMB'LD	1767
BIGHAM, W	1871	RIV. RD S.OF N.C.	1771
BIGHAM, W L	1871	NEW CUMB'LD	1768
BILDERBACH, EPHRIAM JR	1791	DEFENDANT	1556
BIRD, J	1871	MARH'L MAP	1746
BIRD, R	1871	MARH'L MAP	1746
BIRKETT, R / INITIALS R.B.	1871	OH CO. MAP	1742
BIRKETT, R / RES	1871	OH CO. MAP	1742
BIRKHEAD, ABERHAM	1809	DEFENDANT	1599
BISELL, JOHN	1796	DEFENDANT	1556
BISHOP, A	1871	MARH'L MAP	1759
BISHOP, JOHN	1855	DEFENDANT	1596
BISHOP, JOHN	1856	DEFENDANT	1653
BISHOP, JOHN	1857	DEFENDANT	1560
BISHOP, JOHN	1858	DEFENDANT	1560
BISHOP, JOHN	1858	DEFENDANT	1597
BISHOP, WILLIAM	1839	DEFENDANT	1557
BITZER, A	1871	OH CO. MAP	1741
BITZER, A	1871	OH CO. MAP	1742
BK KILN / (?BRICK?) TOMLINSON RUN	1871	HAN MAP	1727
BLACK - SLAVE	1818	PLAINTIFF	1556
BLACK CHILD	1827	MISC	1693
BLACK HORSE FIRE BRICK WORKS	1871	RIV. RD S.OF N.C.	1763
BLACK HORSE FIRE BRICK WORKS	1871	RIV. RD S.OF N.C.	1771
BLACK HORSE LANDING	1871	RIV. RD S.OF N.C.	1771
BLACK, A	1871	MARH'L MAP	1746
BLACK, ABNER	1844	DEFENDANT	1553
BLACK, JOHN	1805	DEFENDANT	1607
BLACK, ROBERT	1784	DEFENDANT	1556
BLACK, SAMUEL F	1855	DEFENDANT	1576
BLACK, SAMUEL F	1858	DEFENDANT	1557
BLACK, THOMAS G	1851	DEFENDANT	1653
BLACKHORSE LANDING	1871	HAN MAP	1730
BLACKS ISLAND - OHIO RIVER	1871	HAN MAP	1730
BLACKSMITH - HINDMANS / ANDREW - HARMONS CREEK	1871	CROSS CRK.BUS.	1772
BLACKSMITH SHOP / ABBREV. B.S.SH.	1871	HAN MAP	1729
BLACKSMITH SHOP / N. OF BLAIR P.O.	1871	HAN MAP	1731
BLACKSMITH SHOP / NEAR GOULD, PEARCH & CO	1871	WELLSBURG	1776
BLACKSMITH SHOP - ALLISONS / JOHN W.	1871	HAN MAP	1731
BLACKSMITH SHOP - BELLTON	1871	BELLTON	1814
BLACKSMITH SHOP - BELLTON P.O.	1871	MARH'L MAP	1761
BLACKSMITH SHOP - BENWOOD IRON WORKS	1871	BENWOOD	1799
BLACKSMITH SHOP - BROOKLYN MILLS	1871	HAN MAP	1726

VIII

'PERSONAL TIME LINE' INDEX TO VOLUME 7 OF THE *OHIO COUNTY INDEX*

ENTRY	YEAR	SUBJECT	PAGE
BLACKSMITH SHOP - BUCHANANS / M (?LIVING NEXT TO SHOP?) - LIMESTONE P.O.	1871	LIMESTONE	1805
BLACKSMITH SHOP - CAMPBELLS / ALEXANDER - MAP#128	1852	BRKE MAP	1844
BLACKSMITH SHOP - COLLEGE ST - BETHANY	1871	BETHANY	1773
BLACKSMITH SHOP - DARES / J	1871	BRKE MAP	1737
BLACKSMITH SHOP - DURBINS / T - NEW MANCHESTER	1871	NEW MANCH.	1763
BLACKSMITH SHOP - E. END OF VALLEY GROVE	1871	OH CO. MAP	1740
BLACKSMITH SHOP - E. OF D.MCCRACKEN	1871	MARH'L MAP	1757
BLACKSMITH SHOP - EDWARDS / J C - NEW CUMBERLAND	1871	NEW CUMB'LD	1762
BLACKSMITH SHOP - EISENNACHS / ? K - SE. OF SHADY VALLEY	1871	MARH'L MAP	1746
BLACKSMITH SHOP - ELDERS / WILLIAM - MOUNDSVILLE	1871	MDSVL BUS.	1796
BLACKSMITH SHOP - ELDERS / WILLIAM - MOUNDSVILLE	1871	MDSVILLE	1807
BLACKSMITH SHOP - ELM GROVE	1871	ELM GROVE	1782
BLACKSMITH SHOP - FAIRVIEW	1871	MARH'L MAP	1758
BLACKSMITH SHOP - FLANEGINS / W - NEW MANCHESTER	1871	NEW MANCH.	1769
BLACKSMITH SHOP - FOWLERS / JOHN - MAP#375	1852	BRKE MAP	1847
BLACKSMITH SHOP - FOWLERS / J	1871	FOWLERS P.O.	1775
BLACKSMITH SHOP - FOWLERS P.O.	1871	BRKE MAP	1735
BLACKSMITH SHOP - FOWLERS P.O.	1871	BRKE MAP	1737
BLACKSMITH SHOP - GREENE ST - CAMERON	1871	CAMERON	1803
BLACKSMITH SHOP - GROVES / S. - RICHLAND TWP	1871	RICHLD TWP-BUS.	1797
BLACKSMITH SHOP - HEDGES / MOSES - MAP#117	1852	BRKE MAP	1844
BLACKSMITH SHOP - HOLLIDAYS COVE	1871	HAN MAP	1733
BLACKSMITH SHOP - HOOTHS / H. - SHERRARD P.O.	1871	SHERRARD	1811
BLACKSMITH SHOP - HUSTERS / NATHANIEL - MAP#458	1852	BRKE MAP	1849
BLACKSMITH SHOP - HUTTON / J - WELLSBURG	1871	WELLSBURG	1778
BLACKSMITH SHOP - JONES / CHARLES	1852	NOT ON MAP	1836
BLACKSMITH SHOP - KIRKS / J. - WEST UNION	1871	W.UNION	1812
BLACKSMITH SHOP - KITTLES / S.G. & SON - 'GRINDSTAFFS RUN'	1871	SAND HILL-BUS.	1797
BLACKSMITH SHOP - KUHNS	1871	WELLSBURG	1777
BLACKSMITH SHOP - LEATHERWOOD	1871	TRIAD.TWP.	1781
BLACKSMITH SHOP - LOUDENSVILLE	1871	MARH'L MAP	1753
BLACKSMITH SHOP - LYCLICKS / WILLIAM	1871	MARH'L BUS.	1796
BLACKSMITH SHOP - LYNNCAMP P.O.	1871	MARH'L MAP	1755
BLACKSMITH SHOP - LYNNCAMP P.O. / NEAR P.KEMP	1871	MARH'L MAP	1759
BLACKSMITH SHOP - M. OF M. CROW	1871	MARH'L MAP	1752
BLACKSMITH SHOP - MAGGOTY RUN	1871	MARH'L MAP	1756
BLACKSMITH SHOP - MARTINS / W - BETHANY	1871	BETHANY	1773
BLACKSMITH SHOP - MCDANELLS / MRS. - FURNACE ST - WEST UNION	1871	W.UNION	1812
BLACKSMITH SHOP - MCDANELLS / MRS. - WEST UNION	1871	W.UNION	1812
BLACKSMITH SHOP - MCGLUMPHYS / A	1871	MARH'L MAP	1747
BLACKSMITH SHOP - MILLERS / J	1852	NOT ON MAP	1836
BLACKSMITH SHOP - N. OF G.R.PORTER	1871	FRE'MAN'S LDG	1764
BLACKSMITH SHOP - N. OF MRS. E. WEIDEMAN	1871	BKE/OH MAP	1739
BLACKSMITH SHOP - N. OF W. CONNELL	1871	MARH'L MAP	1752
BLACKSMITH SHOP - N.E. OF MOUNDSVILLE	1871	MARH'L MAP	1748
BLACKSMITH SHOP - NATIONAL RD	1871	WHG CITY	1787
BLACKSMITH SHOP - NATIONAL RD - NEAR JUDGE THOMPSON	1871	WHG CITY	1787
BLACKSMITH SHOP - NATIONAL ROAD - LEATHERWOOD	1871	WHG CITY	1789
BLACKSMITH SHOP - NE OF PAN-HANDLE P.O.	1871	BRKE MAP	1734
BLACKSMITH SHOP - NE OF S. GROVES	1871	BKE/OH MAP	1738
BLACKSMITH SHOP - NEAR CASTLE ROCK	1871	BRKE MAP	1734
BLACKSMITH SHOP - NEAR G. EDGINGTON	1871	W.LIBERTY	1780
BLACKSMITH SHOP - NEAR G.F.MCGLUMPHY	1871	MARH'L MAP	1761
BLACKSMITH SHOP - NEAR J.ALLISON	1871	HAN MAP	1727
BLACKSMITH SHOP - NEAR M.EDWARDS	1871	NEW CUMB'LD	1768
BLACKSMITH SHOP - NEAR MRS. MCCOLLOCH	1871	BKE/OH MAP	1738
BLACKSMITH SHOP - NEAR S.M.BELL	1871	MARH'L MAP	1761
BLACKSMITH SHOP - NEAR S.R.GARY - CAMERON	1871	CAMERON	1804
BLACKSMITH SHOP - NEAR SYCAMORE GROVE	1871	MARH'L MAP	1756
BLACKSMITH SHOP - NEW CUMBERLAND	1871	NEW CUMB'LD	1767
BLACKSMITH SHOP - OLD / INITIALS OLD B.S.S. - CROSS CREEK	1871	BRKE MAP	1735
BLACKSMITH SHOP - ORUMS / P	1871	MARH'L MAP	1746
BLACKSMITH SHOP - PAN-HANDLE P.O.	1871	BRKE MAP	1734
BLACKSMITH SHOP - PARKS / J	1871	MARH'L MAP	1753
BLACKSMITH SHOP - PETERS / R.S. - SHERRARD P.O.	1871	SHERRARD	1811
BLACKSMITH SHOP - PLEASANT VALLEY	1871	MARH'L MAP	1746
BLACKSMITH SHOP - PLEASANT VALLEY - OHIO CO	1871	OH CO. MAP	1742
BLACKSMITH SHOP - PLEASANT VALLEY P.O.	1871	MARH'L MAP	1749
BLACKSMITH SHOP - REEDS / J - NATL RD	1871	TRIAD.TWP.	1781
BLACKSMITH SHOP - ROBERTS / WILLIAM - HOLLIDAYS COVE	1871	HO'LIDAYS COVE	1762
BLACKSMITH SHOP - ROCK LICK P.O.	1871	MARH'L MAP	1753
BLACKSMITH SHOP - ROGERS / J	1871	MARH'L MAP	1747
BLACKSMITH SHOP - ROGERS / J - SAND HILL	1871	SAND HILL-BUS.	1797
BLACKSMITH SHOP - RONEY POINT STATION	1871	OH CO. MAP	1743
BLACKSMITH SHOP - RONEY POINT STATION	1871	OH CO. MAP	1744
BLACKSMITH SHOP - ROSBBYS ROCK	1871	ROSBBYS RK	1813
BLACKSMITH SHOP - S. OF BURCH VALLEY	1871	MARH'L MAP	1753
BLACKSMITH SHOP - S. OF COLD SPRING	1871	HAN MAP	1732
BLACKSMITH SHOP - S. OF F. MAJOR	1871	MARH'L MAP	1746
BLACKSMITH SHOP - S. OF F. MAJOR - WASH. TWP	1871	MARH'L MAP	1749
BLACKSMITH SHOP - S. OF H. PITTENGER	1871	HAN MAP	1731
BLACKSMITH SHOP - SE OF FULTON	1871	OH CO. MAP	1742
BLACKSMITH SHOP - SE OF G. ELLIOTT	1871	BKE/OH MAP	1739
BLACKSMITH SHOP - SEABRIGHTS / HENRY - RONEY POINT	1871	OH CO.BUS.	1779
BLACKSMITH SHOP - SEABRIGHTS / H - RONEY POINT	1871	RONEY PT	1783
BLACKSMITH SHOP - SHANLEY / W ?	1871	NEW CUMB'LD	1767
BLACKSMITH SHOP - SOUTH BRANCH OF CROSS CREEK	1871	OH CO. MAP	1741
BLACKSMITH SHOP - SW. OF J.YOHO	1871	MARH'L MAP	1758
BLACKSMITH SHOP - TRIADELPHIA	1871	TRIAD.BORO.	1784
BLACKSMITH SHOP - TRIADELPHIA	1871	TRIAD.BORO.	1784
BLACKSMITH SHOP - TRIADELPHIA / NEAR A.F.EBERLING	1871	TRIAD.BORO.	1784
BLACKSMITH SHOP - W. END OF VALLEY GROVE	1871	OH CO. MAP	1740
BLACKSMITH SHOP - W. OF JOHN W. MCCOLLOCH	1871	OH CO. MAP	1741
BLACKSMITH SHOP - WARNAKES / A	1871	OH CO. MAP	1741
BLACKSMITH SHOP - WAYMANS / F. & SON - NEAR FAIRVIEW	1871	FRKLN TWP-BUS.	1797
BLACKSMITH SHOP - WELLS / NATHANIEL - MAP#551	1852	BRKE MAP	1851
BLACKSMITH SHOP - WELLSBURG / NEAR E.H.MOORE	1871	WELLSBURG	1777
BLACKSMITH SHOP - WEST LIBERTY	1871	W.LIBERTY	1780
BLACKSMITH SHOP - WILSONS / DANIEL - LIMESTONE P.O.	1871	WASH.TWP-BUS.	1797

'PERSONAL TIME LINE' INDEX TO VOLUME 7 OF THE *OHIO COUNTY INDEX*

ENTRY	YEAR	SUBJECT	PAGE	ENTRY	YEAR	SUBJECT	PAGE
BLACKSMITH SHOP - WILSONS / DANIEL (?LIVING NEXT TO SHOP?) - LIMESTONE P.O.	1871	LIMESTONE	1805	BOENER, C F	1871	CAMER'N - BUS.	1795
				BOENER, C F / SHOE SHOP	1871	CAMERON	1803
				BOENER, C F / VINEYARD	1871	CAMERON	1803
BLACKSMITH SHOP - WOLFS / HORNBROOK BROTHERS	1871	MARH'L MAP	1754	BOERY, GEORGE	1784	APPENDIX	1874
				BOGGS RUN	1871	MARH'L MAP	1745
BLACKSMITH SHOP #1 - LIMESTONE	1871	MARH'L MAP	1749	BOGGS RUN	1871	LAGRANGE	1794
BLACKSMITH SHOP #2 - LIMESTONE	1871	MARH'L MAP	1749	BOGGS RUN - FERTILE VALLEY	1871	BENWO'D - BUS.	1795
BLAINE, DAVID H	1818	DEFENDANT	1638	BOGGS SCHOOL NO. _ / ELM GROVE DIST	1871	OH CO. MAP	1744
BLAIR	1871	DISTANCES	1815				
BLAIR P.O.	1871	HAN MAP	1731	BOGGS SCHOOL NO.? - ELM GROVE DIST	1871	OH CO. MAP	1742
BLAIR P.O.	1871	HAN MAP	1731				
BLAIR P.O. - CLAY TWP	1871	HAN-CLAY TWP	1763	BOGGS SCHOOL NO.10	1871	OH CO. MAP	1742
BLAIR, - / HOMESTEAD	1871	MARH'L MAP	1749	BOGGS, D B	1871	OH CO. MAP	1742
BLAIR, - / MRS (?MRS.E)?	1871	MDSVILLE	1808	BOGGS, EZECIAL	1789	DEFENDANT	1554
BLAIR, - / MRS (?E.?)	1871	MDSVILLE	1810	BOGGS, EZECIAL	1789	DEFENDANT	1647
BLAIR, A	1871	MARH'L MAP	1746	BOGGS, WILLIAM J	1871	OH CO. MAP	1742
BLAIR, E / MRS	1871	MDSVILLE	1808	BOILERS - BENWOOD IRON WORKS	1871	BENWOOD	1799
BLAIR, E / MRS	1871	MDSVILLE	1810	BOILERS - BENWOOD IRON WORKS	1871	BENWOOD	1799
BLAIR, J M / HOMESTEAD	1871	MARH'L MAP	1749	BOLE, MARGARET	1857	DEFENDANT	1586
BLAKE, - / EST	1871	MARH'L MAP	1748	BOLIVER CLAY / COAL, IRON ORE & BOLIVER CLAY	1871	FRE'MAN'S LDG	1765
BLAKE, G	1871	MARH'L MAP	1745				
BLAKE, H	1871	MARH'L MAP	1749	BOLLINGER, ANN	1860	DEFENDANT	1616
BLAKE, H	1871	MARH'L MAP	1749	BONAR, - / BONERS RUN / (?BONARS?)	1852	BRKE MAP	1840
BLAKE, J	1871	MARH'L MAP	1747	BONAR, A	1871	MARH'L MAP	1756
BLAKE, J	1871	MARH'L MAP	1750	BONAR, A / INITIALS A.B.	1871	MARH'L MAP	1756
BLAKE, J	1871	MARH'L MAP	1760	BONAR, A / INITIALS A.B.	1871	MARH'L MAP	1756
BLAKE, ROBERT	1832	MISC	1703	BONAR, A / INITIALS A.B.	1871	MARH'L MAP	1756
BLAKE, S	1871	MARH'L MAP	1760	BONAR, C	1871	MARH'L MAP	1757
BLAKE, T	1871	MARH'L MAP	1755	BONAR, DAVID	1839	PLAINTIFF	1600
BLAKE, W	1871	MDSVILLE	1807	BONAR, G D	1871	BKE/OH MAP	1738
BLAKE, W	1871	MDSVILLE	1807	BONAR, GEORGE	1871	BKE/OH MAP	1738
BLAKE, W	1871	MDSVILLE	1807	BONAR, GEORGE / INITIALS G.B.	1871	BKE/OH MAP	1738
BLAKE, W / INITIALS W.B.	1871	MDSVILLE	1807	BONAR, J	1871	MARH'L MAP	1752
BLAKE, W / REV	1871	MDSVILLE	1807	BONAR, J	1871	MARH'L MAP	1752
BLAKE, W / REV	1871	MDSVILLE	1807	BONAR, J	1871	MDSVILLE	1808
BLAKE, W / REV	1871	MDSVILLE	1807	BONAR, L / MRS	1871	MARH'L MAP	1752
BLAKEM J	1871	MARH'L MAP	1755	BONAR, M	1871	MARH'L MAP	1752
BLAKEMON, T	1871	MDSVILLE	1807	BONAR, M	1871	MARH'L MAP	1756
BLAKEMORE, B	1871	MDSVILLE	1807	BONAR, R / ? INITIALS R.B -NEAR OTHER BONARS	1871	BKE/OH MAP	1738
BLAKEWAY, HUMPHREY	1839	PLAINTIFF	1651				
BLANCHARD, I Z	1871	OH CO. MAP	1742	BONAR, R / ? INITIALS R.B -NEAR OTHER BONARS	1871	BKE/OH MAP	1738
BLANCHARD, I Z	1871	TRIAD TWP.	1781				
BLANEKNSOP, -	1871	WELLSBURG	1778	BONAR, W N	1871	MARH'L MAP	1756
BLANKENSOP, - / EVERETT & BLANKENSOP - FOUNDRY	1871	WELLSBURG	1777	BONAR,L / MRS	1871	MARH'L MAP	1755
				BONAR'S RUN	1871	MARH'L MAP	1752
BLANKENSOP, - / EVERETT & BLANKENSOPS HARDWARE	1871	WELLSBURG	1777	BOND, BENJAMIN	1797	DEFENDANT	1600
				BONDY, J / ?	1871	MARH'L MAP	1761
BLANKENSOP, G / EVERETT & G. BLANKENSOP	1871	BRKE MAP	1736	BONER, - / MRS	1871	MARH'L MAP	1755
				BONER, GEORGE / MAP#70	1852	BRKE MAP	1840
BLANKENSOP, J	1871	WELLSBURG	1777	BONER, J W	1871	MARH'L MAP	1755
BLANKENSOP, J / CHARLES ST	1871	WELLSBURG	1777	BONERS RUN / (?BONARS?)	1852	BRKE MAP	1840
BLANKENSOP, J / HRS-HEIRS (?INITIALS J.B. - BLANKENSHOP, J?) - NEAR QUEEN ST	1871	WELLSBURG	1777	BONHAM, JOHN L	1858	DEFENDANT	1615
				BONHAM, R C	1841	DEFENDANT	1643
				BONHAM, ROBERT	1857	DEFENDANT	1661
BLANKENSOP, J / HRS - HEIRS	1871	WELLSBURG	1778	BONHAM, ROBERT C	1840	DEFENDANT	1643
BLANKENSOP, P / CHARLES ST	1871	WELLSBURG	1777	BONHAM, ROBERT C	1857	DEFENDANT	1567
BLANKENSOPS, - / EVERETT & BLANKENSOPS	1871	WLSBRG BUS.	1772	BONHAM, ROBERT C	1857	DEFENDANT	1584
				BONHAM, ROBERT C	1857	DEFENDANT	1603
BLAYNEY, A	1871	OH CO. MAP	1740	BONHAM, ROBERT G	1843	DEFENDANT	1643
BLAYNEY, B	1871	OH CO. MAP	1743	BONHAMS RUN	1852	BRKE MAP	1852
BLAYNEY, B / INITIALS B.B.	1871	OH CO. MAP	1743	BONHAMS RUN	1871	BRKE MAP	1734
BLAYNEY, D M	1871	OH CO. MAP	1740	BONLY, J / ?	1871	MARH'L MAP	1761
BLAYNEY, DAVID M	1866	MISC	1683	BONNETT, LEWIS	1825	DEFENDANT	1646
BLAYNEY, E	1871	OH CO. MAP	1740	BONOR, JOHN	1798	DEFENDANT	1647
BLAYNEY, E / INITIALS E.B.	1871	OH CO. MAP	1740	BONOR, WILLIAM	1795	DEFENDANT	1572
BLAYNEY, J	1871	OH CO. MAP	1743	BONSELL, W G	1871	NEW CUMB'LD	1762
BLAYNEY, J	1871	OH CO. MAP	1743	BONSELL, W G / TAYLOR ST	1871	NEW CUMB'LD	1768
BLAYNEY, J / RES & STORE	1871	RONEY PT.	1783	BOOHER, -	1842	PLAINTIFF	1620
BLAYNEY, JOHN	1871	OH CO.BUS.	1779	BOOHER, J	1871	MARH'L MAP	1757
BLAYNEY, S F	1871	OH CO. MAP	1740	BOOHER, J	1871	CAMERON	1803
BLINCOE, M	1871	GLEN EASTON	1801	BOOHER, J / INITIALS J.B.	1871	CAMERON	1803
BLINCOE, MARK / 'CHARLES HOTEL' - GLEN EASTON	1871	GLEN EASTON - BUS.	1796	BOOHER, J / INITIALS J.B.	1871	CAMERON	1803
				BOOHER, J / INITIALS J.B.	1871	CAMERON	1803
BLOCKHOUSE RUN, OH	1852	BRKE MAP	1845	BOOKER, JOHN	1863	DEFENDANT	1615
BLOOM, V	1871	SHERRARD	1811	BOOKER, JOHN	1863	DEFENDANT	1633
BLOWING SPRING / NEAR OHIO RIVER	1871	BRKE MAP	1734	BOON, HUMPHREY	1835	MISC	1705
BLOYD, S L	1871	MDSVILLE	1807	BOON, HUNPHREY	1836	MISC	1705
BLUM, RICHARD	1858	DEFENDANT	1653	BOONE, H	1871	BKE/OH MAP	1738
BLY, DAVID	1880	DEFENDANT	1601	BOONE, H	1871	OH CO. MAP	1741
BOARD TREE RUN	1871	MARH'L MAP	1761	BOONE, HAMILTON	1858	DEFENDANT	1670
BOARD TREE TUNNEL - B&O RR	1871	MARH'L MAP	1761	BOONE, RICHARD	1811	DEFENDANT	1648
BOCKING, EDMUND	1859	DEFENDANT	1602	BOOTH - CHILDREN	1857	MISC	1679
BODLEY, JAMES	1879	DEFENDANT	1654	BOOTH, J	1871	MARH'L MAP	1755
BODLEY, JOSHUA	1871	RITCHIE TWP	1791	BOOTH, J A	1871	MARH'L MAP	1755
BODWELL, WILLIAM	1807	DEFENDANT	1644	BOOTH, J J	1871	MARH'L MAP	1755
BOEHER, - / MR ?	1871	HAN MAP	1728				

X

'PERSONAL TIME LINE' INDEX TO VOLUME 7 OF THE *OHIO COUNTY INDEX*

ENTRY	YEAR	SUBJECT	PAGE
BOOTH, J K / (?JOHN KENT?)	1871	MARH'L MAP	1758
BOOTH, R	1871	MARH'L MAP	1755
BOOTH, SUSANA JANE	1844	MISC	1679
BORAM, SARAH	1843	DEFENDANT	1584
BORGEDIN, -	1828	PLAINTIFF	1625
BORING, ELI / MAP#249	1852	BRKE MAP	1843
BORING, J	1871	BETHANY	1773
BORING, JOHN W	1856	DEFENDANT	1636
BORLAND, JOHN	1836	DEFENDANT	1579
BORLAND, JOHN	1836	MISC	1689
BORMSLEY, PETER	1799	DEFENDANT	1585
BOSHART, J	1871	MARH'L MAP	1759
BOSLEY, WILLIAM / HEIRS - MAP#489	1852	BRKE MAP	1849
BOSMANS BRANCH	1852	BRKE MAP	1843
BOSTLEY, ROBERT	1817	DEFENDANT	1611
BOSTWICH, SAMUEL W	1824	DEFENDANT	1668
BOSTWICK, SAMUEL W	1823	DEFENDANT	1668
BOTSFORD, -	1856	DEFENDANT	1641
BOTTOM FARM	1871	OH CO. MAP	1743
BOTTOM FARM	1871	OH CO. MAP	1744
BOTTS, ADOLPH	1878	DEFENDANT	1560
BOUING, JOHN W	1847	MISC	1674
BOUND IN - DEFINED	2000	APPENDIX	1875
BOUND OUT - DEFINED	2000	APPENDIX	1875
BOUND, A / (?BOUNDS?)	1871	MARH'L MAP	1746
BOUND, JOHN	1807	DEFENDANT	1589
BOUND, JOHN	1807	DEFENDANT	1610
BOUND, WILLIAM	1819	DEFENDANT	1624
BOUNDS, A / ? (?BOUND?)	1871	MARH'L MAP	1746
BOUNDS, JOHN	1806	DEFENDANT	1626
BOUNDS, JOHN	1806	DEFENDANT	1644
BOUNDS, WILLIAM	1807	DEFENDANT	1624
BOUNDS, WILLIAM	1810	APPENDIX	1873
BOUNDS, WILLIAM	1811	DEFENDANT	1599
BOWEN, WILLILAM L	1871	MARH'L MAP	1754
BOWERS, A	1871	CAMERON	1804
BOWERS, C / TINNER	1871	NEW CUMB'LD	1762
BOWERS, JACOB	1871	MDSVILLE	1809
BOWERS, JOHN	1852	DEFENDANT	1561
BOWERS, JOHN	1853	DEFENDANT	1561
BOWERS, N / MRS / W EDGE OF MAP	1871	BRKE MAP	1737
BOWMAN, - / MRS	1871	BRKE MAP	1736
BOWMAN, AB / HEIRS. - MAP#176	1852	BRKE MAP	1843
BOWMAN, E / MRS - RES.	1871	MARH'L MAP	1754
BOWMAN, J / MAP#173	1852	BRKE MAP	1843
BOWMAN, J / & S (MILL) - MAP#175	1852	BRKE MAP	1843
BOWMAN, J / (MILL) - MAP#175	1852	BRKE MAP	1843
BOWMAN, J / MAP#174	1852	BRKE MAP	1843
BOWMAN, J	1871	BRKE MAP	1736
BOWMAN, J / (?JOHN?) COAL BANK	1871	BRKE MAP	1736
BOWMAN, J / COAL BANK / (?JOHN?)	1871	BRKE MAP	1736
BOWMAN, JACOB	1828	DEFENDANT	1649
BOWMAN, JOHN / RES	1871	BRKE MAP	1736
BOWMAN, JOHN / COAL DEALER	1871	BUFF.TWP.BUS.	1772
BOWMAN, N	1871	WHG CITY	1790
BOWMAN, N	1871	WHG CITY	1790
BOWMAN, S / (MILL) - MAP#175	1852	BRKE MAP	1843
BOWMAN, S / MAP#173	1852	BRKE MAP	1843
BOWMAN, S / MAP#174	1852	BRKE MAP	1843
BOWMAN, WESLEY	1879	DEFENDANT	1578
BOWMAN, WILLIAM O	1871	BRKE MAP	1736
BOYD, C	1871	WELLSBURG	1777
BOYD, H	1871	MARH'L MAP	1746
BOYD, P	1871	HAN MAP	1732
BOYD, PRYOR	1877	DEFENDANT	1590
BOYD, PRYOR / & CO	1878	DEFENDANT	1564
BOYD, R	1871	BRKE MAP	1734
BOYD, R	1871	BRKE MAP	1735
BOYD, T	1871	BRKE MAP	1736
BOYERS, LENARD	1797	DEFENDANT	1647
BOYLES, THOMAS	1820	DEFENDANT	1624
BOYLES, THOMAS	1821	DEFENDANT	1624
BRACKSON, ROSS	1840	DEFENDANT	1662
BRADEN, SAMUEL	1877	DEFENDANT	1631
BRADFORD, DAVID	1789	DEFENDANT	1655
BRADFORD, DAVID	1790	DEFENDANT	1571
BRADLEY, BENJAMIN	1812	DEFENDANT	1648
BRADLEY, J	1871	NEW CUMB'LD	1768
BRADLEY, S	1839	DEFENDANT	1651
BRADLEY, T / HRS	1871	NEW CUMB'LD	1767
BRADLEY, W	1839	DEFENDANT	1651
BRADLEY, W H	1871	NEW CUMB'LD	1767
BRADSHAW, GEORGE	1809	DEFENDANT	1659
BRADY SCHOOL NO.8	1871	OH CO. MAP	1740
BRADY, B / B & W	1871	BRKE MAP	1735
BRADY, BERNARD / MAP#445	1852	BRKE MAP	1849
BRADY, BERNARD	1871	BRKE MAP	1735
BRADY, CHARLES	1824	DEFENDANT	1649
BRADY, D / OC	1871	BRKE MAP	1737
BRADY, D / ? UNSURE INITIALS	1871	OH CO. MAP	1740
BRADY, DAVID	1836	MISC	1705
BRADY, H Y / WESTMORELAND CO,PA	1852	HEMPFIELD RR	1817
BRADY, J	1871	BRKE MAP	1736
BRADY, J / INITIALS J.B.	1871	BRKE MAP	1736
BRADY, JOHN	1817	DEFENDANT	1659
BRADY, JOHN	1818	DEFENDANT	1659
BRADY, JOHN	1822	DEFENDANT	1624
BRADY, JOHN	1852	HEMPFIELD RR	1822
BRADY, JOHN / MAP#267	1852	BRKE MAP	1843
BRADY, JOHN / MAP#268	1852	BRKE MAP	1843
BRADY, JOHN / (GONE) - MAP#316	1852	BRKE MAP	1846
BRADY, JOHN / (GONE) - MAP#317	1852	BRKE MAP	1846
BRADY, JOHN / (GONE) - MAP#318	1852	BRKE MAP	1846
BRADY, JOHN	1871	BRKE MAP	1736
BRADY, JOHN / CUT OFF W. SIDE OF MAP	1871	BRKE MAP	1737
BRADY, JOHN / O	1871	BRKE MAP	1737
BRADY, W / B & W	1871	BRKE MAP	1735
BRADY, W S	1871	BRKE MAP	1737
BRADY, WALTER	1824	DEFENDANT	1649
BRADY, WILLIAM P / MAP#20	1852	BRKE MAP	1839
BRADY, WILLIAM P / MAP#77	1852	BRKE MAP	1839
BRAMHALL, JOHN	1834	DEFENDANT	1662
BRANCH OF GARDNERS RUN	1871	HAN MAP	1727
BRANCH OF LITTLE GRAVE CREEK	1871	MARH'L MAP	1748
BRANCH OF LITTLE GRAVE CREEK	1871	MARH'L MAP	1749
BRANCH OF LITTLE GRAVE CREEK / CUT OFF TOP OF MAP	1871	MARH'L MAP	1752
BRANCH OF LITTLE GRAVE CREEK	1871	MARH'L MAP	1753
BRANCH OF LITTLE MILL CREEK / ?	1871	HAN MAP	1728
BRAND, J N	1871	HAN MAP	1726
BRANDT, - / CAPTAIN	1916	NAT'L ROAD	1867
BRANSON, ISAIAH	1825	DEFENDANT	1668
BRANSON, ISAIAH	1829	DEFENDANT	1668
BRANSON, ISAIAH	1830	DEFENDANT	1669
BRANSON, ISIAH	1826	DEFENDANT	1668
BRANSTROOP - EARLIER WRITTEN AS BRANSTRUP	1871	TRIAD.BORO.	1784
BRANSTROOP - SEE ALSO BRANSTROUP OR BRANSTRUP	1871	TRIAD.BORO.	1784
BRANSTROUP, J	1871	TRIAD.BORO.	1784
BRANSTROUP, W	1871	TRIAD.BORO.	1784
BRANSTRUP - LATER WRITTEN AS BRANSTROOP	1871	TRIAD.BORO.	1784
BRANSTRUP, B / (?LISTED AS HUNSTRUP?)	1871	TRIAD.BORO.	1784
BRANSTRUP, B / (?LISTED AS HUNSTRUP?)	1871	TRIAD.BORO.	1785
BRANSTRUP, B / (?LISTED AS HUNSTRUP?)	1871	TRIAD.BORO.	1785
BRASHEAR, B C	1871	NEW CUMB'LD	1768
BRASHEAR, B C / INITIALS B.C.B	1871	NEW CUMB'LD	1768
BRASHEAR, C / DENTIST	1871	WELLSBURG	1778
BRATCKEY, GEORGE	1809	DEFENDANT	1659
BRAY, O C	1874	DEFENDANT	1631
BRENNEMAN, CC	1871	HAN MAP	1726
BRENNEMAN, CC / RES	1871	HAN MAP	1726
BRENNEMAN, J	1871	HAN MAP	1726
BRENNEMAN, R B	1871	HAN MAP	1726
BRENNEMAN, R B	1871	HAN MAP	1726
BRENNEMAN, R B / INITIALS R.B.B	1871	HAN MAP	1726
BRENTLINGER, F A	1874	DEFENDANT	1565
BRENTLINGER, F A	1875	DEFENDANT	1565
BRENTLINGER, JOSEPH	1836	DEFENDANT	1554
BRENTLINGER, SAMUEL	1836	DEFENDANT	1553
BRENTON, JOHN	1858	DEFENDANT	1603
BRIAN, D / MRS	1871	WELLSBURG	1777
BRIAN, S C	1871	NEW CUMB'LD	1768
BRIARLY, THOMAS	1871	NEW CUMB'LD	1767
BRICE, E	1871	HAN MAP	1732
BRICE, R	1871	HAN MAP	1732
BRICE, W	1871	HAN MAP	1732
BRICELAND, T	1871	BKE/OH MAP	1739
BRICELAND, THOMAS	1871	W.LIBRTY.BUS.	1780
BRICELAND, WILLIAM	1860	DEFENDANT	1588
BRICK HOUSE - S. OF PLEASANT HILL FARM	1871	MARH'L MAP	1745
BRICK KILN - BK KILN / (?BRICK?) TOMLINSON RUN	1871	HAN MAP	1727
BRICK YARD / ABBREVIATED YD ?	1871	HAN MAP	1730
BRICK YARD - BARCLAY, LLOYD & CO.	1871	WELLSBURG	1776
BRICK YARD - MORENS	1871	FRE'MAN'S LDG	1764

XI

'PERSONAL TIME LINE' INDEX TO VOLUME 7 OF THE OHIO COUNTY INDEX

ENTRY	YEAR	SUBJECT	PAGE
BRICK YARD - N. OF J.L.FREEMAN & CO	1871	FRE'MAN'S LDG	1764
BRICK YARD - WHEELING ISLAND	1871	WHG ISLAND	1788
BRIDGE	1841	MISC	1678
BRIDGE - CHARTIERS CREEK / WASH CO., PA	1916	NAT'L ROAD	1861
BRIDGE - ELM GROVE	1916	NAT'L ROAD	1865
BRIDGE - ELM GROVE - PHOTO	1916	NAT'L ROAD	1866
BRIDGE - IRON BRIDGE - OHIO RIVER - AT EDGINGTON STATION	1871	BRKE MAP	1734
BRIDGE - OHIO RIVER CHANEL BRIDGE - BALTIMORE & OHIO RR - AT BENWOOD / STONE & IRON	1871	BENWOOD	1799
BRIDGE - S. BRIDGE - E. SIDE OF ELM GROVE	1871	OH CO. MAP	1742
BRIDGE - STEEL BRIDGE - MAP	1916	NAT'L ROAD	1868
BRIDGE - SUSPENSION BRIDGE - WHEELING	1852	HEMP. RR MAP	1826
BRIDGE - SUSPENSION BRIDGE - WHEELING	1871	WHG CITY	1788
BRIDGE - WHEELING ISLAND TO BRIDGEPORT OHIO	1871	WHG ISLAND	1788
BRIDGEPORT, OH	1852	HEMP. RR MAP	1826
BRIDGEPORT, OH	1871	WHG CITY	1786
BRIDGEPORT, OH	1871	WHG ISLAND	1788
BRIDGEPORT, OH	1916	NAT'L ROAD	1867
BRIDGEPORT, WV / NEAR ELM GROVE	1871	OH CO. MAP	1742
BRIDGEPORT, WV / SE OF ELM GROVE	1871	OH CO. MAP	1744
BRIDLE RUN / (?BIDDLE?)	1871	OH CO. MAP	1740
BRIGG, J	1871	MARH'L MAP	1749
BRIGGS & CRAIG	1871	WELLSBURG	1777
BRIGGS, -	1871	WELLSBURG	1776
BRIGGS, - / MISS - WATER ST	1871	WELLSBURG	1777
BRIGGS, W / & BRO	1871	BRKE MAP	1736
BRIGGS, W / & BRO	1871	BRKE MAP	1736
BRIGGS, W / & BRO - OLD DYE HOUSE	1871	BRKE MAP	1736
BRIGGS, W / & BRO - WOOLEN FACTORY	1871	BRKE MAP	1736
BRIGGS, W / & BRO -FACTORY	1871	BRKE MAP	1736
BRIGGS, W / & BRO. WOOLEN HOUSE	1871	BRKE MAP	1736
BRIGGS, W J	1871	WELLSBURG	1776
BRINER, J	1871	MARH'L MAP	1756
BRINER, J	1871	MARH'L MAP	1760
BRINKMIRE, T	1871	MARH'L MAP	1759
BRINTON, JOHN	1860	DEFENDANT	1603
BRINTON, JOHN	1862	DEFENDANT	1603
BRITT, A H	1871	MISC	1690
BROADRICK, CONRAD	1857	DEFENDANT	1582
BRODIE, J M	1875	DEFENDANT	1576
BROGG, M	1871	BRKE MAP	1736
BROGG, M	1871	BKE/OH MAP	1738
BROMAN, V	1871	MDSVILLE	1807
BROMAN, V / INITIALS V.B.	1871	MDSVILLE	1807
BROMER, E	1871	OH CO. MAP	1742
BROMER, E / INITIAL E.B.	1871	OH CO. MAP	1742
BROMER, F	1871	RITCHIE TWP	1793
BROMER, F / INITIALS F.B.	1871	RITCHIE TWP	1793
BROMER, F / INITIALS F.B.	1871	RITCHIE TWP	1793
BRONSON, J	1871	HAN MAP	1727
BRONSON, J	1871	HAN MAP	1728
BROOKE CO	1871	POPULATION	1816
BROOKE CO - BUSINESS NOTICES	1871	BROOKE CO	1772
BROOKE CO - CLINTON	1871	DISTANCES	1815
BROOKE CO - CROSS CREEK TWP	1871	BRKE MAP	1734
BROOKE CO - N. BOUNDARY WITH HANCOCK CO	1852	BRKE MAP	1853
BROOKE CO - ON PANHANDLE MAP	1871	MAP	1713
BROOKE CO - S. BOUNDARY WITH OHIO CO	1852	BRKE MAP	1839
BROOKE CO - S. BOUNDARY WITH OHIO CO	1852	BRKE MAP	1840
BROOKE CO - TOWNSHIPS	1871	MAP	1719
BROOKE CO 1852 LANDOWNER MAP - INDEX TO 'CUT UP' MAP SECTIONS	1852	BRKE MAP	1837
BROOKE CO 1852 LANDOWNER MAP - INDEX TO 'MISSING' NAMES ON MAP	1852	BRKE MAP	1836
BROOKE CO 1852 LANDOWNER MAP - MAP TITLE BLOCK	1852	BRKE MAP	1838
BROOKE CO 1852 LANDOWNER MAP - N. HALF OVERVIEW / SEE DETAIL SECTIONAL MAPS	1852	BRKE MAP	1829
BROOKE CO 1852 LANDOWNER MAP - NUMBERICAL INDEX TO MAP NUMBERS	1852	BRKE MAP	1830
BROOKE CO 1852 LANDOWNER MAP - S. HALF OVERVIEW / SEE DETAIL SECTIONAL MAPS	1852	BRKE MAP	1828
BROOKE CO GENEALOGICAL SOCIETY	2000	PREFACE	1748
BROOKE CO LINE	1871	HAN MAP	1733
BROOKLIN MILLS	1871	HAN-GR'NT TWP	1763
BROOKLYN MILLS	1871	HAN MAP	1726
BROOKLYN SCHOOL NO. 3	1871	HAN MAP	1726
BROOKS, FRANKLIN H	1841	DEFENDANT	1646
BROOKS, JOHN	1818	PLAINTIFF	1595
BROOKS, JOHN	1839	DEFENDANT	1551
BROOKSIDE	1871	HAN MAP	1726
BROOKSIDE	1871	OH CO. MAP	1743
BROOKSIDE	1871	OH CO. MAP	1744
BROOM FACTORY - SAMUEL STRONG & SONS	1871	BRKE MAP	1735
BROOM MAKING SHOP - RIVER ROAD	1871	BKE/OH MAP	1738
BROTHERS, -	1863	PLAINTIFF	1632
BROTHERTON, JOHN	1845	DEFENDANT	1567
BROTHERTON, JOHN	1855	DEFENDANT	1596
BROW, F W	1871	MDSVILLE	1807
BROWN J W	1871	OH CO. MAP	1741
BROWN, -	1839	PLAINTIFF	1625
BROWN, - / HEIRS	1871	MARH'L MAP	1746
BROWN, -	1871	BETHANY	1773
BROWN, -	1871	WELLSBURG	1777
BROWN, - / MRS	1871	TRIAD.BORO.	1784
BROWN, - / WEBSTER, BROWN & CO / 'MOUND CITY FLOUR MILL'	1871	MDSVL BUS.	1796
BROWN, - / WEBSTER, BROWN & CO	1871	MDSVILLE	1808
BROWN, - / WEBSTER, BROWN & CO	1871	MDSVILLE	1810
BROWN, - / HRS - HEIRS	1871	SHERRARD	1811
BROWN, A	1871	MDSVILLE	1807
BROWN, ALEX	1818	DEFENDANT	1596
BROWN, C	1871	HAN MAP	1726
BROWN, D / MAP#349	1852	BRKE MAP	1842
BROWN, D / MAP#349	1852	BRKE MAP	1842
BROWN, D / (MILL) - MAP#352	1852	BRKE MAP	1846
BROWN, D / (MILL) - MAP#352	1852	BRKE MAP	1846
BROWN, D / (MILL) - MAP#352	1852	BRKE MAP	1846
BROWN, D / MAP#349	1852	BRKE MAP	1846
BROWN, D L	1871	WELLSBURG	1777
BROWN, DANFORTH SR / MAP#282	1852	BRKE MAP	1846
BROWN, DANIEL	1802	DEFENDANT	1556
BROWN, GEORGE	1871	HAN MAP	1726
BROWN, J / MAP#274	1852	BRKE MAP	1842
BROWN, J / MAP#275	1852	BRKE MAP	1842
BROWN, J / (MILL) - MAP#350	1852	BRKE MAP	1846
BROWN, J / (MILL) - MAP#351	1852	BRKE MAP	1846
BROWN, J / (MILL) - MAP#352	1852	BRKE MAP	1846
BROWN, J / MAP#278	1852	BRKE MAP	1846
BROWN, J / MAP#349	1852	BRKE MAP	1846
BROWN, J	1871	HAN MAP	1732
BROWN, J / REV	1871	W.LIBERTY	1780
BROWN, J / STORE	1871	BENWOOD	1798
BROWN, J M	1871	MARH'L MAP	1745
BROWN, J N	1871	HAN MAP	1726
BROWN, J N / INITIALS J.N.B.	1871	HAN MAP	1726
BROWN, J N / RES	1871	HAN MAP	1726
BROWN, J W	1871	OH CO. MAP	1742
BROWN, J W	1871	TRIAD.BORO.	1784
BROWN, J W	1871	TRIAD.BORO.	1784
BROWN, JACOB	1831	DEFENDANT	1639
BROWN, JAMES	1808	DEFENDANT	1556
BROWN, JAMES	1814	DEFENDANT	1556
BROWN, JAMES	1821	PLAINTIFF	1646
BROWN, JAMES W	1871	HAN MAP	1731
BROWN, JAMES W	1871	HAN MAP	1732
BROWN, JOSEPH / MAP#114	1852	BRKE MAP	1840
BROWN, JOSEPH / MAP#55	1852	BRKE MAP	1840
BROWN, JOSEPH / MAP#56	1852	BRKE MAP	1840
BROWN, JOSEPH / MAP#113	1852	BRKE MAP	1844
BROWN, JOSIAH	1858	MISC	1694
BROWN, L / CUT OFF W. SIDE OF MAP	1871	MARH'L MAP	1746
BROWN, L	1871	WELLSBURG	1777
BROWN, M / MRS - INITIALS MRS. M.B.	1871	OH CO. MAP	1742
BROWN, M / MRS - SAW MILL ? - PETERS RUN	1871	OH CO. MAP	1742
BROWN, M / MRS - RES - PETERS RUN	1871	OH CO. MAP	1744
BROWN, M / MRS - SAW MILL & DAM ON PETERS RUN	1871	OH CO. MAP	1744
BROWN, MATTHEW	1822	DEFENDANT	1602
BROWN, R	1871	HAN MAP	1731
BROWN, R	1871	MARH'L MAP	1750

XII

'PERSONAL TIME LINE' INDEX TO VOLUME 7 OF THE *OHIO COUNTY INDEX*

ENTRY	YEAR	SUBJECT	PAGE
BROWN, R	1871	MARH'L MAP	1753
BROWN, R H / (O.C.)	1871	HAN MAP	1726
BROWN, ROBERT	1820	DEFENDANT	1572
BROWN, T	1871	MARH'L MAP	1750
BROWN, T	1871	MARH'L MAP	1752
BROWN, T	1871	MARH'L MAP	1753
BROWN, W / RES	1871	HAN MAP	1733
BROWN, W / INITIALS W.B.	1871	HAN MAP	1733
BROWN, W / INITIALS W.B.	1871	HAN MAP	1733
BROWN, W	1871	BRKE MAP	1734
BROWN, W	1871	MARH'L MAP	1750
BROWN, W / DEALER GENERAL MERCHANDISE	1871	HO'LIDAYS COVE	1762
BROWN, W	1871	BENWOOD	1798
BROWN, WILLIAM	1809	PLAINTIFF	1642
BROWN, WILLIAM	1850	DEFENDANT	1608
BROWN, WILLIAM	1851	DEFENDANT	1565
BROWN, WILLIAM	1852	DEFENDANT	1588
BROWN, WILLIAM / STORE	1871	HAN MAP	1733
BROWNING, CLINTON	1875	DEFENDANT	1578
BROWNING, L / (?LEWIS?)	1871	BRKE MAP	1734
BROWNING, LEWIS / MAP#512	1852	BRKE MAP	1849
BROWNING, LEWIS / MAP#514	1852	BRKE MAP	1851
BROWNING, LEWIS / MAP#516	1852	BRKE MAP	1851
BROWNING, LEWIS	1871	BRKE MAP	1734
BROWNING, LEWIS	1871	BRKE MAP	1735
BROWNLEE SCHOOL DIST	1871	OH CO. MAP	1743
BROWNLEE SCHOOL NO. 1	1871	OH CO. MAP	1743
BROWNLEE, J	1871	OH CO. MAP	1743
BROWNLEE, J / INITIALS J.B.	1871	OH CO. MAP	1743
BROWNLEE, J / RES	1871	OH CO. MAP	1743
BROWNS ISLAND	1871	HAN MAP	1732
BROWNS ISLAND - OHIO RIVER	1852	BRKE MAP	1853
BROWNS RUN	1871	OH CO. MAP	1741
BROWNS RUN	1871	OH CO. MAP	1742
BROWNS RUN / NE OF BENWOOD	1871	MARH'L MAP	1745
BROWNSVILLE, PA	1852	HEMP. RR MAP	1826
BRUCE, G W / PHYSICIAN	1871	MDSVL BUS.	1796
BRUCE, G W / DR	1871	MDSVILLE	1806
BRUCE, G W / DR - INITIALS DR.G.BRUCE	1871	MDSVILLE	1806
BRUCE, G W / DR - INITIALS DR.G.W.BRUCE	1871	MDSVILLE	1806
BRUCE, G W / DR	1871	MDSVILLE	1808
BRUCE, G W / DR	1871	MDSVILLE	1808
BRUCE, G W / DR	1871	MDSVILLE	1808
BRUCE, G W / DR - INITIALS DR.G.W.B	1871	MDSVILLE	1808
BRUCE, G W / DR - INITIALS DR.G.W.B	1871	MDSVILLE	1808
BRUCE, G W / DR - INITIALS DR.G.W.B	1871	MDSVILLE	1808
BRUCE, G W / DR - OFFICE	1871	MDSVILLE	1808
BRUCE, ROBERT / AUTHOR - THE NATIONAL ROAD	1916	NAT'L ROAD	1861
BRUEL, LENARD	1840	DEFENDANT	1662
BRUHN, JOHN	1871	MARH'L MAP	1756
BRUHN, JOHN / INITIALS J.B.	1871	MARH'L MAP	1756
BRUICES RUN	1871	MARH'L MAP	1747
BRUNEL, -	1861	PLAINTIFF	1631
BRUNELL, -	1862	PLAINTIFF	1631
BRUNER, J W	1871	OH CO. MAP	1741
BRUNER, J W / INITIALS J.W.B.	1871	OH CO. MAP	1741
BRUNER, JACOB	1840	PLAINTIFF	1670
BRYAN BREWEN FARM	1871	MARH'L MAP	1751
BRYAN BREWEN FARM	1871	MARH'L MAP	1755
BRYAN, J C	1839	DEFENDANT	1672
BRYANS, W	1871	MDSVILLE	1808
BRYSON, I	1871	MDSVILLE	1807
BRYSON, I	1871	MDSVILLE	1807
BRYSON, I	1871	MDSVILLE	1807
BRYSON, I / INITIALS I.B.	1871	MDSVILLE	1807
BRYSON, L	1871	MARH'L MAP	1745
BRYSON, L	1871	MARH'L MAP	1748
BUCHANAN, A M	1871	BRKE MAP	1737
BUCHANAN, A M / INITIALS A.M.B.	1871	BRKE MAP	1737
BUCHANAN, A M / INITIALS A.M.B.	1871	BRKE MAP	1737
BUCHANAN, E	1871	NEW MANCH.	1769
BUCHANAN, ELIZABETH	1855	MISC	1684
BUCHANAN, GEORGE A	1837	DEFENDANT	1662
BUCHANAN, H	1871	OH CO. MAP	1743
BUCHANAN, J	1871	OH CO. MAP	1743
BUCHANAN, J	1871	OH CO. MAP	1743
BUCHANAN, J	1871	MARH'L MAP	1747
BUCHANAN, J	1871	MARH'L MAP	1747
BUCHANAN, JAMES R	1847	DEFENDANT	1670
BUCHANAN, JAMES R	1847	DEFENDANT	1670
BUCHANAN, JOHNATHAN	1852	NOT ON MAP	1836
BUCHANAN, JONATHAN / MAP#120	1852	BRKE MAP	1844

ENTRY	YEAR	SUBJECT	PAGE
BUCHANAN, JONATHAN / MAP#121	1852	BRKE MAP	1844
BUCHANAN, JOSEPH	1848	DEFENDANT	1620
BUCHANAN, JOSEPH	1848	DEFENDANT	1641
BUCHANAN, M / NEAR BLACKSMITH SHOP	1871	LIMESTONE	1805
BUCHANAN, MARY	1871	MARH'L MAP	1749
BUCHANAN, R	1871	MARH'L MAP	1746
BUCHANAN, R E	1871	BKE/OH MAP	1739
BUCHANAN, R S	1871	MARH'L MAP	1747
BUCHANAN, S	1871	OH CO. MAP	1740
BUCHANAN, S	1871	OH CO. MAP	1743
BUCHANAN, S / GRIST MILL ON MIDDLE WHEELING CREEK	1871	OH CO. MAP	1743
BUCHANAN, S / RES	1871	OH CO. MAP	1743
BUCHANAN, T	1871	BRKE MAP	1737
BUCHANAN, T / INITILAS T.B.	1871	BRKE MAP	1737
BUCHANAN, THOMAS / MAP#188	1852	BRKE MAP	1844
BUCHANAN, WILLIAM	1784	APPENDIX	1874
BUCHANAN, WILLIAM	1871	MARH'L MAP	1747
BUCHANAN,T / RES	1871	BRKE MAP	1737
BUCHANNAN, J	1871	HAN MAP	1732
BUCHANON, ALEXANDER	1834	DEFENDANT	1650
BUCHANON, EBENEZER	1813	MISC	1674
BUCHANON, SAMUEL	1811	DEFENDANT	1578
BUCHANON, THOMAS	1877	DEFENDANT	1661
BUCKANAN, JAMES R	1851	DEFENDANT	1663
BUCKEY, JEMIMA	1778	APPENDIX	1874
BUCKEY, JOHN	1778	APPENDIX	1874
BUCKEY, JOHN	1810	APPENDIX	1873
BUCKEY, JOHN / MAP#363	1852	BRKE MAP	1847
BUCKEY, JOHN / COAL BANK - INITIALS J.B.'S COALBANK	1871	BRKE MAP	1735
BUCKEY, JOHN / COAL BANK	1871	BRKE MAP	1737
BUCKEY, JOHN / EMINENCE	1871	BRKE MAP	1737
BUCKEYS RUN	1852	BRKE MAP	1847
BUCKEYS RUN	1871	BRKE MAP	1735
BUCKEYS RUN	1871	BRKE MAP	1737
BUFFALO CREEK / HUMPHREYS LAND	1784	APPENDIX	1874
BUFFALO CREEK	1852	BRKE MAP	1843
BUFFALO CREEK	1871	BRKE MAP	1736
BUFFALO CREEK	1871	BRKE MAP	1737
BUFFALO CREEK	1871	BKE/OH MAP	1739
BUFFALO CREEK - AT BETHANY	1852	BRKE MAP	1844
BUFFALO CREEK - AT BETHANY	1871	BETHANY	1773
BUFFALO CREEK - BRIDGE OVER - WASH. CO., PA.	1916	NAT'L ROAD	1861
BUFFALO CREEK - CLARK BRIDGE - WASH. CO., PA.	1916	NAT'L ROAD	1862
BUFFALO CREEK - MOUTH OF / WELLSBURG	1871	WELLSBURG	1778
BUFFALO CREEK - MOUTH OF AT OHIO RIVER	1852	BRKE MAP	1846
BUFFALO CREEK - S BRIDGE - WASH.CO., PA.	1916	NAT'L ROAD	1863
BUFFALO CREEK - SAW MILL - S.M.	1871	BRKE MAP	1736
BUFFALO TOWNSHIP	1871	WELLSBURG	1778
BUFFALO TOWNSHIP - BETHANY - DETAIL MAP	1871	BETHANY	1773
BUFFALO TOWNSHIP - BROOKE CO	1871	BRKE MAP	1736
BUFFALO TOWNSHIP - BROOKE CO	1871	WELLSBURG	1777
BUFFALO TOWNSHIP - BROOKE CO	1871	POPULATION	1816
BUFFALO TOWNSHIP - BROOKE CO - BUSINESS NOTICES	1871	BUFFALO TWP	1772
BUFFALO TOWNSHIP - BROOKE CO. / E. PART	1871	BRKE MAP	1737
BUFFALO, NY	1916	NAT'L ROAD	1868
BUFFINGTON, - / MRS	1871	MDSVILLE	1806
BUFFINGTON, - / MRS	1871	MDSVILLE	1807
BUFFINGTON, - / MRS - INITIALS MRS.B.	1871	MDSVILLE	1807
BUFFINGTON, - / MRS	1871	MDSVILLE	1809
BUFFINGTON, A R	1871	MDSVILLE	1806
BUFFINGTON, A R	1871	MDSVILLE	1809
BUILDING SITES - ORRS / N	1871	BRKE MAP	1734
BUKEY, - / HEIRS	1824	DEFENDANT	1579
BUKEY, ANA	1827	DEFENDANT	1579
BUKEY, JOHN	1798	PLAINTIFF	1572
BUKEY, WILLIAM	1843	DEFENDANT	1663
BUMGARDNER, H	1871	MARH'L MAP	1745
BUMGARDNER, J	1871	MARH'L MAP	1745
BUNGARD, B	1871	MARH'L MAP	1753
BUNGARD, J / INITIALS J.B.	1871	MARH'L MAP	1750
BUNGARD, J / RES	1871	MARH'L MAP	1750
BUNTING, A	1871	HAN MAP	1726
BUNTING, S	1871	HAN MAP	1726
BUNTINS, A	1871	HAN MAP	1726

'PERSONAL TIME LINE' INDEX TO VOLUME 7 OF THE OHIO COUNTY INDEX

ENTRY	YEAR	SUBJECT	PAGE	ENTRY	YEAR	SUBJECT	PAGE
BURCH VALLEY	1871	MARH'L MAP	1753	BURT, E	1871	OH CO. MAP	1741
BURCH, - / MRS	1871	MDSVILLE	1808	BURT, ISAAC	1840	DEFENDANT	1652
BURCH, JESSE	1784	APPENDIX	1874	BURT, M / HRS -HEIRS	1871	WELLSBURG	1778
BURCH, JESSE	1827	DEFENDANT	1585	BURT, M / MRS	1871	WELLSBURG	1778
BURCH, R T	1871	MARH'L MAP	1758	BURT, NANCY	1820	DEFENDANT	1561
BURCH, R T / INITIALS R.T.B.	1871	MARH'L MAP	1758	BURTON, H / ? - N. OF NEW LEXINGTON	1871	HAN MAP	1730
BURCH, R T / INITIALS R.T.B.	1871	MARH'L MAP	1758				
BURCH, R T / INITIALS R.T.B.	1871	MARH'L MAP	1758	BURTON, H	1871	MARH'L MAP	1754
BURCHES RUN	1871	MARH'L MAP	1749	BURTON, H	1871	MARH'L MAP	1754
BURCHES RUN	1871	MARH'L MAP	1753	BURTON, R J	1871	MARH'L MAP	1755
BURDICK, HENRY	1835	DEFENDANT	1650	BURTON, WILLIAM	1814	DEFENDANT	1635
BURGE, GEORGE	1821	DEFENDANT	1660	BURWINKTZ, -	1871	BENWOOD	1798
BURGE, W	1871	MARH'L MAP	1759	BUSBEY, W	1871	BKE/OH MAP	1738
BURGES, WILLIAM	1808	APPENDIX	1645	BUSHFIELD, - / HEIRS	1871	BENWOOD	1799
BURGESS, W	1871	MARH'L MAP	1749	BUSHFIELD, HOMER A	1863	DEFENDANT	1632
BURGOYNE, J R	1871	BRKE MAP	1735	BUSHFIELD, SAMUEL B	1856	DEFENDANT	1594
BURGOYNE, J R / LIMESTONE QUARRY	1871	BRKE MAP	1735	BUSHFIELD, SAMUEL B	1861	DEFENDANT	1597
				BUSHFIELD, W	1871	OH CO. MAP	1740
BURGOYNE, J R / INITIALS J.R.B.	1871	BRKE MAP	1735	BUSINESS NOTICES - HANCOCK CO	1871	HAN BUS	1762
BURGOYNE, J R / ORCHARD	1871	BRKE MAP	1735	BUSINESS NOTICES - MARSHALL CO	1871	MARH'L BUS.	1796
BURGOYNE, JOSHUA / MAP#485	1852	BRKE MAP	1849	BUSINESS NOTICES ON 18571 MAP - SEE TOWN NAME	1871	MARH'L BUS.	1795
BURGRAFF, -	1856	PLAINTIFF	1630				
BURK, J	1871	BRKE MAP	1734	BUSKIRK, LAWRENCE	1784	DEFENDANT	1554
BURKAM, ISAAC G	1873	DEFENDANT	1609	BUTLER TOWNSHIP - HANCOCK - BUSINESS LISTINGS	1871	HAN-BUTL'R TWP	1763
BURKE, M	1871	MARH'L MAP	1752				
BURKETT, E	1853	DEFENDANT	1594	BUTLER TOWNSHIP - HANCOCK CO	1871	FRE'MAN'S LDG	1764
BURKETT, JACOB	1810	APPENDIX	1873	BUTLER TOWNSHIP - HANCOCK CO	1871	FRE'MAN'S LDG	1765
BURKHAM, ISAAC	1842	DEFENDANT	1577	BUTLER TOWNSHIP - HANCOCK CO.	1871	POPULATION	1816
BURLEIGH, P M	1871	MARH'L MAP	1761	BUTLER TOWNSHIP - HANCOCK CO.	1871	HAN MAP	1732
BURLEIGH, P M	1871	MARH'L MAP	1761	BUTLER TOWNSHIP - HANCOCK CO.	1871	HAN MAP	1733
BURLEY, D	1871	CAMERON	1803	BUTLER, J	1871	BRKE MAP	1734
BURLEY, J / ? (?INITIALS J.B.?)	1871	MARH'L MAP	1748	BUTLER, JAMES	1876	DEFENDANT	1590
BURLEY, J / ? (?INITIALS J.B.?)	1871	MARH'L MAP	1748	BUTLER, JOHN	1798	DEFENDANT	1634
BURLEY, J / EST	1871	MARH'L MAP	1748	BUTLER, JOHN	1800	DEFENDANT	1665
BURLEY, J / HEIRS	1871	MARH'L MAP	1748	BUTLER, WILLIAM / KILLED ACCIDENTLY APRIL 1ST, 1855	1871	MARH'L MAP	1753
BURLEY, J / HEIRS - INITIALS J.B. HEIRS	1871	MARH'L MAP	1748				
				BUTT, JACOB	1850	DEFENDANT	1573
BURLEY, J / EST	1871	MARH'L MAP	1751	BUTTER RUN / AT OHIO RIVER	1871	MARH'L MAP	1748
BURLEY, J / INITIALS J.B.	1871	MARH'L MAP	1753	BUTTER RUN / MOUTH AT OHIO RIVER	1871	MARH'L MAP	1751
BURLEY, J / INITIALS J.B.	1871	MARH'L MAP	1753	BUZZARD, D	1871	MARH'L MAP	1753
BURLEY, J / RES	1871	MARH'L MAP	1753	BUZZARD, D	1871	MARH'L MAP	1757
BURLEY, J F / INTIALS J.F.B.	1871	MARH'L MAP	1745	BUZZARD, T	1871	MARH'L MAP	1753
BURLEY, J F	1871	MARH'L MAP	1748	BUZZARD, T	1871	MARH'L MAP	1757
BURLEY, J F / INITIALS J.F.B	1871	MARH'L MAP	1748	BYARRS, J	1871	MARH'L MAP	1754
BURLEY, L	1871	MARH'L MAP	1750	BYRNE, PATRICK	1875	DEFENDANT	1578
BURLEY, L	1871	MARH'L MAP	1757	BYRNE, PATRICK	1875	DEFENDANT	1627
BURNING WELL	1871	HAN MAP	1730	BYRNES, THOMAS	1879	MISC	1689
BURNING WELL / AT DEEP GUT RUN	1871	RIV. RD N.OF N.C.	1770	C, - / J.R.C. (?CUNNINGHAM, JOHN R?)	1871	HAN MAP	1727
BURNS, -	1861	DEFENDANT	1569	C, - / J.R.C. (?CUNNINGHAM, JOHN R?)	1871	HAN MAP	1727
BURNS, A	1871	MARH'L MAP	1746	C, - / J.R.C. (?CUNNINGHAM, JOHN R?)	1871	HAN MAP	1727
BURNS, C	1871	MARH'L MAP	1746	C, B / NURSERY / UNKNOWN INITIALS	1871	MARH'L MAP	1748
BURNS, DENNY	1841	MISC	1707	C, M / UNKNOWN INITIALS	1871	OH CO. MAP	1742
BURNS, G W	1871	CAMERON	1804	C, R B / R.B.C UNKNOWN INITIALS	1871	MARH'L MAP	1748
BURNS, J R / MRS	1871	NEW MANCH.	1763	C.H. / ABBREV. FOR CUSTOM HOUSE	1871	WHG CITY	1788
BURNS, J R / INITIALS J.R.B. - LOT #77 (?MRS.?)	1871	NEW MANCH.	1769	C.W. / C ST - UNKNOWN INITIALS	1871	MDSVILLE	1809
				CABINET SHOP / SW OF J. BROWNLEE	1871	OH CO. MAP	1743
BURNS, J R / INITIALS J.R.B. - LOT #78 (?MRS.?)	1871	NEW MANCH.	1769				
				CABINS - NE OF J. HARGRAVES	1871	OH CO. MAP	1742
BURNS, J R / INITIALS J.R.B. - LOT#34 (?MRS.?)	1871	NEW MANCH.	1769	CABLE, ANDREW	1840	DEFENDANT	1643
				CABLE, W T	1871	HAN MAP	1732
BURNS, J R / MRS - PROPRIETER - MANCHESTER HOUSE / HOTEL	1871	NEW MANCH.	1769	CAHILL, WILLIAM	1840	DEFENDANT	1643
				CAIDZ, OH	1852	HEMP. RR MAP	1826
BURNS, JAMES	1818	DEFENDANT	1572	CAIN, - / MRS	1871	NEW MANCH.	1769
BURNS, JOHN	1874	DEFENDANT	1627	CAIN, EDWARD	1878	DEFENDANT	1623
BURNS, WILLIAM	1825	DEFENDANT	1604	CAIN, M	1871	NEW MANCH.	1763
BURNSIDE, WILLIAM	1839	DEFENDANT	1625	CAIN, M	1871	NEW MANCH.	1769
BURR, CHRISTOPHER	1805	DEFENDANT	1556	CAIN, M / STORE	1871	NEW MANCH.	1769
BURR, MARY / MRS - BENWOOD HOTEL	1871	BENWO'D - BUS.	1795	CAIN, RICHARD	1810	PLAINTIFF	1645
				CAINS RUN / (?CANES?)	1852	BRKE MAP	1842
BURR, MARY / INITIALS M.B.	1871	BENWOOD	1798	CAIRNES RUN	1852	BRKE MAP	1852
BURR, MARY / MRS - ABBREV. M.BURR	1871	BENWOOD	1798	CAIRNS, JAMES / MAP#644	1852	BRKE MAP	1851
BURRESS, - / MRS	1871	MARH'L MAP	1745	CAIRNS, JAMES / MAP#645	1852	BRKE MAP	1851
BURRIS, DANIEL	1838	DEFENDANT	1580	CAIRNS, MARY / HEIRS - MAP#560	1852	BRKE MAP	1852
BURRIS, ELIJAH	1822	DEFENDANT	1559	CAIRNS, MARY / MAP#612	1852	BRKE MAP	1852
BURRIS, ELIJAH	1823	DEFENDANT	1612	CAIRNS, SARAH / MAP#536	1852	BRKE MAP	1852
BURRIS, ELIJAH	1824	DEFENDANT	1559	CALDWELL, -	1798	PLAINTIFF	1607
BURRIS, ELIJAH	1825	DEFENDANT	1612	CALDWELL, -	1799	PLAINTIFF	1607
BURRIS, ELIJAH	1833	DEFENDANT	1620	CALDWELL, -	1802	PLAINTIFF	1607
BURRIS, ELIJAH	1833	DEFENDANT	1622	CALDWELL, -	1803	PLAINTIFF	1607
BURRIS, ELIJAH	1834	DEFENDANT	1620	CALDWELL, -	1804	PLAINTIFF	1628
BURRIS, ELIJAH	1834	DEFENDANT	1622	CALDWELL, -	1805	PLAINTIFF	1607
BURRIS, JOHN	1859	DEFENDANT	1672	CALDWELL, -	1806	PLAINTIFF	1607
BURROW, J / SAW MILL	1871	MARH'L MAP	1746	CALDWELL, - / MRS	1871	OH CO. MAP	1741
BURROWS, J / SAW MILL - MIDDLE WHEELING CREEK	1871	OH CO. MAP	1743	CALDWELL, - / EST	1871	OH CO. MAP	1742
				CALDWELL, - / MRS	1871	OH CO. MAP	1742
BURRY, J	1871	MARH'L MAP	1745	CALDWELL, - / MRS	1871	MARH'L MAP	1745

XIV

'PERSONAL TIME LINE' INDEX TO VOLUME 7 OF THE *OHIO COUNTY INDEX*

ENTRY	YEAR	SUBJECT	PAGE
CALDWELL, - / OAK HALL	1871	WHG CITY	1790
CALDWELL, - / EST	1871	RITCHIE TWP	1791
CALDWELL, - / EST	1871	RITCHIE TWP	1791
CALDWELL, - / OAK HALL	1871	WHG CITY	1792
CALDWELL, - / EST	1871	RITCHIE TWP	1793
CALDWELL, - / EST	1871	RITCHIE TWP	1793
CALDWELL, A	1846	MISC	1706
CALDWELL, A	1871	BRKE MAP	1734
CALDWELL, A	1871	BRKE MAP	1734
CALDWELL, A H	1871	OH CO. MAP	1740
CALDWELL, ALEXANDER	1805	MISC	1693
CALDWELL, ALEXANDER	1808	DEFENDANT	1635
CALDWELL, ALEXANDER	1823	DEFENDANT	1594
CALDWELL, ALEXANDER	1837	DEFENDANT	1594
CALDWELL, ALF	1844	DEFENDANT	1663
CALDWELL, ALFRED	1842	DEFENDANT	1640
CALDWELL, ALFRED	1846	DEFENDANT	1640
CALDWELL, ANNIE	1873	DEFENDANT	1671
CALDWELL, ANNIE	1874	DEFENDANT	1671
CALDWELL, B	1871	OH CO. MAP	1742
CALDWELL, CHAPLINE	1821	DEFENDANT	1667
CALDWELL, E H / EST - INITIALS E.H.C. EST.	1871	MDSVILLE	1807
CALDWELL, E H / EST.	1871	MDSVILLE	1807
CALDWELL, F / MRS	1871	MARH'L MAP	1745
CALDWELL, F / MISS	1871	MARH'L MAP	1749
CALDWELL, G	1871	MARH'L MAP	1749
CALDWELL, G	1871	RITCHIE TWP	1791
CALDWELL, G	1871	RITCHIE TWP	1793
CALDWELL, G	1871	LIMESTONE	1805
CALDWELL, G W / LAWYER	1871	BRKE MAP	1735
CALDWELL, G W	1871	WELLSBURG	1777
CALDWELL, G W	1871	WELLSBURG	1777
CALDWELL, G W	1871	WELLSBURG	1777
CALDWELL, G W / INITIALS G.W.C.	1871	WELLSBURG	1777
CALDWELL, GEORGE B	1879	MISC	1676
CALDWELL, GEORGE E	1858	DEFENDANT	1584
CALDWELL, GEORGE E	1861	DEFENDANT	1636
CALDWELL, H	1871	MARH'L MAP	1746
CALDWELL, J	1816	MISC	1684
CALDWELL, J / RES	1871	BKE/OH MAP	1738
CALDWELL, J / RES	1871	BKE/OH MAP	1738
CALDWELL, J / INITIALS J.C.	1871	BKE/OH MAP	1739
CALDWELL, J	1871	MARH'L MAP	1745
CALDWELL, J	1871	MARH'L MAP	1746
CALDWELL, J	1871	MARH'L MAP	1746
CALDWELL, J	1871	MARH'L MAP	1748
CALDWELL, JAMES	1784	APPENDIX	1874
CALDWELL, JAMES	1822	DEFENDANT	1668
CALDWELL, JAMES	1842	DEFENDANT	1561
CALDWELL, JAMES	1842	DEFENDANT	1672
CALDWELL, JAMES	1854	MISC	1680
CALDWELL, JAMES Y	1845	DEFENDANT	1600
CALDWELL, JAMES Y	1846	PLAINTIFF	1653
CALDWELL, JOHN	1793	MISC	1682
CALDWELL, JOHN	1800	DEFENDANT	1647
CALDWELL, JOHN	1800	DEFENDANT	1647
CALDWELL, JOHN	1801	DEFENDANT	1647
CALDWELL, JOHN	1803	DEFENDANT	1648
CALDWELL, JOHN	1808	APPENDIX	1873
CALDWELL, JOHN	1809	DEFENDANT	1642
CALDWELL, JOHN	1819	DEFENDANT	1667
CALDWELL, JOHN	1821	DEFENDANT	1668
CALDWELL, JOHN	1825	DEFENDANT	1649
CALDWELL, JOHN	1825	DEFENDANT	1668
CALDWELL, JOHN	1825	DEFENDANT	1668
CALDWELL, JOHN / TAVERN - WASH.CO.,PA.	1916	NAT'L ROAD	1861
CALDWELL, JOHN / TAVERN - WASH.CO.,PA.	1916	NAT'L ROAD	1862
CALDWELL, JOSEPH	1821	DEFENDANT	1574
CALDWELL, JOSEPH	1830	MISC	1702
CALDWELL, O	1871	MARH'L MAP	1746
CALDWELL, R / EST	1871	MARH'L MAP	1749
CALDWELL, R / EST	1871	LIMESTONE	1805
CALDWELL, ROBERT	1812	MISC	1677
CALDWELL, VAN	1823	DEFENDANT	1553
CALDWELL, VAN	1823	DEFENDANT	1587
CALDWELL, WILLIAM	1778	DEFENDANT	1634
CALDWELLS RUN	1871	OH CO. MAP	1742
CALDWELLS RUN	1871	RITCHIE TWP	1791
CALDWELLS RUN	1871	RITCHIE TWP	1793
CALENDINE, HENRY / MAP#378	1852	BRKE MAP	1847
CALHOUN, A	1778	APPENDIX	1874
CALLAN, W	1871	MARH'L MAP	1752
CALLAN, W	1871	MARH'L MAP	1752
CALLAWAY, JOHN	1794	DEFENDANT	1572
CALLENDINE, H	1871	BRKE MAP	1735
CALLENDINE, H	1871	BRKE MAP	1737
CALLENDINE, H	1871	FOWLERS P.O.	1775
CALLEY, F	1871	MARH'L MAP	1757
CALP, ANNA LAURA	1866	MISC	1699
CALP, MARY ANN	1866	MISC	1699
CALVERT, J	1871	MARH'L MAP	1760
CAMBPELL, - / DEAN & CAMPBELL	1871	NEW CUMB'LD	1766
CAMBRIDGE, OH	1852	HEMP. RR MAP	1826
CAMERON	1871	DISTANCES	1815
CAMERON - BUSINESS NOTICES	1871	CAMERON	1795
CAMERON - CAMERON TOWNSHIP - MARSHALL CO	1871	CAMERON	1802
CAMERON - CARPENTER SHOP	1871	CAMERON	1803
CAMERON - CATTLE YARD - AT B&O RR	1871	CAMERON	1803
CAMERON - CENTRE ST	1871	CAMERON	1804
CAMERON - CHURCH ST	1871	CAMER'N - BUS.	1795
CAMERON - CHURCH ST	1871	CAMERON	1803
CAMERON - DETAIL MAP	1871	CAMERON	1802
CAMERON - DETAIL MAP	1871	CAMERON	1803
CAMERON - DETAIL MAP	1871	CAMERON	1804
CAMERON - GREEN ST	1871	CAMER'N - BUS.	1795
CAMERON - GREENE ST	1871	CAMERON	1802
CAMERON - GREENE ST	1871	CAMERON	1803
CAMERON - ICE HOUSE / NEAR W.MCGAHAN	1871	CAMERON	1803
CAMERON - MAIN ST	1871	CAMER'N - BUS.	1795
CAMERON - MAIN ST	1871	CAMERON	1803
CAMERON - MAIN ST	1871	CAMERON	1804
CAMERON - MASONIC HALL	1871	CAMERON	1803
CAMERON - PANORAMIC MAP	1899	CAMERON	1857
CAMERON - POND	1871	CAMERON	1802
CAMERON - POST OFFICE	1871	CAMERON	1803
CAMERON - RIDGE ST	1871	CAMER'N - BUS.	1795
CAMERON - RIDGE ST	1871	CAMERON	1802
CAMERON - RIDGE ST	1871	CAMERON	1803
CAMERON - SOUTH SIDE CREEK	1871	CAMER'N - BUS.	1795
CAMERON - STAVE FACTORY	1871	CAMERON	1804
CAMERON - TELEGRAPH OFFICE	1871	CAMER'N - BUS.	1795
CAMERON - UNION HOUSE	1871	CAMERON	1803
CAMERON - WAREHOUSE AT B&O RR	1871	CAMERON	1803
CAMERON, EXCLUDING TOWN	1871	POPULATION	1816
CAMERON CEMETERY - CAMERON	1871	CAMERON	1804
CAMERON HOUSE - HOTEL - CAMERON	1871	CAMER'N - BUS.	1795
CAMERON HOUSE - HOTEL - CAMERON	1871	CAMERON	1803
CAMERON P.O. - MARSHALL CO	1871	MARH'L MAP	1757
CAMERON TOWNSHIP - MARSHALL CO	1871	POPULATION	1816
CAMERON TOWNSHIP - MARSHALL CO.	1871	MARH'L MAP	1752
CAMERON TOWNSHIP - MARSHALL CO.	1871	MARH'L MAP	1753
CAMERON TOWNSHOP - MARSHALL CO	1871	GLEN EASTON	1801
CAMERON, J	1871	HAN MAP	1731
CAMERON, JAMES / NW OF BLAIR P.O.	1871	HAN MAP	1731
CAMERON, S	1871	HAN MAP	1731
CAMERON, S	1871	NEW CUMB'LD	1768
CAMERON, WV - MAP	1916	NAT'L ROAD	1869
CAMNITZ, JOHN	1811	DEFENDANT	1579
CAMNITZ, JOHN	1811	DEFENDANT	1579
CAMP MEETING GROUND - ON CASTLEMANS RUN	1871	BKE/OH MAP	1739
CAMP, -	1841	PLAINTIFF	1629
CAMPBEL, FRANCIS C	1834	MISC	1680
CAMPBELL & CO FIRE BRICK WORKS	1871	FRE'MAN'S LDG	1765
CAMPBELL, -	1833	DEFENDANT	1551
CAMPBELL, - / FIRE BRICK YARD / CAMPBELL & CO.	1871	HAN MAP	1732
CAMPBELL, - / MRS	1871	BRKE MAP	1737
CAMPBELL, - / DOCTOR	1871	OH CO. MAP	1741
CAMPBELL, - / DOCTOR - INITIALS DR. C.	1871	OH CO. MAP	1741
CAMPBELL, - / DOCTOR - INITIALS DR. C.	1871	OH CO. MAP	1741
CAMPBELL, - / DOCTOR - INITIALS DR. C.	1871	OH CO. MAP	1741
CAMPBELL, - / MRS	1871	MARH'L MAP	1748
CAMPBELL, - / & CO	1871	FRE'MAN'S LDG	1762
CAMPBELL, - / DEAN & CAMPBELL	1871	NEW CUMB'LD	1767
CAMPBELL, - / MRS	1871	NEW CUMB'LD	1768
CAMPBELL, - / MRS	1871	MDSVILLE	1806

XV

'PERSONAL TIME LINE' INDEX TO VOLUME 7 OF THE *OHIO COUNTY INDEX*

ENTRY	YEAR	SUBJECT	PAGE	ENTRY	YEAR	SUBJECT	PAGE
CAMPBELL, A	1871	HAN MAP	1733	CAMPBELL, L P / MRS - INITIALS MRS. C	1871	MARH'L MAP	1754
CAMPBELL, A	1871	BRKE MAP	1737	CAMPBELL, L P / MRS - INITIALS MRS. C	1871	MARH'L MAP	1758
CAMPBELL, A	1871	BRKE MAP	1737				
CAMPBELL, A / RES	1871	BRKE MAP	1737	CAMPBELL, P	1871	MARH'L MAP	1745
CAMPBELL, A / INITIALS A.C.	1871	BRKE MAP	1737	CAMPBELL, P P	1871	MARH'L MAP	1758
CAMPBELL, A / INITIALS A.C.	1871	BRKE MAP	1737	CAMPBELL, P P / INITIALS P.P.C.	1871	MARH'L MAP	1758
CAMPBELL, A / INITIALS A.C.	1871	BRKE MAP	1737	CAMPBELL, P P / INITIALS P.P.C.	1871	MARH'L MAP	1758
CAMPBELL, A / INITIALS A.C. - S. OF SLAUGHTER HOUSE	1871	BRKE MAP	1737	CAMPBELL, P P / INITIALS P.P.C.	1871	MARH'L MAP	1758
CAMPBELL, A	1871	BKE/OH MAP	1739	CAMPBELL, P P / INITIALS P.P.C.	1871	MARH'L MAP	1758
CAMPBELL, A	1871	BKE/OH MAP	1739	CAMPBELL, P P	1871	FRKLN TWP-BUS.	1797
CAMPBELL, A / INITIALS A.C.	1871	BKE/OH MAP	1739	CAMPBELL, R	1871	HAN MAP	1731
CAMPBELL, A / INITIALS A.C.	1871	BKE/OH MAP	1739	CAMPBELL, R	1871	HAN MAP	1732
CAMPBELL, A / INITIALS A.C.	1871	BKE/OH MAP	1739	CAMPBELL, R A	1871	HAN MAP	1732
CAMPBELL, A / RES	1871	BKE/OH MAP	1739	CAMPBELL, TERRENCE	1789	DEFENDANT	1644
CAMPBELL, A	1871	HAN-POE TWP	1763	CAMPBELL, THOMAS / MAP#630	1852	BRKE MAP	1852
CAMPBELL, A	1871	RIV. RD S.OF N.C.	1771	CAMPBELL, W / (?WILLIAM?)	1871	BRKE MAP	1737
CAMPBELL, A	1871	RIV. RD S.OF N.C.	1771	CAMPBELL, W / (?WILLIAM?) INITIALS W.C.	1871	BRKE MAP	1737
CAMPBELL, A	1871	BETHANY	1773				
CAMPBELL, A H	1871	MARH'L MAP	1746	CAMPBELL, W / INITIALS W.C.	1871	BRKE MAP	1737
CAMPBELL, A W	1871	BETHANY	1773	CAMPBELL, W	1871	BKE/OH MAP	1739
CAMPBELL, ALEX / CAPT. - MAP#663	1852	BRKE MAP	1854	CAMPBELL, W / INITIALS W.C.	1871	BKE/OH MAP	1739
CAMPBELL, ALEXANDER / (MILL) - MAP#181	1852	BRKE MAP	1843	CAMPBELL, W D	1871	MARH'L MAP	1746
CAMPBELL, ALEXANDER / MAP#110	1852	BRKE MAP	1843	CAMPBELL, WILLIAM	1871	BRKE MAP	1737
CAMPBELL, ALEXANDER / (MILL) - MAP#130	1852	BRKE MAP	1844	CAMPBELL, WILLIAM	1871	BKE/OH MAP	1739
CAMPBELL, ALEXANDER / (MILL) - MAP#136	1852	BRKE MAP	1844	CAMPBELLS ADDITION / LAND LOTS IN NEW CUMBERLAND	1871	NEW CUMB'LD	1767
CAMPBELL, ALEXANDER / (MILL) - MAP#137	1852	BRKE MAP	1844	CAMPBELLS RUN	1871	MARH'L MAP	1760
CAMPBELL, ALEXANDER / (MILL) - MAP#185	1852	BRKE MAP	1844	CAMPGROUND - OLD CAMPGROUND - CASTLEMANS RUN	1852	BRKE MAP	1840
CAMPBELL, ALEXANDER / (MILL) - MAP#186	1852	BRKE MAP	1844	CANADA NO.2	1871	MARH'L MAP	1759
CAMPBELL, ALEXANDER / (MILL) - MAP#187	1852	BRKE MAP	1844	CANDLE, L	1871	MARH'L MAP	1747
CAMPBELL, ALEXANDER / (MILL) - MAP#191	1852	BRKE MAP	1844	CANDLE, L	1871	MARH'L MAP	1750
				CANE, J / EST.	1871	MARH'L MAP	1760
CAMPBELL, ALEXANDER / (STUDY) - MAP#127	1852	BRKE MAP	1844	CANE, J / EST.	1871	MARH'L MAP	1760
CAMPBELL, ALEXANDER / MAP#125	1852	BRKE MAP	1844	CANES RUN / (?CANES?)	1852	BRKE MAP	1842
CAMPBELL, ALEXANDER / MAP#126	1852	BRKE MAP	1844	CANES RUN	1871	BRKE MAP	1736
CAMPBELL, ALEXANDER / MAP#129	1852	BRKE MAP	1844	CANNON, C	1871	MARH'L MAP	1747
CAMPBELL, ALEXANDER / SMITHSHOP - MAP#128	1852	BRKE MAP	1844	CANNON, C	1871	MARH'L MAP	1747
				CANNON, C / GRIST MILL	1871	MARH'L MAP	1750
CAMPBELL, B	1871	BETHANY	1773	CANNS RUN	1871	BRKE MAP	1735
CAMPBELL, D	1871	HAN MAP	1732	CANON, JOHN	1818	MISC	1709
CAMPBELL, D / INITIALS D.C.	1871	HAN MAP	1732	CAPITOLA, STEAMER	1861	DEFENDANT	1631
CAMPBELL, E	1871	MARH'L MAP	1745	CAPSTACK, J	1857	DEFENDANT	1632
CAMPBELL, EDWARD	1871	HAN MAP	1731	CAPTINA ISLAND - OHIO RIVER	1871	MARH'L MAP	1751
CAMPBELL, F	1871	MARH'L MAP	1749	CARDON, - / MRS	1871	RITCHIE TWP	1791
CAMPBELL, F / INITIALS F.C.	1871	MARH'L MAP	1749	CARIGAN, M / ?	1871	MARH'L MAP	1745
CAMPBELL, GEORGE W / INITIALS G.W.C.	1871	HAN MAP	1732	CARIGAN, M / W. OF M.E. CHURCH	1871	MARH'L MAP	1745
				CARIGAN, M / W. OF M.E. CHURCH	1871	MARH'L MAP	1745
CAMPBELL, GEORGE W / SW OF PLEASANT HILL	1871	HAN MAP	1732	CARLE & PERRY / MAP#404	1852	BRKE MAP	1846
CAMPBELL, ISAAC W	1854	DEFENDANT	1629	CARLE & PERRY / MAP#405	1852	BRKE MAP	1846
CAMPBELL, J	1871	HAN MAP	1730	CARLE, A	1871	WELLSBURG	1777
CAMPBELL, J	1871	HAN MAP	1731	CARLIN, EDWARD G	1822	DEFENDANT	1668
CAMPBELL, J	1871	MARH'L MAP	1746	CARLON, EDWARD G	1822	DEFENDANT	1668
CAMPBELL, J	1871	MARH'L MAP	1749	CARMICHAEL - CHILDREN	1816	MISC	1707
CAMPBELL, J	1871	MARH'L MAP	1749	CARMICHAEL, - / COAL DEALERS - FORBES & CARMICHAEL	1871	BUFF.TWP.BUS.	1772
CAMPBELL, J	1871	MARH'L MAP	1752	CARMICHAEL, - / FORBES & CARMICHAEL	1871	BUFF.TWP.BUS.	1772
CAMPBELL, J	1871	NEW CUMB'LD	1767				
CAMPBELL, J	1871	NEW CUMB'LD	1767	CARMICHAEL, G	1871	MARH'L MAP	1752
CAMPBELL, J / LUMBER YARD	1871	NEW CUMB'LD	1768	CARMICHAEL, G / INITIALS G.C.	1871	MARH'L MAP	1752
CAMPBELL, J / LUMBER YARD	1871	NEW CUMB'LD	1768	CARMICHAEL, G	1871	MARH'L MAP	1756
CAMPBELL, J	1871	BETHANY	1773	CARMICHAEL, G	1871	MARH'L MAP	1756
CAMPBELL, J	1871	BETHANY	1773	CARMICHAEL, G / INITIALS G.C.	1871	MARH'L MAP	1756
CAMPBELL, J	1871	MDSVILLE	1807	CARMICHAEL, HUGH	1815	MISC	1707
CAMPBELL, J C / ESQ. - MAP#142	1852	BRKE MAP	1843	CARMICHAEL, HUGH	1821	MISC	1678
CAMPBELL, J C / ESQ. - MAP#143	1852	BRKE MAP	1843	CARMICHAEL, J	1871	MARH'L MAP	1753
CAMPBELL, J C / ESQ. - MAP#144	1852	BRKE MAP	1843	CARMICHAEL, J	1871	WELLSBURG	1778
CAMPBELL, J C / ESQ. - MAP#145	1852	BRKE MAP	1843	CARMICHAEL, JOHN	1799	PLAINTIFF	1634
CAMPBELL, J C / ESQ. - MAP#147	1852	BRKE MAP	1843	CARMICHAEL, WILLIAM	1821	MISC	1684
CAMPBELL, J C	1871	HAN MAP	1733	CARMICHEL, JAMES	1817	MISC	1685
CAMPBELL, J H	1871	HAN MAP	1731	CARMICLE, ELIZABETH	1811	APPENDIX	1873
CAMPBELL, JAMES	1871	HAN MAP	1732	CARMICLE, HIRAM	1811	APPENDIX	1873
CAMPBELL, JAMES M	1871	HAN MAP	1732	CARMICLE, HUGH	1811	APPENDIX	1873
CAMPBELL, JAMES M	1871	HAN-BUTL'R TWP	1763	CARMICLE, HUGH	1811	APPENDIX	1873
CAMPBELL, JOHN	1810	MISC	1711	CARMICLE, JAMES	1811	APPENDIX	1873
CAMPBELL, JOHN	1871	NEW CUMB'LD	1762	CARNAHAN, J	1871	BRKE MAP	1736
CAMPBELL, L P / MRS	1871	MARH'L MAP	1754	CARNAHAN, J / OC	1871	BKE/OH MAP	1738
CAMPBELL, L P / MRS - INITIALS MRS. C	1871	MARH'L MAP	1754	CARNAHAN, THOMAS / SHORT CREEK COAL BANK	1871	BUFF.TWP.BUS.	1772
				CARNEHAM, W	1871	MARH'L MAP	1745
				CARNES, - / MISS	1871	BRKE MAP	1734
				CARNES, J / HRS	1871	BRKE MAP	1735
				CARNEY, H J / MRS	1871	OH CO. MAP	1741
				CARNEY, J	1871	WHG CITY	1790
				CARNEY, J	1871	RITCHIE TWP	1791

XVI

'PERSONAL TIME LINE' INDEX TO VOLUME 7 OF THE *OHIO COUNTY INDEX*

ENTRY	YEAR	SUBJECT	PAGE
CARNEY, J	1871	MDSVILLE	1808
CARNEY, JAMES	1871	MARH'L MAP	1749
CARNEY, JAMES	1871	WHG CITY	1790
CARNEY, JAMES	1871	RITCHIE TWP	1791
CARNEY, JAMES	1871	WASH.TWP-BUS.	1797
CAROTHERS RUN / SE CORNER OF MAP	1871	HAN MAP	1727
CAROTHERS RUN	1871	HAN MAP	1731
CAROTHERS, D	1871	HAN MAP	1731
CAROTHERS, D	1871	HAN MAP	1732
CAROTHERS, JOHN	1841	DEFENDANT	1582
CAROTHERS, T C	1871	HAN MAP	1732
CAROTHERS, T C	1871	HAN MAP	1733
CAROTHERS, T C	1871	HAN-BUTL'R TWP	1763
CARP, ADAM	1825	DEFENDANT	1612
CARP, ADAM	1827	DEFENDANT	1613
CARP, ADAM	1828	DEFENDANT	1613
CARP, ADAM	1844	DEFENDANT	1615
CARPENTER SHOP / LOT 45	1871	NEW CUMB'LD	1766
CARPENTER SHOP - HALSTEADS / A	1871	BRKE MAP	1734
CARPENTER SHOP - LIMESTONE	1871	MARH'L MAP	1749
CARPENTER, -	1840	PLAINTIFF	1628
CARPENTER, -	1841	PLAINTIFF	1629
CARPENTER, J	1871	MARH'L MAP	1745
CARPENTER, J	1871	MARH'L MAP	1748
CARPENTER, JOHN	1778	DEFENDANT	1644
CARPENTER, JOHN	1779	APPENDIX	1874
CARPENTER, LENARD	1819	DEFENDANT	1577
CARPENTER, LEONARD	1819	DEFENDANT	1577
CARPENTER, SAMUEL	1810	DEFENDANT	1642
CARR, BENJAMIN M	1842	DEFENDANT	1584
CARR, D	1871	MARH'L MAP	1746
CARR, JOHN	1807	DEFENDANT	1659
CARR, JOHN	1807	DEFENDANT	1659
CARR, JOHN	1809	DEFENDANT	1645
CARR, JOHN	1812	DEFENDANT	1610
CARR, JOHN	1813	DEFENDANT	1645
CARR, JOHN D M	1862	DEFENDANT	1564
CARR, L	1871	MARH'L MAP	1753
CARR, M / MRS	1871	MDSVILLE	1807
CARR, WATSON	1857	DEFENDANT	1621
CARR, WATTSON	1857	DEFENDANT	1588
CARR, WATTSON	1857	DEFENDANT	1626
CARR, WILLIAM	1871	MDSVILLE	1807
CARROL & BURNS	1861	DEFENDANT	1569
CARROLL, J	1871	MARH'L MAP	1747
CARROLL, THOMAS	1829	DEFENDANT	1613
CARRUTHERS, GEORGE	1823	DEFENDANT	1555
CARRUTHERS, GEORGE	1825	DEFENDANT	1579
CARRUTHERS, GEORGE	1841	DEFENDANT	1672
CARSON, A	1871	HAN MAP	1731
CARSON, J	1871	OH CO. MAP	1740
CARSON, JAMES	1871	HAN MAP	1731
CARSON, RICHARD	1806	DEFENDANT	1589
CARTER, - / MRS	1871	OH CO. MAP	1742
CARTER, - / MRS	1871	WHG CITY	1786
CARTER, CEPHAS	1871	BRKE MAP	1735
CARTER, CEPHAS / COAL & TIMBERLANDS	1871	BRKE MAP	1735
CARTER, EDWARD	1819	MISC	1677
CARTER, JOSEPH / MAP#435	1852	BRKE MAP	1850
CARTER, L W / INITIALS L.W.C.	1871	BRKE MAP	1734
CARTER, L W	1871	BRKE MAP	1735
CARTER, L W / & MRS. MCFARLAND	1871	BRKE MAP	1735
CARTER, L W / INITIALS L.W.C.	1871	BRKE MAP	1735
CARTER, LEWIS / MAP#524	1852	BRKE MAP	1852
CARTER, R	1871	OH CO. MAP	1741
CARTER, R	1871	OH CO. MAP	1742
CARTER, R / & CO. DISTILLERY NO. 3	1871	OH CO. MAP	1742
CARTER, R / DISTILLER	1871	OH CO.BUS.	1779
CARTER, R R / INITIALS R.C.	1871	OH CO. MAP	1741
CARTER, RICHARD	1802	DEFENDANT	1666
CARTER, RICHARD	1868	MISC	1694
CARTER, S H B	1871	OH CO. MAP	1742
CARTER, S H B / INITIALS S.H.B.C.	1871	OH CO. MAP	1742
CARTER, S L	1871	BRKE MAP	1734
CARTER, SAMUEL	1834	DEFENDANT	1639
CARTER, SAMUEL	1836	DEFENDANT	1640
CARTER, SAMUEL	1838	DEFENDANT	1640
CARTER, SAMUEL	1841	DEFENDANT	1595
CARTER, SAMUEL	1841	DEFENDANT	1640
CARTER, SAMUEL / MAP#539	1852	BRKE MAP	1852
CARTER, SAMUEL / MAP#564	1852	BRKE MAP	1852
CARTER, SAMUEL	1859	DEFENDANT	1586
CARTER, SAMUEL H B	1846	DEFENDANT	1595
CARTER, SAMUEL H B	1846	DEFENDANT	1640
CARTER, SAMUEL H B	1862	DEFENDANT	1597
CARTERS RUN	1871	OH CO. MAP	1742
CARTOR, DANIEL	1794	DEFENDANT	1655
CASCADE RUN	1852	BRKE MAP	1844
CASCADE RUN	1871	BRKE MAP	1737
CASNER, JAMES / HEIRS - (MILL) - MAP#258	1852	BRKE MAP	1843
CASNER, JAMES / HEIRS - (MILL) - MAP#259	1852	BRKE MAP	1843
CASNER, JAMES / HEIRS - MAP#256	1852	BRKE MAP	1843
CASNER, JAMES / HEIRS - MAP#257	1852	BRKE MAP	1843
CASNER, JAMES / HEIRS - (DISTILLERY) - MAP#255	1852	BRKE MAP	1843
CASSAT, DENNIS	1804	PLAINTIFF	1666
CASSAT, DENNIS	1808	DEFENDANT	1610
CASSIDAY, R	1871	NEW CUMB'LD	1767
CASSIDAY, R	1871	NEW CUMB'LD	1768
CASSIDAY, ROBERT / HEIRS - MAP#497	1852	BRKE MAP	1850
CASSIDAY, S	1871	NEW CUMB'LD	1767
CASSIDY, I / MRS	1871	BRKE MAP	1735
CASTARD, - / MRS	1871	MARH'L MAP	1752
CASTLE ROCK	1871	BRKE MAP	1734
CASTLEMAN RIVER	1916	NAT'L ROAD	1863
CASTLEMAN RUN / NE CORNER OF MAP	1871	BKE/OH MAP	1739
CASTLEMAN RUN	1871	OH CO. MAP	1740
CASTLEMANS RUN	1852	BRKE MAP	1840
CASTLEMANS RUN	1852	BRKE MAP	1841
CASTLEMANS RUN - CAMP MEETING GROUND ON	1871	BKE/OH MAP	1739
CASTLEMANS RUN - GRIST MILL ON	1871	BKE/OH MAP	1739
CASTNAR, WILLIAM	1871	BKE/OH MAP	1739
CATFISH RUN / WASH., PA.	1916	NAT'L ROAD	1861
CATHOLIC CEMETERY - CAMERON	1871	CAMERON	1804
CATHOLIC CHURCH - FIFTH ST	1871	WHG CITY	1788
CATHOLIC CHURCH - MARSHALL ST - BENWOOD	1871	BENWOOD	1798
CATHOLIC CHURCH - MOUND ST - MOUNDSVILLE	1871	MDSVILLE	1808
CATHOLIC CHURCH - TRIADELPHIA	1871	OH CO. MAP	1743
CATHOLIC CHURCH - TRIADELPHIA	1871	OH CO. MAP	1744
CATHOLIC CHURCH - TRIADELPHIA	1871	TRIAD.BORO.	1784
CATHOLIC CHURCH - WELLSBURG - COMMERCE ST	1871	WELLSBURG	1778
CATHOLIC PARSONAGE - B ST - MOUNDSVILLE	1871	MDSVILLE	1808
CATHOLIC SCHOOL - WELLSBURG - COMMERCE ST	1871	WELLSBURG	1778
CATLET, NIMROD	1812	DEFENDANT	1585
CATLET, THOMAS	1812	DEFENDANT	1585
CATLET, THOMAS B	1817	DEFENDANT	1638
CATLETT, P B	1871	MDSVILLE	1806
CATLETT, P B	1871	MDSVILLE	1807
CATON, HARRISON	1847	MISC	1674
CATON, THOMAS	1818	DEFENDANT	1624
CATON, THOMAS	1818	DEFENDANT	1624
CATON, THOMAS	1820	DEFENDANT	1624
CATON, THOMAS	1821	DEFENDANT	1624
CATS, CONROD	1832	DEFENDANT	1639
CATTLE YARD - B&O RR - AT CAMERON	1871	CAMERON	1803
CATZ, CONRAD	1816	DEFENDANT	1611
CATZ, CONRAD	1823	DEFENDANT	1612
CAULDWELL, - / S.RIGGS & CAULDWELL	1871	MARH'L MAP	1754
CAULDWELL, A C	1871	MARH'L MAP	1746
CAULEY, JOHN	1833	DEFENDANT	1669
CAVANAUGH, A J	1871	MDSVILLE	1808
CAVANAUGH, A J / INITIALS A.J.C.	1871	MDSVILLE	1808
CAVANAUGH, A J	1871	MDSVILLE	1810
CAVANAUGH, A J	1871	MDSVILLE	1810
CAVANAUGH, A J / INITIALS A.J.C.	1871	MDSVILLE	1810
CAVE, REBECCAH	1808	MISC	1708
CECIL, CHARLES B	1857	MISC	1702
CECIL, H M / (?R.M.?)	1871	MARH'L MAP	1751
CECIL, I	1871	MARH'L MAP	1751
CECIL, I	1871	MARH'L MAP	1755
CECIL, R M	1871	MARH'L MAP	1755
CECIL, W	1871	MARH'L MAP	1755
CECIL, W H	1871	MDSVILLE	1810
CECIL, WILLIAM H	1842	DEFENDANT	1592
CEDAR VALLEY	1871	BKE/OH MAP	1739
CEICLE, W	1871	MARH'L MAP	1755
CEMETERY - BAPTIST CHURCH & GRAVEYARD - FORK RIDGE ROAD	1871	MARH'L MAP	1753

'PERSONAL TIME LINE' INDEX TO VOLUME 7 OF THE *OHIO COUNTY INDEX*

ENTRY	YEAR	SUBJECT	PAGE
CEMETERY - CAMERON CEMETERY - CAMERON	1871	CAMERON	1804
CEMETERY - CAMERON P.O.	1871	MARH'L MAP	1757
CEMETERY - CATHOLIC CEMETERY - CAMERON	1871	CAMERON	1804
CEMETERY - CHRIS. CHURCH & CEM - NEAR SCHOOL NO.7	1871	MARH'L MAP	1756
CEMETERY - CHRIS. CHURCH & CEMETERY - NEAR SCHOOL NO.12	1871	MARH'L MAP	1757
CEMETERY - CHURCH OF GOD - SHERRARD P.O. / & GRAVEYARD	1871	SHERRARD	1811
CEMETERY - CITY CEMETERY / OR PENINSULA	1871	WHG CITY	1787
CEMETERY - CITY CEMETERY / OR PENINSULA	1871	WHG CITY	1788
CEMETERY - DISCIPLES CHURCH & CEMETERY - MAIN ST. - BETHANY	1871	BETHANY	1773
CEMETERY - E. OF SCHOOL NO. 6	1871	BRKE MAP	1735
CEMETERY - EPISCOPAL CHURCH & CEMETERY - NEAR SCHOOL NO. 5	1871	BRKE MAP	1734
CEMETERY - FAIRMONT TURNPIKE / MT.ZION	1871	RITCHIE TWP	1793
CEMETERY - FAIRVIEW - FRANKLIN TWP	1871	MARH'L MAP	1758
CEMETERY - FLEET ST / #1 - WELLSBURG	1871	WELLSBURG	1776
CEMETERY - FLEET ST / #2 - WELLSBURG	1871	WELLSBURG	1776
CEMETERY - FRANKLIN CEMETERY	1871	BRKE MAP	1737
CEMETERY - GRAVE YARD - NW OF SHERRARD / NEAR CHURCH OF GOD	1871	MARH'L MAP	1745
CEMETERY - GRAVEYARD - E. OF J. FOSTER	1871	MARH'L MAP	1753
CEMETERY - GRAVEYARD - W. OF J.CARNEY	1871	WHG CITY	1790
CEMETERY - GRAVEYARD - W. OF ROCK LICK P.O.	1871	MARH'L MAP	1753
CEMETERY - GREENWOOD CEMETERY	1871	OH CO. MAP	1742
CEMETERY - INDIAN GRAVES - N. OF SUGAR BOTTOM	1871	MARH'L MAP	1750
CEMETERY - INDIAN GRAVES - S. OF SUGAR BOTTOM	1871	MARH'L MAP	1750
CEMETERY - J. ALEXANDERS GRAVE YARD - INITIALS GR.YD.	1871	MARH'L MAP	1748
CEMETERY - LOCUST GROVE	1871	BRKE MAP	1734
CEMETERY - MAIN ST - WEST UNION	1871	W.UNION	1812
CEMETERY - MEADE TWP - SW. OF A. BISHOP - MEADE TWP	1871	MARH'L MAP	1759
CEMETERY - METHODIST CHURCH & CEMETERY - SAND HILL	1871	MARH'L MAP	1746
CEMETERY - METHODIST EPISCOPAL CHURCH & CEM / CLAY TWP	1871	MARH'L MAP	1751
CEMETERY - METHODIST EPISCOPAL CHURCH & CEM & PARSONAGE	1871	BKE/OH MAP	1738
CEMETERY - METHODIST EPISCOPAL CHURCH & CEMETERY - NEAR PLEASANT HOME - CLAY TWP	1871	MARH'L MAP	1752
CEMETERY - METHODIST EPISCOPAL CHURCH & CEMETERY - NEW MANCHESTER - N. OF TANNERY	1871	NEW MANCH.	1769
CEMETERY - METHODIST EPISCOPAL CHURCH & CEMETERY - ON FAIRMOUNT ROAD	1871	MARH'L MAP	1745
CEMETERY - METHODIST EPISCOPAL CHURCH & CEMETERY - S. OF BLAIR HOMESTEAD	1871	MARH'L MAP	1749
CEMETERY - METHODIST EPISCOPAL CHURCH & GRAVE YARD - NW. OF R. ZINK	1871	MARH'L MAP	1749
CEMETERY - METHODIST EPISCOPAL CHURCH & GRAVEYARD - WAYNESBURGH ROAD	1871	MARH'L MAP	1749
CEMETERY - METHODIST EPISCOPAL CHURCH AND CEMETERY - E. OF J M. WILSON	1871	BKE/OH MAP	1738
CEMETERY - METHODIST EPISCOPAL CHURCH CEMETERY / E. OF J.M. WILSON	1871	BRKE MAP	1736
CEMETERY - MOUNT ROSE CEMETERY - MOUNDSVILLE	1871	MDSVILLE	1807
CEMETERY - MT. WOOD	1871	WHG CITY	1786
CEMETERY - N OF S. CLELAND	1871	BRKE MAP	1735
CEMETERY - N. END OF WHEELING CITY	1871	OH CO. MAP	1742
CEMETERY - N. OF DEWEY VANCE & CO SPIKE WORKS	1871	WHG CITY	1790
CEMETERY - N. OF GREGGSVILLE / NEAR SCHOOL NO.8	1871	OH CO. MAP	1741
CEMETERY - N. OF J HARGRAVEDS	1871	OH CO. MAP	1742
CEMETERY - N. OF SCHOOL NO. 12	1871	BKE/OH MAP	1739
CEMETERY - N. OF SCHOOL NO.1 - MEADE TWP	1871	MARH'L MAP	1756
CEMETERY - N. OF WILLIAM CAMPBELL	1871	BKE/OH MAP	1739
CEMETERY - N. OF WILLIAM CAMPBELL - E. OF BETHANY	1871	BRKE MAP	1737
CEMETERY - N. OF WILLIAM MCCRARY	1871	MARH'L MAP	1746
CEMETERY - N. SIDE OF MOUNDSVILLE	1871	MARH'L MAP	1748
CEMETERY - NE OF SCHOOL NO. 7	1871	BRKE MAP	1737
CEMETERY - NE. OF SCHOOL NO.2	1871	MARH'L MAP	1753
CEMETERY - NEAR CHURCH OF GOD - LIBERTY TWP	1871	MARH'L MAP	1760
CEMETERY - NEW CUMBERLAND	1871	HAN MAP	1730
CEMETERY - NEW CUMBERLAND	1871	NEW CUMB'LD	1767
CEMETERY - NORNBROOK BROTHERS	1871	MARH'L MAP	1754
CEMETERY - NW. OF HAZELDELL SCHOOL NO.5	1871	MARH'L MAP	1750
CEMETERY - OLD - NEAR CROSS CREEK	1871	BRKE MAP	1735
CEMETERY - PENINSULA	1871	OH CO. MAP	1742
CEMETERY - PENINSULA OR CITY CEMETERY	1871	WHG CITY	1787
CEMETERY - PENINSULA OR CITY CEMETERY	1871	WHG CITY	1788
CEMETERY - PRESBYTERIAN CHURCH / & CEMETERY - PLEASANT HILL	1871	HAN MAP	1732
CEMETERY - PRESBYTERIAN CHURCH - WEST LIBERTY	1871	W.LIBERTY	1780
CEMETERY - PRESBYTERIAN CHURCH & CEMETERY - SHERRARD P.O.	1871	MARH'L MAP	1746
CEMETERY - PRESBYTERIAN CHURCH & CEMETERY - SHERRARD P.O.	1871	SHERRARD	1811
CEMETERY - PRESBYTERIAN CHURCH & CEMETERY - WEST UNION	1871	MARH'L MAP	1747
CEMETERY - PRESBYTERIAN CHURCH & CEMETERY - WEST UNION	1871	W.UNION	1812
CEMETERY - PRISON CEMETERY - MOUNDSVILLE	1871	MDSVILLE	1809
CEMETERY - ROMAN CATHOLIC CEMETERY / NEAR POWER HOUSE	1871	WHG CITY	1789
CEMETERY - S. OF B. SUTTON	1871	MARH'L MAP	1746
CEMETERY - S. OF O.E. GREEN	1871	BRKE MAP	1737
CEMETERY - S. OF QUIET HOME	1871	OH CO. MAP	1740
CEMETERY - S. OF RITCHIETOWN FARM	1871	OH CO. MAP	1742
CEMETERY - SANDERS FAMILY CEMETERY	1871	HAN MAP	1732
CEMETERY - SE OF GEORGE COXS HEIRS	1871	BRKE MAP	1735
CEMETERY - SHERRARD - ACROSS FROM L.CRISWELL	1871	SHERRARD	1811
CEMETERY - SHERRARD P.O.	1871	MARH'L MAP	1746
CEMETERY - ST JOHNS CHURCH / & GRAVEYARD	1871	BRKE MAP	1734
CEMETERY - STATE PENITENTIARY CEMETERY	1871	MDSVILLE	1809
CEMETERY - STONE PRESBYTERIAN CHURCH	1871	OH CO. MAP	1742
CEMETERY - SW. OF SCHOOL NO.5	1871	MARH'L MAP	1754
CEMETERY - SW. OF SCHOOL NO.5 - LIBERTY TWP	1871	MARH'L MAP	1758
CEMETERY - UNION CHURCH & CEMETERY - S. OF LIMESTONE	1871	MARH'L MAP	1749
CEMETERY - W. OF WOLF RUN PRESBYTERIAN CHURCH	1871	MARH'L MAP	1750
CENSUS 1870 POPULATION TOTALS	1871	POPULATION	1816
CENTRAL OHIO RR	1852	HEMP. RR MAP	1826
CENTRE SUMMIT	1871	BKE/OH MAP	1739
CENTRE SUMMIT / UNION TWP	1871	MARH'L MAP	1745
CENTRE TOWNSHIP - OHIO CO	1871	WHG CITY	1788
CENTRE TOWNSHIP - OHIO CO	1871	WHG CITY	1790
CENTRE TOWNSHIP - WHEELING	1871	OH CO. MAP	1742

'PERSONAL TIME LINE' INDEX TO VOLUME 7 OF THE *OHIO COUNTY INDEX*

ENTRY	YEAR	SUBJECT	PAGE
CHADDOCK, R	1871	MDSVILLE	1808
CHAFFANT, WILLIAM	1829	DEFENDANT	1613
CHAMBERLAIN, S	1871	WELLSBURG	1778
CHAMBERLAIN, T / MRS	1871	BRKE MAP	1736
CHAMBERS FARM	1871	HAN MAP	1726
CHAMBERS, - / MRS	1871	OH CO. MAP	1742
CHAMBERS, - / MISS	1871	MARH'L MAP	1757
CHAMBERS, - / MRS	1871	MARH'L MAP	1757
CHAMBERS, A / EST	1871	MARH'L MAP	1757
CHAMBERS, A / EST - INITIALS A.C. EST.	1871	MARH'L MAP	1757
CHAMBERS, C	1871	MARH'L MAP	1753
CHAMBERS, C	1871	MARH'L MAP	1757
CHAMBERS, CATHERINE	1800	DEFENDANT	1583
CHAMBERS, E	1871	MARH'L MAP	1757
CHAMBERS, GEORGE	1871	HAN MAP	1731
CHAMBERS, J	1871	MARH'L MAP	1760
CHAMBERS, J	1871	MARH'L MAP	1760
CHAMBERS, J A	1871	MARH'L MAP	1757
CHAMBERS, J A / INITIALS J.A.C.	1871	MARH'L MAP	1757
CHAMBERS, J A / INITIALS J.A.C.	1871	MARH'L MAP	1757
CHAMBERS, JACOB	1800	DEFENDANT	1554
CHAMBERS, JACOB	1800	DEFENDANT	1583
CHAMBERS, JAMES	1871	OH CO. MAP	1740
CHAMBERS, JAMES	1871	OH CO. MAP	1740
CHAMBERS, M / EST.	1871	MARH'L MAP	1756
CHAMBERS, S	1871	OH CO. MAP	1740
CHAMBERS, S	1871	MARH'L MAP	1756
CHAMBERS, S / INITIALS S.C.	1871	MARH'L MAP	1756
CHAMBERS, S B	1871	OH CO. MAP	1740
CHAMBERS, S B	1871	OH CO. MAP	1743
CHAMBERS, SAMUEL	1871	ELM GROVE	1782
CHAMBERS, T	1871	MARH'L MAP	1756
CHAMBERS, W T	1871	OH CO. MAP	1742
CHAMBERS, W T	1871	OH CO. MAP	1744
CHAMBERS, W T	1871	OH CO. BUS.	1779
CHAMBERS, WILLIAM T	1871	ELM GROVE	1782
CHAMBERS, WILLIAM T	1871	ELM GROVE	1782
CHAMBERS, WILLIAM T / INITIALS W.T.C. - STORE	1871	ELM GROVE	1782
CHAMBERS, WILLIAM T	1875	DEFENDANT	1574
CHAMPION MACHINE WORKS	1871	NEW MANCH.	1763
CHAMPION WORKS / CHAMPION MACHINE WORKS	1871	NEW MANCH.	1769
CHANCERY COURT ENTRIES	2000	APPENDIX	1872
CHANEY, JOHN	1792	DEFENDANT	1647
CHAPEL, KATY'S / MAP#159	1852	BRKE MAP	1842
CHAPLIN, JOSIAH	1831	DEFENDANT	1650
CHAPLINE, -	1840	PLAINTIFF	1628
CHAPLINE, -	1851	PLAINTIFF	1629
CHAPLINE, -	1855	PLAINTIFF	1629
CHAPLINE, -	1857	PLAINTIFF	1630
CHAPLINE, EAZCHELL	1831	DEFENDANT	1669
CHAPLINE, J W	1846	DEFENDANT	1653
CHAPLINE, JONAH	1828	DEFENDANT	1649
CHAPLINE, JOSEPH	1839	DEFENDANT	1662
CHAPLINE, JOSIAH	1808	APPENDIX	1873
CHAPLINE, JOSIAH	1824	DEFENDANT	1585
CHAPLINE, JOSIAH	1828	DEFENDANT	1642
CHAPLINE, JOSIAH	1829	DEFENDANT	1642
CHAPLINE, JOSIAH	1830	DEFENDANT	1628
CHAPLINE, JOSIAH	1832	DEFENDANT	1639
CHAPLINE, JOSIAH	1834	DEFENDANT	1650
CHAPLINE, JOSIAH W	1856	DEFENDANT	1558
CHAPLINE, JOSIAH W	1856	DEFENDANT	1621
CHAPLINE, JOSIAH W	1856	DEFENDANT	1636
CHAPLINE, JOSIAH W	1856	DEFENDANT	1670
CHAPLINE, JOSIAH W	1859	DEFENDANT	1590
CHAPLINE, MOSES	1783	APPENDIX	1874
CHAPLINE, MOSES	1805	DEFENDANT	1554
CHAPLINE, MOSES	1809	DEFENDANT	1555
CHAPLINE, MOSES	1811	DEFENDANT	1667
CHAPLINE, NOAH	1845	DEFENDANT	1652
CHAPLINE, NOAH ZANE	1840	DEFENDANT	1551
CHAPLINE, SAMUEL H	1823	DEFENDANT	1638
CHAPLINE, SAMUEL H	1824	DEFENDANT	1638
CHAPLINE, WILLIAM	1804	DEFENDANT	1637
CHAPLINE, WILLIAM	1805	DEFENDANT	1554
CHAPLINE, WILLIAM	1806	DEFENDANT	1589
CHAPLINE, WILLIAM	1807	DEFENDANT	1554
CHAPLINE, WILLIAM	1807	DEFENDANT	1589
CHAPLINE, WILLIAM	1807	DEFENDANT	1659
CHAPLINE, WILLIAM	1808	DEFENDANT	1637
CHAPLINE, WILLIAM	1808	APPENDIX	1873
CHAPLINE, WILLIAM	1809	DEFENDANT	1555
CHAPLINE, WILLIAM	1809	DEFENDANT	1589
CHAPLINE, WILLIAM	1810	DEFENDANT	1596
CHAPLINE, WILLIAM	1810	DEFENDANT	1642
CHAPLINE, WILLIAM	1810	DEFENDANT	1642
CHAPLINE, WILLIAM	1815	DEFENDANT	1611
CHAPLINE, WILLIAM	1815	DEFENDANT	1624
CHAPLINE, WILLIAM	1816	DEFENDANT	1645
CHAPLINE, WILLIAM	1816	DEFENDANT	1648
CHAPLINE, WILLIAM	1816	DEFENDANT	1667
CHAPLINE, WILLIAM	1817	DEFENDANT	1585
CHAPLINE, WILLIAM	1817	DEFENDANT	1616
CHAPLINE, WILLIAM	1817	DEFENDANT	1632
CHAPLINE, WILLIAM	1817	DEFENDANT	1645
CHAPLINE, WILLIAM	1817	DEFENDANT	1648
CHAPLINE, WILLIAM	1817	DEFENDANT	1659
CHAPLINE, WILLIAM	1818	DEFENDANT	1553
CHAPLINE, WILLIAM	1818	DEFENDANT	1555
CHAPLINE, WILLIAM	1818	DEFENDANT	1585
CHAPLINE, WILLIAM	1819	DEFENDANT	1585
CHAPLINE, WILLIAM	1820	DEFENDANT	1667
CHAPLINE, WILLIAM	1820	DEFENDANT	1667
CHAPLINE, WILLIAM	1822	DEFENDANT	1608
CHAPLINE, WILLIAM	1822	DEFENDANT	1668
CHAPLINE, WILLIAM	1824	DEFENDANT	1608
CHAPLINE, WILLIAM	1824	DEFENDANT	1668
CHAPLINE, WILLIAM	1832	DEFENDANT	1594
CHAPLINE, WILLIAM	1832	DEFENDANT	1618
CHAPLINE, WILLIAM	1837	DEFENDANT	1651
CHAPLINE, WILLIAM	1840	DEFENDANT	1551
CHAPLINE, WILLIAM	1840	DEFENDANT	1614
CHAPLINE, WILLIAM	1840	DEFENDANT	1619
CHAPLINE, WILLIAM	1841	DEFENDANT	1580
CHAPLINE, WILLIAM	1846	DEFENDANT	1580
CHAPLINE, WILLIAM JR	1813	DEFENDANT	1611
CHAPLINE, WILLIAM SR	1821	DEFENDANT	1649
CHAPMAN, - / MRS	1871	NEW CUMB'LD	1767
CHAPMAN, A / W. SIDE OF MAP	1871	HAN MAP	1731
CHAPMAN, A	1871	NEW CUMB'LD	1767
CHAPMAN, B W / DOCTOR	1871	NEW CUMB'LD	1762
CHAPMAN, B W	1871	NEW CUMB'LD	1767
CHAPMAN, EZEKIEL	1830	DEFENDANT	1628
CHAPMAN, G W	1871	HAN MAP	1726
CHAPMAN, G W	1871	HAN MAP	1730
CHAPMAN, J C	1871	NEW CUMB'LD	1768
CHAPMAN, JOHN	1805	DEFENDANT	1574
CHAPMAN, NATHAN	1848	MISC	1680
CHAPMAN, S	1871	NEW CUMB'LD	1768
CHAPMAN, T S	1871	HAN MAP	1732
CHAPMAN, W	1871	NEW CUMB'LD	1768
CHAPMAN, WILLIAM H	1873	DEFENDANT	1560
CHAPMANS LANDING	1871	HAN MAP	1730
CHARLES HOTEL - GLEN EASTON	1871	GLEN EASTON - BUS.	1796
CHARLES, HILDEBRAND	1856	DEFENDANT	1569
CHARLES, WALTER	1824	DEFENDANT	1649
CHARLES, WILLIAM	1841	DEFENDANT	1629
CHARLES, WILLIAM	1851	DEFENDANT	1653
CHARLES, WILLIAM	1851	DEFENDANT	1661
CHARLESTON, VA / (WV)	1852	HEMP. RR MAP	1826
CHARLESTON, WV	1916	NAT'L ROAD	1867
CHARTIERS CREEK - BRIDGE OVER / WASH CO., PA	1916	NAT'L ROAD	1861
CHARTIERS CREEK - WASH CO., PA	1916	NAT'L ROAD	1861
CHARTIERS CREEK - WASH.CO., PA. - THREE SPAN-ARCH BRIDGE OVER	1916	NAT'L ROAD	1862
CHAUFFANT, WILLIAM	1829	DEFENDANT	1602
CHECK HO / (?HOUSE?)	1871	HAN MAP	1730
CHECK HO / (?HOUSE?) - N. OF J LEWIS	1871	BRKE MAP	1736
CHECK HO / HOUSE	1871	BRKE MAP	1736
CHECK HO / HOUSE - ON RIVER ROAD - SW CORNER OF MAP	1871	BRKE MAP	1736
CHECK HO / HOUSE (?SOME SORT OF TOLL OR INSPECTION HOUSE?)	1871	BRKE MAP	1736
CHECK HO / HOUSE	1871	BKE/OH MAP	1738
CHECK HO / (?HOUSE?)	1871	NEW CUMB'LD	1767
CHEEK, - / MRS	1871	BETHANY	1773
CHEEK, JAMES	1871	BKE/OH MAP	1739
CHERRY GROVE - FRANKLIN TWP	1871	MARH'L MAP	1758
CHERRY HILL	1871	BRKE MAP	1734
CHERRY HILL	1871	BKE/OH MAP	1739
CHERRY HILL	1871	OH CO. MAP	1740
CHERRY HILL FARM	1871	MARH'L MAP	1745
CHERRY LANE FARM	1871	MARH'L MAP	1758
CHERRY RIDGE - FRANKLIN TWP	1871	MARH'L MAP	1758

'PERSONAL TIME LINE' INDEX TO VOLUME 7 OF THE *OHIO COUNTY INDEX*

ENTRY	YEAR	SUBJECT	PAGE
CHERRY ROW / S. OF SUNNYSIDE - 'RRY ROW' SHOWING	1871	MARH'L MAP	1745
CHESAPEAKE BAY	1916	NAT'L ROAD	1868
CHESSER, FRANCIS	1856	DEFENDANT	1577
CHESTER, C	1871	WHG CITY	1787
CHESTER, C	1871	WHG CITY	1789
CHESTER, G W	1871	WELLSBURG	1777
CHESTNUT HILL / H.I.MENDEL	1871	BRKE MAP	1736
CHESTNUT HILL	1871	MARH'L MAP	1745
CHESTNUT RIDGE	1871	HAN MAP	1731
CHESTNUT RIDGE	1871	MARH'L MAP	1745
CHILICOTHE, OH	1852	HEMPFIELD RR	1821
CHILICOTHE, OH	1852	HEMP. RR MAP	1825
CHRIS, C	1871	BKE/OH MAP	1739
CHRIS. CHURCH - FISH CREEK	1871	MARH'L MAP	1755
CHRIS. CHURCH & CEM - NEAR SCHOOL NO.7	1871	MARH'L MAP	1756
CHRIS. CHURCH & CEMETERY - NEAR SCHOOL NO.12	1871	MARH'L MAP	1757
CHRIST. CHURCH - RIDGE ST - CAMERON	1871	CAMERON	1803
CHRUCH - PRESBYTERIAN CHURCH & CEMETERY - WEST UNION	1871	MARH'L MAP	1747
CHURCH - BAPTIST / (OLD) - MAP#456	1852	BRKE MAP	1849
CHURCH - BAPTIST / (OLD) - MAP#467	1852	BRKE MAP	1849
CHURCH - BAPTIST CHURCH - CLAY TWP	1871	MARH'L MAP	1751
CHURCH - BAPTIST CHURCH - JOHNSONS RUN	1852	BRKE MAP	1849
CHURCH - BAPTIST CHURCH - MARKET ST	1871	WHG CITY	1788
CHURCH - BAPTIST CHURCH - MARKET ST	1871	WHG CITY	1790
CHURCH - BAPTIST CHURCH - MONROE ST	1871	WHG CITY	1788
CHURCH - BAPTIST CHURCH & GRAVEYARD - FORK RIDGE ROAD	1871	MARH'L MAP	1753
CHURCH - BETHLEHEM METHODIST EPISCOPAL CHURCH / UNION TWP	1871	MARH'L MAP	1745
CHURCH - BETHLEHEM METHODIST EPISCOPAL CHURCH / MARSH. CO.	1871	MARH'L MAP	1748
CHURCH - CATHOLIC CHURCH - FIFTH ST	1871	WHG CITY	1788
CHURCH - CATHOLIC CHURCH - MARSHALL ST - BENWOOD	1871	BENWOOD	1798
CHURCH - CATHOLIC CHURCH - MOUND ST - MOUNDSVILLE	1871	MDSVILLE	1808
CHURCH - CATHOLIC CHURCH - TRIADELPHIA	1871	OH CO. MAP	1743
CHURCH - CATHOLIC CHURCH - TRIADELPHIA	1871	OH CO. MAP	1744
CHURCH - CATHOLIC CHURCH - TRIADELPHIA	1871	TRIAD.BORO.	1784
CHURCH - CATHOLIC CHURCH - WELLSBURG / COMMERCE ST	1871	WELLSBURG	1776
CHURCH - CATHOLIC PARSONAGE - B ST - MOUNDSVILLE	1871	MDSVILLE	1808
CHURCH - CEMETERY PRESBYTERIAN CHURCH - WEST LIBERTY	1871	W.LIBERTY	1780
CHURCH - CHRIS. CHURCH - FISH CREEK	1871	MARH'L MAP	1755
CHURCH - CHRIS. CHURCH & CEM - NEAR SCHOOL NO.7	1871	MARH'L MAP	1756
CHURCH - CHRIS. CHURCH & CEMETERY - NEAR SCHOOL NO.12	1871	MARH'L MAP	1757
CHURCH - CHRIST. CHURCH - RIDGE ST - CAMERON	1871	CAMERON	1803
CHURCH - CHURCH OF GOD - NW OF SHERRARD	1871	MARH'L MAP	1745
CHURCH - CHURCH OF GOD - SHERRARD	1871	MARH'L MAP	1746
CHURCH - CHURCH OF GOD - SHERRARD P.O. / & GRAVEYARD	1871	SHERRARD	1811
CHURCH - DEC. CHURCH - NEAR A. WILSON	1871	MARH'L MAP	1753
CHURCH - DISCIPLES CHURCH / GONE - MAP#401	1852	BRKE MAP	1846
CHURCH - DISCIPLES CHURCH - HOLLIDAYS COVE	1871	HAN MAP	1733
CHURCH - DISCIPLES CHURCH - WEST LIBERTY	1871	W.LIBERTY	1780
CHURCH - DISCIPLES CHURCH & CEMETERY - MAIN ST. - BETHANY	1871	BETHANY	1773
CHURCH - DUTCH CHURCH - S. WHG	1871	SOUTH WHG	1792
CHURCH - EPISCOPAL CHURCH - D & SECOND ST - MOUNDSVILLE	1871	MDSVILLE	1808
CHURCH - EPISCOPAL CHURCH - LIBERTY ST - WELLSBURG	1871	WELLSBURG	1777
CHURCH - EPISCOPAL CHURCH - MARKET ST	1871	WHG CITY	1788
CHURCH - EPISCOPAL CHURCH - MARKET ST	1871	WHG CITY	1790
CHURCH - EPISCOPAL CHURCH - WHEELING ST - MOUNDSVILLE	1871	MDSVL BUS.	1796
CHURCH - EPISCOPAL CHURCH & CEMETERY - NEAR SCHOOL NO. 5	1871	BRKE MAP	1734
CHURCH - EPISCOPAL CHURCH SOCIETY - MOUND & SECOND ST - MOUNDSVILLE	1871	MDSVILLE	1808
CHURCH - GERMAN LUTHERAN CHURCH - 4TH WARD	1871	WHG CITY	1788
CHURCH - GERMAN LUTHERAN CHURCH - NEAR CLAY ST	1871	WHG CITY	1790
CHURCH - LUTHERAN CHURCH - FOURTH ST	1871	WHG CITY	1788
CHURCH - LUTHERAN CHURCH - FOURTH ST & JOHN ST	1871	WHG CITY	1788
CHURCH - LUTHERAN CHURCH - MARKET ST	1871	WHG CITY	1788
CHURCH - LUTHERAN CHURCH - MARKET ST	1871	WHG CITY	1790
CHURCH - M.E. CHURCH / METHODIST EPISCOPAL	1871	HAN MAP	1726
CHURCH - METHODIST CHURCH / MAP#672	1852	BRKE MAP	1854
CHURCH - METHODIST CHURCH - CHAPLINE ST	1871	WHG CITY	1790
CHURCH - METHODIST CHURCH - N.OF HORNBROOK BROTHERS	1871	MARH'L MAP	1754
CHURCH - METHODIST CHURCH - NE. OF WHITE OAK GROVE	1871	MARH'L MAP	1751
CHURCH - METHODIST CHURCH & PARSONAGE - WEST UNION	1871	W.UNION	1812
CHURCH - METHODIST EPISCOPAL - INITIALS M.P. (?M.E.?) PROSPECT ST - WELLSBURG	1871	WELLSBURG	1777
CHURCH - METHODIST EPISCOPAL CHURCH / WEST OF PLEASANT VALLEY	1871	HAN MAP	1727
CHURCH - METHODIST EPISCOPAL CHURCH / E. OF J.M. WILSON	1871	BRKE MAP	1736
CHURCH - METHODIST EPISCOPAL CHURCH / PARSONAGE	1871	BRKE MAP	1737
CHURCH - METHODIST EPISCOPAL CHURCH - BROADWAY ST	1871	WHG ISLAND	1788
CHURCH - METHODIST EPISCOPAL CHURCH - C ST - MOUNDSVILLE	1871	MDSVILLE	1809
CHURCH - METHODIST EPISCOPAL CHURCH - CHAPLINE & SECOND ST	1871	WHG CITY	1790
CHURCH - METHODIST EPISCOPAL CHURCH - CORNER OF PEARL AND WATER STS - NEW CUMBERLAND	1871	NEW CUMB'LD	1767
CHURCH - METHODIST EPISCOPAL CHURCH - COUNCILMANS RUN	1871	BKE/OH MAP	1739
CHURCH - METHODIST EPISCOPAL CHURCH - E. OF SCHOOL NO.9 - LIBERTY TWP	1871	MARH'L MAP	1761
CHURCH - METHODIST EPISCOPAL CHURCH - FERTILE VALLEY	1871	MARH'L MAP	1745
CHURCH - METHODIST EPISCOPAL CHURCH - FIFTH ST - WHEELING	1871	WHG CITY	1788
CHURCH - METHODIST EPISCOPAL CHURCH - FIRST ST - BENWOOD	1871	BENWOOD	1798
CHURCH - METHODIST EPISCOPAL CHURCH - FOURTH ST - WHEELING	1871	WHG CITY	1788
CHURCH - METHODIST EPISCOPAL CHURCH - GREGGVILLE	1871	OH CO. MAP	1741
CHURCH - METHODIST EPISCOPAL CHURCH - N OF PAN-HANDLE P.O.	1871	BRKE MAP	1734
CHURCH - METHODIST EPISCOPAL CHURCH - N. OF BENWOOD	1871	MARH'L MAP	1745
CHURCH - METHODIST EPISCOPAL CHURCH - N. OF SCHOOL NO. 8	1871	BRKE MAP	1737
CHURCH - METHODIST EPISCOPAL CHURCH - N. OF W. CONNELLEY	1871	OH CO. MAP	1741
CHURCH - METHODIST EPISCOPAL CHURCH - NEW MANCHESTER	1871	HAN MAP	1731
CHURCH - METHODIST EPISCOPAL CHURCH - NW OF SHERRARD	1871	MARH'L MAP	1745

XX

'PERSONAL TIME LINE' INDEX TO VOLUME 7 OF THE *OHIO COUNTY INDEX*

ENTRY	YEAR	SUBJECT	PAGE
CHURCH - METHODIST EPISCOPAL CHURCH - PARSONAGE - NEW MANCHESTER	1871	NEW MANCH.	1769
CHURCH - METHODIST EPISCOPAL CHURCH - ROSBY'S ROCK	1871	MARH'L MAP	1752
CHURCH - METHODIST EPISCOPAL CHURCH - S. OF BENWOOD	1871	MARH'L MAP	1745
CHURCH - METHODIST EPISCOPAL CHURCH - S. OF MOUNT ZION	1871	MARH'L MAP	1745
CHURCH - METHODIST EPISCOPAL CHURCH - S. OF THE WHITE HOUSE FARM	1871	MARH'L MAP	1752
CHURCH - METHODIST EPISCOPAL CHURCH - S. OF THE WHITE HOUSE FARM	1871	MARH'L MAP	1755
CHURCH - METHODIST EPISCOPAL CHURCH - SHERRARD P.O.	1871	SHERRARD	1811
CHURCH - METHODIST EPISCOPAL CHURCH - SIXTH ST	1871	WHG CITY	1790
CHURCH - METHODIST EPISCOPAL CHURCH - SIXTH ST - WHEELING	1871	WHG CITY	1788
CHURCH - METHODIST EPISCOPAL CHURCH - SW. OF SCHOOL NO. 15	1871	MARH'L MAP	1756
CHURCH - METHODIST EPISCOPAL CHURCH - TRIADELPHIA	1871	OH CO. MAP	1743
CHURCH - METHODIST EPISCOPAL CHURCH - TRIADELPHIA	1871	OH CO. MAP	1744
CHURCH - METHODIST EPISCOPAL CHURCH - TRIADELPHIA	1871	TRIAD.BORO.	1784
CHURCH - METHODIST EPISCOPAL CHURCH - UNION ST - MOUNDSVILLE / COL'D OR COLD ?	1871	MDSVILLE	1810
CHURCH - METHODIST EPISCOPAL CHURCH - UPPER N.FORK OF GRAVE CREEK	1871	MARH'L MAP	1753
CHURCH - METHODIST EPISCOPAL CHURCH - VALLEY RUN	1871	MARH'L MAP	1760
CHURCH - METHODIST EPISCOPAL CHURCH - WASH. TWP	1871	MARH'L MAP	1748
CHURCH - METHODIST EPISCOPAL CHURCH - WEST LIBERTY	1871	W.LIBERTY	1780
CHURCH - METHODIST EPISCOPAL CHURCH - WEST UNION / NE CORNER OF MAP	1871	OH CO. MAP	1743
CHURCH - METHODIST EPISCOPAL CHURCH - WEST UNION	1871	MARH'L MAP	1747
CHURCH - METHODIST EPISCOPAL CHURCH & CEM / CLAY TWP	1871	MARH'L MAP	1751
CHURCH - METHODIST EPISCOPAL CHURCH & CEM & PARSONAGE	1871	BKE/OH MAP	1738
CHURCH - METHODIST EPISCOPAL CHURCH & CEMETERY - NEAR PLEASANT HOME - CLAY TWP	1871	MARH'L MAP	1752
CHURCH - METHODIST EPISCOPAL CHURCH & CEMETERY - NEW MANCHESTER - N. OF TANNERY	1871	NEW MANCH.	1769
CHURCH - METHODIST EPISCOPAL CHURCH & CEMETERY - ON FAIRMOUNT ROAD	1871	MARH'L MAP	1745
CHURCH - METHODIST EPISCOPAL CHURCH & CEMETERY - S. OF BLAIR HOMESTEAD	1871	MARH'L MAP	1749
CHURCH - METHODIST EPISCOPAL CHURCH & GRAVE YARD - NW OF R. ZINK	1871	MARH'L MAP	1749
CHURCH - METHODIST EPISCOPAL CHURCH & GRAVEYARD - WAYNESBURGH ROAD	1871	MARH'L MAP	1749
CHURCH - METHODIST EPISCOPAL CHURCH AND CEMETERY - E. OF J M. WILSON	1871	BKE/OH MAP	1738
CHURCH - METHODIST EPISCOPAL CHURCH PARSONAGE - TRIADELPHIA	1871	TRIAD.BORO.	1784
CHURCH - METHODIST EPISCOPAL CHURCH PARSONAGE - WALNUT ST	1871	WELLSBURG	1777
CHURCH - METHODIST EPISCOPAL CHURCH PARSONAGE - WEST LIBERTY	1871	W.LIBERTY	1780
CHURCH - MOUNT DE CHANTAL CONVENT / CATHOLIC	1871	TRIAD.TWP.	1781
CHURCH - MOUNT DE CHANTAL CONVENT	1871	WHG CITY	1789
CHURCH - OLD THREE SPRINGS CHURCH / FIRST CHURCH IN COUNTY	1871	HAN MAP	1732
CHURCH - PRESBYTERIAN CHURCH / & CEMETERY - PLEASANT HILL	1871	HAN MAP	1732
CHURCH - PRESBYTERIAN CHURCH	1871	HAN MAP	1733
CHURCH - PRESBYTERIAN CHURCH / INITIALS P. CHURCH - S. OF W. MCKINLEY	1871	BKE/OH MAP	1738
CHURCH - PRESBYTERIAN CHURCH / STONE CHURCH	1871	OH CO. MAP	1742
CHURCH - PRESBYTERIAN CHURCH - CAMERON	1871	CAMERON	1803
CHURCH - PRESBYTERIAN CHURCH - FOURTH ST	1871	WHG CITY	1788
CHURCH - PRESBYTERIAN CHURCH - HAMPDEN ST	1871	WHG CITY	1788
CHURCH - PRESBYTERIAN CHURCH - HARRISON ST - NEW CUMBERLAND	1871	NEW CUMB'LD	1768
CHURCH - PRESBYTERIAN CHURCH - LIMESTONE	1871	MARH'L MAP	1749
CHURCH - PRESBYTERIAN CHURCH - LIMESTONE P.O.	1871	LIMESTONE	1805
CHURCH - PRESBYTERIAN CHURCH - MAIN ST	1871	WHG CITY	1788
CHURCH - PRESBYTERIAN CHURCH - MAIN ST - WHEELING	1871	WHG CITY	1786
CHURCH - PRESBYTERIAN CHURCH - MARKET ST	1871	WHG CITY	1790
CHURCH - PRESBYTERIAN CHURCH - MOUND ST - MOUNDSVILLE	1871	MDSVILLE	1809
CHURCH - PRESBYTERIAN CHURCH - NW OF NEW MANCHESTER / G.Y. PRES. CH. ?	1871	HAN MAP	1731
CHURCH - PRESBYTERIAN CHURCH - ROCK LICK P.O.	1871	MARH'L MAP	1753
CHURCH - PRESBYTERIAN CHURCH - S. WHG	1871	SOUTH WHG	1792
CHURCH - PRESBYTERIAN CHURCH - W. OF MARLOW RUN	1871	OH CO. MAP	1743
CHURCH - PRESBYTERIAN CHURCH - WEBSTER ST	1871	WHG CITY	1788
CHURCH - PRESBYTERIAN CHURCH - WELLSBURG / QUEEN ST	1871	WELLSBURG	1777
CHURCH - PRESBYTERIAN CHURCH - WELLSBURG - PARSONAGE / URANA ST.	1871	WELLSBURG	1777
CHURCH - PRESBYTERIAN CHURCH & CEMETERY - SHERRARD P.O.	1871	MARH'L MAP	1746
CHURCH - PRESBYTERIAN CHURCH & CEMETERY - SHERRARD P.O.	1871	SHERRARD	1811
CHURCH - PRESBYTERIAN CHURCH & CEMETERY - WEST UNION	1871	W.UNION	1812
CHURCH - PRESYTERIAN CHURCH - SECOND ST - MOUNDSVILLE	1871	MDSVL BUS.	1796
CHURCH - PROSPECT ST - DISCIPLES ? - WELLSBURG	1871	WELLSBURG	1777
CHURCH - REFORMED PRESBYTERIAN CHURCH	1871	HAN MAP	1731
CHURCH - REFORMED PRESBYTERIAN CHURCH - SW OF BROWNLEE SCHOOL NO. 1	1871	OH CO. MAP	1743
CHURCH - ROMAN CATHOLIC CHURCH / MEADE TWP - INITIALS R.C.CH.	1871	MARH'L MAP	1759
CHURCH - ROMAN CATHOLIC CHURCH - MARKET ST	1871	WHG CITY	1788
CHURCH - ROMAN CATHOLIC CHURCH - MARKET ST	1871	WHG CITY	1790
CHURCH - SECEDER / MAP#534	1852	BRKE MAP	1852
CHURCH - ST JOHNS CHURCH / & GRAVEYARD	1871	BRKE MAP	1734
CHURCH - ST JOHNS CHURCH - BROOKE CO	1852	BRKE MAP	1852
CHURCH - ST. JOHN'S / MAP#540	1852	BRKE MAP	1852
CHURCH - ST. JOHN'S CHURCH / MAP#540	1852	BRKE MAP	1852
CHURCH - STATE PENITENTIARY - CHAPEL	1871	MDSVILLE	1809
CHURCH - STONE PRESBYTERIAN CHURCH - ELM GROVE	1916	NAT'L ROAD	1863
CHURCH - STONE PRESBYTERIAN CHURCH - ELM GROVE	1916	NAT'L ROAD	1864
CHURCH - UNION CHAPEL - WELLSBURG / (?CHAPEL?) - PROSPECT ST.	1871	WELLSBURG	1777
CHURCH - UNION CHURCH & CEMETERY - S. OF LIMESTONE	1871	MARH'L MAP	1749
CHURCH - UNIV. CHURCH / (?UNIVERSALIST?)	1871	MARH'L MAP	1752

ENTRY	YEAR	SUBJECT	PAGE	ENTRY	YEAR	SUBJECT	PAGE
CHURCH - UNIV. CHURCH & SCHOOL / (?UNIVERSALIST?)	1871	MARH'L MAP	1752	CLARK, SETH / MILL - MAP#450	1852	BRKE MAP	1849
				CLARK, SETH / MILL - MAP#451	1852	BRKE MAP	1849
CHURCH - UNKNOWN DENOMINATION - WASHINGTON ST - NEW CUMBERLAND	1871	NEW CUMB'LD	1767	CLARK, SETH / MILL - MAP#453	1852	BRKE MAP	1849
				CLARK, SETH / MILL - MAP#454	1852	BRKE MAP	1849
				CLARK, SETH / MILL- MAP#452	1852	BRKE MAP	1849
CHURCH - WOLF RUN PRESBYTERIAN CHURCH	1871	MARH'L MAP	1750	CLARK, SETH / (FERRY) - MAP#549	1852	BRKE MAP	1851
				CLARK, SETH / MAP#513	1852	BRKE MAP	1851
CHURCH - ZION'S CHAPEL	1871	MARH'L MAP	1751	CLARK, SETH / MAP#548	1852	BRKE MAP	1851
CHURCH OF GOD - LIBERTY TWP	1871	MARH'L MAP	1760	CLARK, WILLIAM	1825	DEFENDANT	1574
CHURCH OF GOD - MARSHALL CO / MISC.	1871	BENWO'D - BUS.	1795	CLARK, WILLIAM	1827	MISC	1678
				CLARK, WILLIAM	1828	DEFENDANT	1613
CHURCH OF GOD - NW OF SHERRARD / S. OF GR.YD.	1871	MARH'L MAP	1745	CLARKE, HEZEKIAH	1854	MISC	1689
				CLARKE, JAMES A	1845	MISC	1710
CHURCH OF GOD - SHERRARD	1871	MARH'L MAP	1746	CLARKE, JAMES A	1846	MISC	1706
CHURCH OF GOD - SHERRARD P.O. / & GRAVEYARD	1871	SHERRARD	1811	CLARKE, JOHN F	1840	DEFENDANT	1596
				CLARKE, WILLIAM A	1843	DEFENDANT	1599
CHURCH ST - RITCHIE TWP	1871	RITCHIE TWP	1793	CLARYS RUN	1852	BRKE MAP	1843
CHURCH, DAVID	1821	DEFENDANT	1570	CLASE, JAMES G	1832	DEFENDANT	1620
CHURCH, DAVID	1822	DEFENDANT	1587	CLAW, I G	1834	DEFENDANT	1639
CHURCH, DAVID	1834	DEFENDANT	1618	CLAWSON, E / MRS	1871	MARH'L MAP	1753
CHURCH, DAVID	1839	DEFENDANT	1662	CLAWSON, M / MRS	1871	MARH'L MAP	1753
CHURCH, ELIJAH	1818	DEFENDANT	1587	CLAWSON, T	1871	MARH'L MAP	1761
CHURCH, ELIJAH	1820	DEFENDANT	1638	CLAY - E. OF ATKINSON & SHANE	1871	RIV. RD N.OF NC	1770
CHURCH, FRANKLIN / MAP#366	1852	BRKE MAP	1847	CLAY - E. OF J. & A. MANYPENNY	1871	RIV. RD N.OF NC	1770
CHURCHMAN, J / HEIRS - MAP#439	1852	BRKE MAP	1849	CLAY - E. OF M.M.CULLEN & BROS	1871	RIV. RD N.OF NC	1770
CIDER HOUSE	1871	HAN MAP	1731	CLAY - E. OF SMITH, PORTER & CO	1871	RIV. RD N.OF NC	1770
CIDER HOUSE	1871	HAN MAP	1732	CLAY - E. OF T.ANDERSON & CO	1871	FRE'MAN'S LDG	1764
CIGARS - LITEUTZ CIGARS / F.SPRINGARBORN	1871	WELLSBURG	1777	CLAY - N. OF FREEMANS LANDING	1871	HAN MAP	1731
				CLAY - NW. OF D. TROUP / #1	1871	RIV. RD N.OF N.C.	1770
CINCINNATI	1852	HEMPFIELD RR	1818	CLAY - NW. OF NEWELL HALL	1871	HAN MAP	1727
CINCINNATI	1852	HEMPFIELD RR	1819	CLAY - POTTERS CLAY / S. OF LOCUST GROVE	1871	HAN MAP	1726
CINCINNATI	1852	HEMPFIELD RR	1820				
CINCINNATI	1852	HEMPFIELD RR	1821	CLAY AND COAL BANK - NEAR DEEP GUT RUN	1871	HAN MAP	1730
CINCINNATI	1852	HEMP. RR MAP	1825				
CINCINNATI	1852	HEMP. RR MAP	1826	CLAY BED - NE OF COLD SPRINGS	1871	HAN MAP	1726
CINCINNATI / PITTSBURGH, CINCINNATI & ST. LOUIS RR	1871	BRKE MAP	1734	CLAY MONUMENT - ELM GROVE	1916	NAT'L ROAD	1863
				CLAY- NW. OF D. TROUP / #2	1871	RIV. RD N.OF N.C.	1770
CINCINNATI / PITTSBURGH, CINCINNATI & ST. LOUIS RR	1871	BRKE MAP	1735	CLAY ROAD - 923 FROM CLAY ROAD TO [MIDDLE WHEELING] CREEK BY OLD ROAD	1871	OH CO. MAP	1743
CINCINNATI & ST. LOUIS RR	1871	BRKE MAP	1734				
CINCINNATI, CHILLICOTHE & MARIETTA RR	1852	HEMP. RR MAP	1826	CLAY TOWNSHIP - HANCOCK CO	1871	FRE'MAN'S LDG	1764
				CLAY TOWNSHIP - HANCOCK CO	1871	POPULATION	1816
CINCINNATI, WILMINGTON & ZANESVILLE RR	1852	HEMP. RR MAP	1826	CLAY TOWNSHIP - HANCOCK CO - BUSINESS LISTINGS	1871	HAN-CLAY TWP	1763
CIRCUIT COURT - HIGH ST NEW MANCHESTER	1871	NEW MANCH.	1763	CLAY TOWNSHIP - HANCOCK CO.	1871	HAN MAP	1731
				CLAY TOWNSHIP - MARSHALL CO	1871	POPULATION	1816
CIRCUIT COURT - MOUNDSVILLE	1871	MDSVL BUS.	1796	CLAY TOWNSHIP - MARSHALL CO - N. PART	1871	MDSVILLE	1809
CITY CEMETERY / OR PENINSULA	1871	WHG CITY	1787				
CITY CEMETERY / OR PENINSULA	1871	WHG CITY	1788	CLAY TOWNSHIP - MARSHALL CO - N. PART	1871	MDSVILLE	1810
CITY COMMONS - WHEELING CITY	1871	WHG CITY	1788				
CLAGG, ROBERT	1826	DEFENDANT	1668	CLAY TOWNSHIP - MARSHALL CO - ROSBBYS ROCK - DETAIL MAP	1871	ROSBBYS RK	1813
CLARE, I G	1834	DEFENDANT	1639				
CLARE, I G	1836	DEFENDANT	1640	CLAY TOWNSHIP - MARSHALL CO.	1871	MARH'L MAP	1751
CLARE, S G	1838	DEFENDANT	1640	CLAY TOWNSHIP - MARSHALL CO.	1871	MARH'L MAP	1752
CLARINGTON, MONROE CO., OHIO / FORMERLY KNOWN AS SUNFISH	1871	MARH'L MAP	1754	CLAY TOWNSHIP - NEW CUMBERLAND - RIVER ROAD N. OF - DETAIL MAP	1871	RIV. RD N.OF N.C.	1770
CLARK - WIFE	1828	DEFENDANT	1613				
CLARK BRIDGE - BUFFALO CREEK - WASH. CO., PA.	1916	NAT'L ROAD	1862	CLAY TOWNSHIP - NEW CUMBERLAND - RIVER ROAD S. OF - DETAIL MAP	1871	RIV. RD S.OF N.C.	1771
CLARK, BARNABAS	1820	DEFENDANT	1624				
CLARK, GEORGE	1871	MARH'L MAP	1758	CLAY TOWNSHIP - OHIO CO	1871	WHG CITY	1788
CLARK, H	1871	OH CO. MAP	1742	CLAY TOWNSHIP - WHEELING	1871	OH CO. MAP	1742
CLARK, H / INITIALS H.C.	1871	RITCHIE TWP	1791	CLAY, HENRY / MONUMENT ERECTED 18??	1871	OH CO. MAP	1742
CLARK, HENRY	1802	DEFENDANT	1666				
CLARK, HUGH	1871	OH CO. MAP	1742	CLAY, HENRY / MONUMENT ERECTED TO IN 1820	1871	ELM GROVE	1782
CLARK, J	1871	OH CO. MAP	1743				
CLARK, JAMES	1783	DEFENDANT	1610	CLAY, HENRY / KENTUCKY STATESMAN	1916	NAT'L ROAD	1862
CLARK, JOHN	1800	DEFENDANT	1583				
CLARK, JOHN	1803	DEFENDANT	1579	CLAY, HENRY / MONUMENT - ELM GROVE	1916	NAT'L ROAD	1864
CLARK, JOHN	1804	DEFENDANT	1635				
CLARK, JOHN	1817	DEFENDANT	1635	CLAY, HENRY / HISTORY OF MONUMENT	1916	NAT'L ROAD	1865
CLARK, JOHN	1820	DEFENDANT	1642				
CLARK, JOHN	1824	DEFENDANT	1581	CLAY, HENRY / MONUMENT - PHOTO	1916	NAT'L ROAD	1865
CLARK, JOHN	1824	DEFENDANT	1635	CLAYSVILLE, PA / LAID OUT IN 1817	1916	NAT'L ROAD	1862
CLARK, JOHN	1828	DEFENDANT	1613	CLAYSVILLE, PA - MAP	1916	NAT'L ROAD	1863
CLARK, JOHN C / PRINTER OF MAP	1852	HEMPFIELD RR	1817	CLAYSVILLE, PA - MAP	1916	NAT'L ROAD	1869
CLARK, M / MRS	1871	MARH'L MAP	1761	CLAYTON, RICHARD / MAP#412	1852	BRKE MAP	1846
CLARK, P	1871	OH CO. MAP	1742	CLAYTON, STEPHEN / MAP#423	1852	BRKE MAP	1847
CLARK, P	1871	OH CO. MAP	1744	CLAYTON, W	1871	BENWOOD	1798
CLARK, P	1871	BENWOOD	1799	CLEAR VIEW	1871	OH CO. MAP	1740
CLARK, ROBERT R	1829	DEFENDANT	1639	CLEAR VIEW	1871	OH CO. MAP	1743
CLARK, ROBERT R	1831	DEFENDANT	1639	CLEARY, S	1871	BRKE MAP	1736
CLARK, ROBERT R	1831	DEFENDANT	1650	CLELAND, S	1871	BRKE MAP	1735
CLARK, S	1871	NEW CUMB'LD	1767	CLEMANS, ABRAHAM W	1827	DEFENDANT	1613
CLARK, SETH	1852	NOT ON MAP	1836	CLEMENS, -	1858	DEFENDANT	1630
CLARK, SETH / MAP#455	1852	BRKE MAP	1849	CLEMENS, -	1878	DEFENDANT	1568

'PERSONAL TIME LINE' INDEX TO VOLUME 7 OF THE *OHIO COUNTY INDEX*

ENTRY	YEAR	SUBJECT	PAGE
CLEMENS, A W	1856	PLAINTIFF	1641
CLEMENS, ABRAHAM W	1834	DEFENDANT	1618
CLEMENS, ABRAHAM W	1836	DEFENDANT	1628
CLEMENS, ABRAHAM W	1836	DEFENDANT	1662
CLEMENS, ABRAHAM W	1839	DEFENDANT	1614
CLEMENS, ABRAHAM W	1839	DEFENDANT	1619
CLEMENS, ABRAHAM W	1855	DEFENDANT	1641
CLEMENS, J	1871	WELLSBURG	1777
CLEMENS, JAMES	1779	APPENDIX	1874
CLEMENS, JAMES	1843	DEFENDANT	1619
CLEMENS, JEREMIAH	1838	DEFENDANT	1598
CLEMENS, JEREMIAH	1838	DEFENDANT	1651
CLEMENS, JEREMIAH	1838	DEFENDANT	1651
CLEMENS, JEREMIAH	1839	DEFENDANT	1614
CLEMENS, JEREMIAH	1839	DEFENDANT	1619
CLEMENS, JEREMIAH	1841	DEFENDANT	1662
CLEMENS, JERIMIAH	1838	DEFENDANT	1598
CLEMENS, SAMUEL M	1877	DEFENDANT	1558
CLEMENS, SHERRARD	1851	DEFENDANT	1641
CLEMENS, SHERRARD	1852	DEFENDANT	1561
CLEMENS, SHERRARD	1852	DEFENDANT	1623
CLEMENS, SHERRARD	1855	DEFENDANT	1561
CLEMENS, SHERRARD	1855	DEFENDANT	1584
CLEMENS, SHERRARD	1855	DEFENDANT	1603
CLEMENS, SHERRARD	1855	DEFENDANT	1623
CLEMENS, SHERRARD	1855	DEFENDANT	1636
CLEMENS, SHERRARD	1857	DEFENDANT	1663
CLEMENS, SHERRARD	1858	DEFENDANT	1603
CLEMINS, JEREMIAH	1832	DEFENDANT	1618
CLEMMENS, S	1871	MARH'L MAP	1746
CLEMMONS, - / MRS	1871	OH CO. MAP	1743
CLEMMONS, ABRAHAM	1825	DEFENDANT	1649
CLEMMONS, ABRAHAM	1825	DEFENDANT	1649
CLEMS RUN / (?SPELLED CLENS?)	1852	BRKE MAP	1852
CLENCH, -	1854	PLAINTIFF	1623
CLENDENIN, WILLIAM / MAP#156	1852	BRKE MAP	1842
CLENDENIN, WILLIAM / MAP#158	1852	BRKE MAP	1842
CLENDENIN, WILLIAM / MAP#159	1852	BRKE MAP	1842
CLENDENIN, WILLIAM / MAP#159	1852	BRKE MAP	1842
CLENS RUN / (?CLEMS?)	1852	BRKE MAP	1852
CLEVELAND & COLUMBUS & CINCINNATI RR	1852	HEMP. RR MAP	1826
CLEVELAND & WELLSVILLE RR	1852	HEMP. RR MAP	1826
CLEVELAND AND PITTSBURG RR	1871	HAN MAP	1730
CLEVELAND AND PITTSBURG RR	1871	HAN MAP	1732
CLEVELAND AND WHEELING ROAD / RR	1852	HEMPFIELD RR	1820
CLEVELAND, OH	1852	HEMPFIELD RR	1820
CLEVELAND, OH	1852	HEMP. RR MAP	1826
CLIFTON FIRE BRICK WORKS	1871	RIV. RD N.OF N.C.	1763
CLIFTON FIRE BRICK WORKS / SMITH, PORTER & CO.	1871	RIV. RD N.OF N.C.	1770
CLIFTON HOUSE - HOTEL - MOUNDSVILLE	1871	MDSVL BUS.	1796
CLIFTON HOUSE - HOTEL - MOUNDSVILLE / M.C.KEILY	1871	MDSVILLE	1808
CLIFTON HOUSE - PURDY ST - HOTEL	1871	MDSVILLE	1810
CLINE, C	1871	BRKE MAP	1734
CLINE, JOSEPH	1825	DEFENDANT	1660
CLINE, JOSEPH	1825	DEFENDANT	1660
CLINGAN, JOSEPH	1820	DEFENDANT	1563
CLINGAN, JOSEPH	1821	DEFENDANT	1563
CLINKS, - / ?	1871	MARH'L MAP	1745
CLINOR, - / MISS - INITIAL MISS C.	1871	MARH'L MAP	1745
CLINOR, - / MISS	1871	MARH'L MAP	1749
CLINOR, C	1871	MARH'L MAP	1745
CLINOR, C	1871	MARH'L MAP	1749
CLINTON / BROOKE CO	1871	DISTANCES	1815
CLINTON P.O.	1871	OH CO. MAP	1741
CLOGAS, - / (?OR CLOGUS?)	1871	MARH'L MAP	1746
CLOGUS, - / (?OR CLOGAS?)	1871	MARH'L MAP	1746
CLORD, WILLIAM ANN	1826	DEFENDANT	1613
CLOUSTON, - / MRS	1871	MARH'L MAP	1757
CLOUSTON, W	1871	CAMERON	1802
CLOUSTON, W / INITIALS W.C.	1871	CAMERON	1802
CLOVER HILL	1871	MARH'L MAP	1749
CLOVER HILL	1871	MARH'L MAP	1753
CLSCAN, C / MRS - (?OR OLSON?)	1871	MARH'L MAP	1752
CLSCAN, C / MRS - (?OR OLSON?)	1871	MARH'L MAP	1756
CLUNEY, MILES	1821	DEFENDANT	1656
CLUSTER ISLAND / IN OHIO RIVER	1871	HAN MAP	1726
CLUTTER, GEORGE A	1843	DEFENDANT	1629
CLUTTER, GEORGE A	1843	DEFENDANT	1656
COAL / DIRECTIONS LISTED FROM NEAREST LAND	1800	APPENDIX	1738

ENTRY	YEAR	SUBJECT	PAGE
COAL - 6 FEET COAL / NW OF MT PLEASANT	1871	HAN MAP	1732
COAL - B. WELLS JR	1871	BRKE MAP	1736
COAL - CANNEL COAL	1871	HAN MAP	1727
COAL - CEPHAS CARTER	1871	BRKE MAP	1735
COAL - E OF BROWNS ISLAND	1871	HAN MAP	1732
COAL - E OF WHITE OAK FLATS	1871	HAN MAP	1726
COAL - E. OF ATKINSON & SHANE	1871	RIV. RD N.OF N.C.	1770
COAL - E. OF J GROVES	1871	BRKE MAP	1736
COAL - E. OF J. & A. MANYPENNY	1871	RIV. RD N.OF N.C.	1770
COAL - E. OF J.N. MAYHEW	1871	HAN MAP	1731
COAL - E. OF M.M.CULLEN & BROS	1871	RIV. RD N.OF N.C.	1770
COAL - E. OF MAPLE GROVE	1871	OH CO. MAP	1742
COAL - E. OF R BIRKETT	1871	OH CO. MAP	1742
COAL - E. OF SHADE RUN	1871	HAN MAP	1732
COAL - E. OF SMITH, PORTER & CO	1871	RIV. RD N.OF N.C.	1770
COAL - E. OF T. BAKER	1871	BRKE MAP	1735
COAL - E. OF T.ANDERSON & CO	1871	FRE'MAN'S LDG	1764
COAL - E. OF W. BUSBEY	1871	BKE/OH MAP	1738
COAL - E. OF WILLIAM GASTON	1871	OH CO. MAP	1740
COAL - EAST OF RIVERSIDE	1871	HAN MAP	1726
COAL - J. LEWIS	1871	BRKE MAP	1736
COAL - J. WIGGINS	1871	BRKE MAP	1735
COAL - J.B. WIGGINS	1871	BRKE MAP	1735
COAL - JOHN C REEVES	1871	BRKE MAP	1735
COAL - LAZUR HOLLOW	1871	BKE/OH MAP	1739
COAL - LYNNCAMP P.O.	1871	MARH'L MAP	1755
COAL - N OF EUGENE TARR	1871	BRKE MAP	1736
COAL - N. OF A. CAMPBELL	1871	BRKE MAP	1737
COAL - N. OF A. MITCHELL	1871	OH CO. MAP	1741
COAL - N. OF C RYAN	1871	BKE/OH MAP	1738
COAL - N. OF COLD SPRING FARM	1871	HAN MAP	1731
COAL - N. OF COLD SPRING FARM	1871	HAN MAP	1732
COAL - N. OF D. TROUP / #1	1871	RIV. RD N.OF N.C.	1770
COAL - N. OF D. TROUP / #2	1871	RIV. RD N.OF N.C.	1770
COAL - N. OF FARMERS DELIGHT	1871	HAN MAP	1731
COAL - N. OF FREEMANS LANDING	1871	HAN MAP	1731
COAL - N. OF G KEMPLE	1871	MARH'L MAP	1745
COAL - N. OF G.B. MILLER	1871	BKE/OH MAP	1739
COAL - N. OF G.R.PORTER	1871	FRE'MAN'S LDG	1764
COAL - N. OF H. FISHER	1871	BRKE MAP	1737
COAL - N OF J WILSON	1871	BRKE MAP	1737
COAL - N. OF J. SPOON	1871	MARH'L MAP	1752
COAL - N. OF J. WOODS	1871	OH CO. MAP	1741
COAL - N. OF J.SEIDLER	1871	MARH'L MAP	1754
COAL - N. OF J.T.SCOTT	1871	MARH'L MAP	1758
COAL - N. OF JOB LEWIS	1871	BRKE MAP	1736
COAL - N. OF MRS. N.GRAY	1871	MARH'L MAP	1760
COAL - N. OF P. RILEY	1871	OH CO. MAP	1741
COAL - N. OF P.RILEY	1871	OH CO. MAP	1741
COAL - N. OF PLEASANT VIEW	1871	HAN MAP	1726
COAL - N. OF RIVERVIEW	1871	HAN MAP	1726
COAL - N. OF SCHOOL NO.7	1871	OH CO. MAP	1743
COAL - N. OF SCHOOL NO.7 - OHIO CO	1871	MARH'L MAP	1746
COAL - N. OF SPRING HILL	1871	HAN MAP	1726
COAL - N. OF STEENROD	1871	OH CO. MAP	1742
COAL - N. OF T. CRISWELL	1871	MARH'L MAP	1745
COAL - N. OF W. BRICE	1871	HAN MAP	1732
COAL - N. OF WILLIAM A JONES	1871	HAN MAP	1731
COAL - N. OF WILLIAM PORTER	1871	OH CO. MAP	1742
COAL - N. OF WILLIAM RODGERS	1871	BRKE MAP	1737
COAL - N. OF WILLIAM RODGERS	1871	BKE/OH MAP	1739
COAL - N.E. OF C. FORD	1871	MARH'L MAP	1745
COAL - NE OF ALLISON HOMESTEAD	1871	HAN MAP	1727
COAL - NE OF CHERRY HILL FARM	1871	MARH'L MAP	1745
COAL - NE OF G. ELLIOTT	1871	BKE/OH MAP	1739
COAL - NE OF H. KELTZ	1871	MARH'L MAP	1745
COAL - NE OF J. HOOD	1871	HAN MAP	1731
COAL - NE OF J. MAHAN	1871	HAN MAP	1732
COAL - NE OF J.L.FREEMAN & CO	1871	FRE'MAN'S LDG	1764
COAL - NE. OF JUDGE THOMPSON	1871	WHG CITY	1787
COAL - NE. OF MRS. RAMSEY	1871	MARH'L MAP	1755
COAL - NE. OF TRAVIS RIDGE	1871	MARH'L MAP	1754
COAL - NEAR D. CUMMINS	1871	HAN MAP	1731
COAL - NEAR LOCUST ST - S. WHG	1871	SOUTH WHG	1792
COAL - NEAR LOCUST ST - S. WHG	1871	SOUTH WHG	1794
COAL - NEAR MARKS RUN	1871	HAN MAP	1728
COAL - NEAR MIDDLE RUN	1871	HAN MAP	1728
COAL - NEAR OHIO RIVER	1871	HAN MAP	1730
COAL - NNE OF COLD SPRING FARM	1871	HAN MAP	1731
COAL - NORTH OF T. HENDERSON / INITIALS T.H.	1871	BRKE MAP	1737
COAL - NW OF C.C.TARR	1871	BRKE MAP	1736
COAL - NW OF CHAMBERS FARM	1871	HAN MAP	1726
COAL - NW OF ELWOOD GROVE	1871	HAN MAP	1726
COAL - NW OF J. PURDY	1871	HAN MAP	1732

XXIII

'PERSONAL TIME LINE' INDEX TO VOLUME 7 OF THE *OHIO COUNTY INDEX*

ENTRY	YEAR	SUBJECT	PAGE
COAL - NW OF J. STEWART	1871	BKE/OH MAP	1739
COAL - NW OF J. MCINTIRE	1871	BRKE MAP	1736
COAL - NW OF MAPLE GROVE	1871	HAN MAP	1732
COAL - NW OF T. SMITH	1871	HAN MAP	1732
COAL - NW OF ORCHARD SIDE	1871	OH CO. MAP	1744
COAL - NW OF PLEASANT HILL	1871	HAN MAP	1732
COAL - NW. OF ELM GROVE STATION	1871	OH CO. MAP	1744
COAL - NW. OF J. WOODS	1871	OH CO. MAP	1742
COAL - S. OF FORTUNE HILL	1871	HAN MAP	1727
COAL - S OF R. CAMPBELL	1871	HAN MAP	1732
COAL - S OF WHITE OAK FLATS	1871	HAN MAP	1726
COAL - S. OF BROOKLYN SCHOOL NO. 3	1871	HAN MAP	1726
COAL - S. OF CHAMBERS FARM	1871	HAN MAP	1726
COAL - S. OF CHERRY LANE FARM	1871	MARH'L MAP	1758
COAL - S. OF E. CONNER	1871	MARH'L MAP	1745
COAL - S. OF E. COX	1871	BKE/OH MAP	1739
COAL - S. OF FLAG QUARRY	1871	OH CO. MAP	1742
COAL - S. OF FREDERICK BADE	1871	OH CO. MAP	1744
COAL - S OF H.I. MENDEL	1871	BRKE MAP	1736
COAL - S OF HANK SPRING RUN	1871	BRKE MAP	1735
COAL - S. OF J. LEWIS	1871	BRKE MAP	1736
COAL - S. OF J. LEWIS	1871	BRKE MAP	1736
COAL - S. OF J. MAHAN	1871	HAN MAP	1732
COAL - S. OF J. MCDONALD	1871	OH CO. MAP	1742
COAL - S. OF J. MCDONALD	1871	OH CO. MAP	1744
COAL - S. OF J.F. COUNCILMAN	1871	BKE/OH MAP	1739
COAL - S. OF J. FORD	1871	MARH'L MAP	1745
COAL - S. OF J.W. MORGAN	1871	BKE/OH MAP	1738
COAL - S. OF JAMES ARCHER ORCHARD	1871	BRKE MAP	1734
COAL - S. OF MRS B. HARKER	1871	BRKE MAP	1736
COAL - S. OF MRS J.J. ANDERSON	1871	HAN MAP	1731
COAL - S. OF NEW GERMANTOWN	1871	MARH'L MAP	1750
COAL - S. OF PINE GROVE	1871	OH CO. MAP	1740
COAL - S. OF PLEASANT VIEW	1871	MARH'L MAP	1746
COAL - S. OF R.M. WELLS	1871	BKE/OH MAP	1738
COAL - S. OF R. STEWART	1871	OH CO. MAP	1740
COAL - S. OF R. STEWART	1871	OH CO. MAP	1743
COAL - S. OF R.H. MCFARLAND	1871	MARH'L MAP	1751
COAL - S. OF ROBERT MURCHLAND	1871	BRKE MAP	1735
COAL - S. OF ROCK SPRING	1871	HAN MAP	1727
COAL - S. OF SUGAR GROVE	1871	OH CO. MAP	1743
COAL - S. OF T. BRICELAND	1871	BKE/OH MAP	1739
COAL - S. OF W. MARSHALL	1871	OH CO. MAP	1741
COAL - S. OF W. FLETCHER	1871	OH CO. MAP	1741
COAL - S. OF W. RUTHS GRIST MILL	1871	MARH'L MAP	1747
COAL - S. OF W.B. FREEMAN	1871	FRE'MAN'S LDG	1764
COAL - S. OF W.C. MURPHY	1871	HAN MAP	1731
COAL - S. OF W.T. HINKSON	1871	BRKE MAP	1737
COAL - S. OF WHITE COTTAGE	1871	MARH'L MAP	1745
COAL - S. OF WILLIAM CAMPBELL	1871	BRKE MAP	1737
COAL - S. OF WILLIAM CAMPBELL	1871	BKE/OH MAP	1739
COAL - S. OF WILLIAM HUKILL	1871	BRKE MAP	1736
COAL - S. OF WILLIAM SMITH	1871	OH CO. MAP	1742
COAL - S. OF WM. STEWART	1871	HAN MAP	1731
COAL - S. OF WOODLAND	1871	OH CO. MAP	1743
COAL - SE OF FREDERICK BADE	1871	OH CO. MAP	1743
COAL - SE OF JAMES PUNTNEY	1871	BRKE MAP	1735
COAL - SE OF MAPLE HILL	1871	BKE/OH MAP	1739
COAL - SE OF MRS HUNTER	1871	BRKE MAP	1735
COAL - SE OF PINE GROVE	1871	BKE/OH MAP	1739
COAL - SE OF RIVERSIDE	1871	HAN MAP	1726
COAL - SE OF ROCKY POINT	1871	HAN MAP	1731
COAL - SE OF SCHOOL NO. 7 - OHIO CO	1871	MARH'L MAP	1746
COAL - SE OF W. CAMPBELL	1871	BKE/OH MAP	1739
COAL - SE OF WHITE OAK FLATS	1871	HAN MAP	1726
COAL - SE. OF RIVERVIEW - WASH. TWP	1871	MARH'L MAP	1748
COAL - SHIPMENTS	1916	NAT'L ROAD	1867
COAL - SHORT CREEK COAL BANK	1871	BUFF.TWP.BUS.	1772
COAL - SW OF BETHANY COLLEGE	1871	BKE/OH MAP	1739
COAL - SW OF FARMERS DELIGHT	1871	HAN MAP	1731
COAL - SW OF HERRON SCHOOL	1871	HAN MAP	1731
COAL - SW OF ORCHARD HILL	1871	HAN MAP	1732
COAL - SW OF R. CARTER DISTILLERY	1871	OH CO. MAP	1742
COAL - SW OF SUGAR GROVE	1871	OH CO. MAP	1743
COAL - SW OF W. HINKSON	1871	BRKE MAP	1735
COAL - SW OF W.B. MORROW	1871	HAN MAP	1732
COAL - SW OF WHITE OAK FLATS	1871	HAN MAP	1726
COAL - SW OF WILLIAM HUKILL	1871	BRKE MAP	1736
COAL - SW. OF E. ALLY	1871	MARH'L MAP	1747
COAL - SW. OF J. YOHO	1871	MARH'L MAP	1755
COAL - SW. OF MOUNTAINS BROW	1871	MARH'L MAP	1754
COAL - SW. OF UNION BASIN	1871	MARH'L MAP	1754
COAL - SW. OF W. TALBERT	1871	MARH'L MAP	1745
COAL - T. MEYER	1871	TRIAD.TWP.	1781
COAL - W. OF ANDREW HALSTEAD	1871	OH CO. MAP	1742
COAL - W. OF CORVEY LODGE	1871	MARH'L MAP	1745
COAL - W. OF J.W. - LEATHERWOOD	1871	WHG CITY	1789
COAL - W. OF LOCUST GROVE	1871	OH CO. MAP	1744
COAL - W. OF LYNNCAMP P.O.	1871	MARH'L MAP	1759
COAL - W. OF M FISHER	1871	OH CO. MAP	1741
COAL - W. OF M FISHER	1871	OH CO. MAP	1742
COAL - W. OF METHODIST EPISCOPAL CHURCH	1871	BKE/OH MAP	1738
COAL - W. OF OHIO VIEW	1871	HAN MAP	1730
COAL - W. OF R. PROSSER	1871	HAN MAP	1726
COAL - W. OF RIVERVIEW	1871	HAN MAP	1726
COAL - W. OF SCANTLON, J	1871	MARH'L MAP	1745
COAL - W. OF SCHOOL NO. 4	1871	HAN MAP	1731
COAL - W. OF T. GRIMES	1871	BRKE MAP	1737
COAL - WILLIAM PORTER	1871	TRIAD.TWP.	1781
COAL #1 - S OF HAMILTON	1871	HAN MAP	1726
COAL #2 - S OF HAMILTON	1871	HAN MAP	1726
COAL & CLAY - NW OF ORCHARD HILL	1871	HAN MAP	1732
COAL AND CLAY BANK - NEAR DEEP GUT RUN	1871	HAN MAP	1730
COAL BANK - E OF THOMAS DONOVAN	1871	BRKE MAP	1734
COAL BANK - E OF THOMAS DONOVAN	1871	BRKE MAP	1735
COAL BANK - E OF THOMAS WHEELER	1871	BRKE MAP	1735
COAL BANK - E. OF G W STEENROD	1871	OH CO. MAP	1742
COAL BANK - E. OF W. SIMPSON	1871	BRKE MAP	1735
COAL BANK - GEORGE MOONEYS	1871	BRKE MAP	1735
COAL BANK - J BOWMAN / (?JOHN?)	1871	BRKE MAP	1736
COAL BANK - JAMES PATTON	1871	BRKE MAP	1735
COAL BANK - JOHN BUCKEY	1871	BRKE MAP	1737
COAL BANK - JOHN BUCKEYS	1871	BRKE MAP	1735
COAL BANK - N OF J. OR S. MORTON	1871	BRKE MAP	1734
COAL BANK - N OF J WRIGHT SR	1871	BRKE MAP	1734
COAL BANK - N OF R FRESHWATER	1871	BRKE MAP	1734
COAL BANK - N OF T MARSH	1871	BRKE MAP	1734
COAL BANK - N. OF J. WILLIAMSON	1871	BRKE MAP	1735
COAL BANK - N. OF REV WOODS HEIRS	1871	OH CO. MAP	1741
COAL BANK - N. OF W.L. MILLER	1871	BRKE MAP	1735
COAL BANK - NE OF J WRIGHT SR	1871	BRKE MAP	1734
COAL BANK - NE OF J. WIGGINS SR	1871	BRKE MAP	1735
COAL BANK - NW OF A CALDWELL	1871	BRKE MAP	1734
COAL BANK - NW OF R. BOYD	1871	BRKE MAP	1734
COAL BANK - S OF A. STANSBURY	1871	BRKE MAP	1734
COAL BANK - S OF N WELLS	1871	BRKE MAP	1734
COAL BANK - S OF S. WHITE	1871	BRKE MAP	1734
COAL BANK - S OF STATION	1871	BRKE MAP	1734
COAL BANK - S OF T. MARSH	1871	BRKE MAP	1734
COAL BANK - S OF W WILLIAMSON	1871	BRKE MAP	1734
COAL BANK - S OF W. ATKINSON	1871	BRKE MAP	1734
COAL BANK - S. OF BERNARD BRADY	1871	BRKE MAP	1735
COAL BANK - S. OF G. COX	1871	BRKE MAP	1735
COAL BANK - S. OF GEORGE COXS HEIRS	1871	BRKE MAP	1735
COAL BANK - S. OF NEW GERMANTOWN	1871	MARH'L MAP	1750
COAL BANK - S. OF TOMLINSON HEIRS	1871	MARH'L MAP	1748
COAL BANK - SE OF E.N. ROBINSON	1871	BRKE MAP	1734
COAL BANK - SE OF W. SIMPSON	1871	BRKE MAP	1735
COAL BANK - SE. OF MRS. R. DORSEY	1871	MARH'L MAP	1749
COAL BANK - SW OF W.S. MURCHLAND	1871	BRKE MAP	1735
COAL BANK - SW OF W.S. MURCHLAND	1871	BRKE MAP	1735
COAL DEALER - FORBES & CARMICHAEL	1871	BUFF.TWP.BUS.	1772
COAL DEALER - JOHN BOWMAN	1871	BUFF.TWP.BUS.	1772
COAL FARM	1871	BRKE MAP	1735
COAL KENNEL	1871	HAN MAP	1731
COAL PRODUCER - GEORGE ELLIOTT	1871	BUFF.TWP.BUS.	1772
COAL RUN	1852	BRKE MAP	1843
COAL SHOOT - NEAR HEMPFIELD RR CO - LEATHERWOOD	1871	WHG CITY	1789
COAL SPRINGS - S. OF WILLIAM MAXWELL	1871	OH CO. MAP	1740
COAL SPRINGSBECK, L	1871	BKE/OH MAP	1739
COAL TRACK INTO NAIL WORKS - BENWOOD	1871	BENWOOD	1799
COAL WKS / WORKS	1871	BRKE MAP	1736

XXIV

'PERSONAL TIME LINE' INDEX TO VOLUME 7 OF THE *OHIO COUNTY INDEX*

ENTRY	YEAR	SUBJECT	PAGE
COAL YARD - W. MARSHALL	1871	OH CO. MAP	1741
COAL, IRON ORE & BOLIVER CLAY	1871	FRE'MAN'S LDG	1765
COALMAN, JOHN	1786	DEFENDANT	1583
COATS, J	1871	W LIBERTY	1780
COCHRAN, J	1871	HAN MAP	1732
COCHRAN, J	1871	MARH'L MAP	1752
COCHRAN, J	1871	MARH'L MAP	1752
COCHRAN, J	1871	MARH'L MAP	1756
COCHRAN, JAMES A	1834	DEFENDANT	1618
COCHRAN, R H	1879	DEFENDANT	1601
COCHRAN, SAMUEL JR	1830	DEFENDANT	1669
COCHRAN, W	1871	HAN MAP	1732
COCKAYNE, A	1871	MDSVILLE	1809
COCKAYNE, B	1871	MARH'L MAP	1748
COCKAYNE, B / INITIALS B.C.	1871	MARH'L MAP	1748
COCKAYNE, SAMUEL	1818	DEFENDANT	1595
COCKAYNE, SAMUEL	1818	DEFENDANT	1598
COCKAYNE, SAMUEL	1819	DEFENDANT	1598
COCKAYNE, SAMUEL	1823	DEFENDANT	1649
COCKAYNE, SAMUEL	1829	DEFENDANT	1668
COCKAYNE, SAMUEL	1831	DEFENDANT	1555
COCKAYNE, V L	1871	MARH'L MAP	1748
COCKAYNE, V L / INITIALS V.L.C.	1871	MARH'L MAP	1748
COCKAYNE, V L / INITIALS V.L.C.	1871	MARH'L MAP	1748
COCKAYNE, V L	1871	MDSVILLE	1809
COCKAYNE, V L / INITIALS V.L.C.	1871	MDSVILLE	1809
COCKAYNE, WILLIAM	1831	DEFENDANT	1669
COCKE, SMITH	1824	DEFENDANT	1628
CODE OF VIRGINIA - RE: HEMPFIELD RR	1852	HEMPFIELD RR	1821
COE, I	1871	MARH'L MAP	1753
COE, J	1871	MARH'L MAP	1753
COE, J	1871	CAMERON	1802
COE, J	1871	CAMERON	1802
COE, WILLIAM V / VALLEY GROVE	1871	OH CO. MAP	1740
COE, Z	1871	MARH'L MAP	1756
COE, Z	1871	MARH'L MAP	1760
COEN, -	1848	PLAINTIFF	1629
COEN, EDWARD	1787	DEFENDANT	1604
COFFIELD, J	1871	MARH'L MAP	1746
COFFIELD, J	1871	MARH'L MAP	1749
COHN, -	1876	DEFENDANT	1631
COL. MEADE INSTITUTE / MAP#398	1852	BRKE MAP	1846
COLD HOMESTEAD - WASH TWP	1871	MARH'L MAP	1749
COLD METHODIST EPISCOPAL CHURCH / OR COL'D - MOUNDSVILLE	1871	MDSVILLE	1810
COL'D METHODIST EPISCOPAL CHURCH / OR COLD - MOUNDSVILLE	1871	MDSVILLE	1810
COLD SPING - S. OF D. WINTERS	1871	MARH'L MAP	1746
COLD SPRING	1871	HAN MAP	1726
COLD SPRING	1871	HAN MAP	1732
COLD SPRING / #2 - E SIDE OF MAP	1871	HAN MAP	1732
COLD SPRING - S. OF MOUNTAIN SIDE	1871	OH CO. MAP	1743
COLD SPRING FARM	1871	HAN MAP	1731
COLD SPRING FARM	1871	HAN MAP	1732
COLD SPRINGS	1871	HAN MAP	1731
COLD SPRINGS - E. OF NEW LEXINGTON	1871	HAN MAP	1726
COLDWELL, -	1871	NEW MANCH.	1769
COLDWELL, G W	1871	WELLSBURG	1776
COLE, B	1871	MARH'L MAP	1756
COLE, B	1871	MARH'L MAP	1756
COLE, BENJAMIN	1821	DEFENDANT	1585
COLE, BENJAMIN	1822	DEFENDANT	1585
COLE, J	1871	MARH'L MAP	1747
COLE, J	1871	MARH'L MAP	1761
COLE, J W	1871	MARH'L MAP	1746
COLE, T	1871	MARH'L MAP	1760
COLE, W	1871	MARH'L MAP	1756
COLEE, C C	1871	NEW CUMB'LD	1762
COLEE, C C	1871	NEW CUMB'LD	1767
COLEE, T F	1871	NEW CUMB'LD	1762
COLEE, T F	1871	NEW CUMB'LD	1767
COLEMAN, - / MRS	1871	BRKE MAP	1736
COLEMAN, - / MRS - INITIALS MRS. C	1871	BRKE MAP	1736
COLEMAN, - / MRS	1871	BKE/OH MAP	1738
COLEMAN, D J / CUT OFF EDGE OF MAP	1871	BKE/OH MAP	1738
COLL__, - / WEBSTER ST - UNKNOWN (?COLLEGE?)	1871	WHG CITY	1788
COLL__, - / WEBSTER ST - UNKNOWN (?COLLEGE?)	1871	WHG CITY	1790
COLLEGE / BETHANY COLLEGE	1871	BRKE MAP	1737
COLLEGE - COLL__, - / WEBSTER ST - UNKNOWN (?COLLEGE?)	1871	WHG CITY	1788
COLLEGE - COLL__, - / WEBSTER ST - UNKNOWN (?COLLEGE?)	1871	WHG CITY	1790
COLLENDER, JOHN	1812	DEFENDANT	1611
COLLENGER, THOMAS	1813	DEFENDANT	1611
COLLENS & RIGGS	1871	MARH'L MAP	1751
COLLIERS STATION / RR	1871	BRKE MAP	1734
COLLINGS, W	1871	MARH'L MAP	1751
COLLINS, W	1871	MARH'L MAP	1748
COLLVER, L / ?	1871	HAN MAP	1730
COLMAN, MACOM	1788	DEFENDANT	1556
COLORED	1841	MISC	1707
COLORED	1854	MISC	1695
COLTZ, P	1871	MARH'L MAP	1759
COLTZ, PETER CONROD	1826	DEFENDANT	1587
COLUMBUS, OH	1852	HEMPFIELD RR	1820
COLUMBUS, OH	1852	HEMP. RR MAP	1825
COLUMBUS, OH	1916	NAT'L ROAD	1866
COLUMBUS, PIQUA & INDIANA RR	1852	HEMP. RR MAP	1826
COLVIG, J	1871	MDSVILLE	1808
COLVIG, J	1871	MDSVILLE	1810
COLVIG, J B	1871	MDSVILLE	1808
COLWELL, - / MRS	1871	ROSBBYS RK	1813
COLWELL, A	1871	OH CO. MAP	1741
COLWELL, A	1871	OH CO. MAP	1741
COLWELL, A / INITIALS A.C.	1871	OH CO. MAP	1741
COLWELL, M	1871	MARH'L MAP	1746
COMBS, JOHN	1784	DEFENDANT	1647
COMMONS - CITY COMMONS - WHEELING CITY	1871	WHG CITY	1788
COMMONWEATH OF VA	1783	APPENDIX	1874
COMMONWEATH OF VA	1784	APPENDIX	1874
CONALLY, THOMAS	1812	DEFENDANT	1563
CONANT & BEDILION / ICE HOUSSE	1871	OH CO. MAP	1742
CONANT & BEDILION / ICE HOUSE	1871	TRIAD.TWP.	1781
CONANT, - / MRS	1871	BRKE MAP	1736
CONANT, - / MRS	1871	BKE/OH MAP	1738
CONARD, THOMAS	1824	MISC	1693
CONELLY, J	1871	MARH'L MAP	1750
CONELLY, J	1871	MARH'L MAP	1753
CONELLY, J	1871	MARH'L MAP	1753
CONGILL, STEPHTHA	1858	DEFENDANT	1621
CONKEL SPRINGS	1871	MARH'L MAP	1747
CONKEL SPRINGS	1871	MARH'L MAP	1750
CONKEL, - / SPRINGS	1871	MARH'L MAP	1750
CONKEL, B	1871	MDSVILLE	1810
CONKEL, P / RES	1871	MARH'L MAP	1747
CONKEL, P / RES	1871	MARH'L MAP	1750
CONKLE, E	1871	MARH'L MAP	1748
CONKLE, H	1871	MARH'L MAP	1751
CONKLE, HENRY SR	1808	DEFENDANT	1635
CONKLE, P	1871	MARH'L MAP	1751
CONKLE, P	1871	MARH'L MAP	1755
CONLEY, L	1871	MARH'L MAP	1752
CONN, ISAAC J	1857	DEFENDANT	1653
CONN, ISAAC T	1857	DEFENDANT	1590
CONN, ISAAC T	1857	DEFENDANT	1663
CONNELL, W	1871	MARH'L MAP	1751
CONNELL, W B	1871	NEW CUMB'LD	1767
CONNELLEY, E	1871	OH CO. MAP	1740
CONNELLEY, E	1871	OH CO. MAP	1741
CONNELLEY, E	1871	OH CO. MAP	1741
CONNELLEY, E / INITIALS E.C.	1871	OH CO. MAP	1741
CONNELLEY, E / INITIALS E.C.	1871	OH CO. MAP	1741
CONNELLEY, W	1871	OH CO. MAP	1741
CONNELLY, JAMES C	1871	MARH'L MAP	1757
CONNELLY, JAMES C / INITIALS J.C.C.	1871	MARH'L MAP	1757
CONNER, E	1871	MARH'L MAP	1745
CONNER, E / SPRING - INITIALS E.C. SPRING	1871	MARH'L MAP	1745
CONNER, G W	1871	MARH'L MAP	1745
CONNER, J W	1871	MARH'L MAP	1751
CONNER, J W	1871	MARH'L MAP	1755
CONNER, JOHN	1876	DEFENDANT	1609
CONNER, JOSEPH	1830	DEFENDANT	1573
CONNER, P M	1871	MARH'L MAP	1751
CONNER, SILAS	1838	DEFENDANT	1576
CONNER, W	1871	MARH'L MAP	1750
CONNER, W	1871	MARH'L MAP	1750
CONNER, W H	1871	MARH'L MAP	1746
CONNER, W H	1871	MARH'L MAP	1749
CONNERS RUN	1871	MARH'L MAP	1751
CONNERS RUN	1871	MARH'L MAP	1754
CONNOR, M / PAN-HANDLE P.O.	1871	BRKE MAP	1734
CONNOR, M	1871	MDSVILLE	1808
CONNOR, P	1871	MARH'L MAP	1750
CONNOR, WILLIAM	1840	DEFENDANT	1577

'PERSONAL TIME LINE' INDEX TO VOLUME 7 OF THE *OHIO COUNTY INDEX*

ENTRY	YEAR	SUBJECT	PAGE
CONNOR, WILLIAM	1840	DEFENDANT	1617
CONNOR, WILLIAM	1840	DEFENDANT	1652
CONNS RUN	1852	BRKE MAP	1850
CONNS, L / ?	1871	HAN MAP	1730
CONRAD - SEE ALSO CUNRAD	1871	TRIAD.TWP.	1781
CONRAD, THOMAS	1823	MISC	1693
CORNELIUS RUN	1852	BRKE MAP	1849
CONROY, -	1871	BENWOOD	1799
CONROY, D	1871	BENWOOD	1798
CONTENTS - APPENDIX VOL.7	2000	APPENDIX	1712
CONTENTS - VOL.7	2000	CONTENTS	1545
CONVENT - MOUNT DE CHANTAL CONVENT	1871	OH CO. MAP	1742
CONVENT - MOUNT DE CHANTAL CONVENT / CATHOLIC	1871	TRIAD.TWP.	1781
CONVENT - MOUNT DE CHANTAL CONVENT	1871	WHG CITY	1789
CONWELL, WILLIS	1839	DEFENDANT	1619
CONWELL, WILLIS S	1839	DEFENDANT	1640
CONWELL, WILLIS S	1839	PLAINTIFF	1662
COOFER, C C	1871	MARH'L MAP	1746
COOK, -	1833	PLAINTIFF	1628
COOK, -	1834	PLAINTIFF	1628
COOK, J R	1871	TRIAD.BORO.	1785
COOK, LEWIS	1859	DEFENDANT	1616
COOK, PAUL	1855	DEFENDANT	1561
COOKE, W	1871	MARH'L MAP	1749
COOKS FORK	1852	BRKE MAP	1846
COOL SPRING RUN - OHIO	1852	BRKE MAP	1846
COOLEY, N	1871	MARH'L MAP	1752
COOLEY, N	1871	MARH'L MAP	1756
COOLY, F H	1842	DEFENDANT	1557
COON ISLAND / ALSO KNOWN AT VIENNA, PA	1916	NAT'L ROAD	1862
COON ISLAND, PA. - MAP	1916	NAT'L ROAD	1863
COON RUN	1871	MARH'L MAP	1754
COON RUN	1871	MARH'L MAP	1758
COON, J	1871	MARH'L MAP	1746
COONS, MARTIN	1815	DEFENDANT	1566
COOPER - WILLIAM G. SHRIMPLIN	1871	BUFF.TWP. BUS.	1772
COOPER SHOP - HUSTERS / NATHANIEL - MAP#565	1852	BRKE MAP	1852
COOPER SHOP - LOWS / J ?	1871	MARH'L MAP	1759
COOPER SHOP - S. OF CHAMBERS FARM	1871	HAN MAP	1726
COOPER SHOP - S. OF CUNNINGHAM VALLEY	1871	HAN MAP	1726
COOPER SHOP - SE OF D. CORNELIUS	1871	BRKE MAP	1736
COOPER SHOP - SMITHS / A	1871	BRKE MAP	1737
COOPER SHOP - SNIDERS / DAVID - HEIRS - MAP#640	1852	BRKE MAP	1852
COOPER SHOP - TRIADELPHIA	1871	TRIAD.BORO.	1784
COOPER SHOP - WAUGHS / RICHARD - HEIRS - MAP#264	1852	BRKE MAP	1843
COOPER SHP - SMITHS / W.J. & R - MAP#483	1852	BRKE MAP	1849
COOPER, E	1871	BRKE MAP	1736
COOPER, J M / PHYSICIAN	1871	WLSBRG BUS.	1772
COOPER, J M / DOCTOR	1871	WELLSBURG	1777
COOPER, JOHN	1878	DEFENDANT	1595
COOPER, N	1871	MARH'L MAP	1759
COPE, W	1871	WELLSBURG	1777
COPPIN, JOSEPH M	1838	DEFENDANT	1579
COPPINS, JOSEPH M	1839	DEFENDANT	1580
CORBIN, C J / MAP ASSISTANT	1871	MAP	1713
CORDALL, THOMAS	1822	DEFENDANT	1574
CORKLE, A / MRS	1871	MDSVILLE	1810
CORNELIUS, D	1871	BRKE MAP	1736
CORNELIUS, ELIJAH / MAP#466	1852	BRKE MAP	1849
CORNELIUS, ELIJAH / MAP#468	1852	BRKE MAP	1849
CORNELIUS, J	1871	HAN MAP	1729
CORNER, GEORGE L S	1878	DEFENDANT	1593
CORR, - / MRS	1871	GLEN EASTON	1801
CORTES, J	1871	MARH'L MAP	1747
CORTES, J	1871	MARH'L MAP	1750
CORVEY LODGE	1871	MARH'L MAP	1745
CORW, P	1871	MARH'L MAP	1752
COSHCOTON, OH	1852	HEMP. RR MAP	1826
COSS, WILLIAM	1801	DEFENDANT	1610
COSSER, J	1871	BENWOOD	1798
COSSNER, T	1871	BENWOOD	1798
COSTER, RICHARD	1826	DEFENDANT	1599
COTSON, ROBERT H	1862	DEFENDANT	1592
COTTAGE HOME	1871	OH CO. MAP	1741
COTTAGE HOME	1871	OH CO. MAP	1742
COTTAGE HOME	1871	MARH'L MAP	1745
COTTAGE HOME / JOHN SNEDIKER	1871	MARH'L MAP	1750
COTTAGE HOME	1871	MARH'L MAP	1753
COTTAGE HOUSE	1871	OH CO. MAP	1743
COTTS, -	1841	PLAINTIFF	1629
COTTS, CONRAD	1855	DEFENDANT	1582
COTTS, ISAAC	1834	DEFENDANT	1672
COTTS, ISAAC	1863	DEFENDANT	1602
COTTS, ISAAC	1875	DEFENDANT	1641
COTTS, JOHN	1853	DEFENDANT	1661
COUDON, -	1862	PLAINTIFF	1631
COULTER, EDWARD	1853	DEFENDANT	1561
COULTER, F	1871	MARH'L MAP	1754
COULTER, F	1871	MARH'L MAP	1758
COULTERS RUN	1871	OH CO. MAP	1743
COUNCILMAN RUN - OLD GRIST MILL ON	1871	BKE/OH MAP	1739
COUNCILMAN, H / MRS	1871	BKE/OH MAP	1739
COUNCILMAN, J F	1871	BRKE MAP	1737
COUNCILMAN, J F	1871	BKE/OH MAP	1739
COUNCILMAN, L	1871	BKE/OH MAP	1739
COUNCILMAN, L	1871	BKE/OH MAP	1739
COUNCILMAN, L J	1871	BKE/OH MAP	1739
COUNCILMAN, LEWIS J / MAP#105	1852	BRKE MAP	1843
COUNCILMAN, LEWIS J / MAP#106	1852	BRKE MAP	1843
COUNCILMAN, LEWIS J / MAP#107	1852	BRKE MAP	1843
COUNCILMANS RUN - METHODIST EPISCOPAL CHURCH ON	1871	BKE/OH MAP	1739
COUNSELMAN, JOHN F / MAP#115	1852	BRKE MAP	1840
COUNSELMAN, JOHN F / MAP#111	1852	BRKE MAP	1844
COUNSELMAN, JOHN F / MAP#112	1852	BRKE MAP	1844
COUNT HOUSE - ELM GROVE / (?COURT.?) HOUSE	1871	OH CO. MAP	1742
COUNT HOUSE - ELM GROVE / (?COURT.?) HOUSE	1871	OH CO. MAP	1742
COUNTY FORMATION CHART	2000	MAP	1546
COUNTY ROAD - AT ELM GROVE & NATL RD	1871	ELM GROVE	1782
COURT CASE FILES	2000	APPENDIX	1873
COURT HOUSE - ELM GROVE / (?COUNT.?) HOUSE	1871	OH CO. MAP	1742
COURT HOUSE - FOURTH ST - WHEELING	1871	WHG CITY	1788
COURT HOUSE - MARSHALL CO - A ST - MOUNDSVILLE	1871	MDSVILLE	1809
COURTHOUSE / ABBREV CH ?	1871	HAN MAP	1731
COURTNEY, J T	1871	OH CO. MAP	1741
COURTRIGHT, J	1871	MARH'L MAP	1756
COURTRIGHT, T	1871	MARH'L MAP	1757
COURTRIGHT, T / INITIALS T.C.	1871	MARH'L MAP	1757
COUTS, J	1871	MARH'L MAP	1747
COUTS, J	1871	MARH'L MAP	1750
COVALT, J	1871	MARH'L MAP	1761
COVALT, J	1871	MARH'L MAP	1761
COVALT, S / MRS	1871	MARH'L MAP	1761
COVALT, W	1871	MARH'L MAP	1761
COVINGTON, KY	1852	HEMP. RR MAP	1826
COWAN, - / MRS	1871	BETHANY	1773
COWAN, J F	1871	HAN MAP	1732
COWAN, J P	1871	HAN MAP	1733
COWAN, J P	1871	HAN MAP	1733
COWAN, J P / WAGON SHOP	1871	HAN MAP	1733
COWAN, JAMES P	1871	HO'LIDAYS COVE	1762
COWDEN, -	1858	PLAINTIFF	1630
COWDEN, J R	1878	MISC	1695
COWDEN, W J	1874	MISC	1679
COWDEN, W J W	1873	MISC	1695
COWDEN, W J W	1876	MISC	1679
COWDEN, W J W	1876	MISC	1695
COWDEN, W J W	1877	DEFENDANT	1560
COWDEN, WILLIAM	1857	DEFENDANT	1653
COWDEN, WILLIAM	1858	DEFENDANT	1653
COWEL, J	1871	HAN MAP	1726
COWGILL, JEPHSHA	1858	DEFENDANT	1636
COWGILL, JEPTHA	1858	DEFENDANT	1621
COWN, ISAAC T	1857	DEFENDANT	1630
COX, A	1871	BKE/OH MAP	1739
COX, A	1871	BKE/OH MAP	1739
COX, A / RES	1871	BKE/OH MAP	1739
COX, BENJAMIN G	1871	BRKE MAP	1735
COX, D	1871	BKE/OH MAP	1739
COX, E	1871	BKE/OH MAP	1739
COX, ELEANOR	1778	APPENDIX	1874
COX, F	1871	BRKE MAP	1735
COX, F	1871	BRKE MAP	1736
COX, F	1871	MARH'L MAP	1753
COX, FRIEND	1836	DEFENDANT	1628

XXVI

'PERSONAL TIME LINE' INDEX TO VOLUME 7 OF THE *OHIO COUNTY INDEX*

ENTRY	YEAR	SUBJECT	PAGE
COX, FRIEND	1836	DEFENDANT	1651
COX, FRIEND	1852	NOT ON MAP	1836
COX, G	1871	BRKE MAP	1735
COX, GABRIEL	1778	APPENDIX	1874
COX, GABRIEL	1789	DEFENDANT	1658
COX, GEORGE / ESQ. - MAP#408	1852	BRKE MAP	1846
COX, GEORGE / ESQ. - MAP#447	1852	BRKE MAP	1849
COX, GEORGE / ESQ. - MAP#448	1852	BRKE MAP	1849
COX, GEORGE / HEIRS	1871	BRKE MAP	1735
COX, GEORGE / HEIRS	1871	BRKE MAP	1735
COX, GEORGE / SETTLED THIS FARM IN 1774 - NEAR OHIO RIVER	1871	BRKE MAP	1735
COX, H	1871	MDSVILLE	1807
COX, H / (?HARVEY?)	1871	MDSVILLE	1807
COX, H / GREEN HOUSE	1871	MDSVILLE	1807
COX, HARVEY	1871	MDSVL BUS.	1796
COX, HARVEY / HARNES (?HARNESS?) & SADDLE	1871	MDSVILLE	1807
COX, I	1871	BKE/OH MAP	1739
COX, I	1871	MARH'L MAP	1753
COX, ISRAEL	1778	APPENDIX	1874
COX, J T	1871	MARH'L MAP	1748
COX, JAMES W	1871	BRKE MAP	1735
COX, JOHN	1852	NOT ON MAP	1836
COX, JOHN / MAP#449	1852	BRKE MAP	1849
COX, L	1871	OH CO. MAP	1741
COX, L H	1877	DEFENDANT	1661
COX, R W	1871	MARH'L MAP	1751
COX, R W / INITIALS R.C.	1871	MARH'L MAP	1751
COX, U	1871	WELLSBURG	1777
COXS RUN	1852	BRKE MAP	1844
COXS RUN / NE OF WELLSBURG	1852	BRKE MAP	1846
COXS RUN	1871	BRKE MAP	1735
COZADS RUN / OR BRANCH	1852	BRKE MAP	1843
CRACRAFT & SANGSTON	1857	DEFENDANT	1663
CRACRAFT, CHARLES	1799	DEFENDANT	1665
CRACRAFT, D C	1855	DEFENDANT	1629
CRACRAFT, DEWIT C	1856	DEFENDANT	1663
CRACRAFT, G A / DR	1871	TRIAD.BORO.	1784
CRACRAFT, GEORGE A	1857	DEFENDANT	1586
CRACRAFT, GEORGE A	1857	DEFENDANT	1641
CRACRAFT, GEORGE A	1857	DEFENDANT	1663
CRACRAFT, GEORGE A	1858	DEFENDANT	1584
CRACRAFT, GEORGE A	1858	DEFENDANT	1603
CRACRAFT, GEORGE A	1860	DEFENDANT	1580
CRAFT, A	1871	BKE/OH MAP	1739
CRAFT, E / (?ELISHA?)	1871	BRKE MAP	1737
CRAFT, E / (?ELISHA?) - INITIALS E.C.	1871	BRKE MAP	1737
CRAFT, G / (?E.G. - EDWARD?) GILFILLEN	1871	OH CO. MAP	1743
CRAFT, G / (?E.G. - EDWARD GILFILLEN?) - TRIADELPHIA	1871	OH CO. MAP	1744
CRAFT, GEORGE	1850	DEFENDANT	1670
CRAFT, KENNETH FISCHER JR / AUTHOR	2000	TITLE	1544
CRAFT, KENNETH FISCHER JR / AUTHOR	2000	PREFACE	1748
CRAFT, MICHAEL	1801	DEFENDANT	1634
CRAFT, WILLIAM	1871	BKE/OH MAP	1739
CRAG, J	1871	W.UNION	1812
CRAGO, F H / NORMAL SCHOOL	1871	W.LIBRTY.BUS.	1780
CRAIG, - / BRIGGS & CRAIG	1871	WELLSBURG	1777
CRAIG, - / MRS	1871	WELLSBURG	1777
CRAIG, -	1871	RITCHIE TWP	1793
CRAIG, ANDREW	1814	DEFENDANT	1572
CRAIG, ANDREW	1816	DEFENDANT	1642
CRAIG, E B	1871	OH CO. MAP	1742
CRAIG, W	1871	OH CO. MAP	1743
CRAIL RUN	1871	BRKE MAP	1734
CRAMLET, MICHELL	1809	DEFENDANT	1626
CRANE, A S	1853	DEFENDANT	1641
CRANFORD, H	1871	OH CO. MAP	1741
CRANSWICK, RICHARD	1823	DEFENDANT	1638
CRATON, D	1871	MARH'L MAP	1747
CRAWFORD, - / MRS	1871	HAN MAP	1732
CRAWFORD, - / MRS	1871	HAN MAP	1733
CRAWFORD, G H	1871	WELLSBURG	1776
CRAWFORD, G H	1871	WELLSBURG	1777
CRAWFORD, G W	1871	WELLSBURG	1777
CRAWFORD, J	1871	MARH'L MAP	1750
CRAWFORD, J	1871	MARH'L MAP	1761
CRAWFORD, J	1871	BENWOOD	1798
CRAWFORD, J / INITIALS J.C.	1871	BENWOOD	1798
CRAWFORD, J C	1871	HAN MAP	1732
CRAWFORD, JOHN	1803	DEFENDANT	1634
CRAWFORD, R / INITIALS R.C. - CAMERON	1871	MARH'L MAP	1753
CRAWFORD, R / INITIALS R.C. - CAMERON	1871	MARH'L MAP	1757
CRAWFORD, R	1871	CAMERON	1804
CRAWFORD, R	1871	CAMERON	1804
CRAWFORD, T	1871	MARH'L MAP	1761
CRAWFORD, W L	1871	HAN MAP	1732
CRAWFORD, W P	1871	MARH'L MAP	1760
CRAWFORD, W P / PROBABLE OWNER OF - HIGGINS, CRAWFORD & CO. STORE	1871	MARH'L MAP	1760
CRAWFORD, WILLIAM	1796	DEFENDANT	1585
CRAWFORD, WILLIAM	1823	DEFENDANT	1612
CRAWFORD, WILLIAM	1824	DEFENDANT	1612
CRAWLE, J W	1839	DEFENDANT	1569
CRAWLE, L W	1828	DEFENDANT	1625
CREE, H	1871	BRKE MAP	1737
CREE, H	1871	BRKE MAP	1737
CREEK SIDE - WASHINGTON TWP	1871	MARH'L MAP	1748
CREGG, GEORGE	1809	DEFENDANT	1569
CREIGHTON, E / MRS	1871	OH CO. MAP	1742
CREIGHTON, E / MRS	1871	OH CO. MAP	1744
CREIGHTON, J	1871	OH CO. MAP	1743
CREIGTON, JOHN S	1873	DEFENDANT	1609
CREIS, JACOB	1812	MISC	1704
CRELY, J	1871	BRKE MAP	1737
CRESAP, E V / MRS	1871	MARH'L MAP	1751
CRESAP, E V / MRS - INITIALS MRS. C	1871	MARH'L MAP	1751
CRESAP, E V / MRS - INITIALS MRS. C	1871	MARH'L MAP	1751
CRESAP, E V / MRS - INITIALS MRS. C	1871	MARH'L MAP	1751
CRESAP, MICHAEL	1810	DEFENDANT	1642
CRESAP, MICHAEL	1825	MISC	1674
CRESAP, Q	1871	MARH'L MAP	1751
CRESAP, Q / INITIALS Q.C.	1871	MARH'L MAP	1751
CRESAP, Q / INITIALS Q C.	1871	MARH'L MAP	1751
CRESAPS GROVE	1871	MARH'L MAP	1751
CRESCENT IRON WORKS	1871	WHG CITY	1790
CRESCENT MFG CO - THE	1858	DEFENDANT	1590
CRESSON, CALEB	1803	PLAINTIFF	1579
CRESWELL, R	1871	MARH'L MAP	1756
CRIDER, J	1871	MARH'L MAP	1747
CRIER, L	1871	OH CO. MAP	1742
CRIER, L / (?GRIER?)	1871	OH CO. MAP	1742
CRIER, L	1871	OH CO. MAP	1744
CRISPIN, THOMAS	1821	DEFENDANT	1660
CRISPIN, THOMAS	1824	DEFENDANT	1660
CRISPIN, THOMAS	1825	DEFENDANT	1660
CRISS, J O	1871	BRKE MAP	1734
CRISS, N	1871	BRKE MAP	1734
CRISS, T	1871	BRKE MAP	1737
CRISSINGER, A W	1871	NEW CUMB'LD	1768
CRISSON, JOHN	1809	DEFENDANT	1645
CRISWELL - SEE ALSO GRISWELL	1871	MARH'L MAP	1745
CRISWELL & MCCONNELL	1871	MDSVILLE	1808
CRISWELL, - / MISSES - MAP#572	1852	BRKE MAP	1852
CRISWELL, - / MRS	1871	MARH'L MAP	1756
CRISWELL, - / ALEXANDER & CRISWELL	1871	MDSVILLE	1809
CRISWELL, - / OFFICE	1871	MDSVILLE	1809
CRISWELL, - / RES	1871	MDSVILLE	1809
CRISWELL, H	1871	MARH'L MAP	1748
CRISWELL, H	1871	MARH'L MAP	1757
CRISWELL, H	1871	MDSVILLE	1806
CRISWELL, H	1871	MDSVILLE	1807
CRISWELL, H	1871	MDSVILLE	1807
CRISWELL, H	1871	MDSVILLE	1808
CRISWELL, HANSON / ATTORNEY	1871	MDSVL BUS.	1796
CRISWELL, J	1871	MARH'L MAP	1745
CRISWELL, J	1871	MARH'L MAP	1761
CRISWELL, JAMES / MAP#571	1852	BRKE MAP	1852
CRISWELL, L	1871	MARH'L MAP	1756
CRISWELL, L	1871	SHERRARD	1811
CRISWELL, L	1871	SHERRARD	1811
CRISWELL, MARY	1871	MARH'L MAP	1746
CRISWELL, O	1871	MDSVILLE	1808
CRISWELL, T	1871	MARH'L MAP	1745
CRISWELL, W H	1871	MDSVILLE	1807
CROCKSDON, ABRAHAM	1791	DEFENDANT	1665
CROFFORD, JOHN	1803	DEFENDANT	1635
CROFFT, MICHAEL	1798	PLAINTIFF	1634
CRONERON, JAMES / ?	1871	HAN MAP	1731
CROSBEY, HISACIAH	1795	DEFENDANT	1553
CROSS CREEK	1796	MISC	1674
CROSS CREEK	1796	MISC	1676
CROSS CREEK	1871	BRKE MAP	1735

'PERSONAL TIME LINE' INDEX TO VOLUME 7 OF THE *OHIO COUNTY INDEX*

ENTRY	YEAR	SUBJECT	PAGE
CROSS CREEK - AT PA. BORDER	1852	BRKE MAP	1850
CROSS CREEK - MOUTH OF AT OHIO RIVER	1852	BRKE MAP	1849
CROSS CREEK TOWNSHIP - BROOKE CO.	1871	BRKE MAP	1734
CROSS CREEK TOWNSHIP - BROOKE CO.	1871	POPULATION	1816
CROSS CREEK TOWNSHIP - BROOKE CO.	1871	BRKE MAP	1735
CROSS CREEK TOWNSHIP - BROOKE CO.	1871	EDGINGTON STA.	1774
CROSS CREEK TOWNSHIP - BROOKE CO.	1871	WELLSBURG	1776
CROSS CREEK TOWNSHIP - BROOKE CO. - BUSINESS NOTICES	1871	CROSS CRK TWP	1772
CROSS CREEK TOWNSHIP - FOWLERS P.O.	1871	FOWLERS P.O.	1775
CROSS, JACOB	1810	APPENDIX	1873
CROSSON, JAMES	1808	DEFENDANT	1645
CROTHERS, -	1854	PLAINTIFF	1621
CROTHERS, A H	1871	WELLSBURG	1777
CROTHERS, H W	1871	WELLSBURG	1777
CROTHERS, H W / INITIALS H.W.C.	1871	WELLSBURG	1777
CROTY, N	1871	OH CO. MAP	1741
CROUCH, D G	1871	BRKE MAP	1736
CROUCH, D G / INITIALS D.G.C.	1871	BRKE MAP	1736
CROUCH, D G	1871	BKE/OH MAP	1739
CROUCH, D.G.	1871	BKE/OH MAP	1739
CROUP, L	1871	MARH'L MAP	1747
CROUP, L	1871	MARH'L MAP	1750
CROW, A	1871	MARH'L MAP	1748
CROW, A	1871	MARH'L MAP	1753
CROW, B	1871	OH CO. MAP	1740
CROW, B / INITIALS B.C.	1871	OH CO. MAP	1743
CROW, B / RES	1871	OH CO. MAP	1743
CROW, B / INITIALS B.C. - RONEY POINT	1871	OH CO. MAP	1744
CROW, B L	1871	MARH'L MAP	1753
CROW, G	1871	MARH'L MAP	1749
CROW, G	1871	MARH'L MAP	1749
CROW, H	1871	MARH'L MAP	1756
CROW, H	1871	MARH'L MAP	1756
CROW, I	1871	MARH'L MAP	1752
CROW, J	1871	OH CO. MAP	1740
CROW, J	1871	MARH'L MAP	1747
CROW, J	1871	MARH'L MAP	1748
CROW, J	1871	MARH'L MAP	1750
CROW, J	1871	MARH'L MAP	1752
CROW, J L	1871	MARH'L MAP	1750
CROW, J W	1871	MARH'L MAP	1756
CROW, M	1871	MARH'L MAP	1750
CROW, M	1871	MARH'L MAP	1752
CROW, P	1871	MARH'L MAP	1745
CROW, P / INITIALS P.C.	1871	MARH'L MAP	1745
CROW, P / INITIALS P.C.	1871	MARH'L MAP	1745
CROW, P	1871	MARH'L MAP	1748
CROW, P / INITIALS P.C.	1871	MARH'L MAP	1748
CROW, P / INITIALS P.C.	1871	MARH'L MAP	1748
CROW, P	1871	MARH'L MAP	1755
CROW, P / INITIALS P.C.	1871	MARH'L MAP	1756
CROW, P / INITIALS P.C.	1871	MARH'L MAP	1756
CROW, S	1871	MARH'L MAP	1746
CROW, S	1871	MARH'L MAP	1749
CROW, S	1871	MARH'L MAP	1749
CROW, S	1871	MARH'L MAP	1750
CROW, W	1871	MARH'L MAP	1749
CROW, W	1871	MARH'L MAP	1751
CROW, W / SAW MILL	1871	MARH'L MAP	1752
CROW, WILLIAM	1871	MARH'L MAP	1755
CROWL, J C	1838	DEFENDANT	1569
CROWL, J C	1838	DEFENDANT	1569
CROWLEY, JAMES	1816	DEFENDANT	1648
CRUGER, LYDIA L	1862	DEFENDANT	1560
CRUMBACKER, EDWARD C	1839	DEFENDANT	1640
CRUMBACKER, GEORGE	1875	DEFENDANT	1565
CRUMBACKER, GEORGE	1876	DEFENDANT	1580
CRUMBACKER, GEORGE	1878	DEFENDANT	1580
CRUSEN, J	1871	OH CO. MAP	1741
CRUTCHLEY, WESLEY	1877	DEFENDANT	1633
CRUTH, R	1871	BRKE MAP	1737
CRYMBLE, HUGH G & CO	1860	DEFENDANT	1601
CUCKLER, SAMUEL	1818	MISC	1676
CUFF, RICHARD	1815	DEFENDANT	1667
CULBERTSON, -	1841	PLAINTIFF	1629
CULBERTSON, W / ?	1871	HAN MAP	1730
CULLEN, M M / & BROS.	1871	RIV. RD N.OF N.C.	1763
CULLEN, M M / & BROS.	1871	NEW CUMB'LD	1766
CULLEN, M M / & BROS.	1871	NEW CUMB'LD	1767
CULLEN, M M / & BROS - FIRE BRICK WORKS	1871	RIV. RD N.OF N.C.	1770
CULLEY, F	1871	MARH'L MAP	1757
CULP, DANIEL	1784	APPENDIX	1874
CULVER, SIMON	1831	PLAINTIFF	1650
CUMBERLAND	1852	HEMP. RR MAP	1827
CUMBERLAND - MILEPOST - NATIONAL ROAD	1916	NAT'L ROAD	1862
CUMBERLAND MOUNTAINS	1852	HEMPFIELD RR	1819
CUMBERLAND P.O.	1871	HAN MAP	1730
CUMBERLAND RIVER TRAFFIC	1852	HEMPFIELD RR	1817
CUMBERLAND ROAD - HISTORY	1916	NAT'L ROAD	1865
CUMBERLAND TO WHEELING - NATIONAL ROAD MAP	1916	NAT'L ROAD	1869
CUMBERLAND TO WHEELING - TRAVEL ROUTES COMPARED	1916	NAT'L ROAD	1869
CUMBERLAND, MD	1916	NAT'L ROAD	1861
CUMBERLAND, MD - MAP	1916	NAT'L ROAD	1869
CUMMINGS, JOHN	1841	DEFENDANT	1589
CUMMINGS, JOHN	1841	DEFENDANT	1640
CUMMINGS, R	1871	MARH'L MAP	1756
CUMMINS - CHILDREN	1878	MISC	1694
CUMMINS J H	1871	MARH'L MAP	1753
CUMMINS, D / (?DAVID?)	1871	HAN MAP	1731
CUMMINS, D / (?DAVID?)	1871	HAN MAP	1731
CUMMINS, DAVID	1871	HAN MAP	1731
CUMMINS, F A	1871	MARH'L MAP	1753
CUMMINS, JOHN	1871	GLEN EASTON	1801
CUMMINS, JOHN W	1857	MISC	1702
CUMMINS, W	1871	MARH'L MAP	1752
CUMULATIVE INDEX TO VOL. 1-7 / PREVIEW	2000	APPENDIX	1875
CUNNINGHAM VALLEY	1871	HAN MAP	1726
CUNNINGHAM VALLEY	1871	HAN MAP	1727
CUNNINGHAM, - / MRS	1871	W.LIBERTY	1780
CUNNINGHAM, - / MRS - INITIALS MRS.C (OW)	1871	CAMERON	1803
CUNNINGHAM, - / MRS - RES	1871	CAMERON	1803
CUNNINGHAM, A	1871	HAN MAP	1731
CUNNINGHAM, C II / MAP#335	1852	BRKE MAP	1846
CUNNINGHAM, CHRISTOPHER	1801	DEFENDANT	1666
CUNNINGHAM, G	1871	MARH'L MAP	1749
CUNNINGHAM, J R / INITIALS J.R.C. OR J.B.C.	1871	HAN MAP	1727
CUNNINGHAM, J R / INITIALS J.R.C. OR J.B.C.	1871	HAN MAP	1727
CUNNINGHAM, J S	1871	MARH'L MAP	1749
CUNNINGHAM, J S	1871	MARH'L MAP	1749
CUNNINGHAM, J S	1871	MARH'L MAP	1749
CUNNINGHAM, JAMES	1831	DEFENDANT	1650
CUNNINGHAM, JAMES	1850	DEFENDANT	1653
CUNNINGHAM, JAMES	1871	CAMER'N - BUS.	1795
CUNNINGHAM, JAMES JR	1871	CAMERON	1803
CUNNINGHAM, JOHN B	1871	HAN MAP	1726
CUNNINGHAM, JOHN B	1871	HAN MAP	1727
CUNNINGHAM, L	1871	MARH'L MAP	1749
CUNNINGHAM, L / INITIALS L.C.	1871	MARH'L MAP	1749
CUNNINGHAM, L / INITIALS L.C.	1871	LIMESTONE	1805
CUNNINGHAM, P	1871	MARH'L MAP	1749
CUNNINGHAM, W	1871	MARH'L MAP	1750
CUNNINGHAM, WILLIAM	1823	DEFENDANT	1649
CUNNINGHAM, WILLIAM	1823	MISC	1678
CUNNINGHAM, WILLIAM	1829	DEFENDANT	1668
CUNNINGHAM, WILLIAM	1830	DEFENDANT	1559
CUNNINGHAM, WILLIAM	1830	DEFENDANT	1669
CUNNINGHAM, WILLIAM	1832	DEFENDANT	1639
CUNNINGHAM, WILLIAM	1834	DEFENDANT	1618
CUNNINGHAM, WILLIAM	1836	DEFENDANT	1614
CUNNINGHAM, WILLIAM	1836	DEFENDANT	1614
CUNNINGHAM, WILLIAM	1840	DEFENDANT	1587
CUNNINGHAM, WILLIAM	1840	DEFENDANT	1626
CUNNINGHAM, WILLIAM	1840	DEFENDANT	1643
CUNNINGHAM, WILLIAM	1841	DEFENDANT	1567
CUNNINGHAM, WILLIAM	1842	DEFENDANT	1563
CUNNINGHAM, WILLIAM	1842	DEFENDANT	1663
CUNRAD, G / (?CONRAD?)	1871	TRIAD.TWP.	1781
CUNRAD, G	1871	WHG CITY	1787
CUNRAD, G	1871	WHG CITY	1789
CUPPY, G W	1871	RIV. RD N.OF N.C.	1770
CURITS, W B / & SON	1871	W.LIBRTY. BUS.	1780
CURREN J	1871	NEW MANCH.	1769
CURREN, THOMAS	1876	DEFENDANT	1592
CURRENS, J	1871	GLEN EASTON	1801
CURRY, GEORGE	1857	DEFENDANT	1616

'PERSONAL TIME LINE' INDEX TO VOLUME 7 OF THE *OHIO COUNTY INDEX*

ENTRY	YEAR	SUBJECT	PAGE
CURRY, GEORGE	1857	DEFENDANT	1632
CURRY, GEORGE	1857	DEFENDANT	1632
CURRY, WILLIAM	1857	DEFENDANT	1574
CURTIS & PEARSON	1841	DEFENDANT	1640
CURTIS, -	1871	MARH'L MAP	1757
CURTIS, - / & CO.	1871	BETHANY	1773
CURTIS, G D	1871	WASH.TWP-BUS.	1797
CURTIS, J	1871	OH CO. MAP	1740
CURTIS, J A	1871	OH CO. MAP	1740
CURTIS, J E	1871	BKE/OH MAP	1739
CURTIS, J E	1871	BKE/OH MAP	1739
CURTIS, J E	1871	BKE/OH MAP	1739
CURTIS, J E	1871	OH CO. MAP	1740
CURTIS, J E	1871	OH CO. MAP	1740
CURTIS, J E	1871	BETHNY BUS.	1772
CURTIS, J E	1871	BETHANY	1773
CURTIS, J E	1871	BETHANY	1773
CURTIS, J E	1871	BETHANY	1773
CURTIS, J E	1871	BETHANY	1773
CURTIS, J E / & CO. - INITIALS J.E.C.&CO.	1871	BETHANY	1773
CURTIS, J E / INITIALS J.E.C.	1871	BETHANY	1773
CURTIS, J E / INITIALS J.E.C.	1871	BETHANY	1773
CURTIS, J E / INTIALS J.E.C.	1871	BETHANY	1773
CURTIS, J E / INTIALS J.E.C.	1871	BETHANY	1773
CURTIS, J E / INTIALS J.E.C.	1871	BETHANY	1773
CURTIS, J E / INTIALS J.E.C.	1871	BETHANY	1773
CURTIS, J E / LOTS	1871	BETHANY	1773
CURTIS, J E / RES	1871	BETHANY	1773
CURTIS, J M	1871	MARH'L MAP	1749
CURTIS, JAMES	1807	DEFENDANT	1608
CURTIS, L C	1873	DEFENDANT	1586
CURTIS, M / MRS	1871	BETHANY	1773
CURTIS, R B	1871	WASH.TWP-BUS.	1797
CURTIS, R I	1871	MARH'L MAP	1748
CURTIS, R I	1871	MARH'L MAP	1748
CURTIS, R I / INITIALS R.I.C.	1871	MARH'L MAP	1748
CURTIS, SALATHIEL	1822	MISC	1684
CURTIS, W B / & SON - P.O. & STORE	1871	W.LIBERTY	1780
CURTIS, WILLIAM M	1877	DEFENDANT	1631
CURTIS, ZEDEKIAH	1833	DEFENDANT	1628
CURTIS, ZEDEKIAH B	1833	DEFENDANT	1598
CURTIS, ZEDEKIAH B	1833	DEFENDANT	1669
CURTIS, ZEDEKIAH B	1834	DEFENDANT	1669
CURTIS, ZEDEKIAH B	1838	DEFENDANT	1592
CUSHING, DANIEL	1858	DEFENDANT	1653
CUSTOM HOUSE - MARKET ST - WHEELING / ABBREV. C.H.	1871	WHG CITY	1788
CUTHBERT, JOHN / CURATOR	2000	PREFACE	1748
CUTLER, PORTER E	1855	DEFENDANT	1629
CUTLER, PORTER E	1855	DEFENDANT	1663
D, - / MISS D. - PURDY ST - MDSVILLE	1871	MDSVILLE	1808
D. FLAX WHORREY MILLS	1871	MARH'L MAP	1746
D.B. / UNKNOWN INITIALS - (?D.BRADY?)	1871	OH CO. MAP	1740
DAGG, EPHRAIM	1836	DEFENDANT	1574
DAGUE, - / MRS	1871	MARH'L MAP	1747
DAGUE, D	1871	MARH'L MAP	1747
DAGUE, E	1871	MARH'L MAP	1750
DAGUE, W	1871	MARH'L MAP	1747
DAGUE, W	1871	MARH'L MAP	1750
DAILY, M / MRS	1871	ROSBBYS RK	1813
DAINOLD, JOHN	1790	DEFENDANT	1600
DAKIN, ELIZA J	1874	MISC	1703
DALE HALL	1871	OH CO. MAP	1742
DALLAS - DETAIL MAP	1871	W.UNION	1812
DAM - NEAR W. POLLOCK	1871	OH CO. MAP	1740
DAM - OHIO RIVER - N. OF FISH CREEK ISLAND	1871	MARH'L MAP	1754
DAM ON LEFT OR PENN FORK OF FISH CREEK / PENNSYLVANIA FORK	1871	BELLTON	1814
DAM ON RIGHT FORK OF FISH CREEK	1871	MARH'L MAP	1761
DANIELS, J T	1871	NEW CUMB'LD	1762
DANIELS, J T / STORE	1871	NEW CUMB'LD	1767
DANIELS, JOHN	1830	MISC	1674
DANKVIRT, CHARLES	1859	DEFENDANT	1552
DANVILLE	1852	BRKE MAP	1853
DARE, J	1871	BRKE MAP	1737
DARE, J / BLACKSMITH SHOP	1871	BRKE MAP	1737
DARE, JAMES	1841	DEFENDANT	1561
DARE, JAMES	1841	DEFENDANT	1623
DARE, THOMAS	1839	DEFENDANT	1640
DARNELL, PETER	1804	DEFENDANT	1644
DAVES, MICHAEL	1856	DEFENDANT	1588
DAVIDSON, M / MRS	1871	MARH'L MAP	1745
DAVIDSON, M / MRS - INITIALS MRS. M .D.	1871	MARH'L MAP	1745
DAVIDSON, M / MRS - INITIALS MRS. M .D.	1871	MARH'L MAP	1745
DAVIDSON, S P	1871	MDSVILLE	1809
DAVIS, -	1837	DEFENDANT	1583
DAVIS, A	1871	OH CO. MAP	1743
DAVIS, A	1871	MARH'L MAP	1746
DAVIS, A	1871	MARH'L MAP	1746
DAVIS, A K	1871	MDSVILLE	1808
DAVIS, E / MRS	1871	MARH'L MAP	1752
DAVIS, E	1871	MARH'L MAP	1759
DAVIS, E / S. SHOP (?SHOE?)	1871	BETHANY	1773
DAVIS, G	1871	MARH'L MAP	1757
DAVIS, G	1871	CAMERON	1804
DAVIS, H	1871	MARH'L MAP	1747
DAVIS, ISAAC	1840	DEFENDANT	1625
DAVIS, ISAAC	1842	DEFENDANT	1570
DAVIS, ISAAC	1842	DEFENDANT	1625
DAVIS, J	1871	MARH'L MAP	1752
DAVIS, J	1871	MARH'L MAP	1752
DAVIS, J W	1871	OH CO. MAP	1742
DAVIS, J W / QUIET HOME	1871	MARH'L MAP	1746
DAVIS, J W	1871	CAMERON	1804
DAVIS, J W	1871	CAMERON	1804
DAVIS, J W	1871	CAMERON	1804
DAVIS, JAMES	1827	DEFENDANT	1646
DAVIS, JAMES	1871	BETHANY	1773
DAVIS, JOHN	1858	DEFENDANT	1636
DAVIS, JOHN	1858	DEFENDANT	1661
DAVIS, JOHN	1859	DEFENDANT	1616
DAVIS, JOHN T	1858	DEFENDANT	1661
DAVIS, JONATHAN	1840	DEFENDANT	1640
DAVIS, JONATHAN	1840	DEFENDANT	1643
DAVIS, L	1871	MARH'L MAP	1745
DAVIS, M J	1834	DEFENDANT	1650
DAVIS, MICHAEL	1856	DEFENDANT	1588
DAVIS, RICHARD	1818	DEFENDANT	1667
DAVIS, ROBERT	1825	DEFENDANT	1628
DAVIS, S	1871	ROSBBYS RK	1813
DAVIS, S / INITIALS S.D.	1871	ROSBBYS RK	1813
DAVIS, S R	1871	MARH'L MAP	1746
DAVIS, S R / INITIALS S.R.D.	1871	MARH'L MAP	1746
DAVIS, T	1871	MARH'L MAP	1756
DAVIS, T / INITIALS T.D.	1871	MARH'L MAP	1756
DAVIS, THOMAS	1802	DEFENDANT	1583
DAVIS, W	1871	MDSVILLE	1808
DAVIS, W C	1871	CAMERON	1804
DAVIS, W J	1871	MARH'L MAP	1757
DAVIS, W P / WASHINGTON HOUSE - HOTEL	1871	MDSVILLE	1807
DAVIS, WILLIAM	1871	OH CO. MAP	1740
DAVIS, WILLIAM E	1871	BETHANY	1773
DAVIS, WILLIAM J / PASTOR 'CHURCH OF GOD'	1871	BENWO'D - BUS.	1795
DAVISON, S P	1871	MARH'L MAP	1748
DAVON & BRO	1871	BRKE MAP	1734
DAVON & BRO	1871	EDGINGTON STA.	1774
DAWSEY, R	1871	WELLSBURG	1777
DAY & HARKINS	1852	DEFENDANT	1600
DAY & HARKINS	1855	DEFENDANT	1603
DAY, ELIJAH	1838	MISC	1681
DAY, ELIJAH	1840	DEFENDANT	1662
DAY, ELIJAH	1880	MISC	1682
DAY, GEORGE W	1808	DEFENDANT	1594
DAY, JOSEPH	1816	DEFENDANT	1645
DAY, JOSEPH	1818	DEFENDANT	1638
DAYLY	1871	MARH'L MAP	1752
DAYTON, J	1871	WELLSBURG	1778
DAYTON, W	1871	WELLSBURG	1778
DEADY, THOMAS	1788	PLAINTIFF	1637
DEAL, WILLIAM	1824	DEFENDANT	1649
DEAN & CAMPBELL	1871	NEW CUMB'LD	1766
DEAN & CAMPBELL	1871	NEW CUMB'LD	1767
DEAN, CHARLES	1810	DEFENDANT	1638
DEAN, D	1871	OH CO. MAP	1741
DEAN, DANIEL	1855	DEFENDANT	1561
DEATH - ROSENBERGER, JOHN / ACCIDENTLY KILLED NOV 2, 1856	1871	MARH'L MAP	1750
DEATH - WILLIAM BUTLER - KILLED ACCIDENTLY APRIL 1ST, 1855	1871	MARH'L MAP	1753
DEC. CHURCH - NEAR A. WILSON /	1871	MARH'L MAP	1753
DECKERS RUN	1852	BRKE MAP	1849
DECKERS RUN	1871	BRKE MAP	1735
DEDDY, THOMAS	1791	DEFENDANT	1655
DEEMER, A	1871	HAN MAP	1727

'PERSONAL TIME LINE' INDEX TO VOLUME 7 OF THE *OHIO COUNTY INDEX*

ENTRY	YEAR	SUBJECT	PAGE
DEEP GUT RUN	1871	HAN MAP	1730
DEEP GUT RUN	1871	RIV. RD N.OF N.C.	1770
DEEP RUN	1852	BRKE MAP	1843
DEER LICK / SW OF MRS. MARSH	1871	MARH'L MAP	1746
DEER LICK - MEADE TWP	1871	MARH'L MAP	1755
DEETS, C / MRS	1871	MARH'L MAP	1751
DEETS, C / MRS - INITIALS MRS. C.D.	1871	MARH'L MAP	1752
DEFIBAUGH, WILLIAM	1857	DEFENDANT	1588
DEFORD, MERCHANT	1839	DEFENDANT	1584
DEFORD, PERRY	1840	DEFENDANT	1614
DEFORD, PERRY	1840	DEFENDANT	1619
DEFUSSIT, J	1871	WELLSBURG	1777
DEFUSSIT, J / URBANA & YANKEE	1871	WELLSBURG	1777
DEGAN, J	1871	BENWOOD	1798
DEGAN, W	1871	BENWOOD	1798
DEGARMO, HEZEKIAL	1842	DEFENDANT	1578
DEGARMO, M	1871	OH CO. MAP	1743
DEGARMO, M	1871	OH CO. MAP	1744
DEGARMORE, I	1871	OH CO. MAP	1740
DEGARMORE, J	1871	OH CO. MAP	1740
DEGARMORER, HEZIKIAH	1840	DEFENDANT	1578
DEGGE, WILLIAM H F	1841	DEFENDANT	1663
DEHART, CORNELIUS	1812	DEFENDANT	1608
DEIHL, D	1871	WELLSBURG	1777
DELAPLAIN, -	1854	PLAINTIFF	1620
DELAPLAIN, -	1855	PLAINTIFF	1621
DELAPLAIN, -	1856	PLAINTIFF	1621
DELAPLAIN, -	1858	PLAINTIFF	1621
DELAPLAIN, -	1860	PLAINTIFF	1621
DELAPLAIN, -	1862	PLAINTIFF	1621
DELAPLAIN, -	1863	PLAINTIFF	1621
DELAPLAINE, P	1871	BKE/OH MAP	1738
DELAPLAINE, P / INITIALS P.D.	1871	BKE/OH MAP	1738
DELAPLANE, -	1857	PLAINTIFF	1621
DELEPLAIN, -	1855	PLAINTIFF	1621
DELEPLAIN, -	1855	PLAINTIFF	1621
DELEPLAIN, -	1858	PLAINTIFF	1621
DELLAPLAIN, -	1858	PLAINTIFF	1621
DELONGS RUN	1852	BRKE MAP	1841
DEMAPOLIS	1852	BRKE MAP	1854
DEMENT, BENIJAH	1784	APPENDIX	1874
DEMENT, DAVID	1783	APPENDIX	1874
DEMENT, DAVID	1784	APPENDIX	1874
DEMENT, DAVID	1784	APPENDIX	1874
DEMENT, ELIAS	1801	DEFENDANT	1666
DEMENT, GEORGE	1803	DEFENDANT	1589
DEMENT, GEORGE GORDEN	1802	DEFENDANT	1600
DEMENT, J / MRS	1871	OH CO. MAP	1740
DEMENT, SIMMS	1822	DEFENDANT	1579
DEMENT, WILLIAM	1801	DEFENDANT	1610
DEMENT, WILLIAM	1802	DEFENDANT	1572
DEMENT, WILLIAM	1802	DEFENDANT	1607
DEMENT, WILLIAM	1805	DEFENDANT	1635
DEMENT, WILLIAM	1810	DEFENDANT	1596
DEMENT, WILLIAM	1814	DEFENDANT	1596
DENER, F	1871	BETHANY	1773
DENIZOT, NICHOLAS	1858	DEFENDANT	1626
DENNISON, A	1871	OH CO. MAP	1743
DENNISON, M	1871	OH CO. MAP	1743
DENNISON, W	1871	OH CO. MAP	1740
DENNISTON, - / SISTERS	1871	OH CO. MAP	1740
DENTIST - C.BRASHEAR - WELLSBURG	1871	WELLSBURG	1778
DEPOT - HOLLIDAYS COVE	1871	HAN MAP	1733
DEPOT & WAREROOM / POINT MILL STATION	1871	OH CO. MAP	1743
DERDUN, - / MRS	1871	WELLSBURG	1778
DERRINGER, -	1871	OH CO. MAP	1743
DERRINGER, -	1871	OH CO. MAP	1744
DESPADD, -	1835	PLAINTIFF	1626
DESSELL, GURTRUDE	1854	MISC	1679
DEVENNY LANDING / ON OHIO RIVER	1871	BRKE MAP	1735
DEVENNY, C / & BROS	1871	BRKE MAP	1735
DEVENNY, C / & BROS	1871	BRKE MAP	1735
DEVERS, WILLIAM	1871	HAN MAP	1726
DEVINE, HUGH	1855	DEFENDANT	1581
DEVINE, HUGH C	1856	DEFENDANT	1604
DEVINE, HUGH C	1856	DEFENDANT	1632
DEVINNE, JAMES	1836	MISC	1674
DEVOOR, - / MRS	1871	HAN MAP	1732
DEVORE, H	1871	BKE/OH MAP	1738
DEWEY, - / (?DEWEY?) VANCE, DEWEY / & CO. - NAIL WORKS	1871	WHG CITY	1790
DEWEY, - / (?DEWEY?) VANCE, DEWEY / & CO. - SPIKE WORKS	1871	WHG CITY	1790
DEWEY, E C	1853	DEFENDANT	1581
DEWEY, ELIPHALET C	1855	DEFENDANT	1630
DEWEY, ELIPHALET C	1855	DEFENDANT	1670
DEWEY, ELIPHALET C	1856	DEFENDANT	1554
DEWEY, ELIPHALET C	1856	DEFENDANT	1554
DEWITT, -	1788	DEFENDANT	1644
DEXTER, OTIS	1839	DEFENDANT	1602
DICE, HENRY	1855	DEFENDANT	1588
DICK, -	1854	PLAINTIFF	1623
DICKEY, J H / CAPT.	1871	MARH'L MAP	1753
DICKEY, J H / CAPT. - INITIALS CAPT.J H D	1871	MARH'L MAP	1753
DICKEY, J H / CAPT. - INITIALS CAPT.J H D	1871	MARH'L MAP	1753
DICKEY, JOHN H	1871	CAMER'N - BUS.	1795
DICKS BRANCH	1852	BRKE MAP	1849
DICKSON, CHRISTOPHER	1802	DEFENDANT	1666
DICKSON, J	1871	OH CO. MAP	1740
DICKSON, J	1871	MARH'L MAP	1756
DICKSON, LEWIS	1802	DEFENDANT	1655
DICKSON, LITTA	1800	DEFENDANT	1554
DICKSON, THOMAS	1788	DEFENDANT	1572
DIGG, ROBERT F	1830	DEFENDANT	1574
DILLE, DAVID	1808	APPENDIX	1873
DILLE, RICHARD	1818	DEFENDANT	1638
DILLE, SAMUEL	1808	APPENDIX	1873
DILLER, SALATHIAL	1829	DEFENDANT	1613
DILLER, SALATHIEL	1829	DEFENDANT	1632
DILLIE, RICHARD	1818	DEFENDANT	1638
DILLIR, SALATHIEL	1830	DEFENDANT	1602
DILLON, HENRY	1811	DEFENDANT	1599
DILLON, HENRY	1814	DEFENDANT	1599
DILLON, WILLIAM	1860	DEFENDANT	1654
DILWORTH, -	1843	PLAINTIFF	1629
DISCIPLES CHURCH / (GONE) -MAP#401	1852	BRKE MAP	1846
DISCIPLES CHURCH / (GONE) - MAP#362	1852	BRKE MAP	1847
DISCIPLES CHURCH - HOLLIDAYS COVE	1871	HAN MAP	1733
DISCIPLES CHURCH - WEST LIBERTY	1871	W.LIBERTY	1780
DISCIPLES CHURCH & CEMETERY - MAIN ST. - BETHANY	1871	BETHANY	1773
DISTANCES FROM TOWN TO TOWN - TABLE	1871	DISTANCES	1815
DISTILLER - R. CARTER	1871	OH CO.BUS.	1779
DISTILLERY - CASNERS / JAMES - HEIRS - MAP#255	1852	BRKE MAP	1843
DISTILLERY - R.CARTER & CO. DISTILLERY NO. 3	1871	OH CO. MAP	1742
DITWILER, ABRAHAM	1859	DEFENDANT	1653
DIVEN, -	1824	PLAINTIFF	1620
DIVIDING RIDGE FARM	1871	MARH'L MAP	1753
DIXON RUN	1871	OH CO. MAP	1740
DIXON, HUGH	1821	DEFENDANT	1561
DIXON, JONES	1810	DEFENDANT	1587
DIXON, WILLIAM	1808	DEFENDANT	1638
DIXON, WILLIAM	1809	DEFENDANT	1638
DIXON, WILLIAM	1818	DEFENDANT	1649
DIXSON, LEWIS	1801	DEFENDANT	1655
DIXSON, LEWIS	1801	DEFENDANT	1655
DOAK, JAMES	1871	HAN MAP	1727
DOAK, JAMES	1871	HAN MAP	1728
DOASE, EZRA W	1822	DEFENDANT	1581
DOAYE, EZRA W	1822	DEFENDANT	1581
DOBBIN, WILLIAM I	1834	DEFENDANT	1600
DOBBINS, JAMES	1820	DEFENDANT	1624
DOBBS, A	1871	MARH'L MAP	1756
DOCTOR - B.W. CHAPMAN	1871	NEW CUMB'LD	1762
DOCTOR - CAMPBELL	1871	OH CO. MAP	1741
DOCTOR - DR.NEY - MOUNDSVILLE	1871	MDSVILLE	1808
DOCTOR - E.C.THOMAS - MOUNDSVILLE	1871	MDSVILLE	1807
DOCTOR - E.H.MOORE	1871	WELLSBURG	1777
DOCTOR - E.H.MOORE	1871	WELLSBURG	1778
DOCTOR - E.H.MOORE - WELLSBURG	1871	WLSBRG BUS.	1772
DOCTOR - G.A.CRACRAFT - TRIADELPHIA	1871	TRIAD.BORO.	1784
DOCTOR - G.L.BEAUMONT - NEW CUMBERLAND	1871	NEW CUMB'LD	1762
DOCTOR - G.L.BEAUMONT - NEW CUMBERLAND	1871	NEW CUMB'LD	1766
DOCTOR - G.W.BRUCE - MOUNDSVILLE	1871	MDSVL BUS.	1796
DOCTOR - G.W.BRUCE - MOUNDSVILLE	1871	MDSVILLE	1806
DOCTOR - G.W.MCKIMIE	1871	MARH'L MAP	1759

'PERSONAL TIME LINE' INDEX TO VOLUME 7 OF THE *OHIO COUNTY INDEX*

ENTRY	YEAR	SUBJECT	PAGE
DOCTOR - G.W.MCKIMIE - NEAR FAIR VIEW	1871	FRKLN TWP-BUS.	1797
DOCTOR - H.YANT - NEW MANCHESTER	1871	NEW MANCH.	1769
DOCTOR - HOSKINSON / LIBERTY TWP	1871	MARH'L MAP	1761
DOCTOR - I.N.LUCAS - LIMESTONE	1871	MARH'L MAP	1749
DOCTOR - I.N.LUCAS - LIMESTONE P.O.	1871	LIMESTONE	1805
DOCTOR - J. ENGLISH	1871	OH CO. MAP	1741
DOCTOR - J.H.STORER - TRIADELPHIA	1871	OH CO.BUS.	1779
DOCTOR - J.H.STORER - TRIADELPHIA	1871	TRIAD.BORO.	1784
DOCTOR - J.H.STORER - TRIADELPHIA	1871	TRIAD.BORO.	1784
DOCTOR - J.M.COOPER - WELLSBURG	1871	WLSBRG BUS.	1772
DOCTOR - J.M.COOPER - WELLSBURG	1871	WELLSBURG	1777
DOCTOR - J.W. GIST	1871	BRKE MAP	1737
DOCTOR - J.W.PIPES - CAMERON	1871	CAMERON	1803
DOCTOR - JAMES EVANS - NEW CUMBERLAND	1871	NEW CUMB'LD	1762
DOCTOR - JOHN C. HUPP	1871	OH CO.BUS.	1779
DOCTOR - MCCOY / H	1871	MARH'L MAP	1745
DOCTOR - MOORE	1871	BRKE MAP	1736
DOCTOR - MOORE	1871	BRKE MAP	1736
DOCTOR - MOORE	1871	BRKE MAP	1736
DOCTOR - MRS.DR.MOORE - MOUNDSVILLE / ? (?PHYSICIAN OR PHD.)?	1871	MDSVILLE	1810
DOCTOR - NEY / CLAY TWP	1871	MARH'L MAP	1751
DOCTOR - OWINGS / E OF HOLLIDAYS COVE P.O.	1871	HAN MAP	1732
DOCTOR - R. ANDREWS - NEW MANCHESTER	1871	NEW MANCH.	1769
DOCTOR - R. RICHARDSON	1871	BKE/OH MAP	1739
DOCTOR - RICHTER - GLEN EASTON	1871	GLEN EASTON	1801
DOCTOR - S.B. STIDGER / N. OF CAMERON P.O.	1871	MARH'L MAP	1757
DOCTOR - S.B.STIDGER	1871	MARH'L MAP	1753
DOCTOR - S.B.STIDGER - CAMERON	1871	CAMER'N - BUS.	1795
DOCTOR - S.B.STIDGER - CAMERON	1871	CAMERON	1802
DOCTOR - S.C.MCCRACKEN - WEST UNION	1871	W.UNION-BUS.	1797
DOCTOR - S.C.MCCRACKEN - WEST UNION	1871	W.UNION	1812
DOCTOR - S.H.KELLEY - WEST LIBERTY	1871	W.LIBRTY.BUS.	1780
DOCTOR - T.F.MARSHMAN - WEST UNION	1871	W.UNION	1812
DOCTOR - W. SHANKY / NEW CUMBERLAND	1871	NEW CUMB'LD	1767
DOCTOR - W.S.HOWARD	1871	MARH'L MAP	1759
DOCTOR - WILLIAM HUKELL - WEST LIBERTY	1871	W.LIBERTY	1780
DOCTOR - WILLIAM HUKILL - WEST LIBERTY	1871	W.LIBRTY.BUS.	1780
DODD, WILLIAM	1871	MARH'L MAP	1756
DODDRIDGE, N	1871	WELLSBURG	1777
DODDRIDGE, PHILIP	1800	PLAINTIFF	1556
DODDRIDGE, PHILIP	1828	DEFENDANT	1639
DODDRIDGE, PHILLIP	1800	PLAINTIFF	1556
DODGSON, JAMES H	1856	DEFENDANT	1584
DODGSON, JAMES H	1856	DEFENDANT	1603
DODSON, -	1871	MARH'L MAP	1752
DODSON, -	1871	MARH'L MAP	1755
DODSON, C M	1871	MARH'L MAP	1751
DOLAN, M	1871	MARH'L MAP	1753
DOLAN, M	1871	BENWOOD	1798
DOLAN, MARGARET	1860	MISC	1682
DOLAN, MARGARET	1861	MISC	1680
DOLBEUR, A E / (?OR DOLLEUR?) - LOT 161	1871	BETHANY	1773
DOLLEUR, A E / (?OR DOLBEUR?) - LOT 161	1871	BETHANY	1773
DONALDSON, WILLIAM	1824	DEFENDANT	1591
DONALDSON, WILLIAM	1828	DEFENDANT	1587
DONALDSON, WILLIAM	1828	DEFENDANT	1591
DONALDSON, WILLIAM	1838	DEFENDANT	1580
DONALDSON, WILLIAM	1839	DEFENDANT	1580
DONANGAN, J	1871	NEW CUMB'LD	1768
DONANGAN, J	1871	NEW CUMB'LD	1768
DONANGAN, J	1871	RIV. RD S.OF N.C.	1771
DONEHOO, D / DANIEL	1871	NEW MANCH.	1769
DONEHOO, D / DANIEL - LAW OFFICE	1871	NEW MANCH.	1769
DONEHOO, DANIEL / ATTORNEY	1871	NEW MANCH.	1763
DONEHOO, J C / LOTS 57 & 58	1871	NEW MANCH.	1769
DONLEY, M	1871	GLEN EASTON	1801
DONLEY, W M	1858	DEFENDANT	1588
DONNALD, ELIZABETH	1800	DEFENDANT	1598
DONNALD, ELIZABETH	1800	DEFENDANT	1634
DONNALD, PETER	1800	DEFENDANT	1598
DONNOLDSON, WILLIAM	1797	DEFENDANT	1576
DONOVAN, A O	1871	FOWLERS P.O.	1775
DONOVAN, THOMAS / MAP#525	1852	BRKE MAP	1852
DONOVAN, THOMAS / MAP#526	1852	BRKE MAP	1852
DONOVAN, THOMAS	1871	BRKE MAP	1734
DONOVAN, THOMAS	1871	BRKE MAP	1735
DOOLING, JAMES	1878	DEFENDANT	1601
DORNAN, A	1871	MARH'L MAP	1750
DORNAN, A	1871	MARH'L MAP	1753
DORNAN, E	1871	NEW CUMB'LD	1768
DORNAN, M	1871	HAN MAP	1731
DORSEY, B	1871	MARH'L MAP	1749
DORSEY, C	1871	MARH'L MAP	1750
DORSEY, D	1871	MARH'L MAP	1745
DORSEY, D / INITIALS D.D.	1871	MARH'L MAP	1745
DORSEY, E	1871	MARH'L MAP	1757
DORSEY, E	1871	MARH'L MAP	1757
DORSEY, E	1871	MARH'L MAP	1757
DORSEY, E / INITIALS E.D.	1871	MARH'L MAP	1757
DORSEY, ELY	1838	DEFENDANT	1614
DORSEY, ELY	1838	DEFENDANT	1628
DORSEY, ELY	1839	DEFENDANT	1614
DORSEY, ELY	1839	DEFENDANT	1619
DORSEY, ELY	1844	DEFENDANT	1670
DORSEY, MATILDA / MAP#419	1852	BRKE MAP	1847
DORSEY, N L	1856	DEFENDANT	1590
DORSEY, N S	1858	DEFENDANT	1590
DORSEY, NATHANIEL L	1855	DEFENDANT	1636
DORSEY, NATHANIEL L	1856	DEFENDANT	1636
DORSEY, NATHANIEL S	1852	DEFENDANT	1626
DORSEY, R / MRS	1871	MARH'L MAP	1749
DORSEY, T J	1871	MARH'L MAP	1746
DORSEY, T J	1871	MARH'L MAP	1749
DORSEY, W	1871	MDSVILLE	1807
DORSEY, W	1871	MDSVILLE	1807
DOTY, J	1871	MARH'L MAP	1754
DOUGER, J	1871	MARH'L MAP	1746
DOUGHERTY, H	1871	MARH'L MAP	1758
DOUGHERTY, W H	1871	MARH'L MAP	1746
DOUGLAS, E	1871	MARH'L MAP	1746
DOUGLAS, JOHN	1849	DEFENDANT	1590
DOUGLASS, MARK	1821	DEFENDANT	1574
DOUGLASS, W / E. SIDE OF MAP	1871	MARH'L MAP	1746
DOUGLASS, W / N. OF PLEASANT VALLEY	1871	MARH'L MAP	1747
DOVER, PHILIP	1788	DEFENDANT	1610
DOVER, PHILLIP	1799	DEFENDANT	1607
DOWLER, E	1871	MARH'L MAP	1757
DOWLER, E / EST	1871	MARH'L MAP	1757
DOWLER, EDWARD	1816	DEFENDANT	1555
DOWLER, EDWARD	1816	MISC	1707
DOWLER, I / (?L?)	1871	MARH'L MAP	1750
DOWLER, I	1871	MARH'L MAP	1757
DOWLER, J / SAW MILL	1871	MARH'L MAP	1746
DOWLER, J	1871	MARH'L MAP	1749
DOWLER, J	1871	MARH'L MAP	1757
DOWLER, J	1871	CAMERON	1803
DOWLER, J F	1871	MARH'L MAP	1746
DOWLER, J M	1871	OH CO. MAP	1742
DOWLER, J M / TOP OF MAP	1871	MARH'L MAP	1745
DOWLER, J W	1871	MARH'L MAP	1757
DOWLER, M	1871	MARH'L MAP	1745
DOWLER, M / INITIALS M.D.	1871	MARH'L MAP	1745
DOWLER, N	1871	MARH'L MAP	1745
DOWLER, T	1871	MARH'L MAP	1746
DOWLER, W	1871	MARH'L MAP	1746
DOWNER, T	1871	OH CO. MAP	1741
DOWNEY, P	1871	WELLSBURG	1778
DOWNEY, WILLIAM	1808	DEFENDANT	1635
DOWNING, J	1871	MARH'L MAP	1746
DOWNING, JAMES	1813	DEFENDANT	1656
DOWNING, WILLIAM	1807	DEFENDANT	1635
DOWNING, WILLIAM	1808	DEFENDANT	1635
DOWNING, WILLIAM	1812	DEFENDANT	1583
DOWNING, WILLIAM	1813	PLAINTIFF	1648
DOWNS, JEROME	1853	DEFENDANT	1663
DOWNS, JOHN H	1857	DEFENDANT	1586
DOWNS, JOHN H	1860	MISC	1679

'PERSONAL TIME LINE' INDEX TO VOLUME 7 OF THE *OHIO COUNTY INDEX*

ENTRY	YEAR	SUBJECT	PAGE
DOWNS, JOSEPH J	1857	DEFENDANT	1630
DOWNY, WILLIAM	1813	DEFENDANT	1583
DOYLE, J R	1871	BKE/OH MAP	1739
DRAIN = RUN / ?	1871	MARH'L MAP	1751
DRAKE, J B	1876	DEFENDANT	1627
DRAKELY & SWEENEY	1859	DEFENDANT	1621
DRENER, JACOB	1778	APPENDIX	1874
DROVERS ROAD / (?PROVERS?)	1871	BKE/OH MAP	1739
DRUBIN, E	1871	NEW MANCH.	1769
DRUG STORE - CORNER CHESTER AND PEARL	1871	NEW CUMB'LD	1767
DRUG STORE - NEW CUMBERLAND	1871	NEW CUMB'LD	1767
DRY RIDGE ROAD	1871	MARH'L MAP	1750
DRY RUN	1871	HAN MAP	1726
DRY RUN	1871	MARH'L MAP	1750
DRY RUN	1871	MARH'L MAP	1758
DUBOIS, J D	1871	OH CO. BUS.	1779
DUBOIS, J H	1871	WHG CITY	1787
DUBOIS, J H / INITIALS J.H.D.	1871	WHG CITY	1787
DUBOIS, J H	1871	WHG CITY	1789
DUBOIS, J H / INITIALS J.H.D.	1871	WHG CITY	1789
DUBOIS, L / RES	1871	TRIAD.TWP.	1781
DUFFY, B	1871	MARH'L MAP	1755
DUFFY, JOHN	1859	DEFENDANT	1588
DUGAN, WDOLAN, M	1871	BENWOOD	1798
DUKE & DAVIS	1837	DEFENDANT	1583
DULTY, GEORGE	1832	DEFENDANT	1553
DULTY, GEORGE	1834	DEFENDANT	1618
DULTY, GEORGE	1840	DEFENDANT	1643
DULTY, GEORGE	1841	DEFENDANT	1551
DULTY, JOHN	1858	DEFENDANT	1552
DULTY, JOHN	1858	DEFENDANT	1621
DULTY, WILLIAM	1857	DEFENDANT	1582
DUMOND, W R / MAP ASSISTANT	1871	MAP	1713
DUN, DAVID	1788	DEFENDANT	1644
DUNBAR, DANIEL	1861	DEFENDANT	1597
DUNCAN, DAVID	1787	DEFENDANT	1644
DUNKIRK	1852	HEMP. RR MAP	1825
DUNLANY, P	1871	GLEN EASTON	1801
DUNLAP, -	1861	DEFENDANT	1554
DUNLAP, - / MRS - MARSHALL ST - REFERENCE #2	1871	MDSVILLE	1810
DUNLAP, ATKINSON & CO	1862	DEFENDANT	1574
DUNLAP, M M / (?MASON?)	1862	DEFENDANT	1592
DUNLAP, M M / (?MASON?)	1871	BKE/OH MAP	1739
DUNLAP, MARK	1829	MISC	1680
DUNLAP, MARK	1829	MISC	1702
DUNLAP, MASON M	1849	DEFENDANT	1568
DUNLAP, MASON M	1849	DEFENDANT	1623
DUNLAP, MASON M	1857	DEFENDANT	1616
DUNLAP, MASON M	1857	DEFENDANT	1616
DUNLAP, MASON M	1858	DEFENDANT	1592
DUNLAP, MASON M	1861	DEFENDANT	1557
DUNLAP, MASON M	1861	DEFENDANT	1592
DUNLAP, S	1871	OH CO. MAP	1740
DUNLAP, S	1871	W.LIBRTY.BUS	1780
DUNLAP, W / INITIALS W.D.	1871	MARH'L MAP	1748
DUNLAP, W	1871	MARH'L MAP	1749
DUNLAP, W / INITIALS W.D.	1871	MARH'L MAP	1749
DUNLAP, W / INITIALS W.D.	1871	MARH'L MAP	1752
DUNLAP, W / INITIALS W.D. - FAIRVIEW	1871	MARH'L MAP	1752
DUNLAP, W / RES	1871	MARH'L MAP	1752
DUNLAP, WILLIAM	1871	W.LIBERTY	1780
DUNLEVY, -	1857	PLAINTIFF	1630
DUNLEVY, -	1858	PLAINTIFF	1630
DUNLEVY, -	1861	PLAINTIFF	1631
DUNLEVY, - / WILSON, DUNLEVY & CO.	1871	MARH'L MAP	1757
DUNLEVY, - / WILSON, DUNLEVY & CO.	1871	MARH'L MAP	1757
DUNLEVY, - / WILSON, DUNLEVY & CO. - INITIALS W.D. & CO.	1871	MARH'L MAP	1757
DUNLEVY, - / WILSON, DUNLEVY & CO / INITIALS W.D. & CO.	1871	MARH'L MAP	1761
DUNLVEY, - / WILSON, DUNLEVY & CO	1871	MARH'L MAP	1761
DUNLVEY, - / WILSON, DUNLEVY & CO	1871	MARH'L MAP	1761
DUNMORE, / GENERAL	1916	NAT'L ROAD	1867
DUNN, HEZEKIAH	1783	APPENDIX	1874
DUNN, HEZEKIAH	1784	APPENDIX	1874
DUNN, JERIMIAH	1778	APPENDIX	1874
DUNN, M	1871	MDSVILLE	1807
DUNN, M / LOT 66	1871	MDSVILLE	1807
DUNN, M	1871	MDSVILLE	1808
DUNN, M	1871	MDSVILLE	1810
DUNNEVON, WILLIAM	1856	DEFENDANT	1588
DUNWELL, - / MISS - YANKEE ST	1871	WELLSBURG	1777
DURANT, JACOB	1810	DEFENDANT	1572

ENTRY	YEAR	SUBJECT	PAGE
DURBIN, BENJAMIN	1840	DEFENDANT	1628
DURBIN, D	1871	NEW MANCH.	1769
DURBIN, E / INITIALS E.D.	1871	NEW MANCH.	1769
DURBIN, E / INITIALS E.D.	1871	NEW MANCH.	1769
DURBIN, T / BLACKSMITH	1871	NEW MANCH.	1763
DURBIN, T / WITH WAGON SHOP & BLACKSMITH SHOP	1871	NEW MANCH.	1769
DURR, SEBASTION	1796	DEFENDANT	1600
DURRANT, JACOB	1807	DEFENDANT	1572
DUTCH CHURCH - S. WHG	1871	SOUTH WHG	1792
DUVAL, - / GEN (?GENERAL?)	1871	BRKE MAP	1736
DUVAL, - / GENERAL	1871	WELLSBURG	1776
DUVAL, - / GENERAL	1871	WELLSBURG	1777
DUVAL, - / GENERAL OF BARCLAY & LLOYD (GROC) O.C.	1871	WELLSBURG	1777
DUVAL, H	1871	WELLSBURG	1777
DUVAL, W	1871	WELLSBURG	1777
DUVALL, MUNDICAN	1835	DEFENDANT	1587
DUVAULL, G W	1860	DEFENDANT	1621
DWIRE, J	1871	MARH'L MAP	1751
DWIRE, J	1871	MARH'L MAP	1751
DWIRE, J / INITIALS J.D.	1871	MARH'L MAP	1751
DWIRE, T	1871	MARH'L MAP	1751
DWIRE, T	1871	MARH'L MAP	1754
DYE, MARY	1822	DEFENDANT	1559
DYE, MAY	1829	DEFENDANT	1585
E.D. / (?EDUCATION DEPARTMENT?)	1871	NEW MANCH.	1769
E.D. / CONFIRMED - INITIALS FOR E. DURBIN	1871	NEW MANCH.	1769
E.W / UKNOWN INITIALS	1871	OH CO. MAP	1742
EAGLE, WILLIAM	1842	DEFENDANT	1652
EAR MARKS OF STOCK - DEFINED	2000	APPENDIX	1875
EARLIWINE, G C	1871	MARH'L MAP	1746
EARLY SETTLEMENT - CLAY TWP	1871	MARH'L MAP	1751
EARLYWINE, B	1871	MARH'L MAP	1752
EARLYWINE, J	1871	MARH'L MAP	1753
EAST LIVERPOOL	1871	HAN MAP	1727
EAST LIVERPOOL	1871	HAN MAP	1727
EAST ST - RITCHIE TWP	1871	RITCHIE TWP	1793
EASTER, M	1871	WELLSBURG	1778
EASTERN GATE - TOLL GATE ON NATIONAL ROAD - RONEY POINT STATION	1871	OH CO. MAP	1744
EASTERN SLOPE	1871	MARH'L MAP	1753
EASTON, - / MRS	1871	GLEN EASTON	1801
EASTWOOD, AMON	1798	DEFENDANT	1634
EASTWOOD, JOSEPH	1803	DEFENDANT	1569
EASTWOOD, JOSEPH	1807	DEFENDANT	1569
EASTWOOD, SAMUEL	1798	DEFENDANT	1634
EATON, A	1871	HAN MAP	1731
EATON, A	1871	HAN MAP	1732
EBBERT, J	1871	OH CO. MAP	1743
EBBERT, J	1871	OH CO. MAP	1744
EBBERT, JOHN	1878	DEFENDANT	1593
EBBERT, JOHN V K	1850	DEFENDANT	1600
EBERLING, A F	1871	TRIAD.BORO	1784
EBERT, C	1871	MARH'L MAP	1745
EBERTS, JOHN	1848	DEFENDANT	1596
ECHOLS, -	1840	PLAINTIFF	1625
ECHOLS, -	1842	PLAINTIFF	1625
ECHOLS, CHARLES	1842	DEFENDANT	1652
ECHOLS, DAVID	1839	DEFENDANT	1614
ECHOLS, DAVID	1846	DEFENDANT	1551
ECHOLS, HENRY	1835	DEFENDANT	1662
ECHOLS, HENRY	1837	DEFENDANT	1656
ECHOLS, HENRY	1838	DEFENDANT	1563
ECHOLS, HENRY	1838	DEFENDANT	1563
ECHOLS, HENRY	1838	DEFENDANT	1622
ECHOLS, HENRY	1838	DEFENDANT	1622
ECHOLS, HENRY	1838	DEFENDANT	1661
ECHOLS, J	1871	MARH'L MAP	1757
ECHOLS, JEREMICAH	1833	DEFENDANT	1635
ECHOLS, JOHN	1825	DEFENDANT	1649
ECHOLS, THOMAS	1832	DEFENDANT	1604
ECKLES, A	1871	MARH'L MAP	1756
ECKSTIEN, FREDERICK	1821	DEFENDANT	1620
EDDIE, - / MRS	1871	NEW MANCH.	1769
EDGINGTON	1871	DISTANCES	1815
EDGINGTON BRIDGE CO	1871	CROSS CRK.BUS.	1772
EDGINGTON BRIDGE YARD	1871	BRKE MAP	1734
EDGINGTON BRIDGE YARD	1871	EDGINGTON STA.	1774
EDGINGTON STATION	1871	BRKE MAP	1734
EDGINGTON STATION - DETAIL MAP	1871	EDGINGTON STA.	1774
EDGINGTON STATION - IRON BRIDGE ACROSS OHIO RIVER	1871	BRKE MAP	1734
EDGINGTON STATION - ON RR	1871	EDGINGTON STA.	1774

XXXII

'PERSONAL TIME LINE' INDEX TO VOLUME 7 OF THE OHIO COUNTY INDEX

ENTRY	YEAR	SUBJECT	PAGE
EDGINGTON, DANIEL M	1842	DEFENDANT	1586
EDGINGTON, DANIEL M	1857	DEFENDANT	1584
EDGINGTON, DANIEL M	1857	DEFENDANT	1603
EDGINGTON, G / NEAR BLACKSMITH SHOP	1871	W.LIBERTY	1780
EDGINGTON, GEORGE	1795	DEFENDANT	1608
EDGINGTON, GEORGE	1796	DEFENDANT	1608
EDGINGTON, JESSE / ESQ. - MAP#102	1852	BRKE MAP	1843
EDGINGTON, JESSE / ESQ. - MAP#148	1852	BRKE MAP	1843
EDGINGTON, JESSE / ESQ. - (WAREHOUSE) - MAP#604	1852	BRKE MAP	1851
EDGINGTON, JESSE / ESQ. - (WAREHOUSE) - MAP#646	1852	BRKE MAP	1851
EDGINGTON, JESSE / ESQ. - MAP#602	1852	BRKE MAP	1851
EDGINGTON, JESSE / ESQ. - (FERRY) - MAP#603	1852	BRKE MAP	1851
EDGINGTON, SUSAN / MRS	1871	W.LIBERTY	1780
EDGINGTON, T / TAKEN PRISONER BY INDIANS ABOUT 1790 - (?OR1796?)	1871	BRKE MAP	1734
EDIE, - / MRS	1871	NEW CUMB'LD	1768
EDIE, ALEXANDER	1871	HAN MAP	1731
EDIE, ALEXANDER	1871	HAN MAP	1731
EDIE, D	1871	NEW CUMB'LD	1766
EDIE, JOHN / PILOT	1871	NEW CUMB'LD	1762
EDIE, JOHN	1871	NEW CUMB'LD	1768
EDIE, JOHN	1871	NEW CUMB'LD	1768
EDLER, T B	1871	MARH'L MAP	1750
EDNEY, ROBT J	1822	DEFENDANT	1632
EDWARD, A	1871	MDSVILLE	1809
EDWARDS & ROBERTS	1871	MDSVL BUS.	1796
EDWARDS, -	1838	DEFENDANT	1557
EDWARDS, -	1849	PLAINTIFF	1603
EDWARDS, -	1851	PLAINTIFF	1603
EDWARDS, -	1853	PLAINTIFF	1603
EDWARDS, -	1855	PLAINTIFF	1603
EDWARDS, -	1856	PLAINTIFF	1603
EDWARDS, -	1857	PLAINTIFF	1603
EDWARDS, -	1858	PLAINTIFF	1603
EDWARDS, -	1859	PLAINTIFF	1603
EDWARDS, -	1860	PLAINTIFF	1603
EDWARDS, -	1861	PLAINTIFF	1603
EDWARDS, -	1862	PLAINTIFF	1603
EDWARDS, - / MCCONELS & EDWARDS PORTABLE SAW MILL	1871	MARH'L MAP	1749
EDWARDS, E W	1859	DEFENDANT	1672
EDWARDS, EDWARD W	1856	DEFENDANT	1560
EDWARDS, EDWARD W	1856	DEFENDANT	1601
EDWARDS, EDWARD W	1856	DEFENDANT	1630
EDWARDS, G	1871	MARH'L MAP	1748
EDWARDS, G / & CO	1871	MDSVILLE	1807
EDWARDS, G / STORE - MARKET ST - INTIALS G.E.STORE	1871	MDSVILLE	1807
EDWARDS, GEORGE	1871	MDSVILLE	1809
EDWARDS, GRIFFITH P	1835	DEFENDANT	1570
EDWARDS, J C / BLACKSMITH	1871	NEW CUMB'LD	1762
EDWARDS, J C	1871	NEW CUMB'LD	1768
EDWARDS, J D	1871	NEW CUMB'LD	1767
EDWARDS, M	1871	NEW CUMB'LD	1768
EDWARDS, M	1871	MDSVILLE	1807
EDWARDS, MICHAEL	1838	DEFENDANT	1651
EDWARDS, MICHAEL	1838	DEFENDANT	1651
EDWARDS, MICHAEL JR	1858	DEFENDANT	1626
EDWARDS, W	1871	MDSVILLE	1809
EDWARDS, W A & BRO	1861	DEFENDANT	1588
EDWARDS, W L	1871	MDSVILLE	1807
EDWARDS, W L	1871	MDSVILLE	1809
EIMER, HANSEN	1876	DEFENDANT	1603
EISENNACH, K	1871	MARH'L MAP	1746
EISENNACH, K / BLACKSMITH SHOP ?	1871	MARH'L MAP	1746
EISMAN, J	1871	NEW MANCH.	1769
ELDER, S	1871	MDSVILLE	1807
ELDER, S	1871	MDSVILLE	1807
ELDER, S / INITIALS W.E.	1871	MDSVILLE	1807
ELDER, W	1871	MDSVILLE	1807
ELDER, W	1871	MDSVILLE	1807
ELDER, W / INITIALS W.E.	1871	MDSVILLE	1807
ELDER, W / INITIALS W.E.	1871	MDSVILLE	1807
ELDER, WILLIAM / BLACKSMITH - MOUNDSVILLE	1871	MDSVL BUS.	1796
ELDER, WILLIAM / BLACKSMITH SHOP	1871	MDSVILLE	1807
ELDERSVILLE, PA / WASHINGTON CO	1852	BRKE MAP	1852
ELIAS, E / NEAR WAIT FARM	1871	MARH'L MAP	1745
ELKINS, SAMUEL	1839	DEFENDANT	1640
ELKINS, SAMUEL	1841	DEFENDANT	1596
ELLEOT, CHARLES	1809	DEFENDANT	1645
ELLET, CHARLES	1809	DEFENDANT	1645
ELLET, CHARLES	1852	HEMPFIELD RR	1817
ELLET, CHARLES JR / CIVIL ENGINEER ON MAP	1852	HEMP. RR MAP	1825
ELLIFRITZ, S J	1877	DEFENDANT	1565
ELLIFRITZ, SAMUEL J	1866	MISC	1680
ELLIOT, THOMAS / HEIRS - MAP#616	1852	BRKE MAP	1852
ELLIOT, WILLIAM A / MAP#615	1852	BRKE MAP	1852
ELLIOTS BRANCH	1852	BRKE MAP	1852
ELLIOTT, G	1871	BKE/OH MAP	1739
ELLIOTT, GEORGE	1871	BUFF.TWP.BUS.	1772
ELLIOTT, H	1871	MARH'L MAP	1746
ELLIOTT, J	1871	MARH'L MAP	1747
ELLIOTT, J / INITIALS J.E.	1871	MARH'L MAP	1747
ELLIOTT, JAMES	1871	OH CO. MAP	1743
ELLIOTT, JAMES	1871	OH CO. MAP	1743
ELLIOTT, JAMES	1876	DEFENDANT	1627
ELLIOTT, JOHN	1856	DEFENDANT	1575
ELLIOTT, JOHN	1856	DEFENDANT	1580
ELLIOTT, JOHN	1856	DEFENDANT	1604
ELLIOTT, JOHN	1856	DEFENDANT	1632
ELLIOTT, JOHN	1871	OH CO. MAP	1743
ELLIOTT, JOHN A	1857	DEFENDANT	1592
ELLIOTT, S	1871	OH CO. MAP	1743
ELLIOTT, WILLIAM	1838	DEFENDANT	1622
ELLIS, -	1857	PLAINTIFF	1626
ELLIS, -	1858	PLAINTIFF	1626
ELLIS, -	1861	PLAINTIFF	1626
ELLIS, -	1861	PLAINTIFF	1627
ELLSONS RUN	1852	BRKE MAP	1849
ELLSWORTH, - / CUT OFF - W.OF J. DOWLER	1871	CAMERON	1803
ELLSWORTH, -	1871	CAMERON	1804
ELM GROVE / OHIO CO	1871	DISTANCES	1815
ELM GROVE	1916	NAT'L ROAD	1864
ELM GROVE - BLACKSMITH SHOP	1871	ELM GROVE	1782
ELM GROVE - BOGGS SCHOOL NO.? - ELM GROVE DIST	1871	OH CO. MAP	1742
ELM GROVE - BUSINESS CENTER	1916	NAT'L ROAD	1865
ELM GROVE - HENRY CLAY MONUMENT - PHOTO	1916	NAT'L ROAD	1865
ELM GROVE - MAIN ST	1916	NAT'L ROAD	1864
ELM GROVE - MAP	1916	NAT'L ROAD	1863
ELM GROVE - OLD STONE BRIDGE	1916	NAT'L ROAD	1865
ELM GROVE - POST OFFICE	1871	ELM GROVE	1782
ELM GROVE - STORE	1871	ELM GROVE	1782
ELM GROVE - WAGON SHOP	1871	ELM GROVE	1782
ELM GROVE BRIGE - PHOTO	1916	NAT'L ROAD	1866
ELM GROVE DIST	1871	OH CO. MAP	1744
ELM GROVE HOUSE / HOTEL	1871	ELM GROVE	1782
ELM GROVE HOUSE - HOTEL - ELM GROVE	1871	OH CO. BUS.	1779
ELM GROVE P.O.	1871	OH CO. MAP	1742
ELM GROVE P.O.	1871	OH CO. MAP	1742
ELM GROVE P.O.	1871	OH CO. MAP	1744
ELM GROVE STATION	1871	OH CO. MAP	1742
ELM GROVE STATION	1871	OH CO. MAP	1744
ELM GROVE STATION & P.O. - DETAIL MAP	1871	ELM GROVE	1782
ELM GROVE STATION POST OFFICE	1871	ELM GROVE	1782
ELM GROVE STORE	1871	OH CO. MAP	1742
ELM SPRING / S. OF A. DAVIS	1871	OH CO. MAP	1743
ELM SPRING	1871	MARH'L MAP	1746
ELM SPRINGS	1871	OH CO. MAP	1742
ELM ST - RITCHIE TWP	1871	RITCHIE TWP	1793
ELRICK, GEORGE	1852	DEFENDANT	1600
ELSISURE, - / MRS	1871	WELLSBURG	1778
ELSON, ALEX. M / MAP#507	1852	BRKE MAP	1849
ELSON, J	1871	BRKE MAP	1735
ELSON, JOHN / MAP#442	1852	BRKE MAP	1849
ELSON, JOHN C	1871	BRKE MAP	1735
ELSON, JOHN C / INITIALS J.C.E.	1871	BRKE MAP	1735
ELSON, JOHN C / INITIALS J.C.E.	1871	BRKE MAP	1735
ELSONS RUN	1871	BRKE MAP	1735
ELWOOD GROVE	1871	HAN MAP	1726
EMERY, W	1871	MARH'L MAP	1753
EMICK, H / CONFECTIONARY	1871	WELLSBURG	1777
EMICK, H / TAYLOR SHOP ?(TAILOR?)	1871	WELLSBURG	1777
EMIG, P	1871	WELLSBURG	1778
EMIGRATION THROUGH WHEELING	1916	NAT'L ROAD	1866
EMINENCE / JOHN BUCKEY	1871	BRKE MAP	1735
EMINENCE / JOHN BUCKEY	1871	BRKE MAP	1737
EMMICK, J	1871	RITCHIE TWP	1793
EMMICK, J	1871	RITCHIE TWP	1794
EMRICK, W	1871	MDSVILLE	1807
EMSHEIMER, JACOB JR	1874	DEFENDANT	1615
EMSLEY, J / VINEYARD	1871	MARH'L MAP	1745

XXXIII

'PERSONAL TIME LINE' INDEX TO VOLUME 7 OF THE *OHIO COUNTY INDEX*

ENTRY	YEAR	SUBJECT	PAGE
EMSLEY, J W	1871	MARH'L MAP	1745
EMSLEY, JAMES	1839	DEFENDANT	1628
EMSLEY, JAMES / GRAPE GROWER	1871	BENWO'D - BUS.	1795
EMWRICK, J	1871	OH CO. MAP	1742
EMX, L	1871	MARH'L MAP	1752
ENAMEL WARE INDUSTRY - WHEELING	1916	NAT'L ROAD	1865
ENGEL, G	1871	MARH'L MAP	1753
ENGINE HOUSE / N. OF W. BRIGGS & BRO	1871	BRKE MAP	1736
ENGINE HOUSE - HEMPFIELD RR - WHEELING	1871	WHG CITY	1789
ENGLEHARDT, WILLIAM	1873	DEFENDANT	1627
ENGLISH, J / DOCTOR	1871	OH CO. MAP	1741
ENGLISH, JOHN	1852	HEMPFIELD RR	1822
ENOCK, ENOCKS	1800	DEFENDANT	1579
ENSELL & STEWART	1841	DEFENDANT	1577
ENSELL & STEWART	1841	DEFENDANT	1577
ENSELL, CHARLES	1840	DEFENDANT	1551
ENSELL, CHARLES	1840	DEFENDANT	1628
ENSELL, CHARLES	1840	DEFENDANT	1640
ENSELL, CHARLES	1840	DEFENDANT	1656
ENSELL, CHARLES	1841	DEFENDANT	1551
ENSELL, CHARLES	1841	DEFENDANT	1670
ENSELL, CHARLES	1842	DEFENDANT	1551
ENSOR, JOHN / MAP#437	1852	BRKE MAP	1850
ENSOR, JOHN / MAP#471	1852	BRKE MAP	1850
EOFF, - / MRS	1871	TRIAD. TWP.	1781
EOFF, - / MRS	1871	WHG CITY	1789
EOFF, JOHN	1810	APPENDIX	1873
EOFF, JOHN	1852	HEMPFIELD RR	1822
EOFF, JOHN JR	1821	DEFENDANT	1632
EOFF, JOHN JR	1823	DEFENDANT	1632
EOFF, W C	1877	DEFENDANT	1631
EPISCOPAL CHURCH - D & SECOND ST - MOUNDSVILLE	1871	MDSVILLE	1808
EPISCOPAL CHURCH - LIBERTY ST - WELLSBURG	1871	WELLSBURG	1777
EPISCOPAL CHURCH - MARKET ST	1871	WHG CITY	1788
EPISCOPAL CHURCH - MARKET ST	1871	WHG CITY	1790
EPISCOPAL CHURCH - WHEELING ST - MOUNDSVILLE	1871	MDSVL BUS.	1796
EPISCOPAL CHURCH & CEMETERY - NEAR SCHOOL NO. 5	1871	BRKE MAP	1734
EPISCOPAL CHURCH SOCIETY - MOUND & SECOND ST - MOUNDSVILLE	1871	MDSVILLE	1808
EPPLEY, D	1871	OH CO. MAP	1743
EPPLEY, D	1871	OH CO. MAP	1744
ERKONS RUN / (?ERSKINES?)	1852	BRKE MAP	1841
ERLEYWINE, A	1871	MARH'L MAP	1753
ERLEYWINE, A / INITIALS A.E.	1871	MARH'L MAP	1753
ERNST, H	1871	MARH'L MAP	1761
ERNST, M / BAKERY - WATER ST	1871	MDSVILLE	1810
ERNST, M / INITIALS M.E.	1871	MDSVILLE	1810
ERNST, MICHAEL / BAKERY	1871	MDSVL BUS.	1796
ERSKINE, JOHN / RES	1871	OH CO. MAP	1743
ERSKINE, R C	1871	OH CO. MAP	1743
ERSKINE, WILLIAM / MAP#1	1852	BRKE MAP	1841
ERSKINS RUN - ERKONS RUN / (?ERSKINES?)	1852	BRKE MAP	1841
ERWIN HO. / HOUSE (?HOTEL?)	1871	W.LIBERTY	1780
ERWIN, J / WHOLESALE & RETAIL GROCERY	1871	WELLSBURG	1778
ERWIN, W / ERWIN HOUSE (/HOTEL?)	1871	W.LIBERTY	1780
ERWIN, WILLIAM	1810	APPENDIX	1873
ERY, - / MRS (?OR FRY?)	1871	MARH'L MAP	1757
ERYIN, J	1871	WELLSBURG	1776
ESCHEATOR	1810	MISC	1707
ESCHEATOR	1822	MISC	1707
ESTNOOD, JOSEPH	1805	DEFENDANT	1569
'ET AL' - DEFINED	2000	APPENDIX	1875
EUCIL, -	1852	NOT ON MAP	1836
EUREKA HOUSE - MAIN ST	1871	BETHANY	1773
EVAN, WALTER	1871	MDSVILLE	1808
EVANS RUN / G.G.EVANS RUN	1871	HAN MAP	1730
EVANS, ALFRED	1850	DEFENDANT	1629
EVANS, ARNOLD	1786	DEFENDANT	1647
EVANS, EDMOND I	1829	DEFENDANT	1622
EVANS, G W	1871	MARH'L MAP	1752
EVANS, G W	1871	MARH'L MAP	1760
EVANS, I / S.S.MILL	1871	NEW CUMB'LD	1767
EVANS, I C	1871	HAN MAP	1730
EVANS, J	1871	MARH'L MAP	1760
EVANS, J	1871	MARH'L MAP	1760
EVANS, J C	1871	HAN MAP	1730

ENTRY	YEAR	SUBJECT	PAGE
EVANS, J JR	1871	HAN MAP	1730
EVANS, J M D	1871	NEW CUMB'LD	1766
EVANS, JAMES / DOCTOR	1871	NEW CUMB'LD	1762
EVANS, S	1871	MARH'L MAP	1761
EVANS, T	1871	BENWOOD	1798
EVANS, T	1871	BENWOOD	1798
EVANS, T	1871	BENWOOD	1798
EVANS, THOMAS	1808	DEFENDANT	1572
EVANS, THOMAS	1809	DEFENDANT	1572
EVANS, THOMAS	1809	PLAINTIFF	1667
EVANS, THOMAS	1810	APPENDIX	1873
EVANS, THOMAS	1812	DEFENDANT	1572
EVANS, THOMAS	1812	DEFENDANT	1638
EVANS, THOMAS	1812	DEFENDANT	1642
EVANS, THOMAS	1813	DEFENDANT	1645
EVANS, THOMAS	1814	DEFENDANT	1638
EVANS, THOMAS	1816	DEFENDANT	1624
EVANS, W J	1871	HAN MAP	1731
EVERETT & BLANKENSOP / FOUNDRY	1871	WELLSBURG	1777
EVERETT & BLANKENSOP / FOUNDRY	1871	WELLSBURG	1777
EVERETT & BLANKENSOPS	1871	WLSBRG BUS.	1772
EVERETT & BLANKENSOPS HARDWARE	1871	WELLSBURG	1777
EVERETT & G. BLANKENSOP	1871	BRKE MAP	1736
EVERETT, T	1871	WELLSBURG	1777
EVERGREEN COTTAGE	1871	HAN MAP	1730
EVERGREEN HOME	1871	HAN MAP	1726
EVERGREEN HOME	1871	HAN MAP	1731
EVERGREEN VALE	1871	OH CO. MAP	1743
EVERLAND, E	1871	MARH'L MAP	1756
EWETZEL, L / ROCK	1871	OH CO. MAP	1742
EWING, J	1871	HAN MAP	1731
EWING, J D	1871	MDSVILLE	1807
EWING, J DALLAS / ATTORNEY	1871	MDSVL BUS.	1796
EWING, JAMES	1871	HAN MAP	1732
EWING, JOHN	1812	DEFENDANT	1626
EWING, JOHN	1814	DEFENDANT	1645
EWING, JOHN	1820	DEFENDANT	1646
EWING, WALTER / CLERK OF CIRCUIT COURT	1871	MDSVL BUS.	1796
EXCHANGE HOTEL - WATER ST - WELLSBURG	1871	WELLSBURG	1778
EXEMPT FROM MILITARY DUTY OR ROAD WORK - DEFINED	2000	APPENDIX	1875
EXLEY & BICKERTON	1862	DEFENDANT	1673
EXLY & BIGERTON	1859	DEFENDANT	1567
F.L.T. / UNKNOWN INITIALS - SECOND ST	1871	BENWOOD	1798
F.S. / INITIALS UNKNOWN - LAND S. OF MRS.R ACKLES	1871	BKE/OH MAP	1739
F.S. / INITIALS UNKNOWN - LAND SW OF G.B.MILLER	1871	BKE/OH MAP	1739
FACTORY / W. BRIGGS & BRO	1871	BRKE MAP	1736
FACTORY - OLD FACTORY	1871	HAN MAP	1733
FAIR, C	1871	MARH'L MAP	1756
FAIR, C	1871	MARH'L MAP	1760
FAIR, J	1871	BRKE MAP	1736
FAIRCHILD, ARTEMAS O	1852	DEFENDANT	1653
FAIRGROUNDS - NW OF NEW MANCHESTER	1871	HAN MAP	1731
FAIRMONT	1852	HEMP. RR MAP	1826
FAIRMONT TURNPIKE	1871	RITCHIE TWP	1791
FAIRMONT TURNPIKE	1871	WHG CITY	1792
FAIRMONT TURNPIKE	1871	RITCHIE TWP	1793
FAIRMONT, WV - MAP	1916	NAT'L ROAD	1869
FAIRMOUNT PIKE	1871	OH CO. MAP	1742
FAIRMOUNT ROAD - TOP OF MAP	1871	MARH'L MAP	1745
FAIRVIEW	1871	HAN MAP	1727
FAIRVIEW	1871	HAN MAP	1728
FAIRVIEW	1871	HAN MAP	1731
FAIRVIEW	1871	BKE/OH MAP	1739
FAIRVIEW	1871	OH CO. MAP	1743
FAIRVIEW	1871	OH CO. MAP	1744
FAIRVIEW / UNION TWP	1871	MARH'L MAP	1745
FAIRVIEW / TOWN - FRANKLIN TWP	1871	MARH'L MAP	1758
FAIRVIEW - CLAY TWP	1871	MARH'L MAP	1752
FAIRVIEW P.O.	1871	NEW MANCH.	1769
FAIRVIEW P.O. / NEW MANCHESTER	1871	DISTANCES	1815
FAIRVIEW SCHOOL	1871	OH CO. MAP	1743
FAIRVIEW, WV	1871	FRKLN TWP-BUS.	1797
FAIRVIEW, WV	1871	FRKLN TWP-BUS.	1797
FALLS ON UNNAMED CREEK / WATERFALLS	1871	BKE/OH MAP	1738
FAMILY HISTORY CENTER LIBRARY	2000	APPENDIX	1872
FARGUHAR, -	1807	PLAINTIFF	1624
FARIMONT FARM	1871	MARH'L MAP	1755

'PERSONAL TIME LINE' INDEX TO VOLUME 7 OF THE *OHIO COUNTY INDEX*

ENTRY	YEAR	SUBJECT	PAGE
FARIS, -	1861	DEFENDANT	1641
FARIS, ADAM	1820	DEFENDANT	1578
FARIS, ADAM	1822	DEFENDANT	1578
FARIS, J	1871	OH CO. MAP	1740
FARIS, JOHN	1821	DEFENDANT	1578
FARIS, SAMUEL F	1859	DEFENDANT	1672
FARIS, W	1871	OH CO. MAP	1740
FARLENICH, WILLIAM	1841	DEFENDANT	1640
FARLEY, -	1855	PLAINTIFF	1629
FARLEY, JOHN	1818	PLAINTIFF	1591
FARLEY, JOHN	1880	DEFENDANT	1627
FARLINICH, WILLIAM	1841	DEFENDANT	1656
FARMER, A	1871	BENWOOD	1798
FARMER, R	1871	BENWOOD	1798
FARMER, R	1871	BENWOOD	1798
FARMERS DELIGHT	1871	HAN MAP	1731
FARMERS HOME	1871	BRKE MAP	1734
FARMERS HOME	1871	BRKE MAP	1735
FARMERS HOME	1871	OH CO. MAP	1743
FARMERS HOME - LIBERTY TWP	1871	MARH'L MAP	1757
FARNESWORTH, ISAAC	1840	DEFENDANT	1614
FARNESWORTH, ISAAC	1840	DEFENDANT	1619
FARQUHAR, WILLIAM	1810	APPENDIX	1873
FARQUAR, JOHN	1852	NOT ON MAP	1836
FARQUARS RUN	1852	BRKE MAP	1849
FARRELL, P	1871	MARH'L MAP	1752
FARRELLY, P	1871	MARH'L MAP	1745
FARRELLY, P	1871	MARH'L MAP	1749
FARRIER, J W / & CO	1862	DEFENDANT	1567
FARRIS, W R	1871	OH CO. MAP	1740
FARROW, JOHN	1837	DEFENDANT	1582
FARROW, JOHN	1838	DEFENDANT	1614
FARROW, JOHN	1839	DEFENDANT	1614
FATHER OF WATERS / NAME FOR ST.LOUIS	1916	NAT'L ROAD	1866
FAWCETT, JOHN	1823	DEFENDANT	1612
FAY, J / MRS	1871	OH CO. MAP	1743
FEAY, J	1871	OH CO. MAP	1742
FEAY, J	1871	OH CO. MAP	1742
FEAY, J	1871	OH CO. MAP	1744
FEAY, J	1871	OH CO. MAP	1744
FEAY, JOHN	1817	DEFENDANT	1624
FEAY, JOHN	1820	DEFENDANT	1624
FEAY, JOHN	1821	DEFENDANT	1649
FEAY, JOHN	1822	DEFENDANT	1632
FEAY, JOHN	1834	MISC	1702
FEAY, JOHN	1834	MISC	1702
FEAY, JOHN	1847	DEFENDANT	1589
FEAY, JOHN	1850	DEFENDANT	1590
FELDMAN, W	1871	TRIAD.BORO.	1784
FEMALE INS. / INSTITUTE ? - FIFTH ST	1871	WHG CITY	1788
FENWICK, S	1871	WELLSBURG	1778
FERGUS, HUGH E	1840	PLAINTIFF	1554
FERGUSON, J	1871	MDSVILLE	1809
FERNSWORTH, H	1871	NEW MANCH.	1769
FERREL, J	1871	OH CO. MAP	1740
FERREL, J / STORE	1871	TRIAD.BORO.	1784
FERREL, JOHN	1807	PLAINTIFF	1648
FERREL, R	1871	TRIAD.BORO.	1784
FERRELL, J	1871	OH CO. MAP	1742
FERRELL, J	1871	OH CO. MAP	1744
FERRELL, JOHN	1844	DEFENDANT	1577
FERRELL, JOHN	1853	DEFENDANT	1573
FERRELL, JOHN	1856	DEFENDANT	1552
FERRELL, JOHN	1856	DEFENDANT	1621
FERRELL, JOHN	1857	DEFENDANT	1573
FERRELL, JOSEPH	1821	DEFENDANT	1646
FERRELL, ROBERT	1856	DEFENDANT	1552
FERRERAL, J / WATER ST	1871	WELLSBURG	1777
FERRY	1802	MISC	1710
FERRY - BALTIMORE & OHIO RR - FERRY - AT BENWOOD	1871	BENWOOD	1799
FERRY - BELLAIRE FERRY - OHIO RIVER - AT BENWOOD	1871	BENWOOD	1798
FERRY - CLARKS / SETH - MAP#549	1852	BRKE MAP	1851
FERRY - NEW CUMBERLAND / ON OHIO RIVER	1871	HAN MAP	1730
FERRY - OHIO RIVER - AT MOUNDSVILLE	1871	MDSVILLE	1810
FERRY - OHIO RIVER - AT NEW CUMBERLAND	1871	NEW CUMB'LD	1766
FERRY - OHIO RIVER - EAST LIVERPOOL	1871	HAN MAP	1728
FERRY - OHIO RIVER - S. OF MOUTH OF HOG RUN	1871	MARH'L MAP	1751
FERRY - OHIO RIVER - S.OF WELLSVILLE	1871	HAN MAP	1726
FERRY - OHIO RIVER - SLOANS STATION, OHIO TO W.B.FREEMAN FIRE BRICKWORKS	1871	FRE'MAN'S LDG	1764
FERRY - OHIO RIVER AT HAMILTON TO WELLSVILLE	1871	HAN MAP	1726
FERRY - OHIO RIVER TO EAST LIVERPOOL	1871	HAN MAP	1727
FERRY - TO MARTINS FERRY, OHIO	1871	OH CO. MAP	1741
FERRY - TO STEUBENVILLE	1871	BRKE MAP	1734
FERRY - TO WARRENTON, OHIO	1871	BKE/OH MAP	1738
FERRY - WELLS / NATHANIEL - (FERRY & TAV) - MAP#595	1852	BRKE MAP	1851
FERRY LANDING - OHIO RIVER AT MOUNDSVILLE	1871	MDSVILLE	1808
FERRY RUN	1871	BRKE MAP	1737
FERTILE VALLEY	1871	MARH'L MAP	1745
FERTILE VALLEY, BOGGS RUN	1871	BENWO'D - BUS.	1795
FICHNER, JAMES	1851	DEFENDANT	1603
FICKES, W	1871	NEW CUMB'LD	1768
FINCH, J	1871	MARH'L MAP	1759
FINETY, JAMES	1858	DEFENDANT	1661
FINK, JOHN	1819	MISC	1678
FINK, JOHN	1840	DEFENDANT	1628
FINK, MARTIN L	1855	DEFENDANT	1584
FINK, MARTIN L	1855	DEFENDANT	1603
FINK, T	1871	MARH'L MAP	1745
FINK, T	1871	MARH'L MAP	1748
FINK, T	1871	WHG ISLAND	1788
FINKS, S / MRS	1871	MDSVILLE	1810
FINLEY - CHILDREN	1879	MISC	1676
FINLEY, A	1871	BRKE MAP	1735
FINLEY, A	1871	WELLSBURG	1777
FINLEY, G	1871	OH CO. MAP	1740
FINLEY, J	1871	HAN MAP	1727
FINLEY, J	1871	BETHANY	1773
FINLEY, S	1871	OH CO. MAP	1740
FINLEY, W	1871	OH CO. MAP	1740
FINLEY, W / RES	1871	OH CO. MAP	1740
FINN, RICHARD	1802	DEFENDANT	1666
FINN, RICHARD	1807	DEFENDANT	1666
FINN, T	1871	MDSVILLE	1809
FINN, T	1871	MDSVILLE	1809
FINN, THOMAS	1871	MDSVL BUS.	1796
FINNEY, A / CUT OFF BOTTOM	1871	HAN MAP	1726
FINNEY, A	1871	HAN MAP	1730
FINSEL, J	1871	MARH'L MAP	1746
FIRE & MARINE INSURANCE CO	1880	DEFENDANT	1570
FIRE & MARINE INSURANCE CO	1880	DEFENDANT	1576
FIRE & MARINE INSURANCE CO	1880	DEFENDANT	1584
FIRE BRICK	1871	RIV. RD N.OF N.C.	1763
FIRE BRICK COMPANIES	1871	FRE'MAN'S LDG	1762
FIRE BRICK WORKS	1871	HAN MAP	1731
FIRE BRICK WORKS	1871	HAN MAP	1731
FIRE BRICK WORKS - ANDERSON / THOMAS	1871	FRE'MAN'S LDG	1764
FIRE BRICK WORKS - NW. OF D. TROUP	1871	RIV. RD N.OF N.C.	1770
FIRE BRICK WORKS - PORTERS / J.	1871	FRE'MAN'S LDG	1764
FIRE BRICK WORKS - SW. OF J.MANYPENNY	1871	RIV. RD N.OF N.C.	1770
FIRE BRICK WORKS - W. OF G.W.CUPPY	1871	RIV. RD N.OF N.C.	1770
FIRE BRICK YARD / CAMPBELL & CO.	1871	HAN MAP	1732
FIRE CLAY	1871	HAN MAP	1728
FIRE CLAY	1871	HAN MAP	1728
FIRE CLAY - E OF BROWNS ISLAND	1871	HAN MAP	1732
FIRE CLAY - E OF RIVERSIDE	1871	HAN MAP	1726
FIRE CLAY - J. HAMILTON	1871	HAN MAP	1726
FIRE CLAY - S OF FORTUNE HILL	1871	HAN MAP	1727
FIRE CLAY - S. OF ORCHARDDALE	1871	HAN MAP	1726
FIRE CLAY - SW OF FORTUNE HILL	1871	HAN MAP	1727
FIRE ISLAND / (?OR LIME?) - OHIO RIVER	1871	HAN MAP	1728
FIRECLAY - S. OF BLACKS ISLAND	1871	HAN MAP	1730
FIRECLAY I.M. / ABBREVIATION UNKNOWN	1871	HAN MAP	1730
FIRST NATIONAL BANK - WELLSBURG	1871	WLSBRG BUS.	1772
FISCHER, JANUAR	1857	DEFENDANT	1580
FISCHER, JANUAR	1857	DEFENDANT	1580
FISCHER, JANUAR	1857	DEFENDANT	1588
FISCHER, JANUAR	1857	DEFENDANT	1623
FISCHER, JANUARY	1857	DEFENDANT	1588

'PERSONAL TIME LINE' INDEX TO VOLUME 7 OF THE *OHIO COUNTY INDEX*

ENTRY	YEAR	SUBJECT	PAGE
FISH CREEK	1871	MARH'L MAP	1754
FISH CREEK	1871	MARH'L MAP	1755
FISH CREEK	1871	MARH'L MAP	1756
FISH CREEK	1871	MARH'L MAP	1760
FISH CREEK	1871	MARH'L MAP	1761
FISH CREEK	1871	MARH'L MAP	1761
FISH CREEK - A.G. ARNOLDS SAW MILL ON	1871	FRKLN TWP-BUS.	1797
FISH CREEK - SAW MILL ON / (?RALSTON & CO.?)	1871	MARH'L MAP	1761
FISH CREEK - SLIPPERY FORD ON	1871	MARH'L MAP	1755
FISH CREEK ISLAND	1871	MARH'L MAP	1754
FISH CREEK SUMMIT	1871	MARH'L MAP	1754
FISH RUN / MOUTH AT OHIO RIVER	1871	MARH'L MAP	1751
FISH, I N	1871	MARH'L MAP	1755
FISH, I N / INITIALS I.N.F.	1871	MARH'L MAP	1755
FISH, I N / RES	1871	MARH'L MAP	1755
FISH, J	1871	MARH'L MAP	1757
FISH, P	1871	MARH'L MAP	1760
FISH, S	1871	MARH'L MAP	1751
FISH, S SR	1871	MARH'L MAP	1751
FISH, S SR	1871	MARH'L MAP	1751
FISHER, AUGUST	1875	DEFENDANT	1592
FISHER, C	1871	OH CO. MAP	1742
FISHER, CHARLES	1873	DEFENDANT	1552
FISHER, CHARLES	1879	DEFENDANT	1601
FISHER, G	1871	MARH'L MAP	1746
FISHER, HILLARY / MAP#303	1852	BRKE MAP	1847
FISHER, HILLARY / MAP#304	1852	BRKE MAP	1847
FISHER, J	1871	OH CO. MAP	1743
FISHER, J	1871	OH CO. MAP	1744
FISHER, J	1871	MARH'L MAP	1745
FISHER, J	1871	MARH'L MAP	1746
FISHER, JANUAR	1857	DEFENDANT	1566
FISHER, JOHN	1841	DEFENDANT	1602
FISHER, M	1871	OH CO. MAP	1741
FISHER, M / COAL	1871	OH CO. MAP	1742
FISHER, M / MRS	1871	MARH'L MAP	1751
FISHER, PHILIP	1825	DEFENDANT	1594
FISHER, PHILIP	1837	DEFENDANT	1563
FISHER, PHILIP	1837	DEFENDANT	1622
FISHER, ROBERT	1840	DEFENDANT	1614
FISHER, ROBERT	1840	DEFENDANT	1619
FISHER, W	1871	MARH'L MAP	1745
FISHER, W	1871	MARH'L MAP	1745
FITCH, DYER	1820	DEFENDANT	1579
FITCHGIBENS, DAVID	1787	DEFENDANT	1610
FITTON, JOHN	1799	DEFENDANT	1567
FITZGERALD, - / MRS	1871	CAMERON	1803
FITZGERALD, J A	1871	MARH'L MAP	1756
FITZGERALD, J A	1871	MARH'L MAP	1760
FITZGERALD, J B	1871	CAMERON	1803
FITZGERALD, J H	1871	MARH'L MAP	1756
FITZGERALD, JAMES B / 'CAMERON HOUSE'	1871	CAMER'N - BUS.	1795
FITZHUGH, EDWARD H	1840	PLAINTIFF	1661
FITZPATRICK, DENNIS	1848	DEFENDANT	1657
FITZPATRICK, DENNIS	1852	DEFENDANT	1657
FITZPATRICK, JOHN	1877	DEFENDANT	1586
FITZSIMMONS, L	1871	MARH'L MAP	1750
FITZSIMMONS, W	1871	MARH'L MAP	1750
FLACK, JOHN	1818	DEFENDANT	1659
FLACK, JOHN	1819	DEFENDANT	1660
FLACK, JOHN	1822	DEFENDANT	1660
FLAG HO / (?HOUSE?) - ON RR	1871	MARH'L MAP	1752
FLAG HO. / (?FLAG HOUSE ON RR LINE - SIGNAL HOUSE?)	1871	MARH'L MAP	1748
FLAG HO. STONE QUARRY / HOUSE ? (?FLAGSTONE FOR HOMES?)	1871	MARH'L MAP	1752
FLAG HOUSE / ON B&O - SE. OF MOUNDSVILLE	1871	MARH'L MAP	1748
FLAG QUARRY	1871	HAN MAP	1726
FLAG QUARRY	1871	OH CO. MAP	1742
FLAG QUARRY	1871	OH CO. MAP	1742
FLAG QUARRY - CALDWELLS RUN	1871	OH CO. MAP	1742
FLAG QUARRY #2 - N. OF PLEASANT VIEW	1871	HAN MAP	1726
FLAGG QUARRY	1871	WHG CITY	1787
FLAGG QUARRY - N. OF BROWNLEE SCHOOL NO. 1	1871	OH CO. MAP	1743
FLANAGAN, JOHN	1855	PLAINTIFF	1602
FLANEGIN, W	1871	HAN MAP	1731
FLANEGIN, W	1871	NEW MANCH.	1769
FLANEGIN, W / BLACKSMITH SHOP	1871	NEW MANCH.	1769
FLANNAGAN, J	1871	MARH'L MAP	1749
FLANNAGAN, J / INITIALS J.F.	1871	MARH'L MAP	1749
FLANNAGAN, JAMES	1840	MISC	1694
FLANNIAGAN, J	1871	MARH'L MAP	1745
FLANNIAGAN, J / INITIALS J.F.	1871	MARH'L MAP	1745
FLANNIGEN, -	1840	PLAINTIFF	1620
FLAX, D / (?NAME OR FLAX FOR MILL- WHORRY MILL?)	1871	MARH'L MAP	1746
FLEMING, A	1871	OH CO. MAP	1742
FLEMING, JOSEPH / MAP#269	1852	BRKE MAP	1842
FLEMING, M / & M J	1871	WELLSBURG	1777
FLEMING, M J / & M	1871	WELLSBURG	1777
FLEMING, W H	1874	DEFENDANT	1574
FLEMING, WILLIAM H	1873	DEFENDANT	1574
FLEMINGS RUN	1852	BRKE MAP	1852
FLEMINGS, G	1871	MARH'L MAP	1745
FLEMMING, - / MRS	1871	WELLSBURG	1777
FLEMMING, SAMUEL	1823	MISC	1677
FLEMMING, T	1871	MDSVILLE	1808
FLETCHER, J / MRS	1871	MARH'L MAP	1753
FLETCHER, J	1871	W. LIBERTY	1780
FLETCHER, W	1871	OH CO. MAP	1741
FLETCHER, W / INITIALS W.F.	1871	OH CO. MAP	1741
FLINT GLASS WORKS	1871	SOUTH WHG	1792
FLOOD, FRANCIS	1859	DEFENDANT	1672
FLOOD, JOHN	1862	DEFENDANT	1573
FLORACK, DAVID	1818	DEFENDANT	1577
FLORAL HOME	1871	MARH'L MAP	1745
FLORENCE / WELLSVILLE AND FLORENCE ROAD	1871	HAN MAP	1731
FLOUR - WHEELING VALLEY FLOURING MILLS	1871	MARH'L MAP	1746
FLOUR MILL - MOUND CITY FLOUR MILL	1871	MDSVL BUS.	1796
FLOUR MILL - RUTHS / J.&W. RUTHS FLOURING & SAW MILL - NEW GERMANTOWN	1871	SAND HILL-BUS.	1797
FLOUR MILL - WEBSTER, BROWN & CO / MOUNDSVILLE	1871	MDSVL BUS.	1796
FLOUR MILL - WEBSTER, BROWN & CO / MOUNDSVILLE	1871	MDSVILLE	1808
FLOUR MILL - WESBTER, BROWN & CO - PURDY	1871	MDSVILLE	1810
FLOWER, A	1871	HAN MAP	1731
FLOWER, I	1871	HAN MAP	1731
FLOWERS, H	1871	NEW CUMB'LD	1767
FLOWERS, J W	1871	NEW CUMB'LD	1768
FLUCCUS, G	1871	TRIAD. TWP.	1781
FLUHARTY, JAMES	1813	DEFENDANT	1599
FLYNN, M	1871	MARH'L MAP	1757
FO__RS / FOSTERS RUN / (? INCOMPLETE FO__RS?)	1852	BRKE MAP	1842
FOGLE, FREDERICK	1824	DEFENDANT	1649
FOGLE, FREDERICK	1824	DEFENDANT	1649
FOGLE, FREDERICK	1831	DEFENDANT	1639
FOGLE, FREDERICK	1831	DEFENDANT	1650
FOLEY, HEZEKIAH	1856	DEFENDANT	1573
FOLEY, HEZEKIAH	1856	DEFENDANT	1653
FOLMAR, F	1871	WHG CITY	1787
FOLMER, S	1871	OH CO. MAP	1742
FOLWER, J / INITIALS J.F. - FOWLERS P.O.	1871	BRKE MAP	1735
FOOSE, ADAM	1861	DEFENDANT	1552
FOOSE, JOHN P	1873	DEFENDANT	1627
FOOT, STEPHEN	1822	MISC	1704
FORBES & CARMICHAEL	1871	BUFF. TWP. BUS.	1772
FORBES & GARDNER / NAME WRITTEN IN OHIO RIVER	1871	BRKE MAP	1736
FORBES, GEORGE	1842	DEFENDANT	1663
FORBES, GEORGE	1851	PLAINTIFF	1663
FORBES, GEORGE	1852	DEFENDANT	1663
FORBES, GEORGE	1859	DEFENDANT	1552
FORBES, J	1871	WELLSBURG	1778
FORBES, T	1871	WELLSBURG	1778
FORD - SLIPPERY FORD ON FISH CREEK	1871	MARH'L MAP	1755
FORD, -	1879	DEFENDANT	1584
FORD, H T / & CO.	1871	BENWOOD	1798
FORD, H T / & CO.	1871	BENWOOD	1799
FORD, J / OHIO RIVER	1871	MARH'L MAP	1745
FORD, J B / & CO.	1871	MARH'L MAP	1745
FORD, J B	1874	DEFENDANT	1567
FORD, JOSEPH B	1855	DEFENDANT	1629
FORD, MOSES	1833	DEFENDANT	1574
FORD, MOSES	1833	DEFENDANT	1591
FORD, MOSES	1833	DEFENDANT	1613
FORD, MOSES	1833	DEFENDANT	1622
FORD, MOSES	1833	DEFENDANT	1650

'PERSONAL TIME LINE' INDEX TO VOLUME 7 OF THE *OHIO COUNTY INDEX*

ENTRY	YEAR	SUBJECT	PAGE
FORD, MOSES	1833	DEFENDANT	1650
FORD, MOSES	1833	DEFENDANT	1662
FORD, MOSES	1834	DEFENDANT	1622
FORD, MOSES	1834	DEFENDANT	1622
FORD, MOSES	1834	DEFENDANT	1650
FORD, MOSES	1848	DEFENDANT	1641
FORD, MOSES	1850	DEFENDANT	1568
FORD, MOSES	1850	DEFENDANT	1623
FORD, MOSES	1859	DEFENDANT	1575
FORD, PATRICK	1808	DEFENDANT	1620
FORD, ROBERT F	1833	DEFENDANT	1559
FORD, ROBERT T	1833	DEFENDANT	1561
FORD, SAMPLE	1874	MISC	1706
FORDICE, J	1871	OH CO. MAP	1743
FORDYCE, J N	1861	DEFENDANT	1616
FOREMAN & DUNLAP	1861	DEFENDANT	1554
FOREMAN, - / CAP. - CAPTAIN - MONUMNET	1871	MARH'L MAP	1745
FOREMAN, JANE / MRS	1871	W.LIBERTY	1780
FOREMAN, JOSEPH	1833	DEFENDANT	1585
FOREMAN, JOSEPH	1834	DEFENDANT	1585
FOREMAN, R	1871	NEW CUMB'LD	1766
FOREMAN, REUBEN	1810	APPENDIX	1873
FOREMAN, REUBEN	1816	MISC	1701
FOREMAN, RUBEN	1859	DEFENDANT	1664
FOREMAN, STEPHEN	1840	DEFENDANT	1577
FOREMAN, STEPHEN	1840	DEFENDANT	1617
FOREMAN, STEPHEN	1840	DEFENDANT	1652
FOREST HOME	1871	OH CO. MAP	1742
FORK RIDGE ARM	1871	MARH'L MAP	1752
FORK RIDGE ROAD	1871	MARH'L MAP	1752
FORK RIDGE ROAD	1871	MARH'L MAP	1752
FORK RIDGE ROAD	1871	MARH'L MAP	1753
FORLEES, -	1843	DEFENDANT	1565
FORMER, M	1871	MARH'L MAP	1745
FORNEY, DANIEL S	1862	DEFENDANT	1573
FORNEY, J	1871	BRKE MAP	1737
FORNEY, J	1871	BRKE MAP	1737
FORNEY, J	1871	BKE/OH MAP	1739
FORNEY, J	1871	BKE/OH MAP	1739
FORNEY, J	1871	BKE/OH MAP	1739
FORSHA, - / & BROTHERS - SAW MILL ?	1871	HAN MAP	1731
FORSHA, - / SAW MILL - FORSHA & BROTHERS	1871	HAN MAP	1731
FORSHA, - / & BROTHERS - SAW MILL ?	1871	HAN MAP	1732
FORSHA, - / SAW MILL - FORSHA & BROTHERS	1871	HAN MAP	1732
FORSYTH, GIBSON	1809	DEFENDANT	1645
FORSYTH, GIDEON	1805	DEFENDANT	1659
FORSYTH, GIDEON	1806	DEFENDANT	1556
FORSYTH, GIDEON C	1808	DEFENDANT	1610
FORSYTH, GIDEON C	1809	DEFENDANT	1604
FORSYTH, GIDEON C	1813	DEFENDANT	1611
FORSYTH, GIDION	1811	DEFENDANT	1610
FORSYTH, JAMES H	1836	DEFENDANT	1614
FORSYTH, JAMES H	1837	DEFENDANT	1589
FORSYTH, JAMES H	1839	DEFENDANT	1646
FORSYTH, JOSEPH	1859	DEFENDANT	1672
FORSYTH, WILLIAM	1837	DEFENDANT	1618
FORSYTH, WILLIAM	1854	DEFENDANT	1596
FORSYTHE, GIDEON	1811	DEFENDANT	1610
FORSYTHE, GIDEON C	1807	DEFENDANT	1556
FORT - BAKERS FORT	1871	HAN MAP	1726
FORT - WELLS, RICHARD / FORT BUILT BY R.W. FOR PROTECTION FROM INDIANS (?BAMILY MT.?) OR (?FAMILY VLT - VALUT?)	1871	BRKE MAP	1734
FORT FINCASTLE / EARLY NAME FOR FORT HENRY	1916	NAT'L ROAD	1866
FORT HENRY	1916	NAT'L ROAD	1865
FORT HENRY	1916	NAT'L ROAD	1868
FORT HENRY - HISTORY OF BATTLE	1916	NAT'L ROAD	1867
FORT HENRY - NAMED FOR PATRICK HENRY	1916	NAT'L ROAD	1867
FORT HENRY - PREVIOUSLY CALLED FORT FINCASTLE	1916	NAT'L ROAD	1866
FORT HENRY - SITE ON MAP	1916	NAT'L ROAD	1868
FORT NECESSITY - MAP	1916	NAT'L ROAD	1869
FORT, BENJAMIN	1802	DEFENDANT	1666
FORTUNE HILL	1871	HAN MAP	1727
FORTUNE HILL	1871	HAN MAP	1728
FOSBINDER, JOHN	1816	DEFENDANT	1561
FOSERS / FOSTERS RUN / (? INCOMPLETE F0__RS?)	1852	BRKE MAP	1842

ENTRY	YEAR	SUBJECT	PAGE
FOSTER, -	1858	PLAINTIFF	1621
FOSTER, -	1858	PLAINTIFF	1621
FOSTER, J	1871	MARH'L MAP	1753
FOSTER, M	1871	MARH'L MAP	1753
FOSTER, S	1871	MARH'L MAP	1750
FOSTER, WILLIAM M	1849	DEFENDANT	1641
FOSTERS RUN / (? INCOMPLETE F0__RS?)	1852	BRKE MAP	1842
FOUNDRY - BENWOOD IRON WORKS	1871	BENWOOD	1799
FOUNDRY - TAYLOR & WATER STS.	1871	NEW CUMB'LD	1768
FOUNDRY - WHEELING ISLAND	1871	WHG ISLAND	1788
FOUNDS, W	1871	MARH'L MAP	1752
FOUNTAIN, J R	1871	MDSVILLE	1809
FOUR MILE HOUSE / WILLIAM STAMM	1871	OH CO. MAP	1742
FOUR MILE RUN	1871	MARH'L MAP	1757
FOUST, F	1871	MARH'L MAP	1759
FOUST, J	1871	MARH'L MAP	1759
FOUTS, DAVID	1798	DEFENDANT	1647
FOWLER, ALBERT C	1876	DEFENDANT	1604
FOWLER, C H	1871	HAN MAP	1727
FOWLER, J	1871	BRKE MAP	1735
FOWLER, J	1871	BRKE MAP	1735
FOWLER, J	1871	BRKE MAP	1735
FOWLER, J / NE EDGE OF MAP	1871	BRKE MAP	1735
FOWLER, J / SAW MILL & GRIST MILL - ON CROSS CREEK	1871	BRKE MAP	1735
FOWLER, J	1871	BRKE MAP	1737
FOWLER, J	1871	BRKE MAP	1737
FOWLER, J	1871	BRKE MAP	1737
FOWLER, J / INITIALS J.F.	1871	BRKE MAP	1737
FOWLER, J	1871	FOWLERS P.O.	1775
FOWLER, J	1871	FOWLERS P.O.	1775
FOWLER, J / BLACKSMITH & WAGON SHOP & S.SH.	1871	FOWLERS P.O.	1775
FOWLER, J / INITIALS J.F.	1871	FOWLERS P.O.	1775
FOWLER, J / INITIALS J.F.	1871	FOWLERS P.O.	1775
FOWLER, J F	1871	BRKE MAP	1735
FOWLER, J S	1871	CAMERON	1804
FOWLER, JOHN / (SMITHSHOP) - MAP#374	1852	BRKE MAP	1847
FOWLER, JOHN / (SMITHSHOP) - MAP#375	1852	BRKE MAP	1847
FOWLER, JOHN / (TAVERN) - MAP#376	1852	BRKE MAP	1847
FOWLER, JOHN / (TAVERN) - MAP#377	1852	BRKE MAP	1847
FOWLER, JOHN / (TAVERN) - MAP#425	1852	BRKE MAP	1847
FOWLER, JOHN / MAP#355	1852	BRKE MAP	1847
FOWLER, JOHN / MAP#356	1852	BRKE MAP	1847
FOWLER, JOHN / MAP#371	1852	BRKE MAP	1847
FOWLER, JOHN / MAP#372	1852	BRKE MAP	1847
FOWLER, JOHN / MAP#373	1852	BRKE MAP	1847
FOWLER, JOHN / (MILL) - MAP#428	1852	BRKE MAP	1850
FOWLER, JOHN / (MILL)- MAP#429	1852	BRKE MAP	1850
FOWLER, JOSEPH	1856	DEFENDANT	1582
FOWLER, L	1871	MARH'L MAP	1761
FOWLER, L / INITIALS L.F.	1871	MARH'L MAP	1761
FOWLER, R	1871	HAN MAP	1727
FOWLER, W	1871	HAN MAP	1727
FOWLER, W / STORE & RES (OC.)	1871	FOWLERS P.O.	1775
FOWLER, WILLIAM / HEIRS - MAP#368	1852	BRKE MAP	1847
FOWLER, WILLIAM M / OC	1871	BRKE MAP	1735
FOWLER, WILLIAM M	1871	CROSS CRK.BUS.	1772
FOWLER, ZADOC	1871	BRKE MAP	1735
FOWLER, ZADUE / MAP#418	1852	BRKE MAP	1847
FOWLERS / BROOKE CO	1871	DISTANCES	1815
FOWLERS P.O.	1871	BRKE MAP	1735
FOWLERS P.O.	1871	BRKE MAP	1737
FOWLERS P.O.	1871	CROSS CRK.BUS.	1772
FOWLERS P.O. - DETAIL MAP	1871	FOWLERS P.O.	1775
FOX, J	1871	MARH'L MAP	1750
FOX, J	1871	MARH'L MAP	1754
FOX, T	1871	MARH'L MAP	1757
FOX, T	1871	MARH'L MAP	1757
FOX, T	1871	MARH'L MAP	1761
FOX, T	1871	MARH'L MAP	1761
FOX, T / INITIALS T.F.	1871	MARH'L MAP	1761
FRAIL, JOHN	1841	DEFENDANT	1663
FRAIL, JOHN	1841	DEFENDANT	1663
FRANCES, J K	1871	MARH'L MAP	1750
FRANCES, S	1871	MARH'L MAP	1750
FRANCIS, A	1871	MARH'L MAP	1749
FRANCIS, E B	1871	MARH'L MAP	1749
FRANCIS, E B / INITIALS E.B.F	1871	MARH'L MAP	1749
FRANCIS, J T	1871	MARH'L MAP	1753
FRANCIS, S	1871	MARH'L MAP	1750
FRANCIS, W	1871	MARH'L MAP	1751

'PERSONAL TIME LINE' INDEX TO VOLUME 7 OF THE *OHIO COUNTY INDEX*

ENTRY	YEAR	SUBJECT	PAGE
FRANCY, JOHN	1871	NEW CUMB'LD	1767
FRANK, C	1871	OH CO. MAP	1742
FRANK, C	1871	RITCHIE TWP	1791
FRANK, C	1871	RITCHIE TWP	1793
FRANK, CHRISTIAN	1877	DEFENDANT	1654
FRANK, H	1871	BRKE MAP	1736
FRANK, H	1871	WELLSBURG	1777
FRANK, HIGGINS / MAP#333	1852	BRKE MAP	1846
FRANK, HIGGINS / MAP#334	1852	BRKE MAP	1846
FRANK, J D	1871	HAN MAP	1731
FRANK, J D	1871	NEW MANCH.	1763
FRANK, W / INITIALS W.F.	1871	WELLSBURG	1777
FRANKLILN, GEORGE	1871	MARH'L MAP	1760
FRANKLIN CEMETERY	1871	BRKE MAP	1737
FRANKLIN INSURANCE CO	1879	DEFENDANT	1570
FRANKLIN INSURANCE CO	1880	DEFENDANT	1576
FRANKLIN INSURANCE CO	1880	DEFENDANT	1584
FRANKLIN KNOLL	1871	MARH'L MAP	1755
FRANKLIN LANDING - WOODLAND P.O.	1871	MARH'L MAP	1754
FRANKLIN SCHOOL NO. 1	1871	HAN MAP	1727
FRANKLIN SUMMIT	1871	MARH'L MAP	1758
FRANKLIN TOWNSHIP - E.PART - MARSHALL CO	1871	MARH'L MAP	1755
FRANKLIN TOWNSHIP - MARSHALL CO	1871	MARH'L MAP	1754
FRANKLIN TOWNSHIP - MARSHALL CO	1871	POPULATION	1816
FRANKLIN TOWNSHIP - MARSHALL CO - BUSINESS NOTICES	1871	MARH'L BUS.	1797
FRANKLIN TOWNSHIP - W. PART - MARSHALL CO	1871	MARH'L MAP	1758
FRANKLIN TWP - SE. PART - MARSHALL CO	1871	MARH'L MAP	1759
FRANKLIN, - / CEMETERY	1871	BRKE MAP	1737
FRANKLIN, D	1871	MARH'L MAP	1761
FRANKS RUN	1852	BRKE MAP	1844
FRASHER, JOHN	1848	DEFENDANT	1670
FRASUN, -	1830	PLAINTIFF	1622
FRAZIER, D	1871	OH CO. MAP	1743
FRAZIER, JOHN	1837	MISC	1694
FRAZIER, R	1871	OH CO. MAP	1742
FRAZIER, R	1871	OH CO. MAP	1742
FRAZIER, R	1871	OH CO.BUS.	1779
FRAZIER, R / ? LISTED AS FRAZLER, R - RES -	1871	RITCHIE TWP	1792
FRAZIER, R / ? LISTED AS FRAZLER, R - RES -INITIALS R.F.	1871	RITCHIE TWP	1792
FRAZIER, R / ? LISTED AS FRAZLER, R - RES -INITIALS R.F.	1871	RITCHIE TWP	1794
FRAZIER, WILLIAM T	1874	DEFENDANT	1603
FRAZLER, R / RES (?FRAZIER?)	1871	RITCHIE TWP	1792
FRAZLER, R / RES (?FRAZIER?) - INITIALS R.F.	1871	RITCHIE TWP	1792
FRAZLER, R / RES (?FRAZIER?) - INITIALS R.F.	1871	RITCHIE TWP	1794
FRECKMAN, CHARLES	1857	DEFENDANT	1598
FREEBOLT	1871	MARH'L MAP	1745
FREEDOM OF BLACK MAN	1825	MISC	1677
FREELAND, S	1871	MARH'L MAP	1751
FREELAND, S / INITIALS S.F.	1871	MARH'L MAP	1751
FREEMAN, - / ?FIRST NAME ILLEGIBLE	1871	HAN MAP	1731
FREEMAN, E	1871	NEW CUMB'LD	1768
FREEMAN, FRANCIS	1856	DEFENDANT	1565
FREEMAN, J L / ABBREV. J.L.F	1871	HAN MAP	1730
FREEMAN, J L	1871	HAN MAP	1731
FREEMAN, J L	1871	HAN MAP	1731
FREEMAN, J L	1871	HAN MAP	1731
FREEMAN, J L / & CO	1871	HAN MAP	1731
FREEMAN, J L / INITIALS J.L.F.	1871	HAN MAP	1731
FREEMAN, J L / INITLAS J.L.F.	1871	HAN MAP	1731
FREEMAN, J L / & CO - INITIALS J.L.F.& CO.	1871	HAN MAP	1731
FREEMAN, J L	1871	RIV. RD S.OF N.C.	1763
FREEMAN, J L / & CO.	1871	FRE'MAN'S LDG	1764
FREEMAN, J L / & CO. - INITIALS J.L.F.	1871	FRE'MAN'S LDG	1764
FREEMAN, J L / INITIALS J.L.F.	1871	RIV. RD S.OF N.C.	1771
FREEMAN, S	1871	FRE'MAN'S LDG	1764
FREEMAN, W B / INITIALS W.B.F	1871	HAN MAP	1731
FREEMAN, W B / - "FREEMANS LANDING"	1871	FRE'MAN'S LDG	1762
FREEMAN, W B / RES- SLOANS STATION, OHIO	1871	FRE'MAN'S LDG	1762
FREEMAN, W B / FIREBRICK WORKS	1871	FRE'MAN'S LDG	1764
FREEMAN, W B / INITIALS W.B.F	1871	FRE'MAN'S LDG	1764
FREEMAN, W B / INITIALS W.B.F.	1871	FRE'MAN'S LDG	1764
FREEMAN, W B / INITIALS W.B.F.	1871	FRE'MAN'S LDG	1764
FREEMAN, W B / RES. - SLOANS STATION, OHIO	1871	FRE'MAN'S LDG	1764
FREEMANS LANDING	1871	DISTANCES	1815
FREEMANS LANDING - BUSINESS NOTICES	1871	FRE'MAN'S LDG	1762
FREEMANS LANDING - BUTLER TWP - HANCOCK CO	1871	FRE'MAN'S LDG	1765
FREEMANS LANDING - HANCOCK CO - DETAIL MAP	1871	FRE'MAN'S LDG	1764
FREEMANS LANDING - OWNED BY W.B.FREEMAN	1871	FRE'MAN'S LDG	1762
FREEMANS LANDING P.O.	1871	HAN MAP	1731
FREEMANS SUN	1871	HAN MAP	1731
FREESE, ISAAC	1873	DEFENDANT	1566
FREIGHT DEPOT - BELLTON	1871	MARH'L MAP	1761
FREIGHT TONS OF TRAFFIC	1852	HEMPFIELD RR	1819
FREIGHT WAGON STOPS	1916	NAT'L ROAD	1861
FREISMUTH, MICHAEL	1879	MISC	1694
FRENCH RUN	1871	MARH'L MAP	1752
FRENCH, - / MRS	1871	OH CO. MAP	1742
FRENCH, - / MRS - HOTEL - ELM GROVE	1871	ELM GROVE	1782
FRENCH, JOHN	1837	DEFENDANT	1662
FRESHWATER, D	1871	HAN MAP	1732
FRESHWATER, D	1871	BRKE MAP	1734
FRESHWATER, D / INITIALS D.F.	1871	BRKE MAP	1734
FRESHWATER, E A	1871	HAN MAP	1731
FRESHWATER, E A	1871	HAN MAP	1732
FRESHWATER, GEORGE / INITIALS G.F.	1871	BRKE MAP	1735
FRESHWATER, GEORGE / RES	1871	BRKE MAP	1735
FRESHWATER, GEORGE	1871	BRKE MAP	1736
FRESHWATER, GEORGE / RES	1871	BRKE MAP	1736
FRESHWATER, R	1871	HAN MAP	1732
FRESHWATER, R / INITIALS R.F.	1871	HAN MAP	1732
FRESHWATER, R / MT. VERNON	1871	HAN MAP	1732
FRESHWATER, R	1871	BRKE MAP	1734
FRESHWATER, R	1871	BRKE MAP	1734
FRESHWATER, REUBEN / MAP#581	1852	BRKE MAP	1852
FRESHWATER, REUBEN JR / MAP#634	1852	BRKE MAP	1852
FRESHWATER, W	1871	BRKE MAP	1734
FRESHWATER, WILLIAM / MAP#582	1852	BRKE MAP	1852
FRIEND & SON	1876	DEFENDANT	1643
FRISSELL, JACOB	1785	DEFENDANT	1556
FRITKE, ERNESTINE	1872	MISC	1695
FRITSCH, GEORGE	1877	DEFENDANT	1575
FRITZ, C	1871	W.LIBERTY	1780
FRITZ, G	1871	W.LIBERTY	1780
FRITZ, L	1871	MARH'L MAP	1745
FRONEAPPLE, A	1871	MARH'L MAP	1759
FROST, - / DRUG STORE	1871	WELLSBURG	1777
FRUIT HILL	1871	MARH'L MAP	1753
FRUIT HOME	1871	MARH'L MAP	1750
FRUMP, WILLIAM B / & CO	1838	PLAINTIFF	1558
FRUSH, BARBARY	1783	DEFENDANT	1610
FRUSH, GASPOE	1783	DEFENDANT	1610
FRY, - / MRS	1871	MARH'L MAP	1753
FRY, - / MRS - (?OR ERY?)	1871	MARH'L MAP	1757
FRY, C	1871	MARH'L MAP	1753
FRY, M / MRS	1871	MARH'L MAP	1757
FRY, M / MRS	1871	CAMERON	1804
FRY, W	1871	CAMERON	1802
FRYER, GEORGE	1809	DEFENDANT	1648
FUCCUS, WALTER G / GLUE FACTORY	1871	OH CO. MAP	1742
FULERTON, W	1871	CAMERON	1802
FULLER, -	1841	PLAINTIFF	1626
FULLERTON, WILLIAM	1812	MISC	1689
FULLMER, JOHN	1838	DEFENDANT	1662
FULTON	1871	OH CO. MAP	1742
FULTON - BERRY ST / ?	1871	WHG CITY	1789
FULTON - BRIDGE ST	1871	WHG CITY	1787
FULTON - CENTRE ST	1871	WHG CITY	1787
FULTON - CONGRESS DR	1871	WHG CITY	1787
FULTON - FERRY ST / ?	1871	WHG CITY	1789
FULTON - MAP	1916	NAT'L ROAD	1863
FULTON - MERRY ST	1871	WHG CITY	1787
FULTON - MERRY ST / ?	1871	WHG CITY	1789
FULTON - OHIO CO	1871	WHG CITY	1786
FULTON - OHIO CO	1871	WHG CITY	1787
FULTON - SCHOOL - NATIONAL ROAD	1871	WHG CITY	1787
FULTON - SECTION OF TOWN - E. OF WHEELING ON NATIONAL ROAD	1871	WHG CITY	1787
FULTON - TANNERY	1871	WHG CITY	1787
FULTON, ANDREW	1833	MISC	1676
FULTON, JAMES	1797	DEFENDANT	1606

'PERSONAL TIME LINE' INDEX TO VOLUME 7 OF THE *OHIO COUNTY INDEX*

ENTRY	YEAR	SUBJECT	PAGE	ENTRY	YEAR	SUBJECT	PAGE
FULTON, JAMES	1798	DEFENDANT	1606	GARDNER, J C	1871	BRKE MAP	1735
FULTON, JAMES	1801	DEFENDANT	1606	GARDNER, L	1871	HAN MAP	1731
FULTON, JAMES	1801	DEFENDANT	1666	GARDNER, S	1871	HAN MAP	1732
FULTON, SAMUEL	1784	DEFENDANT	1647	GARDNER, S	1871	W.LIBERTY	1780
FULTON, SAMUEL	1796	DEFENDANT	1589	GARDNER, W	1871	MARH'L MAP	1747
FURMER, G	1871	BETHANY	1773	GARDNERS RUN	1871	HAN MAP	1727
FURNACE - OLD BROOK FURNACE / J. ARCHER	1871	HAN MAP	1732	GARDNERS RUN - BRANCH OF	1871	HAN MAP	1727
G, J / INITIALS	1871	HAN MAP	1727	GARFTON, WV - MAP	1916	NAT'L ROAD	1869
G, M / UNKNOWN INITIALS - W. OF THE HOMESTEAD (?GARVIN?)	1871	OH CO. MAP	1742	GARLOW, - / MRS	1871	MDSVILLE	1808
				GARRET STATION - B&O RR	1871	MARH'L MAP	1761
G, W / UNKNOWN INITIALS - BETHANY	1871	BETHANY	1773	GARRET STATION - B&O RR	1871	MARH'L MAP	1757
G, W S / UNKNOWN INITIALS	1871	RITCHIE TWP	1791	GARRET, SAMUEL / MAP#71	1852	BRKE MAP	1839
G. MILL / S. OF CHAMBERS FARM	1871	HAN MAP	1726	GARRETT, J G	1871	MARH'L MAP	1748
G.&S.MILL / GRIST & SAW MILL - NEAR G.ROCKY	1871	OH CO. MAP	1743	GARRISON, -	1871	TRIAD.BORO.	1784
				GARRISON, FRANCES	1875	DEFENDANT	1597
G.G.EVANS RUN	1871	HAN MAP	1730	GARRISON, I	1871	W.LIBERTY	1780
G.H.T / UNKNOWN INITIALS	1871	OH CO. MAP	1742	GARRISON, J	1871	BKE/OH MAP	1739
G.H.T / UNKNOWN INITIALS - ELM GROVE	1871	OH CO. MAP	1744	GARRISON, R / MRS	1871	TRIAD.BORO.	1784
				GARRISON, T	1871	MARH'L MAP	1749
				GARRISON, W	1871	OH CO. MAP	1743
G.M. / NE. OF WOODLAND P.O. - INITIALS UNKNOWN - PERSON OR GRIST MILL ?	1871	MARH'L MAP	1754	GARRISON, W	1871	OH CO. MAP	1744
				GARRISON, W	1871	RONEY PT.	1783
				GARRISONS, FRANCES	1876	DEFENDANT	1597
G.M. / NE OF WOODLAND P.O. (?GRIST MILL?)	1871	MARH'L MAP	1754	GARTNER, PETER	1851	DEFENDANT	1672
				GARVIN, D B / THE HOMESTEAD	1871	OH CO. MAP	1742
G.M. / (?GENERAL MERCHANDISE?) - NEAR MAGGTOTY RUN	1871	MARH'L MAP	1756	GARVIN, J S / QUIET HOME	1871	OH CO. MAP	1742
				GARVIN, J S / QUIET HOME	1871	MARH'L MAP	1746
G.M. / (?GENERAL MERCHANDISE?) - NEAR SCHOOL NO.8	1871	MARH'L MAP	1756	GARVIN, M / UNKNOWN INITIALS - W. OF THE HOMESTEAD (?GARVIN?)	1871	OH CO. MAP	1742
G.M. / INITIALS FOR 'GENERAL MERCHANDISE' STORE ?	1871	MARH'L MAP	1756	GARWOOD, ELIZABETH	1842	DEFENDANT	1663
				GARY, S R	1871	CAMERON	1804
G.M. - NEAR J.McCARDLE / (?GENERAL MERCHANDISE?)	1871	MARH'L MAP	1760	GARY, S R	1871	CAMERON	1804
				GASAWAY, BENJAMIN	1819	DEFENDANT	1611
G.M. - S. OF LYNNCAMP P.O. / (?GENERAL MERCHANDISE?)	1871	MARH'L MAP	1759	GASHEL, E	1871	OH CO. MAP	1743
				GASHEL, E	1871	OH CO. MAP	1744
G.V. / ?	1871	HAN MAP	1731	GASKIN, WILLIAM	1804	MISC	1704
G.Y. / (? PRESBYTERIAN CHURCH ?)	1871	HAN MAP	1731	GASMIER, FREDERICK A	1865	MISC	1698
GABLE, ENGLE	1810	PLAINTIFF	1642	GASMIER, JOHN	1829	DEFENDANT	1565
GABLE, JOHN	1858	DEFENDANT	1630	GASMIRE, AUGUSTUS	1868	MISC	1698
GALE, PETER W	1829	DEFENDANT	1581	GASMIRE, AUGUSTUS	1873	MISC	1698
GALHAGER, D	1871	HAN MAP	1727	GASSAWAY, BENJAMIN	1820	DEFENDANT	1596
GALION	1852	HEMP. RR MAP	1825	GASSWAY, BENJAMIN	1818	DEFENDANT	1589
GALLAHER, J W	1871	MARH'L MAP	1748	GASTON, D	1871	OH CO. MAP	1740
GALLAHER, J W	1871	MDSVL BUS.	1796	GASTON, JOHN	1809	DEFENDANT	1642
GALLAHER, J W / STORE - WATER ST	1871	MDSVILLE	1810	GASTON, W / WILLIAM ?	1871	OH CO. MAP	1740
GALLION, NATHAN	1799	DEFENDANT	1634	GASTON, W	1871	OH CO. MAP	1743
GALLIPOLIS, OH	1852	HEMP. RR MAP	1826	GASTON, WILLIAM	1871	OH CO. MAP	1740
GAMBLE, H	1871	MARH'L MAP	1749	GASTON, WILLIAM	1871	OH CO. MAP	1740
GAMBLE, J	1871	MARH'L MAP	1749	GASTON, WILLIAM / INITIALS W.G.	1871	OH CO. MAP	1740
GAMBLE, JAMES	1809	DEFENDANT	1583	GASTON, WILLIAM / GRIST MILL - POINT MILL STATION	1871	OH CO. MAP	1743
GAMBLE, ROBERT	1812	DEFENDANT	1583				
GAMES, A	1871	MARH'L MAP	1751	GATES, D	1871	MDSVILLE	1808
GAMES, A	1871	MARH'L MAP	1755	GATES, MARTIN	1878	DEFENDANT	1623
GAMES, J / EST	1871	MARH'L MAP	1749	GATTS, A	1871	MARH'L MAP	1751
GAMES, J D	1871	MARH'L MAP	1749	GATTS, A	1871	MARH'L MAP	1754
GAMES, W	1871	MARH'L MAP	1749	GATTS, C	1871	MARH'L MAP	1751
GANON, J	1871	BENWOOD	1798	GATTS, C	1871	MARH'L MAP	1754
GANS, - / MRS	1871	MDSVILLE	1808	GATTS, G	1871	MARH'L MAP	1755
GANS, - / MRS	1871	MDSVILLE	1809	GATTS, G / INITIALS G.G.	1871	MARH'L MAP	1755
GANTS, ANDREW	1827	MISC	1700	GATTS, G / INITIALS G.G.	1871	MARH'L MAP	1755
GANTS, JOSEPH	1827	MISC	1682	GATTS, G	1871	MARH'L MAP	1759
GANTZER, J	1871	MARH'L MAP	1745	GATTS, G / INITIALS G.G.	1871	MARH'L MAP	1759
GANTZER, J	1871	MARH'L MAP	1745	GATTS, M	1871	MDSVILLE	1810
GARDEN, A T	1871	OH CO. MAP	1741	GATTS, N	1871	MARH'L MAP	1751
GARDEN, A T	1871	OH CO. MAP	1741	GATTS, N	1871	MARH'L MAP	1754
GARDEN, A T	1871	OH CO. MAP	1741	GATTS, P	1871	MARH'L MAP	1751
GARDEN, ALEX T	1879	DEFENDANT	1588	GATTS, P	1871	MARH'L MAP	1754
GARDEN, ALEXANDER	1854	DEFENDANT	1594	GATTS, S M	1871	MARH'L MAP	1754
GARDEN, ALEXANDER	1855	DEFENDANT	1594	GATTS, T	1871	MARH'L MAP	1751
GARDNER, - / FORBES & GARDNER / NAME WRITTEN IN OHIO RIVER	1871	BRKE MAP	1736	GATTS, T	1871	MARH'L MAP	1754
				GATTS, T	1871	MARH'L MAP	1759
GARDNER, -	1871	WELLSBURG	1777	GAUS, J	1871	WELLSBURG	1778
GARDNER, -	1871	WELLSBURG	1777	GAUS, J	1871	WELLSBURG	1778
GARDNER, A	1871	OH CO. MAP	1741	GAUS, J	1871	WELLSBURG	1778
GARDNER, D	1871	HAN MAP	1732	GAVERN A / CARP. SHOP	1871	BENWOOD	1798
GARDNER, J	1871	HAN MAP	1727	GAZKE, L	1871	BENWOOD	1798
GARDNER, J / AT OHIO RIVER	1871	HAN MAP	1727	GEARY, D	1871	MDSVILLE	1807
GARDNER, J / INITIALS J.G.	1871	HAN MAP	1727	GEARY, D / INITIALS D.G.	1871	MDSVILLE	1807
GARDNER, J / INITIALS J.G.	1871	HAN MAP	1727	GEER, A	1871	HAN MAP	1726
GARDNER, J	1871	HAN MAP	1728	GEER, A	1871	HAN MAP	1726
GARDNER, J / INITALS J.G.	1871	HAN MAP	1728	GEER, A / S. OF WASHINGTON SCHOOL	1871	HAN MAP	1726
GARDNER, J	1871	HAN MAP	1732				
GARDNER, J	1871	BRKE MAP	1734	GEER, C	1871	HAN MAP	1730
GARDNER, J / (?OR BARDNER?) - PROSPECT & WATER	1871	WELLSBURG	1777	GEER, C	1871	HAN MAP	1730
				GEER, G	1871	HAN MAP	1726
GARDNER, J / INITIALS J.G. ?	1871	WELLSBURG	1777	GEHO, A / MRS	1871	MARH'L MAP	1760

'PERSONAL TIME LINE' INDEX TO VOLUME 7 OF THE *OHIO COUNTY INDEX*

ENTRY	YEAR	SUBJECT	PAGE	ENTRY	YEAR	SUBJECT	PAGE
GEHO, G	1871	MARH'L MAP	1760	GILL, WILLIAM	1837	DEFENDANT	1619
GEHO, J	1871	MARH'L MAP	1760	GILL, WILLIAM	1837	DEFENDANT	1656
GEHO, J	1871	MARH'L MAP	1760	GILLASPIES RUN	1871	OH CO. MAP	1743
GEHO, R	1871	MARH'L MAP	1760	GILLES, THOMAS W	1862	DEFENDANT	1641
GELSLAR, H	1871	MARH'L MAP	1745	GILLESPIE, J T	1856	DEFENDANT	1602
GELSTHORPE, J / (?JOHN - OF "VIRGINIA HOUSE"?)	1871	WELLSBURG	1777	GILLIS, THOMAS W	1861	DEFENDANT	1564
GELSTHORPE, J / INITIALS G.S.	1871	WELLSBURG	1777	GILLMORE, -	1856	PLAINTIFF	1632
GELSTHROPE, JOHN / VIRGINIA HOUSE	1871	WLSBRG BUS.	1772	GILLUS, G	1871	WHG CITY	1786
				GILMER, JOHN	1852	HEMPFIELD RR	1822
GEMMELL, F	1836	DEFENDANT	1591	GILMORE, -	1857	PLAINTIFF	1632
GEMMELL, F / & CO	1838	DEFENDANT	1592	GILMORE, JOHN	1820	DEFENDANT	1579
GENINE, T H / EST.	1871	MARH'L MAP	1757	GILMORE, JOHN	1838	MISC	1676
GENINE, T H / EST. - INITIALS T.H.G.EST.	1871	MARH'L MAP	1757	GILMORE, WILLIAM / FARM	1871	OH CO. MAP	1740
				GIMER, G	1871	BETHANY	1773
GEORGE, - / MRS	1871	MARH'L MAP	1746	GIRTYS RUN	1852	BRKE MAP	1839
GEORGE, S	1871	BRKE MAP	1736	GIRTYS RUN	1871	BKE/OH MAP	1738
GEORGE, S / INITIALS S.G.	1871	BRKE MAP	1736	GIST, CHRISTOPHER / JOURNALS	1916	NAT'L ROAD	1866
GEORGE, S / INITIALS S.G.	1871	BRKE MAP	1736	GIST, GEORGE / MAP#300	1852	BRKE MAP	1847
GEORGE, S / INITIALS S.G.	1871	BRKE MAP	1736	GIST, GEORGE / MAP#301	1852	BRKE MAP	1847
GEORGE, S	1871	BKE/OH MAP	1739	GIST, J C	1871	BRKE MAP	1737
GEORGE, S / INITIALS S.G.	1871	BKE/OH MAP	1739	GIST, J C / INTIALS J.C.C.	1871	BRKE MAP	1737
GEORGE, S / INITLAS S.G.	1871	BKE/OH MAP	1739	GIST, J C / INITIALS J.C.G.	1871	BRKE MAP	1737
GEORGE, S	1871	WELLSBURG	1776	GIST, J C / INITIALS J.C.G.	1871	BRKE MAP	1737
GEORGE, S	1871	WELLSBURG	1777	GIST, J C / RES	1871	BRKE MAP	1737
GEORGE, SAMUEL	1820	DEFENDANT	1635	GIST, J W / DOCTOR	1871	BRKE MAP	1737
GEORGE, THOMAS / MAP#230	1852	BRKE MAP	1844	GIST, J W / DOCTOR	1871	BRKE MAP	1737
GEORGE, THOMAS / MAP#231	1852	BRKE MAP	1844	GIST, J W / DOCTOR - S. OF S.S MILL	1871	BRKE MAP	1737
GEORGES RUN	1871	RITCHIE TWP	1791	GIST, J W / DOCTOR - INITIALS J.W.G.	1871	BRKE MAP	1737
GEORGES RUN	1871	RITCHIE TWP	1793	GIST, JOSEPH / ESQ. - MAP#228	1852	BRKE MAP	1844
GEORGES RUN - OHIO	1852	BRKE MAP	1848	GIST, JOSEPH / ESQ. - MAP#237	1852	BRKE MAP	1844
GERMAN LUTHERAN CHURCH - 4TH WARD	1871	WHG CITY	1788	GIST, JOSEPH / MAP#432	1852	BRKE MAP	1850
GERMAN LUTHERAN CHURCH - NEAR CLAY ST	1871	WHG CITY	1790	GIST, JOSHUA / MAP#238	1852	BRKE MAP	1844
				GIST, T	1871	BRKE MAP	1737
GERMAN SCHOOL - TRIADELPHIA - NATL RD	1871	TRIAD.BORO.	1784	GIST, T / INITIALS T.G.	1871	BRKE MAP	1737
				GISTS BRANCH	1852	BRKE MAP	1847
GERMANTOWN - NEW GERMANTOWN	1871	MARH'L MAP	1747	GLASS CA. / FACTORY NW. OF REILLY EST.	1871	WHG CITY	1789
				GLASS INDUSTRY - WHEELING	1916	NAT'L ROAD	1865
GERMANTOWN - NEW GERMANTOWN	1871	MARH'L MAP	1750	GLASS, A	1871	WELLSBURG	1777
				GLASS, J / MRS	1871	HAN MAP	1731
				GLASSCOCK, JOHN W	1846	DEFENDANT	1570
GEROGE, S / INITIALS S.G.	1871	BKE/OH MAP	1738	GLASSFORD, -	1851	DEFENDANT	1563
GERTNER, PETER	1852	DEFENDANT	1672	GLEN EASTON	1871	DISTANCES	1815
GHOST RUN	1852	BRKE MAP	1843	GLEN EASTON - BUSINESS NOTICES	1871	GLEN EASTON - BUS.	1796
GIBSON, - / MRS	1871	BRKE MAP	1737				
GIBSON, - / MRS	1871	BKE/OH MAP	1739	GLEN EASTON - CAMERON TWP - MARSHALL CO	1871	GLEN EASTON	1801
GIBSON, DAVID W	1876	DEFENDANT	1654				
GIBSON, G	1871	OH CO. MAP	1740	GLEN EASTON - DETAIL MAP	1871	GLEN EASTON	1801
GIBSON, J H	1871	NEW CUMB'LD	1762	GLEN EASTON - GROCERY STORE - MAIN ST	1871	GLEN EASTON	1801
GIBSON, J H	1871	NEW CUMB'LD	1766				
GIBSON, J H	1871	RIV. RD S.OF N.C.	1771	GLEN EASTON - MAIN ST	1871	GLEN EASTON - BUS.	1796
GIBSON, M	1871	OH CO. MAP	1740				
GIBSON, W P	1871	MARH'L MAP	1752	GLEN EASTON - MAIN ST	1871	GLEN EASTON	1801
GIBSON, W P / INITIALS W.P.G.	1871	MARH'L MAP	1752	GLEN EASTON - MECHANIC ST	1871	GLEN EASTON - BUS.	1796
GIESTED, P	1871	OH CO. MAP	1741				
GIESTED, P	1871	OH CO. MAP	1742	GLEN EASTON - MECHANIC ST	1871	GLEN EASTON	1801
GIFFEN, ROBERT	1787	DEFENDANT	1596	GLEN EASTON - ST CHARLES HOTEL	1871	GLEN EASTON	1801
GIFFIN, D A	1871	OH CO. MAP	1740	GLEN EASTON P.O.	1871	MARH'L MAP	1752
GIFFIN, JAMES C	1840	DEFENDANT	1643	GLEN EASTON P.O.	1871	MARH'L MAP	1756
GIFFIN, P M	1871	OH CO. MAP	1740	GLEN ELM	1871	BRKE MAP	1735
GIFFIN, R	1871	OH CO. MAP	1740	GLEN ELM / H.G. LAZEAR	1871	BRKE MAP	1736
GILBERT, A	1871	MARH'L MAP	1760	GLEN MERRY	1871	MARH'L MAP	1759
GILBERT, R	1871	MARH'L MAP	1760	GLENDEAN, WILLIAM / HRS - HEIRS ? NAME WRITTEN IN OHIO RIVER	1871	BRKE MAP	1736
GILBERT, R	1871	MARH'L MAP	1760				
GILBRETH, W L	1871	BETHANY	1773	GLENDEMAN, G	1871	BETHANY	1773
GILCHRIST, J P	1871	WHG CITY	1786	GLENN, S H	1874	DEFENDANT	1562
GILCHRIST, J P	1871	WHG ISLAND	1788	GLENS RUN	1871	OH CO. MAP	1741
GILCHRIST, J P / LEATHERWOOD	1871	WHG CITY	1789	GLICHRIST, JOHN P	1871	TRIAD.TWP.	1781
GILCHRIST, JOHN	1840	DEFENDANT	1661	GLOBE FOUNDRY WAREROOM - KIMBERLAND & KUHN	1871	WELLSBURG	1778
GILCHRIST, JOHN	1840	DEFENDANT	1662				
GILCHRIST, JOHN	1841	DEFENDANT	1551	GLOBER FOUNDRY / NEAR CHARLES ST	1871	WELLSBURG	1777
GILCHRIST, JOHN	1844	DEFENDANT	1558				
GILCHRIST, JOHN P	1871	OH CO.BUS.	1779	GLUE FACTORY - FUCCUS, WALTER G	1871	OH CO. MAP	1742
GILES, HENRY	1835	DEFENDANT	1577				
GILES, HENRY	1835	DEFENDANT	1617	GLUE FACTORY - NATL RD	1871	TRIAD.TWP.	1781
GILES, HENRY	1835	DEFENDANT	1650	GODDARD, J	1871	MARH'L MAP	1755
GILES, W	1871	MARH'L MAP	1754	GODFREY, JAMES	1874	DEFENDANT	1558
GILES, W	1871	MARH'L MAP	1758	GODFREY, JAMES	1874	DEFENDANT	1621
GILFILLAN, EDWARD	1859	DEFENDANT	1584	GODFREY, JOSEPH	1821	DEFENDANT	1612
GILKERSON, JOHN	1840	DEFENDANT	1662	GODWIN, T	1871	NEW CUMB'LD	1768
GILL, A	1871	MARH'L MAP	1756	GOETZ, AUGUST SURV & CO	1859	DEFENDANT	1608
GILL, HARDMAN & STEPHENS	1855	DEFENDANT	1621	GOETZE, AUGUST	1860	DEFENDANT	1608
GILL, HARDMAN & STEPHENS	1861	DEFENDANT	1598	GOETZE, C	1871	MARH'L MAP	1745
GILL, JOHN	1855	DEFENDANT	1588	GOETZE, G	1871	MARH'L MAP	1745
GILL, JOHN W	1856	DEFENDANT	1653	GOLDENBURG, ROBERT	1841	DEFENDANT	1592
GILL, WILLIAM	1837	DEFENDANT	1614	GOLDENBURGH, FREDERICK	1829	DEFENDANT	1591

XL

'PERSONAL TIME LINE' INDEX TO VOLUME 7 OF THE *OHIO COUNTY INDEX*

ENTRY	YEAR	SUBJECT	PAGE
GOOCH, B	1871	BRKE MAP	1737
GOOCH, B	1871	BKE/OH MAP	1739
GOOCH, J	1871	BKE/OH MAP	1738
GOOD INTENT STAGE LINE - RONEYS' POINT	1916	NAT'L ROAD	1864
GOOD, A	1871	MARH'L MAP	1761
GOOD, B S	1871	OH CO. MAP	1742
GOOD, B S	1871	OH CO. MAP	1744
GOOD, JOHN	1826	DEFENDANT	1568
GOOD, JOHN A	1839	MISC	1677
GOOD, MOSES	1841	DEFENDANT	1629
GOOD, MOSES C	1836	MISC	1710
GOOD, T	1871	MARH'L MAP	1761
GOOD, WILLIAM T	1832	DEFENDANT	1600
GOODING, - / MRS - HOUSE ON NATIONAL ROAD	1916	NAT'L ROAD	1865
GOODING, HANNAH	1824	DEFENDANT	1612
GOODING, JACOB	1852	HEMPFIELD RR	1822
GOODING, JACOB	1852	HEMPFIELD RR	1822
GOODING, JACOB	1852	HEMPFIELD RR	1822
GOODING, JOHN	1806	MISC	1688
GOODING, JOHN	1809	DEFENDANT	1667
GOODRICH, WILLIAM	1857	DEFENDANT	1604
GOODRICH, WILLIAM	1857	DEFENDANT	1632
GOODWIN, J	1871	HAN MAP	1728
GOORLEY, J	1871	BRKE MAP	1734
GOORLEY, J M	1871	BRKE MAP	1734
GOORLEY, J M / INITIALS W.S. & J.M.G.	1871	BRKE MAP	1734
GOORLEY, W S	1871	BRKE MAP	1734
GOORLEY, W S / INITIALS W.S. & J.M.G.	1871	BRKE MAP	1734
GORBY, D	1871	MARH'L MAP	1756
GORBY, D	1871	MARH'L MAP	1761
GORBY, E / INITIALS E.G.	1871	MARH'L MAP	1752
GORBY, E	1871	MARH'L MAP	1755
GORBY, E / INITIALS E.G.	1871	MARH'L MAP	1755
GORBY, E / MISS	1871	MARH'L MAP	1761
GORBY, I	1871	MARH'L MAP	1750
GORBY, J E	1871	MARH'L MAP	1756
GORBY, W	1871	MARH'L MAP	1761
GORCLY, - / SCHOOL - MAP#586	1852	BRKE MAP	1851
GORDAN, R G CO	1859	DEFENDANT	1574
GORDON, A B	1871	MARH'L MAP	1752
GORDON, WILLIAM F	1839	DEFENDANT	1596
GORDON, WILLIAM F	1841	DEFENDANT	1585
GORDON, WILLIAM F	1841	DEFENDANT	1643
GORDON, WILLIAM F	1842	DEFENDANT	1663
GORELY, JOHN / CAPT. - MAP#587	1852	BRKE MAP	1851
GORELY, JOHN / CAPT. - MAP#588	1852	BRKE MAP	1851
GORELYS RUN	1852	BRKE MAP	1851
GOSHORN G S	1871	OH CO. MAP	1742
GOSHORN, JOHN	1846	DEFENDANT	1570
GOSHORN, W S	1871	OH CO. MAP	1742
GOSHORN, W S / INITIALS W.S.G.	1871	OH CO. MAP	1742
GOSHORN, WILLIAM	1871	MARH'L MAP	1756
GOSMEY, W	1871	MARH'L MAP	1753
GOSNEY, HENRY	1805	DEFENDANT	1666
GOSNEY, HENRY	1811	DEFENDANT	1595
GOSNEY, HENRY	1811	DEFENDANT	1667
GOSNEY, J	1871	MARH'L MAP	1746
GOSNEY, JOHN	1829	DEFENDANT	1613
GOSNEY, JOHN	1829	DEFENDANT	1632
GOSNEY, JOHN	1830	DEFENDANT	1632
GOSNEY, R	1871	MARH'L MAP	1745
GOSNEY, R	1871	SHERRARD	1811
GOTHIC POINT	1871	MARH'L MAP	1748
GOTTS, CONROD	1866	MISC	1698
GOUDLING, JAMES	1841	DEFENDANT	1661
GOUDY, JOHN	1871	MARH'L MAP	1746
GOUDY, JOHN	1871	MARH'L MAP	1749
GOUDY, JOHN / INITIALS J.G.	1871	MARH'L MAP	1749
GOUDY, JOHN / INITIALS J.G.	1871	MARH'L MAP	1749
GOUDY, JOHN	1871	WASH.TWP-BUS.	1797
GOUDY, R	1871	WELLSBURG	1777
GOUDY, R	1871	WELLSBURG	1777
GOUDY, WILLIAM	1859	DEFENDANT	1636
GOULD, PEARCE & CO	1871	WLSBRG BUS.	1772
GOULD, PEARCE & CO / FLEET ST.	1871	WELLSBURG	1776
GOULD, PEARCE & CO / INITIALS G.P.&CO.	1871	WELLSBURG	1776
GOULD, PEARCE & CO	1871	WELLSBURG	1777
GOULD, PEARCE & CO	1871	WELLSBURG	1777
GOULD, PEARCE & CO / COTTON	1871	WELLSBURG	1777
GOULD, PEARCE & CO / INITIALS G.P.&CO.	1871	WELLSBURG	1777
GOULD, PEARCE & CO / INITIALS G.P.&CO.	1871	WELLSBURG	1777
GOULD, PEARCE & CO / INITIALS G.P.&CO.	1871	WELLSBURG	1777
GOULD, PEARCE & CO. / INITIALS G.P.& CO.	1871	WELLSBURG	1777
GOULD, PEARCE & CO. / INITIALS G.P.& CO	1871	WELLSBURG	1777
GOWAN, W	1871	BRKE MAP	1736
GR YE / (?GRAVEYARD?)	1871	BRKE MAP	1734
GR.YD. / (?ABBREV FOR GRAVE YARD?)	1871	MARH'L MAP	1748
GRACE, J	1871	HAN MAP	1731
GRAFTON, N	1871	HAN MAP	1730
GRAHAM & HELM	1834	DEFENDANT	1650
GRAHAM, -	1858	PLAINTIFF	1626
GRAHAM, G	1871	NEW CUMB'LD	1767
GRAHAM, J	1871	MARH'L MAP	1754
GRAHAM, J S	1831	MISC	1711
GRAHAM, JOHN	1833	DEFENDANT	1613
GRAHAM, JOHN	1834	DEFENDANT	1613
GRAHAM, JOHN	1834	DEFENDANT	1639
GRAHAM, JOHN	1836	DEFENDANT	1614
GRAHAM, JOHN	1836	DEFENDANT	1640
GRAHAM, JOHN	1838	DEFENDANT	1640
GRAHAM, JOSEPH S	1831	MISC	1702
GRAHAM, JOSEPH S	1833	DEFENDANT	1558
GRAHAM, JOSEPH S	1833	DEFENDANT	1650
GRAHAM, JOSEPH S	1834	DEFENDANT	1650
GRAHAM, MICHAEL	1823	DEFENDANT	1656
GRAHAM, PATIENCE	1827	DEFENDANT	1551
GRAND VIEW - CLAY TWP	1871	MARH'L MAP	1752
GRAND VIEW - UNION TWP	1871	MARH'L MAP	1745
GRANDSTAFF, S	1871	MDSVILLE	1808
GRANDSTAFF, S / EST.	1871	MDSVILLE	1810
GRANDSTRAFF, S T	1871	W.UNION	1812
GRANDVIEW - FRANKLIN TWP	1871	MARH'L MAP	1754
GRANT HOUSE HOTEL - WHEELING	1871	OH CO.BUS.	1779
GRANT TOWNSHIP - HANCOCK CO	1871	POPULATION	1816
GRANT TOWNSHIP - HANCOCK CO - BUSINESS LISTINGS	1871	HAN-GR'NT TWP	1763
GRANT TWP - HANCOCK CO. / WEST PART	1871	HAN MAP	1726
GRANT TWP - HANCOCK CO. - EAST PART	1871	HAN MAP	1727
GRANT TWP - HANCOCK CO. - HAMILTON	1871	HAN MAP	1729
GRANT, WILLIAM	1817	DEFENDANT	1638
GRANTSVILLE, MD	1916	NAT'L ROAD	1863
GRASS, J	1871	MARH'L MAP	1759
GRAVE CREEK HEAD	1871	MARH'L MAP	1753
GRAVES, J	1871	BRKE MAP	1736
GRAVEY, LEWIS	1878	DEFENDANT	1593
GRAVEYARD - E. OF J. FOSTER	1871	MARH'L MAP	1753
GRAVEYARD - NW OF SHERRARD / NEAR CHURCH OF GOD - INITIALS GR.YD.	1871	MARH'L MAP	1745
GRAVEYARD - ST JOHNS CHURCH	1871	BRKE MAP	1734
GRAVEYARD - W. OF J.CARNEY	1871	WHG CITY	1790
GRAVEYARD - W. OF ROCK LICK P.O.	1871	MARH'L MAP	1753
GRAVEYARD RUN / AT OHIO RIVER	1871	MARH'L MAP	1751
GRAY BEARD / FARM SETTLED BY RICHARD WELLS, KNOWN AS GRAYBEARD IN 1772	1871	BRKE MAP	1734
GRAY, - / HOMESTEAD	1871	MARH'L MAP	1750
GRAY, C / FISHER, J	1871	MARH'L MAP	1746
GRAY, D	1871	TRIAD.BORO.	1784
GRAY, F W	1871	MARH'L MAP	1760
GRAY, J	1871	MARH'L MAP	1745
GRAY, J	1871	MARH'L MAP	1760
GRAY, J H	1871	MARH'L MAP	1750
GRAY, JAMES	1871	OH CO. MAP	1743
GRAY, JOHN	1805	DEFENDANT	1648
GRAY, JOHN	1807	DEFENDANT	1648
GRAY, M / MRS.	1871	MARH'L MAP	1760
GRAY, P B	1871	MARH'L MAP	1750
GRAY, R	1871	MARH'L MAP	1745
GRAY, S J / MRS	1871	MDSVILLE	1808
GRAY, S J / MRS	1871	MDSVILLE	1808
GRAY, THOMAS	1802	PLAINTIFF	1600
GRAY, THOMAS	1859	DEFENDANT	1552
GRAY, W	1871	MARH'L MAP	1745
GRAY, W	1871	MDSVILLE	1808
GRAYHAM, JOHN	1789	DEFENDANT	1572

'PERSONAL TIME LINE' INDEX TO VOLUME 7 OF THE *OHIO COUNTY INDEX*

ENTRY	YEAR	SUBJECT	PAGE
GRAYHAM, SAMUEL	1793	DEFENDANT	1608
GRAYSON, G	1876	DEFENDANT	1588
GREAT KANAWHA RIVER RR	1852	HEMP. RR MAP	1826
GREAT MEADOWS / FORT NECESSITY	1916	NAT'L ROAD	1869
GREATHOUSE, HARMON	1811	DEFENDANT	1561
GREATHOUSE, HARMON	1818	DEFENDANT	1602
GREATHOUSE, HARMON	1818	DEFENDANT	1660
GREATHOUSE, ISAAC	1817	DEFENDANT	1646
GREATHOUSE, ISAAC	1818	DEFENDANT	1656
GREATHOUSE, ISAAC	1818	DEFENDANT	1660
GREEN RIDGE	1871	MARH'L MAP	1747
GREEN, -	1871	OH CO. MAP	1742
GREEN, -	1871	OH CO. MAP	1744
GREEN, -	1871	ELM GROVE	1782
GREEN, A	1871	HAN MAP	1727
GREEN, E	1871	BRKE MAP	1736
GREEN, ELI / MAP#215	1852	BRKE MAP	1842
GREEN, ELIZABETH	1857	DEFENDANT	1561
GREEN, ELIZABETH	1857	DEFENDANT	1561
GREEN, J F	1871	WELLSBURG	1778
GREEN, JAMES	1820	DEFENDANT	1591
GREEN, JAMES	1821	DEFENDANT	1591
GREEN, JAMES	1830	DEFENDANT	1639
GREEN, JAMES	1830	DEFENDANT	1650
GREEN, JAMES	1831	DEFENDANT	1650
GREEN, JAMES	1837	DEFENDANT	1568
GREEN, JOHN	1784	DEFENDANT	1647
GREEN, JOHN	1799	DEFENDANT	1607
GREEN, O E	1871	BRKE MAP	1737
GREEN, SAMUEL	1810	DEFENDANT	1642
GREEN, WILLIAM / MAP#250	1852	BRKE MAP	1843
GREEN, WILLIAM / MAP#251	1852	BRKE MAP	1843
GREEN, WILLIAM / MAP#252	1852	BRKE MAP	1843
GREEN, WILLIAM / MAP#298	1852	BRKE MAP	1846
GREEN, WILLIAM / MAP#299	1852	BRKE MAP	1846
GREEN, WILLIAM JR	1871	BRKE MAP	1737
GREEN, WILLIAM SR	1871	BRKE MAP	1737
GREENHOUSE	1871	MARH'L MAP	1748
GREENLAND, JAMES	1831	MISC	1678
GREENLEE, M	1871	OH CO. MAP	1742
GREENLEE, M	1871	OH CO. MAP	1742
GREENLEE, M	1871	RITCHIE TWP	1793
GREENLEE, M / INITIALS M.G.	1871	RITCHIE TWP	1793
GREENS FORK	1852	BRKE MAP	1850
GREENSBURG, PA	1852	HEMP. RR MAP	1826
GREENSBURG, PA	1852	HEMP. RR MAP	1827
GREENSBURG, PA - HEMPFIELD RR CONNECTS TO PENNSYLVANIA RR	1852	HEMPFIELD RR	1817
GREENWOOD CEMETERY	1871	OH CO. MAP	1742
GREER, FREDERICK H	1843	DEFENDANT	1652
GREER, JOHN	1788	DEFENDANT	1583
GREER, WILLIAM	1823	DEFENDANT	1612
GREGG & EDWARDS	1838	DEFENDANT	1557
GREGG, -	1857	DEFENDANT	1597
GREGG, BENJAMIN S	1855	DEFENDANT	1561
GREGG, CHARLES	1862	DEFENDANT	1671
GREGG, GEORGE	1810	DEFENDANT	1559
GREGG, GEORGE	1810	DEFENDANT	1656
GREGG, GEORGE	1811	APPENDIX	1873
GREGG, M H / (?MORGAN?)	1873	DEFENDANT	1601
GREGG, M H / (?MORGAN?)	1873	DEFENDANT	1603
GREGG, MORGAN H	1838	DEFENDANT	1557
GREGG, MORGAN H	1854	DEFENDANT	1565
GREGG, MORGAN H	1854	DEFENDANT	1623
GREGG, MORGAN H	1854	DEFENDANT	1629
GREGG, MORGAN H	1854	DEFENDANT	1653
GREGG, MORGAN H	1854	DEFENDANT	1670
GREGG, MORGAN H	1855	DEFENDANT	1564
GREGG, MORGAN H	1855	DEFENDANT	1586
GREGG, MORGAN H	1855	DEFENDANT	1623
GREGG, MORGAN H	1855	DEFENDANT	1630
GREGG, WILLIAM	1833	DEFENDANT	1566
GREGG, WILLIAM	1833	DEFENDANT	1622
GREGG, WILLIAM	1856	DEFENDANT	1559
GREGGSVILLE	1871	OH CO. MAP	1741
GREGGSVILLE / OHIO CO	1871	DISTANCES	1815
GREGGSVILLE POST OFFICE	1871	OH CO. MAP	1741
GREGGVILLE	1871	OH CO. MAP	1742
GREGORY, J / MRS	1871	HAN MAP	1730
GREGORY, W	1871	HAN MAP	1730
GRESHWATER, G / (?GEORGE?)	1871	BRKE MAP	1735
GRETNA GREEN - OLD NAME FOR WEST ALEXANDER	1916	NAT'L ROAD	1862
GRETZENGER, C	1871	NEW MANCH.	1769
GREY, H	1871	TRIAD.BORO.	1784
GRIER, L / (?CRIER?)	1871	OH CO. MAP	1742
GRIESHABER, JOHN	1856	DEFENDANT	1653
GRIESMER, F	1842	DEFENDANT	1663
GRIFFETH, J B	1871	BKE/OH MAP	1739
GRIFFITH, -	1855	PLAINTIFF	1630
GRIFFITH, ASSHAEL	1798	DEFENDANT	1600
GRIFFITH, B	1871	HAN MAP	1732
GRIFFITH, B	1871	MARH'L MAP	1755
GRIFFITH, B	1871	MARH'L MAP	1755
GRIFFITH, B	1871	MARH'L MAP	1759
GRIFFITH, DAVID	1803	PLAINTIFF	1648
GRIFFITH, E	1871	MARH'L MAP	1748
GRIFFITH, J B	1871	BKE/OH MAP	1739
GRIFFITH, JAMES	1791	DEFENDANT	1644
GRIFFITH, JAMES / HEIRS - MAP#492	1852	BRKE MAP	1850
GRIFFITH, LUKE	1830	DEFENDANT	1639
GRIFFITH, NATHAN	1790	DEFENDANT	1644
GRIFFITH, WILLIAM	1871	HAN MAP	1732
GRIFFITHS RUN	1852	BRKE MAP	1853
GRIFFITHS RUN	1871	HAN MAP	1732
GRIMES, J	1871	MARH'L MAP	1756
GRIMES, J	1871	MARH'L MAP	1756
GRIMES, J	1871	MARH'L MAP	1757
GRIMES, T	1871	BRKE MAP	1737
GRIMES, THOMAS P / MAP#354	1852	BRKE MAP	1846
GRIMES, THOMAS P / MAP#382	1852	BRKE MAP	1846
GRINDAGE, -	1825	PLAINTIFF	1628
GRINDSTAFF RUN - S.B. KITTLE'S BLACKSMITH SHOP ON	1871	SAND HILL-BUS.	1797
GRINDSTAFF, S	1871	MARH'L MAP	1746
GRINDSTAFF, W	1871	MARH'L MAP	1746
GRIST MILL	1794	MISC	1710
GRIST MILL	1796	MISC	1674
GRIST MILL	1801	MISC	1707
GRIST MILL / & DAM - S. OF JOB LEWIS	1871	BRKE MAP	1736
GRIST MILL - ANTILLS / BENJAMIN - "CROSS CREEK"	1871	CROSS CRK.BUS.	1772
GRIST MILL - BELLTON	1871	MARH'L MAP	1761
GRIST MILL - BROOKLYN MILLS	1871	HAN MAP	1726
GRIST MILL - BUCHANANS / S - ON MIDDLE WHEELING CREEK	1871	OH CO. MAP	1743
GRIST MILL - CANNONS / C	1871	MARH'L MAP	1750
GRIST MILL - CASTLEMANS RUN	1871	BKE/OH MAP	1739
GRIST MILL - CROSS CREEK / E OF OLD CEMETERY	1871	BRKE MAP	1735
GRIST MILL - E OF PAN-HANDLE P.O.	1871	BRKE MAP	1734
GRIST MILL - E. OF W.A. KNOX	1871	MARH'L MAP	1752
GRIST MILL - FORSHAS / ?	1871	HAN MAP	1731
GRIST MILL - FORSHAS / ?	1871	HAN MAP	1732
GRIST MILL - FOWLERS / J - ON CROSS CREEK	1871	BRKE MAP	1735
GRIST MILL - G.M. / NE. OF WOODLAND P.O. (?GRIST MILL?)	1871	MARH'L MAP	1754
GRIST MILL - GASTONS / WILLIAM - POINT MILL STATION	1871	OH CO. MAP	1743
GRIST MILL - HAMILTONS / J.S.	1871	HAN MAP	1732
GRIST MILL - HIGGINS / JOHN W. - LIBERTY TWP	1871	LIB.TWP-BUS.	1797
GRIST MILL - HINDMANS / S	1871	HAN MAP	1732
GRIST MILL - HINDMANS / S	1871	BRKE MAP	1734
GRIST MILL - HOLLIDAYS COVE	1871	HAN MAP	1733
GRIST MILL - KITTLES / S.B.	1871	MARH'L MAP	1746
GRIST MILL - LYNNCAMP RUN	1871	MARH'L MAP	1759
GRIST MILL - MILL RACE - NEAR J.E. SMITH	1871	NEW CUMB'LD	1768
GRIST MILL - MONUMENT / ELM GROVE	1871	ELM GROVE	1782
GRIST MILL - N. BRANCH OF SHORT CREEK	1871	BKE/OH MAP	1738
GRIST MILL - NE OF SUNNYDALE	1871	HAN MAP	1732
GRIST MILL - NEAR J E SMITH	1871	NEW CUMB'LD	1768
GRIST MILL - NEAR W. POLLOCK	1871	OH CO. MAP	1740
GRIST MILL - NW OF SCHOOL NO. 11	1871	BRKE MAP	1735
GRIST MILL - NW. OF HAZELDELL SCHOOL NO.5	1871	MARH'L MAP	1750
GRIST MILL - OLD GRIST MILL - COUNCILMAN RUN	1871	BKE/OH MAP	1739
GRIST MILL - ON BALL LICK	1871	MARH'L MAP	1757
GRIST MILL - ON HARMONS CREEK	1871	BRKE MAP	1734
GRIST MILL - PORTERS / L. - ROSBBYS ROCK	1871	ROSBBYS RK	1813
GRIST MILL - POTTS / J B	1871	MARH'L MAP	1752
GRIST MILL - PUGHS / G.H. - ON TOMLINSONS RUN	1871	HAN MAP	1731
GRIST MILL - RUTHS / S	1871	MARH'L MAP	1747

'PERSONAL TIME LINE' INDEX TO VOLUME 7 OF THE *OHIO COUNTY INDEX*

ENTRY	YEAR	SUBJECT	PAGE
GRIST MILL - RUTHS / W	1871	MARH'L MAP	1750
GRIST MILL - RYLANDS / HUGH P - "HARMONS CREEK"	1871	CROSS CRK. BUS.	1772
GRIST MILL - S & G MILL / N. OF WHEELING VALLEY FLOURING MILLS	1871	MARH'L MAP	1746
GRIST MILL - S. OF C. CANNON	1871	MARH'L MAP	1747
GRIST MILL - S. OF MRS. E. WEIDEMAN / SHORT CREEK	1871	BKE/OH MAP	1739
GRIST MILL - S. OF WILLIAM GASTON	1871	OH CO. MAP	1740
GRIST MILL - SHORT CREEK	1871	BKE/OH MAP	1738
GRIST MILL - STADIFORDS / A	1871	MARH'L MAP	1748
GRIST MILL - STEAM SAW AND G.MILL / N. OF J.A. RICE	1871	MARH'L MAP	1761
GRIST MILL - SW OF SCHOOL NO. 11	1871	BRKE MAP	1735
GRIST MILL - TRIADELPLHIA	1871	TRIAD.BORO.	1784
GRIST MILL - TRIMBLES / BROS OLD GRIST MILL	1871	BKE/OH MAP	1738
GRIST MILL - W. OF THOMAS H. RALSTON	1871	HAN MAP	1732
GRIST MILL - WHARRYS / JOHN - MOUNDSVILLE	1871	MDSVL BUS.	1796
GRIST MILL - WHARRYS / JOHN - MOUNDSVILLE	1871	MDSVILLE	1810
GRIST MILL - WHEELING CREEK	1871	TRIAD.TWP.	1781
GRIST MILL - WHITE & STILES / BELLTON	1871	BELLTON	1814
GRISWELL - SEE ALSO CRISWELL	1871	MARH'L MAP	1745
GRISWELL, L	1871	MARH'L MAP	1745
GRIZZELL, D B	1871	HAN MAP	1731
GRIZZELL, D B	1871	HAN MAP	1732
GRIZZELL, T	1871	HAN MAP	1732
GROCERY STORE - N. OF J. CAMPBELL	1871	MARH'L MAP	1746
GROE, -	1871	NEW CUMB'LD	1766
GROG RUN	1852	BRKE MAP	1842
GROG RUN	1871	BRKE MAP	1736
GROUND FIRE CLAY COMPANIES	1871	FRE'MAN'S LDG	1762
GROVE - THE GROVE	1871	HAN MAP	1726
GROVE, WILLIAM	1812	DEFENDANT	1611
GROVE, WILLIAM	1812	DEFENDANT	1611
GROVE, WILLIAM	1813	DEFENDANT	1611
GROVERY STORE - HILLS / MRS J	1871	BKE/OH MAP	1739
GROVES, J	1871	BRKE MAP	1736
GROVES, JAMES	1852	NOT ON MAP	1836
GROVES, JOHN / MAP#149	1852	BRKE MAP	1843
GROVES, S	1871	BKE/OH MAP	1738
GROVES, S / BLACKSMITH - RICHLAND TWP	1871	RICHLD TWP-BUS.	1797
GRUPPY, -	1871	MARH'L MAP	1745
GRUS, L	1871	BRKE MAP	1736
GUARDIAN - NEWSPAPER - BETHANY	1871	BETHNY BUS.	1772
GUCKLER, SAMUEL	1825	DEFENDANT	1649
GULLETT, E	1871	BRKE MAP	1734
GUMLY, JOSHUA	1804	DEFENDANT	1628
GUNN, WILLIAM	1818	DEFENDANT	1660
GUNN, WILLIAM	1871	MARH'L MAP	1756
GUNTHER, HENRY	1870	DEFENDANT	1627
GUNTHER, HENRY	1877	DEFENDANT	1580
GURN, G	1871	BENWOOD	1798
GUTLING, NATHAN	1809	DEFENDANT	1658
GUTLING, NATHON	1809	DEFENDANT	1645
GUY, ROBERT	1842	DEFENDANT	1558
GUY, ROBERT	1861	DEFENDANT	1560
H.R.R.CO. / ABBREV. FOR HEMPFIELD RR CO.	1871	OH CO. MAP	1740
H.R.R.CO. / ABBREV FOR HEMPFIELD RR CO.	1871	OH CO. MAP	1743
HABICK, A	1871	BENWOOD	1798
HACKHAM, ANN	1822	MISC	1689
HACKINS, WILLIAM	1830	MISC	1687
HADDEN, -	1836	PLAINTIFF	1628
HADDEN, -	1860	PLAINTIFF	1621
HADDEN, MATILDA	1858	MISC	1683
HADSALL, - / HOMESTEAD	1871	MARH'L MAP	1749
HADSALL, N	1871	MARH'L MAP	1749
HAGEN, J B	1871	WLSBRG BUS.	1772
HAGEN, J B / (O)	1871	WELLSBURG	1778
HAGEN, J B / (O)	1871	WELLSBURG	1778
HAGEN, T	1871	WLSBRG BUS.	1772
HAGEN, T	1871	WELLSBURG	1778
HAGER, JOSEPH D	1839	DEFENDANT	1651
HAGERMAN, J	1871	MARH'L MAP	1749
HAGERMAN, J	1871	MARH'L MAP	1753
HAGERMAN, J	1871	MARH'L MAP	1753
HAHN, LAWRENCE	1859	DEFENDANT	1673

ENTRY	YEAR	SUBJECT	PAGE
HAHNE, JOHN	1878	DEFENDANT	1580
HAHNE, LEWIS	1879	DEFENDANT	1552
HAHNE, LOUIS	1877	DEFENDANT	1564
HAHNE, LOUIS	1877	DEFENDANT	1575
HAINES, CLARK	1839	DEFENDANT	1587
HAINES, JACOB	1800	DEFENDANT	1647
HAIR, JAMES	1816	DEFENDANT	1624
HAIR, JAMES	1817	DEFENDANT	1624
HALEY & KELTZ	1854	DEFENDANT	1592
HALEY, -	1855	DEFENDANT	1653
HALEY, JOHN A	1854	DEFENDANT	1623
HALEY, JOHN P	1852	DEFENDANT	1623
HALEY, JOHN P	1853	DEFENDANT	1623
HALEY, JOHN P	1853	DEFENDANT	1623
HALL - I.O.O.F. - CAMERON	1871	CAMERON	1803
HALL - MASONIC - CAMERON	1871	CAMERON	1803
HALL, -	1871	WELLSBURG	1777
HALL, A / LIME KILN	1871	BRKE MAP	1735
HALL, A / LIME KILM	1871	BRKE MAP	1737
HALL, A C	1871	WELLSBURG	1777
HALL, A C / WATER ST	1871	WELLSBURG	1777
HALL, F P / MRS	1871	WELLSBURG	1778
HALL, F P / MRS	1871	WELLSBURG	1778
HALL, F P / MRS - GROC (OC)	1871	WELLSBURG	1778
HALL, H	1871	MARH'L MAP	1755
HALL, H	1871	MARH'L MAP	1755
HALL, H / INITIALS H.H.	1871	MARH'L MAP	1755
HALL, H / HDWE & GROC. - WATER ST	1871	WELLSBURG	1777
HALL, I D / MAP ASSISTANT	1871	MAP	1713
HALL, J B	1839	DEFENDANT	1632
HALL, JAMES	1791	DEFENDANT	1587
HALL, JOHN	1871	OH CO. MAP	1743
HALL, JOHN E	1856	DEFENDANT	1603
HALL, JOHN R	1834	DEFENDANT	1650
HALL, JOHN R	1839	DEFENDANT	1614
HALL, JOHN R	1839	DEFENDANT	1619
HALL, JOHN W	1835	DEFENDANT	1669
HALL, L	1871	WELLSBURG	1776
HALL, LEWIS	1871	BRKE MAP	1736
HALL, M	1871	WELLSBURG	1777
HALLAM, JOSEPH	1858	DEFENDANT	1552
HALLAM, JOSEPH	1858	DEFENDANT	1621
HALLOCK, H B	1871	BRKE MAP	1734
HALLS RUN	1871	OH CO. MAP	1743
HALSEY, A	1871	BRKE MAP	1734
HALSEY, A / NEAR OHIO RIVER	1871	BRKE MAP	1734
HALSTEAD, A / CARPENTER SHOP	1871	BRKE MAP	1734
HALSTEAD, A	1871	OH CO. MAP	1743
HALSTEAD, A	1871	MARH'L MAP	1746
HALSTEAD, A J / SE OF FAIRVIEW SCHOOL	1871	OH CO. MAP	1743
HALSTEAD, ANDREW	1871	OH CO. MAP	1742
HALSTEAD, ANDREW	1871	OH CO. MAP	1744
HALSTEADS CORNER / SE OF FAIRVIEW SCHOOL	1871	OH CO. MAP	1743
HAMAN, -	1855	DEFENDANT	1570
HAMBLETON, JAMES	1789	DEFENDANT	1655
HAMBLETON, JOHN	1792	DEFENDANT	1563
HAMBLETON, JOHN	1799	DEFENDANT	1598
HAMES, SAMUEL	1852	DEFENDANT	1577
HAMILTON	1871	HAN MAP	1726
HAMILTON / GRANT TWP, HANCOCK CO. / 177 NUMBERED LOTS	1871	HAN MAP	1729
HAMILTON	1871	DISTANCES	1815
HAMILTON - JOHN HUDSON & SONS NEARBY	1871	HAN-GR'NT TWP	1763
HAMILTON - WASHINGTON ST	1871	HAN-GR'NT TWP	1763
HAMILTON - WATER ST	1871	HAN-GR'NT TWP	1763
HAMILTON HEIGHTS	1871	HAN MAP	1726
HAMILTON, -	1832	PLAINTIFF	1622
HAMILTON, -	1833	PLAINTIFF	1620
HAMILTON, -	1833	PLAINTIFF	1622
HAMILTON, -	1833	PLAINTIFF	1650
HAMILTON, -	1834	PLAINTIFF	1622
HAMILTON, -	1836	PLAINTIFF	1622
HAMILTON, -	1838	PLAINTIFF	1622
HAMILTON, -	1841	PLAINTIFF	1623
HAMILTON, -	1848	PLAINTIFF	1620
HAMILTON, - / NE OF WHITEHOUSE HOME	1871	MARH'L MAP	1745
HAMILTON, - / MRS / SW OF A. THOMPSON	1871	MARH'L MAP	1747
HAMILTON, A	1871	TRIAD.BORO.	1784
HAMILTON, ARCHIBALD	1812	DEFENDANT	1585
HAMILTON, ARCHIBALD	1816	DEFENDANT	1642
HAMILTON, ARCHIBALD	1819	MISC	1677

'PERSONAL TIME LINE' INDEX TO VOLUME 7 OF THE OHIO COUNTY INDEX

ENTRY	YEAR	SUBJECT	PAGE
HAMILTON, ARCHIBALD	1821	DEFENDANT	1612
HAMILTON, ARCHIBALD	1822	DEFENDANT	1591
HAMILTON, D	1871	HAN MAP	1726
HAMILTON, J / FIRE CLAY	1871	HAN MAP	1726
HAMILTON, J / NEAR PLEASANT VIEW	1871	HAN MAP	1726
HAMILTON, J C	1871	HAN MAP	1726
HAMILTON, J S / GRIST HILLCOAL - W. OF VALLEY HOMESTEAD	1871	HAN MAP	1732
HAMILTON, J S	1871	HAN-BUTL'R TWP	1763
HAMILTON, JAMES	1835	DEFENDANT	1613
HAMILTON, JAMES	1877	DEFENDANT	1570
HAMILTON, JAMES W	1847	DEFENDANT	1554
HAMILTON, JOHN	1838	DEFENDANT	1558
HAMILTON, N A / MRS	1871	HAN MAP	1729
HAMILTON, ORVILLE	1824	DEFENDANT	1620
HAMILTON, POLLACK	1816	MISC	1700
HAMILTON, ROBERT	1637	DEFENDANT	1602
HAMILTON, ROBERT	1840	DEFENDANT	1551
HAMILTON, SAMUEL	1843	DEFENDANT	1565
HAMILTON, SARY ANN	1826	MISC	1678
HAMMEL - ORPHANS	1838	MISC	1678
HAMMON, G	1871	MARH'L MAP	1748
HAMMON, JOSEPH	1871	MARH'L MAP	1748
HAMMON, JOSEPH / INITIALS J.H.	1871	MARH'L MAP	1748
HAMMON, JOSEPH / INITIALS J.H.	1871	MARH'L MAP	1748
HAMMON, T / INITIALS T.H.	1871	BRKE MAP	1736
HAMMON, T / RES	1871	BRKE MAP	1736
HAMMOND, C	1823	PLAINTIFF	1638
HAMMOND, J	1871	MARH'L MAP	1749
HAMMOND, JACOB	1871	MARH'L MAP	1748
HAMMOND, LAWSON L	1840	DEFENDANT	1643
HAMMOND, T	1871	BRKE MAP	1736
HAMMOND, T / SMITH SHOP	1871	BRKE MAP	1736
HAMMOND, TALBOT / ESQ - MAP#168	1852	BRKE MAP	1842
HAMMOND, W	1871	MDSVILLE	1807
HAMMOND, WILLIAM K	1842	DEFENDANT	1652
HAMON, JOSEPH	1819	MISC	1591
HAMPSON, JAMES B	1837	DEFENDANT	1651
HANCER, JOSEPH / ?	1871	HAN MAP	1731
HANCOCK CO	1871	POPULATION	1816
HANCOCK CO - BUSINESS NOTICES	1871	HAN BUS	1762
HANCOCK CO - ON PANHANDLE MAP	1871	MAP	1713
HANCOCK CO - S. BOUNDARY WITH BROOKE CO	1852	BRKE MAP	1853
HANCOCK CO - S. BOUNDARY WITH BROOKE CO	1852	BRKE MAP	1854
HANCOCK CO - TOWNSHIPS	1871	MAP	1718
HANCOCK CO LINE	1871	HAN MAP	1733
HANCOCK CO. - RIVER ROAD N. OF NEW CUMBERLAND	1871	RIV. RD N.OF N.C.	1770
HANCOCK COURIER - NEWSPAPER - NEW MANCHESTER	1871	NEW MANCH.	1763
HAND, J	1871	MARH'L MAP	1746
HAND, J	1871	MARH'L MAP	1747
HAND, J / INITIALS J H	1871	MARH'L MAP	1747
HAND, SAMUEL	1796	DEFENDANT	1665
HAND, SAMUEL	1797	DEFENDANT	1610
HAND, SAMUEL	1800	DEFENDANT	1665
HAND, SAMUEL	1803	DEFENDANT	1666
HAND, SAMUEL	1803	DEFENDANT	1666
HAND, T	1871	MARH'L MAP	1746
HAND, WILLIAM	1871	OH CO. MAP	1743
HAND, WILLIAM	1871	MARH'L MAP	1746
HANDEL, J	1871	LAGRANGE	1792
HANDEL, J	1871	LAGRANGE	1794
HANES, JACOB	1817	DEFENDANT	1611
HANES, JACOB	1817	DEFENDANT	1632
HANES, WILLIAM C	1862	DEFENDANT	1615
HANEY, H	1871	WELLSBURG	1777
HANEY, J	1871	WELLSBURG	1776
HANEY, M	1871	NEW CUMB'LD	1768
HANEY, M	1871	WELLSBURG	1777
HANK SPRING RUN	1871	BRKE MAP	1735
HANK SPRING RUN	1871	BRKE MAP	1736
HANKE, DANIEL	1838	MISC	1678
HANKS RUN	1852	BRKE MAP	1846
HANLY, JOHN	1778	DEFENDANT	1576
HANNA & CLEMENS	1878	DEFENDANT	1568
HANNA, A / MRS	1871	OH CO. MAP	1740
HANNA, THOMSON / & CO. - MAP#596	1852	BRKE MAP	1851
HANNA, THOMSON / & CO. - MAP#598	1852	BRKE MAP	1851
HANNA, THOMSON / & CO. - MAP#599	1852	BRKE MAP	1851
HANNA, THOMSON / & CO. / (PAPER MILL) - MAP#600	1852	BRKE MAP	1851
HANNA, THOMSON / & CO. / (PAPER MILL) - MAP#601	1852	BRKE MAP	1851

ENTRY	YEAR	SUBJECT	PAGE
HANNAH, WILLIAM	1800	DEFENDANT	1626
HANNAH, WILLIAM	1811	DEFENDANT	1645
HANNAN, J	1871	MARH'L MAP	1760
HANNEL, J	1871	MARH'L MAP	1745
HANNLEIN, - / SCHUCHMAN & HANNLEIN - PITTSBURG, PA / MAP LITHOGR.	1852	BRKE MAP	1838
HANON, NATHANIEL / MURDERED MELISSA MORRIS - JULY 25TH, 1859 (?HANON NAME UNCLEAR - OTHER OPTIONS LISTED?)	1871	MARH'L MAP	1750
HANSON, -	1871	MDSVILLE	1809
HANSON, NATHANIEL / MURDERED MELISSA MORRIS - JULY 25TH, 1859 (?HANSON NAME UNCLEAR - OTHER OPTIONS LISTED?)	1871	MARH'L MAP	1750
HANTHORN, JOHN	1790	DEFENDANT	1577
HAPPY HOME	1871	MARH'L MAP	1756
HARBINGER OFFICE / W.K.PENDLETON - BETHANY COLLEGE	1871	BETHANY	1773
HARD SCRABBLE - OLD NAME FOR WEST ALEXANDER, PA.	1916	NAT'L ROAD	1862
HARDCASTLE, ROBERT	1813	DEFENDANT	1667
HARDESTY, J R L	1875	DEFENDANT	1621
HARDESTY, J R L	1880	DEFENDANT	1621
HARDESTY, JESSE	1811	DEFENDANT	1642
HARDESTY, RICHARD	1821	PLAINTIFF	1646
HARDESTY, RICHARD	1822	DEFENDANT	1587
HARDESTY, THOMAS	1827	DEFENDANT	1668
HARDESTY, THOMAS	1829	DEFENDANT	1668
HARDIN, J	1871	WELLSBURG	1777
HARDIN, NATHANIEL / MURDERED MELISSA MORRIS - JULY 25TH, 1859 (?HARDIN NAME UNCLEAR - OTHER OPTIONS LISTED?)	1871	MARH'L MAP	1750
HARDING, J B	1871	WELLSBURG	1777
HARDING, L	1871	BENWOOD	1798
HARDINS RUN / E. SIDE OF MAP	1871	HAN MAP	1730
HARDINS RUN	1871	HAN MAP	1731
HARDINS RUN	1871	NEW CUMB'LD	1768
HARDINS RUN - MOUTH OF AT OHIO RIVER	1871	NEW CUMB'LD	1767
HARDINS RUN - R. PATTERSONS SAW MILL ON	1871	HAN MAP	1731
HARDINS RUN - S. HOBBS SAW MILL & DAM ON	1871	HAN MAP	1731
HARDINS RUN - STEWARTS VINEYARD ON	1871	HAN-CLAY TWP	1763
HARDISTY, FRANCIS	1788	DEFENDANT	1610
HARDMAN, -	1855	DEFENDANT	1621
HARDMAN, -	1861	DEFENDANT	1598
HARDMAN, GEORGE	1856	DEFENDANT	1552
HARDMAN, GEORGE	1856	DEFENDANT	1621
HARDON, BENJAMIN	1799	DEFENDANT	1647
HARDON, NATHANIEL / MURDERED MELISSA MORRIS - JULY 25TH, 1859 (?HARDON NAME UNCLEAR - OTHER OPTIONS LISTED?)	1871	MARH'L MAP	1750
HARDTIMES	1871	MARH'L MAP	1755
HARDTIMES / LYNNCAMP P.O.	1871	MARH'L MAP	1759
HARDY, - / MRS - MARSHALL ST (?OR PURDY?)	1871	MDSVILLE	1808
HARDY, - / MRS - MARSHALL ST (?OR PURDY?)	1871	MDSVILLE	1810
HARDY, W D	1855	DEFENDANT	1596
HARDY, W D	1855	DEFENDANT	1629
HARGEIRMAN, - / ?	1871	OH CO. MAP	1742
HARGRAVE, J L	1856	DEFENDANT	1575
HARGRAVES, J	1871	OH CO. MAP	1742
HARGRAVES, J	1871	WHG CITY	1789
HARKER, - / MISS	1871	WELLSBURG	1777
HARKER, - / MRS	1871	WELLSBURG	1777
HARKER, B / MRS	1871	BRKE MAP	1736
HARKER, EZEKIEL / MAP#344	1852	BRKE MAP	1846
HARKINS, -	1852	DEFENDANT	1600
HARKINS, -	1855	DEFENDANT	1603
HARKINS, ALFRED	1834	DEFENDANT	1568
HARKINS, WILLIAM	1818	DEFENDANT	1642
HARKINS, WILLIAM	1818	DEFENDANT	1660
HARKINS, WILLIAM	1819	DEFENDANT	1660
HARKINS, WILLIAM	1825	DEFENDANT	1613
HARKLESS, -	1871	OH CO. MAP	1741
HARLEY, FRANCIS T	1833	DEFENDANT	1600
HARMAN, - / MRS	1871	TRIAD. BORO.	1784
HARMONS CREE	1871	HAN MAP	1733

'PERSONAL TIME LINE' INDEX TO VOLUME 7 OF THE *OHIO COUNTY INDEX*

ENTRY	YEAR	SUBJECT	PAGE	ENTRY	YEAR	SUBJECT	PAGE
HARMONS CREEK	1852	BRKE MAP	1851	HARRISON, WILLIAM	1788	DEFENDANT	1571
HARMONS CREEK	1852	BRKE MAP	1852	HARRISS, W	1871	MARH'L MAP	1754
HARMONS CREEK	1871	BRKE MAP	1734	HARRISS, W	1871	MARH'L MAP	1758
HARMONS CREEK	1871	BRKE MAP	1734	HARSH, H	1871	MARH'L MAP	1747
HARMONS CREEK	1871	EDGINGTON STA.	1774	HARSH, H	1871	MARH'L MAP	1750
HARMONS CREEK - ANDREW HINDMAN - BLACKSMITH ON	1871	CROSS CRK.BUS.	1772	HARSH, J	1871	MARH'L MAP	1747
				HARSH, J	1871	MARH'L MAP	1750
HARMONS CREEK - HUGH P RYLANDS SAW & GRIST MILL ON	1871	CROSS CRK.BUS.	1772	HARSH, W	1871	MARH'L MAP	1747
				HARSH, W	1871	MARH'L MAP	1750
HARMONS CREEK - MOUTH OF - IRON BRIDGE OVER OHIO RIVER	1871	EDGINGTON STA.	1774	HART, CHARLES / MAP LITHOGRAPHER - NYC	1871	MAP	1713
	1871	HAN MAP	1731	HART, H D	1838	DEFENDANT	1589
HARPER, J	1787	DEFENDANT	1637	HART, J / E. SIDE OF MAP	1871	HAN MAP	1730
HARPER, JAMES	1871	NEW CUMB'LD	1767	HARTEIL, J	1871	OH CO. MAP	1741
HARPER, R	1871	NEW CUMB'LD	1767	HARTLEIL, J	1871	OH CO. MAP	1742
HARPER, R	1833	DEFENDANT	1573	HARTLEY, D	1871	W.UNION	1812
HARPER, SAMUEL D	1833	DEFENDANT	1575	HARTLEY, WILLIAM	1871	MARH'L MAP	1752
HARPER, SAMUEL D	1871	NEW CUMB'LD	1768	HARTLY, W	1871	MARH'L MAP	1750
HARPER, WILLIAM	1916	NAT'L ROAD	1863	HARTS RUN	1871	MARH'L MAP	1757
HARPERS FERRY, WV	1852	BRKE MAP	1849	HARTS RUN	1871	MARH'L MAP	1761
HARRIS RUN	1871	MARH'L MAP	1752	HARVEY & MANSER / PAPER MILL	1871	WELLSBURG	1776
HARRIS, - / MRS	1871	MARH'L MAP	1749	HARVEY & MANSER / INITIALS H.&M.	1871	WELLSBURG	1777
HARRIS, A	1871	MARH'L MAP	1756	HARVEY & MANSER / INITIALS H.&M.	1871	WELLSBURG	1777
HARRIS, A	1871	CAMERON	1803	HARVEY & MANSER / PAPER MILL	1871	WELLSBURG	1777
HARRIS, A	1871	MARH'L MAP	1752	HARVEY, DAVID	1852	NOT ON MAP	1836
HARRIS, B	1871	MARH'L MAP	1752	HARVEY, DAVID / REV. - MAP#314	1852	BRKE MAP	1847
HARRIS, B	1871	MARH'L MAP	1757	HARVEY, DAVID W	1835	DEFENDANT	1656
HARRIS, C	1871	MARH'L MAP	1757	HARVEY, JOHN	1840	DEFENDANT	1559
HARRIS, E R	1871	MARH'L MAP	1759	HARVEY, JOHN	1848	DEFENDANT	1670
HARRIS, F	1871	MARH'L MAP	1749	HARVEY, JOSIAH	1849	DEFENDANT	1670
HARRIS, G	1871	MARH'L MAP	1752	HARVEY, T L	1871	OH CO. MAP	1740
HARRIS, G	1871	MARH'L MAP	1752	HARVEY, T L	1871	OH CO. MAP	1740
HARRIS, G	1855	DEFENDANT	1636	HARVEY, W H	1871	WELLSBURG	1776
HARRIS, HENRY	1871	MARH'L MAP	1748	HARVEY, W K	1871	WELLSBURG	1776
HARRIS, J	1871	MARH'L MAP	1748	HARVEY, WILLIAM	1853	DEFENDANT	1663
HARRIS, J	1871	MARH'L MAP	1757	HASKINS, ALFRED	1835	DEFENDANT	1618
HARRIS, J / EST.	1871	GLEN EASTON - BUS.	1796	HASLET, JOHN	1816	MISC	1685
HARRIS, J M / FLOURING MILL				HASSNER, C W	1871	WLSBRG BUS.	1772
HARRIS, J M	1871	GLEN EASTON	1801	HASSNER, C W / CIGAR FACTORY (OC.)	1871	WELLSBURG	1777
HARRIS, JAMES	1789	DEFENDANT	1644	HASTINGS, MARGARET	1851	MISC	1688
HARRIS, JOHN	1787	DEFENDANT	1644	HASTINGS, WILLIAM	1858	DEFENDANT	1653
HARRIS, JOSEPH / NURSERYMAN - (?BLURRED - LOOKS LIKE DARRIS?)	1871	MDSVL BUS.	1796	HAUNTED HOUSE - ROBERT SCOTT / HEIRS - MAP#365	1852	BRKE MAP	1847
HARRIS, JOSEPH	1871	MDSVILLE	1806	HAWKINS, J	1871	MARH'L MAP	1755
HARRIS, JOSEPH	1871	MDSVILLE	1806	HAWKINS, JOSIAH H	1838	DEFENDANT	1558
HARRIS, JOSEPH / INITIALS J.H.	1871	MDSVILLE	1806	HAWKINS, JOSIAH H	1838	DEFENDANT	1623
HARRIS, JOSEPH / NURSERY GROUNDS	1871	MDSVILLE	1806	HAWLEY, -	1871	WELLSBURG	1777
HARRIS, JOSEPH / RES	1871	MDSVILLE	1806	HAWLEY, J L	1879	DEFENDANT	1575
HARRIS, JOSEPH / INITIALS J.H.	1871	MDSVILLE	1807	HAWXHURST, H / HARNESS SHOP	1871	ELM GROVE	1782
HARRIS, JOSEPH / INITIALS J.H.	1871	MDSVILLE	1807	HAYDEN, MILES	1784	APPENDIX	1874
HARRIS, JOSEPH / INITIALS J.H.	1871	MDSVILLE	1807	HAYDEN, WILLIAM	1838	DEFENDANT	1567
HARRIS, JOSEPH / INITIALS J.H.	1871	MDSVILLE	1807	HAYMOUNDS, J G	1871	OH CO. MAP	1742
HARRIS, JOSEPH / INITIALS J.H.	1871	MDSVILLE	1808	HAYNES, -	1839	DEFENDANT	1585
HARRIS, LAZARUS	1807	DEFENDANT	1554	HAYNES, J / E. SIDE OF MAP	1871	MARH'L MAP	1749
HARRIS, LAZERUS	1809	DEFENDANT	1554	HAYNES, J	1871	MARH'L MAP	1752
HARRIS, MATHIAS / HEIRS. - MAP#443	1852	BRKE MAP	1849	HAYS RUN	1852	BRKE MAP	1854
HARRIS, MOSES	1823	MISC	1678	HAYS, E	1871	BRKE MAP	1735
HARRIS, MOSES	1827	MISC	1678	HAYS, ENOCH / MAP#503	1852	BRKE MAP	1850
HARRIS, NEHEMIAH T	1855	DEFENDANT	1588	HAYS, HILLERY	1817	MISC	1678
HARRIS, NEHEMIAH T	1862	DEFENDANT	1625	HAYS, J L	1871	OH CO. MAP	1742
HARRIS, NOAH T	1856	DEFENDANT	1584	HAYS, JOHN	1787	DEFENDANT	1606
HARRIS, NOAH T	1856	DEFENDANT	1603	HAYS, NOLLEY	1799	DEFENDANT	1634
HARRIS, REUBEN	1802	DEFENDANT	1607	HAYS, REUBEN	1810	DEFENDANT	1667
HARRIS, S	1871	MARH'L MAP	1756	HAYS, WILLIAM B	1795	DEFENDANT	1596
HARRIS, SAMUEL	1799	DEFENDANT	1576	HAZELDELL SCHOOL NO. 5	1871	MARH'L MAP	1750
HARRIS, SAMUEL	1799	DEFENDANT	1607	HAZLETT & FORD	1879	DEFENDANT	1584
HARRIS, SAMUEL	1800	DEFENDANT	1665	HAZLETT, ISAAC	1859	DEFENDANT	1582
HARRIS, U	1871	MARH'L MAP	1752	HAZLETT, JOHN	1858	DEFENDANT	1570
HARRIS, W	1871	MARH'L MAP	1750	HAZLETTS, JOHN	1858	DEFENDANT	1570
HARRIS, WILLIAM	1830	PLAINTIFF	1573	HEAD, JOHN	1797	PLAINTIFF	1600
HARRISBURG, PA	1852	HEMP. RR MAP	1825	HEADINGTON, ELIZABETH / MRS / MAP#527	1852	BRKE MAP	1852
HARRISBURG, PA	1852	HEMP. RR MAP	1827				
HARRISES RUN	1871	BKE/OH MAP	1738	HEADINGTON, G	1871	BRKE MAP	1735
HARRISES RUN	1871	OH CO. MAP	1741	HEADINGTON, GREENBR'Y / MAP#486	1852	BRKE MAP	1849
HARRISON RUN	1852	BRKE MAP	1842	HEADINGTON, J / EST	1871	BRKE MAP	1735
HARRISON, GEORGE	1835	DEFENDANT	1628	HEADINGTON, JOHN / MAP#430	1852	BRKE MAP	1850
HARRISON, GEORGE	1835	DEFENDANT	1669	HEADLEY, P	1871	NEW CUMB'LD	1766
HARRISON, GEORGE	1840	DEFENDANT	1582	HEADLEY, P G	1871	NEW CUMB'LD	1767
HARRISON, GEORGE	1840	DEFENDANT	1643	HEADLEY, P G	1871	NEW CUMB'LD	1767
HARRISON, JAMES	1792	DEFENDANT	1571	HEADLEY, P G / INITIALS P.G.H.	1871	NEW CUMB'LD	1767
HARRISON, M	1871	MARH'L MAP	1754	HEADY, -	1857	PLAINTIFF	1630
HARRISON, ROBERT	1784	DEFENDANT	1556	HEALY, JOHN	1871	BENWO'D - BUS.	1795
HARRISON, ROBERT	1787	DEFENDANT	1571	HEALY, JOHN / INITIAL J.	1871	BENWOOD	1799
HARRISON, RUSSEL	1813	DEFENDANT	1642	HEALY, JOHN / INITIAL J.	1871	BENWOOD	1799
HARRISON, WILLIAM	1778	APPENDIX	1874	HEBEAU, - / MRS	1871	WELLSBURG	1777

XLV

'PERSONAL TIME LINE' INDEX TO VOLUME 7 OF THE OHIO COUNTY INDEX

ENTRY	YEAR	SUBJECT	PAGE
HEBIN, HENRY	1832	DEFENDANT	1639
HEBRUCKLE, A / BREWERY	1871	WELLSBURG	1778
HECTOR, GILBERT	1800	DEFENDANT	1553
HEDGE, - / MRS	1871	BRKE MAP	1736
HEDGE, - / MRS	1871	W.LIBERTY	1780
HEDGE, D / MRS	1871	W.LIBERTY	1780
HEDGE, J C	1871	W.LIBERTY	1780
HEDGE, L / MRS	1871	BRKE MAP	1736
HEDGE, SAMUEL	1871	W.LIBERTY	1780
HEDGES RUN	1852	BRKE MAP	1843
HEDGES, - / SCHOOL - MAP#36	1852	BRKE MAP	1840
HEDGES, A	1871	BKE/OH MAP	1739
HEDGES, A / INITIALS A.H.	1871	BKE/OH MAP	1739
HEDGES, AARON	1803	DEFENDANT	1589
HEDGES, AARON	1803	DEFENDANT	1644
HEDGES, BURTON	1875	DEFENDANT	1604
HEDGES, C B / INITIALS C.B.H.	1871	BKE/OH MAP	1738
HEDGES, C B	1871	BKE/OH MAP	1739
HEDGES, C B / INITIALS C.B.H.	1871	BKE/OH MAP	1739
HEDGES, HIRAM	1807	MISC	1684
HEDGES, JOHN	1828	DEFENDANT	1602
HEDGES, JOHN	1830	DEFENDANT	1602
HEDGES, JOHN	1840	DEFENDANT	1629
HEDGES, MOSES / (SMITHSHOP) - MAP#57	1852	BRKE MAP	1840
HEDGES, MOSES / (SMITHSHOP) - MAP#58	1852	BRKE MAP	1840
HEDGES, MOSES / MAP#37	1852	BRKE MAP	1840
HEDGES, MOSES / MAP#54	1852	BRKE MAP	1840
HEDGES, MOSES / (SMITHSHOP) - MAP#117	1852	BRKE MAP	1844
HEDGES, O	1871	BKE/OH MAP	1739
HEDGES, OTHO / ESQ. / MAP#27	1852	BRKE MAP	1840
HEDGES, OTHO / ESQ. - MAP#26	1852	BRKE MAP	1840
HEDGES, OTHO JR. / MAP#28	1852	BRKE MAP	1840
HEDGES, REUBEN F	1830	DEFENDANT	1583
HEDGES, REUBEN F	1861	DEFENDANT	1604
HEDGES, S	1871	BKE/OH MAP	1739
HEDGES, SAMUEL / MAP#161	1852	BRKE MAP	1842
HEDGES, SAMUEL / MAP#162	1852	BRKE MAP	1842
HEDGES, SAMUEL / MAP#163	1852	BRKE MAP	1842
HEDGES, SILAS	1778	APPENDIX	1874
HEDGES, SILAS	1778	APPENDIX	1874
HEDGES, SILAS	1783	APPENDIX	1874
HEDGES, SILAS	1795	MISC	1691
HEDGES, SILAS	1798	DEFENDANT	1572
HEGNER, FRANZ	1855	DEFENDANT	1567
HEGNER, FRANZ	1857	DEFENDANT	1630
HEIFENBINE, W	1871	OH CO. MAP	1743
HEIFENBINE, W	1871	OH CO. MAP	1744
HEIM, H	1871	RITCHIE TWP	1793
HEIMBERGER, A / "VIRGINIA HOUSE" HOTEL - RONEY POINT	1871	OH CO.BUS.	1779
HEIMBERGER, A	1871	RONEY PT.	1783
HEIMBERTER, V	1871	RONEY PT.	1783
HEIMER, H	1871	TRIAD.BORO.	1784
HEINBERGER, A	1871	OH CO. MAP	1743
HEINBERGER, A	1871	OH CO. MAP	1744
HEINBERGER, V	1871	OH CO. MAP	1743
HEINBERGER, V	1871	OH CO. MAP	1744
HEINDMARSH, JOHN	1860	DEFENDANT	1588
HEINE, H	1871	OH CO. MAP	1742
HEINSTEIN, PHILIP	1875	MISC	1687
HEISKELL & SWEARINGEN	1861	DEFENDANT	1621
HEITH, HENRY / (?KEITH?)	1784	APPENDIX	1874
HELFENBINE, - / MRS	1871	OH CO. MAP	1743
HELFENBINE, H	1871	ELM GROVE	1782
HELFENBINE, J	1871	TRIAD.BORO.	1784
HELFENBINE, W / "PLEASANT SIDE"	1871	RONEY PT.	1783
HELLEBRAND, HENRY	1877	DEFENDANT	1564
HELLING, HENRY	1874	DEFENDANT	1557
HELLSTERN, M	1871	OH CO. MAP	1742
HELLSTERN, M	1871	RITCHIE TWP	1793
HELLSTERN, M	1871	RITCHIE TWP	1794
HELM, -	1834	DEFENDANT	1650
HELM, HENRY	1840	DEFENDANT	1575
HELM, HENRY	1840	DEFENDANT	1619
HELM, HENRY	1841	DEFENDANT	1672
HELMS, A	1871	ROSBBYS RK	1813
HELMS, LEWIS	1816	DEFENDANT	1656
HELMS, LEWIS	1817	DEFENDANT	1656
HELMS, M B	1871	ROSBBYS RK	1813
HELSTEIN, J	1871	BRKE MAP	1736
HELVEY, H	1871	TRIAD.BORO.	1784
HELWEIG, C	1871	OH CO. MAP	1742
HELWEIG, C	1871	OH CO. MAP	1744

ENTRY	YEAR	SUBJECT	PAGE
HEMPFIELD AND MARIETTA ROADS / RR	1852	HEMPFIELD RR	1821
HEMPFIELD RR CO / MAP & BOND PROSPECTUS	1852	HEMPFIELD RR	1817
HEMPFIELD RR CO / OFFICERS & DIRECTORS	1852	HEMPFIELD RR	1817
HEMPFIELD RR CO	1852	HEMPFIELD RR	1818
HEMPFIELD RR CO / CAPITAL STOCK	1852	HEMPFIELD RR	1822
HEMPFIELD RR CO	1852	HEMPFIELD RR	1824
HEMPFIELD RR CO	1852	HEMP. RR MAP	1825
HEMPFIELD RR CO	1852	HEMP. RR MAP	1826
HEMPFIELD RR CO / CONNECTING ROUTES & RIVALS TO PHILADELPHIA	1852	HEMP. RR MAP	1827
HEMPFIELD RR CO / ABBREV. H.R.R.CO.	1871	OH CO. MAP	1740
HEMPFIELD RR CO	1871	OH CO. MAP	1743
HEMPFIELD RR CO / BLDG RONEY POINT STATION -INITIALS H.R.R.CO.	1871	OH CO. MAP	1743
HEMPFIELD RR CO / BUIILDING N. OF POINT MILL STATION	1871	OH CO. MAP	1743
HEMPFIELD RR CO / INITIALS H.R.R.CO.	1871	OH CO. MAP	1743
HEMPFIELD RR CO	1871	OH CO. MAP	1744
HEMPFIELD RR CO / BLDG AT RONEY POINT STATION	1871	OH CO. MAP	1744
HEMPFIELD RR CO / BLDG AT RONEY POINT STATION	1871	OH CO. MAP	1744
HEMPFIELD RR CO / BLDG AT RONEY POINT STATION	1871	OH CO. MAP	1744
HEMPFIELD RR CO / AT LEATHERWOOD	1871	TRIAD.TWP.	1781
HEMPFIELD RR CO / AT ELM GROVE	1871	ELM GROVE	1782
HEMPFIELD RR CO / PROPERTY	1871	ELM GROVE	1782
HEMPFIELD RR CO / AT RONEY POINT	1871	RONEY PT.	1783
HEMPFIELD RR CO / AT TRIADELPHIA	1871	TRIAD.BORO.	1784
HEMPFIELD RR CO / STATION - TRIADELPHIA	1871	TRIAD.BORO.	1784
HEMPFIELD RR CO / AT PENINSULA	1871	WHG CITY	1787
HEMPFIELD RR CO / BUILDING - FULTON ST - WHEELING	1871	WHG CITY	1788
HEMPFIELD RR CO / AT LEATHERWOOD	1871	WHG CITY	1789
HEMPFIELD RR CO / COAL SHOOT NEAR - LEATHERWOOD	1871	WHG CITY	1789
HEMPFIELD RR CO / ENGINE HOUSE - WHEELING	1871	WHG CITY	1789
HEMPFIELD RR CO / TUNNEL - WHEELING	1871	WHG CITY	1789
HEMPHILL, JOSEPH	1841	DEFENDANT	1629
HEMPHILL, WALLACE	1840	DEFENDANT	1577
HEMPHILL, WALLACE	1840	DEFENDANT	1617
HEMPHILL, WALLACE	1840	DEFENDANT	1652
HENDEERSON, J P	1871	OH CO.BUS.	1779
HENDERSHOT, JOHN S	1830	DEFENDANT	1618
HENDERSHOT, JOHN S	1830	DEFENDANT	1656
HENDERSON, - / MRS	1871	OH CO. MAP	1743
HENDERSON, - / MRS	1871	OH CO. MAP	1743
HENDERSON, - / MRS	1871	OH CO. MAP	1744
HENDERSON, - / MRS	1871	OH CO. MAP	1744
HENDERSON, ARTHUR / HEIRS - MAP#118	1852	BRKE MAP	1844
HENDERSON, ARTHUR / HEIRS - MAP#119	1852	BRKE MAP	1844
HENDERSON, DUNKER	1816	DEFENDANT	1583
HENDERSON, DUNKIN	1817	DEFENDANT	1583
HENDERSON, F M	1871	OH CO. MAP	1743
HENDERSON, J	1871	MARH'L MAP	1754
HENDERSON, J J	1871	W.UNION	1812
HENDERSON, J J	1871	HAN MAP	1733
HENDERSON, J P / (O.C.)	1871	TRIAD.BORO.	1784
HENDERSON, J P / (O.C.)	1871	TRIAD.BORO.	1784
HENDERSON, JOSEPH	1852	HEMPFIELD RR	1817
HENDERSON, T / INITIALS T.H.	1871	BRKE MAP	1737
HENDERSON, T / INITIALS T.H.	1871	BRKE MAP	1737
HENDERSON, T / INITIALS T.H.	1871	BRKE MAP	1737
HENDERSON, T / RES	1871	BRKE MAP	1737
HENDERSON, T / INITIALS T.H.	1871	BKE/OH MAP	1739
HENDERSON, T / INITIALS T.H.	1871	BKE/OH MAP	1739
HENDERSON, T / INITIALS T.H.	1871	BKE/OH MAP	1739
HENDERSON, T / RES	1871	BKE/OH MAP	1739
HENDERSON, W	1871	OH CO. MAP	1743
HENDON, HEZEKIAH	1857	DEFENDANT	1615
HENDRICKS, JOHN	1827	DEFENDANT	1613
HENDRICKS, JOHN	1829	DEFENDANT	1563
HENDRIX, JACOB / MAP#664	1852	BRKE MAP	1854
HENDRIX, JACOB / MAP#665	1852	BRKE MAP	1854

XLVI

'PERSONAL TIME LINE' INDEX TO VOLUME 7 OF THE **OHIO COUNTY INDEX**

ENTRY	YEAR	SUBJECT	PAGE
HENDRIX, JACOB / MAP#666	1852	BRKE MAP	1854
HENDRIX, JOHN / ESQ - HEIRS- MAP#543	1852	BRKE MAP	1852
HENDRIX, TOBIAS / MAP#520	1852	BRKE MAP	1849
HENDRIXS BRANCH	1852	BRKE MAP	1852
HENDRIXS BRANCH	1852	BRKE MAP	1852
HENET, JOSEPHINE	1843	MISC	1674
HENRY CLAY MONUMENT - ELM GROVE	1916	NAT'L ROAD	1864
HENRY, GEORGE	1804	DEFENDANT	1558
HENRY, GEORGE	1807	DEFENDANT	1585
HENRY, PATRICK / FORT HENRY NAMED FOR	1916	NAT'L ROAD	1867
HENRY, R	1871	MARH'L MAP	1758
HENTHORN, J	1871	MARH'L MAP	1754
HENTHORN, J	1871	MARH'L MAP	1758
HENTHORN, JOHN	1794	DEFENDANT	1637
HENTHORN, JOHN	1803	DEFENDANT	1655
HERON, W	1871	HAN MAP	1731
HERP, J	1871	WELLSBURG	1777
HERRICK, H	1871	BENWOOD	1798
HERRICK, H / INITIALS H.H. - STORE	1871	BENWOOD	1798
HERRINGTON, G	1837	MISC	1683
HERRON SCHOOL	1871	HAN MAP	1731
HERRON, CHARLES / MAP#420	1852	BRKE MAP	1847
HERRON, JOHN	1860	DEFENDANT	1599
HERRON, R	1871	HAN MAP	1731
HERRON, ROBERT	1871	HAN MAP	1731
HERRONS RUN	1871	HAN MAP	1731
HERSEY - CHILDREN	1867	MISC	1699
HERSEY, SAMUEL S	1873	MISC	1699
HERVEY D	1871	BRKE MAP	1737
HERVEY, A E	1871	BRKE MAP	1737
HERVEY, H M	1871	OH CO. MAP	1742
HERVEY, H M	1871	OH CO. MAP	1744
HERVEY, H M / INITIALS H.M.H. - ELM GROVE	1871	ELM GROVE	1782
HERVEY, J C	1871	OH CO. MAP	1743
HERVEY, J C	1878	DEFENDANT	1584
HERVEY, JAMES	1871	OH CO. MAP	1742
HERVEY, JOHN C	1871	OH CO.BUS	1779
HERVEY, T Y	1871	OH CO. MAP	1740
HESLER, M	1871	MARH'L MAP	1746
HESLOP, JOHN	1858	DEFENDANT	1661
HESS - ORPHANS	1870	MISC	1695
HEWITT, J	1871	HAN MAP	1726
HEWITT, J / INITIALS J.H.	1871	HAN MAP	1726
HEWITT, R	1871	HAN MAP	1726
HEWITT, R - HEIRS / RES.	1871	HAN MAP	1726
HEWITT, T J	1871	HAN MAP	1726
HEWITT, T J / INITIALS T.J.H	1871	HAN MAP	1726
HIBBARD, -	1877	PLAINTIFF	1621
HIBBERD, -	1878	PLAINTIFF	1621
HICKMAN RUN	1871	MARH'L MAP	1761
HICKMAN, JOHN	1804	DEFENDANT	1666
HICKMAN, JOHN	1805	DEFENDANT	1666
HICKMAN, JOHN	1807	DEFENDANT	1666
HICKS, - / WOODBURN & HICKS / STORE	1871	CAMERON	1803
HICKS, E / MRS	1871	MARH'L MAP	1753
HICKS, G	1871	MARH'L MAP	1753
HICKS, H	1871	MARH'L MAP	1757
HICKS, H	1871	MARH'L MAP	1757
HICKS, J B	1871	CAMERON	1802
HICKS, J B	1871	CAMERON	1803
HICKS, J P C / EST.	1871	MARH'L MAP	1757
HICKS, JOHN	1820	DEFENDANT	1604
HICKS, L / MRS	1871	CAMERON	1804
HICKS, R	1871	MARH'L MAP	1753
HICKS, R	1871	MARH'L MAP	1757
HICKS, W B	1871	CAMERON	1803
HIDER, JOHN P	1817	DEFENDANT	1559
HIDINGER, J	1871	LAGRANGE	1792
HIDINGER, J	1871	LAGRANGE	1794
HIER, F / TRIADELPHIA HOUSE - HOTEL	1871	TRIAD. BORO.	1784
HIER, F / TRIADELPHIA HOUSE - HOTEL	1871	TRIAD. BORO.	1784
HIGGENS, R	1871	BENWOOD	1798
HIGGINS VS POLLOCK	1797	MISC	1701
HIGGINS, CRAWFORD & CO. / PROBABLY J.W.HIGGINS & W.P.CRAWFORD	1871	MARH'L MAP	1760
HIGGINS, J W	1871	MARH'L MAP	1760
HIGGINS, J W / PROBABLE OWNER OF - HIGGINS, CRAWFORD & CO. STORE	1871	MARH'L MAP	1760

ENTRY	YEAR	SUBJECT	PAGE
HIGGINS, JAMES	1829	DEFENDANT	1591
HIGGINS, JOHN W / INITIALS J.W.H.	1871	MARH'L MAP	1760
HIGGINS, JOHN W / RES	1871	MARH'L MAP	1760
HIGGINS, JOHN W / STEAM GRIST & SAW MILL	1871	LIB.TWP-BUS.	1797
HIGGINS, SARAH	1877	DEFENDANT	1621
HIGGINS, SARAH	1877	DEFENDANT	1641
HIGGINSBOTTOM, - / MRS	1871	NEW CUMB'LD	1767
HIGGS, - / MRS	1871	MARH'L MAP	1748
HIGGS, - / MRS	1871	MDSVILLE	1810
HIGGS, J	1871	MARH'L MAP	1754
HIGGS, J	1871	MARH'L MAP	1754
HIGGS, J	1871	MARH'L MAP	1754
HIGGS, JER.	1871	MARH'L MAP	1754
HIGGS, S	1871	MARH'L MAP	1754
HIGHLAND DIST SCHOOL NO. / NO # SHOWN	1871	OH CO. MAP	1741
HIGHLAND HOME	1871	HAN MAP	1732
HIGHLAND HOME	1871	OH CO. MAP	1742
HIGHLAND RUN / SE CORNER OF MAP	1871	BRKE MAP	1736
HIGHLAND RUN	1871	BKE/OH MAP	1739
HILDRAITH, EZEKIEL	1821	DEFENDANT	1672
HILDRAITH, EZEKIEL	1824	MISC	1710
HILL & BELL	1854	DEFENDANT	1629
HILL & BELL	1856	DEFENDANT	1630
HILL & BELL	1857	DEFENDANT	1630
HILL & BELL	1858	DEFENDANT	1630
HILL & BELL	1860	DEFENDANT	1631
HILL & BELL	1862	DEFENDANT	1631
HILL ROAD	1871	OH CO. MAP	1741
HILL, - / MRS	1871	MARH'L MAP	1745
HILL, - / MRS	1871	LAGRANGE	1794
HILL, I	1871	MARH'L MAP	1761
HILL, I	1871	MARH'L MAP	1761
HILL, J / MRS - RES AND GROCERY	1871	BKE/OH MAP	1739
HILL, J	1871	MARH'L MAP	1749
HILL, J A H	1871	MARH'L MAP	1752
HILL, J B	1871	MARH'L MAP	1749
HILL, J B	1871	MARH'L MAP	1749
HILL, RETURN	1850	DEFENDANT	1620
HILL, RETURN W	1853	DEFENDANT	1588
HILL, RETURN W	1853	DEFENDANT	1626
HILL, S A	1871	MARH'L MAP	1749
HILL, S A	1871	MARH'L MAP	1752
HILLSBORO	1852	HEMP. RR MAP	1825
HINCEROTH, H	1871	MARH'L MAP	1752
HINCEROTH, H	1871	MARH'L MAP	1755
HINCEROTH, W	1871	MARH'L MAP	1752
HINCEROTH, W	1871	MARH'L MAP	1755
HINDEMAN, JOHN JR / INITIALS J.H.JR	1871	BRKE MAP	1734
HINDMAN & BROS	1871	BRKE MAP	1737
HINDMAN, - / MRS	1871	HAN MAP	1732
HINDMAN, - / MRS	1871	BRKE MAP	1734
HINDMAN, A	1871	HAN MAP	1732
HINDMAN, A F	1871	HAN MAP	1732
HINDMAN, ANDREW	1871	BRKE MAP	1734
HINDMAN, ANDREW / INITIALS A.H. - PANHANDLE P.O.	1871	BRKE MAP	1734
HINDMAN, ANDREW / BLACKSMITH - HARMONS CREEK	1871	CROSS CRK.BUS.	1772
HINDMAN, F	1871	BRKE MAP	1737
HINDMAN, GEORGE	1871	HAN MAP	1732
HINDMAN, J	1871	HAN MAP	1733
HINDMAN, J	1871	BRKE MAP	1734
HINDMAN, J	1871	BRKE MAP	1734
HINDMAN, JAMES / HEIRS - MAP#565	1852	BRKE MAP	1852
HINDMAN, JAMES / MAP#661	1852	BRKE MAP	1854
HINDMAN, JOHN / (MILL) - MAP#656	1852	BRKE MAP	1854
HINDMAN, JOHN / MAP#655	1852	BRKE MAP	1854
HINDMAN, JOSEPH JR / RES	1871	BRKE MAP	1734
HINDMAN, S	1871	HAN MAP	1732
HINDMAN, S / GRIST MILL	1871	HAN MAP	1732
HINDMAN, S	1871	HAN MAP	1733
HINDMAN, S	1871	BRKE MAP	1734
HINDMAN, S	1871	BRKE MAP	1734
HINDMAN, S / GRIST MILL	1871	BRKE MAP	1734
HINDMAN, S B	1871	BRKE MAP	1735
HINDMAN, SAMUEL	1852	NOT ON MAP	1836
HINDMAN, SAMUEL / MAP#530	1852	BRKE MAP	1850
HINDMAN, SAMUEL / MAP#671	1852	BRKE MAP	1852
HINDMAN, SAMUEL / MAP#657	1852	BRKE MAP	1854
HINDMAN, SAMUEL / MAP#671	1852	BRKE MAP	1854
HINDMAN, SAMUEL JR. / MAP#501	1852	BRKE MAP	1850
HINDMAN, W & SAM'L - MAP#563	1852	BRKE MAP	1852
HINDMAN, W	1871	BRKE MAP	1734
HINDMAN, WILLIAM / MAP#529	1852	BRKE MAP	1850

XLVII

'PERSONAL TIME LINE' INDEX TO VOLUME 7 OF THE OHIO COUNTY INDEX

ENTRY	YEAR	SUBJECT	PAGE
HINDMANS RUN	1852	BRKE MAP	1854
HINDMANS RUN	1871	BRKE MAP	1734
HINDMANS, S / INITIALS S.H.	1871	BRKE MAP	1734
HINE, A / MRS	1871	OH CO. MAP	1741
HINERMAN, -	1871	MARH'L MAP	1757
HINGMAN, E / MIDDLE INITIAL ILLEGIBLE	1871	BRKE MAP	1734
HINKSON, H	1871	BRKE MAP	1737
HINKSON, J / (SAWMILL)	1852	NOT ON MAP	1836
HINKSON, J / (SAWMILL)	1852	NOT ON MAP	1836
HINKSON, JOHN / MAP#313	1852	BRKE MAP	1847
HINKSON, W	1871	BRKE MAP	1735
HINKSON, W T / (C. SHOP)	1852	NOT ON MAP	1836
HINKSON, W T / (C. SHOP)	1852	NOT ON MAP	1836
HINKSON, W T	1871	BRKE MAP	1737
HINKSON, W T / INITIALS W.T.H.	1871	BRKE MAP	1737
HINKSON, WILLIAM T / MAP#358	1852	BRKE MAP	1847
HINKSON, WILLIAM T / MAP#359	1852	BRKE MAP	1847
HINKSTON, W T	1871	BRKE MAP	1737
HINKSTON, W T / INITIALS W.T.H.	1871	BRKE MAP	1737
HINTER, J	1871	BRKE MAP	1734
HINTS FOR INTERPRETING 'MISC.' ENTRIES	2000	APPENDIX	1875
HIRTON, J H / ?	1871	MARH'L MAP	1754
HISEY, JOHN	1813	DEFENDANT	1658
HISHER, H	1871	BRKE MAP	1737
HOAGLANDS RUN	1852	BRKE MAP	1840
HOBBS & BARNES	1862	DEFENDANT	1673
HOBBS, -	1850	PLAINTIFF	1620
HOBBS, C R S	1871	HAN MAP	1730
HOBBS, EDMUND	1856	DEFENDANT	1552
HOBBS, EDMUND	1856	DEFENDANT	1621
HOBBS, G H	1871	HAN MAP	1731
HOBBS, H	1871	HAN MAP	1730
HOBBS, H	1871	NEW CUMB'LD	1767
HOBBS, I. / MRS	1871	HAN MAP	1731
HOBBS, J H	1875	MISC	1685
HOBBS, J R	1871	HAN MAP	1731
HOBBS, J W / & CO	1871	NEW MANCH.	1763
HOBBS, J W	1871	NEW MANCH.	1769
HOBBS, J W / UNKNOWN INITIALS - NEW MANCHESTER (?P=H?)	1871	NEW MANCH.	1769
HOBBS, J W / INITIALS J.W.H.	1871	NEW MANCH.	1769
HOBBS, J W / STORE	1871	NEW MANCH.	1769
HOBBS, L	1871	NEW MANCH.	1769
HOBBS, M / MRS	1871	WELLSBURG	1777
HOBBS, S / HEIRS	1871	NEW CUMB'LD	1768
HOBBS, S / HEIRS - INITIALS S.H.HRS.	1871	NEW CUMB'LD	1768
HOBBS, S - SAW MILL & DAM ON HARDINS RUN	1871	HAN MAP	1731
HOBBS, S - SAW MILL & DAM ON HARDINS RUN	1871	HAN MAP	1731
HOBTITZELL, DENNIS	1839	DEFENDANT	1587
HOCKSHURST, W / ELM GROVE	1871	OH CO. MAP	1742
HODGE, WILLIAM	1841	DEFENDANT	1617
HOFF, CHARLES L	1840	DEFENDANT	1576
HOFF, CHARLES L	1840	DEFENDANT	1626
HOFFMAN, -	1853	DEFENDANT	1641
HOFFMAN, -	1871	MARH'L MAP	1745
HOFFMAN, LIZZIE	1879	MISC	1711
HOG RUN	1871	MARH'L MAP	1751
HOGAN, - / PURDY & HOGAN	1871	MARH'L MAP	1751
HOGAN, - / PURDY & HOGAN	1871	MDSVILLE	1808
HOGAN, - / PURDY & HOGAN	1871	MDSVILLE	1810
HOGAN, J F / RES.	1871	MARH'L MAP	1752
HOGE, W	1871	MARH'L MAP	1757
HOGE, W V	1871	MARH'L MAP	1761
HOGE, W V	1871	MDSVILLE	1806
HOGE, W V	1871	MDSVILLE	1808
HOGE, W Y / AGT (?AGENT?)	1871	MARH'L MAP	1760
HOGG, G	1871	BRKE MAP	1736
HOGG, G	1871	BKE/OH MAP	1738
HOGG, G	1871	BKE/OH MAP	1738
HOGG, G	1871	BKE/OH MAP	1738
HOGG, G	1871	BKE/OH MAP	1738
HOGG, G / INITIALS G.H.	1871	BKE/OH MAP	1738
HOGG, GEORGE	1834	DEFENDANT	1622
HOGG, GEORGE / MAP#74	1852	BRKE MAP	1839
HOGG, GEORGE / MAP#75	1852	BRKE MAP	1839
HOGG, GEORGE / MAP#76	1852	BRKE MAP	1839
HOGG, GEORGE / MAP#98	1852	BRKE MAP	1842
HOGG, THOMAS	1839	DEFENDANT	1656
HOGGS FORK	1852	BRKE MAP	1842
HOLBERTS RUN	1871	HAN MAP	1731
HOLBERTS RUN - J. HOODS SAW MILL ON	1871	HAN MAP	1731
HOLBERTS RUN - MOUTH OF AT OHIO RIVER	1871	FRE'MAN'S LDG	1764
HOLBERTS RUN - NORTH FORK OF	1871	HAN MAP	1731
HOLBERTS RUN - SOUTH FORK OF	1871	HAN MAP	1731
HOLDEN, AMBROS	1879	DEFENDANT	1584
HOLDFAST, DICK	1806	DEFENDANT	1599
HOLIDAY, R C	1871	MDSVILLE	1808
HOLINGSHEAD, E	1871	GLEN EASTON	1801
HOLLAND, S	1871	NEW CUMB'LD	1766
HOLLIDAY, G	1871	W.LIBERTY	1780
HOLLIDAY, JAMES	1846	MISC	1703
HOLLIDAY, WILLIAM	1812	MISC	1709
HOLLIDAY, WILLIAM	1821	DEFENDANT	1628
HOLLIDAYS COVE	1852	BRKE MAP	1853
HOLLIDAYS COVE / MARSHALL CO	1871	DISTANCES	1815
HOLLIDAYS COVE - BUSINESS NOTICES	1871	HO'LIDAYS COVE	1762
HOLLIDAYS COVE - BUTLER TOWNSHIP - HANCOCK CO	1871	HAN MAP	1733
HOLLIDAYS COVE - POST OFFICE	1871	HAN MAP	1733
HOLLIDAYS COVE - WAGON SHOP	1871	HAN MAP	1732
HOLLIDAYS COVE P.O.	1871	HAN MAP	1732
HOLLIDAYS COVE TURNPIKE	1852	BRKE MAP	1851
HOLLIDAYS COVE TURNPIKE	1852	BRKE MAP	1853
HOLLIDAYS COVE TURNPIKE	1852	BRKE MAP	1854
HOLLIDAYS RUN	1871	MARH'L MAP	1746
HOLLIFIELD, WILLIAM	1838	DEFENDANT	1669
HOLLINGSHEAD, A	1871	MARH'L MAP	1751
HOLLINGSHEAD, E	1871	MARH'L MAP	1756
HOLLINGSHEAD, W	1871	MARH'L MAP	1751
HOLLINGSWORTH, JESSE	1796	DEFENDANT	1665
HOLLINGSWORTH, JESSE	1798	DEFENDANT	1665
HOLLINGSWORTH, JOSEPH	1818	DEFENDANT	1649
HOLLISTER, -	1874	DEFENDANT	1621
HOLLOWELL, ALLEN	1859	DEFENDANT	1567
HOLMES RUN	1852	BRKE MAP	1852
HOLMES RUN	1871	BRKE MAP	1734
HOLMES, E E	1871	WELLSBURG	1777
HOLMES, H	1871	MARH'L MAP	1751
HOLMES, H	1871	MARH'L MAP	1751
HOLMES, THOMAS / MAP#626	1852	BRKE MAP	1852
HOLMES, THOMAS / MAP#631	1852	BRKE MAP	1852
HOLMES, THOMAS / MAP#632	1852	BRKE MAP	1852
HOLMS, FELTY	1809	DEFENDANT	1659
HOLMS, VALENTINE	1809	DEFENDANT	1659
HOME FARM / JACKSON TARR	1871	HAN MAP	1732
HOMER / PORT HOMER	1871	HAN MAP	1730
HOMES, J	1871	MARH'L MAP	1755
HOMESTEAD / THE	1871	HAN MAP	1726
HOMESTEAD / THE OLD HOMESTEAD OF 1798	1871	HAN MAP	1732
HOMESTEAD / OLD HOMESTEAD	1871	BRKE MAP	1734
HOMESTEAD / THE HOMESTEAD	1871	OH CO. MAP	1742
HOMESTEAD / SAND HILL TWP	1871	MARH'L MAP	1746
HOMESTEAD - LIBERTY TWP	1871	MARH'L MAP	1756
HOMESTEAD FARM	1871	OH CO. MAP	1743
HOMESTEAD, THE / A.B.MARKS	1871	HAN MAP	1727
HOMESTEAD, THE / A.B.MARKS	1871	HAN MAP	1728
HONEY BEE COTTAGE HOME	1871	MARH'L MAP	1745
HOOD, J	1871	HAN MAP	1731
HOOD, J / SAW MILL ON HOLBERTS RUN	1871	HAN MAP	1731
HOOD, W	1871	MARH'L MAP	1754
HOOD, W / INITIALS W.H.	1871	MARH'L MAP	1754
HOOK, -	1854	PLAINTIFF	1626
HOOK, JAMES	1784	APPENDIX	1874
HOOKER, GEORGE / MAP#533	1852	BRKE MAP	1852
HOOKER, GEORGE / MAP#537	1852	BRKE MAP	1852
HOOKER, GEORGE / LIMESTONE	1871	BRKE MAP	1734
HOOKER, T	1871	HAN MAP	1732
HOOKER, T	1871	HAN MAP	1732
HOOMAN, ROBERT	1859	DEFENDANT	1604
HOOTH, H	1871	MARH'L MAP	1745
HOOTH, H / BLACKSMITH SHOP	1871	SHERRARD	1811
HOOTMAN, CHRISTIAN / MAP#43	1852	BRKE MAP	1841
HOOTMAN, CHRISTIAN / MAP#44	1852	BRKE MAP	1841
HOOTON, J / RES	1871	CAMERON	1803
HOOTON, J E / ATTORNEY	1871	CAMER'N - BUS.	1795
HOOVER, HENRY	1803	DEFENDANT	1607
HOPKINS, MARY	1868	MISC	1695
HOPKINS, R L	1871	OH CO. BUS.	1779
HOPKINS, R S	1871	ELM GROVE	1782
HOPKINS, RICHARD	1834	MISC	1674
HOPKINS, W F	1871	MARH'L MAP	1749
HORAB SCHOOL NO. 2	1871	HAN MAP	1732

'PERSONAL TIME LINE' INDEX TO VOLUME 7 OF THE *OHIO COUNTY INDEX*

ENTRY	YEAR	SUBJECT	PAGE
HORKEIMER, -	1861	DEFENDANT	1626
HORKINSON, ISAAC	1830	MISC	1680
HORN, I	1871	BRKE MAP	1736
HORNBROOK, W P	1871	MARH'L MAP	1754
HORNBROOK BROTHERS	1871	MARH'L MAP	1754
HORNBROOK BROTHERS / TOWN	1871	MARH'L MAP	1754
HORNBROOK BROTHERS / WOODLAND, WV	1871	FRKLN TWP-BUS.	1797
HORNBROOK J	1871	OH CO. MAP	1742
HORNBROOK J P	1871	FRKLN TWP-BUS.	1797
HORNBROOK, E	1871	MARH'L MAP	1754
HORNBROOK, E	1871	MARH'L MAP	1758
HORNBROOK, H C	1871	MARH'L MAP	1754
HORNBROOK, J P	1871	MARH'L MAP	1754
HORNBROOK, J P / RES	1871	MARH'L MAP	1754
HORNBROOK, JOHN	1871	MARH'L MAP	1754
HORNBROOK, RACHEL	1853	DEFENDANT	1561
HORNBROOK, T	1871	OH CO. MAP	1742
HORNBROOK, T P	1871	MARH'L MAP	1754
HORNBROOK, THOMAS	1871	OH CO. BUS.	1779
HORNBROOKS, FRANCIS B	1853	DEFENDANT	1561
HORNISH, A M	1857	DEFENDANT	1630
HORNISH, A M	1857	DEFENDANT	1663
HORRA, P O / STORE	1871	WELLSBURG	1778
HORSESHOE BEND	1871	MARH'L MAP	1755
HORSESHOE BEND / LYNNCAMP RUN	1871	MARH'L MAP	1759
HOSACK & MARTIN	1871	CAMERON	1803
HOSACK, - / HEIRS	1871	OH CO. MAP	1743
HOSACK, -	1871	CAMERON	1803
HOSACK, - / GREENE ST	1871	CAMERON	1803
HOSACK, R P	1871	CAMERON	1803
HOSACK, R P / RES	1871	CAMERON	1803
HOSACK, R P	1871	CAMERON	1804
HOSACK, WILLIAM	1838	DEFENDANT	1662
HOSACK, WILLIAM	1838	DEFENDANT	1662
HOSACK, WILLIAM	1843	DEFENDANT	1594
HOSIE, R	1871	BRKE MAP	1737
HOSIE, R	1871	BRKE MAP	1737
HOSIE, R	1871	BKE/OH MAP	1739
HOSKINSON, - / DR	1871	MARH'L MAP	1761
HOSNER, -	1871	WELLSBURG	1778
HOSOCK, R P	1871	CAMER'N - BUS.	1795
HOTEL - B.WIRT - WEST UNION	1871	W. UNION	1812
HOTEL - BENWOOD HOTEL - BENWOOD	1871	BENWO'D - BUS.	1795
HOTEL - BENWOOD HOTEL - BENWOOD	1871	BENWOOD	1798
HOTEL - CAMERON HOUSE	1871	CAMERON	1803
HOTEL - CAMERON HOUSE - CAMERON	1871	CAMER'N - BUS.	1795
HOTEL - CHARLES HOTEL - GLEN EASTON	1871	GLEN EASTON - BUS.	1796
HOTEL - CLIFTON HOUSE - MOUNDSVILLE	1871	MDSVL BUS.	1796
HOTEL - CLIFTON HOUSE - MOUNDSVILLE	1871	MDSVILLE	1808
HOTEL - CLIFTON HOUSE - MOUNDSVILLE	1871	MDSVILLE	1810
HOTEL - ELM GROVE / MRS.FRENCH	1871	ELM GROVE	1782
HOTEL - ELM GROVE HOUSE	1871	ELM GROVE	1782
HOTEL - ERWIN HOUSE - WEST LIBERTY	1871	W.LIBERTY	1780
HOTEL - EXCHANGE HOTEL - WATER ST - WELLSBURG	1871	WELLSBURG	1778
HOTEL - HOTEL AULD - WASHINGTON, PA	1916	NAT'L ROAD	1861
HOTEL - MARSHALL HOUSE - MOUNDSVILLE	1871	MDSVILLE	1807
HOTEL - MCCLURE - WHEELING	1916	NAT'L ROAD	1868
HOTEL - MORTON HOUSE - MOUNDSVILLE	1871	MDSVILLE	1809
HOTEL - OLD STONE HOTEL - RONEY'S POINT - NATIONAL ROAD	1916	NAT'L ROAD	1866
HOTEL - ST CHARLES - GLEN EASTON	1871	GLEN EASTON	1801
HOTEL - STEENROD HOUSE	1871	TRIAD.TWP.	1781
HOTEL - TRIADELPHIA / F. LAWSON	1871	TRIAD.BORO.	1784
HOTEL - TRIADELPHIA HOUSE	1871	TRIAD.BORO.	1784
HOTEL - TWO MILE HOUSE / NATIONAL RD & BETHANY PIKE	1871	TRIAD.TWP.	1781
HOTEL - VIRGINIA HOUSE - RONEY POINT	1871	RONEY PT.	1783
HOTEL - WASHINGTON HOUSE - MOUNDSVILLE	1871	MDSVILLE	1807
HOTEL - WEST LIBERTY	1871	W.LIBRTY. BUS.	1780
HOTEL - WHITE HOTEL - CAMERON	1871	CAMERON	1803
HOTEL - WHITES HOTEL - CAMERON	1871	CAMER'N - BUS.	1795
HOTEL - WINDSOR - WHEELING	1916	NAT'L ROAD	1868
HOUGH, J	1871	BRKE MAP	1737
HOUGH, J	1871	BKE/OH MAP	1739
HOUGH, JAMES / MAP#116	1852	BRKE MAP	1840
HOUSE, B / (?BOARDING HOUSE?) - GRANT ST - MDSVILLE	1871	MDSVILLE	1807
HOUSE, P	1871	OH CO. MAP	1741
HOUSE, P	1871	OH CO. MAP	1742
HOUSEHOLDER, S	1871	CAMERON	1802
HOUSEHOLDER, S / INITIALS S.H.	1871	CAMERON	1802
HOUSEHOLDER, WILLIAM H	1871	NEW CUMB'LD	1768
HOUSER, G	1871	OH CO. MAP	1742
HOUSER, G	1871	OH CO. MAP	1742
HOUSER, G	1871	OH CO. MAP	1744
HOUSER, G	1871	MARH'L MAP	1759
HOUST, H	1871	BKE/OH MAP	1739
HOUSTON, - / MRS	1861	DEFENDANT	1654
HOUSTON, MATH H	1862	DEFENDANT	1654
HOUSTON, MATHEW H	1863	DEFENDANT	1552
HOUSTON, MATHEW H	1863	DEFENDANT	1621
HOWARD RUN	1871	MARH'L MAP	1750
HOWARD, -	1830	PLAINTIFF	1628
HOWARD, - / MRS	1871	WELLSBURG	1777
HOWARD, A	1871	MARH'L MAP	1756
HOWARD, A P	1871	HAN MAP	1726
HOWARD, B	1871	MARH'L MAP	1757
HOWARD, BRICE	1830	DEFENDANT	1639
HOWARD, J	1871	BKE/OH MAP	1739
HOWARD, J	1871	OH CO. MAP	1740
HOWARD, J	1871	MARH'L MAP	1747
HOWARD, J	1871	MARH'L MAP	1757
HOWARD, J M	1871	MARH'L MAP	1757
HOWARD, J M / INITIALS J.M.H	1871	MARH'L MAP	1757
HOWARD, J M / INITIALS J.M.H	1871	MARH'L MAP	1757
HOWARD, M	1871	MARH'L MAP	1757
HOWARD, R	1871	MARH'L MAP	1757
HOWARD, S	1871	MARH'L MAP	1757
HOWARD, T	1871	MARH'L MAP	1757
HOWARD, THOMAS	1819	DEFENDANT	1667
HOWARD, W S / DR.	1871	MARH'L MAP	1759
HOWARD, WILLIAM	1856	DEFENDANT	1586
HOWARD, WILLIAM	1871	BKE/OH MAP	1739
HOWE, W R	1871	ROSBBYS RK	1813
HOWELL, -	1853	PLAINTIFF	1623
HOWELL, JONATHAN	1799	DEFENDANT	1655
HOWELL, JONOTHAN	1803	MISC	1676
HOWELL, MATTHEW	1807	PLAINTIFF	1666
HOWLET, ANDREW	1817	DEFENDANT	1628
HOWLET, ANDREW	1820	DEFENDANT	1553
HOWLET, ANDREW	1820	DEFENDANT	1620
HOWLET, ANDREW	1820	DEFENDANT	1628
HOWLETT, JOHN	1836	DEFENDANT	1635
HOWLETT, JOHN R	1848	DEFENDANT	1568
HOWLETT, JOHN R	1848	DEFENDANT	1623
HRS. / (?ABBREVIATION FOR HEIRS?)	1871	MARH'L MAP	1753
HUBBARD, DANA	1823	DEFENDANT	1570
HUBBARD, DANA	1824	DEFENDANT	1602
HUBBARD, DANA	1832	DEFENDANT	1583
HUBBARD, DANA	1834	DEFENDANT	1622
HUBBARD, DANA	1834	DEFENDANT	1640
HUBBARD, DANA	1835	DEFENDANT	1598
HUBBARD, DANA	1835	DEFENDANT	1646
HUBBARD, DANA	1835	DEFENDANT	1650
HUBBARD, EDWIN P	1875	DEFENDANT	1636
HUBBARD, G	1871	MARH'L MAP	1752
HUBBARD, G / CUT OFF TOP OF MAP	1871	MARH'L MAP	1756
HUBBARD, WILLIAM B	1838	DEFENDANT	1662
HUBBELL, RICHARD H	1859	DEFENDANT	1597
HUBBELL, STEPHEN	1859	DEFENDANT	1632
HUBBS LANDING - OHIO RIVER - WOODLAND P.O.	1871	MARH'L MAP	1754
HUBBS, E / MARSHALL HOUSE	1871	MDSVILLE	1807
HUBBS, G	1871	MARH'L MAP	1753
HUBBS, G	1871	MARH'L MAP	1756
HUBBS, G	1871	GLEN EASTON	1801
HUBBS, W	1871	MARH'L MAP	1756
HUDGES RUN	1871	BRKE MAP	1736
HUDSON & WILSON	1871	FRE'MAN'S LDG	1762
HUDSON & WILSON FIRE BRICK WORKS	1871	FRE'MAN'S LDG	1765
HUDSON, C B	1871	BRKE MAP	1735
HUDSON, C B	1871	BRKE MAP	1737
HUDSON, C B	1871	BRKE MAP	1737
HUDSON, D	1871	HAN MAP	1732
HUDSON, J	1871	HAN MAP	1726

XLIX

'PERSONAL TIME LINE' INDEX TO VOLUME 7 OF THE *OHIO COUNTY INDEX*

ENTRY	YEAR	SUBJECT	PAGE	ENTRY	YEAR	SUBJECT	PAGE
HUDSON, JOHN	1871	HAN MAP	1732	HUNTER, D	1871	BRKE MAP	1734
HUDSON, JOHN / & SONS - NEAR HAMILTON	1871	HAN-GR'NT TWP	1763	HUNTER, G	1871	BRKE MAP	1734
				HUNTER, J H	1871	BRKE MAP	1737
HUDSON, T	1871	HAN MAP	1726	HUNTER, J S	1871	NEW MANCH.	1763
HUDSON, T / INITIALS T.H.	1871	HAN MAP	1726	HUNTER, JOSEPH / BLAIR P.O.	1871	HAN-CLAY TWP	1763
HUDSON, T / NW OF ORCHARD HILL	1871	HAN MAP	1732	HUNTER, JOSHUA	1836	DEFENDANT	1573
HUDSON, T / (?OF HUDSON & WILSON?)	1871	FRE'MAN'S LDG	1764	HUNTER, R B	1871	MDSVILLE	1809
				HUNTER, T	1871	BRKE MAP	1735
HUDSON, W	1871	HAN MAP	1731	HUNTING, A / ?INGRAM, D	1871	HAN MAP	1729
HUDSON, T M	1871	BRKE MAP	1737	HUOSTON, ANDREW C	1842	DEFENDANT	1551
HUEY, WILLIAM	1829	DEFENDANT	1583	HUPP, - / HEIRS	1871	MARH'L MAP	1750
HUFF, -	1844	PLAINTIFF	1632	HUPP, EVERHART	1871	MARH'L MAP	1757
HUFF, A	1871	OH CO. MAP	1742	HUPP, HENRY	1832	DEFENDANT	1566
HUFF, ELIJAH	1780	DEFENDANT	1600	HUPP, HENRY	1832	DEFENDANT	1622
HUFF, JOHN	1779	APPENDIX	1874	HUPP, ISAAC / & JOSEPH - MAP#10	1852	BRKE MAP	1840
HUFF, JOHN	1779	APPENDIX	1874	HUPP, ISAAC / & JOSEPH - MAP#33	1852	BRKE MAP	1840
HUFF, MICHEL	1790	DEFENDANT	1571	HUPP, J	1871	BKE/OH MAP	1739
HUFF, N	1871	HAN MAP	1727	HUPP, JOHN	1805	DEFENDANT	1655
HUFF, S	1871	HAN MAP	1726	HUPP, JOHN	1832	DEFENDANT	1566
HUFF, S	1871	HAN MAP	1727	HUPP, JOHN C / PHYSICIAN	1871	OH CO. BUS.	1779
HUFF, S	1871	HAN MAP	1727	HUPP, JOSEPH / & ISAAC - MAP#33	1852	BRKE MAP	1840
HUFF, S	1871	BKE/OH MAP	1738	HUPP, JOSEPH / & ISAAC / MAP#10	1852	BRKE MAP	1840
HUFF, T	1871	MARH'L MAP	1747	HUPP, PHILIP	1810	DEFENDANT	1667
HUFF, THOMAS	1819	DEFENDANT	1638	HUSEMAN, -	1873	DEFENDANT	1631
HUFF, WILLIAM	1871	HAN MAP	1726	HUSEMAN, FRED	1877	DEFENDANT	1631
HUGGING, R	1871	BENWOOD	1798	HUSS, JOHN Z	1871	OH CO. MAP	1742
HUGHES & CAMPBELL	1833	DEFENDANT	1551	HUSS, JOHN Z	1871	MARH'L MAP	1745
HUGHES, -	1854	DEFENDANT	1574	HUSS, JOHN Z	1871	OH CO.BUS.	1779
HUGHES, -	1878	PLAINTIFF	1625	HUSTAN, - / KILLED BY AN INDIAN	1871	OH CO. MAP	1740
HUGHES, ENOCH	1879	DEFENDANT	1560	HUSTER, NATHANIEL / (COOPERSHOP) - MAP#463	1852	BRKE MAP	1849
HUGHES, JACOB B	1877	DEFENDANT	1576				
HUGHES, JAMES	1808	APPENDIX	1873	HUSTER, NATHANIEL / (MILL) - MAP#461	1852	BRKE MAP	1849
HUGHES, LOYD	1834	DEFENDANT	1598				
HUGHES, LOYD G	1835	DEFENDANT	1650	HUSTER, NATHANIEL / (MILL) - MAP#462	1852	BRKE MAP	1849
HUGHES, N	1831	MISC	1698				
HUGHES, P	1871	MARH'L MAP	1761	HUSTER, NATHANIEL / (SAWMILL) - MAP#459	1852	BRKE MAP	1849
HUGHES, PATRICK	1854	DEFENDANT	1672				
HUGHEY, THOMAS	1842	DEFENDANT	1594	HUSTER, NATHANIEL / (SAWMILL) - MAP#460	1852	BRKE MAP	1849
HUGHEY, WILLIAM	1858	DEFENDANT	1574				
HUKELL, WILLIAM / DR	1871	W.LIBERTY	1780	HUSTER, NATHANIEL / (SMITHSHOP) - MAP#457	1852	BRKE MAP	1849
HUKIL, WILLIAM / MAP#170	1852	BRKE MAP	1843				
HUKIL, WILLIAM / MAP#196	1852	BRKE MAP	1843	HUSTER, NATHANIEL / (SMITHSHOP) - MAP#458	1852	BRKE MAP	1849
HUKILL, J	1871	BRKE MAP	1736				
HUKILL, M	1871	BKE/OH MAP	1739	HUSTER, NATHANIEL / MAP#440	1852	BRKE MAP	1849
HUKILL, WILLIAM	1871	BRKE MAP	1736	HUSTER, NATHANIEL / MAP#441	1852	BRKE MAP	1849
HUKILL, WILLIAM / RES	1871	BRKE MAP	1736	HUSTER, NATHANIEL / (COOPERSHOP) - MAP#565	1852	BRKE MAP	1852
HUKILL, WILLIAM / PHYSICIAN	1871	W.LIBRTY.BUS.	1780				
HUKLE, - / SCHOOL / MAP#171	1852	BRKE MAP	1843	HUSTON, ROBERT	1807	DEFENDANT	1648
HULL, -	1860	DEFENDANT	1574	HUSTON, WILLIAM	1783	APPENDIX	1874
HULL, DAVID	1840	DEFENDANT	1662	HUTCHINS, - / WOODS & HUTCHINS	1871	MDSVILLE	1807
HULL, HENRY	1808	DEFENDANT	1635	HUTCHINS, - / WOODS & HUTCHINS	1871	MDSVILLE	1809
HULL, JACOB	1854	DEFENDANT	1561	HUTCHINSON, J	1871	MARH'L MAP	1761
HULL, JOHN	1839	DEFENDANT	1670	HUTCHINSON, JAMES	1817	DEFENDANT	1598
HULL, JOHN	1841	DEFENDANT	1557	HUTCHISON, JAMES	1818	DEFENDANT	1598
HULL, JOHN	1841	DEFENDANT	1656	HUTCHISON, JAMES	1820	DEFENDANT	1598
HULL, JOHN C	1835	DEFENDANT	1618	HUTCHISON, RICHARD	1818	DEFENDANT	1559
HULL, WILLIAM	1871	MARH'L MAP	1751	HUTTON, J / WAGON & BLACKSMITH SHOP	1871	WELLSBURG	1778
HULL, WILLIAM / ABBREV WM.H	1871	MARH'L MAP	1751				
HULLIHEN, ALFRED	1858	DEFENDANT	1661	HYDER, V	1871	MARH'L MAP	1758
HULLIHEN, MANFRED	1859	DEFENDANT	1661	HYER, GOTTFRIED	1875	DEFENDANT	1616
HULLIHEN, MANFRED T	1861	DEFENDANT	1552	I.H.M. / UNKNOWN INITIALS (?MAYBE E.H.M.-E.H.MOORE?)	1871	WELLSBURG	1778
HULLIHEN, SIMON P	1838	DEFENDANT	1558				
HUMBERT, MICHAEL	1812	DEFENDANT	1611	I.O. OF O.F. HALL - MOUND ST - MOUNDSVILLE	1871	MDSVILLE	1809
HUMBERT, MICHAEL	1813	DEFENDANT	1611				
HUMES, -	1846	PLAINTIFF	1629	I.O.O.F. HALL - CAMERON	1871	CAMERON	1803
HUMPHREYS, DAVID	1784	APPENDIX	1874	I.O.O.F. HALL - MOUND ST - MOUNDSVILLE	1871	MDSVILLE	1809
HUMPHREYS, GEORGE	1783	APPENDIX	1874				
HUMPHREYS, GEORGE	1784	APPENDIX	1874	I.O.O.F. HALL - NEW MANCHESTER	1871	NEW MANCH.	1769
HUMPHREYS, GEORGE	1784	APPENDIX	1874	IBBITSON, -	1859	PLAINTIFF	1632
HUMPHREYS, GEORGE	1793	DEFENDANT	1572	IBBOTSON, -	1857	PLAINTIFF	1632
HUMPHREYS, JOHN	1784	APPENDIX	1874	IBBOTSON, -	1857	PLAINTIFF	1632
HUMPHREYS, ROBERT	1784	APPENDIX	1874	ICE BREAKER / ON OHIO RIVER	1871	BRKE MAP	1736
HUNGERMAN, -	1871	RITCHIE TWP	1791	ICE HOUSE - 3 MILE ICE HOUSE - WHEELING CREEK	1871	OH CO. MAP	1742
HUNGERMAN, -	1871	RITCHIE TWP	1793				
HUNSTRUP, B / (?PROBABLY BRANSTRUP?)	1871	TRIAD.BORO.	1784	ICE HOUSE - CAMERON / NEAR W.McGAHAN	1871	CAMERON	1803
HUNSTRUP, B / (?PROBABLY BRANSTRUP?)	1871	TRIAD.BORO.	1785	ICE HOUSE - CONANT & BEDILLION - WHEELING CREEK	1871	TRIAD.TWP.	1781
HUNT, D	1871	MARH'L MAP	1757	ICE HOUSE - GEORGE SCHELLHASE - WHEELING CREEK	1871	TRIAD.TWP.	1781
HUNT, G	1871	MARH'L MAP	1752				
HUNT, G	1871	MARH'L MAP	1756	ICE HOUSE - SCHELLHASES / G - ON WHEELING CREEK	1871	OH CO. MAP	1742
HUNT, G	1871	GLEN EASTON	1801				
HUNT, G	1871	GLEN EASTON	1801	ICE HOUSE - THREE MILE ICE HOUSE ON WHEELING CREEK	1871	TRIAD.TWP.	1781
HUNT, G	1871	GLEN EASTON	1801				
HUNT, MORGAN	1799	DEFENDANT	1647	ICE HOUSE - WHEELING CREEK / CONANT & BEDILION ICE HOUSSE	1871	OH CO. MAP	1742
HUNTER, - / MRS	1871	BRKE MAP	1735				

L

'PERSONAL TIME LINE' INDEX TO VOLUME 7 OF THE *OHIO COUNTY INDEX*

ENTRY	YEAR	SUBJECT	PAGE
ILLINOIS	1852	HEMPFIELD RR	1820
ILLINOIS - ROAD MILES	1852	HEMPFIELD RR	1819
IMER, HANSON	1876	DEFENDANT	1627
IMER, HENRY	1876	DEFENDANT	1627
INDEPENDENCE - RIDGE ROAD TO INDEPENDENCE	1871	BRKE MAP	1737
INDEX - CUMULATIVE INDEX TO VOL. 1-7 / PREVIEW	2000	APPENDIX	1875
INDEX CARD FILES TO COURT CASE FILES	2000	APPENDIX	1873
INDEX TO PANHANDLE MAP SECTIONS - BOTTOM HALF	1871	MAP	1717
INDEX TO PANHANDLE MAP SECTIONS - TOP HALF	1871	MAP	1716
INDIAN / PLACE WHERE ADAM POE AND BIG FOOT INDIAN FOUGHT	1871	HAN MAP	1726
INDIAN / HUSTAN KILLED BY AN INDIAN	1871	OH CO. MAP	1740
INDIAN - GRAVE OF JOHN WETZEL - KILLED BY INDIAN	1871	MARH'L MAP	1751
INDIAN - MOUND OLD INDIAN SPRING	1871	RITCHIE TWP	1792
INDIAN - NAMES FOR WHEELING	1916	NAT'L ROAD	1867
INDIAN - OLD INDIAN CAMP	1871	MARH'L MAP	1745
INDIAN - OLD INDIAN SPRING	1871	OH CO. MAP	1742
INDIAN BATLE GROUND	1871	OH CO. MAP	1740
INDIAN BATTLE GROUND / NEAR SUGAR BOTTOM	1871	MARH'L MAP	1747
INDIAN BATTLE GROUND - S. OF SUGAR BOTTOM	1871	MARH'L MAP	1750
INDIAN CAMP RUN	1852	BRKE MAP	1844
INDIAN CAVE WHERE HUMAN SKELETONS WERE FOUND / NEAR OHIO RIVER	1871	BRKE MAP	1734
INDIAN CROSS CREEK - OHIO	1852	BRKE MAP	1848
INDIAN GRAVES - N. OF SUGAR BOTTOM	1871	MARH'L MAP	1750
INDIAN GRAVES - S. OF SUGAR BOTTOM	1871	MARH'L MAP	1750
INDIAN GRAVES #1 / NEAR SUGAR BOTTOM	1871	MARH'L MAP	1747
INDIAN GRAVES #2 / NEAR SUGAR BOTTOM	1871	MARH'L MAP	1747
INDIAN HISTORY - WHEELING - MOUND BUILDERS	1916	NAT'L ROAD	1866
INDIAN KNOLLY	1871	MARH'L MAP	1754
INDIAN MOUND	1871	MARH'L MAP	1754
INDIAN MOUND - N. OF R.N. WELLS	1871	MARH'L MAP	1758
INDIAN MOUND - S. OF MONUMENT PLACE	1871	OH CO. MAP	1742
INDIAN MOUND - S. OF WALNUT FARM - CLAY TWP	1871	MARH'L MAP	1751
INDIAN MOUND - THE MOUND - MOUNDSVILLE	1871	MDSVILLE	1809
INDIAN MOUND - W. OF SCHOOL NO.4 - FRANKLIN TWP	1871	MARH'L MAP	1758
INDIANA	1852	HEMPFIELD RR	1820
INDIANA - ROAD MILES	1852	HEMPFIELD RR	1819
INDIANAPOLIS	1852	HEMPFIELD RR	1820
INDIANAPOLIS & BELLEFONTAINE RR	1852	HEMP. RR MAP	1826
INDIANS - T. EDGINGTON TAKEN PRISONER BY INDIANS ABOUT 1790 - (?OR1796?)	1871	BRKE MAP	1734
INDIANS - WELLS, RICHARD / FORT BUILT BY R.W. FOR PROTECTION FROM INDIANS (?BAMILY MT.?) OR (?FAMILY VLT - VALUT?)	1871	BRKE MAP	1734
INGERSOLL, J	1871	MARH'L MAP	1750
INGERSOLL, J / INITIALS J.I.	1871	MARH'L MAP	1750
INGLEBRIGHT, W	1871	BRKE MAP	1734
INGRAHAM, J / SAW MILL	1871	MARH'L MAP	1753
INGRAM, A	1871	MARH'L MAP	1753
INGRAM, B / (?OR D?)	1871	HAN MAP	1729
INGRAM, D / GROCER	1871	HAN MAP	1729
INGRAM, D	1871	NEW MANCH.	1769
INGRAM, D	1871	NEW MANCH.	1769
INGRAM, DAVID / HAMILTON	1871	HAN-GR'NT TWP	1763
INGRAM, J	1871	MARH'L MAP	1753
INGRAM, J / INITIALS J.I.	1871	MARH'L MAP	1753
INGRAM, J / INITIALS J.I.	1871	MARH'L MAP	1753
INGRAM, SILAS / INITIALS S.I.	1871	MARH'L MAP	1750
INGRAM, SILAS	1871	MARH'L MAP	1753
INGRAM, SILAS / INITIALS S.I.	1871	MARH'L MAP	1753
INGRAM, SILAS / ORCHARD	1871	MARH'L MAP	1753
INIDIAN - MILITARY - FORT HENRY	1916	NAT'L ROAD	1865
INN - FOUR MILE HOUSE / WILLIAM STAMM	1871	OH CO. MAP	1742
INN - SEE ALSO TAVERN & ORDINARY	1916	NAT'L ROAD	1861
INN - TEN HOUSE / S. OF WHEELING IRON WORKS	1871	WHG CITY	1786
INSKEEP, ABRAHAM	1808	APPENDIX	1873
INTENDED ROAD	1871	BRKE MAP	1734
INTYRE, J A	1871	BENWOOD	1799
IRISWONGER, PETER	1807	DEFENDANT	1659
IRON & STEEL INDUSTRY	1916	NAT'L ROAD	1865
IRON BRIDGE - OHIO RIVER - AT EDGINGTON STATION	1871	BRKE MAP	1734
IRON ORE / COAL, IRON ORE & BOLIVER CLAY	1871	FRE'MAN'S LDG	1765
IRON ORE - NE. OF ORCHARDALE	1871	HAN MAP	1727
IRON ORE - NW. OF NEWELL HALL	1871	HAN MAP	1727
IRON ORE - W. OF J.MCDONALD	1871	OH CO. MAP	1742
IRONTON, OH	1852	HEMP. RR MAP	1826
IRWIN, DAVID K	1873	DEFENDANT	1576
IRWIN, DAVID K	1873	DEFENDANT	1580
IRWIN, DAVID K	1873	DEFENDANT	1584
IRWIN, DAVID K	1873	DEFENDANT	1590
IRWIN, JOHN	1826	DEFENDANT	1628
IRWIN, JOHN H	1823	DEFENDANT	1559
IRWIN, JOHN H	1824	DEFENDANT	1559
IRWIN, SAMUEL	1857	MISC	1680
IRWIN, WILLIAM	1790	DEFENDANT	1637
IRWIN, WILLIAM	1819	DEFENDANT	1660
IRWIN, WILLIAM	1858	DEFENDANT	1560
IRWIN, WILLIAM	1880	DEFENDANT	1636
ISETT - ORPHANS	1856	MISC	1702
ISETT, -	1876	PLAINTIFF	1631
ISETT, -	1878	PLAINTIFF	1631
ISHAN, -	1874	PLAINTIFF	1621
ISLAND CREEK - OHIO	1852	BRKE MAP	1853
J J WALKERS TIMERLAND	1871	BRKE MAP	1734
J, S J / INITIALS - J.S.J.	1871	HAN MAP	1727
J.A. / UNKNOWN INITIALS (?J.ATKINSON?) - EDG. STA.	1871	EDGINGTON STA.	1774
J.B. / (?J. BURLEY?)	1871	MARH'L MAP	1748
J.B. / HRS-HEIRS (?BLANKENSHOP, J?) - NEAR QUEEN ST	1871	WELLSBURG	1777
J.B.L. / UNKNOWN INITIALS - BETHANY	1871	BETHANY	1773
J.B.P. EST / ? UNSURE INITIALS J.B.PURDY ?	1871	MARH'L MAP	1752
J.B.P.EST. / (?J.B.PIERCE?)	1871	MARH'L MAP	1748
J.C.R. / UNKNOWN INITILAS - MARKET ST	1871	MDSVILLE	1807
J.G. / INITIALS	1871	HAN MAP	1727
J.L.F. / ABBREV FOR J.L. FREEMAN	1871	HAN MAP	1730
J.L.K. / UNKNOWN INITIALS - BETHANY (?J.KEMP?)	1871	BETHANY	1773
J.McF. / UNKNOWN INITIALS	1871	ELM GROVE	1782
J.P.S. / UNKNOWN INITIALS - ELM GROVE	1871	OH CO. MAP	1744
J.R.C. / (?CUNNINGHAM, JOHN R?)	1871	HAN MAP	1727
J S / ABBERV.	1871	HAN MAP	1731
J.S.J.	1871	HAN MAP	1727
J.T. / UNKNOWN INITIALS	1871	MARH'L MAP	1751
J.W.A. / ALLISON ?	1871	HAN MAP	1727
J.W.P. / UNKNOWN INITIALS - NEW MANCHESTER (?J.W.HOBBS?)	1871	NEW MANCH.	1769
JACKMAN, S	1871	ROSBBYS RK	1813
JACKMAN, S / INITIALS S.J.	1871	ROSBBYS RK	1813
JACKSON, B	1871	HAN MAP	1726
JACKSON, M	1871	CAMERON	1804
JACKSON, W / ON E. EDGE OF MAP	1871	HAN MAP	1726
JACKSON, W	1871	HAN MAP	1727
JACKSON, W	1871	HAN MAP	1727
JACKSON, W L	1871	HAN MAP	1726
JACOB, -	1825	PLAINTIFF	1625
JACOB, - / HRS. - HEIRS	1871	WELLSBURG	1776
JACOB, A	1871	OH CO. MAP	1741
JACOB, A	1871	OH CO. MAP	1741
JACOB, A	1871	OH CO. MAP	1741
JACOB, A R	1871	BKE/OH MAP	1738
JACOB, A R	1871	OH CO. MAP	1740
JACOB, A R / RES	1871	OH CO. MAP	1740
JACOB, ALEXANDER M	1873	DEFENDANT	1560
JACOB, ALEXANDER M	1873	DEFENDANT	1578
JACOB, ALEXANDER M	1874	DEFENDANT	1671
JACOB, D F	1871	OH CO. MAP	1741
JACOB, D F / INITIALS D.F.J	1871	OH CO. MAP	1741
JACOB, D F / RES	1871	OH CO. MAP	1741
JACOB, I / MRS	1871	WELLSBURG	1776
JACOB, I / MRS	1871	WELLSBURG	1776
JACOB, I / MRS - CHARLES ST	1871	WELLSBURG	1777

'PERSONAL TIME LINE' INDEX TO VOLUME 7 OF THE *OHIO COUNTY INDEX*

ENTRY	YEAR	SUBJECT	PAGE	ENTRY	YEAR	SUBJECT	PAGE
JACOB, I / MRS	1871	WELLSBURG	1778	JENKINS, S B	1871	NEW CUMB'LD	1762
JACOB, J	1871	BRKE MAP	1735	JENKINS, S B	1871	NEW CUMB'LD	1766
JACOB, J / EST	1871	BKE/OH MAP	1738	JENKINS, S B / OC	1871	NEW CUMB'LD	1767
JACOB, J	1871	OH CO. MAP	1741	JENNINGS, / HEIRS	1871	MARH'L MAP	1750
JACOB, J G	1871	WELLSBURG	1777	JENNINGS, -	1817	PLAINTIFF	1628
JACOB, J G / (O)	1871	WELLSBURG	1778	JENNINGS, -	1821	PLAINTIFF	1628
JACOB, J J	1871	OH CO. MAP	1740	JENNINGS, - / HEIRS	1871	MARH'L MAP	1747
JACOB, JOHN N	1840	DEFENDANT	1555	JENNINGS, MARTIN	1853	DEFENDANT	1551
JACOB, S	1871	BRKE MAP	1736	JESTER, D	1871	BRKE MAP	1737
JACOB, S	1871	OH CO. MAP	1740	JIMS RUN	1871	MARH'L MAP	1745
JACOB, S / CASHIER - FIRST NATIONAL BANK	1871	WLSBRG BUS.	1772	JOBES, H	1871	MDSVILLE	1810
				JOBES, S	1871	MDSVILLE	1810
JACOB, S	1871	WELLSBURG	1776	JOHNSON, -	1871	BETHANY	1773
JACOB, S S	1871	BKE/OH MAP	1739	JOHNSON, A	1871	HAN MAP	1730
JACOB, S S	1871	BKE/OH MAP	1739	JOHNSON, A	1871	CAMERON	1804
JACOB, S S	1871	BKE/OH MAP	1739	JOHNSON, A	1871	MDSVILLE	1807
JACOB, SAMUEL	1852	NOT ON MAP	1836	JOHNSON, A / INITIALS J.A.	1871	MDSVILLE	1807
JACOB, SAMUEL / (GONE) - MAP#320	1852	BRKE MAP	1846	JOHNSON, AMOS / MAP#493	1852	BRKE MAP	1850
JACOB, SAMUEL / (GONE) - MAP#321	1852	BRKE MAP	1846	JOHNSON, B	1871	MARH'L MAP	1750
JACOB, SAMUEL / (GONE) - MAP#322	1852	BRKE MAP	1846	JOHNSON, DAVID	1830	MISC	1687
JACOB, SAMUEL / (GONE) - MILL - MAP#323	1852	BRKE MAP	1846	JOHNSON, G B	1871	HAN MAP	1726
				JOHNSON, G B / SECOND TRACT IDENTIFIED AS G.B.J.	1871	HAN MAP	1726
JACOB, SAMUEL / (GONE) - MAP#319	1852	BRKE MAP	1846	JOHNSON, J	1871	MARH'L MAP	1750
JACOB, SAMUEL / (GONE) - MILL - MAP#348	1852	BRKE MAP	1846	JOHNSON, J	1871	MARH'L MAP	1752
				JOHNSON, JAMES	1877	DEFENDANT	1582
JACOB, ZACHARIAH	1829	MISC	1680	JOHNSON, JOHN	1825	DEFENDANT	1620
JACOBS, - / ESTATE	1871	RITCHIE TWP	1791	JOHNSON, T	1871	MARH'L MAP	1750
JACOBS, B	1871	WELLSBURG	1776	JOHNSON, WILLIAM	1821	DEFENDANT	1612
JACOBS, J	1871	BRKE MAP	1736	JOHNSONS RUN	1852	BRKE MAP	1849
JACOBS, S	1871	BRKE MAP	1736	JOHNSTON & BERRYHILL	1862	DEFENDANT	1604
JACOBS, S	1871	BRKE MAP	1736	JOHNSTON & GLASSFORD	1851	DEFENDANT	1563
JAGER, J	1871	MARH'L MAP	1759	JOHNSTON, ASA D	1860	DEFENDANT	1567
JAICE, J / HRS -HEIRS	1871	MDSVILLE	1808	JOHNSTON, ASA D	1861	DEFENDANT	1631
JAIL - FIFTH ST - WHEELING	1871	WHG CITY	1788	JOHNSTON, ASA D	1862	DEFENDANT	1631
JAIL - MARSHALL CO	1871	MDSVILLE	1809	JOHNSTON, E	1871	HAN MAP	1727
JAKES RUN	1871	MARH'L MAP	1746	JOHNSTON, E / INITALS E.J.	1871	HAN MAP	1727
JAMES, JANE	1848	DEFENDANT	1670	JOHNSTON, GEORGE W	1840	DEFENDANT	1568
JAMISON, HENRY	1826	MISC	1678	JOHNSTON, J S	1871	HAN MAP	1727
JAMISON, HENRY M	1855	DEFENDANT	1618	JOHNSTON, J S / INITIALS J.S.J.	1871	HAN MAP	1727
JAMISON, J	1871	MARH'L MAP	1747	JOHNSTON, JOHN	1833	DEFENDANT	1620
JAMISON, JOHN / MAP#414	1852	BRKE MAP	1846	JOHNSTON, T	1871	MARH'L MAP	1751
JAMISON, JOHN	1871	BRKE MAP	1735	JOHNSTON, T	1871	MARH'L MAP	1751
JAMISON, WILLIAM W	1834	DEFENDANT	1608	JOHNSTON, THOMAS	1822	PLAINTIFF	1591
JEFFERS, E C	1841	MISC	1697	JOHNSTON, THOMAS	1823	PLAINTIFF	1591
JEFFERS, E C	1850	DEFENDANT	1586	JOHNSTON, W	1871	HAN MAP	1727
JEFFERS, ELIJAH C	1855	DEFENDANT	1558	JOHNSTON, WILLIAM	1820	DEFENDANT	1611
JEFFERS, ELIJAH C	1855	DEFENDANT	1621	JOHNSTON, WILLIAM	1827	DEFENDANT	1602
JEFFERS, JOSEPH	1837	DEFENDANT	1651	JOHNSTON, WILLIAM H	1822	DEFENDANT	1600
JEFFERS, MAT	1853	DEFENDANT	1586	JOHNSTONE, ABLE	1794	MISC	1688
JEFFERS, MATHIAS	1834	DEFENDANT	1618	JOLLY, PETER	1778	APPENDIX	1874
JEFFERS, MATHIAS	1834	DEFENDANT	1622	JONATHANS GUT / OR RUN	1871	WHG CITY	1786
JEFFERS, MATHIAS	1836	DEFENDANT	1650	JONATHANS RUN	1871	OH CO. MAP	1741
JEFFERS, MATHIAS	1837	DEFENDANT	1660	JONATHANS RUN	1871	OH CO. MAP	1742
JEFFERS, MATHIAS	1838	DEFENDANT	1622	JONATHANS RUN / OR GUT	1871	WHG CITY	1786
JEFFERS, MATHIAS	1855	DEFENDANT	1586	JONES RUN	1852	BRKE MAP	1840
JEFFERS, MATHIAS	1856	DEFENDANT	1586	JONES RUN	1852	BRKE MAP	1852
JEFFERS, MATHIAS	1857	DEFENDANT	1603	JONES, - / MRS	1871	MARH'L MAP	1746
JEFFERS, MATHIAS	1858	DEFENDANT	1603	JONES, - / WARD & JONES	1871	NEW CUMB'LD	1767
JEFFERS, MATTHIAS	1837	DEFENDANT	1651	JONES, A	1871	MARH'L MAP	1749
JEFFERS, MATTHIAS	1838	DEFENDANT	1622	JONES, ABRAM / MAP#42	1852	BRKE MAP	1840
JEFFERS, MATTHIAS	1841	DEFENDANT	1623	JONES, C	1871	MARH'L MAP	1753
JEFFERS, MATTHIAS	1841	DEFENDANT	1629	JONES, C	1871	WELLSBURG	1776
JEFFERS, MATTHIAS	1843	DEFENDANT	1619	JONES, C E	1871	BKE/OH MAP	1739
JEFFERS, MATTHIAS	1853	DEFENDANT	1586	JONES, C E	1871	BKE/OH MAP	1739
JEFFERSON CITY, MO	1852	HEMPFIELD RR	1817	JONES, C E / INITIALS C.E.J. - STORE	1871	BKE/OH MAP	1739
JEFFERSON CO, OHIO	1871	FRE'MAN'S LDG	1764	JONES, CHARLES / (SMITHSHOP)	1852	NOT ON MAP	1836
JEFFERSON CO, OHIO	1871	RIV. RD S.OF N.C.	1771	JONES, CHARLES / (SMITHSHOP)	1852	NOT ON MAP	1836
JEFFERSON SCHOOL NO. 5	1871	HAN MAP	1731	JONES, CHARLES / (MILL) - MAP#41	1852	BRKE MAP	1840
JEFFERSON SCHOOL NO. 5	1871	HAN MAP	1732	JONES, CHARLES / MAP#40	1852	BRKE MAP	1840
JEFFERSON, J	1871	MARH'L MAP	1749	JONES, D	1871	OH CO. MAP	1743
JEFFERSON, J / INITIALS J.J.	1871	MARH'L MAP	1749	JONES, D	1871	MARH'L MAP	1747
JEFFERSON, J	1871	MARH'L MAP	1751	JONES, D	1871	MARH'L MAP	1749
JEFFERSON, J	1871	MARH'L MAP	1751	JONES, E	1871	BKE/OH MAP	1739
JEFFERSON, J SR	1871	MARH'L MAP	1751	JONES, E	1871	BKE/OH MAP	1739
JEFFERSON, JOSIAH Z	1841	DEFENDANT	1576	JONES, E / MILL	1871	BKE/OH MAP	1739
JEFFERSON, JOSIAH Z	1841	DEFENDANT	1594	JONES, ELLIS C / MAP#45	1852	BRKE MAP	1841
JEFFERSON, JOSIAH Z	1841	DEFENDANT	1626	JONES, ELLIS JR / MAP#38	1852	BRKE MAP	1840
JEFFERSON, S	1871	MARH'L MAP	1751	JONES, G	1871	BKE/OH MAP	1739
JEFFERY, BENJAMIN	1817	DEFENDANT	1659	JONES, G A	1871	MARH'L MAP	1750
JEFFERY, BENJAMIN	1818	DEFENDANT	1624	JONES, GARRISON	1817	DEFENDANT	1659
JENKINS, D Z	1871	NEW CUMB'LD	1767	JONES, GARRISON	1821	DEFENDANT	1570
JENKINS, J / MRS	1871	ROSBBYS RK	1813	JONES, GARRISON	1821	DEFENDANT	1632
JENKINS, J H	1871	NEW CUMB'LD	1762	JONES, GARRISON	1823	PLAINTIFF	1649
JENKINS, J H	1871	NEW CUMB'LD	1766	JONES, GARRISON	1828	DEFENDANT	1613
JENKINS, J H / OC	1871	NEW CUMB'LD	1767	JONES, GARRISON	1828	DEFENDANT	1632
JENKINS, M	1871	HAN MAP	1731				

'PERSONAL TIME LINE' INDEX TO VOLUME 7 OF THE *OHIO COUNTY INDEX*

ENTRY	YEAR	SUBJECT	PAGE
JONES, GARRISON	1830	DEFENDANT	1620
JONES, J	1871	MARH'L MAP	1749
JONES, J	1871	MARH'L MAP	1757
JONES, J	1871	WELLSBURG	1776
JONES, J P	1871	MARH'L MAP	1752
JONES, J R	1859	DEFENDANT	1588
JONES, JAMES / MAP#380	1852	BRKE MAP	1847
JONES, JAMES / MAP#381	1852	BRKE MAP	1847
JONES, JAMES K / ? S. OF QUEEN ST	1871	WELLSBURG	1777
JONES, JOHN	1787	DEFENDANT	1571
JONES, JOHN	1848	DEFENDANT	1629
JONES, JOHN	1857	DEFENDANT	1588
JONES, JOHN	1859	DEFENDANT	1560
JONES, JOHN	1863	DEFENDANT	1654
JONES, JOHN G	1871	MARH'L MAP	1746
JONES, JOHN G	1871	MARH'L MAP	1749
JONES, JOSEPHINE	1855	MISC	1681
JONES, JOSHUA J	1834	DEFENDANT	1620
JONES, JOSIAH	1852	NOT ON MAP	1836
JONES, MORGAN	1816	DEFENDANT	1645
JONES, MORGAN	1818	DEFENDANT	1642
JONES, MORGAN	1818	DEFENDANT	1660
JONES, MORGAN	1823	DEFENDANT	1649
JONES, MORGAN JR	1832	DEFENDANT	1585
JONES, MORGAN JR	1833	DEFENDANT	1620
JONES, MORGAN JR	1833	DEFENDANT	1639
JONES, MORGAN JR	1834	DEFENDANT	1620
JONES, P	1871	MARH'L MAP	1755
JONES, P / INITIALS P.J.	1871	MARH'L MAP	1755
JONES, ROBERT	1826	DEFENDANT	1565
JONES, S	1871	MARH'L MAP	1745
JONES, S	1871	MARH'L MAP	1745
JONES, S	1871	MARH'L MAP	1749
JONES, S	1871	MARH'L MAP	1749
JONES, S	1871	MARH'L MAP	1749
JONES, S B	1871	MARH'L MAP	1751
JONES, S B	1871	MARH'L MAP	1755
JONES, SAMUEL P	1835	DEFENDANT	1574
JONES, SAMUEL P	1835	DEFENDANT	1600
JONES, W	1871	BKE/OH MAP	1739
JONES, W P	1871	MARH'L MAP	1749
JONES, WASHINGTON / MAP#47	1852	BRKE MAP	1840
JONES, WILLIAM A	1871	HAN MAP	1731
JORDAN, MICHAEL W	1875	DEFENDANT	1567
JOYCE & WARD / OC	1871	BRKE MAP	1736
JOYCE & WARD / OFFICE	1871	BRKE MAP	1736
JOYCE, M	1871	HAN MAP	1733
JUDGE - G.W. THOMPSON	1871	OH CO. MAP	1742
JUDGE - G.W. THOMPSON	1871	TRIAD.TWP.	1781
JUDGE - G.W.THOMPSON	1871	WHG CITY	1789
JUNGMAN, J	1871	BKE/OH MAP	1738
JUNKIN, JOSEPH	1841	DEFENDANT	1563
JUNKIN, JOSEPH	1841	DEFENDANT	1672
JUNKIN, JOSEPH & SONS	1841	DEFENDANT	1672
JUNKINS, D	1844	DEFENDANT	1636
JUNKINS, J	1844	DEFENDANT	1636
JUNKINS, JOSEPH	1840	DEFENDANT	1670
JURGENS, B	1871	MARH'L MAP	1745
JURGENS, B	1871	MARH'L MAP	1745
K, J L / UNKNOWN INITIALS - BETHANY (?J.KEMP?)	1871	BETHANY	1773
KAIN, -	1840	PLAINTIFF	1620
KAIN, JOHN J	1880	MISC	1688
KAIN, WILLIAM	1871	MARH'L MAP	1747
KAISER - ORPHANS	1869	MISC	1686
KAISER, C	1869	MISC	1686
KANAWHA / PROPOSED NEW STATE NAME	1916	NAT'L ROAD	1863
KANE, J	1871	MARH'L MAP	1760
KANE, W	1871	MARH'L MAP	1750
KARR, JAMES	1779	APPENDIX	1874
KEATING, MARTHA JANE	1852	MISC	1697
KEEFE, M	1871	MARH'L MAP	1752
KEENAN, WILLIAM	1834	DEFENDANT	1578
KEER, JOSEPH	1811	DEFENDANT	1583
KEILY, M C / CLIFTON HOUSE	1871	MDSVILLE	1808
KEITH, HENRY / ?	1784	APPENDIX	1874
KEITH, PETER	1849	MISC	1706
KEITH, PETER	1853	MISC	1706
KELLER, - / MILLER & KELLER	1871	BRKE MAP	1734
KELLER, - / MILLER & KELLER	1871	BRKE MAP	1734
KELLER, - / MILLER & KELLER	1871	BRKE MAP	1734
KELLER, - / MILLER & KELLER / OFFICE	1871	BRKE MAP	1734
KELLER, - / MILLER, KELLER & TUTTLE	1871	BRKE MAP	1734
KELLER, - / MILLER & KELLER	1871	EDGINGTON STA.	1774
KELLER, - / MILLER & KELLER	1871	EDGINGTON STA.	1774
KELLER, - / MILLER & KELLER	1871	EDGINGTON STA.	1774
KELLER, - / MILLER, KELLER & TUTTLE PLANING MILL	1871	EDGINGTON STA.	1774
KELLER, C	1871	MARH'L MAP	1753
KELLER, FRANCIS	1792	DEFENDANT	1598
KELLER, J	1871	OH CO. MAP	1743
KELLER, J	1871	MARH'L MAP	1746
KELLEY, - / MRS	1871	BRKE MAP	1735
KELLEY, ISAAC	1791	DEFENDANT	1556
KELLEY, ISAAC	1792	DEFENDANT	1556
KELLEY, J	1871	BENWOOD	1798
KELLEY, J F V	1871	MARH'L MAP	1755
KELLEY, J R	1871	MARH'L MAP	1755
KELLEY, JAMES	1852	HEMPFIELD RR	1822
KELLEY, JAMES	1852	HEMPFIELD RR	1822
KELLEY, N	1871	OH CO. MAP	1742
KELLEY, S H / WEST LIBERTY	1871	W.LIBRTY.BUS.	1780
KELLEY, W	1871	MARH'L MAP	1755
KELLS, LOUIS	1854	DEFENDANT	1563
KELLS, LOUIS	1854	DEFENDANT	1623
KELLY, A	1871	OH CO. MAP	1741
KELLY, A / INITLAS A.K.	1871	OH CO. MAP	1741
KELLY, A / INITLAS A.K.	1871	OH CO. MAP	1741
KELLY, A / INITLAS A.K.	1871	OH CO. MAP	1741
KELLY, AARON	1857	DEFENDANT	1592
KELLY, AARON	1858	DEFENDANT	1657
KELLY, AARON	1860	DEFENDANT	1573
KELLY, AARON	1862	DEFENDANT	1597
KELLY, AARON	1862	DEFENDANT	1631
KELLY, ARON	1857	DEFENDANT	1626
KELLY, BENJAMIN	1826	DEFENDANT	1557
KELLY, BENJAMIN	1827	DEFENDANT	1557
KELLY, BENJAMIN F	1835	DEFENDANT	1576
KELLY, E	1871	MARH'L MAP	1755
KELLY, ELIZABETH	1844	MISC	1688
KELLY, I B / INITIALS L.B.K.	1871	OH CO. MAP	1741
KELLY, I B / INITIALS L.B.K.	1871	OH CO. MAP	1741
KELLY, I B / RES	1871	OH CO. MAP	1741
KELLY, J	1871	BENWOOD	1799
KELLY, M C / 'CLIFTON HOUSE'	1871	MDSVL BUS.	1796
KELLY, N	1871	OH CO. MAP	1744
KELLY, S	1871	MARH'L MAP	1745
KELLY, T B / INITIALS T.B.K.	1871	OH CO. MAP	1741
KELLY, T B / INITIALS T.B.K. - SEE ALSO KELLY, I.B. - SAME PERSON ?	1871	OH CO. MAP	1741
KELLY, THOMAS R / MAP#421	1852	BRKE MAP	1847
KELLY, W	1871	OH CO. MAP	1742
KELLY, W	1871	RITCHIE TWP	1791
KELT, H	1871	MARH'L MAP	1746
KELTY, H / SHERIFF OF MARSHALL CO - UNION TWP	1871	UNION TWP-BUS.	1797
KELTZ, -	1854	DEFENDANT	1592
KELTZ, H	1871	MARH'L MAP	1745
KELTZ, H	1871	MARH'L MAP	1745
KELTZ, H / HEIRS	1871	MARH'L MAP	1753
KELTZ, H	1871	MDSVILLE	1807
KEMP, ADAM	1834	DEFENDANT	1591
KEMP, ADAM	1837	DEFENDANT	1592
KEMP, J	1871	MARH'L MAP	1755
KEMP, J	1871	BETHANY	1773
KEMP, J / UNSURE INITIALS J.L.K. - BETHANY (?J.KEMP?)	1871	BETHANY	1773
KEMP, JACOB	1848	DEFENDANT	1620
KEMP, JACOB	1848	DEFENDANT	1620
KEMP, P	1871	MARH'L MAP	1755
KEMP, P / NEAR BLACKSMITH SHOP	1871	MARH'L MAP	1759
KEMPLE, -	1855	PLAINTIFF	1629
KEMPLE, -	1859	PLAINTIFF	1630
KEMPLE, - / MRS - BELOW M. DOWLER	1871	MARH'L MAP	1745
KEMPLE, - / MRS - S. OF LOCUST GROVE	1871	MARH'L MAP	1746
KEMPLE, CHARLES	1833	MISC	1695
KEMPLE, G	1871	MARH'L MAP	1745
KEMPLE, G	1871	MARH'L MAP	1757
KEMPLE, W	1871	MARH'L MAP	1746
KEMPLE, W	1871	MARH'L MAP	1749
KENADAY, PETER W	1832	DEFENDANT	1639
KENDALL, -	1840	PLAINTIFF	1626
KENDALL, -	1841	DEFENDANT	1586
KENDALL, -	1841	DEFENDANT	1629
KENDALL, ROBERT T / & CO	1841	DEFENDANT	1557

'PERSONAL TIME LINE' INDEX TO VOLUME 7 OF THE *OHIO COUNTY INDEX*

ENTRY	YEAR	SUBJECT	PAGE	ENTRY	YEAR	SUBJECT	PAGE
KENDALL, ROBERT T	1841	DEFENDANT	1585	KINGS CREEK	1871	HAN MAP	1732
KENDALL, ROBERT T	1841	DEFENDANT	1629	KINGS CREEK - MOUTH OF AT OHIO RIVER	1871	FRE'MAN'S LDG	1765
KENDALL, ROBERT T	1841	DEFENDANT	1652				
KENNEDAY, P W	1843	DEFENDANT	1640	KINGS CREEK - NORTH FORK OF	1871	HAN MAP	1732
KENNEDEY, D	1835	DEFENDANT	1553	KINGSTON FIRE BRICK WORKS	1871	FRE'MAN'S LDG	1762
KENNEDY, DAVID	1861	DEFENDANT	1664	KINGSTON FIRE BRICK WORKS	1871	FRE'MAN'S LDG	1765
KENNEDY, GEORGE	1859	DEFENDANT	1673	KINNEY, JOSEPH	1871	HAN MAP	1727
KENNEDY, PATRICK	1877	DEFENDANT	1560	KINNEY, JOSEPH	1871	HAN MAP	1728
KENNEL COAL	1871	HAN MAP	1731	KINNEY, W H	1871	HAN MAP	1727
KENNEL COAL - E OF BROWNS ISLAND	1871	HAN MAP	1732	KINNEY, W H	1871	HAN MAP	1728
				KINNEY, WILLIAM	1871	HAN MAP	1728
KENNIDY, J	1871	MARH'L MAP	1745	KINNEYS RUN	1871	HAN MAP	1727
KENOVA, WV	1916	NAT'L ROAD	1863	KINNEYS RUN	1871	HAN MAP	1728
KENTUCKY	1852	HEMPFIELD RR	1821	KINNYS RUN	1871	HAN MAP	1728
KERNES, J	1871	MARH'L MAP	1753	KIRBY, A	1871	MARH'L MAP	1761
KERNS, J / ?	1871	MARH'L MAP	1753	KIRCHER - CHILDREN	1875	MISC	1711
KERR, / - MRS	1871	FRE'MAN'S LDG	1764	KIRCHER - ORPHANS	1872	MISC	1711
KERR, G	1871	MARH'L MAP	1757	KIRK, J	1871	W.UNION	1812
KERR, JAMES	1813	DEFENDANT	1559	KIRK, J / BLACKSMITH SHOP	1871	W.UNION	1812
KERR, JOHN	1810	DEFENDANT	1642	KIRK, M / MRS	1871	BRKE MAP	1737
KERR, JOSEPH	1805	DEFENDANT	1556	KIRK, MARY / MAP#353	1852	BRKE MAP	1846
KERR, JOSEPH	1811	DEFENDANT	1638	KIRKER, - / A.P. - DRUG STORE / (OC.)	1871	WELLSBURG	1777
KERR, JOSEPH	1811	DEFENDANT	1667	KIRKER, A P	1871	WLSBRG BUS.	1772
KERR, JOSEPH	1811	DEFENDANT	1667	KIRKER, A P	1871	WELLSBURG	1777
KERR, JOSEPH	1812	DEFENDANT	1555	KIRKER, JAMES M	1849	DEFENDANT	1603
KERR, JOSEPH	1814	DEFENDANT	1555	KIRKMAN, GEORGE	1838	DEFENDANT	1635
KERR, JOSEPH	1814	DEFENDANT	1559	KIRKPATRICK, -	1821	PLAINTIFF	1620
KERR, MATTHEW	1784	DEFENDANT	1610	KIRKPATRICK, HENRY	1822	DEFENDANT	1638
KERR, MATTHEW	1805	PLAINTIFF	1648	KIRKPATRICK, HENRY	1829	DEFENDANT	1574
KETLER, CHARLES	1871	MARH'L MAP	1745	KIRKPATRICK, JOHN	1858	DEFENDANT	1616
KEVNS, J / ?	1871	MARH'L MAP	1753	KIRKPATRICK, W	1871	BRKE MAP	1734
KEY, A	1871	OH CO. MAP	1742	KIRKPATRICK, W / INITIALS W.K.	1871	BRKE MAP	1734
KEY, ALEXES	1871	MARH'L MAP	1745	KIRTON, J H / ?	1871	MARH'L MAP	1754
KEYS, -	1840	PLAINTIFF	1620	KIRTON, J N	1871	MARH'L MAP	1758
KEYSER	1871	MARH'L MAP	1749	KISNER, J	1871	MARH'L MAP	1756
KEYSER, -	1871	MARH'L MAP	1746	KISNER, J	1871	MARH'L MAP	1756
KEYSER, A	1871	MARH'L MAP	1746	KITTLE, S B / GRIST MILL	1871	MARH'L MAP	1746
KEYSER, A	1871	MARH'L MAP	1750	KITTLE, S B / & SON - BLACKSMITHS - 'GRINDSTAFFS RUN'	1871	SAND HILL-BUS.	1797
KEYSER, J	1871	MARH'L MAP	1746				
KEYSER, J	1871	MARH'L MAP	1749	KITTLE, S B / & SON - STEAM SAW MILL	1871	SAND HILL-BUS.	1797
KEYSER, P	1871	MARH'L MAP	1752				
KEYSER, W	1871	MARH'L MAP	1750	KITTLE, S S	1871	MARH'L MAP	1753
KHIKINS, J	1871	BENWOOD	1798	KITTLE, S S	1871	MARH'L MAP	1757
KIDD, D	1871	OH CO. MAP	1743	KITTLE, S B / & SON - S.S.MILL	1871	MARH'L MAP	1746
KIERLE, JOHN W	1840	PLAINTIFF	1576	KLEINER, C T	1871	MARH'L MAP	1745
KILE, H	1871	OH CO. MAP	1741	KLEINER, C T / INITIALS C.T.K.	1871	MARH'L MAP	1745
KILE, H	1871	OH CO. MAP	1742	KLEINER, C T / INITIALS C.T.K.	1871	MARH'L MAP	1748
KILLEN, WILLIAM	1826	DEFENDANT	1583	KLEVIS, WILLIAM	1849	DEFENDANT	1600
KILN - BK KILN / (?BRICK?) TOMLINSON RUN	1871	HAN MAP	1727	KLIEVES & KRAFT	1846	DEFENDANT	1592
				KLIEVES, WILLIAM	1874	DEFENDANT	1603
KILN - LIME KILN	1871	OH CO. MAP	1742	KLIEVES, WILLIAM	1874	DEFENDANT	1621
KIMBERLAND, -	1871	WELLSBURG	1776	KLIEVES, WILLIAM	1874	DEFENDANT	1636
KIMBERLAND, -	1871	WELLSBURG	1776	KLINE, -	1857	PLAINTIFF	1626
KIMBERLAND, - / MRS	1871	WELLSBURG	1776	KLINE, JACOB A	1842	MISC	1685
KIMBERLAND, - / GLOBE FOUNDRY WAREROOM - KIMBERLAND & KUHN	1871	WELLSBURG	1778	KLINESBURG, -	1871	OH CO. MAP	1743
				KLINESBURG, -	1871	OH CO. MAP	1744
KIMBERLAND, C	1871	WELLSBURG	1777	KNIGHT, RICHARD	1834	DEFENDANT	1555
KIMBERLAND, C / CHARLES ST ?	1871	WELLSBURG	1777	KNODE, SAMUEL	1830	DEFENDANT	1591
KIMBERLAND, K	1871	WELLSBURG	1777	KNODE, SAMUEL	1833	DEFENDANT	1566
KIMBERLY & CO	1875	DEFENDANT	1592	KNODE, SAMUEL	1833	DEFENDANT	1622
KIMBERLY & CO	1878	DEFENDANT	1592	KNODE, SAMUEL	1839	MISC	1677
KIMBERLY, WILLIAM / MAP#270	1852	BRKE MAP	1842	KNOKE & HAMAN	1855	DEFENDANT	1570
KIMBERLYS RUN	1852	BRKE MAP	1843	KNOKE, HENRY & CO	1876	DEFENDANT	1609
KIMMINS SCHOOL NO. 2	1871	OH CO. MAP	1743	KNOTE, JOHN	1835	MISC	1702
KIMMINS, - / (?INITIAL UNCLEAR?) - NEAR WHITE OAK SPRING	1871	OH CO. MAP	1743	KNOUP, MARY	1810	DEFENDANT	1648
				KNOWLES, R & CO	1852	DEFENDANT	1663
KIMMINS, - / ON BORDER - FIRST INITIALS NOT CLEAR	1871	MARH'L MAP	1746	KNOWLES, RICHARD	1852	DEFENDANT	1608
				KNOWLES, RICHARD	1853	DEFENDANT	1663
KIMMINS, A H	1871	OH CO. MAP	1743	KNOX, -	1817	PLAINTIFF	1632
KIMMINS, A R	1871	MARH'L MAP	1747	KNOX, -	1818	PLAINTIFF	1632
KIMMINS, A R	1871	MARH'L MAP	1747	KNOX, -	1821	PLAINTIFF	1632
KIMMINS, E L	1871	OH CO. MAP	1740	KNOX, -	1822	PLAINTIFF	1632
KIMMINS, J	1871	OH CO. MAP	1743	KNOX, -	1823	PLAINTIFF	1632
KIMMINS, J	1871	OH CO. MAP	1743	KNOX, -	1824	PLAINTIFF	1632
KIMMONS DIST	1871	OH CO. MAP	1743	KNOX, -	1828	PLAINTIFF	1632
KIMMONS, S	1871	MARH'L MAP	1747	KNOX, -	1829	PLAINTIFF	1632
KIMMONS, W	1871	MARH'L MAP	1747	KNOX, -	1844	PLAINTIFF	1632
KING, J	1871	LAGRANGE	1794	KNOX, - / MRS	1871	HAN MAP	1733
KING, JAMES F	1828	DEFENDANT	1649	KNOX, A / (?OR J?)	1871	HAN MAP	1733
KING, JAMES F	1830	DEFENDANT	1622	KNOX, CHARLES	1825	MISC	1710
KING, SOLOMON	1823	DEFENDANT	1581	KNOX, CHARLES D	1818	MISC	1683
KING, SOLOMON	1825	DEFENDANT	1581	KNOX, CHARLES D	1831	MISC	1678
KING, SOLOMON	1835	DEFENDANT	1613	KNOX, CHARLES D	1852	HEMPFIELD RR	1822
KING, WILLIAM H	1843	DEFENDANT	1620	KNOX, CHESTER D	1871	TRIAD.TWP.	1781
KING, WILLIAM H	1843	DEFENDANT	1640	KNOX, D	1871	WHG CITY	1789
KINGS CREEK	1871	HAN MAP	1732	KNOX, GEORGE	1802	MISC	1703

'PERSONAL TIME LINE' INDEX TO VOLUME 7 OF THE *OHIO COUNTY INDEX*

ENTRY	YEAR	SUBJECT	PAGE	ENTRY	YEAR	SUBJECT	PAGE
KNOX, GEORGE	1824	DEFENDANT	1656	LAFFERTY, J	1871	MDSVILLE	1809
KNOX, GEORGE	1826	DEFENDANT	1656	LAFFERTY, J / INITIALS J.L. - THOMPSON ST	1871	MDSVILLE	1810
KNOX, J	1871	HAN MAP	1733				
KNOX, J / (?OR A?)	1871	HAN MAP	1733	LAGRANGE - BEECH ST	1871	LAGRANGE	1792
KNOX, J	1871	MARH'L MAP	1749	LAGRANGE - BEECH ST	1871	LAGRANGE	1794
KNOX, J	1871	MARH'L MAP	1749	LAGRANGE - DETAIL MAP	1871	LAGRANGE	1792
KNOX, J	1871	MARH'L MAP	1750	LAGRANGE - DETAIL MAP	1871	LAGRANGE	1794
KNOX, J	1871	MARH'L MAP	1750	LAGRANGE - ELM ST	1871	LAGRANGE	1792
KNOX, JAMES	1799	DEFENDANT	1591	LAGRANGE - ELM ST	1871	LAGRANGE	1794
KNOX, JAMES	1800	DEFENDANT	1665	LAGRANGE - OHIO CO	1871	WHG CITY	1786
KNOX, JAMES	1801	DEFENDANT	1591	LAGRANGE - PLANK ROAD	1871	LAGRANGE	1792
KNOX, W A	1871	MARH'L MAP	1752	LAGRANGE - PLANK ROAD	1871	LAGRANGE	1794
KNOX, W A	1871	MARH'L MAP	1752	LAGRANGE - POPLAR ST	1871	LAGRANGE	1792
KOBER, F	1871	OH CO. MAP	1742	LAGRANGE - POPLAR ST	1871	LAGRANGE	1794
KOBER, F	1871	OH CO. MAP	1742	LAGRANGE - S. OF SOUTH WHEELING	1871	OH CO. MAP	1742
KOBER, F	1871	WHG CITY	1787	LAGRANGE - SYCAMORE ST	1871	LAGRANGE	1792
KOBER, FRED	1871	OH CO.BUS.	1779	LAGRANGE - SYCAMORE ST	1871	LAGRANGE	1794
KOCH, DOROTHEA	1869	MISC	1711	LAGRANGE - TANNERY	1871	LAGRANGE	1794
KOCH, J	1871	MARH'L MAP	1754	LAGRANGE - WILLOW ST / (?W.WILLOW?)	1871	WHG CITY	1792
KOCH, J	1871	MARH'L MAP	1758				
KOEN, O T	1871	MDSVILLE	1810	LAGRANGE - WILLOW ST / (?W.WILLOW?)	1871	RITCHIE TWP	1794
KOLLMAN - HEIRS	1871	MISC	1698				
KOONTZ, G	1871	MARH'L MAP	1748	LAGRANGE, OH	1871	BRKE MAP	1736
KOONTZ, G	1871	MARH'L MAP	1748	LAGRANGE, OH - ACROSS FROM WELLSBURG	1852	BRKE MAP	1846
KOONTZ, G / INITIALS G.K.	1871	MARH'L MAP	1748	LAIDLEY, ALEXANDER J	1842	DEFENDANT	1586
KOONTZ, G / INITIALS G.K.	1871	MARH'L MAP	1748	LAIRD, HARRISON P / WESTMORELAND CO	1852	HEMPFIELD RR	1817
KOONTZ, G / INITIALS G.K. - SAW MILL	1871	MARH'L MAP	1748	LAKE ERIE	1852	HEMPFIELD RR	1820
KOONTZ, G / INITIALS G.K. - FAIRVIEW	1871	MARH'L MAP	1752	LAKIN, -	1855	PLAINTIFF	1629
KOONTZ, G / INITIALS G.K. - FAIRVIEW	1871	MARH'L MAP	1752	LAKIN, -	1857	PLAINTIFF	1630
KOONTZ, G / SAW MILL - FAIRVIEW	1871	MARH'L MAP	1752	LAKIN, -	1859	PLAINTIFF	1630
KOONTZ, W	1871	MARH'L MAP	1752	LAKIN, -	1860	PLAINTIFF	1630
KOONTZ, W	1871	MDSVILLE	1807	LAKIN, JOHN T	1878	DEFENDANT	1631
KOONTZ, W	1871	MDSVILLE	1807	LALLY, FRANCES	1852	DEFENDANT	1586
KOONTZ, W / CABINET SHOP	1871	MDSVILLE	1807	LAMASTERS, C / MRS	1871	MARH'L MAP	1761
KORN, GEORGE	1871	OH CO. MAP	1740	LAMB, DANIEL	1839	MISC	1705
KORNE, JOHN	1878	MISC	1698	LAMB, FREDERICK	1785	DEFENDANT	1554
KRAFT, -	1846	DEFENDANT	1592	LAMBDIN, - & CO. - MAP#403	1852	BRKE MAP	1846
KRAFT, -	1870	PLAINTIFF	1627	LAMBDIN, - & CO. PAPERMILL - MAP#406	1852	BRKE MAP	1846
KRAFT, JOHN	1842	DEFENDANT	1643				
KRAFT, JOHN	1846	DEFENDANT	1643	LAMBDIN, WILLIAM	1834	DEFENDANT	1669
KRAFT, JOHN	1847	DEFENDANT	1600	LAMBDIN, WILLIAM	1836	DEFENDANT	1591
KRAKENBURG, FREDERICK M	1855	DEFENDANT	1588	LAMBDIN, WILLIAM	1841	DEFENDANT	1670
KREUSCH, PETER	1879	DEFENDANT	1618	LAMBS RUN	1852	BRKE MAP	1842
KRIDER, ISAAC	1834	DEFENDANT	1662	LANCASTER, B W	1871	CAMERON	1802
KRONHART, C / STORE	1871	BENWOOD	1798	LANCASTER, B W / INITIALS B.W.L.	1871	CAMERON	1802
KRUMM, W H	1871	OH CO. MAP	1744	LANCASTER, J	1871	MARH'L MAP	1757
KRUMM, W H	1871	OH CO. MAP	1744	LANCASTER, J	1871	MARH'L MAP	1761
KRUSER, J	1871	OH CO. MAP	1744	LANCASTER, JOSEPH	1858	DEFENDANT	1558
KUCH, H	1871	TRIAD. TWP.	1781	LANDING - ANDERSONS	1871	HAN MAP	1730
KUCH, H	1871	WHG CITY	1787	LANDING - ANDERSONS	1871	HAN MAP	1732
KUCH, H	1871	WHG CITY	1789	LANDING - ANDERSONS - OHIO RIVER	1871	FRE'MAN'S LDG	1764
KUGER, W	1871	BRKE MAP	1737	LANDING - CHAPMANS	1871	HAN MAP	1730
KUHLEMAN, PETER	1873	MISC	1690	LANDING - DEVENNYS / ON OHIO RIVER	1871	BRKE MAP	1735
KUHN, - / PENDLETON & KUHN	1871	WELLSBURG	1776				
KUHN, -	1871	WELLSBURG	1777	LANDING - FRANKLIN LANDING - WOODLAND P.O.	1871	MARH'L MAP	1754
KUHN, - / BLACKSMITH SHOP	1871	WELLSBURG	1777				
KUHN, - / BLACKSMITH SHOP	1871	WELLSBURG	1777	LANDING - HUBBS LANDING - OHIO RIVER - WOODLAND P.O.	1871	MARH'L MAP	1754
KUHN, - / GLOBE FOUNDRY WAREROOM - KIMBERLAND & KUHN	1871	WELLSBURG	1778				
KUHN, A	1871	BRKE MAP	1736	LANDING - OHIO RIVER / EDGE OF MAP	1871	MARH'L MAP	1751
KUHN, A / PRES.- FIRST NATIONAL BANK	1871	WLSBRG BUS.	1772	LANDING - OHIO RIVER - N. OF FISH CREEK ISLAND	1871	MARH'L MAP	1754
KUHN, A / (O)	1871	WELLSBURG	1777				
KUHN, A W	1871	BRKE MAP	1735	LANDING - OHIO RIVER - S. OF FISH CREEK ISLAND	1871	MARH'L MAP	1754
KUHN, A W / RES	1871	BRKE MAP	1735				
KUHN, ADAM / ESQ. - MAP#279	1852	BRKE MAP	1846	LANDING - PORTERS - OHIO RIVER	1871	FRE'MAN'S LDG	1764
KUHN, ADAM / ESQ. - MAP#280	1852	BRKE MAP	1846	LANDING - SIMS / OHIO RIVER	1871	MARH'L MAP	1754
KUHN, ADAM / ESQ. - MAP#345	1852	BRKE MAP	1846	LANDING - STEAMBOAT LANDING - WELLSBURG	1871	WELLSBURG	1778
KULL, DAVID	1855	DEFENDANT	1615				
KULL, DAVID	1875	DEFENDANT	1566	LANE, DAVID	1832	DEFENDANT	1662
KULL, J / EST	1871	MDSVILLE	1810	LANE, EDWARD	1828	DEFENDANT	1649
KULL, R / MRS	1871	MARH'L MAP	1751	LANE, EDWARD R	1829	DEFENDANT	1650
KULLMAN - HEIRS	1873	MISC	1690	LANE, M	1871	WELLSBURG	1777
KYLE, J	1871	MARH'L MAP	1748	LANE, M	1871	WELLSBURG	1777
KYLE, J / INITIALS J.K.	1871	MARH'L MAP	1748	LANE, R	1871	MDSVILLE	1808
L, J B / UNKNOWN INITIALS - BETHANY	1871	BETHANY	1773	LANGFITT, - / MRS	1871	WELLSBURG	1777
L.S. / UNKNOWN INITIALS	1871	MARH'L MAP	1756	LANGFITT, E	1871	HAN MAP	1731
LABELLE IRON WORKS	1871	WHG CITY	1790	LANGFITT, J / MRS - SW CORNER OF MAP	1871	BRKE MAP	1735
LABELLE IRON WORKS	1871	WHG CITY	1792				
LACOCK, J K / PHOTOGRAPHER	1916	NAT'L ROAD	1866	LANGFITT, J / MRS	1871	BRKE MAP	1736
LADLEY RUN	1871	OH CO. MAP	1743	LANGLITT, - / MRS	1871	WELLSBURG	1776
LADY, DANIEL	1840	DEFENDANT	1662	LANGSTON, JEFFERSON	1859	DEFENDANT	1602
LAFAYETTE, MARQUIS DE / NAMESAKE OF LAFAYETTE TAVERN	1916	NAT'L ROAD	1862	LARGE, -	1852	NOT ON MAP	1836
				LARKIN, -	1855	DEFENDANT	1590
LAFFERTY, J	1871	MDSVILLE	1807	LARKIN, - / MRS	1871	OH CO. MAP	1742

LV

'PERSONAL TIME LINE' INDEX TO VOLUME 7 OF THE OHIO COUNTY INDEX

ENTRY	YEAR	SUBJECT	PAGE	ENTRY	YEAR	SUBJECT	PAGE
LARKIN, ED	1876	DEFENDANT	1597	LEASURE, GEORGE R	1874	DEFENDANT	1631
LASH, J	1871	OH CO. MAP	1741	LEATHEM, J	1871	HAN MAP	1727
LASH, JACOB	1879	DEFENDANT	1590	LEATHERWOOD / NATIONAL ROAD	1871	OH CO. MAP	1742
LASHLEY, JOSHUA	1834	DEFENDANT	1591	LEATHERWOOD	1871	WHG CITY	1789
LASKEY, JOSHUA	1832	DEFENDANT	1591	LEATHERWOOD - DETAIL MAP	1871	TRIAD.TWP.	1781
LATHROP, JAMES M / MAP ASSISTANT	1871	MAP	1713	LEATHERWOOD - DETAIL MAP	1871	RITCHIE TWP	1794
				LEATHERWOOD - OHIO CO	1871	WHG CITY	1786
LATIMER, -	1871	WELLSBURG	1777	LEATHERWOOD - SECTION OF TOWN	1871	TRIAD.TWP.	1781
LATIMER, A	1871	WELLSBURG	1777	LEATHERWOOD - TOLL HOUSE - NATIONAL ROAD	1871	TRIAD.TWP.	1781
LATIMER, D	1871	WELLSBURG	1777	LEBAREN, WILLIAM	1838	DEFENDANT	1568
LATIMER, D / & SONS - SADDLER & HARNESS (OC)	1871	WELLSBURG	1778	LEE, A / EST (?ESTATE?)	1871	BRKE MAP	1734
LATIMER, J	1871	BRKE MAP	1734	LEE, ANDREW / HEIRS - MAP#585	1852	BRKE MAP	1851
LATTIMER, R B	1871	BRKE MAP	1734	LEE, DAVID	1837	DEFENDANT	1614
LATTIMORE, BROWN	1852	NOT ON MAP	1836	LEE, DAVID	1837	DEFENDANT	1618
LAUCK, ALFRED S	1840	DEFENDANT	1577	LEE, DAVID	1838	DEFENDANT	1651
LAUCK, ALFRED S	1840	DEFENDANT	1617	LEE, DAVID	1840	DEFENDANT	1640
LAUCK, ALFRED S	1840	DEFENDANT	1652	LEE, ISAAC	1859	DEFENDANT	1641
LAUCK, J T / PROPT BETHANY HOUSE	1871	BETHNY BUS.	1772	LEE, JOHN	1803	PLAINTIFF	1583
				LEE, JOHN	1804	DEFENDANT	1644
LAUCK, J T	1871	BETHANY	1773	LEE, JOHN	1807	DEFENDANT	1556
LAUCK, J T	1871	BETHANY	1773	LEE, JOHN	1808	DEFENDANT	1608
LAUCK, S / REV.HEIRS - MAP#9	1852	BRKE MAP	1840	LEE, JOHN	1809	DEFENDANT	1587
LAUCK, S	1871	BETHANY	1773	LEE, JOHN	1809	DEFENDANT	1608
LAUCK, WILLIAM	1871	BETHANY	1773	LEE, W M	1871	HAN MAP	1733
LAUGHEAD, J / & W (GONE) - (MILL) - MAP#386	1852	BRKE MAP	1846	LEES BRANCH	1852	BRKE MAP	1851
				LEES RUN	1852	BRKE MAP	1850
LAUGHEAD, J / & W(GONE) - MAP#384	1852	BRKE MAP	1846	LEFLER, DAVID / (SAWMILL)	1852	NOT ON MAP	1836
LAUGHEAD, J / & W (GONE) - MAP#385	1852	BRKE MAP	1846	LEFLER, DAVID / MAP#66	1852	BRKE MAP	1840
				LEFLER, DAVID / MAP#69	1852	BRKE MAP	1840
LAUGHEAD, J / & W(GONE) - MAP#383	1852	BRKE MAP	1846	LEFT FORK OF FISH CREEK / ALSO CALLED PENN FORK	1871	MARH'L MAP	1761
LAUGHEAD, W / & J (GONE) - MAP#383	1852	BRKE MAP	1846	LEFT FORK OF MAGGOTY RUN	1871	MARH'L MAP	1756
LAUGHEAD, W / & J (GONE) - MAP#384	1852	BRKE MAP	1846	LEFT OR PENN FORK OF FISH CREEK / (?PENNSYLVANIA FORK?)	1871	MARH'L MAP	1761
LAUGHEAD, W / & J (GONE) - MAP#385	1852	BRKE MAP	1846	LEFT OR PENN FORK OF FISH CREEK / PENNSYLVANIA FORK	1871	BELLTON	1814
LAUGHEAD, W / & J (GONE) - MILL / MAP#386	1852	BRKE MAP	1846	LEFT OR PENN FORK OF FISH CREEK / PENNSYLVANIA FORK - DAM ON	1871	BELLTON	1814
LAUGHLIN, J	1871	MARH'L MAP	1753	LEFT OR PENN FORK OF FISH CREEK / PENNSYLVANIA FORK - DAM ON	1871	BELLTON	1814
LAUGHLIN, J / INITIALS J.L. - ROCK LICK P.O.	1871	MARH'L MAP	1753	LEGHORN, LEMUEL	1810	DEFENDANT	1583
LAUGHLIN, JOHN / ROCK LICK	1871	GLEN EASTON - BUS.	1796	LEIPER, JOHN	1852	NOT ON MAP	1836
				LEIPERS RUN	1852	BRKE MAP	1850
LAUGHLIN, ROBERT	1829	MISC	1705	LELAMSTERS - SEE ALSO LAMASTERS	1871	MARH'L MAP	1761
LAUGHRIDGE, WILLIAM	1822	DEFENDANT	1572				
LAUGHRIDGE, WILLIAM	1822	DEFENDANT	1612	LEMASTERS, LEWIS	1835	DEFENDANT	1591
LAUGHTEN, JOHN	1827	MISC	1684	LEMMON, JOHN	1785	MISC	1701
LAUREL RUN	1871	MARH'L MAP	1756	LEMON, - / MRS	1871	CAMERON	1803
LAUREL RUN	1871	MARH'L MAP	1760	LEPEN, JAMES	1779	APPENDIX	1874
LAW ORDER BOOK ENTRIES	2000	APPENDIX	1872	LEPEN, MARGARET	1779	APPENDIX	1874
LAW, W	1871	BENWOOD	1798	LETTEN, SAMUEL	1797	DEFENDANT	1596
LAW, W	1871	BENWOOD	1798	LETZKUTS, G	1871	WELLSBURG	1777
LAWS, ALEXANDER	1840	DEFENDANT	1640	LETZKUTS, G / INITIALS G.L.	1871	WELLSBURG	1777
LAWS, THOMAS	1840	DEFENDANT	1577	LETZKUZ, R / ?	1871	WELLSBURG	1778
LAWS, THOMAS	1840	DEFENDANT	1617	LETZLEUS, J / NAME WRITTEN IN OHIIO RIVER	1871	BRKE MAP	1736
LAWS, THOMAS	1840	DEFENDANT	1652	LEUKERT, JACOB P	1879	DEFENDANT	1661
LAWSON, - / ESTATE	1871	TRIAD.BORO.	1784	LEWELLEN, H	1871	MARH'L MAP	1756
LAWSON, - / ESTATE	1871	TRIAD.BORO.	1784	LEWIS & WOODMANSEE / GRANT HOUSE - WHEELING	1871	OH CO. BUS.	1779
LAWSON, F / HOTEL - TRIAD.	1871	TRIAD.BORO.	1784				
LAWSON, FRANCIS	1850	DEFENDANT	1586	LEWIS BRANCH	1852	BRKE MAP	1846
LAWSON, FRANCIS	1851	DEFENDANT	1573	LEWIS, G W	1871	OH CO. MAP	1740
LAWSON, FRANCIS	1851	DEFENDANT	1604	LEWIS, G W	1871	OH CO. MAP	1743
LAWSON, FRANCIS	1851	DEFENDANT	1604	LEWIS, HENRY	1841	DEFENDANT	1577
LAWYER - CALDWELL / G W	1871	BRKE MAP	1735	LEWIS, HENRY	1841	DEFENDANT	1617
LAYTON, T C	1856	DEFENDANT	1616	LEWIS, HENRY	1841	DEFENDANT	1652
LAZAER, JESSE / MAP#104	1852	BRKE MAP	1843	LEWIS, J	1871	BRKE MAP	1736
LAZAER, JOSEPH / MAP#164	1852	BRKE MAP	1842	LEWIS, J	1871	BRKE MAP	1736
LAZEAR, H G	1871	BRKE MAP	1735	LEWIS, J	1871	BRKE MAP	1736
LAZEAR, H G / GLEN ELM	1871	BRKE MAP	1736	LEWIS, J	1871	BRKE MAP	1736
LAZEAR, H G	1871	WELLSBURG	1776	LEWIS, J	1871	BRKE MAP	1736
LAZEAR, J	1871	BRKE MAP	1736	LEWIS, J	1871	BRKE MAP	1736
LAZEAR, J	1871	BKE/OH MAP	1739	LEWIS, J / (?JOB?)	1871	BRKE MAP	1736
LAZEAR, J	1871	BKE/OH MAP	1739	LEWIS, J / COAL	1871	BRKE MAP	1736
LAZEAR, J / INITIALS J.L.	1871	BKE/OH MAP	1739	LEWIS, J / SAW MILL	1871	BRKE MAP	1736
LAZEAR, J / INITIALS J.L.	1871	BKE/OH MAP	1739	LEWIS, J	1871	BRKE MAP	1737
LAZEAR, J D	1871	WELLSBURG	1778	LEWIS, J	1871	BKE/OH MAP	1739
LAZEAR, P	1871	BKE/OH MAP	1739	LEWIS, J	1871	MARH'L MAP	1746
LAZUR HOLLOW	1871	BRKE MAP	1736	LEWIS, J	1871	BETHANY	1773
LAZUR HOLLOW	1871	BKE/OH MAP	1739	LEWIS, J	1871	BETHANY	1773
LDS - FAMILY HISTORY CENTER LIBRARY	2000	APPENDIX	1872	LEWIS, JOB / (MILL) - MAP#295	1852	BRKE MAP	1846
LEACH, CLEMENT / RES	1871	MARH'L MAP	1749	LEWIS, JOB / (MILL) - MAP#329	1852	BRKE MAP	1846
LEACH, E	1871	BENWOOD	1799	LEWIS, JOB / MAP#288	1852	BRKE MAP	1846
LEACH, E	1871	BENWOOD	1799	LEWIS, JOB / MAP#293	1852	BRKE MAP	1846
LEACH, J	1871	MARH'L MAP	1749	LEWIS, JOB / MAP#294	1852	BRKE MAP	1846
LEACH, J W	1871	MARH'L MAP	1749				
LEACH, WILLIAM	1878	DEFENDANT	1593				

'PERSONAL TIME LINE' INDEX TO VOLUME 7 OF THE *OHIO COUNTY INDEX*

ENTRY	YEAR	SUBJECT	PAGE	ENTRY	YEAR	SUBJECT	PAGE
LEWIS, JOB	1871	BRKE MAP	1736	LINDSEY, E	1871	MARH'L MAP	1748
LEWIS, JOB	1871	BRKE MAP	1736	LINDSEY, E	1871	MARH'L MAP	1748
LEWIS, JOB	1871	BRKE MAP	1736	LINDSEY, E	1871	MARH'L MAP	1748
LEWIS, JOB JR	1871	WLSBRG BUS.	1772	LINDSEY, E	1871	MDSVILLE	1808
LEWIS, JOB JR / GRAIN & AG. TOOLS	1871	WELLSBURG	1777	LINDSEY, JOSH SR / HEIRS - MAP#124	1852	BRKE MAP	1844
LEWIS, JOHN / MAP#270	1852	BRKE MAP	1842	LINDSEY, JOSHUA / HEIRS - MAP#48	1852	BRKE MAP	1840
LEWIS, JOHN / MAP#271	1852	BRKE MAP	1842	LINDSEY, JOSHUA / HEIRS - MAP#49	1852	BRKE MAP	1840
LEWIS, JOHN / MAP#271	1852	BRKE MAP	1842	LINDSEY, JOSHUA / HEIRS / (SAWMILL) - MAP#50	1852	BRKE MAP	1840
LEWIS, JOHN / MAP#284	1852	BRKE MAP	1846	LINDSEY, JOSHUA / HEIRS / (SAWMILL) - MAP#51	1852	BRKE MAP	1840
LEWIS, JOHN / MAP#285	1852	BRKE MAP	1846				
LEWIS, JOHN / MAP#286	1852	BRKE MAP	1846	LINDSEY, SAMUEL / MAP#210	1852	BRKE MAP	1842
LEWIS, JOHN / MAP#287	1852	BRKE MAP	1846	LINDSEY, WILLIAM	1871	NEW CUMB'LD	1762
LEWIS, JOHN / MAP#336	1852	BRKE MAP	1846	LINDSEY, WILLIAM	1871	NEW CUMB'LD	1768
LEWIS, JOHN / MAP#339	1852	BRKE MAP	1846	LINE FARM	1871	BKE/OH MAP	1739
LEWIS, NICHOLAS	1814	DEFENDANT	1591	LINEBERGER, W	1871	BENWOOD	1798
LEWIS, NICHOLAS	1814	DEFENDANT	1595	LINGEN, HERMANN	1874	DEFENDANT	1603
LEWIS, NICHOLAS	1816	DEFENDANT	1595	LINK, - / MRS	1871	MARH'L MAP	1756
LEWIS, O	1871	BRKE MAP	1736	LINSLEY, W	1871	BENWOOD	1798
LEWIS, T H	1871	WELLSBURG	1777	LINTON P.O.	1871	HAN MAP	1726
LEWIS, WALTER	1807	DEFENDANT	1554	LINTON, - / MRS	1871	BKE/OH MAP	1739
LEXINGTON, KY	1852	HEMPFIELD RR	1820	LINTON, ISAAC	1875	DEFENDANT	1574
LEXINGTON, KY	1852	HEMPFIELD RR	1821	LINTON, J	1871	OH CO. MAP	1742
LEXINGTON, MAYSVILLE & PORTSMOUTH RR	1852	HEMP. RR MAP	1826	LINTONS RUN	1852	BRKE MAP	1842
LIBERTY	1871	MARH'L MAP	1754	LIST, DANIEL C	1850	DEFENDANT	1657
LIBERTY - CLAY TWP	1871	MARH'L MAP	1751	LIST, HENRY K	1854	MISC	1687
LIBERTY - WASHINGTON & LIBERTY PIKE / WEST LIBERTY	1871	BKE/OH MAP	1739	LIST, JOHN JR	1838	PLAINTIFF	1628
				LISTON, JOSEPH	1858	DEFENDANT	1586
LIBERTY HALL / E. WELLS	1871	BRKE MAP	1736	LITEUTZ CIGAR SHOP / F.SPRINGARBORN	1871	WELLSBURG	1777
LIBERTY SCHOOL NO. 3	1871	HAN MAP	1732	LITEUTZ CIGARS / F.SPRINGARBORN	1871	WELLSBURG	1777
LIBERTY TOWNSHIP - BOUNDARY WITH CAMERON	1871	CAMERON	1803	LITTE STAR VILLAGE HOME / (?LITTLE STAR?)	1871	W.LIBERTY	1780
LIBERTY TOWNSHIP - E. PART - MARSHALL CO	1871	MARH'L MAP	1757	LITTLE BISON CREEK / ? BOTTOM OF MAP	1871	MARH'L MAP	1761
LIBERTY TOWNSHIP - E.PART - MARSHALL CO.	1871	MARH'L MAP	1761	LITTLE BRISON CREEK / ? BOTTOM OF MAP	1871	MARH'L MAP	1761
LIBERTY TOWNSHIP - MARHSALL CO - BUSINESS NOTICES	1871	LIB.TWP-BUS.	1797	LITTLE COVE RUN	1871	HAN MAP	1732
				LITTLE GRAVE CREEK	1871	MARH'L MAP	1745
LIBERTY TOWNSHIP - MARHSALL CO - BUSINESS NOTICES	1871	MARH'L BUS.	1797	LITTLE GRAVE CREEK	1871	MARH'L MAP	1748
LIBERTY TOWNSHIP - MARSHALL CO	1871	POPULATION	1816	LITTLE GRAVE CREEK	1871	MDSVILLE	1806
LIBERTY TOWNSHIP - MARSHALL CO - BELLTON - DETAIL MAP	1871	BELLTON	1814	LITTLE GRAVE CREEK - BRANCH OF LITTLE GRAVE CREEK	1871	MARH'L MAP	1749
LIBERTY TOWNSHIP - N. BOUNDARY WITH CAMERON	1871	CAMERON	1804	LITTLE GRAVE CREEK - MOUTH OF - SCHOOL NO.5	1871	MARH'L MAP	1745
LIBERTY TOWNSHIP - OHIO CO	1871	OH CO. MAP	1740	LITTLE MIAMI RR	1852	HEMP. RR MAP	1826
LIBERTY TOWNSHIP - OHIO CO	1871	W.LIBERTY	1780	LITTLE MILL CREEK - BRANCH OF / ?	1871	HAN MAP	1728
LIBERTY TOWNSHIP - OHIO CO	1871	POPULATION	1816	LITTLE STAR VILLAGE HOME / ? SPELLED LITTE STAR	1871	W.LIBERTY	1780
LIBERTY TOWNSHIP - SW. PART - MARSHALL CO	1871	MARH'L MAP	1760	LITTLE TRIBBLE RUN	1871	MARH'L MAP	1751
LIBERTY TOWNSHIP HALL	1871	MARH'L MAP	1761	LITTLE TRIBBLE RUN	1871	MARH'L MAP	1755
LIBRARIAN OF CONGRESS / MAP COPYRIGHT INFO	1871	WHG CITY	1787	LITTLE WHEELING CREEK	1871	OH CO. MAP	1740
				LITTLE WHEELING CREEK	1871	OH CO. MAP	1743
LIBRARY OF CONGRESS - MAP & GEOGRAPHY DIVISION	2000	PREFACE	1748	LITTLE WHEELING CREEK	1871	OH CO. MAP	1744
				LITTLE WHEELING CREEK	1916	NAT'L ROAD	1863
LICK / (?NAME FOR VERY SMALL CREEK?)	1871	MARH'L MAP	1761	LITTLE WHEELING CREEK - BRIDGE AT ELM GROVE - PHOTO	1916	NAT'L ROAD	1866
LICK RUN	1871	MARH'L MAP	1760	LITTLE WHEELING CREEK - RONEY POINT	1871	RONEY PT.	1783
LIDLE, T	1871	WELLSBURG	1777				
LIEBERT - ORPHANS	1856	MISC	1686	LITTLE WHEELING CREEK - SAW MILL ON - AT RONEY POINT	1871	OH CO. MAP	1743
LIGHTCAP, SOLOMON	1824	DEFENDANT	1612				
LIGHTNER, S	1871	MARH'L MAP	1752	LITTLE WHEELING CREEK - SAW MILL ON - AT RONEY POINT	1871	OH CO. MAP	1744
LIME ISLAND / (?OR FIRE?) - OHIO RIVER	1871	HAN MAP	1728				
				LITTLE WHEELING CREEK - TRIADELPHIA	1871	TRIAD.BORO.	1784
LIME KILN	1871	OH CO. MAP	1742				
LIME KILN - A. HALL	1871	BRKE MAP	1737	LITTLE, A	1871	MDSVILLE	1807
LIME KILN - HALLS / A	1871	BRKE MAP	1735	LITTLE, W	1871	OH CO. MAP	1742
LIMESTONE / (?QUARRY?) - N. OF LIMESTONE FARM	1871	MARH'L MAP	1750	LITTLE, W	1871	RITCHIE TWP	1791
				LITTLE, W	1871	RITCHIE TWP	1793
LIMESTONE	1871	DISTANCES	1815	LITTLETON, VW - MAP	1916	NAT'L ROAD	1869
LIMESTONE - GEORGE HOOKER	1871	BRKE MAP	1734	LIVENS, HERCULES	1808	DEFENDANT	1635
LIMESTONE FARM	1871	MARH'L MAP	1750	LLIEWELLYIN, - / MRS	1871	BETHANY	1773
LIMESTONE P.O.	1871	MARH'L MAP	1749	LLOYD, - / BARCLAY & LLOYD	1871	WLSBRG BUS.	1772
LIMESTONE P.O. - BLACKSMITH SHOP	1871	WASH.TWP-BUS.	1797	LLOYD, - / BARCLAY, LLOYD & CO. / BRICK YARD	1871	WELLSBURG	1776
LIMESTONE P.O. - BLACKSMITH SHOP	1871	LIMESTONE	1805	LLOYD, -	1871	WELLSBURG	1777
LIMESTONE P.O. - CARPENTER SHOP	1871	LIMESTONE	1805	LLOYD, - / GENERAL DUVAL OF BARCLAY & LLOYD (GROC) O.C.	1871	WELLSBURG	1777
LIMESTONE P.O. - DETAIL MAP	1871	LIMESTONE	1805				
LIMESTONE P.O. - WASHINGTON TOWNSHIP - MARSHALL CO	1871	LIMESTONE	1805	LLOYD, - / WATER ST	1871	WELLSBURG	1777
				LLOYD, - / HRS - HEIRS (O)	1871	WELLSBURG	1778
LIMESTONE QUARRY - BURGOYNES / J R	1871	BRKE MAP	1735	LLOYD, J D	1871	WLSBRG BUS.	1772
				LLOYD, J D	1871	WELLSBURG	1776
LINCOLN, HARRY	1871	MISC	1681	LLOYD, J D / FUR. (FURNITURE) ROOMS (OC)	1871	WELLSBURG	1778
LINDNER - ORPHANS	1871	MISC	1711				
LINDSAY, J W	1871	BKE/OH MAP	1739	LLOYD, J H	1871	WELLSBURG	1776
				LLOYD, JAMES	1841	DEFENDANT	1614

'PERSONAL TIME LINE' INDEX TO VOLUME 7 OF THE *OHIO COUNTY INDEX*

ENTRY	YEAR	SUBJECT	PAGE
LLOYD, JAMES	1841	DEFENDANT	1619
LLOYD, T M	1871	WELLSBURG	1776
LLOYD, T M	1871	WELLSBURG	1776
LLOYD, THOMAS	1871	NEW MANCH.	1763
LLOYD, THOMAS	1871	NEW MANCH.	1769
LLOYD, THOMAS / TAYLOR SHOP (?TAILOR?)	1871	NEW MANCH.	1769
LLOYD, THOMAS M	1871	WLSBRG BUS.	1772
LLOYD, THOMAS M / VARIETY STORE - (OC.)	1871	WELLSBURG	1777
LOCK, - / MRS	1871	MDSVILLE	1807
LOCKHART, A	1871	NEW CUMB'LD	1767
LOCKHART, A	1871	NEW CUMB'LD	1768
LOCKHART, H / MRS	1871	NEW CUMB'LD	1768
LOCKHART, J	1871	NEW CUMB'LD	1767
LOCKHART, J T	1871	BETHANY	1773
LOCKWOOD, - / MRS	1871	MDSVILLE	1810
LOCKWOOD, J / COL	1871	MARH'L MAP	1751
LOCKWOOD, J / COL	1871	MARH'L MAP	1751
LOCKWOOD, J / COL - INITIALS COL J.L.	1871	MARH'L MAP	1751
LOCKWOOD, J / COL - INITIALS COL J.L.	1871	MARH'L MAP	1751
LOCKWOOD, J H	1871	MARH'L MAP	1748
LOCKWOOD, J H	1871	MDSVILLE	1808
LOCKWOOD, J H / INITIALS J.H.L.	1871	MDSVILLE	1808
LOCKWOOD, J H / INITIALS J.H.L.	1871	MDSVILLE	1808
LOCKWOOD, J H / THE MOUND	1871	MDSVILLE	1809
LOCKWOOD, J H	1871	MDSVILLE	1810
LOCKWOOD, J H	1871	MDSVILLE	1810
LOCKWOOD, J H	1871	MDSVILLE	1810
LOCKWOOD, J H / INITIALS J.H.L.	1871	MDSVILLE	1810
LOCKWOOD, J H / INITIALS J.H.L.	1871	MDSVILLE	1810
LOCKWOOD, J H / INITIALS J.H.L.	1871	MDSVILLE	1810
LOCKWOOD, J H / INITIALS J.H.L.	1871	MDSVILLE	1810
LOCUST GROVE	1871	HAN MAP	1731
LOCUST GROVE	1871	HAN MAP	1732
LOCUST GROVE	1871	BRKE MAP	1734
LOCUST GROVE	1871	OH CO. MAP	1742
LOCUST GROVE	1871	OH CO. MAP	1744
LOCUST GROVE / SAND HILL TWP	1871	MARH'L MAP	1746
LOCUST GROVE	1871	MARH'L MAP	1754
LOCUST GROVE - FRANKLIN TWP	1871	MARH'L MAP	1758
LOCUST GROVE - SAND HILL TWP	1871	MARH'L MAP	1746
LOCUST GROVE CEMETERY	1871	BRKE MAP	1734
LOCUST HILL	1871	OH CO. MAP	1740
LOCUST RIDGE	1871	OH CO. MAP	1740
LOCUST RIDGE	1871	OH CO. MAP	1743
LOCUST ROW	1871	OH CO. MAP	1740
LOCUST ROW - FRANKLIN TWP	1871	MARH'L MAP	1758
LOCUST VALLEY	1871	BKE/OH MAP	1739
LOCUSTGROVE	1871	HAN MAP	1726
LOCUSTRIDGE	1871	MARH'L MAP	1753
LOCUSTVALLEY	1871	HAN MAP	1726
LOG CABIN - WHEELING MAP	1916	NAT'L ROAD	1868
LOGAN RUN	1871	BKE/OH MAP	1739
LOGAN, A	1871	HAN MAP	1727
LOGAN, D	1871	MARH'L MAP	1748
LOGAN, D L	1871	MDSVILLE	1809
LOGAN, EMMA	1879	MISC	1675
LOGAN, J	1871	MDSVILLE	1809
LOGAN, JAMES	1856	DEFENDANT	1616
LOGAN, SAMUEL	1819	DEFENDANT	1582
LOGAN, W / HRS.	1871	HAN MAP	1732
LOGANS RUN	1852	BRKE MAP	1840
LOGDSON, BENNETT	1822	DEFENDANT	1587
LOGE, JOHN / MAP#515	1852	BRKE MAP	1851
LOGSDENS RUN	1852	BRKE MAP	1852
LOGSDON, J	1871	MARH'L MAP	1752
LOGSDON, W D	1871	MARH'L MAP	1752
LOGSTON, - / MRS	1871	MARH'L MAP	1752
LOGSTON, L	1871	MARH'L MAP	1752
LOHMAN, C	1871	MARH'L MAP	1746
LOLLER, S W	1871	W.UNION-BUS.	1797
LOLLER, S W / (OC.) - STORE	1871	W. UNION	1812
LOMBARD, S	1871	MDSVILLE	1807
LONG FLATS	1871	OH CO. MAP	1740
LONG LANE ROAD - TRAIDELPHIA	1871	TRIAD. BORO.	1784
LONG RUN	1852	BRKE MAP	1840
LONG RUN	1871	BKE/OH MAP	1739
LONG RUN	1871	OH CO. MAP	1740
LONG RUN	1871	OH CO. MAP	1741
LONG RUN	1871	MARH'L MAP	1754
LONG RUN DIST	1871	OH CO. MAP	1741
LONG, G	1871	MARH'L MAP	1747
LONGFINGERS, JACK	1812	DEFENDANT	1559
LONGFITT, J / MRS	1871	BRKE MAP	1735
LONGHEAD, J	1871	BRKE MAP	1735
LOOCKHOT, G	1871	MARH'L MAP	1759
LOOMIS, CECILIA R	1842	DEFENDANT	1640
LOOMIS, H G	1860	DEFENDANT	1560
LOOS, C L / PROF.	1871	BETHANY	1773
LOOSE COURT PAPERS	2000	APPENDIX	1873
LOPER, J	1871	CAMERON	1803
LOPER, J / PAINT SHOP	1871	CAMERON	1803
LOPER, JOHN	1871	CAMER'N - BUS.	1795
LORAIN, J	1871	MDSVILLE	1808
LORD, -	1861	PLAINTIFF	1621
LORING A / MAJOR	1871	OH CO. MAP	1742
LORING PLACE - ELM GROVE	1916	NAT'L ROAD	1864
LORING, A / INITIALS A.L. - ELM GROVE	1871	OH CO. MAP	1742
LORING, A	1871	OH CO. BUS.	1779
LORING, A / INITIALS A.L.	1871	ELM GROVE	1782
LORING, A / MAJOR	1871	ELM GROVE	1782
LORING, ABBOT	1876	DEFENDANT	1631
LORING, ALONZO	1841	DEFENDANT	1568
LORING, ALONZO	1863	MISC	1708
LOUDENSLAGER, - / LOUDENSVILLE - (?NAMED FOR LOUDENSLAGER FAMILY?)	1871	MARH'L BUS.	1796
LOUDENSLAGER, J	1871	MARH'L MAP	1753
LOUDENSLAGER, J	1871	MARH'L MAP	1753
LOUDENSLAGER, J / INITIALS J.L.	1871	MARH'L MAP	1753
LOUDENSLAGER, J / INITIALS J.L.	1871	MARH'L MAP	1753
LOUDENSLAGER, J / CUT OFF - E. SIDE OF MAP	1871	MARH'L MAP	1756
LOUDENSLAGER, J	1871	MARH'L MAP	1757
LOUDENSLAGER, J	1871	MARH'L MAP	1757
LOUDENSLAGER, J / CUT OFF W. SIDE OF MAP	1871	MARH'L MAP	1757
LOUDENSLAGER, J / INITIALS J.L.	1871	MARH'L MAP	1757
LOUDENSLAGER, J / INITIALS J.L.	1871	MARH'L MAP	1757
LOUDENSLAGER, J / INITIALS J.L.	1871	MARH'L MAP	1757
LOUDENSLAGER, J / (?JOSEPH?)	1871	CAMERON	1803
LOUDENSLAGER, J / (?JOSEPH?) - INITIALS J.L.	1871	CAMERON	1803
LOUDENSLAGER, JOSEPH / MAIN ST - LOUDENSVILLE	1871	MARH'L BUS.	1796
LOUDENSVILLE	1871	MARH'L MAP	1753
LOUDENSVILLE / (?APPARENTLY NAMED FOR J.LOUDENSLAGER?)	1871	MARH'L MAP	1753
LOUDENSVILLE	1871	MARH'L MAP	1757
LOUDENSVILLE	1871	MARH'L BUS.	1796
LOUDENSVILLE / (?NAMED FOR LOUDENSLAGER FAMILY?)	1871	MARH'L BUS.	1796
LOUDENSVILLE - MAIN ST	1871	MARH'L BUS.	1796
LOUGHEAD, J	1871	BRKE MAP	1737
LOUGHEAD, W	1871	BRKE MAP	1735
LOUGHEAD, W	1871	BRKE MAP	1737
LOUISVILLE, KY	1852	HEMPFIELD RR	1821
LOVE, ALEXANDER	1807	DEFENDANT	1591
LOVE, J	1871	MARH'L MAP	1752
LOVE, JAMES	1800	DEFENDANT	1634
LOW, G W	1871	MARH'L MAP	1757
LOW, GF W	1871	MARH'L MAP	1753
LOW, J	1871	MARH'L MAP	1759
LOW, J / NEAR COOPER SHOP	1871	MARH'L MAP	1759
LOW, L	1871	MARH'L MAP	1759
LOW, L	1871	MARH'L MAP	1761
LOWARY, W K	1871	HAN MAP	1726
LOWE, M A / MRS - LITTE (?LITTLE?) STAR VILLAGE HOME	1871	W.LIBERTY	1780
LOWER BOWMAN RUN	1871	MARH'L MAP	1755
LOWER TWIN (SISTER) ISLAND - OHIO RIVER	1871	OH CO. MAP	1741
LOWRIE, JOHN	1827	DEFENDANT	1613
LOWRY, E	1871	BETHANY	1773
LOWRY, J	1871	MARH'L MAP	1754
LOWRY, J	1871	MARH'L MAP	1758
LOWRY, JOHN	1844	DEFENDANT	1615
LOYONS, CHARLES	1879	MISC	1698
LUCAS, C	1871	MARH'L MAP	1747
LUCAS, C	1871	MARH'L MAP	1750
LUCAS, I N / DOCTOR	1871	MARH'L MAP	1749
LUCAS, I N / DR	1871	LIMESTONE	1805
LUCAS, J	1871	BRKE MAP	1735
LUCAS, J	1871	OH CO. MAP	1740
LUCAS, J	1871	MARH'L MAP	1750

'PERSONAL TIME LINE' INDEX TO VOLUME 7 OF THE *OHIO COUNTY INDEX*

ENTRY	YEAR	SUBJECT	PAGE
LUDGE, L / (?OR LUDGES?)	1871	MARH'L MAP	1747
LUDGES, L / (?OR LUDGE?)	1871	MARH'L MAP	1747
LUDGET, L	1871	MARH'L MAP	1750
LUIKERT, JACOB F	1876	DEFENDANT	1566
LUIKERT, JACOB F	1877	DEFENDANT	1609
LUK, JOHN	1795	DEFENDANT	1634
LUKE, DAVID	1858	DEFENDANT	1584
LUKE, DAVID	1858	DEFENDANT	1603
LUKE, J / ?	1871	HAN MAP	1730
LUKE, J	1871	NEW CUMB'LD	1768
LUKE, ROBERT	1871	OH CO.BUS.	1779
LUKE, W	1871	HAN MAP	1731
LUKE, W	1871	MARH'L MAP	1747
LUKER, J	1871	OH CO. MAP	1741
LUKER, J	1871	OH CO. MAP	1742
LUKERT, J	1871	OH CO. MAP	1742
LUMBER INSPECTOR	1823	MISC	1685
LUNATIC ASYLUM - STAUNTON, VIRGINIA	1834	MISC	1697
LUNDUFF, ISAAC	1871	HAN MAP	1731
LUNSFORD, LEWIS	1871	TRIAD.TWP.	1781
LUNSFORN, L	1871	WHG CITY	1789
LUSTTER, JACOB	1827	MISC	1682
LUTES HOMESTEAD	1871	MARH'L MAP	1751
LUTES, C	1871	MARH'L MAP	1751
LUTES, D	1871	MARH'L MAP	1746
LUTES, D	1871	MARH'L MAP	1746
LUTES, D	1871	MARH'L MAP	1751
LUTES, D	1871	SAND HILL-BUS.	1797
LUTES, E	1871	MARH'L MAP	1746
LUTES, E	1871	MARH'L MAP	1746
LUTES, E	1871	SAND HILL-BUS.	1797
LUTES, H	1871	MARH'L MAP	1751
LUTES, I	1871	MARH'L MAP	1751
LUTES, W	1871	GLEN EASTON	1801
LUTES, WILLIAM / RES	1871	MARH'L MAP	1752
LUTES, WILLIAM / INITIALS W.L.	1871	MARH'L MAP	1755
LUTES, WILLIAM / INITIALS W.L.	1871	MARH'L MAP	1755
LUTES, WILLIAM / RES	1871	MARH'L MAP	1755
LUTHERAN CHURCH - FOURTH ST	1871	WHG CITY	1788
LUTHERAN CHURCH - FOURTH ST & JOHN ST	1871	WHG CITY	1788
LUTHERAN CHURCH - MARKET ST	1871	WHG CITY	1788
LUTHERAN CHURCH - MARKET ST	1871	WHG CITY	1790
LUTZ - CHILDREN	1800	MISC	1697
LUTZ, C	1871	MDSVILLE	1807
LYCLICK, WILLIAM / BLACKSMITH & WAGON MAKER	1871	MARH'L BUS.	1796
LYDICK, J	1871	MARH'L MAP	1756
LYDICK, S	1871	MARH'L MAP	1756
LYDICK, WILLIAM	1871	MARH'L MAP	1753
LYLE, J	1871	OH CO. MAP	1741
LYLE, J B	1871	OH CO. MAP	1741
LYLE, JA	1871	OH CO. MAP	1740
LYLE, JA	1871	OH CO. MAP	1741
LYLE, JA A	1871	OH CO. MAP	1743
LYLE, JAMES	1871	OH CO. MAP	1741
LYLES, THOMAS	1817	DEFENDANT	1611
LYNCH, EDWARD	1804	PLAINTIFF	1635
LYNN CAMP P.O.	1871	MARH'L MAP	1759
LYNN CAMP RUN - HORSESHOE BEND	1871	MARH'L MAP	1759
LYNN, A	1871	MDSVILLE	1810
LYNN, JAMES	1824	DEFENDANT	1612
LYNNCAMP P.O.	1871	MARH'L MAP	1755
LYNNCAMP P.O. - BLACKSMITH SHOP	1871	MARH'L MAP	1755
LYNNCAMP RUN	1871	MARH'L MAP	1759
LYNNCAMP RUN	1871	MARH'L MAP	1760
LYNNCAMP RUN - GRIST MILL ON	1871	MARH'L MAP	1759
LYON, M	1871	HAN MAP	1732
LYONS, J	1871	MARH'L MAP	1749
LYONS, J / INITIALS J.L.	1871	MARH'L MAP	1749
LYONS, JOHN H	1833	DEFENDANT	1618
LYONS, M	1871	HAN MAP	1733
LZAEAR, P	1871	BRKE MAP	1736
M, G / UNKNOWN INITIALS - NE OF WOODLAND P.O.	1871	MARH'L MAP	1754
M, G / (?GENERAL MERCHANDISE?) - NEAR SCHOOL NO.8	1871	MARH'L MAP	1756
M, I H / UNKNOWN INITIALS (?MAYBE E.H.M.-E.H.MOORE?)	1871	WELLSBURG	1778
M, O / UNKNOWN INITIALS - UNION TWP	1871	MARH'L MAP	1745
M.C. / UNKNOWN INITIALS	1871	OH CO. MAP	1742
M.E. CHURCH / METHODIST EPISCOPAL	1871	HAN MAP	1726

ENTRY	YEAR	SUBJECT	PAGE
M.E. CHURCH / ABBREVIATION FOR METHODIST EPISCOPAL CHURCH	1871	WELLSBURG	1777
M.G. / UNKNOWN INITIALS - W. OF THE HOMESTEAD (?GARVIN?)	1871	OH CO. MAP	1742
MACK, J	1871	CAMERON	1804
MACK, WILLIAM	1829	DEFENDANT	1668
MACKEY, B	1871	HAN MAP	1730
MACKEY, JOHN S	1838	DEFENDANT	1651
MACKIN, C H	1871	CAMER'N - BUS.	1795
MACKIN, C H	1871	CAMERON	1803
MACKS RUN	1871	HAN MAP	1727
MAD RIVER & LAKE ERIE RR	1852	HEMP. RR MAP	1826
MADDEN, HENRY	1807	DEFENDANT	1644
MADISON TOWNSHIP - OHIO CO - WHEELING ISLAND	1871	WHG CITY	1786
MADISON TOWNSHIP - OHIO CO - WHEELING ISLAND	1871	WHG CITY	1788
MADISON TOWNSHIP - WHEELING	1871	OH CO. MAP	1742
MADISON TOWNSHIP - WHEELING CITY	1871	WHG CITY	1788
MADISON TOWNSHIP - WHEELING ISLAND	1871	OH CO. MAP	1742
MADISON TOWNSHIP - WHEELING ISLAND	1871	WHG ISLAND	1788
MADISON, JAMES	1828	DEFENDANT	1551
MADISON, JAMES C JR	1828	DEFENDANT	1551
MAGEE & WILSON	1871	FRE'MAN'S LDG	1762
MAGEE & WILSON / STORE AND P.O.	1871	FRE'MAN'S LDG	1764
MAGEE, - / MRS	1871	BRKE MAP	1735
MAGEE, - / MRS	1871	BRKE MAP	1737
MAGEE, JOHN / MAP#422	1852	BRKE MAP	1847
MAGEE, JOHN / MAP#424	1852	BRKE MAP	1847
MAGEE, JOHN / MAP#431	1852	BRKE MAP	1850
MAGEE, JOHN / MAP#434	1852	BRKE MAP	1850
MAGER, ALEXANDER	1831	DEFENDANT	1566
MAGER, ALEXANDER	1831	DEFENDANT	1639
MAGER, FIDEL	1857	MISC	1688
MAGER, FIDEL	1859	MISC	1688
MAGERS, - / MRS	1871	MARH'L MAP	1748
MAGERS, D	1871	MARH'L MAP	1748
MAGERS, GEORGE	1871	MARH'L MAP	1748
MAGERS, J / HRS	1871	MARH'L MAP	1748
MAGERS, J / MRS	1871	MARH'L MAP	1748
MAGGOTY RUN	1871	MARH'L MAP	1756
MAGNOLIA - FRANKLIN TWP	1871	MARH'L MAP	1758
MAHALL, J	1871	BRKE MAP	1735
MAHAN, J	1871	HAN MAP	1732
MAHAN, J L / INITIALS J.L.M.	1871	HAN MAP	1726
MAHAN, J L / INITIALS J.L.M.	1871	HAN MAP	1726
MAHAN, J L / RES.	1871	HAN MAP	1726
MAHAN, J L / RES.	1871	HAN MAP	1726
MAHAN, JOHN L	1871	HAN-GR'NT TWP	1763
MAHAN, T / (?THOMAS?)	1871	BRKE MAP	1735
MAHAN, THOMAS	1871	BRKE MAP	1735
MAHAN, W	1871	HAN MAP	1732
MAHAN, W E	1871	BRKE MAP	1735
MAHAN, WILLIAM	1852	NOT ON MAP	1836
MAHAN, WILLIAM / MAP#511	1852	BRKE MAP	1849
MAHANS RUN	1852	BRKE MAP	1849
MAHEW, J	1871	HAN MAP	1731
MAHONEY, PATRICK	1880	DEFENDANT	1569
MAIN ST. - HAMILTON	1871	HAN MAP	1729
MAIN, C	1871	BETHANY	1773
MAJOR, E	1871	MARH'L MAP	1746
MAJOR, F	1871	MARH'L MAP	1746
MAJOR, F	1871	MARH'L MAP	1749
MAJORS, JOSEPH	1818	DEFENDANT	1551
MAJORS, JOSEPH	1818	DEFENDANT	1660
MALCUM, ALEXANDER	1857	DEFENDANT	1604
MALCUME, ALEXANDER	1857	DEFENDANT	1604
MALEY, WILLIAM	1871	MARH'L MAP	1761
MALIN, JOB	1802	DEFENDANT	1634
MALLORY, JASPER	1814	DEFENDANT	1638
MALONEY, JAMES	1836	DEFENDANT	1656
MALONEY, WILLIAM	1871	BETHANY	1773
MALONY, T	1871	MARH'L MAP	1757
MANARY, JAMES / ESQ. - MAP#633	1852	BRKE MAP	1852
MANCHESTER HOUSE - NEW MANCHESTER / HOTEL	1871	NEW MANCH.	1769
MANCHESTER, I F / MAP ASSISTANT	1871	MAP	1713
MANDEVENDER RUN	1871	MARH'L MAP	1749
MANDEVENDER'S RUN / TOP OF MAP - CUT OFF	1871	MARH'L MAP	1752
MANLY, JAMES	1840	DEFENDANT	1614
MANLY, JAMES	1840	DEFENDANT	1619
MANNING, - / MRS	1871	MARH'L MAP	1756

'PERSONAL TIME LINE' INDEX TO VOLUME 7 OF THE *OHIO COUNTY INDEX*

ENTRY	YEAR	SUBJECT	PAGE	ENTRY	YEAR	SUBJECT	PAGE
MANNING, - / MRS	1871	MARH'L MAP	1760	MARS, S	1871	MARH'L MAP	1745
MANNING, - / MRS	1871	CAMERON	1803	MARSH, - / SCHOOL - MAP#591	1852	BRKE MAP	1851
MANNING, G	1871	MARH'L MAP	1751	MARSH, -	1855	PLAINTIFF	1621
MANNING, G	1871	MARH'L MAP	1751	MARSH, - / MISS	1871	BRKE MAP	1734
MANNING, G / INITIALS G.M.	1871	MARH'L MAP	1751	MARSH, - / MRS	1871	BRKE MAP	1734
MANNINGTON, WV - MAP	1916	NAT'L ROAD	1869	MARSH, - / MRS	1871	MARH'L MAP	1746
MANSER, - / HARVEY & MANSER PAPER MILL	1871	WELLSBURG	1776	MARSH, DAVID / OC	1871	MARH'L MAP	1745
MANSER, - / HARVEY & MANSER / INITIALS H.&M.	1871	WELLSBURG	1777	MARSH, G E	1871	BRKE MAP	1734
				MARSH, J M	1871	WELLSBURG	1777
MANSER, W	1871	WELLSBURG	1776	MARSH, JAMES / MAP#580	1852	BRKE MAP	1852
MANVILL, ADRIAN	1820	DEFENDANT	1600	MARSH, M	1871	MARH'L MAP	1746
MANYPENNY, A	1871	RIV. RD N.OF N.C.	1770	MARSH, MIFFLIN	1854	DEFENDANT	1594
MANYPENNY, A	1871	RIV. RD N.OF N.C.	1770	MARSH, T	1871	BRKE MAP	1734
MANYPENNY, A / INITIALS A.M.	1871	RIV. RD N.OF N.C.	1770	MARSH, T / HRS	1871	BRKE MAP	1734
MANYPENNY, J	1871	RIV. RD N.OF N.C.	1770	MARSH, THOMAS / MAP#590	1852	BRKE MAP	1851
MANYPENNY, J	1871	RIV. RD N.OF N.C.	1770	MARSHAL, JOHN	1804	DEFENDANT	1608
MANYPENNY, T / NEAR OHIO RIVER	1871	HAN-POE TWP	1763	MARSHALL CO	1871	POPULATION	1816
MANYPENY, A	1871	RIV. RD N.OF N.C.	1763	MARSHALL CO - BUSINESS NOTICES	1871	MARH'L BUS.	1795
MANYPENY, J	1871	RIV. RD N.OF N.C.	1763	MARSHALL CO - BUSINESS NOTICES	1871	MARH'L BUS.	1797
MAP - DETAIL INDEX	2000	APPENDIX	1712	MARSHALL CO - N. BOUNDARY WITH OHIO CO.	1871	W.UNION	1812
MAP - NATIONAL ROAD & OLD NORTHWEST TERRITORY	1916	NAT'L ROAD	1870	MARSHALL CO - ON PANHANDLE MAP	1871	MAP	1713
MAP OF OHIO COUNTY	1816	MISC	1707	MARSHALL CO - SHERIFF - H.KELTY	1871	UNION TWP-BUS.	1797
MAP OF THE PANHANDLE	1871	MAP	1713	MARSHALL CO - TOWNSHIPS ON MAP - N. HALF	1871	MAP	1724
MAP OF THE WESTERN RAILROADS TRIBUTARY TO PHILADELPHIA WITH THEIR RIVAL LINES	1852	HEMP. RR MAP	1825	MARSHALL CO - TOWNSHIPS ON MAP - S. HALF	1871	MAP	1725
MAPLE GROVE	1871	HAN MAP	1732	MARSHALL CO - WEBSTER TOWNSHIP	1871	MARH'L MAP	1750
MAPLE GROVE	1871	BKE/OH MAP	1739	MARSHALL CO COURTHOUSE - A ST - MOUNDSVILLE	1871	MDSVILLE	1809
MAPLE GROVE	1871	OH CO. MAP	1742				
MAPLE HILL	1871	BKE/OH MAP	1739	MARSHALL CO JAIL - MOUNDSVILLE	1871	MDSVILLE	1809
MAPLE VALLEY	1871	HAN MAP	1727	MARSHALL CO N. BOUNDARY WITH OHIO CO	1871	RITCHIE TWP	1792
MAPLE, WILLIAM	1839	DEFENDANT	1626				
MAPS - ORIGINAL OHIO COUNTY	2000	MAP	1546	MARSHALL CO N. BOUNDARY WITH OHIO CO	1871	RITCHIE TWP	1794
MAPS - PANHANDLE COUNTIES	2000	MAP	1546				
MARES, -	1818	PLAINTIFF	1620	MARSHALL HOUSE - HOTEL - MOUNDSVILLE	1871	MDSVILLE	1807
MARGIN, A	1871	BKE/OH MAP	1739				
MARIETTA, OH	1852	HEMPFIELD RR	1820	MARSHALL, GEORGE	1859	DEFENDANT	1586
MARIETTA, OH	1852	HEMPFIELD RR	1821	MARSHALL, J	1871	CAMERON	1803
MARIETTA, OH	1852	HEMPFIELD RR	1821	MARSHALL, J / INITIALS J.M.	1871	CAMERON	1803
MARIETTA, OH	1852	HEMP. RR MAP	1825	MARSHALL, J	1871	CAMERON	1804
MARIETTA, OH	1852	HEMP. RR MAP	1826	MARSHALL, J G / JAMES - LAW OFFICE	1871	NEW MANCH.	1769
MARION, R	1871	MDSVILLE	1807	MARSHALL, JAMES	1780	DEFENDANT	1569
MARION, R / INTIALS R.M.	1871	MDSVILLE	1807	MARSHALL, JAMES	1789	DEFENDANT	1655
MARIS, -	1808	PLAINTIFF	1620	MARSHALL, JAMES G / ATTORNEY	1871	NEW MANCH.	1763
MARKE, JAMES	1797	DEFENDANT	1634	MARSHALL, JOHN	1805	DEFENDANT	1608
MARKER, W / ? (?OR MARKES?)	1871	HAN MAP	1729	MARSHALL, JOSEPH	1840	DEFENDANT	1577
MARKER, W / ? (?OR MARKES?)	1871	HAN MAP	1729	MARSHALL, JOSEPH	1840	DEFENDANT	1617
MARKES, W / ?	1871	HAN MAP	1729	MARSHALL, JOSEPH	1840	DEFENDANT	1652
MARKET HO. LOT / (?HOUSE?)	1871	TRIAD.BORO.	1784	MARSHALL, JOSEPH	1875	DEFENDANT	1654
MARKET ST. - HAMILTON	1871	HAN MAP	1729	MARSHALL, LEWIS	1873	DEFENDANT	1641
MARKEY, P	1871	MARH'L MAP	1745	MARSHALL, M F / MRS	1871	HAN MAP	1731
MARKEY, T	1871	MARH'L MAP	1745	MARSHALL, R	1871	OH CO. MAP	1741
MARKS RUN	1871	HAN MAP	1727	MARSHALL, R / INITIALS R.M.	1871	OH CO. MAP	1741
MARKS RUN	1871	HAN MAP	1728	MARSHALL, R / INITIALS R.M.	1871	OH CO. MAP	1741
MARKS, A B / THE HOMESTEAD ?	1871	HAN MAP	1727	MARSHALL, R	1871	MARH'L MAP	1750
MARKS, A B / THE HOMESTEAD ?	1871	HAN MAP	1728	MARSHALL, R	1871	NEW CUMB'LD	1766
MARKS, A G	1871	HAN MAP	1727	MARSHALL, ROBERT	1827	DEFENDANT	1672
MARKS, A J	1871	HAN MAP	1727	MARSHALL, ROBERT	1838	DEFENDANT	1558
MARKS, A.J.	1871	HAN MAP	1728	MARSHALL, S	1871	MARH'L MAP	1746
MARKS, C / WATER ST	1871	WELLSBURG	1777	MARSHALL, S	1871	SHERRARD	1811
MARKS, M	1871	HAN MAP	1733	MARSHALL, T J	1871	NEW MANCH.	1769
MARLIN, E	1871	OH CO. MAP	1740	MARSHALL, W	1871	OH CO. MAP	1741
MARLIN, E JR	1871	OH CO. MAP	1741	MARSHALL, W	1871	OH CO. MAP	1741
MARLIN, E SR	1871	OH CO. MAP	1741	MARSHALL, W / COAL - INITIALS COAL.W.M.	1871	OH CO. MAP	1741
MARLIN, E SR	1871	OH CO. MAP	1741				
MARLIN, E SR	1871	OH CO. MAP	1741	MARSHALL, W / COAL YARD	1871	OH CO. MAP	1741
MARLIN, ELIJAH	1858	DEFENDANT	1671	MARSHALL, W	1871	OH CO. MAP	1742
MARLING FARM	1871	OH CO. MAP	1740	MARSHALL, W	1871	WHG CITY	1787
MARLING, ELIJAH	1858	DEFENDANT	1653	MARSHALL, WILLIAM	1871	MARH'L MAP	1757
MARLING, JOHN	1875	DEFENDANT	1590	MARSHEL, C / & E - MAP#325	1852	BRKE MAP	1846
MARLING, JOHN	1876	DEFENDANT	1584	MARSHEL, E / & C. - MAP#325	1852	BRKE MAP	1846
MARLING, JOHN	1877	DEFENDANT	1584	MARSHEL, THOMAS / MRS - MAP#559	1852	BRKE MAP	1852
MARLOW, PETER	1823	DEFENDANT	1660	MARSHMAN, T F	1871	W.UNION-BUS.	1797
MARLOW, PETER	1823	DEFENDANT	1660	MARSHMAN, T F / DR	1871	W.UNION	1812
MARLOW, THOMAS	1807	DEFENDANT	1606	MARSHMAN, T F / DR - ? - ADJOINING LOT - INITIALS T.M.	1871	W.UNION	1812
MARPLE, B	1871	MARH'L MAP	1745				
MARPLE, B	1871	MARH'L MAP	1745	MARSILLIOT, JACOB	1821	DEFENDANT	1668
MARPLE, B	1871	SHERRARD	1811	MARTIN - CHILD	1810	MISC	1693
MARPLE, G	1871	MARH'L MAP	1745	MARTIN, - / BROS.	1871	BKE/OH MAP	1739
MARPLE, J	1871	MARH'L MAP	1746	MARTIN, - / BROS.	1871	BKE/OH MAP	1739
MARPLE, J H	1871	MARH'L MAP	1745	MARTIN, - / MRS	1871	OH CO. MAP	1740
MARQUIT, J	1871	NEW CUMB'LD	1767	MARTIN, - / BROS.	1871	W.LIBERTY	1780
MARQUIT, J	1871	NEW CUMB'LD	1767	MARTIN, - / BROS.	1871	W.LIBERTY	1780
MARREN, J	1871	NEW CUMB'LD	1767				

LX

'PERSONAL TIME LINE' INDEX TO VOLUME 7 OF THE *OHIO COUNTY INDEX*

ENTRY	YEAR	SUBJECT	PAGE
MARTIN, - / HEIRS	1871	TRIAD.BORO.	1784
MARTIN, - / HOSACK & MARTIN	1871	CAMERON	1803
MARTIN, A	1871	HAN MAP	1727
MARTIN, ABNER	1806	DEFENDANT	1648
MARTIN, ABNER	1814	DEFENDANT	1569
MARTIN, ABSALOM	1802	DEFENDANT	1610
MARTIN, ABSOLOM	1803	DEFENDANT	1572
MARTIN, ABSOLOM	1803	DEFENDANT	1610
MARTIN, ABSOLOM	1803	DEFENDANT	1647
MARTIN, C	1871	OH CO. MAP	1742
MARTIN, C	1871	OH CO. MAP	1744
MARTIN, C	1871	TRIAD.BORO.	1784
MARTIN, DANIEL P	1860	DEFENDANT	1616
MARTIN, EBENEZER	1807	MISC	1710
MARTIN, ESTHER	1876	DEFENDANT	1578
MARTIN, H / W&H - S. BORDER OF OHIO CO	1871	OH CO. MAP	1742
MARTIN, H / W & H	1871	MARH'L MAP	1745
MARTIN, HIRAM	1835	DEFENDANT	1591
MARTIN, HIRAM	1836	DEFENDANT	1592
MARTIN, HIRAM	1842	DEFENDANT	1592
MARTIN, J / MRS	1871	HAN MAP	1727
MARTIN, J	1871	MARH'L MAP	1750
MARTIN, J / INITIALS J.M. ?	1871	MARH'L MAP	1750
MARTIN, J B	1871	MARH'L MAP	1752
MARTIN, J B / INITIALS J.B.M.	1871	MARH'L MAP	1752
MARTIN, JOHN	1811	DEFENDANT	1638
MARTIN, JOHN	1856	DEFENDANT	1592
MARTIN, L	1871	MARH'L MAP	1756
MARTIN, L G	1871	MDSVILLE	1808
MARTIN, P A	1871	MARH'L MAP	1751
MARTIN, P A	1871	MARH'L MAP	1755
MARTIN, R A / MRS	1871	MDSVILLE	1810
MARTIN, REUBEN	1805	DEFENDANT	1559
MARTIN, REUBEN	1808	DEFENDANT	1559
MARTIN, ROBERT C	1838	DEFENDANT	1563
MARTIN, ROBERT C	1838	DEFENDANT	1622
MARTIN, ROBERT G	1837	DEFENDANT	1614
MARTIN, ROBERT G	1838	DEFENDANT	1558
MARTIN, ROBERT G	1838	DEFENDANT	1622
MARTIN, ROBERT G	1838	DEFENDANT	1660
MARTIN, ROBERT L S	1838	DEFENDANT	1558
MARTIN, S	1871	MARH'L MAP	1753
MARTIN, SAMUEL	1812	DEFENDANT	1577
MARTIN, SHIPLEY	1834	DEFENDANT	1669
MARTIN, W / W&H - S. BORDER OF OHIO CO	1871	OH CO. MAP	1742
MARTIN, W / W & H	1871	MARH'L MAP	1745
MARTIN, W	1871	BETHANY	1773
MARTIN, W / BLACKSMITH SHOP	1871	BETHANY	1773
MARTIN, W / WAGON SHOP	1871	BETHANY	1773
MARTIN, WILLIAM	1807	PLAINTIFF	1551
MARTINEN, - / MRS ?	1871	MARH'L MAP	1749
MARTINS FERRY, OHIO - FERRY TO	1871	OH CO. MAP	1741
MARTON, ABSOLAM	1804	DEFENDANT	1610
MARTON, JOHN	1799	DEFENDANT	1665
MARTON, R	1871	MARH'L MAP	1752
MASH, DAVID	1795	DEFENDANT	1644
MASK, ISAAC	1855	DEFENDANT	1577
MASON AND DIXON LINE	1916	NAT'L ROAD	1867
MASON, -	1820	DEFENDANT	1602
MASON, H	1871	MARH'L MAP	1745
MASON, H	1871	MARH'L MAP	1745
MASON, H / INITIALS H.M.	1871	MARH'L MAP	1745
MASON, H	1871	MARH'L MAP	1760
MASON, J	1871	MARH'L MAP	1756
MASON, J	1871	MARH'L MAP	1756
MASON, J / INITIALS J.M.	1871	MARH'L MAP	1756
MASON, J	1871	MARH'L MAP	1759
MASON, J	1871	MARH'L MAP	1760
MASON, J	1871	MARH'L MAP	1760
MASON, J / INITIALS J.M.	1871	MARH'L MAP	1760
MASON, SAMUEL	1778	DEFENDANT	1567
MASONIC HALL - CAMERON	1871	CAMERON	1803
MASONIC HALL - NEW MANCHESTER	1871	NEW MANCH.	1769
MAST, ISAAC	1855	DEFENDANT	1577
MASTERS DRAIN	1871	MARH'L MAP	1751
MASTERS, - / MISS	1871	MDSVILLE	1809
MASTERS, C / MISS	1871	MARH'L MAP	1751
MASWIE, AUGUSTUS	1829	DEFENDANT	1553
MATHERS, E	1839	DEFENDANT	1651
MATHERS, WILLIAM	1822	DEFENDANT	1581
MATHERS, WILLIAM	1830	DEFENDANT	1581
MATHEWS, A R	1871	FRKLN TWP-BUS.	1797
MATHEWS, J	1871	MARH'L MAP	1750
MATHEWS, J	1871	MARH'L MAP	1750
MATHEWS, J	1871	MARH'L MAP	1757
MATHEWS, J / INITIALS J.M.	1871	MARH'L MAP	1757
MATHEWS, W	1871	MARH'L MAP	1757
MATHEWS, W	1871	MARH'L MAP	1757
MATHEWS, WILLIAM	1832	DEFENDANT	1587
MATHEWSON, W / JEFFERSON ST ?	1871	NEW CUMB'LD	1767
MATTHERS, EBENEZER S	1838	DEFENDANT	1651
MATTHEWS, A R	1871	MARH'L MAP	1754
MATTHEWS, C	1871	MDSVILLE	1807
MATTHEWS, J	1871	MARH'L MAP	1756
MATTHEWS, J	1871	MDSVILLE	1807
MATTHEWS, J / INITIALS J.M.	1871	MDSVILLE	1807
MATTHEWS, J / INITIALS J.M.	1871	MDSVILLE	1807
MATTHEWS, L	1871	MARH'L MAP	1752
MATTHEWS, W / ? JEFFERSON ST	1871	NEW CUMB'LD	1767
MATTHIAS, JOSEPH	1828	DEFENDANT	1613
MAULDING - CHILDREN	1834	MISC	1705
MAUNS, PROVIDENCE	1808	APPENDIX	1873
MAWHA - SEE ALSO MCWHA / ?	1871	HAN MAP	1733
MAWHA, G / & R	1852	NOT ON MAP	1836
MAWHA, G / & R - MAP#659	1852	BRKE MAP	1854
MAWHA, G / & R - MAP#662	1852	BRKE MAP	1854
MAWHA, R / & G.	1852	NOT ON MAP	1836
MAWHA, R / & G - MAP#659	1852	BRKE MAP	1854
MAWHA, R / & G - MAP#662	1852	BRKE MAP	1854
MAXWELL, E	1871	MARH'L MAP	1748
MAXWELL, E / INITIALS E.M.	1871	MARH'L MAP	1748
MAXWELL, E	1871	MARH'L MAP	1751
MAXWELL, J / MRS	1871	OH CO. MAP	1740
MAXWELL, J	1871	MARH'L MAP	1746
MAXWELL, J	1871	MARH'L MAP	1749
MAXWELL, J C / (OC.) PROPT	1871	W.LIBERTY	1780
MAXWELL, J C / PROPT OF HOTEL	1871	W.LIBRTY.BUS.	1780
MAXWELL, JOHN L	1851	DEFENDANT	1553
MAXWELL, JOHN L	1851	DEFENDANT	1620
MAXWELL, JOHN SR	1857	DEFENDANT	1578
MAXWELL, R M	1871	OH CO. MAP	1740
MAXWELL, ROBERT	1790	DEFENDANT	1647
MAXWELL, S / MRS	1871	OH CO. MAP	1740
MAXWELL, W H	1871	WELLSBURG	1777
MAXWELL, W M	1871	WELLSBURG	1777
MAXWELL, WILLIAM	1871	OH CO. MAP	1740
MAY, - / SCHOOL - MAP#510	1852	BRKE MAP	1849
MAY, A	1871	BKE/OH MAP	1739
MAY, ALEXANDER / MAP#108	1852	BRKE MAP	1840
MAY, J	1871	BRKE MAP	1735
MAY, J	1871	MARH'L MAP	1756
MAY, JASON / MAP#510	1852	BRKE MAP	1849
MAY, L	1871	MARH'L MAP	1760
MAYERS, A	1871	MARH'L MAP	1745
MAYES, JOSEPH F	1874	MISC	1675
MAYGER, RICHARD	1852	DEFENDANT	1590
MAYHALL, J	1871	MARH'L MAP	1754
MAYHEW, J N	1871	HAN MAP	1731
MAYHEW, J N	1871	HAN MAP	1731
MAYSVILLE	1852	HEMPFIELD RR	1820
MAYSVILLE, KY	1852	HEMP. RR MAP	1826
MAZINGO, S	1871	OH CO. MAP	1740
MCANALL, HUGH	1871	OH CO. MAP	1742
MCARIGAN, - / ?	1871	MARH'L MAP	1745
MCBRIDE, WILLIAM H	1861	DEFENDANT	1646
MCBRIDE, WILLIAM H	1862	DEFENDANT	1646
MCBROOM, R / (?OR P.?)	1871	BKE/OH MAP	1739
MCBROOM, ROBERT / MAP#2	1852	BRKE MAP	1841
MCBROOM, ROBERT / MAP#46	1852	BRKE MAP	1841
MCCABE, R A	1871	OH CO.BUS.	1779
MCCABE, R A	1871	TRIAD.TWP.	1781
MCCABE, R A	1871	WHG CITY	1789
MCCAFFERTY, J	1871	NEW CUMB'LD	1766
MCCAFFERY, J	1871	MARH'L MAP	1745
MCCALL, MARY	1851	MISC	1688
MCCALLAM, A C	1842	DEFENDANT	1663
MCCALLISTER, JOSEPH	1829	DEFENDANT	1581
MCCAN, JAMES	1793	DEFENDANT	1655
MCCANAUGHEY, W	1871	MARH'L MAP	1757
MCCANAUGHY, D	1871	MARH'L MAP	1757
MCCARDLE, C Y	1871	MARH'L MAP	1756
MCCARDLE, D	1871	MARH'L MAP	1756
MCCARDLE, J	1871	MARH'L MAP	1756
MCCARDLE, J	1871	MARH'L MAP	1760
MCCARDLE, J / S.M. STORE (?MEANING UNKNOWN?)	1871	MARH'L MAP	1760
MCCARDLE, J F	1871	MARH'L MAP	1756
MCCARDLE, P	1871	TRIAD.BORO.	1784
MCCARDLE, W	1871	MARH'L MAP	1756
MCCARITHON, A	1871	MARH'L MAP	1747

LXI

'PERSONAL TIME LINE' INDEX TO VOLUME 7 OF THE *OHIO COUNTY INDEX*

ENTRY	YEAR	SUBJECT	PAGE
MCCARRIHER, J	1871	MARH'L MAP	1745
MCCARRIHER, J	1871	MARH'L MAP	1748
MCCARRIHER, J W	1871	MDSVILLE	1807
MCCARTHEY, J	1871	MARH'L MAP	1745
MCCARTHEY, J / TOP OF MAP	1871	MARH'L MAP	1748
MCCARTNEY, ALEXANDER	1839	DEFENDANT	1672
MCCARTY, - / MRS	1871	NEW CUMB'LD	1767
MCCARTY, - / MRS	1871	NEW CUMB'LD	1767
MCCARTY, H	1871	BKE/OH MAP	1739
MCCARTY, S	1871	BKE/OH MAP	1739
MCCARTY, T	1871	WELLSBURG	1777
MCCASH, - / MRS	1871	MARH'L MAP	1753
MCCASKEY, JAMES	1829	DEFENDANT	1668
MCCASKEY, JOHN	1839	DEFENDANT	1662
MCCAUSLAND, E C	1871	OH CO. MAP	1743
MCCAUSLAND, E C	1871	OH CO. MAP	1743
MCCAUSLIN, GEORGE	1871	MARH'L MAP	1747
MCCAUSLIN, J	1871	BKE/OH MAP	1739
MCCDONALD, J	1871	OH CO. MAP	1743
MCCDONALD, J / INITIALS J. MCD.	1871	OH CO. MAP	1743
MCCLAIN, ALEXANDER	1814	DEFENDANT	1563
MCCLANE, DAVID	1855	DEFENDANT	1641
MCCLANE, JOHN	1808	DEFENDANT	1656
MCCLANEY, WILLIAM / MAP#337	1852	BRKE MAP	1846
MCCLEAN, - / S.S MILL ? - OHIO RIVER	1871	MARH'L MAP	1748
MCCLEAN, - / MRS	1871	MDSVILLE	1808
MCCLEAN, -	1871	MDSVILLE	1810
MCCLEAN, ARCHIBALD	1813	DEFENDANT	1555
MCCLEAN, E H	1871	MARH'L MAP	1748
MCCLEAN, E H / INITIALS E.H.MC.C	1871	MARH'L MAP	1748
MCCLEAN, E H / INITIALS E.H.MC.C	1871	MARH'L MAP	1748
MCCLEAN, E H / INITIALS E.H.MC.	1871	MARH'L MAP	1751
MCCLEAN, E H	1871	MDSVILLE	1810
MCCLEAN, H J	1871	MARH'L MAP	1748
MCCLEAN, H J / INITIALS H.J.MC.C	1871	MARH'L MAP	1748
MCCLEAN, H J	1871	MDSVILLE	1810
MCCLEAN, H J / EST.	1871	MDSVILLE	1810
MCCLEAN, JAMES A	1837	DEFENDANT	1614
MCCLEAN, JAMES A	1837	DEFENDANT	1619
MCCLEAN, JAMES A	1839	DEFENDANT	1563
MCCLEAN, JAMES F	1838	DEFENDANT	1619
MCCLEANS RUN	1871	MARH'L MAP	1748
MCCLEANS RUN - TIMBERLAND ON	1871	MARH'L MAP	1748
MCCLEARY, EWING / (GONE) - MAP#498	1852	BRKE MAP	1850
MCCLEARY, EWING	1871	BRKE MAP	1735
MCCLELLAND, J K	1871	BRKE MAP	1735
MCCLELLAND, WILLIAM	1822	DEFENDANT	1612
MCCLOUD, A	1871	NEW CUMB'LD	1766
MCCLOUD, A / INITIALS A.MC.C	1871	NEW CUMB'LD	1766
MCCLOUD, R	1871	HAN MAP	1731
MCCLUNEY, JAMES	1840	DEFENDANT	1643
MCCLUNEY, JAMES	1842	DEFENDANT	1615
MCCLUNEY, JAMES	1875	DEFENDANT	1609
MCCLUNG, W	1871	HAN MAP	1733
MCCLURE HOTEL - WHEELING	1916	NAT'L ROAD	1868
MCCLURE HOTEL - WHEELING -MAP	1916	NAT'L ROAD	1868
MCCLURE, J / MRS	1871	MDSVILLE	1807
MCCLURE, J / MRS - INITIALS J.MC.C	1871	MDSVILLE	1807
MCCLURE, JOHN	1810	APPENDIX	1873
MCCLURE, NANCY	1796	MISC	1707
MCCLURE, ROBERT	1800	DEFENDANT	1598
MCCLURE, ROBERT	1800	DEFENDANT	1665
MCCLURE, ROBERT	1801	DEFENDANT	1598
MCCLURE, S / EST	1871	OH CO. MAP	1741
MCCLURE, SAMUEL	1799	DEFENDANT	1607
MCCLURE, SAMUEL	1810	APPENDIX	1873
MCCLURE, SAMUEL	1814	MISC	1682
MCCLURE, WILLIAM R	1838	DEFENDANT	1616
MCCLURE, WILLIAM R	1839	DEFENDANT	1642
MCCLURE, WILLIAM R	1839	DEFENDANT	1651
MCCLURG, J	1871	HAN MAP	1733
MCCLURG, W K	1871	NEW CUMB'LD	1762
MCCLURG, W K / OC	1871	NEW CUMB'LD	1767
MCCLUSKEY, URIAH	1788	DEFENDANT	1604
MCCLUTCHY, URIAH	1788	DEFENDANT	1644
MCCOEN, A	1871	OH CO. MAP	1740
MCCOLLOCH, -	1844	DEFENDANT	1632
MCCOLLOCH, - / MRS -INITIALS MRS. MC.C	1871	BKE/OH MAP	1738
MCCOLLOCH, - / MRS -INITIALS MRS. MC.C	1871	BKE/OH MAP	1738
MCCOLLOCH, - / MRS	1871	BKE/OH MAP	1738
MCCOLLOCH, - / MRS - INITIALS MRS. MC.C	1871	BKE/OH MAP	1738
MCCOLLOCH, A	1871	BKE/OH MAP	1738

ENTRY	YEAR	SUBJECT	PAGE
MCCOLLOCH, A	1871	OH CO. MAP	1741
MCCOLLOCH, A	1871	OH CO. MAP	1741
MCCOLLOCH, ABRAHAM	1816	DEFENDANT	1648
MCCOLLOCH, ABRAHAM	1817	DEFENDANT	1659
MCCOLLOCH, ANDREW W	1832	DEFENDANT	1585
MCCOLLOCH, ANDREW W	1839	DEFENDANT	1551
MCCOLLOCH, E	1871	BKE/OH MAP	1738
MCCOLLOCH, E / ? - WRITTEN IN OHIO RIVER	1871	BKE/OH MAP	1738
MCCOLLOCH, E / INITIALS E.MC.C	1871	BKE/OH MAP	1738
MCCOLLOCH, GEORGE	1782	MISC	1684
MCCOLLOCH, GEORGE	1806	DEFENDANT	1607
MCCOLLOCH, GEORGE	1811	DEFENDANT	1567
MCCOLLOCH, GEORGE	1811	DEFENDANT	1567
MCCOLLOCH, GEORGE	1823	DEFENDANT	1572
MCCOLLOCH, GEORGE C	1877	DEFENDANT	1654
MCCOLLOCH, IDA	1873	MISC	1687
MCCOLLOCH, IVA	1875	MISC	1687
MCCOLLOCH, IVEA	1871	MISC	1687
MCCOLLOCH, JAMES	1871	OH CO. MAP	1741
MCCOLLOCH, JAMES / INITIALS JAS. MC.C	1871	OH CO. MAP	1741
MCCOLLOCH, JOHN	1777	APPENDIX	1874
MCCOLLOCH, JOHN	1779	APPENDIX	1874
MCCOLLOCH, JOHN	1799	MISC	1689
MCCOLLOCH, JOHN	1805	DEFENDANT	1648
MCCOLLOCH, JOHN	1810	APPENDIX	1873
MCCOLLOCH, JOHN	1821	PLAINTIFF	1570
MCCOLLOCH, JOHN	1821	PLAINTIFF	1570
MCCOLLOCH, JOHN W	1871	OH CO. MAP	1741
MCCOLLOCH, JOHN W / INITIALS J.B.W.	1871	OH CO. MAP	1741
MCCOLLOCH, JOSIAH	1823	DEFENDANT	1570
MCCOLLOCH, S / INITIALS S.MC.C	1871	BKE/OH MAP	1738
MCCOLLOCH, S / INITIALS S. MC. C	1871	OH CO. MAP	1741
MCCOLLOCH, S / RES	1871	OH CO. MAP	1741
MCCOLLOCH, SAMUEL / MCCOLLOCH'S LEAP	1916	NAT'L ROAD	1865
MCCOLLOCH, W J	1871	OH CO. MAP	1741
MCCOLLOCH, W J / INITIALS W.J.MCC.	1871	OH CO. MAP	1741
MCCOLLOCH, WILLIAM	1822	PLAINTIFF	1572
MCCOLLOCH, WILLIAM	1823	PLAINTIFF	1572
MCCOLLOCH'S LEAP - MAP	1916	NAT'L ROAD	1868
MCCOLLOCH'S LEAP - WHEELING	1916	NAT'L ROAD	1865
MCCOLLOCK, GEORGE	1809	DEFENDANT	1626
MCCOLLOCK, GEORGE	1829	DEFENDANT	1639
MCCOLLOCK, JOSIAH	1823	DEFENDANT	1572
MCCOLLOCK, JOSIAH	1825	DEFENDANT	1625
MCCOLLOCK, SAMUEL	1852	HEMPFIELD RR	1822
MCCOLLOUGH, GEORGE	1806	DEFENDANT	1644
MCCOMBS, GEORGE	1876	DEFENDANT	1592
MCCOMBS, J	1871	MARH'L MAP	1746
MCCOMBS, J	1871	MARH'L MAP	1746
MCCOMBS, J	1871	SHERRARD	1811
MCCOMBS, J / STORE & POST OFFICE	1871	SHERRARD	1811
MCCOMBS, J W	1871	MARH'L MAP	1746
MCCOMICK, THOMAS	1833	DEFENDANT	1579
MCCOMMON, J	1871	BKE/OH MAP	1739
MCCOMMON, J	1871	OH CO. MAP	1740
MCCON, J	1871	OH CO. MAP	1740
MCCON, JAMES	1825	DEFENDANT	1639
MCCONAGHEY, D	1871	CAMERON	1802
MCCONAGHEY, D / INITIALS D.MC.C	1871	CAMERON	1802
MCCONAGHEY, D / INITIALS D.MC.C	1871	CAMERON	1803
MCCONAGHEY, D / INITIALS D.MC.C	1871	CAMERON	1803
MCCONAUGHEY, D	1871	MARH'L MAP	1757
MCCONAUGHEY, D	1871	CAMERON	1804
MCCONELS & EDWARDS PORTABLE SAW MILL	1871	MARH'L MAP	1749
MCCONKEY, J	1871	WELLSBURG	1777
MCCONN, A	1871	OH CO. MAP	1743
MCCONN, J	1871	OH CO. MAP	1740
MCCONN, J	1871	OH CO. MAP	1743
MCCONNAL, ARTHUR	1779	APPENDIX	1874
MCCONNALDIS BRANCH	1852	BRKE MAP	1852
MCCONNEL, ALEXR JR	1818	DEFENDANT	1648
MCCONNEL, J	1871	OH CO. MAP	1743
MCCONNEL, M P / MRS - GROC. & P.O.	1871	NEW CUMB'LD	1767
MCCONNEL, P / MRS - GROC. & P.O.	1871	NEW CUMB'LD	1767
MCCONNELL - CHILDREN	1827	MISC	1697
MCCONNELL, - / MRS	1871	OH CO. MAP	1743
MCCONNELL, -	1871	WELLSBURG	1777
MCCONNELL, -	1871	MDSVILLE	1807
MCCONNELL, - / CRISWELL & MCCONNELL	1871	MDSVILLE	1808
MCCONNELL, ALEX	1829	DEFENDANT	1672

LXII

'PERSONAL TIME LINE' INDEX TO VOLUME 7 OF THE *OHIO COUNTY INDEX*

ENTRY	YEAR	SUBJECT	PAGE
MCCONNELL, ALEXANDER	1816	DEFENDANT	1648
MCCONNELL, C	1871	OH CO. MAP	1743
MCCONNELL, D	1871	MARH'L MAP	1746
MCCONNELL, E	1871	OH CO. MAP	1743
MCCONNELL, J	1871	OH CO. MAP	1743
MCCONNELL, J	1871	MDSVILLE	1807
MCCONNELL, JAMES	1786	MISC	1697
MCCONNELL, JAMES	1798	DEFENDANT	1589
MCCONNELL, JAMES	1838	DEFENDANT	1568
MCCONNELL, JAMES	1840	DEFENDANT	1643
MCCONNELL, JAMES	1857	DEFENDANT	1573
MCCONNELL, JOHN	1799	DEFENDANT	1665
MCCONNELL, JOHN	1878	DEFENDANT	1597
MCCONNELL, L	1871	WELLSBURG	1777
MCCONNELL, R	1871	MDSVILLE	1808
MCCONNELL, R / OFFICE	1871	MDSVILLE	1808
MCCONNELL, R / RES	1871	MDSVILLE	1809
MCCONNELL, R	1871	MDSVILLE	1810
MCCONNELL, ROBERT	1800	DEFENDANT	1658
MCCONNELL, ROBERT / ATTORNEY	1871	MDSVL BUS.	1796
MCCONNELL, WILLIAM	1798	DEFENDANT	1598
MCCONNELL, WILLIAM	1800	DEFENDANT	1647
MCCONNELL, WILLIAM	1813	DEFENDANT	1611
MCCONNELL, WILLIAM	1813	DEFENDANT	1611
MCCONNELL, WILLIAM	1815	DEFENDANT	1595
MCCONNELL, WILLIAM	1818	DEFENDANT	1646
MCCONNELL, WILLIAM	1818	DEFENDANT	1660
MCCONNELL, WILLIAM	1834	MISC	1707
MCCONNELL, WILLIAM	1835	MISC	1707
MCCONNELL, WILLIAM	1837	MISC	1707
MCCONNELL, WILLIAM	1839	MISC	1707
MCCONNELL, WILLIAM	1841	MISC	1707
MCCONVILLE, P	1871	BRKE MAP	1735
MCCORD, - / MRS	1871	BRKE MAP	1736
MCCORD, - / MRS	1871	BRKE MAP	1736
MCCORD, - / MRS	1871	BKE/OH MAP	1738
MCCORD, - / MRS	1871	BKE/OH MAP	1738
MCCORD, G W / ESQ. / (OLD CABIN) - MAP#155	1852	BRKE MAP	1842
MCCORD, G W / ESQ. / (OLD CABIN) - MAP#157	1852	BRKE MAP	1842
MCCORD, G W / ESQ. / (OLD CABIN) - MAP#160	1852	BRKE MAP	1842
MCCORD, G W / ESQ. / MAP#97	1852	BRKE MAP	1842
MCCORD, G W	1871	BRKE MAP	1736
MCCORD, JAMES	1807	DEFENDANT	1602
MCCORD, JAMES	1821	DEFENDANT	1570
MCCORD, T	1871	OH CO. MAP	1741
MCCORD, T	1871	OH CO. MAP	1741
MCCORD, T / INITIALS T. MC. C	1871	OH CO. MAP	1741
MCCORKLE, - / MRS	1871	MDSVILLE	1806
MCCORKLE, - / MRS	1871	MDSVILLE	1808
MCCORMACK, ED	1878	DEFENDANT	1646
MCCORMACK, EDWARD	1878	DEFENDANT	1646
MCCORMACKS RUN	1852	BRKE MAP	1844
MCCORMIC, THOMAS	1835	DEFENDANT	1579
MCCORMICK, GEORGE	1819	DEFENDANT	1667
MCCORMICK, POLLARD	1858	DEFENDANT	1561
MCCORMICK, W	1871	WELLSBURG	1777
MCCORNELL, ALEX	1809	DEFENDANT	1626
MCCORTNEY, ALEXANDER	1838	DEFENDANT	1662
MCCORTNEY, ALEXANDER	1839	DEFENDANT	1662
MCCORTNEY, ALEXANDER	1840	DEFENDANT	1585
MCCORTNEY, ALEXANDER	1840	DEFENDANT	1594
MCCORTNEY, ALEXANDER	1840	DEFENDANT	1635
MCCORTNEY, ALEXANDER	1840	DEFENDANT	1643
MCCORTNEY, ALEXANDER	1841	DEFENDANT	1595
MCCORTNEY, ALEXANDER	1841	DEFENDANT	1672
MCCORTNEY, JOHN	1825	DEFENDANT	1573
MCCORTNEY, JOHN	1841	DEFENDANT	1594
MCCORTNEY, JOHN / TAVERN	1916	NAT'L ROAD	1867
MCCORTNEY, JOHN / TAVERN	1916	NAT'L ROAD	1868
MCCORTNEY, JOHN / TAVERN - ON MAP	1916	NAT'L ROAD	1868
MCCOWN, J C	1871	NEW MANCH.	1769
MCCOWN, JOHN	1798	DEFENDANT	1634
MCCOY, A	1871	BKE/OH MAP	1739
MCCOY, EBENEZER	1857	DEFENDANT	1663
MCCOY, H / DOCTOR	1871	MARH'L MAP	1745
MCCOY, J	1871	MARH'L MAP	1745
MCCOY, JAMES	1788	PLAINTIFF	1665
MCCOY, JAMES	1820	DEFENDANT	1660
MCCOY, JAMES	1821	DEFENDANT	1561
MCCOY, JAMES	1821	DEFENDANT	1612
MCCOY, JAMES	1821	DEFENDANT	1649
MCCOY, JAMES	1821	DEFENDANT	1660
MCCOY, JAMES	1840	PLAINTIFF	1652
MCCOY, JOHN	1859	DEFENDANT	1641
MCCOY, S	1871	OH CO. MAP	1743
MCCOY, S	1871	OH CO. MAP	1744
MCCOY, W	1871	OH CO. MAP	1740
MCCOY, WILLIAM	1823	DEFENDANT	1596
MCCOY, WILLIAM	1851	MISC	1694
MCCOY, WILLIAM	1856	MISC	1694
MCCOYS RUN	1871	OH CO. MAP	1743
MCCOYS RUN	1871	OH CO. MAP	1744
MCCOYS STATION	1871	HAN MAP	1730
MCCRACKEN C	1871	MARH'L MAP	1757
MCCRACKEN, D	1871	MARH'L MAP	1757
MCCRACKEN, D / INITIALS D.MCC.	1871	MARH'L MAP	1757
MCCRACKEN, J	1871	MARH'L MAP	1747
MCCRACKEN, J	1871	MARH'L MAP	1757
MCCRACKEN, JAMES	1833	DEFENDANT	1628
MCCRACKEN, S C / M.D.	1871	W UNION-BUS.	1797
MCCRACKEN, S C / DR	1871	W UNION	1812
MCCRACKEN, WILLIAM	1871	MARH'L MAP	1747
MCCRACKIN, JAMES	1834	DEFENDANT	1628
MCCRARY	1871	MARH'L MAP	1747
MCCRARY, -	1871	MARH'L MAP	1750
MCCRARY, T	1871	MARH'L MAP	1746
MCCRARY, WILLIAM	1871	MARH'L MAP	1746
MCCREA, J	1871	HAN MAP	1731
MCCREADY, R	1871	BRKE MAP	1734
MCCREARY, - / MRS	1871	MARH'L MAP	1753
MCCREARY, G	1871	BRKE MAP	1735
MCCREARY, G	1871	BRKE MAP	1737
MCCREARY, G W	1871	FOWLERS P.O.	1775
MCCREARY, JOHN M	1841	DEFENDANT	1614
MCCREARY, JOHN M	1841	DEFENDANT	1619
MCCREERY, S	1871	MARH'L MAP	1746
MCCREERY, S	1871	MARH'L MAP	1746
MCCREERY, S	1871	MARH'L MAP	1750
MCCREERY, S	1871	MARH'L MAP	1750
MCCRERY - CHILDREN	1817	MISC	1693
MCCRUM, J	1871	OH CO. MAP	1741
MCCUEN, WILLIAM	1871	MARH'L MAP	1751
MCCULLEY, A	1871	OH CO. MAP	1742
MCCULLEY, J	1871	MARH'L MAP	1746
MCCULLOCH, JOHN	1821	PLAINTIFF	1570
MCCULLOCH, JOHN	1821	PLAINTIFF	1570
MCCULLOCH, JOHN	1823	PLAINTIFF	1570
MCCULLOCH, JOHN	1823	PLAINTIFF	1570
MCCULLOCHS RUN / OR BRANCH	1852	BRKE MAP	1843
MCCURDY & GREGG	1857	DEFENDANT	1597
MCCURDY, HUGH	1839	MISC	1688
MCCURDY, HUGH	1841	DEFENDANT	1589
MCCURDY, WILLIAM	1857	DEFENDANT	1636
MCCUSKEY, J	1871	MARH'L MAP	1757
MCCUSKEY, J	1871	CAMERON	1803
MCCUSKEY, M	1871	MARH'L MAP	1757
MCCUSKEY, S	1871	MARH'L MAP	1757
MCCUSKY, J / NEAR WHITE OAK SPRING	1871	OH CO. MAP	1743
MCCUSKY, J / ON BORDER	1871	MARH'L MAP	1746
MCCUTCHEN, - / BROS	1871	OH CO. MAP	1743
MCCUTCHEN, J	1871	OH CO. MAP	1743
MCCUTCHEN, JAMES / THE OLD HOMESTEAD	1871	OH CO. MAP	1743
MCCUTCHEN, JOHN H	1871	OH CO. MAP	1743
MCCUTCHEN, W	1871	OH CO. MAP	1740
MCDANELL, - / MRS	1871	W UNION	1812
MCDANELL, - / MRS	1871	W UNION	1812
MCDANELL, - / MRS - BLACKSMITH SHOP - FURNACE ST	1871	W UNION	1812
MCDANELL, - / MRS - BLACKSMITH SHOP - INITIALS MRS.MC.D.	1871	W UNION	1812
MCDANELL, B	1871	W.UNION-BUS.	1797
MCDANIEL, M - MRS	1871	BRKE MAP	1735
MCDONALD, - / MRS	1871	NEW CUMB'LD	1766
MCDONALD, - / MRS	1871	CAMERON	1804
MCDONALD, ANN	1832	DEFENDANT	1573
MCDONALD, ARCHIBALD	1818	DEFENDANT	1599
MCDONALD, BARTHOLAMEW	1821	DEFENDANT	1581
MCDONALD, BARTHOLOMEW	1822	DEFENDANT	1581
MCDONALD, CON	1851	DEFENDANT	1672
MCDONALD, G	1871	BRKE MAP	1736
MCDONALD, G	1871	BKE/OH MAP	1739
MCDONALD, J	1871	OH CO. MAP	1741
MCDONALD, J	1871	OH CO. MAP	1742
MCDONALD, J	1871	OH CO. MAP	1742
MCDONALD, J	1871	OH CO. MAP	1744

'PERSONAL TIME LINE' INDEX TO VOLUME 7 OF THE OHIO COUNTY INDEX

ENTRY	YEAR	SUBJECT	PAGE	ENTRY	YEAR	SUBJECT	PAGE
MCDONALD, J	1871	OH CO. MAP	1744	MCGAVE, SAMUEL	1832	DEFENDANT	1591
MCDONALD, J / INITIALS J.MC.D	1871	OH CO. MAP	1744	MCGAVERN, E T	1871	NEW CUMB'LD	1768
MCDONALD, J	1871	MARH'L MAP	1756	MCGEARY, J	1871	MARH'L MAP	1753
MCDONALD, J	1871	MARH'L MAP	1760	MCGEARY, L / MRS	1871	W.LIBERTY	1780
MCDONALD, J S	1871	MDSVILLE	1809	MCGEE, E	1871	BKE/OH MAP	1738
MCDONALD, JAMES	1827	DEFENDANT	1649	MCGEE, JAMES	1859	DEFENDANT	1597
MCDONALD, JAMES	1831	DEFENDANT	1573	MCGER. , J	1871	MARH'L MAP	1761
MCDONALD, JOHN	1784	DEFENDANT	1568	MCGERARY, J	1871	MARH'L MAP	1750
MCDONALD, JOHN	1788	DEFENDANT	1637	MCGILL, - / MRS	1871	MDSVILLE	1810
MCDONALD, JOHN	1799	DEFENDANT	1563	MCGILL, JAMES	1871	MDSVILLE	1807
MCDONALD, SMITH	1850	DEFENDANT	1616	MCGILL, W	1871	MDSVILLE	1807
MCDONALD, SMITH	1875	DEFENDANT	1615	MCGILL, W / INITIALS W.MC.G.	1871	MDSVILLE	1807
MCDONALD, THOMAS	1854	DEFENDANT	1672	MCGLOUGHLAND, HUGH	1789	DEFENDANT	1655
MCDONALD, W	1871	HAN MAP	1726	MCGLOUGHLAND, JOHN	1789	DEFENDANT	1600
MCDONALD, W	1871	MDSVILLE	1807	MCGLUMPHY, A / BLACKSMITH SHOP	1871	MARH'L MAP	1747
MCDONALD, W E	1871	GLEN EASTON - BUS.	1796	MCGLUMPHY, G F	1871	MARH'L MAP	1761
MCDONALD, W R	1871	CAMER'N - BUS.	1795	MCGLUMPHY, J	1871	HAN MAP	1732
MCDONALD, W R / STORE	1871	GLEN EASTON	1801	MCGLUMPHY, J	1871	MARH'L MAP	1761
MCDONALD, W R / INITIALS W.R.MC.D. (?SR?)	1871	CAMERON	1804	MCGRAWS RUN	1871	OH CO. MAP	1740
MCDONALD, W R SR	1871	CAMERON	1804	MCGREARY, GEORGE	1804	DEFENDANT	1587
MCDONALD, WILLIAM	1834	DEFENDANT	1589	MCGREGGAR, ALLEN	1810	DEFENDANT	1648
MCDONALD, WILLIAM	1852	NOT ON MAP	1836	MCGRUDER, D P	1871	MARH'L MAP	1755
MCDONNALD, JOHN	1797	DEFENDANT	1647	MCGUFFY, A	1871	MARH'L MAP	1761
MCDONNELL, ALLEN	1803	DEFENDANT	1637	MCGUIRE, FRANK / (MILL) - MAP#427	1852	BRKE MAP	1847
MCDONNELL, W	1871	NEW CUMB'LD	1768	MCGUIRE, FRANK / MAP#426	1852	BRKE MAP	1847
MCDONNELL, WILLIAM	1818	DEFENDANT	1646	MCGUIRE, HUGH	1789	DEFENDANT	1655
MCDONNOLD, JAMES	1798	DEFENDANT	1634	MCGUIRE, HUGH	1801	DEFENDANT	1634
MCDOW, M	1871	HAN MAP	1727	MCGUIRE, J B	1860	DEFENDANT	1621
MCDOWELL, D	1871	MARH'L MAP	1760	MCGUIRE, LUKE / MAP#484	1852	BRKE MAP	1849
MCDOWELL, H	1871	MARH'L MAP	1760	MCGUIRE, THOMAS	1778	APPENDIX	1874
MCELHANEY, - / MRS	1871	OH CO. MAP	1742	MCGUIRES RUN	1852	BRKE MAP	1847
MCELHANEY, - / MRS	1871	OH CO. MAP	1742	MCGUYRE, F	1871	BRKE MAP	1735
MCELHANY, - / MRS	1871	RITCHIE TWP	1791	MCHENRY, - / HRS	1871	MARH'L MAP	1745
MCELHANY, - / MRS	1871	RITCHIE TWP	1791	MCHENRY, - / MRS	1871	WELLSBURG	1777
MCELHANY, - / MRS	1871	RITCHIE TWP	1791	MCHENRY, GEORGE	1871	MARH'L MAP	1758
MCELHANY, - / MRS	1871	RITCHIE TWP	1793	MCHENRY, J / HEIRS	1871	MARH'L MAP	1745
MCELHENNEY, W	1871	NEW CUMB'LD	1767	MCHENRY, J	1871	MARH'L MAP	1758
MCELHENNEY, W / INITIALS W.M.	1871	NEW CUMB'LD	1767	MCHENRY, JOHN	1810	DEFENDANT	1635
MCELROY, J R	1871	WELLSBURG	1778	MCHENRY, JOHN	1810	DEFENDANT	1648
MCELVANE, WILLIAM	1871	NEW CUMB'LD	1767	MCHENRY, JOSEPH	1804	DEFENDANT	1587
MCELWAINE, G	1871	MARH'L MAP	1756	MCHENRY, JOSEPH	1805	DEFENDANT	1587
MCELWAINE, G / INITIALS G.MC.E	1871	MARH'L MAP	1756	MCHENRY, ROBERT	1833	DEFENDANT	1669
MCENTEE, THOMAS	1877	DEFENDANT	1576	MCHENRY, S / 'QUIET HOME'	1871	HAN MAP	1727
MCF, J / UNKNOWN INITIALS	1871	ELM GROVE	1782	MCINGTIER, JOHN	1798	PLAINTIFF	1594
MCFADDEN G S	1871	MARH'L MAP	1748	MCINTIER, JOHN	1798	MISC	1710
MCFADDEN, CHARLES	1821	DEFENDANT	1581	MCINTIRE RUN	1852	BRKE MAP	1843
MCFADDEN, CHARLES	1821	DEFENDANT	1594	MCINTIRE, J	1871	BRKE MAP	1736
MCFADDEN, G S	1871	MARH'L MAP	1746	MCINTIRE, J / INITIALS J.MC.I.	1871	BRKE MAP	1736
MCFADDEN, G S	1871	MARH'L MAP	1749	MCINTIRE, ROBERT	1801	DEFENDANT	1598
MCFADDEN, G S / INITIALS G.S.MCF.	1871	MARH'L MAP	1749	MCINTIRE, ROBERT	1801	DEFENDANT	1598
MCFADDEN, G S	1871	MARH'L MAP	1750	MCINTIRE, ROBERT	1801	DEFENDANT	1666
MCFADDEN, G S	1871	MDSVILLE	1808	MCINTIRE, S C	1871	MARH'L MAP	1754
MCFADDEN, G S / INITIALS G.S.MCF.	1871	MDSVILLE	1808	MCINTYRE, I	1871	BRKE MAP	1736
MCFADDEN, G S	1871	MDSVILLE	1809	MCINTYRE, ISAAC / MAP#198	1852	BRKE MAP	1843
MCFADDEN, J / SEE MCF, J - UNKNOWN INITIALS ??	1871	ELM GROVE	1782	MCINTYRE, J	1871	BRKE MAP	1736
MCFADDEN, MERCER	1818	DEFENDANT	1648	MCINTYRE, JOSEPNUS / MAP#272	1852	BRKE MAP	1842
MCFARLAND, - / MRS & L.W. CARTER	1871	BRKE MAP	1735	MCINTYRE, JOSEPNUS / MAP#273	1852	BRKE MAP	1842
MCFARLAND, ANDREW	1800	DEFENDANT	1665	MCINTYRE, JOSEPNUS / MAP#216	1852	BRKE MAP	1843
MCFARLAND, J / SEE MCF, J - UNKNOWN INITIALS ??	1871	ELM GROVE	1782	MCKAY, THOMAS	1831	MISC	1710
MCFARLAND, NATHAN	1789	DEFENDANT	1610	MCKAY, WILLIAM	1848	DEFENDANT	1670
MCFARLAND, R H	1871	MARH'L MAP	1751	MCKEAG, A	1871	OH CO. MAP	1743
MCFARLAND, R H / INITIALS R.H.MCF	1871	MARH'L MAP	1751	MCKEAN, - / MRS	1871	MARH'L MAP	1751
MCFARLAND, T B	1871	MARH'L MAP	1751	MCKEAN, - / MRS	1871	MARH'L MAP	1755
MCFARLAND, WILLIAM	1871	BETHANY	1773	MCKEAN, JAMES	1840	DEFENDANT	1559
MCFLANEGIN, A	1871	NEW MANCH.	1763	MCKEAN, JAMES	1840	DEFENDANT	1573
MCFORSON, JOHN	1784	APPENDIX	1874	MCKEAN, R	1871	MARH'L MAP	1755
MCGAHAN, W / (OC.)	1871	CAMERON	1803	MCKEE, -	1824	PLAINTIFF	1632
MCGAHAN, W / RES	1871	CAMERON	1803	MCKEE, -	1843	DEFENDANT	1672
MCGAHAN, W / RIDGE ST	1871	CAMERON	1803	MCKEE, ARTHUR C	1874	DEFENDANT	1597
MCGAHAN, W T	1871	CAMER'N - BUS.	1795	MCKEE, FRANK	1840	DEFENDANT	1643
MCGANES, - / EST	1871	MARH'L MAP	1751	MCKEE, JOSEPH	1824	DEFENDANT	1579
MCGANNON, DAVID	1858	DEFENDANT	1588	MCKEE, JOSEPH	1825	DEFENDANT	1579
MCGANNON, JAMES	1874	DEFENDANT	1609	MCKEE, REDECK	1831	DEFENDANT	1660
MCGANNON, JAMES	1876	DEFENDANT	1565	MCKEE, REDIC	1841	DEFENDANT	1629
MCGARTY, SAMUEL	1852	NOT ON MAP	1836	MCKEE, REDICK	1835	DEFENDANT	1622
MCGARVY, - / MRS	1871	W.LIBERTY	1780	MCKEE, REDICK	1840	DEFENDANT	1559
MCGARY, A	1871	MARH'L MAP	1752	MCKEE, REDICK	1840	DEFENDANT	1628
MCGARY, A / INITIALS A.MCG.	1871	MARH'L MAP	1752	MCKEE, REDICK	1840	DEFENDANT	1661
MCGARY, A / RES	1871	MARH'L MAP	1752	MCKEE, THOMAS	1847	DEFENDANT	1641
MCGARY, A / INITIALS A.MCG. / CUT OFF EDGE OF MAP	1871	MARH'L MAP	1755	MCKEEN, PATTON & CO	1860	DEFENDANT	1584
				MCKEEVER, WILLIAM / MAP#487	1852	BRKE MAP	1849
				MCKENNAN, J E	1879	DEFENDANT	1609
				MCKENNAN, THOMAS M T	1852	HEMPFIELD RR	1817
				MCKENNAN, THOMAS M T / PRESIDENT - HEMPFIELD RR	1852	HEMPFIELD RR	1824
MCGAUGHY, JOHN	1805	DEFENDANT	1658	MCKIE, R / ?	1871	BKE/OH MAP	1738

LXIV

'PERSONAL TIME LINE' INDEX TO VOLUME 7 OF THE *OHIO COUNTY INDEX*

ENTRY	YEAR	SUBJECT	PAGE	ENTRY	YEAR	SUBJECT	PAGE
MCKIM, - / & CO. - (DIS'Y) - MAP#87	1852	BRKE MAP	1842	MCNALLEY, J B	1871	WELLSBURG	1778
MCKIM, NANCY / MRS - MAP#606	1852	BRKE MAP	1851	MCNALLY, J B	1871	WELLSBURG	1778
MCKIM, NANCY / HRS	1871	BRKE MAP	1734	MCNEAL, P	1871	NEW CUMB'LD	1767
MCKIM, THOMAS / OC	1871	BRKE MAP	1734	MCNEIL, E	1871	NEW CUMB'LD	1767
MCKIMIE, G W	1871	MARH'L MAP	1759	MCNEIL, G	1871	NEW CUMB'LD	1767
MCKIMIE, G W / DOCTOR	1871	MARH'L MAP	1759	MCNULTY, CALEB	1812	DEFENDANT	1599
MCKIMIE, G W / INITIALS G.W.MCK.	1871	MARH'L MAP	1759	MCNULTY, PATRICK	1827	DEFENDANT	1672
MCKIMIE, G W / PHYSICIAN - NEAR FAIR VIEW	1871	FRKLN TWP-BUS.	1797	MCSHERRY, REUBEN	1806	DEFENDANT	1583
				MCSWEGIN, J D	1871	HAN MAP	1729
MCKINLEY, D C	1871	W.LIBERTY	1780	MCSWEGIN, J D	1871	HAN MAP	1729
MCKINLEY, D C / INITIALS D.C.MC.K.	1871	W.LIBERTY	1780	MCSWEGIN, W R	1871	HAN MAP	1729
MCKINLEY, D W C	1856	DEFENDANT	1559	MCVEIGH, -	1858	PLAINTIFF	1630
MCKINLEY, J W / INITIALS J.W.M.	1871	BKE/OH MAP	1738	MCVICKER, JAMES	1811	APPENDIX	1873
MCKINLEY, J W / INITIALS J.W.M.	1871	BKE/OH MAP	1738	MCWHA - SEE ALSO MAWHA / ?	1871	HAN MAP	1733
MCKINLEY, J W	1871	W.LIBERTY	1780	MCWHA, G	1871	BRKE MAP	1734
MCKINLEY, JAMES	1871	HAN MAP	1727	MCWHA, G	1871	BRKE MAP	1734
MCKINLEY, JAMES	1871	HAN MAP	1728	MCWHA, R	1871	HAN MAP	1733
MCKINLEY, JOHN W	1871	W.LIBRTY.BUS.	1780	MCWHORTER, J	1871	BENWOOD	1798
MCKINLEY, W	1871	BKE/OH MAP	1738	MCWHORTER, S	1871	W.UNION	1812
MCKINLEY, WILLIAM	1794	PLAINTIFF	1655	MEADE SUMMIT	1871	MARH'L MAP	1755
MCKINLEY, WILLIAM	1810	APPENDIX	1873	MEADE SUMMIT - CLAY TWP	1871	MARH'L MAP	1751
MCKINLEY, WILLIAM	1819	DEFENDANT	1667	MEADE TOWNSHIP - E. PART - MARSHALL CO.	1871	MARH'L MAP	1756
MCKINLEY, WILLIAM / MAP#29	1852	BRKE MAP	1840	MEADE TOWNSHIP - MARSHALL CO.	1871	POPULATION	1816
MCKINLEY, WILLIAM / MAP#30	1852	BRKE MAP	1840	MEADE TOWNSHIP - MARSHALL CO.	1871	MARH'L MAP	1755
MCKINLEY, WILLIAM	1856	DEFENDANT	1598	MEADE TOWNSHIP - S. PART - MARSHALL CO.	1871	MARH'L MAP	1760
MCKINLEY, WILLIAM	1856	DEFENDANT	1630	MEADE TOWNSHIP - SW PART - MARSHALL CO	1871	MARH'L MAP	1759
MCKINLEYS RUN	1852	BRKE MAP	1840				
MCKINLEYVILLE CREEK	1841	MISC	1678	MEADE, - / COL. INSTITUTE - MAP#398	1852	BRKE MAP	1846
MCKITRICKS RUN	1871	BKE/OH MAP	1739	MEADOW FARM	1871	OH CO. MAP	1740
MCKNIGHT, G	1871	MDSVILLE	1808	MEADOWBROOK	1871	HAN MAP	1732
MCKNIGHT, G M	1871	MDSVILLE	1810	MEAKE, JAMES	1797	DEFENDANT	1634
MCKNIGHT, JAMES	1809	DEFENDANT	1608	MEDER, ALWINA	1879	MISC	1698
MCKOKEY, J G	1871	WELLSBURG	1776	MEDFORD & RICHARDSON / STORE	1871	CAMERON	1803
MCLAIN, D B	1879	DEFENDANT	1595	MEEK, ISAAC	1778	APPENDIX	1874
MCLEOD, -	1825	PLAINTIFF	1622	MEEK, ISAAC	1795	DEFENDANT	1608
MCLURE, JAMES	1852	DEFENDANT	1616	MEEK, ISAAC	1795	MISC	1691
MCLURE, JOHN	1822	PLAINTIFF	1587	MEEK, JOHN	1799	PLAINTIFF	1655
MCLURE, ROBERT	1801	DEFENDANT	1598	MEEK, T / ESTATE	1871	BRKE MAP	1735
MCLURE, ROBERT	1801	DEFENDANT	1666	MEEKS BRANCH	1852	BRKE MAP	1849
MCLURE, ROBERT	1801	DEFENDANT	1666	MEEKS RUN	1852	BRKE MAP	1843
MCLURE, WILLIAM R	1840	DEFENDANT	1628	MELLON, MARK	1857	DEFENDANT	1661
MCLURE, WILLIAM R	1840	DEFENDANT	1661	MELLON, S	1871	MARH'L MAP	1757
MCMACHAN, WILLIAM	1794	DEFENDANT	1606	MELLOR, JAMES	1850	MISC	1680
MCMACHAN, WILLIAM	1794	DEFENDANT	1647	MELVIN, J H	1871	HAN MAP	1731
MCMAHAN, PAPRICK	1806	DEFENDANT	1600	MELVIN, J H	1871	NEW MANCH.	1769
MCMAHANS RUN	1852	BRKE MAP	1851	MELVIN, JAMES	1871	NEW MANCH.	1763
MCMAHON, JOSEPH C	1822	DEFENDANT	1600	MELVIN, JAMES	1871	NEW MANCH.	1769
MCMAHON, JOSEPH C	1822	DEFENDANT	1620	MEMMINGER, W	1871	OH CO. MAP	1742
MCMAHONS RUN	1871	BRKE MAP	1734	MEMMINGER, W	1871	TRIAD.TWP.	1781
MCMEACHEN, S	1871	MARH'L MAP	1745	MENDEL, - / MRS	1871	WELLSBURG	1777
MCMEACHEN, S / INITIALS S.MC.M.	1871	MARH'L MAP	1745	MENDEL, GEORGE	1872	MISC	1690
MCMEACHEN, S / INITIALS S.MC.M.	1871	MARH'L MAP	1745	MENDEL, H I / CHESTNUT HILL	1871	BRKE MAP	1736
MCMEACHEN, S / INITIALS S.MC.M.	1871	MARH'L MAP	1745	MENDEL, HENRY / MAP#347	1852	BRKE MAP	1846
MCMEANS, ANDREW	1844	DEFENDANT	1652	MENDELL, -	1840	PLAINTIFF	1620
MCMECHAN, H	1871	BENWOOD	1798	MENDELS FORK	1852	BRKE MAP	1846
MCMECHAN, H / AGT	1871	BENWOOD	1798	MENDLE, VALENTINE	1787	DEFENDANT	1644
MCMECHAN, H / RES	1871	BENWOOD	1798	MERCER, L	1871	HAN MAP	1727
MCMECHEH, BENJAMIN	1822	DEFENDANT	1646	MERCER, R / RES.	1871	HAN MAP	1727
MCMECHEN PATENT	1871	MARH'L MAP	1745	MERCERS RUN	1871	HAN MAP	1727
MCMECHEN RUN	1871	MARH'L MAP	1745	MERDY, HENRY G	1842	DEFENDANT	1620
MCMECHEN, B	1838	DEFENDANT	1625	MEREDITH, GEORGE L	1834	DEFENDANT	1599
MCMECHEN, B	1839	DEFENDANT	1625	MERKLE, AUGUSTUS N	1847	DEFENDANT	1641
MCMECHEN, BENJAMIN	1810	APPENDIX	1873	MERRICK, WILLIAM	1811	DEFENDANT	1645
MCMECHEN, BENJAMIN	1822	DEFENDANT	1625	MERRICK, WILLIAM	1812	DEFENDANT	1645
MCMECHEN, D	1871	MARH'L MAP	1745	MERRY HOME	1871	MARH'L MAP	1755
MCMECHEN, D	1871	MARH'L MAP	1745	MERRYMAN, J / HEIRS - MAP#488	1852	BRKE MAP	1849
MCMECHEN, D / INITIALS D.MC.M	1871	MARH'L MAP	1745	MERRYMAN, T	1871	WELLSBURG	1777
MCMECHEN, D / INITIALS D.MC.M	1871	MARH'L MAP	1745	MERRYMAN, W	1871	WELLSBURG	1777
MCMECHEN, D / INITIALS D.MC.M	1871	MARH'L MAP	1745	MERRYMANS FORK	1852	BRKE MAP	1849
MCMECHEN, D / INITIALS D.MC.M	1871	MARH'L MAP	1745	MESSEGER, MARY	1826	DEFENDANT	1579
MCMECHEN, DAVID	1817	DEFENDANT	1648	MESSER, JOHN	1806	DEFENDANT	1658
MCMECHEN, H	1871	BENWOOD	1798	MESSEY, J	1871	MARH'L MAP	1759
MCMECHEN, W	1871	MARH'L MAP	1745	METCALF, GEORGE	1860	DEFENDANT	1616
MCMECHEN, WILLIAM	1855	DEFENDANT	1552	METCALF, JACOB G	1858	DEFENDANT	1590
MCMECHEN, WILLIAM	1855	DEFENDANT	1621	METCALF, JACOB G	1859	DEFENDANT	1653
MCMILLAIN, T	1871	MARH'L MAP	1750	METCALF, JOSEPH A	1857	DEFENDANT	1576
MCMILLAN, JOHN	1842	MISC	1683	METHODIST / CHURCH ? - MAP#672	1852	BRKE MAP	1854
MCMILLEN, J	1871	WELLSBURG	1778	METHODIST CHURCH - CHAPLINE ST	1871	WHG CITY	1790
MCMILLEN, WILLIAM	1819	DEFENDANT	1602	METHODIST CHURCH - N.OF HORNBROOK BROTHERS	1871	MARH'L MAP	1754
MCMILLIN, J	1871	MARH'L MAP	1755				
MCMURRAY, - / MRS	1871	BKE/OH MAP	1739	METHODIST CHURCH - NE. OF WHITE OAK GROVE	1871	MARH'L MAP	1751
MCMURRAY, J	1871	MARH'L MAP	1745				
MCMURRY, GEORGE	1830	PLAINTIFF	1669				
MCMURRY, J R	1871	BKE/OH MAP	1739				
MCNALL, H	1871	OH CO. MAP	1742				

'PERSONAL TIME LINE' INDEX TO VOLUME 7 OF THE OHIO COUNTY INDEX

ENTRY	YEAR	SUBJECT	PAGE
METHODIST CHURCH & CEMETERY - SAND HILL	1871	MARH'L MAP	1746
METHODIST CHURCH & PARSONAGE - WEST UNION	1871	W.UNION	1812
METHODIST EPISCOPAL CHURCH / WEST OF PLEASANT VALLEY	1871	HAN MAP	1727
METHODIST EPISCOPAL CHURCH / E. OF J.M. WILSON	1871	BRKE MAP	1736
METHODIST EPISCOPAL CHURCH / PARSONAGE	1871	BRKE MAP	1737
METHODIST EPISCOPAL CHURCH - BROADWAY ST	1871	WHG ISLAND	1788
METHODIST EPISCOPAL CHURCH - C ST - MOUNDSVILLE	1871	MDSVILLE	1809
METHODIST EPISCOPAL CHURCH - CHAPLINE & SECOND ST	1871	WHG CITY	1790
METHODIST EPISCOPAL CHURCH - CORNER OF PEARL AND WATER STS - NEW CUMBERLAND	1871	NEW CUMB'LD	1767
METHODIST EPISCOPAL CHURCH - COUNCILMANS RUN	1871	BKE/OH MAP	1739
METHODIST EPISCOPAL CHURCH - E. OF SCHOOL NO.9 - LIBERTY TWP	1871	MARH'L MAP	1761
METHODIST EPISCOPAL CHURCH - FERTILE VALLEY	1871	MARH'L MAP	1745
METHODIST EPISCOPAL CHURCH - FIFTH ST - WHEELING	1871	WHG CITY	1788
METHODIST EPISCOPAL CHURCH - FIRST ST - BENWOOD	1871	BENWOOD	1798
METHODIST EPISCOPAL CHURCH - FOURTH ST - WHEELING	1871	WHG CITY	1788
METHODIST EPISCOPAL CHURCH - GREGGVILLE	1871	OH CO. MAP	1741
METHODIST EPISCOPAL CHURCH - INITIALS M.P. (?M.E.?) PROSPECT ST - WELLSBURG	1871	WELLSBURG	1777
METHODIST EPISCOPAL CHURCH - N OF PAN-HANDLE P.O.	1871	BRKE MAP	1734
METHODIST EPISCOPAL CHURCH - N. OF BENWOOD	1871	MARH'L MAP	1745
METHODIST EPISCOPAL CHURCH - N. OF SCHOOL NO. 8	1871	BRKE MAP	1737
METHODIST EPISCOPAL CHURCH - N. OF W. CONNELLEY	1871	OH CO. MAP	1741
METHODIST EPISCOPAL CHURCH - NW OF SHERRARD	1871	MARH'L MAP	1745
METHODIST EPISCOPAL CHURCH - PARSONAGE - NEW MANCHESTER	1871	NEW MANCH.	1769
METHODIST EPISCOPAL CHURCH - ROSBY'S ROCK	1871	MARH'L MAP	1752
METHODIST EPISCOPAL CHURCH - S. OF BENWOOD	1871	MARH'L MAP	1745
METHODIST EPISCOPAL CHURCH - S. OF MOUNT ZION	1871	MARH'L MAP	1745
METHODIST EPISCOPAL CHURCH - S. OF THE WHITE HOUSE FARM	1871	MARH'L MAP	1752
METHODIST EPISCOPAL CHURCH - S. OF THE WHITE HOUSE FARM	1871	MARH'L MAP	1755
METHODIST EPISCOPAL CHURCH - SHERRARD P.O.	1871	SHERRARD	1811
METHODIST EPISCOPAL CHURCH - SIXTH ST	1871	WHG CITY	1790
METHODIST EPISCOPAL CHURCH - SIXTH ST - WHEELING	1871	WHG CITY	1788
METHODIST EPISCOPAL CHURCH - SW. OF SCHOOL NO. 15	1871	MARH'L MAP	1756
METHODIST EPISCOPAL CHURCH - TRIADELPHIA	1871	OH CO. MAP	1743
METHODIST EPISCOPAL CHURCH - TRIADELPHIA	1871	OH CO. MAP	1744
METHODIST EPISCOPAL CHURCH - TRIADELPHIA	1871	TRIAD.BORO.	1784
METHODIST EPISCOPAL CHURCH - UNION ST - MOUNDSVILLE / COL'D OR COLD ?	1871	MDSVILLE	1810
METHODIST EPISCOPAL CHURCH - UPPER N.FORK OF GRAVE CREEK	1871	MARH'L MAP	1753
METHODIST EPISCOPAL CHURCH - VALLEY RUN	1871	MARH'L MAP	1760
METHODIST EPISCOPAL CHURCH - WASH. TWP	1871	MARH'L MAP	1748
METHODIST EPISCOPAL CHURCH - WEST LIBERTY	1871	W.LIBERTY	1780
METHODIST EPISCOPAL CHURCH - WEST UNION / NE CORNER OF MAP	1871	OH CO. MAP	1743
METHODIST EPISCOPAL CHURCH - WEST UNION	1871	MARH'L MAP	1747
METHODIST EPISCOPAL CHURCH & CEM / CLAY TWP	1871	MARH'L MAP	1751
METHODIST EPISCOPAL CHURCH & CEM & PARSONAGE	1871	BKE/OH MAP	1738
METHODIST EPISCOPAL CHURCH & CEMETERY - NEAR PLEASANT HOME - CLAY TWP	1871	MARH'L MAP	1752
METHODIST EPISCOPAL CHURCH & CEMETERY - NEW MANCHESTER - N. OF TANNERY	1871	NEW MANCH.	1769
METHODIST EPISCOPAL CHURCH & CEMETERY - ON FAIRMOUNT ROAD	1871	MARH'L MAP	1745
METHODIST EPISCOPAL CHURCH & CEMETERY - S. OF BLAIR HOMESTEAD	1871	MARH'L MAP	1749
METHODIST EPISCOPAL CHURCH & GRAVE YARD - NW. OF R. ZINK	1871	MARH'L MAP	1749
METHODIST EPISCOPAL CHURCH & GRAVEYARD - WAYNESBURGH ROAD	1871	MARH'L MAP	1749
METHODIST EPISCOPAL CHURCH AND CEMETERY - E. OF J M. WILSON	1871	BKE/OH MAP	1738
METHODIST EPISCOPAL CHURCH CEMETERY / E. OF J.M. WILSON	1871	BRKE MAP	1736
METHODIST EPISCOPAL CHURCH PARSONAGE - TRIADELPHIA	1871	TRIAD.BORO.	1784
METHODIST EPISCOPAL CHURCH PARSONAGE - WALNUT ST	1871	WELLSBURG	1777
METHODIST EPISCOPAL CHURCH PARSONAGE - WEST LIBERTY	1871	W.LIBERTY	1780
METZ, ANDREW	1859	DEFENDANT	1588
MEYER, T / COAL	1871	TRIAD.TWP.	1781
MICEANHELTER, C	1871	MARH'L MAP	1745
MIDDLE BOWMAN RUN	1871	MARH'L MAP	1755
MIDDLE FERRY HO	1871	BRKE MAP	1734
MIDDLE GRAVE CREEK	1871	MARH'L MAP	1748
MIDDLE GRAVE CREEK	1871	MARH'L MAP	1752
MIDDLE RUN	1871	HAN MAP	1727
MIDDLE RUN	1871	HAN MAP	1728
MIDDLE WHEELING CREEK	1871	OH CO. MAP	1743
MIDDLE WHEELING CREEK	1871	OH CO. MAP	1743
MIDDLE WHEELING CREEK	1871	OH CO. MAP	1744
MIDDLE WHEELING CREEK	1916	NAT'L ROAD	1863
MIDDLE WHEELING CREEK	1916	NAT'L ROAD	1864
MIDDLE WHEELING CREEK - 888 FROM NEAR CO. LINE TO MIDDLE WHEELING CREEK ROAD BY TURNPIKE	1871	OH CO. MAP	1743
MIDDLE WHEELING CREEK - 923 FROM CLAY ROAD TO [MIDDLE WHEELING] CREEK BY OLD ROAD	1871	OH CO. MAP	1743
MIILL - S.S.MILL - NEAR W. POLLOCK	1871	OH CO. MAP	1740
MILEAGE FROM TOWN TO TOWN - TABLE	1871	DISTANCES	1815
MILEPOSTS - NATIONAL ROAD - OLD DESCRIPTIONS	1916	NAT'L ROAD	1862
MILER, B	1871	HAN MAP	1731
MILES, AMOS	1821	DEFENDANT	1583
MILES, R	1871	MARH'L MAP	1750
MILITARY - BAKERS FORT	1871	HAN MAP	1726
MILITARY - CAP. (CAPT.) FOREMAN MONUMNET	1871	MARH'L MAP	1745
MILITARY - CAPT. ALEX. CAMPBELL / MAP#663	1852	BRKE MAP	1854
MILITARY - CAPT. BRANDT	1916	NAT'L ROAD	1867
MILITARY - CAPT. FRED BEYMER	1916	NAT'L ROAD	1868
MILITARY - CAPT. J H DICKEY	1871	MARH'L MAP	1753
MILITARY - CAPT. JOHN GORELY / MAP#588	1852	BRKE MAP	1851
MILITARY - CAPT. LUDWIG MYERS	1776	APPENDIX	1874
MILITARY - COL. E. BALDWIN	1871	MARH'L MAP	1753
MILITARY - COL. EBENEZER ZANE	1916	NAT'L ROAD	1866
MILITARY - COL. EBENEZER ZANE	1916	NAT'L ROAD	1867
MILITARY - COL. J LOCKWOOD	1871	MARH'L MAP	1751
MILITARY - COL. MEADE INSTITUTE / MAP#398	1852	BRKE MAP	1846
MILITARY - COL. MOSES SHEPHERD	1916	NAT'L ROAD	1864
MILITARY - ENSIGN 1760	1781	MISC	1707
MILITARY - FOREMAN, - / CAP. - CAPTAIN - MONUMNET	1871	MARH'L MAP	1745
MILITARY - FORT FINCASTLE	1916	NAT'L ROAD	1866
MILITARY - FORT HENRY	1916	NAT'L ROAD	1865
MILITARY - FORT HENRY	1916	NAT'L ROAD	1868
MILITARY - GENERAL DUNMORE	1916	NAT'L ROAD	1867
MILITARY - GENERAL DUVAL	1871	BRKE MAP	1736

'PERSONAL TIME LINE' INDEX TO VOLUME 7 OF THE *OHIO COUNTY INDEX*

ENTRY	YEAR	SUBJECT	PAGE
MILITARY - GENERAL DUVAL	1871	WELLSBURG	1776
MILITARY - GENERAL DUVAL	1871	WELLSBURG	1777
MILITARY - GENERAL DUVAL / WATER ST.	1871	WELLSBURG	1777
MILITARY - MAJOR A LORING	1871	OH CO. MAP	1742
MILITARY - MAJOR A. LORING	1871	ELM GROVE	1782
MILITARY - RANGING CO 1758	1780	MISC	1684
MILITARY - REV. WAR - LAST BATTLE OF IN WHEELING	1916	NAT'L ROAD	1867
MILITARY - SERVICE 1760	1781	MISC	1689
MILITARY - SOLDIER 1758	1780	MISC	1684
MILITARY - SOLDIERS REST	1871	MARH'L MAP	1755
MILITARY - SOLDIERS REST - CLAY TWP	1871	MARH'L MAP	1751
MILITARY - WHEELING RIFLE CORPS	1841	PLAINTIFF	1629
MILL - APPLEGATES / MAP#123	1852	BRKE MAP	1844
MILL - ATKINSONS / MAP#4	1852	BRKE MAP	1841
MILL - BAXTERS	1871	HAN-POE TWP	1763
MILL - BOWMANS / S. & J. - MAP#175	1852	BRKE MAP	1843
MILL - BROWNS / J & D - MAP#352	1852	BRKE MAP	1846
MILL - CAMPBELLS / ALEXANDER - MAP#191	1852	BRKE MAP	1844
MILL - CASNERS / JAMES - HEIRS - MAP#259	1852	BRKE MAP	1843
MILL - CLARKS / SETH - MAP#454	1852	BRKE MAP	1849
MILL - D. FLAX WHORREY MILLS	1871	MARH'L MAP	1746
MILL - FLOURING MILL - CAMERON	1871	CAMER'N - BUS.	1795
MILL - FLOURING MILL - HARRIS / J M	1871	GLEN EASTON - BUS.	1796
MILL - FOWLERS / JOHN - MAP#429	1852	BRKE MAP	1850
MILL - GRIST MILL - G. MILL - S. OF CHAMBERS FARM	1871	HAN MAP	1726
MILL - HUSTERS / NATHANIEL - MAP#462	1852	BRKE MAP	1849
MILL - JACOBS / SAMUEL (GONE) - MAP#348	1852	BRKE MAP	1846
MILL - JONES / CHARLES - MAP#41	1852	BRKE MAP	1840
MILL - JONES / E	1871	BKE/OH MAP	1739
MILL - LAUGHEADS / J & W (GONE) - MAP#386	1852	BRKE MAP	1846
MILL - LEWIS / JOB - MAP#329	1852	BRKE MAP	1846
MILL - MILL, J / (?MILL?) - ON WHEELING CREEK	1871	WHG CITY	1787
MILL - MOUNMENT MILL - ELM GROVE	1871	OH CO. MAP	1742
MILL - MOUNMENT MILL - ELM GROVE	1871	OH CO. MAP	1744
MILL - NEAR G. ROCKY / G.&S.MILL / GRIST & SAW MILL	1871	OH CO. MAP	1743
MILL - OLD MILL - NEAR W. POLLOCK	1871	OH CO. MAP	1740
MILL - PARKINSONS / DAVID - MAP#53	1852	BRKE MAP	1840
MILL - PRESBURYS / OCTAY. - MAP#80	1852	BRKE MAP	1839
MILL - RYLAND / HUGH P. - MAP#573	1852	BRKE MAP	1852
MILL - S & G / ON SHORT CREEK	1871	BKE/OH MAP	1738
MILL - S.G. & S.MILL / PROBABLY HIGGINS, CRAWFORD & CO.	1871	MARH'L MAP	1760
MILL - S.G.MILL - GLEN EASTON	1871	GLEN EASTON	1801
MILL - S.G.MILL - WOODLAND P.O.	1871	MARH'L MAP	1754
MILL - S.S. & G. MILL / S.S. & GRIST MILL	1871	MARH'L MAP	1750
MILL - S.S. MILL	1871	HAN MAP	1727
MILL - S.S. MILL	1871	BRKE MAP	1737
MILL - S.S.MILL / MCCLEANS ? - OHIO RIVER	1871	MARH'L MAP	1748
MILL - S.S.MILL - KITTLES / S.B. & SON	1871	MARH'L MAP	1746
MILL - S.S.MILL - N OF MILLER & POLEN	1871	BRKE MAP	1734
MILL - S.S.MILL - NEAR OHIO RIVER	1871	BRKE MAP	1734
MILL - S.S.MILL - NEAR ROCKY POINT	1871	HAN MAP	1731
MILL - S.S.MILL - W. OF T. MARSH	1871	BRKE MAP	1734
MILL - S.S.MILL ON CALDWELLS RUN	1871	OH CO. MAP	1742
MILL - SEE ALSO FLOUR MILL	1871	MDSVL BUS.	1796
MILL - SEE ALSO GRIST MILL	1871	OH CO. MAP	1743
MILL - SEE ALSO S.G.MILL / (?SAW & GRIST?)	1871	MARH'L MAP	1754
MILL - SEE ALSO S.S. MILL / (?ABBREV UNKNOWN?)	1871	OH CO. MAP	1743
MILL - SEE ALSO SAW MILL	1871	OH CO. MAP	1743
MILL - SNIDERS / DAVID - HEIRS - MAP#642	1852	BRKE MAP	1852
MILL - TRIMBLES / M - HEIRS - MAP#17	1852	BRKE MAP	1839
MILL - TWEED & WHITE	1871	WELLSBURG	1777
MILL - WAUGHS / RICHARD - HEIRS - (UPPERMILL) - MAP#262	1852	BRKE MAP	1843
MILL - WAUGHS / RICHARD - HEIRS - (LOWER MILL) - MAP#309	1852	BRKE MAP	1847
MILL - WAUGHS / JAMES	1871	BRKE MAP	1736
MILL - WOOLEN MILL / NW OF P.D.PUGH	1871	HAN MAP	1727
MILL DAM	1796	MISC	1676
MILL DAM & RACE - ON SHORT CREEK	1871	BKE/OH MAP	1739
MILL SITE	1797	MISC	1676
MILL, BENJAMIN	1806	DEFENDANT	1655
MILL, J / (?MILL?) - ON WHEELING CREEK	1871	WHG CITY	1787
MILLER & HAYNES	1839	DEFENDANT	1585
MILLER & KELLER	1871	BRKE MAP	1734
MILLER & KELLER	1871	BRKE MAP	1734
MILLER & KELLER	1871	BRKE MAP	1734
MILLER & KELLER / OFFICE	1871	BRKE MAP	1734
MILLER & KELLER	1871	EDGINGTON STA.	1774
MILLER & KELLER	1871	EDGINGTON STA.	1774
MILLER & KELLER	1871	EDGINGTON STA.	1774
MILLER & KELLER	1871	EDGINGTON STA.	1774
MILLER & POLEN	1871	BRKE MAP	1734
MILLER & POLEN	1871	CROSS CRK.BUS.	1772
MILLER & POLEN	1871	EDGINGTON STA.	1774
MILLER HOUSE - WAGON STAND - WASHINGTON, PA	1916	NAT'L ROAD	1861
MILLER, -	1815	PLAINTIFF	1620
MILLER, A	1871	OH CO. MAP	1742
MILLER, A	1871	MARH'L MAP	1756
MILLER, A	1871	MARH'L MAP	1756
MILLER, A	1871	MARH'L MAP	1759
MILLER, A	1871	MARH'L MAP	1760
MILLER, A	1871	RITCHIE TWP	1793
MILLER, A H	1844	DEFENDANT	1643
MILLER, B	1871	HAN MAP	1731
MILLER, BENJAMIN	1791	DEFENDANT	1571
MILLER, BENJAMIN	1791	DEFENDANT	1572
MILLER, C	1871	BRKE MAP	1736
MILLER, C	1871	WELLSBURG	1777
MILLER, D L / MAP ASSISTANT	1871	MAP	1713
MILLER, DAVID	1820	DEFENDANT	1635
MILLER, DAVID	1821	DEFENDANT	1612
MILLER, DAVID	1822	DEFENDANT	1557
MILLER, DAVID	1823	DEFENDANT	1591
MILLER, DAVID	1824	DEFENDANT	1604
MILLER, DAVID	1824	DEFENDANT	1612
MILLER, DAVID	1825	DEFENDANT	1604
MILLER, DAVID	1825	DEFENDANT	1612
MILLER, DAVID	1828	DEFENDANT	1613
MILLER, DAVID	1835	DEFENDANT	1591
MILLER, F	1871	OH CO. MAP	1740
MILLER, FREDERICK	1859	DEFENDANT	1673
MILLER, G	1871	BRKE MAP	1734
MILLER, G	1871	BRKE MAP	1734
MILLER, G	1871	BRKE MAP	1735
MILLER, G	1871	BRKE MAP	1735
MILLER, G	1871	OH CO. MAP	1743
MILLER, G	1871	TRIAD.BORO.	1784
MILLER, G B	1871	BKE/OH MAP	1739
MILLER, GEORGE	1816	MISC	1703
MILLER, GEORGE / RES - TOP OF MAP	1871	OH CO. MAP	1743
MILLER, GEORGE B / MAP#60	1852	BRKE MAP	1840
MILLER, GEORGE B / MAP#62	1852	BRKE MAP	1840
MILLER, H	1871	MARH'L MAP	1754
MILLER, H / RES	1871	MARH'L MAP	1754
MILLER, H	1871	MARH'L MAP	1755
MILLER, H	1871	TRIAD.TWP.	1781
MILLER, HENRY	1789	DEFENDANT	1577
MILLER, J / (FINISHING HOUSE)	1852	NOT ON MAP	1836
MILLER, J / (SMITHSHOP)	1852	NOT ON MAP	1836
MILLER, J	1871	MARH'L MAP	1747
MILLER, J / CAMERON	1871	MARH'L MAP	1757
MILLER, J	1871	CAMERON	1803
MILLER, J	1871	CAMERON	1803
MILLER, J	1871	CAMERON	1803
MILLER, J	1871	CAMERON	1803
MILLER, J / RES	1871	CAMERON	1803
MILLER, J / STORE	1871	CAMERON	1803
MILLER, J	1871	CAMERON	1804
MILLER, J H	1871	OH CO. MAP	1742
MILLER, J L	1871	HAN MAP	1731
MILLER, J O	1871	NEW CUMB'LD	1762
MILLER, J O	1871	NEW CUMB'LD	1768
MILLER, J O	1871	NEW CUMB'LD	1768
MILLER, JAMES	1785	MISC	1701
MILLER, JAMES	1788	DEFENDANT	1608

'PERSONAL TIME LINE' INDEX TO VOLUME 7 OF THE *OHIO COUNTY INDEX*

ENTRY	YEAR	SUBJECT	PAGE	ENTRY	YEAR	SUBJECT	PAGE
MILLER, JOHN	1790	DEFENDANT	1644	MITCHELL, ISAAC W / WHEELING	1852	HEMPFIELD RR	1817
MILLER, JOHN / (FACTORY) - MAP#327	1852	BRKE MAP	1846	MITCHELL, J	1871	BRKE MAP	1735
MILLER, JOHN / MAP#291	1852	BRKE MAP	1846	MITCHELL, JOHN	1781	MISC	1684
MILLER, JOHN / MAP#292	1852	BRKE MAP	1846	MITCHELL, JOHN	1787	DEFENDANT	1608
MILLER, JOHN / MAP#324	1852	BRKE MAP	1846	MITCHELL, JOHN	1791	DEFENDANT	1587
MILLER, JOHN / MAP#326	1852	BRKE MAP	1846	MITCHELL, JOHN	1792	DEFENDANT	1587
MILLER, JOHN	1871	CAMER'N - BUS.	1795	MITCHELL, JOHN	1799	DEFENDANT	1665
MILLER, JOHN F	1852	DEFENDANT	1670	MITCHELL, JOHN	1803	DEFENDANT	1635
MILLER, JOHN F	1853	DEFENDANT	1670	MITCHELL, W	1871	OH CO. MAP	1741
MILLER, JOSEPH	1779	APPENDIX	1874	MITZ, E	1871	MARH'L MAP	1746
MILLER, KELLER & TUTTLE	1871	BRKE MAP	1734	MIX, AMOS	1819	DEFENDANT	1611
MILLER, KELLER & TUTTLE PLANING MILL	1871	EDGINGTON STA.	1774	MIX, AMOX	1824	DEFENDANT	1672
				MIX, ELIJAH	1838	DEFENDANT	1669
MILLER, M	1871	OH CO. MAP	1742	MIX, JOHN E	1861	DEFENDANT	1592
MILLER, M	1871	BETHANY	1773	MIX, ZEBEDIAH	1816	DEFENDANT	1642
MILLER, M	1871	RITCHIE TWP	1791	MIX, ZEBEDIAH	1817	DEFENDANT	1642
MILLER, M	1871	RITCHIE TWP	1793	MIX, ZEBEDIAH	1818	DEFENDANT	1660
MILLER, R	1871	BRKE MAP	1736	MIX, ZEBEDIAH	1820	DEFENDANT	1587
MILLER, R	1871	BRKE MAP	1736	MIX, ZEBEDIAH	1821	DEFENDANT	1579
MILLER, R / ? - S. OF BEECH BOTTOM RUN	1871	BRKE MAP	1736	MIX, ZEBEDIAH	1821	DEFENDANT	1587
				MIX, ZEBEDIAH	1821	DEFENDANT	1591
MILLER, W L / MAP#395	1852	BRKE MAP	1846	MOAK, JAMES	1800	DEFENDANT	1600
MILLER, W L / MAP#410	1852	BRKE MAP	1846	MOAKE, JAMES	1801	DEFENDANT	1647
MILLER, W L	1871	BRKE MAP	1735	MOFFIT, JOHN	1838	DEFENDANT	1563
MILLER, W L	1871	BRKE MAP	1735	MOFFIT, JOHN	1838	DEFENDANT	1622
MILLER, W W	1871	OH CO. MAP	1741	MOFFIT, JOHN	1838	DEFENDANT	1662
MILLER, WILLIAM	1842	DEFENDANT	1646	MOFFITT, JOHN	1838	DEFENDANT	1558
MILLIGAN, JOHN	1826	DEFENDANT	1570	MOFFITT, JOHN	1838	DEFENDANT	1622
MILLIGAN, JOHN	1827	DEFENDANT	1573	MONEY, A / W. SIDE OF MAP	1871	MARH'L MAP	1747
MILLIGAN, JOHN	1853	MISC	1694	MONEY, J	1871	MARH'L MAP	1746
MILLIGAN, N S / MRS	1871	OH CO. MAP	1743	MONNELL, T	1871	OH CO. MAP	1741
MILLIKAN, THOMAS	1800	DEFENDANT	1634	MONNNELL, T	1871	OH CO. MAP	1742
MILLS - ALASKA	1871	MARH'L MAP	1751	MONONGAHELA CITY, PA	1852	HEMPFIELD RR	1823
MILLS - SEE ALSO S.S. MILL AND S.G. MILL / MEANINGS UNCLEAR	1871	MARH'L MAP	1757	MONONGAHELA RIVER	1852	HEMPFIELD RR	1818
				MONONGAHELA RIVER	1852	HEMP. RR MAP	1826
MILLS, A / EST.	1871	NEW CUMB'LD	1768	MONROE CO., OHIO	1871	MARH'L MAP	1754
MILLS, BENJAMIN	1806	DEFENDANT	1655	MONROE CO., OHIO	1871	MARH'L MAP	1758
MILLS, J	1871	MARH'L MAP	1761	MONTELIUS, -	1823	PLAINTIFF	1628
MILLS, JOHN	1812	DEFENDANT	1563	MONTEZUMA, OH	1852	BRKE MAP	1842
MILLS, JOHN	1813	DEFENDANT	1638	MONTGOMERY, A	1871	W.LIBERTY	1780
MILLS, L	1871	W.LIBERTY	1780	MONTGOMERY, A	1871	W.LIBRTY.BUS.	1780
MILLS, LEVI	1778	APPENDIX	1874	MONTGOMERY, A / RES	1871	W.LIBERTY	1780
MILLS, LEVI	1840	DEFENDANT	1577	MONTGOMERY, D	1871	BRKE MAP	1734
MILLS, LEVI	1840	DEFENDANT	1617	MONTGOMERY, D / NEAR BROOKE CO BORDER	1871	MARH'L MAP	1745
MILLS, LEVI	1840	DEFENDANT	1652				
MILLS, LEVY	1778	APPENDIX	1874	MONTGOMERY, DANIEL / MAP#589	1852	BRKE MAP	1851
MILLS, LEVY	1845	DEFENDANT	1604	MONTGOMERY, J	1871	MARH'L MAP	1755
MILLS, SAMUEL	1834	DEFENDANT	1622	MONTGOMERY, J	1871	WELLSBURG	1777
MILLS, THOMAS	1800	DEFENDANT	1576	MONTGOMERY, J B	1871	MARH'L MAP	1745
MILLS, THOMAS	1801	MISC	1707	MONTGOMERY, J B	1871	OH CO.BUS.	1779
MILLS, WILLIAM	1812	DEFENDANT	1626	MONTGOMERY, J H	1871	BKE/OH MAP	1739
MILTON, J	1799	MISC	1691	MONTGOMERY, J H	1871	OH CO. MAP	1740
MINETT, JULIUS	1856	DEFENDANT	1602	MONTGOMERY, JOSEPH	1822	DEFENDANT	1612
MINGO BOTTOM	1871	BRKE MAP	1734	MONTGOMERY, MARIA	1814	DEFENDANT	1599
MINGO BOTTOM	1871	BRKE MAP	1735	MONTGOMERY, W	1871	MARH'L MAP	1755
MINGO ISLAND - OHIO RIVER	1852	BRKE MAP	1849	MONTGOMERY, W	1871	MARH'L MAP	1755
MINGO ISLAND - OHIO RIVER	1871	BRKE MAP	1735	MONTGOMERY, W	1871	MARH'L MAP	1759
MINGO RUN	1852	BRKE MAP	1844	MONUMENT ERECTED TO HENRY CLAY 1820	1871	ELM GROVE	1782
MINGO RUN	1871	BRKE MAP	1737				
MINISTER - R. WILSON	1871	MARH'L MAP	1747	MONUMENT GRIST MILL	1871	ELM GROVE	1782
MINISTERS - SEE ALSO PASTORS	1852	BRKE MAP	1847	MONUMENT PLACE	1871	OH CO. MAP	1742
MINNIX, WILLIAM	1833	DEFENDANT	1573	MONUMENT PLACE	1871	ELM GROVE	1782
MINOR, - / TROUP & MINOR	1871	RIV. RD N.OF N.C.	1763	MOONEY, GEORGE	1871	BRKE MAP	1735
MINOR, - / TROUP & MINOR - FIRE BRICK WORKS	1871	RIV. RD N.OF N.C.	1770	MOONEY, GEORGE / COAL BANK - INITIALS G.M.	1871	BRKE MAP	1735
MINOR, A	1871	MARH'L MAP	1755	MOONEY, JOHN	1841	DEFENDANT	1577
MINOR, D S	1871	RIV. RD N.OF N.C.	1770	MOONEY, JOHN	1841	DEFENDANT	1617
MINOR, J.B.	1871	HAN MAP	1727	MOONEY, JOHN	1841	DEFENDANT	1652
MINSINGER, D / ?	1871	HAN MAP	1729	MOONEY, PETER / HEIRS - MAP#465	1852	BRKE MAP	1849
MISS D / PURDY ST - MDSVILLE	1871	MDSVILLE	1808	MOONEYS RUN	1852	BRKE MAP	1849
MISSISSIPPI RIVER - AT ALTON	1852	HEMPFIELD RR	1820	MOOR, J	1871	MARH'L MAP	1759
MISSISSIPPI RIVER TRAFFIC	1852	HEMPFIELD RR	1817	MOORE - SEE ALSO MORE / MAP#343	1852	BRKE MAP	1846
MISSISSIPPI ROAD	1852	HEMPFIELD RR	1821	MOORE, -	1829	PLAINTIFF	1628
MITCHEL, A	1823	DEFENDANT	1632	MOORE, - / DR	1871	BRKE MAP	1736
MITCHEL, ALEXANDER	1806	DEFENDANT	1610	MOORE, - / DR	1871	BRKE MAP	1736
MITCHEL, T	1871	MARH'L MAP	1747	MOORE, - / DR	1871	BRKE MAP	1736
MITCHELL, -	1852	PLAINTIFF	1623	MOORE, - / SHAY & MOORE	1871	NEW MANCH.	1769
MITCHELL, -	1853	PLAINTIFF	1623	MOORE, - / MRS	1871	WELLSBURG	1778
MITCHELL, -	1854	PLAINTIFF	1623	MOORE, - / MRS.DR.	1871	MDSVILLE	1810
MITCHELL, -	1854	PLAINTIFF	1623	MOORE, BENTLEY	1855	DEFENDANT	1584
MITCHELL, -	1855	PLAINTIFF	1623	MOORE, BENTLEY	1855	DEFENDANT	1603
MITCHELL, A	1871	OH CO. MAP	1741	MOORE, BENTLEY	1859	DEFENDANT	1603
MITCHELL, ANDREW	1857	DEFENDANT	1584	MOORE, C	1871	MARH'L MAP	1748
MITCHELL, ANDREW	1857	DEFENDANT	1603	MOORE, DAVID	1817	DEFENDANT	1599
MITCHELL, ANDREW	1858	DEFENDANT	1560	MOORE, DAVID	1821	DEFENDANT	1563
MITCHELL, H / MISS	1871	BKE/OH MAP	1739	MOORE, E	1871	BKE/OH MAP	1739

LXVIII

'PERSONAL TIME LINE' INDEX TO VOLUME 7 OF THE *OHIO COUNTY INDEX*

ENTRY	YEAR	SUBJECT	PAGE
MOORE, E H / PHYSICIAN	1871	WLSBRG BUS	1772
MOORE, E H	1871	WELLSBURG	1777
MOORE, E H	1871	WELLSBURG	1777
MOORE, E H	1871	WELLSBURG	1777
MOORE, E H / DOCTOR	1871	WELLSBURG	1777
MOORE, E H / DOCTOR OFFICE - CHARLES ST	1871	WELLSBURG	1777
MOORE, E H / INITIALS E.H.M.	1871	WELLSBURG	1777
MOORE, E H / INITIALS E.H.M.	1871	WELLSBURG	1777
MOORE, E H / INITIALS E.H.M.	1871	WELLSBURG	1777
MOORE, E H / INITIALS E.H.M.	1871	WELLSBURG	1777
MOORE, E H / INITIALS E.H.M.	1871	WELLSBURG	1777
MOORE, E H / LUMBER YARD - INITIALS E.H.M.	1871	WELLSBURG	1777
MOORE, E H / URANA ST	1871	WELLSBURG	1777
MOORE, E H / DOCTOR	1871	WELLSBURG	1778
MOORE, E H / INITIALS E.H.M	1871	WELLSBURG	1778
MOORE, E H / INITIALS E.H.M.	1871	WELLSBURG	1778
MOORE, E H / INITIALS E.H.M.	1871	WELLSBURG	1778
MOORE, E H / MANY LOTS ON EAST ST.	1871	WELLSBURG	1778
MOORE, E H / UNKNOWN INITIALS I.H.M.(?MAYBE E.H.M.-E.H.MOORE?)	1871	WELLSBURG	1778
MOORE, E W	1871	WELLSBURG	1776
MOORE, HENRY	1852	MISC	1711
MOORE, I	1871	MARH'L MAP	1757
MOORE, ISAIAH / HEIRS - MAP#101	1852	BRKE MAP	1842
MOORE, J	1871	HAN MAP	1731
MOORE, J	1871	MARH'L MAP	1746
MOORE, J	1871	MARH'L MAP	1752
MOORE, J G	1871	MARH'L MAP	1749
MOORE, J G / (?OR J.C.?)	1871	MARH'L MAP	1752
MOORE, J G / CUT OFF EDGE OF MAP	1871	MARH'L MAP	1753
MOORE, JAMES	1856	DEFENDANT	1626
MOORE, JAMES	1856	DEFENDANT	1672
MOORE, JAMES	1857	DEFENDANT	1577
MOORE, JAMES	1859	DEFENDANT	1630
MOORE, JOHN	1825	DEFENDANT	1656
MOORE, JOHN	1825	DEFENDANT	1656
MOORE, JOHN	1834	DEFENDANT	1640
MOORE, JOSEPH	1836	DEFENDANT	1561
MOORE, JOSEPH	1836	DEFENDANT	1669
MOORE, JOSEPH	1855	DEFENDANT	1630
MOORE, JOSEPH	1856	DEFENDANT	1630
MOORE, JOSEPH	1857	DEFENDANT	1630
MOORE, JOSEPH	1858	DEFENDANT	1630
MOORE, JOSEPH	1860	DEFENDANT	1631
MOORE, JOSEPH	1862	DEFENDANT	1631
MOORE, O / MRS	1871	CAMERON	1803
MOORE, O / MRS	1871	CAMERON	1804
MOORE, O / MRS	1871	CAMERON	1804
MOORE, P H / RES	1871	OH CO. MAP	1741
MOORE, P H	1878	DEFENDANT	1621
MOORE, R	1871	HAN MAP	1726
MOORE, R	1871	MARH'L MAP	1750
MOORE, R	1871	BETHANY	1773
MOORE, RANDOLPH	1828	DEFENDANT	1573
MOORE, RANDOLPH	1829	DEFENDANT	1573
MOORE, RANDOLPH	1830	DEFENDANT	1573
MOORE, RICHARD	1856	DEFENDANT	1588
MOORE, ROBERT	1789	DEFENDANT	1571
MOORE, ROBERT / MAP#172	1852	BRKE MAP	1843
MOORE, ROBERT / & BRO	1861	DEFENDANT	1602
MOORE, S	1871	NEW MANCH.	1763
MOORE, SHEPHERD	1845	DEFENDANT	1646
MOORE, THOMAS	1803	DEFENDANT	1554
MOORE, THOMAS	1817	DEFENDANT	1579
MOORE, THOMAS	1853	DEFENDANT	1581
MOORE, THOMAS G	1834	DEFENDANT	1579
MOORE, THOMAS G	1840	DEFENDANT	1640
MOORE, W	1871	OH CO. MAP	1740
MOORE, WILLIAM	1798	DEFENDANT	1607
MOORE, WILLIAM	1871	OH CO. MAP	1740
MOORE, WILLIAM / INITIALS WM. M	1871	OH CO. MAP	1740
MOOSE, I / ?	1871	MARH'L MAP	1757
MORAN, ELENOR	1811	DEFENDANT	1578
MORAN, THOMAS	1811	DEFENDANT	1578
MORAN, THOMAS	1811	DEFENDANT	1578
MORAN, WILLIAM	1811	DEFENDANT	1578
MORE, ROBERT / MAP#328	1852	BRKE MAP	1846
MORE, ROBERT / MAP#332	1852	BRKE MAP	1846
MORE, ROBERT / MAP#342	1852	BRKE MAP	1846
MORE, ROBERT / MAP#343	1852	BRKE MAP	1846
MORELAND, ALICE	1824	DEFENDANT	1596
MORELAND, NICHOLAS	1817	DEFENDANT	1624
MORELAND, NICHOLAS	1820	DEFENDANT	1624

ENTRY	YEAR	SUBJECT	PAGE
MOREN & CO BRICK YARD	1871	FRE'MAN'S LDG	1764
MOREN, G W	1871	WELLSBURG	1776
MOREN, G W / INITIALS G.W.M.	1871	WELLSBURG	1776
MOREN, G W	1871	WELLSBURG	1777
MOREN, G W / INITIALS G.W.M.	1871	WELLSBURG	1777
MOREN, J / & CO.	1871	HAN MAP	1731
MOREN, J	1871	WELLSBURG	1776
MOREN, JOHN	1871	RIV. RD S.OF N.C.	1763
MOREN, R R	1871	WELLSBURG	1777
MORESLANDER, - / MRS	1871	MDSVILLE	1808
MORETON, JOHN / MAP#584	1852	BRKE MAP	1851
MORETON, JOSEPH / MAP#583	1852	BRKE MAP	1852
MORETON, THOMAS / MAP#613	1852	BRKE MAP	1852
MORGAN, D	1871	MARH'L MAP	1745
MORGAN, D	1871	SHERRARD	1811
MORGAN, DANIEL	1808	APPENDIX	1873
MORGAN, DANIEL	1853	DEFENDANT	1576
MORGAN, DAVID	1840	DEFENDANT	1643
MORGAN, E	1871	BKE/OH MAP	1738
MORGAN, EDWARD / MAP#24	1852	BRKE MAP	1839
MORGAN, EDWARD	1859	DEFENDANT	1582
MORGAN, HOSEA	1807	DEFENDANT	1594
MORGAN, J W	1871	BKE/OH MAP	1738
MORGAN, JAMES	1823	DEFENDANT	1561
MORGAN, JOHN	1810	DEFENDANT	1604
MORGAN, JOSIAH	1835	MISC	1705
MORGAN, L B	1879	DEFENDANT	1605
MORGAN, M / MRS	1871	BKE/OH MAP	1738
MORGAN, M / MRS	1871	BKE/OH MAP	1739
MORGAN, M / MRS	1871	OH CO. MAP	1740
MORGAN, R	1871	MARH'L MAP	1746
MORGAN, T	1871	MARH'L MAP	1746
MORGAN, T / INITIALS T.M.	1871	MARH'L MAP	1746
MORGAN, T	1871	SHERRARD	1811
MORGAN, W	1871	MARH'L MAP	1745
MORGAN, W	1871	SHERRARD	1811
MORGIANA	1871	MARH'L MAP	1754
MORRIS, E	1871	BENWOOD	1799
MORRIS, E / MRS	1871	CAMERON	1802
MORRIS, FARIS & CO	1861	DEFENDANT	1641
MORRIS, JAMES	1832	DEFENDANT	1596
MORRIS, JOHN	1787	DEFENDANT	1637
MORRIS, MELISSA / MURDERED 25 JULY 1859 NEAR THIS PLACE BY NATHANIEL HANON (?OR HANRON, HANSON, HARDIN, OR OTHER SPELLING?)	1871	MARH'L MAP	1750
MORRIS, P	1871	MARH'L MAP	1757
MORRIS, S	1871	MARH'L MAP	1745
MORRIS, THOMAS	1839	DEFENDANT	1628
MORRIS, THOMAS	1839	DEFENDANT	1640
MORRISON, ALEXANDER	1831	DEFENDANT	1555
MORRISON, ALEXANDER	1831	DEFENDANT	1555
MORRISON, G	1871	OH CO. MAP	1740
MORRISON, ROBERT	1840	DEFENDANT	1640
MORRISON, S G W	1859	DEFENDANT	1590
MORRISON, THOMAS	1791	PLAINTIFF	1665
MORRISON, WILLIAM	1818	DEFENDANT	1599
MORROW, A	1871	HAN MAP	1731
MORROW, A / ALEX.	1871	NEW MANCH.	1769
MORROW, ALEX	1871	NEW MANCH.	1763
MORROW, E	1871	BRKE MAP	1735
MORROW, J R	1871	MARH'L MAP	1745
MORROW, JAMES	1871	HAN MAP	1732
MORROW, JAMES W	1871	HAN MAP	1732
MORROW, JOHN W	1871	HAN MAP	1732
MORROW, R	1871	HAN MAP	1731
MORROW, R	1871	HAN MAP	1732
MORROW, ROBERT	1838	DEFENDANT	1651
MORROW, SAMUEL / MAP#296	1852	BRKE MAP	1846
MORROW, W B	1871	HAN MAP	1732
MORROW, WILLIAM	1871	HAN MAP	1732
MORROW, WILLIAM B	1856	MISC	1694
MORTIN, ALEX	1811	DEFENDANT	1577
MORTIN, SAMUEL	1811	DEFENDANT	1577
MORTON HOUSE - HOTEL - MOUNDSVILLE	1871	MDSVILLE	1809
MORTON, - / MRS	1871	BRKE MAP	1734
MORTON, J / (?OR S.?)	1871	BRKE MAP	1734
MORTON, J	1871	MDSVILLE	1807
MORTON, J	1871	MDSVILLE	1807
MORTON, J / INITIALS J.M.	1871	MDSVILLE	1807
MORTON, J / INITIALS J.M.	1871	MDSVILLE	1807
MORTON, JOSEPH	1798	DEFENDANT	1596
MORTON, JOSHUA	1821	DEFENDANT	1642
MORTON, R	1871	BRKE MAP	1734

LXIX

'PERSONAL TIME LINE' INDEX TO VOLUME 7 OF THE *OHIO COUNTY INDEX*

ENTRY	YEAR	SUBJECT	PAGE
MORTON, R	1871	MARH'L MAP	1748
MORTON, R	1871	MDSVILLE	1807
MORTON, R	1871	MDSVILLE	1807
MORTON, R	1871	MDSVILLE	1807
MORTON, R	1871	MDSVILLE	1809
MORTON, R / MORTON HOUSE	1871	MDSVILLE	1809
MORTON, T	1871	BRKE MAP	1734
MORTON, T	1871	BRKE MAP	1734
MORTONS BRANCH	1852	BRKE MAP	1851
MOSES, N N	1875	DEFENDANT	1616
MOSSLAND, E	1871	MARH'L MAP	1745
MOSSLAND, E / INITIALS E.M.	1871	MARH'L MAP	1745
MOSSLAND, E	1871	MARH'L MAP	1748
MOSSLAND, E / INITIALS E.M.	1871	MARH'L MAP	1748
MOSSLANDER, J	1871	MARH'L MAP	1749
MOUND - THE MOUND - MOUNDSVILLE	1871	MDSVILLE	1809
MOUND BRANCH	1852	BRKE MAP	1842
MOUND CITY FLOUR MILL	1871	MDSVL BUS.	1796
MOUND OLD INDIAN SPRING	1871	RITCHIE TWP	1792
MOUNDSVILLE	1871	DISTANCES	1815
MOUNDSVILLE	1871	POPULATION	1816
MOUNDSVILLE - A ST	1871	MDSVL BUS.	1796
MOUNDSVILLE - A ST	1871	MDSVILLE	1806
MOUNDSVILLE - A ST	1871	MDSVILLE	1808
MOUNDSVILLE - A ST	1871	MDSVILLE	1809
MOUNDSVILLE - B ST	1871	MDSVL BUS.	1796
MOUNDSVILLE - B ST	1871	MDSVILLE	1808
MOUNDSVILLE - B ST	1871	MDSVILLE	1809
MOUNDSVILLE - BAKERY	1871	MDSVL BUS.	1796
MOUNDSVILLE - BAKERY - WATER ST - M.ERNST	1871	MDSVILLE	1810
MOUNDSVILLE - BOARDING HOUSE - GRANT ST / INITIALS B.HOUSE	1871	MDSVILLE	1807
MOUNDSVILLE - BROAD ALLEY	1871	MDSVILLE	1807
MOUNDSVILLE - BUSINESS NOTICES	1871	MDSVL BUS.	1796
MOUNDSVILLE - C ST	1871	MDSVL BUS.	1796
MOUNDSVILLE - C ST	1871	MDSVILLE	1808
MOUNDSVILLE - C ST	1871	MDSVILLE	1809
MOUNDSVILLE - CABINET SHOP	1871	MDSVILLE	1807
MOUNDSVILLE - CENTRE ST	1871	MDSVILLE	1807
MOUNDSVILLE - CENTRE ST	1871	MDSVILLE	1809
MOUNDSVILLE - CLIFTON HOUSE - HOTEL	1871	MDSVILLE	1808
MOUNDSVILLE - D ST	1871	MDSVL BUS.	1796
MOUNDSVILLE - D ST	1871	MDSVILLE	1808
MOUNDSVILLE - D ST	1871	MDSVILLE	1809
MOUNDSVILLE - DETAIL MAP	1871	MDSVILLE	1806
MOUNDSVILLE - DETAIL MAP	1871	MDSVILLE	1809
MOUNDSVILLE - DETAIL MAP	1871	MDSVILLE	1810
MOUNDSVILLE - E ST	1871	MDSVL BUS.	1796
MOUNDSVILLE - E ST	1871	MDSVILLE	1806
MOUNDSVILLE - E ST	1871	MDSVILLE	1808
MOUNDSVILLE - E ST	1871	MDSVILLE	1809
MOUNDSVILLE - FERRY LANDING - OHIO RIVER	1871	MDSVILLE	1808
MOUNDSVILLE - FIRST ST	1871	MDSVILLE	1808
MOUNDSVILLE - FIRST ST	1871	MDSVILLE	1808
MOUNDSVILLE - GATEWAY ST / AT PENITENTIARY	1871	MDSVILLE	1809
MOUNDSVILLE - GRANT ST	1871	MDSVILLE	1807
MOUNDSVILLE - GREEN HOUSE / H.COX	1871	MDSVILLE	1807
MOUNDSVILLE - ICE HOUSE - P.SHARP / EST.	1871	MDSVILLE	1809
MOUNDSVILLE - JACKSON ALLEY	1871	MDSVILLE	1808
MOUNDSVILLE - LIBERTY ST	1871	MDSVL BUS.	1796
MOUNDSVILLE - LIBERTY ST	1871	MDSVILLE	1807
MOUNDSVILLE - LIBERTY ST	1871	MDSVILLE	1810
MOUNDSVILLE - MAIN ST	1871	MDSVILLE	1807
MOUNDSVILLE - MARKET	1871	MDSVILLE	1807
MOUNDSVILLE - MARKET ST	1871	MDSVL BUS.	1796
MOUNDSVILLE - MARKET ST	1871	MDSVILLE	1809
MOUNDSVILLE - MARSHALL ST	1871	MDSVL BUS.	1796
MOUNDSVILLE - MARSHALL ST	1871	MDSVILLE	1808
MOUNDSVILLE - MARSHALL ST	1871	MDSVILLE	1810
MOUNDSVILLE - MECHANIC ST	1871	MDSVL BUS.	1796
MOUNDSVILLE - MECHANIC ST	1871	MDSVILLE	1808
MOUNDSVILLE - MECHANIC ST	1871	MDSVILLE	1810
MOUNDSVILLE - MONROE ST	1871	MDSVILLE	1808
MOUNDSVILLE - MONROE ST	1871	MDSVILLE	1810
MOUNDSVILLE - MOUND ST	1871	MDSVILLE	1808
MOUNDSVILLE - MOUND ST	1871	MDSVILLE	1809
MOUNDSVILLE - NORTH ST	1871	MDSVL BUS.	1796
MOUNDSVILLE - NORTH ST	1871	MDSVILLE	1807
MOUNDSVILLE - NORTH ST	1871	MDSVILLE	1808
MOUNDSVILLE - NURSERY GROUNDS	1871	MDSVILLE	1806
MOUNDSVILLE - PANORAMIC MAP	1889	MOUNDSVL	1858
MOUNDSVILLE - PENITENTIARY	1871	MDSVL BUS.	1796
MOUNDSVILLE - POPLAR ALLEY	1871	MDSVILLE	1807
MOUNDSVILLE - PURDY ST	1871	MDSVL BUS.	1796
MOUNDSVILLE - PURDY ST	1871	MDSVILLE	1808
MOUNDSVILLE - PURDY ST	1871	MDSVILLE	1809
MOUNDSVILLE - PURDY ST	1871	MDSVILLE	1810
MOUNDSVILLE - RIVER ROAD	1871	MDSVL BUS.	1796
MOUNDSVILLE - SECOND ST	1871	MDSVL BUS.	1796
MOUNDSVILLE - SECOND ST	1871	MDSVILLE	1808
MOUNDSVILLE - SECOND ST	1871	MDSVILLE	1809
MOUNDSVILLE - SOUTH ST	1871	MDSVL BUS.	1796
MOUNDSVILLE - SOUTH ST	1871	MDSVILLE	1810
MOUNDSVILLE - STEAMBOAT LANDING	1871	MDSVILLE	1808
MOUNDSVILLE - STEAMBOAT LANDING	1871	MDSVILLE	1810
MOUNDSVILLE - TANNERY	1871	MDSVL BUS.	1796
MOUNDSVILLE - TANNERY / J.C.SIMPSON	1871	MDSVILLE	1807
MOUNDSVILLE - TANNERY - NORTH ST - REFERENCE #1	1871	MDSVILLE	1810
MOUNDSVILLE - THOMPSON ST	1871	MDSVILLE	1810
MOUNDSVILLE - UNION ST	1871	MDSVILLE	1810
MOUNDSVILLE - WASHINGTON ST	1871	MDSVILLE	1807
MOUNDSVILLE - WATER ST	1871	MDSVL BUS.	1796
MOUNDSVILLE - WATER ST	1871	MDSVILLE	1806
MOUNDSVILLE - WATER ST	1871	MDSVILLE	1807
MOUNDSVILLE - WATER ST	1871	MDSVILLE	1808
MOUNDSVILLE - WATER ST	1871	MDSVILLE	1810
MOUNDSVILLE - WHEELING ST	1871	MDSVL BUS.	1796
MOUNDSVILLE - WHEELING ST	1871	MDSVILLE	1806
MOUNDSVILLE - WHEELING ST	1871	MDSVILLE	1807
MOUNDSVILLE - WHEELING ST	1871	MDSVILLE	1809
MOUNDSVILLE - WOOLEN FACTORY - WATER ST	1871	MDSVILLE	1810
MOUNDSVILLE P.O.	1871	MARH'L MAP	1748
MOUNDSVILLE TO WAYNESBURGH ROAD	1871	MARH'L MAP	1748
MOUNDSVILLE TO WAYNESBURGH ROAD	1871	MARH'L MAP	1749
MOUNDSVILLE, WV - MAP	1916	NAT'L ROAD	1869
MOUNMENT MILL - ELM GROVE	1871	OH CO. MAP	1742
MOUNMENT MILL - ELM GROVE	1871	OH. CO. MAP	1744
MOUNT DE CHANTAL CONVENT	1871	OH CO. MAP	1742
MOUNT DE CHANTAL CONVENT / CATHOLIC	1871	TRIAD. TWP.	1781
MOUNT DE CHANTAL CONVENT	1871	WHG CITY	1789
MOUNT LEON	1871	OH CO. MAP	1742
MOUNT NEBO	1871	MARH'L MAP	1746
MOUNT PLEASANT / W, HENDERSON	1871	OH CO. MAP	1743
MOUNT PLEASANT - FRANKLIN TWP	1871	MARH'L MAP	1758
MOUNT ROSE CEMETERY - MOUNDSVILLE	1871	MDSVILLE	1807
MOUNT ZION	1871	MARH'L MAP	1745
MOUNTAIN BROW	1871	MARH'L MAP	1745
MOUNTAIN HOME	1871	OH CO. MAP	1744
MOUNTAIN HOME - FRANKLIN TWP	1871	MARH'L MAP	1758
MOUNTAIN HOMW	1871	OH CO. MAP	1743
MOUNTAIN SIDE	1871	OH CO. MAP	1743
MOUNTAIN VIEW	1871	OH CO. MAP	1742
MOUNTAIN VIEW	1871	OH CO. MAP	1743
MOUNTAINS BROW	1871	MARH'L MAP	1754
MOUNTS, DANIEL	1852	NOT ON MAP	1836
MOUNTS, DANIEL	1852	NOT ON MAP	1836
MOUNTS, DANIEL	1852	NOT ON MAP	1836
MOUREN, J	1871	NEW CUMB'LD	1767
MOYSTEN, WILLIAM A	1848	DEFENDANT	1581
MOZINGO, ROBERT	1860	DEFENDANT	1578
MOZINGO, S	1871	BKE/OH MAP	1739
MOZINGO, S	1871	BKE/OH MAP	1739
MOZINGO, S	1871	OH CO. MAP	1740
MRS.W / UNKNOWN INITIALS	1871	OH CO. MAP	1742
MT PLEASANT	1871	HAN MAP	1732
MT SAVAGE AND SAVAGE MOUNTAIN FIRE BRICKS AND TILES	1871	FRE'MAN'S LDG	1762
MT VERNON - R. FRESHWATER	1871	HAN MAP	1732
MT WOOD CEMETERY	1871	WHG CITY	1786
MT ZION CEMETERY - ON FAIRMONT TURNPIKE / (?NAME ADDED BY AUTHOR?)	1871	RITCHIE TWP	1793
MUCHMORE RUN	1871	HAN MAP	1726
MUCOLLOCH, DAVID	1839	DEFENDANT	1614
MUDGE, -	1856	PLAINTIFF	1630
MULDOON, FRANK	1876	DEFENDANT	1609

'PERSONAL TIME LINE' INDEX TO VOLUME 7 OF THE *OHIO COUNTY INDEX*

ENTRY	YEAR	SUBJECT	PAGE
MULDOON, FRANK	1878	DEFENDANT	1609
MULDREW, A	1871	MARH'L MAP	1752
MULDREW, ANDREW JR	1857	DEFENDANT	1552
MULDREW, ANDREW JR	1857	DEFENDANT	1621
MULDREW, E / MRS	1871	MARH'L MAP	1752
MULDREW, E / MRS	1871	MARH'L MAP	1755
MULDROON, -	1871	TRIAD.BORO.	1784
MULDROON, -	1871	TRIAD.BORO.	1784
MULLICAN, BENJAMIN	1799	DEFENDANT	1634
MULLIGAN, BENJAMIN	1800	DEFENDANT	1634
MULLIGAN, BENJAMIN	1800	DEFENDANT	1655
MULLIGAN, BENJAMIN	1800	DEFENDANT	1655
MULLIGAN, BENJAMIN	1802	DEFENDANT	1647
MULLIGAN, BENJAMIN	1812	DEFENDANT	1611
MULRINE, JOHNSTON	1857	DEFENDANT	1584
MULRINE, JOHNSTON	1857	DEFENDANT	1603
MUNDLE, - / MRS	1871	MARH'L MAP	1752
MUNDLE, A	1871	MARH'L MAP	1752
MUNEL, - / MRS	1871	WELLSBURG	1777
MUNNELL, J M / MRS	1871	OH CO. MAP	1740
MUNTING, A / ?	1871	HAN MAP	1729
MURCHLAND, JAMES / HEIRS - MAP#479	1852	BRKE MAP	1850
MURCHLAND, R	1871	BRKE MAP	1735
MURCHLAND, ROBERT	1871	BRKE MAP	1735
MURCHLAND, ROBERT SR / MAP#481	1852	BRKE MAP	1849
MURCHLAND, ROBERT SR / MAP#494	1852	BRKE MAP	1850
MURCHLAND, ROBERT SR / MAP#495	1852	BRKE MAP	1850
MURCHLAND, ROBERT SR / MAP#502	1852	BRKE MAP	1850
MURCHLAND, W S	1871	BRKE MAP	1735
MURCHLAND, W S	1871	BRKE MAP	1735
MURCHLAND, WILLIAM / (GONE) - MAP#477	1852	BRKE MAP	1850
MURCHLAND, WILLIAM / MAP#475	1852	BRKE MAP	1850
MURCHLAND, WILLIAM / OF R (?ROBERT?) - MAP#480	1852	BRKE MAP	1850
MURCHLAND, WILLIAM	1871	BRKE MAP	1735
MURDECK, G G	1878	DEFENDANT	1574
MURDOCK, G G	1878	DEFENDANT	1584
MURPHY, A / MRS	1871	MARH'L MAP	1756
MURPHY, D	1871	CAMERON	1803
MURPHY, D / INITIALS D.M.	1871	CAMERON	1803
MURPHY, J	1871	WELLSBURG	1778
MURPHY, J A	1871	MARH'L MAP	1757
MURPHY, JAMES	1855	DEFENDANT	1590
MURPHY, JAMES	1855	DEFENDANT	1629
MURPHY, JAMES	1858	DEFENDANT	1584
MURRAY, - / MRS	1871	OH CO. MAP	1740
MURRAY, DANIEL	1835	DEFENDANT	1566
MURRAY, J	1871	NEW CUMB'LD	1767
MURRAY, W C	1871	HAN MAP	1731
MURRAY, W C / ABBREV W.C.M.	1871	HAN MAP	1731
MURRAYS RUN	1871	HAN MAP	1732
MURRY & REED	1841	DEFENDANT	1553
MURRY, - / MRS	1871	MARH'L MAP	1747
MURRY, WILLIAM	1829	DEFENDANT	1628
MURRY, WILLIAM	1829	DEFENDANT	1650
MUSGROVE, ROBERT	1799	DEFENDANT	1647
MUTTON, J	1871	WELLSBURG	1777
MUTTON, J	1871	WELLSBURG	1777
MYER, FREDERICK D	1864	MISC	1683
MYER, H	1871	BRKE MAP	1736
MYER, M	1871	BRKE MAP	1736
MYERS, -	1871	MARH'L MAP	1752
MYERS, LUDWIG / CAPT	1776	APPENDIX	1874
MYERS, THOMAS	1847	DEFENDANT	1561
MYERS, WILLIAM	1847	MISC	1674
MYERS, Z / MISS	1871	W.LIBERTY	1780
MYERS, ZERNIA	1858	DEFENDANT	1552
NADDENBUSH, -	1817	PLAINTIFF	1632
NAEGELE, F	1871	MARH'L MAP	1745
NAGLE, F	1871	OH CO. MAP	1741
NAGLE, F	1871	OH CO. MAP	1742
NAIL FACTORY - BENWOOD	1871	BENWOOD	1799
NAIL WORKS - BENWOOD IRON WORKS	1871	BENWOOD	1799
NARROW HILL FARM	1871	MARH'L MAP	1745
NARROW HILL ROAD	1871	MARH'L MAP	1745
NARROWS RUN	1871	MARH'L MAP	1752
NARROWS RUN / CUT OFF TOP OF MAP	1871	MARH'L MAP	1755
NASHVILLE, LEXINGTON, MAYSVILLE, PORTSMOUTH, MARIETTA AND WHEELING LINE	1852	HEMPFIELD RR	1820
NASHVILLE, TN	1852	HEMPFIELD RR	1821
NATIONAL HIGHWAYS ASSOCIATION	1916	NAT'L ROAD	1861
NATIONAL OR BOW / NEAR WHEELING CREEK	1871	WHG CITY	1786
NATIONAL PIKE - AT VALLEY GROVE	1871	OH CO. MAP	1740
NATIONAL PIKE - FOUR MILE HOUSE - HOTEL -	1871	OH CO. BUS.	1779
NATIONAL ROAD	1916	NAT'L ROAD	1861
NATIONAL ROAD - AT FULTON, OHIO CO	1871	WHG CITY	1787
NATIONAL ROAD - AT TRIADELPHIA	1871	TRIAD. BORO.	1784
NATIONAL ROAD - DETAIL MAP ACROSS PANHANDLE	1916	NAT'L ROAD	1863
NATIONAL ROAD - ELM GROVE	1871	ELM GROVE	1782
NATIONAL ROAD - FULTON	1871	WHG CITY	1789
NATIONAL ROAD - HISTORY	1916	NAT'L ROAD	1865
NATIONAL ROAD - HISTORY OF	1916	NAT'L ROAD	1866
NATIONAL ROAD - OLD NORTHWEST TERRITORY ROAD	1916	NAT'L ROAD	1870
NATIONAL ROAD - RONEY POINT STATION	1871	RONEY PT.	1783
NATIONAL ROAD - TOLL GATE / RONEY POINT - NATIONAL ROAD (?EASTERN GATE?)	1871	OH CO. MAP	1743
NATIONAL ROAD - TOLL GATE - RONEY POINT STATION / (?EASTERN GATE?)	1871	OH CO. MAP	1744
NATIONAL ROAD - TOLL HOUSE - COON ISLAND, PA	1916	NAT'L ROAD	1862
NATIONAL ROAD - TOLL HOUSE - LEATHERWOOD	1871	TRIAD.TWP.	1781
NATIONAL ROAD - TOLL HOUSE - LEATHERWOOD	1871	WHG CITY	1789
NATIONAL ROAD - TOLL HOUSE - TRIAD.TWP / LEATHERWOOD	1871	WHG CITY	1787
NATIONAL ROAD - TOLL HOUSE - WHEELING	1871	WHG CITY	1786
NATIONAL ROAD - TWO MILE HOUSE / AT BETHANY PIKE	1871	TRIAD.TWP.	1781
NATIONAL ROAD - WHEELING	1871	WHG CITY	1786
NATIONAL ROAD - WHEELING CITY MAP	1916	NAT'L ROAD	1868
NATIONAL ROAD - WHEELING SUSPENSION BRIDGE	1871	WHG CITY	1788
NATIONAL ROAD - WHEELING TO BALTIMORE MAP	1916	NAT'L ROAD	1869
NATIONAL ROAD - WHEELING TO CUMBERLAND MAP	1916	NAT'L ROAD	1869
NATIONAL ROAD BOOK / OHIO CO. EXTRACTS	1916	NAT'L ROAD	1861
NATIONAL ROAD MILEPOSTS	1916	NAT'L ROAD	1862
NATIONAL TURNPIKE	1871	OH CO. MAP	1743
NATIONAL TURNPIKE	1871	OH CO. MAP	1744
NAU, GEORGE	1876	DEFENDANT	1671
NAYLER, SAMUEL G	1873	DEFENDANT	1627
NAYLOR, -	1876	PLAINTIFF	1631
NAYLOR, -	1878	PLAINTIFF	1631
NAYLORS RUN	1852	BRKE MAP	1849
NAYLORS RUN	1871	BRKE MAP	1735
NEAFF, HENRY	1808	APPENDIX	1873
NEAL, - / SAWMILL - MAP#476	1852	BRKE MAP	1850
NEAL, G M	1871	NEW CUMB'LD	1768
NEBO - MOUNT NEBO	1871	MARH'L MAP	1746
NEEHOUSE, J C	1871	MARH'L MAP	1745
NEEL, H	1871	OH CO. MAP	1741
NEEL, H	1871	OH CO. MAP	1741
NEEL, SAMUEL / WHEELING	1852	HEMPFIELD RR	1817
NEELSON, JOHN	1808	APPENDIX	1873
NEELY, FLORANNA	1822	DEFENDANT	1646
NEELY, FLORENNA	1812	DEFENDANT	1645
NEELY, FLORENNA	1813	DEFENDANT	1645
NEELY, FLORENNA	1816	DEFENDANT	1645
NEELY, FLORENNA	1817	DEFENDANT	1646
NEELY, HUGH D / MAP#103	1852	BRKE MAP	1843
NEELY, JOSEPH	1790	DEFENDANT	1665
NEFF & BROTHERS	1832	PLAINTIFF	1604
NEFF & SCOTT	1871	MDSVILLE	1808
NEFF, HENRY	1798	MISC	1689
NEFF, HENRY	1798	MISC	1693
NEFF, J	1871	MDSVILLE	1807
NEFF, JESSE / TANNERY	1871	MDSVL BUS.	1796
NEFF, JESSE	1871	MDSVILLE	1807
NEFF, JESSE / INITIALS J.NEFF	1871	MDSVILLE	1807
NEGRO	1788	MISC	1701
NEGRO - FREE	1836	MISC	1677
NEGRO - FREE	1854	MISC	1695
NEGRO SLAVE	1795	MISC	1695
NEGRO SLAVE	1814	MISC	1697

LXXI

'PERSONAL TIME LINE' INDEX TO VOLUME 7 OF THE *OHIO COUNTY INDEX*

ENTRY	YEAR	SUBJECT	PAGE	ENTRY	YEAR	SUBJECT	PAGE
NEGRO SLAVE	1815	MISC	1710	NEW CUMBERLAND - FILLMORE	1871	NEW CUMB'LD	1762
NEGRO WOMAN	1790	MISC	1701	NEW CUMBERLAND - FILLMORE ST	1871	NEW CUMB'LD	1762
NEGRO WOMAN	1822	MISC	1676	NEW CUMBERLAND - FILLMORE ST	1871	NEW CUMB'LD	1768
NEIDEN, CATHARINE	1854	MISC	1686	NEW CUMBERLAND - FIRST ST	1871	NEW CUMB'LD	1766
NEIL, M W / MRS	1871	MDSVILLE	1810	NEW CUMBERLAND - FOURTH ST	1871	NEW CUMB'LD	1766
NEIL, W	1871	MDSVILLE	1810	NEW CUMBERLAND - GRAFTON ALLEY	1871	NEW CUMB'LD	1768
NEIL, W	1871	MDSVILLE	1810				
NEIL, WILLIAM	1871	MDSVILLE	1808	NEW CUMBERLAND - HARRISON ST	1871	NEW CUMB'LD	1762
NEIL, WILLIAM / RES	1871	MDSVILLE	1810	NEW CUMBERLAND - HARRISON ST	1871	NEW CUMB'LD	1768
NEILLY, - / MRS	1871	MARH'L MAP	1760	NEW CUMBERLAND - HIGH ST	1871	NEW CUMB'LD	1762
NEILLY, I	1871	MARH'L MAP	1760	NEW CUMBERLAND - HIGH ST	1871	NEW CUMB'LD	1762
NEILLY, J	1871	MARH'L MAP	1760	NEW CUMBERLAND - HIGH ST	1871	NEW CUMB'LD	1767
NEININGER, JOHN	1859	DEFENDANT	1673	NEW CUMBERLAND - HIGH ST	1871	NEW CUMB'LD	1768
NELSON, A	1871	WELLSBURG	1776	NEW CUMBERLAND - INDIAN ALLEY	1871	NEW CUMB'LD	1768
NELSON, A	1871	WELLSBURG	1776	NEW CUMBERLAND - JACKSON ST	1871	NEW CUMB'LD	1767
NELSON, ANDREW / MAP#402	1852	BRKE MAP	1846	NEW CUMBERLAND - JEFFERSON ST	1871	NEW CUMB'LD	1767
NELSON, H / ?	1871	WELLSBURG	1777	NEW CUMBERLAND - JEFFERSON ST	1871	NEW CUMB'LD	1768
NESBITS, JONATHAN	1826	DEFENDANT	1668	NEW CUMBERLAND - LINE ALLEY	1871	NEW CUMB'LD	1768
NESLY ISLAND / IN OHIO RIVER	1871	HAN MAP	1726	NEW CUMBERLAND - MACHINE SHOP / WASHINGTON ST	1871	NEW CUMB'LD	1767
NESS, A	1871	OH CO. MAP	1742				
NESSLE DALE	1871	HAN MAP	1726	NEW CUMBERLAND - MADISON ST	1871	NEW CUMB'LD	1762
NEVERFAILING SOFT WATER SPRING	1871	OH CO. MAP	1742	NEW CUMBERLAND - MADISON ST	1871	NEW CUMB'LD	1762
NEVERFAILING SOFT WATER SPRING / UNION TWP	1871	MARH'L MAP	1745	NEW CUMBERLAND - MADISON ST	1871	NEW CUMB'LD	1768
				NEW CUMBERLAND - MILL ALLEY	1871	NEW CUMB'LD	1768
NEVERFAILING SOFTWATER SPRING	1871	RITCHIE TWP	1792	NEW CUMBERLAND - MORRIS ST	1871	NEW CUMB'LD	1768
NEVERFAILING SOFTWATER SPRING	1871	RITCHIE TWP	1794	NEW CUMBERLAND - MORRIS ST.	1871	RIV. RD S.OF N.C.	1771
NEVERFAILING SPRING	1871	OH CO. MAP	1743	NEW CUMBERLAND - OAK ALLEY	1871	NEW CUMB'LD	1768
NEVIT, JAMES	1790	DEFENDANT	1589	NEW CUMBERLAND - PEARL ST	1871	NEW CUMB'LD	1762
NEVIT, JAMES	1798	DEFENDANT	1644	NEW CUMBERLAND - PEARL ST	1871	NEW CUMB'LD	1762
NEVIT, JOHN	1783	APPENDIX	1874	NEW CUMBERLAND - PEARL ST	1871	NEW CUMB'LD	1762
NEW ALEXANDRIA, OH	1852	BRKE MAP	1848	NEW CUMBERLAND - PEARL ST	1871	NEW CUMB'BUS	1762
NEW BERRY RUN	1852	BRKE MAP	1847	NEW CUMBERLAND - PEARL ST	1871	NEW CUMB'LD	1762
NEW CUMBEERLAND - GRAPE ALLEY	1871	NEW CUMB'LD	1768	NEW CUMBERLAND - PEARL ST	1871	NEW CUMB'LD	1767
NEW CUMBERLAND	1871	RIV. RD S.OF N.C.	1771	NEW CUMBERLAND - PEAS ALLEY	1871	NEW CUMB'LD	1767
NEW CUMBERLAND	1871	DISTANCES	1815	NEW CUMBERLAND - PINE ALLEY	1871	NEW CUMB'LD	1768
NEW CUMBERLAND - 93 NUMBERED CITY LOTS ON MAP	1871	NEW CUMB'LD	1766	NEW CUMBERLAND - RIVER ROAD N. OF - DETAIL MAP	1871	RIV. RD N.OF N.C.	1770
NEW CUMBERLAND - ADAMS ST	1871	NEW CUMB'LD	1767	NEW CUMBERLAND - RIVER ROAD S. OF - DETAIL MAP	1871	RIV. RD S.OF N.C.	1771
NEW CUMBERLAND - BALL ALLEY	1871	NEW CUMB'LD	1768				
NEW CUMBERLAND - BALLS ADDITION / LAND LOTS	1871	NEW CUMB'LD	1767	NEW CUMBERLAND - SECOND ST	1871	NEW CUMB'LD	1766
				NEW CUMBERLAND - STRAIT ST	1871	NEW CUMB'LD	1762
NEW CUMBERLAND - BUSINESS NOTICES	1871	NEW CUMB'LD	1762	NEW CUMBERLAND - STRAIT ST	1871	NEW CUMB'LD	1767
				NEW CUMBERLAND - SYCAMORE ST	1871	NEW CUMB'LD	1766
NEW CUMBERLAND - CAMPBELL ALLEY	1871	NEW CUMB'LD	1768	NEW CUMBERLAND - SYCAMORE ST	1871	NEW CUMB'LD	1767
				NEW CUMBERLAND - TAYLOR ST	1871	NEW CUMB'LD	1762
NEW CUMBERLAND - CAMPBELLS ADDITION / LAND LOTS	1871	NEW CUMB'LD	1767	NEW CUMBERLAND - TAYLOR ST	1871	NEW CUMB'LD	1762
NEW CUMBERLAND - CEMETERY	1871	NEW CUMB'LD	1767	NEW CUMBERLAND - TAYLOR ST	1871	NEW CUMB'LD	1762
NEW CUMBERLAND - CENTRE ALLEY	1871	NEW CUMB'LD	1766	NEW CUMBERLAND - TAYLOR ST	1871	NEW CUMB'LD	1768
NEW CUMBERLAND - CHAPMAN ALLEY	1871	NEW CUMB'LD	1767	NEW CUMBERLAND - THIRD ST	1871	NEW CUMB'LD	1766
				NEW CUMBERLAND - VALLEY ST	1871	NEW CUMB'LD	1768
NEW CUMBERLAND - CHERRY ALLEY	1871	NEW CUMB'LD	1768	NEW CUMBERLAND - VINE ALLEY	1871	NEW CUMB'LD	1768
NEW CUMBERLAND - CHESNUT ST	1871	NEW CUMB'LD	1768	NEW CUMBERLAND - WASHINGTON ST	1871	NEW CUMB'LD	1762
NEW CUMBERLAND - CHESTER ST	1871	NEW CUMB'LD	1762				
NEW CUMBERLAND - CHESTER ST	1871	NEW CUMB'LD	1762	NEW CUMBERLAND - WASHINGTON ST	1871	NEW CUMB'LD	1767
NEW CUMBERLAND - CHESTER ST	1871	NEW CUMB'LD	1762				
NEW CUMBERLAND - CHESTER ST	1871	NEW CUMB'LD	1762	NEW CUMBERLAND - WATER ST	1871	NEW CUMB'LD	1762
NEW CUMBERLAND - CHESTER ST	1871	MISC	1762	NEW CUMBERLAND - WATER ST	1871	NEW CUMB'LD	1762
NEW CUMBERLAND - CHESTER ST	1871	NEW CUMB'LD	1762	NEW CUMBERLAND - WATER ST	1871	NEW CUMB'LD	1762
NEW CUMBERLAND - CHESTER ST	1871	NEW CUMB'LD	1762	NEW CUMBERLAND - WATER ST	1871	NEW CUMB'LD	1762
NEW CUMBERLAND - CHESTER ST	1871	NEW CUMB'LD	1767	NEW CUMBERLAND - WATER ST	1871	NEW CUMB'LD	1766
NEW CUMBERLAND - CHESTER ST	1871	HAN MAP	1768	NEW CUMBERLAND - WATER ST	1871	NEW CUMB'LD	1767
NEW CUMBERLAND - CHESTNUT ALLEY	1871	NEW CUMB'LD	1766	NEW CUMBERLAND - WATER ST	1871	NEW CUMB'LD	1768
				NEW CUMBERLAND CEMETERY	1871	HAN MAP	1730
NEW CUMBERLAND - CHESTNUT ST	1871	NEW CUMB'LD	1762	NEW GERMANTOWN	1871	MARH'L MAP	1747
NEW CUMBERLAND - CHESTNUT ST	1871	NEW CUMB'LD	1762	NEW GERMANTOWN	1871	MARH'L MAP	1750
NEW CUMBERLAND - CHESTNUT ST	1871	NEW CUMB'LD	1762	NEW GERMANTOWN - RUTHS FLOURING & SAW MILL	1871	SAND HILL-BUS.	1797
NEW CUMBERLAND - CHESTNUT ST	1871	NEW CUMB'LD	1762				
NEW CUMBERLAND - CHESTNUT ST	1871	NEW CUMB'LD	1766	NEW LEXINGTON	1871	HAN MAP	1726
NEW CUMBERLAND - CHESTNUT ST	1871	NEW CUMB'LD	1767	NEW LEXINGTON	1871	HAN MAP	1730
NEW CUMBERLAND - CLAY ST	1871	NEW CUMB'LD	1762	NEW MAHCHESTER - AGRICULTURAL WORKS / J.W. ALLISON	1871	NEW MANCH.	1769
NEW CUMBERLAND - CLAY ST	1871	NEW CUMB'LD	1768				
NEW CUMBERLAND - CLAY TWP - DETAIL MAP	1871	NEW CUMB'LD	1766	NEW MAHCHESTER - WAGON SHOP - DURBINS / T	1871	NEW MANCH.	1769
				NEW MANCHESTER - HIGH ST	1871	NEW MANCH.	1763
NEW CUMBERLAND - CLAY TWP - DETAIL MAP	1871	NEW CUMB'LD	1767	NEW MANCHESTER	1871	HAN MAP	1731
				NEW MANCHESTER - BLACKSMITH SHOP - DURBINS / T	1871	NEW MANCH.	1769
NEW CUMBERLAND - COMMERCE ST	1871	NEW CUMB'LD	1767				
NEW CUMBERLAND - COMMERCE ST	1871	NEW CUMB'LD	1768	NEW MANCHESTER - BOWERY ALLEY	1871	NEW MANCH.	1769
NEW CUMBERLAND - COPPYS ALLEY	1871	NEW CUMB'LD	1767				
NEW CUMBERLAND - DETAIL MAP	1871	NEW CUMB'LD	1768	NEW MANCHESTER - BROADWAY ALLEY	1871	NEW MANCH.	1769
NEW CUMBERLAND - ELM ALLEY	1871	NEW CUMB'LD	1767				
NEW CUMBERLAND - FERRY TO OHIO	1871	NEW CUMB'LD	1766	NEW MANCHESTER - COURIER OFFICE - HIGH ST	1871	NEW MANCH.	1769
NEW CUMBERLAND - FIFTH ST	1871	NEW CUMB'LD	1766				
NEW CUMBERLAND - FIFTH ST.	1871	RIV. RD N.OF N.C.	1770	NEW MANCHESTER - COURT HOUSE / ELM & HIGH STS	1871	NEW MANCH.	1769

'PERSONAL TIME LINE' INDEX TO VOLUME 7 OF THE *OHIO COUNTY INDEX*

ENTRY	YEAR	SUBJECT	PAGE	ENTRY	YEAR	SUBJECT	PAGE
NEW MANCHESTER - CUMBERLAND ALLEY	1871	NEW MANCH.	1769	NEWMAN, L S	1871	MARH'L MAP	1748
NEW MANCHESTER - DETAIL MAP	1871	NEW MANCH.	1769	NEWMAN, LOUIS E / MAP ENGRAVER - NYC	1871	MAP	1713
NEW MANCHESTER - DIAMOND ALLEY	1871	NEW MANCH.	1769	NEWSPAPER - BETHANY - GUARDIAN	1871	BETHNY BUS.	1772
NEW MANCHESTER - ELM ST	1871	NEW MANCH.	1769	NEWSPAPER - HANCOCK COURIER - NEW MANCHESTER	1871	NEW MANCH.	1763
NEW MANCHESTER - FAIRVIEW P.O.	1871	DISTANCES	1815	NEWTON, ENOS	1838	DEFENDANT	1662
NEW MANCHESTER - HANCOCK CO - BUSINESS LISTINGS	1871	NEW MANCH.	1763	NEWTON, ENOS W	1837	DEFENDANT	1568
				NEWTON, ENOS W	1837	DEFENDANT	1595
NEW MANCHESTER - HARNESS SHOP - HIGH ST	1871	NEW MANCH.	1769	NEWTON, ENOS W	1838	DEFENDANT	1583
				NEWTON, ENOS W	1838	DEFENDANT	1628
NEW MANCHESTER - HIGH ST	1871	NEW MANCH.	1763	NEY, - / DR	1871	MARH'L MAP	1751
NEW MANCHESTER - HIGH ST	1871	NEW MANCH.	1763	NEY, - / DR	1871	MDSVILLE	1808
NEW MANCHESTER - HIGH ST	1871	NEW MANCH.	1763	NICE, - / MRS	1871	MARH'L MAP	1758
NEW MANCHESTER - HIGH ST	1871	NEW MANCH.	1763	NICEWARGER, YARNEL PETER	1805	DEFENDANT	1659
NEW MANCHESTER - HIGH ST	1871	NEW MANCH.	1763	NICHOL, WILLIAM M	1849	MISC	1697
NEW MANCHESTER - HIGH ST	1871	NEW MANCH.	1763	NICHOLAS, EDWARD	1806	DEFENDANT	1610
NEW MANCHESTER - HIGH ST	1871	NEW MANCH.	1763	NICHOLLS, HUGH / MAP#203	1852	BRKE MAP	1842
NEW MANCHESTER - HIGH ST	1871	NEW MANCH.	1763	NICHOLLS, HUGH / MAP#204	1852	BRKE MAP	1842
NEW MANCHESTER - HIGH ST	1871	NEW MANCH.	1763	NICHOLLS, HUGH / MAP#205	1852	BRKE MAP	1842
NEW MANCHESTER - HIGH ST	1871	NEW MANCH.	1763	NICHOLLS, HUGH / MAP#206	1852	BRKE MAP	1842
NEW MANCHESTER - HIGH ST	1871	NEW MANCH.	1763	NICHOLLS, HUGH / MAP#207	1852	BRKE MAP	1842
NEW MANCHESTER - HIGH ST	1871	NEW MANCH.	1769	NICHOLLS, HUGH / MAP#208	1852	BRKE MAP	1842
NEW MANCHESTER - HOTEL - HIGH ST	1871	NEW MANCH.	1763	NICHOLLS, ROBERT / ESQ. - MAP#399	1852	BRKE MAP	1846
				NICHOLS, - / HRS - HEIRS - RES	1871	OH CO. MAP	1741
NEW MANCHESTER - HOTEL BARN	1871	NEW MANCH.	1769	NICHOLS, - / COAL	1871	OH CO. MAP	1741
NEW MANCHESTER - I.O.O.F HALL	1871	NEW MANCH.	1769	NICHOLS, - / COAL	1871	OH CO. MAP	1741
NEW MANCHESTER - JAIL / ELM & HIGH STS	1871	NEW MANCH.	1769	NICHOLS, - / HRS	1871	OH CO. MAP	1741
				NICHOLS, - / HRS - HEIRS - RES	1871	OH CO. MAP	1741
NEW MANCHESTER - JERSEY ALLEY	1871	NEW MANCH.	1769	NICHOLS, AUSTIN	1813	DEFENDANT	1553
NEW MANCHESTER - LYNN ST	1871	NEW MANCH.	1769	NICHOLS, E / STORE	1871	HAN MAP	1733
NEW MANCHESTER - MAIN ST	1871	NEW MANCH.	1763	NICHOLS, ED	1871	WELLSBURG	1776
NEW MANCHESTER - MAIN ST	1871	NEW MANCH.	1763	NICHOLS, EDWARD	1812	DEFENDANT	1656
NEW MANCHESTER - MAIN ST	1871	NEW MANCH.	1769	NICHOLS, G W	1871	OH CO. MAP	1741
NEW MANCHESTER - MANCHESTER HOUSE / HOTEL	1871	NEW MANCH.	1769	NICHOLS, G W	1871	OH CO. MAP	1742
				NICHOLS, G W	1871	WHG CITY	1786
NEW MANCHESTER - MARKET ST	1871	NEW MANCH.	1763	NICHOLS, GEORGE / MAP ASSISTANT	1871	MAP	1713
NEW MANCHESTER - MARKET ST	1871	NEW MANCH.	1763	NICHOLS, HUGH	1827	DEFENDANT	1566
NEW MANCHESTER - MARKET ST	1871	NEW MANCH.	1763	NICHOLS, HUGH	1840	DEFENDANT	1643
NEW MANCHESTER - MARKET ST	1871	NEW MANCH.	1769	NICHOLS, JOHN	1795	DEFENDANT	1572
NEW MANCHESTER - MASONIC HALL	1871	NEW MANCH.	1769	NICHOLS, JOHN	1798	DEFENDANT	1634
NEW MANCHESTER - OHIO ST	1871	NEW MANCH.	1769	NICHOLS, JOHN	1803	DEFENDANT	1572
NEW MANCHESTER - ORANGE ALLEY	1871	NEW MANCH.	1769	NICHOLS, JOHN	1803	DEFENDANT	1666
NEW MANCHESTER - PENN ALLEY	1871	NEW MANCH.	1769	NICHOLS, JOHN	1852	DEFENDANT	1602
NEW MANCHESTER - PLUM ALLEY	1871	NEW MANCH.	1769	NICHOLS, JOHN D	1852	NOT ON MAP	1836
NEW MANCHESTER - POE TWP - HANCOCK CO	1871	NEW MANCH.	1769	NICHOLS, R	1871	WELLSBURG	1776
				NICHOLS, REBECCA	1806	DEFENDANT	1600
NEW MANCHESTER - POST OFFICE	1871	NEW MANCH.	1769	NICHOLS, REBECKAH	1814	DEFENDANT	1572
NEW MANCHESTER - SPRUCE ST	1871	NEW MANCH.	1769	NICHOLS, ROBERT JR.	1852	NOT ON MAP	1836
NEW MANCHESTER - STORE / LOT #2	1871	NEW MANCH.	1769	NICHOLS, THOMAS	1778	DEFENDANT	1574
NEW MANCHESTER - STORE - MARKET ST	1871	NEW MANCH.	1769	NICHOLS, W	1871	OH CO. MAP	1741
				NICHOLS, W	1871	OH CO. MAP	1741
NEW MANCHESTER - TANNERY	1871	NEW MANCH.	1769	NICHOLS, W / INITIALS W.N.	1871	OH CO. MAP	1741
NEW MANCHESTER - VINE ALLEY	1871	NEW MANCH.	1769	NICHOLS, W / RES	1871	OH CO. MAP	1741
NEW MANCHESTER - WALL ALLEY	1871	NEW MANCH.	1769	NICHOLS, W	1871	OH CO. MAP	1742
NEW ORLEANS - RIVER TRAFFIC	1916	NAT'L ROAD	1867	NICHOLS, WILLIAM	1871	OH CO. MAP	1740
NEW WASHINGTON	1871	MARH'L MAP	1746	NICHOLSON, - / MRS	1871	HAN MAP	1731
NEW WASHINGTON	1871	MARH'L MAP	1749	NICOLS, W	1871	OH CO. MAP	1741
NEW YORK	1852	HEMPFIELD RR	1820	NIEDERMEYER, KATHERINE	1876	DEFENDANT	1616
NEW, R	1871	HAN MAP	1733	NIENINGER, JOHN	1856	DEFENDANT	1657
NEWBURG / OR SLOANS STATION	1871	HAN MAP	1730	NIGHTLER, J / EST	1871	MARH'L MAP	1751
NEWBY, JOHN L	1838	DEFENDANT	1563	NIPPERGALL, -	1871	BENWOOD	1798
NEWBY, JOHN L	1838	DEFENDANT	1614	NIPPERGALL, D	1871	BENWOOD	1798
NEWELL HALL / JOHN NEWELL	1871	HAN MAP	1727	NISWANGER, E. / MISS	1871	HAN MAP	1728
NEWELL, H	1871	HAN MAP	1727	NISWANGER, G	1871	HAN MAP	1727
NEWELL, H.	1871	HAN MAP	1728	NISWANGER, G	1871	HAN MAP	1728
NEWELL, JOHN / INITIALS J.N.	1871	HAN MAP	1727	NISWANGER, G	1871	HAN MAP	1728
NEWELL, JOHN / NEWELL HALL	1871	HAN MAP	1727	NISWONGER, PETER	1807	DEFENDANT	1659
NEWELL, S	1871	HAN MAP	1727	NIXON & WAY	1871	BRKE MAP	1736
NEWLAND, ISAAC	1800	DEFENDANT	1556	NIXON & WAY	1871	BKE/OH MAP	1738
NEWLAND, ISAAC	1800	DEFENDANT	1556	NIXON, - / MRS	1871	MARH'L MAP	1747
NEWLANDS RUN	1852	BRKE MAP	1839	NIXON, D / PARTIALLY MISSING - CORNER OF WASHINGTON & COMMERCE STS	1871	NEW CUMB'LD	1767
NEWLANDS RUN / BOTTOM OF MAP	1871	BRKE MAP	1736				
NEWLANDS RUN	1871	BKE/OH MAP	1738				
NEWLOVE, WILLIAM	1841	DEFENDANT	1594	NIXON, G	1871	NEW CUMB'LD	1766
NEWLOVE, WILLIAM	1848	DEFENDANT	1670	NIXON, J	1871	MARH'L MAP	1751
NEWLY, JOHN L	1838	DEFENDANT	1651	NIXON, J	1871	MARH'L MAP	1751
NEWMAN, ALEXANDER	1842	DEFENDANT	1663	NOLAN, JOHN	1874	DEFENDANT	1560
NEWMAN, ALEXANDER	1846	DEFENDANT	1663	NOLAN, JOHN	1874	DEFENDANT	1603
NEWMAN, B B	1871	MARH'L MAP	1751	NOLAN, JOHN	1874	DEFENDANT	1636
NEWMAN, E L / MRS	1871	MARH'L MAP	1745	NOLAN, JOHN	1874	DEFENDANT	1654
NEWMAN, E L / MRS	1871	MARH'L MAP	1748	NOLAN, RICHARD	1876	DEFENDANT	1627
NEWMAN, G W	1871	NEW CUMB'LD	1767	NOLAND, - / MRS. - MAP#297	1852	BRKE MAP	1846
NEWMAN, J / MRS	1871	HAN MAP	1726	NOLL, P / MR	1871	OH CO. MAP	1741
NEWMAN, J	1871	MARH'L MAP	1747	NOLL, P	1871	OH CO. MAP	1742
NEWMAN, L S	1871	MARH'L MAP	1745	NOLLER, J C	1871	MDSVILLE	1810

'PERSONAL TIME LINE' INDEX TO VOLUME 7 OF THE *OHIO COUNTY INDEX*

ENTRY	YEAR	SUBJECT	PAGE	ENTRY	YEAR	SUBJECT	PAGE
NOLTE, J	1871	MARH'L MAP	1759	OHIO - ROAD MILES	1852	HEMPFIELD RR	1819
NOREEN, J / & CO. ?	1871	HAN MAP	1731	OHIO & PENNSYLVANIA RR	1852	HEMP. RR MAP	1826
NORMAL SCHOOL - WEST LIBERTY	1871	W.LIBRTY.BUS.	1780	OHIO AND MISSISSIPPI ROAD	1852	HEMPFIELD RR	1821
NORMAN, J / RES	1871	OH CO. MAP	1740	OHIO CO	1852	DEFENDANT	1670
NORMAN, J / RES	1871	OH CO. MAP	1740	OHIO CO	1853	DEFENDANT	1641
NORMAN, R S	1873	DEFENDANT	1578	OHIO CO	1871	POPULATION	1816
NORMAN, W B	1873	DEFENDANT	1578	OHIO CO - HEMPFIELD RR BONDS	1852	HEMPFIELD RR	1822
NORRIS, E	1871	BENWOOD	1799	OHIO CO - LINE - 888 FROM NEAR CO. LINE TO MIDDLE WHEEKING CREEK ROAD BY TURNPIKE	1871	OH CO. MAP	1743
NORRIS, S	1871	MARH'L MAP	1756				
NORTH BRANCH OF LITTLE GRAVE CREEK	1871	MARH'L MAP	1745				
NORTH BRANCH OF LITTLE GRAVE CREEK	1871	MARH'L MAP	1748	OHIO CO - MAP OF ORIGINAL COUNTY	2000	MAP	1546
				OHIO CO - MAP ON NATIONAL ROAD IN	1916	NAT'L ROAD	1863
NORTH BRANCH OF SHORT CREEK	1871	BKE/OH MAP	1738	OHIO CO - N.BOUNDARY WITH BROOKE CO	1852	BRKE MAP	1839
NORTH BRANCH OF TOMLINSONS RUN	1871	HAN MAP	1727	OHIO CO - N.BOUNDARY WITH BROOKE CO	1852	BRKE MAP	1840
NORTH BRANCH OF TOMLINSONS RUN	1871	HAN MAP	1728	OHIO CO - ON PANHANDLE MAP	1871	MAP	1713
NORTH FORK OF HOLBERTS RUN	1871	HAN MAP	1731	OHIO CO - S. BOUNDARY WITH MARSHALL CO	1871	RITCHIE TWP	1792
NORTH FORK OF KINGS CREEK	1871	HAN MAP	1731				
NORTH FORK OF KINGS CREEK	1871	HAN MAP	1732	OHIO CO - S. BOUNDARY WITH MARSHALL CO	1871	RITCHIE TWP	1794
NORTH FORK OF TOMLINSONS RUN	1871	HAN MAP	1731	OHIO CO - S. BOUNDARY WITH MARSHALL CO	1871	W.UNION	1812
NORTH SPRING	1871	HAN MAP	1732				
NORTH, W	1871	OH CO. MAP	1741	OHIO CO - TOWNSHIPS LISTED	1871	MAP	1721
NORTH, W / INITIALS W.N.	1871	OH CO. MAP	1741	OHIO CO - TOWNSHIPS ON MAP	1871	MAP	1720
NORTHERN SLOPE / S. OF MOUNDSVILLE	1871	MARH'L MAP	1748	OHIO CO - WASHINGTON TOWNSHIP	1871	POPULATION	1816
NORTHWESTERN VA	1852	HEMPFIELD RR	1817	OHIO CO BONDS - HEMPFIELD RR - MAP & BOND PROSPECTUS	1852	HEMPFIELD RR	1817
NORTSMAN, AUGT	1878	DEFENDANT	1597				
NORWAY IRON WORKS	1871	SOUTH WHG	1792	OHIO CO MICROFILMS - AT WV. STATE ARCHIVES	2000	APPENDIX	1872
NULL, J	1871	MARH'L MAP	1749				
NULL, J H JR	1871	MARH'L MAP	1749	OHIO CO MICROFILMS - AT WV.UNIV.	2000	APPENDIX	1871
NULL, JER.	1871	MARH'L MAP	1746	OHIO CO ORDER BOOKS ON MICROFILM	2000	APPENDIX	1871
NULL, JER.	1871	MARH'L MAP	1749				
NULL, P	1871	FRE'MAN'S LDG	1764	OHIO COMPANY	1817	PLAINTIFF	1659
NULL, P	1871	WELLSBURG	1778	OHIO COMPANY	1817	PLAINTIFF	1659
NULTY, E	1871	MARH'L MAP	1748	OHIO COMPANY	1817	PLAINTIFF	1659
NUNEMAKER, DANIEL / MAP#302	1852	BRKE MAP	1844	OHIO COMPANY	1818	PLAINTIFF	1659
NUSE, I	1871	MARH'L MAP	1761	OHIO COMPANY	1818	PLAINTIFF	1660
NUSE, J	1871	MARH'L MAP	1761	OHIO COMPANY	1819	PLAINTIFF	1660
O, W H / C ST - UNKNOWN INITIALS	1871	MDSVILLE	1808	OHIO COMPANY	1822	PLAINTIFF	1660
O.M. / UNKNOWN INITIALS - UNION TWP	1871	MARH'L MAP	1745	OHIO COUNTY INDEX - VOL 7A PREVIEW	2000	APPENDIX	1876
OAK ALLEY - HAMILTON	1871	HAN MAP	1729	OHIO COUNTY INDEX - VOL.8 PREVIEW	2000	APPENDIX	1873
OAK HALL - CALDWELL	1871	WHG CITY	1790				
OAK HALL - CALDWELL	1871	WHG CITY	1792	OHIO RIVER	1852	HEMPFIELD RR	1818
OAK HIGHTS	1871	HAN MAP	1731	OHIO RIVER	1852	HEMPFIELD RR	1818
OAK HIGHTS	1871	HAN MAP	1732	OHIO RIVER	1852	HEMP. RR MAP	1826
OAK HILL	1871	OH CO. MAP	1740	OHIO RIVER	1871	HAN MAP	1729
OAK HILL	1871	OH CO. MAP	1742	OHIO RIVER	1871	BRKE MAP	1736
OAK HILL	1871	OH CO. MAP	1744	OHIO RIVER	1871	BKE/OH MAP	1738
OAK HILL / SAND HILL TWP	1871	MARH'L MAP	1746	OHIO RIVER	1871	OH CO. MAP	1741
OAK HILL - CLAY TWP	1871	MARH'L MAP	1751	OHIO RIVER	1871	OH CO. MAP	1741
OAKSIDE / ? - WRITTEN 'OKSIDE' - VANCE	1871	TRIAD.BORO.	1784	OHIO RIVER	1871	MARH'L MAP	1745
				OHIO RIVER	1871	MARH'L MAP	1748
OATH OF ALLEGIANCE	1789	MISC	1680	OHIO RIVER	1871	MARH'L MAP	1751
OATH OF ALLEGIANCE	1789	MISC	1701	OHIO RIVER	1871	MARH'L MAP	1754
OATH OF ALLEGIANCE	1789	MISC	1707	OHIO RIVER	1871	MARH'L MAP	1758
OATH OF ALLEGIANCE	1789	MISC	1710	OHIO RIVER	1871	NEW CUMB'LD	1766
OATH OF ALLEGIENCE / COMMONWEALTH OF VA	1799	MISC	1701	OHIO RIVER	1871	RIV. RD N.OF N.C.	1770
				OHIO RIVER	1916	NAT'L ROAD	1867
OBLY, C	1871	OH CO. MAP	1742	OHIO RIVER - AT BENWOOD	1871	BENWOOD	1798
OBLY, C	1871	RITCHIE TWP	1791	OHIO RIVER - AT BENWOOD	1871	BENWOOD	1799
O'BRIEN, JOHN	1857	DEFENDANT	1616	OHIO RIVER - AT BENWOOD	1871	BENWOOD	1800
O'BRIEN, THOMAS	1880	MISC	1688	OHIO RIVER - AT LAGRANGE	1871	RITCHIE TWP	1794
OC / (?ABBREVIATION FOR BUSINESS OFFICE?)	1871	NEW CUMB'LD	1767	OHIO RIVER - AT MOUNDSVILLE	1871	MDSVILLE	1806
				OHIO RIVER - AT MOUNDSVILLE	1871	MDSVILLE	1808
OGDEN, PETER	1802	DEFENDANT	1604	OHIO RIVER - AT MOUNDSVILLE	1871	MDSVILLE	1810
OGDEN, PETER	1803	DEFENDANT	1607	OHIO RIVER - AT STEUBENVILLE	1852	BRKE MAP	1851
OGLE OR SPRING FARM	1871	MARH'L MAP	1750	OHIO RIVER - AT WHEELING	1871	WHG CITY	1790
OGLE RUN	1871	BKE/OH MAP	1739	OHIO RIVER - BLACKS ISLAND IN	1871	HAN MAP	1730
OGLE RUN	1871	MARH'L MAP	1750	OHIO RIVER - BRIDGE HISTORY	1916	NAT'L ROAD	1866
OGLE, - / OR SPRING FARM	1871	MARH'L MAP	1750	OHIO RIVER - FERRY - AT HAMILTON TO WELLSVILLE	1871	HAN MAP	1726
OGLE, A / HRS - HEIRS	1871	MARH'L MAP	1753				
OGLE, JACOB	1796	DEFENDANT	1644	OHIO RIVER - FERRY - SLOANS STATION TO W.B.FREEMAN BRICK WORKS	1871	FRE'MAN'S LDG	1764
OGLE, JAMES	1799	DEFENDANT	1665				
OGLE, JAMES	1800	PLAINTIFF	1665				
OGLE, JAMES	1802	DEFENDANT	1647	OHIO RIVER - FERRY LANDING - WELLSBURG	1871	WELLSBURG	1777
OGLE, JAMES	1805	DEFENDANT	1658				
OGLE, JAMES	1808	DEFENDANT	1579	OHIO RIVER - FERRY TO EAST LIVERPOOL	1871	HAN MAP	1727
OGLE, JAMES	1809	DEFENDANT	1579				
OGLEBAY, J H	1871	BENWO'D - BUS.	1795	OHIO RIVER - IRON BRIDGE OVER - AT MOUTH OF HARMONS CREEK	1871	EDGINGTON STA.	1774
OGLES RUN	1852	BRKE MAP	1840				
O'HARA, M	1871	MARH'L MAP	1750	OHIO RIVER - MAP	1916	NAT'L ROAD	1868
OHIO	1852	HEMPFIELD RR	1820	OHIO RIVER - MAP	1916	NAT'L ROAD	1869
OHIO - RAILROADS	1852	HEMPFIELD RR	1819				

LXXIV

'PERSONAL TIME LINE' INDEX TO VOLUME 7 OF THE *OHIO COUNTY INDEX*

ENTRY	YEAR	SUBJECT	PAGE
OHIO RIVER - MOUTH OF SHORT CREEK	1852	BRKE MAP	1839
OHIO RIVER - NAVIGATION - HISTORY	1916	NAT'L ROAD	1866
OHIO RIVER - STEAMBOAT LANDING - MOUNDSVILLE	1871	MDSVILLE	1808
OHIO RIVER - STEAMBOAT LANDING - WHEELING	1871	WHG CITY	1788
OHIO RIVER - SUSPENSION BRIDGE - PHOTO	1916	NAT'L ROAD	1867
OHIO RIVER - WELLSBURG	1871	WELLSBURG	1778
OHIO RIVER - WHEELING	1871	WHG CITY	1786
OHIO RIVER - WHEELING - HEMPFIELD RR	1852	HEMPFIELD RR	1817
OHIO RIVER FERRY - S. OF MOUTH OF HOG RUN	1871	MARH'L MAP	1751
OHIO RIVER ROAD - SEE ALSO RIVER ROAD	1871	RIV. RD S OF N.C.	1771
OHIO RIVER VALLEY - VIEW FROM WHEELING HILL	1916	NAT'L ROAD	1865
OHIO VALLEY	1852	HEMPFIELD RR	1820
OHIO VALLEY AUTOMOBILE CLUB - WHEELING / WHEELING HILL PAVING	1916	NAT'L ROAD	1865
OHIO VIEW	1871	HAN MAP	1730
OIHO RIVER / TRAVEL DISTANCE	1916	NAT'L ROAD	1862
OIL DERRICKS - W.VA. PANHANDLE	1916	NAT'L ROAD	1864
OIL DISTRICT & DERRICKS - SW. PA.	1916	NAT'L ROAD	1862
OIL REFINERIES	1871	FRE'MAN'S LDG	1762
OIL WELL - E OF WHITE OAK FLATS	1871	HAN MAP	1726
OIL WORKS / SW. OF HAMILTON	1871	HAN MAP	1726
OIL WORKS - E OF ORCHARDDALE	1871	HAN MAP	1727
OK SIDE / VANCE (?OAKSIDE?)	1871	TRIAD BORO.	1784
OKEEFE, J	1871	OH CO. MAP	1742
OKEEFE, JOHN	1871	OH CO. BUS.	1779
OKEEFE, JOHN	1871	TRIAD TWP.	1781
O'KEEFE, JOHN	1873	MISC	1695
OLD BROOK FURNACE / J. ARCHER	1871	HAN MAP	1732
OLD CAMPGROUND - CASTLEMANS RUN	1852	BRKE MAP	1840
OLD CEMETERY - NEAR CROSS CREEK	1871	BRKE MAP	1735
OLD DYE HOUSE / W. BRIGGS & BRO	1871	BRKE MAP	1736
OLD FACTORY	1871	HAN MAP	1733
OLD GRIST MILL - COUNCILMAN RUN	1871	BKE/OH MAP	1739
OLD HOMESTEAD / THE OLD HOMESTEAD OF 1798	1871	HAN MAP	1732
OLD HOMESTEAD	1871	BRKE MAP	1734
OLD INDIAN CAMP	1871	MARH'L MAP	1745
OLD INDIAN SPRING	1871	OH CO. MAP	1742
OLD MILL - NEAR W. POLLOCK	1871	OH CO. MAP	1740
OLD MILL - XS OF J. SWEARINGEN	1871	BRKE MAP	1734
OLD NORTHWEST TERRITORY & NATIONAL ROAD MAP	1916	NAT'L ROAD	1870
OLD ROAD / RONEY POINT & WEST UNION TURNPIKE	1871	OH CO. MAP	1743
OLD SCHOOL HOUSE - WASHINGTON TWP	1871	MARH'L MAP	1748
OLD STATE ROAD	1871	OH CO. MAP	1740
OLD STATE ROAD - RONEY POINT	1871	RONEY PT.	1783
OLD STATE ROAD - SE OF NATIONAL ROAD - POINT MILL STATION	1871	OH CO. MAP	1743
OLD STONE HOTEL - RONEY'S POINT - NATIONAL ROAD	1916	NAT'L ROAD	1866
OLD THREE SPRINGS CHURCH / FIRST CHURCH IN COUNTY	1871	HAN MAP	1732
OLDENDOFF, E	1871	HAN MAP	1727
OLDHAM, B	1871	OH CO. MAP	1743
OLDHAM, B O / ? SAW MILL (?B IS UNCLEAR?)	1871	OH CO. MAP	1743
OLDHAM, J H	1871	OH CO. MAP	1743
OLDHAM, S	1871	OH CO. MAP	1743
OLDHAM, SAMUEL	1852	HEMPFIELD RR	1822
OLIVER, GEORGE	1866	MISC	1708
OLSON, C / MRS - (?OR CLSCAN - SPELLING UNCLEAR?)	1871	MARH'L MAP	1752
OLSON, C / MRS - (?OR CLSCAN - SPELLING UNCLEAR?)	1871	MARH'L MAP	1756
OMER, M	1871	OH CO. MAP	1742
OMER, N	1871	RITCHIE TWP	1791
OMER, N	1871	RITCHIE TWP	1793
ONEAL, - / EST.	1871	MARH'L MAP	1761
O'NEAL, MARTIN	1855	DEFENDANT	1552
O'NEAL, MARTIN	1856	DEFENDANT	1552
O'NEAL, MARTIN	1857	DEFENDANT	1552
O'NEIL, W J	1871	MARH'L MAP	1755
O'NEIL, W J / INITIALS W.J.O'N.	1871	MARH'L MAP	1755
ONYGOOD, B	1871	MARH'L MAP	1745

ENTRY	YEAR	SUBJECT	PAGE
ORAM - SEE ALSO ORUM	1871	MARH'L MAP	1746
ORAM G	1871	BRKE MAP	1737
ORAM, C	1871	MARH'L MAP	1746
ORAM, C	1871	MARH'L MAP	1749
ORAM, P	1871	BRKE MAP	1736
ORCHARD - ARCHERS / JAMES	1871	BRKE MAP	1734
ORCHARD - ARNOLDS / V ?	1871	MARH'L MAP	1752
ORCHARD - BURGOYNES / J R	1871	BRKE MAP	1735
ORCHARD - CUT OFF TOP OF MAP	1871	MARH'L MAP	1756
ORCHARD - INGRAMS / SILAS	1871	MARH'L MAP	1753
ORCHARD - S. OF BURCHVALLEY	1871	MARH'L MAP	1753
ORCHARD - SE OF BERNARD BRADY	1871	BRKE MAP	1735
ORCHARD BASIN	1871	BKE/OH MAP	1739
ORCHARD HILL	1871	HAN MAP	1732
ORCHARD SIDE	1871	OH CO. MAP	1743
ORCHARD SIDE	1871	OH CO. MAP	1744
ORCHARDDALE	1871	HAN MAP	1726
ORCHARDGROVE	1871	HAN MAP	1732
ORCHARDS - SW OF J. ELSON	1871	BRKE MAP	1735
ORDINARY - SEE ALSO TAVERN	1916	NAT'L ROAD	1861
O'REILLY, -	1871	MARH'L MAP	1750
OREM, GEORGE / MAP#245	1852	BRKE MAP	1843
OREM, GEORGE / MAP#247	1852	BRKE MAP	1843
OREM, GEORGE / MAP#248	1852	BRKE MAP	1843
ORGAN DEALER	1871	NEW CUMB'LD	1762
ORNER, JACOB	1838	DEFENDANT	1595
ORNER, JACOB	1838	DEFENDANT	1640
ORR DIST SCHOOL NO. 4	1871	OH CO. MAP	1743
ORR SETTLEMENT	1871	OH CO. MAP	1743
ORR, - / MISS	1871	OH CO. MAP	1743
ORR, A K	1871	WELLSBURG	1777
ORR, A M / INITIALS A.M.O.	1871	OH CO. MAP	1743
ORR, A M / RES	1871	OH CO. MAP	1743
ORR, ALEXANDER	1794	DEFENDANT	1616
ORR, ALEXANDER	1794	DEFENDANT	1665
ORR, C	1871	OH CO. MAP	1743
ORR, G G	1871	BRKE MAP	1734
ORR, GEORGE G	1871	HAN MAP	1732
ORR, GEORGE G	1871	BRKE MAP	1734
ORR, GEORGE G / TANNERY	1871	BRKE MAP	1734
ORR, J C & CO	1880	DEFENDANT	1603
ORR, JAMES	1826	DEFENDANT	1668
ORR, JAMES	1827	DEFENDANT	1668
ORR, JAMES	1871	OH CO. MAP	1743
ORR, N / TIMBERLAND & BUILDING SITES	1871	BRKE MAP	1734
ORR, S W	1871	HAN MAP	1733
ORR, SAMUEL N	1871	BRKE MAP	1734
ORR, SAMUEL N / INITIALS S.N.O.	1871	BRKE MAP	1734
ORR, SAMVEL / MAP#652	1852	BRKE MAP	1853
ORR, SAMVEL / MAP#653	1852	BRKE MAP	1853
ORR, T J	1871	OH CO. MAP	1743
ORR, THOMAS / ESQ. - MAP#649	1852	BRKE MAP	1853
ORR, THOMAS / ESQ. - MAP#650	1852	BRKE MAP	1853
ORR, THOMAS / ESQ. - MAP#651	1852	BRKE MAP	1853
ORRS OLD ROAD	1871	OH CO. MAP	1743
ORUM - SEE ALSO ORAM	1871	MARH'L MAP	1746
ORUM W / E. SIDE OF MAP	1871	MARH'L MAP	1745
ORUM, P / BLACKSMITH SHOP	1871	MARH'L MAP	1746
ORUM, W / STORE	1871	MARH'L MAP	1746
OSBORN, R / (?OR H?)	1871	HAN MAP	1732
OTL, S / EST.	1871	SOUTH WHG	1792
OTL, S / EST.	1871	SOUTH WHG	1794
OTT, H	1871	MARH'L MAP	1746
OTTARD, R	1871	NEW CUMB'LD	1766
OTTERSON, C	1871	OH CO. MAP	1742
OTTERSON, C	1871	OH CO. MAP	1744
OTTO, H	1871	TRIAD.BORO.	1784
OTTO, H	1871	TRIAD.BORO.	1784
OTTO, H	1871	TRIAD.BORO.	1784
OTTO, H	1871	TRIAD.BORO.	1784
OTTO, HENRY	1855	DEFENDANT	1653
OTTO, HENRY	1860	DEFENDANT	1602
OTTO, J	1871	TRIAD.BORO.	1784
OURAN, H	1871	MARH'L MAP	1745
OURAN, L	1871	SHERRARD	1811
OVER, WILLIAM	1854	DEFENDANT	1582
OVERSEERS OF POOR	1856	MISC	1702
OVERSEERS OF POOR	1861	MISC	1675
OWENS, CHARLES W / MAP#609	1852	BRKE MAP	1851
OWENS, EPHRAIM / MAP#643	1852	BRKE MAP	1852
OWINGS RUN	1852	BRKE MAP	1852
OWINGS, - / DR	1871	HAN MAP	1732
OWINGS, A	1871	NEW CUMB'LD	1768
OWINGS, C W	1871	HAN MAP	1731

'PERSONAL TIME LINE' INDEX TO VOLUME 7 OF THE *OHIO COUNTY INDEX*

ENTRY	YEAR	SUBJECT	PAGE	ENTRY	YEAR	SUBJECT	PAGE
OWINGS, C W	1871	HAN MAP	1732	PARK, ROBERT / MAP#389	1852	BRKE MAP	1846
OWINGS, C W	1871	BRKE MAP	1734	PARKER, HENRY C	1857	DEFENDANT	1630
OWINGS, J S	1871	HAN MAP	1731	PARKER, HENRY E	1853	DEFENDANT	1581
OWINGS, J S / INITIALS J.S.O.	1871	HAN MAP	1731	PARKER, J	1871	MARH'L MAP	1753
OWINGS, J S	1871	HAN MAP	1732	PARKER, J	1871	MARH'L MAP	1753
OWINGS, J S / INITIALS J.S.O.	1871	HAN MAP	1732	PARKER, J	1871	MARH'L MAP	1756
P, J B / ? INITIALS UNSURE - J.B.P.EST. ?	1871	MARH'L MAP	1752	PARKER, J	1871	MARH'L MAP	1756
				PARKER, J	1871	MARH'L MAP	1756
P, J W / UNKNOWN INITIALS - NEW MANCHESTER (?J.W.HOBBS?)	1871	NEW MANCH.	1769	PARKER, JAMES	1784	APPENDIX	1874
P, S B / UNKNOWN INITIALS	1871	MARH'L MAP	1751	PARKER, JOHN E	1879	DEFENDANT	1631
P.A. & CO. / (?ANDERSON?)	1871	HAN MAP	1732	PARKER, JOSEPH N	1878	DEFENDANT	1615
P.A. & CO. / (?ANDERSON?)	1871	HAN MAP	1732	PARKER, P	1871	MARH'L MAP	1752
PAATTERSON, R. / SAW MILL ON HARDINS RUN	1871	HAN MAP	1731	PARKER, ROSIE	1878	MISC	1696
				PARKER, S	1871	WELLSBURG	1777
PADGETT, JAMES	1874	DEFENDANT	1560	PARKER, S C	1871	MARH'L MAP	1753
PADGETT, JAMES	1874	DEFENDANT	1578	PARKER, S C	1871	MARH'L MAP	1756
PAINTER, THOMAS	1858	DEFENDANT	1562	PARKER, THOMAS	1858	DEFENDANT	1565
PAINTER, THOMAS	1858	DEFENDANT	1623	PARKER, THOMAS	1858	DEFENDANT	1590
PAIRSON, J	1871	OH CO. MAP	1740	PARKER, THOMAS M	1857	DEFENDANT	1582
PAIRSON, J	1871	OH CO. MAP	1743	PARKER, THOMAS M	1860	DEFENDANT	1567
PAIRSON, J / INITIALS J.P.	1871	OH CO. MAP	1743	PARKERSBURG	1852	HEMP. RR MAP	1825
PAIRSON, J / INITIALS J.P.	1871	OH CO. MAP	1743	PARKERSBURG	1852	HEMP. RR MAP	1826
PALMER, AMBROSE	1831	DEFENDANT	1553	PARKINSON, BENJAMIN / MAP#183	1852	BRKE MAP	1844
PALMER, J	1871	BRKE MAP	1737	PARKINSON, DAVID / (MILL) / MAP#53	1852	BRKE MAP	1840
PALMER, J	1871	BRKE MAP	1737	PARKINSON, DAVID / MAP#52	1852	BRKE MAP	1840
PALMER, J / E SIDE OF MAP -E. OF D. APPLEGATE	1871	BRKE MAP	1737	PARKINSON, DAVID / MAP#190	1852	BRKE MAP	1844
				PARKINSON, G A	1871	BRKE MAP	1737
PALMER, J C	1871	BRKE MAP	1737	PARKINSON, G A / RES	1871	BRKE MAP	1737
PALMER, J C / RES	1871	BRKE MAP	1737	PARKINSON, J	1871	MARH'L MAP	1753
PALMER, JAMES / MAP#222	1852	BRKE MAP	1843	PARKINSON, J / INITIALS J.P.	1871	MARH'L MAP	1753
PALMER, JAMES / MAP#223	1852	BRKE MAP	1843	PARKINSON, J L / ATTORNEY	1871	MDSVL BUS.	1796
PALMER, JAMES / MAP#224	1852	BRKE MAP	1843	PARKINSON, J L	1871	MDSVILLE	1806
PALMER, JAMES / MAP#193	1852	BRKE MAP	1844	PARKINSON, J L	1871	MDSVILLE	1809
PALMER, JAMES / MAP#241	1852	BRKE MAP	1844	PARKINSON, T	1871	BRKE MAP	1737
PALMER, JAMES H	1830	DEFENDANT	1554	PARKINSON, T / INITIALS T.P.	1871	BRKE MAP	1737
PALMER, JOSEPH	1803	DEFENDANT	1637	PARKS RUN	1871	HAN MAP	1732
PALMER, JOSEPH	1805	DEFENDANT	1579	PARKS, DAVID	1802	DEFENDANT	1596
PALMER, JOSEPH	1806	DEFENDANT	1556	PARKS, G	1871	OH CO. MAP	1742
PALMER, JOSEPH	1807	DEFENDANT	1645	PARKS, G	1871	TRIAD. TWP.	1781
PALMER, JOSEPH	1811	DEFENDANT	1642	PARKS, J	1871	MARH'L MAP	1753
PALMER, JOSEPH THOMAS	1811	DEFENDANT	1642	PARKS, J / BLACKSMITH SHOP	1871	MARH'L MAP	1753
PALMER, T	1871	WELLSBURG	1776	PARKS, J / STORE	1871	MARH'L MAP	1753
PALMER, T	1871	WELLSBURG	1776	PARKS, JAMES	1785	DEFENDANT	1556
PAMER, J	1871	BRKE MAP	1737	PARKS, N	1871	MARH'L MAP	1752
PANHANDLE MAP - BOTTOM HALF OVERVIEW	1871	MAP	1715	PARKS, R	1871	WELLSBURG	1777
				PARKS, R	1871	WELLSBURG	1777
PANHANDLE MAP - NATIONAL ROAD	1916	NAT'L ROAD	1863	PARKS, T	1871	WELLSBURG	1777
PANHANDLE MAP - TOP HALF OVERVIEW	1871	MAP	1714	PARLET, ISAIAH	1820	DEFENDANT	1649
				PARLOR GROVE	1871	BRKE MAP	1737
PANHANDLE MAP INDEX - BOTTOM HALF	1871	MAP	1717	PARMOURS RUN / (?PARMARS?)	1852	BRKE MAP	1850
				PARMOURS RUN	1871	BRKE MAP	1735
PANHANDLE MAP INDEX - TOP HALF	1871	MAP	1716	PARR, NATHAN	1792	DEFENDANT	1591
PAN-HANDLE P O.	1871	BRKE MAP	1734	PARRIOTT, JOHN	1833	DEFENDANT	1551
PANHANDLE POPLUATION 1870 CENSUS	1871	POPULATION	1816	PARRIOTT, JOHN	1834	DEFENDANT	1551
				PARRIOTT, JOHN	1835	DEFENDANT	1559
PANHANDLE ROUTE WAGON ROAD	1871	BRKE MAP	1734	PARRIOTT, RICHARD	1814	DEFENDANT	1599
PANHANDLE RR	1871	HAN MAP	1733	PARRIOTT, S A	1871	MARH'L MAP	1761
PANNELL, GEORGE	1815	DEFENDANT	1600	PARRIOTT, W E	1871	MARH'L MAP	1761
PANNELL, GEORGE	1815	DEFENDANT	1645	PARRISH, JOHN	1790	DEFENDANT	1644
PANNELL, GEORGE	1816	DEFENDANT	1642	PARRISH, JOHN	1792	DEFENDANT	1644
PANNELL, GEORGE	1817	DEFENDANT	1642	PARROTT, - / MRS	1871	MARH'L MAP	1749
PANNELL, GEORGE	1819	DEFENDANT	1642	PARROTT, C	1871	MDSVILLE	1810
PANNELL, GEORGE	1823	DEFENDANT	1594	PARROTT, JOHN	1827	DEFENDANT	1573
PANNELL, GEORGE	1823	DEFENDANT	1638	PARROTT, JOHN	1829	DEFENDANT	1642
PANNELL, GEORGE	1824	DEFENDANT	1594	PARROTT, JOSEPH	1827	DEFENDANT	1649
PANNELL, GEORGE	1824	DEFENDANT	1632	PARROTT, JOSEPH S	1829	DEFENDANT	1567
PANNELL, GEORGE	1824	DEFENDANT	1638	PARROTT, SUSAN	1832	DEFENDANT	1561
PANORAMIC MAPS OF PANHANDLE	2000	MAPS	1855	PARROTT, SUSANNA	1833	DEFENDANT	1555
PANTHER RUN	1852	BRKE MAP	1846	PARROTT, SUSANNA	1833	DEFENDANT	1555
PANTHER RUN / __NEE_THS FORK OF	1852	BRKE MAP	1846	PARROTT, WILLIAM	1818	DEFENDANT	1660
PANTHER RUN / ? INCOMPLETE				PARROTT, WILLIAM	1819	DEFENDANT	1660
PANTHER RUN	1871	BRKE MAP	1736	PARROTT, WILLIAM	1820	DEFENDANT	1624
PANTHER RUN / NW CORNER OF MAP	1871	BRKE MAP	1737	PARRS POINT	1871	MARH'L MAP	1748
PAPER MILL - HARVEY & MANSER	1871	WELLSBURG	1777	PARRS RUN	1871	MARH'L MAP	1748
PARARS RUN / (?SPELLED PARMOURS?)	1852	BRKE MAP	1850	PARRS RUN	1871	MDSVILLE	1807
				PARSHEL, JAMES	1871	OH CO. MAP	1741
PARDY, GEORGE H	1871	MARH'L MAP	1748	PARSON, - / MRS	1871	MARH'L MAP	1759
PARIOTT, E S / ?	1871	MARH'L MAP	1748	PARSON, HENRY	1838	DEFENDANT	1551
PARIOTT, T / MRS	1871	MDSVILLE	1807	PARSON, J	1871	MARH'L MAP	1759
PARIS, PA	1852	BRKE MAP	1854	PARSONS RUN	1852	BRKE MAP	1847
PARISON, JOHN	1811	MISC	1689	PARSONS, J	1871	MARH'L MAP	1759
PARK, R	1871	BRKE MAP	1735	PARSONS, J	1871	WELLSBURG	1777
PARK, R	1871	BRKE MAP	1737	PARSONS, T	1871	MARH'L MAP	1755
PARK, ROBERT / MAP#387	1852	BRKE MAP	1846	PARTIOTT, G W	1871	MARH'L MAP	1760
PARK, ROBERT / MAP#388	1852	BRKE MAP	1846	PASSENGERS OF TRAFFIC	1852	HEMPFIELD RR	1819

'PERSONAL TIME LINE' INDEX TO VOLUME 7 OF THE *OHIO COUNTY INDEX*

ENTRY	YEAR	SUBJECT	PAGE
PASTOR - DAVID HARVEY / MAP#314	1852	BRKE MAP	1847
PASTOR - J. BROWN - WEST LIBERTY	1871	W.LIBERTY	1780
PASTOR - J.F.WOODS - EPISCOPAL CHURCH - MOUNDSVILLE	1871	MDSVL BUS.	1796
PASTOR - JAMES ALEXANDER - MOUNDSVILLE	1871	MDSVL BUS.	1796
PASTOR - REV. S.LAUCK / HEIRS - MAP#9	1852	BRKE MAP	1840
PASTOR - REV. DR. J.ALEXANDER - MOUNDSVILLE	1871	MDSVILLE	1809
PASTOR - W.BLAKE - MOUNDSVILLE	1871	MDSVILLE	1807
PATERSON, -	1871	HAN MAP	1732
PATRICK, FORD	1810	DEFENDANT	1638
PATTEN, T	1871	BRKE MAP	1736
PATTEN, WILLIAM	1825	DEFENDANT	1639
PATTERSON J / HRS	1871	BRKE MAP	1734
PATTERSON J / HRS	1871	BRKE MAP	1734
PATTERSON, A H	1878	DEFENDANT	1573
PATTERSON, FRANCIS	1871	BRKE MAP	1735
PATTERSON, FRANCIS / HIS TIMBERLANDS	1871	BRKE MAP	1735
PATTERSON, J	1871	HAN MAP	1727
PATTERSON, J	1871	HAN MAP	1731
PATTERSON, J	1871	HAN MAP	1732
PATTERSON, J	1871	BRKE MAP	1734
PATTERSON, J	1871	BRKE MAP	1734
PATTERSON, J	1871	OH CO. MAP	1740
PATTERSON, J	1871	WELLSBURG	1777
PATTERSON, J W	1871	BKE/OH MAP	1739
PATTERSON, JAMES / MAP#506	1852	BRKE MAP	1849
PATTERSON, JAMES / MAP#546	1852	BRKE MAP	1851
PATTERSON, JAMES / MAP#557	1852	BRKE MAP	1851
PATTERSON, JAMES / ESQ. - MAP#658	1852	BRKE MAP	1854
PATTERSON, JAMES / MAP#673	1852	BRKE MAP	1854
PATTERSON, JOSIAH	1813	DEFENDANT	1648
PATTERSON, JOSIAH	1816	DEFENDANT	1667
PATTERSON, JOSIAH	1818	DEFENDANT	1660
PATTERSON, R	1871	BRKE MAP	1734
PATTERSON, R	1871	NEW CUMB'LD	1767
PATTERSON, T	1871	OH CO. MAP	1740
PATTERSON, W / (SMITH'P) - MAP#544	1852	BRKE MAP	1852
PATTERSON, W / (SMITH'P) - MAP#545	1852	BRKE MAP	1852
PATTERSON, W	1871	BRKE MAP	1734
PATTERSON, WILLIAM	1808	DEFENDANT	1648
PATTERSON, WILLIAM	1808	DEFENDANT	1667
PATTERSON, WILLIAM	1809	DEFENDANT	1667
PATTERSON, WILLIAM	1871	BKE/OH MAP	1739
PATTON, -	1860	DEFENDANT	1584
PATTON, JAMES	1817	DEFENDANT	1553
PATTON, JAMES	1831	DEFENDANT	1669
PATTON, JAMES	1831	DEFENDANT	1669
PATTON, JAMES / MAP#413	1852	BRKE MAP	1846
PATTON, JAMES	1871	BRKE MAP	1735
PATTON, JAMES / COAL BANK	1871	BRKE MAP	1735
PATTON, JAMES / HRS	1871	BRKE MAP	1735
PATTON, JOHN	1797	DEFENDANT	1553
PATTON, JOHN	1852	NOT ON MAP	1836
PATTON, THOMAS / MAP#330	1852	BRKE MAP	1846
PATTON, WILLIAM	1802	DEFENDANT	1598
PATTON, WILLIAM	1806	DEFENDANT	1666
PATTON, WILLIAM	1807	DEFENDANT	1666
PATTON, WILLIAM	1817	DEFENDANT	1553
PATTON, WILLIAM	1818	DEFENDANT	1638
PATTON, WILLIAM	1819	DEFENDANT	1638
PATTON, WILLIAM	1822	DEFENDANT	1638
PATTON, WILLIAM	1825	DEFENDANT	1639
PATTON, WILLIAM	1828	DEFENDANT	1639
PAUL, -	1823	PLAINTIFF	1628
PAUL, -	1824	PLAINTIFF	1628
PAUL, J	1871	MARH'L MAP	1751
PAULL, -	1824	PLAINTIFF	1628
PAULL, -	1826	PLAINTIFF	1628
PAULL, JAMES / WHEELING	1852	HEMPFIELD RR	1817
PAYTON, J	1871	OH CO. MAP	1741
PEAK, D	1871	HAN MAP	1727
PEAKE, PRESLEY	1791	DEFENDANT	1571
PEARCE - ORPHANS	1821	MISC	1704
PEARCE, - / GOULD, PEARCE & CO	1871	WLSBRG BUS.	1772
PEARCE, - / GOULD, PEARCE & CO / FLEET ST.	1871	WELLSBURG	1776
PEARCE, - / GOULD, PEARCE & CO	1871	WELLSBURG	1777
PEARCE, - / GOULD, PEARCE & CO / COTTON	1871	WELLSBURG	1777
PEARCE, - / GOULD, PEARCE & CO.	1871	WELLSBURG	1777
PEARCE, ARTHUR	1820	DEFENDANT	1577
PEARCE, DANIEL	1797	MISC	1674
PEARCE, DAVID / HEIRS - MAP#570	1852	BRKE MAP	1852
PEARCE, JAMES	1818	MISC	1704
PEARCE, JAMES	1840	DEFENDANT	1643
PEARCE, JAMES J	1838	DEFENDANT	1669
PEARSON, -	1841	DEFENDANT	1640
PEARSON, CURTIS	1840	DEFENDANT	1620
PEARSON, HENRY	1838	MISC	1682
PEAY, AUSTIN	1841	DEFENDANT	1629
PEAY, AUSTIN	1841	DEFENDANT	1661
PECK, - / MRS	1871	MDSVILLE	1810
PECK, DANIEL	1825	DEFENDANT	1649
PECK, DANIEL	1825	DEFENDANT	1649
PECK, DANIEL	1880	MISC	1680
PEGG, J	1871	MARH'L MAP	1758
PEIRCE, A	1871	BKE/OH MAP	1739
PEIRSON, P EDWARD	1875	DEFENDANT	1578
PELLEY, A	1871	MARH'L MAP	1751
PELLEY, C A	1871	MARH'L MAP	1751
PELLEY, G	1871	MARH'L MAP	1749
PELLEY, P	1871	MARH'L MAP	1746
PELLY, G	1871	MARH'L MAP	1745
PELLY, JAMES	1834	DEFENDANT	1669
PEMBERSON, T	1871	OH CO. MAP	1740
PEMBERTON, JAMES	1823	DEFENDANT	1612
PEMBERTON, JAMES	1839	MISC	1685
PEMBERTON, THOMAS	1859	DEFENDANT	1673
PENDLETON, W K / INITIALS W.K.P.	1871	BETHANY	1773
PENDERGAST, P / ?	1871	MARH'L MAP	1761
PENDERGUST, P / (?PENDERGAST?)	1871	MARH'L MAP	1761
PENDLETON / TRACT OF LOTS IN BETHANY	1871	BETHANY	1773
PENDLETON & KUHN	1871	WELLSBURG	1776
PENDLETON, J H	1871	WELLSBURG	1778
PENDLETON, JOHN O	1878	MISC	1679
PENDLETON, JOSEPH H	1861	DEFENDANT	1654
PENDLETON, JOSEPH H	1862	DEFENDANT	1654
PENDLETON, W H / PRES. BETHANY COLLEGE	1871	BETHANY	1773
PENDLETON, W K / MAP#132	1852	BRKE MAP	1844
PENDLETON, W K / PRES. BETHANY COLLEGE	1871	BETHNY BUS.	1772
PENDLETON, W K / HARBINGER OFFICE	1871	BETHANY	1773
PENINSULA CEMETERY	1871	OH CO. MAP	1742
PENINSULA FARM	1871	WHG CITY	1786
PENINSULA FARM	1871	WHG CITY	1787
PENINSULA OR CITY CEMETERY	1871	WHG CITY	1787
PENINSULA OR CITY CEMETERY	1871	WHG CITY	1788
PENITENTIARY - MOUNDSVILLE	1871	MDSVL BUS.	1796
PENITENTIARY - SEE ALSO STATE PENITENTIARY	1871	MDSVILLE	1809
PENN FORK OF FISH CREEK / ALSO CALLED LEFT FORK	1871	MARH'L MAP	1761
PENN OR LEFT FORK OF FISH CREEK / PENNSYLVANIA FORK	1871	BELLTON	1814
PENN, PHILLIPS & CO	1871	CAMER'N - BUS.	1795
PENN, PHILLIPS & CO / STORE	1871	CAMERON	1803
PENNSYLVANIA	1852	HEMPFIELD RR	1817
PENNSYLVANIA CENTRAL RR	1852	HEMP. RR MAP	1827
PENNSYLVANIA RR	1852	HEMPFIELD RR	1817
PENNSYLVANIA RR	1852	HEMPFIELD RR	1818
PENNSYLVANIA RR	1916	NAT'L ROAD	1861
PENNSYLVANIA RR - STATION - WASHINGTON, PA.	1916	NAT'L ROAD	1861
PENNSYLVANIA STATE LINE - WITH OHIO & MARSHALL CO	1871	W.UNION	1812
PENNSYLVANIA RR	1852	HEMP. RR MAP	1825
PENTONEY, -	1830	PLAINTIFF	1618
PENTONEY, -	1831	PLAINTIFF	1618
PENTONEY, -	1832	PLAINTIFF	1618
PENTONEY, -	1833	PLAINTIFF	1618
PENTONEY, -	1834	PLAINTIFF	1618
PENTONEY, -	1835	PLAINTIFF	1618
PENTONEY, -	1836	PLAINTIFF	1618
PENTONEY, -	1837	PLAINTIFF	1618
PENTONEY, -	1837	PLAINTIFF	1619
PENTONEY, -	1838	PLAINTIFF	1619
PENTONEY, -	1839	PLAINTIFF	1619
PENTONEY, -	1840	PLAINTIFF	1619
PENTONEY, -	1841	PLAINTIFF	1619
PENTONEY, -	1843	PLAINTIFF	1619
PERIGO, JAMES	1818	PLAINTIFF	1589
PERIGO, JAMES	1818	PLAINTIFF	1589

'PERSONAL TIME LINE' INDEX TO VOLUME 7 OF THE *OHIO COUNTY INDEX*

ENTRY	YEAR	SUBJECT	PAGE
PERINE, LEWIS	1826	DEFENDANT	1660
PERMILLION, R	1871	OH CO. MAP	1741
PERMILLION, R	1871	OH CO. MAP	1742
PERRIN, -	1871	BETHANY	1773
PERRINE, LEWIS	1829	DEFENDANT	1595
PERRINE, W L / (?WILLIAM?)	1871	W.LIBERTY	1780
PERRINE, W L / (?WILLIAM?) - INITIALS W.L.P.	1871	W.LIBERTY	1780
PERRINE, W L / INITIALS W.L.P	1871	W.LIBERTY	1780
PERRINE, W L / RES	1871	W.LIBERTY	1780
PERRINE, WILLIAM	1804	DEFENDANT	1596
PERRINE, WILLIAM	1805	DEFENDANT	1554
PERRINE, WILLIAM	1806	DEFENDANT	1658
PERRINE, WILLIAM L	1871	W.LIBRTY.BUS.	1780
PERRY, - / CARLE & PERRY - MAP#405	1852	BRKE MAP	1846
PERRY, - / CARLE & PERRY - MAP#405	1852	BRKE MAP	1846
PERRY, JOSEPH	1858	DEFENDANT	1592
PERSONAL TIME LINE INDEX - CUMULATIVE INDEX TO VOL. 1-7 / PREVIEW	2000	APPENDIX	1875
PETERS CREEK	1871	OH CO. MAP	1741
PETERS RUN	1871	OH CO. MAP	1742
PETERS RUN - MRS. M. BROWNS SAW MILL ON	1871	OH CO. MAP	1744
PETERS, R S / BLACKSMITH SHOP	1871	SHERRARD	1811
PETERS, S	1871	MDSVILLE	1807
PETERSON, CHARLES P	1834	DEFENDANT	1635
PETERSON, LEWIS	1822	DEFENDANT	1602
PETERSON, P	1871	MARH'L MAP	1761
PETERSON, P / INITIALS W.P.	1871	MARH'L MAP	1761
PETERSON, PETER	1791	DEFENDANT	1665
PETERSON, PETER	1797	DEFENDANT	1634
PETERSON, PETERS	1788	DEFENDANT	1665
PETERSON, S	1871	HAN MAP	1731
PETERSON, T	1871	HAN MAP	1731
PETERSON, THOMAS	1871	HAN MAP	1731
PETERSON, THOMAS / ABBREV. T.P.	1871	HAN MAP	1731
PETERSON, WILLIAM F	1836	DEFENDANT	1598
PETIT, H	1871	MARH'L MAP	1750
PETIT, H	1871	MARH'L MAP	1753
PETIT, J	1871	MARH'L MAP	1753
PETTICORD, C	1871	BKE/OH MAP	1739
PETTIS, JOHN	1813	DEFENDANT	1642
PETTIS, JOHN	1816	DEFENDANT	1551
PETTIT, JAMES	1806	DEFENDANT	1655
PETTIT, JAMES	1824	DEFENDANT	1639
PEW, G	1871	HAN MAP	1733
PFEISTER, JOHN	1855	DEFENDANT	1672
PFISTER, JOHN	1871	BRKE MAP	1735
PHEPPS, W S	1877	DEFENDANT	1631
PHILABUM, P / (?OR PHILABURN?)	1871	BRKE MAP	1737
PHILABURN, P / (?OR PHILABUM?)	1871	BRKE MAP	1737
PHILABURN, P / (?PHILABUM?)	1871	BRKE MAP	1737
PHILADELPHIA, PA	1852	HEMPFIELD RR	1818
PHILADELPHIA, PA	1852	HEMPFIELD RR	1819
PHILADELPHIA, PA	1852	HEMPFIELD RR	1820
PHILADELPHIA, PA	1852	HEMPFIELD RR	1820
PHILADELPHIA, PA	1852	HEMPFIELD RR	1821
PHILADELPHIA, PA	1852	HEMPFIELD RR	1821
PHILADELPHIA, PA	1852	HEMP. RR MAP	1825
PHILADELPHIA, PA	1852	HEMP. RR MAP	1827
PHILIPS, C	1871	OH CO. MAP	1742
PHILIPS, C	1871	RITCHIE TWP	1791
PHILIPS, L	1871	OH CO. MAP	1744
PHILLIPS, -	1871	WHG ISLAND	1788
PHILLIPS, -	1871	WHG ISLAND	1790
PHILLIPS, - / PENN, PHILLIPS & CO	1871	CAMER'N - BUS.	1795
PHILLIPS, - / PENN, PHILLIPS & CO / STORE	1871	CAMERON	1803
PHILLIPS, A J	1860	DEFENDANT	1604
PHILLIPS, B	1871	MARH'L MAP	1753
PHILLIPS, D	1871	MARH'L MAP	1753
PHILLIPS, H W	1874	DEFENDANT	1615
PHILLIPS, HAN W	1873	DEFENDANT	1615
PHILLIPS, HANS W	1858	DEFENDANT	1552
PHILLIPS, HANS W	1858	DEFENDANT	1621
PHILLIPS, HANS W	1861	DEFENDANT	1552
PHILLIPS, HANS W	1861	DEFENDANT	1597
PHILLIPS, J	1871	OH CO. MAP	1740
PHILLIPS, J	1871	OH CO. MAP	1743
PHILLIPS, J	1871	MARH'L MAP	1750
PHILLIPS, J M	1871	MARH'L MAP	1753
PHILLIPS, JOHN	1860	DEFENDANT	1584
PHILLIPS, L	1871	OH CO. MAP	1743
PHILLIPS, L	1871	OH CO. MAP	1744
PHILLIPS, L	1871	MARH'L MAP	1753
PHILLIPS, M / MRS	1871	MARH'L MAP	1753
PHILLIPS, PETER	1879	DEFENDANT	1673
PHILLIPS, W	1871	MARH'L MAP	1750
PHILLIPS, W / INITIALS W.P.	1871	MARH'L MAP	1750
PHILLIPS, W	1871	NEW MANCH.	1769
PHYSICIANS - SEE ALSO DOCTOR	1871	CAMER'N - BUS.	1795
PIANO DEALER	1871	NEW CUMB'LD	1762
PICCARRA, JOHN / MAP#331	1852	BRKE MAP	1846
PICKER, E	1871	MARH'L MAP	1748
PICKERMAN, J	1871	WELLSBURG	1778
PICKET, E	1871	MARH'L MAP	1745
PICKET, J C	1871	MARH'L MAP	1745
PICKET, J C	1871	MARH'L MAP	1748
PIERCE, A D / RES	1871	MARH'L MAP	1748
PIERCE, A D / RES	1871	MARH'L MAP	1748
PIERCE, A D / CUT OFF TOP OF MAP	1871	MARH'L MAP	1752
PIERCE, A D / CUT OFF TOP OF MAP	1871	MARH'L MAP	1752
PIERCE, ARTHUR	1810	DEFENDANT	1648
PIERCE, J	1871	NEW CUMB'LD	1768
PIERCE, J B / EST	1871	MARH'L MAP	1748
PIERCE, J Q	1871	MARH'L MAP	1752
PIERCE, W S / RES	1871	MARH'L MAP	1752
PIERCEN, J C	1871	OH CO. MAP	1740
PIERCES RUN	1852	BRKE MAP	1844
PIERCES RUN / CUT OFF OF LEFT OF MAP BELOW GISTS BRANCH	1852	BRKE MAP	1847
PIERCES RUN	1871	BRKE MAP	1737
PIERCES RUN	1871	BRKE MAP	1737
PIERCES RUN - SCHOOL / MAP#242	1852	BRKE MAP	1844
PIERSE, ARTHUR	1810	DEFENDANT	1635
PIERSON, DAVID	1818	PLAINTIFF	1667
PIERSON, DAVID / MAP#32	1852	BRKE MAP	1840
PIERSON, JOHN	1831	DEFENDANT	1613
PIERSON, JOHN	1833	DEFENDANT	1553
PIERSON, JOHN	1834	DEFENDANT	1553
PIERSON, P	1871	OH CO. MAP	1740
PIERSON, P	1871	OH CO. MAP	1740
PIG RUN / MOUTH AT OHIO RIVER	1871	MARH'L MAP	1751
PIKARRI, ROBERT	1858	MISC	1690
PIKE ISLAND / OHIO RIVER	1871	BKE/OH MAP	1738
PIKE ISLAND - OHIO RIVER	1871	OH CO. MAP	1741
PIKE, -	1855	PLAINTIFF	1630
PIKE, -	1856	PLAINTIFF	1630
PIKE, -	1857	PLAINTIFF	1630
PIKE, -	1858	PLAINTIFF	1630
PIKE, -	1860	PLAINTIFF	1631
PIKE, -	1862	PLAINTIFF	1631
PILES, ALEX	1837	MISC	1684
PILLINGS, C	1871	WELLSBURG	1777
PINDALE, JAMES	1807	DEFENDANT	1658
PINDALE, JAMES	1809	DEFENDANT	1658
PINE ALLEY - HAMILTON	1871	HAN MAP	1729
PINE ALLEY - HAMILTON	1871	HAN MAP	1730
PINE GROVE	1871	BKE/OH MAP	1739
PINE GROVE	1871	OH CO. MAP	1740
PINE HOLLOW SPRING	1871	HAN MAP	1732
PINE LICK / STREAM	1871	MARH'L MAP	1757
PINE LICK / RUN	1871	MARH'L MAP	1761
PIPER, WILLIAM C	1841	DEFENDANT	1563
PIPER, WILLIAM C CO	1841	DEFENDANT	1584
PIPES & RICKEY / DRUG STORE	1871	CAMERON	1803
PIPES, J M	1871	CAMERON	1803
PIPES, J W	1871	CAMER'N - BUS.	1795
PIPES, J W / DR	1871	CAMERON	1803
PIPES, J W / DR - OFFICE	1871	CAMERON	1803
PIPES, W	1871	CAMERON	1803
PISTOL RUN	1852	BRKE MAP	1839
PITTENGER, A	1871	HAN MAP	1727
PITTENGER, H	1871	HAN MAP	1731
PITTINGER, N	1871	HAN MAP	1727
PITTSBURG	1852	HEMPFIELD RR	1818
PITTSBURG	1852	HEMPFIELD RR	1820
PITTSBURG	1852	HEMP. RR MAP	1825
PITTSBURG	1852	HEMP. RR MAP	1826
PITTSBURG	1852	HEMP. RR MAP	1827
PITTSBURG / CLEVELAND AND PITTSBURG RR	1871	HAN MAP	1732
PITTSBURG - CINCINNATI & ST.LOUIS RR	1871	HAN MAP	1733
PITTSBURG - CINCINNATI & ST.LOUIS RR	1871	EDGINGTON STA.	1774
PITTSBURG - CINCINNATI & ST.LOUIS RR - BLDGS / INITIALS R.R.CO.	1871	EDGINGTON STA.	1774
PITTSBURG - CINCINNATI & ST.LOUIS RR - BLDGS / INITIALS R.R.CO.	1871	EDGINGTON STA.	1774

LXXVIII

'PERSONAL TIME LINE' INDEX TO VOLUME 7 OF THE *OHIO COUNTY INDEX*

ENTRY	YEAR	SUBJECT	PAGE
PITTSBURG - CINCINNATI & ST.LOUIS RR - BLDGS / INITIALS R.R.CO.	1871	EDGINGTON STA.	1774
PITTSBURG - CINCINNATI & ST.LOUIS RR - WATER TANK	1871	EDGINGTON STA.	1774
PITTSBURG, WHEELING & KY RR CO	1874	DEFENDANT	1609
PITTSBURG, WHEELING & KY RR CO	1874	DEFENDANT	1609
PITTSBURG, WHEELING & KY RR CO	1874	DEFENDANT	1633
PITTSBURG, WHEELING & KY RR CO	1875	DEFENDANT	1609
PITTSBURGH	1916	NAT'L ROAD	1868
PITTSBURGH	1916	NAT'L ROAD	1869
PITTSBURGH, CINCINNATI & ST. LOUIS RR	1871	BRKE MAP	1734
PITTSBURGH, CINCINNATI & ST. LOUIS RR	1871	BRKE MAP	1735
PITTSBURGH, PA	1916	NAT'L ROAD	1861
PLACE WHERE ADAM POE AND BIG FOOT INDIAN FOUGHT	1871	HAN MAP	1726
PLANING MILL - EDGINGTON BRIDGE YARD	1871	BRKE MAP	1734
PLANING MILL - J.W. THAYER	1871	NEW CUMB'LD	1768
PLANK ROAD	1871	LAGRANGE	1792
PLANK ROAD - LAGRANGE	1871	LAGRANGE	1794
PLATTENBURG, J W	1871	NEW MANCH.	1763
PLEASANT COVE	1871	OH CO. MAP	1740
PLEASANT HHOME - SAND HILL TWP	1871	MARH'L MAP	1747
PLEASANT HILL	1871	HAN MAP	1731
PLEASANT HILL	1871	HAN MAP	1732
PLEASANT HILL	1871	OH CO. MAP	1740
PLEASANT HILL - CAMERON TWP	1871	MARH'L MAP	1753
PLEASANT HILL - CLAY TWP	1871	MARH'L MAP	1751
PLEASANT HILL FARM	1871	MARH'L MAP	1745
PLEASANT HOME	1871	HAN MAP	1727
PLEASANT HOME	1871	OH CO. MAP	1740
PLEASANT HOME - CLAY TWP	1871	MARH'L MAP	1752
PLEASANT POINT	1871	MARH'L MAP	1745
PLEASANT POINT	1871	MARH'L MAP	1754
PLEASANT POINT	1871	MARH'L MAP	1758
PLEASANT RIDGE	1871	OH CO. MAP	1740
PLEASANT RIDGE	1871	OH CO. MAP	1743
PLEASANT SIDE	1871	OH CO. MAP	1743
PLEASANT SIDE	1871	OH CO. MAP	1744
PLEASANT SIDE / RONEY POINT	1871	RONEY PT.	1783
PLEASANT SPRINGS	1871	HAN MAP	1727
PLEASANT VALE	1871	OH CO. MAP	1740
PLEASANT VALLEY	1871	HAN MAP	1727
PLEASANT VALLEY	1871	OH CO. MAP	1740
PLEASANT VALLEY / 'PLE' LETTERS SHOWING -	1871	MARH'L MAP	1746
PLEASANT VALLEY / MARSHALL CO	1871	DISTANCES	1815
PLEASANT VALLEY - CLAY TWP	1871	MARH'L MAP	1751
PLEASANT VALLEY - DETAIL MAP	1871	TRIAD.TWP.	1781
PLEASANT VALLEY - OHIO CO	1871	OH CO. MAP	1742
PLEASANT VALLEY - POST OFFICE	1871	MARH'L MAP	1749
PLEASANT VALLEY - SAND HILL TWP	1871	MARH'L MAP	1747
PLEASANT VALLEY - SCHOOL NO. 2	1871	MARH'L MAP	1749
PLEASANT VALLEY - STORE IN	1871	MARH'L MAP	1749
PLEASANT VALLEY P.O.	1871	MARH'L MAP	1749
PLEASANT VALLEY P.O. - BLACKSMITH SHOP	1871	MARH'L MAP	1749
PLEASANT VIEW	1871	HAN MAP	1726
PLEASANT VIEW / E. OF NESLY ISLAND	1871	HAN MAP	1726
PLEASANT VIEW	1871	HAN MAP	1727
PLEASANT VIEW	1871	HAN MAP	1732
PLEASANT VIEW	1871	OH CO. MAP	1740
PLEASANT VIEW	1871	OH CO. MAP	1743
PLEASANT VIEW / UNION TWP - MARSHALL CO	1871	MARH'L MAP	1745
PLEASANT VIEW / SAND HILL TWP	1871	MARH'L MAP	1746
PLEASANT VIEW - FRANKLING TWP	1871	MARH'L MAP	1754
PLEASANTDALE	1871	MARH'L MAP	1753
PLEASANTDALE - WASHINGTON TWP	1871	MARH'L MAP	1749
PLEASNAT VIEW - CLAY TWP	1871	MARH'L MAP	1752
PLESSENBURG, J	1871	WELLSBURG	1777
PLUNKETT, FRANCIS	1840	DEFENDANT	1661
POAG, ELIJAH / MAP#31	1852	BRKE MAP	1840
POAK, JOHN	1822	DEFENDANT	1578
POE TOWNSHIP - HANCOCK CO	1871	NEW MANCH.	1769
POE TOWNSHIP - HANCOCK CO	1871	POPULATION	1816
POE TOWNSHIP - HANCOCK CO - BUSINESS LISTINGS	1871	HAN-POE TWP	1763
POE TOWNSHIP LINE - HANCOCK CO	1871	RIV. RD N.OF N.C.	1770
POE, ADAM / PLACE WHERE ADAM POE AND BIG FOOT INDIAN FOUGHT	1871	HAN MAP	1726
POGUE, E	1871	OH CO. MAP	1741
POINT MILL STATION	1871	OH CO. MAP	1740
POINT MILL STATION	1871	OH CO. MAP	1743
POINT MILL STATION - DEPOT & WAREROOM / ?WAREHOUSE?	1871	OH CO. MAP	1740
POINT MILL STATION - DEPOT & WAREROOM / ?WAREHOUSE?	1871	OH CO. MAP	1743
POINT MILLS STATION - MAP	1916	NAT'L ROAD	1863
POINT PLEASANT / SAND HILL TWP	1871	MARH'L MAP	1746
POINT ROCKS	1871	OH CO. MAP	1743
POINT RUN	1871	OH CO. MAP	1740
POINT RUN	1871	OH CO. MAP	1743
POINT RUN	1871	OH CO. MAP	1744
POLEASANT VALE / N. OF RONEY POINT	1871	OH CO. MAP	1743
POLEN, - / MILLER & POLEN	1871	BRKE MAP	1734
POLEN, - / MILLER & POLEN	1871	CROSS CRK.BUS.	1772
POLEN, - / MILLER & POLEN	1871	EDGINGTON STA.	1774
POLL BOOKS	1860	MISC	1698
POLLACK, STEPHEN	1828	MISC	1682
POLLAR, STEVENSON & CO	1860	DEFENDANT	1631
POLLARD & STEPHENSON	1858	DEFENDANT	1630
POLLARD STEVENSON & CO	1862	DEFENDANT	1631
POLLARD, MCCORMICH	1858	DEFENDANT	1626
POLLARD, MCCORMICH	1858	DEFENDANT	1630
POLLARD, MCCORMICH	1858	DEFENDANT	1581
POLLARD, MCCORMICK	1858	DEFENDANT	1602
POLLARD, MCCORMICK	1858	DEFENDANT	1604
POLLARD, MCCORMICK	1858	DEFENDANT	1623
POLLOCH, JOHN	1792	DEFENDANT	1598
POLLOCK, -	1797	MISC	1701
POLLOCK, J N	1871	OH CO. MAP	1740
POLLOCK, J N / INITIALS J N P .	1871	OH CO. MAP	1740
POLLOCK, JOHN	1788	DEFENDANT	1600
POLLOCK, JOHN	1791	DEFENDANT	1556
POLLOCK, JOSEPH	1836	DEFENDANT	1618
POLLOCK, W	1871	OH CO. MAP	1740
POLLY, T	1871	MARH'L MAP	1753
POLLY, T	1871	MARH'L MAP	1756
POLSTON, ASA	1838	DEFENDANT	1672
POMEROY, J S	1871	NEW MANCH.	1769
POMEROY, J S / INITIALS J.S.P.	1871	NEW MANCH.	1769
POMEROY, JOSIAH W	1838	DEFENDANT	1568
POND - CAMERON	1871	CAMERON	1802
POND - NEAR OHIO RIVER	1871	BRKE MAP	1735
POOL BENJAMIN H	1871	BRKE MAP	1734
POOL E	1871	BRKE MAP	1734
POOL, A J	1871	WELLSBURG	1777
POOL, BENJAMIN / MAP#654	1852	BRKE MAP	1853
POOL, R / MISS	1871	BRKE MAP	1734
POOL, R B / (?R.E.?)	1871	BRKE MAP	1734
POOL, R E / (?R.B.?)	1871	BRKE MAP	1734
POOL, WILLIAM / MAP#523	1852	BRKE MAP	1852
POOLE, J B	1871	BRKE MAP	1734
POOR HOUSE - WASHINGTON TWP	1871	MARH'L MAP	1748
POPLAR HILL	1871	OH CO. MAP	1740
POPLAR SPRING	1871	MARH'L MAP	1753
PORT HOMER	1871	HAN MAP	1730
PORTABLE SAW MILL - MCCONELS & EDWARDS PORTABLE SAW MILL	1871	MARH'L MAP	1749
PORTER & BIGHAM	1871	NEW CUMB'LD	1767
PORTER & SMITH	1871	RIV. RD S.OF N.C.	1763
PORTER & SMITH	1871	RIV. RD S.OF N.C.	1771
PORTER & SMITH / INITIALS P. & S.	1871	RIV. RD S.OF N.C.	1771
PORTER & SMITH - BLACK HORSE FIRE BRICK WORKS	1871	RIV. RD S.OF N.C.	1771
PORTER & SMITH - SEWER PIPE & TERRACOTTA WORKS	1871	RIV. RD S.OF N.C.	1771
PORTER AND SMITH COAL	1871	HAN MAP	1731
PORTER, - / MRS - E SIDE OF MAP	1871	HAN MAP	1730
PORTER, - / MRS - W OF MAP	1871	HAN MAP	1731
PORTER, - / SMITH, PORTER & CO.	1871	RIV. RD N.OF N.C.	1763
PORTER, - / SMITH, PORTER & CO.	1871	RIV. RD S.OF N.C.	1763
PORTER, - / SMITH, PORTER & CO.	1871	RIV. RD S.OF N.C.	1763
PORTER, - / SMITH, PORTER & CO.	1871	NEW CUMB'LD	1766
PORTER, - / SMITH, PORTER & CO.	1871	RIV. RD N.OF N.C.	1770
PORTER, - / SMITH, PORTER & CO.	1871	RIV. RD N.OF N.C.	1770
PORTER, - / MRS	1871	RIV. RD S.OF N.C.	1771
PORTER, - / SMITH, PORTER & CO.	1871	RIV. RD S.OF N.C.	1771
PORTER, - / MRS	1871	MDSVILLE	1807
PORTER, A	1871	MARH'L MAP	1746
PORTER, ANDERSON & CO	1871	FRE'MAN'S LDG	1765
PORTER, ANDERSON & CO / INITIALS P.A.& CO.	1871	FRE'MAN'S LDG	1765
PORTER, ANDERSON &CO	1871	FRE'MAN'S LDG	1762
PORTER, E / MRS	1871	NEW CUMB'LD	1768
PORTER, G	1871	MDSVILLE	1807

LXXIX

'PERSONAL TIME LINE' INDEX TO VOLUME 7 OF THE OHIO COUNTY INDEX

ENTRY	YEAR	SUBJECT	PAGE	ENTRY	YEAR	SUBJECT	PAGE
PORTER, G R / RES - ON OHIO RIVER	1871	FRE'MAN'S LDG	1764	POWELL, J	1871	OH CO. MAP	1743
PORTER, H	1871	NEW CUMB'LD	1768	POWELL, JAMES	1799	DEFENDANT	1556
PORTER, J	1871	OH CO. MAP	1740	POWELL, JANE	1849	MISC	1680
PORTER, J	1871	OH CO. MAP	1740	POWELL, L	1871	OH CO. MAP	1743
PORTER, J / & CO.	1871	FRE'MAN'S LDG	1764	POWELL, M / MRS	1871	MDSVILLE	1807
PORTER, J / & CO. - INITIALS J.P. & CO.	1871	FRE'MAN'S LDG	1764	POWELL, T M	1871	MARH'L MAP	1752
PORTER, J	1871	MDSVILLE	1807	POWELL, WILLIAM O	1833	DEFENDANT	1620
PORTER, J C	1871	OH CO. MAP	1740	POWERS, J	1871	MARH'L MAP	1761
PORTER, JASPER M / E SIDE OF MAP	1871	HAN MAP	1730	POWERS, J	1871	MARH'L MAP	1761
PORTER, JASPER M / W SIDE OF MAP	1871	HAN MAP	1731	POWERS, RICHARD	1796	DEFENDANT	1556
PORTER, JASPER M	1871	RIV. RD S. OF N.C.	1771	POYLS, GEORGE	1828	MISC	1678
PORTER, JOHN	1852	DEFENDANT	1581	PRAGER, J D	1879	DEFENDANT	1641
PORTER, JOHN / E SIDE OF MAP	1871	HAN MAP	1730	PRALL, WILLIAM	1839	DEFENDANT	1592
PORTER, JOHN / W SIDE OF MAP	1871	HAN MAP	1731	PRATHER, - / ?	1871	WELLSBURG	1777
PORTER, JOHN / & CO.	1871	FRE'MAN'S LDG	1762	PRATHER, G	1871	WELLSBURG	1777
PORTER, JOHN / AGENT	1871	FRE'MAN'S LDG	1762	PRATHER, JOHN / MAP#400	1852	BRKE MAP	1846
PORTER, JOHN / WORKS AT PORTERS LANDING	1871	FRE'MAN'S LDG	1762	PRATHERS RUN	1852	BRKE MAP	1846
				PRATT, E L	1858	DEFENDANT	1616
PORTER, JOHN / & CO. - FIRE BRICK WORKS	1871	FRE'MAN'S LDG	1764	PRATT, EDWARD L	1856	DEFENDANT	1568
				PRATT, R	1858	DEFENDANT	1616
PORTER, JOHN	1871	RIV. RD S. OF N.C.	1771	PRATT, RICHARD	1837	DEFENDANT	1651
PORTER, L	1871	MARH'L MAP	1752	PRATT, RICHARD	1837	DEFENDANT	1651
PORTER, L	1871	MARH'L MAP	1752	PRATT, RICHARD	1839	DEFENDANT	1651
PORTER, L	1871	MARH'L MAP	1755	PRATT, ROBERT	1839	DEFENDANT	1643
PORTER, L	1871	ROSBBYS RK	1813	PRAVE, LEWIS	1788	DEFENDANT	1665
PORTER, L / INITIALS L.P.	1871	ROSBBYS RK	1813	PREFACE - VOL.7	2000	PREFACE	1547
PORTER, L / INITIALS L.P.	1871	ROSBBYS RK	1813	PRESBURY, OCTAY. / MILL - MAP#15	1852	BRKE MAP	1839
PORTER, L / INITIALS L.P. - GIRST MILL	1871	ROSBBYS RK	1813	PRESBURY, OCTAY. / MILL - MAP#79	1852	BRKE MAP	1839
				PRESBURY, OCTAY. / MILL - MAP#80	1852	BRKE MAP	1839
PORTER, M	1871	MARH'L MAP	1753	PRESBYTERIAN CHURCH / & CEMETERY - PLEASANT HILL	1871	HAN MAP	1732
PORTER, M	1871	MARH'L MAP	1756				
PORTER, R / E SIDE OF MAP	1871	HAN MAP	1730	PRESBYTERIAN CHURCH	1871	HAN MAP	1733
PORTER, R / W. SIDE OF MAP	1871	HAN MAP	1731	PRESBYTERIAN CHURCH - CAMERON	1871	CAMERON	1803
PORTER, R	1871	RIV. RD S. OF N.C.	1771	PRESBYTERIAN CHURCH - FOURTH ST	1871	WHG CITY	1788
PORTER, R	1871	RIV. RD S. OF N.C.	1771				
PORTER, SMITH & CO	1871	NEW CUMB'LD	1766	PRESBYTERIAN CHURCH - HAMPDEN ST	1871	WHG CITY	1788
PORTER, SMITH & CO	1871	NEW CUMB'LD	1766				
PORTER, SMITH & CO / INITIALS P.S. & CO	1871	NEW CUMB'LD	1766	PRESBYTERIAN CHURCH - HARRISON ST - NEW CUMBERLAND	1871	NEW CUMB'LD	1768
PORTER, W	1871	MARH'L MAP	1748	PRESBYTERIAN CHURCH - INITIALS P. CHURCH - S. OF W. MCKINLEY	1871	BKE/OH MAP	1738
PORTER, W	1871	MDSVILLE	1807				
PORTER, WILLIAM	1871	OH CO. MAP	1742	PRESBYTERIAN CHURCH - LIMESTONE	1871	MARH'L MAP	1749
PORTER, WILLIAM / INITIALS W.P.	1871	OH CO. MAP	1742				
PORTER, WILLIAM / INITIALS W.P.	1871	OH CO. MAP	1742	PRESBYTERIAN CHURCH - LIMESTONE P.O.	1871	LIMESTONE	1805
PORTER, WILLIAM	1871	OH CO. BUS.	1779				
PORTER, WILLIAM / COAL	1871	TRIAD.TWP.	1781	PRESBYTERIAN CHURCH - MAIN ST	1871	WHG CITY	1788
PORTER, WILLIAM / INITIALS W.P.	1871	TRIAD.TWP.	1781	PRESBYTERIAN CHURCH - MAIN ST - WHEELING	1871	WHG CITY	1786
PORTERS LANDING	1871	FRE'MAN'S LDG	1762				
PORTERS LANDING - OHIO RIVER	1871	FRE'MAN'S LDG	1764	PRESBYTERIAN CHURCH - MARKET ST	1871	WHG CITY	1790
PORTLAND, OH	1852	BRKE MAP	1839				
PORTSMOUTH, OH	1852	HEMPFIELD RR	1820	PRESBYTERIAN CHURCH - MOUND ST - MOUNDSVILLE	1871	MDSVILLE	1809
PORTSMOUTH, OH	1852	HEMP. RR MAP	1826				
POST OFFICE - BELLTON	1871	MARH'L MAP	1761	PRESBYTERIAN CHURCH - PARSONAGE / URANA ST.	1871	WELLSBURG	1777
POST OFFICE - CAMERON	1871	CAMERON	1803				
POST OFFICE - CLINTON	1871	OH CO. MAP	1741	PRESBYTERIAN CHURCH - QUEEN ST	1871	WELLSBURG	1777
POST OFFICE - ELM GROVE STATION	1871	ELM GROVE	1782	PRESBYTERIAN CHURCH - ROCK LICK P.O.	1871	MARH'L MAP	1753
POST OFFICE - ELM GROVE STATION	1871	ELM GROVE	1782				
POST OFFICE - HOLLIDAYS COVE	1871	HAN MAP	1733	PRESBYTERIAN CHURCH - S. WHG	1871	SOUTH WHG	1792
POST OFFICE - HOLLIDAYS COVE	1871	BRKE MAP	1735	PRESBYTERIAN CHURCH - SECOND ST - MOUNDSVILLE	1871	MDSVL BUS.	1796
POST OFFICE - MAGEE & WILSON / STORE AND P.O.	1871	FRE'MAN'S LDG	1764				
				PRESBYTERIAN CHURCH - W. OF MARLOW RUN	1871	OH CO. MAP	1743
POST OFFICE - NEW MANCHESTER	1871	NEW MANCH.	1769				
POST OFFICE - PLEASANT VALLEY P.O.	1871	MARH'L MAP	1749	PRESBYTERIAN CHURCH - WEBSTER ST	1871	WHG CITY	1788
POST OFFICE - SHERARD / E. SIDE OF MAP	1871	MARH'L MAP	1745	PRESBYTERIAN CHURCH & CEMETERY / STONE CHURCH	1871	OH CO. MAP	1742
POST OFFICE - SHERRARD P.O.	1871	SHERRARD	1811	PRESBYTERIAN CHURCH & CEMETERY - SHERRARD P.O.	1871	MARH'L MAP	1746
POST OFFICE - TRIADELPHIA	1871	TRIAD.BORO.	1784				
POST OFFICE - WELLSBURG	1871	WELLSBURG	1777	PRESBYTERIAN CHURCH & CEMETERY - SHERRARD P.O.	1871	SHERRARD	1811
POST OFFICE - WEST LIBERTY	1871	W.LIBERTY	1780				
POST OFFICE - WHEELING CITY / AT CUSTOM HOUSE	1871	WHG CITY	1788	PRESBYTERIAN CHURCH & CEMETERY - WEST UNION	1871	MARH'L MAP	1747
POTTER, SAMUEL	1807	DEFENDANT	1626	PRESBYTERIAN CHURCH & CEMETERY - WEST UNION	1871	W. UNION	1812
POTTERS CLAY / S. OF LOCUST GROVE	1871	HAN MAP	1726				
				PRESCOTT, LEVI	1829	DEFENDANT	1589
POTTERS RIDGE	1871	MARH'L MAP	1752	PRESCOTT, LEVI	1829	DEFENDANT	1639
POTTERY / FACTORY	1871	FRE'MAN'S LDG	1764	PRESCOTT, WILLIAM W	1838	DEFENDANT	1583
POTTMAN, JACOB	1821	DEFENDANT	1668	PRESCOTT, WILLIAM W	1838	DEFENDANT	1626
POTTS, J B / GRIST MILL	1871	MARH'L MAP	1752	PRESTON, DANIEL	1787	DEFENDANT	1600
POTTS, J B / INITIALS J.B.P.	1871	MARH'L MAP	1752	PRETTYMAN, JOB	1816	DEFENDANT	1656
POTTS, JAMES	1793	DEFENDANT	1567	PRETTYMAN, JOB	1822	DEFENDANT	1635
POTTS, JAMES	1796	DEFENDANT	1587	PRETTYMAN, R	1871	TRIAD.BORO.	1784
POUNDS, J	1871	MARH'L MAP	1755	PRETTYMAN, R / INITIALS R.P.	1871	TRIAD.BORO.	1784
POWDER HOUSE	1871	WHG CITY	1789	PREVIEW - VOL. 7A - CUMULATIVE INDEX	2000	APPENDIX	1875
POWELL, G	1871	MARH'L MAP	1745				
POWELL, G	1871	MARH'L MAP	1748	PRICE, -	1834	MISC	1696

LXXX

'PERSONAL TIME LINE' INDEX TO VOLUME 7 OF THE *OHIO COUNTY INDEX*

ENTRY	YEAR	SUBJECT	PAGE	ENTRY	YEAR	SUBJECT	PAGE
PRICE, -	1836	PLAINTIFF	1628	PURDY, S S / EST.	1871	MARH'L MAP	1751
PRICE, - / MRS	1871	MARH'L MAP	1749	PURDY, SIMON	1832	PLAINTIFF	1573
PRICE, A	1871	MARH'L MAP	1758	PURL, SETH	1832	DEFENDANT	1628
PRICE, A D	1871	MARH'L MAP	1748	PURL, SETH	1834	DEFENDANT	1662
PRICE, A T / MRS	1871	MDSVILLE	1807	PUSEY, C	1871	HAN MAP	1728
PRICE, A T / MRS	1871	MDSVILLE	1807	PUSEY, W C	1871	HAN MAP	1727
PRICE, A T / MRS - INITIALS MRS. A.T.P.	1871	MDSVILLE	1807	PYATT, DAVID	1805	PLAINTIFF	1579
				PYLES, G	1871	MARH'L MAP	1760
PRICE, B W	1871	MARH'L MAP	1748	PYLES, J	1871	MARH'L MAP	1761
PRICE, BUSHROD W	1834	DEFENDANT	1618	PYLES, M	1871	MARH'L MAP	1761
PRICE, BUSHROD W	1834	DEFENDANT	1618	PYLES, M / RES	1871	MARH'L MAP	1761
PRICE, BUSHROD W	1835	DEFENDANT	1577	PYLES, W	1871	MARH'L MAP	1761
PRICE, BUSROD W	1835	DEFENDANT	1626	QUARRIER, WILLIAM	1845	MISC	1674
PRICE, D	1871	MARH'L MAP	1753	QUARRIER, WILLIAM B	1839	MISC	1674
PRICE, E	1871	MARH'L MAP	1758	QUARRY - FLAG HO. STONE QUARRY / HOUSE ? (?FLAGSTONE FOR HOMES?)	1871	MARH'L MAP	1752
PRICE, J	1871	MARH'L MAP	1745				
PRICE, J M	1871	MARH'L MAP	1748				
PRICE, J M	1871	MARH'L MAP	1752	QUARRY - FLAG QUARRY	1871	HAN MAP	1726
PRICE, M B	1871	MDSVILLE	1808	QUARRY - FLAG QUARRY	1871	OH CO. MAP	1742
PRICE, R W	1871	MARH'L MAP	1748	QUARRY - FLAG QUARRY - CALDWELLS RUN	1871	OH CO. MAP	1742
PRICE, S	1871	MARH'L MAP	1749				
PRICE, T J	1871	MARH'L MAP	1749	QUARRY - FLAG QUARRY #2 -N OF PLEASANT VIEW	1871	HAN MAP	1726
PRICE, WILLIAM	1778	MISC	1687				
PRINTICE, F	1871	BENWOOD	1798	QUARRY - FLAGG QUARRY	1871	WHG CITY	1787
PRISON CEMETERY - MOUNDSVILLE	1871	MDSVILLE	1809	QUARRY - FLAG QUARRY - N. OF BROWNLEE SCHOOL NO.1	1871	OH CO. MAP	1743
PRITCHARD, WILLIAM	1819	DEFENDANT	1572				
PROBASCO, J W	1871	MDSVILLE	1810	QUARRY - N OF WHITE OAK GROVE	1871	HAN MAP	1727
PROBASCO, J W / INITIALS J.W.P.	1871	MDSVILLE	1810	QUARRY - STONE QUARRY / CUT OFF TOP OF MAP	1871	MARH'L MAP	1756
PROBASCO, J W / INITIALS J.W.P.	1871	MDSVILLE	1810				
PROBASCO, JOHN	1827	DEFENDANT	1581	QUARRY - STONE QUARRY - AT ANDERSONS LANDING	1871	FRE'MAN'S LDG	1764
PROPOSED ROAD	1871	OH CO. MAP	1743				
PROSPECT HILL	1871	BKE/OH MAP	1739	QUARRY - STONE QUARRY - E. OF SUMMIT FARM	1871	OH CO. MAP	1742
PROSSER, C	1871	NEW CUMB'LD	1767				
PROSSER, E	1871	HAN MAP	1726	QUARRY - STONE QUARRY - N. OF FAIRVIEW	1871	MARH'L MAP	1748
PROSSER, J	1871	HAN MAP	1726				
PROSSER, J	1871	HAN MAP	1726	QUARRY - STONE QUARRY - N. OF J. TRUSSELL	1871	OH CO. MAP	1743
PROSSER, J A	1871	NEW CUMB'LD	1767				
PROSSER, R	1871	HAN MAP	1726	QUARRY - STONE QUARRY - N. OF L.B. PURDY	1871	MARH'L MAP	1752
PROSSER, S	1871	HAN MAP	1726				
PROVERS ROAD / (?DROVERS?)	1871	BKE/OH MAP	1739	QUARRY - STONE QUARRY - N. OF RONEY POINT SCHOOL	1871	OH CO. MAP	1743
PROVIDENCE MOUNTS	1816	MISC	1701				
PRYOR, C J / MRS (?OR G.J.?)	1871	OH CO. MAP	1742	QUARRY - STONE QUARRY - N. OF W. DUNLAP	1871	MARH'L MAP	1749
PRYOR, J	1871	OH CO. MAP	1744				
PUGH, A C	1871	HAN MAP	1728	QUARRY - STONE QUARRY - N. OF W. DUNLAP	1871	MARH'L MAP	1752
PUGH, A G	1871	HAN MAP	1727				
PUGH, A G	1871	HAN MAP	1728	QUARRY - STONE QUARRY - NE. OF GLEN EASTON	1871	MARH'L MAP	1752
PUGH, A.C.	1871	HAN MAP	1727				
PUGH, D	1871	HAN MAP	1731	QUARRY - STONE QUARRY - NW OF RONEY POINT	1871	OH CO. MAP	1744
PUGH, G H / GRIST MILL ON TOMLINSON RUN	1871	HAN MAP	1731				
				QUARRY - STONE QUARRY - NW OF TRIADELPHIA	1871	OH CO. MAP	1743
PUGH, H	1871	HAN MAP	1731				
PUGH, J H	1871	NEW MANCH.	1769	QUARRY - STONE QUARRY - S. OF J. CUNNINGHAM	1871	MARH'L MAP	1749
PUGH, P D	1871	HAN MAP	1727				
PUGH, P D	1871	HAN MAP	1731	QUARRY - STONE QUARRY - S. OF J.S. GARVIN	1871	MARH'L MAP	1746
PUGH, R W	1871	HAN MAP	1731				
PUGH, WILLIAM H	1871	NEW MANCH.	1763	QUARRY - STONE QUARRY - S. OF T.MCMILLIAN	1871	MARH'L MAP	1750
PUMFREY, RESIN	1785	DEFENDANT	1571				
PUMFRY, -	1786	DEFENDANT	1571	QUARRY - STONE QUARRY - SW OF BARTLETT STATION	1871	MARH'L MAP	1752
PUMPHREY & HULL	1860	DEFENDANT	1574				
PUMPHREY, GEORGE	1858	DEFENDANT	1584	QUARRY - STONE QUARRY - SW. OF FIARVIEW - WASHINGTON TWP	1871	MARH'L MAP	1748
PUMPHREY, GEORGE W	1850	DEFENDANT	1629				
PUMPHREY, GEORGE W	1860	DEFENDANT	1588	QUARRY - STONE QUARRY - TRIADELPHIA	1871	OH CO. MAP	1744
PUMPHREY, REASON	1826	DEFENDANT	1554				
PUMPHREY, REASON	1832	DEFENDANT	1589	QUARRY - YACKER, J / STONE QUARRY	1871	OH CO. MAP	1742
PUMPHREY, ZACHARIAH	1830	DEFENDANT	1669				
PUNTNEY, JAMES	1871	BRKE MAP	1735	QUEENS RUN	1871	BRKE MAP	1736
PUNTNEY, JAMES / TIMBERLAND	1871	BRKE MAP	1735				
PURDY & HOGAN	1871	MARH'L MAP	1751	QUEER, M / MRS	1871	NEW CUMB'LD	1767
PURDY & HOGAN	1871	MDSVILLE	1808	QUEST, S S	1871	WELLSBURG	1778
PURDY & HOGAN	1871	MDSVILLE	1810	QUEST, S S / MRS	1871	WELLSBURG	1778
PURDY, - / MRS - MARSHALL ST (?OR HARDY?)	1871	MDSVILLE	1808	QUIET HOME / S. MCHENRY	1871	HAN MAP	1727
				QUIET HOME	1871	OH CO. MAP	1740
PURDY, - / MRS	1871	MDSVILLE	1810	QUIET HOME / J.S. GRVIN	1871	OH CO. MAP	1742
PURDY, - / MRS - MARSHALL ST (?OR HARDY?)	1871	MDSVILLE	1810	QUIET HOME / J.S. GRVIN	1871	OH CO. MAP	1742
				QUIET HOME / J.S. GARVIN	1871	MARH'L MAP	1746
PURDY, GEORGE H	1871	MDSVILLE	1810	QUIET HOME / J.W. DAVIS	1871	MARH'L MAP	1746
PURDY, J	1871	MDSVILLE	1809	QUIGLEY, GEORGE	1813	MISC	1689
PURDY, J B / ? INITIALS J.B.P.EST. ?	1871	MARH'L MAP	1752	QUIGLEY, J	1871	MARH'L MAP	1757
PURDY, JAMES	1871	HAN MAP	1732	QUINLAN - CHILDREN	1861	MISC	1698
PURDY, L B / RES.	1871	MARH'L MAP	1752	QUINLIN - CHILDREN	1859	MISC	1698
PURDY, S B / EST.	1871	MARH'L MAP	1748	QUINN, GEORGE	1809	DEFENDANT	1575
PURDY, S B / EST	1871	MDSVILLE	1808	QUINN, JOHN	1801	DEFENDANT	1634
PURDY, S B / EST.	1871	MDSVILLE	1810	QUINN, JOHN	1803	DEFENDANT	1635
PURDY, S B / EST.	1871	MDSVILLE	1810	QUINN, MATTHEW	1804	DEFENDANT	1635
PURDY, S M / MRS	1871	MDSVILLE	1809	QUINTER, ELI	1824	DEFENDANT	1591
PURDY, S S / EST	1871	MARH'L MAP	1748	R, - / B.R. CO. / PAN-HANDLE P.O.	1871	BRKE MAP	1734

'PERSONAL TIME LINE' INDEX TO VOLUME 7 OF THE *OHIO COUNTY INDEX*

ENTRY	YEAR	SUBJECT	PAGE
R, J C / UNKNOWN INITILAS - MARKET ST	1871	MDSVILLE	1807
R, WILLIAM / ? WILLIAM RODGERS - INITIALS WM. R	1871	BKE/OH MAP	1739
R.B. / INITIALS - R. BONAR ?	1871	BKE/OH MAP	1738
R.B. / INITIALS - R. BONAR ?	1871	BKE/OH MAP	1738
R.B.C / UNKNOWN INITIALS	1871	MARH'L MAP	1748
R.R.CO. / 3 - B&O RR BUILDINGS NEAR FARMERS HOME	1871	MARH'L MAP	1757
R.S. / INITIALS FOR R.SHERFY	1871	MARH'L MAP	1756
R.W. / (?INITIALS FOR RICHARD WELLS?)	1871	BRKE MAP	1734
RADCLIFF, RICHARD	1861	DEFENDANT	1654
RAIL ROAD SYSTEM	1852	HEMPFIELD RR	1819
RAILROAD - GRADIENTS ON MAP	1852	HEMP. RR MAP	1825
RAILROAD - HEMPFIELD RR CO.	1871	OH CO. MAP	1740
RAILROAD - IN OHIO	1852	HEMP. RR MAP	1826
RAILROAD - IN PENNSYLVANIA	1852	HEMP. RR MAP	1826
RAILROAD - IN VA (WVA)	1852	HEMP. RR MAP	1826
RAILROAD BRIDGE MFG	1871	CROSS CRK.BUS.	1772
RAILROAD CO. - EDGINGTON STATION	1871	BRKE MAP	1734
RAILROAD HISTORY - HEMPFIELD RR BOND PROPOSAL WITH RIVAL & TRIBUTARY RR SYSTEMS	1852	HEMPFIELD RR	1817
RAILROAD MILEAGE CHART - PHILADELPHIA TO CINCINNATI	1852	HEMP. RR MAP	1825
RALSTON & CO / (?SAW MILL ON FISH CREEK?)	1871	MARH'L MAP	1761
RALSTON MILLS - BUTLER TWP	1871	HAN-BUTL'R TWP	1763
RALSTON, - / MRS	1871	NEW MANCH.	1769
RALSTON, A	1871	HAN MAP	1732
RALSTON, GEORGE	1871	HAN MAP	1732
RALSTON, GEORGE	1871	HAN MAP	1732
RALSTON, JAMES	1871	HAN MAP	1732
RALSTON, JEREMIAH	1871	HAN MAP	1732
RALSTON, R	1871	HAN MAP	1732
RALSTON, S	1871	WELLSBURG	1777
RALSTON, SAMUEL	1871	HAN MAP	1732
RALSTON, THOMAS H	1871	HAN MAP	1732
RALSTON, THOMAS H	1871	HAN-BUTL'R TWP	1763
RALSTON, W	1871	HAN MAP	1732
RAMAT, ALLAN	1834	MISC	1696
RAMKAY, WILLIAM	1871	MARH'L MAP	1745
RAMSAY, W	1871	HAN MAP	1732
RAMSEY, - / MRS	1871	MARH'L MAP	1755
RAMSEY, J	1871	BENWOOD	1798
RAMSEY, W	1871	MARH'L MAP	1746
RANDALL, R W / & CO	1827	DEFENDANT	1579
RANDALL, R W / & CO	1830	DEFENDANT	1579
RANDALL, R W	1834	DEFENDANT	1579
RANDAM, LEONARD	1842	DEFENDANT	1618
RANEY, - / HRS - HEIRS	1871	WELLSBURG	1777
RANKIN, JOHN	1857	DEFENDANT	1586
RANKINVILLE / NOW WEST WASHINGTON, PA	1916	NAT'L ROAD	1861
RANNEY, - / HRS - HEIRS (O)	1871	WELLSBURG	1777
RANSAM, IRA	1852	DEFENDANT	1565
RANSAM, IRA	1853	DEFENDANT	1565
RANSOM, J	1871	MDSVILLE	1807
RATCLIFF, JOHN A	1850	DEFENDANT	1641
RAVENSCROFT, R / W. SIDE OF MAP	1871	MARH'L MAP	1746
RAWHEELING VALLEY FARM	1871	MARH'L MAP	1746
RAWLAND, JOHN	1811	DEFENDANT	1595
RAY, - / MRS	1871	WELLSBURG	1778
RAY, - / MRS	1871	MDSVILLE	1809
RAY, ABRAHAM	1860	DEFENDANT	1592
RAY, E / RES	1871	OH CO. MAP	1740
RAY, E / RES	1871	OH CO. MAP	1740
RAY, HIRAM	1841	DEFENDANT	1652
RAY, HIRAM	1862	DEFENDANT	1573
RAY, J	1871	MARH'L MAP	1749
RAY, JAMES	1806	DEFENDANT	1637
RAY, JOHN A	1856	DEFENDANT	1621
RAY, MOSES	1877	DEFENDANT	1558
RAY, PATRICK	1810	PLAINTIFF	1599
RAY, PATRICK	1810	APPENDIX	1873
RAY, PATRICK	1812	DEFENDANT	1553
RAY, THOMAS / HEIRS - MAP#415	1852	BRKE MAP	1846
RAY, W	1871	OH CO. MAP	1740
RAYL, G	1871	MARH'L MAP	1753
RAYLOR, R	1871	MARH'L MAP	1747
REAGER, JACOB	1778	APPENDIX	1874
RED POINT FARM	1871	MARH'L MAP	1746
RED, J	1871	MARH'L MAP	1753
RED, JAMES	1871	MARH'L MAP	1757
RED, S	1871	MARH'L MAP	1753
REDFOX, J	1871	MARH'L MAP	1759
REED, -	1841	DEFENDANT	1553
REED, C H	1871	MARH'L MAP	1761
REED, E	1871	NEW MANCH.	1769
REED, J	1871	OH CO. MAP	1740
REED, J	1871	MARH'L MAP	1746
REED, J	1871	MARH'L MAP	1757
REED, J / BLACKSMITH SHOP - NATL RD	1871	TRIAD TWP.	1781
REED, JAMES	1871	OH CO. MAP	1740
REED, JAMES	1871	MARH'L MAP	1761
REED, M / MRS	1871	MARH'L MAP	1761
REED, O	1871	MARH'L MAP	1761
REED, S / EST	1871	MARH'L MAP	1761
REED, THOMAS	1851	DEFENDANT	1629
REED, WILLIAM	1871	OH CO. MAP	1740
REES, - / WOODBURN REES & CO	1871	CAMERON	1804
REES, - / WOODBURN REES & CO. - BLACKSMITH SHOP / INITIALS W.R.& CO.	1871	CAMERON	1804
REES, - / WOODBURN REES & CO - COOPER SHOP / INITIALS W.R.& CO.	1871	CAMERON	1804
REES, - / WOODBURN REES & CO / INITIALS W.R.& CO.	1871	CAMERON	1804
REES, - / WOODBURN REES & CO / S.G.MILL	1871	CAMERON	1804
REES, WILLIAM H / FLOURING MILL	1871	CAMER'N - BUS.	1795
REES, WILLIAM H / INITIALS W.H. - FIRST NAME FROM BUSINESS NOTICES	1871	CAMERON	1804
REESE, J H	1871	BETHANY	1773
REESIDE, JOHN	1840	DEFENDANT	1619
REESIDE, JOHN	1841	DEFENDANT	1619
REESIDE, JOHN E	1841	DEFENDANT	1614
REEVES, -	1871	OH CO. MAP	1742
REEVES, -	1871	OH CO. MAP	1744
REEVES, - / MRS	1871	WELLSBURG	1777
REEVES, -	1871	ELM GROVE	1782
REEVES, CALEB	1800	DEFENDANT	1665
REEVES, CALEB	1814	DEFENDANT	1563
REEVES, E	1871	WELLSBURG	1777
REEVES, E / MRS	1871	WELLSBURG	1777
REEVES, JOHN C / COAL	1871	BRKE MAP	1735
REEVES, JOHN C / TIMBERLANDS & COAL	1871	BRKE MAP	1735
REEVES, JOHN C / WHITE CLOVER	1871	BRKE MAP	1735
REEVES, NATHAN / MAP#444	1852	BRKE MAP	1849
REEVES, REASON / MAP#416	1852	BRKE MAP	1847
REEVES, REASON / MAP#576	1852	BRKE MAP	1852
REEVES, W	1871	WELLSBURG	1777
REFORMED PRESBYTERIAN CHURCH	1871	HAN MAP	1731
REFORMED PRESBYTERIAN CHURCH - SW OF BROWNLEE SCHOOL NO. 1	1871	OH CO. MAP	1743
REHELDAFFER, WILLIAM	1860	DEFENDANT	1636
REICHARD, -	1831	PLAINTIFF	1628
REID, J	1871	OH CO. MAP	1742
REID, J	1871	OH CO. MAP	1742
REID, J / INITIALS J.R.	1871	OH CO. MAP	1742
REID, J / INITIALS J.R.	1871	OH CO. MAP	1742
REID, J	1871	MARH'L MAP	1756
REID, J	1871	MARH'L MAP	1761
REID, J / INITIALS J.R.	1871	MARH'L MAP	1761
REID, J / INITIALS J.R.	1871	MARH'L MAP	1761
REID, J	1871	WELLSBURG	1777
REIDS RUN	1871	BRKE MAP	1735
REIDS RUN - MOUTH OF AT OHIO RIVER / S. OF CROSS CREEK - HARD TO READ ?	1852	BRKE MAP	1849
REILLY, - / EST.	1871	WHG CITY	1789
REILLY, G W	1871	MARH'L MAP	1745
REILLY, J W / ATTORNEY - WELLSVILLE, OHIO	1871	HAN-GR'NT TWP	1763
REILLY, J W / ATTORNEY - WELLSVILLE, OHIO	1871	NEW MANCH.	1763
REILLY, S	1871	MARH'L MAP	1745
REINHARD, -	1832	PLAINTIFF	1628
REISTER - ORPHANS	1848	MISC	1682
RELEASED FROM PAYING COUNTY LEVY - DEFINED	2000	APPENDIX	1875
RELFE, JAMES	1826	DEFENDANT	1563
RELFE, JOHN	1799	DEFENDANT	1556
RELFE, JOHN	1799	DEFENDANT	1647
RELFE, JOHN	1799	DEFENDANT	1655
RELFE, JOHN	1800	DEFENDANT	1634
RELPE, JOHN	1800	DEFENDANT	1634

'PERSONAL TIME LINE' INDEX TO VOLUME 7 OF THE *OHIO COUNTY INDEX*

ENTRY	YEAR	SUBJECT	PAGE
RELPE, JOHN	1800	DEFENDANT	1647
REMHOFF, A / SHOE SHOP	1871	BENWOOD	1798
RENFORTH, - / MRS - HEIRS	1871	OH CO. MAP	1742
RENFORTH, - / MRS - HEIRS - INITIALS MRS.R. HEIRS	1871	OH CO. MAP	1742
RENFORTH, JAMES	1841	DEFENDANT	1636
RENNER, HERMAN	1858	DEFENDANT	1588
RENNER, HERMAN	1858	DEFENDANT	1626
REPP, CHRISTOPHER	1859	DEFENDANT	1673
RES. / (?ABBREV. FOR RESIDENCE?)	1871	MARH'L MAP	1747
RESSEGER, H	1871	MARH'L MAP	1758
RESSEGER, H / FAIRVIEW WV	1871	FRKLN TWP-BUS.	1797
REUFORTH, T	1871	MARH'L MAP	1746
REVEREND WOODS / HEIRS OF	1871	OH CO. MAP	1741
REVOLUTIONARY WAR - LAST BATTLE OF IN WHEELING	1916	NAT'L ROAD	1867
REWFORT, T / MARSHALL CO BORDER	1871	OH CO. MAP	1742
REYMANN, ANTHONY	1869	MISC	1694
REYNOLDS, E M	1871	CAMERON	1803
REYNOLDS, F M	1871	CAMER'N - BUS.	1795
REYNOLDS, F N / (OC.)	1871	CAMERON	1803
REYNOLDS, J	1871	MARH'L MAP	1754
REYNOLDS, M S	1819	DEFENDANT	1602
REYNOLDS, THOMAS	1822	DEFENDANT	1596
REYNOLDS, THOMAS	1823	DEFENDANT	1596
REYNOLDS, THOMAS	1827	DEFENDANT	1668
REYNOLDS, W	1871	MARH'L MAP	1748
REYNOLDS, W / INITIALS W.R.	1871	MARH'L MAP	1748
REYNOLDS, W / INITIALS W.R.	1871	MARH'L MAP	1748
REYNOLDS, W / INITIALS W.R.	1871	MARH'L MAP	1751
REYNOLDS, WILLIAM B	1838	DEFENDANT	1581
RHODES, MOSES	1840	DEFENDANT	1614
RHODES, W P	1871	MDSVILLE	1808
RIC, D	1871	MARH'L MAP	1747
RICE, -	1786	PLAINTIFF	1628
RICE, ALBERT	1862	DEFENDANT	1558
RICE, G / RES	1871	OH CO. MAP	1740
RICE, G / RES	1871	OH CO. MAP	1740
RICE, J A	1871	MARH'L MAP	1761
RICE, J A	1871	MARH'L MAP	1761
RICE, J A	1871	LIB.TWP-BUS.	1797
RICE, JAMES A	1871	MARH'L MAP	1757
RICE, JOSEPH	1805	DEFENDANT	1644
RICE, L	1871	GLEN EASTON	1801
RICE, STEPHEN	1841	DEFENDANT	1580
RICE, STEPHEN	1841	DEFENDANT	1626
RICE, STEPHEN	1841	DEFENDANT	1629
RICE, STEPHEN	1841	DEFENDANT	1656
RICE, STEPHEN	1856	DEFENDANT	1630
RICE, STEPHEN	1856	DEFENDANT	1653
RICE, STEPHEN	1856	DEFENDANT	1670
RICE, WILLIAM	1871	OH CO. MAP	1740
RICE, WILLIAM / RES	1871	OH CO. MAP	1740
RICHARDS, ANN	1841	DEFENDANT	1661
RICHARDS, ANN	1846	DEFENDANT	1661
RICHARDS, ASA	1829	DEFENDANT	1613
RICHARDS, J M	1871	OH CO. MAP	1742
RICHARDS, J M / TOP OF MAP - ONLY J.M. SHOWING	1871	MARH'L MAP	1745
RICHARDS, J M / TOP OF MAP	1871	MARH'L MAP	1746
RICHARDS, R / W (?WAGON?) SHOP	1871	BRKE MAP	1734
RICHARDS, S C	1841	DEFENDANT	1623
RICHARDS, SAMUEL	1834	DEFENDANT	1622
RICHARDS, SAMUEL	1836	DEFENDANT	1622
RICHARDS, SAMUEL C	1834	DEFENDANT	1618
RICHARDS, THOMAS	1800	DEFENDANT	1665
RICHARDSON, - / MEDFORD & RICHARDSON / STORE	1871	CAMERON	1803
RICHARDSON, E S	1871	MARH'L MAP	1754
RICHARDSON, J	1871	HAN MAP	1731
RICHARDSON, R / DOCTOR	1871	BKE/OH MAP	1739
RICHARDSON, ROBERT / MAP#59	1852	BRKE MAP	1840
RICHARDSON, WILLIAM	1878	DEFENDANT	1595
RICHEY, J	1871	MARH'L MAP	1747
RICHEY, J	1871	MARH'L MAP	1750
RICHEY, J	1871	MARH'L MAP	1750
RICHEY, J / INITIALS J.R.	1871	MARH'L MAP	1750
RICHEY, J	1871	MARH'L MAP	1751
RICHIE, C	1871	MARH'L MAP	1760
RICHLAND DIST SCHOOL NO. 6	1871	OH CO. MAP	1741
RICHLAND TOWNSHIP - MARSHALL CO - BUSINESS NOTICES	1871	MARH'L BUS.	1797
RICHLAND TOWNSHIP - OHIO CO	1871	OH CO. MAP	1741
RICHLAND TOWNSHIP - OHIO CO	1871	POPULATION	1816
RICHMAN, B	1871	MARH'L MAP	1747
RICHMAN, I	1871	MARH'L MAP	1756
RICHMAN, J	1871	MARH'L MAP	1747
RICHMAN, J	1871	MARH'L MAP	1750
RICHMAN, J	1871	MARH'L MAP	1756
RICHMAN, J / INITIALS J.R.	1871	MARH'L MAP	1756
RICHMAN, P	1871	MARH'L MAP	1756
RICHMOND, A	1871	MARH'L MAP	1755
RICHMOND, A	1871	MARH'L MAP	1755
RICHMOND, A / INITIALS A.R.	1871	MARH'L MAP	1755
RICHMOND, D	1871	MARH'L MAP	1756
RICHMOND, D	1871	MARH'L MAP	1760
RICHMOND, H	1871	MARH'L MAP	1760
RICHMOND, IN	1916	NAT'L ROAD	1866
RICHMOND, J / RES	1871	MARH'L MAP	1755
RICHMOND, J	1871	MARH'L MAP	1756
RICHMOND, J / RES.	1871	MARH'L MAP	1759
RICHMOND, J	1871	MARH'L MAP	1760
RICHMOND, J JR	1871	MARH'L MAP	1759
RICHMOND, J W	1871	MARH'L MAP	1755
RICHMOND, J W	1871	MARH'L MAP	1755
RICHMOND, JOSEPH	1818	PLAINTIFF	1591
RICHMOND, S	1871	MARH'L MAP	1756
RICHMOND, VA	1852	HEMPFIELD RR	1820
RICHMONT, J	1871	MARH'L MAP	1756
RICHTER, - / DR	1871	GLEN EASTON	1801
RICHTER, A	1871	MARH'L MAP	1756
RICKEY, - / PIPES & RICKEY / DRUG STORE	1871	CAMERON	1803
RICKEY, J W	1871	CAMER'N - BUS.	1795
RIDDEN, JOHN	1828	DEFENDANT	1613
RIDDEN, JOHN	1828	DEFENDANT	1613
RIDDINGS, BENJAMIN	1830	DEFENDANT	1620
RIDDLE, C	1871	WELLSBURG	1778
RIDGE - FORK RIDGE ROAD	1871	MARH'L MAP	1752
RIDGE - POTTERS	1871	MARH'L MAP	1752
RIDGE ROAD - DRY RIDGE ROAD	1871	MARH'L MAP	1750
RIDGE ROAD - FORK RIDGE ROAD	1871	MARH'L MAP	1752
RIDGE ROAD - FORK RIDGE ROAD	1871	MARH'L MAP	1753
RIDGE ROAD - ROBERT RIDGE ROAD/ CLAY TWP	1871	MARH'L MAP	1751
RIDGE ROAD - ROBERTS RIDGE ROAD	1871	MARH'L MAP	1755
RIDGE ROAD - TO INDEPENDENCE	1871	BRKE MAP	1737
RIDGE ROAD - WAYMAN RIDGE ROAD	1871	MARH'L MAP	1749
RIDGE ROAD - WAYMAN RIDGE ROAD	1871	MARH'L MAP	1752
RIDGELEY, H	1871	BKE/OH MAP	1739
RIDGELEY, H / INITIALS H.R.	1871	BKE/OH MAP	1739
RIDGELEY, H / INITIALS H.R.	1871	OH CO. MAP	1740
RIDGELEY, JAMES	1871	BKE/OH MAP	1738
RIDGELEY, JAMES	1871	BKE/OH MAP	1738
RIDGELY, A	1871	OH CO. MAP	1741
RIDGELY, A / INITIALS A.R.	1871	OH CO. MAP	1741
RIDGELY, A JR	1841	DEFENDANT	1617
RIDGELY, A M	1871	W.LIBRTY.BUS.	1780
RIDGELY, A M / STORE	1871	W.LIBERTY	1780
RIDGELY, ABSALOM	1821	MISC	1687
RIDGELY, ABSALOM	1848	DEFENDANT	1629
RIDGELY, ABSALON	1848	DEFENDANT	1626
RIDGELY, ABSOLAM	1816	MISC	1704
RIDGELY, ABSOLOM	1810	APPENDIX	1873
RIDGELY, E M	1871	OH CO. MAP	1741
RIDGELY, FRANKLIN	1852	NOT ON MAP	1836
RIDGELY, FRANKLIN	1852	NOT ON MAP	1836
RIDGELY, FRANKLIN / MAP#109	1852	BRKE MAP	1843
RIDGELY, FRANKLIN / MAP#141	1852	BRKE MAP	1843
RIDGELY, PEREGRINE	1821	DEFENDANT	1638
RIDGELY, PEREGRINE	1822	DEFENDANT	1638
RIDGELY, W C	1871	BRKE MAP	1737
RIDGELY, W C / INITIALS W.C.R.	1871	BRKE MAP	1737
RIDGELY, W C / INITIALS W.C.R.	1871	BRKE MAP	1737
RIDGELY, W C	1871	BKE/OH MAP	1739
RIDGELY, W C / INITIALS W.C.R.	1871	BKE/OH MAP	1739
RIDGELY, W C / INITIALS W.C.R.	1871	BKE/OH MAP	1739
RIDGELY, W C / INITIALS W.C.R.	1871	BKE/OH MAP	1739
RIDGELY, W C / INITIALS W.C.R.	1871	BKE/OH MAP	1739
RIDGELY, WILLIAM	1871	BKE/OH MAP	1739
RIDGLE, D	1871	BRKE MAP	1736
RIDGLY, ABSALOM	1859	DEFENDANT	1560
RIDINGER, J	1871	HAN MAP	1729
RIDINGER, N	1871	HAN MAP	1729
RIELLY, J M	1871	MARH'L MAP	1745
RIGGLE, J	1871	MARH'L MAP	1757
RIGGLE, J	1871	CAMERON	1803
RIGGLE, W	1871	MARH'L MAP	1747
RIGGLE, W	1871	MARH'L MAP	1750
RIGGS T F	1871	MARH'L MAP	1748
RIGGS, - / COLLENS & RIGGS	1871	MARH'L MAP	1751

'PERSONAL TIME LINE' INDEX TO VOLUME 7 OF THE **OHIO COUNTY INDEX**

ENTRY	YEAR	SUBJECT	PAGE	ENTRY	YEAR	SUBJECT	PAGE
RIGGS, H	1871	MARH'L MAP	1751	RITCHIE TWP - CHURCH ST	1871	RITCHIE TWP	1793
RIGGS, J	1871	MARH'L MAP	1748	RITCHIE TWP - DETAIL MAP	1871	RITCHIE TWP	1793
RIGGS, J L	1871	MARH'L MAP	1751	RITCHIE TWP - EAST ST	1871	RITCHIE TWP	1793
RIGGS, J S	1871	MARH'L MAP	1748	RITCHIE TWP - ELM ST	1871	RITCHIE TWP	1793
RIGGS, J S / INITIALS J.S.R.	1871	MARH'L MAP	1748	RITCHIE TWP - FAIRMONT TURNPIKE	1871	RITCHIE TWP	1793
RIGGS, JOHN / INITIALS J.R.	1871	MARH'L MAP	1754	RITCHIE TWP - VINE ST	1871	RITCHIE TWP	1793
RIGGS, JOHN / INITIALS J.R.	1871	MARH'L MAP	1754	RITCHIE, - / MRS	1871	MARH'L MAP	1750
RIGGS, JOHN / RES.	1871	MARH'L MAP	1754	RITCHIE, -	1871	MARH'L MAP	1756
RIGGS, L	1871	MARH'L MAP	1749	RITCHIE, JOHN	1838	DEFENDANT	1662
RIGGS, M	1871	MARH'L MAP	1749	RITCHIE, WILLIAM	1838	MISC	1689
RIGGS, N / (?OR M.?)	1871	MARH'L MAP	1749	RITCHIES RUN	1871	HAN MAP	1732
RIGGS, N	1871	MARH'L MAP	1751	RITCHIETOWN FARM	1871	OH CO. MAP	1742
RIGGS, N S	1871	MARH'L MAP	1751	RITZ, CAROLINE	1873	DEFENDANT	1597
RIGGS, NATHAN	1823	DEFENDANT	1555	RITZ, WILLIAM	1874	DEFENDANT	1594
RIGGS, NATHAN	1823	DEFENDANT	1555	RIVER ROAD - SOUTH OF NEW CUMBERLAND	1871	RIV. RD S.OF N.C.	1771
RIGGS, S	1871	MARH'L MAP	1748				
RIGGS, S	1871	MARH'L MAP	1748	RIVER VALLEY VIEW	1871	HAN MAP	1726
RIGGS, S	1871	MARH'L MAP	1748	RIVER VALLEY VIEW - HAMILTON	1871	HAN MAP	1729
RIGGS, S	1871	MARH'L MAP	1749	RIVERSIDE	1871	HAN MAP	1726
RIGGS, S	1871	MARH'L MAP	1751	RIVERVIEW	1871	HAN MAP	1726
RIGGS, S	1871	MARH'L MAP	1751	RIVERVIEW	1871	HAN MAP	1726
RIGGS, S	1871	MARH'L MAP	1751	RIVERVIEW	1871	MARH'L MAP	1745
RIGGS, S / & CAULDWELL	1871	MARH'L MAP	1754	RIVERVIEW - WASHINGTON TWP	1871	MARH'L MAP	1748
RIGGS, S	1871	MARH'L MAP	1755	ROACH, J	1871	HAN MAP	1731
RIGGS, S E	1871	MARH'L MAP	1746	ROAD - OLD STATE ROAD - RONEY POINT	1871	RONEY PT.	1783
RIGGS, T T F	1871	MDSVILLE	1809				
RIGGS, T T F	1871	MDSVILLE	1809	ROAD DISTANCES - 888 FROM NEAR CO. LINE TO MIDDLE WHEEKING CREEK ROAD BY TURNPIKE	1871	OH CO. MAP	1743
RIGGS, THOMAS	1834	MISC	1705				
RIGGS, W	1871	MARH'L MAP	1748				
RIGGS, W	1871	MDSVILLE	1810	ROAD DISTANCES - 923 FROM CLAY ROAD TO [MIDDLE WHEELING] CREEK BY OLD ROAD	1871	OH CO. MAP	1743
RIGGS, W	1871	MDSVILLE	1810				
RIGGS, W / MRS	1871	MDSVILLE	1810				
RIGHT FISH CREEK / (?RIGHT FORK?)	1871	MARH'L MAP	1761	ROBB, -	1844	DEFENDANT	1623
RIGHT FORK OF FISH CREEK / ?	1871	MARH'L MAP	1761	ROBB, J S	1871	NEW CUMB'LD	1767
RIGHT FORK OF FISH CREEK - DAM ON	1871	MARH'L MAP	1761	ROBB, JAMES	1830	MISC	1682
				ROBB, WILLIAM J	1873	DEFENDANT	1601
RIGHT FORK OF MAGGOTTY RUN	1871	MARH'L MAP	1757	ROBB, WILLIAM M	1839	MISC	1702
RIGHT FORK OF MAGGOTTY RUN	1871	MARH'L MAP	1757	ROBERTS RIDGE FARM	1871	MARH'L MAP	1751
RIGHT, JONATHAN	1802	DEFENDANT	1559	ROBERTS RIDGE ROAD / CLAY TWP	1871	MARH'L MAP	1751
RIHELDAFFER, WILLIAM & CO	1857	DEFENDANT	1552	ROBERTS RIDGE ROAD	1871	MARH'L MAP	1755
RIHELDAFFER, WILLIAM & CO	1857	DEFENDANT	1621	ROBERTS RUN	1871	HAN MAP	1732
RILETER, - / MRS	1871	MDSVILLE	1808	ROBERTS, - / EDWARDS & ROBERTS	1871	MDSVL BUS.	1796
RILEY, - / EST.	1871	OH CO. MAP	1742	ROBERTS, A	1871	MDSVILLE	1808
RILEY, - / EST.	1871	WHG CITY	1789	ROBERTS, C	1871	MDSVILLE	1807
RILEY, - / EST	1871	RITCHIE TWP	1791	ROBERTS, D	1871	MARH'L MAP	1748
RILEY, E	1871	HAN MAP	1727	ROBERTS, D	1871	MARH'L MAP	1748
RILEY, M	1871	GLEN EASTON	1801	ROBERTS, D	1871	MARH'L MAP	1748
RILEY, P	1871	OH CO. MAP	1741	ROBERTS, D	1871	WELLSBURG	1777
RILEY, P	1871	OH CO. MAP	1741	ROBERTS, D	1871	MDSVILLE	1810
RILEY, W	1871	MDSVILLE	1808	ROBERTS, G	1871	OH CO. MAP	1742
RILEY, W	1871	MDSVILLE	1810	ROBERTS, G	1871	RITCHIE TWP	1791
RILEY, WILLIAM	1829	DEFENDANT	1668	ROBERTS, GEORGE	1873	DEFENDANT	1564
RINE, - / MRS	1871	MARH'L MAP	1755	ROBERTS, GEORGE	1874	DEFENDANT	1597
RINE, G	1871	MARH'L MAP	1755	ROBERTS, GEORGE	1874	DEFENDANT	1631
RINE, H	1871	MARH'L MAP	1754	ROBERTS, H / MRS	1871	MARH'L MAP	1748
RINE, H	1871	MARH'L MAP	1754	ROBERTS, I F / (?L.F.?)	1871	MARH'L MAP	1751
RINE, H / INITIALS H.R.	1871	MARH'L MAP	1754	ROBERTS, J D	1871	MARH'L MAP	1751
RINE, H	1871	MARH'L MAP	1759	ROBERTS, J E	1871	MARH'L MAP	1748
RINE, H F	1871	MARH'L MAP	1755	ROBERTS, J J	1878	DEFENDANT	1617
RINE, J	1871	MARH'L MAP	1754	ROBERTS, JAMES	1819	MISC	1688
RINE, J	1871	MARH'L MAP	1755	ROBERTS, JAMES H	1859	DEFENDANT	1574
RINE, J	1871	MARH'L MAP	1755	ROBERTS, JONATHAN	1833	DEFENDANT	1669
RINE, R	1871	MARH'L MAP	1754	ROBERTS, L / HRS - HEIRS	1871	MDSVILLE	1808
RINE, W	1871	MARH'L MAP	1759	ROBERTS, R	1871	WELLSBURG	1777
RINE, W B	1871	MARH'L MAP	1754	ROBERTS, R T	1871	WELLSBURG	1778
RINE, W B	1871	MARH'L MAP	1754	ROBERTS, R T / INITIALS R.T.R.	1871	WELLSBURG	1778
RINE, WILLIAM	1871	OH CO. MAP	1740	ROBERTS, R T / INITIALS R.T.R.	1871	WELLSBURG	1778
RINKES, - / MRS	1871	OH CO. MAP	1742	ROBERTS, S	1871	HAN MAP	1733
RINKES, - / MRS	1871	OH CO. MAP	1744	ROBERTS, SAMUEL / MAP#290	1852	BRKE MAP	1846
RINKES, P	1871	OH CO. MAP	1742	ROBERTS, THOMAS	1788	DEFENDANT	1571
RINKES, P	1871	OH CO. MAP	1744	ROBERTS, W	1871	HAN MAP	1733
RIST, G	1871	MARH'L MAP	1751	ROBERTS, WILLIAM / BLACKSMITH	1871	HO'LIDAYS COVE	1762
RIST, J	1871	MARH'L MAP	1751	ROBERTSON, J M	1871	MARH'L MAP	1760
RITCHARDS, THOMAS	1800	DEFENDANT	1665	ROBERTSON, WILLIAM	1854	DEFENDANT	1623
RITCHEE RUN	1871	FRE'MAN'S LDG	1764	ROBINSON & CLEMENS	1858	DEFENDANT	1630
RITCHIE & WILSON	1837	MISC	1683	ROBINSON & SMART	1871	MARH'L MAP	1749
RITCHIE TOWN FARM	1871	RITCHIE TWP	1792	ROBINSON & SMART	1871	LIMESTONE	1805
RITCHIE TOWNSHIP - BUSINESS NOTICES	1871	OH CO.BUS.	1779	ROBINSON, - / MRS	1871	MARH'L MAP	1760
				ROBINSON, - / MRS	1871	TRIAD.BORO.	1784
RITCHIE TOWNSHIP - DETAIL MAP	1871	TRIAD.TWP.	1781	ROBINSON, A	1871	MARH'L MAP	1760
RITCHIE TOWNSHIP - OHIO CO	1871	OH CO. MAP	1742	ROBINSON, A G / & CO	1856	DEFENDANT	1630
RITCHIE TOWNSHIP - OHIO CO	1871	WHG CITY	1789	ROBINSON, CHARLES	1802	DEFENDANT	1634
RITCHIE TOWNSHIP - OHIO CO	1871	RITCHIE TWP	1793	ROBINSON, CHARLES	1803	DEFENDANT	1634
RITCHIE TOWNSHIP - OHIO CO	1871	POPULATION	1816	ROBINSON, E N	1871	BRKE MAP	1734
RITCHIE TOWNSHIP - OHIO CO - DETAIL MAP	1871	RITCHIE TWP	1791	ROBINSON, ELIJAH / HEIRS - MAP#576	1852	BRKE MAP	1852
				ROBINSON, EZERIAH	1817	DEFENDANT	1659

'PERSONAL TIME LINE' INDEX TO VOLUME 7 OF THE *OHIO COUNTY INDEX*

ENTRY	YEAR	SUBJECT	PAGE	ENTRY	YEAR	SUBJECT	PAGE
ROBINSON, GORDON	1858	DEFENDANT	1636	RODIFFER, JOHN	1805	MISC	1682
ROBINSON, GORDON	1859	DEFENDANT	1608	RODOCKER, W	1871	MARH'L MAP	1751
ROBINSON, GORDON	1860	DEFENDANT	1636	RODOCKER, WILLIAM	1871	MARH'L MAP	1751
ROBINSON, J	1871	OH CO. MAP	1743	ROE, JOHN A	1834	DEFENDANT	1561
ROBINSON, J	1871	OH CO. MAP	1743	ROE, JOHN A	1835	DEFENDANT	1581
ROBINSON, J	1871	MARH'L MAP	1749	ROE, PATRICK	1840	DEFENDANT	1643
ROBINSON, J	1871	MARH'L MAP	1752	ROE, RICHARD	1824	DEFENDANT	1638
ROBINSON, J	1871	MARH'L MAP	1752	ROEMER, JOHN	1875	DEFENDANT	1562
ROBINSON, J H / (OC.) - STORE	1871	MDSVILLE	1809	ROETTGER, A / ELM GROVE HOUSE - HOTEL - ELM GROVE	1871	OH CO. BUS.	1779
ROBINSON, JAMES	1805	DEFENDANT	1637				
ROBINSON, JAMES	1806	DEFENDANT	1583	ROETTGER, A	1871	ELM GROVE	1782
ROBINSON, JAMES	1808	DEFENDANT	1637	ROGER, JAMES P	1880	MISC	1706
ROBINSON, JAMES	1811	DEFENDANT	1626	ROGERS, -	1855	PLAINTIFF	1629
ROBINSON, JAMES	1858	DEFENDANT	1636	ROGERS, ALEXANDER	1833	PLAINTIFF	1561
ROBINSON, JAMES H	1854	DEFENDANT	1551	ROGERS, ALEXANDER	1851	MISC	1688
ROBINSON, JAMES H	1854	DEFENDANT	1559	ROGERS, ALEXANDER	1852	HEMPFIELD RR	1822
ROBINSON, JAMES H	1854	DEFENDANT	1636	ROGERS, CHARLES	1809	DEFENDANT	1645
ROBINSON, JAMES H	1856	DEFENDANT	1552	ROGERS, DAVID	1784	APPENDIX	1874
ROBINSON, JAMES H	1857	DEFENDANT	1636	ROGERS, ELIZABETH	1815	DEFENDANT	1579
ROBINSON, JOHN	1836	MISC	1691	ROGERS, F	1871	OH CO. MAP	1742
ROBINSON, JOHN / MAP#578	1852	BRKE MAP	1852	ROGERS, F	1871	RITCHIE TWP	1793
ROBINSON, JOHN H / 'SHARPS GARDEN'	1871	MDSVL BUS.	1796	ROGERS, F	1871	RITCHIE TWP	1794
				ROGERS, J	1871	HAN MAP	1727
ROBINSON, N	1871	MARH'L MAP	1750	ROGERS, J	1871	HAN MAP	1728
ROBINSON, N	1871	MARH'L MAP	1753	ROGERS, J /BLACKSMITH SHOP	1871	MARH'L MAP	1747
ROBINSON, P	1871	MARH'L MAP	1750	ROGERS, J / BLACKSMITH & WAGON MAKER - SAND HILL	1871	SAND HILL-BUS.	1797
ROBINSON, P	1871	MARH'L MAP	1753				
ROBINSON, SAMUEL G	1836	DEFENDANT	1651	ROGERS, NICHOLAS	1785	MISC	1674
ROBINSON, SAMUEL G	1840	DEFENDANT	1554	ROGERS, SAMUEL	1853	DEFENDANT	1604
ROBINSON, SAMUEL G	1840	DEFENDANT	1620	ROGERS, W	1871	MARH'L MAP	1747
ROBINSON, SAMUEL G	1841	DEFENDANT	1585	ROGERSON, J / HRS - HEIRS	1871	MARH'L MAP	1745
ROBINSON, SAMUEL G	1841	DEFENDANT	1629	ROGERSON, J / HRS - HEIRS	1871	MARH'L MAP	1748
ROBINSON, SAMUEL G	1841	DEFENDANT	1652	ROGERSON, J	1871	MDSVILLE	1807
ROBINSON, SAMUEL L	1841	DEFENDANT	1586	ROGERSON, WILLIAM	1871	MARH'L MAP	1745
ROBINSON, SAMUEL L	1841	DEFENDANT	1629	ROGERSON, WILLIAM	1871	MARH'L MAP	1748
ROBINSON, SAMUEL L	1841	DEFENDANT	1652	ROHAN, -	1839	PLAINTIFF	1632
ROBINSON, SARAH	1820	DEFENDANT	1591	ROHAN, -	1841	DEFENDANT	1551
ROBINSON, SARAH	1821	DEFENDANT	1587	ROHAN, MICHAEL J	1835	DEFENDANT	1662
ROBINSON, T P	1834	DEFENDANT	1553	ROHAN, MICHAEL J	1855	DEFENDANT	1636
ROBINSON, T P	1836	DEFENDANT	1553	ROHAN, MICHAEL J	1855	MISC	1702
ROBINSON, W	1871	BRKE MAP	1734	ROHAN, MICHAEL J	1856	DEFENDANT	1636
ROBINSON, W	1871	OH CO. MAP	1743	ROLF, AUGUST	1876	DEFENDANT	1603
ROBINSON, WILLIAM	1813	DEFENDANT	1556	ROLLING MILL	1871	OH CO. MAP	1741
ROBINSON, WILLIAM	1822	DEFENDANT	1625	ROLSTON, SAMUEL	1791	DEFENDANT	1637
ROBINSON, WILLIAM	1841	DEFENDANT	1672	ROMAN CATHOLIC CEMETERY / NEAR POWER HOUSE	1871	WHG CITY	1789
ROBINSON, WILLIAM / MAP#575	1852	BRKE MAP	1852				
ROBINSON, WILLIAM F	1860	DEFENDANT	1621	ROMAN CATHOLIC CHURCH / MEADE TWP - INITIALS R.C.CH.	1871	MARH'L MAP	1759
ROBINSON, WILLIAM T	1854	DEFENDANT	1636				
ROBINSON, WILLIAM T	1858	DEFENDANT	1602	ROMAN CATHOLIC CHURCH - MARKET ST	1871	WHG CITY	1788
ROBINSON, WILLIAM T	1858	DEFENDANT	1630				
ROBINSON, WILLIAM T	1860	DEFENDANT	1621	ROMAN CATHOLIC CHURCH - MARKET ST	1871	WHG CITY	1790
ROBINSON, WILLIAM T	1861	DEFENDANT	1664				
ROBINSON, WILLIAM T	1862	DEFENDANT	1621	ROMMAGE, JOHN	1790	DEFENDANT	1644
ROBINSON, WILLIAM T	1862	DEFENDANT	1664	RONEY POINT - SAW MILL - ON LITTLE WHEELING CREEK	1871	OH CO. MAP	1743
ROBRECHT, JOSEPH	1877	DEFENDANT	1631				
ROCK LICK	1871	MARH'L BUS.	1796	RONEY POINT - SAW MILL - ON LITTLE WHEELING CREEK	1871	OH CO. MAP	1744
ROCK LICK / MARSHALL CO	1871	DISTANCES	1815				
ROCK OAK	1871	MARH'L MAP	1759	RONEY POINT - TURNPIKE TO WEST UNION	1871	RONEY PT.	1783
ROCK SPRING	1871	HAN MAP	1727				
ROCK SPRING	1871	HAN MAP	1728	RONEY POINT & WEST UNION TURNPIKE	1871	OH CO. MAP	1743
ROCK SPRING FARM	1871	HAN MAP	1727				
ROCK SPRING FARM	1871	HAN MAP	1728	RONEY POINT SCHOOL	1871	OH CO. MAP	1743
ROCKBRANDT, HENRY	1859	DEFENDANT	1673	RONEY POINT SCHOOL	1871	OH CO. MAP	1744
ROCKLICK P.O.	1871	MARH'L MAP	1753	RONEY POINT STATION	1871	OH CO. MAP	1743
ROCKVILLE, OH	1852	BRKE MAP	1849	RONEY POINT STATION	1871	OH CO. MAP	1744
ROCKY POINT	1871	HAN MAP	1731	RONEY POINT STATION - DETAIL MAP	1871	RONEY PT.	1783
ROCKY, G	1871	OH CO. MAP	1743				
ROCKY, G	1871	OH CO. MAP	1743	RONEY POINT STATION - STORE	1871	OH CO. MAP	1743
RODELHEIMER & COHN	1876	DEFENDANT	1631	RONEY POINT STATION - STORE & TICKET OFFICE	1871	OH CO. MAP	1743
RODGERS, ANDREW	1801	DEFENDANT	1579				
RODGERS, B	1871	BKE/OH MAP	1739	RONEY, FRANCES	1852	DEFENDANT	1663
RODGERS, BENJAMIN	1836	DEFENDANT	1554	RONEY, J	1871	MARH'L MAP	1746
RODGERS, DAVID	1777	MISC	1674	RONEY, J H	1871	OH CO. MAP	1743
RODGERS, EZEKIEL	1873	DEFENDANT	1609	RONEY, L / NW OF WEST UNION	1871	MARH'L MAP	1747
RODGERS, J G	1871	BKE/OH MAP	1739	RONEY, S	1871	OH CO. MAP	1740
RODGERS, NANCY / MISS - YJULIA HOME	1871	W.LIBERTY	1780	RONEY, S	1871	OH CO. MAP	1743
				RONEY'S POINT	1802	MISC	1701
RODGERS, P / MRS	1871	BKE/OH MAP	1739	RONEY'S POINT - GOOD INTENT STAGE LINE	1916	NAT'L ROAD	1864
RODGERS, R	1871	BKE/OH MAP	1739				
RODGERS, WILLIAM / MAP#3	1852	BRKE MAP	1841	RONEY'S POINT - NATIONAL ROAD MAP	1916	NAT'L ROAD	1863
RODGERS, WILLIAM / RES	1871	BRKE MAP	1737				
RODGERS, WILLIAM / RES	1871	BKE/OH MAP	1739	RONEY'S POINT - OLD ROAD / RONEY POINT & WEST UNION TURNPIKE	1871	OH CO. MAP	1743
RODGERS, WILLIAM / ? INITIALS WM.R	1871	BKE/OH MAP	1739				
RODGERSON, J	1871	MARH'L MAP	1748	RONEY'S POINT - OLD STONE HOTEL - NATIONAL ROAD	1916	NAT'L ROAD	1866
RODGERSON, J / INITIALS J.R.	1871	MARH'L MAP	1748				
RODIFER, JOHN	1820	DEFENDANT	1624				

'PERSONAL TIME LINE' INDEX TO VOLUME 7 OF THE OHIO COUNTY INDEX

ENTRY	YEAR	SUBJECT	PAGE	ENTRY	YEAR	SUBJECT	PAGE
RONEY'S POINT - OLD STONE TAVERN	1916	NAT'L ROAD	1864	RUSSELL, S D	1843	DEFENDANT	1592
				RUSSELL, W R	1871	OH CO. MAP	1742
RONEY'S POINT - SIMO STAGE LINE	1916	NAT'L ROAD	1864	RUSSELL, WILLIAM E	1857	DEFENDANT	1564
ROOT, WILLIAM	1827	DEFENDANT	1660	RUSSELL, WILLIAM H	1857	DEFENDANT	1575
ROPE WALK - NW OF H. BUMGARDNER	1871	MARH'L MAP	1745	RUSSELL, WILLIAM H	1857	DEFENDANT	1580
				RUSSELL, WILLIAM H	1857	DEFENDANT	1604
ROSBBYS - POND	1871	ROSBBYS RK	1813	RUSSELL, WILLIAM H	1857	DEFENDANT	1625
ROSBBYS ROCK	1871	MARH'L MAP	1752	RUSSELL, WILLIAM H	1857	DEFENDANT	1632
ROSBBYS ROCK	1871	DISTANCES	1815	RUSSELL, WILLIAM H	1858	DEFENDANT	1562
ROSBBYS ROCK - BLACKSMITH SHOP	1871	ROSBBYS RK	1813	RUSSELL, WILLIAM H	1858	DEFENDANT	1623
ROSBBYS ROCK - DETAIL MAP	1871	ROSBBYS RK	1813	RUST, AUGUST	1874	DEFENDANT	1590
ROSBY'S ROCK	1871	MARH'L MAP	1752	RUTH, J / FLOURING MILL & SAW MILL - NEW GERMANTOWN	1871	SAND HILL-BUS.	1797
ROSE COTTAGE	1871	HAN MAP	1731				
ROSE, A	1871	WELLSBURG	1777	RUTH, S / SAW & GRIST MILL	1871	MARH'L MAP	1747
ROSE, H	1871	WELLSBURG	1777	RUTH, W	1871	MARH'L MAP	1747
ROSE, J H	1871	WELLSBURG	1777	RUTH, W	1871	MARH'L MAP	1750
ROSE, J H / LIVERY STA. (?STABLE?)	1871	WELLSBURG	1777	RUTH, W / SAW & GRIST MILL	1871	MARH'L MAP	1750
ROSE, J S	1871	NEW MANCH.	1769	RUTH, W / FLOURING MILL & SAW MILL - NEW GERMANTOWN	1871	SAND HILL-BUS.	1797
ROSE, LEVI	1839	DEFENDANT	1581				
ROSE, LEVI H	1839	DEFENDANT	1563	RUUTH, W	1871	MARH'L MAP	1747
ROSE, R	1871	MARH'L MAP	1745	RYAN, C	1871	BKE/OH MAP	1738
ROSEBERRY, J	1871	MARH'L MAP	1747	RYAN, J	1871	OH CO. MAP	1740
ROSEBERRY, W	1871	MARH'L MAP	1747	RYAN, J	1871	OH CO. MAP	1741
ROSENBARGER, R G	1871	MARH'L MAP	1750	RYAN, J	1871	OH CO. MAP	1742
ROSENBARGER, R G / SAW MILL ?	1871	MARH'L MAP	1750	RYAN, J B	1871	MARH'L MAP	1754
ROSENBARGER, R G / INITIALS R.G.R.	1871	MARH'L MAP	1750	RYAN, JAMES	1810	APPENDIX	1873
ROSENBARGER, R G	1871	MARH'L MAP	1753	RYLAND, HUGH B	1871	BRKE MAP	1734
ROSENBERGER, JOHN / ACCIDENTLY KILLED NOV 2, 1856	1871	MARH'L MAP	1750	RYLAND, HUGH P	1852	NOT ON MAP	1836
				RYLAND, HUGH P / (MILL) - MAP#573	1852	BRKE MAP	1852
ROSENKRANZ, G	1871	TRIAD.BORO.	1784	RYLAND, HUGH P / MAP#574	1852	BRKE MAP	1852
ROSENKRANZ, G	1871	TRIAD.BORO.	1784	RYLAND, HUGH P / SAW & GRIST MILL - "HARMONS CREEK"	1871	CROSS CRK.BUS.	1772
ROSENKRANZ, G / INITIALS G.R.	1871	TRIAD.BORO.	1784				
ROSENTHRAL & HORKEIMER	1861	DEFENDANT	1626	RYLEY, FRANCIS	1786	DEFENDANT	1628
ROSS, -	1806	PLAINTIFF	1626	S & G MILL / ON SHORT CREEK	1871	BKE/OH MAP	1738
ROSS, - / MAP#138	1852	BRKE MAP	1844	S & G MILL / N. OF WHEELING VALLEY FLOURING MILLS	1871	MARH'L MAP	1746
ROSS, ANDREW F	1862	DEFENDANT	1560				
ROSS, ANDREW F	1862	DEFENDANT	1560	S BRIDGE	1871	OH CO. MAP	1742
ROSS, JOSEPH	1793	DEFENDANT	1608	S BRIDGE - BUFFALO CREEK - WASH. CO., PA.	1916	NAT'L ROAD	1861
ROSS, S	1871	MARH'L MAP	1757				
ROSS, W	1871	NEW CUMB'LD	1768	S BRIDGE - BUFFALO CREEK - WASH. CO., PA.	1916	NAT'L ROAD	1863
ROTH, G	1871	OH CO. MAP	1742				
ROTH, G	1871	TRIAD.TWP.	1781	S MILL - BELLTON	1871	MARH'L MAP	1761
ROTHACKER, F & CO	1855	DEFENDANT	1670	S&S / UNKNOWN INITIALS	1871	ELM GROVE	1782
ROTHBURN, EDMUND	1804	PLAINTIFF	1635	S, - / S&S - UNKNOWN INITIALS	1871	ELM GROVE	1782
ROUGH & READY SCHOOL DIST	1871	OH CO. MAP	1740	S, B / UNKNOWN INITIALS	1871	ELM GROVE	1782
ROUGH & READY SCHOOL NO. 7	1871	OH CO. MAP	1740	S, F / INITIALS UNKNOWN - LAND SW OF G.B. MILLER	1871	BKE/OH MAP	1739
ROUSE, E	1871	BKE/OH MAP	1738				
ROUSE, J	1871	BKE/OH MAP	1738	S, G W / INITIALS G.W.S. - (?GEORGE W.STEENROD?)	1871	WHG CITY	1789
ROUSE, THOMAS	1788	DEFENDANT	1637				
ROWLAND, ABRAHAM	1812	DEFENDANT	1596	S, J / ABBREV.	1871	HAN MAP	1731
ROWLAND, JOHN	1812	DEFENDANT	1595	S, J P / UNKNOWN INITIALS - ELM GROVE	1871	OH CO. MAP	1744
RUCKMAN, T / INITIALS T.R.	1871	MARH'L MAP	1754				
RUCKMAN, T	1871	MARH'L MAP	1755	S, L / UNKNOWN INITIALS	1871	MARH'L MAP	1756
RUCKMAN, T / INITIALS T.R.	1871	MARH'L MAP	1755	S, T T / UNKNOWN INITIALS ON GRANT ST - MDSVILLE	1871	MDSVILLE	1807
RUCKMAN, T	1871	MARH'L MAP	1759				
RUCKMAN, T	1871	MARH'L MAP	1759	S, W	1871	HAN MAP	1731
RUCKMAN, T / INITIALS T.R.	1871	MARH'L MAP	1759	S, W & P / W. & P.W. - UNKNOWN INITIALS	1871	MARH'L MAP	1748
RUCKMAN, T / INITIALS T.R.	1871	MARH'L MAP	1759				
RUCKMAN, T / INITIALS T.R.	1871	MARH'L MAP	1759	S. MILL / SAW MILL - VALLEY GROVE	1871	OH CO. MAP	1740
RUDIFORD, WILLIAM	1831	MISC	1681	S. SHOP - ZIELERS / B	1871	BKE/OH MAP	1738
RULE - CHILDREN	1873	MISC	1698	S. SHOP - ZITTERS / D	1871	BKE/OH MAP	1738
RULONG, - / MRS	1871	MARH'L MAP	1751	S. WHEELING	1871	OH CO. MAP	1742
RULONG, AARON	1809	DEFENDANT	1648	S. WHEELING	1871	POPULATION	1816
RULONG, J	1871	MARH'L MAP	1751	S. WHEELING - DETAIL MAP	1871	SOUTH WHG	1792
RULONG, J / RES	1871	MARH'L MAP	1752	S. WHEELING - DETAIL MAP	1871	SOUTH WHG	1794
RULONG, M	1871	MDSVILLE	1809	S. WHEELING - MAP	1871	WHG CITY	1786
RULONG, M	1871	MDSVILLE	1809	S.B.P.EST. / UNKNOWN INTITALS	1871	MARH'L MAP	1751
RULONG, M	1871	MDSVILLE	1810	S.G. & S.MILL / PROBABLY HIGGINS, CRAWFORD & CO.	1871	MARH'L MAP	1760
RURAL HOME - WEST UNION	1871	MARH'L MAP	1747				
RUSH RUN - OHIO / E. OF MONTEZUMA	1852	BRKE MAP	1842	S.G.MILL - GLEN EASTON	1871	GLEN EASTON	1801
RUSH, D	1871	MARH'L MAP	1756	S.G.MILL - HORNBROOK BROTHERS	1871	MARH'L MAP	1754
RUSH, D	1871	MARH'L MAP	1760	S.G.MILL - LOUDENSVILLE	1871	MARH'L MAP	1753
RUSSELL COTTAGE	1871	OH CO. MAP	1742	S.G.MILL - LOUDENSVILLE	1871	MARH'L MAP	1757
RUSSELL, - / MRS	1871	WELLSBURG	1777	S.G.MILL - WOODLAND P.O.	1871	MARH'L MAP	1754
RUSSELL, - / MRS	1871	WELLSBURG	1778	S.M. / (?SAW MILL)? - BUFFALO CREEK	1871	BRKE MAP	1736
RUSSELL, G W / TEACHER	1871	WLSBRG BUS.	1772				
RUSSELL, G W	1871	WELLSBURG	1777	S.M. / (?=SAW MILL?)	1871	MARH'L MAP	1749
RUSSELL, HARRY M	1874	MISC	1698	S.M. / (?UNKNOWN INITIALS - IN VILLAGES - SALES MERCHANDISE?)	1871	MARH'L MAP	1760
RUSSELL, J / HRS - HEIRS	1871	WELLSBURG	1776				
RUSSELL, JOHN	1841	DEFENDANT	1577	S.M. / STORE IN VILLAGE NEAR J.MCCARDLE	1871	MARH'L MAP	1760
RUSSELL, JOHN	1841	DEFENDANT	1617				
RUSSELL, JOHN	1841	DEFENDANT	1652	S.M. / (?ABBREVIATION FOR SAW MILL?)	1871	MARH'L MAP	1761
RUSSELL, JOHN	1859	DEFENDANT	1584				
RUSSELL, JOHN	1860	DEFENDANT	1565	S.M. / ON LITTLE FORK OF FISH CREEK - N. OF W. ADAMS/ (?SAW MILL?)	1871	MARH'L MAP	1761
RUSSELL, JOHN	1862	DEFENDANT	1565				
RUSSELL, S / MRS	1871	WELLSBURG	1777				

'PERSONAL TIME LINE' INDEX TO VOLUME 7 OF THE OHIO COUNTY INDEX

ENTRY	YEAR	SUBJECT	PAGE
S.S / (?ABBREVIATION FOR STEAM SAW MILL?)	1871	MARH'L MAP	1761
S.S. - S. OF PLEASANT VIEW	1871	HAN MAP	1727
S.S. & G. MILL / S.S. & GRIST MILL	1871	MARH'L MAP	1750
S.S. MILL	1871	HAN MAP	1727
S.S. MILL	1871	BRKE MAP	1737
S.S. MILL / MEANING ?	1871	MARH'L MAP	1750
S.S. MILL - / (?ABBREVIATION FOR STEAM SAW?)	1871	MARH'L MAP	1761
S.S. MILL - VALLEY GROVE	1871	OH CO. MAP	1740
S.S. MILL / ABBREVIATIONS UNKNOWN	1871	MARH'L MAP	1746
S.S. MILL / MCCLEANS ? - OHIO RIVER	1871	MARH'L MAP	1748
S.S. MILL / (?STEAM SAW MILL?)	1871	EDGINGTON STA.	1774
S.S. MILL - BELLTON / (?WHITE & STILES?)	1871	BELLTON	1814
S.S. MILL - BELLTON P.O. / (?STEAM SAW?)	1871	MARH'L MAP	1761
S.S. MILL - EVANS / I	1871	NEW CUMB'LD	1767
S.S. MILL - KITTLES / S.B. & SON	1871	MARH'L MAP	1746
S.S. MILL - LOUDENSVILLE	1871	MARH'L MAP	1753
S.S. MILL - LOUDENSVILLE	1871	MARH'L MAP	1757
S.S. MILL - N OF MILLER & POLEN	1871	BRKE MAP	1734
S.S. MILL - N. OF GRAVE CREEK HEAD	1871	MARH'L MAP	1753
S.S. MILL - NEAR OHIO RIVER	1871	BRKE MAP	1734
S.S. MILL - NEAR ROCKY POINT	1871	HAN MAP	1731
S.S. MILL - NEAR W. POLLOCK	1871	OH CO. MAP	1740
S.S. MILL - W. OF T. MARSH	1871	BRKE MAP	1734
S.S. MILL - WHEELING	1871	WHG CITY	1786
S.S. MILL ON CALDWELLS RUN	1871	OH CO. MAP	1742
S.SH / (?SHOE SHOP?)	1871	NEW CUMB'LD	1768
S.SH / (?SHOE SHOP?)	1871	NEW CUMB'LD	1767
S.W. / UNKNOWN INITIALS	1871	MARH'L MAP	1749
S.WHEELING - CALDWELL ST	1871	WHG CITY	1792
S.WHEELING - CHESTNUT ST	1871	SOUTH WHG	1792
S.WHEELING - DENNY ST	1871	SOUTH WHG	1792
S.WHEELING - EIGHTH ST	1871	SOUTH WHG	1792
S.WHEELING - EIGHTH ST	1871	SOUTH WHG	1794
S.WHEELING - ELM ST	1871	SOUTH WHG	1792
S.WHEELING - ELM ST	1871	SOUTH WHG	1794
S.WHEELING - FIFTH ST	1871	SOUTH WHG	1792
S.WHEELING - FIFTH ST	1871	SOUTH WHG	1794
S.WHEELING - FILBERT ST	1871	SOUTH WHG	1792
S.WHEELING - FIRST OR WATER ST	1871	SOUTH WHG	1792
S.WHEELING - FIRST OR WATER ST	1871	SOUTH WHG	1794
S.WHEELING - FOURTH ST	1871	SOUTH WHG	1792
S.WHEELING - HAZEL ST	1871	SOUTH WHG	1792
S.WHEELING - LOCUST ST	1871	SOUTH WHG	1792
S.WHEELING - LOCUST ST	1871	SOUTH WHG	1792
S.WHEELING - LOCUST ST	1871	SOUTH WHG	1794
S.WHEELING - OAK ST	1871	SOUTH WHG	1792
S.WHEELING - OAK ST	1871	SOUTH WHG	1792
S.WHEELING - OAK ST	1871	SOUTH WHG	1794
S.WHEELING - PINE ST	1871	SOUTH WHG	1792
S.WHEELING - SECOND ST	1871	SOUTH WHG	1792
S.WHEELING - SEVENTH ST	1871	SOUTH WHG	1792
S.WHEELING - SEVENTH ST	1871	SOUTH WHG	1794
S.WHEELING - SIXTH ST	1871	SOUTH WHG	1792
S.WHEELING - SIXTH ST	1871	SOUTH WHG	1794
S.WHEELING - THIRD ST	1871	SOUTH WHG	1792
S.WHEELING - VINE ST	1871	SOUTH WHG	1792
S.WHEELING - WALNUT ST	1871	SOUTH WHG	1792
S.WHEELING - WATER OR FIRST ST	1871	SOUTH WHG	1792
S.WHEELING - WATER OR FIRST ST	1871	SOUTH WHG	1794
S.WHEELING - WILLOW ST	1871	SOUTH WHG	1792
S.WHEELING - WILLOW ST	1871	SOUTH WHG	1794
SABIN, -	1838	PLAINTIFF	1626
SAILOR, JACOB	1808	DEFENDANT	1658
SAILOR, JACOB	1809	DEFENDANT	1658
SAINTS REST - OLD NAME FOR WEST ALEXANDER	1916	NAT'L ROAD	1862
SALISBURY, JAMES	1823	DEFENDANT	1596
SALLYARD, JOHN	1840	DEFENDANT	1662
SALT LAKE CITY - LDS FAMILY HISTORY CENTERS	2000	APPENDIX	1872
SALTERS, JAMES	1813	DEFENDANT	1611
SALTWORKS / MAP#283	1852	BRKE MAP	1846
SALYARD, JOSEPH	1859	DEFENDANT	1630
SALYARDS, JOSEPH	1860	DEFENDANT	1630
SAMPLE, - / BROS	1871	OH CO. MAP	1740
SAMPLE, A	1871	OH CO. MAP	1743
SAMPLE, A	1871	OH CO. MAP	1743
SAMPLE, JOSEPH W	1836	DEFENDANT	1581
SAMPSON, U	1871	MARH'L MAP	1757
SAND HILL	1871	MARH'L MAP	1746
SAND HILL TWP - MARSHALL CO	1871	MARH'L MAP	1746
SAND HILL TWP - MARSHALL CO	1871	MARH'L MAP	1747
SAND HILL TWP - MARSHALL CO	1871	POPULATION	1816
SAND HILL TWP - MARSHALL CO - BUSINESS NOTICES	1871	MARH'L BUS.	1797
SAND HILL TWP - MARSHALL CO - WEST UNION, DALLAS, P.O.	1871	W.UNION	1812
SAND HILL TWP - MARSHALL CO.	1871	MARH'L MAP	1746
SANDERS, - / FAMILY CEMETERY	1871	HAN MAP	1732
SANDERS, B	1871	HAN MAP	1732
SANDERS, B D / (SAWMILL GONE) - MAP#618	1852	BRKE MAP	1852
SANDERS, B D / (SAWMILL GONE) - MAP#619	1852	BRKE MAP	1852
SANDERS, B D / (SAWMILL GONE) - MAP#621	1852	BRKE MAP	1852
SANDERS, B D / (SAWMILL GONE) - MAP#622	1852	BRKE MAP	1852
SANDERS, B D / MAP#617	1852	BRKE MAP	1852
SANDERS, B D	1871	BRKE MAP	1735
SANDERS, F A	1871	BRKE MAP	1735
SANDERS, H / (?OR R?)	1871	BRKE MAP	1734
SANDERS, M M	1859	DEFENDANT	1565
SANDERS, R / (?OR H?)	1871	BRKE MAP	1734
SANDUSKY CITY, OH	1852	HEMP. RR MAP	1826
SANGSTON, -	1857	DEFENDANT	1663
SANGSTON, J L	1861	DEFENDANT	1618
SANGSTON, JEFFERSON S	1862	DEFENDANT	1618
SAPPINGTONS RUN	1852	BRKE MAP	1851
SAPPINGTONS RUN	1871	BRKE MAP	1734
SATTER, JAMES	1800	DEFENDANT	1576
SAUNDERS, WILLIAM	1860	DEFENDANT	1575
SAVAGE, R	1877	DEFENDANT	1616
SAVEAGE MOUNTAIN - MT.SAVAGE AND SAVAGE MOUNTAIN FIRE BRICKS AND TILES	1871	FRE'MAN'S LDG	1762
SAW & GRIST MILL - BROOKLYN MILLS	1871	HAN MAP	1726
SAW MILL / (?ABBREVIATION S.M.?)	1871	MARH'L MAP	1761
SAW MILL - ANTILLS / BENJAMIN - "CROSS CREEK"	1871	CROSS CRK.BUS.	1772
SAW MILL - ARNOLDS / I (?OR L?)	1871	MARH'L MAP	1752
SAW MILL - ARNOLDS / A.G. - FISH CREEK	1871	FRKLN TWP-BUS.	1797
SAW MILL - BANES / R - MAP#14	1852	BRKE MAP	1839
SAW MILL - BANES / S - GONE / MAP#78	1852	BRKE MAP	1839
SAW MILL - BERDENS / O ?	1871	MARH'L MAP	1749
SAW MILL - BROOKLYN MILLS	1871	HAN MAP	1726
SAW MILL - BROWNS / ? MRS - PETERS RUN	1871	OH CO. MAP	1742
SAW MILL - BROWNS / MRS. M. BROWN - & DAM ON PETERS RUN	1871	OH CO. MAP	1744
SAW MILL - BURROWS / S - ON MIDDLE WHEEING CREEK	1871	OH CO. MAP	1743
SAW MILL - BURROWS . J	1871	MARH'L MAP	1746
SAW MILL - CROWS / W	1871	MARH'L MAP	1752
SAW MILL - DOWLERS . J	1871	MARH'L MAP	1746
SAW MILL - FISH CREEK / RALSTON & CO. ?	1871	MARH'L MAP	1761
SAW MILL - FORSHA & BROTHERS	1871	HAN MAP	1731
SAW MILL - FORSHA & BROTHERS	1871	HAN MAP	1732
SAW MILL - FOWLERS / J - ON CROSS CREEK	1871	BRKE MAP	1735
SAW MILL - HIGGINS, CRAWFORD & CO. / ?	1871	MARH'L MAP	1760
SAW MILL - HINKSON / J	1852	NOT ON MAP	1836
SAW MILL - HOBBS / S - & DAM ON HARDINS RUN	1871	HAN MAP	1731
SAW MILL - HOLLIDAYS COVE	1871	HAN MAP	1733
SAW MILL - HOODS / J - ON HOLBERTS RUN	1871	HAN MAP	1731
SAW MILL - HUSTERS / NATHANIEL - MAP#460	1852	BRKE MAP	1849
SAW MILL - INGRAHAMS / J	1871	MARH'L MAP	1753
SAW MILL - KOONTZ / G - INITIALS G.K. - SAW MILL	1871	MARH'L MAP	1748
SAW MILL - KOONTZS / G. - INITIALS G.K.- FAIRVIEW	1871	MARH'L MAP	1752
SAW MILL - LEWIS / J	1871	BRKE MAP	1736
SAW MILL - LINDSEYS / JOSHUA - HEIRS - MAP#51	1852	BRKE MAP	1840
SAW MILL - LITTLE WHEELING CREEK & RONEY POINT	1871	OH CO. MAP	1743
SAW MILL - LITTLE WHEELING CREEK & RONEY POINT	1871	OH CO. MAP	1744

LXXXVII

'PERSONAL TIME LINE' INDEX TO VOLUME 7 OF THE OHIO COUNTY INDEX

ENTRY	YEAR	SUBJECT	PAGE
SAW MILL - LYNNCAMP RUN / NEAR E.B.YOUNG	1871	MARH'L MAP	1759
SAW MILL - MCCONELS & EDWARDS PORTABLE SAW MILL	1871	MARH'L MAP	1749
SAW MILL - N. OF MCCUTCHEN BROS	1871	OH CO. MAP	1743
SAW MILL - NEALS / MAP#476	1852	BRKE MAP	1850
SAW MILL - NEAR A.G. ARNOLD	1871	MARH'L MAP	1754
SAW MILL - NEAR H.HALL	1871	MARH'L MAP	1755
SAW MILL - NEAR SCOTTS RUN	1871	BRKE MAP	1735
SAW MILL - OLDHAMS / B O	1871	OH CO. MAP	1743
SAW MILL - ON LITTLE FORK OF FISH CREEK - N. OF W. ADAMS / INITIALS S.M. ?	1871	MARH'L MAP	1761
SAW MILL - P.A. & CO / (?ANDERSON?)	1871	HAN MAP	1732
SAW MILL - PATTERONS / R. ON HARDINS RUN	1871	HAN MAP	1731
SAW MILL - ROSENBARGERS / R G ?	1871	MARH'L MAP	1750
SAW MILL - RUTHS / S	1871	MARH'L MAP	1747
SAW MILL - RUTHS / W	1871	MARH'L MAP	1750
SAW MILL - RUTHS / J.&W.RUTHS FLOURING & SAW MILL - NEW GERMANTOWN	1871	SAND HILL-BUS.	1797
SAW MILL - RYLANDS / HUGH P - "HARMONS CREEK"	1871	CROSS CRK BUS.	1772
SAW MILL - S & G MILL / N. OF WHEELING VALLEY FLOURING MILLS	1871	MARH'L MAP	1746
SAW MILL - S. OF J.G. & J. MOORE	1871	MARH'L MAP	1752
SAW MILL - S. OF L.A.WETZEL	1871	MARH'L MAP	1755
SAW MILL - S. OF T. DAVIS	1871	MARH'L MAP	1756
SAW MILL - S.M. - BUFFALO CREEK	1871	BRKE MAP	1736
SAW MILL - S.S. MILL - / (?ABBREVIATION FOR STEAM SAW?)	1871	MARH'L MAP	1761
SAW MILL - SEE ALSO STEAM SAW MILL	1871	MARH'L MAP	1761
SAW MILL - SEE ALSO STEAM SAW MILL	1871	SAND HILL-BUS.	1797
SAW MILL - STRAINS / EBEN - MAP#505	1852	BRKE MAP	1850
SAW MILL - SW. OF J.MCGLUMPHY	1871	MARH'L MAP	1761
SAW MILL - WHETSTONE CREEK / SW. OF W.L. ALLEY	1871	MARH'L MAP	1759
SAW MILL - WOLF CREEK	1871	MARH'L MAP	1750
SAW MILL & DAM - SE. OF B. GRIFFITH / WHETSTONE CREEK	1871	MARH'L MAP	1759
SAW MILL & DAM ON RIGHT FORK OF FISH CREEK - N. OF J.MILLS	1871	MARH'L MAP	1761
SAW MILL DAM - PETERS RUN	1871	OH CO. MAP	1742
SAWLTER, F W	1871	MARH'L MAP	1749
SAWTELL, G	1871	OH CO. MAP	1741
SAWTELL, G / INITIALS G.S.	1871	OH CO. MAP	1741
SAWYER, B C	1871	BRKE MAP	1735
SAYLOR, SAMUEL	1820	DEFENDANT	1611
SAYLOR, SAMUEL	1820	DEFENDANT	1656
SAYLOR, SAMUEL	1821	DEFENDANT	1570
SAYLOR, SAMUEL	1821	DEFENDANT	1572
SAYLOR, SAMUEL	1821	DEFENDANT	1612
SAYLOR, SAMUEL	1822	DEFENDANT	1642
SCALES - TRIDELPHIA	1871	TRIAD.BORO	1784
SCANTLON, J	1871	MARH'L MAP	1745
SCHADE, A	1871	BENWOOD	1798
SCHAFFER, ED	1859	DEFENDANT	1663
SCHAUBER, JOHN	1879	MISC	1694
SCHELLHASE, G	1871	OH CO. MAP	1742
SCHELLHASE, G / INITIALS G.S. ICE HOUSE	1871	OH CO. MAP	1742
SCHELLHASE, GEORGE	1871	OH CO. BUS.	1779
SCHELLHASE, GEORGE / ICE HOUSE	1871	TRIAD.TWP.	1781
SCHELLHASE, GEORGE / RES	1871	TRIAD.TWP.	1781
SCHELT, J / ?	1871	MDSVILLE	1808
SCHELT, J / ?	1871	MDSVILLE	1810
SCHLAG, D	1871	OH CO. MAP	1742
SCHLERNITZAUER, PETER	1876	DEFENDANT	1657
SCHLOG, E	1871	OH CO. MAP	1742
SCHLOG, E	1871	OH CO. MAP	1742
SCHLOG, E	1871	TRIAD.TWP.	1781
SCHMULBACH, HENRY	1874	DEFENDANT	1553
SCHNEIDER, JANE	1877	DEFENDANT	1560
SCHNEIDER, JANE	1878	DEFENDANT	1560
SCHOL NO. 13	1871	BRKE MAP	1737
SCHOLG, E / GROC	1871	TRIAD.TWP.	1781
SCHOOL / NE OF J.W. MORGAN - NO # SHOWN	1871	BKE/OH MAP	1738
SCHOOL - #1 CLAY ST - WHEELING	1871	WHG CITY	1788
SCHOOL - #1 CLAY ST	1871	WHG CITY	1790
SCHOOL - #1 WALNUT ST - S. WHG	1871	SOUTH WHG	1792
SCHOOL - #2 CLAY ST - WHEELING	1871	WHG CITY	1788
SCHOOL - #2 WALNUT ST - S. WHG	1871	SOUTH WHG	1792
SCHOOL - AGNEWS / MAP#166	1852	BRKE MAP	1842
SCHOOL - BANES / MAP#90	1852	BRKE MAP	1842
SCHOOL - BEACH GLEN SCHOOL NO.8 / (?BEECH GLEN?)	1871	OH CO. MAP	1742
SCHOOL - BEECH GLEN SCHOOL NO.8 / (?WRITTEN AS BEACH GLEN?)	1871	OH CO. MAP	1742
SCHOOL - BETHLEHEM SCHOOL NO.2	1871	OH CO. MAP	1742
SCHOOL - BOGGS SCHOOL NO. _ / ELM GROVE DIST	1871	OH CO. MAP	1744
SCHOOL - BOGGS SCHOOL NO.? - ELM GROVE DIST	1871	OH CO. MAP	1742
SCHOOL - BOGGS SCHOOL NO.10	1871	OH CO. MAP	1742
SCHOOL - BRADY SCHOOL NO.8	1871	OH CO. MAP	1740
SCHOOL - BROOKLYN SCHOOL NO. 3	1871	HAN MAP	1726
SCHOOL - BROWNLEE SCHOOL DIST	1871	OH CO. MAP	1743
SCHOOL - BROWNLEE SCHOOL NO. 1	1871	OH CO. MAP	1743
SCHOOL - C ST - MOUNDSVILLE	1871	MDSVILLE	1809
SCHOOL - CAMERON - RIDGE ST	1871	CAMERON	1803
SCHOOL - CHAPLINE ST	1871	WHG CITY	1790
SCHOOL - CHESTNUT ST - WHEELING ISLAND	1871	WHG ISLAND	1788
SCHOOL - CLAY ST	1871	WHG CITY	1790
SCHOOL - COL. MEADE INSTITUTE / MAP#398	1852	BRKE MAP	1846
SCHOOL - CORNER CHESTNUT & CUPPYS ALLEY - NEW CUMBERLAND	1871	NEW CUMB'LD	1767
SCHOOL - CORNER JEFFERSON & CHESTNUT - NEW CUMBERLAND	1871	NEW CUMB'LD	1767
SCHOOL - ELM GROVE DIST	1871	OH CO. MAP	1744
SCHOOL - FAIRVIEW SCHOOL	1871	OH CO. MAP	1743
SCHOOL - FILBERT ST - S. WHG	1871	SOUTH WHG	1792
SCHOOL - FIRST ST - BENWOOD	1871	BENWOOD	1798
SCHOOL - FRANKLIN SCHOOL NO. 1	1871	HAN MAP	1727
SCHOOL - FULTON - NATIONAL ROAD	1871	WHG CITY	1787
SCHOOL - GERMAN SCHOOL - TRIADELPHIA - NATL RD	1871	TRIAD.BORO.	1784
SCHOOL - GLENS RUN	1871	OH CO. MAP	1741
SCHOOL - GORCLY'S / MAP#586	1852	BRKE MAP	1851
SCHOOL - HAZELDELL SCHOOL NO.5	1871	MARH'L MAP	1750
SCHOOL - HEDGES / MAP#36	1852	BRKE MAP	1840
SCHOOL - HERRON SCHOOL	1871	HAN MAP	1731
SCHOOL - HIGHLAND DIST SCHOOL NO. / NO # SHOWN	1871	OH CO. MAP	1741
SCHOOL - HORAB SCHOOL NO. 2	1871	HAN MAP	1732
SCHOOL - HUKLE'S / MAP#171	1852	BRKE MAP	1843
SCHOOL - JEFFERSON SCHOOL NO. 5	1871	HAN MAP	1731
SCHOOL - JEFFERSON SCHOOL NO. 5	1871	HAN MAP	1732
SCHOOL - KIMMINS SCHOOL NO. 2	1871	OH CO. MAP	1743
SCHOOL - MADISON ST	1871	WHG CITY	1788
SCHOOL - MARKET & HIGH STS. - NEW MANCHESTER	1871	NEW MANCH.	1769
SCHOOL - MARKET ST - WHEELING	1871	WHG CITY	1786
SCHOOL - MARSH'S / MAP#591	1852	BRKE MAP	1851
SCHOOL - MAY'S / MAP#510	1852	BRKE MAP	1849
SCHOOL - MONROE ST	1871	WHG CITY	1788
SCHOOL - N. OF WHEELING IRON WORKS	1871	WHG CITY	1786
SCHOOL - NATIONAL ROAD - LEATHERWOOD	1871	WHG CITY	1787
SCHOOL - NE. OF ORCHARDALE	1871	HAN MAP	1727
SCHOOL - NEAR TOLL HOUSE - NATIONAL ROAD - LEATHERWOOD	1871	WHG CITY	1789
SCHOOL - NO NAME / MAP#64	1852	BRKE MAP	1840
SCHOOL - NO NAME / MAP#305	1852	BRKE MAP	1844
SCHOOL - NO NAME / MAP#610	1852	BRKE MAP	1852
SCHOOL - NORMAL SCHOOL - WEST LIBERTY	1871	W.LIBRTY.BUS.	1780
SCHOOL - NORTH ST - WHEELING	1871	WHG CITY	1786
SCHOOL - NOT FREE - CLAY TWP	1871	MARH'L MAP	1751
SCHOOL - ON SHORT CREEK	1871	BKE/OH MAP	1738
SCHOOL - ORR DIST SCHOOL NO. 4	1871	OH CO. MAP	1743
SCHOOL - PIERCE'S RUN / MAP#242	1852	BRKE MAP	1844
SCHOOL - QUINCY ST	1871	WHG CITY	1788
SCHOOL - RICHARDSON ST. - BETHANY	1871	BETHANY	1773
SCHOOL - RICHLAND DIST SCHOOL NO. 6	1871	OH CO. MAP	1741
SCHOOL - RONEY POINT	1871	OH CO. MAP	1744
SCHOOL - RONEY POINT SCHOOL	1871	OH CO. MAP	1743
SCHOOL - ROUGH & READY SCHOOL NO. 7	1871	OH CO. MAP	1740
SCHOOL - S. OF FLAG QUARRY	1871	OH CO. MAP	1742
SCHOOL - SE OF ELWOOD GROVE	1871	HAN MAP	1726
SCHOOL - SHEPARD SCHOOL - ELM GROVE	1871	OH CO. MAP	1742

'PERSONAL TIME LINE' INDEX TO VOLUME 7 OF THE *OHIO COUNTY INDEX*

ENTRY	YEAR	SUBJECT	PAGE
SCHOOL - SIXTH ST	1871	WHG CITY	1790
SCHOOL - SIXTH ST - WHEELING	1871	WHG CITY	1788
SCHOOL - SYCAMORE / MAP#577	1852	BRKE MAP	1852
SCHOOL - TENT / MAP#535	1852	BRKE MAP	1852
SCHOOL - TRIADELPHIA	1871	OH CO. MAP	1743
SCHOOL - TRIADELPHIA	1871	OH CO. MAP	1744
SCHOOL - UNIV. CHURCH & SCHOOL / (?UNIVERSALIST?)	1871	MARH'L MAP	1752
SCHOOL - VERNON SCHOOL No.4	1871	HAN MAP	1732
SCHOOL - WALKERS / MAP#25	1852	BRKE MAP	1839
SCHOOL - WALLACE'S / (LOUISA OF BROOKE) - MAP#542	1852	BRKE MAP	1852
SCHOOL - WALNUT RIDGE / MAP#213	1852	BRKE MAP	1842
SCHOOL - WARDEN DIST SCHOOL NO.9	1871	OH CO. MAP	1741
SCHOOL - WASHINGTON SCHOOL	1871	HAN MAP	1726
SCHOOL - WAUGH'S / MAP#253	1852	BRKE MAP	1843
SCHOOL - WELLS	1871	BRKE MAP	1736
SCHOOL - WELLSBURG FREE SCHOOL / QUEEN ST	1871	WELLSBURG	1777
SCHOOL - WEST LIBERTY NORMAL SCHOOL	1871	W.LIBERTY	1780
SCHOOL HOUSE - OLD / NAME IN OHIO RIVER	1871	BRKE MAP	1736
SCHOOL HOUSE - OLD / NAME IN OHIO RIVER	1871	BKE/OH MAP	1738
SCHOOL HOUSE NO.1	1871	HAN MAP	1733
SCHOOL NO. 1	1871	HAN MAP	1730
SCHOOL NO. 1	1871	BRKE MAP	1734
SCHOOL NO. 1	1871	BKE/OH MAP	1739
SCHOOL NO. 1	1871	OH CO. MAP	1740
SCHOOL NO. 10 / NE CORNER OF MAP	1871	BRKE MAP	1735
SCHOOL NO. 10	1871	BRKE MAP	1737
SCHOOL NO. 11	1871	BRKE MAP	1735
SCHOOL NO. 12	1871	BKE/OH MAP	1739
SCHOOL NO. 13	1871	BKE/OH MAP	1739
SCHOOL NO. 15 - LIBERTY TWP	1871	MARH'L MAP	1760
SCHOOL NO. 2	1871	BRKE MAP	1734
SCHOOL NO. 2	1871	BKE/OH MAP	1738
SCHOOL NO. 2	1871	OH CO. MAP	1740
SCHOOL NO. 2 - OHIO CO	1871	BKE/OH MAP	1738
SCHOOL NO. 3	1871	BRKE MAP	1734
SCHOOL NO. 3	1871	BRKE MAP	1736
SCHOOL NO. 3	1871	BKE/OH MAP	1738
SCHOOL NO. 3	1871	BKE/OH MAP	1739
SCHOOL NO. 3 - FAIRMOUNT ROAD	1871	MARH'L MAP	1745
SCHOOL NO. 4	1871	BRKE MAP	1734
SCHOOL NO. 4	1871	OH CO. MAP	1740
SCHOOL NO. 4 - WEBSTER TWP - SW. OF WOLF RUN PRESBYTERIAN CHURCH	1871	MARH'L MAP	1750
SCHOOL NO. 5	1871	BRKE MAP	1734
SCHOOL NO. 5	1871	OH CO. MAP	1740
SCHOOL NO. 6	1871	BKE/OH MAP	1739
SCHOOL NO. 6 - W OF FORTUNE HILL	1871	HAN MAP	1727
SCHOOL NO. 7	1871	BRKE MAP	1735
SCHOOL NO. 7	1871	BRKE MAP	1737
SCHOOL NO. 7 / SAND HILL TWP	1871	MARH'L MAP	1746
SCHOOL NO. 7 - N. OF WALNUT SPRING	1871	OH CO. MAP	1743
SCHOOL NO. 8	1871	BRKE MAP	1737
SCHOOL NO. 8	1871	BRKE MAP	1737
SCHOOL NO. 8	1871	OH CO. MAP	1741
SCHOOL NO. 8 - S. OF BENWOOD	1871	MARH'L MAP	1745
SCHOOL NO. 8 - WSH. TWP	1871	MARH'L MAP	1749
SCHOOL NO. 9 - FOWLERS P.O.	1871	BRKE MAP	1735
SCHOOL NO.1 - CLAY TWP	1871	MARH'L MAP	1752
SCHOOL NO.1 - CLAY TWP	1871	MARH'L MAP	1752
SCHOOL NO.1 - EDGINGTON STATION	1871	EDGINGTON STA.	1774
SCHOOL NO.1 - MEADE TWP	1871	MARH'L MAP	1756
SCHOOL NO.1 - MEADE TWP	1871	MARH'L MAP	1759
SCHOOL NO.1 - WASHINGTON TWP - N. OF J.ROBINSON	1871	MARH'L MAP	1749
SCHOOL NO.1 - WEBSTER TWP	1871	MARH'L MAP	1752
SCHOOL NO.1 - WEST UNION	1871	MARH'L MAP	1747
SCHOOL NO.10 - NEAR FAIRMONT FARM	1871	MARH'L MAP	1755
SCHOOL NO.10 - SLIPPERY FORD	1871	MARH'L MAP	1755
SCHOOL NO.11 - CLAY TWP	1871	MARH'L MAP	1751
SCHOOL NO.11 - HORNBROOK BROTHERS	1871	MARH'L MAP	1754
SCHOOL NO.11 - LEATHERWOOD	1871	TRIAD.TWP.	1781
SCHOOL NO.11 - LIBERTY TWP	1871	MARH'L MAP	1761
SCHOOL NO.12 - CLAY TWP	1871	MARH'L MAP	1751
SCHOOL NO.12 - LIBERTY TWP	1871	MARH'L MAP	1757
SCHOOL NO.12 - SAND HILL TWP	1871	MARH'L MAP	1747
SCHOOL NO.12 - SW OF WILLIAM MURCHLAND	1871	BRKE MAP	1735
SCHOOL NO.13 - FRANKLIN TWP	1871	MARH'L MAP	1754
SCHOOL NO.13 - MEADE TWP	1871	MARH'L MAP	1760
SCHOOL NO.13- LIBERTY TWP	1871	MARH'L MAP	1757
SCHOOL NO.14 - LIBERTY TWP	1871	MARH'L MAP	1757
SCHOOL NO.14 - LIBERTY TWP	1871	MARH'L MAP	1761
SCHOOL NO.15 - LIBERTY TWP	1871	MARH'L MAP	1756
SCHOOL NO.16 - LIBERTY TWP	1871	MARH'L MAP	1761
SCHOOL NO.2 - CAMERON TWP	1871	MARH'L MAP	1753
SCHOOL NO.2 - CLAY TWP	1871	MARH'L MAP	1752
SCHOOL NO.2 - FRANKLIN TWP	1871	MARH'L MAP	1758
SCHOOL NO.2 - LIBERTY TWP	1871	MARH'L MAP	1757
SCHOOL NO.2 - MEADE TWP	1871	MARH'L MAP	1756
SCHOOL NO.2 - MEADE TWP	1871	MARH'L MAP	1760
SCHOOL NO.2 - PLEASANT VALLEY P.O.	1871	MARH'L MAP	1749
SCHOOL NO.2 - UNION TWP	1871	MARH'L MAP	1745
SCHOOL NO.2 - WASHINGTON TWP	1871	MARH'L MAP	1749
SCHOOL NO.20 - LIBERTY TWP	1871	MARH'L MAP	1761
SCHOOL NO.3	1871	BRKE MAP	1737
SCHOOL NO.3 - CAMERON TWP	1871	MARH'L MAP	1753
SCHOOL NO.3 - FRANKLIN TWP	1871	MARH'L MAP	1758
SCHOOL NO.3 - MEADE TWP	1871	MARH'L MAP	1756
SCHOOL NO.3 - MEADE TWP	1871	MARH'L MAP	1756
SCHOOL NO.3 - ROCK LICK P.O.	1871	MARH'L MAP	1753
SCHOOL NO.3 - ROSBY'S ROCK	1871	MARH'L MAP	1752
SCHOOL NO.3 - SAND HILL TWP	1871	MARH'L MAP	1747
SCHOOL NO.3 - WASHINGTON TWP	1871	MARH'L MAP	1748
SCHOOL NO.3 - WEBSTER TWP / W. OF CONKEL SPRINGS	1871	MARH'L MAP	1750
SCHOOL NO.4	1871	HAN MAP	1731
SCHOOL NO.4 / SAND HILL TWP	1871	MARH'L MAP	1746
SCHOOL NO.4 - CLAY TWP	1871	MARH'L MAP	1751
SCHOOL NO.4 - FRANKLIN TWP	1871	MARH'L MAP	1758
SCHOOL NO.4 - LIBERTY TWP	1871	MARH'L MAP	1757
SCHOOL NO.4 - LYNNCAMP P.O.	1871	MARH'L MAP	1755
SCHOOL NO.4 - LYNNCAMP P.O.	1871	MARH'L MAP	1759
SCHOOL NO.4 - SAND HILL TWP	1871	MARH'L MAP	1747
SCHOOL NO.4 - WASH. TWP	1871	MARH'L MAP	1749
SCHOOL NO.5 / SAND HILL TWP	1871	MARH'L MAP	1746
SCHOOL NO.5 / SAND HILL TWP	1871	MARH'L MAP	1746
SCHOOL NO.5 - CLAY TWP	1871	MARH'L MAP	1751
SCHOOL NO.5 - FISH CREEK	1871	MARH'L MAP	1755
SCHOOL NO.5 - FRAKNLIN TWP	1871	MARH'L MAP	1754
SCHOOL NO.5 - FRANKLIN TWP	1871	MARH'L MAP	1758
SCHOOL NO.5 - LIBERTY TWP	1871	MARH'L MAP	1757
SCHOOL NO.5 - MOUTH OF LITTLE GRAVE CREEK	1871	MARH'L MAP	1745
SCHOOL NO.5 - WASHINGTON TWP	1871	MARH'L MAP	1748
SCHOOL NO.5 - WASHINGTON TWP	1871	MARH'L MAP	1748
SCHOOL NO.5 - WASHINGTON TWP	1871	MARH'L MAP	1748
SCHOOL NO.6	1871	HAN MAP	1728
SCHOOL NO.6	1871	HAN MAP	1732
SCHOOL NO.6	1871	BRKE MAP	1735
SCHOOL NO.6 - E.OF FRUIT HOME	1871	MARH'L MAP	1750
SCHOOL NO.6 - FRANKLIN TWP	1871	MARH'L MAP	1754
SCHOOL NO.6 - GLEN EASTON	1871	GLEN EASTON	1801
SCHOOL NO.6 - LIBERTY TWP	1871	MARH'L MAP	1757
SCHOOL NO.6 - LIBERTY TWP / NEQAR MRS.MANNING - CUT OFF EDGE OF MAP	1871	MARH'L MAP	1760
SCHOOL NO.6 - PLEASANT VIEW / SAND HILL TWP	1871	MARH'L MAP	1746
SCHOOL NO.6 - S. OF SHERRARD	1871	MARH'L MAP	1746
SCHOOL NO.6 - SW. OF SOLDIERS REST	1871	MARH'L MAP	1755
SCHOOL NO.6 - TRIADELPHIA / (?6?)	1871	TRIAD.BORO.	1785
SCHOOL NO.7 / OHIO CO	1871	MARH'L MAP	1746
SCHOOL NO.7 - LOUDENSVILLE	1871	MARH'L MAP	1753
SCHOOL NO.7 - MEADE TWP	1871	MARH'L MAP	1756
SCHOOL NO.7 - PORTERS LANDING	1871	FRE'MAN'S LDG	1764
SCHOOL NO.7 - S. OF RED POINT FARM	1871	MARH'L MAP	1746
SCHOOL NO.7 - WEBSTER TWP - DRY RIDGE ROAD	1871	MARH'L MAP	1750
SCHOOL NO.7 - WOODLAND P.O.	1871	MARH'L MAP	1754
SCHOOL NO.8 - CAMERON TWP	1871	MARH'L MAP	1753
SCHOOL NO.8 - FRANKLIN TWP	1871	MARH'L MAP	1759
SCHOOL NO.8 - LIBERTY TWP	1871	MARH'L MAP	1760
SCHOOL NO.8 - MEADE TWP	1871	MARH'L MAP	1756
SCHOOL NO.8 - N. OF CHESTNUT RIDGE	1871	MARH'L MAP	1745
SCHOOL NO.9 - BUFFALO CREEK	1871	BRKE MAP	1736
SCHOOL NO.9 - FRANKLIN TWP	1871	MARH'L MAP	1754
SCHOOL NO.9 - LIBERTY TWP	1871	MARH'L MAP	1761

ENTRY	YEAR	SUBJECT	PAGE	ENTRY	YEAR	SUBJECT	PAGE
SCHOOL NO. 9 - MEADE TWP	1871	MARH'L MAP	1756	SEWARD, -	1871	BETHANY	1773
SCHOOL NO. 9 - WEST LIBERTY	1871	W. LIBERTY	1780	SEWER PIPE & TERRACOTTA WORKS	1871	RIV. RD S. OF N.C.	1771
SCHOOLS - COUNTY SUPT OF SCHOOL - WELLSBURG	1871	WLSBRG BUS	1772	SEWRIGHT, JAMES	1808	DEFENDANT	1610
SCHOOLS - WEST LIBERTY	1871	BKE/OH MAP	1739	SEXTON, JOHN	1828	DEFENDANT	1585
SCHOTT, B	1871	LAGRANGE	1792	SEXTON, JOHN	1832	DEFENDANT	1622
SCHOTT, B	1871	LAGRANGE	1794	SEXTON, JOHN	1833	DEFENDANT	1557
SCHROADER, N	1871	MARH'L MAP	1746	SEXTON, JOHN	1833	DEFENDANT	1566
SCHU, - / COAL CO - NAME WRITTEN IN OHIO RIVER	1871	BRKE MAP	1736	SEXTON, JOHN	1833	DEFENDANT	1620
				SEXTON, JOHN	1836	DEFENDANT	1551
SCHUBERT, C	1871	OH CO. MAP	1742	SEXTON, JOHN	1836	DEFENDANT	1591
SCHUCHMAN & HANNLEIN - PITTSBURG, PA / MAP LITHOGR.	1852	BRKE MAP	1838	SEXTON, JOHN	1837	DEFENDANT	1669
				SEXTON, JOHN	1838	DEFENDANT	1563
SCHUCKMAN, JOHN	1852	DEFENDANT	1616	SEXTON, JOHN	1838	DEFENDANT	1622
SCHWENCHBECK - CHILDREN	1872	MISC	1683	SEXTON, JOHN	1839	DEFENDANT	1565
SCHWENCHBECK, LOUISA	1872	MISC	1683	SEYBERT, JOHN	1807	DEFENDANT	1608
SCHWIM, H	1871	BENWOOD	1798	SEYBOLD, JOSEPH	1866	MISC	1690
SCHWIM, H / INITIALS H.S.	1871	BENWOOD	1798	SHABOURDAY, LEEK	1877	DEFENDANT	1595
SCIOTA VALLEY RR	1852	HEMP. RR MAP	1826	SHADDOCK, - / MRS - CUT OFF - E. SIDE OF MAP	1871	MARH'L MAP	1756
SCOTT, - / MRS	1871	NEW MANCH.	1769				
SCOTT, -	1871	WELLSBURG	1777	SHADDOCK, - / MRS - CUT OFF W. SIDE OF MAP	1871	MARH'L MAP	1757
SCOTT, - / NEFF & SCOTT	1871	MDSVILLE	1808				
SCOTT, ALEXANDER / HOMESTEAD - E. SIDE OF MAP	1871	HAN MAP	1730	SHADE RUN	1871	HAN MAP	1732
				SHADY GLEN SCHOOL NO. 2	1871	HAN MAP	1731
SCOTT, ALEXANDER / HOMESTEAD - W. SIDE OF MAP	1871	HAN MAP	1731	SHADY GROVE	1871	HAN MAP	1731
				SHADY ORCHARD	1871	MARH'L MAP	1747
SCOTT, CHAS	1819	DEFENDANT	1624	SHADY VALLEY / N. OF A. BURNS	1871	MARH'L MAP	1746
SCOTT, H	1871	MARH'L MAP	1749	SHAFER, B	1871	WELLSBURG	1778
SCOTT, J C JR	1871	HAN MAP	1730	SHAFFER, -	1871	OH CO. MAP	1743
SCOTT, J R	1871	HAN MAP	1731	SHAFFIELD, J H	1875	DEFENDANT	1664
SCOTT, J R	1871	HAN MAP	1731	SHANE, - / ATKINSON & SHANE	1871	RIV. RD N. OF N.C.	1763
SCOTT, J T	1871	MARH'L MAP	1758	SHANE, - / ATKINSON & SHANE - FIRE BRICK WORKS	1871	RIV. RD N. OF N.C.	1770
SCOTT, JOHN / MAP#340	1852	BRKE MAP	1846				
SCOTT, JOHN / MAP#341	1852	BRKE MAP	1846	SHANE, B F	1871	RIV. RD N. OF N.C.	1770
SCOTT, JOHN	1876	DEFENDANT	1558	SHANE, B F / INITIALS B.F.S	1871	RIV. RD N. OF N.C.	1770
SCOTT, MATTHEW	1818	PLAINTIFF	1638	SHANKY, W / DOCTOR	1871	NEW CUMB'LD	1767
SCOTT, ROBERT / HEIRS - (HAUNTED) - MAP#365	1852	BRKE MAP	1847	SHANLEY, B	1876	DEFENDANT	1627
				SHANLEY, BERNARD	1876	DEFENDANT	1590
SCOTT, ROBERT / HEIRS - MAP#360	1852	BRKE MAP	1847	SHANLEY, W / ? BLACKSMITH SHOP	1871	NEW CUMB'LD	1767
SCOTT, ROBERT / HEIRS - MAP#364	1852	BRKE MAP	1847	SHARP, -	1853	PLAINTIFF	1626
SCOTT, T	1871	MARH'L MAP	1747	SHARP, -	1854	PLAINTIFF	1629
SCOTT, WILLIAM / HOMESTEAD	1871	HAN MAP	1731	SHARP, -	1856	PLAINTIFF	1630
SCOTTS RUN	1852	BRKE MAP	1850	SHARP, -	1857	PLAINTIFF	1630
SCOTTS RUN	1871	BRKE MAP	1735	SHARP, -	1858	PLAINTIFF	1630
SCOTTS RUN - SAW MILL ON	1871	BRKE MAP	1735	SHARP, -	1860	PLAINTIFF	1631
SCOVILL, S	1821	DEFENDANT	1668	SHARP, -	1862	PLAINTIFF	1631
SCRIBNER, ELIAS	1834	DEFENDANT	1563	SHARP, P / EST - ICE HOUSE	1871	MDSVILLE	1809
SEABOARD SYSTEM - FREIGHT	1852	HEMPFIELD RR	1820	SHARP, PEARLEY	1827	DEFENDANT	1649
SEABRIGHT, C	1871	MARH'L MAP	1746	SHARP, PEARLEY	1834	DEFENDANT	1591
SEABRIGHT, H	1871	OH CO. MAP	1743	SHARP, PEARLY	1836	DEFENDANT	1583
SEABRIGHT, H	1871	OH CO. MAP	1744	SHARPS GARDEN	1871	MDSVL BUS.	1796
SEABRIGHT, H	1871	RONEY PT.	1783	SHATTUCK, N K	1871	MDSVL BUS.	1796
SEABRIGHT, H / BLACKSMITH & WAGON SHOP	1871	RONEY PT.	1783	SHATTUCK, N K	1871	MDSVILLE	1809
				SHATTUCK, N K / RES	1871	MDSVILLE	1809
SEABRIGHT, H / RES	1871	RONEY PT.	1783	SHAUBLE, P	1871	NEW CUMB'LD	1767
SEABRIGHT, HENRY / BLACKSMITH	1871	OH CO. BUS.	1779	SHAW, -	1833	PLAINTIFF	1620
SEABRIGHT, L	1871	MARH'L MAP	1745	SHAW, -	1834	PLAINTIFF	1620
SEABROOK, THOMAS	1874	DEFENDANT	1631	SHAW, G	1871	OH CO. MAP	1742
SEABROOK, THOMAS	1874	DEFENDANT	1643	SHAW, G	1871	OH CO. MAP	1744
SEAMAN, JONAH	1787	MISC	1684	SHAW, JOSEPH	1806	DEFENDANT	1659
SEAMON, JOHN D	1823	DEFENDANT	1559	SHAW, JOSEPH	1807	DEFENDANT	1645
SEAMON, JOHN D	1824	MISC	1680	SHAW, JOSEPH	1808	DEFENDANT	1645
SEAMON, JONAH	1784	MISC	1684	SHAW, WILLIAM	1818	DEFENDANT	1589
SEAMON, JONAH	1809	DEFENDANT	1667	SHAW, WILLIAM	1819	DEFENDANT	1589
SEARS, WILLIAM / NE CORNER OF MAP	1871	OH CO. MAP	1743	SHAW, WILLIAM	1820	DEFENDANT	1589
				SHAW, WILLIAM	1821	DEFENDANT	1589
SEARS, WILLIAM / E. SIDE OF MAP	1871	MARH'L MAP	1747	SHAW, WILLIAM	1824	DEFENDANT	1589
SEATON, J B	1871	MARH'L MAP	1750	SHAW, WILLIAM	1840	DEFENDANT	1661
SEBRIGHT, L	1871	LAGRANGE	1792	SHAWAL, WILLIAM	1792	DEFENDANT	1589
SEBRIGHT, L	1871	LAGRANGE	1794	SHAY & MOORE	1871	NEW MANCH.	1769
SECEDER CHURCH / MAP#534	1852	BRKE MAP	1852	SHAY, W	1871	NEW MANCH.	1769
SEEVERS, -	1837	PLAINTIFF	1622	SHEAPHEARD - SEE ALSO SHEPHERD	1871	MARH'L MAP	1748
SEEVERS, -	1838	PLAINTIFF	1622				
SEEVERS, -	1843	PLAINTIFF	1623	SHEAPHEARD, - / MRS	1871	MARH'L MAP	1748
SEIDLER, J	1871	MARH'L MAP	1754	SHEETS, J	1871	MDSVILLE	1808
SELBY, GEROGE	1815	DEFENDANT	1667	SHEFFIELD, -	1856	PLAINTIFF	1630
SELBY, WILLIAM T	1852	HEMPFIELD RR	1822	SHEIB, WILLIAM H	1876	DEFENDANT	1558
SELBY, WILLIAM T	1852	HEMPFIELD RR	1822	SHEIBLEHOOD, J	1871	MARH'L MAP	1759
SELLS RUN	1871	BRKE MAP	1737	SHELBY, -	1857	PLAINTIFF	1621
SELMAN, THOMAS	1787	DEFENDANT	1556	SHELL SPRING - S. OF GRAY HOMESTEAD	1871	MARH'L MAP	1750
SELMON, THOMAS	1787	DEFENDANT	1644				
SEMINARY - WASHINGTON LADIES SEMINARY / WASH., PA.	1916	NAT'L ROAD	1861	SHELLCROSS, ALEXANDER	1837	DEFENDANT	1561
				SHELPER, S / ?(SNOWN AS SHEPLER) - S OF PLEASANT HILL	1871	HAN MAP	1732
SEMORE, ROBERT	1875	DEFENDANT	1657				
SETTLE, JOHN	1834	DEFENDANT	1582	SHEPARD SCHOOL - ELM GROVE	1871	OH CO. MAP	1742
SEVEN WILLOWS	1871	OH CO. MAP	1740	SHEPARD SCHOOL - ELM GROVE	1871	ELM GROVE	1782

ENTRY	YEAR	SUBJECT	PAGE	ENTRY	YEAR	SUBJECT	PAGE
SHEPHEARD, MOSES	1806	DEFENDANT	1666	SHOP - SHOE SHOP - LIMESTONE	1871	MARH'L MAP	1749
SHEPHEARD, MOSES	1807	DEFENDANT	1666	SHOP - WAGON SHOP - COWANS / J P	1871	HAN MAP	1733
SHEPHEARD, NATHAN	1795	MISC	1691	SHORT CREEK	1852	BRKE MAP	1839
SHEPHERD - SEE ALSO SHEAPHEARD	1871	MARH'L MAP	1748	SHORT CREEK	1871	BKE/OH MAP	1738
				SHORT CREEK - GRIST MILL ON	1871	BKE/OH MAP	1739
SHEPHERD, DAVID	1778	APPENDIX	1874	SHORT CREEK - MOUTH OF	1871	BKE/OH MAP	1738
SHEPHERD, DAVID	1778	APPENDIX	1874	SHORT CREEK - MOUTH OF AT OHIO	1852	BRKE MAP	1839
SHEPHERD, DAVID	1778	APPENDIX	1874	RIVER			
SHEPHERD, I	1871	MARH'L MAP	1746	SHORT CREEK - S & G MILL ON	1871	BKE/OH MAP	1738
SHEPHERD, I / INITIALS I.S.	1871	MARH'L MAP	1746	SHORT CREEK COAL BANK	1871	BUFF.TWP.BUS.	1772
SHEPHERD, J	1871	MARH'L MAP	1746	SHORT CREEK HO / HOUSE	1871	BKE/OH MAP	1738
SHEPHERD, J / INITIALS J.S.	1871	MARH'L MAP	1746	SHORT CREEK HOUSE / HOTEL	1871	BUFF.TWP.BUS.	1772
SHEPHERD, JOHN	1811	DEFENDANT	1599	SHORTS, - / BROS	1871	W.LIBERTY	1780
SHEPHERD, LYDIA / HISTORY	1916	NAT'L ROAD	1864	SHORTS, - / HRS - HEIRS	1871	W.LIBERTY	1780
SHEPHERD, LYDIA / HISTORY	1916	NAT'L ROAD	1865	SHORTS, J P & CO - WAGON SHOP	1871	W.LIBERTY	1780
SHEPHERD, MOSES	1805	DEFENDANT	1600	SHOWACRE, S H H	1871	MARH'L MAP	1748
SHEPHERD, MOSES	1806	DEFENDANT	1658	SHOWACRE, W H H	1871	MDSVILLE	1806
SHEPHERD, MOSES	1807	DEFENDANT	1658	SHOWMAN, E W	1878	DEFENDANT	1601
SHEPHERD, MOSES	1809	DEFENDANT	1667	SHRADES, J	1871	BELLTON	1814
SHEPHERD, MOSES	1811	MISC	1682	SHRADES, J / INITIALS J.S.	1871	BELLTON	1814
SHEPHERD, MOSES	1812	DEFENDANT	1635	SHRIER, A	1871	OH CO. MAP	1741
SHEPHERD, MOSES	1812	DEFENDANT	1667	SHRIMPLIN, G	1871	BRKE MAP	1736
SHEPHERD, MOSES	1815	DEFENDANT	1667	SHRIMPLIN, JOHN / MAP#194	1852	BRKE MAP	1843
SHEPHERD, MOSES	1822	DEFENDANT	1612	SHRIMPLIN, L	1871	BRKE MAP	1737
SHEPHERD, MOSES	1826	DEFENDANT	1563	SHRIMPLIN, WILLIAM G / COOPER	1871	BUFF.TWP.BUS.	1772
SHEPHERD, MOSES	1830	DEFENDANT	1650	SHRIVER, HAMPDEN	1880	DEFENDANT	1673
SHEPHERD, MOSES / COL. - HISTORY	1916	NAT'L ROAD	1864	SHRIVER, WILLIAM W	1856	DEFENDANT	1636
SHEPHERD, MOSES / COL. - HISTORY	1916	NAT'L ROAD	1865	SHRODER, J / BELLTON P.O.	1871	MARH'L MAP	1761
SHEPHERD, MOSES / MANSION & HISTORY	1916	NAT'L ROAD	1865	SHUMIRE, BARTHOLD	1825	MISC	1683
				SHUTE, A	1871	MARH'L MAP	1745
SHEPHERD, N	1871	MARH'L MAP	1756	SHUTLER, J	1871	MARH'L MAP	1755
SHEPHERD, N	1871	MARH'L MAP	1760	SHUTLER, J	1871	MARH'L MAP	1759
SHEPHERD, THOMAS	1797	DEFENDANT	1655	SHUTLER, J	1871	MARH'L MAP	1759
SHEPHERD, WILLIAM	1804	DEFENDANT	1637	SIBERT, J	1871	MARH'L MAP	1757
SHEPHERD, WILLIAM	1805	DEFENDANT	1637	SIBERT, J	1871	MARH'L MAP	1761
SHEPHERD, WILLIAM	1806	DEFENDANT	1637	SIBERTS, B	1871	MARH'L MAP	1755
SHEPHERD, WILLIAM	1806	DEFENDANT	1666	SIBERTS, J	1871	MARH'L MAP	1755
SHEPHERD, WILLIAM	1807	DEFENDANT	1666	SIBERTS, W	1871	MARH'L MAP	1755
SHEPHERDS RUN	1852	BRKE MAP	1843	SICKLER, LAWRENCE	1876	DEFENDANT	1631
SHEPLER, S / (?SHELPER?)-S. OF PLEASANT HILL	1871	HAN MAP	1732	SICKLES, W	1871	MARH'L MAP	1750
				SIGAFOOSE, G	1871	MDSVILLE	1808
SHEPPARD, E T	1875	MISC	1688	SIGHTLY HOME	1871	OH CO. MAP	1740
SHEPPARD, JOSEPH	1863	MISC	1699	SIGHTLY HOME	1871	MARH'L MAP	1746
SHERFY, R	1871	MARH'L MAP	1752	SIGHTLY HOME - CLAY TWP	1871	MARH'L MAP	1751
SHERFY, R / INITIALS R.S.	1871	MARH'L MAP	1752	SIGHTS, GEORGE W	1839	DEFENDANT	1614
SHERFY, R	1871	MARH'L MAP	1755	SIGHTS, GEORGE W	1839	DEFENDANT	1619
SHERFY, R / INITIALS R.S.	1871	MARH'L MAP	1756	SIGHTS, GEORGE W	1840	DEFENDANT	1643
SHERMAN, - / MRS	1871	MDSVILLE	1808	SILVER MAPLE RIDGE	1871	MARH'L MAP	1746
SHERRARD / MARSHALL CO	1871	DISTANCES	1815	SILVERS FORK	1852	BRKE MAP	1840
SHERRARD - CEMETERY - ACROSS FROM L.CRISWELL	1871	SHERRARD	1811	SILVERS, JAMES	1852	NOT ON MAP	1836
				SILVERS, JAMES / MAP#67	1852	BRKE MAP	1840
SHERRARD - DETAIL MAP	1871	SHERRARD	1811	SILVEY, A	1852	HEMPFIELD RR	1824
SHERRARD - SEE ALSO SHERRARD P.O.	1871	SHERRARD	1811	SIMMONS, JOHN	1871	MARH'L MAP	1760
SHERRARD - WAGON SHOP	1871	SHERRARD	1811	SIMMONS, JOSEPH	1859	MISC	1698
SHERRARD P.O.	1871	MARH'L MAP	1746	SIMMS - CHILDREN	1823	MISC	1700
SHERRARD P.O. - POST OFFICE	1871	SHERRARD	1811	SIMMS, CLABURN	1802	DEFENDANT	1572
SHERRARD P.O. - UNION TOWNSHIP - MARSHALL CO - DETAIL MAP	1871	SHERRARD	1811	SIMMS, CLABURN	1823	MISC	1704
				SIMMS, CLEABURN	1816	DEFENDANT	1645
SHERROD, DAVID B	1877	DEFENDANT	1586	SIMMS, CLEABURN	1818	DEFENDANT	1646
SHEWELL, -	1792	DEFENDANT	1589	SIMMS, CLEABURN	1818	DEFENDANT	1648
SHIMER, JAMES	1838	DEFENDANT	1662	SIMMS, CLEABURN	1819	DEFENDANT	1660
SHIMP, J	1871	MDSVILLE	1807	SIMMS, CLEABURN	1820	DEFENDANT	1624
SHIMP, J / INITIALS J.S.	1871	MDSVILLE	1807	SIMMS, HEZEKIAH	1824	DEFENDANT	1558
SHIMP, J / INITIALS J.S.	1871	MDSVILLE	1807	SIMMS, RICHARD	1825	MISC	1698
SHIMP, J / INITIALS J.S.	1871	MDSVILLE	1807	SIMMS, RICHARD	1836	MISC	1677
SHIMP, J / INITIALS J.S.	1871	MDSVILLE	1807	SIMMS, RICHARD	1839	MISC	1705
SHIMP, J / INITIALS J.S.	1871	MDSVILLE	1807	SIMMS, RICHARD	1848	MISC	1706
SHIPLER, SAMUEL	1834	DEFENDANT	1589	SIMMS, SAMUEL	1792	DEFENDANT	1572
SHIPLEY, JOHN A	1842	DEFENDANT	1646	SIMMS, SAMUEL	1821	DEFENDANT	1602
SHIPLEY, PETER	1832	DEFENDANT	1553	SIMO STAGE LINE - RONEY'S POINT	1916	NAT'L ROAD	1864
SHIPLEYS BRANCH	1852	BRKE MAP	1854	SIMPSON, J	1871	BRKE MAP	1735
SHIPTON, E / MRS	1871	TRIAD.BORO.	1784	SIMPSON, J	1871	MARH'L MAP	1752
SHITE, S / HRS	1871	OH CO. MAP	1743	SIMPSON, J / HERIS	1871	MARH'L MAP	1753
SHMULBACH, HENRY	1880	DEFENDANT	1580	SIMPSON, J C	1871	MARH'L MAP	1748
SHOE SHOP	1871	MARH'L MAP	1754	SIMPSON, J C / TANNERY	1871	MDSVILLE	1807
SHOE SHOP - HOLLIDAYS COVE	1871	HAN MAP	1733	SIMPSON, L	1871	MARH'L MAP	1747
SHOE SHOP - LIMESTONE	1871	MARH'L MAP	1749	SIMPSON, W	1871	BRKE MAP	1735
SHOOK, H	1871	MARH'L MAP	1746	SIMPSON, W	1871	MARH'L MAP	1756
SHOOK, H	1871	MARH'L MAP	1749	SIMS LANDING / OHIO RIVER	1871	MARH'L MAP	1754
SHOOK, H	1871	MARH'L MAP	1749	SIMS RUN	1871	MARH'L MAP	1754
SHOOK, JOSHUA	1878	DEFENDANT	1597	SIMS RUN	1871	MARH'L MAP	1758
SHOOK, S	1871	MARH'L MAP	1746	SIMS, - / MRS	1871	MARH'L MAP	1754
SHOOK, S	1871	MARH'L MAP	1749	SIMS, - / MRS	1871	MARH'L MAP	1754
SHOP - CARPENTER SHOP - LIMESTONE	1871	MARH'L MAP	1749	SIMS, - / MRS - INITIALS MRS. S.	1871	MARH'L MAP	1754
				SIMS, - / MRS - INITIALS MRS. S.	1871	MARH'L MAP	1754
				SIMS, - / MRS	1871	MARH'L MAP	1758

'PERSONAL TIME LINE' INDEX TO VOLUME 7 OF THE *OHIO COUNTY INDEX*

ENTRY	YEAR	SUBJECT	PAGE	ENTRY	YEAR	SUBJECT	PAGE
SIMS, - / MRS - INITIALS MRS. S.	1871	MARH'L MAP	1758	SMITH, A / COOPER SHOP	1871	BRKE MAP	1737
SIMS, - / MRS	1871	CAMERON	1803	SMITH, A C / PUBLISHER	1871	BETHNY BUS.	1772
SIMS, CLABOURN	1810	APPENDIX	1873	SMITH, ANDREW / MAP#246	1852	BRKE MAP	1843
SIMS, CLABOURNE	1811	DEFENDANT	1599	SMITH, ANDREW / MAP#244	1852	BRKE MAP	1844
SIMS, CLABURN	1812	DEFENDANT	1648	SMITH, ANDREW / MAP#436	1852	BRKE MAP	1850
SIMS, E / MRS	1871	MARH'L MAP	1754	SMITH, B J	1871	HAN MAP	1731
SIMS, J	1871	MARH'L MAP	1754	SMITH, B J	1871	RIV. RD S.OF N.C.	1771
SIMS, J	1871	MARH'L MAP	1758	SMITH, BENJAMIN	1839	DEFENDANT	1651
SIMS, J	1871	MARH'L MAP	1758	SMITH, C	1871	NEW CUMB'LD	1768
SIMS, RICHARD	1810	APPENDIX	1873	SMITH, D B	1871	MARH'L MAP	1754
SINCLAIR, JAMES / MAP#647	1852	BRKE MAP	1853	SMITH, E M / MRS	1871	W.LIBERTY	1780
SINCLAIR, JAMES B	1831	DEFENDANT	1565	SMITH, EDWARD	1840	PLAINTIFF	1551
SINCLAIR, JAMES B	1832	DEFENDANT	1566	SMITH, EDWARD / ESQ. - MAP#312	1852	BRKE MAP	1847
SINGLEMON, JACOB	1834	DEFENDANT	1591	SMITH, EDWARD / ESQ. - MAP#357	1852	BRKE MAP	1847
SINGLETON, JACOB	1832	DEFENDANT	1591	SMITH, EDWARD / ESQ. - MAP#367	1852	BRKE MAP	1847
SIPPLE, WAITMAN	1803	DEFENDANT	1628	SMITH, EDWARD / ESQ. - MAP#369	1852	BRKE MAP	1847
SISSIN, A / (?STORE?)	1871	MARH'L MAP	1752	SMITH, EDWARD / ESQ. - MAP#370	1852	BRKE MAP	1847
SISSON, J E	1871	OH CO. MAP	1740	SMITH, ELISABETH / MISS - MAP#433	1852	BRKE MAP	1850
SISSON, J E	1871	OH CO. MAP	1743	SMITH, ELISABETH / MISS - MAP#472	1852	BRKE MAP	1850
SISSON, J E	1871	OH CO. MAP	1743	SMITH, F	1871	BKE/OH MAP	1738
SISSON, J E	1871	OH CO. MAP	1743	SMITH, F / INTIALS F.S.	1871	BKE/OH MAP	1739
SISSON, J E	1871	OH CO. MAP	1744	SMITH, F / INTIALS F.S.	1871	BKE/OH MAP	1739
SISSON, J E	1871	OH CO. MAP	1744	SMITH, FERGUS / MAP#68	1852	BRKE MAP	1840
SISSON, LEWIS	1817	DEFENDANT	1624	SMITH, FREDERICK	1842	DEFENDANT	1663
SISSON, LEWIS	1832	DEFENDANT	1669	SMITH, G W / HRS	1871	BRKE MAP	1737
SIVERT, - / MRS	1871	MARH'L MAP	1747	SMITH, H	1871	NEW CUMB'LD	1766
SIVERT, J	1871	MARH'L MAP	1756	SMITH, HAMILTON	1841	PLAINTIFF	1568
SIVERTS, D	1871	OH CO. MAP	1743	SMITH, HENRY	1801	DEFENDANT	1567
SKINNER, I L	1821	DEFENDANT	1646	SMITH, HENRY	1805	DEFENDANT	1599
SKINNER, J L	1821	DEFENDANT	1557	SMITH, HENRY	1805	DEFENDANT	1666
SKINNER, WILLIAM	1800	DEFENDANT	1577	SMITH, HENRY	1808	DEFENDANT	1667
SKINNER, WILLIAM	1801	DEFENDANT	1600	SMITH, HENRY	1808	APPENDIX	1873
SKOAF, WILLIAM	1871	MARH'L MAP	1747	SMITH, HENRY	1809	DEFENDANT	1645
SKULL HOLLOW RUN	1871	BRKE MAP	1735	SMITH, J / ELM GROVE	1871	OH CO. MAP	1744
SKULL HOLLOW RUN	1871	BRKE MAP	1736	SMITH, J	1871	MARH'L MAP	1745
SKULL RUN	1852	BRKE MAP	1846	SMITH, J / & CO.	1871	MARH'L MAP	1745
SKULL RUN	1871	WELLSBURG	1776	SMITH, J	1871	MARH'L MAP	1747
SLATER, C E	1871	OH CO. MAP	1740	SMITH, J	1871	MARH'L MAP	1754
SLATER, J E	1871	W.LIBRTY.BUS.	1780	SMITH, J / INITIAL J.S.	1871	MARH'L MAP	1754
SLATER, THOMAS	1853	DEFENDANT	1576	SMITH, J	1871	MARH'L MAP	1756
SLATER, THOMAS	1854	DEFENDANT	1661	SMITH, J	1871	WHG ISLAND	1788
SLAUGHTER HO / HOUSE	1871	BRKE MAP	1737	SMITH, J D	1871	MARH'L MAP	1758
SLAUGHTER HO / HOUSE - BETHANY	1871	BKE/OH MAP	1739	SMITH, J D / INITIALS J.D.S.	1871	MARH'L MAP	1758
SLAVE	1819	MISC	1704	SMITH, J E / NEAR GRIST MILL	1871	NEW CUMB'LD	1768
SLAVE MARKET - WHEELING	1916	NAT'L ROAD	1867	SMITH, J F	1871	OH CO.BUS.	1779
SLAVES	1817	MISC	1678	SMITH, J F	1871	ELM GROVE	1782
SLAVES - IN OHIO CO - IN 1860	1916	NAT'L ROAD	1867	SMITH, J G	1841	DEFENDANT	1629
SLIGER, F	1871	OH CO. MAP	1743	SMITH, J J	1871	MARH'L MAP	1758
SLIGER, P	1871	OH CO. MAP	1744	SMITH, J W	1871	MDSVILLE	1806
SLIPPERY FORD - FISH CREEK	1871	MARH'L MAP	1755	SMITH, J W	1871	MDSVILLE	1807
SLOAN, - / MRS	1871	MDSVILLE	1809	SMITH, J W	1871	MDSVILLE	1807
SLOAN, M	1871	MARH'L MAP	1761	SMITH, JACOB J	1857	DEFENDANT	1570
SLOANS - TOWN IN JEFFERSON CO, OHIO / SLOANS STATION	1871	FRE'MAN'S LDG	1764	SMITH, JACOB T	1857	DEFENDANT	1570
SLOANS STATION / OR NEWBURG	1871	HAN MAP	1730	SMITH, JAMES P	1832	DEFENDANT	1604
SLOANS STATION, OHIO	1871	FRE'MAN'S LDG	1762	SMITH, JESSE C	1829	DEFENDANT	1668
SLOANS STATION, OHIO	1871	FRE'MAN'S LDG	1764	SMITH, JOHN	1819	DEFENDANT	1561
SLOUGHTON, W	1871	MDSVILLE	1810	SMITH, JOHN	1819	DEFENDANT	1561
SMALLY, J	1871	MARH'L MAP	1752	SMITH, JOHN	1829	DEFENDANT	1581
SMART, - / ROBINSON & SMART	1871	MARH'L MAP	1749	SMITH, L	1871	OH CO. MAP	1742
SMART, - / ROBINSON & SMART	1871	LIMESTONE	1805	SMITH, L	1871	OH CO. MAP	1744
SMART, J	1871	MARH'L MAP	1749	SMITH, L R	1871	HAN MAP	1732
SMART, J	1871	MARH'L MAP	1753	SMITH, L R / RES	1871	FRE'MAN'S LDG	1765
SMART, T	1871	MARH'L MAP	1749	SMITH, LEVI	1798	DEFENDANT	1634
SMART, T	1871	MARH'L MAP	1749	SMITH, MAHALA BARNE	1811	MISC	1709
SMITH & FORLEES	1843	DEFENDANT	1565	SMITH, PORTER & CO.	1871	RIV. RD N.OF N.C.	1763
SMITH SHOP - HAMMONDS / T	1871	BRKE MAP	1736	SMITH, PORTER & CO.	1871	RIV. RD S.OF N.C.	1763
SMITH, -	1854	PLAINTIFF	1629	SMITH, PORTER & CO.	1871	NEW CUMB'LD	1766
SMITH, -	1855	PLAINTIFF	1625	SMITH, PORTER & CO.	1871	RIV. RD N.OF N.C.	1770
SMITH, -	1857	PLAINTIFF	1626	SMITH, PORTER & CO.	1871	RIV. RD N.OF N.C.	1770
SMITH, -	1862	PLAINTIFF	1625	SMITH, PORTER & CO.	1871	RIV. RD S.OF N.C.	1771
SMITH, - / PORTER AND SMITH COAL	1871	HAN MAP	1731	SMITH, R / & W.J. / MAP#482	1852	BRKE MAP	1849
SMITH, - / MRS	1871	BKE/OH MAP	1738	SMITH, R / & W.J. (COOPERSHOP) - MAP#483	1852	BRKE MAP	1849
SMITH, - / PORTER, SMITH & CO	1871	NEW CUMB'LD	1766	SMITH, RALPH	1800	DEFENDANT	1576
SMITH, - / PORTER, SMITH & CO	1871	NEW CUMB'LD	1766	SMITH, RALPH	1801	DEFENDANT	1579
SMITH, - / PORTER & SMITH	1871	RIV. RD S.OF N.C.	1771	SMITH, S	1871	HAN MAP	1732
SMITH, - / PORTER & SMITH - BLACK HORSE FIRE BRICK WORKS	1871	RIV. RD S.OF N.C.	1771	SMITH, S	1871	OH CO. MAP	1740
SMITH, - / PORTER & SMITH - SEWER PIPE & TERRACOTTA WORKS	1871	RIV. RD S.OF N.C.	1771	SMITH, S / MRS - EST.	1871	MARH'L MAP	1754
SMITH, - / MISS	1871	MDSVILLE	1809	SMITH, SAMUEL	1784	APPENDIX	1874
SMITH, -	1878	PLAINTIFF	1623	SMITH, SAMUEL	1832	DEFENDANT	1608
SMITH, -. PORTER, SMITH & CO - INITIALS P.S. & CO	1871	NEW CUMB'LD	1766	SMITH, T	1871	HAN MAP	1732
SMITH, A	1871	BRKE MAP	1735	SMITH, THOMAS	1800	DEFENDANT	1598
SMITH, A	1871	BRKE MAP	1737	SMITH, THOMAS	1800	DEFENDANT	1665
				SMITH, THOMAS	1801	DEFENDANT	1647
				SMITH, THOMAS	1802	DEFENDANT	1634

'PERSONAL TIME LINE' INDEX TO VOLUME 7 OF THE *OHIO COUNTY INDEX*

ENTRY	YEAR	SUBJECT	PAGE
SMITH, THOMAS	1822	DEFENDANT	1642
SMITH, THOMAS	1825	DEFENDANT	1642
SMITH, W	1871	MARH'L MAP	1745
SMITH, W J / & R. - MAP#482	1852	BRKE MAP	1849
SMITH, W J / & R. - (COOPERSHOP) - MAP#483	1852	BRKE MAP	1849
SMITH, WILLIAM	1871	OH CO. MAP	1741
SMITH, WILLIAM	1871	OH CO. MAP	1742
SMITH, WILLIAM HENRY	1862	MISC	1689
SMITIR, R / & W J	1852	NOT ON MAP	1836
SMITIR, W J / & R.	1852	NOT ON MAP	1836
SMYLIE, JAMES	1855	DEFENDANT	1573
SMYLIE, JAMES	1855	DEFENDANT	1600
SMYLIE, JAMES	1855	DEFENDANT	1625
SMYLIE, JAMES	1855	DEFENDANT	1653
SMYLIE, JAMES	1856	DEFENDANT	1602
SMYLIE, JAMES	1856	DEFENDANT	1608
SMYLIE, JAMES	1856	DEFENDANT	1641
SMYLIE, JAMES	1856	DEFENDANT	1670
SNEDEKER, C H / TOP OF MAP	1871	MARH'L MAP	1745
SNEDEKER, GEORGE / HEIRS - MAP#35	1852	BRKE MAP	1840
SNEDEKER, ISAAC	1877	DEFENDANT	1562
SNEDEKER, W	1871	BKE/OH MAP	1739
SNEDIKER, JOHN / COTTAGE HOME	1871	MARH'L MAP	1750
SNEDIKER, JOHN	1871	MARH'L MAP	1753
SNEDIKER, JOSEPH / TOP RIGHT OF MAP - CUT OFF	1871	MARH'L MAP	1749
SNEDIKER, JOSEPH	1871	MARH'L MAP	1753
SNEDIKER, L	1871	BKE/OH MAP	1739
SNEDIKER, S / MARSHALL CO BORDER	1871	OH CO. MAP	1742
SNEDIKER, S	1871	MARH'L MAP	1745
SNIDER, DAVID / HEIRS - MAP#638	1852	BRKE MAP	1852
SNIDER, DAVID / HEIRS / (COOPERSHOP) - MAP#639	1852	BRKE MAP	1852
SNIDER, DAVID / HEIRS / (COOPERSHOP) - MAP#640	1852	BRKE MAP	1852
SNIDER, DAVID / HEIRS / (MILL) - MAP#641	1852	BRKE MAP	1852
SNIDER, DAVID / HEIRS / (MILL) - MAP#642	1852	BRKE MAP	1852
SNIDER, FREDERICK	1825	DEFENDANT	1649
SNIDER, H	1871	MARH'L MAP	1748
SNIDER, JOHN C	1842	DEFENDANT	1554
SNIDER, JOHN C	1843	DEFENDANT	1663
SNIDER, W	1871	MARH'L MAP	1746
SNODGRASS, DAVID	1858	DEFENDANT	1653
SNODGRASS, JOHN	1827	MISC	1704
SNODGRASS, JOHN	1841	MISC	1705
SNOWDEN, I	1871	HAN MAP	1731
SNOWDEN, JOHN	1871	HAN MAP	1727
SNOWDEN, JOHN	1871	HAN MAP	1728
SNOWDEN, P A	1871	NEW MANCH.	1769
SNOWDEN, W	1871	HAN MAP	1727
SNOWDEN, W D	1871	HAN MAP	1727
SNOWDEN, W D	1871	HAN MAP	1731
SNYDER, -	1871	BRKE MAP	1734
SNYDER, - / MRS	1871	BRKE MAP	1734
SNYDER, D	1871	BRKE MAP	1734
SNYDER, D	1871	BRKE MAP	1734
SNYDER, J	1871	NEW CUMB'LD	1768
SOAP FACTORY - S. OF S.JACOB	1871	BRKE MAP	1736
SOCKMAN, CATHERINE	1846	DEFENDANT	1672
SOCKMAN, H	1871	MARH'L MAP	1760
SOCKMAN, HENRY	1816	DEFENDANT	1555
SOCKMAN, HENRY	1820	DEFENDANT	1559
SOCKMAN, HENRY	1820	DEFENDANT	1585
SOCKMAN, HENRY	1820	DEFENDANT	1638
SOCKMAN, HENRY	1823	DEFENDANT	1559
SOCKMAN, HENRY	1824	DEFENDANT	1596
SOCKMAN, HENRY	1825	DEFENDANT	1628
SOCKMAN, HENRY B	1844	DEFENDANT	1640
SOCKMAN, JOHN	1821	PLAINTIFF	1587
SOCKMAN, PETER	1811	DEFENDANT	1599
SOLDIERS REST	1871	MARH'L MAP	1755
SOLDIERS REST - CLAY TWP	1871	MARH'L MAP	1751
SOUTH BRANCH OF SHORT CREEK	1871	BKE/OH MAP	1738
SOUTH BRANCH OF SHORT CREEK	1871	OH CO. MAP	1741
SOUTH FORK OF HOLBERTS RUN	1871	HAN MAP	1731
SOUTHERIN, H	1871	HAN MAP	1731
SOUTHERN SLOPE / WASHINGTON TWP	1871	MARH'L MAP	1749
SOUTHERN SLOPE	1871	MARH'L MAP	1752
SOUTHERN, J / MRS	1871	BENWOOD	1799
SOUTHSIDE FARM - CLAY TWP	1871	MARH'L MAP	1751

ENTRY	YEAR	SUBJECT	PAGE
SOUTHWESTERN PA	1852	HEMPFIELD RR	1817
SPAHR, JOHN JR	1808	APPENDIX	1873
SPAHR, JOHN SR	1808	APPENDIX	1873
SPEAKERSBURG, OH	1852	BRKE MAP	1851
SPEAR, RICHARD	1798	PLAINTIFF	1589
SPEARS, A	1871	OH CO. MAP	1742
SPEARS, A	1871	RITCHIE TWP	1793
SPEARS, RICHARD	1798	PLAINTIFF	1594
SPEARS, WILLIAM	1863	DEFENDANT	1631
SPEIGLE, O	1871	OH CO. MAP	1742
SPEIGLE, O	1871	RITCHIE TWP	1793
SPENCER, WILLIAM	1788	DEFENDANT	1589
SPENCER, WILLIAM	1788	DEFENDANT	1637
SPIDLE, - / (O)	1871	WELLSBURG	1777
SPIDLE, C	1871	WELLSBURG	1777
SPIDLE, F / WATER ST ?	1871	WELLSBURG	1777
SPINKS, -	1871	MARH'L MAP	1761
SPINLER, W	1871	OH CO. MAP	1742
SPINLER, W	1871	MARH'L MAP	1746
SPIVEY, N	1871	HAN MAP	1731
SPIVEY, N	1871	HAN MAP	1731
SPIVEY, S	1871	HAN MAP	1731
SPIVEY, W	1871	HAN MAP	1731
SPOON, J	1871	MARH'L MAP	1752
SPRIGG, SAMUEL	1825	DEFENDANT	1574
SPRIGG, ZACHARIAH	1778	APPENDIX	1874
SPRIGG, ZACHARIAH	1790	DEFENDANT	1644
SPRIGGS, J E	1871	MARH'L MAP	1751
SPRING / & STILL HOUSE	1871	HAN MAP	1732
SPRING - BLOWING SPRING / NEAR OHIO RIVER	1871	BRKE MAP	1734
SPRING - COLD SPRING - S. OF MOUNTAIN SIDE	1871	OH CO. MAP	1743
SPRING - CONNER, E / SPRING - INITIALS E.C. SPRING	1871	MARH'L MAP	1745
SPRING - E . OF PLEASANT VIEW	1871	HAN MAP	1726
SPRING - E OF HAMILTON	1871	HAN MAP	1726
SPRING - E OF JOHN W. MORROW	1871	HAN MAP	1732
SPRING - E. OF ALLISON SUMMIT	1871	HAN MAP	1727
SPRING - E. OF C.P.WELLS	1871	MARH'L MAP	1758
SPRING - E. OF FORTUNE HILL	1871	HAN MAP	1727
SPRING - E. OF FORTUNE HILL	1871	HAN MAP	1728
SPRING - E. OF J.R. SCOTT	1871	HAN MAP	1731
SPRING - E. OF JOSEPH KINNEY	1871	HAN MAP	1728
SPRING - E. OF SCHOOL NO.8	1871	MARH'L MAP	1745
SPRING - E. OF W. FARIS	1871	OH CO. MAP	1740
SPRING - ELM SPRING / S. OF A. DAVIS	1871	OH CO. MAP	1743
SPRING - ELM SPRING	1871	MARH'L MAP	1746
SPRING - MOUND OLD INDIAN SPRING	1871	RITCHIE TWP	1792
SPRING - N . OF FORTUNE HILL	1871	HAN MAP	1727
SPRING - N. OF A. BITZER	1871	OH CO. MAP	1741
SPRING - N. OF A. BITZER	1871	OH CO. MAP	1742
SPRING - N. OF A. WAYNE	1871	MARH'L MAP	1758
SPRING - N. OF CHERRY HILL FARM	1871	MARH'L MAP	1745
SPRING - N. OF COLD SPRING	1871	HAN MAP	1726
SPRING - N. OF EVERGREEN HOME	1871	HAN MAP	1726
SPRING - N. OF G.W.C.	1871	HAN MAP	1732
SPRING - N. OF GRANDVIEW	1871	MARH'L MAP	1745
SPRING - N. OF J MCCOY	1871	MARH'L MAP	1745
SPRING - N. OF J. KENNIDY	1871	MARH'L MAP	1745
SPRING - N. OF J.INGRAHAM	1871	MARH'L MAP	1753
SPRING - N. OF J.L.RIGGS	1871	MARH'L MAP	1751
SPRING - N. OF LOCUSTRIDGE	1871	MARH'L MAP	1753
SPRING - N. OF MOUNT PLEASANT	1871	MARH'L MAP	1758
SPRING - N. OF OHIO VIEW	1871	HAN MAP	1730
SPRING - N. OF PLEASANT VIEW	1871	HAN MAP	1726
SPRING - N. OF QUIET HOME	1871	OH CO. MAP	1740
SPRING - N. OF S. GEORGE	1871	BRKE MAP	1736
SPRING - N. OF SCHOOL NO.3 - WEBSTER TWP	1871	MARH'L MAP	1750
SPRING - N. OF SILVER MAPLE RIDGE	1871	MARH'L MAP	1746
SPRING - N. OF SPRING HILL	1871	HAN MAP	1726
SPRING - N. OF W. ARNOLD	1871	MARH'L MAP	1752
SPRING - N. OF W. RALSTON	1871	HAN MAP	1732
SPRING - N. OF WHITE OAK SPRING - CAMERON TWP	1871	MARH'L MAP	1753
SPRING - N. OF WHITEHOUSE HOME	1871	MARH'L MAP	1745
SPRING - N. OF WOODSIDE	1871	HAN MAP	1727
SPRING - NE OF HAMILTON	1871	HAN MAP	1726
SPRING - NE OF J. WHITEHALL	1871	HAN MAP	1731
SPRING - NE OF WHITE OAK GROVE	1871	HAN MAP	1727
SPRING - NE. OF BURCHVALLEY	1871	MARH'L MAP	1753
SPRING - NE. OF FLORAL HOME	1871	MARH'L MAP	1745
SPRING - NE. OF FORTUNE HILL	1871	HAN MAP	1728
SPRING - NE. OF G.W.REILLY	1871	MARH'L MAP	1745

'PERSONAL TIME LINE' INDEX TO VOLUME 7 OF THE *OHIO COUNTY INDEX*

ENTRY	YEAR	SUBJECT	PAGE
SPRING - NE. OF J. DAVIS	1871	MARH'L MAP	1752
SPRING - NE. OF J.T. SCOTT	1871	MARH'L MAP	1758
SPRING - NE. OF SAND HILL ?	1871	MARH'L MAP	1746
SPRING - NEAR L. CONNS / ?	1871	HAN MAP	1730
SPRING - NEVERFAILING SOFT WATER SPRING	1871	OH CO. MAP	1742
SPRING - NEVERFAILING SOFT WATER SPRING / UNION TWP	1871	MARH'L MAP	1745
SPRING - NEVERFAILING SOFTWATER SPRING	1871	RITCHIE TWP	1792
SPRING - NEVERFAILING SOFTWATER SPRING	1871	RITCHIE TWP	1794
SPRING - NEVERFAILING SPRING	1871	OH CO. MAP	1743
SPRING - NW OF HAMILTON HEIGHTS	1871	HAN MAP	1726
SPRING - NW. OF C. SEABRIGHT	1871	MARH'L MAP	1746
SPRING - NW. OF JOHN SNEDIKER	1871	MARH'L MAP	1750
SPRING - NW. OF JOHN SNEDIKER	1871	MARH'L MAP	1753
SPRING - NW. OF MOUNTAIN HOME - FRANKLIN TWP	1871	MARH'L MAP	1758
SPRING - NW. OF SIGHTLY HOME	1871	MARH'L MAP	1751
SPRING - OLD INDIAN SPRING	1871	OH CO. MAP	1742
SPRING - PINE HOLLOW SPRING	1871	HAN MAP	1732
SPRING - S. OF A. BURNS	1871	MARH'L MAP	1746
SPRING - S. OF BROOKSIDE	1871	HAN MAP	1726
SPRING - S. OF C.LUTES	1871	MARH'L MAP	1751
SPRING - S. OF EARLIWINE HOMESTEAD	1871	MARH'L MAP	1746
SPRING - S. OF EARLY SETTLEMENT - CLAY TWP	1871	MARH'L MAP	1751
SPRING - S. OF FISH CREEK SUMMIT	1871	MARH'L MAP	1754
SPRING - S. OF FRANKLIN SUMMIT	1871	MARH'L MAP	1758
SPRING - S. OF G. BAXTER	1871	HAN MAP	1730
SPRING - S. OF G.W. CHAPMAN	1871	HAN MAP	1730
SPRING - S. OF GOTHIC POINT	1871	MARH'L MAP	1748
SPRING - S. OF GRANDVIEW	1871	MARH'L MAP	1745
SPRING - S. OF J. CURTIS	1871	OH CO. MAP	1740
SPRING - S. OF J N POLLOCK	1871	OH CO. MAP	1740
SPRING - S. OF J. CURTIS	1871	BKE/OH MAP	1739
SPRING - S. OF J. ELLIOTT	1871	MARH'L MAP	1747
SPRING - S. OF J.NIXON	1871	MARH'L MAP	1751
SPRING - S. OF L. BECK	1871	BKE/OH MAP	1739
SPRING - S. OF L. BECK	1871	BKE/OH MAP	1739
SPRING - S. OF LOCUST GROVE	1871	HAN MAP	1726
SPRING - S. OF LOCUST VALLEY	1871	HAN MAP	1726
SPRING - S. OF MEADE SUMMIT	1871	MARH'L MAP	1751
SPRING - S. OF MEADE SUMMIT	1871	MARH'L MAP	1755
SPRING - S. OF P A MARTIN	1871	MARH'L MAP	1751
SPRING - S. OF P.A. MARTIN	1871	MARH'L MAP	1755
SPRING - S. OF PLEASANT HILL - CLAY TWP	1871	MARH'L MAP	1751
SPRING - S. OF PLEASANT HOME	1871	HAN MAP	1727
SPRING - S. OF PLEASANT VIEW	1871	MARH'L MAP	1746
SPRING - S. OF R.G.ROSENBARGER	1871	MARH'L MAP	1750
SPRING - S. OF R.G.ROSENBARGER	1871	MARH'L MAP	1753
SPRING - S. OF SHADY ORCHARD	1871	MARH'L MAP	1747
SPRING - S. OF SIGHTLY HOME	1871	OH CO. MAP	1740
SPRING - S. OF T.DOWLER	1871	MARH'L MAP	1746
SPRING - S. OF THE WHITE HOUSE FARM	1871	MARH'L MAP	1752
SPRING - S. OF THE WHITE HOUSE FARM	1871	MARH'L MAP	1755
SPRING - S. OF UNIV. CHURCH	1871	MARH'L MAP	1752
SPRING - S. OF W. JACKSON	1871	HAN MAP	1727
SPRING - S. OF W. POLLOCK	1871	OH CO. MAP	1740
SPRING - S. OF WAIT FARM	1871	MARH'L MAP	1745
SPRING - S. OF WALNUT RIDGE	1871	MARH'L MAP	1752
SPRING - S. OF WHEELING VALLEY FARM	1871	MARH'L MAP	1746
SPRING - S. OF WHITHAM	1871	OH CO. MAP	1740
SPRING - S. OF WILLIAM MOORE	1871	OH CO. MAP	1740
SPRING - S.OF FRANKLIN KNOLL	1871	MARH'L MAP	1755
SPRING - S.OF VALLEY VIEW	1871	HAN MAP	1728
SPRING - SE OF WHITE COTTAGE	1871	MARH'L MAP	1745
SPRING - SE. OF UNION FARM	1871	MARH'L MAP	1755
SPRING - SE. OF VALLEY VIEW	1871	HAN MAP	1727
SPRING - SEE ALSO SPRINGS	1871	OH CO. MAP	1743
SPRING - SHELL SPRING - S. OF GRAY HOMESTEAD	1871	MARH'L MAP	1750
SPRING - SULPHUR SPRINGS	1871	HAN MAP	1732
SPRING - SW OF B. MILLER	1871	HAN MAP	1731
SPRING - SW OF LOCUST GROVE	1871	HAN MAP	1731
SPRING - SW OF PLEASANT HOME	1871	HAN MAP	1727
SPRING - SW OF SOUTHERN SLOPE	1871	MARH'L MAP	1749
SPRING - SW OF W.D. SHOWDEN	1871	HAN MAP	1731
SPRING - SW OF WILLIAM SCOTT	1871	HAN MAP	1731
SPRING - SW. OF A.H. CALDWELL	1871	OH CO. MAP	1740
SPRING - SW. OF CENTRE SUMMIT	1871	MARH'L MAP	1745
SPRING - SW. OF FAIRVIEW	1871	MARH'L MAP	1758
SPRING - SW. OF FRANKLIN KNOLL	1871	MARH'L MAP	1755
SPRING - SW. OF H.MILLER	1871	MARH'L MAP	1754
SPRING - SW. OF HONEY BEE COTTAGE HOME	1871	MARH'L MAP	1745
SPRING - SW. OF SIGHTLY HOME	1871	MARH'L MAP	1746
SPRING - SW. OF SOUTHERN SLOPE	1871	MARH'L MAP	1752
SPRING - W. OF CORVEY LODGE	1871	MARH'L MAP	1745
SPRING - W. OF GRAY HOMESTEAD	1871	MARH'L MAP	1750
SPRING - W. OF W. LUKE	1871	MARH'L MAP	1747
SPRING - W.L.PERRINE - WEST LIBERTY	1871	W.LIBERTY	1780
SPRING - WHITE OAK SPRING	1871	OH CO. MAP	1743
SPRING FARM - OR OGLE FARM	1871	MARH'L MAP	1750
SPRING HILL	1871	HAN MAP	1726
SPRING HOUSE - NE OF ORCHARD HILL	1871	HAN MAP	1732
SPRING HOUSE - S OF WILLIAM MORROW	1871	HAN MAP	1732
SPRING NW. OF MEADE SUMMIT	1871	MARH'L MAP	1755
SPRING RIDGE	1871	MARH'L MAP	1753
SPRING RIDGE - WEBSTER TWP	1871	MARH'L MAP	1750
SPRINGARBORN, F / LITEUTZ CIGAR SHOP	1871	WELLSBURG	1777
SPRINGARBORN, F / LITEUTZ CIGARS	1871	WELLSBURG	1777
SPRINGEBORN, F / (O) LITEUTZ CIGARS	1871	WELLSBURG	1777
SPRINGER, B	1871	OH CO. MAP	1740
SPRINGER, B / INITIALS B.S. - TOP OF MAP	1871	OH CO. MAP	1741
SPRINGER, B	1871	OH CO. MAP	1743
SPRINGER, B	1871	MARH'L MAP	1746
SPRINGER, W S	1871	MARH'L MAP	1745
SPRINGFIELD, OH	1916	NAT'L ROAD	1866
SPRINGS - E. OF FREEBOLT	1871	MARH'L MAP	1745
SPRINGS - E. OF MRS. JONES	1871	MARH'L MAP	1746
SPRINGS - N. OF FAIRVIEW - FRANKLIN TWP	1871	MARH'L MAP	1758
SPRINGS - N. OF GRAND VIEW - FRANKLIN TWP	1871	MARH'L MAP	1754
SPRINGS - N. OF HOURSEHOE BEND	1871	MARH'L MAP	1759
SPRINGS - N. OF J.YARNALL	1871	MARH'L MAP	1751
SPRINGS - N. OF MEADOW FARMS	1871	OH CO. MAP	1740
SPRINGS - N. OF PROSPECT HILL	1871	BKE/OH MAP	1739
SPRINGS - N. OF R. BIRD	1871	MARH'L MAP	1746
SPRINGS - N. OF SCHOOL NO.3 - SAND HILL TWP	1871	MARH'L MAP	1747
SPRINGS - N. OF W. RUTH	1871	MARH'L MAP	1747
SPRINGS - N. OF WILLIAM MOORE	1871	OH CO. MAP	1740
SPRINGS - N.OF HORSESHOE BEND	1871	MARH'L MAP	1755
SPRINGS - NE OF WHITE OAK GROVE - CLAY TWP	1871	MARH'L MAP	1751
SPRINGS - NE. OF MRS. MARSH	1871	MARH'L MAP	1746
SPRINGS - NE. OF SCHOOL NO.8	1871	MARH'L MAP	1745
SPRINGS - NW. OF J.YOHO	1871	MARH'L MAP	1755
SPRINGS - NW. OF PLEASANT POINT	1871	MARH'L MAP	1754
SPRINGS - NW. OF PLEASANT POINT	1871	MARH'L MAP	1758
SPRINGS - NW. OF PLEASANT POINT	1871	MARH'L MAP	1758
SPRINGS - NW. OF W. RUTH	1871	MARH'L MAP	1750
SPRINGS - S. OF CENTRE SUMMIT	1871	BKE/OH MAP	1739
SPRINGS - S. OF CENTRE SUMMIT	1871	BKE/OH MAP	1739
SPRINGS - S. OF CHERRY LANE FARM	1871	MARH'L MAP	1758
SPRINGS - S. OF CHESTNUT RIDGE	1871	HAN MAP	1731
SPRINGS - S. OF COTTAGE HOME	1871	MARH'L MAP	1745
SPRINGS - S. OF D. WINTERS	1871	MARH'L MAP	1746
SPRINGS - S. OF E. BLAYNEY	1871	OH CO. MAP	1740
SPRINGS - S. OF FAIRMONT FARM	1871	MARH'L MAP	1755
SPRINGS - S. OF FRUIT HILL	1871	MARH'L MAP	1753
SPRINGS - S. OF GLEN MERRY	1871	MARH'L MAP	1759
SPRINGS - S. OF GRAY HOMESTEAD	1871	MARH'L MAP	1750
SPRINGS - S. OF H. RIDGELEY	1871	BKE/OH MAP	1739
SPRINGS - S. OF J G ROGERS	1871	BKE/OH MAP	1739
SPRINGS - S. OF J R MCMURRY	1871	BKE/OH MAP	1739
SPRINGS - S. OF J.E.WAYT JR	1871	BKE/OH MAP	1739
SPRINGS - S. OF J.H. CUMMINS	1871	MARH'L MAP	1753
SPRINGS - S. OF J.M. ATEN	1871	HAN MAP	1727
SPRINGS - S. OF LIBERTY - CLAY TWP	1871	MARH'L MAP	1751
SPRINGS - S. OF MAPLE VALLEY	1871	HAN MAP	1727
SPRINGS - S. OF MERRY HOME	1871	MARH'L MAP	1755
SPRINGS - S. OF P.GATTS	1871	MARH'L MAP	1754
SPRINGS - SE OF BURCHES RUN	1871	MARH'L MAP	1753
SPRINGS - SE OF PLEASANT HILL	1871	HAN MAP	1732
SPRINGS - SE. OF HAPPY HOME	1871	MARH'L MAP	1756

'PERSONAL TIME LINE' INDEX TO VOLUME 7 OF THE OHIO COUNTY INDEX

ENTRY	YEAR	SUBJECT	PAGE
SPRINGS - SW OF CHERRY HILL FARM	1871	MARH'L MAP	1745
SPRINGS - SW OF INDIAN KNOLLY	1871	MARH'L MAP	1754
SPRINGS - SW OF TRAVIS RIDGE	1871	MARH'L MAP	1754
SPRINGS - SW. OF FRANKLIN SUMMIT	1871	MARH'L MAP	1758
SPRINGS - SW. OF HAPPY HOME	1871	MARH'L MAP	1756
SPRINGS - W. OF SPRING HILL	1871	HAN MAP	1726
SPROUL, ROBERT	1846	DEFENDANT	1629
SPROUL, ROBERT	1846	DEFENDANT	1652
SPROULE, H	1871	HAN MAP	1726
SPROWL, ANDREW	1801	DEFENDANT	1666
SPROWL, ROBERT	1846	DEFENDANT	1573
SPURNAUGLE, E	1834	DEFENDANT	1553
ST CHARLES HOTEL - GLEN EASTON	1871	GLEN EASTON	1801
ST CLAIR, E J / MRS - MILLINERY	1871	WELLSBURG	1778
ST CLAIR, H J / MRS - MILLINERY	1871	WELLSBURG	1778
ST CLAIRSVILLE, OH	1852	HEMP. RR MAP	1826
ST JOHNS CHURCH / & GRAVEYARD	1871	BRKE MAP	1734
ST JOHNS CHURCH - BROOKE CO	1852	BRKE MAP	1852
ST LOUIS	1852	HEMPFIELD RR	1818
ST LOUIS	1852	HEMPFIELD RR	1819
ST LOUIS	1852	HEMPFIELD RR	1821
ST LOUIS, VINCENNES, CINCINNATI, ZANESVILLE AND WHEELING LINE	1852	HEMPFIELD RR	1820
ST. JOHN'S CHURCH / MAP#540	1852	BRKE MAP	1852
ST. LOUIS / PITTSBURGH, CINCINNATI & ST. LOUIS RR	1871	BRKE MAP	1734
ST. LOUIS / PITTSBURGH, CINCINNATI & ST. LOUIS RR	1871	BRKE MAP	1735
ST. LOUIS - CINCINNATI & ST. LOUIS RR	1871	BRKE MAP	1734
ST.CLAIR, R G / EST	1871	MDSVILLE	1808
ST.CLAIR, R G / EST	1871	MDSVILLE	1808
ST.CLAIR, R G	1871	MDSVILLE	1810
ST.CLAIR, R G	1871	MDSVILLE	1810
ST.LOUIS	1916	NAT'L ROAD	1866
STADIFORD, A / GRIST MILL	1871	MARH'L MAP	1748
STAGE COACH STOPS	1916	NAT'L ROAD	1861
STAIB, J C / WAGON MAKER	1871	MDSVL BUS.	1796
STAIL, J C	1871	MDSVILLE	1810
STALEY, - / MRS	1871	MARH'L MAP	1757
STALEY, D	1871	MDSVILLE	1810
STALEY, D	1871	MDSVILLE	1810
STALEY, J	1871	MDSVILLE	1810
STAMIFORD, E / MRS	1871	MARH'L MAP	1755
STAMM HOUSE / INN - NATIONAL ROAD	1871	OH CO. MAP	1744
STAMM, - / ROAD HOUSE ON NATIONAL ROAD	1916	NAT'L ROAD	1865
STAMM, W / 4 MILE HOUSE	1871	OH CO. MAP	1742
STAMM, WILLIAM	1840	DEFENDANT	1643
STAMM, WILLIAM	1841	DEFENDANT	1643
STAMM, WILLIAM	1844	DEFENDANT	1643
STAMM, WILLIAM / FOUR MILE HOUSE - HOTEL - NATIONAL PIKE	1871	OH CO.BUS.	1779
STAMM, WILLIAM / FOUR MILE HOUSE - HOTEL - NATIONAL PIKE	1871	OH CO.BUS.	1779
STAMM'S ROAD HOUSE ON NATIONAL ROAD	1916	NAT'L ROAD	1865
STANDIFORD - SEE ALSO STAMIFORD / ?	1871	MARH'L MAP	1755
STANDIFORD, J	1871	MARH'L MAP	1749
STANDIFORD, J	1871	MARH'L MAP	1749
STANDIFORD, J	1871	MARH'L MAP	1749
STANDIFORD, P	1871	MARH'L MAP	1756
STANDIFORD, P / INITIALS P.S.	1871	MARH'L MAP	1756
STANDIFORD, V	1871	MARH'L MAP	1754
STANFORD, THOMAS	1808	DEFENDANT	1566
STANLEY, CUTHBERT	1843	DEFENDANT	1663
STANLEY, HENRY	1834	DEFENDANT	1639
STANLEY, S	1871	WELLSBURG	1778
STANSBERRY, - / MAP#624	1852	BRKE MAP	1852
STANSBERRY, - / MAP#625	1852	BRKE MAP	1852
STANSBERRY, JOHN / MAP#623	1852	BRKE MAP	1852
STANSBERRY, NICHOLAS / MAP#635	1852	BRKE MAP	1852
STANSBERRY, NICHOLAS / MAP#636	1852	BRKE MAP	1852
STANSBURY, A	1871	BRKE MAP	1734
STANSBURY, A	1871	BRKE MAP	1734
STANSBURY, J	1871	BRKE MAP	1734
STANSBURY, J	1871	BRKE MAP	1734
STANSBURY, N	1871	BRKE MAP	1734
STANTON, FREDERICK	1862	DEFENDANT	1636
STARR, - / MRS	1871	NEW CUMB'LD	1768
STARRS BRANCH	1852	BRKE MAP	1847
STATE / OLD STATE ROAD	1871	OH CO. MAP	1740
STATE LINE - PA	1802	MISC	1701

ENTRY	YEAR	SUBJECT	PAGE
STATE PENITENTIARY	1871	MDSVILLE	1809
STATE PENITENTIARY - CELLS	1871	MDSVILLE	1809
STATE PENITENTIARY - CEMETERY	1871	MDSVILLE	1809
STATE PENITENTIARY - CHAPEL	1871	MDSVILLE	1809
STATE PENITENTIARY - DINING ROOM	1871	MDSVILLE	1809
STATE PENITENTIARY - ENGINE HOUSE	1871	MDSVILLE	1809
STATE PENITENTIARY - OFFICE	1871	MDSVILLE	1809
STATE PENITENTIARY - SHOPS / 4 SHOPS	1871	MDSVILLE	1809
STATION / RR STATION	1871	HAN MAP	1732
STATION / RR	1871	BRKE MAP	1734
STATION - RONEY POINT STATION	1871	RONEY PT.	1783
STAUNTON ASYLUM	1834	MISC	1697
STEAD, THOMAS	1822	DEFENDANT	1612
STEAM BOAT BOILERS	1871	FRE'MAN'S LDG	1762
STEAM BOAT BUILDER - JOHN L MAHAN	1871	HAN-GR'NT TWP	1763
STEAM SAW AND G.MILL / N. OF J A RICE	1871	MARH'L MAP	1761
STEAM SAW MILL - HIGGINS / JOHN W - LIBERTY TWP	1871	LIB. TWP-BUS.	1797
STEAM SAW MILL - KITTLES / S.B. & SON	1871	SAND HILL-BUS.	1797
STEAMBOAT - "LABELLE"	1854	DEFENDANT	1620
STEAMBOAT LANDING - AT MOUNDSVILLE	1871	MDSVILLE	1810
STEAMBOAT LANDING - MOUNDSVILLE	1871	MDSVILLE	1808
STEAMBOAT LANDING - WELLSBURG	1871	WELLSBURG	1778
STEAMBOAT LANDING - WHEELING	1871	WHG CITY	1788
STEAMBOATS - 230 REGISTERED AT WHARF MASTER IN WHEELING	1852	HEMPFIELD RR	1819
STEEL BRIDGE - WHEELING	1916	NAT'L ROAD	1866
STEEL, G	1871	W.LIBERTY	1780
STEELE, A J	1871	MARH'L MAP	1747
STEELE, MICHEL	1788	DEFENDANT	1559
STEELE, T	1871	MARH'L MAP	1747
STEELE, W	1871	MARH'L MAP	1747
STEEN, W M	1871	BRKE MAP	1735
STEEN, WILLIAM / MAP#499	1852	BRKE MAP	1850
STEEN, WILLIAM / MAP#500	1852	BRKE MAP	1850
STEENROD HOUSE / HOTEL	1871	TRIAD.TWP.	1781
STEENROD, - / EST.	1871	WHG CITY	1789
STEENROD, BRIGG	1803	DEFENDANT	1598
STEENROD, CORNELIUS	1818	DEFENDANT	1638
STEENROD, D / ? LISTED AS STEINROD	1871	MARH'L MAP	1745
STEENROD, DANIEL	1828	DEFENDANT	1613
STEENROD, DANIEL	1854	DEFENDANT	1670
STEENROD, EDWARD S	1829	DEFENDANT	1639
STEENROD, G W	1871	OH CO. MAP	1742
STEENROD, G W	1871	OH CO. MAP	1742
STEENROD, G W	1871	OH CO. MAP	1742
STEENROD, GEORGE	1871	OH CO.BUS.	1779
STEENROD, GEORGE W	1871	TRIAD.TWP.	1781
STEENROD, GEORGE W / ? INITIALS G.W.S	1871	WHG CITY	1789
STEENROD, GEORGE W	1875	DEFENDANT	1643
STEENROD, ZEBULON	1815	DEFENDANT	1620
STEGER, M	1871	MARH'L MAP	1754
STEGER, M / INITIALS M.S.	1871	MARH'L MAP	1754
STEIN, MICHAEL	1875	DEFENDANT	1595
STEINHILBER, EZEKIEL	1840	DEFENDANT	1662
STEINROD, D / (?STEENROD?)	1871	MARH'L MAP	1745
STELLE, W H	1871	OH CO. MAP	1742
STELLE, WILLIAM H	1873	DEFENDANT	1566
STENGEL, FREDERICK	1876	MISC	1711
STENGEL, FREDERICK	1877	MISC	1711
STEORTS, L	1871	BKE/OH MAP	1739
STEPHENS, -	1855	DEFENDANT	1621
STEPHENS, -	1861	DEFENDANT	1598
STEPHENS, -	1877	PLAINTIFF	1631
STEPHENS, J	1871	BRKE MAP	1735
STEPHENS, JACOB / MAP#417	1852	BRKE MAP	1847
STEPHENS, JAMES	1823	MISC	1701
STEPHENS, JOHN	1873	DEFENDANT	1641
STEPHENS, WILLIAM / MAP#315	1852	BRKE MAP	1847
STEPHENSON, -	1858	DEFENDANT	1630
STEPHENSON, JAMES	1841	DEFENDANT	1616
STERLING, W	1871	HAN MAP	1730
STERRATT, J	1871	MARH'L MAP	1749
STERRATT, J	1871	MARH'L MAP	1752
STERRET, HENRY	1809	DEFENDANT	1585

'PERSONAL TIME LINE' INDEX TO VOLUME 7 OF THE OHIO COUNTY INDEX

ENTRY	YEAR	SUBJECT	PAGE	ENTRY	YEAR	SUBJECT	PAGE
STETTS, ISAAC / MAP#65	1852	BRKE MAP	1840	STEWART, M	1871	WELLSBURG	1776
STEUBEN, CHARLES	1842	DEFENDANT	1586	STEWART, P	1871	HAN MAP	1727
STEUBENVILLE	1852	HEMP. RR MAP	1825	STEWART, P	1871	HAN MAP	1728
STEUBENVILLE	1852	HEMP. RR MAP	1826	STEWART, R / RES	1871	OH CO. MAP	1740
STEUBENVILLE	1871	DISTANCES	1815	STEWART, R	1871	OH CO. MAP	1741
STEUBENVILLE - BANK OF	1815	PLAINTIFF	1645	STEWART, R	1871	OH CO. MAP	1742
STEUBENVILLE & INDIANA RR	1852	HEMP. RR MAP	1826	STEWART, R	1871	OH CO. MAP	1743
STEUBENVILLE AND PITTSBURGH TURNPIKE	1871	HAN MAP	1733	STEWART, R / RES	1871	OH CO. MAP	1743
STEUBENVILLE BANK	1813	PLAINTIFF	1645	STEWART, R	1871	OH CO. MAP	1744
STEUBENVILLE BANK	1816	PLAINTIFF	1645	STEWART, R / CUT OFF RIGHT SIDE	1871	MARH'L MAP	1750
STEUBENVILLE BANK	1817	PLAINTIFF	1646	STEWART, R	1871	MARH'L MAP	1753
STEUBENVILLE BANK	1818	PLAINTIFF	1646	STEWART, ROBERT	1811	DEFENDANT	1599
STEUBENVILLE BANK	1822	PLAINTIFF	1646	STEWART, ROBERT	1816	DEFENDANT	1572
STEUBENVILLE, OH	1852	BRKE MAP	1851	STEWART, S	1871	HAN MAP	1726
STEUBENVILLE, OHIO - FERRY TO WV	1871	BRKE MAP	1734	STEWART, S / MRS.	1871	MARH'L MAP	1753
				STEWART, S JR	1871	MARH'L MAP	1752
STEUBENVILLE,OH	1852	HEMPFIELD RR	1818	STEWART, T / EST	1871	OH CO. MAP	1743
STEVENS, A	1871	HAN MAP	1732	STEWART, T / EST	1871	OH CO. MAP	1744
STEVENS, B H	1871	NEW CUMB'LD	1762	STEWART, T	1871	MARH'L MAP	1746
STEVENS, E	1871	OH CO. MAP	1743	STEWART, T	1871	MARH'L MAP	1750
STEVENS, E	1871	OH CO. MAP	1743	STEWART, T	1871	MARH'L MAP	1753
STEVENS, J	1871	BRKE MAP	1737	STEWART, W	1871	MARH'L MAP	1753
STEVENS, R H / MACHINE SHOP	1871	NEW CUMB'LD	1767	STEWART, W / INITIALS W.S.	1871	MARH'L MAP	1753
STEVENS, S S	1871	OH CO. MAP	1743	STEWART, W	1871	NEW CUMB'LD	1768
STEVENS, S S	1871	MARH'L MAP	1746	STEWART, W H	1871	MARH'L MAP	1748
STEVENS, WILLIAM	1871	BRKE MAP	1737	STEWART, WILLIAM	1871	HAN MAP	1731
STEVENSON, -	1860	DEFENDANT	1631	STEWART, WILLIAM	1875	DEFENDANT	1661
STEVENSON, -	1862	DEFENDANT	1631	STGEWART, T	1871	MARH'L MAP	1753
STEVENSON, J / INITIALS J.S. ?	1871	HAN MAP	1731	STICKNEY, CHARLES B	1837	DEFENDANT	1669
STEVENSON, J E / CUT OFF S.E. EDGE	1871	HAN MAP	1726	STIDGER, S B / DR. - RES.	1871	MARH'L MAP	1753
STEVENSON, J E	1871	HAN MAP	1727	STIDGER, S B / DR	1871	MARH'L MAP	1757
STEVENSON, J S	1871	HAN MAP	1731	STIDGER, S B / PHYSICIAN & SURGEON	1871	CAMER'N - BUS.	1795
STEVENSON, JOHN E	1871	HAN-POE TWP	1763	STIDGER, S B / DR - INITIALS DR. S.S.	1871	CAMERON	1802
STEVENSON, THOMAS W	1871	HAN MAP	1731	STIDGER, S B / DR - RES	1871	CAMERON	1802
STEWARD, C	1871	HAN MAP	1727	STILES, - / WHITE & STILES - INITIALS W. & S.	1871	MARH'L MAP	1757
STEWARD, I	1871	BETHANY	1773				
STEWARD, I	1871	BETHANY	1773	STILES, - / WHITE & STILES	1871	MARH'L MAP	1761
STEWART, -	1841	DEFENDANT	1577	STILES, - / WHITE & STILES	1871	MARH'L MAP	1761
STEWART, -	1841	DEFENDANT	1577	STILES, - / WHITE & STILES - INITIALS W & S	1871	MARH'L MAP	1761
STEWART, - / MRS - HOUSE	1871	HAN MAP	1727				
STEWART, - / (?G?) - ON PA. BORDER	1871	HAN MAP	1728	STILES, - / WHITE & STILES - INITIALS W & S	1871	MARH'L MAP	1761
STEWART, - / MRS	1871	HAN MAP	1728				
STEWART, - / MRS	1871	BKE/OH MAP	1739	STILES, - / WHITE & STILES - INITIALS W & S	1871	MARH'L MAP	1761
STEWART, - / MRS	1871	OH CO. MAP	1743				
STEWART, -	1871	NEW CUMB'LD	1766	STILES, - / WHITE & STILES - INITIALS W & S	1871	MARH'L MAP	1761
STEWART, B	1871	HAN MAP	1727				
STEWART, B	1871	HAN MAP	1728	STILES, - / WHITE & STILES - INITIALS W & S	1871	MARH'L MAP	1761
STEWART, EDIE	1843	DEFENDANT	1661				
STEWART, ELIZA	1846	MISC	1711	STILES, - / WHITE & STILES - INITIALS W & S	1871	MARH'L MAP	1761
STEWART, ELIZABETH / MAP#34	1852	BRKE MAP	1840				
STEWART, ELIZABETH / MAP#39	1852	BRKE MAP	1840	STILES, - / WHITE & STILES - NUMEROUS BUILDINGS NEAR BELLTON P.O.	1871	MARH'L MAP	1761
STEWART, G / INITIALS G.S.	1871	HAN MAP	1728				
STEWART, G / INITIALS G.S.	1871	HAN MAP	1728	STILES, - / WHITE & STILES - BELLTON	1871	LIB. TWP-BUS.	1797
STEWART, G W / W. SIDE OF MAP	1871	HAN MAP	1731				
STEWART, G W	1871	NEW CUMB'LD	1762	STILES, - / WHITE & STILES	1871	BELLTON	1814
STEWART, G W / STORE	1871	NEW CUMB'LD	1768	STILES, - / WHITE & STILES	1871	BELLTON	1814
STEWART, G W / INITIALS G.W.S.	1871	NEW CUMB'LD	1768	STILES, - / WHITE & STILES	1871	BELLTON	1814
STEWART, G W / INITIALS G.W.S.	1871	NEW CUMB'LD	1768	STILES, - / WHITE & STILES	1871	BELLTON	1814
STEWART, GEORGE / RES.	1871	HAN MAP	1727	STILL HOUSE / & SPRING	1871	HAN MAP	1732
STEWART, GEORGE	1871	HAN MAP	1728	STILL HOUSE / N. OF SUNNY SLOPES	1871	OH CO. MAP	1743
STEWART, GEORGE W	1871	HAN-CLAY TWP	1763	STILLWELL, E	1871	MDSVILLE	1808
STEWART, GEORGE W.	1871	HAN MAP	1730	STILLWELL, S / MRS	1871	MDSVILLE	1810
STEWART, H	1871	OH CO. MAP	1743	STINE, A	1871	MARH'L MAP	1759
STEWART, HUGH	1821	DEFENDANT	1599	STOBRIDGE, JESSE	1854	DEFENDANT	1551
STEWART, I / CUT OFF RIGHT SIDE	1871	MARH'L MAP	1750	STOBRIDGE, JESSE	1854	DEFENDANT	1621
STEWART, I	1871	MARH'L MAP	1753	STOCKING, PHILO W	1841	DEFENDANT	1587
STEWART, ISAAC	1841	DEFENDANT	1629	STOCKTON COACH LINE STATION - VALLEY GROVE	1916	NAT'L ROAD	1863
STEWART, J	1871	HAN MAP	1727				
STEWART, J	1871	BKE/OH MAP	1739	STOCKTON, DANIEL M	1852	DEFENDANT	1554
STEWART, J	1871	OH CO. MAP	1743	STOETZER, WILLIAM	1874	DEFENDANT	1597
STEWART, J	1871	OH CO. MAP	1744	STOKLER, JOHN	1789	PLAINTIFF	1598
STEWART, J	1871	MARH'L MAP	1753	STONE CHURCH - ELM GROVE - MAP	1916	NAT'L ROAD	1863
STEWART, J	1871	MARH'L MAP	1753	STONE CHURCH - HISTORY OF	1916	NAT'L ROAD	1864
STEWART, J	1871	MARH'L MAP	1760	STONE COAL RUN	1871	OH CO. MAP	1742
STEWART, J F	1871	MARH'L MAP	1753	STONE COAL RUN	1871	RITCHIE TWP	1791
STEWART, J P	1871	OH CO. MAP	1741	STONE PRESBYTERIAN CHURCH	1871	OH CO. MAP	1742
STEWART, JAMES / HEIRS - MAP#61	1852	BRKE MAP	1840	STONE PRESBYTERIAN CHURCH - ELM GROVE	1916	NAT'L ROAD	1864
STEWART, JOHN	1803	DEFENDANT	1553				
STEWART, JOHN	1806	DEFENDANT	1576	STONE QUARRY / RUN	1871	OH CO. MAP	1742
STEWART, JOHN	1813	MISC	1678	STONE QUARRY - AT ANDERSONS LANDING	1871	FRE'MAN'S LDG	1764
STEWART, JOHN / MAP#63	1852	BRKE MAP	1840				
STEWART, JOHN	1860	DEFENDANT	1592	STONE QUARRY - CUT OFF TOP OF MAP	1871	MARH'L MAP	1756
STEWART, JOHN	1871	HAN MAP	1726				
STEWART, JOSEPH M	1857	DEFENDANT	1616				

'PERSONAL TIME LINE' INDEX TO VOLUME 7 OF THE *OHIO COUNTY INDEX*

ENTRY	YEAR	SUBJECT	PAGE
STONE QUARRY - E. OF SUMMIT FARM	1871	OH CO. MAP	1742
STONE QUARRY - N. OF FAIRVIEW	1871	MARH'L MAP	1748
STONE QUARRY - N. OF J. TRUSSELL	1871	OH CO. MAP	1743
STONE QUARRY - N. OF L.B. PURDY	1871	MARH'L MAP	1752
STONE QUARRY - N. OF PLEASANT VIEW	1871	MARH'L MAP	1745
STONE QUARRY - N. OF RONEY POINT SCHOOL	1871	OH CO. MAP	1743
STONE QUARRY - N. OF W. DUNLAP	1871	MARH'L MAP	1749
STONE QUARRY - N. OF W. DUNLAP	1871	MARH'L MAP	1752
STONE QUARRY - NE. OF GLEN EASTON	1871	MARH'L MAP	1752
STONE QUARRY - NE. OF SYCAMORE GROVE	1871	MARH'L MAP	1753
STONE QUARRY - NW OF RONEY POINT	1871	OH CO. MAP	1744
STONE QUARRY - NW OF TRIADELPHIA	1871	OH CO. MAP	1743
STONE QUARRY - S. OF G. FRESHWATER	1871	BRKE MAP	1735
STONE QUARRY - S. OF J. CUNNINGHAM	1871	MARH'L MAP	1749
STONE QUARRY - S. OF J.S. GARVIN	1871	MARH'L MAP	1746
STONE QUARRY - S. OF T. MCMILLIAN	1871	MARH'L MAP	1750
STONE QUARRY - SE OF HAMILTON	1871	HAN MAP	1726
STONE QUARRY - SW OF BARTLETT STATION	1871	MARH'L MAP	1752
STONE QUARRY - SW. OF FIARVIEW - WASHINGTON TWP	1871	MARH'L MAP	1748
STONE QUARRY - TRIADELPHIA	1871	OH CO. MAP	1744
STONE, E J	1875	MISC	1679
STONE, J	1871	WHG ISLAND	1788
STONEY RUN	1871	MARH'L MAP	1761
STONY HOLLOW	1871	MARH'L MAP	1756
STONY HOLLOW	1871	MARH'L MAP	1759
STOOLFIRE, G	1871	OH CO. MAP	1740
STOOLFIRE, G	1871	OH CO. MAP	1743
STORCH, PETER	1871	OH CO. BUS.	1779
STORE - BLAIR P.O.	1871	HAN MAP	1731
STORE - BROWNS / WILLLIAM	1871	HAN MAP	1733
STORE - CHESTNUT & PEARL	1871	NEW CUMB'LD	1767
STORE - E. OF N. CROW / TOP OF MAP	1871	MARH'L MAP	1750
STORE - FAIRVIEW - FRANKLIN TWP	1871	MARH'L MAP	1758
STORE - HORNBROOK BROTHERS	1871	MARH'L MAP	1754
STORE - LOUDENSVILLE	1871	MARH'L MAP	1753
STORE - LOUDENSVILLE	1871	MARH'L MAP	1757
STORE - N. OF L.S. NEWMAN	1871	MARH'L MAP	1748
STORE - N. OF L. SL.NEWMAN	1871	MARH'L MAP	1745
STORE - NEAR A. SISSIN	1871	MARH'L MAP	1752
STORE - NEAR W.H.CONNER	1871	MARH'L MAP	1746
STORE - ORUMS / W - S. OF SHERRARD P.O.	1871	MARH'L MAP	1746
STORE - PARKS / J	1871	MARH'L MAP	1753
STORE - PLEASANT VALLEY P.O.	1871	MARH'L MAP	1749
STORE - ROCK LICK P.O.	1871	MARH'L MAP	1753
STORE - RONEY POINT STATION	1871	OH CO. MAP	1743
STORE - RONEY POINT STATION	1871	OH CO. MAP	1744
STORE - S. OF W H CONNER	1871	MARH'L MAP	1749
STORE - S. OF WAGON SHOP / SAND HILL TWP	1871	MARH'L MAP	1747
STORE - SHERRARD / E. SIDE OF MAP	1871	MARH'L MAP	1745
STORE - WOODLAND	1871	MARH'L MAP	1754
STORE #1 - ELM GROVE	1871	OH CO. MAP	1744
STORE #1 - WOODLAND P.O.	1871	MARH'L MAP	1754
STORE #2 - WOODLAND P.O.	1871	MARH'L MAP	1754
STORE & P.O.	1871	MARH'L MAP	1761
STORE & POST OFFICE - ELM GROVE	1871	OH CO. MAP	1744
STORE & TICKET OF / OFFICE - N. OF W. GASTON	1871	OH CO. MAP	1740
STORE & TICKET OFFICE - RONEY POINT STATION	1871	OH CO. MAP	1743
STOREL, P	1871	OH CO. MAP	1742
STORER, J H / PHYSICIAN	1871	OH CO. BUS.	1779
STORER, J H / DR	1871	TRIAD.BORO.	1784
STORER, J H / DR - OFFICE	1871	TRIAD.BORO.	1784
STORER, J H / DR	1871	TRIAD.BORO.	1785
STOREY, GEORGE	1862	DEFENDANT	1664
STOTTS, GEORGE	1813	DEFENDANT	1556
STOUT, JAMES H	1838	DEFENDANT	1596
STOWBRIDGE, JESSE	1854	DEFENDANT	1551
STRAIGHT RUN	1871	MARH'L MAP	1753
STRAIN, E	1871	BRKE MAP	1735
STRAIN, E G	1871	BRKE MAP	1734
STRAIN, E G	1871	BRKE MAP	1735
STRAIN, EBEN / (SAWMILL) - MAP#505	1852	BRKE MAP	1850
STRAIN, EBENEZER / MAP#522	1852	BRKE MAP	1852
STRAIN, J	1871	BRKE MAP	1734
STRAIN, JOHN / MAP#558	1852	BRKE MAP	1852
STRAIN, T H	1871	BRKE MAP	1735
STRAIN, W P	1871	BRKE MAP	1734
STRAIN, WILLIAM P / MAP#538	1852	BRKE MAP	1852
STREBEL, JOHN	1867	MISC	1711
STREET NAMES - SEE CITY NAME, THEN STREET NAME	1871	NEW CUMB'LD	1767
STRICHLIN, - / MRS	1871	MARH'L MAP	1753
STRICHLIN, - / MRS	1871	MARH'L MAP	1757
STRICKLAND, E	1871	MARH'L MAP	1747
STRIKER, GEORGE	1788	DEFENDANT	1665
STRINGER, GEORGE	1802	DEFENDANT	1624
STROBEL RUN	1871	WHG CITY	1790
STROBEL RUN	1871	RITCHIE TWP	1791
STROBLE, CONRAD	1861	DEFENDANT	1627
STRONG, BENJAMIN	1812	DEFENDANT	1610
STRONG, BENJAMIN	1812	DEFENDANT	1611
STRONG, HENRY S	1839	DEFENDANT	1651
STRONG, NATHAN	1814	MISC	1677
STRONG, SAMUEL / & SONS - BROOM FACTORY	1871	BRKE MAP	1735
STRONG, SAMUEL / & SONS	1871	CROSS CRK. BUS.	1772
STROUP, CONROD	1783	DEFENDANT	1610
STTENROD - DETAIL MAP	1871	TRIAD.TWP.	1781
STUART, JOSEPH M	1857	DEFENDANT	1574
STUART, ROBERT	1789	DEFENDANT	1647
STUART, ROBERT	1801	DEFENDANT	1647
STULSE, MICHAEL	1789	DEFENDANT	1600
SUDDETH, E	1871	BETHANY	1773
SUDDETH, E	1871	BETHANY	1773
SUEDEKER, C H	1871	OH CO. MAP	1742
SUGAR BOTTOM - WEBSTER TWP	1871	MARH'L MAP	1750
SUGAR CAMP RUN	1871	HAN MAP	1726
SUGAR CAMP RUN / W. SIDE OF MAP - S. OF WOODSIDE	1871	HAN MAP	1727
SUGAR CAMP RUN	1871	HAN MAP	1728
SUGAR GROVE / W SIDE OF MAP AT OHIO RIVER	1871	BRKE MAP	1735
SUGAR GROVE	1871	OH CO. MAP	1743
SUGAR GROVE - FRANKLIN TWP / ?	1871	MARH'L MAP	1759
SUGAR RUN	1871	MARH'L MAP	1755
SUGAR RUN / CUT OFF TOP OF MAP	1871	MARH'L MAP	1759
SUGAR TREE RUN	1871	HAN MAP	1732
SUITER, J F SELLS, J	1871	OH CO. MAP	1740
SULIER, A	1871	MARH'L MAP	1755
SULLIVAN, J	1871	MDSVILLE	1808
SULPHUR SPRING	1871	HAN MAP	1731
SULPHUR SPRING HILL	1871	HAN MAP	1732
SULPHUR SPRINGS	1871	HAN MAP	1732
SUMMERVILLE, J	1871	MDSVILLE	1807
SUMMIT FARM	1871	OH CO. MAP	1742
SUMMIT FARM	1871	MARH'L MAP	1745
SUNFISH FERRY - OHIO RIVER / (?SUNFISH IS NOW CLARINGTON, MONROE CO., OHIO?)	1871	MARH'L MAP	1754
SUNFISH FERRY - OHIO RIVER	1871	MARH'L MAP	1758
SUNNY HOME	1871	OH CO. MAP	1743
SUNNY SIDE	1871	OH CO. MAP	1740
SUNNY SIDE / UNION TWP	1871	MARH'L MAP	1745
SUNNYDALE	1871	HAN MAP	1732
SUNNYSIDE	1871	HAN MAP	1726
SUNNYSIDE	1871	HAN MAP	1731
SUNNYSIDE	1871	HAN MAP	1732
SUNNYSIDE	1871	OH CO. MAP	1743
SUPLER, B / RES	1871	OH CO. MAP	1743
SUPLER, E	1871	OH CO. MAP	1743
SUPLER, E	1871	OH CO. MAP	1744
SUPLER, J	1871	TRIAD.BORO.	1784
SUPLIER, E	1871	RONEY PT.	1783
SUPREME COURT OF THE U.S.	1852	HEMPFIELD RR	1818
SURVEYOR'S BOOKS	1788	MISC	1708
SUSPENSION BRIDGE - MAP	1916	NAT'L ROAD	1868
SUSPENSION BRIDGE - WHEELING	1852	HEMP. RR MAP	1826
SUSPENSION BRIDGE - WHEELING	1852	HEMP. RR MAP	1827
SUSPENSION BRIDGE - WHEELING	1871	WHG CITY	1788
SUSPENSION BRIDGE - WHEELING	1916	NAT'L ROAD	1865
SUSPENSION BRIDGE - WHEELING	1916	NAT'L ROAD	1866
SUSPENSION BRIDGE - WHEELING / PHOTO	1916	NAT'L ROAD	1867
SUTER, J T	1871	MARH'L MAP	1759
SUTER, S T	1852	NOT ON MAP	1836
SUTER, STROTHER T / MAP#189	1852	BRKE MAP	1844
SUTER, WILLIAM	1871	MARH'L MAP	1754

'PERSONAL TIME LINE' INDEX TO VOLUME 7 OF THE *OHIO COUNTY INDEX*

ENTRY	YEAR	SUBJECT	PAGE	ENTRY	YEAR	SUBJECT	PAGE
SUTER, WILLIAM / INITIALS WM.S.	1871	MARH'L MAP	1754	TAGGART, J H	1857	DEFENDANT	1626
SUTER, WILLIAM / WOODLAND, WV	1871	FRKLN TWP-BUS.	1797	TAGGART, J H / & CO	1857	DEFENDANT	1626
SUTHERLAND, WILLIAM	1789	DEFENDANT	1655	TAGGART, JAMES	1868	MISC	1675
SUTHERLAND, WILLIAM	1796	PLAINTIFF	1585	TAGGART, JAMES H	1857	PLAINTIFF	1552
SUTOR, R	1871	HAN MAP	1732	TAGGART, MICHAEL	1836	PLAINTIFF	1551
SUTOR, T	1871	HAN MAP	1732	TAGGART, WILLIAM	1879	DEFENDANT	1570
SUTT, JOHN	1797	PLAINTIFF	1553	TAGGERT, HENRY	1846	PLAINTIFF	1551
SUTTON, B	1871	MARH'L MAP	1746	TAIT, WILLIAM	1878	DEFENDANT	1601
SUTTON, B / (?OR R.)	1871	MARH'L MAP	1750	TALBERT, B	1871	MARH'L MAP	1746
SUTTON, J	1871	HAN MAP	1731	TALBERT, E	1871	CAMERON	1803
SUTTON, J JR	1871	HAN MAP	1731	TALBERT, E / MRS	1871	CAMERON	1803
SUTTON, PHILIP	1810	DEFENDANT	1645	TALBERT, J / E. SIDE OF MAP	1871	MARH'L MAP	1745
SUTTON, PHILIP C	1812	DEFENDANT	1626	TALBERT, J	1871	MARH'L MAP	1746
SUTTON, RICHARD	1786	DEFENDANT	1647	TALBERT, J	1871	MARH'L MAP	1746
SWAN, M	1871	WELLSBURG	1776	TALBERT, J / CUT OFF W. SIDE OF MAP	1871	MARH'L MAP	1746
SWAN, P	1871	WELLSBURG	1776	TALBERT, J L	1871	MARH'L MAP	1752
SWANEY, J	1871	NEW CUMB'LD	1768	TALBERT, W	1871	MARH'L MAP	1745
SWARTZ & SONS	1874	DEFENDANT	1631	TALBERT, W / INITIALS W.T.	1871	MARH'L MAP	1745
SWARTZ, CHARLES	1854	DEFENDANT	1616	TALBOT, EUGENE	1874	MISC	1675
SWARTZ, DAVID F	1874	DEFENDANT	1557	TALBOT, UPTON L	1838	PLAINTIFF	1551
SWEARINGEN, -	1861	DEFENDANT	1621	TALBOTT, ELISHA	1840	PLAINTIFF	1551
SWEARINGEN, ANDREW	1796	DEFENDANT	1659	TALBOTT, RICHARD	1839	PLAINTIFF	1551
SWEARINGEN, ANDREW	1797	DEFENDANT	1659	TALCOTT, WILLIAM H	1857	PLAINTIFF	1552
SWEARINGEN, ELLZAY	1798	DEFENDANT	1594	TALCOTT, WILLIAM H / & CO	1857	PLAINTIFF	1621
SWEARINGEN, GEORGE	1840	DEFENDANT	1563	TALLANT & DELAPLAIN	1854	PLAINTIFF	1620
SWEARINGEN, J	1871	HAN MAP	1733	TALLANT & DELAPLAIN	1855	PLAINTIFF	1621
SWEARINGEN, J	1871	BRKE MAP	1734	TALLANT & DELAPLAIN	1855	PLAINTIFF	1621
SWEARINGEN, N / HRS - HERIS	1871	HAN MAP	1732	TALLANT & DELAPLAIN	1856	PLAINTIFF	1621
SWEARINGEN, N / HRS - HERIS	1871	BRKE MAP	1734	TALLANT & DELAPLAIN	1857	PLAINTIFF	1621
SWEARINGEN, TAYLOR & CO	1855	DEFENDANT	1636	TALLANT & DELAPLAIN	1858	PLAINTIFF	1621
SWEARINGENS RUN	1852	BRKE MAP	1852	TALLANT & DELAPLAIN	1858	PLAINTIFF	1621
SWEARINGERN, - / MRS	1871	HAN MAP	1731	TALLANT & DELAPLAIN	1858	PLAINTIFF	1621
SWEARINGERN, - / MRS	1871	HAN MAP	1732	TALLANT & DELAPLAIN	1860	PLAINTIFF	1621
SWEEANY, BARNEY	1825	DEFENDANT	1639	TALLANT & DELAPLAIN	1862	PLAINTIFF	1621
SWEENEY, -	1859	DEFENDANT	1621	TALLANT & DELAPLAIN	1863	PLAINTIFF	1621
SWEENEY, - / & CO.FOUNDRY	1871	WHG CITY	1786	TALLANT, DRURY	1840	PLAINTIFF	1551
SWEENEY, J W	1863	DEFENDANT	1631	TALLANT, DRURY J	1838	PLAINTIFF	1551
SWEENEY, JAMES	1842	DEFENDANT	1551	TALLANT, DRURY J	1840	PLAINTIFF	1551
SWEENEY, JAMES W	1879	DEFENDANT	1597	TALLANT, DRURY J	1840	PLAINTIFF	1551
SWEENEY, M	1847	DEFENDANT	1657	TALLANT, DRURY J	1841	PLAINTIFF	1551
SWEENEY, M	1863	DEFENDANT	1631	TALLANT, DRURY J	1841	PLAINTIFF	1551
SWEENEY, MICHAEL	1855	DEFENDANT	1559	TALLANT, DRURY J	1841	PLAINTIFF	1551
SWEENEY, MICHAEL	1855	DEFENDANT	1566	TALLANT, DRURY J	1842	PLAINTIFF	1551
SWEENEY, MICHAEL	1855	DEFENDANT	1623	TALLANT, DRURY J	1842	PLAINTIFF	1551
SWEENEY, MORGAN	1853	DEFENDANT	1657	TALLANT, DRURY J	1842	PLAINTIFF	1551
SWEENEY, THOMAS	1839	DEFENDANT	1651	TALLANT, DRURY J	1846	PLAINTIFF	1551
SWEENEY, THOMAS	1842	DEFENDANT	1673	TALLANT, HENRY	1855	PLAINTIFF	1552
SWEENEY, THOMAS	1852	HEMPFIELD RR	1822	TALLANT, HENRY	1855	PLAINTIFF	1552
SWEENEY, THOMAS	1871	WHG CITY	1786	TALLANT, HENRY	1856	PLAINTIFF	1552
SWEENEY, W	1853	DEFENDANT	1657	TALLANT, HENRY	1856	PLAINTIFF	1552
SWEITZER, P	1857	MISC	1688	TALLANT, HENRY	1857	PLAINTIFF	1552
SWEURENGEN, G D / HEIRS - MAP#648	1852	BRKE MAP	1853	TALLANT, HENRY	1858	PLAINTIFF	1552
SWEURENGEN, GEORGE / ESQ. - MAP#637	1852	BRKE MAP	1852	TALLANT, HENRY	1858	PLAINTIFF	1552
SWEURENGEN, GEORGE / ESQ. - (GONE) - MAP#660	1852	BRKE MAP	1854	TALLANT, HENRY	1858	PLAINTIFF	1552
SWIFT, SAMUEL	1876	DEFENDANT	1597	TALLANT, HENRY	1859	PLAINTIFF	1552
SWIFT, WILLIAM D	1855	DEFENDANT	1653	TALLANT, HENRY	1859	PLAINTIFF	1552
SWORDS, -	1871	WHG ISLAND	1788	TALLANT, HENRY	1861	PLAINTIFF	1552
SWORDS, -	1871	WHG ISLAND	1790	TALLANT, HENRY	1863	PLAINTIFF	1552
SWYLER, JOHN	1825	DEFENDANT	1622	TALLANT, WILLIAM	1854	PLAINTIFF	1551
SWYLER, JOHN	1829	DEFENDANT	1650	TALLANT, WILLIAM	1855	PLAINTIFF	1552
SYCAMORE GROVE	1871	MARH'L MAP	1753	TALLANT, WILLIAM	1855	PLAINTIFF	1552
SYCAMORE GROVE	1871	MARH'L MAP	1756	TALLANT, WILLIAM	1856	PLAINTIFF	1552
SYCAMORE SCHOOL / MAP#577	1852	BRKE MAP	1852	TALLANT, WILLIAM	1856	PLAINTIFF	1552
SYCAMORE ST - HAMILTON	1871	HAN MAP	1729	TALLANT, WILLIAM	1856	PLAINTIFF	1552
SYMS, CLABURN	1810	DEFENDANT	1635	TALLANT, WILLIAM	1857	PLAINTIFF	1552
SYMS, CLABURN	1810	DEFENDANT	1648	TALLANT, WILLIAM	1858	PLAINTIFF	1552
SYOC, J	1871	MARH'L MAP	1755	TALLANT, WILLIAM	1858	PLAINTIFF	1552
T, F L / UNKNOWN INITIALS - SECOND ST	1871	BENWOOD	1798	TALLANT, WILLIAM	1858	PLAINTIFF	1552
T, G H / UNKNOWN INITIALS	1871	OH CO. MAP	1742	TALLANT, WILLIAM	1859	PLAINTIFF	1552
T, G H / UNKNOWN INITIALS - ELM GROVE	1871	OH CO. MAP	1744	TALLANT, WILLIAM	1859	PLAINTIFF	1552
				TALLANT, WILLIAM	1860	PLAINTIFF	1552
T, J / UNKNOWN INITIALS	1871	MARH'L MAP	1751	TALLANT, WILLIAM	1861	PLAINTIFF	1552
T.M. / INITIALS IN WEST UNION - POSSSIBLY DR. T.F.MARSHMAN	1871	W.UNION	1812	TALLANT, WILLIAM	1863	PLAINTIFF	1552
				TALLMAN & BOOHER	1842	PLAINTIFF	1620
T.T.S. / UNKNOWN INITIALS ON GRANT ST - MDSVILLE	1871	MDSVILLE	1807	TALLMAN, PETER	1873	PLAINTIFF	1552
				TALLON, MICHELL	1790	DEFENDANT	1644
TABLE OF AIR LINE DISTANCES - CITY TO CITY	1871	DISTANCES	1815	TALON, MICHEL	1789	DEFENDANT	1644
				TAN SHOP / TANNERY	1871	NEW CUMB'LD	1768
TADE, ISAAC	1777	MISC	1674	TAN YARD / E. OF NEW MANCHESTER	1871	HAN MAP	1731
TAG, STEWART	1855	DEFENDANT	1602	TAN YARD - WEST UNION	1871	MARH'L MAP	1747
TAG, THOMAS	1878	DEFENDANT	1560	TANEY, WILLIAM H	1877	MISC	1675
TAGGART, ALEX	1834	MISC	1674	TANK HOUSE - BENWOOD IRON WORKS	1871	BENWOOD	1799
TAGGART, ISAAC	1861	PLAINTIFF	1552				

'PERSONAL TIME LINE' INDEX TO VOLUME 7 OF THE *OHIO COUNTY INDEX*

ENTRY	YEAR	SUBJECT	PAGE
TANNANT & DELEPLAIN	1855	PLAINTIFF	1621
TANNER, DEBORAH	1827	PLAINTIFF	1551
TANNER, DEBORAH	1859	PLAINTIFF	1552
TANNER, J	1871	OH CO. MAP	1743
TANNER, J	1871	OH CO. MAP	1744
TANNER, JAMES	1817	MISC	1674
TANNER, JAMES	1827	PLAINTIFF	1551
TANNER, JAMES	1839	PLAINTIFF	1551
TANNER, JAMES	1840	DEFENDANT	1614
TANNER, JAMES	1840	DEFENDANT	1619
TANNER, JAMES	1843	DEFENDANT	1561
TANNER, JAMES	1844	DEFENDANT	1558
TANNER, JAMES	1847	MISC	1674
TANNER, JAMES	1847	MISC	1674
TANNER, JAMES	1851	MISC	1675
TANNER, JAMES	1853	PLAINTIFF	1551
TANNER, JAMES	1855	PLAINTIFF	1552
TANNER, JAMES	1856	PLAINTIFF	1552
TANNER, JAMES	1857	PLAINTIFF	1552
TANNER, JAMES	1858	DEFENDANT	1565
TANNER, JAMES	1859	PLAINTIFF	1552
TANNER, JAMES	1860	MISC	1675
TANNER, MICHAEL	1825	MISC	1674
TANNER, THOMAS	1817	MISC	1674
TANNERY	1871	HAN MAP	1732
TANNERY - COMMERCE ST	1871	WELLSBURG	1777
TANNERY - LAGRANGE	1871	LAGRANGE	1794
TANNERY - MOUNDSVILLE	1871	MDSVL BUS.	1796
TANNERY - NEW MANCHESTER	1871	HAN MAP	1731
TANNERY - ORRS / GEORGE G	1871	BRKE MAP	1734
TANNOR, JAMES	1843	MISC	1674
TAPPAN, BENJAMIN	1818	PLAINTIFF	1551
TAPPAN, BENJAMIN	1833	PLAINTIFF	1551
TAPPAN, BENJAMIN	1834	PLAINTIFF	1551
TAPPAN, JOHN H	1855	DEFENDANT	1584
TAPPE, CHARLES	1879	PLAINTIFF	1552
TAPPE, HENRY	1878	PLAINTIFF	1552
TAPPE, HENRY	1880	MISC	1675
TAPPE, SOPHIA	1879	MISC	1675
TAR, PETER	1828	PLAINTIFF	1551
TARBETT, JAMES B	1878	DEFENDANT	1552
TARBETT, ROBERT A	1878	PLAINTIFF	1552
TARBILL, HOLMER	1805	MISC	1674
TARKER BROTHERS	1878	DEFENDANT	1631
TARR & CROTHERS	1854	PLAINTIFF	1621
TARR MENDELL & CO, C	1840	PLAINTIFF	1620
TARR, - / HRS - HIERS	1871	WELLSBURG	1776
TARR, C / & W - MAP#411	1852	BRKE MAP	1846
TARR, C	1871	BRKE MAP	1735
TARR, C	1871	WELLSBURG	1777
TARR, C	1871	WELLSBURG	1777
TARR, C	1871	WELLSBURG	1778
TARR, CAMPBELL	1840	PLAINTIFF	1551
TARR, CAMPBELL	1840	PLAINTIFF	1551
TARR, CAMPBELL	1854	PLAINTIFF	1551
TARR, CAMPBELL	1871	WLSBRG BUS.	1772
TARR, CAMPBELL SR / MAP#390	1852	BRKE MAP	1846
TARR, CAMPBELL SR / MAP#391	1852	BRKE MAP	1846
TARR, CAMPBELL SR / MAP#392	1852	BRKE MAP	1846
TARR, CAMPBELL SR / MAP#393	1852	BRKE MAP	1846
TARR, CAMPBELL SR / MAP#394	1852	BRKE MAP	1846
TARR, EUGENE	1871	BRKE MAP	1736
TARR, F / MRS	1871	WELLSBURG	1777
TARR, JACKSON / HOME FARM	1871	HAN MAP	1732
TARR, O / (O)	1871	WELLSBURG	1777
TARR, PETER	1833	PLAINTIFF	1551
TARR, PETER JR	1828	PLAINTIFF	1551
TARR, W & C. - MAP#411	1852	BRKE MAP	1846
TARR, W H	1871	WELLSBURG	1777
TARR, WILLIAM / MAP#396	1852	BRKE MAP	1846
TARR, WILLIAM / MAP#397	1852	BRKE MAP	1846
TARR, WILLIAM / MAP#409	1852	BRKE MAP	1846
TARR, C C	1871	BRKE MAP	1736
TARR, C C	1871	BRKE MAP	1736
TARRIES, JOHN	1816	PLAINTIFF	1551
TARRILL, JOHN L	1880	DEFENDANT	1554
TASKER, J	1871	MARH'L MAP	1757
TASKER, STEPHEN P M	1861	PLAINTIFF	1552
TASKER, THOMAS T	1861	PLAINTIFF	1552
TASSEY, JOHN	1840	PLAINTIFF	1551
TATE, JAMES	1807	PLAINTIFF	1551
TATE, JOHN	1790	MISC	1674
TATE, JOHN	1791	MISC	1674
TATE, THOMAS	1807	PLAINTIFF	1551
TAVERN - AMERICAN EAGLE - WEST ALEXANDER	1916	NAT'L ROAD	1862
TAVERN - BEYMERS / CAPT. FRED	1916	NAT'L ROAD	1868
TAVERN - BEYMERS / MRS	1916	NAT'L ROAD	1868
TAVERN - CALDWELLS / JOHN - WASH.CO.,PA.	1916	NAT'L ROAD	1861
TAVERN - CALDWELLS / JOHN - WASH.CO.,PA.	1916	NAT'L ROAD	1862
TAVERN - FOWLERS / JOHN - MAP#425	1852	BRKE MAP	1847
TAVERN - GOODINGS	1916	NAT'L ROAD	1865
TAVERN - LAFAYETTE - WEST ALEXANDER	1916	NAT'L ROAD	1862
TAVERN - MCCORTNEYS / JOHN - MAIN ST - WHEELING	1916	NAT'L ROAD	1867
TAVERN - NATIONAL ROAD - VALLEY GROVE	1916	NAT'L ROAD	1863
TAVERN - OLD STONE HOTEL - RONEY'S POINT - NATIONAL ROAD	1916	NAT'L ROAD	1866
TAVERN - RONEY'S POINT - OLD STONE TAVERN	1916	NAT'L ROAD	1864
TAVERN - TRIADELPHIA	1916	NAT'L ROAD	1864
TAVERN - WELLS / NATHANIEL - (FERRY & TAV) - MAP#595	1852	BRKE MAP	1851
TAVERN - WHITES / HUGH - MAP#379	1852	BRKE MAP	1847
TAVERN NEAR S BRIDGE - BUFFALO CREEK - WASH. CO., PA.	1916	NAT'L ROAD	1861
TAWSEY, JOSEPH	1828	PLAINTIFF	1551
TAYLER & LORD	1861	PLAINTIFF	1621
TAYLER, ALEXANDER	1836	MISC	1674
TAYLER, ISAAC	1778	PLAINTIFF	1634
TAYLER, ISAAC	1778	MISC	1674
TAYLER, ISAAC	1778	MISC	1674
TAYLER, ISAAC	1820	MISC	1674
TAYLER, JOSEPH	1875	PLAINTIFF	1636
TAYLER, LAVINA	1863	MISC	1675
TAYLOR - COLORED	1868	MISC	1675
TAYLOR - WIDOW	1836	PLAINTIFF	1635
TAYLOR & BENNETT	1874	PLAINTIFF	1621
TAYLOR & FOSTER CO	1858	PLAINTIFF	1621
TAYLOR & HAMILTON	1848	PLAINTIFF	1620
TAYLOR & HOBBS	1850	PLAINTIFF	1620
TAYLOR & KAIN	1840	PLAINTIFF	1620
TAYLOR & KEYS	1840	PLAINTIFF	1620
TAYLOR SHELBY & CO	1857	PLAINTIFF	1621
TAYLOR, -	1855	DEFENDANT	1636
TAYLOR, - / MRS	1871	MARH'L MAP	1751
TAYLOR, - / MRS	1871	W.LIBERTY	1780
TAYLOR, ALFRED	1855	PLAINTIFF	1636
TAYLOR, BENJAMIN	1823	MISC	1674
TAYLOR, CHARLES	1796	MISC	1674
TAYLOR, CHARLES E	1880	PLAINTIFF	1636
TAYLOR, CHARLES F	1858	PLAINTIFF	1636
TAYLOR, CHARLES F	1860	PLAINTIFF	1636
TAYLOR, E	1854	PLAINTIFF	1551
TAYLOR, E	1854	PLAINTIFF	1636
TAYLOR, E	1856	PLAINTIFF	1552
TAYLOR, E	1857	PLAINTIFF	1636
TAYLOR, E	1871	MARH'L MAP	1750
TAYLOR, EDWARD	1813	DEFENDANT	1635
TAYLOR, EDWARD	1814	PLAINTIFF	1635
TAYLOR, EDWARD	1825	MISC	1674
TAYLOR, EDWARD	1825	MISC	1674
TAYLOR, EDWARD	1854	PLAINTIFF	1636
TAYLOR, ELIZABETH	1822	PLAINTIFF	1635
TAYLOR, ELIZABETH	1822	MISC	1674
TAYLOR, FOSTER & CO	1858	PLAINTIFF	1621
TAYLOR, G	1858	PLAINTIFF	1636
TAYLOR, G	1871	MARH'L MAP	1751
TAYLOR, G	1871	MARH'L MAP	1751
TAYLOR, GEORGE	1800	PLAINTIFF	1634
TAYLOR, GEORGE	1820	PLAINTIFF	1635
TAYLOR, GEORGE	1820	MISC	1674
TAYLOR, GEORGE	1854	PLAINTIFF	1636
TAYLOR, GEORGE	1858	PLAINTIFF	1636
TAYLOR, GEORGE	1859	PLAINTIFF	1636
TAYLOR, GEORGE R	1855	PLAINTIFF	1636
TAYLOR, GEORGE R	1856	PLAINTIFF	1636
TAYLOR, GEORGE R	1860	PLAINTIFF	1636
TAYLOR, GEORGE R	1861	PLAINTIFF	1636
TAYLOR, GEORGE R	1862	PLAINTIFF	1636
TAYLOR, GEORGE R	1874	PLAINTIFF	1636
TAYLOR, GEORGE R & CO	1874	PLAINTIFF	1621
TAYLOR, GEORGE R & CO	1875	PLAINTIFF	1621
TAYLOR, GEORGE R & CO	1880	PLAINTIFF	1621
TAYLOR, HENRY	1857	PLAINTIFF	1636
TAYLOR, ISAAC	1779	MISC	1674
TAYLOR, ISAAC	1794	MISC	1674

'PERSONAL TIME LINE' INDEX TO VOLUME 7 OF THE *OHIO COUNTY INDEX*

ENTRY	YEAR	SUBJECT	PAGE
TAYLOR, ISAAC	1795	PLAINTIFF	1634
TAYLOR, ISAAC	1797	PLAINTIFF	1634
TAYLOR, ISAAC	1797	MISC	1674
TAYLOR, ISAAC	1798	PLAINTIFF	1634
TAYLOR, ISAAC	1798	PLAINTIFF	1634
TAYLOR, ISAAC	1799	PLAINTIFF	1634
TAYLOR, ISAAC	1799	PLAINTIFF	1634
TAYLOR, ISAAC	1801	DEFENDANT	1610
TAYLOR, ISAAC	1801	PLAINTIFF	1634
TAYLOR, ISAAC	1802	PLAINTIFF	1634
TAYLOR, ISAAC	1803	PLAINTIFF	1634
TAYLOR, ISAAC	1803	PLAINTIFF	1635
TAYLOR, ISAAC	1804	PLAINTIFF	1635
TAYLOR, ISAAC	1805	PLAINTIFF	1635
TAYLOR, ISAAC	1806	MISC	1674
TAYLOR, ISAAC	1807	PLAINTIFF	1635
TAYLOR, ISAAC	1808	PLAINTIFF	1635
TAYLOR, ISAAC	1838	PLAINTIFF	1635
TAYLOR, ISAAC	1844	PLAINTIFF	1636
TAYLOR, ISABEL	1845	MISC	1674
TAYLOR, ISABELLE	1839	MISC	1674
TAYLOR, J / ABOVE PLEASANT HOME	1871	MARH'L MAP	1747
TAYLOR, J	1871	MARH'L MAP	1750
TAYLOR, J	1871	MARH'L MAP	1750
TAYLOR, J	1871	MARH'L MAP	1755
TAYLOR, J E	1856	PLAINTIFF	1552
TAYLOR, J F	1871	MARH'L MAP	1751
TAYLOR, J H	1854	PLAINTIFF	1551
TAYLOR, J N	1854	PLAINTIFF	1636
TAYLOR, J W	1858	PLAINTIFF	1636
TAYLOR, J Z / INITIALS J.Z.T.	1871	MARH'L MAP	1751
TAYLOR, J Z / RES.	1871	MARH'L MAP	1751
TAYLOR, JACOB	1808	PLAINTIFF	1635
TAYLOR, JAMES	1798	DEFENDANT	1665
TAYLOR, JAMES	1798	MISC	1674
TAYLOR, JAMES	1803	DEFENDANT	1635
TAYLOR, JAMES	1804	PLAINTIFF	1635
TAYLOR, JAMES	1810	PLAINTIFF	1635
TAYLOR, JAMES	1817	PLAINTIFF	1635
TAYLOR, JAMES	1818	MISC	1674
TAYLOR, JAMES	1822	MISC	1674
TAYLOR, JAMES	1822	MISC	1674
TAYLOR, JAMES	1824	PLAINTIFF	1635
TAYLOR, JAMES	1833	PLAINTIFF	1635
TAYLOR, JAMES	1840	PLAINTIFF	1635
TAYLOR, JOHN	1785	MISC	1674
TAYLOR, JOHN	1798	PLAINTIFF	1634
TAYLOR, JOHN	1799	PLAINTIFF	1634
TAYLOR, JOHN	1800	PLAINTIFF	1634
TAYLOR, JOHN	1802	PLAINTIFF	1634
TAYLOR, JOHN	1813	PLAINTIFF	1635
TAYLOR, JOHN	1813	MISC	1674
TAYLOR, JOHN	1814	MISC	1674
TAYLOR, JOHN	1815	DEFENDANT	1667
TAYLOR, JOHN	1825	MISC	1674
TAYLOR, JOHN	1830	MISC	1674
TAYLOR, JOHN W	1861	MISC	1675
TAYLOR, JONATHAN	1811	PLAINTIFF	1635
TAYLOR, JOSEPH	1840	PLAINTIFF	1636
TAYLOR, L / MRS	1871	BKE/OH MAP	1738
TAYLOR, L / MRS	1871	BKE/OH MAP	1738
TAYLOR, LEWIS	1868	MISC	1675
TAYLOR, M	1871	MARH'L MAP	1751
TAYLOR, MAHLONE	1858	PLAINTIFF	1636
TAYLOR, MARGARET	1825	MISC	1674
TAYLOR, MARTHA	1825	MISC	1674
TAYLOR, PATTY	1825	MISC	1674
TAYLOR, PATTY	1825	MISC	1674
TAYLOR, R / HRS	1871	MARH'L MAP	1747
TAYLOR, ROBERT	1779	PLAINTIFF	1634
TAYLOR, ROBERT	1797	PLAINTIFF	1634
TAYLOR, ROBERT	1834	PLAINTIFF	1635
TAYLOR, ROBERT G	1842	MISC	1674
TAYLOR, SAMUEL	1784	DEFENDANT	1598
TAYLOR, SAMUEL	1803	PLAINTIFF	1635
TAYLOR, SARAH	1780	PLAINTIFF	1634
TAYLOR, SEPTIMUS	1798	PLAINTIFF	1634
TAYLOR, THOMAS	1798	PLAINTIFF	1634
TAYLOR, THOMAS	1800	PLAINTIFF	1634
TAYLOR, THOMAS	1801	PLAINTIFF	1634
TAYLOR, THOMAS	1816	PLAINTIFF	1635
TAYLOR, THOMAS	1825	MISC	1674
TAYLOR, THOMAS	1825	MISC	1674
TAYLOR, THOMAS	1841	PLAINTIFF	1636
TAYLOR, THOMAS	1842	PLAINTIFF	1636
TAYLOR, THOMAS	1854	MISC	1675
TAYLOR, THOMAS	1855	PLAINTIFF	1636
TAYLOR, THOMAS	1871	W.UNION	1812
TAYLOR, WILLIAM	1812	PLAINTIFF	1635
TAYLOR, WILLIAM Y	1854	MISC	1675
TEABLER, GEORGE	1812	MISC	1676
TEABLER, MICHAEL	1818	PLAINTIFF	1553
TEABLER, MICHAEL	1822	MISC	1676
TEACHER - G.W.RUSSELL	1871	WLSBRG BUS.	1772
TEAGARDEN, ISAAC M	1863	MISC	1676
TEAGARDEN, JACOB	1816	PLAINTIFF	1553
TEAGARDEN, T H	1871	MARH'L MAP	1760
TEAGARDEN, WILLIAM	1857	PLAINTIFF	1553
TEAL, ASEY	1796	MISC	1676
TEAL, CHARLES	1796	MISC	1676
TEAL, CHARLES	1797	PLAINTIFF	1553
TEAL, NICHOLAS	1820	PLAINTIFF	1553
TEAL, NICHOLAS	1832	PLAINTIFF	1553
TEAMSTERS - AT ROAD HOUSES ON NATIONAL ROAD	1916	NAT'L ROAD	1865
TEATER, H	1839	PLAINTIFF	1553
TEATER, HENRY	1836	DEFENDANT	1651
TEATERS, HENRY	1833	MISC	1676
TEDFORD, JOHN	1838	MISC	1676
TEDFORD, JOHN	1839	MISC	1676
TEDFORD, SUSANNA	1839	MISC	1676
TEDFORD, SUSANNA	1841	PLAINTIFF	1553
TEECE, ARTHUR M	1874	PLAINTIFF	1553
TEECE, MARY	1875	MISC	1676
TEECE, SARAH	1879	MISC	1676
TEECE, SARAH A	1875	MISC	1676
TEEL, CHARLES	1797	MISC	1676
TEEL, CLARISSA	1827	MISC	1676
TEESDALE, WILLIAM	1871	NEW CUMB'LD	1762
TEESDALE, WILLIAM / GROCER	1871	NEW CUMB'LD	1768
TEETER, DAVID	1803	MISC	1697
TEETER, GEORGE	1803	MISC	1676
TEETER, MARY	1803	MISC	1676
TEETERS, DAVID	1803	MISC	1676
TEETERS, JOSEPH	1829	PLAINTIFF	1553
TEETERS, JOSEPH	1831	PLAINTIFF	1553
TEETERS, JOSEPH	1832	PLAINTIFF	1553
TEETERS, JOSEPH	1832	DEFENDANT	1650
TEETERS, JOSEPH	1833	PLAINTIFF	1553
TEETERS, JOSEPH	1834	PLAINTIFF	1553
TEETERS, JOSEPH	1834	PLAINTIFF	1553
TEETERS, JOSEPH	1834	PLAINTIFF	1553
TEETERS, JOSEPH	1836	PLAINTIFF	1553
TEETERS, JOSEPH	1836	PLAINTIFF	1553
TEGARDEN, JOHN	1812	PLAINTIFF	1553
TEGARDEN, JOHN	1813	PLAINTIFF	1553
TEGARDEN, JOHN	1814	DEFENDANT	1645
TEGHARDIN, JACOB	1803	PLAINTIFF	1553
TEIRN, LUKE	1820	PLAINTIFF	1553
TEIRNAN, LUKE	1820	PLAINTIFF	1553
TEMPLE & BARKER	1851	PLAINTIFF	1620
TEMPLE, JAMES	1838	DEFENDANT	1669
TEMPLE, JOSEPH E	1851	PLAINTIFF	1553
TEMPLETON, HUGH	1846	DEFENDANT	1653
TEMPLETON, JAMES	1781	MISC	1676
TEMPLETON, JAMES	1795	PLAINTIFF	1553
TEMPLETON, JAMES	1800	PLAINTIFF	1553
TEMPLETON, NATHANL	1778	DEFENDANT	1634
TEMPLETON, THOMAS	1835	PLAINTIFF	1553
TEMPLETON, WILLIAM	1817	PLAINTIFF	1553
TEMPLETON, WILLIAM	1818	DEFENDANT	1624
TEMPLETON, WILLIAM	1818	DEFENDANT	1660
TEMPLETON, WILLIAM	1819	DEFENDANT	1624
TEMPLETON, WILLIAM	1822	DEFENDANT	1612
TEMPLETON, WILLIAM	1823	PLAINTIFF	1553
TEMPLETON, WILLIAM	1843	PLAINTIFF	1553
TEMPLETON, WILLIAM	1844	PLAINTIFF	1553
TEMPLETON, WILLIAM	1844	DEFENDANT	1584
TEN HOUSE / INN - S.OF WHEELING IRON WORKS	1871	WHG CITY	1786
TENNAN, FRANCIS	1830	PLAINTIFF	1554
TENNAN, MICHAEL	1830	PLAINTIFF	1554
TENNESSEE	1852	HEMPFIELD RR	1821
TENNESSEE RIVER TRAFFICE	1852	HEMPFIELD RR	1817
TENNIS, ANTHONY	1826	PLAINTIFF	1554
TENT SCHOOL / MAP#535	1852	BRKE MAP	1852
TENTONEY, THOMAS J B	1842	DEFENDANT	1672
TEREL, JAMES	1789	PLAINTIFF	1554
TEREL, JAMES	1789	PLAINTIFF	1647
TERHUNE & VANMETER	1830	PLAINTIFF	1620
TERRA ALTA, WV - MAP	1916	NAT'L ROAD	1869

'PERSONAL TIME LINE' INDEX TO VOLUME 7 OF THE *OHIO COUNTY INDEX*

ENTRY	YEAR	SUBJECT	PAGE
TERRA HAUTE	1852	HEMPFIELD RR	1820
TERRA HAUTE, IN	1916	NAT'L ROAD	1866
TERRACOTTA / SEWER PIPE & TERRACOTTA WORKS	1871	RIV. RD S.OF N.C.	1771
TERREL, C S	1879	MISC	1676
TERREL, DANIEL	1824	PLAINTIFF	1554
TERREL, EBERT	1807	PLAINTIFF	1554
TERRELL, CALAIN	1818	MISC	1676
TERRELL, CALVIN	1836	PLAINTIFF	1554
TERRELL, DANIEL G	1854	MISC	1676
TERRELL, EDMOND	1809	DEFENDANT	1667
TERRELL, ELIZABETH	1848	MISC	1676
TERRELL, ELIZABETH	1851	MISC	1676
TERRELL, GEORGE	1803	PLAINTIFF	1554
TERRELL, J	1871	OH CO. MAP	1740
TERRELL, J W	1861	PLAINTIFF	1554
TERRELL, JANE	1849	MISC	1676
TERRELL, JOHN	1879	PLAINTIFF	1554
TERRELL, LUCY	1851	MISC	1676
TERRELL, MARY	1818	MISC	1676
TERRELL, MATHEW	1851	MISC	1676
TERRELL, OLIVE	1851	MISC	1676
TERRELL, PETER	1800	DEFENDANT	1583
TERRELL, SARAH	1803	DEFENDANT	1554
TERRELL, SARAH	1851	MISC	1676
TERRIL, C	1871	MARH'L MAP	1753
TERRIL, DANIEL	1847	MISC	1676
TERRIL, JEREMIAH	1847	MISC	1676
TERRIL, WILLIAM H	1865	MISC	1676
TERRILL, A	1871	MARH'L MAP	1749
TERRILL, A	1871	MARH'L MAP	1752
TERRILL, C S	1871	OH CO. MAP	1740
TERRILL, MARY M	1880	PLAINTIFF	1554
TERRY, ELI	1836	PLAINTIFF	1554
TERRY, JAMES	1842	PLAINTIFF	1554
TERRY, JOHN P	1856	PLAINTIFF	1554
TERYTITAN, JACOB	1830	MISC	1676
TERYTITAN, JACOB	1830	MISC	1691
TEUSBURY, R M	1856	PLAINTIFF	1554
TEVIS & FLANNIGEN	1840	PLAINTIFF	1620
TEVIS, JOHN	1840	PLAINTIFF	1554
TEVIS, JOHN	1847	PLAINTIFF	1554
TEVIS, JOSEPH D	1852	PLAINTIFF	1554
TEWHEE, JAMES	1855	PLAINTIFF	1554
THACKER, J / HRS -HEIRS	1871	MARH'L MAP	1745
THALLMANE, JOSEPH	1878	PLAINTIFF	1560
THALMAN, ANDREW	1878	PLAINTIFF	1560
THARP, DANIEL V	1840	PLAINTIFF	1559
THARP, DANIEL V	1860	PLAINTIFF	1560
THARP, DANIEL V	1861	PLAINTIFF	1560
THARPES RUN	1852	BRKE MAP	1847
THATCHER, CHARLES	1823	PLAINTIFF	1559
THATCHER, CHARLES	1824	PLAINTIFF	1559
THATCHER, J / HEIRS	1871	MARH'L MAP	1745
THATCHER, JAMES	1838	MISC	1678
THATCHER, JONAS	1820	PLAINTIFF	1559
THATCHER, JONAS	1823	PLAINTIFF	1559
THATCHER, JONAS	1824	PLAINTIFF	1559
THATCHER, JONAS	1828	MISC	1678
THATCHER, JONAS	1830	PLAINTIFF	1559
THATCHER, JONAS	1833	PLAINTIFF	1559
THATCHER, JONAS	1842	DEFENDANT	1636
THATCHER, JONES	1826	MISC	1678
THAWLEY, DAVID / MAP#561	1852	BRKE MAP	1852
THAWLEY, SAMUEL / HEIRS -MAP#508	1852	BRKE MAP	1849
THAYER, J W	1871	NEW CUMB'LD	1762
THAYER, J W / PLANING MILL	1871	NEW CUMB'LD	1768
THAYER, MILTON H	1871	NEW CUMB'LD	1762
THAYER, MILTON H	1871	NEW CUMB'LD	1768
THAYER, NATHAN	1871	NEW CUMB'LD	1768
THAYER, ZIPHEON	1835	PLAINTIFF	1559
THE GROVE	1871	HAN MAP	1726
THE HOMESTEAD	1871	HAN MAP	1726
THE HOMESTEAD	1871	HAN MAP	1732
THE HOMESTEAD	1871	OH CO. MAP	1742
THE HOMESTEAD / D.B.GARVIN	1871	OH CO. MAP	1742
THE HOMESTEAD	1871	OH CO. MAP	1743
THE MOUND - J.H.LOCKWOOD	1871	MDSVILLE	1809
THE NATIONAL ROAD / BOOK	1916	NAT'L ROAD	1861
THE OLD HOME	1871	OH CO. MAP	1742
THE OLD HOMESTEAD / JAMES MCCUTCHEN	1871	OH CO. MAP	1743
THE OLD HOMESTEAD OF 1798	1871	HAN MAP	1732
THE THREE RIDGES - OLD NAME FOR WEST ALEXANDER	1916	NAT'L ROAD	1862
THE TWO OAKS - FRANKLIN TWP	1871	MARH'L MAP	1758
THE WHITE HOUSE FARM	1871	MARH'L MAP	1752
THE WHITE HOUSE FARM	1871	MARH'L MAP	1755
THERRILL, GEORGE	1802	PLAINTIFF	1559
THIBALETT, FRANCIS	1857	PLAINTIFF	1560
THIERIOT, FERDINAND	1858	PLAINTIFF	1560
THIS FARM WAS SETTLED BY RICHARD WELLS, KNOWN AS GRAYBEARD IN 1772	1871	BRKE MAP	1734
THISTLE, BENJAMAN T	1840	PLAINTIFF	1559
THISTLE, SAMPSON	1822	PLAINTIFF	1559
THISTLE, SAMPSON	1823	PLAINTIFF	1559
THISTLE, THOMAS	1817	PLAINTIFF	1559
THOBURN & HADDEN	1860	PLAINTIFF	1621
THOBURN, ALEXANDER	1877	MISC	1679
THOBURN, ALEXANDER	1877	MISC	1692
THOBURN, JOSEPH	1854	MISC	1679
THOBURN, JOSEPH	1864	MISC	1679
THOBURN, WILLIAM M	1878	DEFENDANT	1617
THOMAS & BALLARD	1871	MDSVILLE	1807
THOMAS, A H	1871	HAN MAP	1731
THOMAS, ANDREAS	1874	MISC	1679
THOMAS, ASAEEL	1837	PLAINTIFF	1559
THOMAS, D	1871	HAN MAP	1732
THOMAS, DANIEL	1859	PLAINTIFF	1560
THOMAS, E C	1871	MDSVL BUS.	1796
THOMAS, E C	1871	MDSVILLE	1807
THOMAS, E C / DR	1871	MDSVILLE	1807
THOMAS, ELLIS	1810	PLAINTIFF	1559
THOMAS, ELLIS	1810	PLAINTIFF	1559
THOMAS, ELLIS	1810	PLAINTIFF	1559
THOMAS, ELLIS	1814	PLAINTIFF	1559
THOMAS, FRANCIS	1805	PLAINTIFF	1559
THOMAS, FRANCIS	1808	PLAINTIFF	1559
THOMAS, HENRY	1818	PLAINTIFF	1559
THOMAS, HENRY E	1854	PLAINTIFF	1559
THOMAS, J	1871	CAMERON	1802
THOMAS, J	1871	CAMERON	1803
THOMAS, J	1871	CAMERON	1804
THOMAS, JACOB	1859	PLAINTIFF	1560
THOMAS, JACOB	1859	PLAINTIFF	1560
THOMAS, JACOB C	1855	PLAINTIFF	1559
THOMAS, JACOB C	1855	PLAINTIFF	1559
THOMAS, JACOB C	1856	PLAINTIFF	1559
THOMAS, JACOB C	1856	PLAINTIFF	1559
THOMAS, JACOB C	1858	PLAINTIFF	1560
THOMAS, JACOB C	1862	PLAINTIFF	1560
THOMAS, JACOB C	1862	PLAINTIFF	1560
THOMAS, JACOB C	1873	PLAINTIFF	1560
THOMAS, JACOB C	1874	PLAINTIFF	1560
THOMAS, JOHN	1859	PLAINTIFF	1560
THOMAS, JOHN M	1859	PLAINTIFF	1560
THOMAS, LOUIS	1869	MISC	1679
THOMAS, MARY E	1875	MISC	1679
THOMAS, P	1871	MARH'L MAP	1760
THOMAS, REASON	1858	PLAINTIFF	1560
THOMAS, THOMAS	1822	PLAINTIFF	1559
THOMAS, THOMAS	1824	PLAINTIFF	1559
THOMAS, WASHINGTON	1856	PLAINTIFF	1560
THOMAS, WILLIAM	1788	PLAINTIFF	1559
THOMAS, WILLIAM	1858	PLAINTIFF	1560
THOMESON, LAWRENCE / & CO	1856	PLAINTIFF	1621
THOMESON, LAWRENCE	1856	PLAINTIFF	1641
THOMPSON & DIVEN	1824	PLAINTIFF	1620
THOMPSON & HIBBARD	1877	PLAINTIFF	1621
THOMPSON & HIBBERD	1878	PLAINTIFF	1621
THOMPSON & KIRKPATRICK	1821	PLAINTIFF	1620
THOMPSON & MARES	1818	PLAINTIFF	1620
THOMPSON & MARIS	1808	PLAINTIFF	1620
THOMPSON, -	1843	MISC	1679
THOMPSON, -	1871	BRKE MAP	1734
THOMPSON, - / MRS - YANKEE ST	1871	WELLSBURG	1777
THOMPSON, - / (?JUDGE?)	1871	WHG CITY	1787
THOMPSON, - / JUDGE	1871	WHG CITY	1787
THOMPSON, - / JUDGE	1871	WHG CITY	1789
THOMPSON, - / JUDGE	1871	WHG CITY	1789
THOMPSON, - / ROAD HOUSE ON NATIONAL ROAD	1916	NAT'L ROAD	1865
THOMPSON, A	1871	MARH'L MAP	1747
THOMPSON, A	1871	MARH'L MAP	1747
THOMPSON, ALEX	1859	PLAINTIFF	1641
THOMPSON, ALEXANDER	1859	PLAINTIFF	1641
THOMPSON, ALEXANDER	1860	PLAINTIFF	1641
THOMPSON, ALEXANDER	1862	PLAINTIFF	1641
THOMPSON, ANDREW	1858	PLAINTIFF	1641
THOMPSON, ARCHIBALD L	1830	PLAINTIFF	1639
THOMPSON, ARMOR	1879	MISC	1679

'PERSONAL TIME LINE' INDEX TO VOLUME 7 OF THE *OHIO COUNTY INDEX*

ENTRY	YEAR	SUBJECT	PAGE	ENTRY	YEAR	SUBJECT	PAGE
THOMPSON, BENJAMIN	1825	PLAINTIFF	1639	THOMPSON, JAMES P	1848	PLAINTIFF	1641
THOMPSON, C	1871	MDSVILLE	1808	THOMPSON, JAMES SR	1829	PLAINTIFF	1639
THOMPSON, C	1871	MDSVILLE	1808	THOMPSON, JAMES T	1853	PLAINTIFF	1641
THOMPSON, C	1871	MDSVILLE	1808	THOMPSON, JOHN	1787	PLAINTIFF	1637
THOMPSON, CATHARINE	1870	MISC	1679	THOMPSON, JOHN	1788	PLAINTIFF	1637
THOMPSON, DAVID H	1847	PLAINTIFF	1641	THOMPSON, JOHN	1790	PLAINTIFF	1637
THOMPSON, DAVID H / & CO	1848	PLAINTIFF	1620	THOMPSON, JOHN	1805	PLAINTIFF	1637
THOMPSON, DAVID H	1848	PLAINTIFF	1641	THOMPSON, JOHN	1808	PLAINTIFF	1637
THOMPSON, EDWARD	1818	PLAINTIFF	1638	THOMPSON, JOHN	1809	PLAINTIFF	1638
THOMPSON, FRANCES	1872	MISC	1679	THOMPSON, JOHN	1810	PLAINTIFF	1638
THOMPSON, G	1871	MARH'L MAP	1757	THOMPSON, JOHN	1812	PLAINTIFF	1638
THOMPSON, G W / JUDGE	1871	OH CO. MAP	1742	THOMPSON, JOHN	1817	PLAINTIFF	1638
THOMPSON, G W / JUDGE - RES.	1871	OH CO. MAP	1742	THOMPSON, JOHN	1818	PLAINTIFF	1638
THOMPSON, G W	1871	MARH'L MAP	1757	THOMPSON, JOHN	1820	PLAINTIFF	1638
THOMPSON, G W / JUDGE	1871	TRIAD. TWP.	1781	THOMPSON, JOHN	1823	PLAINTIFF	1638
THOMPSON, G W	1871	WHG CITY	1787	THOMPSON, JOHN	1824	PLAINTIFF	1638
THOMPSON, G W	1871	WHG CITY	1789	THOMPSON, JOHN	1827	MISC	1678
THOMPSON, G W	1871	WHG CITY	1789	THOMPSON, JOHN	1828	DEFENDANT	1581
THOMPSON, G W / JUDGE - RES	1871	WHG CITY	1789	THOMPSON, JOHN	1832	PLAINTIFF	1639
THOMPSON, G W / INITIALS G.W.T.	1871	CAMERON	1804	THOMPSON, JOHN	1833	PLAINTIFF	1639
THOMPSON, GEORGE	1803	PLAINTIFF	1637	THOMPSON, JOHN F	1861	PLAINTIFF	1641
THOMPSON, GEORGE	1804	PLAINTIFF	1637	THOMPSON, JOHN F	1877	PLAINTIFF	1641
THOMPSON, GEORGE	1805	PLAINTIFF	1637	THOMPSON, JOHN H	1842	PLAINTIFF	1640
THOMPSON, GEORGE	1806	PLAINTIFF	1637	THOMPSON, JOHN H	1851	PLAINTIFF	1641
THOMPSON, GEORGE	1808	PLAINTIFF	1637	THOMPSON, JOHN JR	1823	PLAINTIFF	1638
THOMPSON, GEORGE	1814	PLAINTIFF	1638	THOMPSON, JOHN JR	1824	PLAINTIFF	1638
THOMPSON, GEORGE	1839	MISC	1678	THOMPSON, JOHN N	1847	PLAINTIFF	1641
THOMPSON, GEORGE	1844	MISC	1679	THOMPSON, JOHN SR	1824	DEFENDANT	1660
THOMPSON, GEORGE	1857	MISC	1679	THOMPSON, JONAS	1825	PLAINTIFF	1639
THOMPSON, GEORGE R	1879	DEFENDANT	1671	THOMPSON, JONAS	1829	PLAINTIFF	1639
THOMPSON, GEORGE S	1850	PLAINTIFF	1641	THOMPSON, JONAS	1831	PLAINTIFF	1639
THOMPSON, GEORGE S	1855	PLAINTIFF	1641	THOMPSON, JOSEPH R	1846	PLAINTIFF	1640
THOMPSON, GEORGE S	1857	PLAINTIFF	1641	THOMPSON, JOSIAH	1824	PLAINTIFF	1638
THOMPSON, GEORGE W	1838	PLAINTIFF	1640	THOMPSON, JOSIAH	1829	PLAINTIFF	1639
THOMPSON, GEORGE W	1839	PLAINTIFF	1640	THOMPSON, JOSIAH	1829	MISC	1681
THOMPSON, GEORGE W	1840	PLAINTIFF	1640	THOMPSON, JOSIAH	1831	PLAINTIFF	1639
THOMPSON, H	1871	MARH'L MAP	1747	THOMPSON, JOSIAS	1817	MISC	1678
THOMPSON, H P	1818	PLAINTIFF	1638	THOMPSON, JOSIAS	1821	PLAINTIFF	1638
THOMPSON, HARRIETT	1879	PLAINTIFF	1641	THOMPSON, JOSIAS	1822	PLAINTIFF	1638
THOMPSON, HENRY	1857	DEFENDANT	1608	THOMPSON, JOSIAS	1825	PLAINTIFF	1639
THOMPSON, HILARY	1842	PLAINTIFF	1640	THOMPSON, JOSIAS	1835	MISC	1678
THOMPSON, ISAAC	1841	PLAINTIFF	1640	THOMPSON, LEWIS	1828	DEFENDANT	1604
THOMPSON, J / SE OF JAMES WINTERS	1871	MARH'L MAP	1746	THOMPSON, M R / W - MARSHALL ST (?POSSIBLY W.)	1871	MDSVILLE	1808
THOMPSON, J	1871	MARH'L MAP	1747	THOMPSON, M R / W.	1871	MDSVILLE	1810
THOMPSON, J / W. SIDE OF MAP	1871	MARH'L MAP	1747	THOMPSON, MARY VIRGINIA	1860	MISC	1679
THOMPSON, J	1871	MARH'L MAP	1756	THOMPSON, MOSES	1810	PLAINTIFF	1638
THOMPSON, J / INITIALS J.T.	1871	MARH'L MAP	1757	THOMPSON, MOSES	1813	MISC	1678
THOMPSON, J / INITIALS J.T.	1871	MARH'L MAP	1757	THOMPSON, MOSES	1821	MISC	1678
THOMPSON, J	1871	MDSVILLE	1808	THOMPSON, MOSES	1823	MISC	1678
THOMPSON, J	1871	MDSVILLE	1808	THOMPSON, MOSES	1826	MISC	1678
THOMPSON, J / INITIALS J.T.	1871	MDSVILLE	1808	THOMPSON, MOSES	1827	MISC	1678
THOMPSON, J / INITIALS J.T.	1871	MDSVILLE	1808	THOMPSON, MOSES	1828	MISC	1678
THOMPSON, J	1871	MDSVILLE	1810	THOMPSON, MOSES	1831	MISC	1678
THOMPSON, J M	1830	PLAINTIFF	1639	THOMPSON, MOSES	1832	PLAINTIFF	1639
THOMPSON, J M	1834	PLAINTIFF	1639	THOMPSON, MOSES	1833	MISC	1678
THOMPSON, JAMES / & CO	1832	PLAINTIFF	1620	THOMPSON, MOSES	1834	MISC	1678
THOMPSON, JAMES	1833	PLAINTIFF	1639	THOMPSON, MOSES	1834	MISC	1678
THOMPSON, JAMES	1839	PLAINTIFF	1640	THOMPSON, MOSES	1834	MISC	1678
THOMPSON, JAMES	1840	PLAINTIFF	1640	THOMPSON, MOSES	1839	PLAINTIFF	1640
THOMPSON, JAMES	1843	PLAINTIFF	1640	THOMPSON, MOSES	1840	PLAINTIFF	1640
THOMPSON, JAMES	1856	PLAINTIFF	1641	THOMPSON, MOSES	1841	PLAINTIFF	1589
THOMPSON, JAMES	1859	PLAINTIFF	1641	THOMPSON, MOSES	1841	PLAINTIFF	1640
THOMPSON, JAMES A	1836	MISC	1678	THOMPSON, MOSES	1843	PLAINTIFF	1640
THOMPSON, JAMES M	1817	MISC	1678	THOMPSON, MOSES W	1844	PLAINTIFF	1640
THOMPSON, JAMES M	1820	PLAINTIFF	1638	THOMPSON, MOSEY	1842	PLAINTIFF	1640
THOMPSON, JAMES M	1822	MISC	1678	THOMPSON, O D	1853	PLAINTIFF	1641
THOMPSON, JAMES M	1823	PLAINTIFF	1638	THOMPSON, O D	1873	PLAINTIFF	1641
THOMPSON, JAMES M	1828	PLAINTIFF	1639	THOMPSON, O D	1874	DEFENDANT	1586
THOMPSON, JAMES M	1829	PLAINTIFF	1639	THOMPSON, OSCAR D	1857	DEFENDANT	1653
THOMPSON, JAMES M / & CO	1830	PLAINTIFF	1620	THOMPSON, OSCAR D	1860	DEFENDANT	1597
THOMPSON, JAMES M	1830	PLAINTIFF	1639	THOMPSON, R / WAGON SHOP	1871	WELLSBURG	1777
THOMPSON, JAMES M	1831	PLAINTIFF	1639	THOMPSON, R C	1822	PLAINTIFF	1638
THOMPSON, JAMES M	1831	MISC	1678	THOMPSON, ROBERT	1814	PLAINTIFF	1638
THOMPSON, JAMES M	1832	PLAINTIFF	1639	THOMPSON, ROBERT	1815	MISC	1678
THOMPSON, JAMES M / & CO	1834	PLAINTIFF	1620	THOMPSON, ROBERT	1818	PLAINTIFF	1638
THOMPSON, JAMES M	1834	PLAINTIFF	1639	THOMPSON, ROBERT	1819	PLAINTIFF	1638
THOMPSON, JAMES M	1834	PLAINTIFF	1639	THOMPSON, ROBERT	1819	MISC	1677
THOMPSON, JAMES M	1834	PLAINTIFF	1640	THOMPSON, ROBERT	1819	MISC	1678
THOMPSON, JAMES M	1835	DEFENDANT	1565	THOMPSON, ROBERT	1824	PLAINTIFF	1639
THOMPSON, JAMES M	1836	PLAINTIFF	1640	THOMPSON, ROBERT	1831	MISC	1678
THOMPSON, JAMES M	1838	PLAINTIFF	1640	THOMPSON, ROBERT / & CO	1833	PLAINTIFF	1620
THOMPSON, JAMES M	1839	PLAINTIFF	1640	THOMPSON, ROBERT / & CO	1834	PLAINTIFF	1620
THOMPSON, JAMES M	1841	PLAINTIFF	1640	THOMPSON, ROBERT C	1819	MISC	1678
THOMPSON, JAMES M	1846	PLAINTIFF	1640	THOMPSON, ROBERT C	1821	DEFENDANT	1581

'PERSONAL TIME LINE' INDEX TO VOLUME 7 OF THE *OHIO COUNTY INDEX*

ENTRY	YEAR	SUBJECT	PAGE	ENTRY	YEAR	SUBJECT	PAGE
THOMPSON, S L	1841	PLAINTIFF	1640	THORNBURG, THOMAS	1874	MISC	1679
THOMPSON, SAMUEL	1825	PLAINTIFF	1639	THORNBURG, WILLIAM C	1855	DEFENDANT	1590
THOMPSON, SAMUEL	1828	MISC	1678	THORNBURG, WILLIAM C	1855	DEFENDANT	1629
THOMPSON, SAMUEL	1875	PLAINTIFF	1641	THORNBURGER MILLER & WEBSTER	1815	PLAINTIFF	1620
THOMPSON, SAMUEL L / & CO	1840	PLAINTIFF	1620	THORNBURGH, DANIEL S	1873	PLAINTIFF	1560
THOMPSON, STEPHEN	1853	PLAINTIFF	1641	THORNBURGH, DANIEL S	1874	PLAINTIFF	1560
THOMPSON, THOMAS	1808	PLAINTIFF	1638	THORNBURGH, DANIEL S	1874	PLAINTIFF	1560
THOMPSON, THOMAS	1809	PLAINTIFF	1638	THORNBURGH, DANIEL S	1874	PLAINTIFF	1560
THOMPSON, THOMAS	1811	DEFENDANT	1610	THORNBURGH, DANIEL S	1874	PLAINTIFF	1560
THOMPSON, THOMAS	1811	DEFENDANT	1610	THORNBURGH, DANIEL S	1874	PLAINTIFF	1560
THOMPSON, THOMAS	1811	PLAINTIFF	1638	THORNBURGH, DAVID	1828	MISC	1678
THOMPSON, THOMAS	1818	PLAINTIFF	1638	THORNBURGH, DAVID M	1873	PLAINTIFF	1560
THOMPSON, THOMAS	1819	PLAINTIFF	1638	THORNBURGH, E	1877	PLAINTIFF	1560
THOMPSON, THOMAS	1822	PLAINTIFF	1638	THORNBURGH, H S	1856	PLAINTIFF	1560
THOMPSON, THOMAS	1828	PLAINTIFF	1639	THORNBURGH, H S	1873	PLAINTIFF	1560
THOMPSON, THOMAS	1832	PLAINTIFF	1639	THORNBURGH, H S	1874	DEFENDANT	1560
THOMPSON, THOMAS B	1817	PLAINTIFF	1638	THORNBURGH, H S	1877	PLAINTIFF	1560
THOMPSON, THOMAS B	1822	PLAINTIFF	1638	THORNBURGH, JOHN	1852	HEMPFIELD RR	1822
THOMPSON, THOMAS M	1813	PLAINTIFF	1638	THORNBURGH, JOHN	1873	DEFENDANT	1560
THOMPSON, THOMAS MCKEAN	1803	PLAINTIFF	1637	THORNBURGH, JOHN	1874	MISC	1679
THOMPSON, W / ? - MARSHALL ST. - PROBABLY M.R.	1871	MDSVILLE	1808	THORNBURGH, JOHN	1875	MISC	1679
THOMPSON, W / ? - LISTING IS M.R.THOMPSON W.	1871	MDSVILLE	1810	THORNBURGH, JOHN	1876	MISC	1679
				THORNBURGH, MOSES	1834	DEFENDANT	1613
				THORNBURGH, THOMAS	1818	DEFENDANT	1624
THOMPSON, W. / ? - N. OF BLACKS ISLAND	1871	HAN MAP	1730	THORNBURGH, THOMAS	1820	DEFENDANT	1624
				THORNBURGH, THOMAS	1823	PLAINTIFF	1559
THOMPSON, WILLIAM	1794	PLAINTIFF	1637	THORNBURGH, THOMAS	1852	HEMPFIELD RR	1822
THOMPSON, WILLIAM	1806	PLAINTIFF	1637	THORNBURGH, THOMAS	1852	HEMPFIELD RR	1822
THOMPSON, WILLIAM	1839	MISC	1678	THORNBURGH, THOMAS	1875	MISC	1679
THOMPSON, WILLIAM	1840	MISC	1678	THORNBURGH, W C	1873	DEFENDANT	1560
THOMPSON, WILLIAM	1841	MISC	1678	THORNTON, W H	1879	PLAINTIFF	1560
THOMPSON, WILLIAM	1870	MISC	1679	THREE MILE ICE HOUSE - WHEELING CREEK	1871	TRIAD.TWP.	1781
THOMPSON, WILLIAM B	1849	PLAINTIFF	1641				
THOMPSON, WILLIAM P	1839	MISC	1678	THREE SPRINGS CHURCH - OLD THREE SPRINGS CHURCH / FIRST CHURCH IN COUNTY	1871	HAN MAP	1732
THOMPSON, WILLIAM R / & CO	1843	PLAINTIFF	1620				
THOMPSON'S ROAD HOUSE ON NATIONAL ROAD	1916	NAT'L ROAD	1865				
				THUMB, TOM	1812	PLAINTIFF	1559
THOMSON, - / HANNA, THOMSON & CO. - MAP#599	1852	BRKE MAP	1851	THUMB, TOM	1813	PLAINTIFF	1559
				THURSBEY, EDWARD	1806	PLAINTIFF	1559
THOMSON, - / HANNA, THOMSON & CO. - MAP#599	1852	BRKE MAP	1851	TIBERGAN, CHARLES	1788	PLAINTIFF	1556
				TIBERGAN, CHARLES	1789	DEFENDANT	1598
THOMSON, - / HANNA, THOMSON & CO. - (PAPER MILL) - MAP#601	1852	BRKE MAP	1851	TIBERGHIN, CHARLES	1813	PLAINTIFF	1556
				TIBERGHIN, CHARLES	1813	PLAINTIFF	1556
THOMSON, - / HANNA, THOMSON & CO. / (PAPER MILL) - MAP#601	1852	BRKE MAP	1851	TIBERGIN, CHARLES	1800	PLAINTIFF	1556
				TIBERGIN, LEO	1812	DEFENDANT	1648
THOMSON, - / HANNA, THOMSON / & CO. - MAP#599	1852	BRKE MAP	1851	TIBUGAN, CHARLES	1791	PLAINTIFF	1556
				TIBUGIN, CHARLES	1799	PLAINTIFF	1556
THOMSON, JOHN	1787	PLAINTIFF	1637	TIBUGIN, ISAAC	1800	PLAINTIFF	1556
THOMSON, JOHN	1788	PLAINTIFF	1637	TICE, H	1871	OH CO. MAP	1740
THOMSON, JOHN	1791	PLAINTIFF	1637	TIDDEN, THOMAS E	1838	PLAINTIFF	1557
THOMSON, JOHN	1801	MISC	1678	TIEMAN, H	1871	OH CO. MAP	1742
THOMSON, LAWRENCE & CO	1857	PLAINTIFF	1621	TIEMANN, H	1871	TRIAD.TWP.	1781
THOMSON, NANCY	1791	PLAINTIFF	1637	TIERAN, LUKE	1805	PLAINTIFF	1556
THOMSON, THOMAS	1800	MISC	1677	TIERNAN, ELLA	1874	MISC	1677
THOMSON, WILLIAM	1794	PLAINTIFF	1637	TIERNAN, FRANCIS & CO	1822	PLAINTIFF	1620
THOMPSON, G W / INITIALS G.W.T.	1871	OH CO. MAP	1742	TIERNAN, HENRY	1879	PLAINTIFF	1557
THORLEYS RUN OR BRANCH	1852	BRKE MAP	1849	TIERNAN, J M	1857	DEFENDANT	1552
THORN, - / MRS - LIBERTY ST	1871	WELLSBURG	1777	TIERNAN, LUKE	1807	PLAINTIFF	1556
THORNBERG, THOMAS	1850	MISC	1679	TIERNAN, M J	1862	MISC	1677
THORNBURG, - / MRS	1871	TRIAD.BORO.	1784	TIERNAN, M J	1874	MISC	1677
THORNBURG, C	1871	OH CO. MAP	1743	TIERNAN, MICHAEL	1824	PLAINTIFF	1558
THORNBURG, C	1871	OH CO. MAP	1744	TIERNAN, MICHAEL	1878	MISC	1677
THORNBURG, D	1871	OH CO. MAP	1742	TIERNAN, MILES J	1858	PLAINTIFF	1557
THORNBURG, D	1871	OH CO. MAP	1744	TIERNAN, WILLIAM M	1874	MISC	1677
THORNBURG, DAVID	1828	MISC	1703	TIERNEY, JOSEPH	1874	PLAINTIFF	1557
THORNBURG, H S	1871	OH CO. MAP	1743	TIERS, E	1871	WELLSBURG	1778
THORNBURG, H S	1871	OH CO. MAP	1744	TIFFANY SHAW & CO	1833	PLAINTIFF	1620
THORNBURG, H S	1878	DEFENDANT	1560	TIFFANY SHAW & CO	1834	PLAINTIFF	1620
THORNBURG, HARRIET	1862	PLAINTIFF	1560	TIFFANY, COMFORT	1833	PLAINTIFF	1557
THORNBURG, J	1871	OH CO. MAP	1743	TIFFANY, HENRY	1841	PLAINTIFF	1557
THORNBURG, J	1871	OH CO. MAP	1744	TIFFANY, HENRY	1841	PLAINTIFF	1557
THORNBURG, JOHN	1877	PLAINTIFF	1560	TIFFANY, HENRY	1841	PLAINTIFF	1557
THORNBURG, JOHN	1878	PLAINTIFF	1560	TIFFANY, HENRY	1861	PLAINTIFF	1557
THORNBURG, JOHN	1878	PLAINTIFF	1560	TIFFANY, OSMOND C	1833	PLAINTIFF	1557
THORNBURG, JOHN	1878	MISC	1679	TIFFANY, WEYMAN & CO	1833	PLAINTIFF	1620
THORNBURG, JOHN N	1877	PLAINTIFF	1560	TIFFENY, WEYMAN & CO	1825	PLAINTIFF	1620
THORNBURG, T	1871	OH CO. MAP	1743	TIFFENY, WYMAN & CO	1820	PLAINTIFF	1620
THORNBURG, T	1871	OH CO. MAP	1744	TIFFT, B E	1874	PLAINTIFF	1557
THORNBURG, THOMAS	1813	MISC	1678	TIGART, FRANCIS	1791	PLAINTIFF	1556
THORNBURG, THOMAS	1822	PLAINTIFF	1559	TIGERT, FRANCIS	1792	PLAINTIFF	1556
THORNBURG, THOMAS	1840	PLAINTIFF	1559	TILDEN, SOPHIA	1858	MISC	1677
THORNBURG, THOMAS	1840	PLAINTIFF	1559	TILDEN, THOMAS	1838	PLAINTIFF	1557
THORNBURG, THOMAS	1848	MISC	1679	TILDEN, THOMAS E	1839	PLAINTIFF	1557
THORNBURG, THOMAS	1848	MISC	1687	TILDEN, WILLIAM	1821	PLAINTIFF	1557
THORNBURG, THOMAS	1850	MISC	1679	TILE COMPANIES	1871	FRE'MAN'S LDG	1762
THORNBURG, THOMAS	1871	MISC	1679	TILES FOR GAS HOUSES	1871	FRE'MAN'S LDG	1762

'PERSONAL TIME LINE' INDEX TO VOLUME 7 OF THE *OHIO COUNTY INDEX*

ENTRY	YEAR	SUBJECT	PAGE	ENTRY	YEAR	SUBJECT	PAGE
TILFORD, JAMES	1820	PLAINTIFF	1556	TINGLE, GEORGE R	1879	PLAINTIFF	1558
TILLMAN - COLORED	1873	MISC	1677	TINGLE, GEORGE T	1843	PLAINTIFF	1558
TILLMAN, SUSAN	1873	MISC	1677	TINGLE, GEORGE T	1844	PLAINTIFF	1558
TILS RUN	1852	BRKE MAP	1846	TINGLE, GEORGE T	1855	PLAINTIFF	1558
TILTON, DAVID	1842	PLAINTIFF	1557	TINGLE, WILLIAM	1809	MISC	1677
TILTON, JOHN	1778	PLAINTIFF	1556	TINNY, JAMES	1811	MISC	1677
TILTON, JOHN	1784	PLAINTIFF	1556	TIN-PLATE INDUSTRY - WHEELING	1916	NAT'L ROAD	1865
TILTON, JOHN	1784	PLAINTIFF	1556	TINSON, AARON	1834	PLAINTIFF	1558
TILTON, JOHN	1784	PLAINTIFF	1556	TIPPER, WILLIAM	1858	PLAINTIFF	1558
TILTON, JOHN	1784	DEFENDANT	1589	TIPPETT, WILLIAM S	1860	DEFENDANT	1654
TILTON, JOHN	1784	MISC	1677	TIPPETT, WILLIAM S	1860	DEFENDANT	1671
TILTON, JOHN	1785	PLAINTIFF	1556	TIPPINGS, ELIZABETH	1794	MISC	1677
TILTON, JOHN	1787	PLAINTIFF	1556	TISDALE, MACE	1862	PLAINTIFF	1558
TILTON, JOHN	1787	PLAINTIFF	1556	TITLE PAGE - VOL. 7	2000	TITLE	1544
TILTON, JOHN	1791	PLAINTIFF	1556	TITTLE, LEMUEL	1833	PLAINTIFF	1558
TILTON, JOHN	1796	PLAINTIFF	1556	TITTLE, LEMUEL	1838	PLAINTIFF	1558
TILTON, JOHN	1798	PLAINTIFF	1556	TITTLE, LEMUEL	1838	PLAINTIFF	1558
TILTON, JOHN	1798	DEFENDANT	1600	TITTLE, LEMUEL	1838	PLAINTIFF	1558
TILTON, JOHN	1800	DEFENDANT	1556	TITTLE, LEMUEL	1838	PLAINTIFF	1558
TILTON, JOHN	1802	PLAINTIFF	1556	TITTLE, LEMUEL	1838	PLAINTIFF	1558
TILTON, JOHN	1805	PLAINTIFF	1556	TITTLE, LEMUEL	1838	PLAINTIFF	1558
TILTON, JOHN	1806	PLAINTIFF	1556	TITTLE, LEMUEL	1838	PLAINTIFF	1558
TILTON, JOHN	1807	PLAINTIFF	1556	TITTLE, LEMUEL	1838	DEFENDANT	1623
TILTON, JOHN	1808	PLAINTIFF	1556	TITTLE, SAMUEL	1838	PLAINTIFF	1558
TILTON, JOHN	1814	PLAINTIFF	1556	TITUS, - / MRS	1871	MARH'L MAP	1752
TILTON, RICHARD	1799	PLAINTIFF	1556	TITUS, - / MRS	1871	MARH'L MAP	1756
TILTON, RICHARD	1800	PLAINTIFF	1556	TITUS, ALLEN	1839	MISC	1677
TILTON, RICHARD	1800	PLAINTIFF	1556	TITUS, ELIZABETH	1836	MISC	1677
TILTON, THOMAS	1785	PLAINTIFF	1556	TMITT BROS CO	1859	PLAINTIFF	1621
TILTON, WILLIAM	1796	PLAINTIFF	1556	TOBACCO INDUSTRY - WHEELING	1916	NAT'L ROAD	1865
TILTON, WILLIAM	1806	PLAINTIFF	1556	TOBIN, JOSIAH	1804	PLAINTIFF	1561
TILTONSVILLE, OH	1852	BRKE MAP	1839	TODD & HOWELL	1853	PLAINTIFF	1623
TILTONVILLE, OHIO	1871	BKE/OH MAP	1738	TODD & MITCHELL	1852	PLAINTIFF	1623
TIMBER LAND	1871	HAN MAP	1732	TODD & MITCHELL	1853	PLAINTIFF	1623
TIMBERLAND - E. OF T.M.POWELL	1871	MARH'L MAP	1752	TODD & MITCHELL	1854	PLAINTIFF	1623
TIMBERLAND - J J WALKERS	1871	BRKE MAP	1734	TODD & MITCHELL	1854	PLAINTIFF	1623
TIMBERLAND - ON MCCLEANS RUN	1871	MARH'L MAP	1748	TODD & MITCHELL	1855	PLAINTIFF	1623
TIMBERLAND - ORRS / N & BUILDING SITES	1871	BRKE MAP	1734	TODD & SMITH	1878	PLAINTIFF	1623
				TODD, A S	1854	MISC	1680
TIMBERLAND - WHEELERS / THOMAS	1871	BRKE MAP	1735	TODD, A S	1875	PLAINTIFF	1562
TIMBERLAND - WILSONS / JAMES	1871	BRKE MAP	1735	TODD, ARCHIBALD L	1837	PLAINTIFF	1561
TIMBERLANDS - CARTERS / CEPHAS	1871	BRKE MAP	1735	TODD, ARCHIBALD PAULL	1848	MISC	1680
TIMBERLANDS - PATTERSONS / FRANCIS	1871	BRKE MAP	1735	TODD, ARCHIBALD S	1836	PLAINTIFF	1561
				TODD, ARCHIBALD S	1842	PLAINTIFF	1561
TIMBERLANDS - PUNTNEYS / JAMES	1871	BRKE MAP	1735	TODD, ARCHIBALD S	1843	PLAINTIFF	1561
TIMBERLANDS - REEVES / JOHN C	1871	BRKE MAP	1735	TODD, ARCHIBALD S	1856	PLAINTIFF	1561
TIMBERLANDS - WALLACES / JOHN	1871	BRKE MAP	1735	TODD, ARCHIBALD S	1857	PLAINTIFF	1561
TIMBERLANDS - WIGGINS / J	1871	BRKE MAP	1735	TODD, ARCHIBALD S	1857	PLAINTIFF	1561
TIMBERLANDS - WIGGINS / J.B.	1871	BRKE MAP	1735	TODD, ELIZA JANE	1866	MISC	1680
TIMES PUBLISHING CO - THE	1858	DEFENDANT	1653	TODD, G	1871	MARH'L MAP	1757
TIMMANNS, JACOB H	1861	DEFENDANT	1615	TODD, GENEVIEVE	1880	MISC	1680
TIMMINS, NANCY	1814	MISC	1677	TODD, J M / & CO	1858	PLAINTIFF	1623
TIMMONS - BLACK MAN	1825	MISC	1677	TODD, JAMES	1853	MISC	1680
TIMMONS, AMOS	1818	PLAINTIFF	1556	TODD, JAMES	1871	OH CO. MAP	1743
TIMMONS, CHARLOTTE	1819	MISC	1677	TODD, JAMES C	1853	MISC	1680
TIMMONS, HENRY	1822	PLAINTIFF	1557	TODD, JAMES C	1854	PLAINTIFF	1561
TIMMONS, J M	1871	OH CO. MAP	1740	TODD, JAMES C	1855	PLAINTIFF	1561
TIMMONS, JESSE	1825	MISC	1677	TODD, JAMES C	1857	PLAINTIFF	1561
TIMMONS, JESSE	1826	PLAINTIFF	1557	TODD, JAMES M	1852	PLAINTIFF	1561
TIMMONS, JESSE	1827	PLAINTIFF	1557	TODD, JAMES M	1855	PLAINTIFF	1561
TIMMONS, JOHN	1819	MISC	1677	TODD, JAMES M	1855	PLAINTIFF	1561
TIMMONS, JOHN	1819	MISC	1678	TODD, JAMES M	1855	PLAINTIFF	1561
TIMMONS, LAZARUS	1812	MISC	1677	TODD, JAMES M	1858	DEFENDANT	1552
TIMMONS, LUCINDA	1819	MISC	1677	TODD, JAMES M	1858	PLAINTIFF	1561
TIMMONS, LUCINDA	1819	MISC	1704	TODD, JAMES M	1858	PLAINTIFF	1562
TIMMONS, NANCY	1810	MISC	1677	TODD, JAMES M	1858	PLAINTIFF	1562
TIMMONS, NANCY	1810	MISC	1709	TODD, JAMES M	1858	DEFENDANT	1590
TIMMONS, PETER	1819	MISC	1677	TODD, JAMES M	1858	DEFENDANT	1597
TIMMONS, SHARTOL	1823	MISC	1677	TODD, JAMES M	1858	DEFENDANT	1621
TINGES, GEORGE W	1839	PLAINTIFF	1558	TODD, JAMES M	1858	DEFENDANT	1630
TINGLE & ALMAN	1856	PLAINTIFF	1621	TODD, JAMES M	1859	DEFENDANT	1560
TINGLE & ISHAN	1874	PLAINTIFF	1621	TODD, JAMES M	1859	DEFENDANT	1597
TINGLE & MARSH	1855	PLAINTIFF	1621	TODD, JAMES M	1859	DEFENDANT	1657
TINGLE, EBINEZER	1804	PLAINTIFF	1558	TODD, JAMES M	1874	PLAINTIFF	1562
TINGLE, G R	1871	ELM GROVE	1782	TODD, M C	1871	MARH'L MAP	1753
TINGLE, GEORGE	1842	PLAINTIFF	1558	TODD, M C	1871	MARH'L MAP	1757
TINGLE, GEORGE	1844	PLAINTIFF	1558	TODD, M C / INITIALS M.C.T.	1871	MARH'L MAP	1757
TINGLE, GEORGE	1856	PLAINTIFF	1558	TODD, MARGARET ELIZABETH	1866	MISC	1680
TINGLE, GEORGE	1871	OH CO. MAP	1741	TODD, MARTIN	1829	MISC	1680
TINGLE, GEORGE R	1874	PLAINTIFF	1558	TODD, MARTIN L	1832	PLAINTIFF	1561
TINGLE, GEORGE R	1876	PLAINTIFF	1558	TODD, MARTIN L	1833	PLAINTIFF	1561
TINGLE, GEORGE R	1876	PLAINTIFF	1558	TODD, MARTIN L	1834	PLAINTIFF	1561
TINGLE, GEORGE R	1877	PLAINTIFF	1558	TODD, MARTIN LUTHER	1871	MISC	1680
TINGLE, GEORGE R	1877	PLAINTIFF	1558	TODD, NANCY DEVOL	1853	MISC	1680
TINGLE, GEORGE R	1877	PLAINTIFF	1558	TODD, NANCY DEVOL	1853	MISC	1680
TINGLE, GEORGE R	1878	MISC	1701	TODD, SAMUEL	1811	PLAINTIFF	1561

CIV

'PERSONAL TIME LINE' INDEX TO VOLUME 7 OF THE *OHIO COUNTY INDEX*

ENTRY	YEAR	SUBJECT	PAGE
TODD, SAMUEL	1816	PLAINTIFF	1561
TODD, SAMUEL	1816	DEFENDANT	1659
TODD, SAMUEL	1817	DEFENDANT	1659
TODD, THOMAS	1852	PLAINTIFF	1561
TODD, THOMAS	1852	PLAINTIFF	1561
TODD, THOMAS	1852	DEFENDANT	1663
TODD, THOMAS	1853	PLAINTIFF	1561
TODD, THOMAS	1853	PLAINTIFF	1561
TODD, THOMAS	1872	MISC	1680
TODD, WILLIAM	1819	PLAINTIFF	1561
TODD, WILLIAM	1819	PLAINTIFF	1561
TODD, WILLIAM	1821	PLAINTIFF	1561
TODD, WILLIAM	1821	PLAINTIFF	1561
TODD, WILLIAM	1825	MISC	1680
TODD, WILLIAM	1828	MISC	1680
TODD, WILLIAM	1847	PLAINTIFF	1561
TODD, WILLIAM F	1841	PLAINTIFF	1561
TODD, WILLIAM F / & CO	1841	PLAINTIFF	1623
TODD, WILLIAM T	1867	MISC	1680
TODDS RUN	1871	OH CO. MAP	1743
TOLAND, JAMES	1831	MISC	1680
TOLAND, JAMES	1834	MISC	1680
TOLAND, WILLIAM	1820	PLAINTIFF	1561
TOLAND, WILLIAM	1823	PLAINTIFF	1561
TOLEN, S	1871	MARH'L MAP	1747
TOLEN, THOMAS	1877	PLAINTIFF	1562
TOLFORD, D W	1853	PLAINTIFF	1561
TOLFORD, D W	1853	PLAINTIFF	1561
TOLIVER, JOSEPH	1861	MISC	1680
TOLL GATE - N. OF STEENROD	1871	OH CO. MAP	1742
TOLL GATE - RONEY POINT - NATIONAL ROAD (?EASTERN GATE?)	1871	OH CO. MAP	1743
TOLL GATE - RONEY POINT STATION - NATIONAL ROAD / (?EASTERN GATE?)	1871	OH CO. MAP	1744
TOLL GATE - W. OF BETHANY	1871	BRKE MAP	1737
TOLL GATE - W. OF BETHANY	1871	BKE/OH MAP	1739
TOLL GATE - WAYNESBURGH ROAD - NEAR POPLAR SPRING	1871	MARH'L MAP	1753
TOLL HOUSE	1852	NOT ON MAP	1836
TOLL HOUSE / MAP#346	1852	BRKE MAP	1846
TOLL HOUSE / MAP#362	1852	BRKE MAP	1847
TOLL HOUSE - BETHANY PIKE NEAR NAT'L RD	1871	TRIAD. TWP.	1781
TOLL HOUSE - NATIONAL ROAD - COON ISLAND	1916	NAT'L ROAD	1862
TOLL HOUSE - NATIONAL ROAD - LEATHERWOOD	1871	TRIAD. TWP.	1781
TOLL HOUSE - NATIONAL ROAD - LEATHERWOOD	1871	WHG CITY	1789
TOLL HOUSE - NATIONAL ROAD - TRIAD.TWP / LEATHERWOOD	1871	WHG CITY	1787
TOLL HOUSE - NATIONAL ROAD - WHEELING	1871	WHG CITY	1786
TOLL HOUSE - ROAD TO GREGGSVILLE	1871	OH CO. MAP	1742
TOLLAND, WILLIAM	1827	MISC	1680
TOLLER, A	1871	MARH'L MAP	1755
TOMINISON, LETITIA	1850	MISC	1680
TOMISON, LETITIA	1850	MISC	1680
TOMISON, WILLIAM	1848	MISC	1680
TOMLINSON RUN	1871	HAN MAP	1726
TOMLINSON RUN	1871	HAN MAP	1727
TOMLINSON RUN	1871	HAN MAP	1731
TOMLINSON RUN - BRANCH OF	1871	HAN MAP	1727
TOMLINSON RUN - NORTH FORK OF	1871	HAN MAP	1727
TOMLINSON, - / HEIRS	1871	MARH'L MAP	1748
TOMLINSON, A	1871	MDSVILLE	1807
TOMLINSON, A	1871	MDSVILLE	1807
TOMLINSON, A	1871	MDSVILLE	1807
TOMLINSON, A	1871	MDSVILLE	1807
TOMLINSON, A B	1871	MARH'L MAP	1745
TOMLINSON, A B / INITIALS A.B.T.	1871	MARH'L MAP	1745
TOMLINSON, ALFRED	1830	MISC	1680
TOMLINSON, ALFRED / RES	1871	MARH'L MAP	1748
TOMLINSON, ELISABETH	1831	PLAINTIFF	1555
TOMLINSON, ELIZABETH	1800	PLAINTIFF	1554
TOMLINSON, ELIZABETH	1831	PLAINTIFF	1555
TOMLINSON, ELIZABETH	1831	PLAINTIFF	1555
TOMLINSON, ELIZABETH	1831	PLAINTIFF	1555
TOMLINSON, ELIZABETH	1832	PLAINTIFF	1555
TOMLINSON, ELIZABETH ANN	1824	MISC	1680
TOMLINSON, ELLEN	1830	MISC	1680
TOMLINSON, ISAAC	1804	DEFENDANT	1648
TOMLINSON, ISAAC	1805	PLAINTIFF	1554
TOMLINSON, J	1871	MDSVILLE	1807
TOMLINSON, JAMES	1823	PLAINTIFF	1555
TOMLINSON, JESSE	1823	PLAINTIFF	1555
TOMLINSON, JESSE	1823	PLAINTIFF	1555
TOMLINSON, JOSEPH	1784	PLAINTIFF	1554
TOMLINSON, JOSEPH	1784	MISC	1680
TOMLINSON, JOSEPH	1785	PLAINTIFF	1554
TOMLINSON, JOSEPH	1789	PLAINTIFF	1554
TOMLINSON, JOSEPH	1789	MISC	1680
TOMLINSON, JOSEPH	1789	MISC	1680
TOMLINSON, JOSEPH	1791	DEFENDANT	1655
TOMLINSON, JOSEPH	1795	PLAINTIFF	1554
TOMLINSON, JOSEPH	1796	DEFENDANT	1655
TOMLINSON, JOSEPH	1798	DEFENDANT	1610
TOMLINSON, JOSEPH	1798	DEFENDANT	1647
TOMLINSON, JOSEPH	1799	DEFENDANT	1665
TOMLINSON, JOSEPH	1799	DEFENDANT	1665
TOMLINSON, JOSEPH	1800	PLAINTIFF	1554
TOMLINSON, JOSEPH	1800	PLAINTIFF	1554
TOMLINSON, JOSEPH	1800	PLAINTIFF	1554
TOMLINSON, JOSEPH	1800	DEFENDANT	1655
TOMLINSON, JOSEPH	1801	PLAINTIFF	1554
TOMLINSON, JOSEPH	1803	PLAINTIFF	1554
TOMLINSON, JOSEPH	1805	PLAINTIFF	1554
TOMLINSON, JOSEPH	1807	PLAINTIFF	1554
TOMLINSON, JOSEPH	1807	PLAINTIFF	1554
TOMLINSON, JOSEPH	1807	MISC	1680
TOMLINSON, JOSEPH	1808	DEFENDANT	1554
TOMLINSON, JOSEPH	1808	PLAINTIFF	1554
TOMLINSON, JOSEPH	1808	MISC	1680
TOMLINSON, JOSEPH	1809	PLAINTIFF	1554
TOMLINSON, JOSEPH	1809	PLAINTIFF	1555
TOMLINSON, JOSEPH	1809	PLAINTIFF	1555
TOMLINSON, JOSEPH	1810	DEFENDANT	1667
TOMLINSON, JOSEPH	1810	APPENDIX	1873
TOMLINSON, JOSEPH	1812	PLAINTIFF	1555
TOMLINSON, JOSEPH	1814	PLAINTIFF	1555
TOMLINSON, JOSEPH	1816	PLAINTIFF	1555
TOMLINSON, JOSEPH	1825	MISC	1680
TOMLINSON, JOSEPH JR	1784	DEFENDANT	1610
TOMLINSON, JOSEPH JR	1813	PLAINTIFF	1555
TOMLINSON, MARGARET	1828	PLAINTIFF	1555
TOMLINSON, MARGARET	1829	PLAINTIFF	1555
TOMLINSON, MARGARET	1831	PLAINTIFF	1555
TOMLINSON, MARGARET	1840	PLAINTIFF	1555
TOMLINSON, MARY	1871	MDSVILLE	1810
TOMLINSON, NATHANIEL	1816	PLAINTIFF	1555
TOMLINSON, NATHANIEL	1818	PLAINTIFF	1555
TOMLINSON, NATHANIEL	1823	PLAINTIFF	1555
TOMLINSON, NATHANIEL	1827	MISC	1680
TOMLINSON, NATHANIEL	1828	PLAINTIFF	1555
TOMLINSON, NATHANIEL	1829	PLAINTIFF	1555
TOMLINSON, NATHANIEL	1829	PLAINTIFF	1555
TOMLINSON, NATHANIEL	1829	PLAINTIFF	1555
TOMLINSON, NATHANIEL	1829	MISC	1680
TOMLINSON, ROBERT	1799	PLAINTIFF	1554
TOMLINSON, ROBERT	1810	MISC	1680
TOMLINSON, SAMUEL	1815	MISC	1680
TOMLINSON, SAMUEL	1831	PLAINTIFF	1555
TOMLINSON, SAMUEL	1833	PLAINTIFF	1555
TOMLINSON, SAMUEL	1833	PLAINTIFF	1555
TOMLINSON, SAMUEL	1834	PLAINTIFF	1555
TOMLINSONS RUN - NORTH BRANCH OF	1871	HAN MAP	1728
TOMLINSONS RUN - NORTH FORK OF	1871	HAN MAP	1731
TOMLISON, A B	1871	MARH'L MAP	1748
TOMLISON, A B / INITIALS A.B.T.	1871	MARH'L MAP	1748
TOMPKINS, JAMES L	1860	MISC	1681
TOMPKINS, JOHN H	1838	PLAINTIFF	1563
TOMPKINS, LEWIS L	1861	MISC	1681
TOMPSON, THOMAS	1812	PLAINTIFF	1563
TOMS RUN	1871	MARH'L MAP	1749
TOMS RUN	1871	MARH'L MAP	1749
TOM'S RUN	1871	MARH'L MAP	1748
TONG & SEEVERS	1837	PLAINTIFF	1622
TONG & SEEVERS	1838	PLAINTIFF	1622
TONGE & SEEVERS	1838	PLAINTIFF	1622
TONGE & SEEVERS	1843	PLAINTIFF	1623
TONGE, SAMUEL D	1837	PLAINTIFF	1563
TONGE, SAMUEL D	1838	PLAINTIFF	1563
TONGE, SAMUEL D	1838	PLAINTIFF	1563
TONGE, SAMUEL D	1838	PLAINTIFF	1563
TONGE, SAMUEL D	1838	PLAINTIFF	1563
TONGE, SAMUEL D	1838	PLAINTIFF	1563
TONGE, SAMUEL D	1838	PLAINTIFF	1563
TONGE, SAMUEL D	1841	PLAINTIFF	1563
TONIHILL, ADAMSON	1792	PLAINTIFF	1563
TONINI, JOSEPH	1873	PLAINTIFF	1564

'PERSONAL TIME LINE' INDEX TO VOLUME 7 OF THE *OHIO COUNTY INDEX*

ENTRY	YEAR	SUBJECT	PAGE
TONINI, JOSEPH	1878	PLAINTIFF	1564
TONINI, JOSEPH	1879	MISC	1681
TONINI, MARY	1879	MISC	1681
TONNER, THOMAS	1814	PLAINTIFF	1563
TONNER, THOMAS	1816	PLAINTIFF	1563
TONNER, THOMAS	1816	PLAINTIFF	1563
TONNER, THOMAS	1817	DEFENDANT	1659
TONNER, THOMAS	1820	PLAINTIFF	1563
TONNER, THOMAS	1821	PLAINTIFF	1563
TONNER, THOMAS	1821	PLAINTIFF	1563
TONNER, THOMAS	1821	PLAINTIFF	1563
TONNER, THOMAS	1821	DEFENDANT	1612
TONNER, THOMAS	1826	PLAINTIFF	1563
TONNER, THOMAS	1829	PLAINTIFF	1563
TONNER, THOMAS	1842	PLAINTIFF	1563
TONNER, WILLIAM	1841	MISC	1680
TONNER, WILLIAM	1877	PLAINTIFF	1564
TOOL HOUSE - BENWOOD	1871	BENWOOD	1799
TOOTHACRE, HANNAH L	1873	MISC	1681
TOPE SCHOOL NO. 4	1871	HAN MAP	1731
TOPE, J J	1871	HAN MAP	1731
TOPE, J J	1871	HAN MAP	1731
TOPP, C ERNEST	1877	MISC	1681
TOPP, CARLE EARNEST	1879	PLAINTIFF	1564
TOPP, CHRISTIANA J	1879	PLAINTIFF	1564
TOPPE, CHARLES	1877	PLAINTIFF	1564
TORING, ALONZO	1860	MISC	1690
TORRENCE & MCLEOD	1825	PLAINTIFF	1622
TORREYSON, WILLIAM D	1857	PLAINTIFF	1564
TOTTON, M C / STORE	1871	GLEN EASTON	1801
TOULLERTON, MATTHEW	1814	PLAINTIFF	1563
TOULMAN, CHARLES	1851	PLAINTIFF	1563
TOVRILL, JOSEPH	1799	PLAINTIFF	1563
TOWELL, JAMES F	1861	PLAINTIFF	1564
TOWERS, E W	1862	PLAINTIFF	1564
TOWERS, FLORENCE N	1873	MISC	1681
TOWERS, FLORENCE N	1873	MISC	1706
TOWERS, GEORGE	1825	PLAINTIFF	1563
TOWLES, WILLIAM P	1855	PLAINTIFF	1564
TOWN ROCK	1871	BRKE MAP	1734
TOWN, DAVID A	1834	PLAINTIFF	1563
TOWNSEND & FRASUN	1830	PLAINTIFF	1622
TOWNSEND, ABEL W	1840	PLAINTIFF	1563
TOWNSEND, AMOS	1857	MISC	1680
TOWNSEND, CLENCH & DICK	1854	PLAINTIFF	1623
TOWNSEND, JAMES	1841	DEFENDANT	1615
TOWNSEND, JAMES	1841	DEFENDANT	1619
TOWNSEND, JEREMIAH	1826	PLAINTIFF	1563
TOWNSEND, SOLOMON	1854	PLAINTIFF	1563
TOWNSEND, THOMAS	1838	DEFENDANT	1651
TOWNSEND, THOMAS	1839	PLAINTIFF	1563
TOWNSEND, THOMAS	1839	PLAINTIFF	1563
TOWNSEND, THOMAS	1840	PLAINTIFF	1563
TOWNSEND, THOMAS	1841	PLAINTIFF	1563
TOWNSEND, THOMAS	1841	DEFENDANT	1614
TOWNSEND, THOMAS	1842	DEFENDANT	1661
TOWNSEND, THOMAS	1851	MISC	1680
TOWNSHIPS BY COUNTY	1871	POPULATION	1816
TOWNSHIPS SHOWN ON MAPS	1871	MAP	1718
TOWSEY, JOSEPH	1828	PLAINTIFF	1563
TOWSON, JACOB T	1812	PLAINTIFF	1563
TOZZER, MARY ANN	1849	MISC	1680
TRACEY, ELIZABETH M	1874	PLAINTIFF	1565
TRACEY, JAMES	1874	PLAINTIFF	1565
TRACEY, JAMES	1875	PLAINTIFF	1565
TRACEY, M F	1875	PLAINTIFF	1565
TRACEY, STEPHEN P	1874	DEFENDANT	1565
TRACY, D	1871	MARH'L MAP	1753
TRACY, ERASTUS	1858	PLAINTIFF	1565
TRACY, JULIA	1857	MISC	1681
TRACY, M F	1877	PLAINTIFF	1565
TRACY, MARGARET	1857	MISC	1681
TRACY, PERRY	1855	DEFENDANT	1602
TRACY, W F	1876	PLAINTIFF	1565
TRAIDELPHIA - COOPER SHOP	1871	TRIAD.BORO.	1784
TRAIDELPHIA - MILEPOST - NATIONAL ROAD	1916	NAT'L ROAD	1862
TRAIDELPHIA - S.SH. / (?SHOE SHOP?)	1871	TRIAD.BORO.	1784
TRAIDELPHIA - TROLLEY TO WHEELING	1916	NAT'L ROAD	1864
TRAIDELPHIA - WAGON SHOP	1871	TRIAD.BORO.	1784
TRAIDELPHIA BOROUGH	1871	DISTANCES	1815
TRAIDELPHIA TOWNSHIP - BUSINESS NOTICES	1871	OH CO.BUS.	1779
TRAIL, DANIEL	1831	MISC	1681
TRAIL, EDWARD H	1852	PLAINTIFF	1565

ENTRY	YEAR	SUBJECT	PAGE
TRAIL, EDWARD H	1853	PLAINTIFF	1565
TRAINER, JOHN	1853	MISC	1681
TRAVERS, BRIDGET	1854	MISC	1681
TRAVERS, JAMES	1854	MISC	1681
TRAVIS RIDGE	1871	MARH'L MAP	1754
TRAVIS, J	1871	MARH'L MAP	1755
TRAVIS, J	1871	BENWOOD	1798
TRAVIS, JAMES	1844	MISC	1681
TRAVIS, T	1871	BENWOOD	1798
TRAVIS, WHITE, G	1871	MARH'L MAP	1759
TRAVIS, WILLIAM	1861	DEFENDANT	1673
TRAVIS, WILLIAM	1862	DEFENDANT	1673
TRAWARTHA, WILLIAM	1843	PLAINTIFF	1565
TREADWAY, WILLIAM N	1871	MARH'L MAP	1755
TREESDALE, CALVIN	1831	PLAINTIFF	1565
TREMBLE, MATHEW	1826	PLAINTIFF	1565
TRESTLER, JACOB	1829	PLAINTIFF	1565
TREVER, JOHN B	1835	PLAINTIFF	1565
TRIADELPHIA	1829	MISC	1681
TRIADELPHIA	1871	OH CO. MAP	1743
TRIADELPHIA - BAINBRIDGE ST	1871	TRIAD.BORO.	1784
TRIADELPHIA - BLACKSMITH SHOP	1871	TRIAD.BORO.	1784
TRIADELPHIA - CALHOUN ST	1871	TRIAD.BORO.	1784
TRIADELPHIA - CARPENTER SHOP	1871	TRIAD.BORO.	1784
TRIADELPHIA - CLAY ST	1871	TRIAD.BORO.	1784
TRIADELPHIA - DECATUR ST	1871	TRIAD.BORO.	1784
TRIADELPHIA - GRIST MILL	1871	TRIAD.BORO.	1784
TRIADELPHIA - LONG LANE RD	1871	TRIAD.BORO.	1784
TRIADELPHIA - MARKET HO. LOT / (?HOUSE?)	1871	TRIAD.BORO.	1784
TRIADELPHIA - MONROE ST	1871	TRIAD.BORO.	1784
TRIADELPHIA - MONROE ST	1871	TRIAD.BORO.	1784
TRIADELPHIA - NATIONAL ROAD	1871	TRIAD.BORO.	1784
TRIADELPHIA - NATIONAL ROAD	1916	NAT'L ROAD	1864
TRIADELPHIA - NATIONAL ROAD MAP	1916	NAT'L ROAD	1863
TRIADELPHIA - PHOTO WITH TROLLEY	1916	NAT'L ROAD	1864
TRIADELPHIA - POST OFFICE	1871	TRIAD.BORO.	1784
TRIADELPHIA - SCALES - NATL RD	1871	TRIAD.BORO.	1784
TRIADELPHIA - SHORT CREEK ST	1871	TRIAD.BORO.	1784
TRIADELPHIA - STORE ROOM	1871	TRIAD.BORO.	1784
TRIADELPHIA - STORE ROOM / LOT 33 ?	1871	TRIAD.BORO.	1785
TRIADELPHIA - TAVERNS IN	1916	NAT'L ROAD	1864
TRIADELPHIA - TOWN LAID OUT	1829	MISC	1681
TRIADELPHIA - TURNPIKE ST	1871	TRIAD.BORO.	1784
TRIADELPHIA - WASHINGTON ST	1871	TRIAD.BORO.	1784
TRIADELPHIA BOROUGH	1871	OH CO. MAP	1743
TRIADELPHIA BOROUGH - DETAIL MAP	1871	TRIAD.BORO.	1784
TRIADELPHIA HOUSE / HOTEL	1871	TRIAD.BORO.	1784
TRIADELPHIA P.O.	1871	OH CO. MAP	1743
TRIADELPHIA P.O. BOROUGH	1871	OH CO. MAP	1744
TRIADELPHIA TOWNSHIP - DETAIL MAP	1871	TRIAD.TWP.	1781
TRIADELPHIA TOWNSHIP - ELM GROVE STATION & P.O.	1871	ELM GROVE	1782
TRIADELPHIA TOWNSHIP - OHIO CO	1871	OH CO. MAP	1742
TRIADELPHIA TOWNSHIP - OHIO CO	1871	OH CO. MAP	1743
TRIADELPHIA TOWNSHIP - OHIO CO	1871	WHG CITY	1787
TRIADELPHIA TOWNSHIP - OHIO CO	1871	POPULATION	1816
TRIADELPHIA TOWNSHIP - OHIO CO.	1871	TRIAD.TWP.	1781
TRIADELPHIA TOWNSHIP - RONEY POINT STATION	1871	RONEY PT.	1783
TRIADELPHIA TOWNSHIP - TRIADELPHIA BOROUGH	1871	TRIAD.BORO.	1784
TRIBUTARY RAILROADS TO HEMPFIELD RR	1852	HEMPFIELD RR	1817
TRIMBLE BROS OLD GRIST MILL	1871	BKE/OH MAP	1738
TRIMBLE, - / BANE, WILLIAM & TRIMBLE / INITIALS B & T	1871	BRKE MAP	1736
TRIMBLE, - / BANE, WILLIAM & TRIMBLE - INITIALS B. & T.	1871	BKE/OH MAP	1738
TRIMBLE, - / BANE, WILLIAM / & TRIMBLE	1871	BKE/OH MAP	1738
TRIMBLE, EPHRAIM	1873	DEFENDANT	1567
TRIMBLE, HARRIET A	1871	MISC	1681
TRIMBLE, JOHN	1787	PLAINTIFF	1565
TRIMBLE, JOHN B	1871	MISC	1681
TRIMBLE, M / HEIRS (MILL) - MAP#16	1852	BRKE MAP	1839
TRIMBLE, M / HEIRS (MILL) - MAP#17	1852	BRKE MAP	1839
TRIMBLE, M / HEIRS -MILL - (GONE) - MAP#19	1852	BRKE MAP	1839
TRIMBLE, ROBERT	1871	BKE/OH MAP	1738
TRIMBLE, S / OC	1871	BKE/OH MAP	1738
TRIMBLE, SAMUEL	1859	PLAINTIFF	1565

CVI

'PERSONAL TIME LINE' INDEX TO VOLUME 7 OF THE *OHIO COUNTY INDEX*

ENTRY	YEAR	SUBJECT	PAGE
TRIMBLE, SAMUEL	1871	BUFF.TWP.BUS.	1772
TRIMBLE, WALTER	1851	PLAINTIFF	1565
TRIMBLE, WILLIAM	1843	PLAINTIFF	1565
TRIMMELL, MARIA	1838	MISC	1681
TRIMMELL, SARAH	1838	MISC	1681
TRIPLER, THOMAS	1858	PLAINTIFF	1565
TRIPLER, THOMAS C	1858	PLAINTIFF	1565
TRIPLETT, ISABEL	1856	PLAINTIFF	1565
TRISLER, GEORGE	1855	MISC	1681
TRISLER, JAMES	1840	DEFENDANT	1643
TRISLER, JAMES	1853	MISC	1681
TRISLER, MARTHA	1841	MISC	1681
TRISLER, PHEBE	1841	MISC	1681
TRISLER, SUSAN	1862	PLAINTIFF	1565
TRISSELL, JOHN	1839	PLAINTIFF	1565
TRISSLER, SUSAN	1860	PLAINTIFF	1565
TROLL, VALENTINE	1857	PLAINTIFF	1566
TROLLEY - ALONG NATIONAL ROAD IN PANHANDLE	1916	NAT'L ROAD	1863
TROLLEY - WHEELING TO TRIADELPHIA	1916	NAT'L ROAD	1864
TROOP, D / ?	1871	HAN MAP	1730
TROUP & MINOR	1871	RIV. RD N.OF N.C.	1763
TROUP & MINOR - FIRE BRICK WORKS / (?D.TROUP?)	1871	RIV. RD N.OF N.C.	1770
TROUP, D	1871	RIV. RD N.OF N.C.	1770
TROXWELL, FREDERICK	1815	PLAINTIFF	1566
TROY, ROSANNA	1808	PLAINTIFF	1566
TRUAX & HAMILTON	1832	PLAINTIFF	1622
TRUAX & HAMILTON	1833	PLAINTIFF	1620
TRUAX & HAMILTON	1833	PLAINTIFF	1622
TRUAX & HAMILTON	1833	PLAINTIFF	1650
TRUAX & HAMILTON	1834	PLAINTIFF	1622
TRUAX & HAMILTON	1836	PLAINTIFF	1622
TRUAX & HAMILTON	1838	PLAINTIFF	1622
TRUAX & HAMILTON	1841	PLAINTIFF	1623
TRUAX, - / MISS	1871	BRKE MAP	1734
TRUAX, HAMILTON	1835	PLAINTIFF	1566
TRUAX, JOHN F	1831	PLAINTIFF	1566
TRUAX, JOHN F	1832	PLAINTIFF	1566
TRUAX, JOHN F	1833	PLAINTIFF	1566
TRUAX, JOHN F	1833	PLAINTIFF	1566
TRUAX, JOHN F	1833	PLAINTIFF	1566
TRUAX, JOHN F	1833	PLAINTIFF	1566
TRUAX, JOHN F	1834	PLAINTIFF	1566
TRUAX, JOHN F	1835	PLAINTIFF	1566
TRUAX, JOHN F	1837	MISC	1682
TRUAX, JOHN F	1838	DEFENDANT	1619
TRUAX, JOHN F	1838	DEFENDANT	1619
TRUAX, MARIA	1843	DEFENDANT	1619
TRUAX, NICHOLAS	1876	PLAINTIFF	1566
TRUESCHELL, FERDINAND	1854	MISC	1682
TRUESDELL, CALVIN	1832	PLAINTIFF	1566
TRUESDELL, DAVID JR	1832	PLAINTIFF	1566
TRUESDELL, FRANCIS	1832	PLAINTIFF	1566
TRUITT BROTHERS & CO	1855	PLAINTIFF	1623
TRUITT, CHARLES B	1855	PLAINTIFF	1566
TRUITT, ROBERT W D	1855	PLAINTIFF	1566
TRULL, WILLIAM E	1873	PLAINTIFF	1566
TRULY, SIMON	1839	PLAINTIFF	1566
TRUMAN, - / MRS	1871	MDSVILLE	1809
TRUMP, A / ? LOT 110	1871	NEW CUMB'LD	1768
TRUMP, WILLIAM B / & CO	1838	PLAINTIFF	1622
TRUMP, WILLIAM B / & CO	1838	PLAINTIFF	1623
TRUSCHELL, JOHN P	1873	PLAINTIFF	1566
TRUSELL, W	1871	W.UNION	1812
TRUSSCHEL, FERDINAND	1848	MISC	1682
TRUSSEL, J	1871	OH CO. MAP	1743
TRUSSEL, J	1871	MARH'L MAP	1747
TRUSSEL, W / NE CORNER OF MAP	1871	OH CO. MAP	1743
TRUSSEL, W / E.SIDE OF MAP	1871	MARH'L MAP	1747
TRUSSELL, CHARLES	1831	PLAINTIFF	1566
TRUSSELL, T	1871	MARH'L MAP	1747
TRUSSLE WORK / BUSINESS ?	1871	OH CO. MAP	1740
TRUXEL, CATHARINE	1833	MISC	1682
TRUXEL, JACOB	1827	PLAINTIFF	1566
TRUXEL, JACOB	1833	MISC	1682
TRUXEL, JOHN	1827	PLAINTIFF	1566
TRUXELL, CATHERINE	1842	PLAINTIFF	1566
TRUXELL, JOHN C	1875	PLAINTIFF	1566
TRUXELL, JOHN C	1877	PLAINTIFF	1566
TRUXELL, MARY	1842	PLAINTIFF	1566
TRYON, E W / & CO	1854	PLAINTIFF	1623
TRYON, E W / & CO	1855	PLAINTIFF	1623
TRYON, EDMUND	1854	PLAINTIFF	1565

ENTRY	YEAR	SUBJECT	PAGE
TRYON, FRANCIS	1854	PLAINTIFF	1565
TUBBY, J T	1875	PLAINTIFF	1567
TUCKER - ORPHANS	1868	MISC	1682
TUCKER, CHARLES	1859	PLAINTIFF	1567
TUCKER, D A / & CO	1839	PLAINTIFF	1623
TUCKER, DOUGLASS A	1839	PLAINTIFF	1567
TUCKER, JACKSON	1839	PLAINTIFF	1567
TUCKER, JAMES	1799	PLAINTIFF	1567
TUCKER, JOHN	1860	MISC	1682
TUCKER, JOSHUA	1838	MISC	1682
TUCKER, MARY ANN	1868	MISC	1682
TUCKER, MICHAEL	1854	MISC	1682
TUCKER, WILLIAM	1801	PLAINTIFF	1567
TUMBELSON, JOSEPH JR	1793	MISC	1682
TUMBLETON, JOSEPH	1788	MISC	1682
TUMLINSON, JOSEPH	1778	PLAINTIFF	1567
TUN HILL RUN / ?	1871	HAN MAP	1727
TUNER, J	1871	MARH'L MAP	1749
TUNKILL RUN / ?	1871	HAN MAP	1727
TUNNEL - B&O RR EAST OF ROSBY'S ROCK	1871	MARH'L MAP	1752
TUNNEL - B&O RR SE. OF CAMERON P.O.	1871	MARH'L MAP	1757
TUNNEL - BETHANY PIKE	1871	BRKE MAP	1736
TUNNEL - E. OF G, WHARTON	1871	BRKE MAP	1736
TUNNEL - HEMPFIELD RR CO AT WHEELING	1871	WHG CITY	1789
TUNNEL - JAMES WAUGH	1871	BRKE MAP	1736
TUNNEL - NW. CORNER OF MAP	1871	HAN MAP	1731
TUPPER, EDWARD W	1793	PLAINTIFF	1567
TURK - CHILDREN	1807	MISC	1682
TURK, MARGARET	1807	MISC	1682
TURKEY RUN	1871	MARH'L MAP	1747
TURKEY RUN	1871	MARH'L MAP	1747
TURNBULL, JAMES	1838	PLAINTIFF	1567
TURNBULL, JAMES	1841	PLAINTIFF	1567
TURNER - SEE ALSO TUNER	1871	MARH'L MAP	1749
TURNER & WHEELRIGHT	1844	PLAINTIFF	1623
TURNER, ALEXANDER	1851	MISC	1682
TURNER, ALEXANDER	1862	PLAINTIFF	1567
TURNER, ALFRED	1875	MISC	1682
TURNER, GEORGE	1810	MISC	1682
TURNER, GEORGE	1811	PLAINTIFF	1567
TURNER, GEORGE	1811	PLAINTIFF	1567
TURNER, GEORGE	1811	PLAINTIFF	1567
TURNER, GEORGE	1814	MISC	1682
TURNER, GEORGE	1841	PLAINTIFF	1567
TURNER, J	1871	MARH'L MAP	1757
TURNER, JOHN	1822	MISC	1682
TURNER, JOHN	1824	MISC	1682
TURNER, JOHN	1829	PLAINTIFF	1567
TURNER, JOHN	1833	DEFENDANT	1620
TURNER, JOHN	1833	DEFENDANT	1639
TURNER, JOHN	1880	MISC	1682
TURNER, JOSEPH	1834	PLAINTIFF	1567
TURNER, JOSEPH	1835	DEFENDANT	1618
TURNER, JOSEPH	1845	PLAINTIFF	1567
TURNER, LYDIA A	1875	MISC	1682
TURNER, MARY	1811	PLAINTIFF	1567
TURNER, MARY	1814	MISC	1682
TURNER, MARY	1852	MISC	1682
TURNER, SAMUEL R	1860	PLAINTIFF	1567
TURNER, W	1871	MARH'L MAP	1746
TURNER, W	1871	MARH'L MAP	1747
TURNER, WILLIAM	1859	PLAINTIFF	1567
TURNER, WILLIAM	1874	MISC	1682
TURNER, WILLIAM	1875	MISC	1682
TURNER, WILLIAM A	1857	PLAINTIFF	1567
TURNERS ASSOCIATION	1857	PLAINTIFF	1623
TURNIPSEED, JOHN L	1873	PLAINTIFF	1567
TURNPIKE - 888 FROM NEAR CO. LINE TO MIDDLE WHEEKING CREEK ROAD BY TURNPIKE	1871	OH CO. MAP	1743
TURNPIKE - FAIRMONT TURNPIKE	1871	RITCHIE TWP	1793
TURNPIKE CO	1871	BRKE MAP	1736
TURNPIKE CO / NATIONAL ROAD - RONEY POINT	1871	OH CO. MAP	1743
TURNPIKE CO / NATIONAL ROAD - RONEY POINT STATION	1871	OH CO. MAP	1744
TURNPIKE ST - NATIONAL ROAD	1871	TRIAD.BORO.	1784
TURNPIKE TO WEST UNION / FROM RONEY POINT	1871	RONEY PT.	1783
TURPIN, J	1871	OH CO. MAP	1741
TURPIN, JOHN	1855	PLAINTIFF	1567
TURTEN, JAMES	1858	PLAINTIFF	1567
TURTON, JAMES	1855	PLAINTIFF	1567

CVII

'PERSONAL TIME LINE' INDEX TO VOLUME 7 OF THE OHIO COUNTY INDEX

ENTRY	YEAR	SUBJECT	PAGE	ENTRY	YEAR	SUBJECT	PAGE
TURTON, JAMES	1857	PLAINTIFF	1567	UNION TOWNSHIP - OHIO CO	1871	WHG CITY	1790
TURTON, THOMAS	1860	PLAINTIFF	1567	UNION TOWNSHIP - WHEELING	1871	OH CO. MAP	1742
TURVEY, H L	1879	DEFENDANT	1606	UNIONTOWN, PA	1916	NAT'L ROAD	1863
TUSH, GEORGE	1805	MISC	1682	UNITED STATES	1802	PLAINTIFF	1624
TUSH, GEORGE	1811	MISC	1682	UNITED STATES	1815	PLAINTIFF	1624
TUSTLER, JACOB	1827	MISC	1682	UNITED STATES	1816	PLAINTIFF	1624
TUTTLE, - / MILLER, KELLER & TUTTLE	1871	BRKE MAP	1734	UNITED STATES	1817	PLAINTIFF	1624
				UNITED STATES	1818	PLAINTIFF	1624
TUTTLE, - / MILLER, KELLER & TUTTLE PLANING MILL	1871	EDGINGTON STA.	1774	UNITED STATES	1819	PLAINTIFF	1624
				UNITED STATES	1820	PLAINTIFF	1624
TUTTLE, JACOB	1828	MISC	1682	UNITED STATES	1821	PLAINTIFF	1624
TUTTLE, JESSE	1874	PLAINTIFF	1567	UNITED STATES	1822	PLAINTIFF	1624
TUTTLE, JOSEPH	1828	MISC	1682	UNITED STATES	1838	PLAINTIFF	1625
TWEED & WHITE - MILL	1871	WELLSBURG	1777	UNITED STATES	1839	PLAINTIFF	1625
TWEED, ISAAC	1830	MISC	1682	UNITED STATES HOTEL	1839	MISC	1683
TWEED, J	1871	WELLSBURG	1777	UNITED STATES HOTEL	1842	MISC	1683
TWEEDIE, DAVID	1838	PLAINTIFF	1568	UNIV. CHURCH / (?UNIVERSALIST?)	1871	MARH'L MAP	1752
TWEEHE, JAMES	1852	PLAINTIFF	1568	UNIV. CHURCH & SCHOOL / (?UNIVERSALIST?)	1871	MARH'L MAP	1752
TWIN SISTER ISLAND - OHIO RIVER	1871	OH CO. MAP	1741				
TWINAM, LEONARD	1850	PLAINTIFF	1568	UNKNOWN NAME - SE OF BABBS ISLAND	1871	HAN MAP	1728
TWINAM, LEONARD / & CO	1850	PLAINTIFF	1623				
TWINAM, W	1871	MARH'L MAP	1752	UNMUSSIG, JOSEPH	1859	PLAINTIFF	1569
TWINAM, W	1871	MARH'L MAP	1752	UNMUSSIG, JOSEPH	1860	PLAINTIFF	1569
TWINAM, W	1871	MARH'L MAP	1756	UNTERZUBER, CHARLES	1869	MISC	1683
TWINAM, W	1871	MARH'L MAP	1756	UPDEGRAFF & FARGUHAR	1807	PLAINTIFF	1624
TWINAM, W	1871	MARH'L MAP	1756	UPDEGRAFF, CHARLES	1841	PLAINTIFF	1643
TWINHAM, W	1871	MARH'L MAP	1753	UPDEGRAFF, ISRAEL	1809	PLAINTIFF	1642
TWINHAM, W	1871	MARH'L MAP	1756	UPDEGRAFF, ISRAEL	1810	PLAINTIFF	1642
TWO MILE HO / HOUSE - HOTEL	1871	TRIAD.TWP.	1781	UPDEGRAFF, ISRAEL	1816	DEFENDANT	1563
TWO MILE HOUSE	1871	OH CO. MAP	1742	UPDEGRAFF, ISRAEL	1816	PLAINTIFF	1642
TWO MILE POST - AT WHEELING PARK - NATIONAL ROAD	1916	NAT'L ROAD	1865	UPDEGRAFF, ISRAEL	1816	DEFENDANT	1645
				UPDEGRAFF, ISRAEL	1817	PLAINTIFF	1642
TWO OAKS / THE - FRANKLIN TWP	1871	MARH'L MAP	1758	UPDEGRAFF, ISRAEL	1818	DEFENDANT	1620
TYDINGS & BAILEY	1848	PLAINTIFF	1623	UPDEGRAFF, ISRAEL	1818	DEFENDANT	1638
TYDINGS & BAILEY	1849	PLAINTIFF	1623	UPDEGRAFF, ISRAEL	1818	PLAINTIFF	1642
TYDINGS, LEWIS	1849	PLAINTIFF	1568	UPDEGRAFF, ISRAEL	1819	PLAINTIFF	1642
TYDINGS, LOUIS L	1848	PLAINTIFF	1568	UPDEGRAFF, ISRAEL	1820	PLAINTIFF	1642
TYGART, MICHAEL	1784	PLAINTIFF	1568	UPDEGRAFF, ISRAEL	1821	PLAINTIFF	1642
TYLER, JAMES	1826	PLAINTIFF	1568	UPDEGRAFF, ISRAEL	1822	PLAINTIFF	1642
TYLER, W S	1878	PLAINTIFF	1568	UPDEGRAFF, ISRAEL	1822	PLAINTIFF	1642
TYSON, JOSEPH W	1841	PLAINTIFF	1568	UPDEGRAFF, ISRAEL	1825	PLAINTIFF	1642
TYSON, WILLIAM	1837	PLAINTIFF	1568	UPDEGRAFF, ISRAEL	1825	DEFENDANT	1649
TYSON, WILLIAM B / & CO	1829	PLAINTIFF	1622	UPDEGRAFF, ISRAEL	1825	MISC	1683
TYSON, WILLIAM B	1830	MISC	1682	UPDEGRAFF, ISRAEL	1826	MISC	1683
TYSON, WILLIAM B	1834	PLAINTIFF	1568	UPDEGRAFF, ISRAEL	1828	PLAINTIFF	1642
TYSON, WILLIAM B / & CO	1834	PLAINTIFF	1622	UPDEGRAFF, ISRAEL	1829	PLAINTIFF	1642
TYSON, WILLIAM B / & CO	1835	PLAINTIFF	1622	UPDEGRAFF, ISRAEL	1837	MISC	1683
TYSON, WILLIAM B	1837	PLAINTIFF	1568	UPDEGRAFF, ISRAEL	1840	PLAINTIFF	1643
TYSON, WILLIAM B	1838	PLAINTIFF	1568	UPDEGRAFF, ISRAEL	1841	PLAINTIFF	1643
TYSON, WILLIAM B	1838	PLAINTIFF	1568	UPDEGRAFF, ISRAEL	1842	PLAINTIFF	1643
TYSON, WILLIAM B	1840	PLAINTIFF	1568	UPDEGRAFF, ISRAEL	1843	PLAINTIFF	1643
TYWELL, ROBERT S	1856	PLAINTIFF	1568	UPDEGRAFF, ISRAEL	1844	PLAINTIFF	1643
T-Z INDEX PAGE - FIRMS - OBSOLETE	1807	INDEX	1850	UPDEGRAFF, ISRAEL	1846	PLAINTIFF	1643
T-Z INDEX PAGE - OBSOLETE	1807	INDEX	1549	UPDEGRAFF, ISRAEL	1860	MISC	1683
UBRECHT, CHARLES	1864	MISC	1683	UPDEGRAFF, ISRAEL	1874	PLAINTIFF	1643
UBRECHT, JOHN	1864	MISC	1683	UPDEGRAFF, ISRAEL	1876	MISC	1683
UCHTOLF, HENRY	1838	PLAINTIFF	1569	UPDEGRAFF, ISRAEL	1876	MISC	1683
UCHTOLF, HENRY	1838	PLAINTIFF	1569	UPDEGRAFF, ISRAIL	1817	PLAINTIFF	1642
UCHTOLF, HENRY	1839	PLAINTIFF	1569	UPDEGRAFF, JAMES H	1839	PLAINTIFF	1642
UCHTORF & BORGEDIN	1828	PLAINTIFF	1625	UPDEGRAFF, JONAH	1809	DEFENDANT	1604
UGAR GROVE - FRANKLIN TWP / (?SUGAR GROVE?)	1871	MARH'L MAP	1759	UPDEGRAFF, JOSEPH	1816	PLAINTIFF	1642
				UPDEGRAFF, JOSEPH	1839	PLAINTIFF	1643
UHL, CHARLES P	1861	PLAINTIFF	1569	UPDEGRAFF, JOSIAH	1809	DEFENDANT	1610
UHLRICH, C F	1871	BETHANY	1773	UPDEGRAFF, JOSIAH	1809	PLAINTIFF	1638
ULRICH, ALOES	1868	MISC	1683	UPDEGRAFF, JOSIAH	1809	PLAINTIFF	1642
UMSTADT, RICHARD S	1856	PLAINTIFF	1569	UPDEGRAFF, JOSIAH	1810	PLAINTIFF	1642
UNDERWOOD, JOSEPH	1809	PLAINTIFF	1569	UPDEGRAFF, JOSIAH	1810	PLAINTIFF	1642
UNDERWOOD, SAMUEL	1803	PLAINTIFF	1569	UPDEGRAFF, JOSIAH	1811	DEFENDANT	1604
UNDERWOOD, SAMUEL	1805	PLAINTIFF	1569	UPDEGRAFF, JOSIAH	1811	PLAINTIFF	1642
UNDERWOOD, SAMUEL	1807	PLAINTIFF	1569	UPDEGRAFF, JOSIAH	1812	PLAINTIFF	1642
UNDERWOOD, SAMUEL	1814	PLAINTIFF	1569	UPDEGRAFF, JOSIAH	1813	PLAINTIFF	1642
UNDERWOOD, THOMAS	1814	PLAINTIFF	1569	UPDEGRAFF, JOSIAH	1814	DEFENDANT	1604
UNION BASIN	1871	MARH'L MAP	1754	UPDEGRAFF, JOSIAH	1815	MISC	1683
UNION CHAPLE / (?CHAPEL?) - PROSPECT ST.	1871	WELLSBURG	1777	UPDEGRAFF, JOSIAH	1816	PLAINTIFF	1642
				UPDEGRAFF, JOSIAH	1818	PLAINTIFF	1642
UNION CHURCH & CEMETERY - S. OF LIMESTONE	1871	MARH'L MAP	1749	UPDEGRAFF, JOSIAH	1818	MISC	1683
				UPDEGRAFF, JOSIAH F	1875	PLAINTIFF	1643
UNION FARM	1871	MARH'L MAP	1755	UPDEGRAFF, JOSIAH F	1876	PLAINTIFF	1643
UNION HOME	1871	OH CO. MAP	1743	UPDEGRAFF, JOSIAH F	1876	MISC	1683
UNION HOUSE - CAMERON	1871	CAMERON	1803	UPDEGRAFF, MARY A	1876	MISC	1683
UNION ST. - HAMILTON	1871	HAN MAP	1729	UPDGRAFF, JOSISH	1813	PLAINTIFF	1642
UNION TOWNSHIP - MARSHALL CO	1871	MARH'L MAP	1745	UPDIGRAFF, ISRAEL	1822	DEFENDANT	1632
UNION TOWNSHIP - MARSHALL CO	1871	POPULATION	1816	UPP, FRANCES	1809	PLAINTIFF	1569
UNION TOWNSHIP - MARSHALL CO - SHERRARD P.O. - DETAIL MAP	1871	SHERRARD	1811	UPP, FRANCIS	1811	PLAINTIFF	1569
				UPPER BOWMAN RUN	1871	MARH'L MAP	1756
UNION TOWNSHIP - OHIO CO	1871	WHG CITY	1788	UPPER NORTH FORK GRAVE CREEK	1871	MARH'L MAP	1753

'PERSONAL TIME LINE' INDEX TO VOLUME 7 OF THE OHIO COUNTY INDEX

ENTRY	YEAR	SUBJECT	PAGE
UPPER NORTH FORK OF GRAVE CREEK / CUT OFF TOP OF MAP	1871	MARH'L MAP	1757
URIE, THOMAS SR	1780	PLAINTIFF	1569
URLAMB, GEORGE	1874	MISC	1683
USELTON, GEORGE	1880	PLAINTIFF	1569
USELTON, SAMUEL	1856	PLAINTIFF	1569
USTICK, JOHN	1799	DEFENDANT	1655
USTIE, JOHN	1799	DEFENDANT	1655
UTTER, J	1871	MARH'L MAP	1759
VAAS, FRED	1877	PLAINTIFF	1570
VAAS, WILLIAM	1872	MISC	1683
VACTOR, BOSTON	1835	PLAINTIFF	1570
VAGHLHART, L / ?	1871	WELLSBURG	1778
VAIL, I C	1856	PLAINTIFF	1570
VAIL, JOHN C	1846	PLAINTIFF	1570
VALENTINE, C	1826	PLAINTIFF	1570
VALENTINE, MARY E	1866	MISC	1683
VALENTINE, MARY E	1872	MISC	1683
VALENTINE, MARY E	1873	MISC	1683
VALENTINE, SUSAN	1868	MISC	1683
VALILEY, DANIEL	1816	PLAINTIFF	1570
VALLENTINE, BENJAMIN	1869	MISC	1683
VALLEY FARM / J.YOHO	1871	MARH'L MAP	1755
VALLEY FARM - N. OF MOUNDSVILLE	1871	MARH'L MAP	1748
VALLEY GROVE - MAP	1916	NAT'L ROAD	1863
VALLEY GROVE - NATIONAL ROAD DESCRIPTION	1916	NAT'L ROAD	1863
VALLEY GROVE - OHIO CO	1871	DISTANCES	1815
VALLEY GROVE - STOCKTON COACH LINE STATION	1916	NAT'L ROAD	1863
VALLEY GROVE - TAVERN	1916	NAT'L ROAD	1863
VALLEY GROVE P.O.	1871	OH CO. MAP	1740
VALLEY GROVE P.O.	1871	OH CO. MAP	1740
VALLEY GROVE POST OFFICE / INITIALS P.O.	1871	OH CO. MAP	1740
VALLEY GROVE STORE	1871	OH CO. MAP	1740
VALLEY HOME	1871	OH CO. MAP	1743
VALLEY HOME	1871	OH CO. MAP	1744
VALLEY HOME - FRANKLIN TWP	1871	MARH'L MAP	1758
VALLEY HOMESTEAD	1871	HAN MAP	1732
VALLEY RUN	1871	MARH'L MAP	1760
VALLEY VIEW / CLAY TWP	1871	MARH'L MAP	1751
VALLEYVIEW / N. PART OF MAP NEAR OHIO RIVER	1871	HAN MAP	1727
VALLEYVIEW / N. PART OF MAP NEAR OHIO RIVER	1871	HAN MAP	1728
VALLEYVIEW E.D.	1871	NEW MANCH.	1769
VAMEY, GEORGE M	1857	PLAINTIFF	1570
VAN BONHERST, CHARLES	1833	PLAINTIFF	1573
VAN BUSKIRK, -	1786	PLAINTIFF	1571
VAN BUSKIRK, LAWRANCE	1787	PLAINTIFF	1571
VAN BUSKIRK, LAWRANCE	1788	PLAINTIFF	1571
VAN BUSKIRK, LAWRANCE	1789	PLAINTIFF	1571
VAN BUSKIRK, LAWRANCE	1790	PLAINTIFF	1571
VAN BUSKIRK, LAWRANCE	1790	PLAINTIFF	1571
VAN BUSKIRK, LAWRANCE	1791	PLAINTIFF	1571
VAN BUSKIRK, LAWRANCE	1791	PLAINTIFF	1571
VAN BUSKIRK, LAWRANCE	1792	PLAINTIFF	1571
VAN BUSKIRK, LAWRENCE	1785	PLAINTIFF	1571
VAN BUSKIRK, LAWRENCE	1788	PLAINTIFF	1571
VAN BUSKIRK, SAMUEL	1792	MISC	1684
VAN BUSKIRK, TARRANCE JR	1791	MISC	1684
VAN BUSKIRK, THOMAS	1787	PLAINTIFF	1571
VAN DUSEN, SMITH & CO	1862	PLAINTIFF	1625
VAN METRE, JOSEPH	1780	MISC	1684
VAN SCYOC - SEE ALSO SCYOC & VANSEYOC	1810	PLAINTIFF	1572
VAN SCYOC, ABEL	1808	PLAINTIFF	1572
VAN SCYOC, ABEL	1809	PLAINTIFF	1572
VAN SCYOC, ABEL	1814	MISC	1684
VAN SCYOC, ABLE	1810	PLAINTIFF	1572
VAN SIHN, B	1850	PLAINTIFF	1573
VAN SWEARINGEN, -	1793	DEFENDANT	1589
VANAMAN, GEORGE	1788	PLAINTIFF	1572
VANATA, SAMUEL	1818	PLAINTIFF	1572
VANATA, THOMAS	1846	PLAINTIFF	1573
VANCE & JACOB	1825	PLAINTIFF	1625
VANCE, - / MISS	1871	TRIAD.BORO.	1784
VANCE, - / OK SIDE (?OAKSIDE?)	1871	TRIAD.BORO.	1784
VANCE, A	1871	TRIAD.BORO.	1784
VANCE, A	1871	TRIAD.BORO.	1784
VANCE, A	1871	TRIAD.BORO.	1784
VANCE, A	1871	TRIAD.BORO.	1784
VANCE, A / INITIALS A.V.	1871	TRIAD.BORO.	1784
VANCE, A / INITIALS A.V.	1871	TRIAD.BORO.	1784
VANCE, ANDREW	1874	DEFENDANT	1560

ENTRY	YEAR	SUBJECT	PAGE
VANCE, ANDREW	1876	PLAINTIFF	1573
VANCE, ANDREW	1878	PLAINTIFF	1573
VANCE, DAVID	1803	PLAINTIFF	1572
VANCE, DEWEY / & CO. - NAIL WORKS	1871	WHG CITY	1790
VANCE, DEWEY / & CO. - SPIKE WORKS	1871	WHG CITY	1790
VANCE, HUGHES & CO	1878	PLAINTIFF	1625
VANCE, J	1871	OH CO. MAP	1743
VANCE, J	1871	OH CO. MAP	1744
VANCE, JAMES	1819	PLAINTIFF	1572
VANCE, JAMES	1840	PLAINTIFF	1573
VANCE, JAMES	1851	PLAINTIFF	1573
VANCE, JAMES	1855	MISC	1684
VANCE, JAMES	1857	PLAINTIFF	1573
VANCE, JAMES	1862	PLAINTIFF	1573
VANCE, JAMES	1873	MISC	1684
VANCE, JAMES N	1853	PLAINTIFF	1573
VANCE, JAMES N	1857	PLAINTIFF	1573
VANCE, JAMES N	1861	PLAINTIFF	1573
VANCE, JAMES N	1862	PLAINTIFF	1573
VANCE, JOHN	1821	PLAINTIFF	1572
VANCE, JOHN	1821	MISC	1684
VANCE, JOHN	1832	DEFENDANT	1622
VANCE, JOHN	1833	DEFENDANT	1650
VANCE, JOHN	1833	DEFENDANT	1669
VANCE, JOHN	1834	DEFENDANT	1650
VANCE, JOHN	1834	DEFENDANT	1669
VANCE, JOHN	1856	MISC	1684
VANCE, JOSEPH	1839	DEFENDANT	1614
VANCE, JOSEPH	1839	DEFENDANT	1619
VANCE, WILLIAM	1821	PLAINTIFF	1570
VANCE, WILLIAM	1821	PLAINTIFF	1570
VANCE, WILLIAM	1821	PLAINTIFF	1570
VANCE, WILLIAM	1823	PLAINTIFF	1570
VANCE, WILLIAM	1872	MISC	1684
VANCURLEN, SAMUEL W	1860	PLAINTIFF	1573
VANCYOC, WILLIAM	1833	PLAINTIFF	1573
VANDALIA, IL	1916	NAT'L ROAD	1866
VANDERPOOL, FREDERICK	1855	PLAINTIFF	1573
VANDERPOOL, S	1855	PLAINTIFF	1573
VANDERPOOL, SMITH & CO	1855	PLAINTIFF	1625
VANDINE, WILLIAM	1792	MISC	1684
VANDIVENDER, C	1827	PLAINTIFF	1573
VANDMAN, HENRY	1837	MISC	1684
VANDWORT, JOHN	1807	MISC	1684
VANDYKE, AUGUSTUS C	1860	PLAINTIFF	1573
VANE, JOSEPH C	1836	PLAINTIFF	1573
VANLEAR, MATTHEW	1792	PLAINTIFF	1572
VANLEAR, MATTHEW	1802	PLAINTIFF	1572
VANMEATER, ISAAC	1798	PLAINTIFF	1572
VANMEATRE, MORGAN	1795	PLAINTIFF	1572
VANMETER, -	1830	PLAINTIFF	1620
VANMETER, ABRAHAM	1820	PLAINTIFF	1572
VANMETER, HENRY	1789	PLAINTIFF	1572
VANMETER, JOHN	1814	PLAINTIFF	1572
VANMETER, JOHN	1825	MISC	1684
VANMETER, JOSEPH	1787	MISC	1684
VANMETER, JOSEPH	1814	PLAINTIFF	1572
VANMETER, JOSEPH	1815	PLAINTIFF	1572
VANMETER, JOSEPH	1815	PLAINTIFF	1572
VANMETER, JOSEPH	1816	PLAINTIFF	1572
VANMETER, JOSEPH	1817	PLAINTIFF	1572
VANMETER, JOSEPH	1822	MISC	1684
VANMETER, ROBERT	1822	MISC	1684
VANMETER, VINCENT	1862	PLAINTIFF	1573
VANMETER, VINCENT H	1856	PLAINTIFF	1573
VANMETER, WILLIAM	1825	PLAINTIFF	1573
VANMETERS RUN	1852	BRKE MAP	1849
VANMETRE, ABRAHAM	1801	MISC	1684
VANMETRE, ABRAM	1782	MISC	1684
VANMETRE, ISAAC	1803	PLAINTIFF	1572
VANMETRE, ISAAC	1830	PLAINTIFF	1573
VANMETRE, JOHN	1784	MISC	1684
VANMETRE, JOHN	1784	MISC	1684
VANMETRE, JOHN	1794	PLAINTIFF	1572
VANMETRE, JOSEPH	1781	MISC	1684
VANMETRE, MORGAN	1784	MISC	1684
VANMETRE, MORGAN	1793	PLAINTIFF	1572
VANMETRE, MORGAN	1793	PLAINTIFF	1572
VANMETRE, MORGAN	1796	MISC	1684
VANMETRE, MORGAN	1796	MISC	1684
VANMETRE, V	1871	W.LIBERTY	1780
VANMETRE, V H	1871	BKE/OH MAP	1739
VANMETRE, VINCENT H	1879	PLAINTIFF	1573
VANOSDAL, JOHN	1795	PLAINTIFF	1572
VANOSDLE, JOHN	1791	PLAINTIFF	1571

CIX

'PERSONAL TIME LINE' INDEX TO VOLUME 7 OF THE *OHIO COUNTY INDEX*

ENTRY	YEAR	SUBJECT	PAGE	ENTRY	YEAR	SUBJECT	PAGE
VANOSDLE, JOHN	1791	PLAINTIFF	1572	VENNUM, ABIGAIL	1839	PLAINTIFF	1574
VANSCOYE, LORENZO	1831	PLAINTIFF	1573	VENNUM, DAVID	1850	MISC	1685
VANSCYOC, ABEL	1828	PLAINTIFF	1573	VENNUM, GEORGE	1814	MISC	1685
VANSCYOC, LORENZO	1832	PLAINTIFF	1573	VENNUM, GEORGE	1816	MISC	1685
VANSE, WILLIAM	1822	PLAINTIFF	1572	VENNUM, GEORGE	1816	MISC	1707
VANSE, WILLIAM	1822	PLAINTIFF	1572	VENNUM, GEORGE	1817	MISC	1685
VANSE, WILLIAM	1822	PLAINTIFF	1572	VENNUM, GEORGE	1820	DEFENDANT	1635
VANSE, WILLIAM	1823	PLAINTIFF	1570	VENNUM, GEORGE	1821	PLAINTIFF	1574
VANSE, WILLIAM	1823	PLAINTIFF	1570	VENNUM, GEORGE	1823	MISC	1685
VANSE, WILLIAM	1823	PLAINTIFF	1572	VENNUM, GEORGE	1825	PLAINTIFF	1574
VANSE, WILLIAM	1823	PLAINTIFF	1572	VENNUM, GEORGE	1829	PLAINTIFF	1574
VANSE, WILLIAM	1823	PLAINTIFF	1572	VENNUM, GEORGE	1829	DEFENDANT	1650
VANSE, WILLIAM	1824	PLAINTIFF	1570	VENNUM, GEORGE	1830	PLAINTIFF	1574
VANSES RUN	1852	BRKE MAP	1842	VENNUM, GEORGE	1837	DEFENDANT	1651
VANSEYOC, -	1812	PLAINTIFF	1572	VENNUM, GEORGE	1838	MISC	1685
VANSEYOC, ABEL	1816	MISC	1684	VENNUM, GEORGE	1839	MISC	1685
VANSEYOO, ABLE	1802	PLAINTIFF	1572	VENNUM, MARTHA	1876	MISC	1685
VANSICKLE, - / MRS	1871	WELLSBURG	1777	VENSUS, S / EST	1871	MARH'L MAP	1751
VANSIOCK, ABLE	1802	DEFENDANT	1647	VENUS FARM	1871	MARH'L MAP	1756
VANSWEARINGEN - BASTARD CHILD OF	1784	MISC	1710	VENUS, S / EST	1871	MARH'L MAP	1748
				VENUS, S / EST.	1871	MARH'L MAP	1751
VANSYOC - SEE ALSO SYOC / ?	1871	MARH'L MAP	1755	VENUS, S / RES	1871	MDSVILLE	1810
VANSYOC, A	1871	MARH'L MAP	1755	VENUS, SAMUEL	1835	PLAINTIFF	1574
VANSYOC, ABLE	1801	DEFENDANT	1647	VERMILION, -	1854	PLAINTIFF	1574
VANSYOCK, ABEL	1807	PLAINTIFF	1572	VERMILION, CHARLES	1822	MISC	1685
VANSYOCK, ABEL	1829	PLAINTIFF	1573	VERMILLING, CHARLES	1848	MISC	1685
VANSYOCK, ABEL	1830	PLAINTIFF	1573	VERMILLION, CHARLES	1824	DEFENDANT	1602
VANSYOCK, AREN	1827	PLAINTIFF	1573	VERNER & BROWN	1839	PLAINTIFF	1625
VANSYOCK, JAMES	1827	MISC	1676	VERNER, FEARN S / & CO	1822	PLAINTIFF	1625
VANSYOCK, JAMES	1827	MISC	1684	VERNON SCHOOL No.4	1871	HAN MAP	1732
VARLEY, - / MRS	1871	MARH'L MAP	1751	VESSEL, J	1871	MARH'L MAP	1749
VARLEY, W	1871	MARH'L MAP	1751	VESSELS, J / SHOE SHOP	1871	LIMESTONE	1805
VARNER, JOHN	1861	DEFENDANT	1603	VICK, WILLIAM	1873	PLAINTIFF	1574
VARNER, W	1871	BETHANY	1773	VICK, WILLIAM	1874	PLAINTIFF	1574
VARNEY & ECHOLS	1840	PLAINTIFF	1625	VICK, WILLIAM	1875	PLAINTIFF	1574
VARNEY & ECHOLS	1842	PLAINTIFF	1625	VICK, WILLIAM	1875	PLAINTIFF	1574
VARNEY, AARON	1838	DEFENDANT	1551	VICTOR, D	1836	PLAINTIFF	1574
VARNEY, AARON	1842	PLAINTIFF	1570	VICTOR, DAVID	1832	DEFENDANT	1662
VARNEY, EDWARD	1854	PLAINTIFF	1570	VICTOR, DAVID	1834	DEFENDANT	1650
VARNEY, EDWARD	1858	MISC	1683	VICTOR, DAVID	1836	DEFENDANT	1651
VARNEY, EDWIN	1855	PLAINTIFF	1570	VICTOR, DAVID	1840	DEFENDANT	1614
VARNEY, EDWIN	1855	PLAINTIFF	1570	VICTOR, DAVID	1840	DEFENDANT	1619
VARNEY, EDWIN	1858	PLAINTIFF	1570	VICTOR, DAVID	1840	DEFENDANT	1643
VARNEY, EDWIN	1858	PLAINTIFF	1570	VIENNA, PA / ALSO KNOWN AS COON ISLAND - RELAY FOR EXPRESS DRIVERS	1916	NAT'L ROAD	1862
VARNEY, GEORGE	1854	PLAINTIFF	1570				
VARNEY, GEORGE M	1857	PLAINTIFF	1570				
VARNEY, ROYAL	1838	MISC	1683	VIENNA, PA . - MAP	1916	NAT'L ROAD	1863
VASS, FANNIE	1879	PLAINTIFF	1570	VIERS BRANCH	1852	BRKE MAP	1851
VASSAL, WILLIAM	1846	PLAINTIFF	1570	VIEWIG, C	1878	PLAINTIFF	1574
VASSALL, WILLIAM	1847	PLAINTIFF	1570	VILLAGE HOME - LITTLE STAR VILLAGE HOME / ? SPELLED LITTE STAR	1871	W.LIBERTY	1780
VATES, N / MRS	1871	MDSVILLE	1808				
VAUGHAN, GEORGE	1879	PLAINTIFF	1570				
VAUGHAN, GEORGE	1880	PLAINTIFF	1570	VILLARS, EDWARD	1807	MISC	1685
VAUGHN, S	1871	BRKE MAP	1734	VINCENNES	1852	HEMPFIELD RR	1820
VAUSE, WILLIAM	1821	PLAINTIFF	1570	VINCENT, J A	1857	PLAINTIFF	1574
VAUSE, WILLIAM	1821	PLAINTIFF	1570	VINCENT, JOHN	1859	PLAINTIFF	1574
VAUSE, WILLIAM	1821	PLAINTIFF	1570	VINCENT, JOHN	1859	PLAINTIFF	1574
VAUSE, WILLIAM	1821	PLAINTIFF	1570	VINCENT, JOHN	1859	PLAINTIFF	1574
VAUSE, WILLIAM	1822	PLAINTIFF	1572	VINCENT, JOHN A	1857	PLAINTIFF	1574
VAUSE, WILLIAM	1822	PLAINTIFF	1572	VINCENT, JOHN A	1860	PLAINTIFF	1574
VAUSE, WILLIAM	1823	PLAINTIFF	1570	VINCENT, JOHN A	1862	PLAINTIFF	1574
VAUSE, WILLIAM	1823	PLAINTIFF	1570	VINE ALLEY - HAMILTON	1871	HAN MAP	1729
VAUSE, WILLIAM	1823	PLAINTIFF	1570	VINE ST / RITCHIE TWP	1871	RITCHIE TWP	1791
VAUSE, WILLIAM	1823	PLAINTIFF	1572	VINE ST - RITCHIE TWP	1871	RITCHIE TWP	1793
VAUSE, WILLIAM	1823	PLAINTIFF	1572	VINEYARD - C.F.BOENER - CAMERON	1871	CAMERON	1803
VAUSE, WILLIAM	1824	PLAINTIFF	1570	VINEYARD - EMSLEY, J	1871	MARH'L MAP	1745
VEASY, NOBLE	1811	MISC	1685	VINEYARD - JAMES EMSLEY - GRAPE GROWER	1871	BENWO'D - BUS.	1795
VEAZEY - CHILDREN	1875	MISC	1685				
VEAZEY - ORPHANS	1872	MISC	1685	VINEYARD - N. OF G.W. STEWART	1871	HAN MAP	1730
VEAZEY, RICHARD	1870	MISC	1685	VINEYARD - N. OF G.W. STEWART / W. SIDE OF MAP	1871	HAN MAP	1731
VEAZEY, RICHARD	1872	MISC	1685				
VEAZEY, RICHARD	1873	MISC	1685	VINEYARD - S. OF GOTHIC POINT	1871	MARH'L MAP	1748
VEAZEY, RICHARD	1875	MISC	1685	VINEYARD - STEWARTS / GEORGE W	1871	HAN-CLAY TWP	1763
VEAZEY, RICHARD W	1872	MISC	1685	VINEYARD - WHEELING CITY	1871	WHG CITY	1788
VEERS, ASAHEL	1833	PLAINTIFF	1574	VINYARD, LEWIS	1813	DEFENDANT	1656
VEES, VINCENT	1853	PLAINTIFF	1574	VIRDIN, WILLIAM W	1871	MISC	1685
VEIWIG, C	1858	PLAINTIFF	1574	VIRGIN, RESIN	1778	MISC	1685
VELLENOWETH, OPHIR E / MAP COMPILER	2000	PREFACE	1748	VIRGIN, RIZON	1778	PLAINTIFF	1574
				VIRGINIA HOTEL	1842	MISC	1685
VEMMON, GEORGE	1805	PLAINTIFF	1574	VIRGINIA HOUSE / INN ? - RONEY POINT	1871	OH CO. MAP	1743
VENES, S	1871	MDSVILLE	1809				
VENES, W / EST	1871	MDSVILLE	1810	VIRGINIA HOUSE / INN	1871	OH CO. MAP	1744
VENNIUM, GEORGE	1825	PLAINTIFF	1574	VIRGINIA HOUSE / LIBERTY ST - HOTEL	1871	WELLSBURG	1777
VENNUM, -	1843	DEFENDANT	1670				
VENNUM, ABIGAIL	1838	MISC	1685	VIRGINIA HOUSE - HOTEL / RONEY POINT	1871	RONEY PT.	1783

'PERSONAL TIME LINE' INDEX TO VOLUME 7 OF THE *OHIO COUNTY INDEX*

ENTRY	YEAR	SUBJECT	PAGE
VIRGINIA HOUSE - NEW MANCHESTER / HOTEL	1871	NEW MANCH.	1769
VIRGINIA HOUSE - WELLSBURG / HOTEL	1871	WLSBRG BUS.	1772
VIRGINIA HOUSE HOTEL - RONEY POINT	1871	OH CO. BUS.	1779
VIRGINNIA HOUSE - HOTEL IN NEW MANCHESTER	1871	NEW MANCH.	1763
VIRTUE, SAMUEL	1821	PLAINTIFF	1574
VIRTUE, SAMUEL	1822	PLAINTIFF	1574
VOCKLER, JOHN	1859	PLAINTIFF	1575
VOCKLER, JOHN	1860	PLAINTIFF	1575
VOELKER, CHARLES H	1867	MISC	1686
VOGELSAHNE, MENA	1877	PLAINTIFF	1575
VOGLEMAN, JACOB	1856	PLAINTIFF	1575
VOGLEMAN, JACOB	1859	DEFENDANT	1673
VOGLER - CHILDREN	1880	MISC	1686
VOGLER, ANDREW	1880	MISC	1686
VOGLER, JACOB	1880	MISC	1686
VOGLER, JACOB	1880	MISC	1686
VOGLER, JOHN	1854	MISC	1686
VOGLER, JOHN	1856	MISC	1686
VOGLER, JOHN	1869	MISC	1686
VOLLMER, HENRY	1856	PLAINTIFF	1575
VOLTZ, BRIDGET V	1877	PLAINTIFF	1575
VOLTZ, BRIDGET V	1879	PLAINTIFF	1575
VOLTZ, NICHOLAS	1864	MISC	1686
VON KAPFF & ARONS	1857	PLAINTIFF	1625
VON KAPFF, HERMAN	1857	PLAINTIFF	1575
VOORHEES, ABRAHAM L	1840	PLAINTIFF	1575
VOSMEN, FREDERICK	1842	DEFENDANT	1594
VOSS, H C / EST	1871	MDSVILLE	1810
VOSS, H C / EST	1871	MDSVILLE	1810
VOTO, JACOB	1824	MISC	1686
VOTY, CHARLES L	1833	PLAINTIFF	1575
VOWEL, JOHN	1809	PLAINTIFF	1575
W, - / MRS - UNKNOWN INITIALS	1871	OH CO. MAP	1742
W, C / C ST - UNKNOWN INITIALS	1871	MDSVILLE	1809
W, E P / INITIALS IN CAMERON - PROBABLY R.E.WILLARD ?	1871	CAMERON	1804
W, E P / INITIALS IN CAMERON - PROBABLY R.E.WILLARD ?	1871	CAMERON	1804
W, J / INITIALS - IN LEATHERWOOD (?J.WOODS?)	1871	WHG CITY	1787
W, S / UNKNOWN INITIALS	1871	MARH'L MAP	1749
W, W / UNKNOWN INITIALS - LOT 63	1871	TRIAD.BORO.	1784
W. & P.S. / UNKNOWN INITIALS	1871	MARH'L MAP	1748
W. E / UNKNOWN INITIALS	1871	OH CO. MAP	1742
W.C.A / UNKNOWN INITIALS - WELLSBURG	1871	WELLSBURG	1777
W.G. / UNKNOWN INITIALS - BETHANY	1871	BETHANY	1773
W.H.O. - C ST / UNKNOWN INITIALS	1871	MDSVILLE	1808
W.S.	1871	HAN MAP	1731
W.S.G / UNKNOWN INITIALS	1871	RITCHIE TWP	1791
W.SH. / (?ABBREV. FOR WAGON SHOP?)	1871	BETHANY	1773
WADDLE - ORPHANS	1848	MISC	1679
WADDLE, -	1835	PLAINTIFF	1617
WADDLE, -	1840	PLAINTIFF	1617
WADDLE, -	1841	PLAINTIFF	1617
WADDLE, -	1842	PLAINTIFF	1617
WADDLE, - / MRS	1871	TRIAD.BORO.	1784
WADDLE, A	1871	OH CO. MAP	1742
WADDLE, ARCHIBALD	1873	PLAINTIFF	1578
WADDLE, ARCHIBALD	1874	PLAINTIFF	1578
WADDLE, ARCHIBALD	1875	PLAINTIFF	1578
WADDLE, DAVID	1878	MISC	1687
WADDLE, ELIZABETH	1848	MISC	1687
WADDLE, F	1871	TRIAD.BORO.	1784
WADDLE, F	1871	TRIAD.BORO.	1784
WADDLE, GEORGE	1819	PLAINTIFF	1577
WADDLE, GEORGE	1819	PLAINTIFF	1577
WADDLE, JAMES	1848	MISC	1687
WADDLE, JAMES	1852	PLAINTIFF	1577
WADDLE, JOHN	1820	PLAINTIFF	1577
WADDLE, JOHN	1821	MISC	1687
WADDLE, JOHN	1822	PLAINTIFF	1577
WADDLE, JOHN	1835	PLAINTIFF	1577
WADDLE, JOHN	1840	PLAINTIFF	1577
WADDLE, JOHN	1840	PLAINTIFF	1577
WADDLE, JOHN	1840	PLAINTIFF	1577
WADDLE, JOHN	1840	PLAINTIFF	1577
WADDLE, JOHN	1840	PLAINTIFF	1577
WADDLE, JOHN	1840	PLAINTIFF	1577
WADDLE, JOHN	1840	PLAINTIFF	1577
WADDLE, JOHN	1841	PLAINTIFF	1577
WADDLE, JOHN	1841	PLAINTIFF	1577
WADDLE, JOHN	1841	PLAINTIFF	1577
WADDLE, JOHN	1841	PLAINTIFF	1577
WADDLE, JOHN	1842	PLAINTIFF	1577
WADDLE, JOSEPH	1830	MISC	1687
WADDLE, JOSEPH	1834	MISC	1691
WADDLE, JOSEPH	1871	MISC	1687
WADDLE, JOSEPH	1873	MISC	1687
WADDLE, JOSEPH	1875	MISC	1687
WADDLE, JOSEPH	1878	MISC	1687
WADDLE, MARY	1825	MISC	1687
WADDLE, PAULINE V	1850	MISC	1687
WADDLE, R	1871	OH CO. MAP	1741
WADDLE, RACHEL	1830	MISC	1687
WADDLE, ROBERT	1879	PLAINTIFF	1578
WADDLE, SARAH	1848	MISC	1687
WADDLE, SARAH	1850	MISC	1687
WADDLE, SARAH A	1858	PLAINTIFF	1578
WADDLE, WILLIAM	1811	PLAINTIFF	1577
WADDLE, WILLIAM	1812	PLAINTIFF	1577
WADDLE, WILLIAM	1830	MISC	1687
WADDLE, WILLIAM	1835	MISC	1687
WADDLE, WILLIAM	1842	PLAINTIFF	1577
WADDLE, WILLIAM	1844	PLAINTIFF	1577
WADDLE, WILLIAM	1848	PLAINTIFF	1577
WADDLE, WILLIAM	1848	MISC	1687
WADDLE, WILLIAM	1856	PLAINTIFF	1577
WADDLE, WILLIAM H	1850	MISC	1687
WADDLE, WILLIAM H	1873	PLAINTIFF	1578
WADDLE, WILLIAM SR	1830	MISC	1687
WADE, - / MRS	1871	MDSVILLE	1807
WADE, J H	1871	MARH'L MAP	1755
WADE, N THOMAS	1818	PLAINTIFF	1577
WADE, W K	1871	MDSVILLE	1809
WADEL, JOHN	1818	MISC	1687
WADEN, JOHN	1800	PLAINTIFF	1577
WADLE, J	1871	BKE/OH MAP	1738
WADLE, M	1871	BKE/OH MAP	1738
WADLES RUN	1871	OH CO. MAP	1741
WADLES RUN	1871	OH CO. MAP	1742
WADLES RUN - FALLS OF	1871	OH CO. MAP	1741
WAER, JAMES	1798	MISC	1687
WAER, JANE	1798	MISC	1687
WAESCHE & DESPADD	1835	PLAINTIFF	1626
WAESCHE, GEORGE FREDERICK	1835	PLAINTIFF	1577
WAESCHE, REPOLD	1835	PLAINTIFF	1577
WAGENER & CO	1875	PLAINTIFF	1627
WAGENER, DAVID	1875	PLAINTIFF	1578
WAGENKABT, L / (?WAGONECHT, LUDWIG?)	1871	OH CO. MAP	1742
WAGENKAUCHT, CHARLES	1876	DEFENDANT	1590
WAGENKNECHT, EMILIE	1875	MISC	1687
WAGENKNECHT, MATILDA	1875	MISC	1687
WAGENKNHT, L	1871	OH CO. MAP	1742
WAGENKNHT, L	1871	OH CO.BUS.	1779
WAGENKNHT, L	1871	RITCHIE TWP	1793
WAGENKNHT, L	1871	RITCHIE TWP	1794
WAGNER & SON CO	1861	PLAINTIFF	1626
WAGNER, C	1862	PLAINTIFF	1578
WAGNER, JOSEPH	1875	PLAINTIFF	1578
WAGNER, LOUIS	1879	MISC	1687
WAGNER, MARY E	1879	MISC	1687
WAGNER, MICHAEL	1835	DEFENDANT	1581
WAGNER, MICHAEL	1836	DEFENDANT	1581
WAGON ROAD - PANHANDLE ROUTE	1871	BRKE MAP	1734
WAGON ROAD			
WAGON SHOP - COWANS / J P	1871	HAN MAP	1733
WAGON SHOP - ELM GROVE	1871	ELM GROVE	1782
WAGON SHOP - FOWLERS / J	1871	FOWLERS P.O.	1775
WAGON SHOP - HUTTON / J - WELLSBURG	1871	WELLSBURG	1778
WAGON SHOP - LYCLICKS / WILLIAM	1871	MARH'L BUS.	1796
WAGON SHOP - MARTINS / W - BETHANY	1871	BETHANY	1773
WAGON SHOP - NEAR MAGGOTY RUN	1871	MARH'L MAP	1756
WAGON SHOP - NW OF HONEY BEE COTTAGE HOME	1871	MARH'L MAP	1745
WAGON SHOP - RICHARDS / R ?	1871	BRKE MAP	1734
WAGON SHOP - ROCK LICK P.O.	1871	MARH'L MAP	1753
WAGON SHOP - ROGERS / J - SAND HILL	1871	SAND HILL-BUS.	1797
WAGON SHOP - RONEY POINT STATION	1871	OH CO. MAP	1743
WAGON SHOP - RONEY POINT STATION	1871	OH CO. MAP	1744

CXI

'PERSONAL TIME LINE' INDEX TO VOLUME 7 OF THE *OHIO COUNTY INDEX*

ENTRY	YEAR	SUBJECT	PAGE	ENTRY	YEAR	SUBJECT	PAGE
WAGON SHOP - S. OF W. RUTH	1871	MARH'L MAP	1747	WALKER, JOHN P	1854	MISC	1688
WAGON SHOP - SEABRIGHTS / H - RONEY POINT	1871	RONEY PT.	1783	WALKER, JOSEPH	1820	PLAINTIFF	1576
				WALKER, L	1874	PLAINTIFF	1576
WAGON SHOP - SHORTS / J P	1871	W.LIBERTY	1780	WALKER, L	1874	PLAINTIFF	1576
WAGON SHOP - STAIBS / J.C.	1871	MDSVL BUS.	1796	WALKER, M	1871	BKE/OH MAP	1738
WAGON SHOP - TRIADELPHIA	1871	TRIAD.BORO.	1784	WALKER, MONTGOMERY	1847	PLAINTIFF	1576
WAGONECHT, LUDWIG / ? -WAGONKABT, L	1871	OH CO. MAP	1742	WALKER, MONTGOMYRY / MAP#72	1852	BRKE MAP	1839
				WALKER, MONTGOMYRY / MAP#100	1852	BRKE MAP	1842
WAGONER, CASPER	1841	PLAINTIFF	1577	WALKER, MONTGONERY	1866	MISC	1688
WAGONER, CASPER	1841	PLAINTIFF	1577	WALKER, NATHAN W	1857	PLAINTIFF	1576
WAIER, WILLIAM	1798	MISC	1687	WALKER, NATHAN W	1875	PLAINTIFF	1576
WAIT - ORPHANS	1868	MISC	1687	WALKER, PHILIP A	1880	PLAINTIFF	1576
WAIT FARM	1871	MARH'L MAP	1745	WALKER, PHILIP A	1880	PLAINTIFF	1576
WAIT, ALBERT	1868	MISC	1687	WALKER, ROBERT	1778	PLAINTIFF	1576
WAIT, LORENZO	1857	PLAINTIFF	1577	WALKER, ROBERT	1877	PLAINTIFF	1576
WAIT, SARAH	1868	MISC	1687	WALKER, S D / & CO	1841	PLAINTIFF	1626
WAITE, LORENZO	1855	PLAINTIFF	1577	WALKER, SAMUEL B	1873	PLAINTIFF	1576
WAITS, JOHN	1778	MISC	1687	WALKER, SAMUEL D	1835	PLAINTIFF	1576
WAITS, JOHN	1785	MISC	1687	WALKER, SAMUEL D	1841	PLAINTIFF	1576
WAITS, JOHN	1787	MISC	1687	WALKER, THOMAS	1806	MISC	1688
WAITS, JOHN	1789	PLAINTIFF	1577	WALKER, THOMAS	1853	PLAINTIFF	1576
WAITS, JOHN	1790	PLAINTIFF	1577	WALKER, W	1840	PLAINTIFF	1576
WAITS, JOHN	1790	PLAINTIFF	1577	WALKER, WILLIAM	1842	DEFENDANT	1652
WAITS, JOHN	1803	PLAINTIFF	1577	WALKER, WILLIAM	1855	PLAINTIFF	1576
WAKEMAN, GEORGE	1840	DEFENDANT	1620	WALKERS RUN	1852	BRKE MAP	1839
WAKEMAN, GEORGE A	1840	DEFENDANT	1635	WALKERS RUN / INCOMPLETE - R.SIDE OF MAP NEAR MAP # 425	1852	BRKE MAP	1847
WAKEMAN, GEORGE A	1850	MISC	1687				
WAKEMAN, GEORGE A	1854	MISC	1687	WALKERS RUN	1871	BRKE MAP	1735
WALDEN, JOHN	1834	PLAINTIFF	1579	WALKERS RUN / NE CORNER OF MAP	1871	BRKE MAP	1737
WALDIN, JOHN	1825	PLAINTIFF	1579	WALKERS, - / SCHOOL - MAP#25	1852	BRKE MAP	1839
WALDREN, FRANCIS	1822	PLAINTIFF	1579	WALL, HENRY	1778	MISC	1688
WALGAMUTH, FRANCIS F	1856	PLAINTIFF	1580	WALL, JOEL	1855	DEFENDANT	1586
WALKE, FRANK	1878	PLAINTIFF	1580	WALLACE, - / SCHOOL - (LOUISA OF BROOKE) - MAP#542	1852	BRKE MAP	1852
WALKER - ORPHANS	1866	MISC	1688				
WALKER TANK / (?WATER TANK?)	1871	BENWOOD	1799	WALLACE, - / MRS	1871	TRIAD.BORO.	1784
WALKER TANK / (?WATER TANK?)	1871	BENWOOD	1800	WALLACE, - / MRS	1871	TRIAD.BORO.	1784
WALKER, - / TANK ?	1871	BENWOOD	1799	WALLACE, ALEX JR	1880	PLAINTIFF	1580
WALKER, - / TANK ?	1871	BENWOOD	1800	WALLACE, ALLEN	1834	DEFENDANT	1558
WALKER, - / MRS	1871	MDSVILLE	1810	WALLACE, B E	1871	MARH'L MAP	1747
WALKER, - / MRS - INITIALS MRS.W.	1871	MDSVILLE	1810	WALLACE, B E	1871	MARH'L MAP	1750
WALKER, ALEXANDER	1800	PLAINTIFF	1576	WALLACE, DAVID	1805	PLAINTIFF	1579
WALKER, ALEXANDER	1842	DEFENDANT	1577	WALLACE, DAVID	1811	PLAINTIFF	1579
WALKER, ALEXANDER	1842	DEFENDANT	1617	WALLACE, DAVID	1811	PLAINTIFF	1579
WALKER, ALEXANDER	1842	DEFENDANT	1652	WALLACE, DAVID	1824	PLAINTIFF	1579
WALKER, ALEXANDER W	1841	DEFENDANT	1577	WALLACE, DAVID	1824	PLAINTIFF	1579
WALKER, ALEXANDER W	1841	DEFENDANT	1617	WALLACE, DAVID	1825	PLAINTIFF	1579
WALKER, ALEXANDER W	1841	DEFENDANT	1652	WALLACE, DAVID	1827	PLAINTIFF	1579
WALKER, ANDREW	1797	PLAINTIFF	1576	WALLACE, ELIZA JANE	1851	MISC	1688
WALKER, ANDREW	1799	PLAINTIFF	1576	WALLACE, HENRY	1820	PLAINTIFF	1579
WALKER, ANDREW	1800	PLAINTIFF	1576	WALLACE, HENRY	1821	PLAINTIFF	1579
WALKER, ANDREW	1806	PLAINTIFF	1576	WALLACE, HENRY	1876	PLAINTIFF	1580
WALKER, ANN	1874	PLAINTIFF	1576	WALLACE, HENRY	1878	PLAINTIFF	1580
WALKER, ANN	1874	PLAINTIFF	1576	WALLACE, IRWIN	1820	PLAINTIFF	1579
WALKER, ANNIE	1877	PLAINTIFF	1576	WALLACE, IRWIN	1821	PLAINTIFF	1579
WALKER, CARRIE	1878	MISC	1688	WALLACE, JAMES	1796	MISC	1688
WALKER, CARRIE C	1876	MISC	1688	WALLACE, JAMES	1800	PLAINTIFF	1579
WALKER, CARRIE C	1878	MISC	1688	WALLACE, JAMES	1801	PLAINTIFF	1579
WALKER, DANIEL	1800	PLAINTIFF	1576	WALLACE, JAMES	1801	PLAINTIFF	1579
WALKER, EDWARD	1810	DEFENDANT	1635	WALLACE, JAMES	1801	PLAINTIFF	1579
WALKER, ELENOR	1806	MISC	1688	WALLACE, JAMES	1801	DEFENDANT	1666
WALKER, GEORGE	1840	PLAINTIFF	1576	WALLACE, JAMES	1821	DEFENDANT	1579
WALKER, GEORGE W / & CO	1840	PLAINTIFF	1626	WALLACE, JAMES / MAP#541	1852	BRKE MAP	1852
WALKER, HUGH	1831	MISC	1688	WALLACE, JARED	1821	PLAINTIFF	1579
WALKER, HUGH	1831	MISC	1705	WALLACE, JOHN	1817	PLAINTIFF	1579
WALKER, J J	1871	BRKE MAP	1734	WALLACE, JOHN / MAP#594	1852	BRKE MAP	1851
WALKER, J J / TIMBERLAND	1871	BRKE MAP	1734	WALLACE, JOHN	1860	PLAINTIFF	1580
WALKER, J J	1871	BRKE MAP	1735	WALLACE, JOHN	1871	BRKE MAP	1735
WALKER, J J	1871	BRKE MAP	1735	WALLACE, JOHN / HIS TIMBERLANDS	1871	BRKE MAP	1735
WALKER, JACOB	1796	MISC	1688	WALLACE, LOUISA / SCHOOL - LOUISA OF BROOKE / MAP#542	1852	BRKE MAP	1852
WALKER, JACOB	1796	MISC	1688				
WALKER, JACOB / HEIRS - MAP#517	1852	BRKE MAP	1851	WALLACE, MARY	1835	MISC	1688
WALKER, JACOB / HEIRS - MAP#518	1852	BRKE MAP	1851	WALLACE, PYATT	1805	PLAINTIFF	1579
WALKER, JAMES	1831	MISC	1688	WALLACE, ROBERT	1871	MISC	1688
WALKER, JAMES D	1838	PLAINTIFF	1576	WALLACE, SAMUEL / MAP#562	1852	BRKE MAP	1852
WALKER, JAMES D	1852	PLAINTIFF	1576	WALLACE, SAMUEL C	1872	MISC	1688
WALKER, JANE A	1878	MISC	1688	WALLACE, SPAULDING K	1875	PLAINTIFF	1580
WALKER, JOHN	1788	PLAINTIFF	1576	WALLACE, STEWART	1838	PLAINTIFF	1579
WALKER, JOHN	1800	PLAINTIFF	1576	WALLACE, STEWART	1838	PLAINTIFF	1580
WALKER, JOHN	1840	PLAINTIFF	1576	WALLACE, STEWART	1839	PLAINTIFF	1580
WALKER, JOHN / MAP#519	1852	BRKE MAP	1851	WALLACE, STEWART	1839	PLAINTIFF	1580
WALKER, JOHN / MAP#547	1852	BRKE MAP	1851	WALLACE, T	1871	WELLSBURG	1778
WALKER, JOHN	1853	PLAINTIFF	1576	WALLACE, THOMAS	1839	MISC	1688
WALKER, JOHN	1853	PLAINTIFF	1576	WALLACE, THOMAS	1844	MISC	1688
WALKER, JOHN	1853	DEFENDANT	1603	WALLACE, VOLNEY	1827	PLAINTIFF	1579
WALKER, JOHN	1854	PLAINTIFF	1576	WALLACE, VOLNEY	1830	PLAINTIFF	1579
WALKER, JOHN P	1852	MISC	1688	WALLACE, VOLNEY	1834	PLAINTIFF	1579

CXII

'PERSONAL TIME LINE' INDEX TO VOLUME 7 OF THE *OHIO COUNTY INDEX*

ENTRY	YEAR	SUBJECT	PAGE	ENTRY	YEAR	SUBJECT	PAGE
WALLACE, WILLIAM	1857	PLAINTIFF	1580	WARD, W	1871	NEW CUMB'LD	1767
WALLACES BRANCH	1852	BRKE MAP	1852	WARD, W	1871	NEW CUMB'LD	1767
WALLCE, THEO.	1871	OH CO. MAP	1743	WARD, WILLIAM	1781	MISC	1689
WALLER, ABRAHAM B	1836	PLAINTIFF	1579	WARD, WILLIAM	1798	MISC	1689
WALLER, ELIZABETH	1826	MISC	1688	WARD, WILLIAM	1800	DEFENDANT	1554
WALLER, JESSE	1809	PLAINTIFF	1579	WARD, WILLIAM	1800	PLAINTIFF	1583
WALLER, JESSE	1812	PLAINTIFF	1579	WARD, WILLIAM	1802	PLAINTIFF	1583
WALLER, KESIAH	1826	MISC	1688	WARD, WILLIAM	1803	PLAINTIFF	1583
WALLER, THOMAS	1778	MISC	1688	WARD, WILLIAM	1803	DEFENDANT	1666
WALLIS, BENJAMIN	1835	PLAINTIFF	1579	WARD, WILLIAM	1871	NEW CUMB'LD	1766
WALLIS, BENJAMIN E	1833	PLAINTIFF	1579	WARDELL, MARY	1856	DEFENDANT	1588
WALLIS, JAMES	1794	MISC	1688	WARDELL, SARAH	1828	MISC	1689
WALLOR, JESSE	1801	PLAINTIFF	1579	WARDELL, SOLOMON	1828	MISC	1689
WALLS, JOHN	1868	MISC	1688	WARDEN & EDWARDS	1849	PLAINTIFF	1603
WALN, CALEB CRESSON	1803	PLAINTIFF	1579	WARDEN & EDWARDS	1851	PLAINTIFF	1603
WALN, NICHOLAS	1803	PLAINTIFF	1579	WARDEN & EDWARDS	1853	PLAINTIFF	1603
WALNUT FARM - CLAY TWP	1871	MARH'L MAP	1751	WARDEN & EDWARDS	1855	PLAINTIFF	1603
WALNUT RIDGE	1871	OH CO. MAP	1743	WARDEN & EDWARDS	1856	PLAINTIFF	1603
WALNUT RIDGE	1871	MARH'L MAP	1752	WARDEN & EDWARDS	1857	PLAINTIFF	1603
WALNUT RIDGE - SCHOOL / MAP#213	1852	BRKE MAP	1842	WARDEN & EDWARDS	1858	PLAINTIFF	1603
WALNUT SPRING	1871	MARH'L MAP	1746	WARDEN & EDWARDS	1859	PLAINTIFF	1603
WALNUT ST. - HAMILTON	1871	HAN MAP	1729	WARDEN & EDWARDS	1860	PLAINTIFF	1603
WALRAVIN, ELIAS	1819	MISC	1688	WARDEN & EDWARDS	1861	PLAINTIFF	1603
WALRAVIN, ELIAS	1838	PLAINTIFF	1580	WARDEN & EDWARDS	1862	PLAINTIFF	1603
WALSH, LOUISA	1853	MISC	1688	WARDEN DIST SCHOOL NO.9	1871	OH CO. MAP	1741
WALT, ELIZABETH	1801	PLAINTIFF	1579	WARDEN S	1871	OH CO. MAP	1742
WALT, JAMES	1801	DEFENDANT	1579	WARDEN, CATHERINE	1855	PLAINTIFF	1584
WALTER & KRAFT	1870	PLAINTIFF	1627	WARDEN, JACOB	1855	PLAINTIFF	1584
WALTER, CHARLES	1857	MISC	1688	WARDEN, JACOB	1859	PLAINTIFF	1584
WALTER, CHARLES	1859	MISC	1688	WARDEN, JACOB M	1842	PLAINTIFF	1584
WALTER, CONRAD	1856	MISC	1688	WARDEN, JACOB M	1855	PLAINTIFF	1584
WALTER, E	1871	TRIAD.TWP.	1781	WARDEN, JACOB M	1856	PLAINTIFF	1584
WALTER, F	1871	OH CO. MAP	1742	WARDEN, JACOB M	1857	PLAINTIFF	1584
WALTER, F	1871	TRIAD.TWP.	1781	WARDEN, JACOB M	1858	PLAINTIFF	1584
WALTER, FRAZ	1857	PLAINTIFF	1580	WARDEN, JACOB M	1874	MISC	1689
WALTER, JONATHAN	1826	PLAINTIFF	1579	WARDEN, JACOB W	1853	PLAINTIFF	1584
WALTER, LEWIS	1856	DEFENDANT	1560	WARDEN, JAMES	1799	MISC	1689
WALTER, ROBERT	1855	DEFENDANT	1636	WARDEN, JAMES	1804	MISC	1689
WALTER, STEPHEN	1857	PLAINTIFF	1580	WARDEN, JAMES	1806	DEFENDANT	1658
WALTERMYER, A J	1875	MISC	1688	WARDEN, JAMES	1808	DEFENDANT	1658
WALTERS, CHARLOTTA	1872	MISC	1688	WARDEN, JAMES	1837	PLAINTIFF	1583
WALTERS, FRANK	1878	DEFENDANT	1631	WARDEN, JAMES	1838	PLAINTIFF	1583
WALTERS, FRANK	1879	DEFENDANT	1631	WARDEN, JAMES	1839	MISC	1689
WALTERS, GEORGE	1808	PLAINTIFF	1579	WARDEN, JAMES W	1860	DEFENDANT	1573
WALTERS, GEORGE	1809	PLAINTIFF	1579	WARDEN, JAMES W	1860	PLAINTIFF	1584
WALTERS, GEORGE	1815	PLAINTIFF	1579	WARDEN, JAMES W	1861	DEFENDANT	1584
WALTERS, GEORGE JR	1873	PLAINTIFF	1580	WARDEN, JOHN	1799	MISC	1689
WALTERS, JOHN	1872	MISC	1688	WARDEN, S	1871	OH CO. MAP	1741
WALTERS, JOHN H	1880	MISC	1688	WARDEN, S	1871	OH CO. MAP	1741
WALTERS, ROBERT	1854	DEFENDANT	1636	WARDEN, S W / (?OR WARDER?)	1871	MARH'L MAP	1746
WALTERS, WILLIAM B	1877	PLAINTIFF	1580	WARDEN, SAMUEL	1803	MISC	1689
WALTON & FULLER	1841	PLAINTIFF	1626	WARDEN, SAMUEL	1816	PLAINTIFF	1583
WALTON, A / HEIRS	1871	CAMERON	1803	WARDEN, SAMUEL	1817	PLAINTIFF	1583
WALTON, H	1871	MARH'L MAP	1753	WARDEN, SAMUEL	1820	DEFENDANT	1611
WALTON, THORNTON	1820	PLAINTIFF	1579	WARDEN, SAMUEL	1821	PLAINTIFF	1583
WALTON, WILLIAM	1841	PLAINTIFF	1580	WARDEN, SAMUEL	1822	DEFENDANT	1612
WALTON, WILLIAM	1841	PLAINTIFF	1580	WARDEN, SAMUEL	1830	PLAINTIFF	1583
WALTON, WILLIAM	1846	PLAINTIFF	1580	WARDEN, SAMUEL	1839	MISC	1689
WAME, EDWARD	1855	PLAINTIFF	1581	WARDEN, SAMUEL	1854	MISC	1689
WANCHOPE, ELEANOR	1852	PLAINTIFF	1581	WARDEN, SAMUEL	1873	MISC	1689
WANDELHOR, FREDERICK A	1838	PLAINTIFF	1581	WARDER, S W / (?OR WARDEN?)	1871	MARH'L MAP	1746
WANDELHOUR, FREDERICK A	1835	PLAINTIFF	1581	WARDLE, SARAH	1829	PLAINTIFF	1583
WANDELOHER, FREDERICK A	1836	PLAINTIFF	1581	WARDLE, SARAH	1830	PLAINTIFF	1583
WANDELOHR, FREDERICK A	1836	PLAINTIFF	1581	WARDLE, SOLOMON	1816	DEFENDANT	1563
WARD & JONES	1871	NEW CUMB'LD	1767	WARDLE, WILLIAM	1836	PLAINTIFF	1583
WARD, - / JOYCE & WARD	1871	BRKE MAP	1736	WARDNER & SABIN	1838	PLAINTIFF	1626
WARD, ALLEN	1829	PLAINTIFF	1583	WARDNER, ALLEN	1838	PLAINTIFF	1583
WARD, ANNIE	1879	MISC	1689	WARDS FOR WHEELING CITY LISTED	1871	MAP	1721
WARD, BOLIVAR	1858	DEFENDANT	1597	WARDS OF WHEELING - SEE WHEELING - WARD #	1871	WHG CITY	1786
WARD, D A	1880	PLAINTIFF	1584				
WARD, DAVID	1871	HAN MAP	1731	WARE HO / (?HOUSE?) AT DEVENNY LANDING -OHIO RIVER	1871	BRKE MAP	1735
WARD, EDWARD	1803	MISC	1701				
WARD, EDWARD	1810	PLAINTIFF	1583	WARE HO / WAREHOUSE ? - MOUTH OF SHORT CREEK	1871	BKE/OH MAP	1738
WARD, H	1871	MARH'L MAP	1748				
WARD, H / INITIALS H.W.	1871	MARH'L MAP	1751	WARE HO. / (?HOUSE?)	1871	MARH'L MAP	1754
WARD, J W	1878	PLAINTIFF	1584	WAREHAM, JOHN	1812	PLAINTIFF	1583
WARD, JANE	1862	MISC	1689	WAREHAM, JOHN	1813	PLAINTIFF	1583
WARD, JOSEPH	1800	PLAINTIFF	1583	WARFIELD, B H	1879	PLAINTIFF	1584
WARD, JOSEPH	1809	DEFENDANT	1585	WARFIELD, GERRARD	1786	PLAINTIFF	1583
WARD, JOSEPH	1812	MISC	1689	WARFORD, JOHN	1778	MISC	1689
WARD, JOSEPH	1812	MISC	1689	WARLEY, DAVID	1787	DEFENDANT	1565
WARD, JOSEPH	1826	MISC	1689	WARN, -	1860	PLAINTIFF	1630
WARD, JOSEPH	1827	MISC	1689	WARNAFELDT, JOHN H	1869	MISC	1689
WARD, JOSEPH JR	1822	MISC	1689	WARNAKE, A / BLACKSMITH SHOP	1871	OH CO. MAP	1741
WARD, MATTHYAS	1788	PLAINTIFF	1583	WARNE, EDWARD A	1858	PLAINTIFF	1584
WARD, RACHEL	1859	PLAINTIFF	1584	WARNER, DENNIS	1826	PLAINTIFF	1583

CXIII

'PERSONAL TIME LINE' INDEX TO VOLUME 7 OF THE *OHIO COUNTY INDEX*

ENTRY	YEAR	SUBJECT	PAGE
WARNER, GEORGE	1843	PLAINTIFF	1584
WARNER, GREAGORY	1879	PLAINTIFF	1584
WARNER, GRISWOLD E	1858	PLAINTIFF	1584
WARNER, PETER	1815	PLAINTIFF	1583
WARNER, PETER	1817	PLAINTIFF	1583
WARNER, PETER	1818	PLAINTIFF	1583
WARNER, RICHARD C	1861	PLAINTIFF	1584
WARNER, THOMAS	1832	PLAINTIFF	1583
WARNOCH, JOHN	1806	PLAINTIFF	1583
WARNOCH, REBECKAH	1811	MISC	1689
WARNOCK, JOHN	1844	PLAINTIFF	1584
WARNOCK, REBECKAH	1811	MISC	1689
WARNOCK, WILLIAM	1811	PLAINTIFF	1583
WARNOCK, WILLIAM	1844	PLAINTIFF	1584
WARPENBY, WILLIAM	1795	MISC	1689
WARRANT, JACK	1802	PLAINTIFF	1583
WARRANT, JOHN	1803	PLAINTIFF	1583
WARREN & SON	1857	PLAINTIFF	1626
WARREN & SONS	1857	PLAINTIFF	1626
WARREN, DWIGHT	1876	MISC	1689
WARREN, GEORGE	1860	PLAINTIFF	1584
WARREN, ISIAH	1857	MISC	1689
WARREN, ISIAH	1878	PLAINTIFF	1584
WARREN, JOHN T	1873	PLAINTIFF	1584
WARREN, L MARIA	1876	PLAINTIFF	1584
WARREN, L MARIA	1877	PLAINTIFF	1584
WARREN, MATHEW	1841	PLAINTIFF	1584
WARREN, MATHEW	1858	PLAINTIFF	1584
WARREN, MATTHEW	1837	PLAINTIFF	1583
WARREN, MATTHEW	1839	PLAINTIFF	1584
WARREN, R	1871	NEW CUMB'LD	1767
WARREN, T	1871	HAN MAP	1731
WARRENTON, OH	1852	BRKE MAP	1839
WARRENTON, OHIO / FERRY TO	1871	BKE/OH MAP	1738
WARRING, JOHN	1806	PLAINTIFF	1583
WARSINSKY, THEODORE	1879	PLAINTIFF	1584
WARTENBE, WILLIAM	1809	PLAINTIFF	1583
WARTINBE, WILLIAM	1812	PLAINTIFF	1583
WARWICK, A	1871	HAN MAP	1732
WARWICK, N E & CO	1876	PLAINTIFF	1627
WARWICK, WILLIAM	1806	PLAINTIFF	1600
WASHAM, JOHN	1809	PLAINTIFF	1585
WASHINGTON - CHILDREN	1828	MISC	1691
WASHINGTON - NEW WASHINGTON	1871	MARH'L MAP	1746
WASHINGTON - NEW WASHINGTON	1871	MARH'L MAP	1749
WASHINGTON - WELLSBURG & WASHINGTON TURNPIKE	1852	BRKE MAP	1846
WASHINGTON - WELLSBURG & WASHINGTON TURNPIKE	1852	BRKE MAP	1847
WASHINGTON - WELLSBURG & WASHINGTON TURNPIKE	1871	BRKE MAP	1737
WASHINGTON & JEFFERSON COLLEGE / WASH., PA.	1916	NAT'L ROAD	1861
WASHINGTON & LIBERTY PIKE	1871	BKE/OH MAP	1739
WASHINGTON & WEST LIBERTY PIKE	1871	BKE/OH MAP	1739
WASHINGTON BOROUGH, WASHINGTON CO, PA	1852	HEMPFIELD RR	1823
WASHINGTON CO, PA / POOR HOUSE	1846	MISC	1709
WASHINGTON CO, PA / HEMPFIELD RR - MAP & BOND PROSPECTUS	1852	HEMPFIELD RR	1817
WASHINGTON CO, PA	1852	HEMPFIELD RR	1818
WASHINGTON CO, PA / HEMPFIELD RR BONDS	1852	HEMPFIELD RR	1823
WASHINGTON CO, PA / 1850 AGRICULTURAL STATISTICS	1852	HEMPFIELD RR	1824
WASHINGTON CO, PA	1852	BRKE MAP	1841
WASHINGTON CO, PA	1852	BRKE MAP	1844
WASHINGTON CO, PA	1852	BRKE MAP	1847
WASHINGTON CO, PA	1852	BRKE MAP	1850
WASHINGTON CO, PA	1852	BRKE MAP	1852
WASHINGTON HALL ASSOCIATION	1848	PLAINTIFF	1626
WASHINGTON HALL ASSOCIATION	1852	PLAINTIFF	1626
WASHINGTON HALL ASSOCIATION	1858	PLAINTIFF	1626
WASHINGTON HOUSE - HOTEL	1871	MDSVILLE	1807
WASHINGTON LADIES SEMINARY / WASH., PA.	1916	NAT'L ROAD	1861
WASHINGTON PIKE	1871	WELLSBURG	1777
WASHINGTON SCHOOL	1871	HAN MAP	1726
WASHINGTON ST. - HAMILTON	1871	HAN MAP	1729
WASHINGTON TURNPIKE	1871	BRKE MAP	1735
WASHINGTON TURNPIKE CO - HOUSE AND STORE	1871	BRKE MAP	1736
WASHINGTON TWP - MARSHALL CO	1871	OH CO. MAP	1741
WASHINGTON TWP - MARSHALL CO	1871	MARH'L MAP	1748
WASHINGTON TWP - MARSHALL CO	1871	MARH'L MAP	1749
WASHINGTON TWP - MARSHALL CO	1871	POPULATION	1816
WASHINGTON TWP - MARSHALL CO - BUSINESS NOTICES	1871	MARH'L BUS.	1797
WASHINGTON TWP - MARSHALL CO - LIMESTONE P.O	1871	LIMESTONE	1805
WASHINGTON TWP - MARSHALL CO - MOUNDSVILLE	1871	MDSVILLE	1806
WASHINGTON TWP - MARSHALL CO - S. BOUNDARY LINE	1871	MDSVILLE	1809
WASHINGTON TWP - OHIO CO	1871	WHG CITY	1786
WASHINGTON TWP - OHIO CO	1871	WHG CITY	1787
WASHINGTON TWP - OHIO CO	1871	POPULATION	1816
WASHINGTON TWP - WHEELING CITY	1871	OH CO. MAP	1742
WASHINGTON, DC	1852	HEMP. RR MAP	1827
WASHINGTON, HANNAH	1876	MISC	1692
WASHINGTON, L	1828	MISC	1691
WASHINGTON, LAURENCE A	1835	MISC	1691
WASHINGTON, LAWRANC	1841	PLAINTIFF	1585
WASHINGTON, LAWRENCE	1840	PLAINTIFF	1585
WASHINGTON, LAWRENCE	1842	PLAINTIFF	1586
WASHINGTON, LAWRENCE A	1824	MISC	1691
WASHINGTON, LAWRENCE A	1841	PLAINTIFF	1585
WASHINGTON, LAWRENCE A	1842	PLAINTIFF	1586
WASHINGTON, MARY DORCAS	1824	MISC	1691
WASHINGTON, MARY DORCAS	1828	MISC	1691
WASHINGTON, PA	1852	HEMP. RR MAP	1826
WASHINGTON, PA	1916	NAT'L ROAD	1861
WASHINGTON, PA - BEAU ST	1916	NAT'L ROAD	1861
WASHINGTON, PA - CATFISH RUN	1916	NAT'L ROAD	1861
WASHINGTON, PA - CHESTNUT ST	1916	NAT'L ROAD	1861
WASHINGTON, PA - COLLEGE ST	1916	NAT'L ROAD	1861
WASHINGTON, PA - COURT HOUSE	1916	NAT'L ROAD	1861
WASHINGTON, PA - DETAIL DOWNTOWN MAP	1916	NAT'L ROAD	1861
WASHINGTON, PA - EAST MAIDEN ST	1916	NAT'L ROAD	1861
WASHINGTON, PA - HOTEL AULD	1916	NAT'L ROAD	1861
WASHINGTON, PA - MAIDEN ST	1916	NAT'L ROAD	1861
WASHINGTON, PA - MAIN ST	1916	NAT'L ROAD	1861
WASHINGTON, PA - MAP	1916	NAT'L ROAD	1869
WASHINGTON, PA - TAVERN	1916	NAT'L ROAD	1861
WASHINGTON, PA - WASHINGTON & JEFFERSON COLLEGE	1916	NAT'L ROAD	1861
WASHINGTON, PA - WASHINGTON LADIES SEMINARY	1916	NAT'L ROAD	1861
WASHINGTON, PA - WASHINGTON TRUST CO	1916	NAT'L ROAD	1861
WASHINGTON, PA - WEST CHESTNUT ST	1916	NAT'L ROAD	1861
WASHINGTON, PA - WHEELING ST	1916	NAT'L ROAD	1861
WASHINGTON, W	1840	PLAINTIFF	1585
WASHINGTON, W	1842	PLAINTIFF	1586
WASON, GEORGE	1820	DEFENDANT	1656
WASON, GEORGE	1821	PLAINTIFF	1585
WASON, GEORGE	1822	PLAINTIFF	1585
WASSEMAN, ELIZABETH	1875	MISC	1692
WASSEMANN, CONROD	1873	MISC	1692
WASSEN, THOMAS	1866	MISC	1692
WASSERMEIER, WILLIAM	1869	MISC	1692
WATER GRIST MILL	1796	MISC	1684
WATER GRIST MILL	1812	MISC	1676
WATER ST. - HAMILTON	1871	HAN MAP	1729
WATER TANK	1871	BRKE MAP	1734
WATER TANK / ON B&O - SE OF MOUNDSVILLE	1871	MARH'L MAP	1748
WATER TANK - AT BENWOOD / ?	1871	BENWOOD	1800
WATER TANK ON B&O RR - E. OF P. PARKER	1871	MARH'L MAP	1752
WATERBURY, STEPHEN W	1855	PLAINTIFF	1586
WATERHOUSE, JOHN	1859	PLAINTIFF	1586
WATERHOUSE, JOHN	1877	PLAINTIFF	1586
WATERHOUSE, STEPHEN	1842	PLAINTIFF	1586
WATERHOUSE, STEPHEN	1850	PLAINTIFF	1586
WATERHOUSE, STEPHEN	1853	PLAINTIFF	1586
WATERHOUSE, STEPHEN	1855	PLAINTIFF	1586
WATERHOUSE, STEPHEN	1856	PLAINTIFF	1586
WATERHOUSE, STEPHEN	1859	MISC	1692
WATERS - CHILDREN	1866	MISC	1692
WATERS, HANSON	1811	PLAINTIFF	1585
WATERS, HANSON	1812	PLAINTIFF	1585
WATERS, JOSEPH H	1858	PLAINTIFF	1586
WATERS, JOSEPH H	1859	PLAINTIFF	1586
WATERS, JOSEPH H	1866	MISC	1692
WATERS, MARGARET	1866	MISC	1692
WATERSON, JAMES	1828	PLAINTIFF	1585
WATERSON, ROBERT	1851	MISC	1691
WATERSON, ROBERT W	1838	DEFENDANT	1651
WATES, THOMAS	1850	PLAINTIFF	1586

'PERSONAL TIME LINE' INDEX TO VOLUME 7 OF THE *OHIO COUNTY INDEX*

ENTRY	YEAR	SUBJECT	PAGE	ENTRY	YEAR	SUBJECT	PAGE
WATKINS, ANN	1795	MISC	1691	WAUGH, RICHARD / HEIRS - MAP#179	1852	BRKE MAP	1843
WATKINS, ANN	1798	MISC	1691	WAUGH, RICHARD / HEIRS - MAP#180	1852	BRKE MAP	1843
WATKINS, ELIZABETH ANNA	1795	MISC	1691	WAUGH, RICHARD / HEIRS - MAP#182	1852	BRKE MAP	1843
WATKINS, ENOCH	1832	DEFENDANT	1613	WAUGH, RICHARD / HEIRS - MAP#195	1852	BRKE MAP	1843
WATKINS, ENOCH	1832	DEFENDANT	1618	WAUGH, RICHARD / HEIRS - MAP#218	1852	BRKE MAP	1843
WATKINS, ENOCH	1839	PLAINTIFF	1585	WAUGH, RICHARD / HEIRS- (COOPERSHOP) - MAP#264	1852	BRKE MAP	1843
WATKINS, SARAH	1812	PLAINTIFF	1585				
WATKINS, TAXWELL	1853	MISC	1691	WAUGH, RICHARD / HEIRS- (LOWER MILL) - MAP#265	1852	BRKE MAP	1843
WATKINS, THOMAS	1795	MISC	1691				
WATKINS, TOBIAS	1831	DEFENDANT	1618	WAUGH, RICHARD / HEIRS- (LOWER MILL) - MAP#266	1852	BRKE MAP	1843
WATSON, AARON	1811	MISC	1691				
WATSON, AARON	1811	MISC	1691	WAUGH, RICHARD / HEIRS- (LOWER MILL) - MAP#308	1852	BRKE MAP	1847
WATSON, AARON	1819	MISC	1691				
WATSON, BENJAMIN H	1857	PLAINTIFF	1586	WAUGH, RICHARD / HEIRS- (LOWER MILL) - MAP#309	1852	BRKE MAP	1847
WATSON, CATHARINE	1827	MISC	1691				
WATSON, CATHERINE ANN	1827	MISC	1691	WAY, - / NIXON & WAY	1871	BRKE MAP	1736
WATSON, DANIEL	1799	MISC	1691	WAY, - / NIXON & WAY	1871	BKE/OH MAP	1738
WATSON, DANIEL	1801	DEFENDANT	1579	WAY, ABISHA	1818	PLAINTIFF	1585
WATSON, G	1871	MARH'L MAP	1746	WAY, ABISHA	1819	PLAINTIFF	1585
WATSON, G / INITIALS G.W.	1871	MARH'L MAP	1746	WAY, ABISHAI	1817	PLAINTIFF	1585
WATSON, GEORGE	1873	PLAINTIFF	1586	WAY, JOSHUA	1829	PLAINTIFF	1585
WATSON, GEORGE	1876	DEFENDANT	1627	WAY, T G	1856	PLAINTIFF	1586
WATSON, HUGH	1799	PLAINTIFF	1585	WAYMAN - CHILDREN	1872	MISC	1692
WATSON, JACOB	1855	PLAINTIFF	1586	WAYMAN RIDGE ROAD	1871	MARH'L MAP	1752
WATSON, JACOB	1872	MISC	1692	WAYMAN RIDGE ROAD - WASH TWP	1871	MARH'L MAP	1749
WATSON, JAMES	1796	PLAINTIFF	1585	WAYMAN, F	1871	MARH'L MAP	1758
WATSON, JAMES	1852	PLAINTIFF	1586	WAYMAN, F / & SON - BLACKSMITH - NEAR FAIRVIEW	1871	FRKLN TWP-BUS.	1797
WATSON, JOHN	1824	PLAINTIFF	1585				
WATSON, JOHN	1825	PLAINTIFF	1585	WAYMAN, F M	1871	CAMERON	1802
WATSON, JOHN	1828	DEFENDANT	1591	WAYMAN, F M / INITIALS F.M.W.	1871	CAMERON	1802
WATSON, JOHN	1829	DEFENDANT	1591	WAYMAN, F N	1871	CAMERON	1802
WATSON, JOHN	1839	MISC	1691	WAYMAN, H	1871	MARH'L MAP	1758
WATSON, JOHN	1842	MISC	1691	WAYMAN, J P	1871	MARH'L MAP	1756
WATSON, R	1871	HAN MAP	1726	WAYMAN, J P / INITIALS J.P.W.	1871	MARH'L MAP	1756
WATSON, ROBERT	1836	MISC	1691	WAYMAN, J P	1871	GLEN EASTON	1801
WATSON, SADIE	1880	MISC	1692	WAYMAN, J P / STORE	1871	GLEN EASTON	1801
WATSON, THOMAS	1830	MISC	1676	WAYMAN, J P / STORE	1871	ROSBBYS RK	1813
WATSON, THOMAS	1830	MISC	1691	WAYMAN, MARTIN	1872	MISC	1692
WATSON, THOMAS	1833	PLAINTIFF	1585	WAYMAN, MARTIN F	1857	PLAINTIFF	1586
WATSON, THOMAS	1874	PLAINTIFF	1586	WAYMAN, MARTIN T	1857	PLAINTIFF	1586
WATSON, WILLIAM	1832	PLAINTIFF	1585	WAYMAN, SAMUEL	1827	PLAINTIFF	1585
WATSON, WILLIAM	1833	PLAINTIFF	1585	WAYMAN, SAMUEL	1856	MISC	1691
WATSON, WILLIAM	1834	PLAINTIFF	1585	WAYMAN, SAMUEL	1872	MISC	1692
WATSON, WILLIAM	1853	DEFENDANT	1584	WAYMAN, THOMAS	1809	PLAINTIFF	1585
WATT, -	1841	PLAINTIFF	1629	WAYMAN, THOMAS	1811	MISC	1691
WATT, ANN ELIZ	1877	MISC	1679	WAYMAN, THOMAS	1811	MISC	1691
WATT, ANN ELIZABETH	1877	MISC	1692	WAYMAN, THOMAS	1822	MISC	1691
WATT, ELIZABETH	1801	PLAINTIFF	1585	WAYMAN, THOMAS	1827	MISC	1691
WATT, JAMES	1801	DEFENDANT	1585	WAYMAN, ZACHARIAH	1832	PLAINTIFF	1585
WATT, JAMES	1871	HAN MAP	1732	WAYMAN, ZACHERIAH	1812	PLAINTIFF	1585
WATT, JAMES	1871	BRKE MAP	1734	WAYMAN, ZACHRIAH	1812	PLAINTIFF	1585
WATT, JANE	1820	PLAINTIFF	1585	WAYMER, JOHN	1877	PLAINTIFF	1586
WATT, JOHN	1841	PLAINTIFF	1585	WAYNE, - / MRS	1871	MARH'L MAP	1754
WATT, JOHN	1841	PLAINTIFF	1586	WAYNE, A	1871	MARH'L MAP	1758
WATTERHOUSE, STEPHEN	1853	PLAINTIFF	1586	WAYNE, ANDREW	1831	MISC	1691
WATTERMAN, CHARLES	1807	PLAINTIFF	1585	WAYNE, J L & CO	1858	PLAINTIFF	1626
WATTERS, FRANK	1879	DEFENDANT	1584	WAYNE, JULIUS	1859	PLAINTIFF	1586
WATTERSON, MARY JR	1878	MISC	1692	WAYNESBURG ROAD / BOTTOM OF MAP	1871	MARH'L MAP	1750
WATTERSON, MARY SR	1878	MISC	1692				
WATTS, JOHN S	1854	MISC	1691	WAYNESBURG, PA	1852	HEMP. RR MAP	1826
WATTS, RICHARD	1824	PLAINTIFF	1585	WAYNESBURG ROAD	1871	MARH'L MAP	1753
WAUCHOPE, ELEANOR	1860	MISC	1692	WAYNESBURGH ROAD - FROM MOUNDSVILLE	1871	MARH'L MAP	1748
WAUGH, - / SCHOOL - MAP#253	1852	BRKE MAP	1843				
WAUGH, D	1871	BRKE MAP	1736	WAYNESBURGH ROAD - FROM MOUNDSVILLE	1871	MARH'L MAP	1749
WAUGH, D	1871	BRKE MAP	1736				
WAUGH, DAVID / MAP#234	1852	BRKE MAP	1844	WAYNESBURGH ROAD - TOLL GATE ON - NEAR POPLAR SPRING	1871	MARH'L MAP	1753
WAUGH, J SR	1871	BRKE MAP	1736				
WAUGH, J SR / RES	1871	BRKE MAP	1736	WAYT, A	1856	PLAINTIFF	1626
WAUGH, JAMES	1871	BRKE MAP	1736	WAYT, FANNY	1820	PLAINTIFF	1578
WAUGH, JAMES	1871	BRKE MAP	1736	WAYT, FANNY	1822	PLAINTIFF	1578
WAUGH, JAMES / MILL	1871	BRKE MAP	1736	WAYT, FANNY	1827	DEFENDANT	1578
WAUGH, JAMES / TUNNEL	1871	BRKE MAP	1736	WAYT, FANNY	1830	DEFENDANT	1578
WAUGH, RICHARD	1840	PLAINTIFF	1585	WAYT, H	1871	MARH'L MAP	1746
WAUGH, RICHARD / HEIRS - (UPPERMILL) - MAP#219	1852	BRKE MAP	1843	WAYT, J	1871	OH CO. MAP	1740
				WAYT, J	1871	MARH'L MAP	1756
WAUGH, RICHARD / HEIRS - (UPPERMILL) - MAP#254	1852	BRKE MAP	1843	WAYT, J B	1871	MARH'L MAP	1756
				WAYT, J E JR	1871	BKE/OH MAP	1739
WAUGH, RICHARD / HEIRS - (UPPERMILL) - MAP#260	1852	BRKE MAP	1843	WAYT, JAMES	1840	PLAINTIFF	1578
				WAYT, JAMES	1853	MISC	1691
WAUGH, RICHARD / HEIRS - (UPPERMILL) - MAP#261	1852	BRKE MAP	1843	WAYT, JAMES	1857	PLAINTIFF	1578
				WAYT, JAMES	1858	DEFENDANT	1552
WAUGH, RICHARD / HEIRS - (UPPERMILL) - MAP#262	1852	BRKE MAP	1843	WAYT, JAMES	1858	DEFENDANT	1621
				WAYT, JAMES	1860	DEFENDANT	1552
WAUGH, RICHARD / HEIRS - MAP#146	1852	BRKE MAP	1843	WAYT, JAMES	1860	PLAINTIFF	1578
WAUGH, RICHARD / HEIRS - MAP#177	1852	BRKE MAP	1843	WAYT, JAMES	1862	PLAINTIFF	1578
WAUGH, RICHARD / HEIRS - MAP#178	1852	BRKE MAP	1843	WAYT, JAMES	1879	DEFENDANT	1554

'PERSONAL TIME LINE' INDEX TO VOLUME 7 OF THE *OHIO COUNTY INDEX*

ENTRY	YEAR	SUBJECT	PAGE	ENTRY	YEAR	SUBJECT	PAGE
WAYT, JAMES	1879	DEFENDANT	1578	WEBB, WILLIAM	1846	PLAINTIFF	1595
WAYT, JOHN	1800	PLAINTIFF	1578	WEBB, WILLIAM T E	1841	PLAINTIFF	1595
WAYT, JOHN	1811	PLAINTIFF	1578	WEBER KENDALL & CO	1840	PLAINTIFF	1626
WAYT, JOHN	1811	PLAINTIFF	1578	WEBER, C A	1880	MISC	1690
WAYT, JOHN	1811	PLAINTIFF	1578	WEBER, CHRISTIAN	1860	PLAINTIFF	1588
WAYT, JOHN	1821	PLAINTIFF	1578	WEBER, E A	1856	PLAINTIFF	1588
WAYT, JOHN	1822	PLAINTIFF	1578	WEBER, E A	1880	MISC	1690
WAYT, JOHN	1824	MISC	1691	WEBER, FRANK A	1873	MISC	1690
WAYT, JOHN	1827	MISC	1691	WEBER, FRANK S	1873	MISC	1690
WAYT, JOHN	1829	MISC	1691	WEBER, JOHN	1840	PLAINTIFF	1587
WAYT, JOHN	1829	MISC	1691	WEBER, M O	1880	MISC	1690
WAYT, JOHN	1830	DEFENDANT	1578	WEBER, W H	1880	MISC	1690
WAYT, JOHN	1855	DEFENDANT	1559	WEBSTER TWP - MARSHALL CO	1871	POPULATION	1816
WAYT, JOHN E	1878	DEFENDANT	1631	WEBSTER TWP - MARSHALL CO.	1871	MARH'L MAP	1750
WAYT, JOHN E	1879	DEFENDANT	1573	WEBSTER TWP - OHIO CO	1871	WHG CITY	1790
WAYT, JOHN E	1879	DEFENDANT	1661	WEBSTER TWP - WHEELING	1871	OH CO. MAP	1742
WAYT, JOSEPH	1829	MISC	1691	WEBSTER, -	1815	PLAINTIFF	1620
WAYT, L	1856	PLAINTIFF	1626	WEBSTER, BROWN & CO / 'MOUND CITY FLOUR MILL'	1871	MDSVL BUS.	1796
WAYT, MARTHA	1876	PLAINTIFF	1578	WEBSTER, BROWN & CO / FLOUR MILL	1871	MDSVILLE	1808
WAYT, MARY	1834	MISC	1691				
WAYT, NATHANIEL	1827	PLAINTIFF	1578	WEBSTER, BROWN & CO	1871	MDSVILLE	1810
WAYT, NATHANIEL	1830	PLAINTIFF	1578	WEBSTER, GEORGE	1852	PLAINTIFF	1588
WAYT, NATHANIEL	1830	PLAINTIFF	1578	WEBSTER, GEORGE F	1859	PLAINTIFF	1588
WAYT, NATHANIEL	1834	PLAINTIFF	1578	WEBSTER, JOHN	1809	PLAINTIFF	1587
WAYT, NATHANIEL	1849	MISC	1691	WEBSTER, JOHN PORTER	1791	PLAINTIFF	1587
WAYT, NATHANIEL	1854	MISC	1691	WEBSTER, JOHN PORTER	1796	PLAINTIFF	1587
WAYT, ROBERT B	1879	PLAINTIFF	1578	WEBSTER, JOHN PORTOR	1792	PLAINTIFF	1587
WAYT, S	1871	MARH'L MAP	1756	WEBSTER, JOSHUA E	1835	PLAINTIFF	1587
WAYTS - HEIRS	1820	PLAINTIFF	1578	WEBSTER, SAMUEL	1844	PLAINTIFF	1587
WAYTS EXECTORS	1820	DEFENDANT	1578	WEDDLE, HENRY	1828	PLAINTIFF	1587
WAYTS, ELIZABETH	1818	DEFENDANT	1556	WEDDLE, HENRY	1829	PLAINTIFF	1587
WAYTS, JAMES	1842	PLAINTIFF	1578	WEDDLE, HENRY	1830	PLAINTIFF	1587
WAYTS, JOHN	1818	MISC	1691	WEDICK, SAMUEL	1821	PLAINTIFF	1587
WEAD, JACOB	1855	PLAINTIFF	1588	WEDLE, HENRY	1829	PLAINTIFF	1587
WEAKLY, THOMAS	1810	PLAINTIFF	1587	WEED SEWING MACHINE CO	1873	PLAINTIFF	1627
WEAKS, CORNELIUS	1823	PLAINTIFF	1587	WEED SEWING MACHINE CO	1874	PLAINTIFF	1627
WEALER, JOHN C	1856	PLAINTIFF	1588	WEED, H R	1873	MISC	1690
WEAR, THOMAS	1804	PLAINTIFF	1587	WEED, HENRY R	1871	MISC	1690
WEASNER, THOMAS	1836	MISC	1702	WEED, M	1871	MARH'L MAP	1747
WEASNER, THOMAS H	1836	MISC	1689	WEEDMAN, F	1871	MARH'L MAP	1753
WEATHERLY, J / FLEET ST	1871	WELLSBURG	1776	WEEK, WILLIAM	1793	DEFENDANT	1589
WEAVER & GRAHAM	1858	PLAINTIFF	1626	WEEKLY, THOMAS	1811	PLAINTIFF	1587
WEAVER, EMMOR	1858	PLAINTIFF	1581	WEEKS, CORNELIUS	1822	PLAINTIFF	1587
WEAVER, HANSE	1835	PLAINTIFF	1581	WEEKS, JANE	1798	MISC	1689
WEAVER, HENRY	1813	PLAINTIFF	1581	WEEKS, WILLIAM	1794	PLAINTIFF	1587
WEAVER, HENRY	1815	PLAINTIFF	1581	WEEKS, WILLIAM	1796	PLAINTIFF	1587
WEAVER, HENRY	1821	PLAINTIFF	1581	WEEMS, HENRY	1818	PLAINTIFF	1587
WEAVER, HENRY	1821	PLAINTIFF	1581	WEEMS, HENRY	1821	PLAINTIFF	1587
WEAVER, HENRY	1822	PLAINTIFF	1581	WEEMS, HENRY	1822	PLAINTIFF	1587
WEAVER, HENRY	1822	PLAINTIFF	1581	WEEMS, HENRY	1823	PLAINTIFF	1591
WEAVER, HENRY	1823	DEFENDANT	1628	WEEMS, HENRY	1828	PLAINTIFF	1587
WEAVER, HENRY	1824	PLAINTIFF	1581	WEHLER, WILHELM	1857	PLAINTIFF	1588
WEAVER, HENRY	1827	PLAINTIFF	1581	WEHNER, GEORGE JR	1871	MISC	1690
WEAVER, HENRY	1828	PLAINTIFF	1581	WEHNER, JOHN	1871	MISC	1690
WEAVER, HENRY	1829	PLAINTIFF	1581	WEHNER, JOHN MICHAEL	1853	PLAINTIFF	1588
WEAVER, HENRY	1829	PLAINTIFF	1581	WEHNER, M	1860	MISC	1690
WEAVER, HENRY	1830	PLAINTIFF	1581	WEHNER, MARGARET	1871	MISC	1690
WEAVER, JACOB	1822	PLAINTIFF	1581	WEHNER, MICHAEL	1859	MISC	1690
WEAVER, JACOB	1823	PLAINTIFF	1581	WEIDEBUSH, AUGUST	1855	PLAINTIFF	1588
WEAVER, JACOB	1825	PLAINTIFF	1581	WEIDEBUSH, AUGUST	1858	PLAINTIFF	1588
WEAVER, JACOB	1848	PLAINTIFF	1581	WEIDEBUSH, AUGUST	1859	PLAINTIFF	1588
WEAVER, JACOB	1853	PLAINTIFF	1581	WEIDEBUSH, AUGUST	1860	PLAINTIFF	1588
WEAVER, JACOB JR	1853	PLAINTIFF	1581	WEIDEBUSH, AUGUST	1879	PLAINTIFF	1588
WEAVER, JACOB JR	1853	PLAINTIFF	1581	WEIDEBUSH, JOHN	1858	PLAINTIFF	1588
WEAVER, JOHN	1821	PLAINTIFF	1581	WEIDEBUSH, WILLIAM	1859	PLAINTIFF	1588
WEAVER, JOHN W	1839	PLAINTIFF	1563	WEIDEMAN, E / MRS	1871	BKE/OH MAP	1739
WEAVER, JOHN W	1839	PLAINTIFF	1581	WEIDEMAN, E / MRS - INITIALS E.W. (?MRS?)	1871	BKE/OH MAP	1739
WEAVER, T	1871	BRKE MAP	1734				
WEB, -	1812	MISC	1689	WEIDEMAN, E / MRS - INITIALS E.W. (?MRS?)	1871	BKE/OH MAP	1739
WEBB, JOHN A	1838	PLAINTIFF	1595	WEIDEMAN, E / MRS - INITIALS MRS. E.W.	1871	BKE/OH MAP	1739
WEBB, JOSEPH	1877	PLAINTIFF	1595				
WEBB, JOSEPH	1878	PLAINTIFF	1595	WEIDMAN, J G	1859	PLAINTIFF	1588
WEBB, WILLIAM	1811	PLAINTIFF	1595	WEIGETT, FREDERICK	1857	PLAINTIFF	1588
WEBB, WILLIAM	1812	PLAINTIFF	1595	WEIKEL, GEORGE W	1861	PLAINTIFF	1588
WEBB, WILLIAM	1813	MISC	1689	WEIL, THEODORE & CO	1873	PLAINTIFF	1627
WEBB, WILLIAM	1814	PLAINTIFF	1595	WEIL, THERESA	1855	PLAINTIFF	1588
WEBB, WILLIAM	1815	PLAINTIFF	1595	WEILLER & ELLIS	1858	PLAINTIFF	1626
WEBB, WILLIAM	1816	PLAINTIFF	1595	WEILLER & ELLIS	1861	PLAINTIFF	1626
WEBB, WILLIAM	1818	PLAINTIFF	1595	WEILLER & ELLIS	1861	PLAINTIFF	1627
WEBB, WILLIAM	1829	PLAINTIFF	1595	WEILLER KLINE & ELLIS	1857	PLAINTIFF	1626
WEBB, WILLIAM	1836	MISC	1678	WEILLER, HERMANN	1857	PLAINTIFF	1588
WEBB, WILLIAM	1837	PLAINTIFF	1595	WEILLER, HERMANN	1858	PLAINTIFF	1588
WEBB, WILLIAM	1837	MISC	1682	WEING, F / MRS	1871	MARH'L MAP	1746
WEBB, WILLIAM	1841	PLAINTIFF	1595	WEINS, HENRY	1826	PLAINTIFF	1587
WEBB, WILLIAM	1843	DEFENDANT	1652				

'PERSONAL TIME LINE' INDEX TO VOLUME 7 OF THE *OHIO COUNTY INDEX*

ENTRY	YEAR	SUBJECT	PAGE
WEIR, JOHN	1822	PLAINTIFF	1587
WEIR, JOHN	1827	PLAINTIFF	1587
WEIR, THOMAS	1805	PLAINTIFF	1587
WEIRIG, PETER	1857	PLAINTIFF	1588
WEISCABBER, JOHN	1855	PLAINTIFF	1588
WEISGARBER, JOHN	1871	MISC	1690
WEISGARD & SHARP	1853	PLAINTIFF	1626
WEISGARD, DANIEL	1853	PLAINTIFF	1588
WEISGERBER & HOOK	1854	PLAINTIFF	1626
WEISGERBER, HENRY	1859	MISC	1690
WEISGERBER, JOHN	1857	PLAINTIFF	1588
WEISKE, HERMAN	1874	MISC	1690
WEISS, CATHARINE	1875	DEFENDANT	1616
WEISS, CATHERINE	1880	MISC	1690
WEISS, J / (?JOHN?)	1871	TRIAD.BORO.	1784
WEISS, JOHN	1871	OH CO.BUS.	1779
WEISS, JOHN	1871	TRIAD.BORO.	1784
WEISS, JOHN	1871	TRIAD.BORO.	1784
WEISS, WILLIAM W	1880	MISC	1690
WEISTER, GEORGE	1879	PLAINTIFF	1588
WEITZEL, CHARLES	1878	MISC	1690
WEITZEL, WILLIAM	1879	MISC	1690
WEIZELL, WILLIAM	1839	PLAINTIFF	1587
WELCH, JAMES	1788	PLAINTIFF	1589
WELCH, JAMES	1790	PLAINTIFF	1589
WELCH, JAMES	1794	DEFENDANT	1587
WELCH, JAMES	1796	PLAINTIFF	1589
WELCH, JAMES	1798	PLAINTIFF	1589
WELCH, JAMES	1833	PLAINTIFF	1589
WELCH, JOHN	1859	PLAINTIFF	1590
WELCH, MARGARET	1798	MISC	1693
WELCH, PHILIP	1837	MISC	1694
WELCH, WILLIAM	1789	MISC	1693
WELCH, WILLIAM	1792	PLAINTIFF	1589
WELCH, WILLIAM	1824	MISC	1693
WELCHONS, JOSEPH	1838	PLAINTIFF	1589
WELD, Z A	1841	PLAINTIFF	1589
WELEHHANS, JOSEPH	1842	MISC	1694
WELKINS, TIMOTHY	1799	DEFENDANT	1665
WELL - BURNING WELL / AT DEEP GUT RUN	1871	RIV. RD N.OF N.C.	1770
WELL, N	1871	BRKE MAP	1734
WELLER, J / PAN-HANDLE P.O.	1871	BRKE MAP	1734
WELLER, PETER	1806	PLAINTIFF	1589
WELLER, PETER	1807	PLAINTIFF	1589
WELLER, PETER	1809	PLAINTIFF	1589
WELLER, PETER	1810	PLAINTIFF	1589
WELLER, PETER	1819	PLAINTIFF	1589
WELLER, PETER	1820	PLAINTIFF	1589
WELLER, PETER	1824	PLAINTIFF	1589
WELLER, THOMAS	1778	MISC	1688
WELLIINGTON	1871	OH CO. MAP	1742
WELLING, LEVI	1833	MISC	1694
WELLINGTON	1871	OH CO. MAP	1744
WELLMAN, A	1871	MARH'L MAP	1753
WELLMAN, J	1871	MARH'L MAP	1755
WELLMAN, S	1871	MARH'L MAP	1753
WELLS - NEGRO WOMAN OF	1790	MISC	1701
WELLS & ROSS	1806	PLAINTIFF	1626
WELLS BOTTOM	1871	MARH'L MAP	1758
WELLS RUN	1852	BRKE MAP	1844
WELLS RUN - OHIO	1852	BRKE MAP	1851
WELLS SCHOOL	1871	BRKE MAP	1736
WELLS, - / MRS	1861	PLAINTIFF	1646
WELLS, - / MRS	1862	PLAINTIFF	1646
WELLS, -	1871	MARH'L MAP	1752
WELLS, A W	1871	BRKE MAP	1736
WELLS, A W	1871	BRKE MAP	1736
WELLS, ABSALOM	1807	PLAINTIFF	1644
WELLS, ABSALAM	1792	PLAINTIFF	1644
WELLS, ABSOLOM	1788	PLAINTIFF	1644
WELLS, ABSOLOM	1789	PLAINTIFF	1644
WELLS, ABSOLOM	1790	PLAINTIFF	1644
WELLS, ABSOLOM	1806	PLAINTIFF	1644
WELLS, ALEXANDER	1787	PLAINTIFF	1644
WELLS, ALEXANDER	1788	PLAINTIFF	1644
WELLS, ALEXANDER	1791	PLAINTIFF	1644
WELLS, ALEXANDER	1796	PLAINTIFF	1644
WELLS, ALEXANDER JR	1796	DEFENDANT	1644
WELLS, AMOS	1790	PLAINTIFF	1644
WELLS, B JR	1871	BRKE MAP	1736
WELLS, B JR / COAL	1871	BRKE MAP	1736
WELLS, B P	1878	PLAINTIFF	1646
WELLS, B SR	1871	BRKE MAP	1736
WELLS, B SR / INITIALS B.W. SR	1871	BRKE MAP	1736
WELLS, B T	1871	BRKE MAP	1736
WELLS, BAZALEEL	1813	PLAINTIFF	1645
WELLS, BAZALEEL	1815	PLAINTIFF	1645
WELLS, BAZALEEL	1822	PLAINTIFF	1646
WELLS, BAZEL / (GONE) - MAP#202	1852	BRKE MAP	1842
WELLS, BAZEL / (GONE) - MAP#211	1852	BRKE MAP	1842
WELLS, BAZEL / (GONE) - MAP#212	1852	BRKE MAP	1842
WELLS, BAZEL / (GONE) - MAP#214	1852	BRKE MAP	1842
WELLS, BAZEL / (GONE) - MAP#276	1852	BRKE MAP	1842
WELLS, BAZEL / MAP#169	1852	BRKE MAP	1842
WELLS, BAZEL / MAP#201	1852	BRKE MAP	1842
WELLS, BAZEL / MAP#197	1852	BRKE MAP	1843
WELLS, BAZELEEL	1816	PLAINTIFF	1645
WELLS, BAZELEEL	1818	PLAINTIFF	1646
WELLS, BAZELUL	1817	PLAINTIFF	1645
WELLS, BAZELUL	1817	PLAINTIFF	1646
WELLS, BAZIEL	1792	MISC	1701
WELLS, BENJ	1809	PLAINTIFF	1645
WELLS, BENJAMIN	1795	MISC	1701
WELLS, BENJAMIN	1798	MISC	1701
WELLS, BENJAMIN	1799	MISC	1701
WELLS, BENJAMIN / & SON	1800	PLAINTIFF	1626
WELLS, BENJAMIN	1806	PLAINTIFF	1644
WELLS, BENJAMIN / & SON	1807	PLAINTIFF	1626
WELLS, BENJAMIN	1807	PLAINTIFF	1644
WELLS, BENJAMIN	1807	PLAINTIFF	1645
WELLS, BENJAMIN	1808	PLAINTIFF	1645
WELLS, BENJAMIN / & SON	1809	PLAINTIFF	1626
WELLS, BENJAMIN	1809	PLAINTIFF	1645
WELLS, BENJAMIN / & SON	1810	PLAINTIFF	1626
WELLS, BENJAMIN	1810	PLAINTIFF	1645
WELLS, BENJAMIN / & SON	1811	PLAINTIFF	1626
WELLS, BENJAMIN	1811	PLAINTIFF	1645
WELLS, BENJAMIN / & SON	1812	PLAINTIFF	1626
WELLS, BENJAMIN	1813	PLAINTIFF	1645
WELLS, BENJAMIN	1814	PLAINTIFF	1645
WELLS, BENJAMIN	1816	PLAINTIFF	1645
WELLS, BENJAMIN	1820	PLAINTIFF	1646
WELLS, BEZALEEL	1816	PLAINTIFF	1645
WELLS, BEZALUL	1818	PLAINTIFF	1646
WELLS, BEZULUL	1816	PLAINTIFF	1645
WELLS, C C	1871	MARH'L MAP	1758
WELLS, C C	1871	MARH'L MAP	1758
WELLS, C C / INITIALS C.C.W	1871	MARH'L MAP	1758
WELLS, C P	1871	MARH'L MAP	1758
WELLS, CALAB	1798	PLAINTIFF	1644
WELLS, CALEB	1796	PLAINTIFF	1644
WELLS, CHARLES	1779	MISC	1701
WELLS, CHARLES	1779	MISC	1701
WELLS, CHARLES	1784	DEFENDANT	1556
WELLS, CHARLES	1787	DEFENDANT	1556
WELLS, CHARLES	1787	PLAINTIFF	1644
WELLS, CHARLES	1788	MISC	1701
WELLS, CHARLES	1788	MISC	1701
WELLS, CHARLES	1789	MISC	1701
WELLS, CHARLES	1792	MISC	1701
WELLS, CHARLES	1793	MISC	1701
WELLS, CHARLES	1793	MISC	1701
WELLS, CHARLES	1798	MISC	1701
WELLS, CHARLES	1803	PLAINTIFF	1644
WELLS, CHARLES	1814	DEFENDANT	1569
WELLS, CHARLES	1821	PLAINTIFF	1646
WELLS, CHARLES	1827	PLAINTIFF	1646
WELLS, CHARLES C / RES	1871	MARH'L MAP	1754
WELLS, CHARLES C / RES	1871	MARH'L MAP	1758
WELLS, CHARLES E	1878	DEFENDANT	1646
WELLS, CHAS E	1878	DEFENDANT	1646
WELLS, CLARK	1876	MISC	1701
WELLS, E	1871	BRKE MAP	1736
WELLS, E / LIBERTY HALL	1871	BRKE MAP	1736
WELLS, E	1871	MARH'L MAP	1752
WELLS, E O	1871	MARH'L MAP	1758
WELLS, ELI	1822	PLAINTIFF	1646
WELLS, ENOCH	1784	MISC	1701
WELLS, G / NEAR OHIO RIVER	1871	HAN MAP	1726
WELLS, GREYBEARD / HEIRS - MAP#531	1852	BRKE MAP	1852
WELLS, GREYBEARD / HEIRS - MAP#532	1852	BRKE MAP	1852
WELLS, GREYBEARD / HEIRS - MAP#567	1852	BRKE MAP	1852
WELLS, GREYBEARD / HEIRS - MAP#568	1852	BRKE MAP	1852
WELLS, GREYBEARD / HEIRS - MAP#569	1852	BRKE MAP	1852
WELLS, J	1871	CAMERON	1803
WELLS, JESSE	1871	BKE/OH MAP	1738

'PERSONAL TIME LINE' INDEX TO VOLUME 7 OF THE *OHIO COUNTY INDEX*

ENTRY	YEAR	SUBJECT	PAGE	ENTRY	YEAR	SUBJECT	PAGE
WELLS, JESSE / INITIALS J.W.	1871	BKE/OH MAP	1738	WELLS, WILLIAM	1811	DEFENDANT	1587
WELLS, JESSE / INITIALS J.W.	1871	BKE/OH MAP	1738	WELLS, WILLIAM	1825	PLAINTIFF	1646
WELLS, JESSE	1876	MISC	1701	WELLS, WILLIAM	1840	DEFENDANT	1577
WELLS, JESSE	1876	MISC	1701	WELLS, WILLIAM	1840	DEFENDANT	1617
WELLS, JESSE	1878	MISC	1701	WELLS, WILLIAM	1840	DEFENDANT	1652
WELLS, JESSE SR	1872	MISC	1701	WELLS, WILLIAM	1841	DEFENDANT	1670
WELLS, JESSEE	1835	PLAINTIFF	1646	WELLS, WILLIAM	1871	BRKE MAP	1734
WELLS, JOHN	1790	PLAINTIFF	1644	WELLS, WILLIAM	1879	MISC	1701
WELLS, JOHN	1812	PLAINTIFF	1645	WELLS, ZENAS	1839	PLAINTIFF	1646
WELLS, JOHN	1813	PLAINTIFF	1645	WELLSBURG	1852	BRKE MAP	1846
WELLS, JOHN	1816	PLAINTIFF	1645	WELLSBURG	1871	DISTANCES	1815
WELLS, JOHN	1817	PLAINTIFF	1646	WELLSBURG	1916	NAT'L ROAD	1862
WELLS, JOHN	1822	PLAINTIFF	1646	WELLSBURG - BETHANY PIKE	1871	WELLSBURG	1778
WELLS, JOHN / S. BORDER OF BROOKE CO.	1871	BKE/OH MAP	1738	WELLSBURG - BREWERY	1871	WELLSBURG	1778
				WELLSBURG - BREWERY - HEBRUCKLE, A	1871	WELLSBURG	1778
WELLS, JOHN J	1842	PLAINTIFF	1646	WELLSBURG - BROOKE CO - BUSINESS NOTICES	1871	WELLSBURG	1772
WELLS, JOHN S	1841	PLAINTIFF	1646				
WELLS, JONATHAN	1799	DEFENDANT	1665	WELLSBURG - CARPENTER SHOP	1871	WELLSBURG	1777
WELLS, JOSEPH	1778	PLAINTIFF	1644	WELLSBURG - CARPENTER SHOP	1871	WELLSBURG	1777
WELLS, JOSEPH	1779	MISC	1701	WELLSBURG - CHARLES ST	1871	WLSBRG BUS.	1772
WELLS, JOSEPH	1824	MISC	1701	WELLSBURG - CHARLES ST	1871	WLSBRG BUS.	1772
WELLS, LEVI	1845	PLAINTIFF	1646	WELLSBURG - CHARLES ST	1871	WLSBRG BUS.	1772
WELLS, LEVI	1852	PLAINTIFF	1646	WELLSBURG - CHARLES ST	1871	WLSBRG BUS.	1772
WELLS, M	1871	WELLSBURG	1777	WELLSBURG - CHARLES ST	1871	WLSBRG BUS.	1772
WELLS, MARY	1811	PLAINTIFF	1645	WELLSBURG - CHARLES ST	1871	WELLSBURG	1777
WELLS, MARY	1812	PLAINTIFF	1645	WELLSBURG - CHARLES ST	1871	WELLSBURG	1778
WELLS, MARY W	1879	MISC	1701	WELLSBURG - COMMERCE ST	1871	WELLSBURG	1777
WELLS, MILTON / SUPT OF SCHOOLS	1871	WLSBRG BUS.	1772	WELLSBURG - COMMERCE ST	1871	WELLSBURG	1778
WELLS, N	1871	BRKE MAP	1734	WELLSBURG - DENTIST - C.BRASHEAR	1871	WELLSBURG	1778
WELLS, N	1871	BRKE MAP	1734				
WELLS, N	1871	BRKE MAP	1734	WELLSBURG - DETAIL MAP	1871	WELLSBURG	1776
WELLS, N	1871	BRKE MAP	1734	WELLSBURG - EAST ST	1871	WELLSBURG	1777
WELLS, NATHANIEL	1852	NOT ON MAP	1836	WELLSBURG - EAST ST	1871	WELLSBURG	1778
WELLS, NATHANIEL / (WAREHOUSE)	1852	NOT ON MAP	1836	WELLSBURG - ENG. HO. / (?FIRE ENGINE HOUSE?)	1871	WELLSBURG	1777
WELLS, NATHANIEL / (FERRY & TAV) - MAP#552	1852	BRKE MAP	1851	WELLSBURG - FEDERAL ST	1871	WELLSBURG	1778
WELLS, NATHANIEL / (FERRY & TAV) - MAP#592	1852	BRKE MAP	1851	WELLSBURG - FERRY LANDING - OHIO RIVER	1871	WELLSBURG	1777
WELLS, NATHANIEL / (FERRY & TAV) - MAP#593	1852	BRKE MAP	1851	WELLSBURG - FIRE DEPT / ? ENG.HO. - LIBERTY ST	1871	WELLSBURG	1777
WELLS, NATHANIEL / (FERRY & TAV) - MAP#594	1852	BRKE MAP	1851	WELLSBURG - FIRE HOUSE / WATER & LIBERTY ?	1871	WELLSBURG	1777
WELLS, NATHANIEL / (FERRY & TAV) - MAP#595	1852	BRKE MAP	1851	WELLSBURG - FLEET ST	1871	WLSBRG BUS.	1772
				WELLSBURG - FLEET ST	1871	WELLSBURG	1776
WELLS, NATHANIEL / (SMITHSHOP) - MAP#551	1852	BRKE MAP	1851	WELLSBURG - FLEET ST	1871	WELLSBURG	1777
WELLS, NATHANIEL / MAP#550	1852	BRKE MAP	1851	WELLSBURG - FURNITURE STORE	1871	WELLSBURG	1777
WELLS, NATHANIEL / NEAR OHIO RIVER	1871	BRKE MAP	1734	WELLSBURG - FURNITURE STORE / WATER ST	1871	WELLSBURG	1777
WELLS, NATHANIEL / RES - NEAR OHIO RIVER	1871	BRKE MAP	1734	WELLSBURG - GREEN ST	1871	WELLSBURG	1778
				WELLSBURG - GROCERY - OHIO ST	1871	WELLSBURG	1777
WELLS, NICHOLAS	1821	PLAINTIFF	1646	WELLSBURG - GROCERY - WATER ST	1871	WELLSBURG	1777
WELLS, R M	1871	BKE/OH MAP	1738				
WELLS, R M / INITIAS R.M.W	1871	BKE/OH MAP	1738	WELLSBURG - HIGH ST	1871	WELLSBURG	1777
WELLS, R M / INITIAS R.M.W	1871	BKE/OH MAP	1738	WELLSBURG - HIGH ST	1871	WELLSBURG	1778
WELLS, R N	1871	MARH'L MAP	1758	WELLSBURG - JAIL / LIBERTY ST	1871	WELLSBURG	1777
WELLS, R N	1871	MARH'L MAP	1758	WELLSBURG - LIBERTY ST	1871	WLSBRG BUS.	1772
WELLS, R N / INITIALS R.N.W.	1871	MARH'L MAP	1758	WELLSBURG - LIBERTY ST	1871	WLSBRG BUS.	1772
WELLS, R N / INITIALS R.N.W.	1871	MARH'L MAP	1758	WELLSBURG - LIBERTY ST	1871	WELLSBURG	1777
WELLS, R N / INITIALS R.N.W.	1871	MARH'L MAP	1758	WELLSBURG - MARKET HO. / HOUSE ?	1871	WELLSBURG	1777
WELLS, R N / INITIALS R.N.W.	1871	MARH'L MAP	1758				
WELLS, RICHARD	1789	MISC	1701	WELLSBURG - OHIO ST	1871	WELLSBURG	1778
WELLS, RICHARD	1790	MISC	1701	WELLSBURG - POST OFFICE	1871	WELLSBURG	1777
WELLS, RICHARD	1794	MISC	1701	WELLSBURG - PROSPECT ST	1871	WELLSBURG	1777
WELLS, RICHARD / FARM SETTLED BY RICHARD WELLS, KNOWN AS GRAY BEARD IN 1772	1871	BRKE MAP	1734	WELLSBURG - QUEEN ST	1871	WELLSBURG	1777
				WELLSBURG - STEAMBOAT LANDING	1871	WELLSBURG	1778
				WELLSBURG - UNION ST	1871	WELLSBURG	1778
WELLS, RICHARD / FORT BUILT BY R.W. FOR PROTECTION FROM INDIANS (?BAMILY MT.?) OR (?FAMILY VLT - VALUT?)	1871	BRKE MAP	1734	WELLSBURG - URANA ST	1871	WELLSBURG	1777
				WELLSBURG - WALNUT ST	1871	WELLSBURG	1777
				WELLSBURG - WASHINGTON PIKE	1871	WELLSBURG	1777
				WELLSBURG - WASHINGTON ST	1871	WELLSBURG	1778
WELLS, ROBERT M / MAP#277	1852	BRKE MAP	1842	WELLSBURG - WATER ST	1871	WLSBRG BUS.	1772
WELLS, ROSS	1804	PLAINTIFF	1644	WELLSBURG - WATER ST	1871	WLSBRG BUS.	1772
WELLS, SAMUEL	1808	PLAINTIFF	1645	WELLSBURG - WATER ST	1871	WLSBRG BUS.	1772
WELLS, SAMUEL	1814	MISC	1701	WELLSBURG - WATER ST	1871	WLSBRG BUS.	1772
WELLS, SAMUEL H	1825	DEFENDANT	1612	WELLSBURG - WATER ST	1871	WLSBRG BUS.	1772
WELLS, T	1871	BKE/OH MAP	1738	WELLSBURG - WATER ST	1871	WLSBRG BUS.	1772
WELLS, TEMPERANCE	1796	MISC	1701	WELLSBURG - WATER ST	1871	WLSBRG BUS.	1772
WELLS, THOMAS	1795	PLAINTIFF	1644	WELLSBURG - WATER ST	1871	WLSBRG BUS.	1772
WELLS, THOMAS	1804	PLAINTIFF	1644	WELLSBURG - WATER ST	1871	WLSBRG BUS.	1772
WELLS, WASHINGTON	1834	PLAINTIFF	1646	WELLSBURG - WATER ST	1871	WLSBRG BUS.	1772
WELLS, WILLIAM	1797	MISC	1701	WELLSBURG - WATER ST	1871	WELLSBURG	1777
WELLS, WILLIAM	1805	PLAINTIFF	1644	WELLSBURG - WATER ST	1871	WELLSBURG	1778
WELLS, WILLIAM	1809	PLAINTIFF	1645	WELLSBURG - WATER ST	1871	WELLSBURG	1778
WELLS, WILLIAM	1810	DEFENDANT	1559	WELLSBURG - YANKEE ST	1871	WLSBRG BUS.	1772
WELLS, WILLIAM	1810	DEFENDANT	1656	WELLSBURG - YANKEE ST	1871	WELLSBURG	1777

'PERSONAL TIME LINE' INDEX TO VOLUME 7 OF THE OHIO COUNTY INDEX

ENTRY	YEAR	SUBJECT	PAGE
WELLSBURG - YANKEE ST	1871	WELLSBURG	1778
WELLSBURG & BETHANY TURNPIKE	1852	BRKE MAP	1843
WELLSBURG & BETHANY TURNPIKE / CUT OFF LEFT OF MAP	1852	BRKE MAP	1846
WELLSBURG & WASHINGTON TURNPIKE	1852	BRKE MAP	1846
WELLSBURG & WASHINGTON TURNPIKE	1852	BRKE MAP	1847
WELLSBURG & WASHINGTON TURNPIKE	1871	BRKE MAP	1737
WELLSBURG AND WASHINGTON TURNPIKE	1871	BRKE MAP	1736
WELLSBURG FREE SCHOOL / QUEEN ST	1871	WELLSBURG	1777
WELLSBURG MANUFACTURING CO.	1871	WELLSBURG	1777
WELLSBURG NAT. BANK / WATER & URANA STS.	1871	WELLSBURG	1777
WELLSBURG P.O.	1871	BRKE MAP	1736
WELLSBURG TOWNSHIP - BROOKE CO	1871	POPULATION	1816
WELLSVILLE	1852	HEMPFIELD RR	1820
WELLSVILLE	1871	HAN MAP	1726
WELLSVILLE AND FLORENCE ROAD	1871	HAN MAP	1731
WELLSVILLE, OH	1852	HEMP. RR MAP	1826
WELLSVILLE, OH / ATTORNEY	1871	NEW MANCH.	1763
WELLSVILLE, OH / HOTEL - WHITACRE HOUSE	1871	NEW MANCH.	1763
WELMAN, JOHN	1784	PLAINTIFF	1589
WELMAN, JOHN	1786	MISC	1693
WELSH, -	1792	PLAINTIFF	1589
WELSH, -	1793	PLAINTIFF	1589
WELSH, JAMES	1793	PLAINTIFF	1589
WELSH, JOHN	1879	MISC	1694
WELSH, MICHAEL	1852	PLAINTIFF	1590
WELSH, MICHAEL	1853	PLAINTIFF	1590
WELSH, PHILIP	1852	PLAINTIFF	1590
WELSH, SARAH / (GONE) - MAP#614	1852	BRKE MAP	1852
WELSH, SARAH / (GONE) - MAP#620	1852	BRKE MAP	1852
WELSH, THOMAS	1859	PLAINTIFF	1590
WELSHANS, B G	1871	OH CO. MAP	1741
WELSHANS, O	1871	OH CO. MAP	1741
WELSHAUS, B G	1879	PLAINTIFF	1590
WELSHAUS, MATHILDA	1880	MISC	1694
WELSHHAN, J W	1871	OH CO. MAP	1741
WELSHHANS, JOSEPH	1839	MISC	1694
WELSHONS, DAVID	1821	MISC	1693
WELSHONS, HENRY	1849	PLAINTIFF	1590
WELTE, MARY ANN	1869	MISC	1694
WELTE, MARY CATHARINE	1869	MISC	1694
WELTEY, CHRISTIAN	1854	PLAINTIFF	1590
WELTY, C / & BRO	1873	PLAINTIFF	1627
WELTY, C	1874	PLAINTIFF	1590
WELTY, C / & BRO	1876	PLAINTIFF	1627
WELTY, C / & BROS	1876	PLAINTIFF	1627
WELTY, C / & BROTHER	1876	PLAINTIFF	1627
WELTY, C / & BROTHER	1876	PLAINTIFF	1627
WELTY, CHRISTIAN	1854	PLAINTIFF	1590
WELTY, CHRISTIAN	1870	MISC	1694
WELTY, JOHN	1879	MISC	1694
WELTY, M	1876	PLAINTIFF	1590
WELTY, MARY	1872	MISC	1694
WELTY, P	1877	PLAINTIFF	1590
WELTY, PETER / & BROTHERS	1880	PLAINTIFF	1627
WELTY, S	1877	PLAINTIFF	1590
WELTY, SABASTIAN	1880	DEFENDANT	1673
WENDEL, -	1879	MISC	1695
WENDEL, JACOB	1870	MISC	1695
WENDEL, PETER	1879	DEFENDANT	1557
WENDEL, PETER	1879	DEFENDANT	1564
WENDER, JAMES A	1833	MISC	1678
WENDER, JAMES A	1833	MISC	1695
WENDT, A	1871	MARH'L MAP	1757
WENDT, A	1871	MARH'L MAP	1757
WENDT, E	1871	MARH'L MAP	1757
WENT, ERNST	1858	PLAINTIFF	1592
WENZEL, GEORGE H	1875	PLAINTIFF	1592
WERDEBAUGH SMITH & CO	1857	PLAINTIFF	1626
WERDEBAUGH, HENRY J	1857	PLAINTIFF	1592
WERDEBAUGH, SAMUEL	1833	PLAINTIFF	1591
WERDER, A W	1872	MISC	1695
WERNER, JOSEPH	1875	PLAINTIFF	1592
WERNER, JOSEPH	1878	PLAINTIFF	1592
WERTMAN, PHEBE A	1846	PLAINTIFF	1592
WESBTER TWP - MARSHALL CO.	1871	MARH'L MAP	1752
WESCHLER BROTHERS	1873	PLAINTIFF	1627
WESHART, JOHN	1832	PLAINTIFF	1594

ENTRY	YEAR	SUBJECT	PAGE
WEST ALEXANDER	1916	NAT'L ROAD	1863
WEST ALEXANDER, PA - AMERICAN EAGLE TAVERN	1916	NAT'L ROAD	1862
WEST ALEXANDER, PA - HISTORY	1916	NAT'L ROAD	1862
WEST ALEXANDER, PA - LIST OF OLD TOWN NAMES	1916	NAT'L ROAD	1862
WEST ALEXANDER, PA - MAP	1916	NAT'L ROAD	1869
WEST ALEXANDER, PA. - LAFAYETTE TAVERN	1916	NAT'L ROAD	1862
WEST BRANCH OF LOWER BOWMAN RUN	1871	MARH'L MAP	1755
WEST LIBERTY	1852	BRKE MAP	1840
WEST LIBERTY	1871	DISTANCES	1815
WEST LIBERTY - BUSINESS NOTICES	1871	W.LIBRTY.BUS.	1780
WEST LIBERTY - CABINET SHOP	1871	W.LIBERTY	1780
WEST LIBERTY - CHATHAM ST	1871	W.LIBERTY	1780
WEST LIBERTY - DETAIL MAP	1871	W.LIBERTY	1780
WEST LIBERTY - DRUG STORE	1871	W.LIBERTY	1780
WEST LIBERTY - LIBERTY ST	1871	W.LIBERTY	1780
WEST LIBERTY - LITTLE STAR VILLAGE HOME	1871	W.LIBERTY	1780
WEST LIBERTY - MASONIC HALL	1871	W.LIBERTY	1780
WEST LIBERTY - MONTGOMERY ST	1871	W.LIBERTY	1780
WEST LIBERTY - POST OFFICE	1871	W.LIBERTY	1780
WEST LIBERTY - S.SH/ (?SHOE?)	1871	W.LIBERTY	1780
WEST LIBERTY - SPRING ST	1871	W.LIBERTY	1780
WEST LIBERTY - TANNERY	1871	W.LIBERTY	1780
WEST LIBERTY - VILLAGE HOME	1871	W.LIBERTY	1780
WEST LIBERTY - WALNUT ST	1871	W.LIBERTY	1780
WEST LIBERTY - WASHINGTON & WEST LIBERTY PIKE	1871	BKE/OH MAP	1739
WEST LIBERTY - WASHINGTON ST	1871	W.LIBERTY	1780
WEST LIBERTY - WATER TROUGH	1871	W.LIBERTY	1780
WEST LIBERTY ACADEMY	1859	DEFENDANT	1608
WEST LIBERTY ACADEMY	1860	DEFENDANT	1608
WEST LIBERTY ACADEMY TRUSTEES	1839	PLAINTIFF	1626
WEST LIBERTY NORMAL SCHOOL	1871	W.LIBERTY	1780
WEST LIBERTY P.O.	1871	BKE/OH MAP	1739
WEST LOUDENSVILLE	1871	MARH'L BUS.	1796
WEST NEWTON, PA	1852	HEMP. RR MAP	1826
WEST NEWTON, PA	1852	HEMP. RR MAP	1827
WEST UNION	1871	MARH'L MAP	1747
WEST UNION	1871	DISTANCES	1815
WEST UNION - ALEXANDER ST	1871	W.UNION	1812
WEST UNION - BUSINESS NOTICES	1871	MARH'L BUS.	1797
WEST UNION - CEMETERY - MAIN ST	1871	W.UNION	1812
WEST UNION - DETAIL MAP	1871	W.UNION	1812
WEST UNION - FURNACE ST	1871	W.UNION	1812
WEST UNION - MAIN ST	1871	W.UNION-BUS.	1797
WEST UNION - MAIN ST	1871	W.UNION	1812
WEST UNION - OLD ROAD / RONEY POINT & WEST UNION TURNPIKE	1871	OH CO. MAP	1743
WEST UNION - POST OFFICE	1871	ROSBBYS RK	1813
WEST UNION - RONEY POINT & WEST UNION TURNPIKE	1871	OH CO. MAP	1743
WEST UNION - SHOE SHOP - FURNACE ST	1871	W.UNION	1812
WEST UNION - STORE	1871	ROSBBYS RK	1813
WEST UNION - WASHINGTON ST	1871	W.UNION-BUS.	1797
WEST UNION - WASHINGTON ST	1871	W.UNION	1812
WEST UNION - WHEELING ST	1871	W.UNION-BUS.	1797
WEST UNION - WHEELING ST	1871	W.UNION	1812
WEST UNION TURNPIKE - FROM RONEY POINT	1871	RONEY PT.	1783
WEST VIRGINIA & REGIONAL HISTORY COLLECTION	2000	APPENDIX	1871
WEST VIRGINIA & REGIONAL HISTORY COLLECTION - CARD INDEX TO COURT PAPERS	2000	APPENDIX	1873
WEST VIRGINIA AND REGIONAL HISTORY COLLECTION AT WVU	2000	PREFACE	1748
WEST VIRGINIA PANHANDLE	1916	NAT'L ROAD	1861
WEST VIRGINIA PANHANDLE	1916	NAT'L ROAD	1862
WEST VIRGINIA STATE ARCHIVES	2000	APPENDIX	1872
WEST VIRGINIA STATEHOOD	1916	NAT'L ROAD	1863
WEST WASHINGTON, PA / FORMERLY RANKINVILLE	1916	NAT'L ROAD	1861
WEST, A	1871	WELLSBURG	1778
WEST, A H	1875	PLAINTIFF	1595
WEST, AMOS	1807	PLAINTIFF	1594
WEST, AMOS	1808	PLAINTIFF	1594
WEST, HENRY	1874	PLAINTIFF	1594
WEST, J	1871	TRIAD.BORO.	1784
WEST, J W	1878	PLAINTIFF	1595
WEST, JOHN	1827	MISC	1695

'PERSONAL TIME LINE' INDEX TO VOLUME 7 OF THE *OHIO COUNTY INDEX*

ENTRY	YEAR	SUBJECT	PAGE	ENTRY	YEAR	SUBJECT	PAGE
WEST, SAMUEL	1806	PLAINTIFF	1594	WHEAT, CONROD	1781	MISC	1697
WEST, WALTER	1854	MISC	1695	WHEAT, GEORGE K	1857	PLAINTIFF	1663
WESTBROOK, ELIZA	1854	MISC	1695	WHEAT, GEORGE K	1857	PLAINTIFF	1663
WESTBROOK, ELIZA	1868	MISC	1695	WHEAT, GEORGE K	1861	PLAINTIFF	1664
WESTBROOK, GEORGE	1854	MISC	1695	WHEAT, GEORGE K	1861	PLAINTIFF	1664
WESTCOTT, SAMUEL	1825	PLAINTIFF	1594	WHEAT, GEORGE K	1862	PLAINTIFF	1664
WESTCOTT, SAMUEL A	1833	MISC	1695	WHEAT, GEORGE K	1874	PLAINTIFF	1664
WESTERN RAILROADS	1852	HEMPFIELD RR	1817	WHEAT, GEORGE W	1866	MISC	1698
WESTERN RR	1852	HEMP. RR MAP	1826	WHEAT, H BRADLEY	1875	PLAINTIFF	1664
WESTERN RR	1852	HEMP. RR MAP	1827	WHEAT, H BRADLEY	1877	PLAINTIFF	1664
WESTMODE, J	1871	MARH'L MAP	1745	WHEAT, ISETT & NAYLOR	1876	PLAINTIFF	1631
WESTMORELAND CO, PA.	1852	HEMPFIELD RR	1817	WHEAT, J M & SONS	1858	PLAINTIFF	1630
WESTMORELAND CO, PA.	1852	HEMPFIELD RR	1818	WHEAT, JAMES	1839	PLAINTIFF	1662
WESTON, ISABEL	1837	PLAINTIFF	1594	WHEAT, JAMES	1840	PLAINTIFF	1662
WESTON, SARAH	1874	PLAINTIFF	1594	WHEAT, JAMES	1841	DEFENDANT	1629
WESTWOOD, A	1879	PLAINTIFF	1595	WHEAT, JAMES	1841	DEFENDANT	1652
WESTWOOD, E	1853	PLAINTIFF	1594	WHEAT, JAMES	1844	PLAINTIFF	1663
WESTWOOD, EDWARD	1855	DEFENDANT	1592	WHEAT, JAMES	1859	MISC	1698
WETHEL, L / ROCK - WETZEL	1871	OH CO. MAP	1742	WHEAT, JAMES A	1842	PLAINTIFF	1663
WETHERED, RICHARD	1804	MISC	1695	WHEAT, JAMES A	1842	MISC	1697
WETSELL, JOHN	1799	MISC	1695	WHEAT, JAMES M	1835	PLAINTIFF	1662
WETSELL, JOHN	1799	MISC	1695	WHEAT, JAMES M	1838	PLAINTIFF	1662
WETSELL, THOMAS	1799	MISC	1695	WHEAT, JAMES M	1839	PLAINTIFF	1662
WETSELL, THOMAS	1799	MISC	1695	WHEAT, JAMES M	1840	DEFENDANT	1551
WETZEL - SEE ALSO WHETZAL	1871	MARH'L MAP	1749	WHEAT, JAMES M	1840	DEFENDANT	1576
WETZEL CO. - NORTHERN BOUNDARY LINE	1871	MARH'L MAP	1758	WHEAT, JAMES M	1840	DEFENDANT	1594
WETZEL, F	1871	OH CO. MAP	1742	WHEAT, JAMES M	1840	DEFENDANT	1620
WETZEL, F	1871	OH CO. MAP	1744	WHEAT, JAMES M	1840	DEFENDANT	1628
WETZEL, JOHN / GRAVE OF - KILLED BY INDIAN	1871	MARH'L MAP	1751	WHEAT, JAMES M	1840	DEFENDANT	1636
WETZEL, L / L. WETHEL ROCK	1871	OH CO. MAP	1742	WHEAT, JAMES M	1840	PLAINTIFF	1662
WETZEL, L A	1871	MARH'L MAP	1755	WHEAT, JAMES M	1841	DEFENDANT	1557
WEYMAN, -	1825	PLAINTIFF	1620	WHEAT, JAMES M	1841	PLAINTIFF	1662
WEYMAN, -	1833	PLAINTIFF	1620	WHEAT, JAMES M	1841	PLAINTIFF	1663
WEYMAN, GEORGE	1854	PLAINTIFF	1594	WHEAT, JAMES M	1841	PLAINTIFF	1663
WEYMAN, JOHN	1852	MISC	1695	WHEAT, JAMES M	1841	PLAINTIFF	1663
WEYMER, ADAM	1846	MISC	1695	WHEAT, JAMES M	1874	DEFENDANT	1664
WHALEN, PATRICK	1823	PLAINTIFF	1596	WHEAT, JAMES M SR	1865	MISC	1698
WHALIER, GEORGE	1852	DEFENDANT	1623	WHEAT, JAMES S	1838	PLAINTIFF	1662
WHALLY, FEARGUS	1879	MISC	1698	WHEAT, JAMES S	1838	PLAINTIFF	1662
WHALON, PATRICK	1823	PLAINTIFF	1596	WHEAT, JAMES S	1839	PLAINTIFF	1662
WHALTMAN, ADAM	1856	PLAINTIFF	1597	WHEAT, JAMES S	1840	PLAINTIFF	1662
WHARF MASTER AT WHEELING	1852	HEMPFIELD RR	1818	WHEAT, JAMES S	1840	PLAINTIFF	1662
WHARF MASTER AT WHEELING - STEAMBOATS - 230 REGISTERED AT WHARF MASTER IN WHEELING	1852	HEMPFIELD RR	1819	WHEAT, JAMES S	1840	PLAINTIFF	1662
				WHEAT, JAMES S	1840	PLAINTIFF	1662
WHARF, -	1851	MISC	1696	WHEAT, JAMES S	1840	PLAINTIFF	1662
WHARRY, J	1871	MDSVILLE	1808	WHEAT, JAMES S	1840	PLAINTIFF	1662
WHARRY, J	1871	MDSVILLE	1810	WHEAT, JAMES S	1841	MISC	1697
WHARRY, J	1871	MDSVILLE	1810	WHEAT, JAMES S	1842	PLAINTIFF	1663
WHARRY, JOHN / GRIST MILL	1871	MDSVL BUS.	1796	WHEAT, JAMES S	1842	PLAINTIFF	1663
WHARRY, JOHN	1871	MDSVILLE	1810	WHEAT, JAMES S	1842	PLAINTIFF	1663
WHARRY, JOHN / WOOLEN FACTORY & GRIST MILL	1871	MDSVILLE	1810	WHEAT, JAMES S	1842	PLAINTIFF	1663
				WHEAT, JAMES S	1842	PLAINTIFF	1663
WHARRY, MARY A	1878	PLAINTIFF	1597	WHEAT, JAMES S	1842	PLAINTIFF	1663
WHARTON & GRINDAGE	1825	PLAINTIFF	1628	WHEAT, JAMES S	1843	PLAINTIFF	1663
WHARTON, ANDREW	1813	PLAINTIFF	1596	WHEAT, JAMES S	1843	PLAINTIFF	1663
WHARTON, BAILEY	1856	MISC	1697	WHEAT, JAMES S	1844	PLAINTIFF	1663
WHARTON, E W	1871	OH CO. MAP	1744	WHEAT, JAMES S	1846	PLAINTIFF	1663
WHARTON, G	1871	BRKE MAP	1736	WHEAT, JAMES S	1862	PLAINTIFF	1664
WHARTON, GIBSON	1857	PLAINTIFF	1597	WHEAT, JAMES S	1873	DEFENDANT	1592
WHARTON, JAMES E	1839	DEFENDANT	1567	WHEAT, JAMES S	1874	MISC	1698
WHARTON, JAMES E	1839	DEFENDANT	1623	WHEAT, JAMES S	1874	MISC	1698
WHARTON, JAMES E	1840	DEFENDANT	1619	WHEAT, JESSE	1832	PLAINTIFF	1662
WHARTON, JAMES E	1841	DEFENDANT	1567	WHEAT, JESSE	1833	PLAINTIFF	1662
WHARTON, JAMES E	1841	PLAINTIFF	1596	WHEAT, JESSE	1834	PLAINTIFF	1662
WHARTON, JAMES K	1840	DEFENDANT	1614	WHEAT, JESSE	1836	PLAINTIFF	1662
WHARTON, L	1871	OH CO. MAP	1742	WHEAT, JESSE	1837	PLAINTIFF	1662
WHARTON, L	1871	ELM GROVE	1782	WHEAT, JESSE	1838	PLAINTIFF	1662
WHARTON, LANDON	1868	MISC	1695	WHEAT, JESSE	1838	PLAINTIFF	1662
WHARTON, LANDON	1869	MISC	1698	WHEAT, JESSE	1838	PLAINTIFF	1662
WHARTON, LANDON	1873	MISC	1698	WHEAT, JESSE	1838	PLAINTIFF	1662
WHARTON, LEWIS	1873	PLAINTIFF	1597	WHEAT, JESSE	1838	PLAINTIFF	1662
WHARTON, MEREDITH	1838	MISC	1697	WHEAT, JESSE	1838	PLAINTIFF	1662
WHARTON, SILAS W	1862	DEFENDANT	1578	WHEAT, JESSE	1843	PLAINTIFF	1663
WHAT, PRICE & CO	1834	MISC	1696	WHEAT, JESSE	1851	PLAINTIFF	1663
WHEAT & CHAPLINE	1851	PLAINTIFF	1629	WHEAT, JESSE	1852	DEFENDANT	1561
WHEAT & CHAPLINE	1855	PLAINTIFF	1629	WHEAT, JESSE	1852	PLAINTIFF	1663
WHEAT & CHAPLINE	1857	PLAINTIFF	1630	WHEAT, JESSE	1853	PLAINTIFF	1663
WHEAT & KEMPLE	1855	PLAINTIFF	1629	WHEAT, JESSE	1853	PLAINTIFF	1663
WHEAT & KEMPLE	1859	PLAINTIFF	1630	WHEAT, JESSE	1856	PLAINTIFF	1663
WHEAT & KENDALL	1841	DEFENDANT	1586	WHEAT, JESSE	1857	PLAINTIFF	1663
WHEAT & SONS	1857	PLAINTIFF	1630	WHEAT, JESSE	1857	PLAINTIFF	1663
WHEAT FARM - WEBSTER TWP	1871	MARH'L MAP	1750	WHEAT, JESSE	1857	PLAINTIFF	1663
WHEAT ISETT & NAYLOR	1878	PLAINTIFF	1631	WHEAT, JESSE	1857	MISC	1697

'PERSONAL TIME LINE' INDEX TO VOLUME 7 OF THE *OHIO COUNTY INDEX*

ENTRY	YEAR	SUBJECT	PAGE
WHEAT, JESSE S	1868	MISC	1698
WHEAT, JESSE S	1873	MISC	1698
WHEAT, JESSEE	1832	PLAINTIFF	1662
WHEAT, JESSEE	1834	PLAINTIFF	1662
WHEAT, JESSEE	1834	PLAINTIFF	1662
WHEAT, JESSEE	1835	PLAINTIFF	1662
WHEAT, JESSEE	1838	PLAINTIFF	1662
WHEAT, JESSEE	1857	PLAINTIFF	1663
WHEAT, JESSIE S	1865	MISC	1698
WHEAT, M	1839	DEFENDANT	1558
WHEAT, PRICE & CO	1836	PLAINTIFF	1628
WHEAT, THOMAS	1837	PLAINTIFF	1662
WHEAT, Z	1853	PLAINTIFF	1663
WHEAT, Z	1861	DEFENDANT	1632
WHEAT, Z	1862	DEFENDANT	1632
WHEAT, ZACHARIAH	1859	PLAINTIFF	1664
WHEATE, GEORGE K	1855	PLAINTIFF	1663
WHEATE, JESSE	1852	PLAINTIFF	1663
WHEATE, JESSE	1852	PLAINTIFF	1663
WHEATE, JESSE	1852	PLAINTIFF	1663
WHEATE, JESSEE	1853	PLAINTIFF	1663
WHEATLEY, GEORGE	1841	DEFENDANT	1617
WHEATLEY, SAMUEL G	1839	PLAINTIFF	1596
WHEATLEY, WARREN	1832	PLAINTIFF	1596
WHEATLEY, WARREN	1840	DEFENDANT	1551
WHEATLEY, WILLIAM	1846	MISC	1697
WHEATLY, GEORGE	1814	MISC	1697
WHEATS, JESSE	1859	PLAINTIFF	1663
WHEELER & LAKIN	1855	PLAINTIFF	1629
WHEELER & LAKIN	1857	PLAINTIFF	1630
WHEELER & LAKIN	1859	PLAINTIFF	1630
WHEELER & LAKIN	1860	PLAINTIFF	1630
WHEELER & LARKIN	1855	DEFENDANT	1590
WHEELER & STEPHENS	1877	PLAINTIFF	1631
WHEELER, - / MRS	1871	NEW CUMB'LD	1768
WHEELER, - / MRS	1871	NEW CUMB'LD	1768
WHEELER, A P	1854	MISC	1697
WHEELER, ALBERT	1855	PLAINTIFF	1596
WHEELER, ALBERT P	1848	PLAINTIFF	1596
WHEELER, ALBERT P	1858	PLAINTIFF	1597
WHEELER, C H	1854	PLAINTIFF	1596
WHEELER, CHARLES	1861	PLAINTIFF	1597
WHEELER, CHARLES H	1861	PLAINTIFF	1597
WHEELER, CHRISTIAN	1874	MISC	1698
WHEELER, ELIAS H	1822	PLAINTIFF	1596
WHEELER, ELIAS H	1823	PLAINTIFF	1596
WHEELER, GARRITT	1828	MISC	1697
WHEELER, HAYDEN W	1858	PLAINTIFF	1597
WHEELER, HENRY & CO	1832	PLAINTIFF	1628
WHEELER, J	1861	DEFENDANT	1573
WHEELER, JAMES	1874	PLAINTIFF	1597
WHEELER, JAMES	1878	PLAINTIFF	1597
WHEELER, JAMES	1879	PLAINTIFF	1597
WHEELER, JARED	1834	MISC	1697
WHEELER, JOHN	1822	PLAINTIFF	1596
WHEELER, JOHN	1832	DEFENDANT	1553
WHEELER, L / INITIALS L.W.	1871	TRIAD.BORO.	1784
WHEELER, L / STORE	1871	TRIAD.BORO.	1784
WHEELER, LOUIS	1871	OH CO. BUS.	1779
WHEELER, LOUIS	1875	PLAINTIFF	1597
WHEELER, LOUIS	1876	PLAINTIFF	1597
WHEELER, P	1855	PLAINTIFF	1596
WHEELER, SAMUEL	1859	PLAINTIFF	1597
WHEELER, SAMUEL P	1860	PLAINTIFF	1597
WHEELER, SAMUEL P	1861	PLAINTIFF	1597
WHEELER, SAMUEL P	1862	PLAINTIFF	1597
WHEELER, THOMAS	1829	MISC	1697
WHEELER, THOMAS	1859	MISC	1698
WHEELER, THOMAS	1868	MISC	1698
WHEELER, THOMAS	1871	BRKE MAP	1735
WHEELER, THOMAS / HIS TIMBERLANDS	1871	BRKE MAP	1735
WHEELER, THOMAS C / HEIRS - MAP#528	1852	BRKE MAP	1852
WHEELER, Z	1871	BRKE MAP	1734
WHEELER, Z	1871	BRKE MAP	1735
WHEELING	1916	NAT'L ROAD	1861
WHEELING - & OLD NORTHWEST TERRITORY	1916	NAT'L ROAD	1870
WHEELING - CITY OF	1827	PLAINTIFF	1672
WHEELING - CITY OF	1827	PLAINTIFF	1672
WHEELING - CITY OF	1827	PLAINTIFF	1672
WHEELING - CITY OF	1829	PLAINTIFF	1672
WHEELING - CITY OF	1834	PLAINTIFF	1672
WHEELING - CITY OF	1838	PLAINTIFF	1672
WHEELING - CITY OF	1839	PLAINTIFF	1672
WHEELING - CITY OF	1839	PLAINTIFF	1672
WHEELING - CITY OF	1841	PLAINTIFF	1672
WHEELING - CITY OF	1841	PLAINTIFF	1672
WHEELING - CITY OF	1841	PLAINTIFF	1672
WHEELING - CITY OF	1841	PLAINTIFF	1672
WHEELING - CITY OF	1841	PLAINTIFF	1672
WHEELING - CITY OF	1841	PLAINTIFF	1672
WHEELING - CITY OF	1842	PLAINTIFF	1672
WHEELING - CITY OF	1842	PLAINTIFF	1672
WHEELING - CITY OF	1843	PLAINTIFF	1672
WHEELING - CITY OF	1846	PLAINTIFF	1672
WHEELING - CITY OF	1851	PLAINTIFF	1672
WHEELING - CITY OF	1851	PLAINTIFF	1672
WHEELING - CITY OF	1852	DEFENDANT	1568
WHEELING - CITY OF	1852	DEFENDANT	1590
WHEELING - CITY OF	1852	DEFENDANT	1618
WHEELING - CITY OF	1852	PLAINTIFF	1672
WHEELING - CITY OF	1853	DEFENDANT	1574
WHEELING - CITY OF	1853	DEFENDANT	1576
WHEELING - CITY OF	1853	DEFENDANT	1588
WHEELING - CITY OF	1853	DEFENDANT	1590
WHEELING - CITY OF	1853	DEFENDANT	1618
WHEELING - CITY OF	1853	DEFENDANT	1663
WHEELING - CITY OF	1854	DEFENDANT	1576
WHEELING - CITY OF	1854	DEFENDANT	1590
WHEELING - CITY OF	1854	DEFENDANT	1594
WHEELING - CITY OF	1854	DEFENDANT	1626
WHEELING - CITY OF	1854	DEFENDANT	1653
WHEELING - CITY OF	1854	DEFENDANT	1670
WHEELING - CITY OF	1854	PLAINTIFF	1672
WHEELING - CITY OF	1854	PLAINTIFF	1672
WHEELING - CITY OF	1855	DEFENDANT	1554
WHEELING - CITY OF	1855	DEFENDANT	1567
WHEELING - CITY OF	1855	DEFENDANT	1588
WHEELING - CITY OF	1855	DEFENDANT	1618
WHEELING - CITY OF	1855	PLAINTIFF	1672
WHEELING - CITY OF	1856	DEFENDANT	1597
WHEELING - CITY OF	1856	DEFENDANT	1604
WHEELING - CITY OF	1856	DEFENDANT	1608
WHEELING - CITY OF	1856	DEFENDANT	1632
WHEELING - CITY OF	1856	DEFENDANT	1653
WHEELING - CITY OF	1856	PLAINTIFF	1672
WHEELING - CITY OF	1857	DEFENDANT	1567
WHEELING - CITY OF	1858	DEFENDANT	1567
WHEELING - CITY OF	1858	DEFENDANT	1641
WHEELING - CITY OF	1859	DEFENDANT	1582
WHEELING - CITY OF	1859	PLAINTIFF	1672
WHEELING - CITY OF	1859	PLAINTIFF	1672
WHEELING - CITY OF	1859	PLAINTIFF	1672
WHEELING - CITY OF	1859	PLAINTIFF	1672
WHEELING - CITY OF	1859	PLAINTIFF	1672
WHEELING - CITY OF	1859	PLAINTIFF	1672
WHEELING - CITY OF	1859	PLAINTIFF	1672
WHEELING - CITY OF	1859	PLAINTIFF	1673
WHEELING - CITY OF	1859	PLAINTIFF	1673
WHEELING - CITY OF	1859	PLAINTIFF	1673
WHEELING - CITY OF	1859	PLAINTIFF	1673
WHEELING - CITY OF	1859	PLAINTIFF	1673
WHEELING - CITY OF	1859	PLAINTIFF	1673
WHEELING - CITY OF	1859	PLAINTIFF	1673
WHEELING - CITY OF	1860	DEFENDANT	1582
WHEELING - CITY OF	1861	PLAINTIFF	1673
WHEELING - CITY OF	1861	PLAINTIFF	1673
WHEELING - CITY OF	1861	PLAINTIFF	1673
WHEELING - CITY OF	1862	DEFENDANT	1582
WHEELING - CITY OF	1862	PLAINTIFF	1673
WHEELING - CITY OF	1862	PLAINTIFF	1673
WHEELING - CITY OF	1862	PLAINTIFF	1673
WHEELING - CITY OF	1871	OH CO. MAP	1742
WHEELING - CITY OF	1874	PLAINTIFF	1673
WHEELING - CITY OF	1875	DEFENDANT	1654
WHEELING - CITY OF	1879	PLAINTIFF	1673
WHEELING - CITY OF	1880	PLAINTIFF	1673
WHEELING - CITY OF	1880	PLAINTIFF	1673
WHEELING - CUMBERLAND TRIP	1916	NAT'L ROAD	1868
WHEELING - DESCRIPTION OF NATIONAL ROAD	1916	NAT'L ROAD	1865
WHEELING - DETAIL MAP OF NATIONAL ROAD AND SOME LANDMARKS	1916	NAT'L ROAD	1868
WHEELING - EARLY TOWN NAMES	1916	NAT'L ROAD	1866
WHEELING - EMIGRATION THROUGH - SOME HISTORY	1916	NAT'L ROAD	1866
WHEELING - FOUNDRY - JOHN ST	1871	WHG CITY	1788
WHEELING - HISTORY OF NAME	1916	NAT'L ROAD	1867

'PERSONAL TIME LINE' INDEX TO VOLUME 7 OF THE *OHIO COUNTY INDEX*

ENTRY	YEAR	SUBJECT	PAGE	ENTRY	YEAR	SUBJECT	PAGE
WHEELING - INDIAN HISTORY - MOUND BUILDERS	1916	NAT'L ROAD	1866	WHEELING CITY - BIDDLE ST	1871	WHG CITY	1788
WHEELING - INDUSTRIES	1916	NAT'L ROAD	1865	WHEELING CITY - BIDDLE ST	1871	WHG CITY	1790
WHEELING - LOG CABIN - MAP	1916	NAT'L ROAD	1868	WHEELING CITY - BOLTON ST	1871	WHG CITY	1790
WHEELING - MAYOR & COMMON ATTY	1826	PLAINTIFF	1672	WHEELING CITY - BOLTON ST	1871	WHG CITY	1792
WHEELING - MAYOR AND COMMON ATTY	1824	PLAINTIFF	1672	WHEELING CITY - BUSINESS NOTICES	1871	OH CO. BUS.	1779
WHEELING - MILEPOST - NATIONAL ROAD	1916	NAT'L ROAD	1862	WHEELING CITY - BY WARDS	1871	POPULATION	1816
				WHEELING CITY - CALDWELL ST	1871	WHG CITY	1790
				WHEELING CITY - CALDWELL ST	1871	WHG CITY	1790
WHEELING - NATIONAL ROAD MAP	1916	NAT'L ROAD	1863	WHEELING CITY - CALDWELL ST	1871	WHG CITY	1792
WHEELING - PANORAMIC MAP	1870	WHG CITY	1859	WHEELING CITY - CALDWELL ST	1871	WHG CITY	1792
WHEELING - S.S.MILL	1871	WHG CITY	1786	WHEELING CITY - CARROLL ST	1871	WHG CITY	1787
WHEELING - SCHOOL - MARKET ST	1871	WHG CITY	1786	WHEELING CITY - CARROLL ST	1871	WHG CITY	1788
WHEELING - SCHOOL - NORTH ST	1871	WHG CITY	1786	WHEELING CITY - CATHERINE ST	1871	WHG CITY	1790
WHEELING - SEARGANT OF	1842	PLAINTIFF	1673	WHEELING CITY - CATHERINE ST	1871	WHG CITY	1792
WHEELING - STEEL BRIDGE	1916	NAT'L ROAD	1866	WHEELING CITY - CENTRE ST	1871	WHG CITY	1788
WHEELING - STRATEGIC HISTORY	1916	NAT'L ROAD	1866	WHEELING CITY - CHAPLINE ST	1871	WHG CITY	1790
WHEELING - SUSPENSION BRIDGE	1916	NAT'L ROAD	1865	WHEELING CITY - CHESTNUT ST	1871	WHG CITY	1789
WHEELING - TAVERNS	1916	NAT'L ROAD	1867	WHEELING CITY - CITY COMMONS	1871	WHG CITY	1786
WHEELING - TOWN HISTORY	1916	NAT'L ROAD	1867	WHEELING CITY - CITY COMMONS	1871	WHG CITY	1788
WHEELING - TRAVEL TIMES	1916	NAT'L ROAD	1868	WHEELING CITY - CITY MAYOR	1821	PLAINTIFF	1672
WHEELING - WHARF MASTER AT	1852	HEMPFIELD RR	1818	WHEELING CITY - CLAY ST	1871	WHG CITY	1788
WHEELING - WHIPPING POST	1916	NAT'L ROAD	1867	WHEELING CITY - CLAY ST	1871	WHG CITY	1790
WHEELING & BELMONT BRIDGE CO	1859	MISC	1696	WHEELING CITY - CLEVELAND AND WHEELING ROAD / RR	1852	HEMPFIELD RR	1820
WHEELING & BETAHNY PIKE	1871	OH CO. MAP	1740	WHEELING CITY - COAL ST	1871	WHG CITY	1790
WHEELING & BETHANY PIKE	1871	OH CO. MAP	1741	WHEELING CITY - COAL ST	1871	WHG CITY	1792
WHEELING & BETHANY PIKE	1871	OH CO. MAP	1741	WHEELING CITY - CONGRESS DR	1871	WHG CITY	1787
WHEELING & BETHANY TURNPIKE	1852	BRKE MAP	1840	WHEELING CITY - CONVENTION HALL	1916	NAT'L ROAD	1867
WHEELING & BETHANY TURNPIKE	1852	BRKE MAP	1844	WHEELING CITY - CORPORATION LINE / NORTHERN BOUNDARY	1871	WHG CITY	1786
WHEELING CITY	1852	HEMPFIELD RR	1818				
WHEELING CITY	1852	HEMPFIELD RR	1819	WHEELING CITY - CORPORATION LINE - S. BOUNDARY	1871	WHG CITY	1790
WHEELING CITY	1852	HEMP. RR MAP	1825				
WHEELING CITY	1852	HEMP. RR MAP	1826	WHEELING CITY - COURT HOUSE - FOURTH ST	1871	WHG CITY	1788
WHEELING CITY	1852	HEMP. RR MAP	1827				
WHEELING CITY	1871	DISTANCES	1815	WHEELING CITY - CUSTOM HOUSE / ABBREV/ C.H.	1871	WHG CITY	1788
WHEELING CITY - 10TH ST	1916	NAT'L ROAD	1865				
WHEELING CITY - 10TH ST	1916	NAT'L ROAD	1867	WHEELING CITY - DENNY ST	1871	WHG CITY	1790
WHEELING CITY - 10TH ST	1916	NAT'L ROAD	1868	WHEELING CITY - DETAIL MAP	1871	WHG CITY	1792
WHEELING CITY - 11TH ST	1916	NAT'L ROAD	1867	WHEELING CITY - DETAIL MAP	1871	RITCHIE TWP	1793
WHEELING CITY - 11TH ST	1916	NAT'L ROAD	1868	WHEELING CITY - DETAIL MAP	1871	RITCHIE TWP	1794
WHEELING CITY - 12TH ST	1916	NAT'L ROAD	1868	WHEELING CITY - DIVISION ST	1871	WHG CITY	1790
WHEELING CITY - 13TH ST	1916	NAT'L ROAD	1868	WHEELING CITY - EIGHTH ST	1871	WHG CITY	1789
WHEELING CITY - 14TH ST	1916	NAT'L ROAD	1867	WHEELING CITY - ELIZABETH ST	1871	WHG CITY	1789
WHEELING CITY - 14TH ST	1916	NAT'L ROAD	1868	WHEELING CITY - ELLET ST	1871	WHG CITY	1789
WHEELING CITY - 15TH ST	1916	NAT'L ROAD	1868	WHEELING CITY - EOFF ST	1871	WHG CITY	1790
WHEELING CITY - 16TH ST	1916	NAT'L ROAD	1868	WHEELING CITY - EOFF ST	1871	WHG CITY	1790
WHEELING CITY - 17TH ST	1916	NAT'L ROAD	1868	WHEELING CITY - FAIRMONT RD	1871	WHG CITY	1790
WHEELING CITY - 1822 MAP - ORIGINAL STREET LAYOUT DESCRIPTION	2000	APPENDIX	1712	WHEELING CITY - FAIRMONT RD	1871	WHG CITY	1792
				WHEELING CITY - FEMALE INS. / INSTITUTE ?	1871	WHG CITY	1788
WHEELING CITY - 1822 MAP - WITH ORIGINAL STREETS LAYOUT	2000	APPENDIX	1860	WHEELING CITY - FIFTH ST	1871	WHG CITY	1788
				WHEELING CITY - FILLMORE ST	1871	WHG CITY	1790
WHEELING CITY - 1870 CENSUS POPULATION	1871	POPULATION	1816	WHEELING CITY - FILLMORE ST	1871	WHG CITY	1792
				WHEELING CITY - FIRST ST	1871	WHG CITY	1790
WHEELING CITY - 1ST WARD	1871	WHG CITY	1786	WHEELING CITY - FOURTH ST	1871	WHG CITY	1788
WHEELING CITY - 1ST WARD	1871	WHG CITY	1788	WHEELING CITY - FRANKLIN ST	1871	WHG CITY	1786
WHEELING CITY - 1ST WARD	1871	POPULATION	1816	WHEELING CITY - FRANKLIN ST	1871	WHG CITY	1788
WHEELING CITY - 2ND WARD	1871	WHG CITY	1788	WHEELING CITY - FREIGHT DEPOT - B&O RR	1871	WHG CITY	1788
WHEELING CITY - 2ND WARD	1871	POPULATION	1816				
WHEELING CITY - 3RD WARD	1871	WHG CITY	1788	WHEELING CITY - FULTON ST	1871	WHG CITY	1786
WHEELING CITY - 3RD WARD	1871	POPULATION	1816	WHEELING CITY - FULTON ST	1871	WHG CITY	1786
WHEELING CITY - 4TH WARD	1871	WHG CITY	1788	WHEELING CITY - FULTON ST	1871	WHG CITY	1788
WHEELING CITY - 4TH WARD	1871	POPULATION	1816	WHEELING CITY - FULTON ST	1871	WHG CITY	1788
WHEELING CITY - 5TH WARD	1871	WHG CITY	1790	WHEELING CITY - GEORGE ST	1871	WHG CITY	1790
WHEELING CITY - 5TH WARD	1871	POPULATION	1816	WHEELING CITY - GEORGE ST	1871	WHG CITY	1792
WHEELING CITY - 6TH WARD	1871	WHG CITY	1790	WHEELING CITY - GERMAN ST	1871	WHG CITY	1790
WHEELING CITY - 6TH WARD	1871	POPULATION	1816	WHEELING CITY - GLASS CA. / FACTORY NW. OF REILLY EST.	1871	WHG CITY	1789
WHEELING CITY - 7TH WARD / WHEELING ISLAND	1871	WHG CITY	1788				
				WHEELING CITY - GRANDVIEW ST	1871	WHG CITY	1786
WHEELING CITY - 7TH WARD	1871	POPULATION	1816	WHEELING CITY - GRANDVIEW ST	1871	WHG CITY	1788
WHEELING CITY - 7TH WARD - WHEELING ISLAND	1871	WHG ISLAND	1788	WHEELING CITY - HALL - MARKET & JEFFERSON ST	1871	WHG CITY	1788
WHEELING CITY - ADAMS ST	1871	WHG CITY	1786	WHEELING CITY - HAMPDEN ST	1871	WHG CITY	1788
WHEELING CITY - ADAMS ST	1871	WHG CITY	1788	WHEELING CITY - HAZEL ST	1871	WHG CITY	1790
WHEELING CITY - ALLEY B	1916	NAT'L ROAD	1867	WHEELING CITY - HIGH ST	1871	WHG CITY	1788
WHEELING CITY - ALLEY B	1916	NAT'L ROAD	1868	WHEELING CITY - HIGH ST	1871	WHG CITY	1790
WHEELING CITY - AUDITORIUM	1916	NAT'L ROAD	1868	WHEELING CITY - HOSPITAL - MAIN ST	1871	WHG CITY	1786
WHEELING CITY - BAKER ST	1871	WHG CITY	1787				
WHEELING CITY - BAKER ST	1871	WHG CITY	1788	WHEELING CITY - JACOB ST	1871	WHG CITY	1790
WHEELING CITY - BALTIMORE & OHIO RR PASSENGER STATION	1916	NAT'L ROAD	1868	WHEELING CITY - JACOB ST	1871	WHG CITY	1792
				WHEELING CITY - JAIL - FIFTH ST	1871	WHG CITY	1788
WHEELING CITY - BALTIMORE ST	1871	WHG CITY	1789	WHEELING CITY - JAMES ST	1871	WHG CITY	1790
WHEELING CITY - BALTIMORE TRIP	1916	NAT'L ROAD	1868	WHEELING CITY - JAMES ST	1871	WHG CITY	1792
WHEELING CITY - BANK ST	1871	WHG CITY	1786	WHEELING CITY - JEFFERSON ST	1871	WHG CITY	1788
WHEELING CITY - BELMONT ST	1871	WHG CITY	1788	WHEELING CITY - JOHN ST	1871	WHG CITY	1788

'PERSONAL TIME LINE' INDEX TO VOLUME 7 OF THE *OHIO COUNTY INDEX*

ENTRY	YEAR	SUBJECT	PAGE
WHEELING CITY - LEE ST	1871	WHG CITY	1790
WHEELING CITY - LIND ST	1871	WHG CITY	1788
WHEELING CITY - LINDSLAY ST	1871	WHG CITY	1790
WHEELING CITY - LINDSLEY ST	1871	WHG CITY	1788
WHEELING CITY - LIST ST	1871	WHG CITY	1786
WHEELING CITY - LOCUST ST	1871	WHG CITY	1790
WHEELING CITY - MADISON ST	1871	WHG CITY	1788
WHEELING CITY - MAIN ST	1871	WHG CITY	1786
WHEELING CITY - MAIN ST	1871	WHG CITY	1788
WHEELING CITY - MAIN ST	1871	WHG CITY	1788
WHEELING CITY - MAIN ST	1871	WHG CITY	1790
WHEELING CITY - MAIN ST	1871	WHG CITY	1790
WHEELING CITY - MAIN ST	1916	NAT'L ROAD	1867
WHEELING CITY - MAIN ST	1916	NAT'L ROAD	1867
WHEELING CITY - MAIN ST	1916	NAT'L ROAD	1867
WHEELING CITY - MAIN ST	1916	NAT'L ROAD	1868
WHEELING CITY - MAP	1871	WHG CITY	1786
WHEELING CITY - MARKET ST	1871	WHG CITY	1786
WHEELING CITY - MARKET ST	1871	WHG CITY	1788
WHEELING CITY - MARKET ST	1871	WHG CITY	1790
WHEELING CITY - MARKET ST	1916	NAT'L ROAD	1865
WHEELING CITY - MARKET ST	1916	NAT'L ROAD	1867
WHEELING CITY - MARKET ST	1916	NAT'L ROAD	1867
WHEELING CITY - MARKET ST	1916	NAT'L ROAD	1868
WHEELING CITY - MARSHALL ST	1871	WHG CITY	1790
WHEELING CITY - MCCLURE	1871	WHG CITY	1786
WHEELING CITY - MONROE ST	1871	WHG CITY	1788
WHEELING CITY - MOYSTON ST	1871	WHG CITY	1790
WHEELING CITY - MOYSTON ST	1871	WHG CITY	1792
WHEELING CITY - NATIONAL OR BOW / STREET ? - ON WHEELING CREEK	1871	WHG CITY	1786
WHEELING CITY - NEW ST	1871	WHG CITY	1790
WHEELING CITY - NEW ST	1871	WHG CITY	1792
WHEELING CITY - NORTH ST	1871	WHG CITY	1786
WHEELING CITY - NORTH ST	1871	WHG CITY	1790
WHEELING CITY - NORTH ST	1871	WHG CITY	1792
WHEELING CITY - OHIO VALLEY AUTO CLUB	1916	NAT'L ROAD	1868
WHEELING CITY - OLD MARKET HOUSE SITE	1916	NAT'L ROAD	1868
WHEELING CITY - PALO ALTO ST	1871	WHG CITY	1788
WHEELING CITY - POST OFFICE	1871	WHG CITY	1788
WHEELING CITY - PRESTON ST	1871	WHG CITY	1790
WHEELING CITY - QUINCY ST	1871	WHG CITY	1788
WHEELING CITY - RESERVOIR	1871	WHG CITY	1786
WHEELING CITY - RESERVOIR	1871	WHG CITY	1788
WHEELING CITY - S. CORPORATION LINE BOUNDARY	1871	WHG CITY	1792
WHEELING CITY - SECOND ST	1871	WHG CITY	1790
WHEELING CITY - SEVENTH ST	1871	WHG CITY	1788
WHEELING CITY - SITE OF FORT HENRY	1916	NAT'L ROAD	1868
WHEELING CITY - SIXTH ST	1871	WHG CITY	1788
WHEELING CITY - SOUTH ST	1871	WHG CITY	1788
WHEELING CITY - SOUTH ST	1871	WHG CITY	1790
WHEELING CITY - SOUTH ST	1871	WHG CITY	1790
WHEELING CITY - SPRUCE ST	1871	WHG CITY	1788
WHEELING CITY - ST CHARLES ST	1871	WHG CITY	1788
WHEELING CITY - STREET LAYOUT - 1822	2000	APPENDIX	1712
WHEELING CITY - STREET LAYOUT - 1822	2000	APPENDIX	1860
WHEELING CITY - STREET NAMING PATTERN	1916	NAT'L ROAD	1867
WHEELING CITY - TAYLOR ST	1871	WHG CITY	1790
WHEELING CITY - THIRD ST	1871	WHG CITY	1788
WHEELING CITY - THIRD ST	1871	WHG CITY	1790
WHEELING CITY - TOWNSHIPS & WARDS LISTED	1871	MAP	1721
WHEELING CITY - UNION ST	1871	WHG CITY	1788
WHEELING CITY - VINEYARDS	1871	WHG CITY	1788
WHEELING CITY - WALNUT	1871	WHG CITY	1789
WHEELING CITY - WALNUT ST	1871	WHG CITY	1790
WHEELING CITY - WALNUT ST	1871	WHG CITY	1792
WHEELING CITY - WARDS 1-5 & 7 ON MAP	1871	MAP	1722
WHEELING CITY - WARDS 6 ON MAP	1871	MAP	1723
WHEELING CITY - WASHINGTON ST	1871	WHG CITY	1786
WHEELING CITY - WASHINGTON ST	1871	WHG CITY	1788
WHEELING CITY - WATER WORKS	1871	WHG CITY	1786
WHEELING CITY - WATER WORKS	1871	WHG CITY	1788
WHEELING CITY - WEBSTER ST	1871	WHG CITY	1788
WHEELING CITY - WEBSTER ST	1871	WHG CITY	1790
WHEELING CITY - WOOD ST	1871	WHG CITY	1786
WHEELING CITY - WOOD ST	1871	WHG CITY	1790
WHEELING CITY - ZANE ST	1871	WHG CITY	1788
WHEELING CITY - ZANE ST	1871	WHG CITY	1790
WHEELING CITY BUILDING -MARKET ST	1871	WHG CITY	1788
WHEELING CREEK / NEAR NATIONAL OR BOW	1871	WHG CITY	1786
WHEELING CREEK	1916	NAT'L ROAD	1867
WHEELING CREEK - AT FULTON	1871	WHG CITY	1787
WHEELING CREEK - AT LEATHERWOOD	1871	TRIAD.TWP.	1781
WHEELING CREEK - AT WHEELING CITY	1871	WHG CITY	1788
WHEELING CREEK - GEORGE SCHELLHASE - ICE HOUSE	1871	TRIAD.TWP.	1781
WHEELING CREEK - GRIST MILL ON	1871	TRIAD.TWP.	1781
WHEELING CREEK - ICE HOUSE / CONANT & BEDILION ICE HOUSSE	1871	OH CO. MAP	1742
WHEELING CREEK - MAP	1916	NAT'L ROAD	1868
WHEELING CREEK - MOUTH OF AT OHIO RIVER	1871	WHG CITY	1788
WHEELING CREEK - RUTHS FLOURING & SAW MILL ON	1871	SAND HILL-BUS.	1797
WHEELING CREEK - THREE MILE ICE HOUSE ON	1871	TRIAD.TWP.	1781
WHEELING CREEK - WHEELING	1871	WHG CITY	1786
WHEELING CREEK - WHEELING	1871	WHG CITY	1789
WHEELING EASTERN CORPORATION LINE	1871	WHG CITY	1790
WHEELING FEMALE ACADEMY	1853	MISC	1696
WHEELING FEMALE ACADEMY	1878	PLAINTIFF	1631
WHEELING FEMALE ACADEMY	1879	PLAINTIFF	1631
WHEELING FEMALE SEMINARY	1850	PLAINTIFF	1629
WHEELING GAS CO	1856	MISC	1696
WHEELING GAS CO	1860	MISC	1696
WHEELING HILL - MAP	1916	NAT'L ROAD	1868
WHEELING HILL - NATIONAL ROAD	1916	NAT'L ROAD	1865
WHEELING HOSPITAL	1859	MISC	1696
WHEELING HOSPITAL	1861	MISC	1696
WHEELING HOSPITAL	1878	MISC	1696
WHEELING HOTEL CO	1856	MISC	1696
WHEELING IRON & NAIL CO	1876	PLAINTIFF	1631
WHEELING IRON WORKS	1871	OH CO. MAP	1741
WHEELING IRON WORKS	1871	WHG CITY	1786
WHEELING ISLAND	1871	WHG CITY	1786
WHEELING ISLAND / IS MADISON TOWNSHIP	1871	WHG CITY	1786
WHEELING ISLAND	1871	WHG CITY	1790
WHEELING ISLAND - BRICK YARD	1871	WHG ISLAND	1788
WHEELING ISLAND - BROADWAY ST	1871	WHG ISLAND	1788
WHEELING ISLAND - CHESTNUT ST	1871	WHG CITY	1786
WHEELING ISLAND - CHESTNUT ST	1871	WHG ISLAND	1788
WHEELING ISLAND - DETAIL MAP	1871	WHG ISLAND	1788
WHEELING ISLAND - ELM ST	1871	WHG ISLAND	1788
WHEELING ISLAND - FIFTH ST	1871	WHG CITY	1786
WHEELING ISLAND - FIFTH ST	1871	WHG ISLAND	1788
WHEELING ISLAND - FOUNDRY	1871	WHG ISLAND	1788
WHEELING ISLAND - FOURTH ST	1871	WHG CITY	1786
WHEELING ISLAND - FOURTH ST	1871	WHG ISLAND	1788
WHEELING ISLAND - FRONT ST	1916	NAT'L ROAD	1868
WHEELING ISLAND - GOODRICH ST	1871	WHG ISLAND	1788
WHEELING ISLAND - HISTORY	1916	NAT'L ROAD	1866
WHEELING ISLAND - HURON ST	1871	WHG ISLAND	1788
WHEELING ISLAND - LANE ST	1871	WHG ISLAND	1788
WHEELING ISLAND - LOCUST ST	1871	WHG CITY	1786
WHEELING ISLAND - LOCUST ST	1871	WHG ISLAND	1788
WHEELING ISLAND - MADISON TOWNSHIP	1871	OH CO. MAP	1742
WHEELING ISLAND - MAP	1916	NAT'L ROAD	1868
WHEELING ISLAND - OHIO AVE	1916	NAT'L ROAD	1868
WHEELING ISLAND - OHIO ST	1871	WHG ISLAND	1788
WHEELING ISLAND - PANORAMIC MAP	1870	WHG CITY	1859
WHEELING ISLAND - PARK	1871	WHG CITY	1786
WHEELING ISLAND - PARK	1871	WHG ISLAND	1788
WHEELING ISLAND - PARK AVE	1916	NAT'L ROAD	1868
WHEELING ISLAND - PENN ST	1871	WHG ISLAND	1788
WHEELING ISLAND - PENN ST	1916	NAT'L ROAD	1868
WHEELING ISLAND - PINE ST	1871	WHG ISLAND	1788
WHEELING ISLAND - SECOND ST	1871	WHG CITY	1786
WHEELING ISLAND - SECOND ST	1871	WHG ISLAND	1788
WHEELING ISLAND - SOUTHERN END	1871	WHG ISLAND	1790
WHEELING ISLAND - THIRD ST	1871	WHG CITY	1786
WHEELING ISLAND - THIRD ST	1871	WHG ISLAND	1788
WHEELING ISLAND - VIRGINIA AVE	1916	NAT'L ROAD	1868
WHEELING ISLAND - VIRGINIA ST	1871	WHG ISLAND	1788
WHEELING ISLAND - WABASH ST	1871	WHG ISLAND	1788
WHEELING ISLAND - WALNUT ST	1871	WHG CITY	1786

'PERSONAL TIME LINE' INDEX TO VOLUME 7 OF THE OHIO COUNTY INDEX

ENTRY	YEAR	SUBJECT	PAGE	ENTRY	YEAR	SUBJECT	PAGE
WHEELING ISLAND - WALNUT ST	1871	WHG ISLAND	1788	WHETZELL, JACOB	1802	MISC	1697
WHEELING ISLAND - WATER ST	1871	WHG ISLAND	1788	WHETZELL, JACOB	1806	PLAINTIFF	1658
WHEELING ISLAND - YORK ST	1871	WHG ISLAND	1788	WHETZELL, JACOB	1807	PLAINTIFF	1658
WHEELING ISLAND - ZANE AVE	1916	NAT'L ROAD	1868	WHETZELL, JACOB	1807	PLAINTIFF	1658
WHEELING ISLAND - ZANE ST	1916	NAT'L ROAD	1866	WHETZELL, JAMES	1807	DEFENDANT	1551
WHEELING LANCASTRIAN ACADEMY	1825	PLAINTIFF	1628	WHETZELL, JOHN	1797	MISC	1697
WHEELING LIBRARY ASSOCIATION	1874	PLAINTIFF	1631	WHETZELL, JOHN	1797	MISC	1697
WHEELING MANUFACTURING CO INC	1828	MISC	1696	WHETZELL, MARTIN	1797	MISC	1697
WHEELING OMNIBUS CO	1877	PLAINTIFF	1631	WHETZELL, MARTON	1803	MISC	1676
WHEELING PARK - MAP	1916	NAT'L ROAD	1863	WHETZELL, MARTON	1803	MISC	1697
WHEELING PARK - NATIONAL ROAD	1916	NAT'L ROAD	1865	WHETZELL, MARY	1788	PLAINTIFF	1658
WHEELING PIKE	1871	BKE/OH MAP	1739	WHIMS, E	1871	NEW MANCH.	1769
WHEELING PITTSBURGH & B R R CO	1876	DEFENDANT	1573	WHIMS, J	1871	NEW MANCH.	1763
WHEELING PITTSBURGH & CINCINNATI TRANS	1874	PLAINTIFF	1631	WHINN, MICHAEL	1876	PLAINTIFF	1597
				WHIPKEY, A	1871	MARH'L MAP	1750
WHEELING RIFLE CORPS	1841	PLAINTIFF	1629	WHIPKEY, A	1871	MARH'L MAP	1753
WHEELING SAVING INSTITUTION	1857	MISC	1696	WHIPPING POST - WHEELING	1916	NAT'L ROAD	1867
WHEELING SAVINGS INSTITUTION	1838	PLAINTIFF	1628	WHIPPLE, H D	1871	BENWO'D - BUS.	1795
WHEELING SAVINGS INSTITUTION	1839	PLAINTIFF	1628	WHISSEN, J	1871	OH CO. MAP	1740
WHEELING SAVINGS INSTITUTION	1841	PLAINTIFF	1629	WHISSEN, JOSEPH	1855	PLAINTIFF	1596
WHEELING TO BALTIMORE - NATIONAL ROAD MAP	1916	NAT'L ROAD	1869	WHISSON - ORPHANS	1841	MISC	1697
				WHISSON, ELIZABETH	1841	MISC	1697
WHEELING TO CUMBERLAND - TRAVEL ROUTES COMPARED	1916	NAT'L ROAD	1869	WHITACRE HOUSE - HOTEL - WELLSVILLE, OHIO	1871	HAN-GR'NT TWP	1763
WHEELING TOWN COUNCIL MEETINGS	1916	NAT'L ROAD	1868	WHITACRE, T W / WELLSVILLE, OHIO	1871	HAN-GR'NT TWP	1763
				WHITACRE, T W / WELLSVILLE, OHIO	1871	NEW MANCH.	1763
WHEELING VALLEY FLOURING MILLS	1871	MARH'L MAP	1746	WHITAKER & COUDON	1862	PLAINTIFF	1631
WHEELING VALLEY FLOURING MILLS	1871	SAND HILL-BUS.	1797	WHITAKER IRON CO	1874	PLAINTIFF	1631
WHEELING WAGON & CARRIAGE CO	1873	PLAINTIFF	1631	WHITAKER, GEORGE	1862	PLAINTIFF	1597
WHEELING WAGON & CARRIAGE CO	1877	PLAINTIFF	1631	WHITAKER, GEORGE P	1874	PLAINTIFF	1597
WHEELING WEST LIBERTY & BETHANY TURNPIK	1848	PLAINTIFF	1629	WHITAKER, HENRY G	1868	MISC	1698
				WHITAKER, JOSEPH	1859	PLAINTIFF	1597
WHEELING WINDOW GLASS CO	1874	PLAINTIFF	1631	WHITAKER, JOSEPH	1862	PLAINTIFF	1597
WHEELING, IRON & NAIL CO	1877	PLAINTIFF	1631	WHITAKER, LEVI	1818	PLAINTIFF	1596
WHEELING, MARIETTA, CHILICOTHE AND CINCINNATI	1852	HEMPFIELD RR	1821	WHITAKER, SAMUEL	1811	DEFENDANT	1599
				WHITE & CHAPLINE	1840	PLAINTIFF	1628
WHEELOR, LEVY	1797	MISC	1697	WHITE & COEN	1848	PLAINTIFF	1629
WHEELRIGHT, -	1844	PLAINTIFF	1623	WHITE & COTTS	1841	PLAINTIFF	1629
WHEELWRIGHT & MUDGE	1856	PLAINTIFF	1630	WHITE & STILES / INITIALS W. & S.	1871	MARH'L MAP	1757
WHEELWRIGHT, JEREMIAH	1856	PLAINTIFF	1597	WHITE & STILES	1871	MARH'L MAP	1761
WHEET, Z	1853	PLAINTIFF	1663	WHITE & STILES	1871	MARH'L MAP	1761
WHELAN, CATHARINE	1852	MISC	1697	WHITE & STILES / INITIALS W & S	1871	MARH'L MAP	1761
WHELAN, R V	1871	WHG CITY	1786	WHITE & STILES / INITIALS W & S	1871	MARH'L MAP	1761
WHELAN, RICHARD B	1859	MISC	1698	WHITE & STILES / INITIALS W & S	1871	MARH'L MAP	1761
WHELAN, RICHARD V	1856	MISC	1697	WHITE & STILES / INITIALS W & S	1871	MARH'L MAP	1761
WHELAN, RICHARD V	1856	MISC	1697	WHITE & STILES / INITIALS W & S	1871	MARH'L MAP	1761
WHELAN, RICHARD V	1861	MISC	1698	WHITE & STILES / INITIALS W & S	1871	MARH'L MAP	1761
WHELAN, RICHARD V	1873	PLAINTIFF	1597	WHITE & STILES / NUMEROUS BUILDINGS NEAR BELLTON P.O.	1871	MARH'L MAP	1761
WHELAN, RICHARD V	1873	MISC	1698				
WHELAN, RICHARD V	1874	MISC	1698	WHITE & STILES / BELLTON	1871	LIB. TWP-BUS.	1797
WHELLIER, GEORGE	1853	MISC	1697	WHITE & STILES	1871	BELLTON	1814
WHELLIER, GEORGE	1860	MISC	1698	WHITE & STILES	1871	BELLTON	1814
WHERRY, JAMES	1871	OH CO. MAP	1740	WHITE & STILES	1871	BELLTON	1814
WHERRY, JOHN	1810	PLAINTIFF	1596	WHITE & STILES	1871	BELLTON	1814
WHERRY, JOSEPH	1810	PLAINTIFF	1596	WHITE & STILES / INITIALS W & S	1871	BELLTON	1814
WHETSAL, JACOB	1806	PLAINTIFF	1658	WHITE & STILES / INITIALS W & S	1871	BELLTON	1814
WHETSAL, JACOB	1806	PLAINTIFF	1658	WHITE & STILES - GRIST MILL - BELLTON	1871	BELLTON	1814
WHETSAL, JACOB	1806	PLAINTIFF	1658				
WHETSAL, JACOB	1807	PLAINTIFF	1658	WHITE & STILES - S.S MILL - BELLTON / ?	1871	BELLTON	1814
WHETSTONE CREEK	1871	MARH'L MAP	1755				
WHETSTONE CREEK	1871	MARH'L MAP	1759	WHITE CLOVER / JOHN C REEVES	1871	BRKE MAP	1735
WHETSTONE CREEK - SAW MILL & DAM ON	1871	MARH'L MAP	1759	WHITE COTTAGE	1871	MARH'L MAP	1745
				WHITE HOTEL - CAMERON	1871	CAMERON	1803
WHETSTONE CREEK - SAW MILL ON - SW. OF W.L. ALLEY	1871	MARH'L MAP	1759	WHITE HOUSE FARM / THE	1871	MARH'L MAP	1752
				WHITE HOUSE FARM / THE	1871	MARH'L MAP	1755
WHETZAL - SEE ALSO WETZEL	1871	MARH'L MAP	1749	WHITE OAK FLATS	1871	HAN MAP	1726
WHETZAL, JACOB	1800	MISC	1697	WHITE OAK GROVE	1871	HAN MAP	1727
WHETZAL, JACOB	1805	PLAINTIFF	1658	WHITE OAK GROVE	1871	HAN MAP	1731
WHETZAL, JACOB	1805	PLAINTIFF	1658	WHITE OAK GROVE - CALY TWP	1871	MARH'L MAP	1751
WHETZAL, JACOB	1805	PLAINTIFF	1658	WHITE OAK RUN	1871	HAN MAP	1726
WHETZEL, L	1871	MARH'L MAP	1749	WHITE OAK SPRING	1871	OH CO. MAP	1743
WHETZEL, J	1871	MARH'L MAP	1752	WHITE OAK SPRING	1871	MARH'L MAP	1746
WHETZEL, JACOB	1806	DEFENDANT	1559	WHITE OAK SPRING - CAMERON TWP	1871	MARH'L MAP	1753
WHETZEL, JACOB	1808	PLAINTIFF	1658	WHITE, -	1786	PLAINTIFF	1659
WHETZEL, JACOB	1808	PLAINTIFF	1658	WHITE, - / TWEED & WHITE - MILL	1871	WELLSBURG	1777
WHETZEL, JACOB	1808	PLAINTIFF	1658	WHITE, ALEXANDER	1815	MISC	1701
WHETZEL, JACOB	1808	DEFENDANT	1667	WHITE, ALEXANDER	1832	MISC	1702
WHETZEL, JACOB	1809	PLAINTIFF	1658	WHITE, ALEXANDER	1834	MISC	1702
WHETZEL, JOHN	1804	MISC	1697	WHITE, ANDREW	1790	DEFENDANT	1577
WHETZEL, JOHN	1808	PLAINTIFF	1658	WHITE, ANDREW	1805	PLAINTIFF	1659
WHETZEL, MARTIN	1813	PLAINTIFF	1658	WHITE, ANDREW	1805	MISC	1701
WHETZEL, MARTON	1800	MISC	1697	WHITE, ANDREW	1807	PLAINTIFF	1659
WHETZEL, MARTON	1808	MISC	1697	WHITE, ANDREW	1807	PLAINTIFF	1659
WHETZEL, MARY	1804	MISC	1697	WHITE, ANDREW	1822	DEFENDANT	1660
WHETZEL, MORTON	1806	MISC	1697	WHITE, ANDREW	1823	MISC	1701
WHETZELL, JACOB	1800	MISC	1697	WHITE, ANDREW	1827	PLAINTIFF	1660

'PERSONAL TIME LINE' INDEX TO VOLUME 7 OF THE *OHIO COUNTY INDEX*

ENTRY	YEAR	SUBJECT	PAGE	ENTRY	YEAR	SUBJECT	PAGE
WHITE, ANDREW	1840	PLAINTIFF	1661	WHITE, JOHN	1807	PLAINTIFF	1659
WHITE, ANDREW	1841	PLAINTIFF	1661	WHITE, JOHN	1809	PLAINTIFF	1659
WHITE, ANDREW	1856	MISC	1702	WHITE, JOHN	1809	PLAINTIFF	1659
WHITE, ANDREW J	1835	MISC	1702	WHITE, JOHN	1810	PLAINTIFF	1659
WHITE, ARLENA	1873	MISC	1702	WHITE, JOHN	1810	APPENDIX	1873
WHITE, BENNET	1806	PLAINTIFF	1659	WHITE, JOHN	1811	PLAINTIFF	1659
WHITE, CHARLES	1808	MISC	1701	WHITE, JOHN	1817	PLAINTIFF	1659
WHITE, CHARLES	1875	PLAINTIFF	1661	WHITE, JOHN	1817	PLAINTIFF	1659
WHITE, DAVID	1829	DEFENDANT	1583	WHITE, JOHN	1817	PLAINTIFF	1659
WHITE, DAVID	1830	DEFENDANT	1583	WHITE, JOHN	1818	PLAINTIFF	1659
WHITE, DAVID	1831	PLAINTIFF	1660	WHITE, JOHN	1818	PLAINTIFF	1660
WHITE, DAVID	1832	DEFENDANT	1594	WHITE, JOHN	1819	PLAINTIFF	1660
WHITE, DENNIS	1858	PLAINTIFF	1661	WHITE, JOHN	1820	PLAINTIFF	1660
WHITE, E / MRS	1871	MARH'L MAP	1760	WHITE, JOHN	1821	PLAINTIFF	1660
WHITE, EBENEZER	1822	PLAINTIFF	1660	WHITE, JOHN	1822	PLAINTIFF	1660
WHITE, EDWARD	1816	PLAINTIFF	1659	WHITE, JOHN	1829	MISC	1702
WHITE, EDWARD	1817	PLAINTIFF	1659	WHITE, JOHN	1831	MISC	1702
WHITE, EDWARD	1817	PLAINTIFF	1659	WHITE, JOHN	1833	MISC	1702
WHITE, EDWARD	1817	PLAINTIFF	1659	WHITE, JOHN	1834	MISC	1702
WHITE, ELANOR	1857	MISC	1702	WHITE, JOHN	1838	PLAINTIFF	1660
WHITE, ELEANOR	1857	MISC	1702	WHITE, JOHN	1839	MISC	1702
WHITE, ELIZABETH	1871	MISC	1702	WHITE, JOHN	1854	PLAINTIFF	1661
WHITE, G	1871	MARH'L MAP	1755	WHITE, JOHN	1875	MISC	1702
WHITE, G	1871	MARH'L MAP	1759	WHITE, JOSEPH	1840	PLAINTIFF	1661
WHITE, GEORGE	1817	DEFENDANT	1632	WHITE, JOSEPH	1841	PLAINTIFF	1661
WHITE, GEORGE	1819	DEFENDANT	1594	WHITE, JOSEPH	1846	PLAINTIFF	1661
WHITE, GEORGE	1820	DEFENDANT	1556	WHITE, JOSEPH	1855	MISC	1702
WHITE, GEORGE	1821	DEFENDANT	1594	WHITE, LOUISA	1873	MISC	1702
WHITE, GEORGE	1821	PLAINTIFF	1660	WHITE, MARY	1839	MISC	1702
WHITE, GEORGE	1821	PLAINTIFF	1660	WHITE, MARY	1852	MISC	1700
WHITE, GEORGE	1822	DEFENDANT	1572	WHITE, MARY	1852	MISC	1702
WHITE, GEORGE	1822	DEFENDANT	1658	WHITE, MARY	1877	PLAINTIFF	1661
WHITE, GEORGE	1823	DEFENDANT	1612	WHITE, N	1871	MARH'L MAP	1745
WHITE, GEORGE	1823	DEFENDANT	1658	WHITE, N	1871	BENWOOD	1800
WHITE, GEORGE	1824	PLAINTIFF	1660	WHITE, NANCY	1873	MISC	1702
WHITE, GEORGE	1824	PLAINTIFF	1660	WHITE, NANCY	1874	DEFENDANT	1661
WHITE, GEORGE	1825	PLAINTIFF	1660	WHITE, NEWKIRK & CO	1838	PLAINTIFF	1628
WHITE, GEORGE	1825	PLAINTIFF	1660	WHITE, NORMAN	1857	PLAINTIFF	1661
WHITE, GEORGE	1825	PLAINTIFF	1660	WHITE, NORMAN	1858	PLAINTIFF	1661
WHITE, GEORGE	1861	DEFENDANT	1673	WHITE, NORMAN	1858	PLAINTIFF	1661
WHITE, GEORGE	1873	MISC	1702	WHITE, NORMAN	1859	PLAINTIFF	1661
WHITE, GEORGE W	1831	MISC	1702	WHITE, P / S. BORDER OF OHIO CO	1871	OH CO. MAP	1742
WHITE, H S / RES	1871	BELLTON	1814	WHITE, P	1871	MARH'L MAP	1745
WHITE, HENRY	1853	PLAINTIFF	1661	WHITE, R / MRS	1871	BRKE MAP	1737
WHITE, HUGH / (TAVERN) - MAP#379	1852	BRKE MAP	1847	WHITE, R	1871	BKE/OH MAP	1739
WHITE, ISABELLA	1873	MISC	1702	WHITE, R	1871	OH CO. MAP	1743
WHITE, J	1871	MARH'L MAP	1750	WHITE, R / ?	1871	MARH'L MAP	1745
WHITE, J	1871	MARH'L MAP	1750	WHITE, R	1871	W.LIBERTY	1780
WHITE, J	1871	MARH'L MAP	1753	WHITE, ROBERT	1803	MISC	1701
WHITE, J H	1871	HAN MAP	1732	WHITE, ROBERT	1832	MISC	1702
WHITE, J H / INITIALS J.H.W.-NW OF PLEASANT HILL	1871	HAN MAP	1732	WHITE, ROBERT	1838	PLAINTIFF	1660
WHITE, ROBERT					1840	PLAINTIFF	1661
WHITE, J H / 'WHITES HOTEL' - CAMERON	1871	CAMER'N - BUS.	1795	WHITE, ROBERT	1858	PLAINTIFF	1661
WHITE, J H / WHITE HOTEL (OC.)	1871	CAMERON	1803	WHITE, ROBERT	1858	PLAINTIFF	1661
WHITE, J W	1871	MARH'L MAP	1750	WHITE, ROBERT	1871	MISC	1702
WHITE, JACKSON	1830	MISC	1702	WHITE, ROBERT	1879	PLAINTIFF	1661
WHITE, JACOB	1816	MISC	1701	WHITE, ROBERT	1879	PLAINTIFF	1661
WHITE, JACOB	1816	MISC	1701	WHITE, S	1871	HAN MAP	1732
WHITE, JACOB	1873	MISC	1702	WHITE, S / INITIALS S.W.	1871	HAN MAP	1732
WHITE, JACOB	1874	PLAINTIFF	1661	WHITE, S	1871	BRKE MAP	1734
WHITE, JAMES	1826	PLAINTIFF	1660	WHITE, S / INITIALS S.W.	1871	BRKE MAP	1734
WHITE, JAMES	1829	MISC	1680	WHITE, S / HRS	1871	OH CO. MAP	1744
WHITE, JAMES	1829	MISC	1702	WHITE, S / MRS	1871	NEW CUMB'LD	1767
WHITE, JAMES	1830	MISC	1702	WHITE, SAMUEL	1778	APPENDIX	1874
WHITE, JAMES	1873	MISC	1702	WHITE, SAMUEL	1785	MISC	1701
WHITE, JAMES	1877	PLAINTIFF	1661	WHITE, SAMUEL	1834	MISC	1702
WHITE, JAMES H	1836	MISC	1702	WHITE, SAMUEL	1857	PLAINTIFF	1661
WHITE, JAMES H	1837	PLAINTIFF	1660	WHITE, SAMUEL	1858	PLAINTIFF	1661
WHITE, JAMES H	1841	MISC	1702	WHITE, SAMUEL	1859	PLAINTIFF	1661
WHITE, JAMES H	1842	PLAINTIFF	1661	WHITE, SARAH	1839	MISC	1702
WHITE, JAMES H	1842	MISC	1702	WHITE, SHEFFIELD & CO	1856	PLAINTIFF	1630
WHITE, JAMES H	1843	PLAINTIFF	1661	WHITE, SOLOMON	1823	PLAINTIFF	1660
WHITE, JAMES SR	1871	OH CO. MAP	1743	WHITE, SOLOMON	1823	PLAINTIFF	1660
WHITE, JAMES SR	1871	OH CO. MAP	1744	WHITE, SOLOMON	1849	MISC	1702
WHITE, JEMINA	1778	APPENDIX	1874	WHITE, T	1871	WELLSBURG	1777
WHITE, JOHN	1797	PLAINTIFF	1659	WHITE, THAYORD	1851	PLAINTIFF	1661
WHITE, JOHN	1799	MISC	1701	WHITE, THOMAS	1809	PLAINTIFF	1659
WHITE, JOHN	1802	MISC	1701	WHITE, THOMAS	1809	PLAINTIFF	1659
WHITE, JOHN	1804	PLAINTIFF	1659	WHITE, THOMAS	1855	MISC	1702
WHITE, JOHN	1804	PLAINTIFF	1659	WHITE, THOMAS T	1873	MISC	1702
WHITE, JOHN	1805	PLAINTIFF	1659	WHITE, W / NEAR BROOKE CO BORDER	1871	MARH'L MAP	1745
WHITE, JOHN	1805	PLAINTIFF	1659				
WHITE, JOHN	1807	PLAINTIFF	1659	WHITE, W	1871	MARH'L MAP	1746
WHITE, JOHN	1807	PLAINTIFF	1659	WHITE, W	1871	MARH'L MAP	1746
WHITE, JOHN	1807	PLAINTIFF	1659	WHITE, W	1871	MARH'L MAP	1749
				WHITE, W	1871	MARH'L MAP	1752

'PERSONAL TIME LINE' INDEX TO VOLUME 7 OF THE OHIO COUNTY INDEX

ENTRY	YEAR	SUBJECT	PAGE	ENTRY	YEAR	SUBJECT	PAGE
WHITE, WASHINGTON	1856	MISC	1702	WHITSELL, LOUIS	1789	PLAINTIFF	1658
WHITE, WASHINGTON	1857	MISC	1702	WHITSETT, J E	1871	BETHANY	1773
WHITE, WILLIAM	1796	PLAINTIFF	1659	WHITSON, R	1871	HAN MAP	1732
WHITE, WILLIAM	1797	PLAINTIFF	1659	WHITTAKER, J	1871	MARH'L MAP	1745
WHITE, WILLIAM	1838	PLAINTIFF	1661	WHITTAKER, JOSEPH	1858	PLAINTIFF	1597
WHITE, WILLIAM	1838	PLAINTIFF	1661	WHITTAKER, P	1871	MARH'L MAP	1745
WHITE, WILLIAM	1839	MISC	1702	WHITTAKER, P	1871	BENWOOD	1799
WHITE, WILLIAM	1840	PLAINTIFF	1661	WHITTAKER, P	1871	BENWOOD	1800
WHITE, WILLIAM	1840	PLAINTIFF	1661	WHITTAKER, W	1871	BENWOOD	1800
WHITE, WILLIAM	1841	PLAINTIFF	1661	WHITTAKERS & COWDEN	1858	PLAINTIFF	1630
WHITE, WILLIAM	1842	DEFENDANT	1640	WHITTAM, BENJAMIN	1800	MISC	1703
WHITE, WILLIAM / (GONE) - MAP#225	1852	BRKE MAP	1844	WHITTAM, JOSEPH	1846	MISC	1703
WHITE, WILLIAM / (GONE) - MAP#226	1852	BRKE MAP	1844	WHITTAM, WILLIAM	1849	MISC	1703
WHITE, WILLIAM / (GONE) - MAP#227	1852	BRKE MAP	1844	WHITTAN, BENJAMIN	1802	MISC	1703
WHITE, Z G	1871	MARH'L MAP	1753	WHITTEN, JOSEPH	1824	PLAINTIFF	1596
WHITE, Z G	1871	MARH'L MAP	1757	WHITTEN, PHILLIP	1791	MISC	1703
WHITEFORD, HUGH	1787	PLAINTIFF	1596	WHITTINGHAM - ORPHANS	1832	MISC	1703
WHITEFORD, HUGH	1797	PLAINTIFF	1596	WHITTINGHAM J / HRS - HEIRS	1871	MDSVILLE	1807
WHITEFORD, JOHN	1797	PLAINTIFF	1596	WHITTINGHAM, GEORGE	1832	MISC	1703
WHITEHEAD, E & SON	1830	PLAINTIFF	1628	WHITTINGHAM, JAMES	1820	PLAINTIFF	1596
WHITEHEAD, ELISHA	1832	PLAINTIFF	1596	WHITTINGHAM, JAMES	1828	MISC	1678
WHITEHEAD, ELISHA	1862	MISC	1698	WHITTINGHAM, JAMES	1828	MISC	1703
WHITEHEAD, SAMUEL	1827	MISC	1697	WHITTINGHAM, JAMES	1828	MISC	1703
WHITEHEAD, SAMUEL H	1824	MISC	1697	WHITTINGHAM, JAMES	1828	MISC	1703
WHITEHEAD, SAMUEL H	1832	PLAINTIFF	1596	WHITTINGHAM, JAMES	1830	MISC	1703
WHITEHEAD, WILLIAM	1791	DEFENDANT	1637	WHITTINGHAM, JOANNA	1832	MISC	1703
WHITEHILL, J	1871	HAN MAP	1731	WHITTINGHAM, JOANNA	1846	MISC	1703
WHITEHILL, JOHN	1786	MISC	1697	WHITTINGHAM, R C	1871	MARH'L MAP	1748
WHITEHOUSE HOME	1871	MARH'L MAP	1745	WHITTINGHAM, RICHARD	1846	MISC	1703
WHITEKER, A O / INITIALS A.O.W.	1871	MARH'L MAP	1754	WHITTINGHAM, SARAH E	1828	MISC	1678
WHITEKER, A Q / INITIALS A.Q.W - EDGE OF MAP	1871	MARH'L MAP	1751	WHITTINGHAM, SARAH ELIZ	1828	MISC	1703
				WHITTOCK & ANDERSON	1878	PLAINTIFF	1631
WHITEKER, A Q	1871	MARH'L MAP	1754	WHITTOM, JOSEPH	1804	PLAINTIFF	1596
WHITEKER, A Q / INITIALS A.Q.W.	1871	MARH'L MAP	1754	WHITTON, JOSEPH	1810	PLAINTIFF	1596
WHITELASH, CHARLES	1798	PLAINTIFF	1596	WHITTON, THOMAS	1802	PLAINTIFF	1596
WHITELOCK, BENJAMIN F	1849	MISC	1697	WHITTUM, ELIZABETH	1803	PLAINTIFF	1577
WHITELOCK, CHARLES	1795	PLAINTIFF	1596	WHITTUM, ELIZABETH	1803	PLAINTIFF	1596
WHITELOCK, CHARLES	1811	MISC	1697	WHITZEL, JACOB	1803	DEFENDANT	1607
WHITELOCK, HANNAH	1812	PLAINTIFF	1596	WHITZEL, JACOB	1809	PLAINTIFF	1658
WHITEMAN, E / & CO	1855	PLAINTIFF	1629	WHITZEL, JACOB	1809	PLAINTIFF	1658
WHITEMAN, EZRA	1855	PLAINTIFF	1596	WHITZEL, JOHN	1809	PLAINTIFF	1658
WHITEMAN, LEWIS	1840	PLAINTIFF	1596	WHITZELL, ADAM	1823	PLAINTIFF	1658
WHITEMAN, MICHAEL	1866	MISC	1698	WHITZELL, GEORGE	1834	DEFENDANT	1669
WHITES HOTEL - CAMERON	1871	CAMER'N - BUS.	1795	WHITZELL, JACOB	1809	PLAINTIFF	1645
WHITES RUN	1852	BRKE MAP	1844	WHORREY, - / MILL (?D. FLAX?)	1871	MARH'L MAP	1746
WHITESIDE, R J	1871	BENWO'D - BUS.	1795	WHYTE, JAMES	1858	PLAINTIFF	1661
WHITESIDE, R J	1871	BENWOOD	1798	WHYTE, JAMES G	1858	PLAINTIFF	1661
WHITESIDE, S M	1876	PLAINTIFF	1597	WICARD, THOMAS	1874	MISC	1690
WHITESIDE, SAMUEL M	1872	MISC	1698	WICK, JAMES R	1855	PLAINTIFF	1588
WHITESIDE, VIRGINIA	1872	MISC	1698	WICKHAM - CHILDREN	1860	MISC	1690
WHITHACRE HOUSE - HOTEL / WELLSVILLE, OHIO	1871	NEW MANCH.	1763	WICKHAM, C W / (?CONRAD?)	1875	MISC	1690
				WICKHAM, C W / (?CONRAD?)	1875	MISC	1700
WHITHAM, -	1871	OH CO. MAP	1740	WICKHAM, CATHERINE	1855	MISC	1689
WHITHAM, D	1874	MISC	1703	WICKHAM, CHARLES	1859	PLAINTIFF	1582
WHITHAM, ELIZABETH	1800	DEFENDANT	1578	WICKHAM, CONRAD W	1877	PLAINTIFF	1582
WHITHAM, EMILY C	1849	MISC	1703	WICKHAM, EMMA C	1866	MISC	1690
WHITHAM, GEORGE D	1849	MISC	1703	WICKHAM, GEORGE A	1873	MISC	1690
WHITHAM, J	1871	OH CO. MAP	1740	WICKHAM, GEORGE A	1873	MISC	1690
WHITHAM, JOSEPH	1800	DEFENDANT	1578	WICKHAM, GEORGE A	1873	MISC	1700
WHITHAM, JOSEPH	1814	PLAINTIFF	1596	WICKHAM, GEORGE E	1854	PLAINTIFF	1582
WHITHAM, JOSEPH	1824	PLAINTIFF	1596	WICKHAM, GEORGE E	1859	PLAINTIFF	1582
WHITHAM, JOSEPH D	1878	PLAINTIFF	1597	WICKHAM, GEORGE E	1862	PLAINTIFF	1582
WHITHAM, M	1871	OH CO. MAP	1740	WICKHAM, GEORGE E	1872	MISC	1690
WHITHAM, M	1871	OH CO. MAP	1740	WICKHAM, GEORGE E	1872	MISC	1700
WHITHAM, PEREGRINE	1816	MISC	1703	WICKHAM, GEORGE E	1876	MISC	1690
WHITHAM, R	1871	OH CO. MAP	1740	WICKHAM, HENRY C	1838	MISC	1689
WHITHAMS - ORPHANS	1801	MISC	1703	WICKHAM, HENRY C	1840	DEFENDANT	1563
WHITHAMS, BENJAMIN	1801	MISC	1703	WICKHAM, HENRY C	1840	PLAINTIFF	1582
WHITHAMS, ELIZABETH	1801	MISC	1703	WICKHAM, HENRY C	1841	PLAINTIFF	1582
WHITHAMS, ELIZABETH	1801	MISC	1703	WICKHAM, J	1871	TRIAD.BORO.	1784
WHITHAMS, ELIZABETH	1801	MISC	1703	WICKHAM, LEVI	1828	MISC	1689
WHITHAMS, PERRYWINE	1801	MISC	1703	WICKHAM, MARY	1855	MISC	1689
WHITHAMS, PERRYWINE	1801	MISC	1703	WICKHAM, MARY ANN SR	1860	MISC	1690
WHITHAMS, WILLIAM R	1801	MISC	1703	WICKHAM, MARY ANNE JR	1860	MISC	1690
WHITHAN, JOSEPH	1818	PLAINTIFF	1596	WICKHAM, REBECCA	1860	MISC	1690
WHITILOCK, CHARLES	1814	DEFENDANT	1596	WICKHAM, ROBERT	1839	MISC	1689
WHITILOCK, HANNAH	1814	PLAINTIFF	1596	WICKHAM, ROBERT	1839	MISC	1689
WHITING, JOHN	1814	MISC	1697	WICKHAM, SARAH	1863	MISC	1690
WHITING, JOHN L	1874	PLAINTIFF	1597	WICKHAM, WARNER	1819	PLAINTIFF	1582
WHITMAN, PETER	1839	PLAINTIFF	1596	WICKHAM, WILLIAM	1856	MISC	1690
WHITNEY, D	1871	MARH'L MAP	1749	WICKHAM, WILLIAM	1859	PLAINTIFF	1582
WHITNEY, D	1871	MARH'L MAP	1752	WICKHAM, WILLIAM	1860	MISC	1690
WHITNEY, JOHN H	1842	MISC	1697	WICKHAM, WILLIAM P	1860	MISC	1690
WHITNEY, JOSEPH	1838	PLAINTIFF	1596	WICKHAM, WILLIAM S	1834	PLAINTIFF	1582
WHITSELL, ADAM	1822	PLAINTIFF	1658	WICKHAM, WILLIAM S	1837	PLAINTIFF	1582
WHITSELL, JACOB	1800	PLAINTIFF	1658	WICKHAM, WILLIAM S	1839	MISC	1689

'PERSONAL TIME LINE' INDEX TO VOLUME 7 OF THE *OHIO COUNTY INDEX*

ENTRY	YEAR	SUBJECT	PAGE	ENTRY	YEAR	SUBJECT	PAGE
WICKHAM, WILLIAM S	1839	MISC	1689	WILLARD, ADALINE	1876	PLAINTIFF	1590
WICKHAM, WILLIAM S	1841	PLAINTIFF	1587	WILLARD, EMMA	1854	MISC	1694
WICKHAM, WILLIAM S	1848	PLAINTIFF	1582	WILLARD, R E / CAMERON	1871	MARH'L MAP	1757
WICKHAM, WILLIAM S	1854	PLAINTIFF	1582	WILLARD, R E / (?OR P.E.?)	1871	CAMERON	1804
WICKHAM, WILLIAM S	1855	PLAINTIFF	1582	WILLARD, R E / ? - INITIALS SAY P.E.W. (?IS IT R OR P?)	1871	CAMERON	1804
WICKHAM, WILLIAM S	1856	PLAINTIFF	1582	WILLARD, R E / ? - INITIALS SAY P.E.W. (?IS IT R OR P?)	1871	CAMERON	1804
WICKHAM, WILLIAM S	1857	PLAINTIFF	1582				
WICKHAM, WILLIAM S	1860	PLAINTIFF	1582				
WIDABUSH, WILLIAM	1858	PLAINTIFF	1588	WILLCOXON, H / ABBEV. H.W.	1871	HAN MAP	1731
WIDABUSH, WILLIAM	1860	PLAINTIFF	1588	WILLCOXON, H H	1871	HAN MAP	1731
WIDDLE, HENRY	1828	PLAINTIFF	1587	WILLCOXTON, HENRY HARDY	1793	MISC	1693
WIDECH, SAMUEL	1820	PLAINTIFF	1587	WILLCOXTON, HENRY HARDY	1801	MISC	1693
WIEDEBUSCH, AUGUST	1876	PLAINTIFF	1588	WILLEKE, JOHN	1874	MISC	1694
WIEDEBUSCH, H	1871	MDSVILLE	1808	WILLER, PETER	1808	APPENDIX	1873
WIEDEBUSCH, H / INITIALS H.W.	1871	MDSVILLE	1808	WILLER, PETER	1821	PLAINTIFF	1589
WIEDEBUSCH, H / INITIALS H.W.	1871	MDSVILLE	1808	WILLETS, J A	1875	MISC	1694
WIEDEBUSCH, H	1871	MDSVILLE	1810	WILLETS, JESSE	1807	PLAINTIFF	1589
WIEDEBUSCH, H / INITIALS H.W.	1871	MDSVILLE	1810	WILLEY, HENRY	1823	DEFENDANT	1612
WIEDEBUSCH, H / INITIALS H.W.	1871	MDSVILLE	1810	WILLHELM, -	1871	MARH'L MAP	1757
WIEDEBUSH, WILLIAM	1858	MISC	1690	WILLIAM, -	1827	MISC	1693
WIEDMAN, BERNARD	1828	DEFENDANT	1551	WILLIAM, ISAAC	1801	PLAINTIFF	1655
WIEDMAN, BERNARD	1828	DEFENDANT	1563	WILLIAM, JAMES	1818	PLAINTIFF	1656
WIER, - / MRS	1871	WELLSBURG	1777	WILLIAM, JOHN	1799	PLAINTIFF	1655
WIER, JANE	1875	MISC	1690	WILLIAM, JOHN	1806	PLAINTIFF	1655
WIER, MARTHA	1856	PLAINTIFF	1588	WILLIAM, JOHN	1806	PLAINTIFF	1655
WIER, THOMAS	1832	PLAINTIFF	1587	WILLIAM, ROBERT	1858	DEFENDANT	1603
WIER, THOMPSON	1856	PLAINTIFF	1588	WILLIAM, WILLIAM W	1858	PLAINTIFF	1657
WIESEL, HENRY J	1873	MISC	1690	WILLIAMS & DILWORTH	1843	PLAINTIFF	1629
WIESEL, MARY H	1874	MISC	1690	WILLIAMS BROTHERS	1876	PLAINTIFF	1631
WIESEL, MICHAEL	1874	MISC	1690	WILLIAMS CAMP & ABBE	1841	PLAINTIFF	1629
WIGGANS, PHILIP	1802	DEFENDANT	1655	WILLIAMS, -	1793	PLAINTIFF	1655
WIGGANS, PHILIP	1803	DEFENDANT	1655	WILLIAMS, - / MRS	1871	MARH'L MAP	1758
WIGGINS, ELY	1839	PLAINTIFF	1587	WILLIAMS, -	1871	CAMERON	1803
WIGGINS, J	1871	BRKE MAP	1735	WILLIAMS, - / MRS	1871	CAMERON	1804
WIGGINS, J / SR	1871	BRKE MAP	1735	WILLIAMS, ALEXANDER	1841	PLAINTIFF	1656
WIGGINS, J JR / HRS - HEIRS	1871	BRKE MAP	1735	WILLIAMS, ANN LUCRETIA	1856	MISC	1694
WIGGINS, J JR / HRS, COAL & TIMBERLAND	1871	BRKE MAP	1735	WILLIAMS, AUSTIN F	1841	PLAINTIFF	1656
				WILLIAMS, AZRA	1800	MISC	1693
WIGGINS, J SR	1871	BRKE MAP	1735	WILLIAMS, B E	1871	WELLSBURG	1777
WIGGINS, JOHN JR / & W - MAP#469	1852	BRKE MAP	1850	WILLIAMS, B E / LIVERY STA. (?STABLE?)	1871	WELLSBURG	1777
WIGGINS, JOHN JR / & W - MAP#470	1852	BRKE MAP	1850				
WIGGINS, JOHN JR / MAP#674	1852	BRKE MAP	1854	WILLIAMS, B E	1871	WELLSBURG	1778
WIGGINS, JOHN SR / MAP#473	1852	BRKE MAP	1850	WILLIAMS, BENJAMIN	1824	PLAINTIFF	1656
WIGGINS, JOHN SR / MAP#474	1852	BRKE MAP	1850	WILLIAMS, BENJAMIN	1826	PLAINTIFF	1656
WIGGINS, W / & JOHN JR - MAP#469	1852	BRKE MAP	1850	WILLIAMS, CHARLES	1789	PLAINTIFF	1655
WIGGINS, W / & JOHN JR / MAP#470	1852	BRKE MAP	1850	WILLIAMS, CHARLES	1791	PLAINTIFF	1655
WIGGINS, W B	1871	BRKE MAP	1735	WILLIAMS, CHARLES	1803	PLAINTIFF	1655
WIGGINS, W B / COAL & TIMBERLAND	1871	BRKE MAP	1735	WILLIAMS, CHARLES H	1858	MISC	1694
WIHTERS, R	1871	MARH'L MAP	1753	WILLIAMS, CHARLES MORTIMER	1840	MISC	1694
WIKOFF, JACOB C	1804	PLAINTIFF	1587	WILLIAMS, CHARLOTTE	1876	PLAINTIFF	1657
WILCOCK, ROGERS & FARLEY	1855	PLAINTIFF	1629	WILLIAMS, DALELIFF	1825	MISC	1693
WILCOCK, WILLIAM	1855	PLAINTIFF	1590	WILLIAMS, DAVID	1794	PLAINTIFF	1655
WILCOX, ALFRED	1834	PLAINTIFF	1589	WILLIAMS, DAVID	1871	MISC	1694
WILCOX, IMRI	1834	PLAINTIFF	1589	WILLIAMS, E	1871	MARH'L MAP	1757
WILCOX, LOYD	1832	PLAINTIFF	1589	WILLIAMS, E	1871	MARH'L MAP	1761
WILCOX, WILLIAM T	1855	PLAINTIFF	1590	WILLIAMS, ELIZABETH	1805	MISC	1693
WILCOXEN, C	1871	HAN MAP	1732	WILLIAMS, ENOCH	1785	MISC	1693
WILCOXON, ANTHONY	1812	MISC	1693	WILLIAMS, FREDERICK	1855	MISC	1694
WILCOXON, C A	1871	HAN MAP	1733	WILLIAMS, GEORGE	1875	PLAINTIFF	1657
WILCOXON, HENRY HARDY	1803	PLAINTIFF	1589	WILLIAMS, H	1871	MARH'L MAP	1752
WILCOXON, S / MISS	1871	HAN MAP	1733	WILLIAMS, H	1871	MARH'L MAP	1756
WILCOXON, S	1871	NEW MANCH.	1769	WILLIAMS, H	1871	MARH'L MAP	1756
WILCOXSEN, S	1871	HAN MAP	1732	WILLIAMS, H H	1871	HAN MAP	1726
WILCOXSON, R / MRS	1871	HAN MAP	1730	WILLIAMS, HARRISON	1841	PLAINTIFF	1656
WILD ROSE - FRANKLIN TWP	1871	MARH'L MAP	1758	WILLIAMS, HENRY	1856	PLAINTIFF	1657
WILDE & BRO	1857	PLAINTIFF	1630	WILLIAMS, HUGH	1797	PLAINTIFF	1655
WILDEN, SHUBAL	1858	PLAINTIFF	1590	WILLIAMS, HUGH	1800	PLAINTIFF	1655
WILDER, SHUBAL	1858	PLAINTIFF	1590	WILLIAMS, HUGH	1813	PLAINTIFF	1656
WILDS, GEORGE	1806	PLAINTIFF	1589	WILLIAMS, ISAAC	1789	PLAINTIFF	1655
WILDS, ISAAC	1844	MISC	1694	WILLIAMS, ISAAC	1802	PLAINTIFF	1655
WILEY, - / MRS	1871	WELLSBURG	1778	WILLIAMS, ISAAC HARRISON	1878	MISC	1694
WILEY, D O & CO	1878	PLAINTIFF	1631	WILLIAMS, J	1871	MARH'L MAP	1758
WILEY, JOSHUA C	1837	PLAINTIFF	1589	WILLIAMS, J	1871	MARH'L MAP	1760
WILEY, THOMAS	1841	PLAINTIFF	1589	WILLIAMS, JAMES	1789	PLAINTIFF	1655
WILEY, WILLIAM	1847	PLAINTIFF	1589	WILLIAMS, JAMES	1789	PLAINTIFF	1655
WILEY, WILLIAM	1850	PLAINTIFF	1590	WILLIAMS, JAMES	1793	MISC	1693
WILHELM, G	1871	HAN MAP	1726	WILLIAMS, JAMES	1793	MISC	1693
WILHELM, LUDWIG	1876	PLAINTIFF	1590	WILLIAMS, JAMES	1830	PLAINTIFF	1656
WILIE, WILLIAM	1829	PLAINTIFF	1589	WILLIAMS, JEREMIAH	1791	PLAINTIFF	1655
WILKIN, L / MRS (?WILKINS?)	1871	NEW CUMB'LD	1767	WILLIAMS, JEREMIAH	1800	PLAINTIFF	1655
WILKINS, JOSEPH & CO	1879	PLAINTIFF	1631	WILLIAMS, JEREMIAH	1802	PLAINTIFF	1655
WILKINS, LEFFERTS	1858	PLAINTIFF	1590	WILLIAMS, JEREMIAH	1802	PLAINTIFF	1655
WILKINS, WILLARD C	1873	PLAINTIFF	1590	WILLIAMS, JEREMIAH	1804	PLAINTIFF	1655
WILKINSON, NATHAN	1875	PLAINTIFF	1590	WILLIAMS, JEREMIAH	1805	PLAINTIFF	1655
WILKINSON, NATHANIEL	1858	DEFENDANT	1661	WILLIAMS, JEREMIAH	1810	PLAINTIFF	1656
WILKINSON, S	1871	NEW MANCH.	1769	WILLIAMS, JEREMIAH	1810	PLAINTIFF	1656

'PERSONAL TIME LINE' INDEX TO VOLUME 7 OF THE *OHIO COUNTY INDEX*

ENTRY	YEAR	SUBJECT	PAGE	ENTRY	YEAR	SUBJECT	PAGE
WILLIAMS, JEREMIAH	1810	PLAINTIFF	1656	WILLIAMSON, ELIZABETH	1800	PLAINTIFF	1598
WILLIAMS, JEREMIAH	1811	MISC	1693	WILLIAMSON, ELIZABETH	1801	PLAINTIFF	1598
WILLIAMS, JESSE	1801	PLAINTIFF	1655	WILLIAMSON, ELIZABETH	1803	MISC	1693
WILLIAMS, JOHN	1789	PLAINTIFF	1655	WILLIAMSON, ELIZABETH	1805	MISC	1693
WILLIAMS, JOHN	1789	PLAINTIFF	1655	WILLIAMSON, ELIZABETH	1880	MISC	1694
WILLIAMS, JOHN	1793	PLAINTIFF	1655	WILLIAMSON, FRANKLIN	1850	DEFENDANT	1608
WILLIAMS, JOHN	1796	PLAINTIFF	1655	WILLIAMSON, ISABEL	1811	PLAINTIFF	1599
WILLIAMS, JOHN	1800	PLAINTIFF	1655	WILLIAMSON, ISABELLA	1811	PLAINTIFF	1599
WILLIAMS, JOHN	1800	DEFENDANT	1665	WILLIAMSON, ISABELLA	1812	PLAINTIFF	1599
WILLIAMS, JOHN	1813	PLAINTIFF	1656	WILLIAMSON, J	1871	BRKE MAP	1735
WILLIAMS, JOHN	1816	PLAINTIFF	1656	WILLIAMSON, JAMES	1782	MISC	1693
WILLIAMS, JOSEPH	1792	PLAINTIFF	1655	WILLIAMSON, JAMES	1803	PLAINTIFF	1598
WILLIAMS, L D	1879	DEFENDANT	1615	WILLIAMSON, JAMES	1805	PLAINTIFF	1599
WILLIAMS, LAMUEL	1820	PLAINTIFF	1656	WILLIAMSON, JAMES	1809	PLAINTIFF	1599
WILLIAMS, LEMUEL	1820	PLAINTIFF	1656	WILLIAMSON, JAMES	1812	PLAINTIFF	1599
WILLIAMS, LEWIN	1799	PLAINTIFF	1655	WILLIAMSON, JAMES	1814	PLAINTIFF	1599
WILLIAMS, LEWIS	1800	PLAINTIFF	1655	WILLIAMSON, JAMES / MAP#490	1852	BRKE MAP	1849
WILLIAMS, LEWIS	1800	PLAINTIFF	1655	WILLIAMSON, JAMES / MAP#491	1852	BRKE MAP	1849
WILLIAMS, M	1871	MARH'L MAP	1753	WILLIAMSON, JANE	1878	PLAINTIFF	1599
WILLIAMS, MARY	1825	PLAINTIFF	1656	WILLIAMSON, JEREMIAH	1788	DEFENDANT	1576
WILLIAMS, MARY	1825	PLAINTIFF	1656	WILLIAMSON, JOHN	1789	PLAINTIFF	1598
WILLIAMS, MATTHEWS	1808	PLAINTIFF	1655	WILLIAMSON, JOHN	1793	PLAINTIFF	1598
WILLIAMS, MATTHEWS	1808	PLAINTIFF	1656	WILLIAMSON, JOHN	1795	MISC	1693
WILLIAMS, MORDECAI	1806	PLAINTIFF	1655	WILLIAMSON, JOHN	1798	PLAINTIFF	1598
WILLIAMS, MORGAN	1859	PLAINTIFF	1657	WILLIAMSON, JOHN	1800	PLAINTIFF	1598
WILLIAMS, MOSES	1793	MISC	1693	WILLIAMSON, JOHN	1801	PLAINTIFF	1598
WILLIAMS, P	1871	MARH'L MAP	1745	WILLIAMSON, JOHN	1805	MISC	1693
WILLIAMS, P	1871	SHERRARD	1811	WILLIAMSON, JOHN	1810	DEFENDANT	1559
WILLIAMS, PETER	1821	PLAINTIFF	1656	WILLIAMSON, JOHN	1810	DEFENDANT	1656
WILLIAMS, POLLY	1823	MISC	1693	WILLIAMSON, JOHN	1812	DEFENDANT	1626
WILLIAMS, R / MRS	1871	MARH'L MAP	1752	WILLIAMSON, JOHN	1813	MISC	1693
WILLIAMS, ROBERT	1823	PLAINTIFF	1656	WILLIAMSON, JOHN D	1852	MISC	1694
WILLIAMS, ROBERT	1835	PLAINTIFF	1656	WILLIAMSON, JOSEPH	1802	PLAINTIFF	1598
WILLIAMS, ROBERT	1841	PLAINTIFF	1656	WILLIAMSON, M	1871	OH CO. MAP	1743
WILLIAMS, ROBERT	1841	PLAINTIFF	1656	WILLIAMSON, M	1871	OH CO. MAP	1744
WILLIAMS, ROBERT	1842	PLAINTIFF	1656	WILLIAMSON, M H / INITIALS M.H.W.	1871	BRKE MAP	1734
WILLIAMS, ROBERT	1846	PLAINTIFF	1657	WILLIAMSON, MARGARET	1851	MISC	1694
WILLIAMS, ROBERT	1847	PLAINTIFF	1657	WILLIAMSON, MARGARET	1853	MISC	1694
WILLIAMS, ROBERT	1848	PLAINTIFF	1657	WILLIAMSON, MARY	1794	MISC	1693
WILLIAMS, ROBERT	1852	PLAINTIFF	1657	WILLIAMSON, MARY	1811	PLAINTIFF	1599
WILLIAMS, ROBERT	1853	PLAINTIFF	1657	WILLIAMSON, MORGAN	1851	MISC	1694
WILLIAMS, ROBERT	1853	PLAINTIFF	1657	WILLIAMSON, MORGAN	1856	MISC	1694
WILLIAMS, S	1817	MISC	1693	WILLIAMSON, MORGAN	1858	MISC	1694
WILLIAMS, SAMUEL	1803	PLAINTIFF	1655	WILLIAMSON, MORGAN	1868	MISC	1694
WILLIAMS, SARAH	1837	PLAINTIFF	1656	WILLIAMSON, MOSES	1792	MISC	1693
WILLIAMS, SWAN	1799	PLAINTIFF	1655	WILLIAMSON, MOSES	1826	PLAINTIFF	1599
WILLIAMS, SWAN	1799	PLAINTIFF	1655	WILLIAMSON, N H	1871	BRKE MAP	1734
WILLIAMS, T	1871	MARH'L MAP	1752	WILLIAMSON, R S	1871	OH CO. MAP	1740
WILLIAMS, T	1871	MARH'L MAP	1752	WILLIAMSON, ROBERT	1811	DEFENDANT	1599
WILLIAMS, THEODORE	1833	PLAINTIFF	1656	WILLIAMSON, ROBERT	1821	MISC	1693
WILLIAMS, THEODORE	1834	PLAINTIFF	1656	WILLIAMSON, ROBERT	1835	MISC	1694
WILLIAMS, THOMAS	1812	PLAINTIFF	1656	WILLIAMSON, S	1871	BKE/OH MAP	1738
WILLIAMS, W / MAP ENGRAVER - PHILADEPHIA	1852	HEMP. RR MAP	1825	WILLIAMSON, SALLY	1810	PLAINTIFF	1599
				WILLIAMSON, SAMUEL	1852	NOT ON MAP	1836
WILLIAMS, WILLIAM	1816	PLAINTIFF	1656	WILLIAMSON, SARAH	1823	MISC	1693
WILLIAMS, WILLIAM	1817	PLAINTIFF	1656	WILLIAMSON, THOMAS	1811	DEFENDANT	1599
WILLIAMS, WILLIAM	1836	PLAINTIFF	1656	WILLIAMSON, THOMAS	1814	PLAINTIFF	1599
WILLIAMS, WILLIAM	1837	PLAINTIFF	1656	WILLIAMSON, THOMAS	1818	PLAINTIFF	1599
WILLIAMS, WILLIAM	1839	PLAINTIFF	1656	WILLIAMSON, W	1871	BRKE MAP	1734
WILLIAMS, WILLIAM	1850	PLAINTIFF	1657	WILLIAMSON, W / INITIALS W.W.	1871	BRKE MAP	1734
WILLIAMS, WILLIAM H / & CO	1840	PLAINTIFF	1628	WILLIAMSON, W / INITIALS W.W.	1871	BRKE MAP	1734
WILLIAMS, WILLIAM H	1840	PLAINTIFF	1656	WILLIAMSON, W	1871	OH CO. MAP	1743
WILLIAMS, WILLIAM H	1843	PLAINTIFF	1656	WILLIAMSON, W	1871	OH CO. MAP	1744
WILLIAMSBURG, PA / WASHINGTON CO	1852	BRKE MAP	1847	WILLIAMSON, WILLIAM	1799	PLAINTIFF	1598
				WILLIAMSON, WILLIAM	1810	MISC	1693
WILLIAMSON & WARN	1860	PLAINTIFF	1630	WILLIAMSON, WILLIAM	1810	MISC	1693
WILLIAMSON, -	1806	PLAINTIFF	1599	WILLIAMSON, WILLIAM	1811	DEFENDANT	1599
WILLIAMSON, ALEX	1802	PLAINTIFF	1598	WILLIAMSON, WILLIAM	1813	PLAINTIFF	1599
WILLIAMSON, ANN	1787	MISC	1693	WILLIAMSON, WILLIAM	1813	MISC	1693
WILLIAMSON, B	1843	PLAINTIFF	1599	WILLIAMSON, WILLIAM	1817	DEFENDANT	1608
WILLIAMSON, BASIL	1834	DEFENDANT	1646	WILLIAMSON, WILLIAM	1818	PLAINTIFF	1599
WILLIAMSON, BAZEL	1834	PLAINTIFF	1599	WILLIAMSON, WILLIAM	1821	PLAINTIFF	1599
WILLIAMSON, BAZIL	1834	PLAINTIFF	1599	WILLIAMSON, WILLIAM	1824	DEFENDANT	1585
WILLIAMSON, D	1871	BRKE MAP	1735	WILLIAMSON, WILLIAM	1825	DEFENDANT	1585
WILLIAMSON, D	1871	MDSVILLE	1807	WILLIAMSON, WILLIAM	1829	MISC	1693
WILLIAMSON, D	1871	MDSVILLE	1809	WILLIAMSON, WILLIAM	1849	MISC	1694
WILLIAMSON, DAVID	1779	DEFENDANT	1634	WILLIAMSON, WILLIAM	1860	PLAINTIFF	1599
WILLIAMSON, DAVID	1780	DEFENDANT	1634	WILLIAMSON, WILLIAM	1871	OH CO. MAP	1740
WILLIAMSON, DAVID	1784	PLAINTIFF	1598	WILLING, JOHN	1803	PLAINTIFF	1589
WILLIAMSON, DAVID	1792	PLAINTIFF	1598	WILLIS, ISAAC	1818	PLAINTIFF	1589
WILLIAMSON, DAVID	1800	PLAINTIFF	1598	WILLIS, JAMES	1858	PLAINTIFF	1590
WILLIAMSON, DAVID	1806	PLAINTIFF	1599	WILLIS, JAMES C	1856	PLAINTIFF	1590
WILLIAMSON, DAVID	1811	PLAINTIFF	1599	WILLIS, PETER	1818	PLAINTIFF	1589
WILLIAMSON, DAVID	1814	PLAINTIFF	1599	WILLIS, ROBERT	1818	PLAINTIFF	1589
WILLIAMSON, DAVID	1817	PLAINTIFF	1599	WILLIS, ROBERT	1818	PLAINTIFF	1589
WILLIAMSON, DAVIDSON	1792	PLAINTIFF	1598	WILLISALIAN SOCIETY	1831	MISC	1694

'PERSONAL TIME LINE' INDEX TO VOLUME 7 OF THE *OHIO COUNTY INDEX*

ENTRY	YEAR	SUBJECT	PAGE	ENTRY	YEAR	SUBJECT	PAGE
WILLISON, ANDREW	1857	PLAINTIFF	1590	WILSON, ALEXANDER	1837	MISC	1705
WILLISON, JOHN	1800	MISC	1693	WILSON, ALEXANDER	1837	MISC	1705
WILLISON, JOSEPH	1806	DEFENDANT	1644	WILSON, ALEXANDER	1837	MISC	1705
WILLISTON, WILLIAM G	1858	PLAINTIFF	1590	WILSON, ALEXANDER	1837	MISC	1705
WILLITTS, JOHN S	1875	MISC	1694	WILSON, ALEXANDER	1838	PLAINTIFF	1651
WILLITTS, JOSEPH A	1875	MISC	1694	WILSON, ALEXANDER	1838	PLAINTIFF	1651
WILLITTS, JOSEPH A	1875	MISC	1695	WILSON, ALEXANDER	1838	MISC	1705
WILLLIAMS, JEREMIAH	1810	APPENDIX	1873	WILSON, ALEXANDER	1838	MISC	1705
WILLOW SPRING	1871	OH CO. MAP	1742	WILSON, ALEXANDER	1839	PLAINTIFF	1651
WILLOW SPRING	1871	RITCHIE TWP	1793	WILSON, ALEXANDER	1840	PLAINTIFF	1652
WILLOW SPRINGS	1871	MARH'L MAP	1745	WILSON, ALEXANDER	1841	PLAINTIFF	1652
WILLS CREEK - AT SPEAKERSBURG, OH	1852	BRKE MAP	1851	WILSON, ALEXANDER	1842	PLAINTIFF	1652
				WILSON, ALEXANDER	1842	MISC	1705
WILLS, ABSOLOM	1806	PLAINTIFF	1644	WILSON, ALEXANDER	1846	PLAINTIFF	1652
WILLS, BENJAMIN	1807	PLAINTIFF	1645	WILSON, ALEXANDER	1846	MISC	1706
WILLS, BENJAMIN	1809	PLAINTIFF	1645	WILSON, ALEXANDER	1848	PLAINTIFF	1653
WILLS, BENJAMIN	1820	PLAINTIFF	1646	WILSON, ALEXANDER	1851	PLAINTIFF	1653
WILLS, LEVE	1879	MISC	1694	WILSON, ALEXANDER	1852	PLAINTIFF	1653
WILLSON, HUGH	1801	PLAINTIFF	1647	WILSON, ANDREW	1784	PLAINTIFF	1647
WILLSON, HUGH	1803	PLAINTIFF	1647	WILSON, ANDREW	1786	PLAINTIFF	1647
WILLSON, J	1871	MARH'L MAP	1754	WILSON, ANDREW	1789	PLAINTIFF	1647
WILLSON, J	1871	MARH'L MAP	1754	WILSON, ANDREW	1793	DEFENDANT	1655
WILLSON, J J	1871	MARH'L MAP	1752	WILSON, ANDREW	1822	PLAINTIFF	1649
WILLSON, JAMES	1799	PLAINTIFF	1647	WILSON, ANDREW	1855	PLAINTIFF	1653
WILLSON, JAMES	1802	PLAINTIFF	1647	WILSON, ANDREW	1856	PLAINTIFF	1653
WILLSON, JAMES	1804	PLAINTIFF	1648	WILSON, ANDREW	1857	PLAINTIFF	1653
WILLSON, JOHN	1801	PLAINTIFF	1647	WILSON, ANDREW	1858	PLAINTIFF	1653
WILLSON, JOHN	1801	PLAINTIFF	1647	WILSON, ANDREW	1859	PLAINTIFF	1653
WILLSON, JOHN	1802	PLAINTIFF	1647	WILSON, ANDREW	1862	MISC	1706
WILLSON, JOSEPH	1810	PLAINTIFF	1648	WILSON, ANDREW	1863	PLAINTIFF	1654
WILLSON, JOSEPH	1821	PLAINTIFF	1649	WILSON, ANDREW	1874	PLAINTIFF	1654
WILLSON, JOSEPH	1824	DEFENDANT	1570	WILSON, ANDREW	1877	PLAINTIFF	1654
WILLSON, S	1871	MARH'L MAP	1758	WILSON, ANDREW	1879	DEFENDANT	1597
WILLSON, SAMUEL	1800	DEFENDANT	1666	WILSON, ANDREW J	1877	PLAINTIFF	1654
WILLSON, SAMUEL	1802	PLAINTIFF	1647	WILSON, ANN	1844	PLAINTIFF	1652
WILLSON, STEPHEN R	1803	PLAINTIFF	1648	WILSON, BENJIMIN	1798	PLAINTIFF	1647
WILMINGTON	1852	HEMP. RR MAP	1825	WILSON, CATHARINE	1832	MISC	1705
WILSON - INFANTS	1832	MISC	1705	WILSON, CATHARINE	1849	MISC	1706
WILSON - ORPHANS	1874	MISC	1706	WILSON, CATHERINE	1837	MISC	1705
WILSON & HADDEN	1836	PLAINTIFF	1628	WILSON, CATHERINE E	1837	MISC	1705
WILSON & HEADY	1857	PLAINTIFF	1630	WILSON, CATHERINE E	1838	MISC	1705
WILSON & HUMES	1846	PLAINTIFF	1629	WILSON, CHARLES	1818	PLAINTIFF	1648
WILSON & MOORE	1829	PLAINTIFF	1628	WILSON, CHARLES G	1829	PLAINTIFF	1649
WILSON & WADDLE	1835	PLAINTIFF	1617	WILSON, CHARLES M	1851	PLAINTIFF	1653
WILSON & WADDLE	1840	PLAINTIFF	1617	WILSON, COLIN	1835	PLAINTIFF	1650
WILSON & WADDLE	1841	PLAINTIFF	1617	WILSON, COLIN	1840	PLAINTIFF	1652
WILSON & WADDLE	1842	PLAINTIFF	1617	WILSON, COLIN	1841	PLAINTIFF	1652
WILSON & WATT	1841	PLAINTIFF	1629	WILSON, COLLIN	1841	PLAINTIFF	1652
WILSON CULBERTSON CO	1841	PLAINTIFF	1629	WILSON, COLLIN	1842	PLAINTIFF	1652
WILSON RUN	1871	BKE/OH MAP	1738	WILSON, DANIEL	1804	MISC	1704
WILSON, -	1786	DEFENDANT	1659	WILSON, DANIEL	1806	MISC	1704
WILSON, -	1800	PLAINTIFF	1647	WILSON, DANIEL	1811	MISC	1704
WILSON, -	1801	PLAINTIFF	1647	WILSON, DANIEL	1871	MARH'L MAP	1749
WILSON, -	1837	MISC	1683	WILSON, DANIEL / BLACKSMITH - LIMESTONE P.O.	1871	WASH. TWP-BUS.	1797
WILSON, -	1840	PLAINTIFF	1628				
WILSON, -	1840	PLAINTIFF	1629	WILSON, DANIEL / NEAR BLACKSMITH SHOP	1871	LIMESTONE	1805
WILSON, -	1841	PLAINTIFF	1629				
WILSON, -	1854	PLAINTIFF	1629	WILSON, DAVID	1837	MISC	1705
WILSON, -	1856	PLAINTIFF	1630	WILSON, DAVID E	1838	MISC	1705
WILSON, - / HUDSON & WILSON	1871	FRE'MAN'S LDG	1762	WILSON, DAVID E	1844	MISC	1705
WILSON, - / MAGEE & WILSON	1871	FRE'MAN'S LDG	1762	WILSON, DAVID E	1848	MISC	1706
WILSON, - / (S.W.?) SADDLER	1871	NEW MANCH.	1763	WILSON, DAVID JR	1812	MISC	1704
WILSON, - / MAGEE & WILSON	1871	FRE'MAN'S LDG	1764	WILSON, DUNLEVY & CO	1857	PLAINTIFF	1630
WILSON, - / HUDSON & WILSON FIRE BRICK WORKS	1871	FRE'MAN'S LDG	1765	WILSON, DUNLEVY & CO	1858	PLAINTIFF	1630
				WILSON, DUNLEVY & CO	1861	PLAINTIFF	1631
WILSON, A	1845	PLAINTIFF	1652	WILSON, DUNLEVY & CO	1871	MARH'L MAP	1757
WILSON, A / & CO	1863	PLAINTIFF	1631	WILSON, DUNLEVY & CO	1871	MARH'L MAP	1757
WILSON, A	1871	BRKE MAP	1736	WILSON, DUNLEVY & CO / INITIALS W.D. & CO.	1871	MARH'L MAP	1757
WILSON, A / INITIALS A.W.	1871	BRKE MAP	1736				
WILSON, A	1871	BKE/OH MAP	1738	WILSON, DUNLEVY & CO	1871	MARH'L MAP	1761
WILSON, A / INITIALS A.W.	1871	BKE/OH MAP	1738	WILSON, DUNLEVY & CO	1871	MARH'L MAP	1761
WILSON, A / BOTTOM OF MAP	1871	MARH'L MAP	1747	WILSON, DUNLEVY & CO / INITIALS W.D. & CO.	1871	MARH'L MAP	1761
WILSON, A	1871	MARH'L MAP	1750				
WILSON, A	1871	MARH'L MAP	1753	WILSON, E / RES	1871	MARH'L MAP	1760
WILSON, A J	1871	BKE/OH MAP	1738	WILSON, ELIZABETH	1837	MISC	1705
WILSON, A J / INITIAS A.J.W.	1871	BKE/OH MAP	1738	WILSON, ELIZABETH	1838	MISC	1705
WILSON, A J / INITIAS A.J.W.	1871	BKE/OH MAP	1738	WILSON, ELIZABETH ANN	1849	MISC	1706
WILSON, ABRAM	1869	MISC	1706	WILSON, ELLEN	1849	MISC	1706
WILSON, ADAM	1789	PLAINTIFF	1647	WILSON, EMILY	1841	MISC	1705
WILSON, ADAM	1790	PLAINTIFF	1647	WILSON, EMILY	1854	MISC	1706
WILSON, ALEXANDER	1834	PLAINTIFF	1650	WILSON, EUGENIUS	1831	MISC	1705
WILSON, ALEXANDER	1835	PLAINTIFF	1650	WILSON, FRANCES	1871	MISC	1706
WILSON, ALEXANDER	1836	PLAINTIFF	1650	WILSON, FREDERICK	1834	MISC	1705
WILSON, ALEXANDER	1836	PLAINTIFF	1651	WILSON, FREDERICK A	1830	DEFENDANT	1669
WILSON, ALEXANDER	1837	PLAINTIFF	1651	WILSON, FREDERICK A	1834	PLAINTIFF	1650
WILSON, ALEXANDER	1837	MISC	1705	WILSON, FREDERICK A	1834	MISC	1705

CXXIX

'PERSONAL TIME LINE' INDEX TO VOLUME 7 OF THE *OHIO COUNTY INDEX*

ENTRY	YEAR	SUBJECT	PAGE	ENTRY	YEAR	SUBJECT	PAGE
WILSON, G W	1874	DEFENDANT	1594	WILSON, JOB	1818	PLAINTIFF	1648
WILSON, GEORGE	1821	PLAINTIFF	1649	WILSON, JOB	1822	MISC	1704
WILSON, GEORGE	1827	PLAINTIFF	1649	WILSON, JOB	1828	MISC	1705
WILSON, GEORGE	1829	DEFENDANT	1555	WILSON, JOB	1831	MISC	1705
WILSON, GEORGE	1829	DEFENDANT	1555	WILSON, JOHN	1784	PLAINTIFF	1647
WILSON, GEORGE	1829	DEFENDANT	1555	WILSON, JOHN	1792	PLAINTIFF	1647
WILSON, GEORGE	1832	DEFENDANT	1555	WILSON, JOHN	1798	PLAINTIFF	1647
WILSON, GEORGE	1833	PLAINTIFF	1650	WILSON, JOHN	1799	PLAINTIFF	1647
WILSON, GEORGE	1841	PLAINTIFF	1652	WILSON, JOHN	1800	PLAINTIFF	1647
WILSON, GEORGE	1846	PLAINTIFF	1652	WILSON, JOHN	1803	MISC	1704
WILSON, GEORGE	1854	PLAINTIFF	1653	WILSON, JOHN	1804	PLAINTIFF	1648
WILSON, GEORGE	1855	PLAINTIFF	1653	WILSON, JOHN	1805	PLAINTIFF	1648
WILSON, GEORGE	1856	PLAINTIFF	1653	WILSON, JOHN	1811	MISC	1704
WILSON, GEORGE	1857	DEFENDANT	1630	WILSON, JOHN	1817	DEFENDANT	1659
WILSON, GEORGE	1857	PLAINTIFF	1653	WILSON, JOHN	1819	MISC	1704
WILSON, GEORGE	1858	PLAINTIFF	1653	WILSON, JOHN	1823	MISC	1704
WILSON, GEORGE	1866	MISC	1706	WILSON, JOHN	1832	PLAINTIFF	1650
WILSON, GEORGE G	1830	PLAINTIFF	1650	WILSON, JOHN	1839	PLAINTIFF	1651
WILSON, GEORGE MICHAEL	1831	DEFENDANT	1555	WILSON, JOHN	1842	PLAINTIFF	1652
WILSON, GEORGE W	1831	DEFENDANT	1555	WILSON, JOHN	1845	PLAINTIFF	1652
WILSON, GEORGE W	1833	PLAINTIFF	1650	WILSON, JOHN	1846	PLAINTIFF	1653
WILSON, GEORGE W	1833	MISC	1702	WILSON, JOHN	1856	MISC	1706
WILSON, GEORGE W	1834	PLAINTIFF	1650	WILSON, JOHN	1859	MISC	1706
WILSON, GEORGE W	1834	MISC	1705	WILSON, JOHN	1869	MISC	1706
WILSON, GEORGE W	1835	PLAINTIFF	1650	WILSON, JOHN B	1839	PLAINTIFF	1651
WILSON, GEORGE W	1837	PLAINTIFF	1651	WILSON, JOHN B	1855	DEFENDANT	1598
WILSON, GEORGE W	1838	PLAINTIFF	1651	WILSON, JOHN B	1855	DEFENDANT	1630
WILSON, GEORGE W	1846	MISC	1706	WILSON, JOHN B	1856	PLAINTIFF	1653
WILSON, GEORGE W	1849	MISC	1706	WILSON, JOHN B	1874	MISC	1706
WILSON, GEORGE W	1876	DEFENDANT	1654	WILSON, JOHN E	1875	MISC	1706
WILSON, H	1871	MARH'L MAP	1747	WILSON, JOHN L	1834	PLAINTIFF	1650
WILSON, HANS	1823	PLAINTIFF	1649	WILSON, JOHN S	1833	PLAINTIFF	1650
WILSON, HENRY	1799	PLAINTIFF	1647	WILSON, JOHN V	1854	PLAINTIFF	1653
WILSON, HENRY	1818	PLAINTIFF	1648	WILSON, JOHN W	1837	PLAINTIFF	1651
WILSON, HENRY	1835	MISC	1705	WILSON, JOHN WILLIAM	1849	MISC	1706
WILSON, HENRY	1852	PLAINTIFF	1653	WILSON, JOSEPH	1778	MISC	1704
WILSON, HENRY	1878	MISC	1706	WILSON, JOSEPH	1784	PLAINTIFF	1647
WILSON, HUGH	1794	PLAINTIFF	1647	WILSON, JOSEPH	1788	DEFENDANT	1600
WILSON, HUGH	1825	PLAINTIFF	1649	WILSON, JOSEPH	1788	DEFENDANT	1658
WILSON, HUGH	1879	PLAINTIFF	1654	WILSON, JOSEPH	1788	DEFENDANT	1665
WILSON, ISAAC	1820	PLAINTIFF	1649	WILSON, JOSEPH	1805	PLAINTIFF	1648
WILSON, ISAAC	1847	DEFENDANT	1576	WILSON, JOSEPH	1806	PLAINTIFF	1648
WILSON, J	1827	PLAINTIFF	1649	WILSON, JOSEPH	1807	DEFENDANT	1644
WILSON, J	1843	MISC	1705	WILSON, JOSEPH	1807	PLAINTIFF	1648
WILSON, J	1846	PLAINTIFF	1653	WILSON, JOSEPH	1808	PLAINTIFF	1648
WILSON, J / RES	1871	BRKE MAP	1737	WILSON, JOSEPH	1809	PLAINTIFF	1648
WILSON, J / RES	1871	BRKE MAP	1737	WILSON, JOSEPH	1810	PLAINTIFF	1648
WILSON, J / HRS - HEIRS	1871	BKE/OH MAP	1738	WILSON, JOSEPH	1816	DEFENDANT	1553
WILSON, J	1871	MARH'L MAP	1747	WILSON, JOSEPH	1818	PLAINTIFF	1649
WILSON, J	1871	MARH'L MAP	1747	WILSON, JOSEPH	1822	DEFENDANT	1572
WILSON, J	1871	MARH'L MAP	1747	WILSON, JOSEPH	1822	DEFENDANT	1625
WILSON, J	1871	MARH'L MAP	1747	WILSON, JOSEPH	1822	DEFENDANT	1649
WILSON, J	1871	MARH'L MAP	1749	WILSON, JOSEPH	1823	PLAINTIFF	1649
WILSON, J	1871	MARH'L MAP	1753	WILSON, JOSEPH	1824	DEFENDANT	1554
WILSON, J	1871	MARH'L MAP	1756	WILSON, JOSEPH	1824	PLAINTIFF	1649
WILSON, J	1871	NEW MANCH.	1769	WILSON, JOSEPH	1825	DEFENDANT	1649
WILSON, J / RES.	1871	NEW MANCH.	1769	WILSON, JOSEPH	1825	PLAINTIFF	1649
WILSON, J / CAPR SHOP ?	1871	LIMESTONE	1805	WILSON, JOSEPH	1825	PLAINTIFF	1649
WILSON, J B	1871	OH CO. MAP	1741	WILSON, JOSEPH	1825	MISC	1704
WILSON, J M	1871	BRKE MAP	1736	WILSON, JOSEPH	1827	MISC	1704
WILSON, J M	1871	BKE/OH MAP	1738	WILSON, JOSEPH	1830	PLAINTIFF	1650
WILSON, J O	1860	PLAINTIFF	1654	WILSON, JOSEPH	1830	MISC	1705
WILSON, JAMES	1797	PLAINTIFF	1647	WILSON, JOSEPH	1841	MISC	1705
WILSON, JAMES	1799	PLAINTIFF	1647	WILSON, JOSEPH	1843	MISC	1705
WILSON, JAMES	1800	PLAINTIFF	1647	WILSON, JOSEPH	1869	MISC	1706
WILSON, JAMES	1808	PLAINTIFF	1648	WILSON, JOSEPH JR	1816	PLAINTIFF	1648
WILSON, JAMES	1811	PLAINTIFF	1648	WILSON, JOSEPH JR	1818	MISC	1704
WILSON, JAMES	1812	PLAINTIFF	1648	WILSON, JOSEPH JR	1825	PLAINTIFF	1649
WILSON, JAMES	1817	PLAINTIFF	1648	WILSON, JOSEPH JR	1825	PLAINTIFF	1649
WILSON, JAMES	1821	PLAINTIFF	1649	WILSON, JOSEPH SR	1818	PLAINTIFF	1649
WILSON, JAMES	1823	PLAINTIFF	1649	WILSON, L	1871	OH CO. MAP	1740
WILSON, JAMES	1825	PLAINTIFF	1649	WILSON, LAVINA	1840	MISC	1705
WILSON, JAMES	1841	PLAINTIFF	1652	WILSON, LEWIS	1819	PLAINTIFF	1649
WILSON, JAMES / MAP#220	1852	BRKE MAP	1843	WILSON, LEWIS	1828	MISC	1705
WILSON, JAMES / MAP#221	1852	BRKE MAP	1843	WILSON, LEWIS	1829	MISC	1705
WILSON, JAMES	1855	MISC	1706	WILSON, LEWIS	1835	MISC	1705
WILSON, JAMES	1858	PLAINTIFF	1653	WILSON, LEWIS	1844	MISC	1705
WILSON, JAMES	1860	PLAINTIFF	1654	WILSON, LEWIS D	1837	PLAINTIFF	1651
WILSON, JAMES	1861	PLAINTIFF	1654	WILSON, M	1844	MISC	1705
WILSON, JAMES	1862	PLAINTIFF	1654	WILSON, M / MRS	1871	MARH'L MAP	1749
WILSON, JAMES	1871	BRKE MAP	1735	WILSON, MARCUS	1824	PLAINTIFF	1649
WILSON, JAMES / HIS TIMBERLAND	1871	BRKE MAP	1735	WILSON, MARCUS	1825	PLAINTIFF	1649
WILSON, JAMES / INITIALS J.W.	1871	BRKE MAP	1735	WILSON, MARCUS	1827	PLAINTIFF	1649
WILSON, JAMES	1875	MISC	1706	WILSON, MARCUS	1828	PLAINTIFF	1649
WILSON, JAMES P	1843	PLAINTIFF	1652	WILSON, MARCUS	1829	PLAINTIFF	1650
WILSON, JOB	1816	PLAINTIFF	1648	WILSON, MARCUS	1830	PLAINTIFF	1650

'PERSONAL TIME LINE' INDEX TO VOLUME 7 OF THE *OHIO COUNTY INDEX*

ENTRY	YEAR	SUBJECT	PAGE	ENTRY	YEAR	SUBJECT	PAGE
WILSON, MARCUS	1831	PLAINTIFF	1639	WILSON, WILLIAM	1819	MISC	1704
WILSON, MARCUS	1831	PLAINTIFF	1650	WILSON, WILLIAM	1821	MISC	1704
WILSON, MARCUS	1833	PLAINTIFF	1650	WILSON, WILLIAM	1822	MISC	1704
WILSON, MARCUS	1834	PLAINTIFF	1650	WILSON, WILLIAM	1828	DEFENDANT	1555
WILSON, MARCUS	1835	PLAINTIFF	1650	WILSON, WILLIAM	1829	MISC	1705
WILSON, MARCUS	1836	PLAINTIFF	1651	WILSON, WILLIAM	1831	MISC	1688
WILSON, MARCUS	1837	PLAINTIFF	1651	WILSON, WILLIAM	1831	MISC	1705
WILSON, MARCUS	1837	MISC	1705	WILSON, WILLIAM	1834	MISC	1705
WILSON, MARCUS	1838	PLAINTIFF	1651	WILSON, WILLIAM	1835	MISC	1705
WILSON, MARCUS	1839	MISC	1705	WILSON, WILLIAM	1836	PLAINTIFF	1651
WILSON, MARCUS	1847	MISC	1706	WILSON, WILLIAM	1836	MISC	1705
WILSON, MARGARET	1841	MISC	1705	WILSON, WILLIAM	1839	MISC	1705
WILSON, MARGARET	1844	MISC	1705	WILSON, WILLIAM	1842	PLAINTIFF	1652
WILSON, MARGARET	1875	PLAINTIFF	1654	WILSON, WILLIAM	1843	PLAINTIFF	1652
WILSON, MARY	1848	MISC	1706	WILSON, WILLIAM	1853	MISC	1706
WILSON, MARY	1856	PLAINTIFF	1653	WILSON, WILLIAM	1861	PLAINTIFF	1654
WILSON, MARY	1857	PLAINTIFF	1653	WILSON, WILLIAM A	1875	PLAINTIFF	1654
WILSON, MARY	1859	PLAINTIFF	1653	WILSON, WILLIAM A	1876	PLAINTIFF	1654
WILSON, N / MRS	1871	BRKE MAP	1737	WILSON, WILLIAM A	1877	PLAINTIFF	1654
WILSON, OLIVER	1825	PLAINTIFF	1649	WILSON, WILLIAM H	1858	PLAINTIFF	1653
WILSON, PAXTON	1836	PLAINTIFF	1651	WILSON, WILLIAM M	1880	MISC	1706
WILSON, PETER	1838	MISC	1695	WILSON, WILLIAM P	1850	PLAINTIFF	1653
WILSON, PETER	1838	MISC	1705	WILSON, WILLIAM P	1873	MISC	1706
WILSON, R / REVEREND	1871	MARH'L MAP	1747	WILSONS RUN	1852	BRKE MAP	1843
WILSON, R H	1858	PLAINTIFF	1653	WILSONS RUN	1871	MARH'L MAP	1745
WILSON, RACHEL	1841	MISC	1705	WILSONS RUN	1871	MARH'L MAP	1749
WILSON, RACHEL	1847	MISC	1706	WILY, J	1871	MARH'L MAP	1758
WILSON, RACHEL	1856	MISC	1706	WIMMS, HENRY	1820	PLAINTIFF	1591
WILSON, REBECCA	1841	MISC	1705	WIMMS, HENRY	1828	PLAINTIFF	1591
WILSON, REBECCA	1848	MISC	1706	WIMMS, HENRY	1834	PLAINTIFF	1591
WILSON, RITCHIE	1836	MISC	1705	WIMMS, HENRY	1838	PLAINTIFF	1592
WILSON, ROBERT	1816	PLAINTIFF	1648	WIMS, GEORGE	1836	PLAINTIFF	1591
WILSON, ROBERT	1819	MISC	1704	WIMS, HENRY	1822	PLAINTIFF	1591
WILSON, ROSANA	1841	MISC	1705	WIMS, HENRY	1823	PLAINTIFF	1591
WILSON, ROSANNAH	1843	MISC	1705	WIMS, HENRY	1824	PLAINTIFF	1591
WILSON, ROXALINE	1849	MISC	1706	WIMS, HENRY	1829	PLAINTIFF	1591
WILSON, S W / ? - NEW MANCHESTER	1871	HAN MAP	1731	WIMS, HENRY	1830	PLAINTIFF	1591
				WIMS, HENRY	1832	PLAINTIFF	1591
WILSON, S W	1871	NEW MANCH.	1763	WIMS, HENRY	1835	PLAINTIFF	1591
WILSON, S W	1871	NEW MANCH.	1769	WIMS, HENRY	1835	PLAINTIFF	1591
WILSON, S W	1871	NEW MANCH.	1769	WIMS, HENRY	1836	PLAINTIFF	1591
WILSON, S W	1871	NEW MANCH.	1769	WIMS, HENRY	1836	PLAINTIFF	1592
WILSON, SAMUEL	1798	PLAINTIFF	1647	WIMS, HENRY	1847	MISC	1695
WILSON, SAMUEL	1799	DEFENDANT	1665	WIMS, MARTIN E	1860	PLAINTIFF	1592
WILSON, SAMUEL	1800	PLAINTIFF	1647	WIMS, THOMAS	1835	PLAINTIFF	1591
WILSON, SAMUEL	1817	PLAINTIFF	1648	WIMS, THOMAS	1836	PLAINTIFF	1591
WILSON, SAMUEL / HEIRS - MAP#217	1852	BRKE MAP	1843	WIMS, THOMAS	1837	PLAINTIFF	1592
WILSON, SAMUEL MCC	1876	PLAINTIFF	1654	WIMS, THOMAS H	1842	PLAINTIFF	1592
WILSON, SARAH	1810	MISC	1704	WIMS, WILLIAM H	1854	MISC	1695
WILSON, SARAH	1812	MISC	1704	WIN., E / ?	1871	WELLSBURG	1777
WILSON, SARAH	1816	MISC	1704	WINANS, THOMAS	1873	PLAINTIFF	1592
WILSON, SARAH	1855	MISC	1706	WINCHEL, CHARLES	1838	MISC	1695
WILSON, SARAH A	1869	MISC	1706	WINCHEL, CHARLES	1838	MISC	1705
WILSON, SARAH R	1869	MISC	1706	WINCHER, AUGUST	1875	MISC	1694
WILSON, SETH	1839	PLAINTIFF	1651	WINCHER, AUGUST	1875	MISC	1694
WILSON, STEPHEN	1817	PLAINTIFF	1648	WINCHER, AUGUST	1875	MISC	1695
WILSON, STEPHEN R	1817	PLAINTIFF	1648	WINCHER, CHRISTIAN E	1875	MISC	1695
WILSON, T	1871	MARH'L MAP	1752	WINCHESTER, O W / & CO	1855	PLAINTIFF	1630
WILSON, T / INITIALS T.W.	1871	MARH'L MAP	1752	WIND, HENRY	1854	PLAINTIFF	1592
WILSON, T / INITIALS T.W.	1871	MARH'L MAP	1756	WINDSOR HOTEL - WHEELING	1916	NAT'L ROAD	1868
WILSON, T	1871	GLEN EASTON	1801	WINDSOR HOTEL - WHEELING - ON MAP	1916	NAT'L ROAD	1868
WILSON, THOMAS	1825	PLAINTIFF	1649				
WILSON, THOMAS	1831	DEFENDANT	1628	WINDSOR, ANN	1879	MISC	1696
WILSON, THOMAS	1839	PLAINTIFF	1651	WINDSOR, ELLEN	1879	MISC	1696
WILSON, THOMAS	1839	PLAINTIFF	1651	WINDSOR, ELLEN	1879	MISC	1696
WILSON, THOMAS	1840	PLAINTIFF	1652	WINDSOR, J R	1871	BRKE MAP	1736
WILSON, THOMAS	1871	GLEN EASTON - BUS.	1796	WINDSOR, J R / RES	1871	BRKE MAP	1736
				WINDSOR, J R / RES	1871	BKE/OH MAP	1738
WILSON, THOMAS	1873	MISC	1681	WINDSOR, JOSHUA	1862	PLAINTIFF	1592
WILSON, THOMAS	1873	MISC	1706	WINDSOR, JOSHUA R / MAP#92	1852	BRKE MAP	1842
WILSON, THOMAS A	1832	DEFENDANT	1628	WINDSOR, JOSHUA R	1876	PLAINTIFF	1592
WILSON, VIRGINIA	1837	MISC	1705	WINDSOR, R	1862	PLAINTIFF	1592
WILSON, VIRGINIA	1838	MISC	1705	WINDSOR, SAMUEL G	1879	MISC	1696
WILSON, W	1871	MARH'L MAP	1747	WINDSOR, THOMAS	1807	PLAINTIFF	1591
WILSON, W / INITIALS W.W.	1871	MARH'L MAP	1747	WINDSOR, THOMAS I	1814	PLAINTIFF	1591
WILSON, W	1871	MARH'L MAP	1751	WINESBURG - CHILDREN	1869	MISC	1698
WILSON, WILLIAM	1793	MISC	1704	WINESBURG, ADALINE	1873	MISC	1695
WILSON, WILLIAM	1803	MISC	1704	WINESBURG, ADALINE	1873	MISC	1698
WILSON, WILLIAM	1808	MISC	1704	WINESBURG, ELIZABETH	1869	MISC	1695
WILSON, WILLIAM	1812	PLAINTIFF	1648	WINESBURG, GEORGE	1856	MISC	1695
WILSON, WILLIAM	1812	MISC	1704	WINESBURG, GEORGE	1868	MISC	1695
WILSON, WILLIAM	1813	PLAINTIFF	1648	WINESBURG, GEORGE	1878	MISC	1695
WILSON, WILLIAM	1816	PLAINTIFF	1648	WINESBURG, JACOB	1852	DEFENDANT	1646
WILSON, WILLIAM	1817	DEFENDANT	1648	WINESBURG, MARY	1878	MISC	1695
WILSON, WILLIAM	1818	MISC	1704	WINESBURG, MARY	1878	MISC	1708
WILSON, WILLIAM	1819	MISC	1677	WINESBURG, NANCY	1868	MISC	1695

'PERSONAL TIME LINE' INDEX TO VOLUME 7 OF THE OHIO COUNTY INDEX

ENTRY	YEAR	SUBJECT	PAGE	ENTRY	YEAR	SUBJECT	PAGE
WINESBURG, NANCY	1876	MISC	1695	WITHRUP, JOHN	1823	PLAINTIFF	1594
WINESBURGH, GEORGE	1873	MISC	1695	WITHURUP, JOHN	1821	PLAINTIFF	1594
WINESBURGH, NANCY	1873	MISC	1695	WITTEN, ARTHUR	1854	PLAINTIFF	1594
WING, ISAIAH	1821	PLAINTIFF	1591	WITTEN, ARTHUR	1855	PLAINTIFF	1594
WING, JOSIAH	1820	PLAINTIFF	1591	WITTEN, JOHN	1821	PLAINTIFF	1594
WINGARD & SHARP	1854	PLAINTIFF	1629	WITTEN, JOSEPH	1828	PLAINTIFF	1594
WINGARD & SHARP	1856	PLAINTIFF	1630	WITTEN, REBECCA	1859	DEFENDANT	1641
WINGARD & SHARP	1857	PLAINTIFF	1630	WITTEN, REBECCA	1860	DEFENDANT	1641
WINGARD & SHARP	1858	PLAINTIFF	1630	WITTENBROCK, RODOLF	1839	MISC	1695
WINGARD & SHARP	1860	PLAINTIFF	1631	WITTENBROK, E	1842	PLAINTIFF	1594
WINGARD & SHARP	1862	PLAINTIFF	1631	WODLAND P.O.	1871	MARH'L MAP	1754
WINGARD, ADAM	1842	PLAINTIFF	1592	WOEBER, FRANK A	1871	MISC	1698
WINGERTER, FERDINAND	1862	PLAINTIFF	1592	WOHERTON, THOMAS	1800	PLAINTIFF	1598
WINGERTER, FERDINAND	1867	MISC	1695	WOHERTON, THOMAS	1800	PLAINTIFF	1634
WINGRAVE LODGE	1871	MARH'L MAP	1754	WOHLERT, HENRY	1876	MISC	1698
WINGRAVE LODGE	1871	MARH'L MAP	1758	WOHUHAS, JOHN	1879	MISC	1698
WINGROVE, HENRY	1878	PLAINTIFF	1593	WOLF CREEK	1871	MARH'L MAP	1750
WINGROVE, S	1878	PLAINTIFF	1593	WOLF CREEK	1871	MARH'L MAP	1753
WINONES, THOMAS	1873	PLAINTIFF	1592	WOLF CREEK - SAW MILL ON	1871	MARH'L MAP	1750
WINSDOR, JOSHUA	1861	PLAINTIFF	1592	WOLF RUN	1871	MARH'L MAP	1750
WINSDOR, R	1861	PLAINTIFF	1592	WOLF RUN PRESBYTERIAN CHURCH	1871	MARH'L MAP	1750
WINSHIP, F C / & CO	1875	DEFENDANT	1580	WOLF SCALPS BOUNTY - DEFINED	2000	APPENDIX	1875
WINSHIP, F C	1878	PLAINTIFF	1593	WOLF, - / BLACKSMITH SHOP	1871	MARH'L MAP	1754
WINSHIP, FRANKLIN	1855	PLAINTIFF	1592	WOLF, C	1871	OH CO. MAP	1742
WINSHIP, FRANKLIN	1857	PLAINTIFF	1592	WOLF, C	1871	RITCHIE TWP	1793
WINSHIP, FRANKLIN	1858	PLAINTIFF	1592	WOLF, CHRISTIAN JR	1857	PLAINTIFF	1598
WINSHIP, FRANKLIN	1860	PLAINTIFF	1592	WOLF, CHRISTY	1779	APPENDIX	1874
WINSHIP, FRANKLIN	1878	MISC	1695	WOLF, J / INITIALS J.W. - EDGE OF MAP	1871	MARH'L MAP	1751
WINSHIP, T	1856	PLAINTIFF	1592				
WINSINDER, D / ?	1871	HAN MAP	1729	WOLF, J	1871	MARH'L MAP	1754
WINSON, E / & CO	1848	PLAINTIFF	1629	WOLF, J / INITIALS J.W.	1871	MARH'L MAP	1754
WINTENGER, JOHN	1839	PLAINTIFF	1592	WOLF, JACOB	1861	PLAINTIFF	1598
WINTER, JAMES	1799	PLAINTIFF	1591	WOLF, JOHN	1831	MISC	1698
WINTER, JAMES	1800	MISC	1695	WOLF, JOHN	1835	PLAINTIFF	1598
WINTER, JOHN	1795	MISC	1695	WOLF, JOHN	1836	PLAINTIFF	1598
WINTERS & RICE	1786	PLAINTIFF	1628	WOLF, JOHN	1838	PLAINTIFF	1598
WINTERS, A	1871	MARH'L MAP	1746	WOLF, JOHN	1856	DEFENDANT	1569
WINTERS, BENJAMIN	1819	PLAINTIFF	1591	WOLF, PETER	1817	PLAINTIFF	1598
WINTERS, D	1871	MARH'L MAP	1746	WOLF, PETER	1818	PLAINTIFF	1598
WINTERS, DANIEL	1821	PLAINTIFF	1591	WOLF, PETER	1820	PLAINTIFF	1598
WINTERS, DAVID	1843	PLAINTIFF	1592	WOLF, PETER	1821	DEFENDANT	1563
WINTERS, ELISABETH	1861	PLAINTIFF	1592	WOLFE, BALLARD & CO	1855	PLAINTIFF	1630
WINTERS, FRANK	1876	PLAINTIFF	1592	WOLFE, ERASMUS D	1833	PLAINTIFF	1598
WINTERS, HENRY	1792	PLAINTIFF	1591	WOLFE, ERASMUS D	1855	PLAINTIFF	1598
WINTERS, HENRY	1818	PLAINTIFF	1591	WOLFE, ERASMUS D	1856	PLAINTIFF	1598
WINTERS, J	1871	MARH'L MAP	1747	WOLFE, JOHN	1834	PLAINTIFF	1598
WINTERS, J / RES	1871	MARH'L MAP	1761	WOLFE, JOHN	1838	PLAINTIFF	1598
WINTERS, J F	1871	MARH'L MAP	1746	WOLFES, BALLARD & CO	1856	PLAINTIFF	1630
WINTERS, J P	1871	MARH'L MAP	1749	WOLFF, ANDREW	1861	MISC	1698
WINTERS, J W	1871	MARH'L MAP	1746	WOLFF, HARRY	1878	MISC	1698
WINTERS, JAMES	1871	MARH'L MAP	1746	WOLFOOT, ADAM	1819	PLAINTIFF	1598
WINTERS, JOHN	1801	PLAINTIFF	1591	WOLFORD, ADAM	1818	PLAINTIFF	1598
WINTERS, JOHN	1841	PLAINTIFF	1592	WOLFORD, ADAM	1818	MISC	1698
WINTERS, JOSEPH	1871	MARH'L MAP	1746	WOLFORD, ADAM	1825	MISC	1698
WINTERS, L D	1871	MARH'L MAP	1746	WOLLENWEBER, WILLIAM F	1877	MISC	1698
WINTERS, VALENTINE	1838	PLAINTIFF	1592	WOOD & CO	1855	PLAINTIFF	1630
WIRT, A	1871	W.UNION	1812	WOOD & COOK	1833	PLAINTIFF	1628
WIRT, B	1871	W.UNION-BUS.	1797	WOOD & COOK	1834	PLAINTIFF	1628
WIRT, B / HOTEL	1871	W.UNION	1812	WOOD & SMITH	1854	PLAINTIFF	1629
WIRT, W M	1871	MARH'L MAP	1747	WOOD, -	1854	PLAINTIFF	1629
WISE, ADAM	1832	PLAINTIFF	1594	WOOD, -	1856	PLAINTIFF	1630
WISE, G	1840	PLAINTIFF	1594	WOOD, A	1856	PLAINTIFF	1670
WISE, G	1841	PLAINTIFF	1594	WOOD, A	1856	PLAINTIFF	1670
WISE, M	1841	PLAINTIFF	1594	WOOD, A	1857	PLAINTIFF	1670
WISEGERBER, -	1854	PLAINTIFF	1594	WOOD, A	1857	PLAINTIFF	1670
WISEGERBER, WILLIAM	1854	PLAINTIFF	1594	WOOD, ALBERT	1855	PLAINTIFF	1670
WISELY, WILLIAM	1845	MISC	1695	WOOD, ANDREW	1808	PLAINTIFF	1667
WISHART, JOHN	1841	PLAINTIFF	1594	WOOD, ANDREW	1810	PLAINTIFF	1667
WISHART, JOHN	1842	PLAINTIFF	1594	WOOD, ANDREW	1831	MISC	1707
WISINALL, JOHN	1821	DEFENDANT	1612	WOOD, ARCHD	1824	MISC	1691
WISTER, BARTHOLAMUS	1819	PLAINTIFF	1594	WOOD, ARCHE	1810	MISC	1707
WISTER, RICHARD JR	1823	PLAINTIFF	1594	WOOD, ARCHIBALD	1806	DEFENDANT	1599
WITERHOLTER, JOHN	1880	MISC	1695	WOOD, ARCHIBALD	1822	PLAINTIFF	1668
WITHERHEAD, RICHARD	1804	DEFENDANT	1655	WOOD, ELIJAH	1800	PLAINTIFF	1665
WITHERS & CARPENTER	1840	PLAINTIFF	1628	WOOD, ELIJAH	1807	PLAINTIFF	1666
WITHERS & CARPENTER	1841	PLAINTIFF	1629	WOOD, ELIJAH	1808	PLAINTIFF	1667
WITHERS, CHARLES A	1840	PLAINTIFF	1594	WOOD, FRANKLIN	1822	PLAINTIFF	1668
WITHERS, EZEKIEL D	1841	PLAINTIFF	1594	WOOD, GEORGE	1823	PLAINTIFF	1668
WITHERS, EZEKIEL D	1843	PLAINTIFF	1594	WOOD, GEORGE	1856	PLAINTIFF	1670
WITHERS, JOSEPH N	1856	PLAINTIFF	1594	WOOD, GEORGE L	1860	PLAINTIFF	1671
WITHERSPOON, - / BROTHERS	1871	HAN MAP	1731	WOOD, HAMILTON	1841	PLAINTIFF	1670
WITHERUP, JOHN	1824	PLAINTIFF	1594	WOOD, J / CUT OFF ON EDGE	1871	EDGINGTON STA.	1774
WITHROE, ROBERT	1798	PLAINTIFF	1594	WOOD, J	1871	TRIAD.TWP.	1781
WITHROU, ROBERT	1798	PLAINTIFF	1594	WOOD, J	1871	TRIAD.TWP.	1781
WITHROW & CALDWELL	1804	PLAINTIFF	1628	WOOD, J / NATL RD	1871	TRIAD.TWP.	1781
WITHRUP, JOHN	1819	PLAINTIFF	1594	WOOD, J / RES	1871	TRIAD.TWP.	1781

'PERSONAL TIME LINE' INDEX TO VOLUME 7 OF THE *OHIO COUNTY INDEX*

ENTRY	YEAR	SUBJECT	PAGE	ENTRY	YEAR	SUBJECT	PAGE
WOOD, JAMES	1816	PLAINTIFF	1667	WOODMANSEE, LOUIS	1879	PLAINTIFF	1601
WOOD, JAMES / & CO	1833	PLAINTIFF	1628	WOODMANSEE, T J	1879	DEFENDANT	1601
WOOD, JAMES	1833	PLAINTIFF	1669	WOODMUNSY, JAMES	1820	PLAINTIFF	1600
WOOD, JAMES	1834	PLAINTIFF	1669	WOODROW, SIMEON	1834	MISC	1699
WOOD, JAMES	1834	PLAINTIFF	1669	WOODROW, SIMEON	1854	MISC	1699
WOOD, JAMES	1855	PLAINTIFF	1670	WOODROW, SIMEON D	1855	DEFENDANT	1552
WOOD, JOE	1873	PLAINTIFF	1671	WOODROW, SIMEON D	1855	DEFENDANT	1621
WOOD, JOSEPH	1837	PLAINTIFF	1669	WOODROW, SIMON	1833	MISC	1699
WOOD, JOSEPH	1848	DEFENDANT	1653	WOODRUFF, EDWARD D	1855	PLAINTIFF	1600
WOOD, JOSEPH	1854	PLAINTIFF	1670	WOODRUFF, H / MRS	1871	MARH'L MAP	1747
WOOD, JOSEPH	1856	PLAINTIFF	1670	WOODRUFF, H / MRS	1871	MARH'L MAP	1750
WOOD, JOSEPH	1874	PLAINTIFF	1671	WOODRUFF, MARY	1829	MISC	1699
WOOD, PHOENIX N / & CO	1835	PLAINTIFF	1628	WOODRURN, R / INITIALS R.W.	1871	MDSVILLE	1807
WOOD, PHOENIX N	1835	PLAINTIFF	1669	WOODRURN, R / INITIALS R.W.	1871	MDSVILLE	1807
WOOD, ROBERT	1788	PLAINTIFF	1665	WOODRURN, R / INITIALS R.W.	1871	MDSVILLE	1807
WOOD, ROBERT	1788	PLAINTIFF	1665	WOODRURN, R / INITIALS R.W.	1871	MDSVILLE	1807
WOOD, ROBERT	1790	PLAINTIFF	1665	WOODRURN, R / INITIALS R.W.	1871	MDSVILLE	1807
WOOD, ROBERT	1800	PLAINTIFF	1665	WOODS & CALDWELL	1798	PLAINTIFF	1607
WOOD, ROBERT	1801	PLAINTIFF	1666	WOODS & CALDWELL	1799	PLAINTIFF	1607
WOOD, ROBERT	1803	DEFENDANT	1583	WOODS & CALDWELL	1802	PLAINTIFF	1607
WOOD, ROBERT	1807	PLAINTIFF	1666	WOODS & CALDWELL	1803	PLAINTIFF	1607
WOOD, ROBERT	1808	PLAINTIFF	1667	WOODS & CALDWELL	1805	PLAINTIFF	1607
WOOD, ROBERT	1809	PLAINTIFF	1667	WOODS & CALDWELL	1806	PLAINTIFF	1607
WOOD, ROBERT	1809	PLAINTIFF	1667	WOODS & HALEY	1855	DEFENDANT	1653
WOOD, ROBERT	1809	PLAINTIFF	1667	WOODS & HOWARD	1830	PLAINTIFF	1628
WOOD, ROBERT	1810	PLAINTIFF	1667	WOODS & HUTCHINS	1871	MDSVILLE	1807
WOOD, ROBERT	1811	PLAINTIFF	1667	WOODS & HUTCHINS	1871	MDSVILLE	1809
WOOD, ROBERT	1812	PLAINTIFF	1667	WOODS & MONTELIUS	1823	PLAINTIFF	1628
WOOD, ROBERT	1815	MISC	1707	WOODS & PAULL	1824	PLAINTIFF	1628
WOOD, ROBERT	1816	PLAINTIFF	1667	WOODS HRS	1871	OH CO. MAP	1741
WOOD, ROBERT	1820	PLAINTIFF	1667	WOODS HRS / (?WAREHOUSE?)	1871	OH CO. MAP	1741
WOOD, ROBERT	1824	PLAINTIFF	1668	WOODS PAULL & CO	1826	PLAINTIFF	1628
WOOD, ROBERT	1826	PLAINTIFF	1668	WOODS RUN	1871	OH CO. MAP	1741
WOOD, ROBERT	1834	MISC	1707	WOODS RUN	1871	TRIAD.TWP.	1781
WOOD, SAMUEL	1781	MISC	1707	WOODS, -	1829	PLAINTIFF	1632
WOOD, THOMAS	1821	PLAINTIFF	1668	WOODS, -	1830	PLAINTIFF	1632
WOOD, THOMAS	1821	PLAINTIFF	1668	WOODS, - / HRS -HEIRS	1871	OH CO. MAP	1741
WOOD, THOMAS	1822	PLAINTIFF	1668	WOODS, - / REV. - HEIRS	1871	OH CO. MAP	1741
WOOD, WILLIAM	1791	PLAINTIFF	1665	WOODS, - / MRS	1871	CAMERON	1804
WOOD, WILLIAM	1841	MISC	1707	WOODS, A	1821	PLAINTIFF	1668
WOOD, WILLIAM	1842	DEFENDANT	1652	WOODS, A	1825	PLAINTIFF	1668
WOOD, WILLIAM	1845	DEFENDANT	1652	WOODS, A P	1834	PLAINTIFF	1669
WOOD, WILLIAM	1852	DEFENDANT	1653	WOODS, A P	1841	DEFENDANT	1616
WOOD, WILLIAM	1852	DEFENDANT	1653	WOODS, A P	1841	DEFENDANT	1616
WOOD, WILSON & WOOD	1854	PLAINTIFF	1629	WOODS, ALEXANDER	1856	PLAINTIFF	1670
WOOD, WILSON & WOOD	1856	PLAINTIFF	1630	WOODS, ALEXANDER O	1858	PLAINTIFF	1670
WOODBORTH & BRUNEL	1861	PLAINTIFF	1631	WOODS, ALFRED	1862	PLAINTIFF	1671
WOODBURN & HICKS / STORE	1871	CAMERON	1803	WOODS, AME	1832	MISC	1707
WOODBURN REES & CO	1871	CAMERON	1804	WOODS, AMELIA S	1878	PLAINTIFF	1671
WOODBURN REES & CO / BLACKSMITH SHOP - INITIALS W.R.& CO.	1871	CAMERON	1804	WOODS, ANDREW	1788	MISC	1707
				WOODS, ANDREW	1794	PLAINTIFF	1665
				WOODS, ANDREW	1795	PLAINTIFF	1665
WOODBURN REES & CO / COOPER SHOP - INITIALS W.R.& CO.	1871	CAMERON	1804	WOODS, ANDREW	1795	MISC	1707
				WOODS, ANDREW	1799	PLAINTIFF	1665
WOODBURN REES & CO / INITIALS W.R.& CO.	1871	CAMERON	1804	WOODS, ANDREW	1799	PLAINTIFF	1665
				WOODS, ANDREW	1799	PLAINTIFF	1665
WOODBURN REES & CO / S.G.MILL	1871	CAMERON	1804	WOODS, ANDREW	1800	PLAINTIFF	1665
WOODBURN, J	1871	MARH'L MAP	1753	WOODS, ANDREW	1802	PLAINTIFF	1666
WOODBURN, JAMES	1834	MISC	1699	WOODS, ANDREW	1802	PLAINTIFF	1666
WOODBURN, JAMES	1843	MISC	1699	WOODS, ANDREW	1803	PLAINTIFF	1666
WOODBURN, JOHN	1802	PLAINTIFF	1600	WOODS, ANDREW	1803	PLAINTIFF	1666
WOODBURN, R / BLURRED - ON NORTH ST & GRANT ST	1871	MDSVILLE	1807	WOODS, ANDREW	1807	PLAINTIFF	1666
				WOODS, ANDREW	1816	MISC	1685
WOODBURN, W / RES	1871	CAMERON	1803	WOODS, ANDREW	1816	MISC	1707
WOODCOCK, BANCROFT	1840	DEFENDANT	1551	WOODS, ANDREW	1826	PLAINTIFF	1668
WOODCOCK, BANCROFT	1840	MISC	1699	WOODS, ANDREW	1827	PLAINTIFF	1668
WOODCOCK, BANCROFT	1844	DEFENDANT	1663	WOODS, ANDREW	1831	PLAINTIFF	1669
WOODCOCK, BANCROFT	1848	DEFENDANT	1582	WOODS, ANDREW	1834	PLAINTIFF	1669
WOODCOCK, JAMES M	1846	DEFENDANT	1652	WOODS, ANDREW	1835	PLAINTIFF	1669
WOODFORD, OLIVER	1835	PLAINTIFF	1600	WOODS, ANDREW	1841	PLAINTIFF	1670
WOODIAN, JOHN	1800	MISC	1699	WOODS, ANDREW JR	1802	PLAINTIFF	1666
WOODLAND	1871	OH CO. MAP	1744	WOODS, ANDREW P	1831	PLAINTIFF	1669
WOODLAND	1871	MARH'L MAP	1754	WOODS, ANDREW P	1831	PLAINTIFF	1669
WOODLAND, WV	1871	FRKLN TWP-BUS.	1797	WOODS, ANDREW P	1838	PLAINTIFF	1669
WOODLAND, WV	1871	FRKLN TWP-BUS.	1797	WOODS, ANDREW P	1838	PLAINTIFF	1669
WOODLAND, WV	1871	FRKLN TWP-BUS.	1797	WOODS, ANDREW P	1839	PLAINTIFF	1670
WOODLAND, WV	1871	FRKLN TWP-BUS.	1797	WOODS, ANDREW P	1850	PLAINTIFF	1670
WOODMANSE, LEWIS	1860	PLAINTIFF	1601	WOODS, ANDREW P	1852	PLAINTIFF	1670
WOODMANSEE, - / LEWIS & WOODMANSEE / GRANT HOUSE - WHEELING	1871	OH.CO.BUS.	1779	WOODS, ANDREW P	1852	PLAINTIFF	1670
				WOODS, ANDREW P	1852	HEMPFIELD RR	1822
				WOODS, ANDREW P	1853	PLAINTIFF	1670
WOODMANSEE, JOSEPH	1845	PLAINTIFF	1600	WOODS, ANDREW P	1854	PLAINTIFF	1670
WOODMANSEE, LEWIS	1878	PLAINTIFF	1601	WOODS, ANDREW P	1858	PLAINTIFF	1671
WOODMANSEE, LEWIS	1879	PLAINTIFF	1601	WOODS, ANDREW SR	1829	PLAINTIFF	1668
WOODMANSEE, LEWIS	1880	PLAINTIFF	1601	WOODS, ARCHEBALD	1826	PLAINTIFF	1668
WOODMANSEE, LOUIS	1878	PLAINTIFF	1601	WOODS, ARCHIBALD	1788	PLAINTIFF	1665

CXXXIII

'PERSONAL TIME LINE' INDEX TO VOLUME 7 OF THE *OHIO COUNTY INDEX*

ENTRY	YEAR	SUBJECT	PAGE	ENTRY	YEAR	SUBJECT	PAGE
WOODS, ARCHIBALD	1793	DEFENDANT	1572	WOODS, JEREMIAH	1815	MISC	1707
WOODS, ARCHIBALD	1799	MISC	1707	WOODS, JEREMIAH	1816	MISC	1707
WOODS, ARCHIBALD	1800	MISC	1707	WOODS, JOHN	1829	PLAINTIFF	1668
WOODS, ARCHIBALD	1801	PLAINTIFF	1606	WOODS, JOHN	1874	PLAINTIFF	1671
WOODS, ARCHIBALD	1801	PLAINTIFF	1666	WOODS, JOHN F	1876	PLAINTIFF	1671
WOODS, ARCHIBALD	1801	PLAINTIFF	1666	WOODS, JOHN F	1878	PLAINTIFF	1671
WOODS, ARCHIBALD	1801	MISC	1707	WOODS, JOHN F	1880	PLAINTIFF	1671
WOODS, ARCHIBALD	1801	MISC	1707	WOODS, JOSEPH / & CO	1803	PLAINTIFF	1628
WOODS, ARCHIBALD	1805	PLAINTIFF	1666	WOODS, JOSEPH	1841	MISC	1707
WOODS, ARCHIBALD	1806	PLAINTIFF	1666	WOODS, LYDIA	1832	MISC	1707
WOODS, ARCHIBALD	1808	PLAINTIFF	1667	WOODS, MARTHA	1802	PLAINTIFF	1666
WOODS, ARCHIBALD	1809	PLAINTIFF	1667	WOODS, N / MRS	1871	OH CO. MAP	1742
WOODS, ARCHIBALD	1811	DEFENDANT	1659	WOODS, N / MRS	1871	OH CO. MAP	1744
WOODS, ARCHIBALD	1814	PLAINTIFF	1667	WOODS, PAUL & CO	1823	PLAINTIFF	1628
WOODS, ARCHIBALD	1816	MISC	1707	WOODS, PAUL & CO	1824	PLAINTIFF	1628
WOODS, ARCHIBALD	1817	DEFENDANT	1648	WOODS, R / HRS	1871	OH CO. MAP	1741
WOODS, ARCHIBALD	1818	PLAINTIFF	1667	WOODS, ROBERT	1784	APPENDIX	1874
WOODS, ARCHIBALD	1818	PLAINTIFF	1667	WOODS, ROBERT	1788	PLAINTIFF	1665
WOODS, ARCHIBALD	1819	PLAINTIFF	1667	WOODS, ROBERT	1789	MISC	1707
WOODS, ARCHIBALD	1819	PLAINTIFF	1667	WOODS, ROBERT	1792	MISC	1707
WOODS, ARCHIBALD	1819	PLAINTIFF	1667	WOODS, ROBERT	1796	PLAINTIFF	1665
WOODS, ARCHIBALD	1821	PLAINTIFF	1667	WOODS, ROBERT	1796	PLAINTIFF	1665
WOODS, ARCHIBALD	1822	DEFENDANT	1625	WOODS, ROBERT	1796	MISC	1707
WOODS, ARCHIBALD	1822	MISC	1707	WOODS, ROBERT	1798	PLAINTIFF	1665
WOODS, ARCHIBALD	1826	PLAINTIFF	1668	WOODS, ROBERT	1798	PLAINTIFF	1665
WOODS, ARCHIBALD	1827	PLAINTIFF	1668	WOODS, ROBERT	1799	PLAINTIFF	1665
WOODS, ARCHIBALD	1829	PLAINTIFF	1668	WOODS, ROBERT	1799	PLAINTIFF	1665
WOODS, ARCHIBALD	1829	PLAINTIFF	1668	WOODS, ROBERT	1799	PLAINTIFF	1665
WOODS, ARCHIBALD	1830	MISC	1707	WOODS, ROBERT	1799	PLAINTIFF	1665
WOODS, ARCHIBALD	1832	PLAINTIFF	1669	WOODS, ROBERT	1799	PLAINTIFF	1665
WOODS, ARCHIBALD	1832	PLAINTIFF	1669	WOODS, ROBERT	1799	PLAINTIFF	1665
WOODS, ARCHIBALD	1832	MISC	1707	WOODS, ROBERT	1799	PLAINTIFF	1665
WOODS, ARCHIBALD	1834	PLAINTIFF	1669	WOODS, ROBERT	1799	MISC	1701
WOODS, ARCHIBALD	1835	PLAINTIFF	1669	WOODS, ROBERT	1800	PLAINTIFF	1665
WOODS, ARCHIBALD	1836	PLAINTIFF	1669	WOODS, ROBERT	1800	PLAINTIFF	1665
WOODS, ARCHIBALD	1838	DEFENDANT	1625	WOODS, ROBERT	1800	PLAINTIFF	1665
WOODS, ARCHIBALD	1839	DEFENDANT	1625	WOODS, ROBERT	1800	PLAINTIFF	1665
WOODS, ARCHIBALD	1840	PLAINTIFF	1670	WOODS, ROBERT	1800	PLAINTIFF	1666
WOODS, ARCHIBALD	1842	PLAINTIFF	1670	WOODS, ROBERT	1801	PLAINTIFF	1666
WOODS, ARCHIBALD	1847	PLAINTIFF	1670	WOODS, ROBERT	1801	PLAINTIFF	1666
WOODS, ARCHIBOLD	1804	PLAINTIFF	1666	WOODS, ROBERT	1801	PLAINTIFF	1666
WOODS, ARCHIBOLD	1821	PLAINTIFF	1668	WOODS, ROBERT	1801	PLAINTIFF	1666
WOODS, EDGAR	1832	MISC	1707	WOODS, ROBERT	1801	PLAINTIFF	1666
WOODS, ELIJAH	1800	PLAINTIFF	1665	WOODS, ROBERT	1802	PLAINTIFF	1666
WOODS, ELIJAH	1801	PLAINTIFF	1666	WOODS, ROBERT	1803	PLAINTIFF	1572
WOODS, ELIJAH	1804	PLAINTIFF	1666	WOODS, ROBERT	1803	PLAINTIFF	1666
WOODS, ELIJAH	1805	PLAINTIFF	1666	WOODS, ROBERT	1803	PLAINTIFF	1666
WOODS, ELIJAH	1811	PLAINTIFF	1667	WOODS, ROBERT	1803	PLAINTIFF	1666
WOODS, ELIJAH	1818	DEFENDANT	1596	WOODS, ROBERT	1805	PLAINTIFF	1666
WOODS, ELIZA	1832	MISC	1707	WOODS, ROBERT	1806	PLAINTIFF	1666
WOODS, ELIZABETH	1848	PLAINTIFF	1670	WOODS, ROBERT	1806	PLAINTIFF	1666
WOODS, ELIZABETH	1848	PLAINTIFF	1670	WOODS, ROBERT	1806	PLAINTIFF	1666
WOODS, ELIZAL	1809	PLAINTIFF	1667	WOODS, ROBERT	1807	PLAINTIFF	1666
WOODS, F H	1871	MARH'L MAP	1757	WOODS, ROBERT	1807	PLAINTIFF	1666
WOODS, FRANKLIN	1825	MISC	1707	WOODS, ROBERT	1807	PLAINTIFF	1666
WOODS, HAMILTON	1841	PLAINTIFF	1670	WOODS, ROBERT	1808	DEFENDANT	1658
WOODS, HAMILTON	1841	PLAINTIFF	1670	WOODS, ROBERT	1809	DEFENDANT	1658
WOODS, HAMILTON	1847	PLAINTIFF	1670	WOODS, ROBERT	1809	PLAINTIFF	1667
WOODS, HAMILTON	1848	PLAINTIFF	1670	WOODS, ROBERT	1810	PLAINTIFF	1667
WOODS, HAMILTON	1849	PLAINTIFF	1670	WOODS, ROBERT	1811	PLAINTIFF	1667
WOODS, HAMILTON	1854	PLAINTIFF	1670	WOODS, ROBERT	1811	PLAINTIFF	1667
WOODS, HAMILTON	1856	PLAINTIFF	1670	WOODS, ROBERT	1813	PLAINTIFF	1667
WOODS, HENRY	1832	MISC	1707	WOODS, ROBERT	1815	PLAINTIFF	1667
WOODS, J	1871	OH CO. MAP	1741	WOODS, ROBERT	1815	PLAINTIFF	1667
WOODS, J	1871	OH CO. MAP	1741	WOODS, ROBERT	1815	PLAINTIFF	1667
WOODS, J	1871	OH CO. MAP	1741	WOODS, ROBERT	1815	PLAINTIFF	1667
WOODS, J	1871	OH CO. MAP	1741	WOODS, ROBERT	1819	PLAINTIFF	1667
WOODS, J	1871	OH CO. MAP	1741	WOODS, ROBERT	1820	PLAINTIFF	1667
WOODS, J / INITIALS J.W.	1871	OH CO. MAP	1741	WOODS, ROBERT	1822	PLAINTIFF	1668
WOODS, J	1871	OH CO. MAP	1742	WOODS, ROBERT	1825	PLAINTIFF	1668
WOODS, J	1871	OH CO. MAP	1742	WOODS, ROBERT	1825	PLAINTIFF	1668
WOODS, J / INITIALS J.W.	1871	OH CO. MAP	1742	WOODS, ROBERT	1825	MISC	1707
WOODS, J / INITIALS J.W. ?	1871	WHG CITY	1787	WOODS, ROBERT	1826	PLAINTIFF	1668
WOODS, J / INITIALS J.W.	1871	WHG CITY	1789	WOODS, ROBERT	1827	PLAINTIFF	1668
WOODS, J F / PASTOR - EPIS. CHURCH	1871	MDSVL BUS.	1796	WOODS, ROBERT	1829	DEFENDANT	1668
				WOODS, ROBERT	1829	PLAINTIFF	1668
WOODS, J F	1871	MDSVILLE	1806	WOODS, ROBERT	1830	PLAINTIFF	1669
WOODS, J F	1871	MDSVILLE	1807	WOODS, ROBERT	1830	PLAINTIFF	1669
WOODS, J F	1871	MDSVILLE	1809	WOODS, ROBERT	1830	PLAINTIFF	1669
WOODS, JAMES	1838	PLAINTIFF	1669	WOODS, ROBERT	1831	MISC	1707
WOODS, JAMES	1843	PLAINTIFF	1670	WOODS, ROBERT	1832	MISC	1707
WOODS, JAMES W	1837	PLAINTIFF	1669	WOODS, ROBERT	1833	PLAINTIFF	1669
WOODS, JEREMIAH	1800	PLAINTIFF	1665	WOODS, ROBERT	1834	PLAINTIFF	1669
WOODS, JEREMIAH	1800	PLAINTIFF	1665	WOODS, ROBERT	1835	MISC	1707
WOODS, JEREMIAH	1800	PLAINTIFF	1665	WOODS, ROBERT	1839	MISC	1707

'PERSONAL TIME LINE' INDEX TO VOLUME 7 OF THE *OHIO COUNTY INDEX*

ENTRY	YEAR	SUBJECT	PAGE	ENTRY	YEAR	SUBJECT	PAGE
WOODS, ROBERT	1841	MISC	1707	WORNOCH, WILLIAM	1806	PLAINTIFF	1600
WOODS, ROBERT	1845	DEFENDANT	1615	WORNOCK, REBECCA	1796	MISC	1699
WOODS, ROBERT B	1878	DEFENDANT	1671	WORNOCK, REBECCAH	1796	MISC	1699
WOODS, ROBERT C	1824	MISC	1709	WORNOCK, WILLIAM	1796	MISC	1699
WOODS, ROBERT C	1829	PLAINTIFF	1668	WORRELL & JENNINGS	1821	PLAINTIFF	1628
WOODS, ROBERT C	1829	MISC	1707	WORRELL JENNINGS & CO	1817	PLAINTIFF	1628
WOODS, ROBERT C	1830	PLAINTIFF	1669	WORRELL, EDWARD	1822	PLAINTIFF	1600
WOODS, ROBERT C	1831	PLAINTIFF	1669	WORTH, JOHN	1790	PLAINTIFF	1600
WOODS, ROBERT C	1832	MISC	1707	WORTH, RICHARD	1789	PLAINTIFF	1600
WOODS, ROBERT C	1833	PLAINTIFF	1669	WORTH, RICHARD	1792	MISC	1699
WOODS, ROBERT C	1837	MISC	1707	WORTHEN, E E	1873	PLAINTIFF	1601
WOODS, ROBERT C	1838	PLAINTIFF	1669	WORTHINGTON, MARY ANN	1806	PLAINTIFF	1600
WOODS, ROBERT C	1838	PLAINTIFF	1669	WORTHINGTON, S J G / MAP#269	1852	BRKE MAP	1842
WOODS, ROBERT C	1839	PLAINTIFF	1670	WORTHINGTON, THOMAS	1779	MISC	1699
WOODS, ROBERT C	1839	MISC	1707	WORTHINGTON, THOMAS	1805	PLAINTIFF	1600
WOODS, SAMUEL	1830	PLAINTIFF	1669	WORTMAN, PHEBE A	1847	PLAINTIFF	1600
WOODS, T	1871	MARH'L MAP	1749	WORTMAN, PHEBE A	1849	PLAINTIFF	1600
WOODS, T	1871	MARH'L MAP	1752	WORTONS RUN	1871	MARH'L MAP	1747
WOODS, THEODORE	1832	MISC	1707	WORTS, JOHN	1800	PLAINTIFF	1600
WOODS, THEODORE	1844	PLAINTIFF	1670	WOSLEY, JOSEPH	1797	PLAINTIFF	1600
WOODS, THEODORE	1848	PLAINTIFF	1670	WOSLEY, JOSEPH	1820	DEFENDANT	1611
WOODS, THEODORE	1848	PLAINTIFF	1670	WRAY, ROBERT	1876	PLAINTIFF	1603
WOODS, THOMAS	1819	MISC	1707	WRAY, ROBERT	1876	PLAINTIFF	1603
WOODS, THOMAS	1821	PLAINTIFF	1668	WRIGHT & CO	1858	PLAINTIFF	1630
WOODS, THOMAS	1822	PLAINTIFF	1668	WRIGHT PIKE & CO	1856	PLAINTIFF	1630
WOODS, THOMAS	1824	PLAINTIFF	1668	WRIGHT PIKE & CO	1857	PLAINTIFF	1630
WOODS, THOMAS	1826	PLAINTIFF	1668	WRIGHT PIKE & CO	1858	PLAINTIFF	1630
WOODS, THOMAS	1827	PLAINTIFF	1668	WRIGHT PIKE & CO	1860	PLAINTIFF	1631
WOODS, THOMAS	1829	PLAINTIFF	1668	WRIGHT PIKE & CO	1862	PLAINTIFF	1631
WOODS, THOMAS	1832	PLAINTIFF	1669	WRIGHT, AMOS	1816	MISC	1700
WOODS, THOMAS	1832	MISC	1707	WRIGHT, AMOS	1823	DEFENDANT	1600
WOODS, THOMAS	1833	PLAINTIFF	1669	WRIGHT, AMOS	1827	MISC	1700
WOODS, THOMAS	1833	PLAINTIFF	1669	WRIGHT, AMOS	1829	MISC	1700
WOODS, THOMAS	1834	PLAINTIFF	1669	WRIGHT, AMOS	1830	PLAINTIFF	1602
WOODS, WILLIAM	1791	PLAINTIFF	1665	WRIGHT, AMOS	1861	MISC	1700
WOODS, WILLIAM	1829	PLAINTIFF	1668	WRIGHT, ANN MARIA	1846	MISC	1700
WOODS, WILLIAM	1829	PLAINTIFF	1668	WRIGHT, AUGUSTUS	1866	MISC	1700
WOODS, WILLIAM H	1879	PLAINTIFF	1671	WRIGHT, AUGUSTUS	1866	MISC	1711
WOODSIDE	1871	HAN MAP	1726	WRIGHT, AUGUSTUS	1869	MISC	1700
WOODSIDE / W. SIDE OF MAP	1871	HAN MAP	1727	WRIGHT, AUGUSTUS	1869	MISC	1711
WOODSIDE	1871	OH CO. MAP	1743	WRIGHT, BENJAMIN C	1832	DEFENDANT	1596
WOODWARD, C A	1871	CAMERON	1803	WRIGHT, FRANCIS W	1859	DEFENDANT	1661
WOODWARD, JOHN	1863	MISC	1699	WRIGHT, GEORGE W	1859	PLAINTIFF	1602
WOODWARD, S H	1854	MISC	1699	WRIGHT, GRIFFITH & CO	1855	PLAINTIFF	1630
WOODWARD, S H	1867	MISC	1699	WRIGHT, HELEN A	1872	MISC	1690
WOODWARD, S H	1873	MISC	1699	WRIGHT, HELEN A	1872	MISC	1700
WOODWELL, JOSEPH	1850	PLAINTIFF	1600	WRIGHT, HELEN A	1873	MISC	1690
WOODWELL, JOSEPH	1852	PLAINTIFF	1600	WRIGHT, HELEN A	1873	MISC	1700
WOODWORD, WILLIAM H	1879	PLAINTIFF	1601	WRIGHT, HELEN A	1875	MISC	1690
WOODWORTH & BRUNELL	1862	PLAINTIFF	1631	WRIGHT, HELEN A	1875	MISC	1700
WOOKMAN, BENJAMIN	1815	PLAINTIFF	1600	WRIGHT, HELEN A	1876	MISC	1690
WOOL GROWER - WEST UNION	1871	W.UNION-BUS.	1797	WRIGHT, HELEN A	1876	MISC	1700
WOOLEN FACTORY / W. BRIGGS & BRO	1871	BRKE MAP	1736	WRIGHT, J JR	1871	BRKE MAP	1734
				WRIGHT, J SR	1871	BRKE MAP	1734
WOOLEN FACTORY	1871	HAN-POE TWP	1763	WRIGHT, JACOB / MAP#627	1852	BRKE MAP	1852
WOOLEN FACTORY	1871	HAN-POE TWP	1763	WRIGHT, JACOB / MAP#629	1852	BRKE MAP	1852
WOOLEN HOUSE / W. BRIGGS & BRO	1871	BRKE MAP	1736	WRIGHT, JACOB	1871	BRKE MAP	1734
WOOLEN MILL / CUT OFF S.E.EDGE	1871	HAN MAP	1726	WRIGHT, JESSE	1824	PLAINTIFF	1602
WOOLEN MILL / NW OF P.D.PUGH	1871	HAN MAP	1727	WRIGHT, JOHN	1852	PLAINTIFF	1602
WOOLLE, MELLON	1796	PLAINTIFF	1600	WRIGHT, JOHN	1852	MISC	1700
WOOSTER, F	1873	PLAINTIFF	1601	WRIGHT, JOHN	1852	MISC	1702
WORDEN, JOHN	1801	PLAINTIFF	1600	WRIGHT, JOHN	1858	MISC	1700
WORHER, -	1798	PLAINTIFF	1600	WRIGHT, JOHN	1858	MISC	1700
WORK, ALFRED D	1865	MISC	1699	WRIGHT, JOHN	1874	PLAINTIFF	1603
WORK, ALFRED D	1866	MISC	1699	WRIGHT, JOHN C	1822	PLAINTIFF	1602
WORK, JOHN A	1852	PLAINTIFF	1600	WRIGHT, JOHN J	1855	PLAINTIFF	1602
WORK, SAMUEL M	1865	MISC	1699	WRIGHT, JOHN R	1873	PLAINTIFF	1602
WORKHOUSE, -	1855	MISC	1699	WRIGHT, JOSEPH	1817	DEFENDANT	1602
WORKMAN, HUGH JR	1823	PLAINTIFF	1600	WRIGHT, JOSEPH	1863	PLAINTIFF	1602
WORKMAN, JAMES	1833	PLAINTIFF	1600	WRIGHT, LLOYD	1834	DEFENDANT	1639
WORKMAN, JAMES	1834	PLAINTIFF	1600	WRIGHT, LLOYD	1834	DEFENDANT	1650
WORKMAN, JOSIAH	1837	PLAINTIFF	1600	WRIGHT, LLOYD	1839	DEFENDANT	1574
WORKMAN, JOSIAH	1839	PLAINTIFF	1600	WRIGHT, LOYD	1827	PLAINTIFF	1602
WORKMAN, L	1871	MARH'L MAP	1759	WRIGHT, M L	1880	PLAINTIFF	1603
WORKMAN, SAMUEL	1787	PLAINTIFF	1600	WRIGHT, MOSES B	1874	PLAINTIFF	1603
WORKMAN, SAMUEL	1788	PLAINTIFF	1600	WRIGHT, MOSES B C	1874	PLAINTIFF	1603
WORKMAN, SAMUEL	1789	PLAINTIFF	1600	WRIGHT, NANCY	1817	PLAINTIFF	1602
WORLEY, DAVID	1794	MISC	1699	WRIGHT, PETER / & CO	1858	PLAINTIFF	1630
WORLEY, JOSEPH	1780	PLAINTIFF	1600	WRIGHT, PETER F / & CO	1860	PLAINTIFF	1631
WORLEY, JOSEPH	1821	DEFENDANT	1612	WRIGHT, PETER T	1858	PLAINTIFF	1602
WORLEY, JOSEPH	1822	PLAINTIFF	1600	WRIGHT, PETER T / & CO	1862	PLAINTIFF	1631
WORLEY, JOSEPH	1822	DEFENDANT	1612	WRIGHT, PIKE & CO	1855	PLAINTIFF	1630
WORLEY, JOSEPH	1832	PLAINTIFF	1600	WRIGHT, R	1874	PLAINTIFF	1603
WORLEY, SAMUEL	1798	PLAINTIFF	1600	WRIGHT, RICHARD	1859	PLAINTIFF	1602
WORMSER BURGRAFF & CO	1856	PLAINTIFF	1630	WRIGHT, ROBERT	1856	PLAINTIFF	1602
WORMSER, EPHRIAM	1856	PLAINTIFF	1601	WRIGHT, S	1871	BRKE MAP	1734

'PERSONAL TIME LINE' INDEX TO VOLUME 7 OF THE *OHIO COUNTY INDEX*

ENTRY	YEAR	SUBJECT	PAGE
WRIGHT, SARAH	1828	PLAINTIFF	1602
WRIGHT, SARAH	1830	PLAINTIFF	1602
WRIGHT, THOMAS	1839	PLAINTIFF	1602
WRIGHT, THOMAS	1858	MISC	1700
WRIGHT, THOMAS	1858	MISC	1700
WRIGHT, ZADOE	1807	PLAINTIFF	1602
WROTH, M	1871	MARH'L MAP	1745
WUNDERLICH, SIMON	1865	MISC	1700
WUNDERLICK, SIMON H	1855	PLAINTIFF	1602
WURSTER, FRED	1873	PLAINTIFF	1603
WURTEZ & REICHARD	1831	PLAINTIFF	1628
WURTS & REINHARD	1832	PLAINTIFF	1628
WURTS, CHARLES	1858	PLAINTIFF	1602
WURTZ AUSTIE & MCVEIGH	1858	PLAINTIFF	1630
WUSTHOFF, FREDERICK	1874	PLAINTIFF	1603
WV & REGIONAL HISTORY COLLECTION - AT WVU	2000	PREFACE	1748
WYAT, ROBERT	1820	PLAINTIFF	1602
WYATT, -	1871	MARH'L MAP	1757
WYCART, FRANCES	1824	PLAINTIFF	1602
WYCART, FRANCIS	1818	PLAINTIFF	1602
WYCART, FRANCIS	1821	PLAINTIFF	1602
WYCART, FRANCIS	1822	PLAINTIFF	1602
WYCART, FRANCIS	1823	MISC	1700
WYCART, NICHOLAS	1824	PLAINTIFF	1602
WYKART, FRANCIS	1825	MISC	1700
WYKART, NICHOLAS	1830	MISC	1700
WYKART, SAMUEL M	1855	PLAINTIFF	1602
WYKOFF, WILLIAM	1852	NOT ON MAP	1836
WYKOFF, WILLIAM / MAP#93	1852	BRKE MAP	1842
WYKOFF, WILLIAM / MAP#94	1852	BRKE MAP	1842
WYKOFF, WILLIAM / MAP#95	1852	BRKE MAP	1842
WYKUFF, - / MRS	1871	HAN MAP	1731
WYLIE & WILSON	1840	PLAINTIFF	1628
WYLIE & WILSON	1840	PLAINTIFF	1629
WYLIE & WILSON	1841	PLAINTIFF	1629
WYLIE, W / (?WILLIAM?)	1871	OH CO. MAP	1742
WYLIE, W / S. OF ELM GROVE STATION ON MAP	1871	OH CO. MAP	1743
WYLIE, W / S. OF ELM GROVE STATION ON MAP	1871	OH CO. MAP	1744
WYLIE, WILLIAM	1841	PLAINTIFF	1602
WYLIE, WILLIAM	1856	MISC	1700
WYLIE, WILLIAM	1860	PLAINTIFF	1602
WYLIE, WILLIAM	1873	MISC	1700
WYMAN & CO	1820	PLAINTIFF	1628
WYMAN, -	1820	PLAINTIFF	1620
WYMAN, SAMUEL	1837	PLAINTIFF	1602
WYMAN, SAMUEL G	1861	PLAINTIFF	1602
WYMS, HENRY	1819	PLAINTIFF	1602
WYMS, HENRY	1819	PLAINTIFF	1602
WYMS, NANCEY	1819	PLAINTIFF	1602
WYNKOOP, FRANCIS S	1856	PLAINTIFF	1602
WYNKOOP, FRANCIS S	1856	PLAINTIFF	1602
WYNKOOP, HANNAH	1829	MISC	1700
WYNKOOP, HANNAH	1831	MISC	1700
WYNKOOP, HANNAH	1831	MISC	1700
WYNSMAN, HENRY	1829	PLAINTIFF	1602
XENIA RR	1852	HEMP. RR MAP	1826
Y, G / PRESBYTERIAN CHURCH ?	1871	HAN MAP	1731
YACKE, A	1871	OH CO. MAP	1742
YACKE, A	1871	OH CO.BUS.	1779
YACKER, J / STONE QUARRY	1871	OH CO. MAP	1742
YAGER, C	1871	WHG CITY	1789
YAGER, F	1871	OH CO. MAP	1741
YAGER, JOHN	1857	PLAINTIFF	1604
YAGER, JOHN	1857	PLAINTIFF	1604
YAGER, JOHN F W	1875	MISC	1708
YAGER, NICHOLAS	1872	MISC	1708
YAGLE, FRANCIS	1873	MISC	1708
YAHRLING, CHARLES	1857	MISC	1708
YAHRLING, ELIZABETH	1857	MISC	1708
YAHRLING, FRED	1862	PLAINTIFF	1604
YAHRLING, FREDERICK	1858	DEFENDANT	1565
YAHRLING, MARGARET	1857	MISC	1708
YANCEY, WILLIAM	1832	PLAINTIFF	1604
YANCY, W	1871	MARH'L MAP	1745
YANT, D H	1871	NEW MANCH.	1763
YANT, H / DOCTOR	1871	NEW MANCH.	1769
YARD, EDMUND	1856	PLAINTIFF	1604
YARD, EDMUND	1856	PLAINTIFF	1604
YARD, EDMUND	1857	PLAINTIFF	1604
YARD, GILLMORE & CO	1856	PLAINTIFF	1632
YARD, GILMORE & CO	1857	PLAINTIFF	1632
YARDLEY, KERKBRIDE	1832	PLAINTIFF	1604
YARHLING, FREDERICK	1859	PLAINTIFF	1604

ENTRY	YEAR	SUBJECT	PAGE
YARHLING, FREDERICK	1860	PLAINTIFF	1604
YARLING, THOEDORE	1854	MISC	1708
YARNALL & BOTSFORD	1856	DEFENDANT	1641
YARNALL, EMILY Y	1858	MISC	1708
YARNALL, EMMA	1849	MISC	1708
YARNALL, J	1871	MARH'L MAP	1751
YARNALL, J J	1855	DEFENDANT	1602
YARNALL, J J	1855	DEFENDANT	1630
YARNALL, J J / & CO	1856	PLAINTIFF	1632
YARNALL, J J / & CO	1857	PLAINTIFF	1632
YARNALL, JOHN J	1852	DEFENDANT	1618
YARNALL, JOHN J	1854	MISC	1708
YARNALL, JOHN J	1856	PLAINTIFF	1604
YARNALL, JOHN J	1856	DEFENDANT	1621
YARNALL, JOHN J	1856	DEFENDANT	1641
YARNALL, JOHN J / & BRO	1857	DEFENDANT	1582
YARNALL, JOHN J	1861	MISC	1708
YARNALL, MORDACIA	1800	PLAINTIFF	1604
YARNALL, MORDECAI	1809	PLAINTIFF	1604
YARNALL, MORDECAI	1811	DEFENDANT	1585
YARNALL, MORDECAI	1811	DEFENDANT	1635
YARNALL, MORDECAI	1811	MISC	1708
YARNALL, MORDECAI	1814	PLAINTIFF	1604
YARNALL, MORDECEI	1809	PLAINTIFF	1604
YARNALL, MORDICAE	1825	PLAINTIFF	1604
YARNALL, MORDICAI	1810	PLAINTIFF	1604
YARNALL, PETER	1814	PLAINTIFF	1604
YARNALL, PETER	1820	PLAINTIFF	1604
YARNALL, PETER	1822	MISC	1708
YARNALL, PETER	1824	PLAINTIFF	1604
YARNALL, PETER	1825	PLAINTIFF	1604
YARNALL, PETER	1825	PLAINTIFF	1604
YARNALL, PETER	1826	MISC	1708
YARNALL, PETER	1846	DEFENDANT	1657
YARNALL, PETER	1849	MISC	1708
YARNALL, PETER	1852	HEMPFIELD RR	1822
YARNALL, PETER	1856	PLAINTIFF	1604
YARNALL, PETER	1858	PLAINTIFF	1604
YARNALL, Z S	1855	DEFENDANT	1602
YARNALL, Z S	1855	DEFENDANT	1630
YARNALL, Z S / & CO	1856	PLAINTIFF	1632
YARNALL, Z S / & CO	1857	PLAINTIFF	1632
YARNALL, ZACHARIAH	1856	PLAINTIFF	1604
YARNALL, ZACHARIAH S	1847	MISC	1708
YARNALL, ZACHARIAH S	1853	PLAINTIFF	1604
YARNALL, ZACHARIAH S	1863	MISC	1708
YARNEL, MORDICO	1802	PLAINTIFF	1604
YARNELL - CHILDREN	1858	MISC	1708
YARNELL, E / & CO	1857	PLAINTIFF	1632
YARNELL, E F C	1857	PLAINTIFF	1604
YARNELL, ELLIS	1857	PLAINTIFF	1604
YARNELL, EMMA	1858	PLAINTIFF	1604
YARNELL, F C & CO	1857	PLAINTIFF	1632
YARNELL, MORDECAI	1808	DEFENDANT	1637
YARNELL, MORDECAI	1811	PLAINTIFF	1604
YARNELL, MORDECAI	1843	MISC	1708
YARNELL, MORDECAI	1847	MISC	1708
YARNELL, MORDECIA	1808	MISC	1708
YARNELL, MORDECIA	1809	DEFENDANT	1638
YARNELL, MORDECIA	1809	DEFENDANT	1642
YARNELL, PETER	1811	PLAINTIFF	1604
YARNELL, PETER	1858	PLAINTIFF	1604
YARNELL, PETER SR	1858	DEFENDANT	1604
YATER, FLORENCE A	1875	PLAINTIFF	1604
YATER, MATTHEW	1866	MISC	1708
YATER, R	1871	MARH'L MAP	1756
YATER, R	1871	MARH'L MAP	1760
YATER, R / INITIALS R.Y.	1871	MARH'L MAP	1760
YATES HOMESTEAD	1871	OH CO. MAP	1740
YATES, A	1871	OH CO. MAP	1740
YATES, ADAM	1837	MISC	1708
YATES, ANDREW	1842	MISC	1708
YATES, ANDREW	1852	HEMPFIELD RR	1822
YATES, ANDREW	1859	MISC	1708
YATES, ANDREW F	1877	DEFENDANT	1605
YATES, B T	1871	OH CO. MAP	1740
YATES, BYEN T	1876	PLAINTIFF	1604
YATES, BYERS T	1879	PLAINTIFF	1605
YATES, DAVID	1822	DEFENDANT	1596
YATES, HETTY	1828	PLAINTIFF	1604
YATES, HUGH	1859	MISC	1708
YATES, JOSEPH	1845	PLAINTIFF	1604
YATES, M / MRS	1871	OH CO. MAP	1740
YATES, RICHARD	1788	PLAINTIFF	1604
YATES, RICHARD	1788	MISC	1708
YATES, THOMAS	1822	MISC	1708

'PERSONAL TIME LINE' INDEX TO VOLUME 7 OF THE OHIO COUNTY INDEX

ENTRY	YEAR	SUBJECT	PAGE	ENTRY	YEAR	SUBJECT	PAGE
YATES, THOMAS	1851	PLAINTIFF	1604	YOUNG & HUSEMAN	1873	DEFENDANT	1631
YATES, THOMAS	1851	PLAINTIFF	1604	YOUNG & McCOLLOCH	1844	DEFENDANT	1632
YATES, THOMAS	1855	MISC	1708	YOUNG, ALBERT	1874	PLAINTIFF	1609
YATES, THOMAS	1859	MISC	1708	YOUNG, ALBERT / & CO	1874	PLAINTIFF	1633
YATES, THOMAS G	1861	PLAINTIFF	1604	YOUNG, ALEXANDER	1788	PLAINTIFF	1608
YATES, THOMAS G	1875	MISC	1708	YOUNG, ALICE B	1876	PLAINTIFF	1609
YATES, THOMAS G	1877	PLAINTIFF	1605	YOUNG, ANDREW	1832	PLAINTIFF	1608
YATES, THOMAS G	1877	MISC	1708	YOUNG, BROTHERS & CO	1863	PLAINTIFF	1632
YATES, THOMAS STOCKTON	1859	MISC	1708	YOUNG, C	1871	MARH'L MAP	1755
YATES, W	1871	BKE/OH MAP	1738	YOUNG, C E	1871	MARH'L MAP	1759
YATES, WILLIAM	1857	MISC	1708	YOUNG, CATHERINE	1812	MISC	1709
YATES, WILLIAM	1874	MISC	1708	YOUNG, CATHERINE	1846	MISC	1709
YATES, WILLIAM L	1875	MISC	1708	YOUNG, E B / CUT OFF EDGE	1871	MARH'L MAP	1755
YATES, WILLIAM LESTER	1877	MISC	1708	YOUNG, E B	1871	MARH'L MAP	1759
YAUND, SILAS	1787	PLAINTIFF	1604	YOUNG, E B	1871	MARH'L MAP	1759
YAUS - CHILDREN	1878	MISC	1695	YOUNG, E B / INITIALS E.B.Y.	1871	MARH'L MAP	1759
YAUS, ANDREW	1878	MISC	1708	YOUNG, E B / INITIALS E.B.Y.	1871	MARH'L MAP	1759
YEAGER, THEODORE	1878	MISC	1709	YOUNG, ED B	1876	MISC	1709
YEAMAN, AGNES	1787	PLAINTIFF	1606	YOUNG, EDWARD B	1873	DEFENDANT	1631
YEARBY, JOHN	1837	DEFENDANT	1559	YOUNG, EDWARD B	1874	PLAINTIFF	1609
YEASTEP, G	1871	MARH'L MAP	1759	YOUNG, EDWARD B	1876	PLAINTIFF	1609
YEATER - FEMALE CHILD	1850	MISC	1709	YOUNG, ELIJAH B	1835	PLAINTIFF	1608
YEATES, THOMAS	1818	MISC	1709	YOUNG, GEORGE	1795	PLAINTIFF	1608
YEATS, RICHARD	1778	MISC	1709	YOUNG, GEORGE C	1856	MISC	1709
YEATS, RICHARD	1789	DEFENDANT	1554	YOUNG, HENRY	1793	PLAINTIFF	1608
YEATS, RICHARD	1793	PLAINTIFF	1606	YOUNG, HENRY	1807	PLAINTIFF	1608
YEATS, RICHARD	1794	PLAINTIFF	1606	YOUNG, HENRY	1807	PLAINTIFF	1608
YEATS, RICHARD	1797	PLAINTIFF	1606	YOUNG, HENRY	1810	MISC	1709
YEATS, RICHARD	1798	PLAINTIFF	1606	YOUNG, J	1871	MARH'L MAP	1755
YEATS, RICHARD	1801	PLAINTIFF	1606	YOUNG, J / INITIALS J.Y	1871	MARH'L MAP	1755
YEATS, THOMAS	1807	PLAINTIFF	1606	YOUNG, J	1871	MARH'L MAP	1759
YELLOW CREEK / IN OHIO - RUNS INTO OHIO RIVER	1871	HAN MAP	1726	YOUNG, J	1871	MARH'L MAP	1759
YELLOW CREEK STATION	1871	HAN MAP	1726	YOUNG, J / INITIALS J.Y.	1871	MARH'L MAP	1759
YINGLING, R H	1879	PLAINTIFF	1606	YOUNG, J / INITIALS J.Y.	1871	MARH'L MAP	1759
YJULIA HOME / MISS NANCY RODGERS	1871	W.LIBERTY	1780	YOUNG, J / INITIALS J.Y.	1871	MARH'L MAP	1759
				YOUNG, JAMES	1793	PLAINTIFF	1608
YOCKE, A	1859	PLAINTIFF	1608	YOUNG, JAMES	1793	MISC	1709
YOCKE, A	1876	PLAINTIFF	1609	YOUNG, JAMES	1795	PLAINTIFF	1608
YOCKE, ADOLPH	1873	PLAINTIFF	1609	YOUNG, JAMES	1802	MISC	1709
YOCKE, ADOLPH	1873	PLAINTIFF	1609	YOUNG, JAMES	1871	MISC	1709
YOCKE, ADOLPH	1874	PLAINTIFF	1609	YOUNG, JOHN	1787	PLAINTIFF	1608
YOCKE, ADOLPH	1874	DEFENDANT	1615	YOUNG, JOHN	1856	PLAINTIFF	1608
YOCKE, ADOLPH	1875	PLAINTIFF	1609	YOUNG, JOHN	1857	DEFENDANT	1616
YOCKS, ADOLPH	1860	PLAINTIFF	1608	YOUNG, JOHN GOODMAN	1796	PLAINTIFF	1608
YODER, J	1871	MARH'L MAP	1761	YOUNG, JOHN N	1827	MISC	1709
YODER, Z	1871	MARH'L MAP	1761	YOUNG, JUDY	1850	PLAINTIFF	1608
YOHO & HUFF	1844	PLAINTIFF	1632	YOUNG, JUDY	1850	PLAINTIFF	1608
YOHO, A	1871	MARH'L MAP	1759	YOUNG, LOUIS	1875	PLAINTIFF	1609
YOHO, F	1871	MARH'L MAP	1754	YOUNG, MARY E	1876	DEFENDANT	1609
YOHO, G	1871	MARH'L MAP	1755	YOUNG, MORGAN	1804	PLAINTIFF	1608
YOHO, G	1871	MARH'L MAP	1759	YOUNG, MORGAN	1805	PLAINTIFF	1608
YOHO, H	1871	MARH'L MAP	1759	YOUNG, P	1871	W.LIBRTY.BUS.	1780
YOHO, H / INITIALS H.Y.	1871	MARH'L MAP	1759	YOUNG, P / STORE	1871	W.LIBERTY	1780
YOHO, H B	1871	MARH'L MAP	1755	YOUNG, PETER B	1877	PLAINTIFF	1609
YOHO, H B	1871	MARH'L MAP	1755	YOUNG, PHILIP	1857	PLAINTIFF	1608
YOHO, H P	1871	MARH'L MAP	1754	YOUNG, PHILIP	1873	PLAINTIFF	1609
YOHO, HENRY	1799	MISC	1709	YOUNG, PHILIP	1876	PLAINTIFF	1609
YOHO, HENRY	1811	PLAINTIFF	1608	YOUNG, PHILIP	1878	PLAINTIFF	1609
YOHO, HENRY	1813	PLAINTIFF	1608	YOUNG, PHILLIP	1879	PLAINTIFF	1609
YOHO, HENRY	1824	PLAINTIFF	1608	YOUNG, SAMUEL	1808	PLAINTIFF	1608
YOHO, HENRY SR	1822	PLAINTIFF	1608	YOUNG, SAMUEL	1809	PLAINTIFF	1608
YOHO, I	1871	MARH'L MAP	1758	YOUNG, SIMON	1859	PLAINTIFF	1608
YOHO, I	1871	MARH'L MAP	1759	YOUNG, SIMON	1860	PLAINTIFF	1608
YOHO, I	1871	MARH'L MAP	1759	YOUNG, THOMAS	1856	PLAINTIFF	1608
YOHO, J / INITIALS J.Y.	1871	MARH'L MAP	1754	YOUNG, THOMAS P	1875	PLAINTIFF	1609
YOHO, J	1871	MARH'L MAP	1755	YOUNG, WILLIAM	1809	PLAINTIFF	1608
YOHO, J	1871	MARH'L MAP	1755	YOUNG, WILLIAM	1812	MISC	1709
YOHO, J / INITIALS J.Y.	1871	MARH'L MAP	1755	YOUNG, WILLIAM	1814	PLAINTIFF	1608
YOHO, J / INITIALS J.Y.	1871	MARH'L MAP	1755	YOUNG, WILLIAM	1823	DEFENDANT	1570
YOHO, J	1871	MARH'L MAP	1758	YOUNG, WILLIAM	1823	DEFENDANT	1572
YOHO, J	1871	MARH'L MAP	1758	YOUNG, WILLIAM	1823	DEFENDANT	1632
YOHO, J	1871	MARH'L MAP	1759	YOUNG, WILLIAM	1823	DEFENDANT	1632
YOHO, L	1871	MARH'L MAP	1759	YOUNG, WILLIAM	1829	DEFENDANT	1632
YOHO, P	1871	MARH'L MAP	1759	YOUNG, WILLIAM H	1876	PLAINTIFF	1609
YOHO, PATRICK	1834	DEFENDANT	1613	YOUNG, WILLIAM JR	1834	PLAINTIFF	1608
YOHO, PETER	1823	MISC	1709	YOUNG, WILLIAM T	1859	PLAINTIFF	1608
YOHO, PETER	1824	MISC	1709	YOUNGER, HUMPHREY	1817	PLAINTIFF	1608
YOHO, T	1871	MARH'L MAP	1759	YOUNGER, MARY	1817	PLAINTIFF	1608
YOHO, W	1871	MARH'L MAP	1759	YOUNGER, NEHEMIAH	1811	MISC	1709
YOHO, W	1871	MARH'L MAP	1759	YOUNGER, NEHEMIAH	1812	PLAINTIFF	1608
YOHO, W JR	1871	MARH'L MAP	1754	YOUNGER, UMPHREY	1810	MISC	1677
YOHO, W JR	1871	MARH'L MAP	1758	YOUNGER, UMPHREY	1810	MISC	1709
YOHO, W JR / INITIALS W.Y.	1871	MARH'L MAP	1758	YOUNGMAN - SEE ALSO JUNGMAN	1871	BKE/OH MAP	1738
YOIOGENY STREAM	1852	HEMPFIELD RR	1818	YOUNGMAN, C	1871	BENWOOD	1798
YONKER, LEWIS	1852	PLAINTIFF	1608	YOUNGMAN, W	1871	BENWOOD	1798

'PERSONAL TIME LINE' INDEX TO VOLUME 7 OF THE *OHIO COUNTY INDEX*

ENTRY	YEAR	SUBJECT	PAGE	ENTRY	YEAR	SUBJECT	PAGE
YUENGLING, LUCAS	1870	MISC	1709	ZANE, EBENEZER	1801	PLAINTIFF	1610
ZANE & CO	1863	PLAINTIFF	1633	ZANE, EBENEZER	1801	PLAINTIFF	1610
ZANE & KNOX	1817	PLAINTIFF	1632	ZANE, EBENEZER	1802	MISC	1710
ZANE & KNOX	1818	PLAINTIFF	1632	ZANE, EBENEZER	1810	PLAINTIFF	1610
ZANE & KNOX	1821	PLAINTIFF	1632	ZANE, EBENEZER	1810	PLAINTIFF	1659
ZANE & KNOX	1822	PLAINTIFF	1632	ZANE, EBENEZER	1811	PLAINTIFF	1610
ZANE & KNOX	1823	PLAINTIFF	1632	ZANE, EBENEZER	1811	PLAINTIFF	1610
ZANE & KNOX	1828	PLAINTIFF	1632	ZANE, EBENEZER	1811	PLAINTIFF	1610
ZANE & KNOX	1829	PLAINTIFF	1632	ZANE, EBENEZER	1811	PLAINTIFF	1610
ZANE & KNOX	1844	PLAINTIFF	1632	ZANE, EBENEZER	1811	MISC	1710
ZANE & PENTONEY	1830	PLAINTIFF	1618	ZANE, EBENEZER	1812	PLAINTIFF	1610
ZANE & PENTONEY	1831	PLAINTIFF	1618	ZANE, EBENEZER	1812	PLAINTIFF	1611
ZANE & PENTONEY	1832	PLAINTIFF	1618	ZANE, EBENEZER	1813	PLAINTIFF	1611
ZANE & PENTONEY	1833	PLAINTIFF	1618	ZANE, EBENEZER	1813	MISC	1710
ZANE & PENTONEY	1834	PLAINTIFF	1618	ZANE, EBENEZER	1830	DEFENDANT	1620
ZANE & PENTONEY	1835	PLAINTIFF	1618	ZANE, EBENEZER	1832	PLAINTIFF	1613
ZANE & PENTONEY	1836	PLAINTIFF	1618	ZANE, EBENEZER	1833	PLAINTIFF	1613
ZANE & PENTONEY	1837	PLAINTIFF	1618	ZANE, EBENEZER	1834	DEFENDANT	1567
ZANE & PENTONEY	1837	PLAINTIFF	1619	ZANE, EBENEZER	1834	DEFENDANT	1599
ZANE & PENTONEY	1838	PLAINTIFF	1619	ZANE, EBENEZER	1834	PLAINTIFF	1613
ZANE & PENTONEY	1839	PLAINTIFF	1619	ZANE, EBENEZER	1835	PLAINTIFF	1613
ZANE & PENTONEY	1840	PLAINTIFF	1619	ZANE, EBENEZER	1835	DEFENDANT	1650
ZANE & PENTONEY	1841	PLAINTIFF	1619	ZANE, EBENEZER	1836	PLAINTIFF	1614
ZANE & PENTONEY	1843	PLAINTIFF	1619	ZANE, EBENEZER	1837	PLAINTIFF	1614
ZANE & ROHAN	1839	PLAINTIFF	1632	ZANE, EBENEZER	1838	DEFENDANT	1558
ZANE, ANDREW	1780	MISC	1710	ZANE, EBENEZER	1838	DEFENDANT	1563
ZANE, ANDREW	1783	PLAINTIFF	1610	ZANE, EBENEZER	1838	PLAINTIFF	1614
ZANE, ANDREW	1783	PLAINTIFF	1610	ZANE, EBENEZER	1838	DEFENDANT	1622
ZANE, ANDREW	1784	APPENDIX	1874	ZANE, EBENEZER	1838	DEFENDANT	1662
ZANE, ANDREW	1788	PLAINTIFF	1610	ZANE, EBENEZER	1839	PLAINTIFF	1614
ZANE, ANDRW	1784	DEFENDANT	1589	ZANE, EBENEZER	1842	PLAINTIFF	1615
ZANE, BENJAMIN	1828	DEFENDANT	1613	ZANE, EBENEZER	1843	MISC	1710
ZANE, C L / & CO	1861	PLAINTIFF	1632	ZANE, EBENEZER	1855	PLAINTIFF	1615
ZANE, C L	1862	PLAINTIFF	1615	ZANE, EBENEZER	1868	MISC	1711
ZANE, C L / & CO	1862	PLAINTIFF	1632	ZANE, EBENEZER / COL.	1916	NAT'L ROAD	1866
ZANE, C L	1871	WHG ISLAND	1788	ZANE, EBENEZER / COL.	1916	NAT'L ROAD	1867
ZANE, C L	1874	PLAINTIFF	1615	ZANE, EBENEZER / COL.	1916	NAT'L ROAD	1867
ZANE, C L	1875	PLAINTIFF	1615	ZANE, EBENZER	1801	PLAINTIFF	1610
ZANE, C LEANDER	1863	PLAINTIFF	1615	ZANE, EDMUND G	1852	MISC	1711
ZANE, C LEANDER	1866	MISC	1700	ZANE, EDWARD E	1874	MISC	1711
ZANE, C LEANDER	1866	MISC	1711	ZANE, EDWIN	1873	PLAINTIFF	1615
ZANE, C LEANDER	1869	MISC	1700	ZANE, EDWIN E	1877	PLAINTIFF	1615
ZANE, C LEANDER	1869	MISC	1711	ZANE, EDWIN E	1878	PLAINTIFF	1615
ZANE, CAROLINE V	1880	MISC	1711	ZANE, EDWIN E	1879	PLAINTIFF	1615
ZANE, CLARK LEANDER	1857	PLAINTIFF	1615	ZANE, ELIZA J	1873	DEFENDANT	1597
ZANE, CLARK LEANDER	1861	PLAINTIFF	1615	ZANE, ELIZA J	1874	PLAINTIFF	1615
ZANE, CORNELIUS	1840	PLAINTIFF	1614	ZANE, ELIZABETH	1784	MISC	1710
ZANE, CYNTHIA	1825	PLAINTIFF	1612	ZANE, ELIZABETH	1812	PLAINTIFF	1611
ZANE, DANIEL	1811	MISC	1710	ZANE, ELIZABETH	1814	MISC	1710
ZANE, DANIEL	1812	PLAINTIFF	1610	ZANE, ELIZABETH	1840	PLAINTIFF	1614
ZANE, DANIEL	1812	PLAINTIFF	1611	ZANE, ELIZABETH / FORT HENRY HISTORY	1916	NAT'L ROAD	1867
ZANE, DANIEL	1812	MISC	1710	ZANE, FANNY	1828	PLAINTIFF	1613
ZANE, DANIEL	1813	PLAINTIFF	1611	ZANE, HAMPDEN	1834	MISC	1710
ZANE, DANIEL	1815	PLAINTIFF	1611	ZANE, HAMPDEN	1843	PLAINTIFF	1615
ZANE, DANIEL	1815	MISC	1710	ZANE, JANATHAN	1788	PLAINTIFF	1610
ZANE, DANIEL	1820	PLAINTIFF	1611	ZANE, JOEL	1798	MISC	1710
ZANE, DANIEL	1821	PLAINTIFF	1612	ZANE, JOEL	1806	MISC	1710
ZANE, DANIEL	1824	DEFENDANT	1591	ZANE, JOEL	1824	MISC	1710
ZANE, DANIEL	1824	PLAINTIFF	1612	ZANE, JOEL	1826	DEFENDANT	1668
ZANE, DANIEL	1825	PLAINTIFF	1612	ZANE, JOEL	1826	DEFENDANT	1668
ZANE, DANIEL	1825	PLAINTIFF	1612	ZANE, JOEL	1832	DEFENDANT	1618
ZANE, DANIEL	1826	PLAINTIFF	1613	ZANE, JOEL	1834	DEFENDANT	1669
ZANE, DANIEL	1827	PLAINTIFF	1613	ZANE, JOHN	1803	PLAINTIFF	1610
ZANE, DANIEL	1828	PLAINTIFF	1613	ZANE, JOHN	1806	MISC	1710
ZANE, DANIEL	1833	PLAINTIFF	1613	ZANE, JOHN	1808	PLAINTIFF	1610
ZANE, DANIEL	1851	MISC	1696	ZANE, JOHN	1818	DEFENDANT	1611
ZANE, DANIEL	1860	MISC	1711	ZANE, JOHN	1839	PLAINTIFF	1614
ZANE, DANIEL	1874	DEFENDANT	1673	ZANE, JONATHAN	1802	PLAINTIFF	1610
ZANE, DANIEL F	1879	DEFENDANT	1558	ZANE, JONATHAN	1804	PLAINTIFF	1610
ZANE, E	1871	WHG ISLAND	1788	ZANE, JONATHAN	1806	PLAINTIFF	1610
ZANE, E B	1784	PLAINTIFF	1610	ZANE, JONATHAN	1808	PLAINTIFF	1610
ZANE, E E	1874	PLAINTIFF	1615	ZANE, JONATHAN	1811	PLAINTIFF	1610
ZANE, E J / MRS	1871	OH CO. MAP	1742	ZANE, JONATHAN	1811	PLAINTIFF	1610
ZANE, E J / MRS	1871	TRIAD TWP.	1781	ZANE, JONATHAN	1812	PLAINTIFF	1611
ZANE, E P	1858	PLAINTIFF	1615	ZANE, JONATHAN	1812	MISC	1710
ZANE, EBENEAZER	1798	PLAINTIFF	1610	ZANE, JONATHAN	1815	DEFENDANT	1611
ZANE, EBENEAZER	1803	PLAINTIFF	1610	ZANE, JONATHAN	1815	PLAINTIFF	1611
ZANE, EBENEAZOR	1794	MISC	1710	ZANE, JONATHAN	1816	DEFENDANT	1611
ZANE, EBENEZAR	1778	MISC	1710	ZANE, JONATHAN	1816	PLAINTIFF	1611
ZANE, EBENEZAR	1806	PLAINTIFF	1610	ZANE, JONATHAN	1817	PLAINTIFF	1611
ZANE, EBENEZER	1784	MISC	1710	ZANE, JONATHAN	1817	PLAINTIFF	1611
ZANE, EBENEZER	1789	PLAINTIFF	1610	ZANE, JONATHAN	1818	DEFENDANT	1667
ZANE, EBENEZER	1789	MISC	1710	ZANE, JONATHAN	1819	PLAINTIFF	1611
ZANE, EBENEZER	1797	PLAINTIFF	1610	ZANE, JONATHAN	1820	PLAINTIFF	1611
ZANE, EBENEZER	1799	PLAINTIFF	1610	ZANE, JONATHAN	1820	PLAINTIFF	1611
ZANE, EBENEZER	1801	DEFENDANT	1554				

'PERSONAL TIME LINE' INDEX TO VOLUME 7 OF THE *OHIO COUNTY INDEX*

ENTRY	YEAR	SUBJECT	PAGE	ENTRY	YEAR	SUBJECT	PAGE
ZANE, JONATHAN	1821	PLAINTIFF	1612	ZANE, SILAS	1784	PLAINTIFF	1610
ZANE, JONATHAN	1823	MISC	1710	ZANE, VIRGINIA F C	1853	PLAINTIFF	1615
ZANE, JONATHAN	1825	PLAINTIFF	1612	ZANE, VIRGINIA F C	1857	PLAINTIFF	1615
ZANE, JONATHAN	1825	MISC	1710	ZANE, VIRGINIA F C	1861	PLAINTIFF	1615
ZANE, JONATHAN	1826	PLAINTIFF	1613	ZANE, W	1871	WHG ISLAND	1788
ZANE, JONATHAN	1827	PLAINTIFF	1613	ZANE, WILLIAM	1787	PLAINTIFF	1610
ZANE, JONATHAN	1828	PLAINTIFF	1613	ZANE, WILLIAM	1810	DEFENDANT	1599
ZANE, JONATHAN	1829	DEFENDANT	1649	ZANE, WILLIAM	1859	DEFENDANT	1569
ZANE, KNOX & MCKEE	1824	PLAINTIFF	1632	ZANE, WILLIAM	1860	DEFENDANT	1569
ZANE, M S	1843	PLAINTIFF	1615	ZANE, WOODS & CO	1829	PLAINTIFF	1632
ZANE, MARIAM	1784	MISC	1710	ZANE, WOODS & CO	1830	PLAINTIFF	1632
ZANE, MARY L	1834	MISC	1710	ZANESBURG / EARLY NAME FOR WHEELING	1916	NAT'L ROAD	1866
ZANE, NANCY	1831	MISC	1710	ZANESVILLE, OH	1852	HEMPFIELD RR	1820
ZANE, NOAH	1807	PLAINTIFF	1610	ZANESVILLE, OH	1852	HEMP. RR MAP	1825
ZANE, NOAH	1807	MISC	1710	ZANESVILLE, OH	1852	HEMP. RR MAP	1826
ZANE, NOAH	1808	PLAINTIFF	1610	ZANESVILLE, OH	1916	NAT'L ROAD	1866
ZANE, NOAH	1808	PLAINTIFF	1610	ZEAGLER, JOHN	1838	PLAINTIFF	1616
ZANE, NOAH	1809	PLAINTIFF	1610	ZECKKLER, PETER	1860	PLAINTIFF	1616
ZANE, NOAH	1810	APPENDIX	1873	ZEDIKER, N	1871	MDSVILLE	1807
ZANE, NOAH	1811	MISC	1710	ZEIGLER, BENJAMIN	1841	PLAINTIFF	1616
ZANE, NOAH	1812	PLAINTIFF	1610	ZEIGLER, F ERNEST	1858	PLAINTIFF	1616
ZANE, NOAH	1812	PLAINTIFF	1611	ZEIGLER, FREDERICK	1856	PLAINTIFF	1616
ZANE, NOAH	1812	MISC	1710	ZEIGLER, FREDERICK	1856	DEFENDANT	1670
ZANE, NOAH	1813	PLAINTIFF	1611	ZEIGLER, LEONARD	1858	DEFENDANT	1616
ZANE, NOAH	1814	PLAINTIFF	1611	ZEIGLER, LEWIS	1859	PLAINTIFF	1616
ZANE, NOAH	1815	PLAINTIFF	1611	ZELCH, JOHN	1857	PLAINTIFF	1616
ZANE, NOAH	1815	PLAINTIFF	1611	ZENGLEIN, BARBARA	1875	PLAINTIFF	1616
ZANE, NOAH	1816	PLAINTIFF	1611	ZENGLEIN, DANIEL	1876	PLAINTIFF	1616
ZANE, NOAH	1816	MISC	1710	ZEOCKLER, ERNEST	1857	PLAINTIFF	1616
ZANE, NOAH	1818	PLAINTIFF	1611	ZEOCKLER, JOHN	1861	MISC	1711
ZANE, NOAH	1819	PLAINTIFF	1611	ZEPHFORD, PETER	1794	PLAINTIFF	1616
ZANE, NOAH	1820	DEFENDANT	1611	ZIBREGIN, CHARLES	1793	DEFENDANT	1598
ZANE, NOAH	1820	PLAINTIFF	1611	ZIEGENDFELDER, JOHN M	1873	MISC	1711
ZANE, NOAH	1820	PLAINTIFF	1611	ZIEGLER, ERNEST F	1858	PLAINTIFF	1616
ZANE, NOAH	1820	PLAINTIFF	1611	ZIEGLER, F E	1858	DEFENDANT	1630
ZANE, NOAH	1821	PLAINTIFF	1612	ZIEGLER, F E	1867	MISC	1711
ZANE, NOAH	1822	PLAINTIFF	1612	ZIEGLER, LEONARD	1858	DEFENDANT	1616
ZANE, NOAH	1823	PLAINTIFF	1612	ZIELER, B / S. SHOP	1871	BKE/OH MAP	1738
ZANE, NOAH	1823	PLAINTIFF	1612	ZIEROWICH, GOTTLIEB	1878	PLAINTIFF	1617
ZANE, NOAH	1824	PLAINTIFF	1612	ZILLIS, GEORGE	1857	PLAINTIFF	1616
ZANE, NOAH	1825	PLAINTIFF	1612	ZILLIS, JACOB	1857	DEFENDANT	1616
ZANE, NOAH	1825	DEFENDANT	1613	ZILLUS, J	1871	OH CO. MAP	1741
ZANE, NOAH	1826	DEFENDANT	1672	ZIM NADDENBUSH & CO	1817	PLAINTIFF	1632
ZANE, NOAH	1827	DEFENDANT	1613	ZIM, DANIEL	1817	PLAINTIFF	1616
ZANE, NOAH	1827	PLAINTIFF	1613	ZIMMER & IBBITSON	1859	PLAINTIFF	1632
ZANE, NOAH	1828	PLAINTIFF	1613	ZIMMER & IBBOTSON	1857	PLAINTIFF	1632
ZANE, NOAH	1829	PLAINTIFF	1613	ZIMMER & IBBOTSON	1857	PLAINTIFF	1632
ZANE, NOAH	1830	PLAINTIFF	1613	ZIMMER, J N	1861	MISC	1711
ZANE, NOAH	1831	PLAINTIFF	1613	ZIMMER, J N	1863	MISC	1711
ZANE, NOAH	1833	PLAINTIFF	1613	ZIMMER, JOHN N	1852	PLAINTIFF	1616
ZANE, NOAH	1833	DEFENDANT	1656	ZIMMER, JOHN N	1857	PLAINTIFF	1616
ZANE, NOAH	1833	MISC	1710	ZIMMER, JOHN N	1858	PLAINTIFF	1616
ZANE, NOAH	1834	PLAINTIFF	1613	ZIMMER, JOHN N	1860	PLAINTIFF	1616
ZANE, NOAH	1834	DEFENDANT	1656	ZIMMER, N	1880	DEFENDANT	1671
ZANE, NOAH	1834	MISC	1710	ZIMMER, NICHOLAS	1878	DEFENDANT	1671
ZANE, NOAH	1834	MISC	1710	ZIMMER, WILLIAM	1875	PLAINTIFF	1616
ZANE, NOAH	1835	MISC	1710	ZIMMERMAN, AUGUST	1857	MISC	1711
ZANE, NOAH	1836	PLAINTIFF	1614	ZIMMERMAN, FREDERICK	1879	MISC	1711
ZANE, NOAH	1836	MISC	1710	ZIMMERMAN, GEORGE	1859	PLAINTIFF	1616
ZANE, NOAH	1840	DEFENDANT	1620	ZIMMERMAN, GUIDO	1851	MISC	1711
ZANE, NOAH	1841	MISC	1710	ZIMMERMAN, LEONARD FREDERICK	1871	MISC	1711
ZANE, NOAH	1841	MISC	1710	ZIMMERMANN, MARY	1871	MISC	1711
ZANE, NOAH	1842	PLAINTIFF	1615	ZIMMIES, LAZERUS	1810	MISC	1711
ZANE, NOAH	1844	PLAINTIFF	1615	ZINC, JOHN / MAP#7	1852	BRKE MAP	1840
ZANE, NOAH	1845	PLAINTIFF	1615	ZINC, JOHN / MAP#8	1852	BRKE MAP	1840
ZANE, NOAH	1845	MISC	1710	ZINK, J	1871	BKE/OH MAP	1739
ZANE, NOAH	1849	MISC	1710	ZINK, MARY	1841	PLAINTIFF	1616
ZANE, ORLOFF A	1843	DEFENDANT	1558	ZINK, R	1871	MARH'L MAP	1749
ZANE, ORLOFF A	1853	DEFENDANT	1615	ZINK, WILLIAM	1861	PLAINTIFF	1616
ZANE, ORLOFF A	1857	DEFENDANT	1615	ZINK, WILLIAM	1878	PLAINTIFF	1617
ZANE, ORLOFF A	1861	DEFENDANT	1615	ZINK, WILLIAM & SON	1877	PLAINTIFF	1633
ZANE, PLATOFF	1837	PLAINTIFF	1614	ZINN & ROHAN	1841	DEFENDANT	1551
ZANE, PLATOFF	1839	PLAINTIFF	1614	ZINN, ANN	1879	MISC	1711
ZANE, PLATOFF	1840	PLAINTIFF	1614	ZINN, GEORGE E	1831	MISC	1711
ZANE, PLATOFF	1841	PLAINTIFF	1614	ZINN, GEORGE E	1848	DEFENDANT	1629
ZANE, PLATOFF	1841	PLAINTIFF	1615	ZINN, GEORGE E	1856	DEFENDANT	1561
ZANE, PLATOFF	1841	DEFENDANT	1670	ZINN, GEORGE E	1857	DEFENDANT	1616
ZANE, PLATOFF	1842	DEFENDANT	1670	ZINN, P E / (?PETER?)	1875	DEFENDANT	1609
ZANE, PLATOFF	1874	PLAINTIFF	1615	ZINN, P E / (?PETER?)	1877	DEFENDANT	1616
ZANE, SAMUEL	1812	PLAINTIFF	1610	ZINN, PETER E	1846	MISC	1711
ZANE, SAMUEL	1812	PLAINTIFF	1611	ZINN, PETER E	1850	PLAINTIFF	1616
ZANE, SAMUEL	1813	PLAINTIFF	1611	ZINN, PETER E	1854	PLAINTIFF	1616
ZANE, SAMUEL	1817	PLAINTIFF	1611	ZINN, PETER E	1857	PLAINTIFF	1616
ZANE, SAMUEL	1817	PLAINTIFF	1611	ZINN, PETER E	1858	PLAINTIFF	1616
ZANE, SAMUEL	1817	PLAINTIFF	1632	ZINN, PETER E			
ZANE, SILAS	1783	PLAINTIFF	1610	ZION'S CHAPEL	1871	MARH'L MAP	1751

'PERSONAL TIME LINE' INDEX TO VOLUME 7 OF THE OHIO COUNTY INDEX

ENTRY	YEAR	SUBJECT	PAGE
ZITTER, D / S. (?SHOE?) SHOP	1871	BKE/OH MAP	1738
ZOECKLER, AUGUST	1876	MISC	1711
ZOECKLER, AUGUST	1877	MISC	1711
ZOECKLER, CASPER	1852	PLAINTIFF	1618
ZOECKLER, CASPER	1853	PLAINTIFF	1618
ZOECKLER, F E	1855	PLAINTIFF	1618
ZOECKLER, GEORGE	1869	MISC	1711
ZOECKLER, JOHN	1842	PLAINTIFF	1618
ZOECKLER, JOHN	1852	PLAINTIFF	1618
ZOECKLER, JOHN	1861	PLAINTIFF	1618
ZOECKLER, JOHN	1862	PLAINTIFF	1618
ZOECKLER, JOHN	1863	MISC	1711
ZOECKLER, JOHN	1872	MISC	1711
ZOECKLER, JOHN	1875	MISC	1711
ZOECKLER, PETER	1855	PLAINTIFF	1618
ZONKLER, LEUS	1835	PLAINTIFF	1618
ZOOK, J	1871	BRKE MAP	1734
ZULAUF, JOHN	1879	PLAINTIFF	1618

www.ingramcontent.com/pod-product-compliance
Lightning Source LLC
Chambersburg PA
CBHW081145290426
44108CB00018B/2442